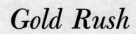

Gold Rush

THE MOUNTAIN LODGE IN PROSPERITY

Gold Rush

THE JOURNALS, DRAWINGS, AND
OTHER PAPERS OF
J. GOLDSBOROUGH BRUFF

Captain, Washington City and California Mining Association

April 2, 1849—July 20, 1851

Edited by GEORGIA WILLIS READ
and RUTH GAINES

With a Foreword by F. W. Hodge

CALIFORNIA CENTENNIAL EDITION

New York: COLUMBIA UNIVERSITY PRESS
1949

The California Centennial Edition contains Bruff's records forming a continuous account of his journeys, together with a selection of his drawings. It does not include his earlier diaries or some other material appearing in the two-volume edition published in 1944 and now out of print. Critical notes and comment have been abbreviated, but fresh information on persons and routes will be found.

FOREWORD

MY boyhood memory of Joseph Goldsborough Bruff, which harks back to the early eighties, is that of a white-bearded patriarch with three daughters and two grandchildren, one of whom, George Jackson, was my special playmate, the other, Nellie, now Mrs. W. J. Procter. It was through my friendship with George that I was permitted to enter the holy of holies of the grandsire, the large lower front room of the family residence at 1009 Twenty-fourth Street in the National Capital. This room was the Bruff museum, consisting in the main of a heterogeneous collection of Indian and other primitive artifacts which caught my fancy, as well as a skull from the old Spanish fort at Saint Augustine, Florida, a carved tusk of a walrus, geological specimens, and various other objects, many of which were evidently gathered during the wanderings of their owner. I have a feeling that my own latent boyhood interest in Indian things was enlivened by the collections in Mr. Bruff's private museum.

The Bruff residence was a large one, more worthy of being called a mansion than many others of lesser size that were so designated; and it was about as venerable, I imagine, as any of Washington's homes of the time—contemporary, it would seem, with the noted "Six Buildings" on Pennsylvania Avenue between Twenty-first and Twenty-second Streets, only about three blocks away, in one of which Joseph Goldsborough Bruff first saw the light on October 2, 1804.

The family home was of brick, three stories and attic, if I remember correctly, painted buff with white trimmings, and with a wide dark-green door quite in keeping with the style of the period. In front were two giant silver poplars, the kind that littered the pavements with their pollen in springtime. Evidently such were the favorite trees in the streets of Washington in its earlier days, for they were of rapid growth and the pollen helped to temper the mud of unpaved streets after spring rains enticed the frost from the oozing soil. In one of the trees were two iron rings, used for hitching horses before an intrusive public sidewalk made this no longer consistent with police regulations. We youngsters did not know the original purpose of the rings at that time; all we cared to know was that they provided adequate means for "skinning the cat." Indeed it was difficult to pass the Bruff poplars without taking a turn at these gymnastics. But the house and the trees have long since passed, the former razed to make room for two or three residences of the kind that meet more modern desires.

When, a few years ago, I was privileged to examine the Bruff notebooks then belonging to Mrs. Procter, I was impressed by the charm of the artist's sketches and by the potential value of them and of the narrative to the history of a thrilling period that ended with the elimination of the western frontier. The thought that I suggested the combination of Mrs. Procter's material with the extended but later Bruff collection in the Henry E. Huntington Library afforded me no small degree of pleasure. This consolidation of data prepared by an artist-traveler born one hundred and forty-five years ago, whom I had actually known, adds more to my sense of satisfaction than I know how to express.

F. W. HODGE

Los Angeles
April, 1948

ACKNOWLEDGMENTS

THANKS are due Dr. Frederick Webb Hodge, Director of the Southwest Museum, Los Angeles, California, who first suggested the editing and publication of the Bruff records; to Mrs. W. J. Procter, of Washington, D. C., granddaughter of Captain Bruff, then owner of many of the sketches and of the diaries designated by the symbol "P" in this volume, who concurred; to the Henry E. Huntington Library and Art Gallery, San Marino, California, which generously permitted the use of its Bruff material in this work—various sketches and the documents designated by the symbol "H"—to supplement that of Mrs. Procter; to Mr. Frederick Coykendall, President, Columbia University Press, who kindly interested himself in bringing about this arrangement; and to Dr. Herbert E. Bolton, then Chairman, Department of History, and Director, Bancroft Library, University of California, who graciously took time to examine the Bruff documents and to give them his endorsement.

In addition, so many libraries, historical societies, other institutions, and individuals have helped us that we are at a loss to know how to thank them. To list them seriatim here, in the second edition, seems unnecessary. Mr. James Anderson, Dr. James T. Babb, Dr. Kate L. Gregg, Dr. George P. Hammond, The National Archives, Mrs. James H. Rea (granddaughter of Joseph B. Chiles), and Miss Caroline Wenzel should, however, be noted for special courtesies. We have merely to add that our gratitude extends to all who have helped us in any way.

G. W. R.
R. G.

South Acworth
New Hampshire
April, 1948

CONTENTS

ILLUSTRATIONS

Some of the drawings have been reduced in size. [P] indicates Procter material, [H] Huntington. All captions are Bruff's, unless enclosed within square brackets. The wagons of the Washington City Company and sometimes some of its members afoot or on horseback are to be seen in some of the sketches. Some of the drawings extend across the double page; some are in several sections, the junction indicated by crosses.

MAPS AND DIAGRAMS OF THE ROUTE

INTRODUCTION

I. THE GOLD RUSH

ONE of the most amazing aspects of the discovery of gold in California is the initial lethargy with which the news was received in the eastern states, to be equaled only by the delirious abandon which followed. Perhaps the slowness of communications then partly accounts for this, perhaps the fact that we credit an incredible truth only after it has been proved. California history in the making, whether in the East or in the West, did tax credulity. Seward, on the floor of the United States Senate on March 11, 1850, epitomized the period which immediately concerns us:

Four years ago, California, a Mexican Province, scarcely inhabited and quite unexplored, was unknown even to our usually immoderate desires, except by a harbor, capacious and tranquil, which only statesmen then foresaw would be useful in the oriental commerce of a far distant, if not merely chimerical, future.

A year ago, California was a mere military dependency of our own, and we were celebrating with unanimity and enthusiasm its acquisition, with its newly-discovered but yet untold and untouched mineral wealth, as the most auspicious of many and unparalleled achievements.

To-day, California is a State, more populous than the least and richer than several of the greatest of our thirty States. This same California, thus rich and populous, is here asking admission into the Union. . . . Shall California be received? . . . Yes. Let California come in ["California, Union, and Freedom"].

In December, 1848, the Secretary of War, in Washington, received from Colonel Mason, in California, specimens of California gold; about the same time the Philadelphia mint issued a report on "the first deposits of gold from California," and the gold fever began to spread. The magnitude of the Gold Rush is not always appreciated. It is perhaps not too much to say that hardly a community in the thirty states then forming the Union — stretching from the Atlantic seaboard to the frontier in Missouri — was left untouched. Brothers, fathers, sons, sweethearts, neighbors, hastened westward, many of them never to return. Bancroft (*Chronicles*, V, 159) estimates the number of homes broken by the deaths of the Argonauts to be "but little less than that inflicted by the civil war ten years later. It was the first general disruption of home circles since our government was formed, the effects of which are destined to reach down to distant generations"; while John S. Hittell, himself a Forty-Niner, declared in 1869, in a speech before the Society of California Pioneers, that "none of the great battles of the late war broke so many heartstrings and caused such widespread pain as did the California gold migration."

While its manifestations were similar throughout the East, our special concern is with Washington, the home of J. Goldsborough Bruff, draftsman to the Bureau of Topographical Engineers and author of the journals and sketches reproduced in this volume.

"At present the people are running over the country and picking it [gold] out of the earth here and there, just as a thousand hogs let loose in a forest would root up the ground-nuts," wrote the Rev. Walter Colton, alcalde of Monterey, on August 29, 1848 (Washington *Daily National Intelligencer*, Dec. 11, 1848). Perhaps the simile was not flattering, but no one's attention focused on that. While the sober-minded of Washington discussed the petrified forests in Egypt and listened to lectures on Athens and Attica, and on the discovery of America by the "Northmen," or the frivolous were lured to "*Something Grand and Magnificent. . . . The Mammoth of Mammoths and King of Lotteries,*" unverified rumors of the discovery of gold in Texas, in North Carolina, in Kentucky, in Maryland, in New Jersey were in the air — if one were true, why not another? But these false fires flickered out, and all the while the glamor of that something really grand and magnificent, that true mammoth of mammoths and king of lotteries across the continent, increased. Preachers preached on gold, in Boston, in New York, in many other cities. "Everybody now talks of gold, dreams of it, or digs for it," wrote one correspondent in the *Intelligencer* (Jan. 6, 1849).

Every time that Bruff looked about him in the shops or in the streets, every time he opened his newspaper, it was the same story — California gold — from first to last. Besides the news items there were the advertisements: "To Companies going to California. — Slakin's celebrated six-barrelled Revolvers"; "California Goods . . . which are particularly recommended to gentlemen about starting for California: Colt's and Allen's Revolving Pistols Allen's Self-cocking do . . . Bowie Knives, assorted qualities and prices . . . Belt Hatchets and Axes . . . Jenk's Patent Carbines and Rifles"; "Money Belts, made exclusively for gold"; "superior Wax Taper Matches, in round wooden boxes perfectly safe and portable"; "California Maps, by Distournel, Mitchell. Emory's Expedition, . . . Abert's Expedition." Taylor and Maury might add below this: "Just received . . . The Heroines of Shakespeare, with 45 superbly engraved portraits, richly bound"; but Fortune was the heroine of the hour, and all intent on her pursuit. There were accounts of vessels lading for California, advice on different routes and equipment, stories from the diggings. The Washington *Globe* published on March 13 an account of "Mr Atherton's Gold Lecture at the Tabernacle" (from the New York *Express*):

The reports concerning the gold mines were not exaggerated in the newspapers; that the supply of gold was absolutely inexhaustible; and that, in his opinion, *one hundred thousand persons* could not exhaust it in *ten or twelve years.* The gains of miners varied from one ounce to one thousand dollars per day. Mr. Atherton said that the largest lump of gold he ever saw was seven pounds weight; it was assayed, and found to be 19¾ carats fine. He also saw it stated, a few days before he left San Francisco, that one man had got $12,000 in six days. Another had obtained 36 pounds in one day. Of the truth of this story he had no more doubt than he had of his own existence. He said that the gold region was as large as New York State, and that a hundred thousand persons would be only two to the square mile. One handful, he said, of the earth where gold is found yields half an ounce of pure gold, on an average.

Perhaps the wonder is, not that so many went, but that so many stayed at home! Such restrained comment as that of Maj. William Tell Poussin, Envoy Extraordinary from the French Republic to the United States, in the *Courier des Etats Unis* (reprinted in the Washington *Daily Globe*, March 3, 1849), that "there is without doubt some gold on the shores of the Sacramento, but it requires a good deal of silver to come at it," received but passing notice.

For one such there were many of the opposite tenor:

The valleys of the Sacramento, w[h]ich but a short time since were hardly known, are now wide and dusty roads. Half of the houses in Monterey are empty, and at least two-thirds of those in San Francisco. The hotels and stores have all closed, and many farms have no occupants whatever.

So wrote an unnamed correspondent from California on August 1, 1848 (Washington *Daily National Intelligencer*, by way of the New York *Intelligencer* and the Boston *Journal*, Dec. 20, 1848). Eastern ports showed unwonted stir, as all available bottoms prepared to take advantage of the California trade. Baltimore, New York, and Boston were especially active, and trade in all lines was brisk. The *New-York Daily Tribune*, as early as January 30, 1849, complained that the California trade had transformed the town. On that day forty-nine ships, schooners, barks, steamers, and brigs were "on the point of sailing" for San Francisco, besides twelve for Chagres and seven for Vera Cruz; and from other Atlantic ports for San Francisco, sixty-five.

And all this time J. Goldsborough Bruff found that even his work kept his mind on the West. A fragment of manuscript, in his hand, laid in with his papers, tells how his idea grew, leading to the formation of the Washington City and California Mining Association:

Having made duplicate drawings of all of Fremont's Reports, maps, plates, &c. for the two houses of Congress — it revived the Spirit of adventure So long dorment, and I was anxious to travel over, and see what my friend had so graphically and scientifically realized: more particularly when a golden reward appear'd to be awaiting us at the nether end of the route. At first, I had mentioned it to a few friends whom I thought might desire to try it also: they told others, and we were nearly resolved on forming a Company of 12 or 15, for the occasion, when some citizens called a meeting to be held at "Apollo Hall" — (between 12 & 13 Sts), to consider about forming an emigrating party. I went, was unanimously called to the Chair, organized by election of a Secretary, and adjourned to meet at my residence a few days later. Regular weekly meetings ensued, the organization was perfected; members signed the Articles, Committee on Supplies &c appointed, and the men regularly drilled as light infantry — A Committee was sent to Pittsburgh, to contract for manufacture of the 14 company wagons, as many large tents, and the purchase of provisions and Stores of all kinds: whilst another committee proceeded far ahead — to procure mules — some 70 being needed. The Company, mostly young men, was 66 strong, neatly uniformed in grey frock and pants, and felt hats — Armed with rifles, muskets, and a few large fowling pieces, all necessary accoutrements, Canteens, &c gum suits & blanket, pair of revolvers in belt, large bowie knives, and belt hatchet — and lots of ammunition. Of Stores, we had a supply of all necessary mechanical tools and appliances: a travelling forge, obtained here from government — and were well-prepared for any emergency that might happen.

Monday, April 2, was the day set for the company's start. On the previous Saturday, March 31, the *Tri-Weekly Intelligencer* reported:

California Emigration Overland. For some time past we were aware that a number of young and enterprising citizens of Washington, Georgetown, and Alexandria, as well as from the surrounding country, contemplated an expedition for the purpose of trying their fortunes in the gold regions of California.

We understand that the organization of the corps is now completed, and from the subjoined list [which did not appear in this issue of the paper], it will be perceived, is composed of a portion of the talent, enterprise, and respectability of the cities the members hail from. It is truly a well-chosen band, handsomely uniformed and well equipped for all the dangers they may have to encounter.

The great principle upon which they are bound, by solemn obligation, to operate, is contained in one of the articles of the constitution, to wit: "Labor shall be the true and legitimate capital of the association; but if, after arrival at California, it shall be found advantageous to trade, a majority of the association may so order it."

The uniform is a short gray frock coat, single-breasted, with gilt eagle buttons; pantaloons the same color, with black stripe; glazed forage-cap, with the initials in front, W.C.C.M.A.

Each member will be armed with a rifle, pair of pistols, bowie-knife, and belt hatchet, with accoutrements.

The Association will leave here on Monday afternoon next, in the cars, under an escort through the city by our volunteer companies. We heartily wish them all success, and a safe return.

Unfortunately, no copy of the Company constitution has come to light.

2. J. GOLDSBOROUGH BRUFF

Joseph Goldsborough Bruff or, as he generally signed himself, J. Goldsborough Bruff, was born in the city of Washington, October 2, 1804. He was the son of Dr. Thomas Bruff, physician and dentist (born in "Chester Town, Md"), and Mary Oliver Bruff (daughter of Charles Oliver Bruff and Mary Letellier, of New York City, and a cousin of the man she married), one of eighteen children born to this couple. In one of his notebooks containing various entries of a genealogical and personal nature, Bruff lists eleven "Brothers & Sisters," the eldest born in 1794 and the youngest in 1810, but this list is obviously incomplete.

Bruff was descended from a line of Bruffs or, as he spelled the name on a drawing of his coat of arms, "Brough (Bruff since 1792)." The words "Quo fata vocant" appear below the drawing. The latest of the original records of Bruff's western experience, so far as known, is a small leather-backed notebook bearing on the cover in the owner's neat lettering, "Summary of events in 1850. J. G. Bruff. California. Quo Fata Vocant," a motto that must have seemed to him singularly appropriate. The notebook with the genealogical entries mentions the "Town of Bruff, in Bruff Co — 60 m. from Cork, on the road to Limerick — Ireland." The same notebook lists "Lieut. Captain Jno. Brough" as appearing in the list of those making the second voyage to Virginia with John Smith; "Richard Brough appointd a Capt. of Marines, B. Navy, 1755"; and a Captain Bruff commanding the first American troops who took possession of Fort Niagara in 1796. Whether J. Goldsborough Bruff was in direct line of descent from these is not clear. He also mentions William Bruff, of Queen Annes County, Md., as a "member of the Maryland Convention framing the Constitution of the States, 1776"; and his "Maternal Uncle, James Bruff — 2d Lieut 6th Battn Regulars, Mar. 27th, 1777.

Oct. 7th 1st Lieut. A member of the Society of the Cincinnati, as a Captain of 6 yrs Service, when it was reform'd 1783 — Queen Ann's Co. Md."

Bruff states, in his genealogical jottings, that his "Mother's grand father commanded the Duke of York's Yacht. Her father Oliver [Bruff], owned all of the Country known as S. Amboy, N.J. was tory in Revn land confiscated — He went to Halifax." He also speaks of "Sophia Goldsborough — (her mother a Bruff) cousin to my parent — owned an immense estate in Talbot Co. Md. A Methodist preacher named Weston was entertained by her for a long time, and though she was very aged proposed marrying her, (for her property) caused her to destroy a Will she had made in favor of myself (named after her by her request)."

He records the fact that two of the family, "Peter Bruff, and his son, . . . were superior Civil Engineers"; also that John Bruff, one of the sons of William Bruff, of Maryland, "was portrait painter, Chiefly in Crayons My cousins 2d degree." This is of interest in view of his own ability as artist and draftsman. General Schuyler "of Revolutionary fame, N.Y. a relative of my Mother." Marooned in the Sierra Nevada in the winter of 1849–50, Bruff was visited one day by four young prospectors, one of whom was Nicholas Schuyler, of New York. In his journal (March 5, 1850) Bruff writes: "Strange how we meet, in this world. The old Schuyler family of New York, and my Mother's family, were related, which has given that name to my only brother living, now in Baltimore Md. Old Genl Schuyler, of Revolutionary memory, and my maternal [grand]father, I think, were related." No brother named Schuyler is included in Bruff's list of his "Brothers & Sisters," unless it be "Charles Schuyler Bruff."

Among the Bruff papers are a few penciled sheets in a feminine hand, believed by Mrs. Procter, Captain Bruff's granddaughter, to be the work of Bruff's wife:

An infant was born on October 9th, 1841 — to a rather unmated couple. The father [J. Goldsborough Bruff], a man of medium height, about thirtyseven years old, with a military bearing, but his yellow hazel eyes under their long black lashes, twinkled with merriment. Laughter and merry jokes, pretty speeches to the fair sex, and a general light hearted view of life, made him good company with all. He did not look his age by ten or more years. His hair was b[l]ack as jet and fell coarse as indians to his shoulders. A fine acquiline nose, gave a distinguished appearance and the mobile mouth, ready for smile or laughter reppartee, or witticism, made him very lovable.

Those were the days of adventure, but he had had an unusual share of it since his fourteenth yeard. Born on Oct — 2nd 1804 in Washington, D.C., he was nearly seven years old when the English invaded the city in 1812 [1814, Bruff would then have been ten] — He was a remarkably precocious child and every event of that period made a lasting impression on his mind. His father was a physician and inventor, of dental instruments, and later, through his interest in these inventions, gave up his general practice entirely, for dentistry. His wife [i.e., Bruff's mother] was a cousin, once removed, of the same name. They were both old time orthodox Methodists. They had eighteen children, but only five boys and girls lived "to grow up." They all were unusually intelligent. The girl was undoubtedly the most brilliant of them all. At the age of eleven she was writing for periodicals. By the age of fourteen she was an accomplished young lady, painted in water-color played on the spinnet (the piano of that period), the harp, and accompanied her sentimental songs of the day, on the guitar. She was the wit of her set and a poetess. She married at eighteen a brilliant man, who worshipped her, but she died a year later leaving a broken-hearted husband. . . . He never married again. [This, according to Mrs. Procter, was Susanna Maria, born in 1798, who became Mrs. Rhine.] One of the boys [the Bruff boys] was sent to West-Point, graduated and entered the Army but his health having been impaired by hard study, he was transfered to the Navy in hopes a cruise would benefit him, but it was of no avail, he died at Portsmouth of an acute attack of bronchitis in his twenty-fifth year. His brothers loved him dearly, his had been a most lovable nature. The other boys had gone to Portsmouth because their brother was stationed there, and being litterary, opened a printing office and published a newspaper.

This was Thomas Oliver Bruff. According to West Point records (letter from Headquarters, Dec. 14, 1934), he entered the Military Academy on October 12, 1814, appointed from the District of Columbia. In 1818 "his name appears in the Official Register of the United States Military Academy, at which time he stood No. 18 in the Third Class. A notation in this Register states that he was 'allowed to proceed until further orders subject to be put back.' We have no further record of him and I presume he was discharged before publication of the Official Register for 1819." This indicates that he did not graduate at West Point; Hamersly confirms this (*Army Register*, Part I, p. 198), in "Cadets Admitted into Military Academy": "Bruff, Thomas O., D.C., 1814. Bruff, Joseph G., D.C., 1820," both listed as nongraduates.

The father of the family — the doctor had died in New York, where he had gone in regard to a patent. He died very suddenly and under circumstances that led people to suspect foul play, poison probably, by a person interested with him in this invention. The model and all the drawings were missing. There was no proof, and no money to probe the matter or to prosecute a suspected person. The wife died a few years later of broken heart, for she and her husband were truly as one and the loss of her much loved daughter was another sad blow.

This probably concerns information referred to in the Washington *Evening Star*, April 8, 1889: "Dr. Bruff, the father, before the war of 1812, invented a machine for making bullets by compressing them from cold lead, and a machine having been built and tried at the Washington navy-yard, an agent of Great Britain offered the inventor a large sum of money to take it to Great Britain, and the offer, though tempting, was indignantly refused." Dr. Bruff died in New York City in 1816, Mrs. Procter says, and his wife in Georgetown, D.C., April 14, 1821. The United States Patent Office says (letter, Oct. 3, 1933, to Dr. F. W. Hodge) that the records disclose "a patent issued to Thomas Bruff on October 5, 1808 for Shot, manufacturing by pressure and patent issued June 4, 1813 to Thomas Bruff for Shot, Manufacturing by pressure."

Shortly before his brother's death, the object of this article [J. Goldsborough Bruff] had been sent to West Point, at the age of fourteen — Being particularly fond of mathematics he soon made himself liked by his teachers. He stood high in his classes, but he had a violent temper. He took umbrage at a trifling insult from one of his class, fought a duel with him, slightly wounded him and was put into the black hole (Dueling was forbidden) As he was a favorite and the fellow who provoked the duel was not, they sent him to an adjacent island — rusticated him — till his case could be determined by the War Department. Instead of a disgraceful dismissal, he was permitted to resign.

According to the records of the Military Academy, Bruff "entered the Military Academy in 1820 having been appointed from the District of Columbia" (letter from Headquarters, Dec. 14, 1934). He would therefore have been sixteen years of age, not fourteen, as his wife states, at that time. His treatment by the authorities, if indeed he issued a challenge or fought in a duel, was lenient in the extreme, severe penalties being prescribd by the military regulations at that time. The Military Academy states (letter to Dr. F. W. Hodge, Sept. 14, 1933) that "It is unknown at this time who sponsored his appointment. . . . Nothing is known as to the circumstances incident to his resignation from the Corps of Cadets in 1822." However, official records in Washington do not bear out the information in Mrs. Bruff's statement.

His mother died at this time, her death possibly hastened by his misconduct. There was no home for him to go to, no one to advise him except the brother-in-law, who had given employment to the three other boys in his printing office. This one smarting under his disgrace, his blighted career, and always acting upon impulse, embarked upon a merchant vessel sailing from Georgetown, as a cabin boy, without consulting the remnants of his family.

The life of a cabin boy of that day might have been a tough experience for the young man, but for the bright, happy nature that drew friends to him everywhere — The captain took especial interest in him and saved him from many hardships and illtreatment. Therefore his first trip across the ocean instead of curing him of roving, gave him a love for it, and so for years he roved, all the ports of Europe and South America. He was seeing the world, it is true, but the life he led threw him with an objectionable class of people, which lowered his standard materially. Early teachings and training made him noticeably better than his companions, but were not strong enough to make him disgusted with such associations. The love of pleasure of freedom absorbed the finer qualities. After many wonderful adventures, full of thrilling escapes, the call of nature, the brother love, the love of home, country, brought him back to his native land to join his brothers in Portsmouth, or rather at Gosport Navy-Yard [now the Portsmouth Navy Yard, at Norfolk, Va.] where he soon obtained a position as draughtsman, a Government position, where his mathematical and designing abilities were appreciated and he consequently enjoyed a fair salary. His erect figure slight and finely proportioned, combined with a disposition that drew all men to him — His brain was stored with anecdotes of his travels.

Here the account ends, at the beginning of a blank page. We have here a good picture of Bruff and a key to the causes of his failure and his success. He was a conspicuously able leader of his company across the plains. He spared himself no effort in the discharge of what he conceived to be his duties; indeed he almost forfeited his life by his self-sacrifice for the company in California. But the fact remains that his company, profiting by his self-sacrifice, left him to starve in the Sierra Nevada with casual indifference, and one of them at least with out-and-out treachery, although it must be said that everybody seems to have deserted to the gold fields in 1849. The answer, it would seem, lies in the fact that Bruff was by training and by taste an army officer, though he never wore the army uniform. The sixty-five other members of the company — or most of them — were to him so many enlisted men — "my company" he says again and again and, being private citizens unused to such restraints, they may have resented military discipline and military point of view, especially as they probably did not appreciate their necessity.

Two fragments in Bruff's handwriting tell in brief of his life at sea and in the years immediately following his return home:

Having from childhood had a strong desire of travelling to distant parts, an opportunity occurred in the fall of 18 . The Ship E. — Capt. M. was at Georgetown D.C. and was ready to sail for the North of Europe; I quickly embraced the chance to gratify my desires, and as I was unable to pay passage, I could only go as a landsman or boy before the mast, which I did.

The Ship soon passed down the Potomac, and entered upon that emblem of eternity, the open ocean — I looked back upon the receding land of my child-hood's happy days, for the first time bidding it adieu, and wept copiously: but the novelty and excitement of my new life, with its promise of adventure in fu-turity, soon composed me: and before I saw old England I was perfectly at home in my floating abode.

We arrived at Cowes, Isle of Wight, and remained there several days, affording me an opportunity of seeing and Sketching castles, &c. There is a very handsome modern Castle here, the residence of Lord Henry Seymour.

From Cowes we proceeded to the Texal, and found the Dutchman's Home cov-ered with Snow. On Christmas day we experienced a violent gale and Snow Storm, which compelled us to throw out every anchor, to preserve the Ship from going ashore. Many vessels and lives were lost that fatal and terrible night. This I may say was the commencement of my hardships: — Standing watch upon a deck all night, bathed with the Spray which froze as it fell, and covered with snow, with-out a fire to comfort me, I thought on the comforts of home, and would then gladly have exchanged my situation for that of the Cow or Dog at home.

Daylight brought more moderate weather, and showed us the disastrous effects of this terrible wintry Storm. — The beach strewed with fragments of wrecks, vessels on Shore, others dismasted, &c — and our own Ship in a most unseamanlike trim, with every thing foul, and covered with Snow and ice. As soon as the weather was sufficiently moderate our task of putting to rights commenced by beating the ice off the rigging, and sending up Topmasts, yards, &c. and ended with rousing in our spare Anchors, and hauling ahead, as we had dragged some distance during the fury of the storm, in Spite of four large Anchors and a small one. We dis-charged our Cargo of Tobacco, and I had then a chance of visiting Nieu Diep and the Helder, to pass over *Buonaparte's Walk*, view the embankment raised by the hardy and persevering dutch to reclaim terra firma from the ocean, and to enjoy a pipe, Schnaps, and a dance with the fat, round, and lively dutch lasses.

Having taken in Sand ballast and got all ready, we bid the industrious Dutch-men farewell, and Steered for home. *Home, home*, what enchantment accompanies that word! How delightful, after such trials and hardships, to know that we are retracing our track homeward!

On returning to my native place, I found my only sister ill, and for several days she was too much indisposed to see me — When admitted, I saw her propped up in bed pale and ill: She was very glad to see the wanderer return, and bade me relate my adventures, which I did briefly, as she was too weak to sit up long. For several days we flattered ourselves that she would soon recover, but suddenly the complaint took and [an] unfavorable turn; and She departed for that bourne from whence no traveller returns! I followed her to the grave, and resolved to for-sake my native place, and while I gratified my thirst for travel, would also banish grief from my bosom.

One morning early, with a small wardrobe enclosed in a handkerchief, which also contained some crackers and Cheese, I started on a pedestrian tramp for Baltimore, where I arrived at sun set. I found a Schooner ready for sea, bound to the W. Indies, and entered on board her as a seaman. The Schooner was leaky, and as the sailors said, We pumped our way out to the Island of Barbadoes, which we made after the usual passage, and hauled into the canal at Bridgetown. Here we discharged cargo, and mended our bottom, and after remaining long enough to afford me an opportunity of visiting the interior, seeing a black regiment, and admiring the beautiful Islands, we sailed for the Grand Turk, for Salt. We passed the sail rock, near St. Thomas's — and it may well be so termed, for nothing could resemble a small Sloop under sail more than it did, till we were quite near it. Passing St. Thomases I had a view of Bluebeard's Castle, built, so said, by a celebrated Buccanneer of that cognomen.

At the Grand Turk Island we took in a cargo of salt: while there, I strolled round to see this lump of Sand and salt; for there is no sign of vegetation here, except the prickly pear: — the inhabitants depending on the importation of provisions entirely. The negroes here are great divers, as they are all through the W. Indies: and for a *bit* will dive down into 6 fathom water to bring you up a sea fan or coral. The inhabitants ornament large Chonch shells with flowers cut out of callico and pasted all over their exterior, which gives them a very pleasing appearance. These they generally sell for 50 ¢ a pair. The meat of the Chonk though very tough is well stewed with savory herbs, and is quite palateable: at least to those who have long fed on salt provisions, with no other change than Pork and bread one day, and bread and pork the next. Of course the only water they have here for drink and culinary purposes, is rain water. This Island has a singular appearance from the Sea, it is perfectly white, and the houses are white washed so that at a little distance they are scarcely discernable from the sand: — and the piles or stacks of salt, of a brown color, looks like hay mounds; for they are piled up in large piles like hay-stacks, and covered with sea-oar which gives them

Here the story of his life as a sailor breaks off.

The narrative of Bruff's wife states that on his final return from wandering, he went to work in the Gosport Navy Yard as draftsman. He himself dates the beginning of this service as June 2, 1827:

Employed by the Commandant of Gosport Navy Yard, June 2nd 1827, as a clerk to execute the writing for the Master's Department of that Naval Station. As the Navy Department had made no provision for such a Clerkship, I performed the duty at the rate of a Rigger, and was so paid — viz: 1.37½ cts per day, for 2 years (till June 1st 1829) From June 1st 1829 to June 1st 1836, I received the pay of 1.50 per day, and the remaining 7 months, up to Sept. 3rd, 1837, of 1.75 cts per day.

Soon after commencing my duties as clerk to the Master, my abilities as Draughts man were called into requisition, for the important purposes of rigging and fitting the Ships of War, &c — Added to which my duties otherwise were greatly increased. — The Gunners and Boatswains, books and writings I had to keep, and Surveys of Stores of every description, receiving of stores and munitions, selling at auction, and collecting the money for the Government, were all required of me — All these duties, laborious and important as they were, I performed, to the entire satisfaction of the U.S. Naval Officers; thinking that the Navy Department would consider my services and grant me more adequate compensation for all these services — In this, I was mistaken, — it had not the power to do so, and I left Gosport Navy Yard after performing $9\frac{1}{4}$ years of such services as are herein set forth. Travelling, and various other incidents have —

Here this fragment ends, but a short entry in one of the personal notebooks adds "1836 — Sep. 3^d Went to Fortress Monroe & engaged by Capt Eliason, Eng. U.S.A. as draughtsman at \$2 pr day — with quarters & 9 chords of wood pr Ann. Commenc'd on 5th. Reported on 7th & . . . 30th moved family & effects in a Sch^r from Portsmouth Va."

Another entry on the same page reads "July 6, 1844 — In Schr. Breeze — geologizing down river."

From this point one of Bruff's personal notebooks continues the résumé of his activities:

2 yrs: Cadet, U.S.M.A. West Point — resign'd to enter Navy. Fail'd to get in Navy. A lapse of 9 yrs. 3 of which devoted to travelling over the World, and being in the Venezuelian Service, as an Officer in some engagements. 6 yrs studying, drawing, and completg educątion.

3 years, acting Master's Mate in Navy, U.S.

9 ” clerk, draughts man, and Superintend work in Navy Yard, Norfolk — (Gosport)

2 ” Drawing for Engineer Dep^t Fortress Monroe. (A lapse of 4 months, on private work)

11 ” The Draughts man to the Bureau of Topographical Engineers — comes up to Spring of 1849. Organiz'd and Commanded an overland expedition to California, via the South pass of the Rocky Mountains: which, with engagements of drawing for the Tehantepec Survey, and working up Genl. Stevens overland surveys, &c. would make a labor of $2\frac{1}{2}$ yrs. &

3 ” miscellaneous Gov't work.

15 ” In Architect's Office, Treasy Dept engag'd Sept 14th, 1853, up to July 1 — 1869. I left — and rec^d a Commiss^n in the Tonnage Division of Register's Office, Treasy Dept &

7 ” Service therein to Sept 1876. Lapse of 2 months — and thro' numerous friends and Mr. Hill reemploy'd in Architect's Office —

2 ” Therein to Oct. 1878.

——

54 Years in the Service of the Government: 49 years of which steadily em-

ployed in designing, and executing every description of drawing, for nearly every branch of public service. $\frac{1}{3}$ of all to the Treasury. to the perfect satisfaction of my employers, and having their respect and esteem. Ample testimonials and record.

Apparently this summary was drawn up by Bruff in 1878. His appointment to the Office of the Supervising Architect, Treasury Department, continued without interruption to the day of his death, the Treasury Department stating (letter to Dr. F. W. Hodge, Sept. 21, 1933): "according to the records, Mr. Joseph G. Bruff was appointed in this office as a draftsman under date of October 16, 1876, and his services were discontinued at the close of business on April 14, 1889."

While on his deathbed, Bruff was accorded a brief account in the Washington *Evening Star* (April 8, 1889):

Capt. Bruff, when a small boy, left Alexandria in a sailing vessel, and for some years traveled in many foreign lands. He early developed a taste for drawing and painting, and on reaching manhood he found employment in the engineer bureau as a draughtsman, where he continued for many years. While in this service he was employed on many of the defenses of the sea coast, among them the rip-raps near Fort Munroe. Mr. Bruff, when a youth, engaged the attention of General Jackson, and when the latter became President he recognized in the draughtsman at the Rip Raps the boy who, ten years before, had, by some of his sketches, attracted the General's attention, who presented him with a box of paints. He was also, in his younger days, brought into contact with many of the leading men of the day, including Gen. W. H. Harrison, who was elected President in 1840, President Adams, and a host of others. For many years he has been engaged in the office of the architect of the Treasury, and notwithstanding his advanced age he had been able to perform his work up to a few months since. Much of the ornamentation of the Treasury building is from his designs.

The (Norfolk?) *Herald* wrote of his drawing in the Gosport days:

Views of the Gosport Dry Dock. — We were yesterday shown two handsome lythograph prints, from drawings by Mr. Joseph G. Bruff, of the Navy Yard: the first representing the U. States ship *Delaware*, 74, going into Dry Dock at Gosport, on the 17th June, 1833, with a view of the scenery on the opposite shore, the galleries on each side of the dock crowded with spectators, and from other localities; the second exhibiting the ship propped up in her position in the dock, ready for the operations of the carpenters. These prints will doubtless revive the interest excited by the event which they are intended to commemorate, and find a ready sale. They are accurate almost to a fault in their delineations, as will readily be seen by any one who was present on the occasion.

The last pages of his personal notebook contain a summary of certain of his pursuits other than his work for the government:

Scientific and Art Matters

Was a delegate to the National Congress of Artists, held 3 days at the Smithsonian Building, many years ago, on the subject of American Art generally. Was one of the memorialists and corporations, named in the Act of Congress, incorporating "The National Art Association" in this City, which existed over 4 yrs, when the War of the Rebellion broke it up. Its members were all the principal artists of the U.S. and in fact, all the art-loving men of distinction in the Country; and among the Honorary Members, were many European Artists. It had perment [permanent] exhibitions of Sculpture, painting, drawing, &c. The contributions for the purpose of Artists, and others possessing such works, Lectures, and papers read before it, (always well attended by crowds of ladies & gentlemen) and published. I was an Academician, and the Recording Secretary & gave two addresses on Art Subjects. Before this, however, I was a member of the National Institute of Arts and Sciences, which existed over 4 yrs. when its collections were turned over to the Smithsonian Institute. Of its members were all the learned men of this Country, and many of Europe. It published Bulletins. I read a paper before it, and contributed to its large and valuable collection Prof. Jameson of Edinburgh sent me a copy of his work   A Member also, of the Metropolitan Mechanics Institute here: lasted about 4 years. Had work on exhibition, — for which awarded a Silver Medal, and a Diploma — and was appointed One of the Judges on Art Matters.

According to the *Bulletin of the Proceedings of the National Institution for the Promotion of Science* (I [1841], 3), this society "was organised at the seat of Government on the 15th of May, 1840." The Secretary of War (Joel Poinsett) and the Secretary of the Navy (J. K. Paulding) were the directors; J. Q. Adams, Colonel Abert, and others, councillors. At the meeting of January 22, 1841, "Hon. Joel R. Poinsett in the Chair . . . The following donations were received: Copy of a sketch from actual survey of several ancient fortifications, situated on the Little Miami river, Green county, Ohio: by J. G. Bruff. — *From J. G. Bruff*" (*ibid.*, pp. 30-32). At the meeting, May 10, 1841, Peter Force in the chair, Bruff donated "Journal of a Voyage to New South Wales, with engravings, by White, 1 vol. 4to.; London" (*ibid.*, pp. 80-81). And on August 9, 1841, Bruff gave a collection of marine shells, 313 specimens, divided among 19 species (*ibid.*, p. 97).

A paper of mine, on mural antiquities, and Monumental Art, and another on Primitive Art, and an illustrated essay on Curvillinear Ornaments, elicited much commendation from the National Institute, and the Art Association. Lord Napier thanked me personally, and it would fill a large volume to enumerate what I have done for the government during such long services. But some special and general relations may be mentioned.

1st — Made the rigging draughts for all classes of ships of war, from an anchor-hoy up to the gun-ship — and designed, drew, and painted, a considerable amount of fancy and decorative work, for naval service.

2nd. — In Engineer Dept. Fortification Drawings, &c.

3rd — Topographical Office — Maps: — and lettering those executed by Officers of the Corps. Drew all the plates for the 3 vols. of Cavalry Tactics. (twice) Designed sword, button, insignias and uniform of the Officers of said Corps. Designed Seals and Medals. Worked up all the numerous maps, sketches, and drawings, of scenery, natural history, &c. of explorations — (Ingraved from my drawings.) Made all the maps and route plans for the Service, of the Florida and Mexican Wars: & duplicated every thing for Congress, (printed) — Designs, maps, and other drawings, for the Indian and Post-Office Departments. Designed, and drew for engraving, (colored also) for the Navy Dep^t the sword, button, &c. of uniform For the State Dep^t several medals, &c.

4th — Treasury Dept: Designs and drawings of all ornamental work, in and about the Treas^y build^g besides much for other buildings. see volume of pub. build^s — for which I prepared the plates. Several Seals and Medals: Vignettes for Treasury Warrants. The Register for American Ships: the handsomest one of all the Nations. (the old one running from foundation of the government was the meanest) Designed the sword, button, &c. of the Uniform of U.S. Rev: [enue] Officers: and supplied the Dept. with a complete set of all the Customs Districts of the U.S. uniform size. And manifold miscellaneous designs and drawings. I compiled and drew, the first Map of the State of Florida. Engraved Bronze Gallery Railing of Cash Room And done some important work on Maps of the N.E. Boundary. White Marble Mantel in Secretary's Room. N.B. The extra hours and days, given to the Service, gratuitously, would aggregate nearly 2 years of time. Complimented by the Danish Antiquarian Soy

According to E. L. Yonge, Map Curator, American Geographical Society, New York, "The full title of the map of Florida . . . is as follows: 'The State of Florida, compiled in the Bureau of Topographical Engineers, from the best authorities, 1846. By J. Goldsborough Bruff. D. McClelland sc. Washn. . . .' This map appears to be the first official map made of the State after being admitted as a state in 1845."

Bruff was an ardent Mason, a charter member of the Federal Lodge in Washington, and a signatory of the dispensation which William H. Van Voorhies, newly appointed Assistant Postmaster General for California, carried with him for California Lodge No. 13, afterwards renumbered California Lodge No. 1, to San Francisco in 1848. This fact throws light on many particulars of Bruff's life on the route and in California. His narrative in its entirety bears out the Masonic claim made in *Fifty Years of Masonry* (I, 53):

> The Masonic Lodges all over the Union [at the time of the Gold Rush] were set to work like so many mills running at their full capacity in grinding out Masons to meet the demand for human sympathy and brotherhood that might be required for mutual aid and assistance on their journey. . . . It is said that there were as many as sixteen Fellow Craft candidates seen at the altar of Masonry at one time in the same Lodge, assuming the obligation of that degree, and from five to nine Master Masons were made in one night by the same Lodge of men who were on the eve of starting for California. Human kindness and the simple modes of recognition among Brethren were deemed of more importance than proficiency in the knowledge of the ritual of the degrees. . . . Applicants for Masonic light and Brotherhood, which was to be severely tested to their fullest extent in the hour of trial — in sickness, misfortune and suffering — and most nobly did Masonry prove that the Mystic Tie was not a mere rope of sand when rightly tested.

Bruff owed his very life to the fraternal aid of a man named Poyle, whom he had never seen until he encountered him casually on the Long March, but who, obedient to his Masonic vows, halted in the Sierra for months, at imminent danger to himself, to assist Bruff. Some of the grave inscriptions copied by Bruff bear the Masonic emblem, and investigation shows that many of the associates chosen and the friends mentioned by him in California belonged to the Masonic order. Indeed the number of Masons who were prominent in the making of California history of that period is amazing. To mention only a few: Lieut. Joseph Warren Revere of the "Portsmouth" (grandson of Paul Revere), who ran up the Stars and Stripes in Upper and Lower California in 1846; Dr. Robert Semple, known for many early activities, including the publication of the California *Star;* Dr. John F. Morse, famous in California annals; Dr. J. D. B. Stillman, who together with Morse opened a hospital in Sacramento in the autumn of 1849; Lieut. George H. Derby, of the Topographical Engineers, known for his "Phœnixiana" papers, as well as for his surveys; last but not least, Peter Lassen. California owed much to the Masons in the early days. Never, we may add, were such obligations more humanely met than by Bruff himself at his "Lodge in the Wilderness" in the Sierra.

This is Bruff's life, and there remains only to tell of its close. The Washington *Evening Star,* April 16, 1889, published his death notice:

> BRUFF On Sunday, April 14, 1889, at 7:45 P.M. at his residence 1009 24th Street, Joseph Goldsborough Bruff in the 85th year of his age.
> Friends are respectfully invited to attend the funeral Wednesday April 17, at 4:30 P.M.

Two days later, the *Evening Star* stated:

Funeral services were held yesterday afternoon over the remains of J. Goldsborough Bruff at his late residence. Reverend Dr. Sunderland conducted the service and the members of the Washington Commandery, no. 1 Knights Templar
were present. A large representation from the Oldest Inhabitants association were
present. The interment was at the Congressional cemetery.

The Washington *Weekly Star* on April 18 printed a fuller account:

Death of J. Goldsborough Bruff.

Sunday night, shortly before eight o'clock, Mr. J. Goldsborough Bruff, whose
illness has been mentioned in The Star, passed away. His illness, while prolonged,
was painless, and the end was not unexpected. Mr. Bruff had nearly attained the
advanced age of eighty-five years, but such was the vigor of his constitution that
he did not give up the active pursuit of his profession as draughtsman until about
four months ago. Mr. Bruff was born October 2, 1804, within a few hundred
yards of the residence, 1009 24th street, where he died, his father being an owner
of one of the famous six buildings on Pennsylvania avenue, between 21st and 22d
streets. For the past sixty-three years Mr. Bruff has been in government employ,
and there was only one interregnum, when, in 1849, with other young men, he was
stricken with the gold fever and started for California to amass a fortune. He was
unsuccessful, and in 1851 he returned to Washington and resumed his work in
the Treasury department. He was a member of the Oldest Inhabitants association
and the Washington Monument association. Mr. Bruff leaves a wife and five children. The funeral will take place at 4:30 P.M. Wednesday, and the arrangements
will be under the direction of Federal lodge of Masons, of which the deceased was
a charter member.

3. THE WASHINGTON CITY AND CALIFORNIA GOLD
MINING ASSOCIATION

Now that we know something of Bruff's life and what manner of man he
was, let us turn to the closing months of 1848 and the opening of 1849. The
lethargy with which the news of Marshall's discovery had been received in
the East had vanished. The country was aflame over the discovery of gold.
"We are all fairly afloat upon one or the other of the three great C's of
excitement — Congress, Cholera and California," wrote a Washington correspondent to the *New-York Tribune* in December, 1848, and articles in the
press fanned the flame.

The Gold Mines in California [*New York Herald*, November 28]. . . . The
excitement in that territory on the subject is increasing, too; old and young, male

and female, the lame, the halt, and we verily believe the blind, too, are on their way to the land of promise and gold, cup and tin kettle in hand. . . . The men of the sea vie with those of the land in pursuit of the treasure — the occupant of the bench is capsized in endeavoring to outrun the sheriff — the lawyer jostles against his client — the farmer and mechanic throw aside their implements, and there is nothing but a busy, exciting race, each on his own account, and the devil to the hindmost, to reach the gold region first. This picture is not too highly colored. It is beyond all question that gold, in immense quantities, is being found daily in this part of our territory, and that every pursuit of trade or business is abandoned.

A few days later (Dec. 11) a writer in the same journal reported:

The gold mania rages with intense vigor, and is carrying off its victims hourly and daily. . . . Ships, freighted with all the necessary articles of life, are being got in readiness. . . . Vessels are about to sail from all Atlantic ports, and our young men — including mechanics, doctors, lawyers, and we may add, clergymen — are taking leave of old associations, and embarking for the land of wealth, where the only capital required for making a fortune is a spade, a sieve, or tin colender, and a small stock of patience and industry.

At this time Bruff was a married man, with several children. He states in his genealogical notebook that his daughter Mary Ann died September 10, 1832, aged four years, three months, and twenty-one days. She must therefore have been born in May, 1828, and it seems reasonable to assume that Bruff married shortly after his return from the sea — probably soon after his establishment in the Gosport Navy Yard. He had therefore strong incentives toward keeping in the beaten track — lucrative and interesting employment and family responsibilities. Nevertheless, his love of adventure prevailed.

The following letter, addressed by him to Col. Peter Force and now in the Peter Force Collection in the Library of Congress, shows the growth of his plan:

Washington, D.C.
Jany 30th 1849

Dear Sir,

The 'Washington City Mining Company' may be said to have been formed. — At least 25 energetic honorable men have determined to go, and in the mode, and under the rules I have advised. — It will be much augmented, no doubt to 50; — but of the same character — material, as the nucleus.

We go via the plains and South Pass of the Rocky Mountains, with wagons, provisions, and implements & tools: each man efficiently armed and equiped. — On arrival at the Nevada Mountains, we purpose selecting an eligible site for mining, trading, water, health, &c. and there construct a log stockade, both for protection and comfort. Common Stock & equal dividends throughout. Shares for the general outfit of wagons, animals, tools, provisions, &c. not yet fully ascertained, but supposed to be about $300. Share-holders may supply an active substitute, with their own mutual understanding about the profits.

A correct and precise journal will be kept en route, for which I shall furnish sketches and meteo[ro]logical observations. This, when published, will not only be interesting, but a perfect guide in every respect to all future travellers on that route. We go as a body of energetic gentlemen, to enrich ourselves, if possible, by every honorable means. I, perhaps, will be worse off, pecuniarily, than any other one of the party; a speculation I am engaged in may yield me, by 1st. April, sufficient, and it may not. My family (whom I love as much as any husband & father can) I shall be compelled to leave on credit, awaiting probably 8 months, ere I will be enabled to send a remittance to them. In a few days I shall commence packing up my valuable collection ["Cabinet" of minerals, coins, etc., many now in the National Museum], and such articles as the family will not need: — these I must store somewhere. — This will afford me the opportunity of giving you many maps. The association will continue in active operation from 10 to 18 mos.

Acquainted with nearly all the officers of the U.S.A. I can-not be very unfortunate in California, and if the gold shall have vanished, my abilities will guarantee a handsome salary.

I take with me all the Maps and works on the country, mineralogical works, tests, &c. — So you see that our principles are of the best character to insure security, comfort, and success.

I am very truly

Yours

[Signed] J. Goldsborough Bruff

To
Col. P. Force
　　present

Bruff's impulse had thus matured.

It therefore suffice[d] [he tells us further] to whisper my intended expedition among a few acquaintances for them to arouse our great rural city of Washington with glowing visions of its great magnitude and prospects. . . . Until, despite my own views and apprehensions, a company of sixty-six men, representing a joint stock fund of $11,000 was the smallest that could be harmoniously organised, where almost every man had a comrade whom he wished to include.

A company had been formed "in the mode, and under the rules" advocated by him, and he had evolved the further idea of compiling a "perfect guide" to the Overland Trail, illustrated with the maps and sketches which his training so richly qualified him to prepare and further enlivened by such interesting experiences as the journey might afford. Early in April was the time set for the departure from Washington.

The company had decided to go by the Oregon-California Trail, but the matter was not so simple, especially for the leader. Probably Bruff's efforts to inform himself as to routes and route hazards were neither understood nor appreciated by the majority of his company. Even before crossing the frontier, such problems arose. At St. Joseph, Missouri, in April, 1849, the company found only one ferry and already hundreds of wagons waiting to be carried across. The wagons in the long line, stretching up into the heart of the town, held their place, day and night, and altercations and even fatal shootings occurred over questions of place and precedence. The *New-York Daily Tribune* (May 9, 1849, from the Independence [Mo.] *Expositor* of April 21) predicted that there were then as many emigrants in St. Joseph as could be ferried over by July 1!

Bruff boldly decided to travel up the eastern side of the Missouri to old Fort Kearny, near the present Nebraska City, and cross there. A few miles south of that point he found a boatman with a scow, and, with the expenditure of considerable engineering skill on his part and of almost incredible physical exertion on the part of all, he crossed the company over the Missouri, then in flood stage. Thence to new Fort Kearny, near Grand Island on the Platte, the route, as Bruff knew, was superior to that between St. Joseph and Fort Kearny, being firmer ground with only one stream difficult to cross—Salt Creek.

The journey up the Platte was fairly easy. The road in general was good; indeed there was no better way. With certain minor variations, the route was the same for all, and travel here, while arduous for those unaccustomed to a vigorous out-of-door life, presented fewer hardships and difficulties than in the later parts of the journey. Horn, in his *Overland Guide*, speaks of the trail across the plains as "the route designed by nature for the great thoroughfare to the Pacific. This was the road selected by *nature's civil engineers*, the buffalo and the elk, for their Western travel. The Indians followed them in the same trail; then the traders; next the settlers came."

From Fort Laramie on, however, things wore a different aspect. The country and the trails were not so well known, and there was more choice as to the route to be followed. That these things were understood and had been considered by Bruff is evidenced not only by his statement to Colonel Force — "I take with me all the Maps and works on the country" — but by the abstracts of routes and distances and the guides found in his notebooks.

Among other things, before leaving Washington he had secured from the Adjutant General's office a copy of a letter to Brig. Gen. R. Jones from J. J. Myers, then in Missouri, offering to guide any party to California and discussing the routes. Four pages of penciled notes, in Bruff's hand, written painstakingly small, cover the route from Grand Island on the Platte to Fort Hall and thence to the head of the Humboldt, not including Sublette's Cut-off. These were an abstract, for that part of the route, of the now-rare *Emigrant's Guide to the Gold Mines, of Upper California, Illustrated with a Map,* by E. Sanford Seymour, Chicago, 1849. Seymour, who seems to have been a seasoned traveler in the Far West, attached himself to Bruff's company on the Platte and doubtless permitted Bruff to examine the manuscript of his *Guide.* Bruff's notes check in every detail — distance, description, and even phrasing — with the comparable portions of Seymour's published work.

In one of Bruff's notebooks appears an account of Sublette's Cut-off, with the words "Thornton says:" in the margin. It is an accurate abstract of the pages of J. Quinn Thornton's *Oregon and California* (published that year) which relate to this cut-off. It is clear from Bruff's notes that he consulted Clayton's *Emigrants' Guide,* Ware's *Emigrants' Guide* (which he called "generally very correct"), Jefferson's Map and the *Accompaniment,* Frémont's *Report* (for which he had drawn the maps), and Hastings' *Emigrants' Guide.* A close-penciled memorandum "from L. W. Hastings Book (a resident of Cal^a)" covers the ground from the Black Hills to the South Pass, Sublette's Cut-off (unnamed), Bear River, Fort Hall, and thence to the Sacramento River, this abstract concluding:

From Ft. Hall to the Bay of S^n Francisco 800 miles. Wagons can be as easily taken from F^t Hall to the Bay of S^n Francisco, as they can from the States to F^t Hall, and in fact, the latter part of the route is the best.

This airy disregard of the Sierra Nevada, not to mention lesser obstacles, is of course now understood to be characteristic of Hastings, but it may have helped to induce in Bruff's mind an unfortunate underestimation of the difficulties of the latter part of the Trail.

It was in the hope of getting more definite information on this part of the route that Bruff determined to visit Fort Hall — a hope not realized — while his company proceeded through the Emigrants' Cut-off. Undoubtedly there was general lack of reliable knowledge as to the western end of the Trail and a widespread dread of it. Shively, of the Oregon emigration, wrote vaguely but grandly in his guide (published in 1846): "I left you at the sink of Mary's river, — take a due west course 40 miles to the foot of the Cascade mountain.

This mountain is a smasher." And Jefferson, who went to California with wagons in 1846, crossing the "Desert of Utariah" by Hastings' Cut-off, which he labeled "The fearful long drive   83 miles no grass nor water," wrote on his Map at the Truckee, where he crossed into California: "The western descent of these mountains is the most rugged and difficult portion of the whole journey."

At the City of Rocks Bruff purchased from a young Mormon and copied into his notebook a brief handwritten "Best Guide to the Gold Mines" over the Carson route — the "Mormon route," "pioneered" from the California side with what courageous toil by himself and other homefaring members of the disbanded Mormon Battalion in the summer of 1848, Bigler records in his "Diary of a Mormon" (MS, Bancroft Library). This guide we have identified as that described by Mrs. Sarah Royce, who has preserved in her *Frontier Lady* the name of the author and sufficient information to demonstrate that it is the one copied by Bruff. She states that it was written by "Ira J. Willes [Willis], GSL City." Bigler, at work under Marshall at Coloma when gold was discovered January 24, 1848, states that Ira Willis and his brother Sidney were at the flouring mill near Sutter's Fort at the time, that they visited Coloma late in February, and that on their return they prospected down the American River, locating the celebrated Mormon Island on March 4 ("Diary," *passim*). The existence of a Mormon guide of this character has been known for some time and has been a puzzle to many. Bruff's is the first copy to be located, but we have now found another, in the "Journal of Philip Badman" (MS, Coe Collection, Yale University), and doubtless others may come to light.

Bruff's copy of Willis' guide, designed to be sold on the California Trail at that hub of intersections where the Oregon Trail, the California Trail, and the Great Salt Lake City road converge, begins there, at the City of Rocks. As a matter of fact, this trail continued from the City of Rocks to GSL City (about 170 miles), a route unknown until the summer of 1848. Samuel J. Hensley, whom Bigler met near Gravelly Ford on the Humboldt, returning from Washington where he had been a witness at Frémont's court-martial, gave the Mormons a "waybill" of his route, and this they followed, turning right at the City of Rocks into his trace.

Hensley had left Salt Lake City intending to take Hastings' Cut-off. Missing his way, he returned to the City and, to avoid a north travel of nearly 300 miles to Fort Hall via Fort Bridger and Soda Springs and a corresponding though shorter southward journey over the old trail to regain his same latitude, he struck boldly north, northwest from GSL City, hoping to intersect the California Trail by traversing the short base of the tall triangle apexed by Fort Hall. This he did at the "Twin Sisters" (City of Rocks). The returning Mormons, likewise dreading the extra "8 or ten days travel" to Fort Hall and down, searched, found, and made their own the short cut pioneered by Hensley — a short cut so timesaving that its very genesis was soon lost sight of. Like water seeking its level, settlers, gold seekers, and Mormons poured over it, making it a vital link in reaching the West.

Hastings' Cut-off, itself a valuable short cut to California when compared to the alternate route from GSL City via Fort Hall, lost that advantage when Hensley opened the trail from Salt Lake City to the City of Rocks. Thus to Hensley belongs the credit of outmoding the Fort Hall route from GSL City and Hastings' Cut-off as well; but even Stansbury, visiting GSL City in 1849, attributed the newer shorter route exclusively to the Mormons (*Exploration . . . of the Valley of the Great Salt Lake*, pp. 75-76).

Joseph B. Chiles, likewise returning to California from the Frémont trial, also shortened the road to California. Setting out, like Hensley, to take Hastings' Cut-off, he led his forty-eight wagons over a modified and shortened version of this trail and likewise met Bigler, at or near Martin's Fork on the Humboldt. He too gave the Mormons a waybill of his route, but this they were unable to find. Apparently they supplied in return information as to the road they had just made over the Carson Pass, for Chiles took his wagons into California over this route. When he reached the Sink of the Humboldt, instead of following the trail to the Truckee River and thence south along the foot of the Sierra to the Carson — the Battalion route — Chiles opened a road direct from the Sink to the Carson River — again the base of a triangle instead of two sides. Like the Salt Lake City–City of Rocks link, this short cut became absorbed into the Mormons' route (as in the Willis guide), and over it in the next few years passed thousands of travelers unconscious of their debt to Chiles.

Peter Lassen, a major figure in Bruff's narrative, also went East for Frémont's court-martial and, on his return in 1848, like Chiles and Hensley pioneered a new route, the Lassen Trail, into California.

At the turn-off from the Humboldt to the Lassen Trail, Bruff copied into his journal (P 5) "The Cherrokee Guide" — perhaps borrowed from one of his fellow travelers. This is practically identical with Jesse Applegate's "Way Bill from Fort Hall to Willamette Valley," printed in *The Oregon Spectator*, April 6, 1848, and entered by Israel F. Hale in his diary as the route taken by him from the *New York Herald* (not published with his diary in the *Quarterly of the Society of California Pioneers*, but kindly made available to us by Mrs. H. P. Van Sicklen). This route was of interest to all Forty-Niners who took the Lassen Trail — which Hale, with unconscious humor, refers to as "the rout" — since the Lassen Trail followed this southern Oregon route as far as the foot of Goose Lake.

The latter part of the Lassen Trail was especially wearing. Shortly before Bruff and his company reached Goose Lake, Lieut. R. S. Williamson, second in command of the ill-fated Warner expedition to the sources of Pit River and beyond, wrote and posted near the lake, over his signature, a true account of distances and difficulties from that point to Lassen's Rancho. Bruff, finding this notice tacked to a tree, promptly copied it into his notebook.

In addition to these sources of information, many pages of routes and distances, gathered from fellow emigrants and from travelers returning from California (notably Lieut. Hawkins, eastward bound from Oregon; and Thomas Rhoads, "of Brannan's Mormon party," returning to Great Salt Lake, both of whom Bruff met on the Humboldt) were set down by him in his notebooks. All of this goes to show that Bruff spared himself no pains in his study of the route and its variants. A cartographer himself, maps and descriptions of natural features bore for him especial significance.

Much of his material is fugitive. All is of value. We regret that, owing to limitations of space, it has been impossible to include most of it in this edition. Students of the overland routes of 1849 will find in Bruff's shorter accounts and in Appendix VIII of the first edition information of interest.

To summarize, Bruff showed marked acumen in his choice of routes until the Lassen Trail was reached. Here he decided like the majority of the emigration about him, a decision caused, perhaps, by a belief that those who laid out this Trail from Goose Lake to the mines intended to follow the Cow Creek route to the Sacramento. Army officers and government appointees, as well as emigrants of intelligence, chose the Lassen route in preference to the more southern routes, believing it to be the shortest and best way to the mines, the Sacramento, and the Golden Gate, and, so far as the crossing of the Sierra was concerned, they were right. Lassen's, or Fandango Pass, is incomparably easier than either the Truckee or the Carson Pass. It was the desert stretches after leaving the Humboldt and the difficult terrain beyond Goose Lake, as well as its length, that made this Trail so hard and brought it into disrepute. Even so, Maj. Rucker, in charge of the Government relief on all the incoming trails, reported to Gen. Persifor F. Smith (Dec. 20, 1849): "Although the distance [via the Lassen Trail] is much greater than by the old routes, and some of the emigrants were much longer in getting in, I cannot but think it a fortunate circumstance they did so, for the loss of property would have been greater on the old trail, as the grass would all have been eaten off long before they could have arrived."

Bruff's company was called "The Washington City and California Gold Mining Association." He also speaks of it as the Washington City Mining Company and the Washington City Company. A revised list of its members appeared in the *Intelligencer* (April 2):

The California Mining Association

Some correction being necessary in the List of Members of the "Washington City and California Mining Association," which we published a day or two ago, a friend has furnished us with the following, which is in every respect a correct list, designating the officers and giving the names and ages of all the members, together with the place of their late residence   The company will leave here this evening:

John M. Farrar, director, aged 59, Washington.

John Cameron, director and committee, 50, Georgetown.

Richard I. A. Culverwell, 48, Washington.

James Wardell, 48, Georgetown.

William H. Dietz, director, 43, Washington.

William Franklin, 43, Washington.

J. Goldsborough Bruff, president, 43, Washington.

Charles Fenderich, lithographer, 43   do.

William J. Stoops, 41, Georgetown.

Josias B. Hills, 40, Washington.

William Pope, 40   do.

John Bates, 34   do.

Edwin D. Slye, director and committee, 33, Washington.

David Fowble, 32, Washington.

C. Columbus McLeod, 32, Washington.

Robert Slight, 31,   do.

Josias C. Willis, 31, Baltimore.

Henry Vermillion, 31, Washington county, Md.

Joseph Thaw, 30, Washington.

Stephen J. Cassin, 30, Georgetown.

Gideon Brooke, vice president, 29, Washington.

George A. Young, 28, New Jersey.

Asaph H. Parish, secretary, 38, Washington.

B. Brooke Edmonston, treasurer, 27, do.

Wm. Jewell, jr., director and committee, 27, Georgetown.

William Barker, 27, Washington.

Charles Reed, 26, Boston.

Thomas B. Scott, 26, Washington.
L. A. Iardella, 26,   do.
Charles Bishop, 25,   do.
John V. Ennis, 25,   do.
Oscar B. Queen, 25,   do.
Thomas J. Griffeth, 25, do.
Joseph C. Riley, 25,   do.
Thomas Williams, 25,   do.
Augustus S. Capron, 25, Laurel, Prince George's co. Md.
H. C. Dorsey, artist, 25, Alexandria, Va.
Charles G. Alexander, 24, King George county, Va.
B. Franklin Burche, 24, Washington.
Daniel R. Wall, 24,   do.
Thos. P. Kingsbury, 24, do.
John T. Coumbs, 24,   do.
Alex. Garratt, ensign, 23, do.
Stephen S. Culverwell, 22, do.
Wm. W. Lloyd, 22,   do.
Joseph Murphy, 22,   do.
Gregory J. Ennis, 22,   do.
Henry J. Queen, 22,   do.
Wm. P. Hilleary, 22,   do.
Richard Washington, 22, Westmoreland county, Va.
C. G. Moxley, 21, Anne Arundel county, Md.
J. W. Marden, 21, Prince George's county, Md.
Fielder M. Magruder, 21, Washington.
James Foy, blacksmith, 21, do.
Samuel D. Lewis, 20,   do.
William Truman, 20,   do.
F. R. Windsor, 20, Alexandria, Va.
John Young Donn, 19, Washington.
Isaac E. Owen, 19,   do.
James H. Barker, 18,   do.
James A. Ennis, 17,   do.
George Byington, 15,   do.
Henry Austin, physician, 32, Maryland.
Matthew M. Treppnell, — , Boston.

Sixty-four members, consisting of twelve carpenters and mechanics of different kinds.

Similar lists of the company members, with negligible differences in spelling, but all substantially correct, appeared in the *New-York Tribune*, April

4, 1849; the St. Louis *Daily Missouri Republican*, April 16; the St. Joseph *Gazette* and the St. Joseph *Adventure*, May 4; and in Haskins' *Argonauts* (p. 405). In one of Bruff's notebooks is a "Roll" of the company, dated August 4, 1849, and containing sixty-three names. That of Bishop, who died of cholera on the Platte, is of course omitted; also that of Culverwell, Senior, left at Fort Kearny on account of ill health. The name of Matthew M. Trepnell (or Tepprell, or Teprell) and that of W. J. Stoops do not appear in the Roll, and we may assume that they were not with the party at that time. Perhaps these men left the company before the start from St. Joseph, or even earlier. Bruff's Roll contains the names [Thadeus] Provost and [Henry] Wright, both of which appear in the Missouri lists, though not in the *Intelligencer*, and in addition the name of Totten, which appears nowhere else. We can only suppose that a few last-minute adjustments occurred. In fact, Bruff wrote, before leaving St. Joseph: "One of our members who is in rather bad health left to-day to return home: and a young man well known to the Company, from St. Louis, is elected in his place." This new member may have been Totten, or perhaps Provost or Wright, replacing Trepnell or Stoops.

On April 15, before leaving St. Louis, Bruff wrote of another unexpected change in personnel:

Here too, a friend of mine, a member of our company, expected to meet his son, who was in government employ at Fort Leavenworth. The father soon returned from the appointed place of meeting in an agony of grief, for his son was dead, a victim of cholera but a few days previous; and I advised the broken-hearted parent to return to his afflicted family, but he resolved to go on.

The name of father and son is nowhere mentitoned, but the following (*New-York Tribune*, April 17, 1849) may afford a clue to their identity:

We make the following extracts from a letter in the *St. Louis Republican*: St. Joseph, Mo. April 2, 1849 — A young man by the name of John B. Dietz, formerly of Washington City, suddenly died at Weston a few days sidce [since], under circumstances painful in the extreme. A wager was laid with a friend that he could drink the most liquor, to test which he filled a pint glass with brandy and drank it down; scarcely had the last mouthful been swallowed before he fell back senseless, and in a few minutes was a corpse. The deceased is of highly respectable connexion, to whom his untimely end will cause much suffering.

Presumably "William H. Dietz, director, 43, Washington," was the bereaved father. This surmise is borne out by the fact that the *Register of All Officers and Agents, Civil, Military, and Naval* for the year 1847 lists John Y. B. Dietz, place of birth unknown, War Department, paymaster's clerk, employed in Missouri, at a salary of $500 per annum. Bruff notes later:

The member who lost his son, is conducting himself singularly, and I am afraid his bereavement has affected his intellect. — This I have communicated to some of my friends, who concur with me, but many of the men are much irritated, in consequence of his conduct towards them.

Dietz persisted in making the trip to California, though later in the journey separating himself to some extent from the company and traveling with a comrade to the rear of the rest.

A memorandum on the company formation, in one of Bruff's notebooks (probably worked out by him in St. Joseph) indicates a total membership at the time of 64 — "6 messes of 11 men each," this reduced to 64 since there were only 9 in Bruff's mess, No. 1.

No 1 Mess, Bruff, Brooks, Edmonston, Parish, Bates, McLeod, Griffith, Owen, Stinson

Sentinels, as many as requisite, on duty 2 hours, day & night, throughout the roll, consecutively. Those on night guard, in Tents, must sleep next the door, so as to prevent disturbance of those not on guard.

Each member of the company was to stand guard once in twenty-four hours. Bruff's name appears in the first watch. Although his other duties were heavy, he took his turn in the early part of the trip, to encourage the others.

Nine months after the start from Washington, stormstaid and sick on the western slope of the Sierra Nevada, deserted by his company, Bruff wrote a request for aid, which his comrade, a chance traveler and fellow Mason who had tarried for weeks to help him, was to carry down to the Settlements. The only member of his company included there is the surgeon, Dr. Henry Austin, and Bruff adds significantly: *"Note* — I want no assistance, only as far as information of others, from members of old Compy except Dr. Austin — " Thus were his hopes for the party shattered by the trip across the plains.

However, on the April day set for the start from Washington, Bruff was as yet ignorant of the miseries before him, pleasurably engaged in launching the great enterprise. A further and final paragraph of the document in Bruff's handwriting cited above (pp. xviii, xxxiii) gives us a glimpse of the company's departure:

The 2nd day of April, 1849, was one of the most eventful, perhaps, to many, than any other circumstance in the City's history, since its occupancy by the British troops in August, 1814 — (of which, though only 10 yrs of age then, I recollect much) At 9 A.M. Sharp, by order, and advertisement, my Company was paraded, armed and equipped, (according to law,) on the pavement of Lafayette Square, opposite to the White House, and soon after, the gallant Light Infantry, Capt. Tait,* who had most courteously tendered us their services as an escort, with a fine band, came up and took post on our right. Some instructions to my squad about breaking into columns of 6, and we shouldered, broke into columns, and crossed over to the Executive Mansion, formed line in front and ordered arms. Then the conjoined officers and friends proceeded up the steps and into the great hall, and were presented to his excellency "Old Zac Taylor" — I explained the situation and circumstances, and informed him of the strength and character of my Company, its destination &c. and that many of my men had held positions here, in the executive department. That as we were on the eve of an extraordinary journey, of great extent, and which must be fraught with ardious trials, seasoned, perhaps with a due quantum of perils, &c and that most probably many of us, would never again have the pleasure of greeting him; I considered it a duty to make the call, bid him farewell, and with our fervent wishes for his continued good health. Pressing my hand warmly in both of his, he thanked me,

*[Joseph B. Tate, founder, Washington *Star*.]

Here this document breaks off, but Bruff gives the conclusion in the opening chapter of his later account:

Old "Rough and Ready" received us in his blandest and frankest manner, but expressed regret that there had been no pre-announcement [of] our visit, as he would otherwise have addressed the whole company from the portico; but as it was, he could only shake me heartily by the hand, and request that I would assure my company of his best wishes for their success in an enterprise at once so adventurous in spirit and laudable in its object. With this we withdrew, alas! never to see the gallant old General again.

The *Register of All Officers* has been consulted, with disappointing results. This, a biennial publication, appeared in the years 1847 and 1849. Apparently the names of government employees in Bruff's company had been dropped before the issue of the 1849 edition. In the 1847 issue Bruff appears as a "clerk" in the War Department, Bureau of Topographical Engineers, compensation $1,000 per annum; William N. Barker, born in Pennsylvania, clerk, Treasury Department, salary $1,150 per annum; William H. Dietz, born in Pennsylvania, one of the clerks of the surveys, Treasury Department, General Land Office, salary $1,260 per annum; Samuel Lewis (no middle initial), born in England, clerk, Treasury Department, $1,000; Asaph H. Parish, born in New York, clerk, Treasury Department, salary $1,000 per annum. These salaries seem at first thought pitifully small. However, if one considers the scale of payment then prevailing (in other words, before California gold lowered the value of the dollar) — $5,000 per annum for the Chief Justice of the Supreme Court, $1,500 for the Librarian of the Library of Congress — Bruff's reference to his remunerative employment is understandable.

The Washington City directories for the period are equally barren of information. Bruff is listed in 1846 as "draughtsman & artist," north side of Louisiana Avenue, between 9th and 10th Streets West. The names of Gregory Ennis, John M. Farrar, Chas. Fenderich (lithographer, east side of Pennsylvania Avenue, between 10th and 11th Streets West, north center), David Fowble, William Pope, Thomas Williams, and W. H. Dietz (north side of F Street, between 11th and 12th Streets West) appear in the 1846 or 1850 issues. In both issues, however, appear individuals with names like those of company members except for a different middle initial or similar slight change, suggesting, as Bruff implies, that various relatives of his associates in government employ were members of the Washington City Company.

Only one man on the company roster — Charles Fenderich, "lithographer, 43," of Washington, was known to fame in 1849. According to Bruff, Fenderich was a Swiss and had been long resident in this country. His series of portraits of political celebrities of the time had attracted considerable attention, and his lithographic skill had long been recognized. Mr. Harry T. Peters, in *America on Stone* (pp. 185–86), says:

Besides doing many excellent portraits for Lehman & Duval and P. S. Duval of Philadelphia, and portraits, military and naval views for E. Weber of Baltimore, Fenderich himself lithographed and issued at the first address above [8 North 3d Street, Philadelphia]: "Sergeant Ands. Wallace, aged 104 years. A Veteran of the Revolution, the Rescuer [of] Lafayette's at the Battle of Brandywine. . . . Philada. published and sold for the Benefit of Mr. Wallace. Fenderich del. 1833." . . . In 1837–1841 Fenderich made and issued a series of political portraits at Washington, bound in yellow paper with a printed cover, and title-page. The cover reads: "Fenderich's Port Folio of Living American Statesmen: embracing the Executive Officers of Government, Distinguished Members of Both Houses of Congress, and others of All Parties. Drawn from Life and Lithographed by Charles Fenderich. . . . The Lithographic Repository, on Pennsylvania Avenue." He seems to have done both good and interesting work. Little seems to be recorded of him.

The New York Public Library reports, in its Print Collection, twenty-one lithographs by Fenderich, all portraits bearing dates between 1837 and 1848.

Fenderich reached California with the company and late in the fall of 1850 lay ill of a fever in San Jose, at one time his death being reported. Bruff, the following May, met him in San Francisco: "I was much gratified to-day, to meet my worthy friend Fenderich, the artist, recently arrived from San Jose

. . . nearly recovered from his severe illness." He is listed in the San Francisco directories, 1858-84, as "artist," but his work during this period seems to have been small in quantity. While unrecorded in *California on Stone*, Fenderich did execute some portraits in California, notable among these being that of "Peter Lassen. Chas Fenderick, del." in *The Hesperian*, August, 1859. The same volume contains a portrait of Isaac J. Sparks, "Chas Fenderick del.," and Wagner records the making of a "crayon likeness" of Ferdinand C. Ewer in 1859. "The artist was a Mr. Fenderich" (see *Calif. Hist. Soc. Quart.*, Dec., 1934).

One of the company, Charles Bishop, referred to above, succumbed to cholera on the march, after a few hours' illness, and was buried in the Platte River country, near Horse Creek, July 8, 1849. The company paused for twenty-four hours — a tribute not always paid to death on the march to California, where haste was the order of the day — and, in recognition of Bishop's service in the Mexican War, accorded him a military funeral.

The two Culverwells, Richard I. A. (or J.?) Culverwell, the father, forty-eight years old, and Stephen S. Culverwell, the son, twenty-two years old, both of Washington, are intriguing figures. Stephen Culverwell, the son, had previously visited California. According to William Heath Davis (*Seventy-Five Years in California*, pp. 111-12), young Culverwell was a powder boy on the frigate "United States," commanded by Commodore Thomas ap Catesby Jones, at the time of the abortive capture of Monterey in 1842. Culverwell says in his account (incorporated by Davis) that he was then a lad of sixteen, which would make him in 1849 twenty-three years old (given on the company list as twenty-two). He completed a three-year cruise to various Pacific ports under Commodore Jones, this being in 1842 about half done. Davis states that at the time Stephen Culverwell gave him the story (1889), he resided in San Francisco. Bancroft (*Chronicles*, VI, 311) mentions "S. S. Culverwell," chosen vice president "at the first annual election of officers of the San Diego and San Bernardino company," 1872, when the railway was being organized. It is believed that Stephen Culverwell left descendants in California, but so far this has not been established. Tentative support for this theory may be found in *Fifty Years of Masonry in California*. This work lists a Stephen Richard Culverwell as Grand Master of California Lodge No. 1 in San Francisco in 1898. It would be reasonable to infer that this might be Stephen Culverwell's son, uniting in his name those of his father and grandfather.

Richard Culverwell, the father, fell ill early on the march to California and was left by the company at Fort Kearny. Bruff says:

One, I find, I must leave, a too elderly man is in such feeble health that he cannot proceed, with us. (Mr. Culverwell) and we shall leave him here. I proposed to the company to vote him $75 with sufficient rations, which they have done. I advised him to remain till he recovered, and then to accompany the first train in to Missouri, and so get home. — His son, a hearty and intelligent man, (a good carpenter,) continues with us.

In March, 1851, the son called upon Bruff in San Francisco and informed him that the father had recovered from his illness, had proceeded to Salt Lake City with a Mormon family, "and from thence — with many others, accompanied some Mormons to come here [California], by a new southern route; and that his father and others perished on a desert."

This scene of Culverwell's death, this "desert," was Death Valley, though Bruff nowhere uses that name, even in his later version or on his map. Culverwell is a familiar figure in the 1849 records of Death Valley and one about whom tantalizingly little has been known. As one student of Death Valley history wrote: "Culverwell is one of the unexplained characters." Manly, perhaps the best-known of the Death Valley Forty-Niners and of course personally acquainted with Richard Culverwell, tried in vain to find the Culverwell family in the East. Returning to California by the Isthmus of Panama in the spring or early summer of 1851, he paused in New Orleans where he was to take ship for Chagres, and

went on board the steamer Falcon, in command of a government officer, to try to learn something about the family of Capt. Culverwell who perished alone in Death Valley. He [Culverwell] told me he had once belonged to the Navy and had his life insured, and as I was an important witness for his family I wanted to learn where they lived. The Captain looked over a list of officers, but Culverwell's name was not there. I then wrote a letter to Washington stating the facts of his death, and my own address in Sacramento. . . . I never received an answer.

In Salt Lake City Culverwell allied himself with five other men California-bound — Fish, Hadapp, Isham, Nusbaumer, and Smith. Their story is told by one of them, Louis Nusbaumer ("Adventures of a Trip to the Gold Fields of California. May 20, 1849 to June 19, 1850," MS, Bancroft Library), first cited in connection with Death Valley in the first edition of *Gold Rush*. Nusbaumer's original diary, written in German (photostat, Bancroft Library) confirms our surmise (1st ed., p. 1228) that "Graham" in the translation should read "Isham."

Leaving Salt Lake City October 7, 1849, the six men overtook Capt. Jefferson Hunt, pilot of the Mormon train, left him, followed Smith, left Smith, traveled with Town, left Town, and joined forces with the Bennetts — names all famous in the annals of Death Valley. On December 28 Nusbaumer, Hadapp, and Culverwell, "der zu krank ist um mit den and. weit zu gehen," Nusbaumer wrote, remained in camp (near Furnace Creek); they reached Bennett's Camp January 13, 1850. Fish, Isham, and Smith went on, in the wake of the Jayhawkers, to their death.

The Death Valley Forty-Niners, the shifting memberships of the various parties and their crisscrossing trails, present problems not all of which have been solved. Suffice it to say here that the Nusbaumer account introduces new figures into the tragedy — the make-up of his party and Schlögel being hitherto unmentioned in Death Valley history — and new data for the computation of the dates of Manly and Rogers' journey to the Settlements for help and their classic rescue of the few survivors. As Manly says, "the accuracy of the calendar was among the least of our troubles," and Nusbaumer's day-by-day entries serve as a check, indicating that Manly in his recollections placed the journeys about fourteen days too early.

February 7, 1850, Nusbaumer, Hadapp, Anton Schlögel, and six other men, among them probably the Earharts, left their camp (below Bennett's Camp), on the Wade trail, the Wades having gone ahead "on foot to help" presumably followed by Culverwell from Bennett's Camp (L. Burrell, "Across the Plains in 1849," 1894). The next day's entry — unfortunately mutilated — reads: "sah ich den im Anfange . . . Colwerwell von Washing[ton] . . . Gegen 5 Uhr Abends hatt . . . zurückzubleiben da . . . seiner nahen Auflösung . . . ohne etwas zu essen n . . . andern Tags ging ich . . . wo der Rest unserer . . . geschlagen hatte."

One gains the impression that Nusbaumer, himself without food or water, finding Culverwell in extremis, stayed with him to the end, and, it may be, carried the news of his death to the son in California, since Nusbaumer records, March 10, 1850: "In Pueblo de los Angeles die Nachricht erhalten dass Fish & Isham der Hunger erlegen sind & Smith von den Peyuths getödtet wurde & so wären von den sechsen [Culverwell, Fish, Hadapp, Isham, Nusbaumer, and Smith] Niemand als Hadapp & ich selbst über."

This place of Culverwell's death tallies with Manly's finding of the body about ten miles from Bennett's Camp and with Almira Wade's recollection of Culverwell overtaking the Wades at a dry camp: "As they could not help him, he went on." Manly, in his incomparable account, says:

He did not look much like a dead man. He lay upon his back with arms extended wide, and his little canteen, made of two powder flasks, lying by his side. . . . I afterwards learned that he could not keep up with them [the Wades?] and turned to go back to the wagons again, and perished, stretched out upon the sand as we saw him. . . . Not a morsel to eat, and the little canteen by his side empty.

Bruff on his large map, at a point far out on the desert, wrote: "Death of Culverwell, Feby 10, 1850." Thus Captain Culverwell, a derelict, wandering from party to party, his last despairing quest for food and water denied, came to rest.

Piloting the Bennett and the Arcane families out, on their long, slow march to the Settlements, Manly made the first night's camp a mile before reaching Culverwell's body.

The second morning Manly climbed the mountain slope with Bennett and Arcane, to view the limitless panorama of desert and mountain behind and before them. Culverwell's body, entombed in the sands by Rogers and Bennett, lay but a few miles below. Who shall say that that sad burial was not in Manly's mind when, as he says, he gave Death Valley the name it bears today? "Just as we were ready to leave and return to camp," he writes, "we took off our hats, and then overlooking the scene of so much trial, suffering and death spoke the thought uppermost saying: — '*Good bye Death Valley!*' "

With a sort of intellectual perversity, the charge is sometimes made that the hardships of the Overland Trail are unduly emphasized, that the Argonauts, as a well-known historian put it, were having the time of their lives. There is a certain superficial truth in this that arrests the attention: no doubt in general it was the adventurous, the questing, those of whom it could rightfully be said

> Out with great mirth that do desire
> Hazard of trackless ways

who were especially drawn to the undertaking. But there the verisimilitude ends. Starvation was as painful; extremes of heat, cold, and dust as wearing; and cholera, scurvy, dysentery, and Indian arrows as deadly to them as to other human beings. As Chittenden says: "If the Trail was the scene of romance, adventure, pleasure, and excitement, so it was marked in every mile of its course by human misery, tragedy, and death."

Brier, a child of six in the Death Valley emigration, spoke more than sixty years later of "the protracted rage of thirst"; and Manly, reliving in memory the sufferings of the Forty-Niners in Death Valley, wrote: "People who have always been well fed, and have never suffered from thirst till every drop of moisture seemed gone from the body, so that they dare not open their mouth lest they dry up and cease to breathe, can never understand, nor is there language to convey the horrors of such a situation."

Of the initiates of such hard fortune, to its fatal end, was Captain Culverwell.

Several emigrants traveled with the company up the Platte. On June 24, 1849, Bruff wrote (H 3): "A gentleman, known to many of my men, came up, desiring to join the company: I called a meeting, and he was permitted, on certain terms, to accompany us." This may have been one "Hume Young," mentioned by Bruff in his notebooks as being with the company for a time, or it may have been "E. S. Seymour," whose *Emigrant's Guide* we referred to above.

A family named Thomas was also permitted to travel up the Platte under the protection of the company and joined it before the Fourth of July. The committee in charge of the company's celebration for that day requested that "each member will appear in uniform, (if not too much defaced) at all events dress neat, as Ladies will be present."

The company suffered the usual vicissitudes of such overland travel: day after day of monotonous marching — Bruff himself said at the Soda Springs on Bear River that he had walked from the frontier, a distance of 1,200 miles; camp at the close of each day's march, with sometimes game, or fish seined from the rivers; heat and cold, dust and storm; and always the anxiety as to grass and water. A wagon capsized, the stock stampeded, an overcharged gun exploded, a man run over by a wagon, a death from cholera, a hunter unhorsed in a buffalo hunt — such were the common incidents of the California Trail.

Disaffection and dissension split the company, as it did practically every band that crossed the plains. Guard duty, which Bruff, with his military training, insisted upon rigorously — and properly — as a precaution against Indian attack, was the principal cause of complaint. Many companies dissolved their bonds soon after crossing the frontier, and few organizations continued to function as a unit until they reached California. Bruff records (H 3) that at Fort Kearny his friend, Colonel Bonneville, the commandant, of Washington Irving fame, predicted trouble for him:

Col. Bonneville kindly insisted on my being his guest while here. . . . Dined with my friends, at the fort. The colonel has related some amusing anecdotes, illustrative of the effects of the march on the pious gold pilgrims. As thousand[s] were camped opposite the fort — on the plain, he had an excellent opportunity of observing them. — Several joint stock companies, with sworn "Constitutions," have dissolved, fought, d——d every thing, and divided their property. . . . He says I have a most trying, thankless, and unenviable task in this matter myself, and he thinks, that if with extraordinary patience, forbearance, and determination, I succeed in keeping the Company together, to California, I shall do wonders.

Nevertheless, by October 21, 1849, Bruff had brought the Washington

City and California Gold Mining Association to the western outpost of the Sierra Nevada, at a point barely thirty-five miles from the Sacramento River. Its members, compared with many in the emigration, had fared well. None was as yet starving, none ill of scurvy or fevers. None had been killed by Indians. At this point Bruff became convinced of the futility of trying to get the remaining company wagons into the Settlements, so bad was the road — or trail — and so reduced the mules. The company, like all the emigrants on the Lassen Trail, were practically out of provisions and much worn down. Indeed the lot of the emigrant on the latter part of the Trail — whatever the route he chose into California — was hard.

Bruff here resigned his leadership to the second in command (George A. Young, elected vice-president August 14, to replace Gideon Brooke, or Brooks), and settled down on this spot, later known as Bruff's Camp, to guard the company property until it could be sent for. Here terminated his official connection with the Washington City Company. Bruff's Camp is on the ridge above Mill Creek, in the western part of the present Tehama County, California. The Forest Service, whose members were helpful to us in locating this spot, have erected a temporary marker, giving some of this information, in commemoration of Captain Bruff, and once more the hilltop camp where he spent so many weary weeks bears his name.

Conditions of transcontinental travel have changed inconceivably in the past hundred years. In 1849 two natural factors, gentle but inexorable, limited movement across the western half of our continent — the spring growth of grass from the Missouri frontier westward for the sustenance of stock, in late April or early May; and the down-drifting Sierra snow, in late October or early November — leaving barely six months for oxen, cows, mules, horses, and "shank's mare" to cover 2,000 miles of practically virgin terrain. The utter strangeness of this no-man's land is attested even by the inscriptions on the graves that lined the route: "May he rest peaceably in this savage unknown country," read one, recorded by Bruff. Thousands of wagons and scores of thousands of animals cut the prairie sod and churned the sandy desert, until, as Wistar said, emigrant trains became moving canopies of dust. They crawled up mountains, forded streams, and crept down slopes such as Ash Hollow, that "hung a little past the perpendicular." Many emigrants knew nothing about the handling of animals. "A wild, unbroken mule," remarked Kimball Webster, whose company and that of Bruff passed and repassed on the Trail, "is the most desperate animal that I have ever seen." But thousands who had never coped with such conditions before learned to shape their lives in accordance with them. Out of the fullness of his experience, in these respects the common lot of the emigration of '49, Bruff wrote:

> To travel o'er the rocky ridge,
> And down the rugged mountain side;
> To sleep within a jungle hedge, —
> Or on the grassy prairie wide. —
> With fire blazing at his feet,
> To scare away the panther bold; —
> To eat, by mountain brook, his meat, —
> To suffer heat, fatigue, and cold; —
> These the advent'er's certain fate, —
> Who travels o'er, from sea to sea, —
> Columbia's continent-estate, —
> The sea-girt homestead of the free.

Thus the generation of today, that has been granted the psalmist's prayer for the wings of a dove, even to the silver lining, that may breakfast in New York and dine in San Francisco, that has seen the country between the Pacific and the Missouri spanned in non-stop flight in less than six hours, may be pardoned for not realizing that less than a hundred years ago four months from the Missouri to the Sacramento was good time, three months speedy, and that Captain Bruff, setting out from Washington at the head of his company on April 2, 1849, did very well to arrive with them at the Sierra rim above the Sacramento on October 21 of that year.

On looking over my notes [says Bruff], I find that we have travelled a distance of 2,061 miles, from the Missouri river, in 120 days (20 days halting, on the route) being $17\frac{1}{6}$ miles per day, very nearly. We have lost only 2 men, — one died with cholera, and one left at Grand Island, too sick to proceed. No accident, of any consequence has occurred to the men, nor have we been molested by Indians, though so many emigrants have. Our mules were too young, hence their failing so rapidly at this end of the route.

Truly a record to be proud of, and one indicative of the energy and ability of the commander.

But the company's sufferings, and especially those of the man who had captained it across the continent, were by no means terminated by arrival in California. The miner's life, seen close to, was not so full of ease as some accounts in the East had drawn it. Stillman, in his *Golden Fleece*, pictures the situation of such as these, from the physician's point of view, and declares that soon "nearly all were anxious to return, whether successful or not; but few were willing to go by the way they came," a commentary on the hardship of that travel.

The members of the company seem to have tried their luck at mining in many localities. We have not made undue effort to trace the histories of these individuals or of their descendants, except in cases of special interest. After all, Bruff's canvas is greater than the activities of the Washington City and California Gold Mining Company; it embraces the whole Great Migration, as he sometimes calls it, in its abounding variety and infinite detail. Except as they fit into this larger background, the company members possess no especial claim to attention. Furthermore, in some cases — as for instance that of the company member who treacherously left Bruff to die, as he must have thought, in the mountains — their descendants, if any, might not welcome the attention.

But the treachery of one or the ill-behavior of a few did not prejudice Bruff against the members of his company — "most of them sensible and well-intentioned men." Even his grim and protracted sufferings at Bruff's Camp in the winter of 1849-50, while he waited for the help that never came, did not seem to embitter him — except perhaps temporarily — against the members of his company. Here on Barclay Mountain, in the late fall of '49, he saw the latter part of the migration pass, warmed it at his fire, and fed it when he had food. Here, as the winter passed, he suffered near-starvation, storm, and cold.

Before he left California, in June, 1851, Bruff had again met many of his men, most of these having gone to some pains to seek him out. Burche, Byington (who came to apologize for his behavior on the Trail), Marden and Slight (on their way out from the Trinity), Windsor (on his way in to the Trinity mines), Parish and Henry Queen, and Wright came to Davis' or Lassen's Rancho to see him. In November, 1850, he read in a newspaper of the death of Bates in San Francisco; in December of that year he came upon Cassin and Murphy in the hospital at Sutter's Fort. At the beginning of December, 1850, he found Coombs "engaged in a store" in Sacramento and, from him or from some other acquaintance, learned that Farrar, Foible, Pope, and Truman had returned to "the States." In Sacramento, where he shared the living quarters of his friend, Dr. Austin, the company surgeon, he saw Marden, Riley, Windsor, and others. At Redwood Lake, in January, 1851, he met Williams, on his way from Klamath to Trinidad. In San Francisco, in the early part of 1851, Barker, Culverwell, Jr., Dorsey, Ennis, and others called at his lodgings.

The history of the company members seems to have resembled that of most other gold seekers, so far as the attainment of their immediate objective was concerned. Theodore T. Johnson, who made one of the shortest visits to California on record, arriving April 1, 1849, visiting Sacramento, Coloma, and points north, and returning to San Francisco in time to sail for home May 1, 1849, on the first southbound voyage of the "California," says in his *California and Oregon,* "In short, California is one vast lottery office — we hear of all the prizes, and of but few of the innumerable blanks."

Nor did Bruff fare better in this respect than his men. Regarding what must have been his deep disappointment, he is reticent, recording only a very unpleasant dream, in which he thought he was "abandoned by my family, my friends, and the whole world, because I had not found a gold mine."

4. THE BRUFF RECORDS

As indicated above, the Bruff records constitute an immense amount of material, some of which was inherited by Mrs. W. J. Procter, Captain Bruff's granddaughter (now part of the Coe Collection, Yale University Library), and some of which is the property of the Henry E. Huntington Library. For convenience, the documents in each of these two series have been numbered by us and further designated by the symbol "P" or "H" to indicate their source. This gives us the following records for the period from April 2, 1849, when Bruff left Washington, to July 20, 1851, when he got home: P 1, P 2, P 3, P 4, P 5, P 6, P 7, P 8, P 8 A, P 9, P 10, P 11, Supplementary A and Supplementary B (two larger notebooks which Bruff carried with him, in his luggage, but not in his pocket; they contain interesting information and many sketches, a number of which are reproduced in this volume); H 1, H 2, and H 3.

In addition, the P material includes a notebook with genealogical information, various papers in Bruff's handwriting, and other family documents. With these are several separate drawings, among them a panorama of Acapulco harbor, drawn by Bruff on the spot, June 23, 1851, and 8 feet $11\frac{3}{8}$ inches in length by $8\frac{1}{2}$ inches high. The Huntington Library, in addition to the three accounts mentioned above, has two series of drawings: 40 large ones in color and 224 in black and white, some of which are reproduced here. Many of these were evidently elaborated by Bruff from his cruder, earlier sketches in the P journals. Some of them have no prototypes there, and some of the earlier subjects are not found in the Huntington sketches, but there is a close correspondence between the two series.

In studying the wealth of combined Bruff material, sorting it by dates, arranging and rearranging, one fact at last assumed sudden importance — the four longer early records (P 1, H 1, P 7, and H 2) formed one continuous account, the shorter early records (P 2, P 3, P 4, P 5, P 6, P 8, P 8 A, P 9, P 10, and P 11) being the basis for these. In the first edition each of the longer early accounts was followed by the shorter, source accounts for the same period. In the present edition these shorter, pocket-notebook accounts, written on the march, have been omitted, resulting in an uninterrupted narrative of perhaps greater general appeal. Yet the student of early overland routes, of day-by-day life on the Trail, of the rosters of emigrant companies, of the Gold Rush in all its ramifications, will find the most rewarding information in the shorter, earliest accounts and in the notes and Appendices of the first edition. The P 9 record, for instance, a small thin leather-covered booklet which rested in Bruff's haversack when he came down to the Settlements, reflects in its pages the extremity of his physical condition, verging on collapse. It is almost illegible in places, the most difficult of all the Bruff documents to decipher, but it gives a far sharper and more truthful picture than the florid verbiage of his later versions (H 2 and H 3). It is axiomatic, of course, that the earlier such records, the more valuable historically.

We have no doubt that the text as presented in this edition — P 1, H 1, P 7, and H 2 — constituted for Bruff his satisfactory record, as prepared by him before sailing from San Francisco in June, 1851, and upon which in turn he based his elaborate 1853 version, written after his return to Washington.

For the period from October 9, 1850, to July 20, 1851, no comparable early records — either short or long — are known, except that part of the fragmentary "Summary of Events in 1850" (P 11) falls within this time. Probably — indeed we believe certainly — such records were made by Bruff, but their present whereabouts, if they are extant, is unknown. Were we to hazard a guess, it would be that a number of briefer records were made by Bruff in the field, upon which he perhaps based two fuller accounts, one from October 10, 1850, to June 14, 1851, when he sailed for home; the other from June 14 to July 20, covering the journey from San Francisco to Washington by the Isthmus of Panama. Since H 3, the later version (1853), is the only record known for this time, we have, by courtesy of the Huntington Library, used this as our text between the dates mentioned.

In addition, the H 3 account, from the beginning, April 2, 1849, to October 10, 1850, has been collated with the P and H records, significant differences and additional information being cited in the notes. Bruff thus virtually annotates the early records himself, furnishing in some cases identifying names and details.

The P 1 record, the earliest of all, was completed, we believe, not much, if any, after its closing date. The H 1 and the P 7 journals we place almost certainly in the winter of 1849–50, before Bruff came into the Settlements; and the H 2 record not later than Bruff's sojourn in San Francisco between his return from Trinidad on March 4, 1851, and his sailing for home on June 14, and possibly earlier.

In reducing to print any such longhand records, some changes must be made in the arrangement, unless one declines on a photostatic medium. We have tried to keep such compromises to a minimum. Bruff's spelling, punctuation, and capitalization have been followed, to the best of our judgment, great care having been taken in deciphering the records. Occasional marginal notes by him we have inserted in the text — at what we assume to be suitable points — in italic type within round parentheses. Abbreviations so contracted or unusual as to puzzle the reader and mystifying misspellings have been amplified or corrected by us, these insertions appearing in the text in roman type within square brackets. This has seemed to us more practical than to put the information into notes, separated in most cases by many pages from the text in question; nor has it seemed necessary to sign such brief insertions, their source and import being clear. These arrangements will, we trust, enable the reader to identify without trouble Bruff's marginal notes and our own slight emendations and will facilitate the reading of the records. To recapitulate, material in the text proper within round parentheses is Bruff's; that within square brackets, ours. At Bruff's Camp, in the winter of 1849-50, Bruff inked over some of the shorter P records and sketches. Apparently for his own convenience, he then lightly underscored certain proper names. This we have interpreted as nothing more than a mechanical timesaving device on his part, when searching for particular data. In the H 1 record some place and proper names and some events are underlined by a different hand — perhaps that of Elliott Coues. These we have not italicized, feeling that the placing of Bruff's marginal notes in italics, within parentheses in the text, already complicated the system. Otherwise no changes have been made in Bruff's text. In short, it has been our wish to present Bruff's records with precision, but without pedantry.

Bruff's map, to which he refers several times, was not among Mrs. Procter's papers which came to us. We early realized its potential value in connection with the plotting of his course and the editing of his records and determined to locate it. Unfortunately, this proved difficult. The Smithsonian Institution found no trace of it, though Bruff mentions it in his article on Indian petroglyphs in the Institution's *Annual Report* for 1872. The Huntington Library reported no copy in its possession. The Bancroft Library, that grand repository of Californiana, could throw no light on its whereabouts. The Society of California Pioneers, to which Bruff sent the map with his 1853 version, believed this to have been destroyed in the earthquake and fire of 1906, supposing it to have remained in the Society's possession after the manuscript was returned to Bruff. The Corps of Engineers (the heir of the Topographical Engineers), United States Army, examined its files, but to no avail.

As a last resort, recalling that Mr. Lathrop C. Harper had suggested that either the late Philip Lee Phillips or the late General Chittenden had brought the 1853 version to his brother's attention, we decided to ask the Library of Congress whether, in view of Mr. Phillips' well-known interest in such records, he might not have secured this map for that institution. To this inquiry Colonel Martin replied in due course that the files had been searched without success. He stated, however, that the Office of Indian Affairs had recently transferred to The National Archives "a manuscript sketch map of the Sierras that shows a route and may have been made in 1849," the authorship of which had not been established.

This proved to be Bruff's field map for the western end of the Trail. It shows the lower portion of Mary's River, with the turn-off to the Lassen Trail (a smaller sketch map of this, Mud Lake, Black Rock, and other points on the Lassen Trail appearing in the lower right-hand corner), and may well be the earliest and the only 1849 map of the Lassen Trail in its entirety. Upon this map Bruff also plotted his 1850 Gold Lake exploration, which terminated with the visit of his party to Honey Lake (the discovery of which he claims on the map), as he recounts. This map (see p. 562) was described by The National Archives as follows:

There is in The National Archives a map which lacks a title. . . . It appears to be a partially inked-in sketch map. There is marked on it an irregular route between the Lofty Hills turn of the Marys River in approximate Latitude 40°45′ North and Longitude 118°27′ West to Lawson's Rancho at the confluence of Deer Creek with the Sacramento River in approximately Latitude 39°55′ North and Longitude 121°55′ West. The map bears annotations. . . . Near the middle of the bottom appears the statement: 'Double Fremont's Scale.' The scale of the map is approximately 1:1,400,000, and the size is 12½ inches by 14½ inches. It is a colored manuscript map on paper.

In The National Archives this map was designated: "Records of the Office of Indian Affairs, Unnumbered map. [Portfolio C-368. Manuscript sketch map showing route of unidentified expedition in Sierra Nevada of California.]"

In addition to the above The National Archives contain the following:

Map of the United States and Their Territories between the Mississippi and the Pacific Ocean; and of Parts of Mexico. Compiled in the Bureau of the Corps of Topogl Engs. . . . 1850. Scale, 1 inch to 50 statute miles. Size, 49 x 40¼ inches to edge of the sheet. 42¼ x 37⅝ inches between the neat lines. Annotated colored printed map on paper.

This map has annotations initialed "J.G.B." It bears the official designation "Records of the Office of Indian Affairs, Map No. 228½, Tube No. 408½." (The official description of each of these maps has now been amended to include its identification as Bruff's work, with a reference to *Gold Rush* ["See especially the Introduction"]).

Also a later, finished map incorporating data from both the large map and the sketch map, bearing the endorsement "Topographic map of area from 106° to Pacific Ocean and from 38° to 44°N. probably associated with J. G. Bruff's Surveys," having been received from the Office of Indian Affairs at the same time as the two mentioned above. "Cantonment Loring," "Camp" above Mill Creek, "Lake Derby," and "Gold Bluffs," with other notations personal to Bruff, mark it indubitably his.

At first thought it seems odd that these maps, certainly the work of Bruff, found their way to the Office of Indian Affairs. Yet it was not until March, 1849, that that Office was separated from the War Department, where Bruff for many years had been attached to the Bureau of Topographical Engineers. In the Library of Congress and in The National Archives are identical MS Maps:

Map exhibiting the position of the Lands occupied by the Indian Tribes in amity with the United States; The Lands ceded to the United States by Treaty with various Indian Tribes. Compiled in the Bureau of Topographical Engineers from the Maps of Capt: W. Hood, T. E. and I. McCoy, Esq: (additions, in compliance with a Resolution of the Senate. 1839.) J. Goldsborough Bruff, Delinr

Indeed Bruff mentions in his work for the government: "Designs, maps, and other drawings for the Indian and Post-Office Departments." Furthermore, in a letter written in 1876 Bruff speaks of "a friend of mine, in the Indian Bureau," a circumstance which may help to explain the disposition of his maps. His Map of Indian lands, basic to this day, might explain too how Bruff came by his understanding of government relations with the Indians whose lands he traversed in 1849 — knowledge of great practical value in dealing with them.

The large map No. 228½ is undoubtedly that prepared by Bruff to accompany his 1853 version, which he sent with the manuscript to the Society of California Pioneers, and contains various entries in his hand. Near Fort Hall is inserted the notation: "With 4 men left the Compy & went to Fort Hall & reg [Cantonment Loring and the Mounted Riflemen]". The route of the company, as it proceeded through Emigrants' Cut-off, across to the Humboldt, down that stream, and into California by the Lassen Trail, is delineated, with the inscription: "Route of an expedition taken across in 1849 by J. G. Bruff." "Bruff's Camp winter 1849" is marked at the correct point on the ridge above Mill Creek in the Sierra Nevada. Bruff's journey to Trinidad is shown, with the words: "Route up in 1851 by J. G. Bruff and back," and Gold Bluffs, Upper, Middle, and Lower Stations, are indicated on the coast between

Klamath River and Trinidad. South from San Francisco the route follows the coast line: "Returning home in 1851." At the bottom of the map, off the Mexican coast, Bruff wrote: "To panama — 3 days of 1st week of July in panama; rode over the Isthmus to Chagres, took steamer to N.Y. via Island of Jamaica —" Many other notations of interest in Bruff's hand appear on this map, especially those relating to his 1850 exploration in California and information acquired by him, probably from Culverwell, Jr., on Death Valley.

Interesting as all his route maps are and valuable in connection with his narrative, they are likewise disappointing, for they incorporate errors which cannot but confuse any effort to plot Bruff's course in the localities affected. This is particularly true in the region between the Humboldt River and the Sierra Nevada, a district then but partly explored and thus not correctly mapped. Here we should bear in mind that scarcely five years had elapsed since Frémont led his men down from Winter Ridge and Summer Lake, through Surprise Valley, impatiently looking for the fabled Buenaventura River, which, he believed, would lead him very shortly to the Humboldt. Pyramid Lake lies roughly thirty miles east of Honey Lake; yet such were the cramping restrictions of geography as then understood that had Bruff plotted Honey Lake on his field map, based on that of Frémont, by his own dates and courses it would have lain directly north of Pyramid and would have coincided with part of "Lower Mud Lake."

Certainly the Topographical Engineers, in compiling their map of 1850, had the benefit of the latest information. But none knew better than Bruff the difficulties of map-making and its perils. "Subsequent explorations have established the topography of this country," he wrote on this large map, "and corrected errors that were unavoidable Due to compilations from mere hearsay incomplete reconnoisances." All in all, however, Bruff's maps enrich and complete his record.

Hulbert ("Crown Collection of American Maps," Series IV, Vol. IV, No. 3) considers the relative scarcity of Gold Rush records disappointing and a "striking commentary on the exceeding hardship of the journey." The majority of the surviving records — with some notable exceptions, of course — are, for reasons understandable but regrettable, brief — many of them bone-brief. They were designed to quicken the memory of the writer later or to preserve for his family the bare facts of his experience. But to Bruff, with a different purpose, all information was pertinent, all effort justified. He looked to a wider audience, and this, coupled with a naturally active mind and a sociable disposition, qualified him in an exceptional way.

On August 3, 1849, for instance, he and his company entered the desert stretch of Sublette's Cut-off, leading from the western summit of the Rocky Mountains to Green River, the "great Colorado of the West." After a morning's travel of twelve miles — a punishing march — the company halted at "10½ A.M." in the blazing sun and the deep dust "to noon." As they ate their lunch, a wagon drove up from the west. Nobody but Bruff was interested enough to investigate this chance arrival. "On going over, found Mr. Babbitt, with 2 lads, from Salt Lake, for the States, with the Mail, and the Mormon Memorial and Constitution, to submit to Congress." Before he left them, Bruff had examined the constitution, drawn up by the "provisional government of the territory of Deseret," found it beautifully engrossed, discussed its provisions with Babbitt, looked at some California gold from Salt Lake, inquired about the road ahead, and written a letter to his family in Washington for Babbitt to carry back. Government documents support Bruff's account.

On October 3, 1849, Bruff, emerging with his train through Lassen's Pass to the western side of the Warner Range of the Sierra Nevada, learned of the death of his friend, Capt. William H. Warner, U. S. Topographical Engineers, killed seven days before by hostile Indians some miles to the northeast, while conducting a government reconnaissance in search of a practicable railroad route through the Sierra Nevada. Bruff later encountered the remainder of Warner's party at several points and the next year met the Army detachment sent to avenge his death. Except for some errors in the initial statement given him by others regarding Warner's death, every entry of Bruff's checks, to the last detail, with government reports.

On October 6, 1849, Bruff and his company, traveling down the upper Pit River, met the government relief, sent out by Gen. Persifor F. Smith, commander of the Army in California, to bring in starving emigrants on the overland routes. Mindful of the terrible fate of the Donner party, the General, hearing of the sufferings of incoming emigrants, appropriated $100,000 from the Civil Fund for the relief, with the approval of General Riley, the Governor of California, and detailed Maj. Daniel Rucker, First Dragoons, to execute it (Fariss and Smith, *Illustrated History of Plumas, Lassen and Sierra Counties*, p. 87; and other sources). Bruff met the party again and again. His record tallies with the government reports of the relief and with the manuscript rolls of those succored. Most diarists tossed a passing reference to such events as Warner's death or the government relief. Bruff got the details down in black and white.

The scope of his work is extended. Besides detailed descriptions of the route and what happened while he passed over it, he mentions about 500 individuals, some 50 companies he encounters, and over 30 vessels — though he went overland. He also copied the perishable inscriptions on 100 graves, carefully describing their location. In the introduction to H 3 he says:

In none will that interest [in his narrative] amount to so intense and profound a sympathy, as in those who will here receive, probably for the first time, authentic tidings of the melancholy fate of lost relatives and friends, and of their final resting place in the remote wilderness of their weary travel. The graves of the lamented dead, and the hurried way-side inscriptions . . . may have been erased and destroyed by beasts of prey or the sacrilegious savage. Yet, not a few of them will be found as faithfully preserved . . . as though . . . memorized in marble, in the grave-yard of their native village.

On September 10, 1849, Bruff, traveling down the Humboldt, entered in his notebook the grave inscription of "H. Biddle, Died Aug: 6th 1849, Aged 22." In H 3 "Biddle" is changed to "Riddle," a note in Bruff's hand explaining: "March 30th 1858 A brother of Mr Riddles seeking to know where and when he died, gave me the correction."

Our annotation has been primarily for the purpose of identifying important individuals, places, and events and of supplying information as to the background where this is essential to intelligent comprehension of Bruff's account. So far as possible, contemporaneous records and government documents have been used, supplemented of course by later works. Newspapers of the day have been heavily drawn on for information, as well as unpublished early journals and government reports. Many Indians shuttle in and out of Bruff's picture, from the Missouri River to the Klamath. The background and customs of the various tribes have been depicted — chiefly through government documents and accounts of the time — in an effort to illuminate the relations between the Indians on one hand, and emigrant trains, miners, and settlers on the other, a subject too seldom viewed from both sides.

For several reasons we set ourselves the above limits. The length of Bruff's account was one. His canvas stretches from the Atlantic to the Pacific. After all, the end of the world *is* coming, and fifteen years of toil and two journeys to California are perhaps enough, although a lifetime would be too short. It is our belief — indeed our hope — that the last lines of annotation to the Bruff records will not be written for months or even years to come, and that they will be added by many individuals, in different places, who may have the unique bits of knowledge — preserved in journals, old letters, or even family tradition — to answer every query left unsolved.

Identification of individuals is not always possible. As in other records of the period but to a lesser degree than in most, some persons lack identifying Christian names or initials. This could hardly have been otherwise in a society constantly shifting, its members largely ignorant of one another's background, and since, moreover, there must have been a number of occasions on which it would be neither tactful nor wise to ask personal questions. Even government reports speak of "Mr. Peoples," "Mr. Rogers," "Mr. Hicks," and the like, without further identification. Degroot ("Six Months in '49," *Overland Monthly*, XIV [1875], 321) comments on a reverse phase of the same phenomenon:

They were queer affairs, those partnerships of that day. Two entire strangers would meet, and without preliminaries go to work, living and toiling together, for weeks and even months, trusting each other with their joint earnings, and dividing the same without trouble; never perhaps learning anything more of each other than simply the Christian name.

The P notebooks, aside from the two supplementary volumes, contain many sketches, some in pen, some in pencil, made on the route. Some of these are reproduced below. They include views of striking objects on the Trail, contour maps and diagrams, and portrayals of varied incidents. They depict with spirit and precision life on the plains in '49. One comic series, "Seeing the Elephant," in Supplementary Notebook A (see pp. 533, 545), follows the gold seeker, from the start in the East to the mines, with delightful humor. Scattered through the volume, one gains the impression that Bruff added the drawings one by one, as his experience grew. Merely to have executed all the drawings he made on the march, exclusive of the written records, is a major feat.

Of these drawings Bruff says:

Such a perfect series of Illustrations have never been, nor can be again produced. Every thing of consequence or interest, on the long route over; the Sierra Nevada Country; the Valley of the Sacramento; Events in Sⁿ Francisco; its harbor, — the Golden Gate; the Coast, — and up to the Gold Bluffs; Humboldt Bay; Trinidad; and the Indians, beasts, &c. and in fact, every thing remarkable, to illustrate from life what I noticed. . . . My coast-views are equal to the best of those on the Coast Survey Charts, and more numerous: — and with bearings and distances to all — I may refer, especially, to a long panoramic view from Trinidad hills, looking out upon the ocean, and taking in Humbold Bay and Cape Mendocino — The Indian Village, burial place, &c. and town of Trinidad [for the latter sketches see pp. 558, 559, 560, 561].

Bruff wrote with a quill, in a script characteristic of the period. Sick and miserable, in the mountains of California in January, 1850, he still had his mind on his journals, noting "Rafen [raven] quills fine for writing." The wonder is that under such varied handicaps his records should be so extraordinarily neat and full. On the march they were written under punishing conditions. In camp on Bear River, where the company halted several days to recruit the mules after the desert stretch of Sublette's Cut-off, Bruff wrote:

This rest afforded me a fine opportunity to correct my notes, and also to wash some articles of clothing. — For the charge and care of the company made my task a very hard one. — I had less repose than any one else, — requiring the Sergeant having the morning guard to call me always at 4, — sometimes earlier; — and [at night] every one in camp, except the sentinels, were snooring some time, ere I could do so. — When all was quiet, by my fire, or lantern, I corrected the day's rough notes, and made my memorandums for the morrow's march. — Whilst my mess-mates sat down comfortably, and eat their meals, I had to snatch a mouthful any how.

On August 2, in camp near Pacific Spring, he noted:

I sat up late to night, writing notes and plotting down memorandums for several day's march ahead: At last, having completed my memorandums, by the light of the flickering camp-fire, and chilled with the cool air, I button'd my over coat close about me, rolled up in a blanket, with my head on an old saddle for a pillow, and went off, also, to the land of Nod.

And on October 20, the night before he made the last camp for the company, at Bruff's Camp, in the Sierra Nevada:

Sun Set clear, calm, Temp. 70° Put a wagon wheel on the fire, and the tar and grease in hub gave me a good light to write up my notes by.

Before starting across the plains, each company member was limited to a minimum amount of baggage. But on July 25, traveling up the Sweetwater, the Washington City Company, like many around them, found they still had too much cargo. They held a meeting and voted, among other things, to decrease each member's personal baggage to fifty pounds' weight. Yet Bruff never discarded journals or drawings, whatever else may have had to go. He had an abiding sense of the value of his records. More than once he risked his life to preserve them. At Bruff's Camp he lingered, in the fall of '49, until trapped by the deep snow, partly on account of these records:

I cannot abandon my notes and drawings, instruments, &c. nor would I like to lose a choice collection of minerals, books, &c. and have no means of getting them in, unless I can procure some animals from the Settlements.

In December, after a heavy snowfall had crushed his tents, he wrote:

Now we cannot enjoy a good comfortable fire; nor sit at our table, as the sides of the tent are pressed in on it. This is a great deprivation to me, about writing.

Two days later matters had grown worse:

The wagons [abandoned by emigrants, about his camp ground] appeared to be high masses of snow. With axes we knocked a wagon bed of one of my old company wagons to pieces. My old comrade across the Continent, No 12, had now to contribute towards warming me; How could I have entertained such an idea, when, all hands full of glee, put it on board the Steamer Robert Fulton at Pittsburgh! . . . Our lodge [two tents connected by a canvas fly] is a complete wreck, the snow drifts in much through the N. side, and the opening at top. . . . If we live to see the morning, we will have to dig our way in.

For, the tents now being uninhabitable, he and his comrade, Poyle, and a little boy of four, whose father had deserted him and whom Bruff was charitably trying to care for, were forced to sleep in wagons. After tucking the child into one and fastening up the back so that no wolves or other wild animals could enter, Bruff and Poyle prepared to retire:

On going into our bed-chamber (wagon) the bedding was white with drift snow. We stood outside, at the back of the wagon, (snow level with the bed) took off our gum coats and laid them on the tail-board, then sat on them, and took off our leggings, (legs of old cloth pants, tied at the knee) and shoes, which we deposited in the corners, under our heads, shook the snow off as well as we could, got under cover, closed all the crevices we could with clothes, and hung the lantern up to a hook above. Poyle lay some time reading "De Toqueville's Democracy of America", while I wrote up my notes.

The only thing he does not tell us is where he balanced the inkpot, for the notes are written in ink.

Ten days later the storm had raged itself out, but the snow was deep and life had become literally almost insupportable on Barclay Mountain. Bruff prepared to shift his quarters to a cabin a few miles down the mountain. The start was made about one o'clock in the afternoon:

I had a large knapsack, filled with note books, drawings, &c. a haversack with various articles in it, wore a belt with cartridge-box, hatchet and knife, Poyle's Pouch and horn, a small camp kettle, lantern, double-gun, and my pockets full of small articles. . . . We did not reach the cabin till 7 at night, and I fainted at the door.

Several months later Bruff left the cabin to try to reach the Settlements. The child was dead, Poyle had long been absent seeking help, and an old hunter who stopped with Bruff for a time had failed to return from one of his lonely hunts:

I see but one chance of saving myself [Bruff entered carefully in his journal]. . . . I am determined to attempt going in to-morrow, let the issue be what it may. . . . I commenced making the necessary preparations. — Collected my note-books, & papers, — quite a parcel. — put ammunition, the two tallow candles [all he had by way of provisions], matches, flint & steel, a memorandum book [P 9] & pencil in a haversack. A clean shirt, pair of socks, comb, towel, soap, pouch of tobacco & pipe — which I have not dared to smoke since I gave Clough up, as lost; my journal-books, my watch, one belonging to Mr Goodrich, and his draught; a gold chain and seal, found in Dr Caldwell's wagon, and a case of sewing materials, made by my wife, I put in a knapsack.

Elsewhere he says: "Labeled my papers and drawings so that they may possibly reach my family if I am lost." Five days later — and the total distance covered was less than thirty miles — he had reached the plain of the Sacramento, a few miles from Lassen's Rancho.

I looked around over the broad plain, not a living thing to be seen! I now loosed my knapsack, and knowing that I could send for it, if I lived to get in, — unless the indians found it, I put my quilt on it, and piled stones over all, forming a small pyrimid. — I also piled up a little pyrimid of stone, in the road opposite, to indicate the locale.

It was at this point, we surmise, that his first entry in the P 9 notebook was written — his record up to date, if he failed to get in. Learning, a few days after he reached the Settlements, that Bruff's Camp had just been looted and his possessions there — clothing, books, instruments, guns, and other material — carried off or damaged, he wrote laconically in his diary: "& well I brot away my journals & notes —"

On the night of May 3, 1851, fire broke out in San Francisco — the fifth conflagration in the history of the town. It burned for ten hours, consuming more than eighteen blocks of buildings, and ceased for "want of further fuel to consume." Of this Bruff wrote:

At a few minutes past eleven o'clock, at night, a fire broke out in Clay Street, above Kearney, on the E. side of the plaza, sweeping down and spreading with fatal irris[is]tibility. . . . I lodged in rear of the plaza. . . . I had barely time to rescue my papers and drawings, from the burning building on Montgomery Street, at much personal hazard. I assisted some French lithographers to save their effects, and in mistake they carried off a carpet bag of mine, containing notes, and other papers. I had then to hasten through the mass of people, goods, vehicles, &c. amidst smoke and cinders, some distance up a street, to find them, recovering my property, fortunately. My bedding, however, was burnt.

In the confusion Bruff was knocked down by a dray and stunned. At eight o'clock the next morning, "completely exhausted by fatigue," he was taken in by friends and put to bed. His papers, however — the records and the sketches in this work — were safe.

There was still another hazard. On July 17, 1851, the "Brother Jonathan," bearing Bruff from Chagres, berthed in New York. In harbor, thieves went through Bruff's baggage and robbed him "of every thing of value I possessed except my books and drawings."

How valuable he considered these is shown by his statement in 1869 (letter to the Society of California Pioneers) that "In Sacramento [1850] I was offered Ten Thousand dollars cash, for my rough sketches of the overland Travel: but declined it, for obvious reasons," referring to the "proposal" of McNairn and Young "for Panorama of [Overland] route & country" based on Bruff's drawings. Panoramas were the movies of the period, some of them amazing in scope and size and extremely profitable. Bruff adds (P 11): "Young offers me 1 share in Panorama Compy." Instead, he returned home "pennyless."

Among Mrs. Procter's papers is the following:

The original M.S. written from my rough notes, under numerous disadvantages, was not broken into Chapters, with proper synoptical headings: — somehow, I made such an extraordinary omission; and retained much matter interesting to those of the emmigration, but unimportant to the public at large. — In its crude state, it was submitted to the Mess Harpers, publishers, of N. York City, by the Honl. W. H. Gwin, Senator from California, who received the following opinion from the reader of the firm: —

"This is a detailed narrative of a journey across the plains, to the Gold Regions, &c. made in 1849-50-51. — It is full of romantic and thrilling adventures. The author is very observing, always on the Alert, of good sound sense, and with excellent talents for description. He has embodied in his journal a good deal of curious, original, and important information. I should advise the author to condense his M.S. give it a thorough revision, and divide it into Chapters, with regular headings; with these improvements there could be no doubt of its success when published."

I had not time to revise and correct it, but had the good fortune to engage the services of one of our most talented literary men — Dr Richd A. Locke, of Staten Isd N.Y. Author of the celebrated "Moon Hoax", many years ago. I am indebted to him for the thorough revision and correction, &c — for which I paid 200 dolls. . . .

If I had given the M.S. and illustrations to our publishers, to whittle down to what is called a *popular edition* — i e 300 pages small 8vo. interspersed with a few miserable wood-cuts, it would have been out long ago. But I preferred being the Author of what I had accomplished in the most creditable form, or not at all. . . .

I had thought of publishing the work, with all the smaller illustrations interspersed, in wood cuts, and the larger ones in a volume of plates, with the map, in style of Morier's plates to his "Persia." . . .

I have the pleasure of knowing Lord Napier, and he was interested in some extracts from my M.S.

This is perhaps a preliminary draft of the letter to the Society of California Pioneers.

The latter document details one more misfortune:

A publisher in N. York, heard of it, and the difficulties I had to contend with, and suggested that if I obtained a certain number of subscribers, at 5 dolls: per copy, he would undertake the publication. Thereupon I was at the expense of having printed a small edition of the Prospectuses of which the one accompanying this, is the last complete copy left me. After some further time, I found a friend going to California, who took charge of a number of these, disposed of them in Sn Fran: and Sacramento, for subscribers; and in a couple of months found four times the amount of subscription required. Coming home, with such a flattering list for me, he lost them all on the Isthmus of Panama! I boxed the M.S. up with the hope that I might, ultimately, dispose of it in London.

Dr. Richard A. Locke, to whom Bruff entrusted the revision of his 1853 account, was a picturesque figure. According to the *Dictionary of American Biography* (XI, 338), he was born in East Brent, Somersetshire, England, and was a collateral descendant of John Locke. He became editor of the *New York Sun* and in 1853 (*Appleton's Cyclopædia*, III, 751) "created a sensation by the publication of what purported to be the astronomical observations, especially on the moon, of Sir John Herschel, the younger, at the Cape of Good Hope, describing in detail, among other things, the discovery of lunar inhabitants." This was published serially in the *Sun* and is said to have increased its circulation. It became known as the Moon Hoax. Dr. Locke's editing of Bruff's H 3 account consisted largely in crossing out portions of Bruff's text which he thought not of general interest or an impediment to the narrative. He thought of Bruff's record, not as source material which it now is, but as something to be turned into an interesting travel account in the manner of the 1850's. Fortunately it is possible to read the portions crossed out, except in a few instances where he pasted something else over the passage. Bruff says humbly, of Dr. Locke's work: "He done so very thoroughly, without interfering with my own style; — so that, exclusive of Title, headings of Chapters, &c. it is all my own."

In 1869, at the suggestion of Dr. James C. Palmer, United States Navy retired (a member of the Wilkes Exploring Expedition, 1838-42, and of the first expedition to lay the Atlantic cable, 1857), Bruff sent his manuscript with map and illustrations to the Society of California Pioneers. (See 1st ed., Appendix I, for his letter of transmittal, together with other documents pertaining to H 3.) The Society returned Bruff's manuscript to him. Subsequently it was lost sight of for a time, but about 1909 appeared in the market and was purchased by the late Francis P. Harper. According to Lathrop C. Harper (letter, Dec. 18, 1934), as indicated above, this came about through either the late Philip Lee Phillips, of the Library of Congress, or the late Gen. Hiram H. Chittenden. The material was seen and examined by the late George Henry Sargent, internationally known bibliographer of the *Boston Evening Transcript*, who wrote a long review which appeared in the *Transcript* July 12, 1911. This began:

> There has recently come to light one of the most valuable additions to the history of early California in the days of Forty-Nine. This is an unpublished illustrated manuscript diary of an overland journey from Washington to California, extending nearly two years and a half, made by Captain J. Goldsboro Bruff at the head of a party styling themselves "The Washington Military Company." . . . Captain Bruff's manuscript is closely written on 420 large folio leaves.
>
> [The account concluded:] It is probable that there has never been penned by any other California emigrant of 1849 a narrative so full of interest, so true to detail, so concise in descriptions and yet so graphic and full of the most valuable scientific interest as this diary of Captain Bruff.

Apparently the late Elliott Coues also examined some of the Bruff material. On the flyleaf of the H 1 notebook appears the following:

> Itinerary of J. Goldsborough Bruff, of Washington, D. C., commanding a party on the Overland Route to California in 1849.
> This book opens abruptly, and is apparently Vol. II — *Vol. I. missing.*
> Elliott Coues, Dec. 1898.

According to our reckoning, this is correct. The P 1 record formed Part One, the H 1 record Part Two.

One of the most interesting portions of Bruff's narrative and one which adds surprisingly to the known history of California is that of the Gold Lake hunt of himself and his comrades in the summer of 1850, in the Sierra Nevada, their eastern slopes, and the adjacent basin region. There has long been speculation as to the identity of the first white men to visit Lassen County and to see Honey Lake and Elysian Valley, but there has been lack of definite information. Beckwourth, the discoverer of the Beckwourth Pass in 1851, claimed to have visited this lake in 1845, but his known propensity to amplify and embroider his own exploits discredited his story. Fariss and Smith (*op. cit.*, pp. 338-39) report that Peter Lassen is said to have been in the valley in 1848, but disparage the idea.

Fairfield (in his valuable *Pioneer History of Lassen County*, pp. 16, 22, 28) believed that too much credit had been given Peter Lassen:

Honey Lake and Honey Lake valley were named from the honey-dew found on the grass and some of the trees and bushes, but it is not certain who gave them the name. After much research in the pioneer literature relating to northern California the writer is satisfied that June, 1852, is the first time the name ever appeared in print and that Mr. Noble, or some member of the party with him at the time, named them in the spring of 1852, or possibly in the spring of 1851. . . . It is also uncertain what white men discovered the valley, or when that event took place. . . . Very few, perhaps none, of the pioneers of this county went through Honey Lake valley before Roop came in here [June, 1853]. . . . It is hard to understand why F. and S. [Fariss and Smith] call Lassen and his five companions the pioneers of Lassen county. Just before that, they say that some of the Roop crowd stayed in the valley during the winter of 1854-5. Roop claimed land in the county two years before Lassen did. . . . Why wasn't Roop the pioneer of the county?

The answer to Fairfield's question would seem to be that, as Bruff's records reveal, Peter Lassen was the pioneer, and perhaps also the white discoverer, of Honey Lake and Elysian Valley, and some living knowledge of this fact must have prevailed. According to Bruff's records, Lassen and his comrades visited the lake twice in the summer of 1850, Bruff being one of the party on the second visit, October 4-5 (and also discovered Eagle Lake):

Lassen was here once before, — then for the first time, and some of the party called it Honey Lake, from a sweet dew distilled from some plants they found in the bottom.

And on November 7, 1850, in the H 3 version, he says:

The elder Hough related to me their first visit to Honey Lake, as they called it, from the sweet substance which they found exuding from the heads of wild oats in the basin. (I have named it L. Derby)

Bruff's tiny memorandum book for 1850, which we may suppose him to have carried when he visited Honey Lake, contains for October 4 the words:

"9 A.M. mov'd on E. of N. enter'd Honey or Hot Spring Basin & Lake". One of the striking features of Honey Lake is the large boiling spring on its northeast shore. This spring, of great volume, enveloped in a cloud of steam, and tossing a constant jet of boiling water several feet into the air, is so spectacular that had Bruff seen it, it seems certain he would have described it at length. The logical inference is that Lassen, having seen or heard of it on his previous visit to Honey Lake, told Bruff about it, possibly while they smoked their pipes and rested, after their midday meal, on a grassy bench above the lake (H 2, Oct. 5), previous to their ascent of Diamond Mountain in the afternoon. This was near the site of the present Janesville. Bruff's various sketches of Honey Lake and the surrounding mountains, most of them dated, correspond to his descriptions of the country and to the contours of the hills as viewed today from these points, notably Shaffer Mountain from the vicinity of Janesville (pictured, with the noon-day bivouac referred to, at p. 554).

In November, 1942, just as we were about to go to press with the first edition, the United States Forest Service, Lassen National Forest, checked in the field our interpretation of Bruff's route in this region, using Bruff's records and sketches. Mr. Philip B. Lord, of the Susanville branch of the Service, who visited Snowstorm Cañon (Bruff's "Hieroglyphic Defile") for the purpose, on horseback and with compass, writes (letter, Nov. 14, 1942):

We entered Snowstorm Canyon about a mile above the place that Bruff's party must have left it and went up the canyon for about 3 miles and then back over into Pete's Valley. The terrain in Snowstorm is just about as described in the diary, the stream, small meadows, and willows, but the walls on the right hand side are not regular all the way down the canyon but broken in several places, the left hand wall, (going down the canyon) is just as he described it. There is a certain amount of picture writing on the right hand wall but no more than there is in Willow Cr or Pete's Valley. Time may have obliterated some of it and time and the elements may have broken down the right hand wall to some extent. The picture writings sometimes show up much more in different lights and if a person was there all day he would discover more of them I am sure.

The distances and compass directions given by Bruff are very accurate and his description of the balance of the trip to Honey lake is very clear and easily traced. I took his drawings and went to Big Mud Flat and vicinity and the outlines of the various mountains are unmistakable and the distances he gives check very closely. Bruff's party must have hit the lake somewhere near the present Fleming Ranch as he does not mention the Hot Springs which are a little east of there. After leaving Snowstorm [stream] the party must have crossed it again somewhere below Karlo but they could have done so without knowing it as the country is very flat there and most of the water has sunk into the ground.

Fairfield adds (*op. cit.*, p. 29): "It is probable that the information gathered by Mr. Dodge for F. and S. together with that obtained by the writer, is all that will ever be known of the history of this [Lassen] county previous to 1856." But even as he wrote, Bruff's notebooks, ink unfaded, sketches fresh and bright, were laid away, to await another term before they saw the light. Their testimony, though delayed, is clear.

It is to be regretted that it has not proved feasible to identify in entirety Bruff's wanderings in 1850, even with the help of his maps. Experts familiar with the terrain would probably find this difficult, if not impossible, in places, so great have been the changes wrought in the face of the country in a hundred years. Earthquakes, erosion, changes in drainage systems, hydraulic mining, building of roads and railroads, deforestation, grazing, farming, and the like have all helped to confuse the trail. Except for cataclysms and hydraulic mining, this holds true for all the California Trail. According to the Nebraska State Historical Society, for instance, the Missouri River, at the point where Bruff crossed his company in 1849, has shifted its bed nearly one mile to the eastward. Hulbert says, of the difficulty of locating the old trail in the region directly east of Fort Hall (*op. cit.*, Vol. III, Nos. 16-17): "the changing drainage conditions of the section . . . have also contributed; it ["T.S. Rs. 33 and 32"] contains upwards of 1200 springs. With the passing years old streams have disappeared; new ones formed." Large artificial reservoirs at Soda and Steamboat Springs, on Bear River; at American Falls, on the Snake River; on the Sacramento; and at Lassen's Depot Camp, in the Big Meadows, as well as the artificial diversion of Pit River in the vicinity of Fall River Valley, have all helped to change the country. The cutting down of the noble Sierra forests may be expected to crown these man-made changes.

The California end of the Trail is complicated, in places, by the appearance, disappearance, and reappearance of playa lakes, of which Honey Lake itself is one. Russell (*Geological History of Lake Lahontan*, pp. 55-56) says:

The area of the lake [Honey] varies with the seasons, as well as from year to year, as is common with all inclosed lakes. As mapped by the survey in charge of Captain Wheeler, in 1867 it covered an area of approximately 90 square miles. In the summers of 1859 and 1863 it is reported by the settlers in the valley to have become completely desiccated, leaving a broad smooth plain of cream-colored mud. . . . The outline of the lake is indefinite. . . . The name "playa-lake" [says Russell, *ibid.*, pp. 81, 82] has been applied to inclosed water bodies of dry climates which have little depth and frequently evaporate to dryness, leaving mud-plains, or playas. . . . Lakes of this class exhibit great variety, and are the most irregular of water bodies. In many instances they hold their integrity for a number of years, and only evaporate to dryness during exceptionally arid seasons. Again, desiccation is apparently the normal condition, and the basins are only flooded during times of unusual humidity. . . . Their outlines consequently fluctuate with the humidity of the season, and, owing to the extreme shallowness of their basins, a variation of an inch or two in depth may make a difference of many square miles in area. . . . The mud-plains originating in the manner described above are characterized by the evenness of their surfaces and their light creamy-yellow color, which is independent of the nature of the surrounding rocks.

In 1931 Goose Lake was dry, and in 1937 motor maps again marked it "dry." In 1939 it was an extended sheet of water, reaching northward beyond the limit of vision, though it was not so high as in 1849. Gazing over its blue expanse toward the enclosing mountains, one could understand how emigrants might mistake it, as some are said to have done, for an arm of the sea. In 1939, likewise, Grasshopper Lake was a sizable body of water, though it was not indicated, even by hatchings, on the maps. There may have been playa lakes in 1849 not to be seen now, or a different combination of them. Where Bruff saw lakes may now be dry land and vice versa. Russell indicates another possible source of confusion (*ibid.*, p. 83): "mirages may be seen every day on these heated deserts [playas]. Similar optical illusions give strange fanciful forms to the mountains, and sometimes transfigure them beyond all recognition."

The fact that some of Bruff's earliest records for Part Four of his account and practically all such records for Part Five are lacking has likewise increased the difficulty.

Some time after he had completed the 1853 version, Bruff wrote an introductory chapter:

As a topographical itinerary [he said], this journal will be found a correct and reliable guide to future travelers, even if, in acquiring this value, it should incur the imputation of tediousness in description. For there is scarcely a mile of the whole Long Route that is not particularly described, not only in regard to its obstacles and facilities, but to its remarkable and often stupendously magnificent scenery, its geology, and its diversified natural productions. The original drawings in which many of these are depicted, together with the occasional sketches of personal situations and important stations, have at least the merit of accuracy and authenticity, and, it is hoped, will prove acceptable for their unquestionable novelty.

The protracted delay which has occurred in the publication of this work [alas, he had then no idea how protracted], has arisen, partly, from subsequent travels and pressing occupations which prevented its early transcription from multitudinous notes; but, principally, from the slow progress of its revision and preparation for the press, while in the possession of another person, to whom it had been submitted for that purpose. It is confidently hoped, however, that since it is the only circumstantial record of the most astonishing enterprise in colonization that has been accomplished in any period or portion of the world, it possesses more than a transient interest, and may become its popular memorial.

Let Bruff's introduction serve for the earlier records also. The drawings and sketches, as he hoped, cannot but prove acceptable. We know of no record of the route comparable to his for length and historical fact and, with Bruff, we believe "it possesses more than a transient interest." In his pages the Great Migration unrolls, not as portrayed in romance and in movies, but as lived by thousands of brave, determined Forty-Niners — the slow westward thrust of men and wagons; the clouds of dust beat up by patient hoofs; the Great West, almost fresh from the hand of God, so far as the white man was concerned, its natural features both novel and arresting; the herds of bison; the traveling bands of red men; always the unknown, until life itself became fluid, no longer set within known bounds; the daily life of the Trail — the smashed wagons, the worry about grass and water, the discarded goods, the sudden deaths from cholera, the deaths from dysentery, the company dissensions, the deaths and disabilities from scurvy, the storms, the deaths from Indian arrows, the babies born, the emigrants' quarrels, sometimes their murders, the hunger, the thirst, the stench of putrid animals, the fiddles squeaking out "Zip Coon" and "Carry Me Back to Old Virginny" to celebrate the arrival at Pacific Springs or some other key point; emigrants, crippled by scurvy, set out by the roadside by their comrades and brutally left to die; emigrants sharing their last bit of food and water with fellow travelers in the desert; the Stars and Stripes floating over South Pass and Fandango — all the remarkable medley of it, the light and the shade.

G. W. R.
R. G.

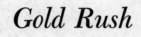

Gold Rush

APRIL 2, 1849 - AUGUST 27, 1849

Washington City to Raft River

1849. APRIL 2^{d1} At 5.15 P.M. left Washington City in the cars for the Relay House,[2] which was reach'd in[3]   Many went on to Baltimore and staid there all night.[4]

[APRIL] 3. 8½ A.M. left in train, the Relay House, and at 5½ P.M. reach'd Cumberland,[5] after ½ hour's Stop at Harper's Ferry to dine. Embarked at once in a crowd'd boat and same evening arrived at Pittsburgh,[6] and engaged the Steamer ["Robert Fulton"] to take all the freight — wagons, &c & company on to St. Louis. Visited the Theatre to hear Booth.[7]

[APRIL] 4 — Getting wagons & freight on board . . .

[APRIL] 10. — On the Ohio river. . . .

MAY 5   At St Joseph's Mo. Rouse camp every morn. at 4 o'clk. Weigh 16 lbs more than ever. Sleep in a log cow-house, forge in it — bedstead a hollowed log — feedtrough. In every direction, as far as can be seen, the country is speckled with the white tents & wagons of the emmigrants. The crowd at the ferry is a dense mass — fighting for precedence to cross. 2 teamster kill'd each other on one of these occasions, with pistols, at the head of their wagons. 2 crazy scows very insufficient for the occasion, as soon as a wagon enters the boat, the next moves close down to the edge of the bank, and the long mass of wagons in rear close down, while companies are falling in the rear, and this goes on from earliest dawn till midnight day after day.[8] Got 2 wagons in line, taking 24 hours to get within 100 yds of the bank — with the hope of entering the boat in 5 or 6 hours more. This slow process I found would occupy about a fortnight to get my train in the line and cross them, so I gave it up, & resolved to go up the Missouri 90 miles, to Ft. Kearney,[9] and cross there. Besides, after crossing here, for a considerable distance, the ground opposite is marshy, grass indifferent, and little corn to be had, many Streams intervening[10] between the Mo. and the Platte, cholera[11] in the immense crowd on the other side, &c. And in Missouri, I had at least a tolerable road, corn & other necessaries could be purchased at reasonable rates, and lastly, but a broad prairie intervening between Mo. & Platte. . . .[12]

[MAY] 10. Our camp (Washington) 3 miles above St Jose.

Grand Island is 100 m. off

1849. APRIL 2^d. The Washington City Emmigrating Co^y 66 men for California, Left Washington, for Pittsburgh P. [Pa.] from thence to takes [take] their wagons, &c. on board a Steamer for St Louis, and up the Missouri river to St Jose, — (*the point I had selected as*) our rendezvous & starting-point for the tedious march across the continent — (*a Committee had gone ahead some weeks, to make contracts, purchase mules, &c. &c.*)

3 days consumed at Pittsburgh in getting wagons &c together and on board the Steamer Robert Fulton[13]

13 Company wagons, known as light Santa Fé wagons — for 6 mules each. An ambulance — (large family carryall) — and 2 small private carryalls = 16 wagons & 84 mules, several spare mules, and about 14 horses, ponies, &c — belonging to the members.

The Commander, Clerk, and 1st Officer of the Robert Fulton, were sons of Coll. Collier, then appointed Collector of S^n Francisco, and on his way thither.[14] The gentlemanly & kind conduct of those officers will long be remembered by us.

Occasionally, on board the Robert Fulton I mustered my men on the hurricane deck, in the morning at 10 o'clock & drilled them at the light infantry manual.

[APRIL] 15 — Reach'd St Louis,[15] and in the afternoon placed the company in 2 detachments on board a couple of Steamers for St Jose — Steamers all crowded,[16] and we could not freight one boat for the purpose without paying too dear for the accomodation; As several articles of importance, including the tents, were in the rear, and some purchases were necessary here, I remain'd with several of my men to attend to the same, and hurry them up. I had also to have an Odometer[17] made.

[APRIL] 18. At 4 P.M. I went on board the steamer Belle Creole,[18] — crowded with emmigrants from all sections of the union, though principally Illinoisians & New Englanders. At night had to lay alongside the bank, as snags rendered night navigation very hazardous — and the river was at a very low stage, and the Steamer a larger class than usually ran up. Left a man to bring missing articles up.

[APRIL] 19 — In the afternoon reach'd the mouth of the Gasconade, where the Steamer Saluda lay, with broken shaft. — We increased the crowd on board by a number of her passengers, & proceeded

[APRIL] 20. Great skill displayed by the pilot, but it was evident the boat could not get much higher up. — We stoped a few minutes at Jefferson City; whose State House, about 3 miles above, looked like a small edition of our Capitol, at Washington. The state prison, is a fine building also — City looks very neat — High round hills about it, while the opposite banks are low & thickly wooded.

[APRIL] 21 — We wooded, on the right bank Paroquets numerous. Stopped at Middleton, Lexington, & Camden; and at 8 P.M. came too, nearly opposite the latter, with rudder unhung, by grounding.

[APRIL] 22. — At 8 A.M. we hauled alongside the landing at Camden,[19] unable to proceed higher, as I expected. Here the emigrants desired a meeting, and waited on me to preside.[20] The meeting was accordingly organized, and a committee of one from each state represented by a company on board, drew up certain propositions, in regard to the deduction proper, on freight & fare, for the inability of the vessel to proceed to St Jose. Some went ashore here, with their freight, but most remained, to be landed back at Lexington, which place we reached at 4 P.M, and the passengers with their freight went ashore, excepting my little party, who slept on board.[21]

[APRIL] 23. At 3½ A.M. we went ashore [at Lexington], with our freight, and in half an hour after, the Steamer proceeded down for St. Louis.

[APRIL] 24. At 5 A.M. the Steamer Meteor, no. 3,[22] came up, and we went on board, and once more started up river for St Jose. Heard of much Cholera[23] on the river   Left some passengers at Camden, & continued on.

[APRIL] 25. at 3½ A.M. reached Independence Landing, where one of our Committee who had been sent on, some time ago, to purchase mules, came on board, reported his purchases, &c. and returned to take them up by land.[24] We were all night grounding on bars & running foul of snags.

[APRIL] 26. At 10 A.M. our boat had to stop 5 miles below F^t Leavenworth, to repair the supply-pump. Saw here 3 Delaware Indians,[25] old woman, daughter, & her little son, — the boy spoke English very well At merdian we moved on — Landed passengers at the Fort, and others at Weston, and at dusk wooded at bank 40 ms. below St Jose, & remained there all night.

[APRIL] 27 — At 5 P.M. reached St Jose[26] — and repaired to the Camp, 2 miles in rear of the town. In consequence of rain and non-arrival of the tents, the boys were very much discon-*tent* ed — poor fellows! — they were like young bears, all their troubles ahead of them.

Regulating matters in Camp, and breaking mules, the latter quite a task for many who had seldom seen a mule.[27] Rouse the camp every morning at 4 o'clock.

[APRIL] 30. — Ke-ro-ich, a Nemahaw[28] half-chief,[29] came into camp: he wore a silver medallion with bust of president Van Buren on it.[30] — A drunken emigrant several days afterwards, jerked it off his neck, and kept it the greater part of a day, but had to restore it on the old Chief kicking up a rumpus: — threatening to look out for the emmigrant when he should cross the river & pass through their country — Ke-ro-ich told me in a very broken way, that his tribe was more than 100, but not quite 200 strong.

MAY 1st Cloudy and cool, Wind N.E.

At night a storm of rain, with thunder & lightning, peculiarly disagreeable as all the tents had not arrived, and the wagon-covers were too thin, — not in conformity with contract.[31]

[MAY] 2^d — Cloudy and disagreeable. The company thought a guide very important, and hired a fellow for that purpose who knew about as much of the plains as the plains knew of him.[32] Dr Austin, our Surgeon, arrived.[33]

[MAY] 3^d & 4th — Repacking freight, breaking mules, &c. &c. weather same as yesterday. Tents & odometer arrived.[34]

[MAY] 5th — a log cow house, near our camp answered an admirable purpose; — we set up the forge in it, for making small iron-work, &c. Across one end there was a hollow log or feed-trough, which I cleaned out, and spread my blanket in, for my sleeping apartment. Sent 2 wagons to ferry.

MAY 6th. Our Camp is situate on Black Snake Hill;[35] from whence there is a fine view of the town & surrounding country.[36] Close by is the camp of a large family, — Mr Abbot, an aged Swiss, who sits in the shade with a large book on the Philosophy of Nature, and peruses its abstruse pages, undisturbed by the din and confusion around.[37] His son-and-law, Mr Keller, a German, has his wife and three small children, a son of old man Abbot has his wife and children, and several other grown relatives and connections, with their tents, wagons, oxen, &c. make a considerable company.

MAY 7th — As but one of the wagons I had sent down, was able to get into line, and would then have to wait several hours before it could be got in the boat,[38] I ordered them back to Camp: and immediately called a meeting of the company, and represented the delay and disadvantages of attempting to cross here, and the advantages, on the other hand, of proceeding 90 ms. up the river, to Fort Kearney;[39] so they resolved on the latter route. As far as we could see, over a great extent of vallies & hills, the country was speckled with the white tents and wagon-covers of the emmigrants. There were but two very indifferent scows at the ferry, and these were being plied from earliest day till midnight, every day; had been so for weeks, and from the mass here, would continue for several weeks more. From the principal street in St Jose, down 300 yds. crossing a bridge, to the river bank, was one dense mass of wagons, oxen, and people, and as soon as a wagon entered the scow, the next moved down to the water's edge, and the mass in the rear closed up to the front, affording the opportunity to one or more lucky wagons to fall in the extreme rear, &c. Fighting for precedence was quite common, and a day or two since, 2 teamsters, in one of these disputes, killed each other with pistols. This slow mode of crossing the river, would, I thought, take my train of 14 Company and 2 private wagons, to gradually get into place and cross, — in a very disjointed way, about a fortnight.[40] I knew that the opposite side for a considerable distance was marshy, there were many streams to cross, forage was scarce, and besides there was plenty of Cholera there. Whereas, by going up the river, corn &c could be had, on reasonable terms, a tolerable road laid before us, and lastly, a country of high rolling prairie intervening between the Missouri & Platte rivers.

[MAY] 8. — Hazy and pleasant. I purchased a common thermometer, the only one left for sale, in St Jose, for $2. Hired a man for $1.50 per day to assist in mule breaking, as he was an old hand at that business.
    Merdn flyg clouds and cooler. Temp. 85°
    Sun Set ditto. Temp. 70° [41]

MAY 9 — Cloudy, Wind E. Temp. 51°

Moved camp 3 miles ahead, better ground; experienced difficulty with several teams of mules, very refractory, and bad places in the road increased the trouble.

Merdn hazy & calm. Temp. 75°

Sun Set cloudy, light airs from the N.E. Temp. 70°

[MAY] 10. Clear, light wind from S. Temp. 62°.

Apportioned the mules to the several wagons. Some guard delinquencies. Am quite sick to-day. Men employed making tent pins, packing wagons, and bringing the mules up to camp.

Merdn hazy & calm. Temp. 88°

Sun Set do light breeze S.W. 70°

[MAY] 11. — Flyg clouds. Wind S.E. Temp. 64°

Completing the arrangements of the wagons. Merdn hazy, Wind S.E. Temp. 90°   From Sun Set till 9 at night, rain, thunder, and lightning. Wind S.E. Temp. 60°

[MAY] 12. — Hazy, light airs from the S. Temp. 54°   Fitting harness, making reins, &c. Called a meeting in reference to superfluous stores, and resolved on disposing of some bacon, whiskey, iron, bar lead, coffee, salt, &c.[42]

(*Frost at night*)

On the 7th — I had to swear 4 men to the constitution of the company, in accordance with said constitution, but which I had intimated, at the meeting which adopted said constitution, how many of the men would regard the obligation about as much as singing pslams [sic] to a dead horse, or whistling jigs to a mile-stone. This like many other matters I had told them of, they found out in the sequel. As the ceremony out here was rather novel, I will relate it. — I went with the men down town, and soon saw the *Shingle* of a lawyer at side of a door, — I step'd up, and asked where I could find a magistrate? — A gentleman replied, that around the corner, in a log house, a Squire resided; — we visited the house, and a colored man there said the Squire was out, — probably in the P. Office. At the P.O. they said he might be found in the Street, but on walking about some time & enquiring of the inhabitants, I could not find him — However, I was told that a Squire Tracy lived in a certain 2 story cabinet maker's Shop, close by. — Thither we hastened, passed through the front room, filled with furniture, and found a man in the back room astride a large block of oak, with mallet & chissel, fashioning the block into a half female screw for a hemp-press. — He was the squire! I told him my business, when he desired me to repeat the form, which I did from my memorandum book; he then requested the men severally to say that they swore to said obligation, holding up his hand. This done, he charged 25 cents, which I paid, & bid him good morning, and left him chisseling his screw. (*This should be date 7th —*)

Merd. Sun shine and rain, alternately — Wind S.E. Temp. 74

Sun Set clear, wind N.W. Temp 62° While spreading my blanket upon the damp ground, for repose, a member of the company was performing "Home, sweet home," upon the Key-bugle. — And caused me to think of the friends and comforts we had bade a long farewell to and to which some of us might never return.

MAY 13. — SUNDAY   Clear, light wind from the N. Temp. 42°

Merd. flyg clouds, light air from N.W. Temp. 74°. Sun Set and night, Rain, thunder and lightning, Temp. 50°

[MAY] 14. — Cloudy. Wind E. Temp. 52°. Loaded 2 wagons with the store condemned to be sold, and sent them to town; Sent 6 pioneers ahead to repair the roads.

Merd. cloudy. Wind N.E. Temp. 65°

[MAY] 15 . . Cloudy, Wind E. 50°   weighing private baggage, &c. Moved ahead 3 miles.

Merd. drizzly. Wind E. Temp. 57°. Roads very muddy & slippery. Sun Set same weather, Temp. 54°

MAY 16. — Commences clear, wind S.E. Temp. 64°. put the train in motion early, for Savannah.[43] Merd. cloudy, Wind S.E. Temp. 78°. many settlements alongside the road, — some quite neat frame houses, but mostly log cabins. Very fertile country. proceeded about 5 miles, and camp'd.

[MAY] 17. — clear and calm. Very bad road, fractious mules, and very green teamsters. One wagon broke its fore axle, and another one, the hinder axle. The last was promptly replaced by a spare one, and the former had to be sent to Savannah to repair   I took the precaution to have several spare axles, tongues, & wheels, which amused the mountaineers, but was most fortunate for the Company, saving trouble, expense, and time. Merd. clear, & calm, Temp. 78°

At 5 P.M. made 5 miles, and camp'd within a mile of the town of Savannah — (13 miles from St Jose, and 75 from Fort Kearney:) in a pleasant oak and walnut grove, close by a handsome farm-house, the proprietor of which, his good lady told me, had gone off some weeks ago, with the Savannah Compᵞ for Calᵃ A well at the house afforded us good clear, cool water. Sun set clear & calm. Temp. 70° (*Here we heard of Duncan's Ferry;*[44] *so I determined to call and see it, and perhaps cross there.*)

MAY 18. — Clear, Wind S.E. Temp. 58°
Repaired damaged wagon, and purchased a very fine new ox wagon, with 3 yoke of large good-looking oxen, for $230. for a commissary wagon.
Merd. clear, Wind S.   Temp. 75°
Sun Set do   ” S.E.   ”   64°.

[MAY] 19. — Hazy, light airs from the S.E. —
Temp. 54°. (At 6 A.M. drizzles, thunder & lightning)   Adjusting the commissary wagon & other freight. Merdⁿ drizzles, Wind S.E. Temp. 68°   After dinner moved on through the town & several miles beyond, to Riggen's farm and house of accomodation. Afternoon and night rain, thunder, & lightning. I slept at the farm-house.

[MAY] 20. At 3 A.M. called in the mules, and at 9 A.M. moved ahead again only an hour's march, when the storm of rain, thunder & lightning compelled us to camp.

[MAY] 21. — Cloudy, with a strong breeze from S.W. Temp. 65°   Moved on a few miles further, when a wagon broke its tongue, and the miserable state of the road, with indications of squalls, made us halt and prepare to meet it.
Merdⁿ same as sun rise, Temp. 76°   Passed, in the woods, on the right, a small log cabin, where resided Moses Payne, of Tenn: wife & two children & squalid poverty.
Afternoon & night squalls of rain, thunder; & lightning. Temp. 66°. This weather very amusing to the sentinels. — I take my turn at guard duty, to stimulate the men, and shall continue it till we cross the Missouri.

MAY 22. — Commences clear. Wind N.W. Temp. 52°. Roused the Camp at 3 and moved on at 5 A.M. Careless driving caused some delay. — A wagon broke the hind axle in the woods, near Polly's Ferry. — it was soon replaced with a spare one, which in half an hour was also broken, and I had to get a new one made and fitted.[45] Crossed Polly's Ferry, 12 miles beyond Savannah, in a scow, drawn over by a line —across the Nodaway river, which is here a pretty stream, and quite broad. We drove up a tolerable steep hill to the right of Hollister's mill, — a stone building, and where good flour could be bought cheap. Here I saw a member of the Pittsburgh Coy who informed me that there was so much threatening with Bowie knives and revolvers in the Company, and particularly in his mess, that he was afraid of his life, and left them here, some 18 days ago.[46] A wagon broke its tongue, which I had replaced at Newark. At 11 A.M. passed through the Village of Newark.[47] log & frame houses lined either side of the road for about 200 yards. Merd. clear, wind light, from the N.W. Temp. 70°   Camp'd 2 miles beyond Polly's Ferry on the "Round prairie," near some farm-houses, a marsh and rill. Beautiful green undulating country.[48] Cattle, hogs, sheep, &c grazing around. Ox wagon & the unfortunate one, came up late. Sun Set clear, light airs from the N.W. Temp. 60°. Mounted guard with charged arms. (*Paid $1 pr wagon crossing Ferry*)

[MAY] 23. — Commences clear, with light airs from the N. N W. Temp. 42° (*I adopted bugle sounds for calling in the mules, moving, and assembly of the men, &c.*)

Camp aroused at 3 A.M. and moved on at 9. Merd. clear, wind same, Temp. 72°   Had to leave the unfortunate N° 2 wagon with the 3ᵈ axle broken, 10 miles from Ferry to repair the damage. Afternoon reached a narrow stream,[49] with deep soft banks — very brushy, over which was a very loose log bridge, against a large tree, inclining over it. — I cautioned the train, and 2 wagons passed safely, when the 3ᵈ kept too near the left, and was precipitated into the muddy brushy stream. The driver leap'd off the saddle mule, and 2 sick men jump'd out behind, as the wagon went over, & saved themselves a concussion. — The mules were cut loose & extricated, getting off with scratches only: and a broken axle, bolsters, & bows, and wetting some of the freight, was the extent of the damage. Wagon hauled out & repacked, mules hitch'd up again, bridge repair'd, and in half an hour we moved on again, the teamster cracking his whip, and singing out "let her rip". — This is 15 mi. from Polly's Ferry.

At 5 P.M. we reached Jackson's, Bluff Post office, Holt Co. 42 miles from St Jose., and Camped.[50] No 2 wagon came up. Sun-Set flying clouds, Wind S.E. Temp. 68°

This is a beautiful & remarkable country: has evidently. been once a large lake or stream — a long, low, and very level plain extends to the   as far as the eye can see: bounded by heights with points & capes, and occasional islands as it were in the bottoms. 8 P.M. Rain, thunder, and lightning.

MAY 24. — Clear, Wind N.E. Temp. 50°

Men employed repairing the damaged wagons, and putting arms and ammunition in order for service. We had some good meals at Mr Jacksons, — fine corn-bread, fresh butter, and plenty of milk.

Merd^n clear, Strong breeze from the E. Temp. 72°   2 P.M. strong gales from the N.E. thunder & indications of rain. Night set in squally, with heavy rain, vivid lightning, and crashing peals of thunder. I was on post from 8 to 10. and only when a flash of lightning enabled me, could I see the mules picketed in a bottom and on the sides of a hill. Several times in the dark, I ran foul of them. The luminous matter of an *ignius fatius* fell in my path, and on my moustache —

MAY 25. Cloudy & drizzly, Wind light from the S.W. Temp. 60°

On calling in the mules, found we had lost no. [number] — stolen no doubt, last night, in the darkness. 8 A.M. we gave up search for the mules & moved on.

[MAY] 26. —Drizzly, Strong breeze from N.W. Temp. 50   At 5 A.M. moved on for Duncan's Ferry. Most of the day spent in getting over a wet prairie.

Merd. clear, light airs N.W. Temp. 68°   Passed through a considerable forrest,[51] interspersed with wet places, and late in the afternoon reached the Ferry, where was quite a neat log & frame house, containing the families of Mr Duncan and his connections—[52]

Sun Set clear, Strong breeze N.W. Temp. 54°

[MAY] 27 — Clear, light breeze from N.W. Temp. 52°   Found a small company here, with ox-wagons, heavily laden with dry-goods, &c. for California, and as they had the precedence, we agreed, to facilitate the crossing, to assist them over, after which they would assist us. So a squad at once took hold, and helped them to get all their wagons down, ¾ mile to the landing.

Merd. clear, strong breeze from the N-N.W. Temp. 70°   Several boats of the Fur trading company passing down the rappid stream.[53]

Sun Set clear, with a light breeze from the N.N.E. Temp. 66°

MAY 28. — Clear & calm, Temp. 55°

The gang detailed for ferrying took over early, a load of oxen, and returned: then took in 4 oxen and a loaded wagon, Six men of the other company, and 8 of ours — On the other side near where they intended to land, the Scow ran on a Sawyer,[54] capsized & sank, in pretty deep water. Mr Duncan, the worthy proprietor of the Ferry, — steering the boat, was most unfortunately drowned. The wagon & many of the goods were lost; the oxen swam ashore,[55] as did several of the men, at great peril; and the others remained on the Sawyer till relieved by a canoe sent for them —

Merd. clear, light airs from the S. Temp. 82°

Sun Set ditto — Temp. 72°

[MAY] 29. — Clear and calm, Temp. 56°

Sent a canoe over, and brought the men across belonging to my company. Merd. clear; Wind S.E. Temp. 88° The disaster on the river necessarily caused much delay, and we could not, in consequence, move on, till 3 P.M.

On emerging from the low woody river bottom, about 2 miles from Camp, at an angle in the road, on the right, stands quite a neat frame house, being the drinking house & store of Robert Hawk, of Ohio.

Sun Set clear Wind S.E. Temp. 70° Spent half an hour at supper, mules in harness, and at 7 P.M. crossed the Nishnabotona Ferry,[56] — in a scow, cordelled across, for which we paid 50 ¢ pr wagon, and 25 ¢ per private animal. Banks steep and soft. Public house kept by the Ferryman. As the soil here is a very light black loam, the roads are easily disturbed by rain, and rendered miry, slippery, and almost impassable in very wet weather. So I resolved here to get over the worst ground by a forced march, while it was passable, — before another rain should interfere; — and we travelled all night.

[MAY] 30. — Early in the morning reach'd a stream, head of the Tarkio Ck,[57] which here makes a sudden short bend; in the bend stood quite a neat frame house, with empty whisky barrels scattered about, and every indication of the place being very recently vacated. In front of the house, lay upon the ground, a long pole & swinging sign, on which was painted a hand pointing — (in direction of a very Chinese-looking bridge 50 yards off) and the following legend; — "TO DUNCAN'S FERRY, 9 MILES, the nearest and best route to the GOLD REGIONS."[58] Moved over this queer log bridge, 2 hours to rest & breakfast, and spent most of the forenoon in getting through the "Willow Slew" (slough) a large and very wet prairie: having to unlade and double-team several wagons.[59] Merd. indications of rain, strong breeze S. Temp. 70°

(*sent 2 men ahead, about 10 ms. to F^t Kearney, to engage the Ferry*)

MAY 31. — Moved on 4 miles, to the Lake House."[60] — a log cabin on the convex edge of a narrow crescent-shaped lake of fresh water. This lake is fringed with willows, and contains fish. Day commenced drizzly, Wind S.E. Temp. 61° Breakfast and dinner at the Lake House, which is 8 miles below F^t Kearney, and 6 ms. above Nishnabotona Ferry. The 2 men I sent ahead, returned, informing me that the June freshet of the Mo. had set in, and was running fuller, and with more drift in it, than had been known for several years, in consequence of which, the ferry there had been a week ago discontinued, as highly dangerous, if not impracticable. My men were accompanied by a Mexican, who told me, in Spanish, that it was not possible to cross the river unless I proceeded up to Council Bluffs, and even there was very bad —

When the Company learnt this Statement, it created a great sensation, and some of the weakest minds thought it would be best to sell out, and return to St Jose. But I had conversed with a man,[61] now here, who, a month ago, ferryied successfully, over the river, opposite here, and about 4 miles off; I called him, and he had 3 hands, also there, and desired them to lead off, and I would follow with the Company, & must and would cross the river there. — So we hitched up and moved on, which was soon reached, and camp'd near the bank, by a rill.

JUNE 1. — Drizzly, strong breeze from the S.E. Temp. 60° Found truly an awful stream: — banks oerflow'd, running like a mill-race, and thick with drift, much of which was large trees. Set mechanicks to work, raising the sides of the Scow, fitting iron thole-pins, making new oars,[62] &c — while others were engaged repairing a portion of the old trail, and cutting a new one, to gain the bank higher up, so as to compensate for the great drift.[63] Merd. fly. clouds. Wind N.W. Temp. 74° We cut a tow path nearly a mile long, through submerged willows & very thick brush, and warped the Scow up to the new landing. At 3 P.M. started the Scow on an experimental trip, with 12 men, and 6 mules; — they drifted about 2 miles, and with great difficulty got up to the proper landing, — Indian Point, and had to remain there. without blankets. Sun Set clear, light variable airs, Temp. 64° Sent a canoe over, with provisions and blankets, and she returned with 2 of our party, and the Ferry-man and his assistants brot the scow over some time after dark. At dusk, the Spanyard rode into Camp, and fell drunk, from his mare, and there slept: — I had the animal removed and tied to a tree. As there were several deserted willow wig-wams, about, and other signs of indians, I had the mules picketed close into Camp.[64]

JUNE 2. — Clear and calm, Temp. 62°. Sent a wagon and 4 mules over. — Men had to stand on the side, with poles, and bear off the drift logs and trees. Cut a tow-path, on the opposite side of the river, in the perpendicular face of a clay cliff, about 2 feet wide, one hundred yards long, and averaging 20 feet above the boiling current — The cliff was rubbed bright, with the elbows of the men engaged in towing the boat up.[65] At 4 P.M. Crossed 2 wagons & 4 mules; until we had successfully ferried over 7 wagons and 12 mules to-day. (*Merd. Strong breeze S.E.*) Sun Set clear, Wind Strong from S.E. Temp. 64°

[JUNE] 3. — Clear, Strong breeze from the S.E. Temp. 62° To-day we crossed 7 wagons more and 12 mules. I accompanied the last boat. A mule chocked to death at his picket this night. — Result of carelessness —

JUNE 4. — Commences clear, wind N.N.E. Temp. 62° (*Merd. clear, Wind N.E. Temp. 82°*) Crossing 2 private vehicles & the remainder of the mules; all successful accomplished by 3 P.M.

This was an extraordinary feat, and exhibited great enterprise, patience and energy of the company. (*Officer rode down*) While eating a lunch of fried bacon & hard bread, on a fallen tree, an officer of the U.S. Army rode down; he had come from Grand Island to Fort Kearny, where he could not cross, and was there inform'd that our company were trying to get over, down here. He participated with us, in our rough lunch, and kindly took charge of some very hastily written letters, for home: And the ferryman took him and his faithful charger over. As the wind was blowing strong up stream, most of the time, I took advantage of it to assist in towing up, from the opposite or Wn shore[66] — A ridge-pole of a tent answered for a mast, another one for a yard, and a tent-fly made a square-sail: lines answered for braces, and thus we were helped up much each trip — The Ferryman said, that as he had only steered, taken upon himself no responsibility, and we had taught him a great *wrinkle*, he would only charge us half the usual price.

6 P.M. moved the train up upon the prairie, N.N.W. 3 miles, to a water hole, and camped. 7 P.M. Sun Set clear, light airs from the N.E. Temp. 70°

[JUNE] 5. — Commences clear, Wind S.E. Temp. 70°   At 3 A.M. we moved on 12 miles, to a pool, in the prairie, breakfasted there, and rolled on to a run,[67] — head waters of the Nemaha river, making 23¼ miles march to-day. Indians seen on the right, at a great distance, — supposed to be Pawnees   Merdn clear, with strong breeze from the S.E. Temp. 82°   Sun Set same 23¼

$$23\tfrac{1}{4}$$
$$14\tfrac{3}{4}$$
$$14$$
$$\overline{}$$
$$53$$

[JUNE] 6. — Cloudy, light breeze from the S.E. Temp. 68°   Moved on at 3 A.M. W. 14½ miles, and halted to breakfast at a stream, — Weeping water?[68] M. [Main] Fork Nemaha. At 11 A.M. moved on again. Merd. clear, Wind S. Temp. 86°   Met a government wagon, 7 days from Ft Childs, Grand Island, going to Ft Kearny, Mo.[69] 2 wagons and 3 gentlemen desired to accompany us, which we permitted — The proprietors of one of the wagons, 2 brothers, were gentlemanly clever fellows.

At 2 P.M. bad gulch, marsh, and mud. 4 P.M. met 3 deserters, from Grand Island, in a starving condition,[70] and relieved them, for which they seemed very grateful.

Afternoon showers, with thunder & lightning. Sun Set squall of rain, Wind S.W. heavy thunder & vivid lightning, Temp. 66° (*8 A M drizzles 9 A M met Gov. wag. 7 day from G. Is. At 9½ A M halted till 11½ Weeping Water Made 14½ m. & moved on again.*)

[JUNE] 7. — Clear and calm, Temp. 52°

At 10 A.M. a wagon broke an axle crossing Willow Ck. — a very bad place.

Merd. clear, light airs from N.W. Temp. 76° Repaired damage, noon'd, and at 1 P.M. moved on. — crossed a broad and very marshy bottom, of Salt Creek, full of small rattlesnakes, and late in the afternoon reached the bank of Salt Creek. This we found rather an interesting place, and calculated to afford us some past-time, by way of an ernest of what might be ahead e're we should reach the land of gold. A Stench, of gasses from the Creek, smelt exactly like putrid carcasses, and we had to hold our noses. — A descent cut at an angle of about 45°, and 10 ft. broad, with a large stump of a tree, worn smooth by ropes, at the head, lead to the upper end of a bridge, which was about 50 feet long, supported on several slender trees, for sleepers, and floored over with loose logs and sticks. No rail, and drift trees, lodging under the upper edge, forced by the torrent below, had raised the upper side and end of the bridge, while it sagged in the middle, and was much twisted.

The mules were taken out of gear, and very carefully lead down and over, in pairs: then a large white rope was fastened to the hind axle of a wagon, 2 men guided the tongue, while the rest of the company, with a round turn of rope, over the stump, lowered the wagon down, about 40 yds. to the bridge; the rope was then transferred to the tongue, and the hands very cautiously drew it across the warped, narrow, and oscillating structure, intended for a bridge. After which they had to double-team to get each wagon up the opposite bank. Here was a trial, and I had to meet it. I told the men that if they would work energetically and safely, to get the train over, as soon as possible, I would treat them, each to a *horn* of whiskey: — this stimulated them to an extraordinary exertion, so that by midnight we had crossed the whole train in safety.[71]

(*Sun Set same as Merd. Temp 70°*)

JUNE 8. — At 1 A.M. moved on 2 miles, beyond stench of the creek, and rested till 3. when we resumed the march. Sun rise clear, Wind N.E. Temp. 73°. — Course N.N.W. 9 A.M. reach'd Cotton Wood Ck. and camp'd, as there was excellent grass and water here, and mules and all wanted a little rest This forenoon we passed a government train with the mail, for Mo. Merd. clear, Wind N. Temp. 84° Here were numerous pretty wild flowers, gooseberries, strawberries, onions, prairie peas,[72] &c. Heard that the Sioux were at war with, and hunting the Pawnees.[73]

Sun Set clear, Wind W. Temp. 74°

After dark, a small lean wolf-dog came into camp, exciting my suspicion that some thieving Pawnee might be crawling around to steal mules, so visited the sentinels & cautioned them; one said he had seen something like a man crawling along the crest of a low ridge, close by, which I visited, but saw nothing. The dog very snapish, and sat outside the sentinels, yelping all night, like a wolf.

JUNE 9. — Clear, with light airs from the W. Temp. 52° At 4 A.M. the train moved.

At 9 A.M. met 7 government wagons, and 2 returning emmigrant wagons, 6 days from Grand Island. At 10 A.M. we halted & noon'd on the prairie. Found fragments of felspar, carnelian, semi-opal, iron-geodes, and lime formations, scattered over the plain. Merd. clear, Wind strong from the N. Temp. 69°

Mr. Bennet,[74] another man, and an old pawnee chief slept in camp.

JUNE 10 — Flyg clouds & calm, Temp. 52°.

At 4½ A.M. put the train in motion, at 8 A.M. a young man fell, and a wagon wheel passed over his leg without injuring him. — his leg happened to lay in a soft indentation of the plain when it occurred. The Pawnees commenced gathering around us, they seem to rise from the earth, on both sides, as far as the eye can distinguish them. I divided my mounted men in two parties, one as an advance guard and the other as a rear guard: and required a man on each side of each wagon, with his gun ready, in case of mischief. I believe the company was a good fighting party; the blackguards, who are generally cowards, were but few. If the pawnees had made a demonstration, we would most assuredly have *made* some ponies, But Alas! the great warriors, arabs, and terror of the plains, turned out to be a sadly reduced, starving, contemptable race![75] They begg'd me for bread, opened their dingy robes, and exhibited their prominent ribs and breastbones. As they were actually starving, famine might drive them to rob and break up some small party, maybe family, in the rear, and we had plenty; so I order'd a halt, gave the indians about a peck of hard bread, half a middling of bacon, and hat full of tobacco.[76] —They spread a skin on the plain, by the road side, on which was placed the bread, &c some of my boys threw in bells & other trinkets: and the chief[77] desired me to sit on his left, like the rest, — cross-legged, — forming a circle around the skin, the chief lit his long pipe, gave 3 whiffs, handed it to me, and I done the same, passing it around, in the same way, till it returned to the

Chief.[78] At 10½ a.m. corralled and nooned in road. Merd. fly. clouds. Wind Strong from the N.E. At 1 p.m. we moved on again, and at 5 p.m. camp'd in the Platte bottom.[79] At night some straggling pawnees, who had followed us, left. 9¾ = 19¾

[JUNE] 11. — Cloudy, Wind S.E. rain, thunder and lightning.

Temp. 56° Roused the camp at 3 a.m. but on account of the squally weather, laid by till after breakfast. 8 a.m. moved on. — Cloudy, Wind N.W. Temp. 60° Passed a grave on a small hill, with a cross on it, formed by pieces of tent-poles. Met Mr Hughes, with 4 wagons and 5 men, on government service, bound to Mo. He said that 2 days ago a little above the old Pawnee Village,[80] he was attacked by a War party of 500 Cheyennes,[81] who robbed him of all his provisions. I sold him 30 lbs of flour, 20. . bacon, and 6. . sugar. He stated that they came down on him, when he halted, closed his wagons, and with his men stood to their arms. — perceiving this, the chief, with 3 or 4 other Indians rode over, with a white flag tied to a rifle, and he went out & met them. The chief spoke Spanish, and said it was folly for that little party of white men to attempt repelling the indians by force, and he might just as well give up his provissions, and save their lives — This he had to do, — as the Indians rode up, and pillaged the wagons. — After which they threw down some bead-work, mocasins, sashes, &c — telling Mr Hughes, that there was pay for the provissions they had taken.[82] He said the indians were well mounted, armed, and caparison'd. He camp'd within a mile of us.[83]

(*Merd. fly. clds, Wind W. Temp. 72°*)
Sun Set clear, Wind N. Temp. 67°

JUNE 12 — Hazy, Wind S.W. Temp. 57°.
Moved early, as usual, — and in 15 miles passed through the deserted Pawnee Village,[84] No regularity in the disposition of the houses here — the trail passes to the left, and close alongside the outer houses, or lodges. In the open spaces between the huts, are scattered about circular pits, filled with rubbish, and are dangerous to fall into. — They were the indian's graneries. — Wooden mortars & pestles, muscle-shells, mats — old & new, worn out mocasins, dried herbs, willow sticks & poles, bones of animals, deer horns, pieces of saddle trees, &c. scattered around. The entrance to a lodge is by a door and sort of porch, the bottom of which descends at an angle of about 4 inches to the foot. — The floor of the lodge, is of course several feet below the surface of the ground. These circular habitations, are well fitted and secured, with upright crotches, and horizontal ridge poles running around, and radiating rafter poles, from the high central post, frame the connicle roof — They are fitted

[PLAINS INDIANS, DRAWN BY BRUFF AS DECORATIONS FOR A
CHANDELIER IN THE TREASURY BUILDING, DESIGNED BY HIM]

in all around and covered over with rushes and straw, and dirt over all. No doubt are very comfortable winter quarters.[85] In the largest lodge, about the centre of the village, I noticed a tier of bunks around, and a broken Mexican bridle and bit, and a straw-stuff'd cormorant. This I thought was the Council Hall. 4 miles further we discovered a small party of indians approaching, from the hills, and displaying a white flag. A squaw and two male indians, the latter arm'd with fusees, and 3 other men, and a boy on foot, with bows & arrows. They had a mule packed with a heavy load of buffalo meat. The principal man said that he was Chi-ri-Cherish's nephew,[86] and a half-chief, and embraced me with the warmth of an affectionate bear, and smelling just as odoriferous. He was tattooed, and told me that in 2 days more we would find buffalo. I gave him a biscuit & some tobacco. Very deep trails here in various directions, formed by the lodge poles dragged by horses, with heavy loads on them — cutting into the soft loam. Saw a very large hare, which some of my horsemen rode after, but it escap'd. In all the hollows, for a couple of miles, were corn-stalks, bean vines, sun-flower stalks, lambs quarter, and rank weeds. Beautiful prairie flowers. plenty of snipes, plovers, killdeer, curlews, grouse, &c —

Merd. hazy, Wind S.W. Temp. 65°.

Stop'd about 15 minutes, and moved on, making 22½ miles to camp, on the banks of the Platte. Sun Set cloudy, Wind strong from the S.E. Temp. 60° Some Antelope[87] & elk seen in the distance.

An ox-wagon, with a family, camp'd near us, they were quarreling all night about a stray ox. At night rain, thunder & lightning.

JUNE 13. — Cloudy, Wind N.E. Temp. 58° —

Our camp-ground of the last night, is a fine position for a prospect — on the top of a pretty high plateau, The broad and silvery Platte, sprinkled with numerous small grassy islets, some of which, in the sun's first rays, look like small sail-vessels — The willowy foot of Grand Island, a little ways above, the broad expanse of blue plains on the north side of the river, and below, looks like the ocean, bounded by the dim blue mountains — Merd. cloudy, Wind N. Temp. 70°. Sun Set cloudy, Wind W. Temp. 64° = 11 miles

[JUNE] 14 — Commences clear, with a light breeze from the N.W. Temp. 52°

At 4 A.M. we moved on, and at 8 A.M. through carelessness, Wagon No 1, was capsized:— it ran over a knoll, and tossed the loaded bed upside down, in the road, while the mules ran off with the running-gear. The smashing of bows and a standard or two, was all the injury. Mules brought back, freight taken out & repacked, after replacing the bed, and the cover thrown over, and we were soon rolling on again. Halted at 9 A.M. — making 9½ miles, breakfasted, and resumed the march. — Merdn clear, with strong breeze from the N.W. Temp. 68° At 12.15 P.M. again moved on, 18¼ miles, camping at 5.25 P.M. having made to-day, 27¾ miles. Camp between the river and trail. Sun Set clear, light airs from the N.N.E. Temp. 60° At night, 3 wagons from Grand Island, bound to Ft Kearney, Mo, camp'd near us, and I wrote by a teamster.

JUNE 15. — Commences clear, light airs from the S. Temp. 60° At 4 A.M. rolled on, halted at 7 A.M. to breakfast, and at 9½ resumed the march. Sent 2 men ahead to Fort Childs,[88] to inform my friends there that we were close by. Merd. hazy, Strong breeze S.E. Temp. 70°

At 2.25 P.M. camp'd, having made 15 miles.

3 Mormons,[89] — one a sick youth, supped and rested with us, and proceeded, going into Mo. from the Salt Lake. They had been robbed by the Crows.[90]

Sun Set fly. clouds, Strong breeze N.E. Temp. 65° 2 Pawnees desired to sleep in camp, putting them under surveilance of the guard, I permitted them to do so.

JUNE 16. Commences hazy, with a strong breeze from the S.E. Temp. 50° Moved again early. A sprightly Pawnee youth followed us, amusing us by chasing and shooting at a sparrow, with arrows, often hitting right under it; at last he fairly ran it down, & knock'd it on the head with his bow — He went to the fort.

Merd. Clear, very strong breeze from the S. Temp. 70° Passed several trains from St Jose. A grave near the fort had the following on the headboard, — "— (name obliterated) Died June 3d 1849, Of Van Buren, Aged 27 years." (*12½ mi —*)

[JUNE] 17 — Cloudy, with strong breeze from S.E. Temp. 52° occasional showers.

I visited the Fort after breakfast, and was most kindly received by Coll Bonneville,[91] Lieuts. Boots[92] & Davis,[93] &c —

This place is as yet merely the site of an intended fort; it has some adobe embankments, quarters — &c. of adobe & frame, and a number of tents & sheds.[94] Is on the bank of the Platte, where Grand Island makes a narrow branch of the river between it and the shore. They had, somehow, at the Fort got a rumor of my death, by Cholera, and knew no better till my card was handed the commandant by the 2 men I sent ahead. On the back of the card I pencilled:—

> "Our banner flutters in the breeze,
> In spite of Sioux and black pawnees".

Officers,[95] — Coll Bonneville, comd^t

Major Chilton (with family)

Capt. Van Vliet, Drag^s Q.M.

Lieuts { Ths. Davis, Levi Boots, Ogle } Inft.

Donaldson

Dr Hammond U.S.A.

(about 170 men here. Drag^s & Inft.)

Had to send a cart several miles, to the hills, for cedar wood fuel. Water we obtained from a *slew*, (I use the technicality of the plains) This part of the plains abound in deer, antelope, wolves, hares, rattlesnakes, Grouse, plovers, Snipes, curlew, ducks, &c —

Held a meeting of the Company, and equalized the private baggage — disgarding [discarding] a great deal of superfluous weight[96] — Sold a wagon to the Sutler for $30 — and the Ambulance to the Officers for $50. — a perfectly useless article, except to encourage lazy men to ride— Forge, Anvil, bellows, some lead & iron, we sold to a Mormon family here for $32.

Merd. flyg clouds, with strong breeze from the S. Temp. 80°

Sun Set do. fresh breeze from the S.E. Temp. 78°

[JUNE] 18. — clear, with strong breeze from S.E. Temp. 68°   Merdⁿ same.

Engaged repacking freight.[97]

Sun Set clear, strong S.E. 76°

[JUNE] 19 — Strong breeze S.E. Temp. 65°.

Moved early, noon'd $1\frac{1}{2}$ hours and continued on. Merdⁿ same weather, temp. 80 —. Made $21\frac{1}{4}$ miles and Camp'd. near river. Grave, close to the Camp:—

> "C. H. Cornwell,
> of Waukeshaw, Wis:
> Died June 10, 1849,
> Aged 26 Years."

Sun Set the same weather, Temp. 76°.

[JUNE] 20   Commences cloudy light S.E. 65

Moved on 12¾ miles to Plum Creek. No. 7 broke the tongue, and replaced it with a spare one. Merdⁿ flying clouds, Temp. 80°— Squalls of rain, thunder & lightning, soon reduced the temp: 20°. Between camp and creek a grave:—

> "J. A. Parks,
> Died June 4, 1849,
> Aged 34 Years,
> from Pontotoc, Miss."

JUNE 21 — Commences hazy, with light airs from the W. Temp. 66°

Recruiting mules, and men washing clothes, and a party out for buffalo.[98] A Mississippi and a Missouri Ox-train co. passed us. Saw a black wolf. Prairie dogs numerous.[99] cactus here — small species. Merdⁿ clear, wind light from the W. Temp. 74°

[JUNE] 22. — Clr. & calm, temp. 62°   At 7 A.M. moved 15 ms. — to 1.15 & noon'd. At 3 P.M. moved 8¾ m. to 6½ P.M. & camp.

Merdⁿ clear, calm, 86°[100]
Sun Set clear, light airs S. 76°
Fairy Rings   23¾ ms.[101]

[JUNE] 23   Clear & calm. Merdⁿ do. Lewis kill'd a buffalo. Their remains in every direction. Trails also. Wolves numerous. Noon'd at 1 P.M. 15 ms.[102] 3½ P.M. moved 7¾ = 22 — Half way, on left, a new grave. Sun Set fly. clds. light airs S.E.

A false alarm of indians at night.

JUNE 24. — Moved off at 6, but halted at 11 A.M. as a wagon had got in a deep gulch, and broken its tongue — Sent a spare one to the rear.

     (*Commences clr. & calm, 68°*   7 A.M. *moved on* —)

Merd. clear, very light airs from the S. Temp. 90°[103]   At 2 P.M. moved on — and made but 12 miles.[104]

Sun Set clear, light airs from S. Temp. 80° [105]   I dined & supped with Capt. McNulty commandg a New York Compy called the Colony Guards. Here I was treated to superior strong coffee. — A New Orleans Ox train compy. close by, among whom I found an old acquaintance, formerly of Washington, and several ladies.[106] A delightful cool spring near us. Clay bluffs ahead, on the left, & half a mile below, on the right are the forks of the Platte[107] —

[JUNE] 25. — Hazy & calm. Temp. 62°   Musquitoes numerous and annoying. Started at 5 A.M. At 7, passed a grave, on right of trail: —

"Lemuel Lee,
of Vandalia, Ill:—
Died June 3, 1849,
at 4 P.M. Aged
64 Years: Died of
prostration consequent
upon Cholera after an
illness of 2 weeks."

Merd. clear, strong breeze from the S. Temp. 86°—Another grave on left of trail:

"Captain Pleasant Gray,
of Huntsville, Walker Co.
Texas:
Died June 9, 1849, of Cholera,
After an illness of 3 days,
Aged 43 years."

Made 10 miles to noon halt.

Buffalo descried on the left,—hunters sent out by the different companies. Crossed a deep and bad hollow. Camped near a Slew, making 23 miles, to Poko Ck.

Sun Set clear, Wind S.E. Temp. 76°. (22¾ ms)

I supped with Capt. Brown, of a Tenn. Company.[108]

[JUNE] 26 — Commences clear, with light airs from the N.W. Temp. 61° Our 2 hunters return'd unsuccessful, having only wounded a buffalo.

Merd. clear, light breeze S.S.E. Temp. 84°. The casualties of buffalo hunting are very common. Men charg'd by wounded bulls, unhorsed, & many badly hurt — the horses generally running off with the band of buffaloes, for the indians to pick up hereafter. Lots of rifles and pistols lost, as well as horses: and many a poor fellow, after a hard day's hunt, on an empty stomach, unhorsed some distance from camp, has a long & tiresome walk, after night, to his own, or the nearest camp he can make. And some have been lost for days, at the imminent risk of their lives[109] —

A grave on the right of the trail:—

"——— (obliterated) Goodwin,
of Ala:
Died June 9th— 1849,
Aged 24 Years.

A little further another; on a bluff, 3 ms. above the Ford of the platte.

> "S. W. Moore,
> Died June 11th . . .
> ——— (obliterated)

I walked ahead with Dr Austin, and 3 men of my Company, 5 ms. As the company had pushed on by the bluff road, instead of fording below, at the forks, owing to the chap they called a *guide,* whom I had cautioned to look out for the ford, as we were close to it, had gone after a buffalo, and left the Company to follow the beaten trail on that side, while I was half a mile in the rear, conversing with a friend. — We met 2 of our men on mules, who said that the Company had proceeded so far that they thought best to keep on and ford higher up, saving time in retrograding.[110] The D^r and 2 others kept on, and myself with the other two, return'd to the Camp of the Tennessessians, where we supped and slept.[111] Dr Austin killed a rattle-snake, & prairie-dog, and chased a deer. To day we cut up a buffalo, (see plate)   4 graves, close together, on right of trail, 1 mile above the Ford, South fork of the Platte. —

"C. Taylor; Tenn: Cholera & Typhus."	"David Amick, Aged 35, Mo."
"Dr. J. T. Boon, Aged 29 yrs. Mo."	"J. Smith, Cholera, Aged 24. Mo."

JUNE 27 — Commences hazy, light airs from the N. Temp. 60°   Early this morning, Capt. McNulty tendered me a mule, and I forded the Platte, with them[112] — Found 2 of men with a St. Louis Comp. on crossing. My New York friends got all their train over without accident, except one wagon, which sank so in the sand that they had to leave it for the day. I [It] was about 50 yds from shore, and about 400 below the landing & camp, and contained a sick man. It looked queer to see a man wading down stream, waist deep, in the rapid river, with a pot of coffee in one hand and a plate of bread and meat in the other, going to the wagon, to the relief of his comrade. On the opposite shore could be seen a pointer dog, at the water's edge, howling for his lost master, on this side. My friends had to double team a heavy wagon to get it out of the river. — (*12 mules to drag wagon out. Forsaken hound on opposite shore. Commencing Clear, Wind N. beautiful view from hill of tongue about 6 ms.*) Dined with them, on buffalo pot-pie, rolls, and strong coffee. Parties were crossing the stream all day. Clear, Wind N. 3 P.M. moved on.

Beautiful prospect from an eminence. — The forks of the Platte, and its tongue of land, for about 6 miles. A grave on divide; —

"J. M. McClanahan,
of Morgan Co. Mo.
Died 13th June '49."

It was thought that the emigrants had made many semblances of graves, which were actually caches of goods.[113]

Another grave:—

"In memory of
Daniel Maloy,
of Gallitin Co. Ill.
Died June 18th
1849, of Cholera,
Aged 48".

Drove 12 miles to noon & lunch; where the road crosses a ridge, with a Slew below it. Saw numerous buffalo, opposite, on the South branch; 2 ahead of us, and chased, but escaped. (*Hunting accidents frequent   Clear & pleasant wind N.*)

Merd. Clear. Wind S. temp. 88°

Ox camp in rear ¼ m. 2 mule trains from Mass.[114] Made 22 m & C. [camped] left bank N. fork. Late at night 4 hunters, from a N. Orleans Compy. lost in a buffalo chase, came into Camp.

JUNE 28. — At 2 A.M. one of my men, with me, who had a mule, and the strangers left, to overtake their companies. Sun-rise flyg clouds, wind light from the E.N.E. At 7 A.M. we moved on the N. fork 22 miles above the ford, & C. [Camped]   About 1 mile from the train, I saw on a high ridge, left of road, 3 dark human figures, who soon disappeared from view: suppose they were indians.

Merd. clear, Wind S. Temp. 88°

A Camp of Ox wagons ¼ mile in rear of us. 2 packed mule companies of Mass. with drove oxen for meat, passed us, never saw such jaded and chafed set of animals in my life.[115] Made to-day about 22 miles, and camped on left bank of N. fork of the Platte. Clear & pleasant, Wind N. Magnificent view (*Saw party of mounted inds on high ridge to left   Passed Cheyenne hunts party*)[116]

[JUNE] 29. — Commences foggy & calm.[117]

[JUNE] 30. — Sandy road

Found a note in a cleft stick, on the side of the road, from my Company, to me.[118]

Merd^n fly. clouds, Wind S.E.

At 4 P.M. met a return wagon, the teamster enquired for me, and handed me another note from the company, to hurry up.

Through the forenoon and middle of the day, our road laid over a very high and level table-land, with dried & drying mud marshes. — Near one of these we nooned. A grave close by, on the right: —

> "Jno: Waugh,
> of Scott Co. Mo.
> June 17. 1849,
> Aged 20 Years."

(*Found Com. at 9 P.M.*) Night reached Co. at Ash Hollow[119]
140 m from F^t Larimie

JULY 1. — Sunday. Noon'd opp. a train on N. side riv. Slye waded across.[120] Grave on end of bluff terminating Ash Hollow. above, — left of trail leavg hollow —

> "Rachel E. Pattison,
> Aged 18, June 19, 49"

Heavy sand   In 5 ms. a grove of cedars on edge of a hill. 11 A.M. 3 horsemen & 2 pack mules passed, from F^t Larimie, express. Pass'd sev^l companies Drove 14 ms. & 1 P.M. camp'd   Fly clds strong E.S.E. Ind. lodges on opp. side

JULY 2. — Commences cloudy, light breeze E. — 68°

From 9¼ to 11 A.M. Rainy. Very light N.E. breeze, temp. 86°   Buffalo scull pillow

Noon halt, on the Platte, is 429 miles from where we left the Missouri river.

Hazy, very light airs N.E. 86° (*conical mount.*)

> "Jno Hoover, died, June 18. 49
> Aged 12 yrs. Rest in peace,
> sweet boy, for thy travels are over."

9¼ m. to 11 A.M.[121]

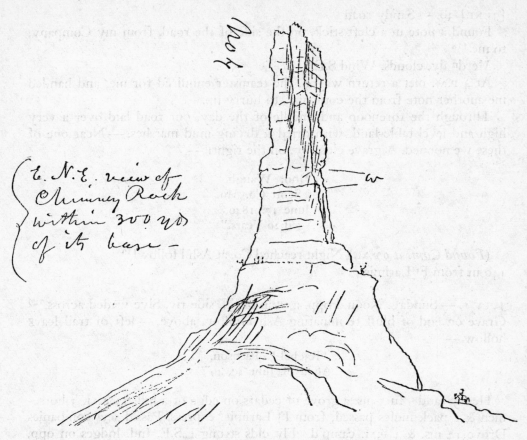

(E. N.E. view of
Chimney Rock
within 300 yds
of its base —

JULY 3 — Started at 9 A.M. — made 12 miles, & noon'd near bad water & alkaline pits, on right of trail.[122] I found an old company Roll-book, of the Army.

Clear, wind light, from E.N.E. Temp. 70°

Merd. ditto — Temp. 90° 3 P.M. moved on, to Dry Ford, a small marshy stream, near Court House Rock.[123]

(*N.T. Phillips Aged 35, Dep. this life July 11, '49, Cholera Bristol*) Frenchman alarmed Camp at night.

JULY 4. Commences cloudy, with showers, thunder, & lightning, and a strong breeze from the E. Temp. 62°.

(*13 guns sunrise*)

Merd. clear, with a strong breeze from the S.S.W. Temp 82°.

(Beyond spring, grave — Ellis Russell   Grave on left of 2 sand hills. Sam P. Judson ⚹ E. Morse Aged 30 y)

At 2 P.M. marshalled the company, fired a feu-dejoi[124] — visited by a squad of our N. York friends, whom we received with military honors, and filed in between 2 wagons, covered over and arranged for dinner; where, by request, I delivered an address, and at 3 sat down (on the ground) to a sumptious repast, — of pork & beans, buffalo meat, sort of rolls, hard bread, bean soup, & stewed dried apples. Dessert — apple pies. After removal of the ———— tin platters & iron spoons, the medical stores of brandy and port-wine, were used up in drinking a set of regular, and some volunteer toasts. The ladies honored us with their presence on the occasion; and to them we were indebted for several pounds of dried apples, and decent pastry. From this camp Cathedral rock bears W. by S. about 6 ms. off. Chimney-Rock[125] W. by N. about 3 miles distant. This humble attempt to celebrate the day, with the most limited means, 3,470 miles from our homes.[126]

JULY 5. — Clear and calm, Temp. 64°

Efflorescences of nitre on the plain, and particularly in the perpendicular banks of the Platte. Started early; 2 miles below Chimney-Rock, on the plain, left of trail, a grave:—

> "G. McBeth, M. D.
> Died June 21. 1849,
> Of Buffalo, N. Y."

near this another: —

> "Wm K. Colly, of Ray Co. Mo.
> Died of Cholera, June 18.
> 1849, Aged 49 years.
> Has 1 brother in Compy"

On small emminence, left of trail, 4 or 5 miles below Chimney Rock, another: —

> "P. W. Totle [Tolle]
> of Marion Co. Mo.
> Died June 14.
> 1849, of Cholera,
> Aged 38 years,
> At 2 P.M."

Graves on N.W. side of Chimney Rock: —

"M. Dade
of Buffalo,
N.Y."

"J. Griffith,
of Buffalo,
N.Y."

One mile below the rock, on the left of trail: —

"Wm Witt,
of Mackin Co. Mo.
Died June 21. 1849,
Aged 29 years."

Merd. Clear, with light airs from E. Temp. 84° Grave 2 ms. in rear of noon halt, on the left: —

"Jno. Campbell,
of Lafayette Co. Mo.
came to his death by the
accidental discharge
of his gun, while riding
with a friend, June 21.
1849. Aged 18 years."

(*noon'd in road, edge of stream*[127]   *Afternoon 12 ms*)
made 14¾ miles, and camp'd near the river. — Chimney Rock bears S.S.E. Sun-set fly. clouds and a strong breeze from S.E. Temp. 70°

JULY 6 — noon'd in road, at edge of stream. Grave, in the heart of Scott's Bluffs: — right of trail: [128] —

"James Roby,
of Comp. I, Mounted
Riflemen; Died
June 19, 1849
of cholera.
Born in the state
of Ohio, Aged 20
years." [129]

Merd. Clear, Strong breeze from S.E. Temp, 88° made 26 miles, to camp near a clear run, and about 1 mile from a trading-post of Rubedeaux's.[130]

Sun-Set flyg clouds, thunder & indications of a squall. Wind strong from the S.E. Temp. 76°

JULY 7 — Clear and calm, Temp. 78°

This basin, among the singular and romantic bluffs, is a beautiful spot. It appears to extend E. & W. about 5 ms. and about 3 ms. wide.[131] In a deep gulch lies a cool clear spring and brook. — Close by is a group of Indian lodges & tents,[132] surrounding a log cabin, where you can buy whisky for $5 per gallon; and look at the *beautiful* squaws, of the traders.[133] Flour here sells for 10¢ per lb   At W. end of the Bluffs you have the 1st sight of Larimie peak, about 60 miles off.[134] Small cactii, with white, and also with red flowers, and plums, are here

3 Graves near the Spring: —

"Jesse Galen,	"F. Dunn,
Independence, Mo."	Aged 26"
"Joseph Blake."	

Beautiful large orange colored poppys, and a small animal of the Lemur genus — with cheek pouches filled with grass-seed.

Merd. fly. clouds, strong breeze from the S.W. Temp. 92°   Made 13¾ ms. to noon halt, on Horse Creek. Saw a dead mule in the road. Sandy barren country. Gofers numerous.[135] Extensive patches of dwarf sun-flowers, and poppys of a red color. The N. York company about ¼ m. ahead. Passed 2 men, one of them mounted, from a camp 10 miles ahead, going back to the bluffs for a stray animal. Horse Creek is very shallow, — 3 to 6 inches only, and sandy bottom. Scattered Sage (Artemesia) in the plains. I killed a large rattle snake.

Sun Set cloudy & calm, Temp. 80°

Afternoon's march 8¾, making for the day, 22½ miles. Camp'd on the banks of the Platte.

The country passed over to-day was generally, sandy and barren, with sand stone. Met 2 wagons, 4 yoke of oxen, each, from Ft. Larimie, bound in to Missouri. An old silver-headed man drove one of them, and lied as though he had followed it all his life. — He told me that he had been 60 ms. west of Larimie, where the chief proprietor of the wagons died, it was the last request of the dying man that he would take them and his family back, to Missouri; He said that the widow and children were in one of the wagons. — This old sinner told another man, that the cause of his return was, because the indians, emmigrants, & drought, had used up the grass W. of that 300 miles; and to another, he stated that insufficiency of provisions was the cause. As my men were very anxious to hear all they could about the country ahead, and generally believed the statements of return parties, they had, in this instance, a queer account to reconcile.

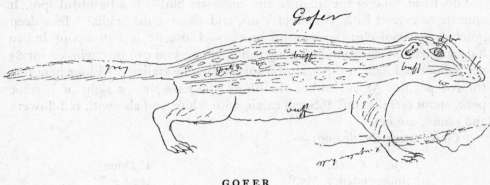

GOFER

[JULY] 8. — Commences clear, strong breeze from the W.S.W. Temp. 72° at 7 A.M. — we moved on, and the train had only gone its length, when I was called, and informed that a member, who had, last night complained of indisposition was now dangerously ill: This was strange, as no report had been made to me of his illness, and the mules were called in, hitched up, and the train put in motion before I was told of the disaster. I immediately wheeled the train to the right, moved down a few hundred yards, and corralled, on the banks of the river. On walking back to the tent of the unfortunate man, I found the wagon of his messmates standing there, and the Surgeon attending him. The D^r told me he had all the symptoms of Asiatic cholera. His messmates said that for several days he had complained of indisposition, and had also drank of *Slew* water, which I had cautioned the men against using. At 11 A.M. he was deranged, saying he was not afraid to die, and requesting his friends to shoot him.

Merd. Clear, Strong breeze from the W.S.W. Temp. 82°

At 1 P.M. poor Bishop died, of Cholera. — The first casualty in the Company, sudden and astounding, was this very mysterious and fatal visitation. Yesterday, in presence of the deceased, I remarked how very fortunate we had been, in all respect[s], and trusted we might continue so. The messmates of the deceased laid him out, sewed him up in his blue blanket, and prepared a bier, formed of his tent-poles. I had a grave dug in a neighboring ridge, on left of the trail, about 400 yards from it. Dry clay and gravel, and coarse white sand-stone on the next hill, afforded slabs to line it with, making a perfect vault. I sat 3 hours in the hot sun, and sculptured a head and foot stone; and filled the letters with blacking from the hub of a wheel.

I then organized a funeral procession, men all in clean clothes and uniforms, with music, (a key-bugle, flute, violin and accordian) and two and two, with the Stars & stripes over the body, we marched to the measured time of the dirge, deposited the body of our comrade in the grave, an elderly gentleman read the burial service, and we filled up the grave, erected the stones, and returned to camp. Capt. McNulty, his Lieutenant, and a firing party of 8 men in uniform (N.Y.Comp) came back some distance & participated in the last rites over the adventurer's grave.[136] The sun shed his declining rays over the closing scene. (*Lowered the body into the grave with bridle-reins.*)

Sun Set clear, light breeze from the W.S.W. Temp. 72°

The adventurer's train, —
On the Platte river plain, —
Was halted at early hour; —
For a comrade was ill,
Whom no medical skill,
Could save from a Higher power! —

On the banks of the Platte, —
With its flow'ry mat, —
A corral and Camp were made; —
And the sick was borne,
To his tent that morn, —
To die on that distant glade! —

The Surgeon's skill —
And his messmate's will —
Were exerted, alas! in vain! —
For the hour of noon,
Came Sorrowing, Soon,
When the faded Corse was lain!

With mournful look, —
For a Shroud they took, —
His blanket, — and sew'd him round; —
And that banner bright, —
Once his soul's delight, —
O'er his breathless form was bound!

The manly tear,
Fell on the bier, —
Of the poles of his vacant tent;
And breath'd they a sigh, —
When they saw him lie, —
In deaths embraces pent! —

Then came from Camp,
The measur'd tramp, —
Of his comrades, — in fun'ral array; —
And they bore his remains,
Across the plains, —
At the dusky close of the day! —

And the bugle's wail,
Was borne on the gale, —
Far, over plain and hill:
And the wolf did howl, —
And seek his hole, —
At a sound so mournful & shrill!

They delved a tomb, —
In a rocky womb, —
Of a hillock, — near the trail; —
And a tear did trace,
Each sun-burnt face,
As they closed his earthly goal!

The isolated range of hills here are of sand, gravel, & clay, and contain varieties of quartz — chalcedony, semi-opal, Carnelian, phrase, berryl, and jasper, of various colors, and fragmentary felspar. I found a yellow granular quartz pebble, size of a black walnut, which was very heavy, and contained a white metal which I thought was silver. Hollows of standing-water emitted a disagreeable effluvia. Musquitoes in abundance. No wild animals or game seen. Buffalo-chips[137] scarce, grass good, fuel drift-wood from the river. Northern side of the river, as far as we could see, white sand-hills. Many ox-trains on the opposite shore. After the funeral hitched up and moved ahead 3 ms. and Camped. River hears [here] appears to be generally very shallow, with numerous small sand islands, covered with some kind of dwarf bush.

During the night a deer ran close by a Sentinel, who imprudently fired at it, and thereby alarmed the camp; I went out and repremanded him.[138]

JULY 9 — Commences clear and calm.

Temp 54°   At 6 A.M. we moved on, and made 14¾ miles to noon halt, — at 11 A.M. on right of the trail, and on the side of a grassy hollow, with willows & small cotton-wood trees. — Here plenty of grass, fuel, musquitoes, flies, and gnats. A guard-sergeant struck one of the men violently in the face, upon which I immediately convened the Company into a drum-head court, tried the offender, broke him of his office, and inflicted 4 extra-guards on him.[139]

Merd. Clear, with light airs from the S.W. Temp. 94°   (1 P.M. *resumed the march*)

The march, this forenoon, was exceedingly warm & dusty. The dust here is very annoying, an impallpable powder, put in motion by the trains, and blowing directly in our faces. On our left coarse brown sand-stone cliffs and sand-hills. In the bottom, — on our right, scattered cotton-wood, willow, and brush. The river is about ¼ mile off — on the right.

(*Grave on left of trail, ½ mile in rear of the noon halt, —*
"*Levi Smith, Died June 19, 1849, Lawrence Co. Mo.*")

Opposite shore sandy & barren, and clouds of dust indicate the march there, of long heavy ox-trains.[140] Sent 3 men ahead to Fort Larimie.

In the afternoon's march, the road turned abruptly to the left, over barren sandy heaths, and hills, — coarse grey sandstone occasionally cropping out of the latter.

Once and a while patches of dwarf sun-flowers gilded acres, with their yellow hues. At our noon halt, the [road?] runs close to the foot, (on our left,) of brown sand stone, blocks of which lay in in [sic] masses and scattered about. All the accessible faces of blocks & cliffs, were marked and inscribed with names, initials, & dates. This peculiar vanity has been displayed all along the route, from our frontier down into the valley of the Sacramento. Nothing escapes that can be marked upon. — Buffalo-sculls, stumps, logs, trees, rocks, etc. even the slab at the heads of graves, are all marked by this propensity of *"pencilling by the way."* The singular feature is that of marking initials; for instance A. S. S. as if every one should know who he was.[141] We had just commenced our noon lunch, when the swarms of biting & stinging insects in the hollow, on our right, where the mules were left to graze, drove them up on the road, in a great hurry, switching their tails furiously, very abruptly spoiling their dinners.

We are close on the rear of our worthy friends, — the N. Yorkers. Foothills of the Rocky Mountains ahead. Some few prairie flowers. Afternoon drive, — 12¾ ms. making 27½ miles to the Ford of Larimie river,[142] by 6 P.M. Here we had to block some of the wagon-beds up, to keep the contents dry, as there was a deep place in the ford. And we immediately crossed over. The bar on which we drove over — extended nearly across, and was composed of coarse pebbles and stones: current — rapid. — About 100 yds. over. Several hundred yards back from the river's bank, on the right, stood the old adobe walls of Fort Platte, the original post of the fur traders, now in ruin; and looks like an old Castle. — It is rectangular[143]

Sun Set cloudy, with a strong breeze from the S.S.E. Temp. 80°

After crossing, I directed the train to continue on to the left, on the trail to Fᵗ Larimie[144] a couple of miles off, and camp in the bottom close by: (Tolerable grass) and proceeded to the right to a Camp of American Fur trade[r]s, & indians. Here I was welcom'd very kindly, and most courteously, by Mr. Husband — the superintendant of the Fur Trading post.[145] Mr. H. informed me that he had had a letter for me, but which some 10 days ago, he had turned over to the Officer at the Fort, who was acting as Post Master. After the luxury of a *cigar*, I walked over to my Camp.

JULY 10   (*Commences clear, light airs from S. Temp* 70°)

We rest to recruit the mules, &c — for 2 days.

I spent the forenoon at the Fort. Maj. Simons[146] treated me most kindly; and on enquiry for the letter, Mr. Husband said was there for me, found that some days ago, a man belonging to a Company from Tennesse or Kentucky, had enquired for and obtained it! Had to send the mules up the Larimie river, 5 miles, under a guard, to graze.

Here we sold our ox-wagon. Mr. Husband, very politely, ordered his black-smith to drop all other work, and cut and shorten our tires. Held a meeting in relation to two men who had travelled some time in the company, whether they should proceed with us or not: — decided in the affirmative.[147]

Merd. Clear & Calm, Temp. 96°
Sun Set flyg clouds, Temp 80°

[JULY] 11. — Grazing mules & repairing wagons. Dined at the Fort, with the Major. Had the pleasure of seeing Lt Woodbury of the Engineers.[148] Sketch'd the Fort. 11 A.M. my train moved on over the sand-hills, to right of and near the Fort, fairly entering the mountains.

Fort Larimie, purchased by our Government, from the American Fur Comp^y is an extensive rectangular structure of adobie. It forms an open area within — houses & balconies against the walls. Heavy portals and watch tower, and square bastions at 2 angles, infilading the faces of the main walls. It has suffered much from time and neglect.[149] (*We bought a small seine here for $10. A very useful article.*) After bidding my kind friends farewell, I shouldered my gun, to walk over the hills alone, to reach the camp of my company. (*12½ P.M.*) A few hundred yards from the fort, after rising a sand hill, the trail passes through a burial ground of the Traders, and mountaineers. Several picketed rectangular enclosures contained one or more graves: several had crosses erected on them, and one, in particular, on the right, containing a single grave, was filled in with buffalo scules [skulls], and deer-horns, and also embellished with a rude wooden cross, — This I presumed was the grave of some Mountain Nimrod. 2 of my friends, who owned a small spring wagon, remain'd at the Fort to repair the broken iron axle.

Larimie Peak stood up boldly on my left. After I had walked 5 or 6 miles, the trail turned abruptly. — with the stream, to the left: and opposite was a small willowy island. In this bend — about 200 yds. from the bank, was a grave, — on right of trail, and a large grey wolf[150] standing close to it, looking down, upon it; and stood so till I was within 50 yds of him, and then looked towards me as unconcerned as if he thought me *nobody*. I fired, striking under his belly, which made him leap, run off slowly about 200 yds. and stop and look at me again. I halloe'd and pointed my gun at him, and at last he sulkily moved over the plain for the hills. I found a board at head of the grave, inscribed with pencil-marks: —

"T. Green.
of Cholera,
Jackson Co. Mo.
20. June."

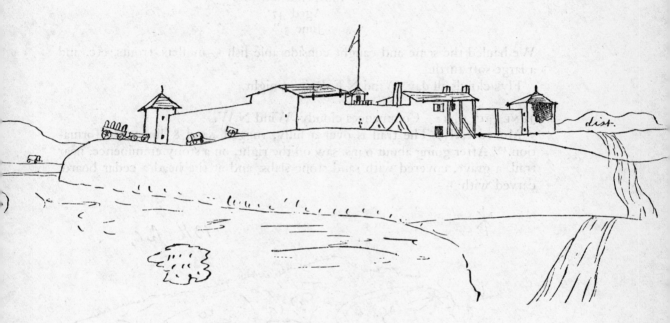

Fort Laramie

dist.

A steep and rugged hill to descend beyond this. High perpendicular white Sand Stone cliffs in an acute angle of the river, where it turns left then right, and the trail descends to a grassy bottom, where, alongside a large island, thick with willows, a short distance below the bend, my Company were camped. This I reached by 3½ P.M. quite tired.

Near by was a grave: —

> "Nathan Noland,
> of Independence, Mo.
> Aged 47
> June 3."

We hauled the seine and caught considerable fish — mullets, trouts, etc. and a large soft turtle.

Flyg clouds all day, Wind N.E. Rain at night.

JUNE [JULY] 12 Commences cloudy, Wind N.W.

Moved early: The trail is over a hilly, rugged, sand & limestone formation.[151] After going about 6 ms. saw on the right, on a stony emminence, near trail, a grave, covered with sand stone slabs, and at the head a cedar board, carved with: —

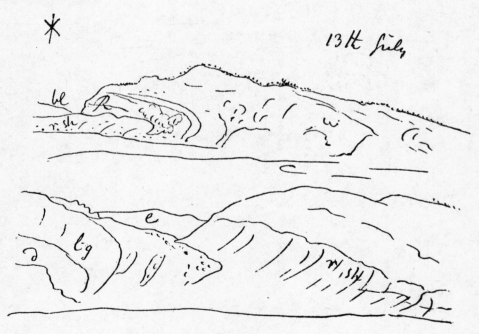

"Mrs. Mildred Moss,
wife of D. H. T. Moss,
late of Galena, Ill:
Died July 7. 1849,
Aged 25 years."

A stick nailed to the head-board, had a white cotton rag attached, — like a flag: intended, no doubt, to attract the attention of some acquaintances in the rear.

Soon reached the "Warm-Sp'g." brook, government wagon & men there, and lime-kilns close by.[152]

In the stream noticed the remains of a dead horse, — and those singular metamorphosis — horse-hair snakes, in various stages of transformation. — Some the worm was only about 2 inches long, with a tail of 10 or 14 ins. of horsehair, others longer, &c.[153] Passed a camp of 5 wagons, one of the party was in a tent dying of Cholera.

Merd. Clear & very warm, light airs from the S.E. very dusty.

The N. Yorkers passed us.

At noon a man on a mule, who was going to Ft Larimie in search of a stray mule belonging to his company, — some short distance ahead, rested with us, and I wrote by him to the Fort. Grass scarce — fish plenty. Here we abandoned some superfluous articles.

At 3 P.M. we moved on among the Black Hills, abreast of Larimie Peak.[154] The road generally good, but tedeous — up & down hill. The Scenery grand.

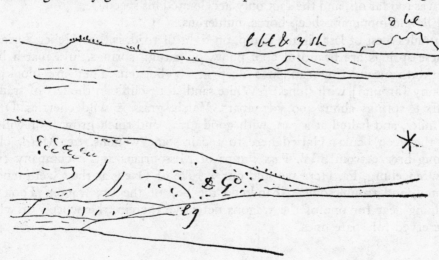

Found some moist places in the road, from the rain last night — every where else the thirsty sands had absorbed it. Passed numerous places where emigrants had camped — thickly strewn with discarded effects.

On descending a rough rocky hill, one of the wagons, was, for a short time, placed in a very perilous position: the right fore-wheel was run over the edge of a steep and high cliff. — We quickly discharged the cargo, extricated it & moved on again. crossed a small run,[155] and watered [stock], — turned immediately to the right, to gain the river bottom. Twice crossed the deep, dry, & serpentine bed of a run. At Sun Set passed several dry beds of streams, and at dusk corralled,[156] on the road, between cliffs and the river (Larimie) 2 ms. from the latter, after a day's march of 23¼ miles.

Sun Set flyg clouds, Wind S.E.

JULY 13. — clear, light breeze from the S.

I ordered the mules in, and train to move on as soon as ready and started ahead, about 4 A.M. I had gone on over a pretty valley country, bounded by low hills on the right, stream on the left, and close behind it rugged hills, morning air delightful, and proceeded about 3 ms. when I perceived a large black wolf coming down the trail, towards me. — He was then about 200 yards off — I had a double-barrel, charged with buck-shot, and I jumped off to the left — down a bank, behind a bush, awaiting the approach of the wolf, to give him a *blizzen*; but he had either seen or smelt me, and on raising my head, saw him sneaking up a hill to the right, I fired at him, but he was too far off, and the shot only accelerated his speed.

Elk and mountain-sheep horns, numerous.

3 miles west of last night's Camp, on right of road, is the "Heber Springs." These springs are beautiful cool pools, or natural springs, in a marsh by a sparkling meandering run, in a deep grassy bottom. They are block[ed] arouny [around] with stone.[157] White sand-stone cliffs on the left of trail, — cliffs & springs about 400 yds. apart. Marsh, grass, & wild cherries. Drove 9½ miles, and halted at a run, with good grass, and thick growth of willows on the deep banks. Halted here to repair some wagons, &c. Merd. clear, strong breeze from S.W. Pass camps of Missourians and a company from Lawrenceburg, Pa. Here we sold our 3 yoke of Oxen, as they were tender-footed, and troublesome. Abandon'd the bed of the Ox wagon. Took the running-gear for one of the wagons defective therein, the wheels of which I reserved for spare ones.

Boston pack'd mule Co.
July 13th

pale dusky olive

RED CLIFFS & EARTH NEAR HEBER SPRINGS [RED BLUFFS, JULY] 15TH

A beautiful undulating road. Sun-Set clear, strong breeze from S.E. Camp'd at Sun-Set, in the Platte bottom, ¼ mile from the edge of stream,[158] in a hollow of a very remarkable bend, where the stream runs through a deep, narrow, short, and crooked cañon.

Found numerous camps here. — Drove 14½ miles

Grass good. Here was a Boston pack company.

DIAGRAM OF THE CAMP
GROUND AND VICINITY

[JULY] 14. — Commences flying clouds, wind light from the E. Road rather bad — hilly, with cobble-stones. A thirsty drive of 15 miles, and halted on the bank of a deep hollow, with a brook, and poor grass. (*Horse Shoe Ck*) Passed 2 very extensive patches of sun-flowers.

Merd^n Flyg clouds, warm, light airs from the S.

On side of a hill of the mountain range on left, about two-thirds of the distance of the morning drive, a grave: —

> "Ths. M. Rankin,
> Of Lewis Co. Mo.
> Died June 25th '49
> Aged 28 years."

Afternoon's drive brought us to "La Bonté Creek," good water, but rather low. Plenty of timber and brush in the bottom Close by the Camp lay a large trunk of a Cotton-wood tree; inscribed all over with names, initials, dates, &c as usual. On leaving Larimie peak in rear and left, saw an indian about 2 miles off, making towards the peak. Road very dusty, but solid & smooth.[159]

A wagon broke a hind wheel, which was speedily replaced. Plenty of snakes and Elk & deer horns in the bottom. Made fires and re-set some tires. No grass here, so sent the mules off under guard, about 2 miles, to where there was. 24½

JULY 15. Commences clear & calm, very warm, wind S.

I feel quite indisposed, — several of my men also unwell.

One mule missing and one had the colic.

We had rather a late start this morning, as there was considerable repairs to complete.[160] Moving now over a very rugged and hilly country: — Red earth and cliffs. Cedars on the hills to the left. — The road soon sweep[s] around the base of a very tall conical hill, crowned with a pile of dingy yellow rock & earth, and resembles much such scenes on the Rhine, — a great eminence, with a ruined tower on top. Here we found horn-frogs.[161] Saw some very pretty tabular white quartz, resembling much fine hard marble. No grass or water during the morning drive. Reached a branch of 'La Bonté.'[162] Steep sandy & sand-stone banks. By going down the dry bed a little, right of trail, found a spring & pool of water. A wagon descending here broke a wheel, detaining us some time to repair. Under the shade of some large willows, was a wagon & tent, — and a colored man & woman; on going up, I had the pleasure of making the acquaintance of Mr. Pickering & lady, from S[t] Louis.[163] (They had a cow,) and most kindly invited to lunch. (They had just dined & put away their provissions, &[c].) Being very hungry & fatigued, I accepted their polite invitation, and had a nice white roll of bread, and a cup of good coffee, with *milk*.

Merd[n] flyg clouds & light showers.

Another broken wheel, and having only spare fore-wheels, had to use them — the wagon thus running on 4 small wheels. At 5 P.M. descending a long stony hill, our little mess wagon, broke down, a perfect wreck. — A short detention here to distribute the load. Found to-day fibrous gypsum, Calcedony, carnelians, green horn-stone, pink-colored also. At 7 P.M. turned down the bank of ⎯⎯ Creek,[164] ¼ miles from the road, and camped. Sent the mules down the creek 3 ms. under guard to graze, as the grass is all gone here. Showers, with thunder & lightning.

JULY 16. Cloudy and calm, very warm. Rugged and irregular road, over continual rolls of mountain spurs & deep vales[165] — Latter part, when near the edge of the Platte, 2 Mormons came up, and desired me to cross there, and informing me what companies they had taken over. But I knew what sort of a ferry they had, and that the country, on the other side was a deep sand-drag, and where the proper ferry and conveyance was: And declined. — Going on, I found the train halted, and on going back to see what was the matter, found that the Mormons had had the impudence to stop them, to persuade the men to cross there; and the teamster of the lead wagon actually said that he thought the *Sense of the company should be taken about it*. I order'd him preremptorily to vacate his seat, or drive on at once, and handling a pistol in my belt, told the Mormons to be off, or I'd blow them to blazes. — So the train promptly moved ahead.[166] This hard tramp for the mules, 27½ miles, brought us to Deer Creek, which we crossed, passing through hundreds of tents, wagons, camp fires, and people of every age & sex, congregated on its banks,[167] and turned down to the right, camped on the banks of the Platte, at the Ferry, ⅓ of a mile above the mouth of the Creek.[168] This drive was without grass. Here was a little grass. The ferry here kept by 3 men. It was night when we camped.

[JULY] 17. — (*Commences clear & very warm Calm.*) Very early this morning I sent the mules 7 miles up Deer Creek, under guard of 20 men — to graze, and a party to cut grass & bring down. Hauled the seine, in Platte, a [&] caught a number of fine fish. A Company with ox-wagons, crossed the ferry this morning. Our wheels much shrunk — repairing & strengthening them.

The abandonment and destruction of property here — at Deer Creek, is extraordinary: true, a great deal is heavy cumbrous, useless articles: A Diving bell and all the apparatus, heavy anvils, iron and steel, forges, bellows, lead, &c. &c. and provisions; — bacon in great piles, many chords of it — good meat. Bags of beans, salt, &c. &c. Trunks, chests, tools of every description, clothing, tents, tent-poles, harness, &c. &c.

I took advantage of the piles of bacon here, and had all mine trimmed of fat and the rusty exterior and the requisite amount of pounds replaced by choice cuts from the abandoned piles. Was told of a man here, who a few days ago offered a barrel of sugar for sale, for about threble its cost, price — and unable to obtain that, he poured Spirits of turpentine in it, and burnt it up. The spirit of selfishness has been here beautifully developed — Discarded effects generally rendered useless: — Camp utensils & vessels broken, kegs & buckets stove, trunks chopped with hatchets, & saws & other tools all broken. A considerable accumulation of ox-chains & yokes. I dined at 1 P.M. with Dr Pegrim and his little company, who are camped ¼ mile above us, on the river bank. They have 3 wagons and mules. Fish cooked every way and rolls and good coffee. Merdⁿ clear, calm, & very warm.

Trains of ox-wagons hourly coming up, among some of them Mr. Pickering & lady. At Deer Creek there is a camp of 3 wagons & several Missourians, who have 2 wagons heavily laden with Alcohol, for California. This they dilute, and with dried apples, peaches, &c. manufacture all kinds of liquors. They sell a dilute whiskey at 50¢ per pint, and expect that on the route, and in California they will realize a fortune from the proceeds: but I doubt much that they will ever get a gallon of it into California.

The Ferry-boat here, made and tended by 3 or 4 men, is composed of 8 *dug-outs*, or canoes, — of cotton-wood; and grooved timber pinned over, connecting them, and forming a rail-way to run the wagons on.[169]

JULY 18   Clear, with fresh breeze from the E. Very dusty. Sent out 2 wagons to grass-camp. Merd. clear. Wind moderate, N.W.

Saw a large buffalo on the edge of a high cliff $\frac{1}{4}$ mile off, on S. Side of our camp. At Sun Set the mule guard drove in the mules & brought the 2 wagons loaded with fine grass: likewise buffalo-meat, having shot one up the Creek. Repaired our wagons to-day 175 miles from this Ferry to the South Pass, Rocky Mts.

[JULY] 19. Several trains of ox-wagons crossed the ferry: — the animals are swum over. Cloudy all forenoon, Strong breeze from the S.E. Crossed the company after dinner, and camped a little above the landing, with springs in a hollow. Country generally sandy. At night it blew fresh, drizzly, and disagreeably cool. Paid $1 per wagon for crossing. Left a guard on S. side, with the mules.

JULY 20. Cloudy, light airs from the N.E. Crossed all the mules over early. Distributed the hay among the wagons, completed some slight repairs and greased all the axles.

Merd^n cloudy, Wind N.E.

At 2 P.M. we rolled on, over a chain of sand-hills, heavy travelling. Sand stone formation, with singular nodules of sand-stone of larger size; — Calcedony, and coarse silecified wood.

The road occasionally runs near the river. Passed many old camping spots, with the usual vestiges and abandoned property. In a bottom, close to the edge of the river, under the willows, had been a large camp, and in the midst was a hole in the earth, fresh cut, like a grave, and a board with fragments of an inscription, "to the memory of "x x x x "Died June "x x x x 1849." All the rest obliterated. Over the quondam grave, a board was nailed to a tree, on which was pencilled this inscription: — *"The fools are not all dead yet."* — This was a cáche, no doubt, formed to resemble a grave, which some cute chaps had opened & emptied. A beautiful prospect on the opposite side of the river. — The dark Black Hills,[170] with bright spots of sun-shine on them, and the rest partially enshrouded in mist and clouds, while around us it was murky and drizzling. Travelled $11\frac{1}{2}$ miles, corralled & camped on the trail, in a bottom with a gentle inclination to the river, $\frac{1}{3}$ mile off. Opposite a bend, and on our right a basin among hills, containing wild-oats, about 300 yds. off, where I sent my mules to graze. Groves of willow and cotton-wood on river bank. Several sand islands, on one was the fragments of a raft. We passed to-day, the camp of a company with ox wagons, who crossed the ferry early in the day, and were apparently holding a meeting. We also passed another ox-train, in motion, which had crossed the ferry an hour before us. Another Compy with ox wagons was camped not far from us.

4 Horse men, in dark clothes, looking in the distance like soldiers, were seen all the afternoon, travelling up the river, on the opposite (S) side. Wolf and badger holes numerous. Saw many dead oxen to-day, and occasionally the remains of buffalo recently killed.

The Platte is rapidly narrowing. Grass very scarce. Camp'd near, my particular friends Wm Poyle, Allen, Young, & Peck, clever, intelligent & worthy men.[171]

A great many women and children in the companies More beans discarded than any other article of provissions. — often disagree with the bowels, and are heavy freight.[172] Sheet-iron stoves, which every mess of the emmigrants had, were gradually drop[p]ed, as useless & troublesome. Sugar & liquors are now scarce

Many of the large companies, from the West, — Ioway, &c — with ox-wagons, were laid off in Divisions, each Division under a captain, and the Senior Captain a Major, and the whole under command of a Colonel.[173] These, like the humbler arrangements, were gradually divided, subdivided, &c. till at last only families or particular friends, travelled together.

It seems, by the report of my men who had been up Deer Ck. that the buffalo they shot there was the same fellow who came down to the edge of the cliff and stood looking over towards the ferry. — They had trailed him. They also killed a deer, there. Saw several mountain-sheep, and numerous wolves, saw bear tracts, and heard panthers, at night. They described the glen in the hills, as very picturesque and beautiful. Plenty of cold springs. A great many parts of wagons & wheels, many trunks, and much iron-work, scattered over this camp ground. An emmigrant took a pair of fore wheels, axle, & tongue, and secured a chest on it, to drag on with a yoke of oxen[174] Ends clear weather.

[JULY] 21. — Commences cloudy, with light airs from the E. pleasant.

Drove from 7 A.M. till 11 A.M. and nooned. 2 P.M. moved on again, over a high and steep sand-hill, very heavy drag, ascended higher, and gained the level mountain top, and fairly in line, on the summit, when, at 3 P.M. two dark clouds one from the S.W. and the other from the N.W. met over head, and (*Hail Storm*) discharged their contents on our devoted heads. Rain fell in a perfect sheet, blinding and appalling lightning, and crashing thunder. In a few seconds from the commencement of this tempest, the hail suddenly descended, like large gravel in immense quantities, thrown down upon us. — then Hail-stones of extraordinary size, not only cut and bruised the men, whose faces and hands were bleeding, but it also cut the mules. I thought that in my younger days, in the tropics, and at sea, I had seen some tall storms, but this one beat all my experience.

It was a perilous position for men & wagons; — in the rear, and on either side of the trail, precipitous and rugged descents. — I was in my shirt-sleeves, as the day was very sultry, before the storm, and my back was as sore from the thrashing given me by the hail as if it had been done with a big stick. As soon as the storm struck us, I ordered the mules turned off, with the rear of the wagons to the gale, and the men to hold them firmly by their heads. — They seemed inclined to stampede, but the intrepidity of the men prevented disaster; and $\frac{1}{2}$ an hour, did they stand in the dreadful tempest, and at the eminent hazard of being run over, keep the mules steady. — No accident happened, except to one wagon, which turned short, in the first of the storm, and broke its tongue. I was holding on to the bridle of a wheel mule, blinded with the avalanche of hail-stones and rain, and the vivid lightning, when the mules dragged us about 20 paces: I lost my hold, and was struck on the back, as the wagon went over me. I found that it was the water keg, hanging to the coupling-pole which had struck my back. In so brief a period the temperature had fallen about 40° and the the [sic] hot mountain top, ancle-deep in ice and ice-water, in pools, and running down in cataracts through every crevice & gulch.

Some ox wagons ahead of us, unyoked and let their oxen stampede down the hill.[175]

Sent a spare tongue to the disabled wagon, which had to remain here, on the hill, to repair, and we moved on, as soon as we had put on dry clothes.

During the fore-noon we passed old camping places, a fire still burning on one, and lots of discarded beans, bacon, &c.

Soon we descended towards the Platte again, reached the bottom. Cotton-wood, willows, &c. plum trees & wild cherries. Magpies numerous, flying about and chattering. River bank close to trail, on the left, steep and deep, containing much coal, — in some places it had been dug out, and in one place, they had used it in strata, for a forge.

Saw where there had been several ferries, and old rafts on the shores & islands.[176] A grave on the heights: — and another one at foot of the hills.

Inscribed sand stone blocks. Numbers of wild geese in the stream (Platte) and flying about. Dead cattle numerous, and several worn out oxen and cows deserted. (*Axes & pickaxes scattered about, discarded.*)

At Sun Set camped in a bottom of good grass. A large camp below us, of ox wagons. Just above, a small camp of mule wagons. Many trains & camps

on the opposite bank, all ox wagons. On the hill above our camp could see
Larimie peak —

JULY 22   (*The wagon which broke tongue on the height, came down very
early, repaired.*) At 6 A.M. moved on, over 2 very high hills, of deep sand;
laborious to the team. and camped. One mile below, in the bottom, where
had been a Camp, was a grave: —

> "Adison Laughlin
> Died July 2nd '49,
> A member of the Spartan
> Band, organized at
> Trader's Point,
> Aged 17 years."[177]

Last night Capt. Duncan U.S.A.[178] with a man and boy, mounted, came to
our camp: and said that he was in search of 4 deserters, from Ft Larimie, and
that one of them was suspected of having ravished an emigrant's wife, in
the absence of her husband, and robbed the tent of considerable money; and
that they had also stolen a box of Colts' revolvers. The Capt. desired fresh
horses, as those of his party were nearly exhausted by the forced march he
had made. I regretted my inability to serve him, but called for 3 vollunters
who had animals, and obtained them. And the party, thus increased, pushed
on. I told the Captain of the 4 men in dark clothes riding close together on
the opposite side of the river, day before yesterday.

This is a fine morning, with strong breeze from the S.

A German compy with ox-wagons, and several other ox trains passed during the day. A party with mule-wagons camped near us: they were packing, and discarding their wagons. We gave them a couple of indifferent common saddles for a fine wagon. And I made a similar bargain with another
company. Company busy drying and packing goods, fitting the wagons, &c.
and cleaning arms.

Merdn flyg clouds, pleasant, light breeze from the S.E.

Late in the afternoon another ox train came down & camped near us. They
reported, that during the great hail-storm, lightning struck and shivered a
couple of trees under which I camped the night before.

Afternoon cloudy, occasional showers, wind variable. (*Dead oxen plenty*)

The Platte is muddy; we hauled the seine, and caught some fish. From
Grand Island on, the trail is like that of a discomfitted army. — In this extensive bottom, are the vestiges of Camps: — Clothes, boots, shoes, hats, lead,

iron, tin-ware, trunks, meat, wheels, axles, wagon-beds, mining-tools, &c. a few hundred yards from my camp I saw an object, which reaching, proved to be a very handsome and new *Gothic bookcas*e! It was soon dismembered to boil our coffee kettles.

Gave a bag of indian meal to a neighboring company, for about 2 bushels biscuit.

Good Grass here.

The Black hills are opposite.

JULY 23. Clear, with a moderate breeze from the N.E. pleasant.

At 8 A.M. enabled to move on, and drove 14½ miles to the bed of a creek with springs in it: ("Mineral Springs") which we reached by 2 P.M. and nooned one hour.[179]

Saw on the road many abandoned water-kegs, very imprudently thrown away. Passed over a rolling & broken country. A slaty district.

Large isolated masses of grey sand stone scattered about. The road generally good. The hills on the W. side of the creek are bare, blue color, & slaty. — Seem to contain coal, a few dwarf cedars are here & there seen. The level country is a parched hether [color], and barren. A few dusty sage bushes show that they can live where no other plant can. Latter part [of day's journey] smooth firm road, with fine sand stone and indurated clay. Fortunely for us the weather is cool, with a strong breeze from the N.W. as all the intermedial watering places are dry. — Passed through a very singular defile, called "Rock Avenue" about 50 ft. wide, and some 200 long.[180] As the Mineral Springs were supposed to be poisonous,[181] I would not allay the mule's thirst at the risk of their lives, and they suffer much. After emerging from the Defile, the road descended a very steep hill (*had to double lock the wheels*), here a wagon broke the fore-axle, and 4 of the mules exhausted: so they had to camp on a barren waste till morning, without feed [for animals] or water. At base of these hills was the "Alkali Swamp & Spring," 2 miles from the Defile, and 7½ from the Mineral Spring.[182] The water here — strong ley, was the color of coffee.[183] And piled around were hundreds of dead animals, chiefly oxen. Ox geering lay about in profusion. We had, now, at dark to move on 4 miles to a small stream & spring of good water. First mile after leaving the Alkali pond, very rough — At this brook we camped, after an ardious march of 13½ miles only;[184] because we were disappointed in finding water intermediate. (*13½*) From Alkali Swamp, to our camp, the road was lined with dead oxen — these all killed by exhaustion and effects of drinking the Alkali water. After passing the Alkali swp. [swamp] I observed, on left of trail, 5 yoke of dead oxen, just as they had fallen in geer: and was told that a stroke of lightning, from the great hail storm, had killed them. A sick mule died.

This rill-water is a little sulphurious, very little grass. Ox trains passing all night.[185] Late at night I sent a number of canteens of water to the wagons on the eminence in rear.[186]

JULY 24. Clear, light airs from the N.E. and pleasant. The wagons all came into camp this morning, when I served out 1 quart of barley to each mule.

Many ox trains passed. Found that the wagon with weak team had discarded the spare axle hung underneath, sent back & recovered it. Great dissention in the company about weight of cargoes. All the bad traits of the men are now well-developed, — their true character is shown, untrammelled, unvarnished. Selfishness, hypocricy, &c. Some, whom at home were thought gentlemen, are now totally unprincipled.[187] All this I was prepared to see and encounter. Threw away our beans.

Last night and this morning I supped & breakfasted in the rear of my Camp, with my mess, detained there.

At 10 A.M. we moved on, to a *Slew*, Willow Spring, 2¾ ms. rill and cool springs.[188] Plenty of young grass, but rather dry. Rested 3 hours, and moved on 4¾ (4½) miles, where finding good grass, in a bottom, camped.[189]

Clear, light breeze S.W. Disaffected men of the Company talking about the propriety of a division; brought about by a certain *aspirant* for office, who wishes a command, but can never command any portion of this company while I remain in position.[190] Excellent grass, and water cold as ice. Numerous striped and speckled, brown squirrels.

Passed over a fine smooth road.[191] Rattlesnakes quite numerous, occasionally amuse myself by putting my foot on one, while I deprive him of his rattles; have a pocket-full.

Dead oxen occasionally, on the trail. Vestiges of women's visit, pieces of calico, a bonnet, &c.

Rocks of the hills a conglomerate in which felspar predominates. Serpentine, and various species of quarts, in angular particles.

The packed company of which I bought a wagon, passed. Many oxen grazing below, — and around the base of a hill in advance, are camps.

A singular pebble conglomerate, with a light colored cement. Also found Beryl. [Day] Ends clear and cool, Wind N.W.

[JULY] 25. Commences clear and cool, Wind strong from the N. Obtained a thermometer from my friend Bates, of the Compy   Held a meeting to decrease the amount of personal baggage, and ascertain what else we could, with propriety, discard: resulting in reducing the weight, pr. man, of personal effects, 50 lbs. And discarding our india-rubber boat, (of no use in the present low stage of all the streams) and a very heavy article. A lot of iron implements. 2 large kegs of gun-powder, which we put in a wolf-hole, on a hill, close by, and blew up.[192]

Lots of dead oxen here, chiefly in a marsh, by us.

A grave near by, on left of trail, neatly sodded, but nothing to tell who the lucky traveller is.

Merd[n] clear, calm, Temp. 84°. We now moved on again, going over an elevated plain, and descending; sandy, with some scattered small sage bushes. This extensive inclined plain, is bounded N W. by hight [high] dark mountains, through gaps in which, can be seen the blue peaks of more distant ranges.[193]

Kept rolling on, in the night, as the mules had rested and fed well. And camped about 9 P.M. on "Grease Wood Creek."[194] Swift rill of cool mineral water, but poor grass.

Evening cloudy, with fresh gale from the N. Temp 58°

Stinson (guide) who went ahead with Capt. Duncan, returned to the Camp, and reported that the Capt. and party were pushing for the "South Pass" and that there was snow there. Very cold night, frost. Slept in the sand, and quite cold, particularly my feet. Drizzly near morning.

[JULY] 26. Commences with flyg clouds, light breeze from the N.E. Temp. 62°

Made an early start, (6 A M)[195] and reached "Independence Rock" by noon, sent the mules across the Sweet Water river, (here very shallow)[196] to a wet marsh opposite, under guard, to graze. Morning's march sandy.

Company seem in good spirits. Independence Rock at a distance looks like a huge whale. It is painted & marked every way, all over, with names, dates, initials, &c — so that it was with difficulty I could find a place to inscribe on it: — "The Washington City Compy   July 26, 1849."[197]

Cast the seine here, and caught a few fish — (mullets)

Merd[n] clear, strong breeze from the N.E. Temp 84°   11¼ miles.

At 3 P.M. we moved on again, forded the stream, in about 4 miles the trail enters a narrow level plain, bounded by piles of rocks & hills, with dwarf cedars scattered over them, and in the crevices.[198] First half mile very sandy. Rocks on left of trail, inscrib'd all over; near the outlet a grave attracted my attention, and I pictured it. (*Grave:* — *Painted on stone at head;* — "*Frederic Richard, son of James M. and Mary Fulkerson   Died July 1, 1847 Aged 18 years*" *on rock above grave* "*J. M. Fulkerson, June 26, '47.*")[199] And leaving this pretty defile, and turning down a short distance to the right, we were again on the banks of the Sweet Water, just above the "Devil's Gate."[200] Made this afternoon 6½ miles, to-day 18 miles, and camped, at Sun-Set.

Sent the mules over the stream, under guard, to graze. Some of the boys clambered up the rocks on the N side of the Gate, and reached some cavernous places, where they fired pistols, and threw down rocks, pleased with the reverberation, which was great. I made a careful sketch of this remarkable gorge.

Procured an old wheel, which made good fuel to cook our supper by, and the hub gave plenty of light, so that I easily wrote up my rough notes. Night clear & serene, early part the moon shone bright. I spread my blanket on the plain, near my camp-fire and slept till awakened by a shot, which quickly bro't me to my feet, gun in hand; and on sending the guard Sergeant across to learn the cause, found that a sentinel had imprudently fired at a bear. 2 men reported for refusing guard duty.

JULY 27. Commences clear, very light airs, from the S.E. Temp 60°

Moved off at 6 A.M. The road generally, heavy sand, for about 5 ms. Passed a bad pond & marsh. Hills on the left are covered with a small growth of pines or cedars, very dense, and in the distance look like velvet moss. (*Commencement of the Rattlesnake Mts. See plate*) Dead oxen scattered on the trail. Halted to noon, on a bank ½ mile below a Cañon, where the road leaves the river and turns S over sand-hills,[201] 10½ A.M. having marched 10½ ms. A large ox-camp near us, their oxen all sick from Alkali water, for which they administered fat pork, or lard and vinegar. Mer^d clear, strong breeze from the S.E. Temp. 92°. (*In the river, at noon, is a small oval sand island, with scattered bushes & few small trees.*)

At 2 P.M. In motion again on road. At 4½ P.M. a mule belonging to one of the wagons failed, and was abandoned.

Dead cattle marking the trail, as usual.

At 7 P-M, having driven 8¾ ms; rather slowly, making 19¼, we reached the bank of the Sweet Water, about 400 yds. above a high gravel bluff, and camped.[202] (River on right.)

A range of hight [high] rocky bluffs about 300 yds. on our left, are the foot hills of the Rattlesnake mountains, and a continuation of the range we passed and noon'd by. The mountains on the right are bare, and of a dun clay color.

A road lays before us, and near the river, and is said to be the shortest & best.

Sun Set clear, with light breeze from the S.E. Temp 64°

The march to-day, was a heavy sandy dusty affair. A German, with his son, — about 12 yrs. of age, on a mule, came into camp, to remain till morning. Had gone ahead some distance, in search of a stray poney; but the boy was taken sick, and his party being several miles in rear of us, he was compelled to stop here. We invited him to supper, and gave him the privilege of a bed on the *first floor*. —

I recollected having passed an ox-wagon in the road, without cattle, and a female sitting alone, on the tongue, weeping: I asked her the matter, and she informed me that her husband & son had gone ahead some distance to look for a stray poney, and she was afraid they could not get back before night. On enquiring about her oxen, she said they were below, in the river bottom. I would have left her a guard, but other companies were coming along, & I thought her husband would not be so imprudent as to leave his poor wife alone on the road, in this wild country.

I was quite lame from chafe. — (Here it will be proper to remark, that the Company had given me a horse on the frontier, but I preferred walking, to cure me of dyspepsia, which I had had for many years.)

A creek, laid down as "Sage Creek,"[203] in to-day's march, I did not see, nor any bottom which could be taken for its bed. And the "2d Ck." of the "Mormon Guide", was but the dry, dusty bed of a run, at the base of a very steep sandy hill. Passed a range of long low gravel bluffs, on left of road near camp. At their upper end is an isolated large rocky hill, with a few stunted pines growing in the crevices.

A beautiful night.

[JULY] 28. — 8 A.M. moved on. Clear, with a light breeze from the S.W. Temp. 56°. A heavy sandy road. In 1½ miles passed the dry bed of "Bitter Cotton Wood Ck." — seems to be at proper season, a considerable and rapid stream.[204]

Just before crossing, and a little lower down, in an area of deep white sand, encompassed in sand-hills, was a sand stone pile, looking like a ruined square tower, which I walked over to see; though it was ½ mile from the trail, and the sand toilsome to walk in. (*Sand stone Tower & interior*) I found it to be earthy friable sand-stone — uncovered by winds.[205] And the shape actually very different from what it appeared at a distance. It was the abode of bats, owls & swallows. And the resort of wolves, antelope, &c. from the signs in and about it. It had been marked with names of earlier travellers, but the elements had eradicated most & left feeble traces of others. — Among the names I made out one "*Greenwood*, and a "*Soublette*" This pile is about 30 feet high, interior an irregular oval, say 40 by 50 feet, and full of concavities, — doubtless the effect of the elements. Near by was a considerable platform of the same rock, cropping out of top and side of a sand-hill. Plenty of dead cattle, as usual. Innumerable hillocks & holes (villages) of the prairie dogs: the little fellows sitting up & yelping furiously at us. I fired at one, and hit him, with buck-shot, but he found the bottom of his hole in a second after.

The large crickets very numerous.

(*A broad strip of very close sage-buses [bushes] line the creek bank.*)

Hot sun, and a strong breeze blowing the fine sand & dust full in our faces, rendered this one of the disagreeable days, both to man and beast. After crossing the Creek bed, turned to the left, and a few hundred yards above crossing, on right of the trail, about 200 yds, from it, was another sand stone pile, like a ruin'd castle: in a hollow also of sand hills, but unlike the locale of the tower on the other side, it had scattered sage bushes. And the pile like the other, had been uncovered & corroded by the elements (*natural castle*). We now have a long sandy ascent. On our left rise the rugged, bare, and harsh looking Rattle Snake Mts.[206] A few miles more brought us on an arid elevated plain, and a low grassy plain on left, extended to a great distance. A large isolated pile of rocks, about 400 yds. on right of trail, attracted my attention, and I visited it through curiosity, and to rest there — the train coming along, below — It is granite, with narrow veins of white felspar sticking up, in some places, several inches; the softer rock worn away by ages of elementary action. This great mass of hard rock was worn smooth as glass, in some prominent parts, by the action of the elements over this exposed and elevated region.

Found among these rocks old horse-manure, several rattlesnakes, and sweet red currents growing in the crevices & shade. On the upper portion, running along a shelf of rock, was a small pine tree growing: the tree was not over 12 feet high, and trunk about 10 inches diameter, while the principal root, lay exposed, along the angle of the narrow shelf, at right angle with the trunk, for about 20 feet, and its diameter little less than that of the trunk. Cavernous hollows, which appeared to have been the asylum of bears and wolves in bad weather. After a good rest I scrambled down, and soon reached the rear of my train, in the road.

About half-way of forenoon's drive, just after reaching the train, from visit to the rock, I descried, about 2 miles off, in the low plain on our left, a lone buffalo, apparently grazing; and sung out for the hunters. Several horsemen took after him, and got pretty near before he noticed them. A young man by the name of Wright being in advance, discharged his piece into the bull's flank, wounding him, — when he charged, causing his horse to throw him & run off: the bull tossed him on his blunt horns, — made a circuit, came up, and put his head down to gore him, when with great presence of mind, he drew a heavy bowie-knife, and chopped the enraged animal across the snout, — causing him to throw up his head, snort, and run off, pursued by another hunter, close down on him. Wright lay on his left elbow, when the buffalo made the 2d demonstration on him, and put his left hand on the curly forehead of the bull. He was bruised & cut in the hand. In $6\frac{1}{2}$ ms. from Bitter Cotton-Wood Ck. we forded the Sweet-Water river.[207] — Gravelly bottom & swift current. Now a broad road, clouds of sand & impallpable dust: — dimming the atmosphere, and covering and penetrating every thing, over rolling sand hills, covered with sage. The river and road now enters a gorge of the mountains. (*4 ox-wagons nooned $\frac{1}{4}$ m. above the ford. Gorge of Rattle-Snake Mts. & Sweet-Water river.*)[208] Perpendicular rock walls, from 400 to 600 ft. hight [high] on our right. This is a very narrow and rugged pass, — or cañon, we crossed and recrossed the stream again, in $1\frac{1}{2}$ miles. Whirlwind of sand blowing through with a fresh breeze. The rocks here, wherever accessable, are marked all over with inscriptions, as usual. Thick growth of willows on the banks. Plenty of remains of broken & burnt wagons here, as well as some dead oxen. Made 11 miles to 1 P.M. and nooned, for 3 hours, in this gorge. 2 of my men went back a few miles, to purchase a horse, they had heard of. Tolerable grass here. Merdn clear, fresh breeze from the S.W. Temp 90° Passed 2 miles below, — on left, a small alkali Lake — white incrustations of it every where around, and on every substance. This pass is $1\frac{3}{4}$ miles long. — After leaving it, we immediately enter a broad bottom, of great extent, with numerous *slews*, and good grazing.

Just before entering the gorge, I passed a wagon in the road, with the poor German woman whom I saw and conversed with, alone on the road, yesterday morning, and who it seems is the wife of the fellow who slept last night at my camp. She was again sitting on the wagon-tongue weeping, and said that her son was sick in the wagon, and her husband had gone back some distance, and the oxen were several miles below, in a bottom, with no watch over them. This poor woman sees hard times indeed; the son will probably die, the indians or emmigrants, some of whom are little better than the savages, (though the emmigration, generally, is intelligent & respectable) will carry off their oxen, and finally the husband take care of himself.

Wheels, axles, hubs, tires, ox-chains, bows, yokes, &c. &c. mark old camping grounds. Made 15¼ miles to-day, and camped near a rill.

Sun-Set the gale abated some; clear, Temp. 72°

[JULY] 29. Commences clear, with light breeze from N.E. Temp. 46°

6 A M. train in motion, crossed the Sweet Water at 4th. ford,[209] and drove on, over a high sandy, arid plain. Saline incrustations at one place on right of trail: At another place, on left, a slight indentation in the plain, with alkali and tall grass: — in wet seasons marshes and pools. — On right of trail, the hill declines to a much lower and swampy plain, which sweep round across the road and to the left — rounding off the Western edge of the hill. —

Merd[n] clear, strong breeze from W. Temp. 74°   very dry & dusty. 5¾ miles from the last ford, on right, in the low ground, by digging a couple of feet, ice is obtained. The surface is dug up all about by the travellers — as much from curiosity as to obtain so desirable a luxury in a march so dry and thirsty — this is called the "Ice-Springs."[210] — Passed down and over the hollow, or marshy ground, making 10 miles, and noon'd. Hot and dusty; I had taken the precaution to bring a supply of water for this dry stretch: — gave each mule 1 quart — On the height, in rear, could see snow-capped mountains ahead.[211]

At 2 P.M. were again in motion: — over plains and sand-hills. Sage-hens (large grouse) very numerous. Among the greasewood & sage bushes on left, I killed 5 and wounded many others — my buck-shot too large for such game — a great number were slain by the men. They were so astonished at the report of guns, that often, they would stand still, within 10 feet of us, and receive another shot, staring at us with apparent astonishment. Few of them flew far away from the spot where fired at. A great many hares here also, affording us much sport, at chasing them among the bushes, and sand-hills on the left, and shooting them. Late in afternoon arrived at the brow of steep bluffs,[212] which with the usual precautions was descended without accident, and at 1 mile below, near bank of the Sweet Water, making 11½ miles this afternoon, (21½ to-day) and camped. From the edge of the bluff above, we had a beautiful view of the Stream, meadow, and camps below, and the mountains around, in every shade of distance.[213] I was informed here, that a few miles below, on the other side of the Stream, were plenty of buffalo and antelope.

Sun Set clear, light wind from the S.W. Temp. 50° (*Wolves numerous at night*)

Night cold; towards morning frost. Saw a buffalo to the left, but the 2 men who went in pursuit, could not shoot him. An island here.

JULY 30　Commences clear, with light airs from the S. (ice $\frac{1}{2}$ inch thick in the pots, this morng)

Moved on at 6 A.M. over deep sandy ridges.[214] The Sweet Water river, here, is very sinuous; with bottoms of good grass; willows on banks. In 1 mile crossed the river at the 5th ford.[215] River is here about 3 rods wide. (A short distance above the last camp) The river and an indian trail, runs through a rugged gorge, while the road keeps to the right, over hills. With a comrade, I followed the river, to get ahead of the train. — They had the dry bed of a stream to cross, in $\frac{1}{4}$ m. and in $\frac{1}{4}$ ms. further a hill to rise $1\frac{1}{2}$ ms. up and steep in places: and in $3\frac{1}{2}$ ms. more, to ford the river the 6th time, as it is shorter & better than another trail, over a sandy ridge.

The river gorge was a very wild looking place. Narrow, and on the left the rocks were piled up ragged and red. On the right were high short hills with the red granular quartz cropping out, and at their bases in blocks & great masses; some having rolled down to the steep banks of the stream, making the travel over them troublesome.

Dense willows along the banks of the Stream. I shot a hare, and saw a very *wild* duck. Our sandy trail was mottled with foot-prints of bears and wolves, made last night, but we saw none. Turning round to the right, soon reached the river bottom, where it keep[s] on till the road crosses it, a couple of miles higher up. Vestiges of old camps — wheels & other parts of wagons, clothing, log-chains, yokes, dead oxen, &c — Made about 12 miles and camped, as the next stretch to grass & water is 9 miles, some portion of the distance are bad ridges to cross, and several mules are quite weak for want of good grass, so I determined to spend the day here for their benefit. Sent them down Stream, a short distance, where the best grass is. Camped in bottom, at entrance to a cañon, which the river goes thro' Plenty of willows here. A German Compy from N. York State, camp'd here. The man who had some distance back put a chest on wheels, was here, with his vehicle; said the Germans had robbed him. Several ox trains coming along.

(*Merdⁿ clear, with a strong breeze from the S. Temp. 81°*)

A rude grave here, with a rough stone at the head, on an eminence, right of trail; river on our left. A short distance before reaching the camp, and intervening is a very rocky ravine, with water holes in it — a bad place for wagons. On our right and ahead, is a long high dusty hill, over which ascends the trail. The Sweet Water river has here become a very small stream, (at this season). — The bottom is generally visible, very clear, white sand, stones, and long green moss in it. Rather rapid, seldom over 2 ft. deep, and generally only a few inches. I am much chafed to-day. The hill before us is a pearl-colored lime-stone, lamillar, the plates thin & smooth on top, and the under side papillary.

Some of my men seem to be perfectly stupid and childish, and it is with difficulty I can make them attend to certain duties for their own welfare — Neglecting the mules. To-day we saw a great many prairie-dogs, several shot & eat. The small striped squirrel also numerous.

Served out meal to the weakest mule.

Sun Set clear, with a light breeze from the S.W. Temp. 66°

Quite indisposed at night.

[JULY] 31. I awoke this morning still indisposed, but kept it to myself —

Commences clear, with a light breeze from the W.S.W. Temp. 50°

At 6 A.M. we left camp and ascended the high hill, moved over it, and ascended another, very stony and rough, requiring care of the teamsters: — then over some hard level road, and minor stony ridges, but mostly sandy and dusty; and descended to the dry stony bed of "Strawberry Creek."[216] Alkali lakes on the left.[217]

Passed the camp of a small party with an ox cart, — a family, they said that the indians were after their cattle, and had given them great trouble. I saw no indians; no doubt they saw or heard my sentinels.

A large pack-train passed. No game but grouse.

Drove 12¼ miles to "Omaco Ck."[218] and nooned. Merdn clear, with a

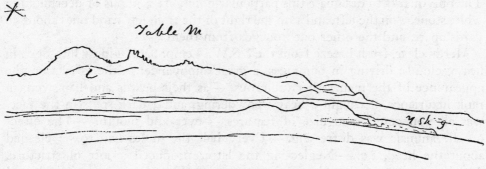

TABLE MOUNTAIN

strong breeze from the W.S.W. Temp. 86°. We descended into the bed of the Creek, its water only in pools just here. Willows here large and thick, and the stream below rippling clear: — a pretty place. Basaltic-looking cliffs on the lower side, rising several hundred feet in perpendicular stria's [striae]. A man belonging to an ox-train, told me that in the bed of Strawberry Creek, some distance from trail, a man was camped with a family, and that his oxen were some distance lower down the creek, and intervening was a body of indians, preventing him from driving them up. — I had seen the top of a tent and wagon there, as I passed, and if I had then known their situation, would very soon have extricated them. Afternoon's trail, over level hills, of sand & fine gravel. Crossed "Willow Creek,"[219] bed (dry) and a ravine, also once filled with water. — Drove 8¼ miles in afternoon, making 20½ to-day, and camped in a hollow, with grass & water, a few miles below the "Table Rocks."

Sun Set clear, with a strong breeze from the S.S.W. Temp. 77°.

AUG. 1. — (*Commences clear, with a light breeze from S.S.W. Temp. 34° — had frost*)

6 A.M. rolled on; cross'd the Sweet Water again, — here a mere brook, (at this season) over sandy hills and plains, sprinkled with scattering dwarf dusty sage bushes. Along the trail, generally on the right side, saw 1 mule & many dead oxen. Seen, at a distance, some deer, and wolves; and a black bear, — which I fired at, but he was too far to hit, and the ball striking the ground near him, caused his speedy retreat. Made 10¼ miles, to noon halt, — just about the length of the train beyond the culminating point of the SOUTH PASS of the Rocky Mountains,[220] and threw our banner to the breeze, on this elevated and notable back-bone of Uncle Sam's. — Elevation above the Gulf of Mexico, 7,489 feet. (*S. Pass is 900 ms. from Independence Mo.*) The only marks to designate this particular point, are 3 knolls of decripitating white stone, 2 on the left, and 1 on the right of the trail; left hand ones about 50 yards apart, and the other one 100 yds from them.

Merd^n clear, fresh breeze from the S.S.W. Temp. 84° Fine white dust, in heavy clouds, driving in our faces, a great annoyance: — the effects on the appearance of the men rather ludicrous, — as their beards and hair were in rank luxuriance, it caught a heavy powdering, and 3 dark spots in the face, was all you could recognize of features, — eyes and mouth. — The effect on the animals was distressing. — Every halt the mules had to be cleaned about the head, &c. — Neglecting the latter produced a sort of stricture. Another man[221] of the advanced party, with Capt. Duncan, returned, and

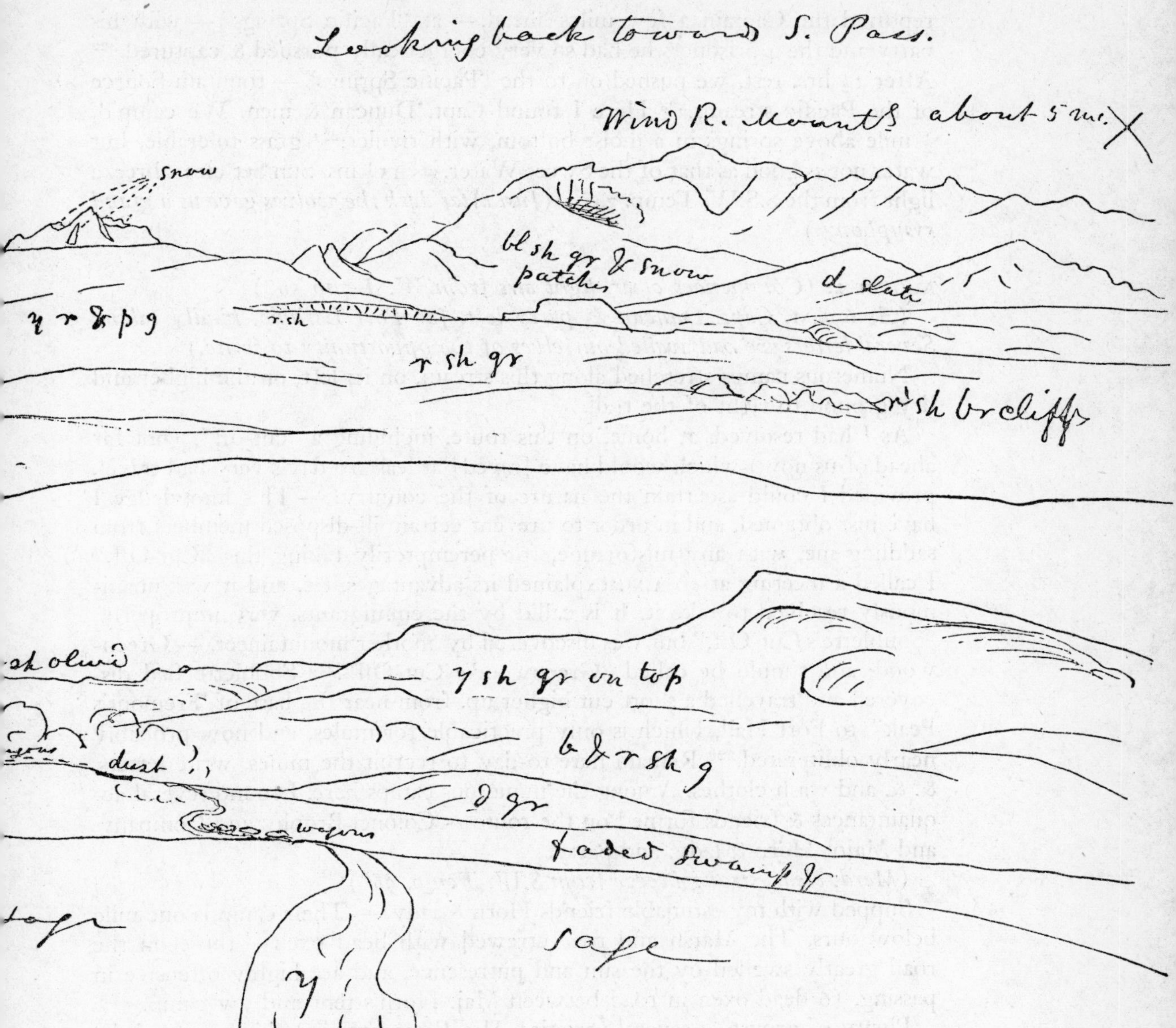

Looking back toward S. Pass.

Wind R. Mounts about 5 mi. X

snow

bl sh gr & snow
patches

d slate

y r & p g

r sh

r sh gr

r sh br cliffs

ak olwd

y sh gr on top

b & r sh g

snow

dust

d gr

wagons

& faded swamp y

top

safe

y

**JUST ON DIVIDING RIDGE BETWEEN WATERS OF PACIFIC
AND ATLANTIC OCEANS WIND R. MOUNTS ABOUT 15 MS.**

reported the Captain a few miles ahead, — at "Pacific Springs" — with his party and the 4 prisoners he had so very energetically pursued & captured.[222] After 1½ hrs. rest, we pushed on to the "Pacific Springs" — fountain Source of the Pacific streams.[223] Here I found Capt. Duncan & men. We camp'd, ½ mile above springs in a moist bottom, with rivulet;[224] grass tolerable, but water not as good as that of the Sweet Water. = 15½ ms. Sun Set clear, breeze light from the S.S.W. Temp. 74°   (*Just after dark the wolves gave us a grand symphony.*)

AUGUST 2. (*Commences clear, light airs from W. Temp 58°*)
   (*At 6 A.M. Capt. Duncan & party left, for Fort Larimie, kindly taking Several letters we had availed ourselves of the opportunity to write.*)
   Numerous camps stretched along this stream, on its left, on the higher and dry ground to right of the trail.
   As I had resolved, at home, on this route, including a "cut-off", (not far ahead of us now) which would have [saved] at least 10 day's very bad travel, provided I could ascertain the nature of the country: — This knowledge I have just obtained, and in order to prevent certain ill-disposed members from saddling me, with any misfortune, for peremptorily taking this "Cut-Off," I called a meeting at 10 A.M. explained its advantages, &c. and it was unanimously resolved to take it. It is call'd by the emmigrants, very improperly, "Soublette's Cut-Off," but was discovered by another mountaineer, — Greenwood; and should be called "Greenwood's Cut-Off".[225] Soublette had discovered and travelled a short cut higher up, from near the base of 'Fremont's Peak", to Fort Hall, which is only practicable for mules, and now probably nearly obliterated.[226] Remain here to-day to recruit the mules, write letters, &. &. and wash clothes. Among the numerous camps here, I found several acquaintances & friends formed on the route — Colonel Brophy and Company, and Major Horn & lady, and party.
   (*Merd. clear, strong breeze from S.W. Temp. 96°*)
   Supped with my estimable friends Horn & lady. — Their camp is one mile below ours. The Marsh and road strewed with dead oxen — those on the road greatly swelled by the sun and putresence, and are highly offensive in passing. (6 dead oxen in road between Maj. Horn's tent and my camp.
   Plenty of grouse — several varieties. My Treasurer made his report of the fiscal affairs of the Company, to date, which I submitted to the meeting, and approved. The other companies, camped here also resolved on the "Cut-Off" route. Maj. Horn was from Lexington, Ky, and intimate with my esteemed friends at Washington, from Lexington, Genl. McCalla and Col. Bradford.[227]

But he immigrated from Ioway — where he has been long residing, and practising law.[228]

Sun Set clear, light breeze from the E. Temp. 64°

The night clear & delightful; dark misty blue hills around us, full moon and stars shining very brightly; camp all still except the occasional snore of the weary sleeper, or the hearty laugh of the sentinels below, watching the mules grazing, at some joke to while away the hour, had caused their mirth to break upon the stillness of the night. Strange that no wolves have seranaded us to night! Where are they? The men were lively on striking these waters, & sat up some time after supper, spinning yarns, singing, and performing on various instruments of music.

I sat up late to night, writing notes and plotting down memorandums for several day's march ahead: At last, having completed my memorandums, by the light of the flickering camp-fire, and chilled with the cool air, I button'd my over coat close about me, rolled up in a blanket, with my head on an old saddle for a pillow, and went off, also, to the land of Nod. The Pacific spring, to the source of a N.E. branch of the great Colorado of the Gulf of California; and the flat table of the South pass, — only about $2\frac{1}{2}$ milves [miles] over, separate the extreme sources of this, and a small branch of the Sweet Water, — running W.

AUG. 3. — Commences clear, light breeze from N.E. Temp 36° (frost early) A beautiful morning. Moved down the "Pacific Branch" about 3 ms: watered the mules, and crossed. — The road generally level & sandy, some low places, and deep sand. After crossing, on our right, about 300 yds. distant, some low clay bluffs, of a dark dingy red hue, and singularly plume-formed projections on top, from the effects of elements. (*see plate*) On our left, opposite this clay ridge, a steep gravel bluff, about $1\frac{1}{4}$ ms. from trail, where I obtained beautiful fragmentary red-felspar. — This bluff recedes as we advance, into a semi-circular hollow, about 4 miles from the crossing of Pacific branch, and 3 left of trail & stream.

(*Half way between Pacific Springs & Little Sandy, we crossed the bed of 'Dry Sandy,' containing pools of Alkali water only.*) — Crossed 4 dry sandy ravines, and reached a tank, within 10 paces of the trail, on the right; — It was dug square, containing good cool water, with probably a fine clay held in suspension, giving it much the appearance of cream tartar water (solution) A pearl-colored micacious clay. (*2 ft. down to surface of water, water 1 foot deep, well 3 ft. square*) At $10\frac{1}{2}$ A.M. we had made 12 ms. and noon'd, in a hot dusty plain, on the road, where was no vegetation except

I obtain'd felspar fragments Clay: Banks opp. the gravel Bluff where

On right — d r sh A M

A

crsh

fwdh

d. olive

pale olive g

& bare knobs & places

g

r sh   r sh

sage

RANGE OF LOW HILLS JUST W^Y BEYOND S. P. [SOUTH PASS] IN WHICH OPP. STREAMS RISE

S. [Sweet] Water empti[es] into N.F. [North Fork] Platte & Pacific Sp^g & br. source of a fork of Green R or Colorado.

stunted sage-bushes, white with dust.[229] The drive fatiguing, from heat &
dust, though the road is a good one.

Merd[n] —

While lunching, in the narrow shade the wagons afforded, a spring wagon,
with 2 mules, from the Westward, came up, and halted near us to noon, also.
On going over, found Mr. Babbitt, with 2 lads, from Salt Lake, for the States,
with the Mail, and the Mormon Memorial and Constitution, to submit to
Congress.[230] He showed me the Constitution, which was beautifully written,
and very neatly put up. — He pointed out particularly, a clause, wherein all
religious denominations are tolerated in the State of "Desertia,"[231] as they
have called their settlement. Several of us scratched off hasty pencil'd letters
for him to take on to Washington, to our relatives. One of his boys was quite
sick. One of these lads, had, a year ago, walked, alone, into Missouri, from
Salt Lake, during the winter! And had since been to California, digging with
the Mormons. Babbitt showed me 2 heavy finger-rings, of California gold,
made at Salt Lake, of the pure oro. also a $10 piece, coined by the mormons,
of California gold, with some of their peculiar emblems on it. He said that
the Mormons, at the Lake, had a barrel of gold dust, as church tithes, from
the Mormon-Diggings, in California[232] — That gold existed in the Bear-
Mountains, The boy who had been to California confirmed all the statements
we had learnt by the papers, of the California mines. Babbitt said that Capt.
Bridger and 2 sons, at F[t] Bridger, had a fine store there, with necessaries and
indian goods, and very good whisky for only $1. per pint. — And that he
had horses, ponies & mules for sale.

Our large yellow cur dog "Bull," holds out well, but has suffered much
with his feet.[233] He is very cunning, and understands the ropes, of this travel,
perfectly. — He visits the messes, in morning, and picks up a breakfast, then
watches for the mules to come in, and while they are being hitched up, he
starts on ahead, continuing on till he finds some shady spot to rest on, and
when the advance gets pretty close on him, he jumps up, and trundles on
again. And so on, he continues from day to day, picking up his meals among
the messes, and travelling ahead. When the train happens to make some unusual halt, he returns to them, and watches the movements, understanding
perfectly if we remain or move on, and governs himself accordingly. Col.
Brophy has a similar dog, but very tender-footed; they had to make mocasins
& tie over his feet, as they have often to do with lame oxen, &c.[234] Drove on,
afternoon, 9½ miles to "Little Sandy", — a Northern tributary of the N.E.
fork of the Colorado; a beautiful mountain stream, a little brackish, but cooled
by the melted snows at its source, in the "Wind river Mountains" On its

western bank, in a bend, we camped in a meadow, having drove, to-day, $21\frac{1}{2}$
miles. This bottom, here, is about $\frac{1}{4}$ mile wide, bounded by clay hills, and cliffs
25 or 30 ft. high. A high hill opposite, at its base thick willows; and running
some distance above, steep cliff banks of the Stream. Stream shoal, and rapid.
A short distance above us, a willowy island.

Above, on the right of road, are 2 graves; no inscriptions. Missed a mule
this morning, and sent a man to rear, in search of him — found him in the
Marsh of Pacific Springs, dead.

Observed, about $\frac{1}{4}$ mile below, on the left edge of the trail, 4 large buffalos grazing; several horsemen put after them, when arrived nearly within
gun-shot, they raised their shaggy heads, stared a few seconds at the horsemen, wheeled, and scampered away to the N.E. over the hills;[235] and after
a short pursuit, the horsemen turned about and rejoined the train. Told of a
grave, in the rear, inscribed with the death of a "Dr. — of St. Louis, died of
Cholera." — it seems that this was a *càche*, — and where the aforesaid Doctor,
had deposited $500 worth of Medicines, on his way to the [Salt] Lake Set-
tlement. — Had sent a mormon wagon out for it, but found, on reaching it,
that some knowing one had abstracted about $200 worth, and left a note to
that effect. Snow-tipped peaks of the Bear river chain ahead, and on our right
and rear those of the Wind-river Mts.

A mule, at noon, had the cholic badly, but relieved by a dose of lard-oil.
— His indisposition caused by the water of Little Sandy, no doubt.

No game to be seen.

A large black Newfoundland and a small spotted dog, lost or deserted, were
seen to day, near the trail, exceedingly wild, being often fired at, by mistake sometimes for wolves, and from deviltry by others.

(*Forks of road 4 or 5 miles before reaching "Little Sandy"*)

The road forks, — left branch to Fort Bridger, Salt Lake, &c. and the right
is the cut-off route.[236] At the Forks of the road, the emmigrants had a meeting, when all of them followed me on the 'Cut-off' except 2 ox wagons, who
turned off to the left, on the other route bidding us all adieu, as they rolled on.
A great many trains have already preceeded us on this route — broad & well
beaten trail.

Major Horn gave me an account of Babbitt. — Knew him well, in Ioway;
was a great politician there; turned Mormon Attorney or advocate, and fills
that office yet.

At the Forks there was a stick driven in the ground, with a board nailed
on it, plastered with notices, of what companies, men, &c. and when, they
had passed, on either route; & desiring friends in the rear to hurry up, &c.

A notice requested travellers to throw stones up against the base, to sustain the stick.

The weather to-day has been fine, and the road good, but the dust awfully bad. Horn's camp close by, and he step'd over to my camp and took me to his to supper. — And it was a supper! his good lady had made nice white light hot rolls, baked a prairie hen, stewed dried peaches, and fine coffee, with *sugar* in it! We ate a hearty supper and talked about *the lodge in the wilderness*.[237]

Counted 46 dead oxen in to-day's march. — A number are scattered about the meadows surrounding the Camp. — Indeed, it is difficult to find a camping ground, destitute of carcases.

(Sun-Set clear, light airs N.N.E. Temp 74°)

Night flying clouds and cold. I never could like coffee without sugar, fond as I am of the decoction, and notwithstanding old mountaineers say to the contrary. Horn, most kindly and generously, in this dearth of *sweetening*, gave me a few pounds, promising me some more, if he could spare it, on another meeting, ahead.

Just before making camp we passed the grave of

> "Robert Gilmore
> and wife,
> Died of Cholera,
> July 18th. 1849."[238]

AUG. 4. — *(Sun rise clear, calm, Temp. 46°)*

At 6 A.M. we rolled on over Little Sandy, & Westerly, till we soon reached a point where the road forks — the right branch leads to a grove of timber about a mile off.[239] I kept the left hand trail, following it on a S.S.W. course 6½ miles, when we struck "Big Sandy," — (another tributary of the Colorado, also of Wind-river birth, and parallel with the "Little Sandy.") which at 9½ A.M. we forded. This stream is a larger edition of Little Sandy: Wider bottoms, bounded by cliffs, — above the road: and having long low banks of sand. The grass in the bottoms grazed off. So I sent the mules 1 m. lower down to graze. Found here a camp of 6 ox-wagons. Thomas & his family are camped 1 mile below us.[240] Passed 4 dead oxen, and there are several here.

The Wind-river chain of Mts' trending off to the N.W. their dark jagged and lofty snow-patch'd fronts within 25 ms. and their northern portion fading away in the blue distance.

The "Wolverine Rangers", Capt. Potts,[241] had been camp'd on the opposite side of us, in the bottom, just above the road, and had broken up a wagon, leaving the sides, &c. for the benefit of our cooks. We also found on their campground several hundred weight of fat bacon, beans, lead, iron, tools, a cast-iron stove, &c.

Merd^n clear, Strong breeze from the W. Temp 84°

Having filled up our water kegs and canteens, at 4 P.M., we left, for the *long drive,* variously estimated, from 35 to 55 ms. without water, and in only one spot a little grass; I thought, from the map,[242] that the distance would be found 40 miles, and having water along, and judging that midway grass could be found off to the right, at the base of the hills, a few miles from trail; and the greater portion of the route level and good. Also, that by the way of Fort Bridger and around, over rugged gorges, down steep hills, and passage of very rough cañons, making by that route, at least 15 days longer, and with all its perils, certainly renders this worth the deprivation.

Quite a sandy & dusty trail; first few miles level, latter part rolling, and perfectly arid. White clay formation. dusty sage bushes scattered over the country. And hosts of dead oxen.

About Sun-Set a mule in wagon next to rear failed, he had been sick, and we left him to the tender mercy of the wolves. Ox trains rolling along, enveloped in a cloud of dust. Men & oxen suffering much from dust, heat, and sandy trail. On right of the trail, to-day, and near it, passed a singular clay mount,[243] of buff colored clay and soft sand-stone, which I found contain'd fossils: digging out, with the point of my bowie-knife, a fragment of a bone & piece of madrepore.

Sun-Set hazy, strong breeze from the N.W. Temp. 76° The wind lulled after Sun-Set, with flying clouds, and the moon rose brightly: —

15 ox wagons had preceded us from the creek, but we soon passed them.

(I have suffered much to-day, from chafe) Another mule fell, in harness, and finding that plunging the blade of a penknife into his shoulder, created no sensation, we left him also, as a tribute to the lean lank wolves.

The temperature fell rapidly after night — at midnight down to 55° A small German Co^y had halted, on right of trail, and were burning greasewood bushes to warm themselves; I went up, and found it very comfortable indeed.[244] Dead oxen numerous.

[AUG.] 5. — At 1 A.M. having driven 17 ms. without water, halted to rest, &c. Sent the mules to the Northward, about 4 miles, under a guard, where they obtained some bunch grass, and wild oats. (*Gave each mule 1 quart of water.*) Some of us, eat a hasty bite of bread, but many were too fatigued to do that, and were all soon down under and about the wagons, rolled up in

[HAYSTACK BUTTE]

their blankets, in the deep dust—'*dust to dust*", soon sound asleep, — I caught a flitting nap on the tongue of a wagon, afraid to lay down, — and sleep too long. The position and cold, in spite of tire and chafe, kept me on guard; and after the men had snoosed a couple of hours, I aroused them, and ordered the mules in. About 4 A.M. we were again en route, on our thirsty and dusty route. Calm and cold weather. (*Commences clear, wind light N.W. Temp. 66° Merd. do. strong W.N.W. Temp. 80°*)

Road trended generally, W.S.W. — occasionally S.W. Country now becomes more irregular, sand deep, crossed several ravines and deep hollows; and over high round hills of sand and slate. — At 8 A.M. reached the brow of a tall and steep descent, of slate, sand, & shingle stone　By double-locking, and carefully leading the mules, who had, most of the way down, to sit on their haunches, the train reached the bottom without accident.[245] — After we had all fairly reached the bottom, I found that our so-called *guide*, had taken this precipitous descent, instead of one to the right of it, a few hundred yards, and quite gentle. — He said he did not notice the branch of the trail.

This basin seems to be a deep dell, without outlet, and must be filled with considerable water in the winter. Sage and grease-wood here. Gave each mule a quart of water, and arose from the barren dell; by an inclined plane considerably less than the one on the other side. The route now quite serpentine, with deep hollows, & high round hills. Clay, with imperfect sand stone, and slate; indications of coal.[246]

Late in the afternoon we arrived at a range of very high and steep clay & sand bluffs, some parts perpendicular, and even oerhanging, ending in this sort of bold rugged promontory, the base of which rests in the bottom of Green River valley. — This termination of the high land — so abrupt, makes a sweep from N. round to S.W. Most of these last hills were truncated cones: — worn in fantastic hollows, the sand stone projecting in rude horizontal strata & lumps, and is scattered all down the sides, and piled up at the base, and rolled into the deep & rough furrows cut down by the winter torrents. From this elevated pinnacle, I looked S.W. down stream, (its nearest part distant $\frac{1}{2}$ m.) and it appeared like a curved silver thread, patches of green willows, distant hills, &c. was a grand sight. Then to turn to the S. and look down on the perrilous descent the wagons had to make. (*Steep descent terminating "Greenwood's cut off"*)[247] It was however deep sand, lumps of clay, and loose stones & fragments of slate. From the crest, down to base, right and left, were fragments of disasters, in the shape of upset wagons, wheels, axles, running-geer, sides, bottoms, &c. &c. — Nothing daunted, we double-locked, and each teamster held firmly to the bridle of his lead mules, and led down, in succession, till the whole train reach'd the valley below, about $\frac{1}{3}$ of a mile, without accident. We followed the base of these tall heights, for some distance, and on a S.S.W. course, generally, for 5 or 6 ms. over deep dusty irregular small hills, on left side of the river, and then turned down Wy to the river; drove in, on its pebbly bottom, — hub deep, and rapid, turned down stream about 150 yds. to a gravel bank, above water, crossed that in about the same distance, and then across the stream again, obliquely 50 yds. to the opposite shore. We drove down the valley $\frac{1}{4}$ mile, and camped, after one of the hardest tramps I ever took, and extremely hard on the mules. — Making 43 miles, from Camp to Camp. (The Mormons swore it was 55 miles)[248] — Here was another instance of the ignorance and inconvenience of the *guide*. I was unable to get ahead, or this error would not have occurred. Instead of turning left, some $\frac{1}{2}$ or $\frac{1}{4}$ mile to the steep descent, a trail branched straight ahead to the Westward, & lead down gently to an old ferry; which if we had taken it, would have saved at least 3 miles, making the "cut-off," actually but 40 miles — and throwing out the 2 steep descents which are so easily avoided, is an excellent road; and if provided with water and forage, there is no difficulty at all in crossing it.

I sent the mules, under guard, 1 m. below, to graze — the grass there being better. Mules near exhausted — 1 wagon in rear.

Sun Set hazy (had been thunder & rain drops)

Light airs from the W.N.W.

Temp 70°

AUG. 6   Commences with flying clouds, and light airs from the N.W. Temp. 62°. Recruiting mules, washing clothes, &c. The wagon left in rear, came in by $11\frac{1}{2}$ A.M. mules exhausted & wagon much damaged. Left 1 mule across creek, which died. Sent Stinson (the *guide*) up the river 7 miles to find better grass. He found some rather better at 3 ms. but interspersed with alkaline incrustations. — At the Ferry, numerous dead oxen and wrecks of many wagons.

Thomas and 2 other mountaineers came into camp. — Said that from here to F^t Hall the grass was plentiful, but beyond that probably scarce. He was from F^t Bridger, and with a party of traders, was speculating in horses.[249] Said that he knew Col. Fremont, who was once anxious to employ him.

The Missouri whisky cart, got down here, and some of my men obtained Alcohol from it; particularly a party, faction, or clique, who were electioneering very strong to change the Presidency of the Association.

When the association was formed, with its constitution, civil officers, &c.

[P 2]

for mining purposes, I told them, at home, that it was all of no importance, and would never go into operation in California; well assured in my own mind, that the hardships of the tramp, and its consequent development of bad spirits, and selfishness particularly, would combine to scatter the members, as soon as they struck the Sacramento valley, in all directions: — but they all knew better than me, and I was compelled to preside over all these proceedings, and see men swear, on the Holy Evangelist, &c. to abide by and uphold the same, who often after d——d it; and but few cared one cent for, ere they had gone half across the continent.

The traders have a fine band of horses and ponies. Brophy's train passed through

Occasional light showers. Abandoned the broken wagon & distributed the freight, &c. Cast the seine here, and caught several mullets & small salmon.

Sun Set cloudy, indications of rain, with a moderate breeze from N.N.W. Temp. 72°.

AUG. 7. About day-break, showers of rain and hail.

Commences cloudy, with light airs from the N. Temp 54°

A grave, in the bottom, 300 yds. below the camp: —

"S. R. Webb,
Died Aug. 1. 1849,
from Selma, Ala:"

For about 3 ms. the mean course of this stream is S. then it turns short to the E. about 1 m. and afterwards resumes its South course. (*Indian map.*) The mules must have good grass, which cannot be obtained here, so at 6 A.M. we moved on: and winding down the bottom, in about $2\frac{1}{2}$ ms. reached an ascent, rather steep, but not high, and just at the foot, on right of trail — 20 paces from it, vertical cliffs of a mouse-colored sand-stone, on the face of which was engraved with a fine-pointed instrument, an Indian diagram, representing 43 rifles, nearly vertical, and a chief and horse, apparently separated from 4 other indians and a horse laying down, by a stream with a small fork to it.[250] This I accidentally discovered, by going close to the cliff, and at once drew it.

IND: MAP SCRATCHED ON THE FACE OF SANDSTONE C[L]IFFS, ON RIGHT, ASCENDING FROM VALLEY [OF GREEN RIVER]

["43 rifles" is written on the picture, but only 32 appear here, although in the finished sketch published in the *Annual Report* of the Smithsonian Institution, 1872, the full number is to be found.]

Sand-hills next to the river. On the Plateau, above, on left of trail, a grave, with sand-stone slab, engraved thus: —

> "Mary, consort of J. M.
> Fulkerson, Died July
> 14. 1847"

The grave was covered with sand-stone slabs, and by the names, it will be seen that the lady is the mother of the youth, buried in the Rattle-snake Pass, [195] ms. back, which I visited July 26th. The youth died on the 1st. and

13 days after his mother died here. (It seems the family was in the pass of the Rattle-snake mountains, at least a week. Doubtless emigrants for Oregon.

A march of 9 miles, about double of what a straight line would be, over high, narrow, and very crooked ridges of grey & brown sand-stone, we reached the beautiful valley of La Fontenelle a tributary of Green river. A diagram will explain a crooked part of this route, better than I can describe it in writing.

A delightful fertile valley the creek very sinuous, here about 10 ft. wide, and 3 ft. deep; sparkling and rapid.

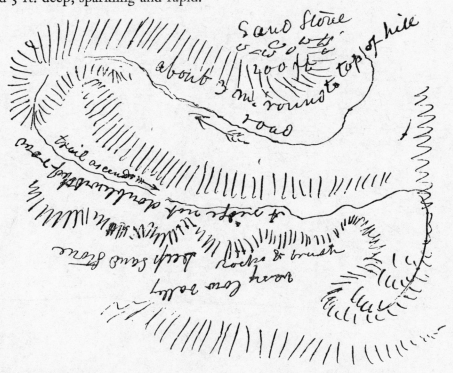

[DIAGRAM OF TRAIL, GREEN RIVER, AUGUST 7]

The train descended the bluffs, and entered the valley about 1 m. above the French traders camp; and here camped, I visited the camp of the French-men, composed of conical skin lodges, tents, bush houses, and about 10 blue ox-wagons. Here was a mixture, white women, and squaws & children, of every age and hue. The men were in a tent, playing Monte, on a skin, for silver. Sitting on a Skin, stretched over sticks, to form a seat, was a *yellow*

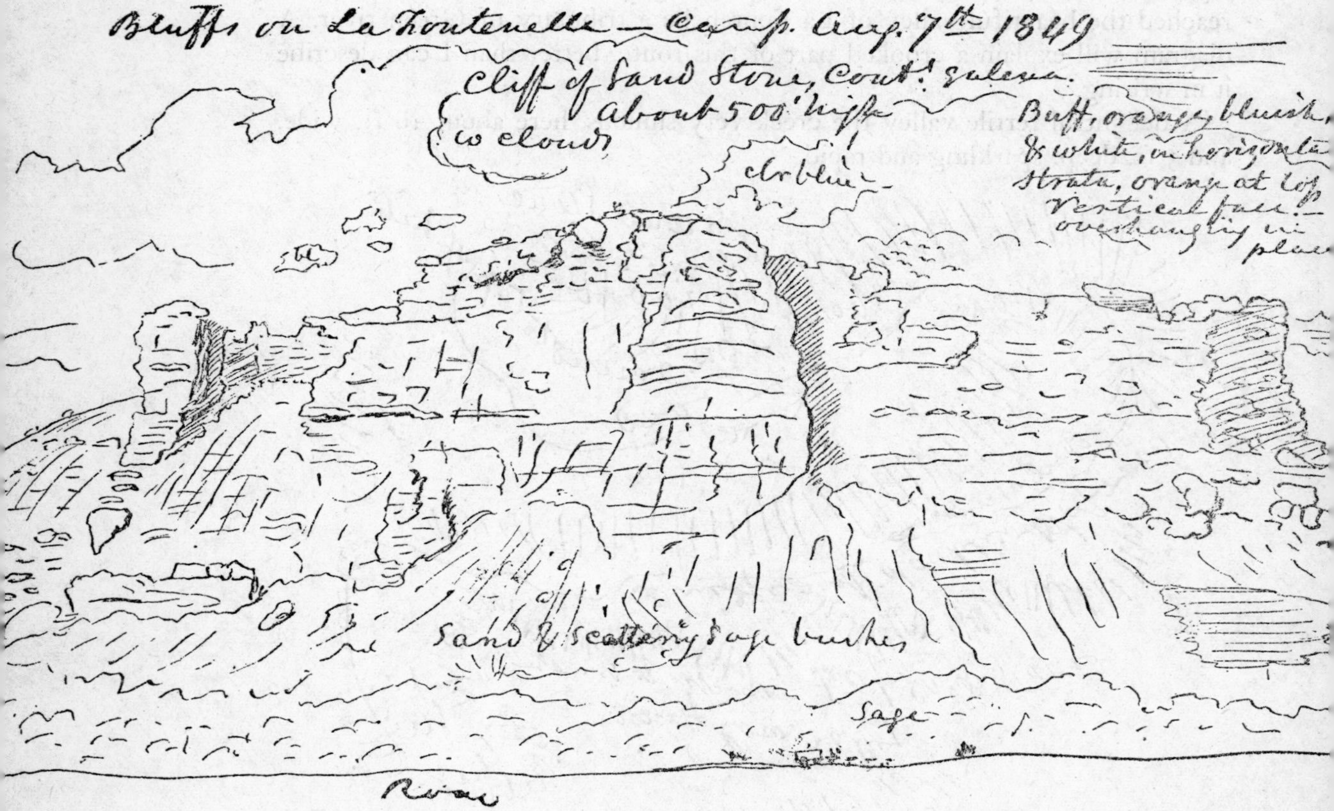

Bluffs on La Fontenelle — Camp. Aug. 7th 1849

Cliff of Sand Stone, Cont.ᵍ galena.
About 500' high
(w clouds)

dr blue

Buff, orange, bluish
& white, in horizontal
strata, orange at top
Vertical face,
overhanging in
place

Sand & scattering sage bushes

Sage

River

indian girl, about 7 yrs. old, dandling an infant, which was nearly white; and another small child was thumping on a common U. S. tenor drum. Indian goods, of every description, mingled with horse-trappings, were scattered around amongst the wagons. In the fine meadow, on the opposite side, was a large band of fat horses & ponies.

I saw a half-breed woman take a very young infant by its legs & hands, and plunge it under, head & heels, in the rippling cool stream: — it did not squall, probably too much chocked to do so.

Some squaws were highly rouged with vermillion, and one of the Frenchmen, had several stripes of it, à la sauvage, across his nose & cheeks. About $1\frac{1}{2}$ mile higher up the creek is another camp of these traders, of 4 ordinary canvass tents, 3 skin lodges, & 2 booths. They all have a number of dogs of various kinds. They ask high prices for their horses, few less than $300. These chaps have been sent here by old Bridger, to trade with the emmigrants, who have mostly come this way; thus trying to cut off the "cut-off" folks.

Merd^n clear, with strong breeze from the S.S.W. Temp 82°

This portion of the valley & stream runs E. & W. 6. P.M. a meeting of the Company, to punish guard delinquents, &c.

Sun Set clear, light and variable airs, Temp. 66°

Plenty of grouse, hares, and hawks, seen. Great feats of horsemanship by the French traders, riding at full speed, over plain, stream, ditches, and irregular & elevated places in pursuit of a run-away poney.

AUG: 8. — Commences with fly^g clouds, & light airs from the S.W.

Temp 44°   Much dew this morning.

Yesterday, the Frenchman — Thomas was thrown from his horse, — had a *brick in his hat*, at the time, injuring his back and spine much.[251]

Having heard that a company a few miles higher up, in the valley, had flour to spare, and fearing my stores were rather under than over, I sent a couple of men up, to purchase some.

Innumerable large black mice here, living in holes in the bank of the stream, generally under bushes: they are fat and very soft & silky: not at all shy, probably unacquainted yet with man's destructive propensity, of which I, however, convinced one by knocking it over, roasting & eating it. — Found it very tender & sweet.

Cast seine & caught some salmon & trout. (*Cliff on La Fontenelle*)   There is An immense perpendicular, clay cliff alongside our camp, which, with some trouble and danger, I managed to scale; and was well compensated by the magnificent, bird's-eye view of the stream & valley. The scene reminded me of prints I had seen of some Prince's estate, where the combined efforts of nature & art had produced the most charming effect. — The beautiful silvery creek, meandering in every variety of curve, and islands mostly of an oveal [oval] shape, filling up, nearly, the concavities of the bank, with bright green grass & willows, and little groves of bright willows interspersed along the grassy edge of the stream. Cattle grazing; the camps; — and people; and blue smoke curling up in delicate and graceful spirals from the camp-fires; the warm tints of the bluff, darker hills above, and the distant blue mountains; made a picture I gazed on with admiration, for some time. — I returned to the camp, after collecting some mineralogical specimens from the cliff, and told my enthusiastic friend, — Fenderich, to mount the cliff at once, and feast his eyes. — He done so.

Merd^n clear, with a strong breeze from the S.W. by W. Temp. 83°

Graves in the valley: —

> "Henry French,
> 20 yrs. July 5th. 1849.
> Michigan; Adrian,
> Lenaway Co."

and

> "J. Merrill,
> died July 9th. 1849,
> Aged 23. Mo."

10 A.M. We moved on out of this beautiful valley.

While the train was wending its way along the valley on left of the creek, I passed up on the right side, to call at Thomas's camp & see how he was. — Found him lying on his back, on a buffalo robe, in a tent, and very pale and ill. — Besides the injury to his spine, he had his left arm, and several ribs broken. — Doct^r McDonald, of another Comp^y of emmigrants, was attending him. Dr Austin, of my company, accompanied me, not knowing that any other physician was in attendance. The unfortunate mountaineer, like the generality of the French mountaineers, was a Bashaw of many tails: — he had 3 squaws, Shoshonees, and several light-colored papooses. The squaws were fat, of the different shades, of light, darker, and dark mulatoe complexions; good features, and fine black eyes, the lightest-colored one very good-looking. They were very attentive to him, and two of them showed great concern, particularly the lightest one. — She sat by his head, wiped the perspiration from his brow, looked mournfully in his face, and quickly attended to any thing required, for her unfortunate lord.[252]

I understood from a person who knew Thomas — the trapper; that his father was a Canadian Frenchman & his mother an Iroquois Indian. And an assistant he had with him — a sort of protegèe, quite a handsome lad of about 18 yrs. with very long and black hair, and wearing Mexican pantaloons; informed me, in very good English, that his father, also, was a French Canadian, and his mother a Santa Fé lady. — He said that he intended to visit California the next season.

Fine weather, but fine dust annoying. Appearance of the country improving. Beautiful ridges, covered with very large sage, &c Hollows filled with willows and groves of tall spiry spruce, often reminding one of some manor residence at home, with its old lombardy-poplars around, and hiding the house from view. On this ridge, we had a fine view of the country. The soft green tints of Spring, and the warm autumnal hues, were blended in the shrubbery, which clustered on the hills and filled the vales & glens. The train had gone on, while the D^r and myself had spent more time at the Frenchman's tent, than we intended; and as we could not possibly overtake it before noon, without too fatiguing exertion, we resolved to take it rather easy; so amused our selves hunting the numerous grouse, among the large sage-bushes. Noon had already passed, ere we reached the declension of this long crooked ridge, and from the brow, where it descends to the narrow valley of a mountain brook, we could just see the company, apparently hitching up to move on. They were about 2 miles ahead, at the base of hill, in a grove of spruce: from our high position the wagons looked like a collection of white cottages, — a pretty country village, beautifully situated.

Tired, hungry, and thirsty, we walked hard to reach them in time, but alas! their long line was stretching away over the hills before we could get in rifle shot: and the camping ground being known, and presuming we were amusing ourselves, they kept on.

Very tired, we reached the ravine, which the company had just left; — A prostrate pine-trunk, where a mess had cooked their dinner, was blazing furiously, fanned by the strong breeze blowing down the vale. After quenching our thirst in the cool, leaping, & babbling, brook, and threw ourselves down on a sloping moss-covered bank, between the roots of a large pine, with the sparkling rill at our feet, and rested, while I smoked a pipe, — one of the times when it was a great luxury.

The train had gone on 6 miles, to better grass than is here. The trees and herbage is different from what we have before seen, on the route: numerous new species of flowers, among them a delicate vermillion color, — a Geranium, and some blue bell-shaped ones. Boxwood, a small creeping variety of Holly, covering portions of the hills; however evergreens predominating.

We ascended a small hill, rather tall, and round, with gravel and flesh-colored clay, and coarse hard sand-stone, — from small fragments to large blocks; — occasionally large stratas cropping out nearly vertical. — The next stretch was in a Westerly direction, pretty level, on top of a ridge, and a good road; then descended into a vale, in which was a brook, embosomed in dense willows and cotton-wood:[253] Crossed this shallow stream, and ascended another hill, — higher and longer than those we had just left; and from the apex, I looked back with delight and astonishment, — at the singularly beautiful landscape in the rear. — The last rays of the declining sun were gilding the peaks and spurs of the very distant, and nearer mountains, while the rest of them were softened down, from light to dark in every tint of purple and blue. —

The hills of the middle ground, were of an autumnal green, and the nearest of a warm flesh color. (color of the clay) The shades of evening warned us to hasten on, and we resumed our tedious walk. — The trail was of deep fine dust, as before, but of a much darker hue. An oblique road, now, up a still taller ridge, on the top of which, though so late, I could not but look back; — and found that night had thrown her sable mantle over the scene; and only the nearest hills were seen, in bold relief against the starry sky. The descent from this hill proved its great height, and very long and steep descent, where the train had to double lock their wheels, and lead down carefully. The trail was in many places winding, of deep sand, with loose slaty stones.[254] — We crossed a rocky rivulet in a quarter of an hour more, rippling through this deep glen, and whose source was in the snow-patches on the hills, near our right. In this vale, I noticed the axles and wheels, of a broken wagon, attesting the perils of the descent — They were not of my train. We were guided in descending the hill, and getting out of the vale, by the lighter color of the trail, than the unbroken ground. After crossing the brook, we turned left, down it some 400 yds, and then to the right, up a slight indentation in a ridge, till we reached the top of another hill, rather lower than the opposite one, and not very level on top. The descent from this elevation, was very long, but not quite so steep as the last; — Long oblique windings, deep sand & dust, loose stones, and projecting rocks. It seemed to me, tired as I was, and in the night, to be the longest descent I had ever made. On reaching the bottom, we found another deep vale, rill,[255] willows, &c. and 2 dead oxen on trail. — Now up again, over a hill of less altitude, and up a higher one, and across its flat top. — Soon like the weary mariner greeted with the twinkling star of the light-house, was I gratified to see the light of our camp-fires, in a meadow below. — We were soon among them, and I found a cup of hot coffee, some corn-cakes, and fried bacon were very palatable. — After which, a pipe, and sound repose.

AUG. 9. — Clear, Temp. 40°. light airs W.

Camp near trail, a spring, cold as ice, on our right. At 6 A.M. Train in motion. — Road winds westerly, over a high ridge, and as our predecessors had all taken a left hand road, along the top of long high ridges, to the left, I took a right hand branch trail, to the right, to ascertain the difference; and found, on striking the valley of "Smith's fork," that it was much the short-est, though there was a pretty steep but short place in it, to ascend. My com-rades, and friends, — Moxley & Washington, were highly pleased with this very romantic country. In a jungle of willows, ascending a hill, found a willow lodge — and in a narrow swampy passage, with streams, springs, and willows, saw a large cart abandoned, and near it, on the ground, a small piece of apple-pie, and fragments of light wheat-bread: I ate the piece of pie, and found it good.

Merd. Fly. clouds, light win[d]s S.W. Temp. 86°

We descended into the valley of "Smith's Spring", and in a small open space, surrounded with willows, near the stream, a small company camped, of 2 wagons from Cincinnati Ohio, and 1 from Arkansas, with a family. Stream here, about 20 feet wide, and not over 3 ft. deep. We waded the stream, and proceeded down the valley on the other side, at least 4 miles, to camp. On our way down, we passed through an extensive camp, or place where the Indians had had a village, probably last winter. At least 60 willow lodges, in various stages of delapidation.[256] I here shot 3 grouse, wounded and lost 4 others, and killed 2 prairie-dogs, which are very numerous. A number of the red-shouldered hawk flying about, and lighting on bushes. I struck a light & broiled one of the prairie-dogs, and we had a bite.

When near the Camp I had to wade across the creek again, and found it very cold. The wagons were little ahead of me, in reaching the valley, though I had travelled very leisurely, and we had loitered much in hunting. Where I struck the valley, was several miles nearer the egress from it. But I soon found out how this came about; — Another detachment of Old Bridger's traders were camped here, and had put up a notice at the branching of the road, for the emmigrants to take the left one, as the best. They had horses, &c. to sell. Their camp within 200 yds. of mine. The traders told me that during the month of June, 3,200 wagons passed through this valley.

The Chief of this party is named Greenwood,[257] (which must be assumed, as he is a Bavarian. — He is a fine tall, well-formed, and handsome fellow:

Our Riv. about 2 m¹. plain between

S. OF CAMP—9TH AUG '49 SMITH'S FORK OF BEAR RIV.

about 35 years of age, and dressed in a full suite of smoked deer-skin: — frock, pantaloons, mocasins, &c. — He, also, has a harem of 3 dark Shoshonee damsels — two of whom I saw, were as black & ugly as mud. Ox wagons, skin-lodges, tents, squaws, papooses, saddles, &c. &c — as usual.

The stream, here, is rapid, clear, and cool; and from 4 to 6 feet deep. We caught some salmon in it.

(*Sun Set clear, light breeze from W.S.W. Temp.* 74°.)

At night, being fine & clear, a party of our musical boys went over to the traders' camp; with a violin, accordian, bugle, &c. and were politely invited into a skin lodge. I accompanied them, — and our party of a dozen, and the Frenchmen & squaws, all crowded around the interior of the lodge, made it rather uncomfortable. They performed several lively airs, such as "Dan Tucker," "Carry me back to old Virginia," "Zip Coon", &c — accompanied by singing, which delighted the traders much, and particularly the indians.[258] Drop'd rain during the night.

AUG. 10. — Commences cloudy, with light airs from the W. Temp 44°

Mien direction of the stream, within view, is about N.W. — (a distance of about 5 miles)

Moved at 6 A.M. At the foot of the ascent from the valley, on left of the trail, a grave: — scratched on a sand-stone slab, which was at the head, but is now prostrate & broken: — This grave has been opened & filled in again. —

> "Died July 21st. 1847,
> Mr. Beverly Appron,
> x x x (obliterated)

And on the heights, about 5 miles beyond, another, on left, & close to the trail. — On a board. —

> "Sacred to the memory
> of Alfred Corum,
> Who died July 4th,
> 1849. Aged 22 years."

And 300 yds further, also on left, —

> "Margaret Campbell,
> departed, July 28,
> 1848, Aged
> 36 yrs: 4 mos. 23 days."

Merd. Flying clouds, with a strong breeze from the W.S.W. Temp 84°

Travelled over very lofty and rugged ridges, requiring great caution; on

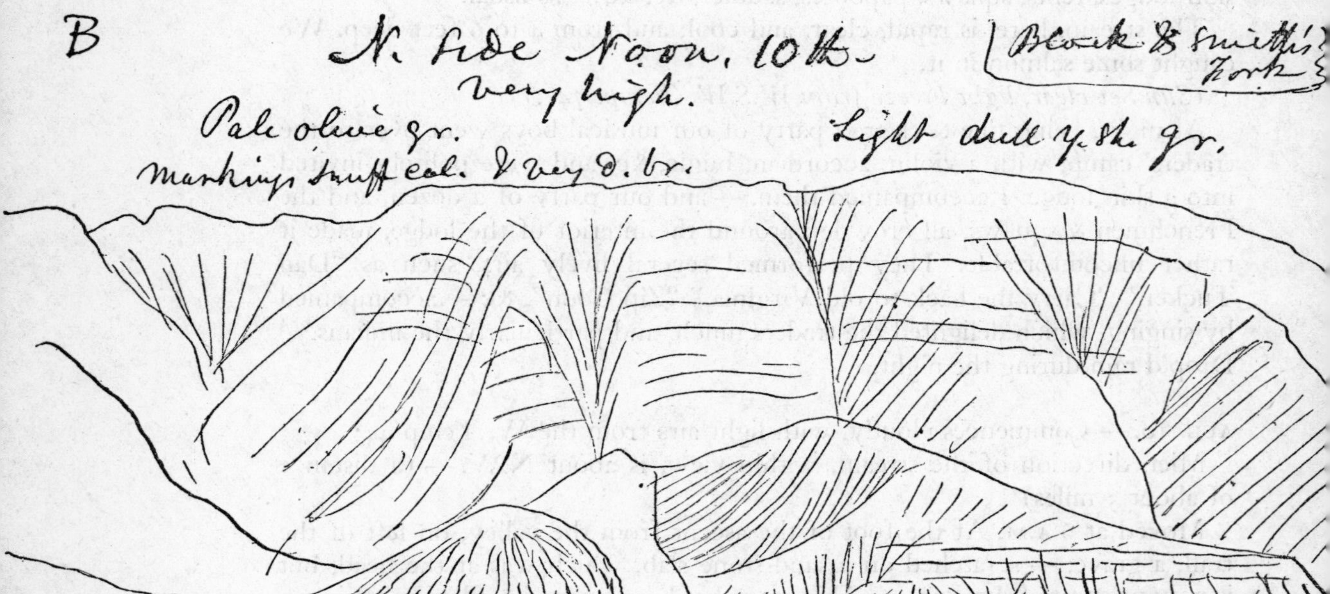

B

N. Side Noon, 10th.
very high.

Pale olive gr.
markings snuff col. & very d. br.

Light dull y.sh gr.

[Block & Smith's Fork]

Streaks nearly W.

near

Straw col.

d g

y.sh. W

r sh

approaching a stream — to left of us, where the trail descends, Mr. Alexander and myself struck through a deep gorge, while the train went off to the right. Here is a pretty brook, sometimes pent up in narrow bounds by masses of rock; now and then disappearing in a subteranean passage for several 100 yards, and then spreading out broad and shallow, with islands, marshes, & grassy bottoms, in the hollows formed by the ravines and spurs of the hills, on left as we descended it. We were compelled to scramble over rocks, leap and wade the stream, and over fallen trees, right and left, for some time. At length while going down the right side, I perceived, through the thick willows, the head and horns of a deer, and cautiously attempted to cross: I waded through brush, mud & water, and at length reached a point where the deer was hid from view by a clump of willows; I steped out, and found he had heard or smelt me, and was standing looking right at me. The grass was up to his knees. He was about 100 yds off, and I fired a charge of buckshot at him. He made two or three leaps, and ran up the neighboring ridge, followed by some 30 antelope, who were hid before in the grass. On reaching the spot where they had been laying down, I saw blood on a stick, which of course was the effect of the shot, and caused the buck to leap so when I fired. Saw a buff colored weasel.

Entering the gorge, dark rugged precipices, with overhanging rocks, rose high on our right, on the left were tall & steep pine-clad mountains, with much fallen timber, — a great deal of it old and decayed, but several large green trees & fragments, as if prostrated by a gale. The willows & quaken [quaking] aspen very thick in the bottom. Passed down, on a narrow indian path, with occasional signs of their visit to the gorge. — Places where they had fires, lodge-poles, &c. Deer and wolf-tracks. This stream is a small tributary of Bear river. And after a very tedious tramp, hemmed in, on the right by the precipices, we at length turned right, up a branch of the stream, over tall spurs, and marshes interve[n]ing bottoms, and reached the Camp, — in a meadow, at the spring-source of this branch, just in time to get a bite and a short rest, before the train moved on again, after dinner. The company had some very rough travelling over high and very rocky ridges, and 2 narrow winding & dangerous descents, from the last, into this bottom where they had nooned and rested themselves.

Later in the afternoon we moved on again, soon ascending a succession of ridges, — higher and higher, to the greatest elevation of the divide; — the descent from which was a series of precipitous places: — deep sand, with loose stones: and dangerous, without great care. We choose what appeared to be the best of two trails, in descending; A Dutch party, who had taken the other, had a wagon upset and smashed, but fortunately no one hurt. We suffered no other accident than the breaking of an axle and some spokes of one wagon. The damage soon repaired. My teamsters are experienced and careful, have got the hang of bad roads, perfectly. At dusk we reached the most elevated point, and by 9 P.M. reached "Smiths Spring,"[259] — the head of a branch, 3 miles below "Smith's fork" of Bear river, after a very toilsome & dusty drive, — nearly suffocated with dust, and camped. Found numerous ox companies here. Passed several dead oxen on road & 1 horse.

Sun Set flying clouds, with very light breeze from the W.S.W. Temp. 70° 18 miles to noon, and 6½ to camp. = 24½.

AUG. 11. Commences clear, wind light from the S.W. Temp 34°.

Moved down, at 6 A.M. 4 miles, to the banks of "Bear river", a beautiful stream: Level and broad bottoms, with plenty of grass. Caught a number of fine large fish. Banks of stream lined with willows. Found here, many ox-camps, and many others, driving on.

Visited a neighboring camp, and a man there told me, that about a week since, an emmigrant went out in the Bear river mountains, from this place, to hunt, and was lost; he met some indians, to whom he gave his rifle to conduct him back to his comrades. — Finding them gone, he desired to be conducted to Salt Lake, and off they started, over the mountains for that settlement.[260]

At at the Camp on Green river, a trader informed me, of another emmigrant, near there, also out hunting, no great distance from his camp, when he was beset by a party of Snake indians,[261] who took his rifle from him, tied him to a tree, and shot him in the back, — and killed him. — His comrades missing him too long, went on a search, and found him fast to the tree, a corpse. — They then got on the indian trail, and found their camp, and demanded redress. The chief held a counsel, detected the murderer, and had him tied to a tree; and then told the emmigrants, that he was at their disposal. — The emmigrants replied that he had taken the life of one of us all, — friends, and that they, the indians, must punish him, in such manner as should be decreed. The old chief then called the brother of the culprit, and ordered him to cut the offender's throat, which he instantly done; and the emmigrants returned, satisfied with the old chief's justice.[262] This would be a magnificent spot for a Settlement, apparently; but timber is distant, and the traders say that snow falls here to the depth of 4 feet.

My men hunting, fishing, and washing clothes; and the mules grazing and resting. The large mice here, quite numerous.

Merd^n clear, with a light wind from the S.W. Temp. 70°

A committee of teamsters waited on me, desiring that I would remain here till the 14th on account of the fine grass for the mules, and game for the men &c. I consented.

Sun Set clear, & calm, Temp 62°

This rest afforded me a fine opportunity to correct my notes, and also to wash some articles of clothing. — For the charge and care of the company made my task a very hard one. — I had less repose than any one else, — requiring the Sergeant having the morning guard to call me always at 4, — sometimes earlier; — and every one in camp, except the sentinels, were snoring some time, ere I could do so. — When all was quiet, by my fire, or lantern, I corrected the day's rough notes, and made my memorandums for the morrow's march. — Whilst my mess-mates sat down comfortably, and eat their meals, I had to snatch a mouthful any how. — Then a few villains in the company, had formed a clique, who threw obstacles in the way of my operations, and evaded the correct performance of duty, while they were too cowardly to openly oppose me. — I say a few, for ¾ of my comp$y$ were intelligent good men, and but for their co-operation, and obedience I could never have succeeded as I did, in keeping them together.

As my camp was close to the edge of the stream, I spread my blanket under the concavity formed in a group of willows, and at midnight laid down, and slept soundly, till a little before day, when some animal about the size of a pointer dog, ran hastily over me, treading on my breast & awakening me. — I presumed it was only a small wolf, and drew my blanket over my face, and finished my repose — till 6 A.M. when called to breakfast. Cold night.

AUG. 12. SUNDAY   Commences hazy & calm, Temp. 60°

3 Pañack indians,[263] each with a large yellow wolf dog, came into camp to barter horses.

Merd. Clear, with moderate breeze from the N.W. by W. Temp. 74°.

After dinner, the Panacks came again; said their camp was among the hills, across the river, not far off. They spoke several words of English, — as *good*, m*uu*le, (mule) *schwap, no schwap*, (swap) &c. Remains of their old camps all through this valley. I found a board on which the squaws strap their infants, and carry thus on their backs. Several of the indians had on blue cloth caps, one wore a teamster's linen frock, with U. S. buttons on it. A party of these chaps: a young man on a very fine poney, a youth and old man on a fat black mule, and a middle age'd sqaw on a mare. — They offered the squaw to us for a copper powder-flask.

Hauled the seine, and caught a number of suckers & trout.

Captured several of the sweet black mice, and had a pie.

Brophy's train came down into the valley to-day, and I had the pleasure of dining with Major Horn and lady.

I strolled down banks of the stream, and shot a large hawk, and wounded 2 ducks, but lost them. My men shot red-shoulder'd hawks, blue-wing & shoveller ducks, mud-hens, curlews, plovers, grouse, &c.

They say that coal has been found in the ridge in rear of this. An Illinois company, of 5 or 6 wagons came in & camped.

This broad bottom, for miles, is a scene of animated life, enough to make one forget that it is a wild country, upwards of a thousand miles from our western frontier. — Bands of oxen and mules grazing about, and cows among them, the tinkling of their bells, improving the semblance to a domestic scene. The bushes and grass covered with washed clothes; men, in groups conversing or reading; others rambling across the meadows and hill sides; and some bathing, fishing, and gunning.

A man and his wife, with tin pails, went from an adjacent camp, over the plain a mile, to a band of cattle, and returned with their buckets full of milk. — A delightful lively scene, — and only needed 2 or 3 cottages to complete the picture.

A young man of my company (Donn) put the charges intended for 2 barrels, by mistake into one barrel of his double-gun, and when discharged, it burst, and hurt his left hand badly.

The beautiful evening was enlivened with instrumental and vocal music.

A small party of Shoshoney came into camp, and amusing us by firing at a mark with rifles and arrows.

Sun Set clear, light airs from the N.W. Temp 63°.

Cold at night, with frost. I slept quite cold.

AUG. 13. Commences clear, with a light wind from N.N.W. Temp 32° plenty of ice.

After breakfast I moved on 9¼ miles. Beautiful day.

Numerous trails, of travellers, and indians. — While my train was winding along, diagonally, from the river, to the higher ground on the right, I followed the bank as close as I could. Other trains were in motion also, some in the rear, and others further back at the base of the hills, some distance off; horsemen — white and red, galloping about, — men driving loose animals, camps, smoke, hunters, &c. all tended to make a fine picture of animation. I wagon was stalled by keeping too near the river, but soon extricated. Passed the Government Express, from Fort Hall, for F^t Larimie.[264]

Merd. clear, with light breeze from the W. Temp. 94°.

Hauled the seine & caught many fish. Clear cold stream Replaced, with a new one, a defective axle.

Sun Set clear, light airs from the S. Temp. 72°

AUG. 14. Commences clear & calm. Temp. 36° (frost)

Merd. Clear, light airs from the S. W. Temp. 80°

I shot several ducks, and lost 2 of them, — they dived & holding on to the grass at the bottom, in pretty deep water, I had to leave them.

A marshy lake — near the stream, in which I found several fine shells, and a *Proteous*, which I drew.

Moved on 9 miles, to "Thomas' fork".

4 P.M. I held a meeting of the Company, *in accordance with the constitution of the Association, for the election of officers*, (6 months' from the organization.)[265]

Sun Set clear & calm, Temp. 75°

AUG 15. Flying clouds, light airs from the S. W. Temp 46° (slight frost) Annoyed with headache —

At 6 A.M. we moved dow[n] a short distance, to cross the stream (Thomas' fork) Found the banks deep and soft, and narrow inclined planes in different places, where the wagons had forded, and worn them in deep bad ruts. Some delay in getting the wagons into the stream. After crossing we drove along an ascending gorge, with ocsasionally [occasionally] a large stone in the way. Saw a grave on the 3^d hill side on left, about 3 ms. from creek. On the head was a rude wooden cross, on which was pencilled: —

"An Indian Squaw;
June 27th. 1849,
Kill'd by a fall from
a horse, near this place:
Calm be her sleep, and sweet
her rest.
Be kind to the Indian."

After getting over this range of hills, we reached a bottom with a stream, then up a steep long spur, across the top of this, and up and over higher mountains, then down a circuitous trail, — sandy, & steep in places, and over several long rolls of hills, into the valley of Bear river. Crossed the plain, to the edge of the river, and nooned. 14 ms.

Willowy banks and islands. The stream here is crooked, with many small branches & numerous marshes & *slews*, and a bottom plain [10] miles broad, on this side. The old mountaineer, — "Peg Leg Smith," came into camp: he has a cabin on the bank, some distance below, and trades with cattle, whisky, &c.[266]

His leg was injured and he out knife & amputated it himself, and afterward dressed, and fortunately recovered.

About 200 yds. above, — on the hill side, over the squaw's grave, I shot a fine fat badger, mortally wounding him with buck-shot, and carried him down & threw him in a wagon.

Merd^n cloudy, light wind from the W. Temp. 82°. We baked the badger, — meat dark red, solid & sweet. At 4 P.M. moved on, over a level and very dusty road, Westerly, then W.N.W. nearly, — in the bottom, near the river, and crossed a small creek, — down that some distance, and over the plain, to a bend in the river, near a large island, and camped, (corralled wagons) by a dam, of bad water, giving us bad coffee at supper. But plenty of fine tall grass. The dust along this drive was very annoying, as the strong breeze blew blinding clouds of this fine powder right in our faces. 24 miles.

Sun Set cloudy, with light wind from the W. Temp. 70° (another instance of the guide's sagacity & knowledge — a miserable camp, except for the mules.)

AUG. 16. Clear and calm, Temp. 42° (slight frost) Beautiful morning, moved off at 6 A.M. Crossed 5 small streams — 2 small ridges between the 2 last ones. Road excellent. Many geese, ducks, owls, hawks, and large blue cranes. Deer started up from plain & ran up into the hills. Patches of snow on the Bear river mountains, to the W^d

Merd. clear, with strong breeze from W.S.W. Temp. 91° Made 17 ms. & noon'd at a cool spring a little saline, embosomed in willows, and about 2 miles from the river. 1½ hrs. rest, and moved on again, trail N.E. up ridges; patches of white coarse lime-stone. Near the road, on the left, a grave, covered with blocks of this stone, and a piece of a barrel-head placed at the head; on which was written

"Jno: Clawson,
of Savannah, Andrew Co.
Mo. Aged about 50 yrs:
Died July 11th 1849"

During the afternoon squalls from the S.E. — rain, thunder, & lightning. In about 3 miles crossed "Tullick's fork", over a small ridge, & camp'd near a brook & the river, 7 ms. = 24 miles.

Sun Set cloudy, light wind from N. Temp. 70° indications of rain. Rain at night.

[AUG.] 17. Commences cloudy, light airs N. Temp. 64°

On opposite side of the creek are 2 indian lodges, about 200 yards off. The indians are continually wading over. Want to trade, have service berrys, dressed skins, &c Children, squaws, ponys, dogs, &c. These Shoshones are riding and walking around thro' camp, trading and begging.

A great many skunks here — Several dead ones about, and live ones running across the plain. A dog chased one and gave us some sport. At 9 A.M. we rolled on. Character of the country very interesting and picturesque to me. Volcanic formations, tufa, &c. Made 10½ miles, and noon'd near the celebrated "Soda and Beer Springs"[267] — Merd^n cloudy, wind light from the W.S.W. Temp 74°

Camps and moving bodies of Shoshonees, in all directions, plenty of fine horses, colts, &c. squaws, papooses, warriors — old & young, dogs, &c. The young men continually begging for "*powdree*," *baalle*", The[y] stand & sit around the messes, while dining, anxiously waiting for a morsel, and picking up every crumb.

Our nooning was beyond the regular 'Soda Springs', — or range of them: — just across a beautiful clear brook, with basaltic banks, and several of these springs were within my corral.[268] — One near my mess-fire. — The water was fine, only needed lemon syrup, to render it perfect soda water. These mineral springs are very numerous, many wells & springs boiling up & shooting jets.

After a short rest, we rolled on — Passed the "Steamboat spring," named from the resemblance of the sound it gives, to that of a steamboat's paddles, under water. It is a circular tumuli of about [5] ft. diam. and about [3] ft. high; bubbling & jetting clear sparkling water, as the hissing gases escape. The mound is of a dark flesh color. (*S. B. Spring is near the bank of stream*)[269]

An old cedar stands near the spr'g, the trunk & branches of which are carved and pencilled all over, as high up as can be reached, with names, &c. These springs are really worth a travel so far to see.

The good-humored trafficking Shoshones speak many English words, as "good," "very good", "horse," powdree, 'baalee", "bad, &c.

We passed through a considerable band of these indians, — moving, to establish a village, some where; and as they stoped, near the trail, to look at us, I walked among them. — An old man and a young one, well-mounted, and accouterd with savage finery, having long rifles, quivers, and bows, stood near me, and I took out my book & pencil, to sketch the young man, and had just taken down his face, when the elder saw me, rode round, so as to look over my shoulder, and spoke abruptly to me; on looking up, he shook his head, frowned, and cried "no schwap!" that is, I must not draw the indian; and made signs, signifying that if I had drawn him, at night he would die. He must have told the youth, for upon interrupting me, the young man rode rapidly away. This party had all their possessions with them. Horses and mules, with long poles attached, & trailing on the ground, loaded with mats, skins, and other luggage. Mares loaded with sacks of parched corn, meat, &c. and some black withered old hag, or a girl sitting on top. A little girl sat on such a pile, with a puppy hugged up in her arms, while her little brother lead the old mare by a raw-hide halter. A squaw passing on horseback, had quite a pretty infant in her arms, which I touched, and made signs that it was a pretty child, — when the little thing nestled up to its mother, & screamed with fright. The squaw pacified it, and I gave her a small bell to hang to its neck.[270]

Drove on 10½ miles & noon'd. After dinner we moved on 5 miles more to the brink of Bear river, within ¼ mile of its abrupt turn, and opposite the "Sheep-Rock",[271] and camped. = 15½ miles.

The bank on this side, by our camp is very precipitous and deep, and across — the opposite is a perpendicular face of a mountain, [1,000] feet high; forming a narrow cañon, through which the stream runs with much rapidity. This rock, I believe is basaltic, The top of this immense wall, is crowned with pine-clad hills, of great altitude. The stream, at this stage, is shallow.

An indian came in, and traded some fine trout, for an old cotton shirt. They are very fond of cloth fancy caps; one had the perforated tin door of a lantern attached to a Scotch-bonnet, for a visor. Another had a fine silver-mounted Bowie-knife, and held in his hand a new and bright claw hammer, — no doubt stolen from some of the emmigrants. — I warned my men to beware of their pilfering.

While sketching the "Steam-boat spring," &c. the train passed on, and 3 miles start of me; and observing a squall arising I walked hard to reach shelter at Camp, but caught a ducking. The gust came on, it blew heavy, and rain'd in torrents, while the forked ligh[t]ning flashed about, in the most apalling manner, — seeming to strike the earth, several times, very near me: and the crashing thunder made the earth tremble, and it reverberated among the

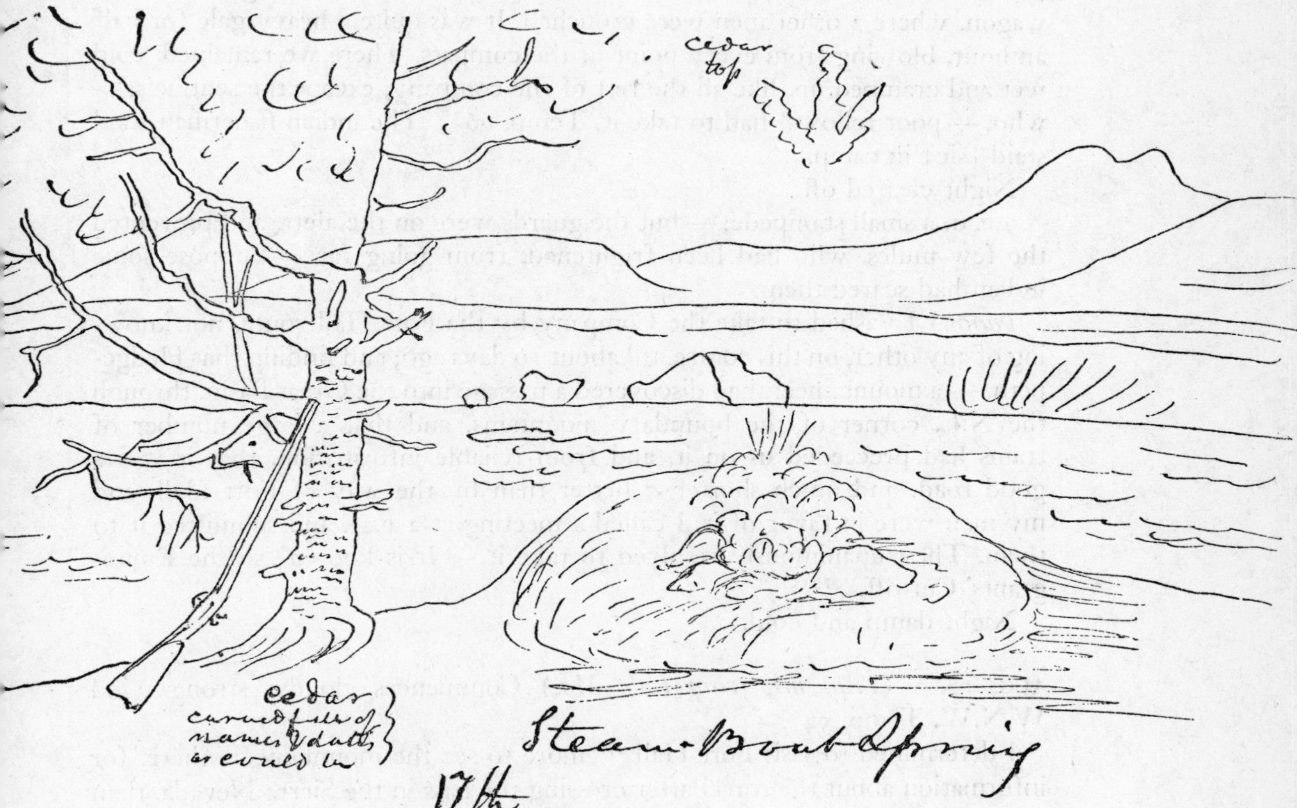

cedar
top

cedar
curved full of
names & dates
as could be

Steam Boat Spring

17th

lofty cliffs & hills, around. I felt some apprehension — running across the plains in this thick demonstration of electricity, with my bright double-barrel'd gun, gleaming in the flashes.

I reached the corral, breathless, and sought shelter from the gust, under a wagon, where 2 other men were crouched, It was quite a heavy gale for half an hour, blowing from every point of the compass. There we remained, cold wet and cramped up, like all the rest of the company, except the sentinals, — who, — poor fellows! had to take it. Temp. 66°　The indian fisherman staid staid [sic] in camp.

Night cleared off.

9 P.M. a small stampede; — but the guards were on the alert, and prevented the few mules, who had been frightened, from going far. — Suppose some indian had scared them.

(*noon*) I wished to take the Company by the Fort Hall route, not knowing of any other, on this course, till about 10 days ago; and finding that Hedgepeth, — a mountaineer, had discovered a passage into the Great Basin, through the N.E. corner of the boundary mountains, and that a large number of trains had preceeded us on it, and from reliable information, that it was a good road, and much shorter & better than by the way of Fort Hall, and my men were in favor of it, I called a meeting at 2 P.M. and submitted it to them. They unanimously resolved to take it. — It is known as "the Emmigrants' Cut-off."[272]

Night damp and cold.

AUG. 18. — (*1140 ms. from Ind*ᵉ *Mo.*) Commences cloudy, strong wind W.N.W. Temp. 54°.

I determined to visit Fort Hall,[273] more to see the mountaineers there, for information about the travel after crossing the pass in the Sierra Nevada, than any thing else. For I could get on to the Pass, I think, without a trail, but beyond that I had no information. However, it was all a well-beaten track, — and marked by relics of the route, and scarcely a day out of sight of fellow voyageurs.

The company gave me an old broke-down bay horse, and offered me 2 men for an escort, one of whom was to be Stinson, (*the guide*) whom I determined to get rid of at Fort Hall. —

(To this point, from Sᵗ Jose, Mo. I had walked.)[274] At 6 A.M. we moved on, and in an hour reached the turn of the river and forks of the road; — the left-hand trail, going over Westerly, by an extinct crater, and the right N.W., up a valley, and over a very tall divide,[275] 50 miles, to Fort Hall. Two other men now increased my little party, — consisting of Messrs. Wm Barker, Provost, Capron, and the Guide. —

We took one day's rations for each, from the commissary, mounted our animals, with rifles across our saddles, and at $7\frac{1}{2}$ A.M. exchanged salutations and good wishes with the train, as it wended its way in one direction, and we in another.

I did not think, from the nature of the mountains, the company had to go over, that this "cut-off", actually could shorten the trip much: and told my men, that in 10 days I would overtake them, on the Humboldt river, — which they seemed to think I could not do.

(*A grave, on left of trail.* — "*D. Porter, aged 69, died July 14. 1849, of Apoplexy, of Pike Co. Ill.*")

Our little party proceeded over a level & pretty road, and in about [8 or 10] ms. nooned amongst very extraordinary volcanic formations, and singularly weather worn tufarous rocks. The trail led through this singular formation, at some elevation above the plain on the left, which was grassy with marshy places. Fine grass and water.

Basaltic cliffs on our right, and grotesque groups & fragments, several detached blocks resembled much the decayed hulls of vessels, being weather worn exteriorly to give the form, and hollow on top: — rather bottom up; — These rocks were on both side[s] of the trail, full of holes, chasms, &c. doubtless the dens of wild beasts. On the right, at foot of the volcanic cliffs, were shelves, containing basins of water, — variously shaped, — round, oval, and irregular — containing holes and springs of soda & sulphur water, very clear, and dripping over their basins, coloring the rocks, orange, blue, &c. and making little marshy places occasionally across the road.

Many Badger holes in and on the edge of the trail; rather awkward for our animals. The road seems to have been travelled a few weeks since, maybe in 10 days, by several small companies of wagons.

An antelope sprang up on left, which my friend Barker attempted to shoot with a large revolver; resulting in the antelope's hasty retreat, performed by many long leaps, and bounds, and then turning round, at about 300 yds. and stared at us.

Discove[re]d in the road, the fresh track of an unshod horse, with a lariet, (halter rope) and 2 wolves following it. Stinson followed it about 2 miles — to right of the trail, — over a plain, to near clumps of willows & a branch [stream], and there lost it.

Merdn clear, Moderate breeze from the N.W. Temp 82°

At about 1 P.M. we halted at a small, shallow, and clear stream of water —

some tributary of Bear river.[276] Good grass here. — Struck a light, broiled a slice of bacon each, which with a handful of biscuit & cup of good water, form'd our dinner. — Smoked our pipes, and in ½ hr. mounted and rode on. After crossing this branch, and proceeding a short distance, we perceived an indian village on the right and another on the left, 2 or 3 miles apart, and horses grazing near them.[277] The village on the right, when abreast of it, was about ½ mile off. Two indians from this, rode at full speed towards us, and were mounted on beautiful fat horses. — Asking the usual question, "Schwap?" and pointing over to the band of horses. But refused to *schwap* those they rode, making signs to us, of taking aim with a gun, &c. that they were their hunters, and they vallued them highly. Stinson gave a small circular pewter mounted looking-glass, worth 6¼¢ in St Louis, for a pair of new half-boot shaped mocasins; and also gave the indian his old broken boots, when he had put on the mocasins. The indian sat down beside the trail, to try them on, but could not get his foot down — his instep too high; I showed him how to split them open; which he did, and mounted his horse, quite proud of wearing boots. We shook hands, and said "good bye", and parted, the indians racing towards their village. We had not proceed[ed] over ¼ m. when another indian, from the same village, also at full speed, making for the road ahead of us: — which reaching, he awaited our approach. The salutation of "how do?," and a shake-hand around, and then he wanted to *schwap* a dressed deer-skin, for tobacco and ammunition. He had a fine green-hide lariet, which I wanted, & offered him a pair of very fine-looking brass bracelets for it: but he declined. As he was in want of "*tabac*" (tobacco) we gave him a few ounces of fine-cut, and separated.

One of those first met, had on a tolerably decent black summer-cloth frock coat, a blue-striped cotton shirt, blue nankeen pants, and cotton *suspenders*, with an old black hat, — decorated with a broad red worsted band. The 2d was attired in deer skin — frock, leggings, & mocasins; and the 3d wore a very tall straw hat, a tatter'd Marsaile's vest, no shirt, & leggings, with mocasins.

They presumed we were the advance party of a train of wagons, and enquired, (by signs of wheels revolving, &c.) if wagons were coming. As our party was so small, and these fellows so numerous, I thought they might follow and steal a horse or so, and therefore made signs that 10 wagons were on the road. We proceeded[278] till near Sun-Set, when Stinson's horse became obstinate and would not proceed, so we had to stop awhile.

Sun Set clear & calm, Temp 80°

Made a cup of coffee, supp'd, and soon were in the saddle again.

Passed 4 dead oxen on the road to-day.

At dusk we reached a considerable creek, deep soft banks, stream about 30 ft. broad and at least 3 feet deep, rapid and very cold. — Here we experienced considerable difficulty. Our animals refused to enter, and nearly $\frac{1}{2}$ hour was consumed ere we could force and pull them over. We got spattered and our feet wet, and it was very cold, — the temperature havi[n]g fallen many degrees since Sun-Set.

We now commenced the ascent of the long and very tall divide, which separated from the waters of the Pacific. Road good, and gentle in ascent, for about $2\frac{1}{2}$ miles, then circuitous, with vales, and numerous brooks intersecting the trail, though we generally followed the stream on our right, up and near it. (source of a tributary of Bear) The road a very good one, though not very broad, and the dense and tall willows, particularly on our left, as the hill rose in that direction from the road, rendered this night travelling rather obscure business, and we had to proceed in single file. When about 2 miles from the summit, a very large panther set up a yell, in the willows on our left, — and followed, us half an hour, screaming continually. — Judging from the sound of his breaking considerable sticks, and crowding through the brush, &c. and the distinctness of his voice, that he was large, and thus keeping along with us, and as near as 20 paces often. — In the day time we could easily have shot him, but he was now invisible in the black forrest. I thought he might be fool enough to attempt a caper, and desired the men not to open out too much.

Reached nearly the Summit about 11 P.M. very cold, — but there was plenty of fine dry willow logs, pieces of a broken wagon, and any quantity of dead brush, on our left, in the woods. So we soon had a rousing fire, in the middle of the road. — Smoked our pipes, drew straws for guard, spread our blankets on the sloping bank on left, feet to the fire, and heads against the trees, the sentinel sat on the end of a large log near the fire, and the others threw themselves, with saddles under their heads, on their pallets & were soon snoring.

The hill on right of the road, was steep— descending about 50 yds. to mountain brook, rattling over rocks and through branches of the thick brush enclosing it. In the woods on left, the grass was very luxuriant & tall, but the forrest was thick; in this we had to tie our animals; and I directed the men, that just before calling the relief, each one should change the position of each animal; affording them a better chance to graze with advantage, and also to clear their lariets, and see that they were not loose. I had the watch, and when I went into the thicket to change the locale of each horse, it was so dark that I had to feel my way, and ran against them several times. Frose [froze] considerably towards morning.

AUG. 19. Commences clear, moderate breeze from the W.N.W. Temp 44°. Awaken'd at earliest dawn, and soon after each one had made his cup of coffee, broiled a slice of bacon on point of a stick, and with crackers, completed breakfast, then saddled up, mounted and proceeded.

This morning, as I desired, I was awakened at the crack of dawn, and the one I relieved lay down & quickly fell asleep. So as soon as it was light enough to see clearly around, I shouldered my gun, and proceeded down the western inclination of the road, to see how it was. For 300 yds. it was nearly level, very smooth, and covered with a very fine powder.[279] Ju[d]ge my surprise, when about 20 yds. from the camp-fire I saw the tracks of an enormous panther — judging from size of the feet — This track came down from the hill and turned into the road, about 50 yards further on. — From where it approached camp the nearest and apparently stood there awhile, it went back on the road, to near a rill — probably 200 yds from our fire, & there were signs in the dusty road here, where a very young bear-cub had reached the road from the gulch on the right, and the panther had crept along and then bounded upon it. — As the trails were lost in confusion, — the dust scratch'd up & scatter'd around, and rolled in one place and hair in it. So Mr *Painter,* as Stinson called him, had made a circuit over the hill, come down beyond our fire, approached it, and looked at the Sentinel, then turned off, disappointed by the big fire, and finally clutched the poor little cub![280] On returning, my comrades had prepared the breakfast, — Coffee, broiled bacon & crackers, which we speedily dispatched, and were about to saddle up, when one of the indians we met yesterday afternoon, wearing the conical straw hat, made his appearance, we exchanged the courtesies of the morning, gave him some fragments of bread, mounted & moved on. This fellow must have followed us last night, — he was a Panack.

After descending a couple of miles, saw basaltic parapets, occasionally on the heights, over the brook, on our right.

Our yellow friend accompanied us, running alongside our horses. — An hour's ride brought us to the crest of the ridge, and through a gap in the mountains near us, beheld a magnificent and extensive landscape. The plains of Snake-river of various shades of blue, and green, stretched far away to the westward, and looked very much like the ocean; in the misty background, — apparently baseless, were dim blue mountains, the 3 Tetons (buttes) seemed like high islands in the ocean;[281] while midway a blue streak indicated the willowly line of the Panak river. A comrade, at my side, enjoying with me, the view, enquired what that dark line was? I pointed down towards it, and replied "the Panak river." — The indian, close by, raised himself on his toes & looked, and when he heard me name the river, he screached out "Panak!," and bounded off down the road like a deer. We had bade farewell to our eastern brook, a short distance, and were among Springs and rills — Sources of the Port Neuf river, on the western side, — some of the fountain-heads of the great Columbia river. — sparkling and rippling amid fringes of dwarf willows. Our Panak friend was soon lost to our view in the sinuous descent of the mountain; the character of the mountain, being now, rocks, precipices, hills, vales, brooks, willows, cedars, ravines, &c. though the road is good.

Merd. clear, light winds W.N.W. Temp. 90°

Road excellent, fuel in abundance, as well as tall green grass.

Winding down a declivity, I noticed a small flat valley ahead, between small eminences, where rows of light-colored stumps appeared like pailings; and a plant scattered about, like the plantain, looked like garden vegetables, and altogether bore a strong resemblance to a garden at home.

Tracks in the road, of a large panther, wolves, a small bear, a grizzly bear, and of 2 unshod mules — the last ascending. — Besides deer, grouse, &c. When we had descended the mountain about half way, on left of the road, apparently not over ¾ m. from us, arose a high peak, with patches of snow on the top & in hollows, looking like linen spread out on a dark green hill to dry. Reached a rivulet, running across the road; — pure and cold, from those snow-patches. And several clear cool springs also. We halted to rest — soon near the foot of the mountain, just below a sudden bend in the river (Port Neuf) in a grove of wild cherry trees, full of robins. — Shot several, as our bacon was out, and being near Sun Set, kindled a fire, made coffee, broiled 2 robins each, and dividing our last bread (dust) supp'd. While saddling, to move on a Shoshone, on a fine horse, rode up, and made signs, that if we pushed hard, we might reach the tents, (cantonment) by dark.[282] But we could not ride fast, for my horse had long since given out, and I had to drag him the most of the way down the mountain, by the bridle; and a comrade's animal was little better. Soon after, a very old Panak, rode up, and enquired of the other, about a stray animal, as we thought, and on his replying, the old man rode hurriedly up the mountain. No doubt he was after the runaway mules whose tracks we saw this morning. Little after Sun Set we were fairly at foot of the hills, and observed, on our left, in a clump of willows, by a stream, a skin lodge, where stood a very dark young indian; his wife, apparently, lighter complection, and of a beautiful figure — about 18 yrs. of age, but with a face as ugly as mud; and old withered hag, — the mother of one of them; and 3 or 4 dirty black papooses of a small size, who seemed to take particular interest in the contents of a small camp-kettle — hanging over the fire. — On examining the said kettle, I found it contained very *savory* broth, of 4 antelope feet, — hairs, hoofs, dirt, &c.

Across the stream — in a meadow, were some fine horses; and I wanted one, and signified it to this Panak family. — The man waded the stream and brought over a beautiful cream-colored poney, but the Squaws rais'd a row with him, and he had to take it back; he then brought over a fine large white horse, with very long tail and main; and then we bartered. — For this animal I gave my used up old brown horse, a broken-stock gun, a striped shirt, and an old coat. — He, of course, wanted much more. Then for fine braided lariet, I gave him 1 pr brass bracelets, end of a plug of tobacco, several charges of powder, and about 50 percussion caps. Transferred the saddle &c to the whitey, and moved on. At nearly dark, we met a very genteel-looking Panak, well mounted; and the old man offered to guide us to the Cantonment; which was, as we understood him, by signs, nearly surrounded by *slews* & marshes, and therefore difficult to reach after dark. Rode several miles over very deep sand, interspersed with sage brushes; then across a long grassy bottom, and finally reached the water & marsh, and rode around — as it appeared to me, in the dark, several times, and at length reach'd some wagons and a tent, among willow bushes. — Here we dismounted, and my worthy old guide informed me that he (the indians) were not allowed to go in at night. So I went on a few paces, met a soldier and enquir'd who commanded the post, and he informed me that it was Col. And^w Porter,[283] of the Mounted Rifles. I was quickly at his Markee,[284] and received in the kindest manner by the Col. and his brother officers.[285] — My comrades introduced, a very hearty supper, a toddy, pipe, recital, and a good bed & sound repose.

Our animals were, by order of the kind colonel, taken to the grazing camp.

"Cantonment Loring" — as this post is called, is situated 6 ms. above Fort Hall, — on the Snake river.[286] A quadrangular Picket-Fort is laid off here. — (*330 by 136 feet*) The cotton-wood logs are laid down, for the commencement of the bastions — intending to build them up of logs, and the curtain — or walls, of picket, or perpendicular logs, close together. At present, the command is sheltered in tents & a few rough sheds. Admirable neatness & discipline observed.[287]

The adjacent hills afford common black-tail deer, Elk, antelope, hares, sheep, &c — and the plains abound with grouse and innumerable flocks of black-birds, curlews, plover, &c. streams, with geese & duck, salmon, trout, &c. —

Col¹ Porter has been most indefatigable — came here but a few days ago, with a small command, and has done so much, is astonishing. Guard mounting & all the regular duties of a garrison, applicable to such a position are strictly observed.

AUG. 20. Commences clear & pleasant I persuaded Stinson to enlist at the Post for a mule driver, and so got rid of him.

Indians, all Panaks, are seen every where. Many of the mean [men] wear the common plaid Scotch bonnet, such as sailors use; given them by the Hudson Bay Compy.

Squads of dirty ill-looking squaws, and dirtier papooses, and mounted men, are riding or walking in all directions, or squatted outside the camp, looking with great curiosity at everything.

[AUG.] 21. Clear & pleasant

Indisposed, with severe headache, had to take medicine.

Merd. & afternoon. same as commencement²⁸⁸

[AUG.] 22. Commences hazy & calm. Indisposition of a comrade, as well as myself, prevented me from moving off today.

Dr. Pegrim, (whom I dined with at the Platte Ferry, on fish, and several others — on horses & mules, came in here, about 12 M. [meridian] out of provissions. They had joined the large Boston pack-Company, under a Capt Thing, who attempted to cut over W. from about Fremonts' Peak, into the Snake Valley, and were lost in the mountains, for a while and with great difficulty extricated themselves.²⁸⁹ — This Capt. Thing was a trapper, about 15 yrs. ago, and then built Fort Hall for the Hudson Bay Comy and Commanded it. — He made a picket fort of it, — since built of adobe.²⁹⁰

Col. Porter supplied the party with fresh beef, &c. although his stores were short. The Col. informed me that Capt. Stansbury, U. S. T. Eng. & party were expected here soon.²⁹¹ And he was also in daily expectation of a supply train from Oregon, under command of Lieut. Hawkins, U.S.A.²⁹²

[AUG.] 23. Commences clear & calm. Temp. 68°

The Officers most kindly supplied me, on application to the Col¹ with 40 days [i.e., ten days' each for four men] rations, bread, bacon, coffee & sugar, charging it to their mess — rejecting pay for it. I am also indebted to the Col. for a military saddle & holsters.

Pegrim & party — chiefly S. Carolinians & Alabamians are shoeing their animals, &c —

My comrade — Barker — quite sick, — too unwell to proceed

[AUG.] 24.

Commences cloudy. Col. Porter & some other officers rode out to look for lime-stone. We dined with our kind friends, and at 2 P.M. bade them adieu, and started for F^t Hall,[293] which we reached at 5 P.M. Road level, but crooked & marshy, with several gravelly bed[s] of streams to cross. Proceeded ½ m. beyond the fort, picketed our animals, spread our blankets & prepared supper.—

While this was in progress (a very simple operation) I walked back to the Fort, entered the Great Portal, walked across the open square, and up a pair of stairs, to a balcony, and at a door of an upper apartment met Capt Grant, the former Hudson Bay commander. Grant is a Scotchman, from Canada, a fine looking portly old man, and quite courteous, for an old mountaineer. His wife is an Iriquois woman, good looking, very neat, and polite.[294] She is, of course dark skin. — Her handywork, — of bead embroidered articles are very ingenious and beautiful: — pouches, sashes, mocasins, &c. &c. adorn the apartment, or office of her husband. I enquired if he had any of them to dispose of, but he said no, all spare things of that kind, had been sold, and that those I saw, were his own reservation. Mrs. G. made a pitcher of fine lemonade, and I found it very refreshing. He said that his whisky was out, and apologized for the deficiency.

I mentioned Capt. Thing, to him, observing that T. said he once commanded this post. "Yes," said Grant, "he was the original builder and commander, — then a mere picket-work, which he presided over for several years, during which he, (T) was guilty of a most extraordinary piece of folly, for one who held such a peculiar position, and who ought to have known the indian character. — Late one day, a party of Black-Feet Indians[295] rode up, and desired to enter; Thing not only invited them in, but feasted them, and also permitted those mountain arabs to sleep within the fort! At dawn, the next morning, the gate was wide open, and his guests were not only *oph*, but they had carried away every animal from the post, &c. and the whites were most lucky that on waking up they did not find their throats cut! Grant relieved him, by order of the Comp^y and rebuilt the fort, as it now stands, of adobes, &c.[296]

Fort Hall = adoobie walls

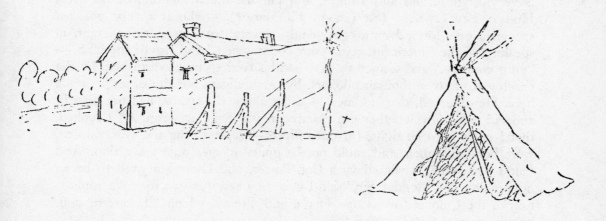

Grant has made himself rich, no doubt, by trading with the indians and emmigrants with horses, &c. and his store: — the latter going to Oregon & California, and this is the first time that the California adventurers by the Northern route, have entered the Great Basin to the South of this. Some few, very early, this year, passed here. I enquired about the "Emmigrants' Cut-Off." — He said he could not find out any thing about it; that he sent one of his sons out to the hills to discover it, but he failed to do so, & only noticed that for a great distance on the southern slope of the mountains, that the grass was burnt off. He thinks the trail must be a very rugged one, and cannot abreviate the distance much. G. says that the discovery of it is attributed to certain mountaineers, whom he knows — Greenwood, Hedge-peth, &c — but he thinks that it was found thus: — "That early, last season, a gentleman, from the States, on his way to California, stop'd at the Fort, introduced himself to him, and exhibited letters from the most prominent men of the country, and desired a loan of Grant, of (I think) $250, which he (G) from the gentleman's manners & supposed standing, readily advanced him; promising to repay it on his return to the States, — the next Season. Well, the aforesaid gentleman did return to the States, but not by the way of Fort Hall; and therefore, Grant concludes, that he sought to evade the call & payment, and seeking a lower exit from the Great Basin, found this Pass, and made it known home![297]

Grant is permitted, by Col. Porter to retain his old home, and gives him charge of some stores in the lower apartments of the Fort. The old Captain is very English, and anti-Yankee, and put me much in mind of his great Hudson Bay Chief, — (Sir George Simpson[298]) — who is a very *polished* speciman of a low adventurer suddenly elevated to a great title. Grant, in speaking of the Americans, says "your countrymen," and also of the U. S. — "your country," and seemed to have had his feelings much disturbed, by the exactment of some thousand dollars, by our Officers, for duties on his trade here. He observed, that he knew nothing about the treaty, had not seen it, and did not know whether the exactment was right or wrong.[299] I replied, that I knew it to be right; for our officers — representing the Government, were honorable men, and could not be guilty of any unjust exaction: And that I was well acquainted with Col. Porter, and knew him well to be an honorable man. "Besides, Sir," said I it is very easy for you to make application to the Colonel for a Copy of the said Treaty, which I'll warrant you, he will most cheerfully furnish."

Grant has a son here, about 18 yrs of age, quite a pretty youth, but seems to be in delicate health. An older son, and a very fine fellow, has a couple of tents in the plain below, with a corral, and band of horses & cattle. — He is married to a lady formerly of St. Louis, (I believe with him) and 2 or 3 children. I understand that the old man was vexed with his son for marrying a white woman, as he wished him to take an indian wife. — And the disagreement causes the younger family to live & trade independently.

While conversing with Grant, sitting opposite the entrance from the balcony, a young indian Squaw came up, and leaned against the railing opposite the door — looking in at me. I was struck with her beautiful and graceful figure, and very neat dress. — She was about 18 yrs of age, rather tall, and slender, of a very light yellow complexion, glossy black hair, done up in long braids, with ribbons, — like our school-girls, black eyes & long silken lashes: Her dress was pure white deer-skin — A frock, reachinging [sic] a little below the knees; pantaloons — to the ancle, — mocasins, and a purple figured Merino shawl, thrown gracefully around her waist, and over one arm. The skirts of her dress, pants, and top of the mocasins, had a very neat vine worked on them — more like the taste of ladies at home, than the rude attempts at ornamental work of the indians. Pretty black eyes, and handsome Grecian nose; but alas! her mouth interfered with perfection! — very thin lips, — merely a long straight line!

Having so often seen those "*Parlor Albums*," &c. in which examples are given, of female beauties of every nation, executed in the best style of the arts, &c. where a Bedoin arab girl, — black, ugly and dirty, as they no doubt are, are here represented, as "Rebecca at the Well," — most fair and beautiful, and attired like the favorite Sultana. — So with the "Indian Princess" — Instead of a faithful portrait, — as far as I have observed thousands, of various tribes, — of every shade, from brown to black, and of a cast of beauty which can only please indians, Hottentots, and the depraved appetites of mountaineers; you see a most charming tawny beauty; bedecked in tasty & neat habiliments.

I had wondered how it was, that so far I had not seen a good-looking Squaw; and this damsel astonished me. I told Grant that she was the only decidedly good looking, neat, and cleanly female indian I had ever seen. — He informed me that she was the wife of his herdsman — a Frenchman I think — and resided in one of the black, dirty, and smoky skin-lodges near by the Fort.

Mrs. G. went out and spoke in the Snake language to the Squaw, and they went to another part of the building together. Of course the Grants are familiar with all the indian languages here & in Oregon. Grant generally pays a visit annually to Fort Vancouver, trading, bringing up supplys, &c.

I enquired if the road all the way down, to Oregon, was good for wagons; he replied tolerable, — had some bad places in it: but, said he, "There is no place where you Yankees cannot carry a wagon, that I ever saw!" (I can almost endorse that, from my own experience)

Accompanied by the old Scotchman, I descended the steps into the court-yard, and when we had reached the well, — in the centre, (a square wooden structure about 3 ft. above ground — with a hinged scuttle to it.) some Shoshonees entered the gate — They had dried salmon to barter. The party were a very old wrinkled black hag, a couple younger squaws, — quite as homely, an old black fellow, and dirty greasy papooses — The bundles of dried fish were deposited on the well platform, and then, between Grant & the old hag, commenced the chaffering about the price, till at last Grant obtained them at his price, and went into his store-room to deposit them & pay the poor indians, with some necessaries. The fish looked nice — though very thin, and I enquired if he could spare me a few, which he did, — giving me 4 for 50 cents. I bade Grant farewell, and proceeded to my very small camp. — We drew lots for guard; and in spite of the strong and cold wind obtained tolerable repose.

AUG. 25. Commences clear, Moderate breeze from the W.S.W. (Temp. 36° (frost early)

At 5 A.M. we had breakfasted, & were in the saddle. Saw Grant's young son, attending to the stock. The other folks at the Fort were yet in bed. We rode off, on a slight trail in the grass, in a S.E. direction — trending to the S. & S. by E. over rich plains of tall beautiful grass, to a bend of the Panack river. — Here it is broad and shallow, with little current, and luxurient green grass & willows kissing its beautiful bosom. —

A short distance back we passed a *slew* which contain'd some varieties of shells, but they were fragile, and I could not take care of them. Continued on, till meridian, and dined on the edge of the stream, a little to the left of the narrow trail. We picketed our animals on the grassy slope above — by trail, struck a light, and soon enjoy'd the luxuries of coffee, biscuit, broiled salmon, — and the usual dessert — a pipe. Made about 12 miles. Clear and calm, Temp. 70°. While examining the marshy lagoon (or *slew*) for shells, a Panak young man, on a fine dark poney, rode up, shook hands, & said "how do?" and continued on towards the fort. He wore a blue striped shirt, & blue nankeen pants.

While nooning, a very clean light colored, clever Wallawallah youth[300] rode up, on a pretty cream-colored poney. He had a very decent dark coat on, shirt & trowsers, a blanket over his saddle, and was armed with a quiver full of arrows, and a bow, and flint-lock fusee. — He was very lively, and spoke many English words. He told us — principally by signs, how he killed buffaloes, with arrows, and that he was now going to the "Big Captain," — (Grant) to trade his blanket and coat & shirt. off. for a horse, which he intended then to trade off, with advantage. We offered him a snack — which he readily accepted of, and when I poured out a tin cup of coffee for him, he said "*Suuger*," and on handing him the small bag of sugar, I found he had

[DIAGRAM OF CAMP AND TRAIL, PANAK RIVER, AUGUST 25, 1849] "A SNUG POSITION"

quite a *sweet tooth*. Barker bought quite a fine buffalo robe of him for a silver dollar. We gave him some tobacco, and he readily cut it up, filled a small American made pipe, and smoked well. On separating he said "good bye, Sir," very distinctly. A half-hour's rest, and again we were mounted & on the mere indian trail, — as I wished to keep nearer the mountains than the road, — and have smoother travel and a shorter distance. Though there are traces along this trail, of the travel of horses, oxen, and wagons. Crossed some rather bad *slews*. — our course about S.S.W. — Crossed the Panack and several branches of it, and late in the afternoon — steering S.S.E. after crossing the streams, reached a creek (branch of Panack) crossed and found a snug position at base of a table-land, with bluffs, — about 40 feet high, and ranging S.W. & N.E. as far as we could see. — These are the outlayers of the mountains. — Here we camped, in so secure and comfortable a spot, that we needed no guard out. — The diagram explains the position. 12 ms = 24 ms It will be seen that S.W. of us, the stream washed the foot of the bluff, and that on the other side a large spring, of clear cool water was so near the foot of the bluff, that we could just lead the animals by it, on firm ground; along the spring rivulet & the creek it was marshy, with dense willows; and within the space chosen, we could not be approached without interruption.

As our friends — Pegrim & party, said that they would soon overtake us, we were disposed to wait awhile, only 4 of us, and half the number sick. Messrs Barker & Provost quite ill. I gave them some laudanum. Near Sun Set, Capron mounted, and rode up the inclined plane, on the trail, and up the plateau to the N.E. — He returned at dark, and reported having rode about 6 ms. and found a camp of French traders & indians. Received no information; nor could he see, — riding along the edge of the bluff, our expected friends, — in the valley below.

Provost quite ill with cholera morbus. Barker much better, after a cup of coffee.

During the afternoon's march, we passed over a perfectly wild country, — generally very level, with excellent grass, but much marsh, in narrow stripes. Indications of indians in all directions. — A few miles back, at a very muddy ford of the Panack stream narrow and deep, and locked in with willows, we had some difficulty, but soon splurged through it, with no other disaster than wetting my feet and gun muzzle. After crossing, found relics of an old camp of indians; & and [sic] among them an iron dragoon picket. Saw antelope and lots of water-fowl, and Barker shot a fine grouse.

Sun Set clear & calm, Temp. 62°.

Our camp afforded all the requisites of a good camping ground; plenty of good grass, sweet clear water, and abundance of fuel. Shells in the stream.

In the edge of the stream, near camp was a red hind wheel of a wagon. — which we rolled & Above us, on the bluffs are remains of several burnt wagons. (Here, no doubt is one of those singular instances of the selfish dispositions so oft elicited on these long travels.

The party, intended to abandon their wagons, and pack into California, Grant either did not want, or would only give a very trifling sum for the wagons; so rather than he should get them for so insignificant a sum, or any body have the benefit of them gratuitously, they broke them up and destroyed them).

Night quite cold, Ducks quacking in the creek all night like fowls in a farm-yard at home.

When we prepared to snoose, spreading our blankets & saddle-pillows, side by side: we picketted our animals above us, in the long dry grass, at foot of the bluffs, and soon were all sound asleep. — We were asleep probably only an hour when awakened by a howling serrenade of a band of wolves, right over us, — on the brow of the bluff. — The horses & mules drew their pickets & stampeded across us, with fright, and remained in the wet grass below. Luckily none of us were hurt, though besprinkled with dust, as an iron picket, flying about, might hurt a fellow in the face or ribs. We jumped up, and finding out the cause of the fuss, laid down again, leaving our animals to graze where they were.

[AUG.] 26. — Very cold morning — frost.
    Commences clear & calm; Temp. 36°

At break of day, we were aroused in the like gentle manner we had been last night; The same, or another set of similar musicians, came to the opposite bank of the creek, below us, and sounding another full blast, sent our animals over us again, to the foot of the bluffs. — We thought then it was time to get up. Our 6 animals, with wood & iron pickets attached to their long lariets, had stampeded over us twice, merely scattering dust in their flight. So we *built* a fire, and made breakfast. Barker nearly well, and Provost much better; the contents of my medicine chest, (a small vial of laudanum & little piece of camphor, carried in my holster) judiciously administered, followed by coffee and broiled salmon, was very beneficial.

Wild water fowl, magpies numerous, ravens, crows, large blue cranes, black birds, &c —

After breakfast & a smoke, we packed, mounted, and rode up the bluff. — Here, we looked down over the expanse of green & blue plains & dark lines of willows, for our friends; — and thus waited an hour. While standing here, a fat square built little old yellow Panack rode up, very suddenly. He was well mounted on a spirited poney. — And directly commenced begging: wanted "Knifeè", "powdrie", "ba*a*le", "tabac", &c. — I was afraid we had none to spare, so gave him only 3 charges of powder, another contributed a *chaw* of *tabac*, and 5 or 6 buck-shot, and he returned to the hills. At length we descried a dim line of moving objects below, — they gradually became more distinct, — and still more so, — pack'd mules, mounted men, guns, &c — till we were assured of their being our friends. And so they proved to be and soon galloped up the bluffs and shook hands. One of them had unfortunately lost a valuable gold watch, and another a mule. Hunting for these missing articles, had detained them.

    This bluff road is sandy — quite deep in places.
    Merd. clear, light airs from the N.E. Temp. 100°

In 5 or 6 miles more, we turned down into the Valley of the Columbia, reached the bank of the river, about 1 mile above the "American Falls", and there nooned.[301]

    Lava & black obsidian fragments scattered all over the plain.

American Falls. 26th looking back

one of the Thod Buttes –
very misty blue

y cliffs

Home Stead
Rock

grey. th. gr sage thick
None ground

Grey rocks & sage

Met 2 Wah-lah-Wah-lah lads, perfectly nude, with fresh salmon, crying out laughingly, "Schwap, feesh?" With 4 rifle-balls we purchased 5 large fresh salmon.

Country volcanic, sandy, rocky, and very irregular.

A wagon trail in the road, and I picked up an infants fine white flannel undershirt.

Our snack of bread & water done, we filled our pipes, mounted & rode on.

(*American Falls Columbia River.*) The "American Falls" of the Columbia are very pretty cascades, but with more rapids and froth than fall of water, at this season.[302] (*On N. side the falls, saw 2 or 3 indians with horses.*) A short distance below, sitting on my horse, I sketched the Falls & scenery.[303] Near Sun Set we passed over a plain, enclosed apparently circularly, with high and very crude volcanic rocks, — and seemed like the mouth of a large Crater — filled up. (*Basaltic Walls Columbia river.*) On our right, outside this walled up area, we could see the perpendicular basaltic banks of the river; the high dark wall very regular, with a rock at an angle — looking like the turret sentry box, on the walls of a castle. Between this, and the rocks near our right, the river had a narrow passage — a sort of Cañon.[304] At dusk we crossed a rapid rocky brook. (Beaver dam Ck) and after dark camped on left of the road 1½ miles from the Ck. near a Spring. Sage the only fuel, grass poor.

DIAGRAM OF
ROAD

Passed 1 mule & several ox carcases to day.

[AUG.] 27. — Commences hazy, light wind S.E. by S. Temp. 27°. (early frost)

Early breakfast, and moved on at Sun rise. Road uninteresting. Sandy and sage-plains. In 1½ hours we reached "Fall river",[305] the stream is small, deeply cut in an abrupt rocky ravine, with dense cedars. It is a brisk stream — leaping and sparkling over beaver-dams, rocks, and cedar-limbs. The perpendicular basaltic walls of the Columbia, on the N. side, are still seen. We crossed a deep gulch of the Strm [Stream], and proceeded towards the Columbia, till about 10 A.M. when a large island crowded the river through a narrow passage, forcing the trail over the bluffs. — Continued along the heights till we reach'd Raft-river,[306] forded it, and just over, on our right, a grave. (Just where the Oregon trail turns off right, over basaltic cliffs. —

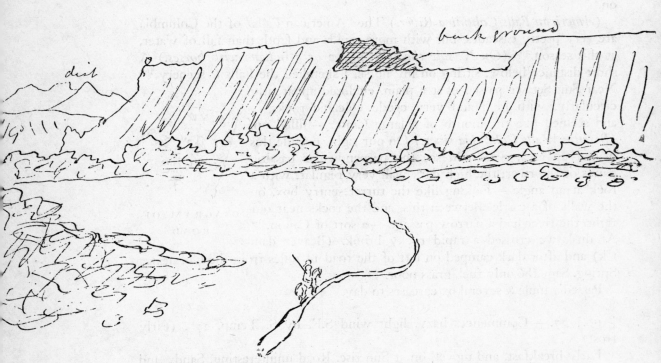

Basaltes Walls. vertical nearly, & very hight — river running at base

back ground

dist

[THE SNAKE RIVER, BELOW THE AMERICAN FALLS]

> "To the Memory
> of
> Lydia Edmonson,
> who died Aug. 15. 1847,
> Aged 25 years."

Merd. clear, with light & variable airs. Temp. 98°

Country passed over this forenoon next river, all volcanic origin   On the left sand & suppressed hills, with sage.

Passed 6 dead oxen and 2 mules.

Rested one hour, and at 2 P.M. rode on again. In 1 mile — from ford, another grave: — (covered with blocks of basaltes.)

> "In Memory
> of
> R. N. Rubey,
> who died Aug. 13.
> 1846. Aged 32"

The river now runs through deep alluvial banks, fringed with thick willows and tall reeds.

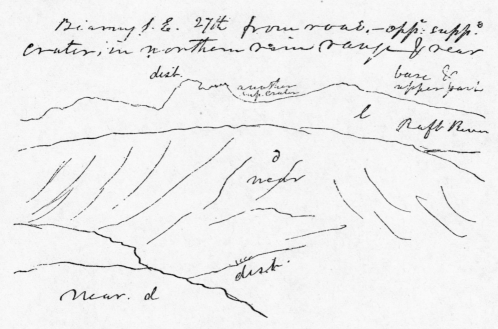

[VOLCANIC FORMATIONS NEAR RAFT RIVER]

We here struck across the plains, towards the mountains, through several miles of deep sand and stunted sage bushes, over hard & smooth, and lastly rich soil and grass. (*Sketch here*)

Passed, this afternoon, 3 dead oxen.

Sun Set clear, light airs from W. Temp. 76°

In river bottom, 1 mile before camping, saw a grave on left of trail. —

"In memory of
Henry Gardiner
Aged 21 years,
Died July 19th 1849."

Camped close to the brink of Raft river, in a bottom of long grass & reeds. Stream here very crooked, deep earth banks, and about 4 feet deep. and 5 to 15 ft. wide. Wild oats here abundant Cut rushes, grass, & wild oats, and had most comfortable beds. After a hearty supper we slept well, excepting the usual disturbance of our lupine serrenaders.

AUGUST 28, 1849 - NOVEMBER 5, 1849

Raft River to Bruff's Camp

AUG. 28. 1849 *Commences* — at Sun-rise meteological rem'ks

Commences hazy, with a strong breeze W. Temp. 54°

The wind increased to a fresh breeze, soon; though otherwise a fine morning. We breakfasted and rode on early. — The sun rose from a hazy bed, and gilded the edges of the clouds beautifully. — The mountains in our front, (the northern boundary of the Great Basin, and divide between the waters of the Basin and the Columbia — Pacific) were of a soft blue, and in places, a flesh-colored tint.[1] The road a good one, on a S. course, in about 2 hour's ride, brought us to a slight table-land, — the outlayer of the mountains: — very near the Stream; then along the stream, thickly fringed with willows, S.W. — Along here the trail seems to have been muched [much] travelled by emigrants, and indians also. We noon'd in a fine grassy bottom, bounded by high sedgy hills, those on the left — across the stream, and the nearest, were the tallest. The river here, is a mere brook, and trends round to the S. Willows and reeds mark its sinuous course, as far back in the plain as I could see. After dinner, the road runs across the plateu, and small hills, and a very fine white dust on it is quite annoying.

Merd[n] slightly hazy, a fresh breeze from the W. Temp. 86

Passed, this forenoon, 4 dead oxen & 1 mule. Little young grass, and moist roads. One of the party had a small indian-dog, who had abandoned his dark master for the chance of being better fed with the whites.

Course S.W. by S. about 3 ms. then S. — a couple of ms, and S.W. by W. till we, in a short distance struck the stream again, and were compelled, by the branches and marshes, to cross it several times. The fresh breeze nearly suffocated us with clouds of blinding, stifling dust — right in our faces. We camped on the bank of the stream, (head of Raft river) here a cold mountain brook; and such objects! such beards & faces! — all white with dust — our animals ditto. A wash was quite refreshing. Here we had dense willows to shelter us from the cold mountain blast. — We beat down the rose-bushes and grass, close to the willows, and spread our blankets, and arranged our saddle-pillows for repose, after a hasty supper, picketing our animals, & setting guard.

A few hundred yards below, we passed the place of an indian bivouac, burnt sticks, roasted muscle-shells, &c — On halting here, I observed ahead, and on our right, columns of blue smoke, curling up from nitches in the mountains: — probably Digger indians.[2]

The head of the stream trends to the S.S.W. The surrounding country of volcanic origin. — Ranges of dark basaltes, and evidently several extinct craters, — one on our left very conspicuous

Sun Set clear, fresh breeze from the W. Temp. 56°. Rained a little at night

AUG: 29   Commences clear and calm, Temp. 28°   (frost early)   Patches of snow on the adjacent mountains. We were all white this morning on awakening, with frost, and my hair being very long, the ends were froze to the saddle and ground, so that I had to pull it loose, but had to leave some, as a memento for the wolves to examine. — I thought of the picture in Gulliver's travels, where the Liliputians had *picketed* his hair down while he slept. We had to look out sharp last night about the indians.

A pack of wolves, this morning, at day-break, saluted us with a *reveillèe*. Early breakfast, & soon on the trail again, — which winds up this deep valley, from S. by E. round to N.W. — An entire range on our left, of volcanic hills, for about 15 miles: and on our right, similar formations for about 10 ms. when we entered a very extraordinary valley, called the "City of Castles." — (*City of Castles*)   A couple of miles long, and probably ½ mile broad, A light grey decripitating granite, (probably altered by fire) in blocks of every size, from that of a barrel to the dimensions of a large dwelling-house; groups, Masses on Masses, and Cliffs; and worn, by the action of ages of elementary affluences, into strange and romantic forms. — The travellers had marked several large blocks, as their fancy dictated the resemblance to houses, castles, &c. — On one was marked (with tar) "NAPOLEON'S CASTLE," another "CITY HOTEL," &c.[3] We nooned among these curious monuments of nature. I dined hastily, on bread & water, and while others rested, I explored and sketched some of these queer rocks. A group, on left of the trail, resembled gigantic fungii, petrified, other clusters were worn in cells and caverns; and one, which contrasted with the size and hight of the

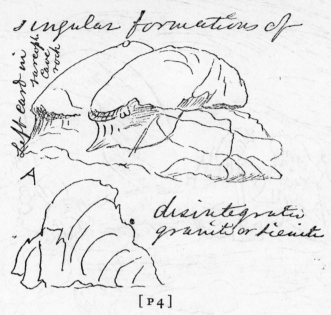

singular formations of

Left end in Sarcophagus Cave rock

A

disintegrating granite or sienite

[P4]

adjacent rocks, seemed no larger than a big chest, was, to my astonishment, when close to it, quite large, hollow, with an arch'd entrance, and capable of containing a dozen persons. (*Sarcophagus rock*) This, from its peculiar shape, I named the "Sarcophagus Rock."[4] While nooning, 2 Mormon young men, on horses, with Mexican equipment, came up; said they were trading for broken-down cattle, and had a camp and wagon not far off, in a small valley. They of course were from Salt Lake. I enquired if they had travelled, by this route, to California, to which they replied in the affirmative; and on desiring some information, one of them took out of his pocket a sort of Guide book, formed of a sheet of paper folded small, miserably written, and worse spelling, which he said was the last he had, & I might take it for 50¢, but that he had sold a number, to the emigrants for $1 each. I purchased it more for a curiosity than any idea of its serving me en route.[5] I have discovered no sign of my train having passed here, and conclude that they are ahead, yet must have passed through this valley. Left my card in Sarcophagus Rock

Merd. clear, with light breeze from S.E. Temp. 80°

(*Pinnacle Pass.*) After dinner a ride of 2 miles brought us to the outlet of this romantic vale, a very narrow pass — just wide enough for a wagon, and on either side very high, jagged, and thin walls of granite, — with cedar

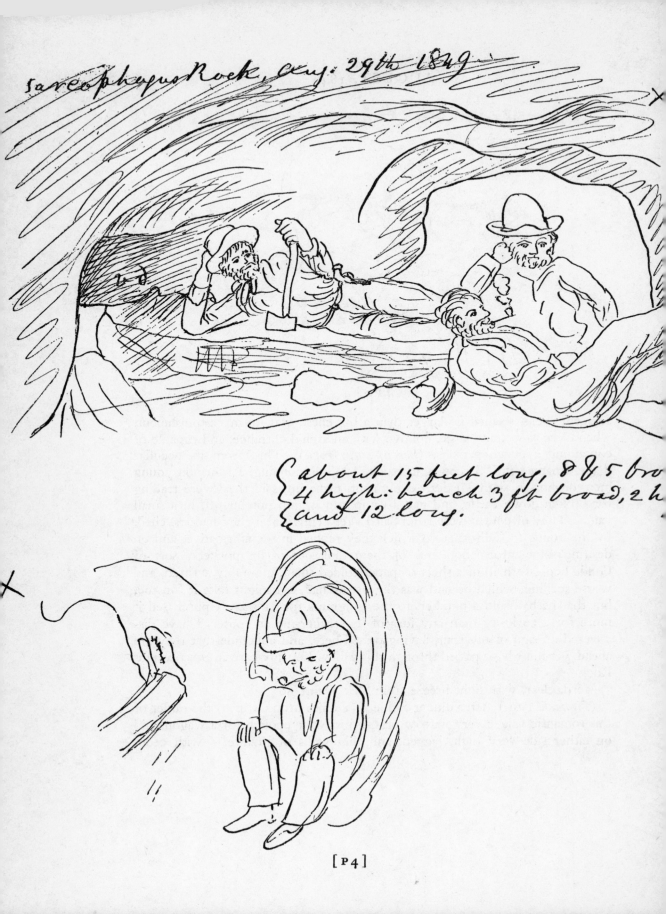

sarcophagus Rock, Aug: 29th 1849.

{ about 15 feet long, 8 & 5 bro
{ 4 high: bench 3 ft broad, 2 h
{ and 12 long.

Near Sunset. — Grove on right. — "Wm. Chenoweth
(remainder abliterated) — in a bottom near a small
river)

X

Sap

Pinnacle —

Pass — outlet of Valley, 29th Aug

bl sh grey, ¼ m off

with cedar
bushes

bushes in the crevices. — This is called the "Pinnacle Pass," and the tall rock on right, — the "Spire rock." On leaving the Gate, we descended a steep hill, and in $\frac{1}{2}$ mile reached where the Salt Lake road joins this, — the Oregon and California road. Overtook a party of 7 Illinoisians — mounted, & 1 mule wagon, from Salt Lake, they informed me that the New York Company was there.

Still no signs of my Company.

Passed 3 dead oxen this afternoon, and travelled till after Sun Set, and camped near an old spring, and stream, surrounded by groves of willows.[6] 8 ms. from Pass.

(*Craters*) Crater in rear of Camp, and another on our left.

Dark brown lava Mcadamized the road, and the brown dust of it rose in a fine powder.

Sun Set clear, Wind moderate, from the W. Temp. 58° The night was very cold, so with standing guard, the cold, and indisposition, I slept very little, though I took a dose of laudanum.

Aug. 30. Plenty of frost and ice. Sun rise clear, with a light breeze from the N.W. Temp. 30°.

An early start. Travelled generally a little N. of W. over ranges of short and steep hills, with deep narrow vales. Just after leaving camp saw an indian running down a hill from our right, towards us: Mr Provost and myself being in the rear, halted & he came up. — a smiling good looking Shoshonee. He had a long rifle & powder-horn, quiver of arrows and bow; and wished to trade a dressed deer-skin, on his arm, for powder and ball, but we neither wanted the skin, nor had ammunition to spare him.

In 2 hours more, we met a Shoshonee family, — an old man, a youth, and little boy on foot, and an old and young squaw, each with a papoose, mounted. Mr Barker gave to the old man, a few charges of powder and ball, for a fine dressed Antelope skin. Latter part of the forenoon we rode over chalk hills, the white impallpable powder choking us as we proceeded. Near the head of "Goose Creek" — a tributary of the Columbia. Long ranges of high chalk cliffs on the right of G. ck. bottom. Relics of old camps are here numerous; — broken wagons; &c. and 1 ox wagon packing. Passed 9 dead oxen, 4 do mules, and 2 do horses.

Noon'd in the bottom, at head of Goose Ck. Clear, light wind N.W. Temp. 80°. (7 *ms.*)

No sign of the company yet.

After dinner, we followed Goose Creek up, about 10 ms. passing 3 dead oxen, 1 do mule, and 1 dying mule.

Overtook Mr. Provost, of Ala. wagon and 6 men, and camped near, on the creek after crossing it. Very poor grass, small willow-bushes. Sage and grease-wood scattered about. Hills and rocks come close down to our camp — in the bottom left of Stream. Wide level bottom, grass dead.

Sun Set clear, light variable wind, Temp. 58° During the night it was freezing cold.

[AUG.] 31st Arose at break of day with cold, white with frost, and hair again *picketted* with frost. Plenty of ice in stream. Breakfasted and moved on early. Sun rise clear with very light airs from the N.W. Temp. 30° A rugged, hilly, dusty, and thirsty ride. Overtook several ox trains, among them a St Louis Coy recognized several old acquaintances on the Platte.

Volcanic formations, basaltes, &c. about 11 A.M. we reached the gorge of Goose Ck, where road and stream goes through a narrow Pass. (*22 ms.*) Here was a notice from my Company, informing me that all are well, and where gone on to, date of passing here, &c —

On the left of the road, a stick, with the following notice on it, written in a fair hand. —

Public Sale.

"Will be sold, on Sunday, 2d Sept. on the head of Mary's River, Stores, and a lot of merchandize. Emigrants in the rear will do well to be there, as great bargains will be sold." Aug. 29th 1849. (signed) Wm Mullin & Co.

Passed 8 dead oxen, 6 do mules, 1 dying horse, and 1 do lame & abandon'd Quite unwell. — Overtook Mr Hunt, — of Peoria, Ill. who kindly invited me to get in his wagon, where I slept soundly till he halted, late in the afternoon, at a beautiful stream gushing out from under a rocky cliff, where the road descends a considerable & stony hill, & turns suddingly to the left. — After which, in a few hundred yards, it turns to the right. Several Ox companies here — Men, women, children, and animals enjoying the clear cool water. This is the valley of the "Hot Springs" — (several hot springs farther along). (*13 ms.*) I supped with my kind Illinoisian friends, — and the pleasure of ladies company, to-boot. After supper and a short chat, I lit my pipe, bade my friends adieu, and rode on, after night, to overtake my old comrades — ahead. Road very deep in dust. Passed a camp, on left — near the bed of the stream, of an ox-wagon & 5 Illinoisians. — 50 yds further another small Co^y of Illinoisians, with a tent; then Mr. Provosts' tent and horse wagon; and at last reach'd our camp — about 5 ms. from the spring. (*5 ms.*) — All dust, very little good grass, — plenty of long dead stuff, sage, & small cedar bushes. Ox trains continually coming in.

Sunset clear, with a strong breeze from the E.N.E. Temp. 72°

Messrs Barker & Provost had ridden with the wagon I was in, and they accompanied me here. The former having missed his pack mule, on the road, turned back to hunt it, and slept at the Illinois camp.

The spring at the head of road, first struck on descending a rugged hill, is the source of a Great Basin stream, at this season dry a short distance below the spring. The water we used is from pits dug in the bed of the stream, and is muddy and bad. This spot is the summit plain of the divide. — No hill nigh us 100 ft. higher than this plain.

Made my bed under a large sage bush, and cut others & formed a barrier against the cold wind.

The fine powdery ground here, at night very cold.

SEP^r 1. — Commences clear, with light variable airs, Temp. 28°   The cold awakened us very early. Upon looking around for our horses and mules, which we did not picket last night, affording them a chance to pick up some fodder, found they had strayed about in a circuit of two miles, browsing for the little green grass there was under the dusty sage-bushes.

At 6 A.M. our Southern friends, Messrs Capron & Provost, and myself proceeded: and after a short ride, halted a couple of hours for Mr Barker, who was with the Illinoisians, about 5 ms. in the rear; — as he did not make his appearance, we moved on again. Our course lay S. — a short distance; then E.S.E. a mile, then S.E. — as far; and lastly S.W. — through a valley of marshes, sinks, and ponds, and artificial tanks; alkaline waters predominating. — Some of these springs cool and remarkable, and some warm springs in soft elevated mounds, surrounded with wet turf, and very dangerous for animals.

Mer^{dn} Hazy, strong wind S.S.W. temp 90°

No good water and the grass either dead, or grazed off. Our forenoon's ride was over a very dusty road. The stone here a fine white volcanic sand stone, the dust of which lies deep in the road. Country all volcanic. Travelled on till 4 P.M. when we came up with some acquaintances — part of the squad of southerners. — They were just mounting their horses, after dinner. This was on the left of the trail, and right of and close to a stream, fringed with willows. A small company from St Louis, with ox-wagons, also came up, and camped here. Passed 8 dead oxen, 2 do mules, & 2 do horses. We loosed our animals to graze & rest, & we foddered and rested also, a short while. A grave on the left: —

> "W. Maxwell, died Aug. 24th 1849,
> Cholera, Teamster in "Pioneer line," —
> Took Cholera on the Platte, then
> Scurvy; from Independence."[7]

We now continued our day's journey, on the same disagreeable road, — the wind increased to a strong breeze, and half-stifled us with the white powdery earth, full of alkaline matter. At Sun-Set we reached the camp of the whole party, choked with dust and thirst, and as hungry as wolves.

Sun Set hazy, sky and moon red, and a strong breeze from the N.W. Temp. 68°

Some young grass here, but mostly tall and dry. Our meat being exhausted, we contented ourselves with a supper of hard bread and coffee. Alkaline earth here, and very dusty. Cut sage bushes, and constructed bulwarks against the cold night breeze. A marsh and deep gully on our left, and the trail at foot of sterile bare hills, on the right, where I picked up some carnelian & agate pebbles.

SEP. 2. — Jack frost aroused us this morning, at $3\frac{1}{2}$ o'clock, so by 4 o'clock we had breakfasted. Last night was *"one of em"* — enveloped every thing in frost. Dr Pegrim invited me to breakfast with his mess, which I accepted most gratefully, as their stores were rather better than ours, and it afforded me much pleasure to associate with them. — They had a *Meat Stew!* Temp. at breakfast time 18°. Sun-rise hazy & calm, Temp. 29°.

Was informed that the Washington City Company was a very little distance ahead, and had laid by yesterday, for me. We therefore urged our animals, and at Merdn overtook them, in a deep vale, about to cross a rivulet branch of the Humboldt.[8] When I appeared, close above them, on the edge of a short eminence, they rais'd a shout of "There's the Captain"! and I was soon in the midst of them, and greeted by my friends. Found them all well.[9]

Merdn hazy, with a strong breeze from the S.S.W. Temp. 80°.

Grave of a German on the left of the road, the inscription was pencilled, and nearly obliterated. On the same side, a little further, another: —

> "Jno. Beerd,
> of Charleston, Mo.
> Aged 40.
> Died Aug. 12th. 1849."

A few days since my company found a discarded ox and cow, and killed them for meat.

Passed to-day, 10 dead oxen, 6 do mules, and 2 do horses.

AUG. [SEPT.] 3. — Commences hazy, light & variable airs, Temp. 34°

(*32 ms from com: of Hot Sp. Vally*) [10]

6 A.M. we rolled on; over a good road, short rolling hills, and S. and S.W. course 10 A.M. entered a moist flat valley, trending round to the Westward, with springs, and a grassy and willowy rivulet; — one of the heads of the Humboldt — (This stream was first known by the name of Ogden's river, — after a celebrated mountaineer, who first visited it, so they say; afterwards called Mary's river, probably in honor of the Blessed Virgin; and continued by that name, till Col. Fremont re-christened it, in honor of Baron Humboldt. Some travellers adopt the last name, but it is generally called "Mary's river".) [11]

Drove to this — 9½ miles, and nooned 2 hours. The plutonic-looking range of the Humboldt Mountains on our left. This valley runs about S.W. Low table land on each side. Distant mountains in all directions.

Passed 4 dead oxen, 1 do mule, 1 do horse, and 1 discarded ox — exhausted.

While breakfasting, this morning, two miserable, half clad, shivering indians came into camp. They were armed with full quivers and bows, and very different and inferior to any indians I had before seen; and was confident that they were the "Diggers", — who use poisoned arrows. [12] — So I steped up to one, took hold of an arrow, and made signs that I wished to look at it; but he objected so strenuously, that I could only get one by force, which I declined, convinced that the arrows were poisoned. And warned my men of them. These brutal wild wretches had committed so many rascalities upon the emigrants, that the least pretext would have been sufficient to ensure their destruction. I said to one of them, "*Digger?*" — he replied with a shake of the head, and downcast look, "*Shoshonee.*" — but I knew he lied. They went around among the messes, and looked wishfully at the men eating, but in vain, There was no charity for them: and they went off.

Road strewed with broken wheels, hubs, tires, &c. An ox train following us, and my late friends — the southerners, close by. At dinner another indian rode in to us: — neatly clad, and on a fine little yellow mare; he was armed with a long old fashioned flint rifle, quiver of arrows, bow, &c. I at once perceived that the smiling, good looking fellow, was one of our old friends, — a Shoshonee. — He readily permitted us to examine his arms, and gave several arrows to the men, they were pointed with yellow quartz. He dined with us.

On a lofty plateau in the mountains on our left, pale blue smoke curling up in a slender column, showing the presence of Diggers, — watching the camps below, to steal or kill animals. — My sentinals on the *qui vive*.

Afternoon's drive 10 miles, to the brink of the stream, (Humboldt) alluvial banks, — pretty deep, grass & willows, on the right hand side of it: where the bottom is 1½ miles wide. One mile back another company is camped. The grass below, — in the bottom, is tolerable, fuel scarce, and water good.

Keeping on the right bank, — where the stream makes a short bend to the left, in a rather rocky road, I observed a good wagon standing, with cover, geer, &c. and a card pinned on the side, to this effect: —

"Aug: 3, 1849. This wagon and plunder is left for the use of the emigrants: Please dont destroy this wagon, for it might be of great service to some poor Emigrant like ourselves." (Signed) Barnet R. Light.[13]

My indian horse — "Panak", quite lazy.

Although I appreciated the benevolence of Mr. Light, (almost amounting to magnanimity, in this very selfish travel), I had to molest the wagon; consoling myself with the idea that he left it for the benefit of "some poor emigrant," and in this instance it would most certainly be so appropriated. — So I took the fore wheels, axle, and tongue, to replace the same parts of one of my wagons, defective therein, & another party wanted other portions for repairs also; so it was not wantonly *used up.*

Sun Set clear and calm, Temp. 70°

Wrecks and fragments of broken up & burnt wagons numerous, — of which our cooks availed themselves. (*19½ miles*)

[SEPT.] 4th   Commences clear and calm, Temp. 32°, (plenty of ice) 6 A.M. rolled on. — Road following the River, S.W. and W.S.W. The Humboldt range appear to run S.S.W. Noon'd on the banks of the river, right hand side, where the stream is about 12 feet wide, and 1 ft. deep, with gravelly bottom, and earthy banks 3 to 4 ft. deep. Thick willows, alluvial bottom, and good grass. Made 12½ miles.

Merd. clear, light wind S.S.W. Temp. 86°.

½ mile in rear of noon-halt, a grave: —

> "Saml A. Fitzzimmons, died from
> effects of a wound received from a
> bowie-knife in the hands of
> Geo: Symington,
> Aug: 25th 1849".

Passed, this forenoon, 6 dead oxen, 6 do mules, and 2 dying oxen.

Was taken quite ill with headache, could not dine, and had to get in a wagon for the afternoon. Still following the river, — on a S. course. Afternoon's drive, to camp on river bank, 10 ms. An Ioway ox company camp'd near us. (*22½ ms.*)

Sun Set clear, light airs from the S.W. Temp. 80°   Good grass & water, but poor fuel.

COURSE [OF ROAD AND STREAM, SEPTEMBER 4, 1849] [P4]

[SEPT.] 5. — Commences clear and calm, Temp. 30°   (plenty of ice again) 6 A.M. moved on, — over a deep sand and dusty road, and in a few miles reached a valley running N.N.W. giving passage to a fork of the river, which we crossed, and ascended a considerable hill. This branch valley runs about N.N.W. and has Alkali ponds[14] on both sides; — our road now proceeded over hills and dry plains, to left of the stream, on courses of several miles each, — W.S.W.; W; and W.N.W. while the stream ran through a crooked narrow gorge, — the first length of which seemed to extend N.E. Passed 4 dead oxen, and 2 do mules. Noon'd on bank of the river, near the road, after a drive of 12¼ miles.

Merdn clear and calm, Temp. 86°

1½ hour's rest, and we were again on the road, — along the river bottom, and very dusty. Road level and generally good. Passed 3 dead oxen, 1 do mule. River getting broader, with numerous islands, and very crooked. Drove 10 ms. to camp, on margin of the stream, and on the right of it. — close to the brink, near a marshy place. Found camped near us, a Mormon train of 8 wagons, several women and children, and plenty of stock, among them some very fine California horses, and Mexican equipments. Brannon commanded them; they were from California, bound to the Salt Lake Settlement.[15]

Good grass, water, and willow fuel.

Sun Set clear, with light airs from the N. Temp. 70°.[16]

After tea I walked over to the Mormon Camp, and obtained much information about California, from an aged man, who seemed to be an honest fellow.[17] He recolled [recalled] several names of acquaintances of mine in the mines, with whom he was acquainted One of them [i.e., one of the Mormons encamped here] had a fine large specimen of crude gold, which he exhibitted to one of my men —

SEPT. 6. Commences clear, with light airs from the N. Temp. 28°. (frost) Last night 2 of my mules got mired in the cold marsh; Extricating them this morning, caused much delay, and we had, at last, to abandon one of them, as he could not stand. I told the Mormons to look after him, as he might, in course of the day revive so as to get along, if attended to.

Travelled about 6 miles S.W.; then S. to a gorge — through which runs the river and road, — in the gorge W. — along an elevated bank, and down to the bottom, — bank of river, 16¾ miles; — thick willows. Very high Cliffs of yellow sand-stone & clay on the right. The road was miserably dusty and cut up. Passed 2 dead oxen, and 1 do mule.

Merd^n clear, light wind S.W. Temp. 90°

Noon'd, and moved on. — Came up with Major Horn and company. Road over a hill, to avoid the wet bottom; crossed the river twice, and campd on river bank; poor grass, tolerable water, and plenty of fuel. 8 miles, making 24¾ miles to-day.

A hundred yards below our camp, in the clay cliff, of river bank, in curve of a bend, a large boiling-spring gushes out. — A fowl had been cleaned there. As a small set of evil-disposed & turbulent fellows in the company would take advantage of anything to affect my reputation, and to annoy me, I determined not to insist arbitrarily on conducting the company by the Oregon or Northern route, but content myself with explaining the character of that, and the Trucky, or middle route, — (within 60 ms. of the sink, where the river makes a sudden bend to the South, the northern route leaves the river, and goes nearly W. 12 miles to a spring, in the mountains —) and therefore I called a meeting, at this camp, explained the two routes, & that I conceived it to be more advantageous, in every respect, to take the northern one; They unanimously approved of my choice.[18]

[SEPT.] 7. — Commences clear, with light wind from the E. Temp. 40°. I went over, by invitation 300 yds to Horn's camp, and breakfasted with him and his lady. The road and stream, early this morning's drive, entered a gorge, called the "Wall defile," — it was a rough and crooked passage, in which we had to ford the river, 4 times in a couple of miles. Short nooning in Defile, and moved on. Course, this forenoon, through the Cañon, N.W. by W. ¼ m, and sweeping around several hundred yards S.E., — W. ¼ mile; S. 100 yds;

"WALL DEFILE" [MOLEEN CAÑON] ROAD ON HUMBOLDT.
[MARTIN'S FORK, SEPTEMBER 7, 1849] [P4]

W. and S.W. 5 or 6 miles; then W. by S. down to the crossing of Robin Creek and 1 mile over it, on N. side, to the camp.

Passed in the Cañon, an abandoned wagon, many wheels, tires, hubs, &c. 1 dead ox, and 1 do horse. The grass dry & scarce

Merd^n clear, with light airs from W. Temp. 100°.

Tiresome dusty drive. Several ox-wagons noon'd in the defile. About the middle of forenoon's march, we passed 2 dry beds of brooks, about $1\frac{1}{2}$ ms. apart, — running S.E. to river. This gorge is walled in, on the right, by lofty orange-colored clay and sand-stone cliffs. On the left, not so high and precipitous, but some places abrupt; and appeared to be inferior granite.

We emerged from the pass, soon forded "Robin's Creek", or "Martin's Fork", of the Humboldt, and 1 mile beyond, in a grassy bottom, close to the River, (— on our left) I camped. The river here is shallow, and divided into many parts by numerous low islands, sandy and covered with dead grass and thick willows. A considerable island close by us, — as branch of the river about [15] ft. broad and [4] deep, separates it from the bank on which we are camped. This island abounds with alkali ponds and warm springs. The stream, a short distance below us, runs S.W. then S.S.W. through another gorge, too abrupt for a road to follow: — the trail or road therefore ascends a considerable hill $\frac{1}{3}$ mile ahead of us, (W.) Martin's fork and valley, run N.E. The water here is cool, but too alkaline to be agreeable. Hot springs in the river-bank, sulphur, &c —. Had to remain here remainder of afternoon, to repair wagon wheels. — Soaked and wrapped them with rags. Grass poor.

Sun Set clear and calm, Temp. 80°

[SEPT.] 8. — Clear and calm, Temp. 32° (ice)

Made an early move, and in less than half a mile, reach the foot of an ascent $\frac{3}{4}$ mile to the top, — W.S.W: then S. a couple of ms — then trending round to the W. a few miles, till we halted, in all about 12 ms. at a spring & small marsh, on left of road, in half a mile another, and 300 yds beyond that another, with a considerable branch; this is the "valley of Fountains". Sage and willows plentiful. Passed 2 dead oxen and 1 do mule. At the 3rd spring we noon'd. I found a very poor and sore-footed ox, standing in the willows, shortly after I noticed him going back to the next spring to drink, and on reaching it, fell in, — to remain there till the wolves pulled his carcase away.

Merd[n] clear, with a moderate breeze from the S. Temp. 89° [10] miles. Maj. Horn 2 wagons and St. Louis ox-train 1 mile in rear. Passed both in the morning. On left of these springs the hills are round and short, rising back higher and higher. Fragments of agates, carnelians, chalcedony & semi-opal, and pieces of arrow-heads, formed of these stones, abundant. On the hill on our left I found many, and the large quartz rock and minute fragments around, with place of a fire near by each big stone, where the indians had spent some days manufacturing arrow-points. — Collected a few of the finest specimens. I had the mules driven W. over this hill, into a depression in the hills, for good grass; under a guard, about 1 mile off. After a good noon rest of $2\frac{1}{2}$ hours, we brought our mules in and soon were descending the valley. Passed several more springs, (the water of all these is good)

A strong breeze now from the W. annoys us much with the fine dust driven in clouds right in our faces. In a few miles, where the valley spread out to the left, I saw the government supply train, from Oregon, for Fort Hall, under command of L[t] Hawkins, U.S.A. They had just arrived, and came by the same pass in the Sierra Nevada, as we were steering for.[19] Learnt that the Pitt river (main fork of the Sacramento, — its source near the pass) indians had killed one of his men, and wounded 2 others;[20] and that many of his men had deserted at the forks of the road, where the California branch turns down S. on the Western slope of the Sierra Nevada. (*Told L[t] Hawkins that Col. Porter was anxiously awaiting him.*)

Continued on — road stony and very dusty, — the train proceeded to a very long and stony descent into the Humboldt valley again, on the left, some distance, and I, with a comrade, rode down a trail in a gulch and ravine,[21] to the S. — being, as I thought, a short cut to the river, affording me the advantage of selecting a good camping ground ahead of the company. This was a difficult route, but had been travelled by horse and foot. Pass a great deal of fine grass. It was near Sun Set ere I reached the Humboldt — and while attempting to ride down into a dry gulch, close by its debouch into the river, my horse became alarmed, and refused to move down, and snorted and evinced much fright; some willows below conceiled the cause, till my voice, urging my horse, had started a large Couger, of a dark gray color, out, and a couple of leaps put him under cover in the willows on my left, — edge of stream. I was compelled to go a hundred yards up the gulch, then dismount and lead my horse before he would descend and cross it: and after crossing he increased his speed considerable.

I saw a large rattle-snake, alive and writhing, impaled to the ground with a stick, near the trail. Striped snakes numerous. My comrade pushed ahead, as I desired him, to reach the train, and halt where there was good grass, but they went on till near dusk, — determined to make as much headway as possible, and in consequence camped on a bare place, near an island, on edge of the river. A branch of the river makes a long detour here to the left. There were two descents into this valley, from the hills on the right, and the company should have taken the 1st rather than the second one, but took advice of a few evil disposed fellows, in order doubtless to bother me. A broad bottom here. — N. side islands, slews, and branches, and immense groves of willows. All the grass here burnt and grazed off. A little above had to ford the river, where it was broad, shallow, and sandy. Sent the animals out S. Westerly, about 2 miles, to good grass, under guard. About here is a dreary looking place. Made 19¾ miles.

Sun Set clear, light breeze from the S.W. Temp. 80°

[SEPT.] 9. — Commences with flying clouds & calm, Temp. 50° Weather quite pleasant now.

Moved on early. — Soon came to a grave, on left of trail & river: —

"Wm Welty,
Aug. 4th. 1849,
Aged 22."

and a notice written also on the same head board, to the rear division of the Nemahaw Co. from their advance, notifying them that the indians had stole all their cattle, and wounded a man in the arm, but they had recovered the cattle.

Here I turned off, to right, alone, to the camp of the "Wolverine Rangers," an ox company from [Michigan],[22] and conversed with some very respectable & intelligent people, there; several ladies, among whom was a Mrs Chandler, from Boston, whose husband was with her. — All well, and looked so. Several camps near them, of 2 and 4 wagons.

About 10 A.M. the trail branched, — a ridge branch on the left, (for wet seasons) and bottom branch, near river, on the right. I took the latter; they branched at foot of bluffs on left. — Soon crossed the bottom, & forded the river.

Several trains took the bluff road, which sent a long and heavy cloud of white dust flying. We passed numerous remains of broken wagons, ox chains, yokes, bows, &cc — 2 dead oxen and 1 do mule. The hills are volcanic, with red and yellow earth. The river, beneath the bluffs, is about 40 ft. wide, and from 6 to 30 ins: deep; with gravel and pebble bottom; little current. — Noon'd close to the stream, 100 yds. from ford, on a short bend; banks 3 to 5 ft. deep, and of a straw-color'd soft earth, very dry.

Merd^n clear, with strong Wind W. Temp: 88°

Drove 11½ ms. Heard of many losing their cattle, doubtless by the indians. — Met a man on a mule, going back, in search of cattle belonging to an Ioway comp^y As the grass was fair, I gave 3 hours nooning, and moved on again, making in afternoon's drive, 6¾ ms: = 18¼ miles. (*18¼ ms:*) Proceeded to a 2^d and prominent bend of the river, with considerable short new grass, and camped in a pretty semi-circular flat, on the bank of the stream, enclosed by willows, through which there was an opening for us to enter, just large enough, and about 200 yds. from the road. Passed the camps of several small companies, one of them, from Wiskonsin, had kill'd an ox for meat; — several ladies with them, appearing prosperous & happy. Saw 2 dead oxen.

Willows, long dry grass, reeds, rushes, & green grass, interspersed among the other growth. River about 60 feet wide, and from 6 ins: to 3 ft. deep here: and a bare sand-bar in the centre.

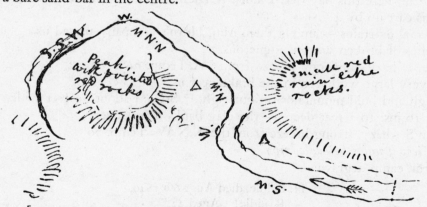

[CAMP ON THE HUMBOLDT, FIRST FORD AFTER
GRAVELLY FORD, SEPTEMBER 9, 1849]

Sun Set clear, moderate breeze from the W. Temp. 82°. Heard some more Mormon lies, intended to beguile the emigrants down to the Salt Lake Settlement, where they might leave their wagons & oxen, for the benefit of the Mormons.[23] — I happened to be wide awake for these chaps, nearly as far back as Grand Island of the Platte. I found that the whole tenor of their statements, and probably the main reason of their travel back, was to induce emigrants to visit their settlement. — The story they had promulgated, of 75 to 100 miles of this route, where we have been several days travelling, is devastated, with fires, sun, and grazing; — whenever such tales were told to me, I gave them this reply, — "We can travel wherever any other two-leg'd animals can.

A bear heard in the jungle at night.

[SEPT.] 10th Commences hazy & calm, Temp. 30° Saw, in the willows, several dilapidated wigwams, or willow-lodges. Passed Col. Brophy's Co. and several other small companies from Ioway. — In one they had a sick man. While a member of my company was riding by my side, his mule suddenly made a perfect summer-set, striking the ground with its nose, and turning over on back, feet up. — The rider was not hurt. We drove 9¾ miles, to a sharp bend in the river — to the N^d and noon'd   (9¾ ms:) Grass fine, plenty of fuel, and a dense growth of willows, reeds, &c   The members bagg'd many grouse this morning; and Barker killed a small spotted Lemur.[24] As the wheels of several wagons were defective, and Dietz & Young were 3 miles in rear, with their small private wagon, — their mules exhausted, I concluded best to remain here this day out. I lent Mr Dietz a mule, which enabled him to get his cart up by 4 P.M.

Several ox trains — among them Maj. Horn's company passed us.

Relics of broken wagons numerous.

Merd^n hazy, moderate breeze from W. Temp. 76°.

A very large wolf seen in the brake near us.

High and bold mountains on our right.[25] Stream about 40 feet wide, and from 10 ins: to 3 feet deep: — the clay banks 6 feet deep.

Sun Set hazy, strong breeze from the N.N.W. Temp. 70°

(*View 3 miles below camp*)

Near camp a grave: —

H. Biddle, died Aug: 6th 1849,
R[iddle]   Aged 22."

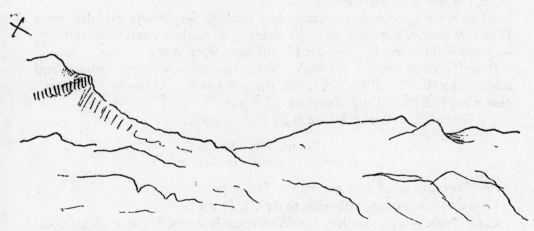

Near camp Grove — 10th 3 ms. below Camp
"H. Biddle, died Aug. 6th 1849.
Aged 22. below it these
emblems)

light

Mary's Riv. Mary's River

[SHOSHONE MESA, FORMERLY BATTLE MOUNTAIN] [P4]

[SEPT.] 11th — Commences hazy, light airs from the N.W. Temp. 32° (frost) (*Breakfast with Maj: Horn*)   Forenoon's drive across a broad alkali desert; face of it glazed and cracked white earth, (had been, in wet season, mud) filling the road with an impallpable white powder. Dwarf sage bushes, white with dust, were scattered over this arid plain. Early, noticed the mountains on our right, a lofty range, and about a mile distant. The very crooked river, on our left 5 to 8 ms. A retiring range of mountains, on the left, 10 or 15 ms. distant.[26]

Passed 3 dead Oxen and 1 do mule: First part of drive over a very rocky & dusty road, and *sideling*, going close to the brink of the stream, where it bends to the N. We shot several grouse and I picked up some fragile shells in a *slew* — Within 2 ms. of our noon halt, on right of road, a grave: —

> "Henry H. Robinson,
> Died Aug: 13.
> Age 26. years.
> of Dysentary, &c.
> Union Co. Ohio."

And ¾ mile lower, in a bend of the river, close to the edge: —

> "Phillip Haller,
> of Independence, Mo.
> Died Aug: 25.
> A.E. 24."

Drove 11 miles, to a bend, with tolerable grass. A mule fell in a marshy place, but was soon extricated.

After nooning, our drive was over a trail of deep white powder, on a Westerly course, generally near the river; close to the stream some fertility, — green willows, reeds, grass, &c. but off from it, all dusty barrens.

Passed 3 dead oxen, 1 do mule. Numerous trains, — some camped and others in motion. Near Sun Set passed the camp of the "Wolverine Rangers," near a large circular damp depression of Alkali.

3 miles before camping, where trails fork, a grave: —

> "In memory of
> E. A. Bryan — " (remainder obliterated)

Sun Set hazy, wind light & variable, Temp. 60°
Drove 7¾ ms: making 18¾ miles to day. (*18¾ ms.*)
Capt. Potts, — commanding the Wolverine Rangers,[27] and 2 of his com-

pany, called and introduced themselves, and very politely invited me to dine with them to-morrow, should we noon near each other.

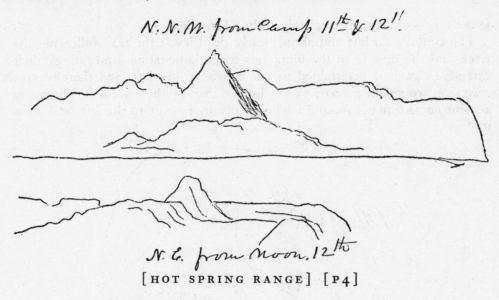

N. N. W. from Camp 11th & 12"

N. E. from noon, 12th

[HOT SPRING RANGE] [P4]

[SEPT.] 12. — Commences clear, calm, (frost) Temp. 33°.

Early move. Passed many ox-trains, and 3 dead oxen. Very dusty drive. A defective wheel caused us to halt at $5\frac{3}{4}$ miles, and repair. I reconnoitred a point of mountains & bend of the river, for a shorter cut than the travelled trail; ascertained that there was no trail, but the wagons could easily travel it, and plenty of grass: but the company objected, (like all other first travellers, afraid to go off the beaten track) and I did not insist on it. (Ascertained afterwards that 8 ox wagons had taken this pass, found a good drive, and excellent grass and water through it.)

Merd^n hazy, Wind light & variable, Temp. 84°

Afternoon we crossed a narrow low hill, Road deep white dust. Very extensive bottom — plains to the N.E. and N. Trail runs on a mein course N. — drove $9\frac{1}{2}$ miles, to a fine level field of grass, between bends of the river, and camped. ($15\frac{1}{4}$ *ms.*)

Squalls at the E. partially obscuring the mountains in that direction

Sun Set cloudy, strong breeze S.W. Temp. 70°.

Held a meeting of the company at their very urgent solicitation, and Resolved to send 6 men ahead into California, to make arrangements for meeting us with provisions, &c, &c. I remonstrated, and explained the folly of

the measure, but silly counsil prevailed, and I gave them the chance of proving it.

[SEPT.] 13. — Commences cloudy, calm, Temp. 64°
The country on left and ahead nearly dead level; the trail following the
river, and the dust from the numerous trains indicitating [indicating] their
extensive circuit, I determined to cut across, to my left, and thereby save
travelling around an arc 6 or 7 miles longer, than by this chord. — There was
a slight horse trail across, and I wheel'd my train short to the left, and went
it.[28]

[CONTOUR MAP, BEND OF THE HUMBOLDT,
ABOVE PAUTA PASS, SEPTEMBER 13, 1849]
[P 4]

Made 10¼ miles, to the bank of the stream, at a saving of 6 or 7 miles,
and the crossing of a rugged spur.
Delayed nooning, by a weak-team'd wagon, — the mules refused to pull
up a little sand hill, where it was rather steep and deep sand: A gentleman
very kindly lent them his oxen, to get over the difficulty. Merdn cloudy,
showers with hail, moderate wind from W. Temp. 80°   Forded the stream,
very well, except banks rendered slippery by the rain. Soon after crossing,
saw a grave: —

"W. Collins,
Died Aug. 27, 1849.
Of the Jefferson
City Mo. Compy"

(Noon'd 3 hours)
The road now runs 1 or 2 miles in a W.N.W. direction, entering the
"Pauta Pass," of the "Blue Mountains", — (a range running about N. by W.

& probably about 60 miles in extent)   Before the circuitous trail reaches the point where I [?] forded, it branches, — the left passing over a rough foot of the mountain & winds up this gorge, while the right hand trail ascends the high mountain and across it into the valley beyond. (This trail is intended for the wet season, no doubt). — (*Pautah Pass.*)   We wound along over an irregular surface about 3 ms. W. (*This is the extent of the narrow part of pass, & its direction.*) (Mountain on right very tall). Crossed the stream, and when about the middle of the gorge, had to recross, to gain the left bank [29] — In the gorge, where the trail was narrow, rugged, sideling, & devious, a lead ox, in a wagon ahead of my train, fell dead, and for a short time blocked the travel. We drove, this afternoon, a rugged travel of 6¼ miles, making 16¾ to-day   (*16½ ms.*)

Grass good, — refreshed by the late shower, a pleasant afternoon. — clouds and sunshine.

The Wolverines forced their wagons through the Sage bushes across the mountain spur, — thereby making a trail, to avoid the lower one, this morning, to enter the Pass, followed by numerous other companies: One horse-wagon ascended the mountain trail; which I imagine is a very tedious dry route. — This wagon I observed ascending the mountain, as I was mounting my horse to ford the river, and examine the road to the Pass. At which time my company was nooning. I rode very leasurely, examining the character of the rocky walls on the right, as I proceeded; — alighting often, and when through, — (about 8 miles from the halt,) and rested on a bank 15 minutes, on looking up to the top of the mountain, — not over ½ mile off, the said horse-wagon made its appearance, having just turned the crest, and descending.

Passed 2 more dead oxen.

Volcanic formations, gathered specimens. Sun Set cloudy, light airs from W. Temp. 70°   We are now 41 miles from that point on the river where we are to cut grass for the desert stretches, and 59 ms. from the bend of the river, where our road branches to the W^d over 3 small deserts.

Our camp ground is about the spot where a man named Jefferson, in 1846, had a fight with the Pauta indians, who succeeded in carrying off the greater part of his stock. He has published a small map, of the route through by "Trucky Pass", — a good Guide.[30]

Slight showers at night.

SEP. 14.   Commences cloudy and calm, Temp. 56°
Started at 6½ A.M. and drove 10¾ ms.[31] — Showery all the forenoon. Road

on left   14th *about 8 miles on the*
                          road, in forenoon

[SONOMA RANGE] [P4]

fine. Noticed trains travelling on the opposite side of the river, where the plains swell out N. Westerly, to a great distance, and the marshy bottoms next to the river force the trails back several miles from it.

Our course, this morning lay about W.S.W. mien. The faction of bad men in the company, evinced some mutinous conduct, this morning, for being called *so early*. At 9 A.M. on right of the trail, saw a camp of Missourians, whom I was inform'd had bacon to sell. — I directed our Commissary to procure 100 lbs, which we paid 15 cts pr lb for. While turning off from the train towards this camp — 100 yds, Dr Austin accompanied me, on a mule, his mule stumbled and fell, throwing the D^r over his head, and hurting him some.

Merd. cloudy, rain, Calm, Temp. 70°

Noon on banks of river a little beyond the Camp. The Mo. Comp^y was detained by a lady of their party, in the last stage of consumption. (She died a few days after)   Rain detained us 3 hours at noon-halt, when we proceeded, and had driven but 1½ miles, when I observed a stick on road-side, with a board attached, on which was pencilled a note to a member of my company, informing, informing [sic] him *that 10 miles lower down the river the grass had been all cut off by the emigrants; but that we should turn down to the right, from there, and in about ½ mile, by the river, we would find plenty fit for mowing*. This was dated the 12th. — So I immediately turned, as directed, on a sandy wagon-trail, and camp'd close to the edge of the river, in good grass, with plenty of tall grass on the opposite side. Drizzled till 3 P.M. when it cleared off to a pleasant afternoon. (*12¾*)   Picked up, in road, this afternoon a piece of paper, on which was written, quite neatly, as follows: —

"The Magnetic Telegraph Company[32] passed here on Friday Aug. 31st — 1849, at 7 O'Clock A.M. All well, come on Boys." (signed)

W. & H. Kilbourn,	Thos Jones,—Ioway,
Edwd Mansfield,	J. Vaughan,—Do
H. C. McClure,	Jno. Banor.

Jno. Putman.

At this camp, we have to cut, dry, and bundle sufficient hay to serve our animals 3 days forrage.

D^r O'Brian and family, clever folks, camp'd close by; the D^r introduced him self and friend, and politely invited me to visit his camp. — He has connexions & acquaintances in the City of Washington.

Sun Set clear, with light breeze from the E. Temp. 60°

About 300 miles from "*Lassin's Pass*" of the Sierra Nevada. The emigrants have named it "*Lassin's*", but it should be "*Myer's Pass*"; for J. J. Myers, an old California settler and mountaineer, is the author of this discovery, and he first took (*piloted*, as the mountaineers say) a Missouri train of emigrants over on it, the opening of this very season; after advertising it, and writing an account of it to the Adjutant General, at Washington; in which he offers to conduct any Government trains over if required. I had determined to take a northern route if practicable, to avoid the long deserts, bad water at Sink of Mary's river, long and heavy sand-drag beyond it, a long and very bad Cañon, and last, tho' not least, a very elevated rugged, and dangerous Pass. The aforesaid letter confirmed me: (Lassin followed Myers, having been on a visit to Missouri.)[33]

[SEPT.] 15. — Commences hazy and calm, Temp. 32°　All hands busy here. — Repairing wagons and geer, cutting & spreading hay, washing clothes, &c. &c.

Merd. clear and calm, Temp. 68°.

An Ioway company with 2 families, camped close by. Maj. Horn's little compy came down and camped. Dr OBrian, lady & 2 beautiful little girls, and friends, with several ox wagons, camped ½ m. above; Brophy's compy camped about 2 ms. below, on the N. side. The Wolverines are camp'd about 2 ms. above us. Ducks, in the stream, numerous. Many small snakes. Fuel willows. Sun Set clear, calm, Temp. 52°.

[SEPT.] 16. — Cloudy, light airs from N.W. Temp. 34°.

Getting our hay into camp, from across the river. After breakfast I took my gun and walked several miles down the river. Saw many remains of Pauta lodges, — Willow sticks, mats, &c, and old beds of rushes. Found some black obsidian arrow-points, also. Passing near a dense hammock of willows, close to the stream, a low growl, and sound of crowding thro' the brush, warned me that my fowling piece was not the arm to encounter a bear with.

Merd. clear and calm, Temp. 76°

Shot 3 grouse, and scared up number. On my way back to camp, I met Dr McDonald,[34] returning from a visit to his brother-in-law, Dr O'Brian. The Dr was mounted, and conversing about some of the extraordinary scenery in the rear, he took out his memorandum book, and read to me a beautiful description he had written of that extraordinary place, — the "City of Castles".

Sun Set clear & calm, Temp. 50°

SEP. 17. Commences clear & calm, Temp. 24°.

The useless project of the company, — the *Evant Courier*, of 6 men, started

this morning early; — they are Messrs. W^m and James Barker, Jerome Totten,
    Burche,   Capron, and Wm Jewell.

At 7 A.M. the train moved on. Our course led W.S.W. about 6 ms. (leaving
the river on our right a short distance,) over sandy rolling country and dusty
sage-bushes — The plane of this road is some 20 or 30 feet above the bottom
plain of the river. The road now trends to the S. — a short drive, then S.S.W.
— to a point where a sharp bend of the stream and the trail are within a few
feet of each other.[35] — There noon'd, having driven 11¼ miles.

Merd. clear, breeze moderate from the W.N.W. Temp. 76°. Pass'd 2 dead
oxen, and 1 do mule. Remains of indian lodges near our halt. Grass and fuel
abundant.

Afternoon's drive, first part sandy, courses S.W. — S.S.W. — and S.W.
again. Latter part, a bend of the river washed the base of a high sandy cliff,
forcing the trail up an ascent of heavy sand, and about ¼ mile over a high
plateau of sand, and down a deep sand descent, to the plains, where we found
good alluvial soil. While riding along this level bottom, I had observed a pack
company travelling down the opposite side of the stream, about ¼ mile off,
where the mountains were crowding them off: and soon saw the advance
fording the stream. — These I thought might be my esteem'd friends — the
Pegrims and party: But turned out to be my New York friends McNulty,
Fowler, Glynn, & 8 comrades; the others — some 12 or 15, were strangers,
but intelligent gentlemen, from Milwaukeè. McNulty informed me, that he
had gone to Salt Lake, where the [they] left many of his old company — the
"Colony Guards", sick; and had come from there by the central route, and
experienced great sufferings, on the long desert of "Utaria". He had heard of
us in the morning, and seeing the blue wagons of my train, thought it was. —
We had a very cordial greeting. The remainder of the Colony Guards were
to remain and take a Southern route from Salt Lake into California, under
the guidance of some Mormons.[36]

We camped on the bank of the river, after a drive of 9¼ miles, making
(20½ ms.) 20½ miles to-day.

Sun Set clear, light wind from the W. Temp. 64°

SEP. 18. — Commences clear, light airs from the N. Temp. 26°   (ice plenty
this morning)

Moved early, road generally very dusty, and crooked, following the river
bottom; the stream crooked, with numerous islands, — all covered with dense
growth of willows, reeds, rushes, &c — Forded, & soon reached a small bend,
where the bottom was narrow, with a hight [high] sandy bluff on the right,

and a trail ascending the bluff, — leading W. along foot of the mountains on an elevated arid plain, (wet season trail) and nearly parallel with the mien course of the river, for [16] miles, terminating at the great bend, where the river runs down nearly S. to the "Sink", (in the Great Basin) about   miles; and at the bend the trail branches, the right stretches a W^ly course over the first Desert, on the route we are to take, while the left follows the Humboldt down to the sink, then over, to the Sierra Nevada. Some emigrants had taken this bluff road for the true *"turn off"* route, and on ascending to the high plain, I saw their trains, enveloped in a cloud of dust wending their way along the rugged and droughthy trail at the base of the mountains. At the foot of the inclined plane, where the trail ascended, was a stick, split at top, and stuck full of notices; and a piece of paper fastened on it, said, *"This is the turn off road."* The emigrants knew that where the road left the river, for the desert, the latter [that is, the river] turned down S. and as there was a bend here, going S, for only a mile or so, they were at a stand; and a number of trains were halted, awaiting my arrival to set them right. — This I did, explaining to them their error; that my odometer registered every inch of the way, and that we had now at least a day's travel to *the* bend proper; also, that this short bend could not answer, nor the description of country; which soon satisfied them. I also informed them, that I would prefer the river road, being easier for the animals' feet, and along-side grass and water all the way, though it might be 5 or 6 miles longer than the ridge trail, which last kept along from 3 to 6 miles, from water. — They drove on, by the river trail, my train and a host of others following. Many of them found the advantage of this trail, for their weary and thirsty oxen.

Merd^n clear and calm, Temp. 72°

Early this forenoon we encountered some small but troublesome hills of deep sand: — drove 9 miles, & noon'd on the river bank. Capt. McNulty and company came up and noon'd with us. Passed 2 dead oxen and 1 do horse. In afternoon the trail followed the meanderings of the stream. — on stretches of S. — S.S.W. — and W. The sandy bluffs occasionally interfering, and throwing the trail & travel out of the bottom. The grass occasionally good. A large ox train and our New York friends in company. Passed another dead ox. Early in the day, with a couple of comrades, I rode over the river, on the left side, up steep sand bluffs, keeping as near the river as I could for the dense willows, &c near its margin, over a perfect sand desert, for about 5 ms. — There was no trail, but vestiges of indian visits, obsidian arrow points, circles of stones where they had had fires, &c. Saw several very large hares. High sand hills and rocky spurs close by, on our left. A few scatt[er]ed dwarf sage bushes. From one point, on the edge of this elevated sand plateu, I had a fine view of the sinuous stream, branches, islands, &c — and the long line of wagons, horse and foot, dust, &c. in the bottom on the other side. Wolf-tracks very numerous; and a large dark colored fox sprang over a ledge of rocks, near us, and secreted himself. As our mules were much fatigued with the *sand-drags,* when I reached decent grass, having drove 9½ ms. I camped near the edge of the stream. (*18½ ms.*) N. Yorkers also camped close by. Valley and stream, here, run a mien W. course. High mountains on our left; stream very shallow, banks deep and friable.

Sun Set clear, light airs from the N. Temp. 70°

Held a meeting to inflict penalties, (extra guards, generally) for guard and other delinquencies: when Mr. Wardell, of my company, desired to read an address to the men, which he had written. — Its general purport was the suppression of evil passions, congratulatory remarks on the extraordinary good luck of the company, thus far; and enjoining strict subordination and obedience to orders. — On concluding, the company gave him 3 cheers, and dispersed to cooking supper, &c. After supper, (in the night) I visited the camp of my esteemed friends, the N. Yorkers, about ½ mile off, & received in their usual cordially friendly way.[37]

SEP. 19. Commences clear and calm, Temp. 24° very cold last night, ice plentiful this morning.

Made an early start, for the *"forks"*. Passed over many ridges of heavy sand. Saw 1 dead ox. River very crooked, and shoaling. This morning some mounted men, and an ox-teamster, fired at a large grey wolf, among sage bushes on our right; none touching him; I tried to *head* him, but he eluded me among the large sage and grease-wood bushes, and I follow'd his track a mile and a half from the road, and halted to look about for him. I soon perceived him scrambling up a low bluff, about 400 yds. off; and as soon as he had ascended, he turned round and barked furiously, while I retraced my steps back to the road. Lost my bowie-knife — (a very valuable article to me, a present from Mr Ames, the sword cutler,)[38] this morning before starting, but recovered it among rushes in the river bottom near the camp, after delaying me ½ hour, after the train had moved off.

Lofty mountains at S.E. — and range stretches to the N.N.W. in the distant S.W. Poor grass here noon'd, after a drive of 9¾ miles, — within 2 ms. of the "Bend" and "turn off," trail. Merdn clear, light wind N.W. Temp. 76° An hour's rest, and we moved off for the "Desert drive." In less than an hour we reached the "Forks"[39] — The river here makes a short bend to the South — and in [58½] ms. — nearly that course, is lost in the pestellencial marshes and alkali pools of the "Sink".

A broad and perfectly level semi-circular area, very dusty, sweeps around the bend — and the two trails, or roads, are broad and as well beaten as any travelled thoroughfare can be. On the right, about a hundred yds. from the Bend, the Desert route branches off, and in the forks of the road, I observed a red painted barrel standing. — I rode up, to examine it. — It was a nice new barrel, about the size of a whisky-barrel, iron hoops, and a square hole cut in the head; and neatly painted in black block letters, upon it, "POST OFFICE".[40] On looking in, I found it half-full of letters, notes, notices, &c. — Near this was a stick and bill-board, also filled with notices. — These were chiefly directed to emigrants in the rear, hurrying them along, giving information about route, telling who had taken this or the southern route, &c. By these I ascertained that few had taken the Southern[41] road. I inscribed a card and left, here, *for the benefit of all whom it might concern*, as follows: —

> "The Washington City Company,
> Capt Bruff, pass'd, — on the
> right-hand trail, Septr
> 19th. 2 P.M. 1849."

The area here, of white earth, extends to the N.W. about ¾ mile, bounded, on the left, by an elevated plain, and long spurs and bluffs of sand.

On the right hand of the bend, looking W. is a remarkable range of sand covered Mountains, the spur of one blends with the dust of this bottom area, and over the end of it, runs the ridge road, before spoken of. (View, looking back, from the 'desert'.[42]

At the "turn off," between sand ranges, a new grave, on left of trail: —

> "Mary Jane McClelland,
> departed this life, Aug.
> 18th, 1849, aged 3 yrs. 4 mos."

A single wagon was camped just around the bend of the river. Now for the terrible desert! Who's afraid of fire? The first 4 miles was over a plain as level as a marble-tablet, and nearly as smooth; firm, where not cut into by the travel, white, and sun-cracked. — Of course, this plain, in the wet season receives the dreinage of the surrounding mountains, and is then a sea of fine mud; the dry season comes on, absorption and evaporation take place, and the hot suns dries & cracks it.[43] On the trail it is deep impallpable powder. We now are gradually ascending, and have to pass over a more irregular plain, of a redish clay, and numerous small stones, with scattered dusty sage

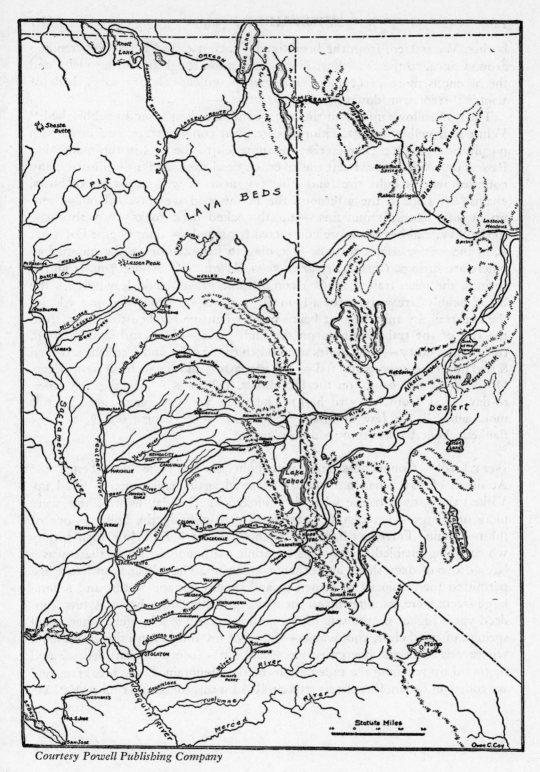

THE LASSEN TRAIL, FROM THE HUMBOLDT RIVER TO
LASSEN'S RANCHO AT THE MOUTH OF DEER CREEK
From Owen C. Coy's *The Great Trek*

bushes. We started, from the bend, on a W. course, and have been trending around since, to the S^d a short distance over the rough bordering plain, and the ascent is more perceptible, and ravines, gulches, & dry stony beds of winter torrents run down in every direction. —

The trail follows up one of these dry conduits, along a sandy pebbly bed;[44] White and yellow quartz, chlorite slate, iron conglomerate, and dust, with porphyritic pebbles, characterise the approach to the pass in the mountains. Passed, on road, since we left the river, 22 dead oxen, and 2 dead horses, any countless wheels, hubs, tires, and other fragments of wagons; ox-yokes, bows, chains, &c. Late in the afternoon the ravine-road we travelled on, — pent up in lofty sterile mountains, — mostly naked dark rocks, turn abruptly, to the S.W. and became more contracted & rugged, — along the bed of what is, in the wet season, a torrent, — leading to indentations in the mountains: where are springs. (*Sun Set clear & calm, Temp.* 65°) About ¾ m. from the springs, the main trail, ascends a considerable gravel bank, leaving here the broad pebbly stream bed, for a high plain. 2 wagons proceeded 100 yds. up the bed-trail, by mistake — it being night when we reached this point. And the rest of the train went up on the high plain. — Men and animals tired, thirsty, and dusty — The mules were taken to the sp'gs and watered, returned & tied up to the wagons and fed — A hasty snack, and we were all soon asleep. Drove, from our camp, on the Humboldt, 15½ miles. — Making 25¼ miles, to-day. (13½ from forks to here) There are 3 spring places here, in this mountain-dell — a few hundred yards apart; — the centre one ¾, and the flankers about ½ mile from road on plateau.[45]

[SEPT.] 20. — Commences hazy, with light airs from the N.E. Temp. 38° At dawn of day I had our animals watered again, and canteens filled up. Visited the springs to see what they looked like by day-light. These were mere drippings — percolating from small clay cliffs in the hollow slope of the mountain. Travellers had dug out hollow reservoirs below each spring, which filling enabled the animals to drink. Although so early, there was a large drove of oxen there, and others coming up. The selfish proprietors had permitted their animals to crowd in and muddy up the water; and several large steers were standing up to their knees, in the larger basin. A few hundred yards higher up the side of the mountain, in a gulch, were other, small springs, of good clear, cool water. — Some of my mules were driven up here; where was also some fine green grass; and I was informed that plenty could be found by pursuing the indentations of the mountain. Early breakfast, and we rolled on for another desert stretch. Road went, for about 1 mile W.N.W.

then over irregular ground, among the hills, several miles S.W. — W. — W.N.W. — into another elevated valley; then over long high rolls, of brown volcanic detritus and rocks, to another pass. Fragments of broken wagons numerous. In this pass the formation had every indication of gold-bearing formation. A block of wood, apparently part of an axle, had written on it, *"This is the place of destruction to team."* It lay on the hill side, left of road, near by lay several dead oxen, & a broken wagon, yokes, &c.

Passed 14 dead oxen, and 1 dying, this forenoon.

Merd^n clear, light breeze N.W. Temp. 70°

Fatigue and heat causes the train to move slowly. We continued on, I directed the teamsters not to urge the mules; and entered a very extraordinary looking country. — Road N.W. through several hundred yards of high clay bluffs and hills, of the most delicate and beautiful warm tints, in horizontal strata. Road-powder blinding & chocking one. Afternoon the road branched around a low bluff to the right; where, in 200 yds, I found, near an orange colored clay spur, a well, or tank, of water,[46] and a crowd of thirsty men and animals surrounding it. — A few yards to left of this another — similar hole, filled up with a dead ox, his hind-quarters & legs only sticking out, — above ground. Dead oxen thick about here, and stench suffocating. The road here sweeps round westerly, a few hundred yards, then S.W. — descending very gradually, to a level white clay hill, beat perfectly bare of every thing but dust, carcases, and relics of used up wagons, &c, by innumerable travellers and camps. — (*Rabbit Hole Springs*) Making 16¾ miles, from the 1st Springs in Gap, to these, — the "Rabbit-Hole Springs". and the Second Desert Stretch.

Passed in afternoon, (including those at the wells ¾ mile in rear) 30 dead oxen. This Table-land descends and projects, from the hollow of the mountains, and is about 40 feet above a sandy arid sage and grease-wood plain, which last is traversed by a deep gulch, serving as a drain for the hills to the Eastward: in which direction the narrow dry deep valley extends several miles. S. of these Springs, about 5 or 6 ms. where there is a gorge from the low narrow valley before us, are Hot-Springs and good grass. So says a mountaineer; and he further remark'd, "that if the road could be carried that way, it would be better, but probably longer." Probably a road might be made from the Humboldt, say a day's travel below the bend, W. to these springs and grass-valley, provided there is a practicable pass in the mountains, — which cannot be far from the river. Along the edge of this Plateau are a number of springs as they are called, but are actually wells, dug from 3 to 6 feet deep, and from 4 to 5 feet diameter; containing cool, clear water but a little saline, — about half filling the wells. Two of these springs were about 4 feet apart; in one was a dead ox, — swelled up so as to fill the hole closely, — his hind-legs and tail only above ground. Not far from this was another spring similarly filled. There was scarcely space for the wagons to reach the holes, for the ox-carcasses. W. of the plateau springs, the road follow'd an indentation formed by winter floods, down into the plain; and close on the right of it was a deep rugged gulch, containing 2 spring-holes, choked up with oxen; while the ravine for 100 yds. was thickly strewn with their carcasses. Here, and around the other springs, I counted 82 dead oxen, 2 dead horses, and 1 mule; — in an area of $\frac{1}{10}$ of a mile. Of course the effluvia was any thing but agreeable. On the spring bluff we halted for the night, watered, and served out grass to the mules. In the very heart of this Golgotha, was a fresh grave, on the head board of which, (piece of a broken wagon), was this inscription: —

> "M. De Morst,
> of Col: Ohio,
> died Sep. 16th. 1849,
> Aged 50 years,
> Of Camp Fever."

Several lame and abandoned oxen here, and the wreck of a wagon

My train came up slowly, from 4 P.M. till dusk. 1 mule exhausted, and we consigned him to this depôt of carcasses. The high rugged mountains opposite, appeared perfectly sterile; and no other growth below, but sage & grease-wood.

Sun Set clear, light airs N.E. Temp. 66°

On first reaching the brink of this plateau, and looking down, to where the bluff road descends into the valley, I espied Maj. Horn's tent & wagons; and rode down to his camp; He had neglected to provide grass for his cattle, and was therefore compelled to bake flour bread for them. When I dismounted he enquired if I was hungry? I replied in the affirmative: He then asked me if I would eat horse-rations? I said that being as hungry as a wolf, I would eat any thing. He pointed to a large warm loaf of bread, and desired me to help my self, which I did; and it was excellent bread. Mrs Horn kindly gave me a slice of fried pork fat, and a cup of Coffee, so I made a very hearty meal: rested 15 minutes, and rode back, to the bluff, to see to the company; leaving Mrs Horn very busy baking a number of large loaves of bread, to serve out to the horses & oxen[47] At night the Maj. moved on. All the Illinois companies, and some other moved off at dusk. I threw down my saddle and blanket, amongst the carcases, as did my men, and we slept as well as the effluvia would permit.

Sun Set clear, light wind N.E. by N. Temp. 66°.

SEPT. 21. — Commences clear, with a moderate breeze from the N.E. Temp. 34° A young man of the company, as reckless as unprincipled, backed by several scoundrels, attempted this morning to take my horse, prompt determination frustrated them. — The recollection of their parents stayed my hand, as I was on the eve of making a bloody example. — Glad that I checked myself.

Mr Richard Washington, who owned a riding animal, yesterday afternoon very philanthropically went back several miles with canteens of water, from the Springs, to relieve some thirsty souls in the rear. We moved early to get out of this miserable spot, and to hasten over the next, and longest desert stretch. —

Course N. of W. and very crooked; but generally level white earth, and small dusty sage bushes scattered over it.

Small clay mounds in various directions. Found nodules of lava and tufa. In about 5½ ms. from Springs, passed a camp of people from the Cherokee country;[48] who had sent their cattle back to the Springs, to water. — Thus far, counted on either side the trail, and some on it, 40 dead oxen, and 1 do horse. 3 ms. further we reached a plain slightly elevated above the last, over which we travelled, still N. of W. a couple of miles, & noon'd, on right of the trail, surrounded by carcasses, and wrecks of wagons, and every kind of property. Gave mules a bite of grass and quart water each. Passed, and about the spot where we halted to rest, 66 dead oxen, and 1 do. mule. 3 abandoned wagons and 3 carts. — Burnt remains of several wagons; and innumerable ox yokes, chains, bows, &c. Dead oxen often in groups, particularly around an abandoned or burnt vehicle.

Merdn clear, light airs from the N. Temp. 88°

Course, after halt, for 6 or 8 miles, N.W. the plain generally level. A plain apparently more elevated, ahead of us, is very level and smooth, and in the sun, looks like a vast field of ice; however, the appearance has no cooling effect on my feelings. — Now 3 miles a S.E. course, — N. quarter of a mile, and then N.W. around a sand ledge. The mountains ahead look like baked clay, yellow, orange, and red.[49] When we reached the white plain, I found that it was not elevated above the other, but was cover'd with a smooth white encrustation, probably alkaline. — This smooth white plain is narrow, but appears to extend to the S. a considerable distance: and in the wet season is

Mirage

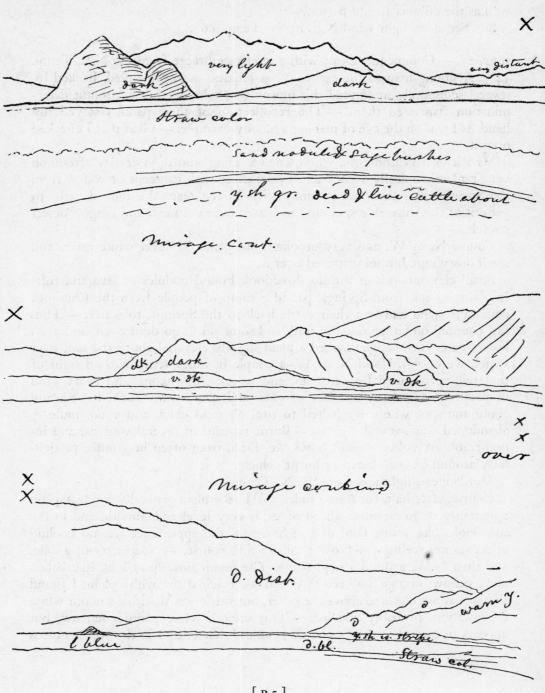

X

very light

dark

dark

very distant

Straw color

Sand nodules & Sage bushes

y. sh gr. dead & live cattle about

Mirage. cont.

X

dk   dark
v. dk

v. dk

X
X
over

X
X

Mirage continued

d. dist.

warm y.

d

d

l blue

d. bl.

y. sh w. stripe

Straw col.

a vast mud lake, now baked by the sun. (*Mirage*)   A very beautiful Mirāge in the S.S.W. on this plain, at base of some mountains. In which appeared a long lagoon of light blue water, bordered with tall trees, small islands and their reflection in its delightful looking bosom. One of my men asked me if it was possible that that apparent lake was *not water?* — I explained it, and informed him that not only was it such a plain as we here stoon [stood] on, but that those pretty cedar-looking trees were only dusty dwarf sage bushes; and the whole landscape was aerial except the outline of the mountains. He was astonished, and an uninformed person might well be. Oxen had stampeded for it, hoping to quench their burning thirst, and left their swelled-up car- casses over the plain in that direction, as far as we could descern them. Passed since noon-halt, not counting those just mentioned, to the South, 103 dead oxen, 3 do horses, and 1 mule. Saw also 3 abandoned oxen, lying down, anx- iously looking back on the road, in vain, for succor from suffering and a slow death. — One of these nearest to the road, I shot, terminating its suf- ferings. — The wolves, to-night will finish the others.[50] Saw 2 more aban- doned wagons, and several fragments of others. Passed several pits, dug down to moist clay, where travellers had tried for water; a little more digging, in one place, would have succeeded — near end of this stretch. Around these attempted wells, were a number of dead oxen, chains, yokes, &c   One of these pits was right in the middle of the trail. A little after Sun Set we reached, on our right, a hight [high] volcanic promontory, and went over knolls of sand, ravines, volcanic rock, &c. around this extraordinary head-land,[51] $\frac{3}{4}$ of a mile, to the "Great Boiling Spring," and a grass valley, a distance of 21 miles from the "Rabbit Hole Springs," and terminating the great desert stretch, so much dreaded. So it will be seen, that there are 2 points on this stretch, of moderate drives between, where good water can be had, and grass, by a little trouble and time; though travellers can provide forage, as we did, on the Humboldt. Water in kegs, for the animals, can be filled up at each station, and taken along.

Some traveller states the entire desert stretch at 40 miles only, a printed Guide-book, some one had, makes it 45 ms.[52] The Mormons said it was 60, but I proved it to be exactly $51\frac{3}{4}$ miles!

Last of route, and scattered about here, are 150 dead oxen, 2 horses & 2 mules: 1 wagon, and numerous remains of others, also a dead cow and calf: to which we add here, 3 mules, and 1 horse.

Sun Set clear, light airs from the N.W. Temp. 70°

[SEPT.] 22. Commences clear and calm, Temp. 40°

Ox trains coming in from the desert, since 3 A.M. (travelled all night, in preference to the day, on account of the heat)   Dr. O'Brian and family, & the New Yorkers here. Dietz & Young obtained assistance of a yoke of oxen most kindly loaned them, and brought their little wagon in this morning.

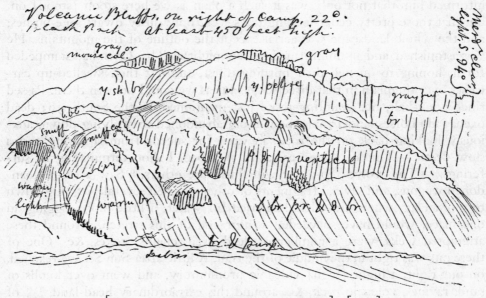

[BLACK ROCK PROMONTORY] [P 5]

This is a very remarkable place. — All volcanic, and in combustion no extraordinary depth below ground. Marshes and plains of poor grass: Streams, or spring rivulets of saline, sulphur, & warm water. The Great Boiling Spring, is like all others I have seen, — a raised circular tumola, about 30 feet diameter on top, basin shap'd within, dark bubbling water, overflowing one edge, and received into a circular reservoùr, dug some yards lower down, and from that into a 3ᵈ reservoùr, in which last it is cool enough to use for ordinary purposes. — The Spring is too hot to put your hand in, and the 1st reservoùr is quite warm. Looking into the great basin I could see, apparently about 4 ft from surface, a black hole, about the size of my head. The diagram will give a better idea of this singular Spring and the tanks. — A grouse had been boiled done in this spring. Coffee also, by immersing the pot containing it.

The water in the 1st receiver is of various bright colors, like sea-water often appe[ar]s, and the clays colored with effects of sulphur and other mineral substances: The ground sounded hollow, exactly like the Soda Springs on Bear river. And the descent grew softer and more wet, till in 100 yds. it became a morass. This valley of Hot Springs, is here about 10 ms. wide, some 2 or 3 miles, on this side marsh, on the other desert, and a beautiful Mirāge is seen there.

[BOILING SPRING AT BLACK ROCK]

Clambered up the pile of volcanic detritus, commencing in a few yards of the Boiling Spring, and gradually ascending probably ¼ mile from it, 40 or 50 feet, to the base of the extraordinary Volcanic Cliffs, called the "Black Rock —" the upper portion of which is a perfect rookery, filled with thousands of crows and ravens. (*It is about 450 ft. high*) At a distance, on this side, it appears of a purplish brown color, and on the desert face looks red and yellow, — much like a brick kiln after it has been burnt. But on a near approach, I found various shades of brown, — from light snuff-color to very dark: yellow, orange, light blue, grey, and purple, — the darker tints predominating.

A hunt over the mounds and piles of detritus gave me possessions of fragmentary calcedony, agates, precious serpentine, obsidian, — black as well as smoky colors. Lance heads & arrow-points, also, of these materials: and several small discs of very hard dark purple slate, thin & sharp at the edges, which the indians use to shape the arrow-points with. — The largest was 3½ inches diameter, about an inch thick, in the middle — flat part, and probably would weigh ½ lb. the others were much smaller, but formed in the same proportion. I saw a rock, about the size of a bushel-measure, with one of these *hammers* on it, and around were fragments of broken quartz and obsidian, and imperfect arrowheads.[53] There are at least 50 head of carcases near us, in the immediate vicinity of this Spring, the air noxious from them. I can see a great many in the adjacent marsh, — probably foundered. Mr Wright's horse gave out here, and was left to the great wolf larder. We here traded off a useless wagon. Having been informed that good grass could be had west of this, a few miles left of the trail, and I determined to give my mules the advantage of it, so at a late hour this morning gradually moved off, leaving 2 wagons to rest their weak team a couple of hours more, and then come on. Continued on the usual trail some distance, passing many square cut tanks, containing cool but rather sulphurous water; in one of these holes I perceived the tail and 1 hind foot of an ox sticking out. Passed by 2 graves.

Dead cattle numerous along the line of travel, principally oxen, but some horses, and fewer mules. Passed the camp of a pack-company & 1 ox wagon. Plain very level, except an undulating strip we passed over, of naked white earth, and a narrow depression of salt and soda encrustations, looking like snow, at a distance. Dr O'Brian and family, and several other companies, with ox wagons, remained at the Black Rock Spring to come on in the afternoon. We proceeded but 3 miles, rested and lunched, an hour; giving the mules a bite of grass, and proceeded. Here where we nooned, was plenty of very dry grass, much grazed down.[54] Remains of old camps, and the usual accompaniment, — dead oxen, &c. Merd. clear, light S. wind, Temp. 94°. We now took the camp trail, travelling W.N.W. — N.W. — and W. In the first part we reached a pretty clear sparkling rill, about 6 ft. broad, and a few inches deep: when to my astonishment the mules halted short at the edge, and refused, in spite of the whip and shouting, to put a foot in! — I guessed there might be a vapor from it, but on putting my hand in, found it quite hot — not sufficiently to scald, however. So we had much trouble here, pulling and urging the teams over; and when they did go, it was accomplished by each pair of mules, in succession, leaving [leaping?] over like deer, and thus jerking the wagons after them. Next, on left, observed a cluster of hot Spring mounds, with their circlets of marsh and tall green grass. —

In one lay a dead ox, apparently fell there yesterday; one hind leg in the basin of hot water, which had so well cooked it, that nought but white bones and tendons were left, of that limb, as high as the water had influence. Now we go over white glazed earth again, with clusters of thick dead bunch-grass, — trail trending to the S.W. Camp relics, broken wheels, tires, chains, ox-yokes, and carcases. The trail now goes N.N.W. & W.N.W. over very level dark brown volcanic debris, sprinkled over with small fragments of calcedony, obsidian, and arrow-points. — Lastly N.W. to a slight elevation, near base of the bounding hills, and plenty of pretty good grass, — on the sides of a considerable brook of good clear water. W. of our camp, very close to us, is the edge of a broad strip of very large grease-wood bushes. They are very resinous, and burn as fiercely as turpentine, with a crackling noise. Our rear wagons came in at dark, having deferred crossing till afternoon. another wagon was late getting in, on account of the obscurity of the trail. As the wind blew in the direction away from any camp, at dusk we fired some grease-wood bushes, and the bright flames ran, from bush to bush, a great distance, bringing out the hills near us, from their evening curtain.[55]

Sun Set clear and calm, Temp. 68°. Dusk a light breeze sprang up N.

Next to the strip of grease-wood, — running length of valley, is an elevated plateau, parrallel, and at the base of the hills. The indentations in it afford plenty of good grass, in patches. Here are also some tanks and springs of sulphur water. 8¾ ms. from noon-halt to this camp, making 11¾ miles to day. — The trail was a circuitous one, on account of springs and marshes. A straight line, from this to Black Rock, Boiling Spring about 8 ms. — The rock bears S.E. by E. from this camp. There are many companies camped here, — 10 P.M. Dr O'Brian & family came up, and camped close by, with Dr McDonald & lady. Here are Missourians, Illinoisians, Cherokees, &c — A small compy of Missourians, close to us, lost a member to day — board at head of grave: —

> "John Chancellor,
> of Lexington, Mo.
> Died Sept. 22. '49,
> of Typhoid Fever."

SEPT. 23. Commences clear and calm, Temp. 46°

The springs and tanks of sulphur water are cool.

On inspection, find we have 1,925 lbs bread-stuffs, which at 60 lbs pr day, allows us 32 days' rations. Some of the mules are very poor and weak, and several wagons require repairs. I condemned one, and distributed the cargo and team.

Merdn clear and calm, Temp. 90°

A few hundred yards below our camp is is [sic] a levil white sun-baked mud plain, sprinkled over with fragments of black volcanic scoriae, lava, pumice, & obsidian. In many spots, in an area of ½ mile, are dark brown volcanic stones, in lumps from size of a man's head to that of a barrel, evidently had been projected from some volcanoe near this. — they are all more or less buried, — according to their weight, and surrounded by fragments and minute particles of the same rock. And the indentations in the neighborhood, and the cracks and dreins therefrom are filled with granular fragments wased [washed] away by the rains.

Found on the surrounding plain, fragments of beautiful agates, and some arrow-heads of quartz and obsidian.

The companies camped here, moved off to-day, except the Cherokees, and an Arkansas company.

Some of the travellers, among other rascalities, are in the habit of putting up erroneous notices to mislead and distress others. I had the pleasure of correcting some of these statements, and thereby prevented misfortune. (*Fremonts'*

Castle.) From our position at noon across the valley to the N. by W. was a very remarkable resemblance of a castle or fortress, of a white substance, (probably clay), in the face of a brownish hill, resting on a shelf of the rock, about ⅓ from the plain; This I sketch'd, and named it Fremont's Castle[56]   It is about N.W. by W. from Black-Rock. Completed our repairs.

Sun Set clear & calm, Temp. 78°

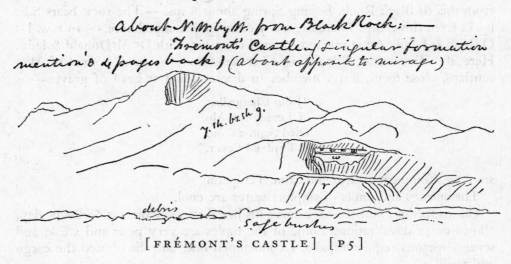

[FRÉMONT'S CASTLE] [P5]

[SEPT.] 24. At 4 A.M. we moved on again, first 2 miles N. 1 mile W. by N, 2 ms. N. and W. by W. 2½ ms. = 7½ miles — Black-rock bearing S.E. by S.

Sun rise clear, moderate wind N. Temp. 58°

Here we are opposite the natural fortress, and near the S.W. side of the valley, and we here noon. Here found the 2 Doctors & their families, I dined with the Cherokees.

Merd[n] flying clouds, light breeze from the E. Temp. 90°

The mountains on our left, are much broken, with short hills, deep vallies, and ravines.

Country tolerably level, of alternate spaces of baked clay, and deep sand, with sage and grease wood bushes. Here again I saw numerous projected rocks, and larger than those in the rear, as though nearer the crater which projected them. — Sizes from 50 to 250 lbs. surrounded by their own fragments, and dark brown detritus. This snuff colored detritus, from coarse gravel to minute granules, cover the knolls and elevations in the plain; and in some places, unaffected by the floods, saw fine powder or ashes, also of a dark brown color. (Fremont's Castle appears to rest on a projection of a tall mountain, whose top looks much like an extinct crater. (see plate) Here also is quartz, in considerable blocks, blackened, cracked, buried, & fragmentized, also, as if projected from a volcanoe.

Here the selfishness of some of my men was exhibited to such a degree, in reference to the baggage of 2 of their comrades, that I had to interfere in a peremptory manner. Two of the most disorderly, are talking about leaving, the quicker they do so, the better.

At 4 P.M. we moved on again, northerly about 6 ms. then Westerly half a mile, and as there was probably 8 miles more without water, and I was informed of good and grass, said to be but about 3 ms. to the left, I consulted with the teamsters, and we concluded that the weakest team might advantageously turn off here, and move off very early in the morning to the "Great Mud Lake" basin, while the other portion of the train should keep on thence; and find a good camping-ground. — So I desired my second to look after the division going on, while I would make the short detour, as my horse was very tired, and I had to hunt out the trail here. So with 3 wagons, and several pedestrians belonging to them, we struck off on a slight wagon trail, to the N.W. over deep sand and gravel, hills and hollows. (The main trail, we had just left, on which the others travel to Mud Lake, is deep sand and fine powder, with occasional stony places.) At last we made a devious and steep sand descent, among large sage and grease-wood bushes, into a narrow bottom, in which is a brook running through a deep and very rocky gulch, passing through a sort of cañon below into Mud Lake. It is very crooked, and in the wet season is a large rapid stream. Thick willows, cedars, &c. Very tall old & new bunch grass here. Near the stream on its western side, was a small dug tank of good cool water, several pools of good water, and a marsh. It was dusk when we reached this, and on a pretty level grassy spot, surrounded by trees and bushes, in this deep narrow vale, stood a tent, a wagon and cart, and a couple of rush-bottom'd chairs, by the dying embers of a fire, around which were some cooking utensils, &c — The folks, (a family with them) were in the tent and wagon asleep. Their cattle were grazing above ¼ mile off, and the tinkling of the cow-bell sounded very domestic.

Sun Set clear, strong breeze from the N.W. Temp. 80°

We passed, in to-day's travel, on the main trail, 20 dead oxen, and 2 do horses.

The main road, on the other side, after I left the train, ran close by the base of the mountains, a dry and very sandy travel for them — Night before they camped.

I was tired, the night cold, and I had no bedding with me but a thin horse-blanket, but a couple of clever lads, of the company, Messrs. Truman and

Ennis, pressed me to share their bed, which I accepted, and we dozed off the cold night very well.

SEP. 25. Commences clear, light wind, W. Temp. 60°

After a very early breakfast we hitched up, to gain the main road. — I rode up the sand heights enclosing this deep nook, to find a shorter and better egress than by the trail we entered: the result being the selection of a flat-bottomed gulch, one of the winter drains of the hills, and pursued it up N.W. It[s] character was deep sand, stones, and slates and such ascent continued, curving a little to the Northward, about 300 yards, then over sand & sage hills, some miles, to the main trail, on the opposite side of the valley.

The vale where we were camped, last night was covered with volcanic ashes, and sprinkled with fragmentary basaltes, tufa, pumice, lava, — red, yellow, and grey, (similar specimens, from Eatna and Vesuvius, in my cabinet, Washington City.) Pretty white calcedony, and obsidian arrow heads numerous; found here, among the willows, near the brook, decayed remains of an indian-lodge, in which was a wolf's scull, and several flint and obsidian arrow heads.

On reaching the main road, found it went N. and in 2 or 3 miles more, opposite the centre of a very high peak, — close on our right, the trail trended around to the W. probably a mile; then W.N.W. a short distance, to a level bottom full of grass, of a ravine, opening out, in a few hundred yards, into the flat grassy basin of the "Mud Lake." Where we turned to the W.N.W. — At our left was the embsoure of a cañon, — outlet of the waters from the deep vale of last night's camp. We turned short, around the point of a low volcanic spur, to our left, and in 200 yds. from the point, found the balance of the company camped. —

singular volcanic formations, 25th. right of road rising hills, bound! Mud Lake bottom.

[MUD LAKE BOTTOM] [P 5]

Plenty of tolerable and abundance of dry grass; springs and rills of pretty fair water, same of mineral and hot water, marshes, efflorescence of alkali and salt; grease-wood, and some few green willows. (*14½ ms.*) The distance, from "Grass-Camp.' to this, pr the main road, 14½ miles.

Merd^n clear and calm, Temp. 100°

Numerous camps here, — among them, the folks who were camped in the deep vale by us, last night, — a mother and 2 very young children of that party. And here to our astonishment and gratification, I found Mr Keller and family, who informed me of old Mr Abbots' death, far back on the Platte. — So the silver headed Swiss philosopher found a romantic grave in the wilds of the Platte. One of his little girls knew me, as I rode by, and called me. First time we had met since they left our camp at St Jose, and crossed the river there, some time before we started up the Missouri.

The large peak which I noticed on our right, coming here, stands up black and prominent, and throws out spurs, which gradually descend, and form the northern side of the entrance into this peculiar basin. — It looks much like an extinct crater, and must have been the great author of all the volcanic phenomena in Black Rock Valley, and the adjacent country. The boundary mountains to the W. (on our left) range about N.E. About 2 miles beyond the entrance here, on right of the road — mere trail, — on a small elevation, surrounded by marsh, is a grave, the board enscribed thus: —

"C. H. Bintly,[57]
from Yorkshire, England,
Died Sep. 9th, 1849,
Aged 43 years."

Relics of camps and discarded effects, carcases, &c. around.

After nooning we pushed on, — over a badly diversified and crooked a trail as could be found. In fact, to avoid the marshes, there were many trails, and we adopted that most travelled. About a mile of alternate marsh and level baked earth; then over volcanic powder and surfaces — generally level, but McAdamiz'd with crude sharp volcanic fragments, resembling broken cast iron, mixed with scoriae from a furnace exceedingly bad for the animal's feet, and racking to vehicles, and annoying to pedestrians. First portion the trail ran N.W. after which it curved around, to avoid marshes, to the S.W. some few hundred yards; then very sinuous, but on a mien Westerly direction, gradually ascending, to the base of the hills. Passing 6 dead oxen, 1 do horse, and 1 do. mule. Temp. at 3 P.M. (in shade) 105° My old friend, Mr. Farror felt much concern about his mules giving out, but I advised him not to urge them beyond their strength, and in advance of the train, we travelled side by side some distance. The entire face of this large basin is sprinkled with volcanic fragments of every size. In the afternoon we reached a depression, running S.W. across the trail; to our right and in front hills rapidly ascended; and this depression became a deep rugged gulch, on our left, probably to the distance of a mile, when it opened into a deep narrow cañnon — the outlet of the Mud Lake Basin,[58] in that direction. From the elevated and rugged part of the hills on our right ¼ mile, and extending down, in a slight curve — crossing the road, and along the declivity of the hill in front, just beyond the Western edge of the deep ravine, and running down, left to the cañon — a distance of 2 miles from the road, was a very singular barrier, formed by the indians, to pen in, probably, large hares when these hunt them. (for there is no other game here) This fence was close and regular, except where travel on the road had prostrated and scattered it. — was composed of sage and grease-wood bushes, torn up by the roots, and placed close together, roots up.[59] (*Volcanic country & casms leaving Mud Lake*) Crossed the stony bed of the winter's torrent, and descended S.S.W. a long hill, tolerably smooth — While ascending this elevation, I had a fine view around, but the harsh angularly ruptured country close on my right, attracted my particular attention, and extorted a sketch. All volcanic. The road terminated, as it were, at the edge of the very apex of this hill, and from a big rock on the left of trail, at crest, I looked down, and for a while thought it must be "*the jumping-off place*"! (*Descent from Mud Lake Basin*) Here, down this very steep descent, must our wagons roll! (I observed to friend Barker, that I

Descent into pass. 25 ft —

⁂ The spiry rock — highest of this ex-
traordinary wall, in the base of which
is this cavern, gives name to the
cañon "High Rock".

[DESCENT INTO HIGH ROCK CAÑON] [P 5]

thought it a very de *scent*, road.) Well, it was only about 200 yards, very deep sand, and loose stones. we double locked the wheels, and teamsters and assistants carefully lead the mules, and one after the other, slowly, and successfully, was the entire train taken down on the plateau below. On looking back; it seemed amazing that wagons and teams could descend in safety. — 100 yards S. out from the descending road, the cliff formed an acute angle, and side of the yawning mouth of a cañon, an immense narrow rugged chasm, rent in the hills. The declivity, and its base, retained vestages of unfortunate travelling, in the shape of broken wagons, wheels, hubs, tires, axles, &c and 3 dead oxen. A small flat circular sweep of the road to the right, from the base of the steep sand bluff, and we ascended a very stony roll of ground, to the brow of another deep descent, — not so steep, yet far more dangerous, on account of rock in it, — a longe ledge cropping out, and forming a step, some 30 feet long, and the lower or Southern end, several feet deep, whilst the upper end was lost in the short curve of the hill. — Around this, keeping *sideling* along this shelf we drove, then as gradually as we could, turned left, — very sideling, we accomplished the turn of a short curve, and double-locked, carefully made the long descent, landing in a low grassy bottom, where the road turned left, a short distance in a sort of gorge, then W. across a broad low level basin; near us on right, semicircular head of this basin, immense piles of rocks. — The greatest extent of this basin appeared to be to the S. — in which direction there seemed to be much green grass and water, — 2 or 3 miles distant. The upper part of this basin is thickly filled with tall dry grass, rushes, willows & weeds. A mile or so over the head of the basin, bro't us to the entrance of the grand cañon — High Rock Cañon", and 2 miles up in it, we found water holes dug in the bottom of a gulch. on the right hand side, and here camped.[60] Road deep dust but otherwise good.

Some of the N. Yorkers here — Capt McNulty, and the greater part of his company, with many sick, turned off, on the Hun [Humboldt][61]

The New Yorkers here. Water here scarce; plenty of dry bunch grass.

Sun Set clear, light breeze from the W. Temp. 70°. 10¾ ms. from Mud Lake Camp. The 2 wagons with weak team did not come up till quite late.

In these deep sheltered gulches, — beds of winter torrents, water can almost any where be obtained by digging pits 2 or 3 feet deep. — often cool and pure.

(*10¾*)

SEPT. 26. — Commences clear, with a strong breeze from the W.N.W. Temp. 48°.

The Cherokees came up this morning. At an early hour I walked ahead, some 2¾ miles, where this narrow and lofty portion of the cañon swelled out in a *cul-de-sac,* on left, and the main cañon — in a much more irregular form (with the road in it) turns to the right. On reaching this circular area, with its cool spring and rill, and green grass, I at once determined to give the mules a day here, and also to settle some irregularities in the company. And on my return, we hitched up, and proceeded, — after dinner.

Merdⁿ clear, moderate wind from W. Temp 74°

This cañon road is quite level and good: the bottom is traversed by a narrow rugged ditch, full of dry cotton wood & willow scrub. At about 1½ miles beyond the water-holes, the cañon expands, and the road turns around to the right, and then almost at right angles, to the left, in 300 yds. In the face of the perpendicular wall of the right side, at base, is a singular cave,[62] just where the road quirks right and then left — in a short bend. The entrance is a low flat arch, 4 ft. high, in the centre, about 25 ft. spring; the chamber oval, & vaulted ceiling: 12 ft. high, (deepest) 35 ft. long, and 18 ft. broad. Much smoked inside. Level earth floor, much covered with fragments from the ceiling. Names and dates scratched all over the outer wall around the mouth of the cave, and numbers within. I wrote the name of the company and date of passing, signed it, and pinned it up in the roof of this grotto. The part of the wall in which this cave is, gave name to the cañon: (High Rock) as over the cave it rises in a vast spire, I judge to be 400 feet high; however not over 50 feet higher than the adjoining continuation. The rock appears to be basaltic.[63]

(*2¾*)　2¾ ms. brought us out into the grassy area I had previously inspected. From cañon, across a grassy level, with pretty rill on left, — (sinks in the earth close by) probably 200 yards, and we reached a tall gateway of volcanic rock. — Road sweeping around to the right, entering a continuation of High Rock Cañon, where it expands to a large gorge; and a slight trail, turning left, led us into the rocky gateway, passing which, the plain spread out into a beautiful grass plot, of probably ¾ m. circuit. — an irregular oval, and surrounded by immense walls and masses of dark volcanic rocks. In the centre of this beautiful nook, was a small circular spring, about 2 ft. deep, & with white sand bottom; the water clear and cool as ice. — It fed a rill which spread out into a marsh and considerable brook, and then, in about ¾ mile was lost amongst rocks and sand.[64]

At the head of this *cûl de sac* of the Cañon, was another chasm — rent by volcanic action, about 300 feet high, and entrance not over 8 feet wide. On entering, over a pile of fallen rock, found that it was most irregular, and a short distance above was exceedingly narrow and dark, filled with cotton wood trees, — many prostrate ones, and masses of the fallen rock, and in its bottom a shallow rivulet, coursing from the Westward. This narrow cañon, is about 50 yards from our camp. To the S.W. and 100 yds. off, commence clay slopes, sprinkled with rock and sage-bushes. Ascending them a few 100 yds. and the ascent by gulches & weatherworn indentations, is rugged and steep to the top of the mountain; and once up, I was paid for the exertion, by the extraordinary prospect it gave me. — On one of many large mountain plains, of great elevation, as though numberless mountains had been evenly truncated. —

Looking to the S.W. observed the slightly undulating summit plains, and shallow valleys, seemingly adorned with green grass and marshes. To the N.W. through the opening in the neighboring mountains, could discern the faint blue peaks of the "Sierra Nevada" — probably in a straight line 60 miles off.[65] In a northerly direction, could trace the black, fading away to deep blue, line of the zigzag High rock cañnon. And the sharp angular black line of our little cañnon, to the S.S.W. Red and white earth up here, volcanic particles and ashes — fragmentary agates and obsidians very pretty. On the clay slope ascending the mountain, found great quantities of fine agatized wood, with streaks of opal in it. white and blue calcedony, semi-opal, and carnelians.

These mountain plains are covered with an open growth of sage.

In the narrow cañon, near camp, I noticed the correspondence of the two sides, as I had done in some other volcanic chasms.

SEP. 27   Commences cloudy and calm, Temp 40°

Rode ahead this morning, (back, and in the continued High rock cañon) about 6 miles, to examine the road. After leaving the camp plain, and turning short around to the left, of the entrance, the trail run W.N.W. about 1 mile, N.E. 1½ ms. N. by E. 1 m. N.W. ¼ m, — in a narrow cañon, W.N.W. ½ m. through a large open area, S.W. 100 yds, N.E. 300, N.N.W. 100 yards, and N.W. 2 ms. through a large open space; the road generally good. About ¾ m. from camp, is a stony rise. Grass and water all through. The walls of the gorge — first part, after re-entering cañon, are encrusted with white vitreous enamel in blotches, — and are in curved horizontal veins, and full of small holes and some large caves, most of which are many feet above the road level; and the whole range shows strongly, the action of fire. Willow, cotton-wood, and sage scatterd about, the former along rivulets and moist places; and some dwarf cedars on the heights,

Merdⁿ cloudy, light breeze from N. Temp: about 70°   (lost my thermometer — broken)

Held a meeting to inflict penalties for guard and other delinquencies, and to consider an application from 2 members of the Company, and of a mess, who produced much disturbance in the company, and were disposed to do any thing but right. This application, respectfully written, from 2 of the most obnoxious men in the company, prayed that we would grant them the 2 lead mules of their wagon, (mediocre animals) 6 days rations of bread, and a full discharge from the company. Some members were opposed to it at first, as a bad precedent, but when I told them how cheaply we should thus rid ourselves of these troublesome fellows, and that it must be a peculiar case, expressly for that, and no other occasion, it unanimously passed, with 3 cheers. — Such was the company's opinion of the men, and such their joy at the riddance.

Sun Set cloudy, light N. wind. Temp. about 50°

At night the disaffected gang, or 5 of them, stole the wine, reserved for medical purposes, and a conceited ass of a fellow, who aspired to command, told them that the company was too large, and it should be divided in *2 separate* commands. — 2 of these men were the fellows we got rid off with cheers. They turned the bung of the keg down and swore the wine leaked out, though I noticed great laughter & hilarity in their wagons at night.

[SEPT.] 28. Commences hazy, light N.W. wind.

Moved quite early, as I described yesterday's reconnoisance — beyond which the trail continued N.W. ¾ m. W.N.W. 1 m. N.N.W. ¾; then 2 miles, in short reaches, of alternate N. and N.W. directions, from ½ to ¾ ms. each. The road ascending, and the enclosing walls and hills are dipping as we advance, till we reached a spreading opening, bounded by very low hills. Just where the gorge expanded suddenly, was a considerable brook running in direction of the pass, and an immense mass of fire-altered granite, from the high pile on our right, had rolled down into the stream, on our left, and had there turned the stream suddenly to the left, the road hugging around the big rock, as the masses of rock on our right came down close, and narrowed the trail. In a N.W. direction, ½ mile further, is a valley, with cool pure water. Amongst the rocks on our right, I found mouse colored fragments of a porous rock, in thin plates, — the faces enamelled with a beautiful blue vitrification. Lavas and pumice in abundance — some fragments of black obsidian. Innumerable minute particles of vitreous matter. (*Oven-looking rocks.*) On the left, my attention was attracted to very singular oven-looking

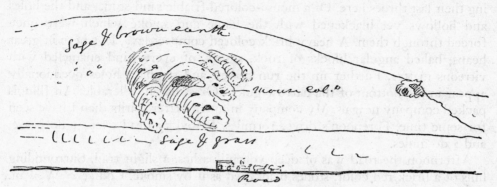

Sage & brown earth

Mouse col.^d

Sage & grass

Road

OVEN EXCRESSENCES [ROCKS] ON HILL SIDE APPEARS,
IN GENERAL FORM LIKE AN IMMENSE COLOSSAL HAND
[P 5]

These friable, clay
oven looking
projections
are very
friable.

Mouse col. earthy furnaces

[SINGULAR VOLANIC ROCKS, DETAIL OF SKETCH ABOVE]
[P 5]

volcanic excrescences on the hill side. These blown out excrescences, appear to have been where the volcanic fires exerted their dying powers, — breathing their last throes here. Of a mouse-colored friable sand-stone, and the holes and hollows yet blackened with the flame and smoke which were once forced through them. A heavy brick colored compact lava, lays here in great heaps; baked angular blocks of rock, stones, of every kind enameled with vitreous matter, Further up the run ceases, and stagnant holes occasionally appear in the bottom of the narrow gulch. Grass barely tolerable. An Illinois packed company near us. My company in much better spirits than I have seen for some time. Forenoon's drive, 10 miles. Passed 15 dead oxen, 1 do horse, and 2 do mules.

Afternoon the road was of deep volcanic ashes, a slight trail. Surrounding hills of a brick red color, stones blackened as if by smoke. Course N.W. ½ m. S.W. ¼, W. 2 m. through a salt-valley, then W. ¼ mile. — a slight smooth ascent brought us to a broad sparkling mountain brook, crossing the road from a nook in the mountain on our right; very shallow and sweet cool water. — This is called the "Spring Branch"[66] near "Little Mountain Pass"[67] — We crossed, and camped below the road, to the left of it, alongside a considerable brook which descends from a cañon 300 yds ahead, and so far is nearly parallel with the slightly ascending and sideling road. Passed, in afternoon's march, 10 dead oxen, 1 do horse, and 1 do mule; & several abandoned live oxen. The grass down here considerably grazed off, but above, in the indentation of the hills — near the spring, it was green and fine; there I sent my mules, under guard. I walked up to examine the spring, — following its meandering streamlet up. The ascent was considerable, and about 400 yds. from the road. Tall grass and willows, with small cotton-wood, marked the line of this rill; and grantic [granitic] blocks were picturesquely piled about. When I reached the Mountain Spring I was delighted: — A pool, at the base of a large rock, circular margin of pebble-stones, pebbly bottom, and the clearest, coolest, and sweetest water I ever drank. The beautiful reservoùr was supplied by a large fountain, gushing from a fissure in the large block above it, and delightfully shaded by a surrounding grove of willows & poplars. The rim, of about 6 ft. diameter of rock-work. After slaking my thirst in this limpid and and romantic fountain, I clambered higher up, following hollows, filled with grass & wild rose bushes, till I gained the nearly flat top of the Mountain. Walked over several hundred yards, to its highest part, — on the edge of the deep narrow cañon, through which we had yet to wend our rugged & devious way; and looked down with astonishment, — that such a pass could be prac[t]icable for wagons. Mein course of the cañon was N.W. There were several fissures over the mountain top, parallel with the cañon, opening at su[r]face a few inches, and choked with volcanic stones, but black and deep where they could be seen into. The stones in these fissures were closely wedged and packed, as though the hill had been rent by an earthquake (as it doubtless was) and suddenly closed again. — In fact the sides of all these, as well as those of the cañon corresponded, to prove them rent asunder by such a phenomena.

I descended to the camp gratified, but very tired.

2 of my men went back to a plain, some 2 miles, and drove up an abandoned ox, and shot him for the meat. The *Packers* came up and camped. This afternoon's drive 10¾ ms. Broken pieces of wagons & camp relics here. (*20¾ ms.*)

[SEPT.] 29. Commences clear, light W. breeze, Tempt. 50°

Started early. When we reached the entrance to the cañon, — turning short to the right, we found that generally the bed of the stream was unavoidably the line of travel through this very rugged mountain pass.[68] This pass, for trail there was none — was filled with stum[p]s of cotton-wood trees, large, fallen trees, stones and rocks of every size, Dead cattle, broken wagons & carts, wheels, axles, tires, yokes, chains, &c &c. — testimonials of its difficult character. Occasionally, a small grassy bottom, or a level earth ledge, on either side, gave the poor animals some chance — to rest and blow. Trees — principally cotton-wood, and quaken Aspen, grew closely in the cañon, where not cut away for the travel, and those cut layed where they fell, the tops still green;[69] The grass where the trail ran was barely broke down, so recent has this route been. — Thank Jupiter! this incomparable (road) route, was only about 2 ms. through! Now we breath free; ascending ground; — narrow valley, and low green hills; — a brook, and fresh green marsh, in a hollow of the hill top. — A great relief to eyes and feet. About a mile and a half from the cañon, on left, where some granite, covered with moss, formed a pretty point on hill-side, was beautiful and cool spring called the bench spring.[70] — Moist and green all around. — At this point the trail turns from the N.N.W. to a W. course: — Then over several low hills, — rather stony, thought not decidedly bad; on a main course N.W. — though somewhat serpentine.

Being a mile in advance of my train, early this morning, walking, with a double-barrel'd gun on my shoulder, just on emerging from the cañon, I descried ahead of me, some 200 yds. a large grey wolf, and hastened up and discharged a charge of buck-shot at him, when within 100 yds, sending him off, to the right, up a hill, on 3 legs, and his tail between his legs, like a

29th Sept

Singular Rock on left of road

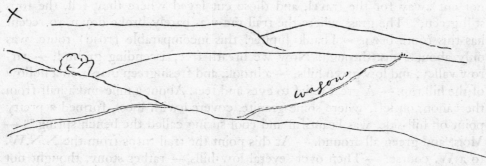

sage

road

wagon

[P 5]

whipped dog. I stopped to watch him; and when he had reached an elevated point, some 300 yds. off, he turned around, and barked very furiously.

15 dead oxen, 3 horses, and 1 mule, in the cañon; and 3 ox carcases this side of it.

Saw, over on right, in a meadow, an ox and 2 fine horses grazing, & met an old man coming back for the latter.

Merd. clear, light airs from the N.E. Temp. 86°

Descended a gentle hill, over a ridge, & and [sic] reached a stream, with tolerable grass, and many companies camped, and also camp'd here. 13 miles (*13 ms.*)

Sun Set hazy, calm, Temp. 60°

Here was friend Horn and lady, camped

[SEPT.] 30. — Commences hazy, light airs from the S. Temp. 34°. We early ascended the sandy hill side, thick-set with sage bushes. — Course N.W. about

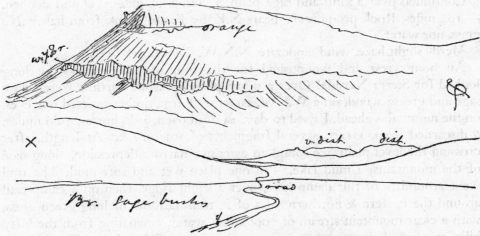

"D" TERMINATING PROMONTORY OF VOLANIC
DISTRICT JUST LEFT [P5]
Bearing N.E. by E. about 5 ms. 30th Sep. from Noon Halt, in Road.
(No Water, Grass Dead)

2 miles, W. 1 m. N.W. 1 m. N.N.W. another, — and then over low ridges of sand & lava, besprinkled with sage bushes: Then the trail trended around W.S.W. to a small hill, with higher ones on either side, — showing a depression in the outline of the mountain. — ("*Little Mtⁿ Pass.*") W. through this, ("The little Mountain Pass")[71] descended serpentine trail, in a mein S.W.

course, with occasional plateus of table land, 1 m: low hills on our left, and higher ones on the right; (see sketch) On reaching the W^n side of this pass, we saw the evant couriers of the Sierra Nevada, close by, — 10 ms. distant,[72] (see plate)

LITTLE MOUNTAIN PASS [FROM THE EAST] [P 5]
The Sierra Nevada 1st Distinct View of Bearing S.W. from Top of Hill, about 10 ms:?
(Broad Level Plain Intervening.) [Forty-Nine Cañon, View of the Warner Range across
Surprise Valley]

Continued over a sand and sage plain, a couple of miles, W^l and nooned, — 10$\frac{1}{2}$ miles. Rock promontery bears N.E. by E. abt^t 5 ms. from halt.[73] No grass, nor water.

Merd^n slight haze, wind moderate, N.N.W. Temp. 70°

An hour's rest and we pushed for the foot of mountains — the long looked for Sierra Nevada! Over a dusty plain, of white earth, covered with sage and grease-wood, on a W.S.W. course.[74] Large timber greeted our eyes, on the mountains ahead. Passed to-day, 14 dead oxen, 2 do horses, 2 do mules; 6 discarded oxen, 1 cart, several fragments of wagons, &c. At length, after crossing the level plain, we found an extensive narrow depression, along base of the mountains; a mud lake, — in one place wet and soft mud; The trail went around S. of this damp hole, over a slight ridge, then on a camp-trail around the Eastern & northern sides of it, to a meadow of long green grass; with a clear mountain stream of cool sweet water, emenating from the lofty hills, at whose base we were now to camp, in a delightful spot. Found here, several Missouri companies, the Cherokees, &c. Major Horn and Coy and Dietz & Young came up late in the afternoon. 4$\frac{1}{2}$ miles since noon. (*15 ms.*) [P 5: This camp still in eastern boundary range, Surprise Valley.]

People here much alarmed, and I felt much concern, myself, from a statement, set up in camp, of the distances on the route, on the western side, down to the Settlements. — Showing it to be farther than I or any body else ever dreampt of. I felt confident that it followed Fremont's trail in: — striking the Valley of the Sacramento in 60 or 70 miles from the Pass, but this shows it to be otherwise![75]

The Mountain road follows a hollow up, S.S.W. from camp. The Volcanic promontory we left this morning, bearing E. by N. abt 5 ms. The hills near us, are green and garnished with cedars, relieved by cliffs and rocks of warm-tinted stones. Plenty of plum-trees here. Much scurvy among the emmigrants, a little girl's mouth badly effected with it. A man in the Missouri compy has the camp-fever.

Sun Set clear, moderate breeze from the W.N.W. Temp. 64°

oct 1st. Commences clear, light breeze from S. Temp. 28°

Some of the folks here, pointed out a man to me (*Symington*) who had killed his comrade with a Bowie knife. (probably the one named on the tomb-board Fitzzimmons) and that he had also *stolen a calf*, here.

Last night the ladies were singing, and some of my boys were performing on musical instruments.

We missed 11 mules this morning, owing to the carelessness of the sentinels, — they had strayed, and 2 hours delay to find them. Nearly all the camps here moved off when we did. The trail ascended a steep sand drag, very crooked, around a huge block of rocks, another trail — longer, went around the other side of it, and they met on top, and in a few yards descended into a pretty grassy vale, with a small brook in it. Had the pleasure of overtaking Mr Pickering & lady here & well, — 3 ms. from last camp   The trail meanders with the descending valley, sometimes following a dry ravine, (the stream having sank in the ground) then over small sandy & stony ridges, on courses S. — S.W. — and N.W. This ravine is bounded by moderate hills, capp'd with basaltic parapets, & projections, for about 6 miles: it then winds to the S.W. and S. and finally, N.W. — over deep sand & shingley hills and deep hollows. We crossed a deep dry sand ravine, and entered an irregular plain, with a "warm spring", marsh, and indifferent grass. The base of the great Sierra Nevada about 6 miles, in a direct line opposite. — Patches of snow on some of the highest points.[76] On a lofty shelf, a bright fire and thick smoke: work of the Digger indians, — watching the emmigrants. There appeared about 10 ms. off, in the S.W. on an alkali plain, a *Mirage*.

6 miles back, in a valley, on left of the trail, a grave; inscribed: —

> "W. Lugo,
> Of Lancaster,
> Erie, Co. N. Y.
> Died Sept. 3, 1849,
> Aged 27, of
> an epeletic fit."

Singular formations of clay & app.ᵈ lime stone

Road

Zore ground. br. & y. sage bushes.

Road

[LITTLE MOUNTAIN PASS FROM THE WEST,
OCTOBER 1, 1849] [P5]

In this same valley, about 8 ms. back, a notice, in a cleft stick: "10 ms. from *small dry branch*" 2 ms. up good grass & water, no more till at base of Sierra Nevada, 15 ms. from *dry branch*." Good at base & up it for 10 ms: — mountain 3 ms. over."

At the "Warm-Spring," near noon halt, another, inscribed: —

"Jno: Bell,
of St Louis,
Sep. 27. '49,
Aged 70."

Morning's drive 15½ ms. Merdn clear, with moderate N. wind, Temp. 82°. (*15½ ms.*)

Passed 21 dead oxen, 2 do horses, & 1 do mule. Cedars abundant. 3 ox wagons nooning by deep "dry branch," — no water there, grass dead and dry, and their oxen were very thin. "Lassin's Pass," as it is called, in the Sierra Nevada,[77] bears about N.W. distant 15 ms.

At 6 P.M. we moved, on a mien N.W. course, from the "Warm-Spring" & marsh, over a sandy road, occasionally turning short distances W. a couple of miles, then over a strip of very level dry mud, beautiful road, ⅔ of which was on a N.W. and the other third Westerly course: to the base of the mountains. — at a spot said to be 6 miles below the Pass. A beautiful clear and cool mountain rill, willows and plumb trees, and stately firs on the sides of the hills. Plenty of fine grass. The mountains appear low here, — in fact are, on this side; the plain ascends to the Northward, while the mountains descent here, in the same direction. Camped at 10 P.M. mules very tired, — drive of, 9½ ms: making 25 miles to-day.

Temp. 50°.

[OCT.] 2. Commences clear, light breeze N. W. Temp. 28°

The long mud lake plain, we crossed last night, and which then appeared as white as if covered with frost, is of a pale dusky green color, with spots of mirage, in the distance. Tall grass all along the inner margin. This range of salt mud, skirted next to the mountains, with moisture and verdure, extends N. and S. as far as I can see, from an elevated spot on the side of the mountains.

Merdn clear, light breeze N.W. Temp. 80°. Sun Set hazy, strong breeze N. Temp. 50°

A little before Sun-Set I put the train in motion for the pass, evening cool, and old Boreus blew a blinding cloud of dust right in our teeth the whole way — 5⅓ ms. to the Western [Eastern] foot of the Pass. A most disagreeable march. (5⅓ *ms.*)   At base of the hills, where we crossed the branch, to come N. along the mountain's base, was a grave: — Name, &c. obliterated, only this remaining: — x x x "Died Aug: 3ᵈ"

[OCT.] 3ᵈ — Commences clear, light breeze from the N. Temp. 26°. (Much frost & ice)

Found here, last night, a mule wagon, belonging to two brothers Beans, of Md. one of them ill with the scurvy. Mr. B. very kindly gave me a piece of bacon, for my own use: ours long since out.

We moved up very early to ascend the Pass. — up a steep, hard, sandy, and winding road.[78] — The first ascent, of about ¼ m. was gentle enough, and brought us to a sort of valley, with a spring and rill in it, and some bunch grass. — Here was a grave, thus enscribed: —

> "Jno. A. Dawson,
> St. Louis, Mo.
> Died Oct. 1ˢᵗ 1849,
> from eating a poisonous
> root at the spring."

The spring just below — In this 1st valley, or platform, above the base, saw numerous ox-camps, breaking up & moving forward. — Some had a team of 10 yoke of oxen.

Mein course to the top, N.W. In the 2ᵈ valley, or rise, more ox trains moving ahead. — Reached the foot of the big hill, — a long and smooth sand drag, pretty steep ascent. — 10 dead oxen marked the trail. Across the road, about midway up this hill, lay an ox on his knees, — dying, and covered with old gum coat, by his compassionate owner; but it was unavailing, — the dust was suffocating, and the animals and wheels went over him, in the haste and trouble of the steep ascent. The first wagon of my train, which reach'd the top of the Pass, displayed the Stars and stripes, to encourage those in the rear.[79] Found many ox-wagons on the flat top of the Pass. Temp. on top the Pass at 8 A.M. 44°.

The Western descent was long and smooth, about 1 ms. and continued on the inclined plain below, to a small rill of very cold & clear water, and fine grass. (— This is one of the fountain sources of Pitt River — head of the Sacramento —) 2 miles from the summit. (*ms. 2*)   The hills around are thickly timbered with firs and other kinds of tall pine trees.

While on top of the Pass, looking down the Eⁿ side, at the bustle, and directing the ascent, I was amused. —

I thought the infirm ox in the road below, occupied rather an unenviable position. — In the centre of a very broad, sandy, and dusty road, men urging their heavy ox-trains up the steep hill, with lashes, imprecations, & shouts, some riding up on horses & mules, and clouds of blinding dust & sand flying. There rode up, an old man, on a jaded horse; a matress covered the horse, the sick man astride and laying over on his breast, with a coverlid thrown over him, and a corner trailing in the dust, he looked pale and haggard; had his arms around the neck of the old horse. He was afflicted with the flux and scurvy. Another unfortunate followed him, on a mule, enveloped in a blue blanket, and barely able to retain his seat; he had the fever and ague. Some small boys, not over 10 years of age, were leading jaded animals up. Women were seen, with the trains, occupied at chocking the wheels, while the oxen were allowed to blow, on the ascent. A man had a baby in his arms, and in midst of the thick dust, was urging up his team. Some wagons had as many as 12 yoke of oxen in them. One wagon, with women and children in it, when near the summit, became uncoupled, and down hill it ran, — *stern-foremost*, with great rapidity. — The women and children screamed, men shouted, and with all the rest of the fuss, there was a great clamor. A dead ox, a short distance in front of a heavy team, and men by them, brought up the backing out vehicle, most luckily without damage to any one.[80]

Merd^n clear, strong breeze N. Temp. 70°

It was near 3 P.M. before we could all reach the top, — 2⅜ ms. from the E^n base.

The W^n descent sand & volcanic detritus. Descent of mountain, 1 m. — to camp another, making 4¾ miles from E^n base. (*4¾ ms*)

Sun Set clear, light wind N. Temp. 34°

On an elevated shelf of the mountains, to the N.W. of camp, about 3 miles distant, an indian fire was brightly blazing; and as my mules were grazing about a mile off, at base of the same range of hills, I warned the sentinels particularly about those thieving red-skins.[81]

It seems that nearly the entire emigration are now short of provisions, we would have plenty, if the road struck into the Sacramento Valley, where I previously supposed it did; as it is we must purchase what we can, and on short rations spin it out.

Here I learnt that my friend Lieut. Warner, of the Top^l Engineers, and his guide, were killed, 2 days since, about 6 ms. north of this, in a cañon; and several of his party wounded; and that they were making their way down to the Settlements.[82]

The emmigrants have such a reluctance to guard-duty, or neglect it so, that they are constantly losing their animals. The indians about here [Pit Rivers], and all along Pitt river, several days march below, are known to be most hostile, — occasionally murdering people, and continually shooting and stealing the animals. — The same disposition and and acts characterized the Diggers of the Humboldt — (Pyutes). Yet no indian has attempted any hostility with my company, for the reason that we are always ready, and keep strict guard —, night and day. I believe that the company, with the exception of a few turbalent braggarts, are a good fighting party. I know many in it, who would have been pleased to have had a fight with the indians of the plains, — the Pawnees, Sioux; &c — in which event we'd most certainly have *made* some horses. I could have had no objection, as its effects on the company, would have been beneficial

The men are quite fagged, and become very impatient, particularly since they have learnt the extension of the route. in the Sierra Nevada[83]

OCT. 4th   Commences clear, strong breeze from E. Temp. 32° (ice)

Grass, water, and fuel abundant.

Moved early, Course W. over low stony spurs, winding amongst tall pines. In 2½ hours, we marched N.N.W. — N.W., — W. — and round to S.W. — and came in sight of "Goose Lake", From the brow of a high hill, I look'd down through the trees and rocks, on this sheet of mud and water. With wet mud, water, Saline or Alkali efflorescence around its margin, and Mirāge together, it seemed a little ocean.[84] Descent of this mountain, a very rocky and dusty road, and through a pine forrest, reached a a lower hill, short steep & stony descent, in a narrow grassy vale, with a rivulet. Now W^{ly} up a hill, steep, sandy and rocky, — requiring double-teaming for the weaker.

On left of the trail, at commencement of this hill, a grave, in the woods, inscribed thus: —

"E. H. Hartsfield,
Ga: Died Aug:—1849."

Course over the hill-top, S.W. thro', a pine forest, sandy and stony, and at descent, winding around irregularly to the westward; then down a sandy and stony descent ¼ mile, to the lake plain. — The beach, or bottom is ½ mile wide here, —and in the winter, the water overflows the lake to a considerable extent. The trail runs down S. along the base of the hills, and I found here, numerous agates, carnelians, and large pebbles of black and smoky obsidian. Immense rocks & cliffs of quartz, &c. altered by fire — containing veins of beautiful white calcedony, and semi-opal, and a pretty red carnelian. Course, between lake and cliffs on left, S. and S.E. — around a rocky point,[85] under high cliffs of a brick-colored volcanic rock, to springs and grass, — 10 miles, where we nooned.

A grave close by, inscribed: —

"J. B. Spencer,
of Jacksonville, Ala
Died Sept. 17th. 1849."

A man who had been a few miles lower down the valley, informed me, that he had been to a camp, below, of a government party, and a wounded man, of Warner's command was there in charge of a Surgeon and non-commissioned officer.[86]

Merdn clear, Strong breeze from the S.E. Temp. 70°.

I dined hastily, and started in advance of my train, to ascertain about poor Warner. — Road S.S.W. 3 ms. then sandy, 3 ms. S.S.E. — and lastly S.E. near the hills, at the ford of a considerable creek, coming down from the E.S.E.[87] On left of the ford road, on bank of stream stood an oak tree, on which was nailed a board, with a neatly written card on it, for the information of the emigrants, as follows: —

"From here, to where the road leaves Pitt R. . . . . 78 ms.
(To valley with water and grass ½ m. beyond)
    ”   Where the road crosses a brook 13
    ”   Spring of water, on right of road, ⎱
    ”   grass in wood close to ⎰ 12
    ”   Valley, with springs and grass 14
    ”   Lake, a mile to left of road, ... 11
    ”   Water & grass, 1 m. East of road, ... 13
    ”   E. branch of Feather Riv: grass ½ m. up stream . . 6
    ”   Next grass & water, very miry bad road, ... 6
    ”   Where there is grass & water, for 5
    ”   Būtte Creek 6
    ”   To where there is grass & water, for 10
    ”   Last water on the road, ... 15
    ”   Crossing of Deer Ck. in Sacramento Valley . . . 36
    ”   Lassin's house 3
From Lassin's to nearest Diggings 40
    ”   ”   ”   Sutter's Fort 115
    ”   Sutter's Fort to Sacramento City 3
    ”   Sacramento City to Sn Francisco 100

Where the road leaves Pitt Riv: it passes over the hills, and is very rough for 20 ms. Mr Lassen recommends keeping to the right, & going around these hills, over a longer, but smoother road. With the above exception, the road is generally good, except the last 40 ms. where it is *very* rough and hilly.

During this 40 miles, the road follows down a ridge, through a pine forrest, and descends 5000 feet. Water may be found by going a mile or 2 down a steep hill, on left of road; no grass. Recruit animals, and cut grass, in the 10 m. valley. After striking Butte Creek camp this side.

Beef, at Lassen's, is $50 a head, and Flour $50 per hundred.

Plenty of provisions & clothing in Sacramento City, and cheap. Pork $35 per bbl. and flour $10 per hundd   Coffee 20¢, Sugar 15¢. In the mines provisions may be bought at prices the same, or higher than at Lassen's."

(Signed) R. S. Williamson,[88]
Lt U. S. Army

Well, here are the facts, and they *are* stubborn things! — The distance from here to Pitt river turn off, is 8 or 10 ms. more than I expected, a week ago, to travel in the mountains on this side, with the company. And at least 150 ms. longer than we all thought it would be, on this side, to the nearest settlement from Pass.[89] We drove across, reached another stream running Westerly, and camped. 7 miles. = (17 ms:)

Sun Set clear, wind light N.E. Temp. 46°[90]

[OCT.] 5. — Commences clear and calm, Temp. 20°   ice plentiful. An early start, on a S. course, 2 ms. then S.S.E. 2 ms. and S.S.W. 2 more, to a lava ridge, which we crossed. In the first distance, we crossed 3 branches,[91] from the mountains. and reached a camp, by a 4th — where was a couple of tents and a wagon, and a man of Warner's party, severely wounded with arrows by the indians. Camp in charge of Corporal Sheckels, U.S.I. (says that he is a native of Washington City.). The corporal related all the circumstances of the affair, and told me that a slightly wounded man was ahead, travelling in, and that Lt Williamson was pushing in to the settlements with the party and effects.[92]

The road now runs S. over spurs of volcanic rocks, to a low vale, and stream, which enters a gorge, 9½ ms. and nooned.

Merdn clear and calm, Temp. 78°

Gorge on the right deep and zig-zag, a noisy stream in it, with willows and tall pines.[93] — Mein course S.S.E. The walls at top, are parapetted with basaltic rocks. Top of the hill is flat. On the road lava, ashes, fragments & nodules of obsidian, — black, smoky, red and yellow striped.

The road leaves the creek, and on a S.S.E. course, passes over a low hill, to avoid a deep narrow gorge on the right. — Then over a very stony and hilly road, S.S.E. — S.W. — W. — and S. and lastly following a ravine, and dry bed of a stream, to the valley of Pitt river,[94] and camped on its banks, right of the road, 6¾ ms: = 16¼ ms. (*16¼ ms.*) A good camping place. A cleft stick stands up near us, with a notice, by a Dr Collins, that *indians a few days ago, attempted to steal their cattle.* On a small ridge below, at rise of the road, 300 yards S.E. of camp, is another, card on a stick, warning the emigrants to beware of the indians, by the *Charleston Va. Compy of being attacked 3 or 4 days since by the indians.*[95] — Our sentinels on qui vive. Passed, on the left, several clusters of conical rocks, (sugar loaf shaped,) some 40 ft. high, on hill side. They were of a light color, and appeared to be volcanic sand-stone. On the opposite side the hills were crowned with parapets and circular bastions, as it were, of basalt.[96] Volcanic sand and obsidian on trail. 2 dead oxen in stream above, and 1 in the road. Remains of several *used up* wagons, signs of indian visits, places of fires, and roasted muscles, arrow-tips, &c. B'ot 40 lbs of flour at 25 cents, of a Missouri company.

Sun Set clear, wind light, from the N.E. Temp. 46°.

[OCT.] 6. — Commences hazy and calm. Temp. 26°

Road, this morning leads S.S.W. about 2 ms. to a hill, at the foot of which is a grave, inscribed: —

> "Mr Eastman; —
> The deceased was killed by
> an Indian arrow;
> Octr 4th. 1849".

In the breast of the grave an arrow was sticking, on which was a card, written: —

> "This is the fatal arrow."

A card also, on the head board, written: —

> "The mules tied up in camp;
> man shot, and 1 mule stolen".

Ascended the hill, and over low spurs and bottoms, S.S.W. and Westerly, — Indian vestiges all about. — They had, also, in one spot, burnt off the grass.

We passed the Batavia and an Illinois Company, — last had killed an ox, and we bought some meat of them. Road deep volcanic dust. Crossed a branch of the river, and the main stream twice. Saw 3 dead oxen. Noon'd 9½ ms: Merdn hazy, with very light breeze from the E. Temp. 86° The river here, makes a bend to the S. about 2 miles, in that direction, washing the base of clay cliffs, stratified horizontally, with beautiful bright color, — red, orange, yellow, blue, and brown. Wrecks of travel, — wheels, axles, &c &c profuse.

Afternoon ascended the cliff-hills, on top a notice, in a cleft stick: —

"Beware of Indians,
they have shot several
animals & wounded a
man just below this."

An ox train asked 35 cents pr. lb. for flour. Ascertained that we have on hand 11 days rations, of bread-stuff.

Afternoon's course, W.S.W. 3 ms: — then a mein S.W. course over hills and valleys, into an extensive plain, (valley of Pitt river) Met a government party sent out to relieve the suffering emigrants, by Genl Smith.[97] A packed company of that employ, with beeves, passed us. —   Peoples,

7th. mountain in plain.

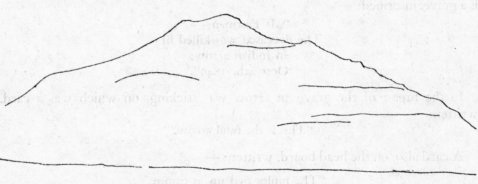

[C E N T E R V I L L E   B U T T E] [P 5]

Esq, commander.[98] Relics of broken wagons all along. In a lower portion of this bottom, were many deep water holes & *slews*. Fine grass abundant. Continued down the plain, on left of the valley through vast fields of very large grease-wood & sage. Pitt river, close to a bend and ford, — (latter 200 yds. below) making miles 8, and camped, by the thick willowy bank (17½ *ms.*) A few hundred yards N.W. of our camp, a tall, symetrical butte, or isolated mountain, rises from the level plain, like a tent. (*Butte on Pitt riv:*)[99] Passed 2 dead oxen, and remains of 2 which had been recently killed for meat. Water and grass good, but dry fuel scarce. Extensive camps here. Sun Set clear, light breeze from the E. Temp. 56°. (180½ ms. to Lassens rancho).

OCT. 7. Commences flying clouds, calm, Temp. 30. (frost). We made an early ford, and 1 mile N.W. forded a *slew*, followed by a compy called the "San Francisco",[100] and numerous ox trains. A short distance beyond the *slew*, on left of trail, a fresh grave, and penciled on a board at head, this: —

> *"The remains of a dead person,*
> *dug up by wolves, and reburied,*
> *by the San Francisco Company,*
> *Octr 7th — 1849"*

This was at about 2 hours drive from camp, but a teamster who thought he knew better than others happened to take an erroneous trail over a marsh, and whilst being extricated, the San Francisco Company passed us, found the corps[e], and reburied it. We now crossed a small ridge, a bottom, then W. over a low stony ridge again, with deep dust, — S. to the base of the mountains, — where, at a bend of the river, — making N.W. we forded. — To the N. — on opposite side of the river, saw indian fires.

Passed a dying mule, just abandoned by 2 men, one of them stuck his rifle through the saddle, and shouldered it. Many packed pedestrians. 4 dead oxen. 300 yds. E. of ford, we crossed a *slew* and rather bad marsh, after passing over loose sand hills. — 2 more dead oxen. — Continued over the bottom, a low stony ridge, down into a meadow, — at the river; — forded, and S.S.W. ascended and passed over a low plateau, or table-land, to a point ¼ mile between bends of stream, — and nooned. — 2 dead oxen, 1 do mule. 11 miles.

Notice written to a man in the rear:—dated 2 days since, informing him, *that the dead horse & mule, in the bottom, had been shot by the indians, and belonged to Mr.* (obliterated) As the murdered animals were close by, I examined them, satisfied of the fact.

Merdn flying clouds, light wind E. Temp. 78°

This seems to have been a favorite resort of the *Diggers*. Roasted muscles, burnt bones of birds & fish, arrow heads, — of quartz, but mostly of black obsidian, — and *chips* of the latter around a quartz rock, where their armorers had been employed.[101] Capt. Peoples, very sick with fever, had to return to us, for medical aid. — My surgeon, Dr Austin au fait on fevers. P. brought 2 mules with him.[102]

At 3 P.M. we moved on, — around the bend, ascended the cliff-hill here, and then ascended a very stoney hill, — thence through a river gorge,[103] on a mien of W.N.W. but very crooked and rocky, and rough for wagons. — narrow bottoms. It soon expanded, and the hills on the left, — in the back ground were tall and thickly timbered with pine. Crossed a branch, and several dangerous places for weak wagons. About $1\frac{1}{2}$ hour's drive, brought us to a small bottom plain, — on the left, — on which was an arrangement of the indians, for jerking (curing) meat. 4 crotch-poles, a staging of willow sticks about 3 ft. square,[104] muscle-shells, &c. A short distance beyond were vestiges of a recent camp of emigrants, — accompanied by the usual garnish, of wheels, hubs, tires, chains, yokes, clothes, old boots; and lastly, — an *empty* liqùor-case Crossed the river and We soon reached a narrow marshy ridge, the river on our left, with large rocks, a rocky hill on right, road crooked with rocks projecting in it, and to complete its difficulties, springs in the banks on the right continually oozing across the road, converting the deep loose soil and dust, into beds and holes of marsh and thin mud. — A really bad place. — 3 mules fell here, one we extricated, but the others had to be left, for the wolves.

Passed an ox company, camped on left, in the bottom. Good grass. Hills thickly timbered with spruce and other pines, and an undergrowth of what the Spanyards call '*Mansanita*' (little apple) an evergreen, with small dark green leaves, and large, angularly crooked stalk and branc[h]es of a dark red color. The berries when ripe, are black, very thick, about the size of an $\frac{1}{2}$ oz. ball, and pleasant, — but said to be astringent.[105] —

The road now turns with the stream — W.N.W. On our left is the river, with hills and pine forests to their summits; on our right are steep hills; also *pined* to their crests. While ascending, we reached a point where the road was very narrow, and descended on left rugged and steep; on right a huge rock projected; considerable rocks also in the road. — The 2nd. wagon of my train ran foul of the big rock, — driving the fore wheel under the head, to the great peril of the axle-tree: however we soon extricated & rolled on. The others experienced no extraordinary difficulty, — (were accustomed to narrow and difficult navigation.) At length we descended into a narrow bottom — greatest extent W[ly] the river bending short over to the S. and the trail passes through this bottom — The level spot here is not over 100 yards broad, and 400 long. Here we corralled the wagons & camp'd Remains of several burnt wagons, and part of a brass Odometer, in the road. 6 ms: aft[n] making 17 miles (*17 ms.*) Sun Set cloudy and calm, Temp. 70° This camp is as delightfully situated for an indian attack, as they could wish: — Blocks and massses of rocks, knolls, and ridges, thickly timbered, surrounding us, affording fine ambuscades, and safe retreats for them. I gave the most particular cautions to the guard-sergeants, and the compy slept on their arms.

At 9 P.M. mules alarmed, but guards on the qui vive. Towards day a mule slipped over the bank, into the river, and was drowned.

[OCT.] 8. — Commences hazy, light airs from W. Temp. 44° Moved early, and shortly forded the river, in cañon. — Rain, wind N.W. shifting to N. — Course, now, N.W. 1 mile, over rocky ridges, and in ¼ mile more, forded stream again: then S. ¼ m. — around a bend of the stream, 1 m. S.W. — over rocks, and through a forrest, to a deep and rocky ford, — crossed, and in 100 yds. more forded back, — at a worse place, where 1 mule fell, in the stream, but recovered. — And in 100 yds further, had to re-cross the stream, where it was very rocky, and the mules of one wagon were near perishing; great exertion in the cold rapid stream saved that team. Then we proceeded ½ m. S.W. and reached a very bad road for 100 yds. — close to a creek; — deep soft mud, with large rocks in it; then a short and steep ascent, where the previous difficulties had so weakened the teams, that we could scarcely overcome this ascent, by double teaming, pushing, and cursing. We repaired some of the worst places in the road, as well as we were able. A good bottom road now for ½ m. — then N. — over a high round hill, descended that to the S.W. and finally reached a considerable valley on the right side of the stream.[106] only 6½ miles, and noon'd.

Merd[n] clear, light breeze from the N.E. Temp. 80°.

(10 dead oxen testified to the bad road).

The hills on both sides, here, are beautiful — some of them very high, and *pined* to their summits.

Capt. Peoples is much better to-day.

Basalt and other volcanic rocks, & lava here: latter generally red & purple. In afternoon, our course lay S.E. following the right bank of the stream, on a generally good road, — after which, it ran S.W. 1½ ms. W. a short distance; then S.W. — over stony ridges and level bottoms, alternating. —

Saw 1 dead horse on the road. The road turns now E. about 300 yards, and forded the stream. — Steep earth banks, shallow water, and pebbly bottom.[107] (about 40 feet wide, and 2 ft deep) 200 yards from the ford, we corralled and camped. Made 6¼ ms: = 13 ms. to-day (*13 ms. 12¾*) Tolerable grass on the gentle foot hills, to the left. — On our right the stream and trail are — running to the south[d]. The carcase of a dead wolf, lays close by, — recently shot. Signs here of a very recent indian visit; — roasted muscles, fire-places, a wicker fish-scoop. Green leaves of some plant — tops cut off, &c. Sandy, with a few sage and some other bushes, and bunch grass. Willows thick on margin of the stream. Plenty of dry fuel. An indian fish-dam in the stream.[108] Our teams have become poor & weak, for want of a regular supply of good nourishing grass. The boys shot plenty of grouse.

Sun Set clear, light variable airs, Temp. 70°.

OCTOBER 9. — Peoples informs me, that at 2 or 3 miles ahead of us, and about 5 ms. left of the road, is a Digger village. — to gain which one must cross a steep hill, and pass through a very narrow and deep defile. — (in the foot hills of the Sierra Nevada mountains). — That they muster several hundred warriors, all well-mounted, (horses & mules stolen from the emigration) and that 3 days ago, when opposite that place, they attacked him, and carried off several mules.[109]

Commences cloudy and calm, Temp 40°

Road runs, about 2 ms. S.E. — then a short distance, S. — another short stretch S.E. — several miles S.S.W. = 4 miles; a few hundred feet S.E. ascended to a higher plain, & over that S.S.E. During the first 6 ms. some low hills, on the right, near the road; and at ½ m. on left others. Plains & river between. Good road.

Mocasin'd feet [footprints] and wolf tracks seen. Passed a camp of several ox-wagons, and a company of 3 ditto on the road, — in which were several females. Latter part of road ran S.W. — S.S.W. — and S. — to a bend of the river, and we turned right, and within 2 or 3 ms. of the bend noon'd. Grass plenty and tolerable. — Close to the brink of the stream, near a grave, on a very smooth dusty place: —

> "Samuel McFarlin,
> of Wright Co Mo. died
> 27th Sep. 1849, of fever,
> Aged 44 years.—
> *May he rest peaceably*
> *in this savage unknown*
> *country.*"

Sage plains here, as well as that passed over. Green willow only, dry fuel scarce, (had to cross river for fuel)   Merdn hazy, moderate breeze from the S.E. Temp. 70°. made 13½ miles.

In 1½ hours we rolled on again; road running S.E. — as the river makes a great sweep around to the right, with a few bends in it, the road only touches 2 of these bends, from camp to the "turn-off," — or where it leaves Pitt river, for the hills. — We reached the end of Pitt valley here — the hills enclose it in gorges and cañons now for some distance,[110] and we have our choice of ascending a very steep hill close by, or crossing the stream,[111] pass through a short narrow vale, and turn left — joining the other road, to proceed along through the mountains.[112] — 10 miles — making 23½ miles to-day (*23½ ms*) Company shot a discarded ox for meat. During the afternoon march exposed to a cold rain, and strong S.E. breeze. Sun Set drizzly, wind S.E. more moderate, Temp. 46°. Rain during the night. This spot, for some distance around, has been swept, by the emigrants, of fuel, and grass, and beaten to a broad expanse of deep dust. After a considerable search, some of the messes obtained sage, &c — sufficient to boil coffee.

[OCT.] 10. Commences cloudy, wind light & variable, Temp. 40°.

I submitted the roads to the Company, pointing out the big hill-road as the most rugged, and the shortest, while the ford road was the longest and smoothest; probably a couple of miles difference.[112] They desired to take the former, and so on we went for it. We ascended Easterly, a long stony hill, very elevated. — A magnificent prospect from the top. (*On top*) The Snow Būtte (St. Joseph)[113] about 50 ms. below Tschastes, being S. about 40 ms. distant, clothed with snow, and truncated with clouds. — Surrounded by high peaks, deep valleys, and silvery thread-like streams. A slight depression, very stony, and we ascend now still higher, — course S.E. and E. A winding, rocky, and deep dust descent — S.W. to a sort of rough plateu, then a still longer and higher ascent — S. & S.E. courses, same character of rough road, and are now on the tall apex of the divide, — between Pitt waters & those at the head of the northern branches of Feather river.

What a scene, from here! The Snow Butte, and his blue neighbors, deep vales, silver-thread like streams, near mountains, dense forrests, bright deep valleys, &c. in every tint of one of natures most extensive landscapes! Pshaw! — enraptur'd with a landscape! — how ridiculous! I have seen many, and some nearly as grand; besides I must look out for the train, or there will be some accidental capsizements, maybe a broken neck or leg! — No time now for the Fine arts, we must patronize the *rough* ones, just now!

We descend now, on a rough rocky road, into a shallow stony vale, & here found a broken & abandoned wagon. On our right can see the Pitt river, descending S. through a very deep, narrow, and dark cañon; its vertical walls, apparently basaltic, and in a curve a rock curtain ran across, in appearance, like the great dam of Niagara Falls. Another descent now, down a very steep and rugged hill, — S.S.W., along a low ridge, — to a vale S.S.E., where lay parts of another broken wagon. We now entered a very rocky ravine, — its mien course being S. — along its narrow flat bottom, on a pretty good road, a short distance; then ascended a small and very stony hill, — S.W. Over a rocky road S.W. and about 1 mile the road comes in — S.W. from the longest & best route, after fording Pitt river, where we ascended the hill, instead of taking that.[114] Flat hill side, on right of hollow, winding to the left, then turning S.S.W. then S. to the top of stony hill — level top; short turn S.S.W. sweeping to S.E. over meadows, — (once marsh) then E.S E. & S. around the slope of a high hill, then S.E. up a flat rocky hill, and S. descending a large hill. Here were the remains of a burnt wagon. and here we abandoned a *used up* mule. Now S.E. course, and very rocky. Numerous small oak trees among the pines. — Now we descended S. into a deep valley, then ascended a hill S.W., and then an awful descent: — A long and rather steep, winding road, deep dust, and volcanic stones, and rocks; Broken wheels, capsized wagons, tires, hubs, &c broken wagons, profusely strewn all the way down, — At the bottom, deeply seated amongst large rocks, ran a clear, cold, and rapid mountain stream. Stony bottom, and steep bank to ascend on the other side. This stream runs to the N.W. Some trouble fording,[115] but greater at the ascent of the opposite bank — Mules very weak, and we had to double-team each wagon successively, and bang and shout the mules up. Bank rocky and slippery. From thence we immediately ascended a hill — W.N.W. — and then, in $\frac{1}{2}$ mile, turned to the left & descended into the bottom of another mountain stream, Here was good grass and *elevated marsh* knolls. Here we found an abandoned wagon, and pieces of others: discarded clothing &c. 3 dead oxen, and 1 horse.

There has been many camps here. Several ox-trains leaving as we arrived.

Sun Set cloudy, moderate breeze from the W. Temp. 60° Made 13 miles, of very hard travel: and camped. (*13 ms.*) A grave, near the brook: —

> "B. W. Buckner,
> Jackson Co. Mo. —
> Died Sep. 24th 1849,
> Aged 29 years."

Held a meeting to punish delinquents, neglecting guard or other duty, &c.

At night saw numerous fires in the mountains around us. — Drizzly, with spits of snow.

[OCT.] 11 — Commences cloudy & calm, Temp. 36°

Moved on at $7\frac{1}{2}$ A.M. — N.W. and winding round more to the W. on a good road, till we reached a hill, ascended S.W. — over it S. and S.W. road alternately good & very stony: we followed a ridge hollow some distance, then S. — up a high long rocky hill, — doubling team to overcome it. Passed a broken wagon. the woods alight and crackling with the many fires, burning the huge dry pines. An ox train ahead of us. Holly,[116] Laurel,[117] &c. Drizzly & cold. Capt Peoples improving rapidly.

Road winding to avoid large rocks and immense fir trees. A cart following, with a yoke of small and very lean oxen; these steep ascents are almost too much for them. — Road W.S.W. over a level mountain-top, ¾ ms. A mule fell, but raised, and proceeded. A tedious road for the poor mules. Passed a *house*-wagon, drawn by 3 yoke of oxen & 2 small cows. — 3 ladies with them. — This wagon was termed by the emigrants, — the 'Steam-boat', — The body had side projections, above the wheels, and in front was a stove, the pipe sticking out of the top. — A family of the name of Allford, were the proprietors.[118]

Scott, one of my men, sick.

Here is a small hollow, and on the right, somewhere — (I did not stop) a spring. We moved from here 1 m. S.W. then made a rocky descent, to another step of this ridge descent. Here were large fires, and remains of recently broken wagons. — From here we wind up another ascent, several hundred yards, to a plateau — A mule comp^y halted here.

We now wound around to the N.W. a very crooked, very rocky, and dangerous for wagons, — then following a very rocky and irregular ravine, a few hundred yards. Now Westerly, over ridges, into a valley, and trail trends to the Westward: — where the road turns, on the right, an upset & broken wagon, — the wheels smashed. — From here we could see, through a glen, to the N.W. mountains, in every shade of distant blue — blending their heads with the clouds; And in front, to the Westward, — the dark clouds and mountains were a mingled mass. Patches of rocks and trees seen here and there, to a great height among the clouds.

We descended S. Westerly, to a brook, in a narrow vale, — running Northerly, with marsh, grass, and willows.

Passed 10 dead oxen. Here we noon'd, after a hard march, for the mules, of 8¼ ms. (*8¼ ms.*) Killed an abandoned ox for meat. Merd^n cloudy, strong breeze from the N. Temp. 60° Some of my team so weak, that they could not keep up, and did not reach us for some time after I halted. A lady in the "*Steam-boat*" wagon, has an infant born a month since, in these mountains. Here I was compelled, on account of the mules, to camp. Condemned a defective wagon, & distributed the cargo and mules. Sun Set cloudy, light Wind N. Temp. 56° While grazing, at night, a mule fell over a rock, and was jamed, keel-up, between a couple of parallel rocks. With great difficulty extricated the *critter*, — bruised & skinned. — A horse also bruised by the rocks, 1 mule died.

[OCT.] 12. Commences clear, with light airs from the S. Temp. 30 (ice)

Discovered that we have lost 2 mules, — the neglect of the sentinels. — night cold, & they hovered around a fire, permitting the mules to fall into the hands of the indians, while they exposed themselves a beautiful mark for the indians.[119] had to leave a small worthless mule here, for the benefit of the wolves and vultures. Moved early, in a Southerly direction, and soon reached a marshy hollow, water over a hill to the right of trail; A spring here, about 200 yds. distant, little grass. An Arkansas Co. and some others here. We watered and proceeded. The trail crosses a hollow, & sweep around to the S.E. is very good, passing over level tops of hills. On this mountain plain saw an abandoned wagon, & several remains of oxen killed for meat. Saw the *Ark* wagon,[120] rode up and enquired how the lady & *young mountaineer* were, they said they were much better. Their wagon was on right near a spring — which I did not see. The summit of the mountain is an extensive plain, — quite level, and a good road. A mountain on our left, about 1 m. distant, (to the E.N.E.) seems to be about 1000 ft. higher than this one. Passed 4 dead oxen, bottom, sides, tires, &cc of a burnt wagon, — about 3 ms. beyond the spring & wagon. A grave in the woods on right of trail: —

"John Hensley,
Aged 73.
Sept. 22d 1849,
Washington Co. Mo."

On the left, a short distance lower, were 2 other graves, no inscriptions
    Blackbirds exceedingly numerous.

We now make a slight descent, and proceed Easterly, over slight elevations and depressions. Passed the remains of a black-tail deer, on left. — Over another mountain plain, — generally E. and observed the wheels, tongue, &c of another wagon. — Road now meandering and descending. On the descent, 100 yds from the trail, saw what appeared to be an open grave. — On visiting the spot, found that it was a cāhce [cache] — and had been formed to resemble a grave; where a lot of medicines had been deposited. — An old chest, broken bottles, scattered pills, powders, papers, & shavings. They had been exhumed through cupidity. Passed 7 dead oxen, and remains of 1 slaughtered for meat. A long descent, not steep, but rather rocky, along a narrow bushy vale, — all easterly; Here we nooned. Tolerable grass, valley full of small sage bushes. 1 dead ox here. (Am quite sick, from want of at least the repose that others can enjoy. An ox and several mule wagons passing. Some nooned here, while others proceeded. Drove 11 ms.

Merdn slightly hazy, strong breeze from N. Temp. 62°.

In 1½ hours we were again in motion; Mien direction of the trail, Easterly. In 1½ ms. saw a grave, on our left: —

"Allen McLane,
Octr 9th. 1849,
Platte Co. Mo. Aged 36 yrs: —
Disease Gastro Enterites Typhoid." [121]

Ascending and passing over low hills, for about 5 ms. and then turn'd N.E^{ly} following the descent and along a valley, which in 1½ ms. expanded to a considerable level: Now the road turned N.W. nearly 2 miles, to springs and a small branch, in a broad level grassy valley.

10 dead oxen, during afternoon's march. The grass near spring is grazed off, higher up stream is better, sent the mules, under guard there. The only fuel near us, is sage bushes. Several camps here.

Sun Set clear, moderate breeze from the N. Temp. 50°   Reached this in the night; afternoon's drive 7¾ ms: = 18¾ ms. (*18¾ ms*)

A cold night, and our long accustomed bed-stead, — old mother earth, is damp.

OCTOBER 13. — Commences clear and calm, Temp. 18°. plenty of ice about, this morning. On looking around this morning, very early, (the frost turned me out to warm my toes by a camp-fire.) Observed some graves fifty yards in rear of my camp, and visited them. 4, — in a row, close together; inscribed as follows: —

"David Myers, of Mo.
Died Oct. 4. 1849, Aged 53."

———

"B. M. Prewitt, of Mo.
Died Sep. 30. 1849, aged 38."

———

"In Memory of Abner Needham,
Of Morrow, Co. Ohio,
Died Sep. 27. 1849."

———

"In Memory of Joel Lock,
Died Oct. 1. 1849,
Aged 33.
From Southport, Wisconsin."

These all seemed to have been very neatly arranged. A long crooked brook here, deeply cut through the soft black alluvial soil.

Last night the indians carried off 16 head of oxen from this camping-ground. A party started out in pursuit, this morning, trailed them up the valley, and were so close on them, that they found the meat of several oxen, hanging on limbs of trees, — in process of drying.

Here we leave 2 more mules, exhausted & unable to proceed.

We started early, preceeding S, — 2 ms. after crossing the brook; over the level bottom, and a gentle, though stony swell; then S.S.W. over a stoney plateau, to the ascent of a hill, thickly timbered with pines, and firs, Westerly. Across a level summit, some hundred yards; and noticed on our left, here, a singular natural granitic pier. It was about 50 yds. long, and at the end some 30 feet hight [high], and laid with even face, of very square blocks, apparently, as if so piled for building purposes. From this summit, saw a snow-capp'd peak bearing S.W. by S. which can only be the "Snow Būtte", before seen. Passed 2 dead oxen. Several ox trains following.

We now make a short and stony ascent, — S.W. then, on an irregular level, thickly timbered, 1 m. S. and turned left, (Easterly) crossed a hollow — where was an Irishman & his wife, with an ox-wagon, to the rear of which was attached a large hen-coop, full of *chickens* and *roosters*. And Pat swore by the "*howly mother of Moses*," that he'd starve before he'd kill one of 'em: intending to make a grand speculation in California on them. Success Pat! Pat has his wife along, sharing all the *programme* of the route, assi[s]ting to drive, yoke and unyoke, water, feed chickens, cook, &c. Over a level table, now, about 300 yds. then descended a gradual slope, — S.E: — the latter part very stony & bad. S.S.E. over head of the valley, about ¼ m. tolerably level, with stony places. Now up and over a slight elevation. The valley and road now sweep around to the W. — expanding, and stretching to the S. Very level, with dry grass & sage. Groups of dark Plutonic rocks lined the left banks of this vale, disposed in piles, of various sizes & lengths. — One of these piles, on entering the vale, I thought look[ed] much like a great pile of Lehigh coal, which had been thrown there by the cart load, of some fifty loads. — At this end, — of the valley, the bottom across, is very level — and smooth, then we ascend and cross a small ridge, a narrow depression, ascend a small hill, across another depression, — grassy and level; then S.S.W. over a level, but very stony, mountain plain, a slight depression, over another mountain top, — long, crooked, and stony, all on a mien S.S.E. course: then gradually descended, S.S.E. to a deep valley, and around Southerly, to an extensive plain, with abundant grass. Cut across the plain, S.E. to a brook which traverses this valley, and camped, to rest & graze the mules. Travelled to-day, a pretty rough, up and down 9¾ miles. This valley seems to extend N.E. and S.W. about 3 ms. and its greatest breadth 1 m. (9¾).

Merd^n clear, with a strong breeze from the N. Temp. 76°   Pass'd 12 dead oxen. Found several companies with ox-wagons, camped or nooning here.

Mr. Barge, (inventor of a very ingenious instrument — serving as an odometer, on his wagon, and which answered all the purposes he needed)   A small mule packed party, among whom was Col^l Ely & servant. — and several ox-wagons, came in, and camped.

One of my company, owning a small carryall, with a pair of mules, was so attached to the vehicle, in spite of my advice to abandon it, that with weak mules, he was continually falling to the rear; and with emergency, of short provissions, & exhausted animals, and impatient men, I could do no more than advise him, and push on. Learnt that he was a day's march in the rear.

We here shot an abandoned ox again, for meat: and soon the remains of an abandoned wagon was in requisition, to fry liver, broil steaks, and boil soup.

A recruited ox train moved off, this afternoon.—This is the 'Nodaway Comp^y from Mo.[122] They sold bread at 50¢ pr. lb, sugar at 75, and bacon at 50 cts — We made some purchases of them. They sold, this morning several hundred pounds of flour to a pack company, and it was said, that at the same time they were selling provisions at such high rates, they recruited their stores, by begging from the Government relief party. Sun Set clear, strong breeze from the N. Temp. 60°.

OCT^r 14. Commences clear, light variable wind, Temp. 29 (ice)   Sent a man ahead to overtake a company, and purchase some provisions, we heard they had to spare. Moved on early, — Grave on a ridge, left of trail; —

✝

"In Memory of
Bartholomew Faherty,
from
Randolph Co. Illinois,
who departed this
life, Sep. 1st. 1849,
Aged 38 years."
He *may* rest in peace."

Mein course S.E. over a winding rocky road, slightly undulated — then S. slightly descending to a large pond, or lake, — (4¾ *ms. from camp*, left of trail) of ⬭⬭ this shape, probably ½ m. long. Passed 6 dead oxen. Met here another   packed party of "*Relief men*. We watered and proceeded.

Much mud and some marsh here — In wet season it is doubtless a lake of some magnitude   It is "Little Goose Lake'.[123]

Valley of lake bottom, grassy, with volcanic rocks, and compact lava. The trail leaves the lake and joins the main road in a mile, and runs then S.E. up a piny ridge. Plenty of company here, mule and ox-wagons, packers — both mounted & pedestrians. My highly esteemed friend, Fenderich, here lost his horse, — he fell in the road, and the Swiss philosopher steped off and moved forward, on shank's mare.

I became acquainted along here, with a Mr. Wm Ashford, of Upper Canada, one acquainted with and who endeavored to act up to the *five points of fellowship*. Mr A. had a cart and yoke of oxen, & a friend with him. — He very ingeniously constructed a simple odometer, and attached it to a wheel of his cart. It was quite correct on level ground, and answered all its ingenious author's desires. — A rough wooden box contained a tin canteen (circular & flat) within which was a tap, brass plumb, and 2 wood cog wheels. Course Southerly, a few hundred yds, over a rocky ridge, and descended to another basin-valley, which ran S.E. and N.W. about $\frac{3}{4}$ ms. and was about $\frac{1}{8}$ m. broad. Road S.S.E. across this bottom, of dead grass, and then ascended a steep, and very rocky hill. Passed, at lake, along route, and in this last vale, numerous remains of wagons. This last vale has a small pond of mud and water at the upper end. (Winter a lake of some extent)   Passed 8 dead oxen, and 1 do mule, 1 abandoned worn out ox at last vale. Ascending this high hill, thick set with the largest and tallest kind of pines, saw an exhausted abandoned ox, and remains of one which had been killed for meat, — on the left; and on the right a large prostrate pine tree, burning furiously, throwing dense pitchy smoke smoke across the road. Saw a white lump, on a rock, and picked it up, being a beautiful fungus-looking specimen of *Volcanic tufa*, about 6 ins: diameter, and hollow, with a projection, underneath, like a stem. On the hill, we travelled S. Westerly, through a dense growth of very small pines, cedars, and bushy undergrowth, under the shade, with 4 comrades, I rested. Camp-fires all around. The train came up, and we proceeded; — in 200 yds. we reached a large pine, where the trails branched. — The tree was stuck full of cards and notices: — directing acquaintances, and travellers in general, *to take the right-hand road*, — which led *to grass and water in 2 miles, and the left, or main road was very rocky and for some distance destitute of either*. We, of course took the most desirable trail — leading S.W. the first few hundred yards beset with rocks (compact grey lava) then over a grassy bottom — (dead grass) with a stream, through a cedar thicket, & descended into the valley of grass & water. This is one of the numerous sources of Feather river. The stream runs in a S.S.E. course over on the N.E. side of the valley: Valley runs S.E. and N.W. — generally, 3 or 4 ms. long, about ¾ ms. broad. Plenty of pretty good grass around the margin. In skirts of the cedars, left of road, descending to the valley, is a grave: —

> "Jackson Newton,
> Of Linn Co. Mo.
> Died of fever,
> Octr 12th 1849,
> Aged 26 years."

Axles, wheels, and other parts of broken wagons, old clothes, and smoking embers of camp-fires, near it. This road is only a few days old, cedar bushes, in the middle of trail, scarcely *barked* by the travel. 300 yards beyond the above grave, another: —

> "S. M. Thompson,
> Hickman, Ky.
> Died Oct. 7th. 1849,
> Aged 36."

4 dead oxen. By this brook we noon, having marched 9¾ miles. Here are the remains of a wagon, and an ox train and company with mules camped.

Merdn clear, strong breeze from the N. Temp. 80° This deep vale, is pent in with the thickest forests of cedars and pines, in all directions, we can see. After a snack and rest, including of course a good pipe-smoke, we rolled on; passed a small lake, or expansion of the stream, by which was a grave: —

> "In Memory of
> J. M. Smiley
> who was shot by ac-
> cident, Oct. 3d
> 1849, aged 22."

The trail now goes S. through the bottom, then up and through a forrest trail, of deep dust and stones, and very crooked, on account of the large trees, but on a mien course of S.E. — in 5 miles, we saw a notice on a tree, (which Capt. Peoples had informed me of) directing the emigrants *to a new right-hand road,* leading to fine grass and water; so we drove on, to an open space in the forrest and camped; and sent our mules Westerly, ¾ mile, under guard, (through thick set pines) into a deep grassy bottom, with a stream and marsh. A considerable camp of emigrants there, with women and children. — and on a neighboring hill Maj. Rucker, U.S.A.[124] was camped, with his wagons, provisions, & men, of the "Relief party, sent out by Genl Smith

— The Major commanded the expedition. Peoples was now nearly recovered, under the skillful treatment of Dr Austin, We proceeded together to the Major's tent, and was introduced to him. — found him to be a very friendly, man, and perfect gentleman. He was surrounded by begging emmigrants, men, women, & children. The Maj. had killed an ox the day before, and he had to serve out the fresh beef, pork, flour, bread, &c. as judiciously as possible, — subject of course, to much imposition. — The importunity of the begging emigrants, was annoying; some greatly in need, some meanly bent on an increase of stores, and others, who would steal a dying man's shoes. His stores were insufficient to serve those actually in want, but how was he to discriminate? Then he had to contend with impudence, &c. from the disappointed and rude applicants. It was one of the most delicate, and troublesome duties ever entrusted to any one!

We passed 4 dead oxen, & 1 do horse on the road. Made 9 miles, = 18¾ ms.

Sun Set clear, moderate breeze from the W. Temp. 60°   (*18¾ ms:*)

An old man, wife, and several children — mostly girls, and 2 other families in the valley.[125]

OCT. 15 — On our camp-ground was an ox-wagon, in which was a widow, with 8 children, She buried her husband on the Platte. and there were 2 other families, with several children each.

Commences clear, calm, temp. 28 (frost) Mules grazing below. I discarded 2 wagons here. The company very anxious for me to make application to Major Rucker for supplies; — I told them that we had enough to take us in on short allowance, and that those stores were sent expressly for starving families — *women and children*, some of whom were now here, but most in the rear, all along Pitt riv: and at the Pass. — but it was of no avail, there were some who would take a biscuit out of a woman's mouth, and I accordingly stated matters to the Major, who very kindly gave us 31 lbs. pork, and 14 lbs crackers.[126] — The latter taken to camp in a sack, while I was attending to other matters, divided, and immediately devoured, not reserving me an oz: We purchased 14 lbs of pork of a Missourian for 50¢ pr. lb.

The Irish chicken-coop wagon here.

We here abandon another mule.

Merd^n clear, Moderate breeze N.E. Temp. 80°

We packed some spare mules.

A thin man on a mule, applied to Maj. R. for some bread, or flour: said that he had a little sour flour, and the only meat he and his comrades had for 3 days, was beef of a discarded ox. The Major enquired of whom the party consisted, &c. &c. Man replied they were 3 men, on mules. Then said the Maj. 'you are well off; — no incombrance, some sour flour, and a chance at ox meat, can push ahead, and as a last recourse have good meat in your mules. The man became very indignant, and told the Maj. that he was sent out to relieve those in want, and that he demanded such relief as his wright, the Maj. cooly told him, he should be the judge of that, and the fellow slowly rode off.

I bade adieu to Maj. R. & Capt People's,[127] and walked over to my camp, where I was taken ill, with a fever — headache — but ordered the train to proceed, and I would rest awhile till able to follow. Mr. Ashford kindly came to the tree under which I was reclining, and invited me to dine with him — I consented to go and get a cup of tea, which relieved me much, and I made out a dinner with these kind friends. About 3 P.M. I mounted my horse, and proceeded, alone, but some travellers not far ahead. The route through the woods was dusty & rocky, meandering in a mean S.E. direction — about $2\frac{1}{2}$ miles, and there joined the main road — After which, for 100 yds it ran S. Passed by a deep narrow cañon — some few hundred yards on the right, A great deal of laurel, and many green plants entirely new to me. Mien course now S.E. occasionally making a short stretch to the S. and W. — the 2 last miles about S. — crossing a small plain, and dry pebbly bed of a stream. Gradually descending, we entered a flat valley, passed Easterly, over it, for a few hundred yards, and saw 3 graves: — on left.

1st paper label on board at the head: —

"Lewis —— (obliterated)
Died Sept. 17th 1849,
Of Jackson Co. Mo."

2nd.

"James Young,
Sept. 16th 1849,
Aged 19 yrs,
Of Mo."

3d   Had no inscription, a rough log was placed at the head, and they were dug in any direction, without regard to the compass. We now went over a slight elevation, into another flat valley, in which was a lake, and camped — Made $7\frac{1}{2}$ ms: ($7\frac{1}{2}ms$)   The latter part of this afternoon's travel, was through an open pine woods, over a very crooked and rough road, and quite dark till occasionally lighted by a camp-fire, left burning, or a tall dry pine in flames. The edge of this valley is lined with blazing fires, showing dark groups of men and wagons, in all directions. These fires are finely reflected on the bosom of the lake.

Sun Set clear, with light, W. wind   Temp. 70°
Abandoned another mule, here.

[OCT.] 16. — Commences clear and calm, ice, Temp 30°

3 dead oxen here. The pond is about 200 yds. long, connected with a marsh by a small stream running Easterly. Remains of broken wagons, fires, &c — around.

Started early, on a mien course of S.W — about 4 miles, then S. and S.E. over a hill and plain, very stony & dusty. Passed 2 dead oxen and parts of several broken wagons. — through open pine timber. stripped cedar bushes on the trail, unbroken by the travel. Many fires burning along the route. Passed 2 ox wagons en route, and some drove oxen, tired out, oxen packed with bedding, &c. Dr Austin accompanying me, on a very refractory mule. We now descend S.W. — a short steep and rugged hill-side, close to the brink of Feather river; — coming from the E^d and running S.W. here. A rapid, cold, sparkling stream. — all rapids. — About 50 ft. broad. Banks a mass of granite rocks, crowned with stately pines. Watered, by clambering down the rocks, close on the left, and then proceeded. The bed of the stream full of large rocks. On the hill, which we just descended, 3 ox wagons were camped, several women & children there. Saw a little girl and boy ascending the hill, each with a tin pail of water. I washed the thick dust from my hands and face, in the cool stream — quite refreshing. Lit my pipe, and rode on. At foot of the hill lay a smashed wagon, and yokes, bows, and ox chains were scattered about. We soon reached a rugged hill, of short ascent, leaving the river on our left; then a slight descent to a small grassy bottom, and in 300 yds. from foot of the last height, forded a small tributary of the river, — coming from the N. and running, below ford, to the S.W. We now ascended another eminence, and on a hill to our left, saw a considerable camp, — wagons, tents, women, children, &c   About 400 yds over the rocky rise, and we reached & crossed another shallow & pebbly tributary of Feather river. A fallen tree, here, formed a bridge for the pedestrians. We now travelled S. over low pine land, sweeping around to the S.W. In the woods, on left of the trail, a grave, inscribed: —

"In Memory of
James Tyler,
Died Octr 11th. 1849,
Aged 69 years,
Of San Francisco Coy Mo."

On a large pine tree, close to head of the grave, was neatly marked, "J. Tyler."

Road now ran W. a short distance, then turned S.W. — very rough, and in all, about 2 ms. from Feather river, it turned short round S.S.W. and then descended S.W. a very steep and rugged hill; — but short, thank God! Next over the rocky, dry bed of a stream, which ran N. & S.: — now along the margin of the right hand — Weste[r]n, hills, — Southerly, & S.W. up a steep tho' not very rocky hill, yet tiresome to our mules; About 50 yds. from the trail a grave; remains of a fire, and 2 pine poles leaning against a tree. Then over a flat hill-top, S.W. $\frac{1}{2}$ mile, Descended S. to a lower one; S.W. over the top of the 2nd step; — passing a very long pine on fire, on the left. Now descend, by a winding trail, a stony hill S. — a mile: 3 mules exhausted & fell, raised them, replaced the team with better, and drove the weak ones along. At bottom we turned E. over another step, and descended S. — to an extensive bottom & stream. This is "Butte Creek" Valley.[128] It is surrounded by green hills, Mountains, trees and rocks. The clear creek meanders below: The valley bottom extends S.E. and N.W. about 10 miles and several miles broad. We entered its N.W. end. The stream comes in here from the W., and continues down the N. side, — in a Southerly direction. The dark firs, pines, and cedars of the adjacent surrounding hills, contrast finely with the light green and yellow and soft willows. Passed, this forenoon, 16 dead oxen. Purchased of the Nodaway Company, 40 lbs flour, at 35 cents pr lb. Fine grass here, but bad marshy places.

Merdn clear, light breeze from N. Temp. 92°.

I served out the flour just purchased, to the messes. Some of my men in the rear, hunting.

A hill to the Eastward of this nooning place, very high, top bare rock, but of an olive green cast. 11$\frac{1}{4}$ miles. After nooning, we moved on, about 300 yds. Westerly from halt, then S.W. — S. — and S.E. along the upper margin of the valley, up a short stony ascent, and winding around edges of hills, ascending — short distance S.W. then S.E. — through thick pines; then S.W. a couple of miles, — S. — W, — N.W. — around S.S.W, — skirting the basin, at foot of hills, (a beautiful green marshy plain on our left. (in basin) On our right, gently sloping hills, pines & rich verdure. Fires numerous. Passed a camp of ox wagons, — women & children playing. Great place for deer, cracking of rifles heard in the hills & woods, in every direction. We keep on at base of the hills, and skirting the marshy basin, occasionally passing over a gentle spur. — (The first position of the route around is rocky and bad, but most of it is level and fine. The pine forests, nearest road are quite open.)

Now we proceed a crooked but mien course S.E. then a couple of miles E. keeping close to the marsh, passing many camps, in the bottom, and camped in an open pine timber, near rills and marsh. Passed 10 dead oxen — many of these were stalled in marshy holes. Around the edge of this basin are many raised springs, which are very soft around, and exceedingly dangerous to animals. Scott and his comrades returned late at night, with a lot of grouse, hares, &c — 5½ ms: This is the valley of a Northern branch of Feather River, and here we have to cut and pack hay for forrage, as very little grass is to be obtained between this and the Settlements. And we must also recruit our mules some. (16¾ ms.)

Sun Set clear, light breeze from S. Temp. 65°. Part of the Nodaway Coy a Virginia, and several other companies are here: — cutting hay & recruiting stock. The plain is covered with cattle, horses, & mules. — Margin of the hills sprinkled with tents, and about 50 wagons. Mr Rodgers, — an old acquaintance of mine, from Norfolk, Va. has charge, here, of Maj. Rucker's depôt, — a tent, mule corral, 2 wagons, & a few men. ½ m. below camp is a grave: —

> "Sacred to the Memory
> of Dr W. W. Freeman,
> who died Oct. 7th 1849,
> Aged 38 yrs. Mo.
> (Wright Coy)"

I had just copied the above inscription, when a party close by completed the last ceremonies over a comrade, and gave me this, to put on a board at his head: —

> "A. J. McDaniel,
> from Laclede Co. Mo.
> Aged 22.
> 17th Oct. 1849."

McDaniel and Freeman were particular friends on the route.

Counted 30 more dead (stalled) oxen here, and one dying. The grass nearest the hills is very dry, and some careless person set it on fire; I assisted Mr Rodgers and his men to extinguish it, which after hard work, beating it down with pine branc[h]es, we succeeded in doing, but not till it had surrounded the poor dying ox, and gave him a considerable scorch.

The water of Feather river, ½ mile below, as clear as crystal, bottom small pebbles, and beautiful plants and long choralline looking grass in it, adhering to the flat rocks. — Numerous fish swiming about as leisurely as gold fish in a vase.

Women in groups, sitting by their wagons, children playing about, in the grass, Mowers busy cutting hay, others tinkering on wagons, clothes drying on the green grass; stately pines and furs, with their dark green foliage and bright brown trunks, the broad grassy bottom — every shade of green and yellow, the pale green willows marking the course of the stream and its branches; The tall mountains on the opposite side, clothed with dark timber to their summits; the tents, wagons, &c. make a beautiful and animated scene.

One of Warner's men was here, in an ox-cart, — he was wounded with 2 arrows.[129] I informed Dr Austin, who visited him. Rodgers has the fever & ague, our Doctor visited him also. The wounded man's leg bleeds a good deal, the arrow passed through the calf of his leg, & another stuck in his back — The latter has healed up. The arrow had obsidian point. (He preserves a small black obsidian point, extracted from his back, and says if he recovers, he intends having it set for a breastpin) This man, as well as his more unfortunate companion, is a Missourian. Rogers related some anecdotes of Grizzly bears, — An emigrant, with rifle coming down from the "Trucky Pass," saw a Grizzler, fired at & wounded him, — he immediately made after the man, who stumbled & fell, when the bear jumped on him, and commenced mutilating him. — The man's comrade was not far behind, and he had a pick-axe, — he ran up and sank the pick in the bear's head, and killed him; but his unfortunate friend was so injured that it was tho't he could not survive. Mr. R. had an adventure himself about 10 days ago, a few miles beyond this. —

He was in company with another man, and had been hunting. Their arms U.S. rifles, each charged, and but 2 cartridges left. Night overtook them, they made a fire, and prepared to lay down, when a huge grizzly made his appearance. They knew the difficulty of soon killing him, and their ammunition so short, they thought to scare him off; so each took a fire brand, and walked slowly towards bruin, who sulkily walked around the fire, side-ways, snorting and showing his teeth, and at last went off.[130]

[OCT.] 17th   Commences clear, light airs S. Temp. 27°

Held a meeting in regard to provisions, &c. Agreed to divide and distribute the remaining provisions, among the members, (about 6 days rations of bread-stuffs).

I breakfasted and dined with friend Rodgers.

Merd^n clear, strong breeze from N. Temp. 72°.

Tried a member for a violent assault with a Bowie-Knife, on his messmate; and turned off a man for slandering the company — who had been travelling some time with us.[131]

Sun Set clear, light breeze from the S.W. Temp. 62°

The wounded man told me that Capt. Warner's command was, including the Captain 12 men. At the time he fell, they were riding through a narrow, deep, and rugged defile; — the guide was ahead, Capt. Warner next, &c — Suddenly a flight of numerous arrows were among them; Capt. Warner reeled and fell from the saddle, the guide was mortally wounded, but they kept him in the saddle; and as Capt Warner was full of arrows, through his breast, and the indians above ready to annihilate the small crippled party, they hastened out of the defile, bearing away the wounded guide and 2 others — one dangerously, and himself, slightly. The guide soon died, but just before he expired, while writhing in agony, offered any one $500 to blow his brains out. As they were retreating, an indian raised head above the basaltic parapets, and made a short vehement speech. One of the men fired a pistol at him.

OCT. 18. Commences clear, light wind W.S.W. Temp. 30° (ice)   We stowed our grass, and moved early. — along base of hill, E. ½ m. to where the river turns down W — by Rodgers Camp. — We followed the river, on the right of it, about 1 m. and forded. Many ox trains fording, much delay. 7 dead oxen (3 at ford) Banks steep and slippery. Several of my mules fell, but recovered. The stream is about 60 feet wide here, generally only a few inches of water, but some deep holes. My men in good spirits. 15 ox wagons crossed. Current rapid —, a gravel bank in centre of stream, at ford. In 5 miles from Grass Camp came to the last ford of F.R.   A lead ox fell on getting the wagon up, the teamster unyoked him & drove on, and one of my men applied a pistol to his forehead and terminated his troubles. About W. from the ford the Snow Butte, patched with snow, seems about 10 ms. distant: — in a range running N. & S. — head of this branch of the valley. Left the ford & proceeded over a level of dead grass, S.W. to foot of the hills, and pine timber; a grave on the right — close to marsh, where we turn up hill to the left: —

> "Sacred to the Memory
> of W. Brown,
> of the Rough & Ready Coy
> of Platte Co. Mo.
> Died with *skervy,*
> Sep. 19th. 1849,
> Aged 35 years."

Road through the pines, edge of hill, skirting the valley, — W. — N.W. — then ascending Westerly the hill. Pass 6 dead & 1 live abandon'd oxen Road stony, running S.W. and Westerly, over the ridge — about $1\frac{1}{2}$ miles. — Now a rocky and rugged descent, tho' short. 8 ox-wagons had greatly difficulty descending the hill; we passed them. Now over a table hill, through thick pine forrest, a little S. of W. — good road. Then down another short stony descent, thro' thick forrest, — Westerly; to a level plateau, up a very stony hill, over the flat top — Westerly; trending around to the S. — a short distance; W, — about 400 yds; Then S.W. up a high and rather stony hill; S.W. — over a very stony hill; winding a short distance to S.E. — W — N.E. — Over stony hills & level places, — then descended hill S.W. to the banks of Būtte Creek 4 miles from last ford. (*4 ms*) General course of stream N. & S.

Most of the way thick forrest of stately pines and dense undergrowth Hills covered with creeping Holly,[132] giving the appearance of green grass at a little distance.

(A few miles back, on the heights, a father with 2 children, a boy & girl were driving a lot of lame oxen along. The children were very small, and the little girl said to her brother, "Never mind, Buddy, tàint far to *grass* and *water*.") We drove 11 miles and camped here. (*11 m.*) Merdⁿ clear, with light variable airs, Temp. 70° A capsized & broken wagon on the hill-side back of this. 3 dead oxen here. Had to drive the mules down creek $1\frac{1}{2}$ ms. on the other side, under guard, to graze — Grass nearly grazed quite off here. The Virginia & several other companies here. Stream clear and rapid.

Trail runs to the right of the creek —

Sun Set clear, wind light & variable, Temp. 63°. (*15 ms: to-day*)

We lost 2 mules strayed & stolen & 1 horse here.

[OCT.] 19. — Commences clear and calm, Temp. 26°. (Ice $\frac{1}{4}$ inch thick, continued unthawed till 8 A.M.)

When we moved on, continuing up stream, on the right of it. On hitching up, we missed another mule, lent my horse to a member to ride back, in search of the lost mule. The train proceeded, and I remained on the ground, awaiting the return of the man gone back for mule. Messrs Murphy and Thaw remained with me. In half an hour Mr Queen returned after an ineffectual search at the grazing place, for the mule, when I mounted and we proceeded. Course W. — N.N.W. — and W. again, for about 3 ms. the valley here spreads out in a low & level pine bottom; tall mountains with patches of snow on them bearing W.S.W. and distant. Saw 10 dead oxen, and many horns and heads of recently killed deer. We now travelled W.S.W. about 4 ms: then S.W. and W. about 3 ms: and by a very gradual descent entered the beautiful valley of "Deer Creek." and camped in the 1st good spot — 10 miles. (*10 ms.*)

About ⅓ of the distance to-day, brought us to where the valley contracted; — and stream, road, & mountains close together on the left. — The long low spurs of the hills gradually receding and rising back to about 1 m. in tall hills: — thickly timbered with pines, cedars, &c. some oaks on the spurs & in the valley, and thick willows along the stream. a slight divide, between Butte & Deer Ck. 3 or 4 miles from the last valley the stream runs W. Saw a very singular spotted fox, on the road-side, dead. Plenty of tolerable grass, but much marsh — some dangerous for animals. Numerous camps here. Children laying and playing on the green sward, happily unconscious of the troubles of others. — Cattle, &c grazing, tinkling cow-bells, clothes drying on the grass. Numerous small ground squirrels.[133]

Merd^n clear, light breeze N.W. Temp. 90°

Head, horns, skins, and feet of deer all about.

Abandoned 1 mule here.

Sun Set clear & calm, Temp 60°

OCT. 20. Commences clear and calm: Temp. 30° (ice) Started at 7 A.M. Course S.W. for 2 ms. over marshy bottom, where the trails forked, and by advice, took the right hand branch, soon after that forked, and we again took the right hand trail; and in a few hundred yards reached the creek, 5 ms. miles [sic] from camp, where it makes a bend under a hill, to the left, muddy banks: forded it, and in ½ m. came to another ford of the stream, close to the foot of the hills — stony bottom; kept on the left side about 100 yds. then recrossed it; here the road and ford was very bad; the hills had so encroac[h]ed, with trees, stumps, logs, & stones, steep muddy banks, stony bottom, swift current, but narrow stream. 6 dead oxen at the 2nd. ford, and 8 here. This ford was very bad for wagons to rise from; very narrow, steep, and slippery banks to ascend; Above and below, near the ford, were fallen trees and drift wood & brush. The close-set trees were scored at the ascent, to permit the wagon-hubs to pass. — Much chafed by the wheels. 20 yds. directly in front of the ford was a deep marsh & mud holes, filled with stumps, logs, and dead cattle. — Hardly before the hind-wheels of the wagons had cleared the trees on the edge of the bank, the lead mules had to be turned short to the left, to prevent their foundering in the mud — Straight ahead from the ford. — Then dash through willow-bushes, green and dead, logs, and stumps; — the slender green willows — (very tough), on this short and newly made trail, switch'd the bellys & legs of the mules as they passed over them, causing them to jump and stumble, for about 50 feet: then turned right over a marshy place, full of logs and brush, & well garnished with dead oxen, the wheels passing over legs and necks, burrying them in the wet soil. for 50 yards. Now over dryer ground, with logs and drift, and stumps, for about 50 yds; then left, up a hill. On this ascent, a mule fell, in the traces, and was with difficulty raised, to renew his exertions. — A few hundred yards more, over slight ridge, and we reached another ford, crossed, and winding around the edge of a small hill, in a Southerly direction, descended to a very rocky margin of a stream, after a rough descent — (Deer Ck.)   Creek about 20 ft. wide, from 9 ins: to 3 ft. deep, bottom stony, and full of logs. — Forded, and ascended a steep hill, winding short to the right as we ascended, (a branch road ascended left, but it was too rough and full of trees to use) This is a very new trail, — full of stumps, and the green trees, cut therefrom, laying right and left, unwithered. 8 ox wagons following. Course, on top the hill S. — over a rocky road, for about ¼ mile, to a double ford, caused by a scrubby tongue between main stream and branch. Steep and muddy descents; Beyond, a rocky and winding road ascends a hill. 3 dead oxen, yokes, pieces of wagons, and fires, remains of yesterday's travel of our illustrious prede- scessors. Mr. Dunn, and some other gentleman, formerly of the Lawrenceburg Coy — with packed mules, passed us. — Also Dr Param and his friend — Mr Kennedy, with a mule wagon, also came up. — Road now over the hill, mostly good, but with some very bad places in it, — grazing the trees with our hubs, on one side, and running foul of large rocks on the other; — endeavoring to avoid *Scylla* we often ran foul of *Charybdis*, — yet sustained no damage of importance. — General S. course. The trail was of an ash- colored powder, — ground, by the travel, from a kind of decrepitating gran- ite, which was scattered around in every shape and size. In about 6 miles we reached a spring, close to the trail, on the right; On the left was a very deep & thickly wooded ravine. — Here we watered the mules, filled kegs, and canteens, and drove on a short distance below, in a vale, and nooned. (*5 m:*)   3 Dead Oxen here; yokes, chains, &c. numerous. Pines very tall, slender, and straight — a very thick pine forrest here. Pine cones from 10 to 18 ins. long. (*10 miles*)[134]   My friend Geo. Young, came up, — he was compelled to leave his partner, who stuck to his old carryall, and was a long way in the rear. — Poor fellow, he was thin and jaded, but in good health. Abandoned a wagon here, & packed the mules   Short rest and a lunch and we moved on again. In a few hundred yards we began ascending, over a tolerable road, — to a plateau, with marsh and run, where we drank, re-plenished canteens, & continued on, — over a succession of rugged ascents and descents, on a mien W. course, and in a few miles, about 3 P.M. met a party sent to the rear to bring forward the wounded men of Warner's command.[135]

6 dead and 1 abandoned ox on road. Merd^n clear, light airs from the S. Temp. 88°. Pine here 10 ft diam: and 200 ft. high, and straight as arrows. Saw on the road side a small black & yellow fox, dead, also a dead deer, and numerous remains of them. Shot a large very dark brown Vulture, measuring 9 feet from tip to tip.[136]

3 mules failed, and we had to abandon them to the tender mercies of the wolves.

Passed 3 more dead oxen.

The road now has a slight descent, occasionally, with considerable ascents, rising to the culminating ridge, from whence, in 40 ms. it descends 5000 feet. — Reached a very rugged hill, with short and steep ascent, and 2 mules failed; on which occasion I had to loan my horse to the weakened team, to complete this ascent. This sturdy animal, drew with such energy, assisted by the men pushing, that he actually roused the wagon and mules up. A mule in another wagon fell & left. 13 dead oxen on this ascent.

Course over the first hill, and to foot of steep one, W.N.W. across the big Hill S. — We descended to a mere indentation where was a good spring and large reservoir hole for animals, 6 ms: Several companies of 6 ox wagons here, and with them families, and children playing and crying, — ragged and dirty, of course. 5 of my wagons on the abrupt hill 50 yards ahead, — and the remaining one here, — in hollow, with me. Lost 2 more mules, exhausted, here. Plenty of broken wagon fragments here. (*5 + 10: 15 miles*)

Sun Set clear and calm, Temp. 70°

A very rocky dusty place; I took a hearty draught of cold mountain water, eat a handful of crackers, smoked my pipe, and made a fire. At the foot of an immense fur tree, where the rocks in the road were so irregular that I might lay in dust in a hollow, with some ease, in shape of letter S, and there spread my blanket & placed my saddle-pillow; some fragments of a wagon — and a wheel, — hub on flame, soon afforded me warmth and light, by which I wrote up my brief notes, buttond up my over coat, and quickly slept sound. Report of rifles, in the adjacent hills, answered by people here, — hunters lost.

[OCT.] 21. Commences clear and calm, Temp. 34°   (frost)

Jack frost and the rocks awakend me very early with sore hips and ribs.

Abandoned a wagon here, packed the mules, and transfered wheels, beds, &c. to render a defective wagon more perfect, an early breakfast, and we rolled on again.[137]

We continue ascending S.W. on a tolerable road. A pack mule fell from exhaustion & was abandoned, soon after another one declined proceeding, and they were left for Messrs. Wolf & Co? In 3 miles drive to a depression in the hills, where is a spring, we passed 5 dead oxen. Watered our mules, filled canteens, and moved on. Course now, over a plain, about 500 yds. W[ly] — then up hill; (all pines) S.W[ly]. Continuing to rise successive heights, till we gained the summit of greatest elevation, about 5 ms. from last camp, (5 m.)[138] Here we found 8 dead oxen, 2 discarded wagons, pieces of others, clothing, &c. scattered around. Deer heads, horns, skins, &c told of game being plentiful.

We now descend, — occasionally ascending a slight elevation, rapid descent very perceptible — Mien course S.W. — reach'd a considerable hill-top, — a long good road, 6 dead oxen, 1 abandoned wagon. A splendid deep valley on our right, — in which meanders "Mill Creek" — nearly parallel with the road. The edge of this mountain is only about 50 ft. on right of the road, where the descent is precipitous, for several thousand feet. Can here look down on the thick pine forrest, and deep down in the dell below, great furs of 300 ft. height, look like small garden plants.[139] The deep vale, or rather gorge, of Mill Creek, is not over 2 ms. wide here; — the rocky bases of the steep and tall mountains, on either side, meeting at the brink of the thread-like stream, much of which is hid by the intervening rocks and trees.

I engaged an ox-cart to carry Messrs Barkers baggage. 2 mules exhausted, can hardly keep up. At $11\frac{1}{2}$ A.M. — rested — The squad or mess, of mounted men, I had recently attached myself to, belonging to the company, and now resting with me as the train proceeds, are Messrs. Edmonston, Marden, G. Ennis, Windsor, O. B. Queen, and Willis.

Merd[n] clear, light breeze from N. Temp. 70°

Moved on, Course S.W. — in $\frac{1}{2}$ m. found oaks numerous, among the pines. Good road, and descending rapidly, by successive descents and inclined plains, till we reached a narrow vale, the[n] ascended a hill, through thick forests of pines and oaks, and reached a narrow curved ascent, gradually curving around to the left, in the hollow of that side it was precipitous, and very deep, — the head of an extensive gorge. On the convex side it was also deep, but not so precipitous, and appeared like a natural semicircular connection between 2 mountains. — Probably the gorge once ran around between these hills, and some subsequent convulsion filled in this natural causeway. On the sides of these abrupt declivities were some of those oven-looking concretions, as I have represented at the termination of High-rock Cañon. — Of a mouse-colored volcanic sand-stone, in crude and fantastic forms. The causeway is about 300 yds. over: the road after leaving it, leads S.W. up a long and steep hill.[140] Passed 4 dead oxen, 1 do mule, and 1 abandoned wagon. On hill-top 6 dead oxen, 2 do horses, and 1 abandoned ox. Here we added 2 exhausted mules. A man was endeavoring to urge 2 weak oxen up the hill, but they would not attempt the laborious ascent, in spite of kicks, banging and stoning. — All their rising aspirations were over. Noticed, on the hill, a very tall spruce tree, on left of the road, with a narrow ribbon of bark stripped off, from tip to base; by lightning. A thick forest here of pines and oak. Here we camped.[141] — 10¾ miles (*10 ms:*) On the right, down a considerable declivity, is a spring, and hole for watering animals, about ¼ m. distant. ("*Bruff's Camp Hill & Spring*")   This is exactly 32 ms. from Lassens Rancho, — which is situated on Deer Creek, about 2 miles above its debouch into the Sacramento river (:From Lassen's to Sacramento City, is about 112 miles. And San Francisco — (down the Sacramento river and the Bay,) is 100 ms. below Sacramento City. The latter is only   ms. below the junctions of the Sacramento and the American Fork.) Here we have to cut down oak trees & browse our animals on the leaves and tops. A great many travellers camped here.[142] Found a large coral of wagons, and accumulation of property, by a party of men who were ostensably engaged in felling timber & getting out pine shingles,[143] for Lassen. One of these chaps said that Lassen paid them, (4 men) $10 per diem each. And to others they said that they were to be paid by the thousand, &c. They were exceedingly prompt in visiting the newly arrived wagons, and advise the proprietors to abondon or leave them in their charge, &c. And were particularly anxious to take stock to recruit, all of which they branded with an eye-bolt, and sent below, in the Mill-Creek gorge, and with some mysterious assistance, were transferred from one gorge to another, and finally *the indians stole them.*[144] These fellows, (whose names and entire history I have) would tell folks, (on arriving here, with weak animals, fagged out themselves with the long & ardious travel, and short of provisions,), that it was 40 or 50 ms. into the Settlements; and over the most rugged and difficult road ever travelled by Christians. The poor emigrants were at once disheartened, and in despair, left wagons, cattle, and all their effects, except such as they could pack on their backs, and pushed on. These men had been emigrants themselves, yet they were determined to prey on the misfortunes of their brethren; and make a harvest of their calamities. —

I enquired what was the yield of the mines, when they informed me that they could make from 1 to 2 oz. gold pr day. *but that mining did not agree with them.*

Grapes[145] in abundance in the gulches on either side of this hill, a couple of miles down. Black-tail deer quite numerous.[146] — Continually being brought in. Tracks of grizzlers frequent.

Mr Seymour quite ill.

This hill looks like what is called home a *clearing* — oak stumps and withered limbs, in all directions. Sun Set clear & calm, Temp. 72°.

Our mules are so reduced, that I am determined to pack the team of two wagons; and in order to get the company into the settlements, in a body, after so difficult and troublesome a task as I have had, thus to have brought them to this point, together, and more prosperous than any company of men in this vast emigration, I shall direct the wagons left here with all their contents, except actual necessaries the men can conveniently take in with them. Some one take charge of these wagons, till either recruited or hired team be brought out for them. And then a proper division of the company property can be made, and the members act as they please: As very few can be found who will keep together as a party, longer than shall serve their individual selfishness.[147]

I am informed that it is difficult travelling down the Sacramento Valley, on account of the moisture; and that there is no river conveyance, and the stream is very rapid, and obstructed with bars and snags. And that the mines are exceedingly unhealthy.

At dark, sitting by the camp fire smoking our pipes, I mentioned to my comrades my resolve; which they all approved of. But who would remain here? there was the rub! — I agreed to do so, make it known, early in the morning, put my assistant, — Young, — (a very worthy gentleman) in charge of the company, and take them down to the Settlements, while they had sufficient provinder to take them in. And to keep as many together afterwards as he could. My kind friend Ashford had given me some days since, a few pounds of flour, and this was deposited in the mess sack, as common stock.

[OCT.] 22 — Commences clear and calm, Temp. 56°   (*The company and I parted company. They go in.*)

I very early informed the company of my resolve, for *their* welfare. And that in order that they might get in soon and successfully, I would not only volunteer to remain here and take charge of the company and private property they should leave in the wagons, Untill they could send out for them, but that I would also lend them my fine strong horse, (who had already served them well, on several hard rubs) to pack also, and thus assist them. They were delighted, and several thanked me — And they immediately set about the task, selecting indispensable articles, to pack in, &c —

The[y] promised me most faithfully to come out in a few days with team, and my horse, but with my horse, anyhow. My mess-mates, already packed passed on, after breakfast, and though my horse was packed principally with *Friend* Edmonston's effects, *he entirely forgot to offer me either flour or bread as he rode by.*

I was aware that certain men and messes in the company had purchased flour, and were well provisioned, but most of the men had scarcely sufficient to take them in. I told the company to push in and have no concern about me, for although I had not a pound of provisions of any kind, yet I could not suffer, as deer were abundant, and I had good arms and plenty of ammunition. Dr Austin came up and gave me a double-handful of rice. And Mr Fenderich added 2 small biscuits. And Bates contributed some pipe-tobacco. At 8 A.M: 4 wagons and all the company, except the men belonging to the 2 wagons and teams packing, moved off. Assorting repacking, &c. &c detained the packers till near noon; when, after rolling the 2 wagons up, near my tent, they also moved off. Mr Willis stepped up, as they were about to leave, and expressed a wish to remain with me, which I accepted of, as we could assist one another, and I believed him to be a clever fellow. So here terminated my trials, and command of the company.[148] —

Some I shall never see again, and there are a few whom I never wish to see again: But therere's many of that company, yes, most of them, I shall ever be happy to meet with, or travel with, again. And my sincerest and best wishes accompany them, wheresoever they go.

The company left 3 infirm mules here At 9 A.M. Mr Brush, a young Illinoisian, with a pack and rifle, was about to go in to the settlements, (from an ox train in the rear) I wrote 2 notes by him, to convey to Sⁿ Francisco, to two officers of my acquaintance, one of the Top^l Engineers, and the other in the Revenue Marine.[149]

Merdⁿ clear and calm, Temp. 74°

Willis and myself closed our wagon up tight, and drove the mules down to water, cut an oak down to browse them on, pitched our tent, and made ourselves contented for the time being. A wagon, with 2 yoke of oxen came up, from the rear, and a family of En[g]lish folks: they looked thin, and complained of hunger, — had barely sufficient provisions to get in on.

Willis has a small cake of bread, and I have a few ounces of parched coffee, and about 2 lbs of beef of an old steer, shot a few days since, given me by Mr Dorsey so we were enabled to get up quite a supper, smoke our pipes, and hoped, devoid of care for once, to get a good *whole* night's repose.

Sun Set clear, light winds S. Temp. 60°

One of our mules died here.

Grizzly bears and deers are quite abundant close around this hill. A couple of the emigrants camped here, brought in a deer they shot this morning, and sold the meat very readily, to their starving fellow travellers, for 50 cts per lb.

Some Illinoisians disposed of their superfluous baggage to charge of the "*Shingle men*," packed provissions, &c on a pair of weak steers, and their own backs, & left a small wagon in my charge, to be sent for in a few days. Ox wagons, packed oxen, mules, cows, and pedestrians, — Men, women, & children, coming up, halting, nooning, watering, passing on, & camping all day. Saw one poor couple with their personal effects, goods & chattel, packed on a poor ox, — the man, with shouldered rifle, led the brute, while the wife, with a stick, followed and urged it ahead.

Women and small children seen driving loose cattle; the little ones seem to stand the hardships & exposure well. All, more or less, Men, women and children, are dirty and tattered — All look alike, one class of rough looking, hairy, dirty, ragged, jaded men. — No discriminations except by acquaintance. — Preachers, Doctors, Lawyers, Editors, & mountaineer, mechanic, educated or ignorant.

Early in the night, Messrs. Magruder and Washington returned, with heavy packs on their backs; 5 miles ahead their mules had failed, so they left the mules to rest, and they came here to do likewise. They said the company was getting along very well. I soon provided them with sleeping apartments.

An elderly gentleman, who has a family on this camp-ground, came in at dusk, and stopping at my tent, told me how he had just returned from a quail-hunt, and that on the edge of the hill, to our left (S.) about 100 yds distant, he fired at a catamount or panther which was following him.

A couple of oxen, tied to tree close by, awoke us with awful bellowing, late in the night, and we thought a grizzler had jumped on them; but learnt since, that it was occasioned by a fight between themselves.

It seems that I can hardly realize the fact, of having the privilege of laying down — early, on a good bed, — (*at least 3 blankets under me!*) and with no present care of mind, can sleep just as long as I please!

OCT. 23. Commences clear, Moderate wind S.E. — Temp. 46°.

After an early breakfast, Magruder and Washington went on.

A clever fellow, whose name I have lost, very kindly gave me 1 lb. tea and 3 lb. coffee, and desired me to take care of a box of small articles which he would try to come out for. He had a cart and an old ox. Willis managed to purchase, of some one, 6 lb. of flour, at 50¢ per lb. for us, and made a similar purchase for Mr Washington.

We have, occasionally, to use muddy water here; the vast number of cattle continually at the spring use up the water and muddys it too.

The great enquiry, here, by the Emmigrant, is *"how far is it to Lassen's?" "Has Lassen flour to sell?" "What does he charge?," (or ax) for it?"* &c. So old Pete Lassen, the honest old Danish Missourian settler of California, is one of the most celebrated men of the country; in fact, he is *the* man.[150] Meridan same as commencement, Temp 80° Sun Set ditto Temp. 66°

The Wyandots came in late, and camp'd above us, for the night.[151] A Frenchman, (clever fellow) whose name I have forgot, was with them, has his wagon & tent, a son and 2 daughters. Another of my mules died.

OCT. 24. — Commences clear, light wind S.E. Temp. 44°

A small Missouri compy having a large family, of sick women & several little girls. These people condens'd their property, and left 2 wagons, with effects in them, in charge of Messrs William Grissom, of Mo. and brothers J.P. and C.B. Bohannon, of Ky, — the latter, and younger, quite sick, with scurvy and consequent debility. These clever fellows, had sufficient flour and pork, to wait a few days for team to come out, and very kindly proposed to make a mess of all of us, for comfort, convenience, &c — I shall ever cherish great regard for these good men. 2 cows and 2 oxen disappeared from the hill to-day. — *Shingle-men* think *the indians stole them.* The Wyandots, and Frenchman, with his 3 sons & 2 daughters, moved off early, with their ox wagon. (Several half-breed, and I think, 2 full-blooded, Wyandots, of that Compy) I was sick all day with headache, and some fever, and took rhubarb.

Just after sunset, I was surprised by the return of Mr Bates, of my company; he was mounted on his pony, — had been 18 ms. ahead, and assisted in getting the wagons up the steep hill of "Steep Hollow," but having missed his baggage, returned, to see if it was here. It was. He said that 8 miles ahead, there was a steep hill, and water on this side of it; — 2 of the wagons had reached the top of the hill, another one broke a fore-wheel trying to get up; they then sawed the wagon in half and made a cart of it, and failed in that experiment; they then abandoned the vehicle, and packed their mules, and their own backs, and proceeded, leaving the *razee*, at the foot of the hill. Another wagon, deeming the mules incapable of surmounting the hill, with it, also packed their team, and abandoned the wagon, to accompany its old, but reduced companion. The[y] also left some baggage in charge of a camp of ox wagons. The company were 2 days travelling 16 miles, (of course had another day's travel to settlements)

A gentleman kindly gave me a couple pounds of bacon, and about 1 pk. of salt.

[OCT.] 25. — Commences clear, light wind S.E. Temp 46° Bates breakfasted with us, packed his poney and bade us adieu, taking a message about my horse.[152] Willis, Grissom, and Bohannon, went hunting after breakfast, the 2 latter returned at 11 A.M. with a fine doe.

A packed mule company, — remains of of [sic] a company with wagons, 2 mule wagons, 8 ox-wagons, and numerous packed pedestrians, passed on during the forenoon

My comrades sold considerable venison to-day. All the travellers here, watered and moved on. A small party left their wagon and contents to the *Shingle men* — and loaned their oxen to another wagon, to carry some articles in for them.

Merd[n] clear, light wind N.E. 66°

About 2 P.M. 5 pedestrian packers came up, recognized and saluted me: set their rifles against a prostrate pine, drop'd their budgets & rested. They purchased some venison of my friend Grissom, for 25¢ pr lb. Grissom is an excellent hunter, — a perfect Nimrod, and brings in a deer almost every day. — So we have plenty of the sweetest meat the forrest affords. The pedestrians also purchased some hard bread, at 50¢ per lb. All the wagons ready to travel, have left the hill. At 3 P.M. it was too late for the 5 men to travel 8 miles, hungry and weary as they were, so they concluded to cook their meat and make a hearty meal, rest, and proceed after night.

About 4 P.M. a wagon with one yoke of oxen and a pair of mules, and a lady walking, the lady recognized by some of my friends, as an old acquaintance on the Platte. — This party had a worn-out ox with them. They watered and camped. A Government party, of the relief expedition, of 8 men, passed, going to the rear.

After dinner, Willis & Grissom proceeded down Mill Ck gorge to hunt deer.

Fuel abundant, affording us a fine fire at all times, generally kept a large log fire all night.

About 5 P.M. a wagon, with 3 yoke of oxen, came up, followed by a drove cow and very poor ox. One of their middle steers looked as though he could not long sustain his share of the yoke.

The dead animals near us, particularly a red ox, near my tent, are becoming rather oderous, during the hot part of the day. The lead wagon of the Nodaway train came up, and drove their cattle down to water. Near Sun-Set 3 wagons with 3 yoke oxen each, came up and camped. — With these were Dr Boone and lady, of Missouri, the Dr. formerly of N. Carolina.[153]

Sun Set clear, light variable airs, Temp. 56°

At dark 10 pedestrians, heavily packed, came up, purchased some venison, and proceeded down to the spring & camped. Our hunters returned with another deer. Willis informed me, that low down in the Mill CK. gorge, he reached a beautiful narrow grass valley, about 2 miles below, and there were a number of oxen grazing there, and ascending, he met one of the *Shingle men*, driving another ox down. They had also a poney, lost by Mr Bryant,[154] whom they said, employed them to hunt for it. — These animals were all branded by them. These men informed me that they intended remaining here till the Knoxville Company arrived, when they would move in. 3 of them were from Knoxville,[155] the other was an Englishman. They had 9 fine wagons at their camp.

After night, a man visited my tent, and enquired if we owned a certain grey mule, to which I replied in the affirmative. He desired me to tie him up, as he was annoying his oxen, by stealing their hay. I accordingly tied the poor fellow up.

Our hunters reports to day stand thus: — killed 2
Wounded .. 2
Missed 2
Saw 5

Total 11 Deer

It is a queer sight now, to observe the straggling emigrants coming up and going in. Wagons of every kind, oxen, horses, mules, bulls, cows, and people, — men, women, & children, all packed. A few weeks travel has wrought a great change in their circumstances. — Many of them I recognized as old acquaintances as far back as Pittsburgh, and all along our western waters, and over the long travel. Large companies, fine animals, a great amount of provisions & stores, and smiling faces; were now a scattered, broken, selfish stragglers, dusty in faces and dress, and many of them, thin with hunger, as well as anxiety.

I try all in my power, to cheer up young Bohannon, his infirmaties, accompanied with deafness, has made him rather desponding.

Mr. Grissom had lived near the celebrated Chief — Black Hawk, was well acquainted with the old chief and his family. — (wife & grown son) He attended the old man in his last illness, and in accordance with his last request, dug his grave, buried him, and picketted the grave around, and piled stones on it, *to keep the whites from digging him up.*[156] Mr G. had swam the Platte, at the lower ford, thrice, and was an experienced hunter.

Our camp is a great convenience to the weary pilgrims, constantly coming up. Here they find a comfortable fire, axes, fuel, cooking utensils, &c, and a comfortable bed in a wagon. Many travellers will recollect the "Lodge in the wilderness."

A beautiful moonlight night.

[OCT.] 26 — Commences clear, strong breeze N.N.W. Temp. 54°

The Nodaway's sent their oxen back on the road ½ mile, and brought up a wagon they had left there. After breakfast the travellers all moved forward, except Dr Boone & lady, with their wagon, and Dr Hervey, sick with the scurvey.[157]

At 8 A.M. 8 pedestrians came up, to rest and breakfast; followed by another, larger party, and 3 packed mules, (remains of companys with trains) After resting, all moved ahead. 3 of my comrades started on a deer-hunt. *Shingle men* brought in a doe to-day — (they killed one yesterday)

11 A.M. Mr Pickering and lady[158] came up, his lady mounted on a horse, while their effects were packed on his. Merdn clear, moderate wind N. Temp. 68° About 2 P.M. Mr & Mrs Pickering bade me adieu and moved on. — followed by others.

Our hunters returned, unsuccessful, had followed the trail of a grizzler and cubs, some distance.

A wagon & mules came up, rested, & moved on. — In this wagon was the man, slightly wounded with Capt Warner. He was rapidly recovering, and quite cheerful, had crutches.[159]

One of the travellers informed me, that about 30 miles back, he saw an old man, on the road-side, nearly dead with the scurvy, his *friends* had ejected him from their wagon, and abandoned him to his fate. A Dutchman here, was discarding some tools, which he could carry no further: and was busy breaking saws, &c. over a stump. Willis asked him why he done so, he replied; "Dey cosht me plendy of money, in St. Louis, and nopoty shall have de goot of dem, py Got!"

Animals of every party constantly and *mysteriously* disappearing from this camp-ground.

Straggling pedestrians, at least 60, passed to-day.

A wagon with 2 yoke of oxen and a lead mule, — Mr. Ford, and a dozen pedestrians, came up and camped.

Sun Set hazy, strong wind N. Temp. 66°

A wagon with 3 yoke of oxen, with 3 women & several children, among them a lady with sick infant, 9 mos. old, from Illinois, short of provissions, came up & camped. At dusk 2 wagons, with 2 & 3 yoke of oxen, also short of provissions, came up and camped.

Mr Bohannon informed me that some emigrants, expelled from the company he was attached to, set fire to the grass, in the "Emigrants' Cut-Off", and burnt a considerable space, and were caught at this diabolical act.[160] They had a wagon.

A sick lady made application for some venison, and Mr Grissom gave her a quarter. 8 ox wagons and a cart, came up in the night and camped. They had about 16 women and 20-odd children, in company. 2 pedestrians came up, and desired to sleep by my camp-fire, which of course I granted.

Dr Boone and several other friends, sat up with me, quite late, telling our experience in travelling, hunting, &c. and then retired. I was about to light my pipe, for the last smoke before laying down, when I heard the tread of an animal on one side, about 50 yards off: I threw some dry stuff on the fire, and looking in the direction of the sound, perceived the glistening eyes of either a large wolf or a panther; and stepped into my tent for a rifle, but when I came out, he was gone. I put my gun away, smoked out my pipe, and soon slept soundly.

[OCT] 27. Commences clear, light airs S. Temp. 50°

2 wagons and 1 cart, and several oxen, left at the shingle-camp.

By 10 A.M. all the parties left the ground except 3 wagons and 1 cart.

A wagon of 4 yoke, and 1 of 3 yoke oxen, came up.

Dr Boone & lady still here.

Our hunters out early.

2 ox-wagons, 1 spring wagon, 2 government mules, and a man on a poney, came up. Among these Mr. Tyler, wife, and infant; Mrs T. cured by the journey of fits, to which she was before subject. Mr. T. buried his aged parents and a child, on the Platte. (Recorded 15th died 11th buried on Feather river

The 2 government men, who arrived on mules, reported that Maj. Rucker had returned to the Feather river Depôt, and would soon be along.

I cannot abandon my notes and drawings, instruments, &c. nor would I like to lose a choice collection of minerals, books, &c. and have no means of getting them in, unless I can procure some animals from the Settlements — I desired Mr Ford to tell the members of the company at Lassen's how I was situated, and wished soon to get in, with my effects.

Merd^n clear, light wind N.W. Temp. 84°

The government employees nooned & proceeded in.

2¼ P.M. 2 ox and 1 mule wagon, — (Dr. Wilder's), and a gang of pedestrians, came up, halted, awhile, and proceeded. A man came along, with a rifle & knapsack on his shoulder, driving a small white cow, — packed with bedding, provisions, grass, cooking-utensils, &c, followed by 2 packed oxen, driven by a couple of men, with rifles and packs.

Was told of an accident which happened 20 miles from Deer Creek; — Dr Bascomb's children were playing near some gun-powder, on the ground, and they ignited it with a match, by which, one of the children was seriously burnt in the face and breast. 3 P.M. 4 ox wagons came up & camped, and another string of packed oxen & men. Soon after another ox wagon. A party of the government men, — horsemen and packed mules, came up, Dr Williams with them, sick.[161] I tendered my pallet to the Doctor, and he reposed awhile there. Dr. Smith also with them.[162]

Sun Set hazy & calm, Temp. 66°

After dark 16 ox, 2 mule, & 1 spring wagon, came up and camped, and 2 ox and 2 mule wagons, moved on. A lively scene here at night; crowded with wagons and animals, and busy throngs of every age and sex, around their bright camp-fires. The glare of the fires on all, — tents, wagons, &cc. and tall pines, made one of the prettiest night-scenes I ever beheld. Then the arms, saddles, trunks, bags, harness, &c. sitting up or piled around the huge trees. People singing, laughing, whistling, & some quarreling,[163] Around us dense forrests, deep black glens, and dark mountains, and now and then the howl of a wolf-pack was borne up the glen by the night breeze.

Dr Boone's lady is a daughter of the celebrated artist Smith, of Philadelphia.[164] The D^r graduated at Pennsylvania. The Government party proceeded, after dark.

One of the travellers told me, that on Pitt river the indians continued their rascalities, — killing and stealing animals; and had recently killed an emigrant, shooting 18 arrows in him.

Grissom, after night, brought in a young buck.

[OCT.] 28. — Commences clear, moderate breeze S.E. Temp. 56°

The Batavia and some other companies moved on early. — (I say *companies*, but these are only portions of what they were)   3 ox wagons from

Oscaloosa Co. —, And about 9 A.M. 2 ox wagons and 8 men on mules, came up, One of the mounted men looked very pale and ill, and carried a pair of crutches with him, he had the scurvy. A man came along on a very poor horse, driving before him a small black bull, packed with bedding, tin pans, &c.

Several animals lost this morning from the hill — camp-ground.

A lady, belonging to one of the partys, here, was asking for beans, said that her child craved some. — poor thing, about 5 yrs. old, was very pale, thin, & weak; the mother said that it was taken sick, and she gave it Calomel, which had salivated it.

11 A.M. A Sergeant of Maj. Rucker's command, passed, driving a mule packed with bedding. And I enquired where the Major was, he replied "ahead," and one of my mess, told him that it could not be so, perhaps they had gone down to the spring, as he saw 2 mounted men go that way; so the Sergeant returned, and proceeded down to the spring. I also proceeded down, a few hundred yards in the same direction, to meet the Major, who was in company with Mr Hicks, the Cherokee.[165] I seated myself under the shade of a balsam fur, smoking my pipe, when a pretty little boy came down, and passing near me, I called him, to come and tell me his name, but he objected; I told him I had a little boy, of his size at home, whose name was Billy; — this brought him up, & he said that his name was Billy too — and amused me much with his volubility and intelligence. — Said he was 6 years old, the 8th of this month; and, said he, "My father had a red horse, — he was a race-horse, and he could run fast *if he was poor!*, and he had a sore back, but he died when we *struck* Goose Creek, and I saw him, poor fellow, — dead! On Pitt river, the indians stole all our cattle, but we got 40 *head* back again, — My uncle is only a boy, but he aint afraid of indians. — He took a pistol and chased one indian, and made him drop his blanket; and the indians fired plenty of arrows at him, but none of 'em hit him. Father has a sword, and 2 holster pistols, and a double-gun besides, and I guess if he had gone after 'em, he would have killed nearly all of 'em! "I 'aint afeard of the indians, if I aint got no gun, nor pistols; but I've got a knife, — here it is." (producing a small pocket-knife) "and I could kill one with that." "I'm a great hand for walking; I walked all day yesterday — last night; and when we camped here, — on the hill, I said I was'nt tired, and I was'nt! We left 3 steers here for 2 men to take care of for us, and they're going to send up from Lassen's for them: — they just now branded em. At home, in Burlington, (Ioway) we had as nice a house as you ever saw: there 'aint any much better: but I guess all the house we'll have in the *Diggings,* will be our tent. — Well, I

dont care much, so we dont stay too long. At our house at Burlington, we had a nice yard, and plum trees, and peaches, and gooseberries: and we could go a little ways, and get blackberrys & grapes, and all them things." "Oh, how I miss em! he said, with a sigh, and ran down the hill, to meet his father, who went down to water his animals. I afterwards found out that this pretty intelligent little fellow, was the son of Dr Walker, of Ioway.

Merdn clear, light wind S.E. Temp. 83°

Mr Bean,[166] with his mule-wagon, came up. Some Ioway people left their wagon here, packed the oxen, and moved on.

Pedestrians, in squads of from 4 to 12 continually passing.

A lady and 3 children, with an ox wagon, came along; She told me that her husband died on the Platte, and was buried at "Chimney Rock", — his name Smith. A pedestrian told me that a few days since, at "Little Goose Lake" he buried a friend, who died of scurvy. The lady (widow) with 8 children, whom I mentioned as seeing at Maj. Rucker's camp on the 14th. was here also. — She had a son along, in a most deplorable condition, — emaciated, feeble, and as ragged as a beggar. He could scarcely speak, and had to be led about. She said she did not know what was the matter with him, nor had any medical attention. I thought it was scurvy. 3 P.M. 5 ox wagons came up, among these a Mr and Mrs Hyatt and Mr. Dickerson. — their wagon and tent close by.

The St Louis company were nearly used up on Pitt river, by the indians; who killed and stole all their cattle.[167] (Indians looking out for winter)

4 P.M. 10 ox wagons and 1 cart, with more women & children, came up & camped.

Dr Boone killed a fine buck, came over, and joined our little party.

About 8 P.M. being a fine night, I walked over 100 yds. to an adjacent camp-fire. I found these good people were all "*Hoosiers*. They were sitting around the fire, and upon and between the tongues of their wagons. — A family party, — an aged couple, a married daughter and her child, 3 grown daughters besides, and 2 grown boys. I bid them 'good evening,' and asked how they were? They received me kindly, & said they were all well, except the baby and old *omen*. — the latter was troubled with dizziness. They desired me to be seated, so I joined the old man, and we sat on the ground, leaning against a wagon-tongue, and had a long talk, about our homes, the troubles of the route, the true and certain development of character, &c. The old gentleman was unletterd, but very intelligent: the folks were clever, agreeable people. I bade them good night, lit my pipe, and retired to my cotton-house.

The camps are all very still to-night, the few here are fatigued, sick, and short of provissions.

Mr & Mrs. Ireland and son here.[168]

[OCT.] 29. Commences cloudy, Strong wind S.E. Temp. 50°

The ox-trains all moved off early.

About 7 A.M. A prussian, his family & a friend, came along: — this was an odd party. — first came a poney, heavily packed with bedding, &c. and a couple of bales of dry-goods, the beast was very poor, and driven by the Prussian, next a cow, packed with sundries, — driven by the Prussian's friend: then a very poor, and heavily packed steer, laden with provissions, frying pan, camp-kettles, platters, axe, &c — driven by the old man's son, — a smart handsome boy, about 12 years old, and he had an infant tied on his back, — indian fashion. And the old woman brought up the rear, with a bruised face, and budget on her arm. I recollected the woman, and that she applied for Dr Austin's services to relieve a *black eye* and cut face, attributed by the husband, to being thrown from a cart. The Doct. said it looked more like the effects of a *love-lick*, inflicted by her lord. — Some one had said he was in the habit of *licking* his wife.[169]

8 A.M. A large ox wagon & a small spring wagon came up & camped.

After breakfast, Dr Boone, Bohannon, and myself, started down Mill-creek gorge, to hunt deer, and look for team oxen. Willis & Grissom went back on the road for the same purposes. We proceeded down a long, narrow, and steep spur; on a good narrow trail, winding between rocks and trees, occasionally reaching plateaus of oak, of small extent;[170] Many bushes of   (Buck eyes) very large nuts, — looked much like large fig bushes and figs on them.[171] This sort of descent, most irregular and irksome, for 2 miles, brought us to a ravine & delightful spring of cool water. The trees and bushes shrouded with grape-vines full of delicious grapes. We ate heartily of them, and collected a quantity to take up to young Bohannon.

The D^r and I then descended, cross'd the ravine, and ascended the foot of another spur, and soon struck on the well beaten trail, leading from the camp of the *Shingle-men*, on the brow of the Hill, down the valley, to a grazing bottom, where, some distance below were a small band of indians. — We followed this trail: — It was well-marked, with tracks of oxen, cows, horses, mules, naked indian feet, coarse shoes of a man; bears, deer, wolves, rabbits, &c. — all leading S.W.[172] From the point where we obtained the grapes, Bohannon left us, to go right, around an abrupt point, to look in a long narrow vale up-stream. We proceeded over rocky spurs, hills, and ravines, till in about 3 miles we struck into a beautiful little vale, with plenty of grass and rushes:[173] and soon were beside the rapid flowing "Mill-Creek." Stream nearly hid by the willows, grape-vines, oaks, and scrub growth. A few hundred yards above where we struck the stream, is a very remarkable rock. — This is a Mountain-rock: — appears to have been thrown into what was once the bed of the creek, by some extraordinary power of nature. It is a lofty pyramid, of at least 500 feet. and its base, on the longest side must be about 150 ft. The top, on the broad front, is hollowed like a saddle, with 2 projections, and is smooth moss-covered granite.[174] It appears to have forced the stream around through another channel, causing it to descend, close in front, from a high bed of large rocks, in a roaring, foaming cascade.

[BLACK] ROCK IN MILL CREEK

Looking down from the high hill-side, as we descended, we noticed this, and observed that there was a cascade, and a *large rock* by it. A short distance below the falls and rapids, the stream is clear, cold, and deep, and very swift. Many large rocks in it. We walked down several hundred yards, till we reached a bend, and a trail led to a fallen tree across the stream, serving as a bridge for the indians, bears, &c. We would not venture on it, on account of its smoothness, and the rapid deep stream below, full of stumps, roots, &c. would afford a fellow a very small chance for his life, should he get in it. Several places here where the indians had made fires, &c. Saw blue smoke curling up, from the valley, some 3 miles below, where it expanded into a considerable plain of grass. The steep hills across the creek, near us, have patches of long green grass, growing in hollows where there is moisture; much of it appears to have been cut; and looks like green wheat.[175] Oaks low down, and higher up, to their summits, pines of every sort and size.

(*Tower looks rocks Mill Ck.*) Where we drank & culled grapes, a short distance down, my attention was drawn to a couple of tower-looking rocks, on the declivity of another ridge; we here could look up to them, and we

Oct. 29th '49   D

[TOWERLIKE ROCKS, UPPER SLOPE, MILL CREEK CAÑON] [P6]

resolved, if not out of our way, to pass by them — Ascending, we noticed pine cones crushed by the indians, on rocks near some tall tree., and hulls of the broken nuts scattered around.[176] The trail ran so near one of those tower-rocks, that it was not over 100 yds. from our right, when half way up the mountain. A grizzly trail led to it, and in the broad base the double mouth of a cave. It seemed to be formed with an arcade, or vestibule, and the smaller dark entrance within was distinctly seen. As we were much fatigued, late in the day, and a considerable and very rough ascent yet to overcome, we though[t] it imprudent to investigate this den of grizzlers, as doubtless it was. Besides we were only prepared for deer hunting. — Night overtook us ere we reached the camp, having in the darkness of the forrest lost the trail, and gone around too far to the left, and struck the emigrant road 1 mile in the rear of the camp. Here we found 10 ox wagons camped. We pushed on to our camp, and there to my surprise, found a squad from the Company, who had come out from Lassen's for the wagons. They were, Messrs Brooks (Treasurer.) Scott, Hilleary, Donn, and the brothers Queen. They brought out 8 mules. Bohannon had reached camp at dusk, he had killed a grouse and quail, but neither of us shot a deer, though we saw many.

My old comrades, for whom I had done so much, did not ask me how I fared, or how I had subsisted? cooked their meals close by, nor did one of them ask me to take a cup of coffee with them. On asking for my horse, I was told in a tone of indifference, that some one had him in the valley, looking for a mule. I then observed that I expected my horse brought out, or I would not have loaned him; At which one of the men was disposed to be impudent: — retorting, that he promised, on his *honor to return for me,* and had kept his word, and this was the thanks for it. *"You came for me!"* said I, *"you came to afford me the priviledge of walking in beside you, eh!"* *"No sir! you came for those wagons, and their contents, that's what you came, for! — take the plunder, and roll on; I'll not disgrace myself by further companionship with you! I shall go in when it suits me!"* Queen the younger was however an exception; he behaved courteously and friendly, and was glad to find me well. — He is a gentleman.

Merd[n] clear, light wind S.E. Temp. 90°
Sun Set hazy, Strong wind S.E. " 62°

[OCT.] 30. Commences hazy, Strong wind S.E. Temp 48°
8 ox-wagons moved off early. 4 others came up, watered and followed on. These were followed by packed oxen and mules, and a string of pedestrians. After breakfast, the 6 men of my old company found that there was

more than they could draw with 8 mules, and avariciously piled one wagon heavily, put 6 mules in, pack'd the other 2, and went off slowly and sulkily. (At Steep hollow they had to throw away more than half the freight they started with, besides sacrificing the wagon. At camp, I observed to young Queen, that as there were several sets of mule harness, they might leave me one, as I expected to obtain team, and in that event would probably take in the wagon they had left. After they had gone, on gathering up the things they had scattered, I observed a lot of mule harness, with the principal leathers cut off; and one of my comrades assured me that he saw one of my men cutting the leathers off, after stowing the wagon. Besides the set of geer used, they took away several spare ones. Mr Hilleary, who was very officious in enquiring for company property, observed that *my tent belonged to the Company*: to which I replied *"Yes, but you dont take it away!"*

Thus ends my connection with the Washington City Company, as an organized body; and with a few of them, all future acquaintance;

As the interest of the company as an association, was properly represented by a *sworn* officer, I did not hesitate to turn over to him all the effects of the association.

Merdidian cloudy, fresh breeze from the S.E. Temp 61° Willis & Grissom returned: the latter had a pheasant (short tail'd variety) They had gone back some miles, and found Maj. Horn encamped, and spent the night with him. 4 ox wagons came up, one of which was Major Horn, and his lady; we were glad to meet.

A sick man, with scurvy, in one wagon.

I exchanged a light wagon, to accommodate a gentleman, for a very heavy Pennsylvania wagon.

Afternoon cloudy, indications of rain, Wind fresh from S.E.

Sun Set rain, fresh breeze from S.E. Temp. 40°

(When I reached Lassen's Rancho, and became acquainted with the old man, and familiar with the place, I notic'd property of the Company piled up there, in a loft, with individual baggage — clothing, &c. also of members of the company. Capt. Lassen informed me that Brooks and a small party of my company, (when they went in, the last time) contracted a debt of $75, for provisions, &cc — for which they pledged this property, — company and individual, and endorsed it, The effects, only to be delivered by the order of   G. Brooks   ⎤
                         O. B. Queen, ⎦

In posting books, and settling accounts, for the worthy old Dane, I found this note, and read it. In consequence, to this day, the property lies there covered with dust, and the clothing, &c. of individuals spoiling.

I appeal to the respectable and intelligent portion of the Company, if it was not, in all respects, more more [sic] prosperous and fortunate, than any other, on that long and ardious travel? With the exception of 3 or [4?] mules, strayed, through the negligence of the guard, in one instance, and in 2 others by unforseen and unavoidable circumstances, and lost, we sustained no loss or interruption by the indians; who, on the Humboldt and Pitt rivers, the latter particularly, not only stole and shot animals frequently, but murdered men, and stole the entire stock of some companies, and that several times very near our camp. Did I not protest against their selling breadstuff in Missouri? And finally, had they followed my advice, would they not have prospered to the end? All the plans of operations, organization for the route, &c were mine. True, there were some who could only be kept in subjection like slaves; and they produced disorder, and trammelled greatly the harmonious & successful operations of the company. Still, all were kept together, and were all managed, in spite of ignorance, vanity, and recklessness.)

(While I remained in the Sierra Nevada, several unprincipled members of the company, wrote home, the most false, and ridiculous statements, in reference to myself. They even wrote word of the certainty of my death, as though it would afford them satisfaction to alarm and grieve my family, then in a state of anxiety to hear from me.

These miscreants I afterwards found out, were such as I had had occasion to speak sharply to, reprimand, or punish, for delinquencies, or to gratify the depravity of their mean souls. It was only for my family, that I apprehended these things; I knew they would occur. For myself I cared not; I was beyond their reach: — Numerous friends, in that vast emigration, of '49, and an extensive circle at home, who had long known me, and who could not credit statements from such sources. The opinion of the vulgar and envious, I cared not a whit for. The good men, the respectable, and intelligent, — a large majority, of my company, knew me, and they could be referred to.)

[OCT.] 31st (Commences rainy, strong breeze S.E. Temp. 38°) A late and hearty supper last night, rendered my first slumbers uneasy, I had the nightmare, which awakened my comrade, Willis, — who called me and awakened me. I soon fell asleep again, and had slept soundly till about 1 o'clock, this morning, when we were awakened by a man, *crying at top of his voice,* — *"Hallo, here! turn out and assist, a tree has fallen on a couple of tents, and killed and wounded several persons!"* We promptly turned out, in the rain, lit a lantern, aroused our friends, and proceeded to the fatal spot. About 100 yds. in rear of my tent, a large oak tree, decayed near the ground, became heavy with the moisture, and probably a gust of wind assisted, and it fell, partially over a tent close to its base, and directly across another tent, 20 paces further, in which lay 4 men, side by side. A large limb, capable of making a couple of cords of fuel, had to be cut off, and then the long heavy trunk pryed with levers and rolled off, consequently mutilating the lower extremities of the unfortunate wretches beneath it. Then we raised the blood-stained tent, cut it off from the chords, and extricated the broken tent-poles, &c. and there lay a shocking sight! — An aged, grey headed man, and his grown son, with their hips buried in the ground, and their ghastly eyes turned up in death! next another son, and beside him, a young man, his comrade, slowly dying in agony, with broken legs and mutillated bodies. — groaning, and uttering the name of God, in acute suffering! The screaming of the females, the grey-headed mother kissing their pallid brows while her silver hairs swept their faces, and then she would groan & scream. — and her 2 grown daughters stood, with clasped hands, choking sobs, and eyes upraised to Heaven, regardless of the bleak storm and rain. While the few men, to succor them, were moving around with lanterns. Whilst extricating the tent from over these unfortunate men, some attended to the tent, at the foot of the tree; it was soon cleared away, while a little girl within, was crying, saying her stomach was hurt, and another that her feet were hurt. — These two were slightly bruised and sprained, while several other little children, with them, escaped any injury. A large limb of the tree, had first struck the ground, twisting the lower end of the tree over, so as merely to knock over the tent, & slightly hurt the children; while the same cause, projected the body of the tree, across the tent of the men. The old man and one son died in half an hour after the accident.[177]

The old lady and daughters wished me to enquire if any of the medical men here, could amputate the boy's leg. I saw that not only were his legs broken, but his hip was crushed, and abdomen contused. — but to gratify them, I applied to Dr Boone, who had no instruments.[178] I then found Dr Crane, who had no instruments, and was besides too ill to walk without assistance;[179] in fact I thought his earthly career seemed nearly terminated I struck a small tent I had, and carried it to the fatal camp, and pitched it over the dead & dying, to protect them from the weather. We now laid the dead out, — the old man was placed on the fallen tree, and an old coat thrown over him; In the tent, beside the tree, the son was laid out, on the side next to the tree, lay his dying brother, and comrade. The young women were constantly going from one to the other, looking in their faces, parting their hair, and sobbing. One of them washed the faces of the dead.

Their wagon, was the one we called the "Steamboat," and they had also one of my company wagons they picked up on the road in the rear. The former stood within 5 feet of the tent, and in it lay the mother & daughters, at the time of the accident.

Near the foot of the tree, only about 4 feet from it, stood another wagon, in which were the parents of the small children.

Meridian drizzly, strong breeze S.E. Temp 44°

In the afternoon, with mattox and shovels, we commenced digging a double grave, for the 2 already dead, on a slight elevation, 50 yds. in rear of the fatal spot: the ground was rocky and hard gravelly clay, with large pine roots, and we had barely made a commencement when the rain and sleet compelled us to desist. Sun Set, rain & hail, strong variable wind, Temp. 40°

Busy with the dead & dying all day. At dusk we chopped wood, and built up a good fire for these unhappy people. About 1 hour after dark, the 2nd son died. Willis and Grissom sat up with them. They said it was a shocking sight, to witness. The dying son turning his head in agony, — on one side saw his dead brother, and on the other his dying friend. The young man died about day-break.

4 ox wagons proceeded in to-day. My tent leaked some, had to shift the position of my pallet, and make a trench through the tent. The rain nearly extinguished our fire. A number of packed pedestrians, (9 white & 1 back [black] man) and 3 ox-wagons, passed on.

There was a lady travelling with these unfortunate females, who gave birth to a child, on the Humboldt river; the child died, and the mother recently went in.

Snow and rain nearly all night.

Dr Boon, and Mess. Grissom, Willis, and Bohannon, will sit up to-night with the unfortunates, keep up their fire, &c. &c —

NOV: 1st: Commences clear, light variable airs, Temp. 34°

Large blotches of snow in all directions, and the distant range beyond Mill Creek is white.

The remains of the Weston and another Missouri company, and numerous pedestrians passed on.

We resumed our labors on the grave, and I resolved now, as the ground was so difficult, and all the circumstances combined to render it proper, instead of 2 graves, to undercut this, so as to accommodate the 4 bodies. The grave finished, we procured an old wagon cover, and laid it with the middle across the bottom of the grave, and stones on the ends, on either side above. I rolled each corpse in a sheet, & tied it up at the ends and middle. Then 3 men assisted me, and we bore the bodies to the grave, one at a time, in a coverlid, slid them down to 2 men standing in the grave, who received and placed them, the old man on the right, oldest son next, the other son, and then their comrade, on the left, fitting very close. I now informed the females I was ready to close the grave, when they asked, if I would read the service, I procured a Presbyterian prayer book, and read the burial service at the head of the [grave] while our rough party stood around uncovered.

The poor woman now wished a last look on their faces, and I had the disagreeable task of getting down in the grave, treading between their necks, as well as I could, and standing in the middle, supporting myself with one hand on the breast of a corpse, while I loosened the sheet & exposed the face of another; till I had open'd and exposed the old man & 2 sons. Their eyes were wide open; and she was very vehement in her grief; — crying out, with clasped hands, *"Why did He take them all at once?"* — and *not leave me one!"* I threw the sheets over as well as I could, scrambled out, and we prepared to fill in. We had laid down pine slabs at first, in bottom of the grave; and now cut a hole at the foot, and a gro[o]ve at the head, centrally, and put in a stout ridge pole, about 18 ins: above the breasts of the bodies. The wagon-cover was thrown in over the dead, pine slabs laid along, from the sides to the ridge pole, the ends up, so as to form a roof, and we then filled in and smoothed over the grave.

I procured the tail-board of a wagon, and scratched and painted together the following inscription, and put it up.

"Ormond Alford, aged 54 yrs.
and his sons. —
William M., aged 19,
and Lorenzo D. aged 15 years
And John W. Cameron, aged 22 yrs.
The 3 first of Kendall Co. Ill.:
formerly of Peru, Clinton Co. N. Y.
and the last, of Will Co. Ill:
Killed by the falling of an oak tree
upon them, while asleep in their
tent, near this spot, about
1 A.M. Oct. 31st. 1849."

Epitaph. —
"Their journey is ended, their toils are all past,
Together they slept, in this false world, their last:
They here sleep together, in one grave entombed,—
Side by side, as they slept, on the night they were doom'd!"

The young women told me that they had an elder brother in the settlements, who had gone in ahead several days before they came up: and their eldest brother, with a family, in Illinois.

The Weston Company, very benevolently gave them some additional provisions, and one of the company volunteered to drive their wagon in for them.

I advised them to abandon their old uncouth wagon, and a great quantity of useless lumber, and only take actual necessaries, conveniences & valuables, in the light wagon, (one of mine) We assisted, overhauled, and packed their freight, and got all ready for them to start early to-morrow. They lost a cow and a poney here.[180] Capt. Pierce, of the Weston Company, with a party of his men, and some Cherokees, returned from their camp, to hunt about the neighboring vales for lost cattle.

In the afternoon 17 ox-wagons came up, all their team weak.

Dr Austin came up, from the settlements, with despatches to Rodgers, on Feather river.[181] I told him of the sad accident, and at my suggestion, [he] visited & prescribed for the little girls.

This morning Mr Dietz came up with his carryall, and proceeded on with Capt Pierce and some of his party.

Grissom killed a deer, and many others were brought in by the hunters. — The top of this hill is fairly covered with skins, heads, legs, &cc — The worn-out cattle are constantly dying here, from cold & exhaustion.

Pedestrians passing all day.

Dr Austin, and the cattle hunters returned and spent the night with me: I lent them a tent which they pitched before my fire, and I made them as comfortable as contracted circumstances would permit.

[NOV.] 2nd   This morning the Weston and Cherokee party, started off early to look for cattle and hunt deer. The Allfords moved off also.[182]

Sunrise cloudy, Strong breeze S.E. Temp. 34°

The family with the little girls have to remain another [day] to search for a stray ox. D^{rs} O'Brien and McDonnald,[183] came up; the former said he was going in for team, and he desired that I would go back, about ¾ mile, to his wagon, and console his family. M^{c}D's wagon, and his lady, on a poney, passed in the afternoon.

Exchanged another light for a heavy wagon

Merd^n rain, strong wind S.E. Temp. 40°

Noticed a number of miserable looking, thin, oxen, tied up to trees, to freeze and starve. I dined on venison with Mr Weed & party. Another abandoned wagon turned over to my camp. Wind increased to a gale, and steady rain. Several deer brought in.

Sun Set same Temp. 44°

Dr Boone gave his wagon and lent a yoke of oxen to Mr Keller to carry in some effects for him.

About 9 P.M. a strong gale, and all is discomfort on the hill. I thought, when 3 of us huddled together in wet covering that there were many that night in the mountains, much worse off —

Our canvass house oscillates in the gale, but trust it will stand till day break. About 11 P.M. Dr Boone made some coffee, with muddy rain water, and it was most grateful.

The dense forrest near, and scattering pines here, break off much of the gale, but it roars like the angry surges on a stormy coast. Alas for the sick & helpless, in these hills, to-night!

NOV. 3 — Commences rainy, strong breeze from the S.S.E. Temp. 36°. Have a severe attack of rheumatism. The cold rain has prostrated many of the poor debilitated cattle, tied up last night, without food, or shelter.

Messrs Hage Hague and Barnham left with me 3 wagons, with some effects. During the morning, drizzle and hail.

Merd^n Drizzly, Moderate wind N. Temp. 46°

2 ox-wagons came up, with them 2 men sick of scurvy. Grissom brought in a young buck, and lost another — mortally wounded, but escaped in deep brush. The Bohannons finding some friends going in, with whom they made arrangements, and they left us — I wish them well. 3 ox-wagons passed this forenoon. It cleared off late in the afternoon.

Sun Set clear, light breeze from the N. Temp. 38° The family with the children, who so narrowly escaped death by the falling tree, started off.

2 ox-wagons came up, and camp'd close to my tent. An elderly and a young man with them, sick with scurvy. Introduced to Mr. Fairchilds, from St. Louis, who politely invited me to call at his camp, ½ m. in the rear, and become acquainted with his family.[184] I am anxiously awaiting the result of applications sent in to Davis & Lassen for succor, — particularly team; that I may get in as soon as possible. The distance in is only 32 miles, but the road is dreadfully rugged and muddy, and rheumatism and hermarhoyd forbid my

attempting it on foot; and I have failed, in several applications to emigrants, to take me in, they are generally too selfish. I will content myself, however; a good spell of weather, abatement of my infirmities, or the means of riding in, without sacrificing my notes, sketches, &c. must soon occur. Then I have the consolation to know, that if I only had a store of breadstuffs, I am probably as well off here, as in the valley of the Sacramento, where all is wet, bustle, and discomfort; and charges are enormous; and a very slim chance of getting down to the cities.[185] Besides, I have the opportunity here, which I could not have below, of correcting my notes and drawings, and the additional information of the rear of the emigration.

[NOV.] 4th   Commences clear, Temp. 34°   (frost) light Wind E. The small party near me have put the sick men and provissions, &c — in one wagon, to drive in;[186] the other wagon, with some effects they cannot now haul, they wish to leave here till they can send out for it. They have flour to sell, at 40 cts pr. lb. measured by a tin pint cup, *a pint = 1 lb.*

Merd^n cloudy, Mod: wind S.E. Temp. 44°

About 3 P.M. the wagon and sick men moved on, leaving 2 young men to hunt for a stray poney, and sleep in the abandoned wagon.

Near Sun Set Rodgers and a small party of men in government employ, came up. R. quite sick, I put him in my bed. 2 ox wagons passed; 2 women and a little girl; on foot, called, to warm their feet, at my camp-fire. I had just prepared my dinner, of roast venison & coffee, (no bread) and invited them to partake, which they did. They had just dined, when a young man, apparently the husband of one of the ladies, came in; — he had been to the spring. — They bade me adieu and proceeded. One of these ladys had a very appropriate volume in her hand, — "Pilgrim's Progres."[187]

Sun Set snow, Strong Wind S.E. Temp. 40°   (Late in the afternoon, I walked back, in the snow, but protected by leggings & a gum poncho and tarpaulin, to visit the Fairchilds. — Became acquainted with them, a very intelligent and friendly family, I shall ever respect them and wish them health & prosperity. At their camp I found Mrs O'Brian, with 2 beautiful little curly-headed girls, and a *mountaineer, 3 weeks old only!* I remained till night, and then walked with Mrs. O'B. back 200 yds. to her wagon & camp-fire. I carried young *Nevada*, under my poncho, to protect the little fellow from the snow, the mother held on to the folds, to assist her in walking over the wet & slippery trail; and the poor little girls, hand & hand, followed, slipping & tottering, and crying with cold and wet. Quite a snow storm   The young man Dr. O'B. had employed as a teamster, was asleep in the wet, under the wagon; and the fire was nearly out. I saw Mr. [Mrs.] ensconced, with her beautiful children, handed in the *young mountaineer*, made the young man turn out, get limbs and sticks, and build up the fire, and bade them good night. In order to urge the young man to keep up a good fire, and have plenty of fuel on hand, I told him that the grizzlers were quite thick about here, (in fact they were) and some night, when they should find the fire very low, might pounce on him, as well as the wagon, and kill all hands. (A hungry grizzler might attack him). Returning, near the top of the hill — where my camp was, the large fire of an Indiana Company attracted me, to light my pipe. Here lay a very large and long dry pine tree trunk. — it was afire & blazing finely, for some forty feet, in front and close to a couple of tents, & several wagons. Several ladies with 5 or 6 little girls, and the men. I believe one of the families was the Atchinsons.[188] They are friendly clever people, asked me in, but I declined, promising them I would try to call in the day-time. I lit my pipe, and a large pine-torch, to enlighten the way, & proceeded. This was on right of the trail 100 yards. A little beyond, on the left, passed a wagon and tent, and heard children there also.

On returning to camp, I found there Mr. and Mrs. Jenkins, their daughter, Allice, nearly grown; her little sister, 2 brothers, — smart boys, probably 12 & 14 yrs. of age. They had an ox and a mule packed with bedding, &c The poor old man had scurvy. They were all wet, cold, tired, hungry, & disheartened. I bade them be seated by the fire, and threw an india-rubber blanket over the heads and shoulders of the females, to protect them from the snow, while they dryed and warmed their feet. The mother sat, with her elbows on her knees, and her face in her hands, weeping; Allice sat, close to her, with her little sister in her lap, looking very pensive into the fire. The old man stood opposite, sighing and despondent, while the 2 brave little boys were endeavoring to cheer them up, and encourage them. They were afraid their ox & mule would perish to-night, and I fastened a blanket over each, and tied them close up to a wagon, under a tree. With old clothing and coverlids & blankets, (plenty here) I made the females a comfortable bed in a wagon, to which they retired after warming themselves. And prepared another wagon for the old man and sons. The Indianians, very benevolently gave them a peck of flour for themselves and animals.

Rogers slept with me, and his men in a wagon.

Some of the families had several small children, nearly bare-foot, and I divided an indian-dressed Elk skin among them, to make mocasins, for the little ones. I was indebted to Col. Porter for that skin.

For several days I have been collecting the abandoned clothing, boots, &

shoes, scattered around this camp-ground, & in the wagons, which I dry and hold in reserve for the unfortunates coming along. Many a poor, wet, tired, and ragged hombre, will recollect the benefits of those things; and how comfortable a good warm dry coat, or pantaloons, and a whole pair of brogans were, after he had thrown away the wet and ragged ones.[189]

Night cold and stormy. And in this night-storm there arrived wagons, with women & children. — Their situations were indeed pitiable. — Dr Boone, Grimson [Grissom], and Willis assisting me to aid these unfortunate people, as far as my limited abilities permitted, till quite late in the night. The distress & sufferings in the rear, must be very great, at this time. I trust there are but few there, and that they will be along, with Peoples, in a few days.

I wrote my notes, late at night, at a temperature of 34°, with a blanket around me, and my fingers became so chilled, I was compelled to *douse the glim*, and try to sleep.

[NOV.] 5th   Commences rain and snow, — latter predominating; fresh wind S.E. Temp. 34°

Walked back, to see my friends there. — The Fairchilds all as lively and agreeable as ever. Mrs. O'Brian and her little family, comfortable in the wagon, had breakfasted. Their man had gone in search of a stray mule. I procured fuel and made up their fire, &c. One of her little girls said, "Ma, I dreampt, last night, that Pa had come back, without any mules." Mr. Fairchilds and Goodrich,[190] and others camped here, had cattle grazing down the steep valley of Mill Ck. and being watched there; but difficult & bad to get them up. The Indianians were all lively and seemed to be doing well; and the other camp contained 1 lady and 3 little girls, and by them a wagon and 2 tents, full of young men.

On return to camp, I found the Jenkins more composed, — Dr Boone had consoled them with the loan of an ox, and we purpose cutting some light wagon in half — make a cart, and with their yoke of oxen and mule, can travel in successfully. — The Dr will accompany them. Rodgers and party started early.

Merdn same as commencement, Temp. 38°

6 pedestrians came in, warmed themselves, and proceeded. We constructed a lodge, with poles and wagon-covers, connected with my tent; under which we could have our fire, the smoke escaping from the top. Grissom & Willis said, that as soon as a dry spell occurred, they would hunt up sufficient team, and we could all go in to the settlements then. Hear that General Wilson &

family are in the rear, in wretched circumstances. Mr Goodrich introduced me to Dr Robertson, — lame with scurvy. (The Doctor had been employed in the U. S. Mint).[191]

3 more wagons came up and camped.

Sun Set — rain & some snow, strong breeze S.E. Temp. 34°. At dusk many pedestrians came in, and warmed themselves; I provided them comfortable sleeping apartments in wagons. — One of these brought to Mrs. Jenkins, a parasol and bonnet, which they had drop'd, in the snow, and the gentleman knew them, and kindly brought them along. Another night of wet gales. Rodgers promised to return soon, and bring me relief. Genl Rowe introduced himself and his friend to me, at request of Dr. Austin, whom he left in Deer Valley. He said that the Doctor's mule had given out there. There is a story among the Emigrants, about a lady and her young daughter, and a Reverend gentleman and his son; their plot for Father & son to run off with mother and daughter; and to accomplish this with greater facility, they had attempted to kill the old man, — husband of the woman & father of the daughter, said one of the men had shot the old man in the neck, and the Company to which they were attached, had tried them, on circumstantial evidence, and expelled the said reverend gentleman & son, and they had gone from thence, (on the Platte) over to Salt Lake. The old man referred to, does carry his head on one side.[192]

A gentleman gave me a very young bull-terrier, born in these mountains, which I shall name *Nevada*.

Hear that General Wilson's family consists of 2 young ladys, the mother, 2 sons young men, and a little boy, and that they have been compelled to abandon every thing, even their carriage, for want of animals. — That they have cached, in Pitt and Feather river valleys, an extensive and valuable law library, and many valuable goods, including silks, &c — and the *relief party*, are assisting them forward, having furnished the females and children with mules. In one of the wagons at my camp, is a large circular tent; this I shall pitch, and with pine branches and old clothes, bags, &c. can make them a comfortable lodging place, when they come up.[193]

Messrs Hague and Burnham most kindly gave me about ⅕ bbll. bread, 1½ side bacon, ¼ sack salt, and ¼ do coffee. And gave me a description list of 5 steers, which they lost here, and suppose to be down in Mill Creek bottom, with the privellige of using them, and besides will reward me, if I get them in. I trust they are safe, but I apprehend that the *mysterious dealers in cattle, &c* have secured them.

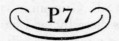

NOVEMBER 6, 1849 - MARCH 16, 1850

Bruff's Camp and Roberts' Cabin in the Sierra Nevada

NOV^R 6th 1849 Commences with rain, strong breeze S.E. Temp. 40° Dr O'Brien returned, with 3 yoke Oxen and a poney, and soon after took his family in: forgot to say 'how di do?' 'good bye,' or any thing else to me.

We rigged up a cart for the Jenkins, and I supplied them with mule-harness, so that by 11 A.M. they rolled on, rejoicing. The old man had a very long and heavy rifle, which he prized exceedingly, but could not conveniently take it, so left it with me, observing that he would give any one $10 to carry it in for him.

Dr Austin came in, from the rear, where he had suffered much, and told of of People's energetic philanthropy — how he carried females over the cold mountain Streams, in some places to his waist, &c.[1]

The D^r breakfasted with me, Stragglers continually passing. A couple of men ask'd me for the loan of a camp-kettle and axe, as they were about to cook a meal close by. I readily loaned them the articles & they made a fire against a trunk of a tree. I had worn a gum poncho & tarpaulin hat, but the rain held up for a while, and I took them off, and threw them in my tent, while I went to a camp near by; on returning the strangers were gone, with the loaned articles, my poncho & hat. I hope their gratitude will meet its reward.

Called over to see my friends, the Fairchilds, whom I found well and lively; then over 200 yds. to Mr. Goodrich's[2] camp, and Miss Fairchild being there, introduced me to Mrs. G. — Mrs. G. is very talented, a poetess and botanist, &c.

A wagon & 3 yoke oxen came up, & camp'd beyond, on the top of the hill. A Man of the party told me of the suffering, in the rear. That he saw a widow & several small children, with effects packed on their backs, on foot, in snow 2 ft. deep.

Merd^n rain, wind moderate S.E. Grissom is half-determined to stay a while longer. Dr Robertson's tent is close by, and has a young man in it, sick and pale, with scurvy. Was told of a man thus afflicted, about 10 ms. ahead, in a wagon, too sick to move, and all alone. Dr Austin saw one on a mule, some miles back, and the mule had nearly failed. Capt. Bousard[3] slept in the lodge, by the fire, and Doct. Austin with me, in tent. The rain and falling twigs, pattering on the tent, roar of the wind, among the trees, and drip in our faces, awoke us near day.

[NOV.] 7th — Awakened, by the elements, I put on a gum coat & hat, lit the lantern, and went into the other tent, — all asleep and fire low. — Threw on fuel, and returned to my own tent. Dr Austin complained of a severe cold, and I found a bottle of sour syrup of squills, from which he took a dose. I fixed a board to throw the water from my head, smoked my pipe, and soon slept soundly.

Sun rise rain, wind S.E. Temp 40°

During the forenoon 6 females of various ages, rode up on government mules, and proceeded.[4] Numerous pedestrians, with packs & rifles. The widow, with a little girl and boy, all with packs, who had plodded along in 2 ft. snow, also passed, Animals of every kind, packed with every thing, and driven by all sorts of people, continually passing. A female on foot with a blanket over her, and rifle on shoulder, looked hearty and cheerful. Peoples and his party soon came up; a corporal's mule exhausted, which he stripped, and turned loose. Peoples in company with me, visited the Fairchilds'. Remainder of the Wolverine Ranger's Comp^y came up, & camp'd near me. — Only 1 wagon of theirs had gone in.[5] They made a large fire, dried bedding & clothing, cooked supper, and seemed lively. 1 wagon to-day pushed on. Grissom and his friends, accompanied by Dr Boone, with their effects, moved off. — We parted reluctantly.

Government party dined and moved on. — Peoples took a note in for me, and promised to send me succor, &c.

Dr. Harvy, of Pike Co. Mo. came up, on an exhausted mare, him self nearly exhausted, with scurvy. Turn'd the mare loose and I took the poor man in my lodge. Dr Austin also pushed in. We repaired our abode. Have only 2 days' bread, and venison short. Made my bed in a wagon, accommodated a gentleman & his son, with another — (Wolverines Co^y) Put 2 Germans in another, and an old man, with a sore foot, who had served under Napoleon, I put in the 4th. This old Guard man carried an old rusty cavalry sabre with him.

Peoples gave me permission to get any of the numerous government mules left along the road and use them. Rather difficult to find any capable of bearing more than themselves. The last stragglers, now coming along, are many of them indifferent & unprincipled people, many of them will appropriate any thing they want to their own purposes. And are mostly those whose want of energy, or plundering propensity detained them in the rear.

(*Merdⁿ drizzly, light wind E. Temp. 44° Sun Set clear, wind same. 40°*)

[NOV.] 8th   Commences clear, wind light & variable, Temp. 34°

Several parties passed, with many packed oxen, and a lady on horse-back, her brother walking. After breakfast the Wolverines passed on. Willis went in search of cattle.

Merdⁿ flying clouds, light variable wind, Temp 50°

Visited Fairchilds' camp. The men had gone down the gorge for their cattle. Pedestrians & oxen, all packed, went by, also a cart and one yoke oxen Willis returned in afternoon, unsuccessful.

The health of Dʳ Harvy seems to be improving.

We spread out our effects to dry. The old guard man proceeded on.

Sun Set fly. clouds, wind variable. Temp 46°

Many pedestrians passed, and a small party of these came up, dried & warmed themselves by my fire & remained for the night. Some of these men I knew & dined with on the Platte. We related our subsequent adventures. Told of a fight People's party had with the Pitt River indians.[6]

[NOV.] 9th   Cloudy, moderate wind S.S.E. Temp. 44°

Soon after sunrise rain. Part of the Indiana company left a wagon & some property with me, and proceeded on with one wagon. Mrs Achinson kindly invited me to dine with them on venison pot-pie. I complied, and enjoyed an excellent dinner with these clever people — a couple of ladies and several young men there   2 Ox wagons came up, one of them proceeded   Fairchilds & Achinson got their oxen up from Mill creek valley   1 carriage & mules came up & camped.

Merdⁿ rain, Strong wind S.E. Temp 48°

Willis and the party who staid with us last night, went off for deer.

Obtained some grapes for Dʳ Harvey, Sun Set same weather, Temp 46° Found an old sheet-iron stove which we put in a large tent for our guests.

Amused myself cleaning my double barrel gun.

Willis & hunting party returnd at night disappointed, wet and hungry.

Looking for Rodgers or Peoples to come out soon. The party now stopping here, are Messrs Wm Poile,[7]

Delighted with the sound of a violin at night.

The Indianians brought in to-day, on a mule and their own shoulders, 4 deer.

Miss Fairchilds regaled me with a piece of grape-pie.

Snow & rain at night

[NOV.] 10th   Commences with rain & snow, strong S.E. wing [wind], Temp. 36°

Merd^n rain, wind same, Temp 44°

Sun Set ditto do   "   43°

Achisons & squad of Indianians moved off. an ox wagon came & passed on 4 of our party went hunting Some men came up from Lassen's, reported the road below almost impassable. Mules were on the road dead, and erect, in mud to the girths, Capt. Peoples' mare in that predicament   3 men had tried in vain to extricate her.[8] — Sacramento Valley, from the City to Lassin's overflowed.[9] Another party of grateful men stole a haversack from me for the loan of some cooking utensils. Some stole a trunk of effects out the rear of one of my wagons. A large party of pedestrian gentlemen came up, supped, & I gave them wagon apartments.

[NOV.] 11th   Commences clear, light variable wind, Temp. 46°

Merd^n Ditto   "   52°

Sun Set Ditto   "   48°

Young Wilson and some government men, on mules, for relief of the General & family, came up, breakfasted, and proceeded back on the road.[10] I sent compliments to the Genl to come on.

Mrs Chandler,[11] on a mule, indisposed, *in charge of Capt. Henly*,[12] came up in the afternoon. Gave them a wagon to sleep in. Visited my friends in the rear, and dined with the Goodrich family, a fine venison pot-pie, pinola[13] bread, coffee, grape-pie, grapes, poetry and botony. — Enjoyed my self much.

A man drove up a team of oxen from 12 ms. in rear, to grase [graze] them here, in Mill Ck. valley. Left their wagon & family in the rear; slept at my camp. A wagon and 3 yoke oxen came up & camped.

A considerable system of robbing wagons left in rear, and men who are known seen to go with packed mules from a wagon, down into the valley of

Mill ck, several miles back. Boxes & trunks of dry-goods, &c. &c. broken open, & contents strewed along the muddy road.[14]

A gentleman told me, that on pitt river, the indians had opened a grave, and taken the corpse out, tied a rope around the neck, dragged it about some time, then impaled it with a stake. And about 20 ms. back he saw a grave partly open, and half of a female corpse protruding, one leg gone, and a large stick under the remaining leg. My informant, Mr Poile, said that he tried to get at the head and re-inter it, but could not. He judged that it was a female from the small delicate foot & form of the body. The indians no doubt had exhumed the body and the wolves carried off the leg.

Wild geese & ducks flying over, quite low all night, to the S.

The track of a large grizzler near our camp, one of my comrades followed it a few miles back, where he [the bear] had dragged an ox-carcase some distance & then torn out the entrails.

Unsuccessful hunt to day, meat getting low. The sick men are improving, except myself.

[NOV.] 12th   Commences clear, light variable wind, Temp. 48°
    Merdn clear & calm, Temp. 60°
    Sun Set ditto   "   48°
The deer seem to be leaving, descending the hills, numbers are seen far off, in the low valleys.

Late in the afternoon some families came up. 2 packed mules, and another with paniers of carpeting on each side, from which protruded the chubby faces of 2 small children. — Father led, and the mother & others followed. — I offered them a wagon to sleep in, but they [went?] off some distance, built a fire & camped out. Near Sun Set Genl. Wilson's family & company came up,[15] and I accommad[at]ed them with lodgings, — circular tent for the ladies, large square one for General & soms [sons], and wagons for the others, though several preferred sleeping around the camp-fire.

Fairchilds & others preparing to move in. Dined with the Fairchilds.

A young man on a deer hunt saw a large grizzler in a deep gulch, not far off, going up hill for some cavernous rocks.

A Dutch woman here, is out of provissions, her child is crying for bread — they have fasted 24 hours: but some good folks are going to help them.

[NOV.] 13th   Commences drizzly & calm, Temp 44°
    Merdn   do   do   "   46°
    Sun Set moderate S.E. wind   "   42°

After breakfast Genl. Wilson & family and party; Capt. Henly and Mrs. Chandler, and Messrs Allen, moved off; Mr Poyle most kindly agreed to remain with me

At Merdⁿ my good neighbors the Fairchilds left, and about 5 P.M. the Goodrich family came up, and I advised them, in consideration of the hour, to remain to-night: which they did.

At night an elderly man, young man & wife, with 2 children, and a very long cart, drawn by 1 yoke oxen, came up, to camp. I invited them to warm & dry themselves. The old man's name is Symington,—the person who killed his comrade Fitzzimmons, on the 25th of August last, (grave noted at Sept. 4th)[16] Their children crying for food. While these people were sitting in my lodge, drying themselves, the husband said to me, "Stranger, I thought that I was pretty rugged, but this little omen is just as rugged as I am!" (slapping her on the shoulder) she replied, "well, I be!"

I put them in a large tent, and they kept the little sheet iron stove red hot all night, risking much a quarrel between it and several kegs of gun-powder, near by.

This young man, (named Cox) told me of the numerous grizzler tracts in the rear, on road, near this; saw where they had dragged dead oxen & horses some distance from the road, after digging them out of the snow.

A young man, Mr Shepherd who had been grazing oxen in the adjacent deep valley, starts to drive them back 10 miles to the family camp: He thinks his folks are in want, as he left them only a little bacon to subsist on. A man here told me that he had fed his oxen 2 days on green coffee. Fairchilds left a cow & young calf below, in the deep vale of Mill Ck. Mrs. F most kindly left me some dried venison.

A man driving oxen up from the deep valley, slip'd down a rocky declivity, cutting his face badly, and injuring his left arm. He came along, with bloody rags about his face, & arm, in sling, and driving an ox wagon, in which was his family.

[NOV.] 14th Commences hazy, variable and light breeze   Temp. 38°
    Merdⁿ do. mod. breeze S.E.   Temp. 40°
    Sun Set rain, wind same   Temp. 36°
    9 A.M. drizzly. During forenoon some snow and rain.
    Goodrich's & family started very early. Young Fairchilds returned to my camp, intends hunting for a stray mule. The cart, with the [Cox] family and Symington, moved off late this morning, leaving very dirty clothes in my tent & the tent much burnt.

I have a very severe headache to-day.

Willis & Poile with some others, started on a deer hunt — Dr. Harvey quite smart now, walks about considerable. During afternoon sun & showers. Hunters returned unlucky. Quite ill to-night, with headache & fever — An ox awakend me in the night, tearing the cover of the wagon I sleep in.

Mr. Goodrich left a large trunk which he wished me to take care of till he could send for it, or otherwise càche it for him.

Strong breeze — cold night —

[NOV.] 15th Drizzly and calm,   Temp 34°
Merdn cloudy, strong breeze N.E   ”   37°
Sun Set rain,   ”   ”   ”   34°

Mr Seymour,[17] with a comrade, and friend Poile, started off to hunt deer 6 miles ahead, and then get one, they killed yesterday & hung up to a tree.

Mr. Shepherd, who day before yesterday took oxen back on the road, came up to-day, with a wagon, in which were 3 married ladies & several children, and camped near us. Came 16 miles. The men here, with a red cart, are in search of their oxen below. The *Shingle men* have heavily packed 3 large wagons. A small wagon is left in their charge, to be sent for, belonging to a Mr Vestal.[18] It is full of family effects, &c. Dr. Harvey still convalescing; has lost his mare, — gone with all the other animals from this hill, but not before it was *branded* Young Fairchilds called this morning, he wishes to get his father's cow and calf up, from the hollow. I feel somewhat better to-day. — A good pot of tea & some boiled venison, for breakfast, was very palatable.

The brothers Seymour invited me to dine with them, and I thereby secured another good meal — coffee & broiled venison. Capt Henly's brother came up this morning from the rear.

A wagon containing several trunks, a number of old rifles, blacksmith's tools, cooking utensils, a circular tent, &c. was left here, on the 3d ulto — and the following card stuck up in it, by the proprietors. —

> "This wagon I leve in care of
> Capt Bruff, I intend to make
> a Return trip for it".
> (signed) G. W. Bower
> or Wm Neele

Dr. Robertson told me all about the man Symington, and his murder of Fitzzimmons, as follows: — That the latter was in the habit of abusing the former, who appeared to be a very easy chap, and continued his persecution, till S. thought it was time for forbearance to cease. A few days before he killed his persecuting comrade, he went amongst the emigrants, complaining of the ill treatment he received, abuse, kicks, cuffs, &c. and solicited their advice. Some replied, "D — n him! Kill him!" Others said they'd d — n soon settle his case, if he treated them so; &c &c. The sense of the majority with [whom] he had conversed on the subject, was for violent retaliation. — One evening, when the companies, with whom he was travelling, were camping, on the Humboldt, he, with the wagons and 2 comrades (one of them Fitz-simmons) camped, off — one side from the others; and that night he killed F. — whom they buried next morning, and the 2 men shared all the property between them. Some thought that F. had money. — Dr R. was ahead, some distance, when the transaction occurred, and heard of it, from some person of the same company. — Not long after, S. made his appearance at the Doc-tor's camp, saluted the D^r and his friends, and observed, "the scene has changed since I saw you last, Fitzsimmons will no more ill use me; my *wife* (signifying a large knife he then held, naked) finished him!" On enquiry how he done it, he said, "he was cooking, and I went around behind him, and plunged the knife in his ribs, under the arm, and he fell on his face!" and added, "he is now in his grave." A man asked him if he had used the knife since? he said "No," "there's some of his blood on it yet!" and added, "Oh, I only wiped it off on the grass!"

Mr Henly told me of the difficulties in getting along in the rear, from snow. — That for about 4 ms. the snow was above the hubs of the wheels, and up to the oxen's bellys, and the wheels became immense circular blocks of snow, and the poor oxen could drag with the greatest exertion but a few feet at a time, and then stop & blow. On reaching a hill, men women and chil-dren were compelled to assist, and transport the contents of the wagon to the top, & then push the empty vehicle up to assist the jaded oxen. They saw where a grizzler had dragged an ox about in the snow, near the trail, while devouring him.

2 young men of Seymour's camp, out hunting, and lost, for to-night. Young Fairchilds found his cow dead, and shot the calf.

Willis discovered a càche, containing a trunk & tools, not over 200 yds. from our camp; it was open, and full of mud & water; had been rifled.

Poyle and his comrades returned late, unsuccessful. Shot nothing, nor ob-tained the deer left hanging to a tree; the eagles & vultures had left nothing but the skeleton & skin; an officious and disagreeable interferance with our rights.

[NOV.] 16th   Commences with rain, strong S.E. wind   Temp. 38°
    Merdⁿ ditto   ”   42°
    Sun Set do. variable wind   ”   40°

A wagon and 2 men proceeded   About 11 A.M. a portion of the relief expedition, under Ford,[19] arrived from the settlements, — Ford handed me a note from Capt. Peoples, dated Davis Rancho, 12th Nov. in which he sends me some flour, pork, and a bottle of whiskey. —Ford gave me a small bottle of sour wine, and told me that the provissions were on a mule, as they left him, pack & all, in the mud nearly to his back, in "Steep Hollow, 10 miles below. He could not extricate him; and left *all standing,* as the sailor says.

In the afternoon another detachment of the same party came up, A Mexican with them. They had meat oxen & packed mules, for the sufferers in the rear. They said they were obliged to leave several mules, standing up in the mud, with their packs of bread, flour, wheat, &c.

There is an inhuman wretch camped here, by the name of *Lambkin,* as perfect a misnomer as was ever bestowed on any thing.

The emigrants who traveled along with him, were all familiar with his notorious character; and one who said he knew the family in St Louis, related the following: — That L. left a reputable wife in that City, whom he had long abused, then stole the only consolation she had remaining, a tender boy, of about 4 yrs. old, and with some woman came off on this journey. There were 2 other men with him. She had an infant, on the latter part of the march, the mother died on the Humboldt, and the infant died, when 4 mos. old. While the females of the adjacent camp were preparing his infant for the grave he was busy in his tent, playing cards for a rifle. His little boy he treated in the most brutal manner, suffering it to want for every thing, and then beating him most unmercifully, for crying. This wretch was camped near me. he had a comrade, and a cart with a yoke of oxen.

He set 2 crotched posts in the ground, laid a pole across, and with slats and old canvass, formed a Shelter, on the weather side, to sleep under. In front of this, he had a log fire. Here slept the unfortunate little boy, exposed to the inclement weather and wet, and half-starved. I heard the poor little fellow crying, as I was passing, with a limb of a tree on my shoulder, and went up to quiet him. He was laying on damp blankets and endeavoring to pull a wet buffalo robe over him, but it was too heavy for his feeble strength. He complained of hunger & cold; I asked him where his father was? He lispingly replied, "I dont know". The fire was out, and the weather wet and bleak. I covered the little fellow up, and told him to be quiet, I would find his father and send to him, with bread.

Soon after I visited Seymour's camp, where they night & day keep up a large log fire. There stood Lambkin, laughing & talking. I told him his little boy was *crying*, "Yes, d — n him," says he, "let him cry!" "he's always crying!" — I felt very indignant at his brutal conduct, as the child was quite pretty, with curly light hair, and the father's conduct appeared so unnatural. I said it was a thundering shame to treat a poor little child so, and if I had the means to take care of it, I would protect it myself. We had a few rough words, and he went off.

Was told of a man, helpless with scurvy, left in a sort of tent, with very little provissions, about 10 miles back, near the road, amongst the Snow, and all alone. — about 10 days ago he was seen.[20]

The *Shingle men* made a move to-day, starting a wagon on the road, heavily laden, with 6 yoke of oxen. A little distance below, where a trail intersects the road, they drove up from the gorge, several packed animals.[21]

Late in the afternoon, to my astonishment, Lambkin brot his little son William, to my lodge, & said if I wanted him I could take him, as he was going in to the settlements for provisions, and would return in a few days. I ask'd for provisions for the child, he said he had none, and considering it a humane action to take care of the child as well as I could, till its father bro't out bread, which he certainly would soon do, and then take it in, from this wild inhospitable hill. — Our store of provissions quite short, some mildewed pinola bread, and a few days rations of venison. I made the boy a comfortable bed in a dry wagon.

The *Shingle men* wished me to take charge of 2 wagons and contents left at their camp, some 300 yds. off. I told them that if they brought said wagons up to my camp, I would watch over them as well as I could, while I remained here, which I hoped would not be much longer.

[NOV.] 17th Commences cloudy, calm, Temp. 42° Merd^n sun & clouds, light wind N. Temp. 44° Sun Set cloudy, wind same, Temp. 40° Midnight drizzles. Temp. 30°

The Government party proceeded, on their march to the rear, accompanied by Willis; to whom they lent a mule. Henly and the party with females moved ahead, and 3 men with packed oxen, and a negro. Dr. Robertson loaned his oxen to the Shingle men, to transport some effects for him. He accompanied them. They carried off a wagon from here by a circuitous route, over a hill. Poyle spent the day unsuccessfully hunting. Lambkin found his oxen in the gorge. I could procure no provissions for the child, more than I have.

The hill is now cleared of the camps except Seymour's and mine. A party of pedestrians camp at the old Shingle camp. As I had a considerable store of gunpowder, I placed it all in a box attached to the rear of a wagon close to my lodge, and threw an old gum coat over, to protect it from moisture.

We caught plenty of rain water to-day Dined on venison and coffee, and bread formed of flour scraped out of old bags.

Poyle sat up at night cooking venison bones and a pint of beans, for to-morrow's dinner. Hope to obtain a deer soon.

Night very still here.

[NOV.] 18th   Commences hazy, moderate N.E. Temp 42°
    Merd. fly. clouds, strong wind S.   ”   44°
    Sun Set cloudy, strong wind. S.E.   ”   42°

Poyle spent another weary day, chasing deer in vain. Only observed a few, at a distance. Baked a cake of some mildewed pinola, (left by Dr. Harvey) and gave it to the child through the day, in small bits.

Our breakfast to-day, is venison bone soup, some beans in it, and a piece of bacon skin; with coffee. The Seymours invited me over to dine with them, about 2 P.M. They also had venison bone-soup, but in addition cold boiled venison, tea, and a *fragment of cheese*! Dr. Harvey, at my request, for his welfare, shouldered his pack, & staff in hand, bade me adieu, hoping to see me soon. He observed, on parting, "*Capt. Bruff, I am a humble individual, but I shall ever gratefully appreciate your kindness to me here, and if it is ever in my power to serve you, I beg you will command me.*"

Late in the afternoon one of the Shingle men came up, with 2 government mules, to go back on the road, (as he said,) for some *provissions left in a wagon*. Mrs. Chandler saw one of these men the other day, (Hartman, an Englishman) and recognised him as the fellow she had seen on the road in the rear, with pack animals, carrying the contents of a wagon down into the deep valley here. This party kept one man stationed 7 miles ahead, in a deep hollow, two looked for and attended to cattle, while 1 was camp-keeper, and shingle-maker. Once a while they would split out a few shingles.

Anticipating a storm, I dried the clothing, and tightened up the tent and lodge.

Young Seymour found the remains of one of his father's oxen in a ravine, close by, devoured by grizzlers. The Seymour hunters unsuccessful to-day. Constant shooting, and bad weather has driven the deer away — lower down.

Trust Willis will obtain some sort of provisions on the road, if nothing better than some musty beans.

One of the *Shingle*-gang, told an old man, at my lodge, that it was impossible to get either a wagon or animals down into the Sacramento Valley: Or from Lassens down the valley to the cities. That he intended to work over the ridges, and get as near the valley as he could, and there wait till he could go further, and try to raft down the Sacramento river. He said that old Lassen remarked that if this weather continued much longer, flour would rise to $25 per lb. on account of the impractibility of getting it up, & the number of sick & other emigrants in the upper part of the valley. Flour is now there $1 per lb. and not much on hand.

Miss Fairchilds sent compliments desiring me to spare them a little salt. They are camped 10 miles ahead.

The Seymours are appreciable neighbors — The old man has been a Santa Fé trader: he has a son, 2 lads, a wagon & carryall; 3 oxen and a horse: (lost 1 ox here)　The old man sick with diarohea — gave him some cholera mixture.

At night strong gales with snow and rain.[22]

[NOV.] 19th

Commence drizzly, Strong S.E. wind　Temp 36°
Merdn occasional drizzle,　do　　　”　40°
Sun Set　do　　do　　do　　　”　38°

In forenoon a sick lady on a mule & her husband on foot, and a sick man on another mule, came up from the rear. The lady warmed herself and exchanged her wet for a dry side saddle　Mrs. Todd left here, and they proceeded.

3 pedestrians came along, going in.

Mrs. Frink came up, in charge of one of the Government employees, on mules. Tied their mule, to a wagon, and made fire, and got supper close to my lodge. I gave *each* a wagon to sleep in. They dried & warmed themselves, and went to bed.

The *Shingle man* returned with only one mule, the other had fallen, exhausted. He tied his mule to a wagon, and walked down the hollow below their old camp, returned in night, & slept in a wagon. At night Willis returned from the government party's camp, 2 miles back, very wet & tired. The indians had come into Feather and Deer Valleys, on the route, plundered wagons, and carried the articles over the hills. What the indians, bears, & wolves had not molested, wanton unprincipled emigrants had. Open trunks & chests, clothing, dry-goods, of every kind, arms, &c &c. buffalo robes, blankets, tents, harness, &c. &c strewed the trail. Lambkin has been absent a day or so, and no one but himself knows where. He had caught his 3 oxen. A yoke he would keep, and the odd, thin, worn-out one, we might kill and eat. Poyle thought it might not be his, and desired him to shoot him himself, which he done. He [Lambkin] reluctantly and awkwardly complied, so Poile had to finish him by another shot. For some of the meat, Seymours young man assisted, to skin & cut up the meat. Poyle, bro't a sack full of meat up from the ravine ½ mile down, and we had liver & coffee for dinner — After dinner P. returned for balance of the meat, and reached the spot just in time to save it, as the eagles & vultures were gathering apace, and commenced operations. He brought up another bag of meat, & left 2 in a tree, hoping that the bears & wolves will not rob us of it. P. was careful to cut all the meat off the skeleton.

Child very troublesome, crying to go to bed, then to get up, was cold, — set him by the fire, he then cried to go to bed.

Occasional rain at night, with strong flaws from the S.E.

[NOV.] 20th   Commences flyg clouds, Mod. breeze. S.E. (Temp. 32°   Soon clouded over.

Merd. cloudy. Strong Wind E. Temp. 38°
Sun Set rain,   "   "   S.E.   "   34°

Mrs. Frink and her *escort* moved on early. Young Wilson, and another man, came up from the rear. I wrote a note to his brother William, to have sent out to me by the first chance, some provissions and 2 yoke oxen, and I would settle it when I should get in. They soon moved on.[23]

Poile & Willis brought up the two sacks of meat, from hollow. P. immediately went to work salting up the beef, while Willis walked back on road.

The *Shingle man* from deep hollow station, came back, enquiring about 2 sacks he had left in my tent, which I gave him. Said he had lost a mule. I had a considerable stock of coffee, which to-day I put in tin canisters and boxes, — over ½ bushel: and not quite ½ bush. salt. Willis, last night brought a heavy black flour cake with him, affording us this morning the luxury of bread at breakfast.

Lambkin visited my lodge, when I took him to task for being so apathetic about his son, who was suffering for want of bread, and that he might have gone in and back again, bringing out relief for his child long ago; but the manner in which I spoke to him aroused his temper, and he told me that he did not allow any man to talk that way to him; when I seized a holster-pistol, to *straighten* him there, and he *put* before I could get a sight. He has a cart, and appears to be employed by the *shingle-men*.

The Seymours informed me that he wished them to take his child. Seymour is making a cart out of a wagon-bed.

Mr. James Douglass, of the same party as Bowers & Neele, came back from his camp 10 ms. below for the circular tent. He told me that there was nothing to be sold at less than 75 cts per lb. at the settlements.

2 sick men, from the rear, on mules, came up. One of them, with crutches, Mr. Jas. Irvine, of Arkansas, wished to stop as he could not urge his mule further. I accommodated him with lodgings and a comfortable fire. He hired Lambkin to go back to the Government camp for another mule. Mr. Douglass supped with us, and added a biscuit apiece to our suppers. I gave the sick men coffee. Willis returned late in the afternoon, with about 1 lb flour. The *Shingle-man* who had been back on the road, came up, had a mule heavily packed, with a buffalo robe over all, 2 rifles on his shoulder, and a pair of boots hanging to them, and a pack on his back. I gave him the salt to take my esteemed friends, the Fairchilds. He told me that he heard Peoples had hired a man to take him down the Sacramento in a canoe: which is very hazardous, on account of snags, rapids, &c. Travelling down the Sacramento valley impracticable.[24] Struck the circular tent & gave it to Mr. Douglass. Willis is quite unwell, from fatigue & exposure. He tells many anecdotes of the laziness, &c. of the emigrants in the rear. — How a tent blew down in the night, and exposed a little girl to the wet storm & snow, but her father would not get up, and assist. Night snow, rain, & squalls

[NOV.] 21st   Commences snow, light wind S.S.E. Temp 33°   This morning every thing looked truly wintry: — The pines and other evergreen trees bending their heads under the weight of snow, and ground covered several inches.

About 9 A.M. 2 young women, a lad and boy, sisters & brothers, with packs on backs & arms, came up from the government camp. They warmed & dried themselves at my fire, & proceeded. Lambkin came up with them, and I told him he must do something for the boy, at once, that I could stand a large amount of suffering, but it was very hard to inflict it on so young a child, when he could soon bear him beyond it. He said he would attend to it at once, & went off. The females who warmed themselves at my lodge, are Germans, I gave them a pair of yarn mits between them, to keep at least one hand protected from cold. The snow gave place to fine drizzle: Willis is better.

11 A.M. The Government relief party came up [from the rear], with 2 wagons of 3 yoke each, and filled with women & children; prin[c]ipally

infirm & helpless creatures. A small boy jumped out of one of the wagons, towards my lodge, crying & saying he was cold, and wished to warm his feet; one of the men caught him, after a scuffle, & put him back in the wagon, and they proceeded. Soon after, there came up a tall hearty good-looking man, with his 2 daughters, about 10 and 12 yrs of age; looking quite hale. The little girls had frock coats of their father on, and each carried on her back a very heavy pack, strapp'd across the breast in the manner of a knapsack, and the lazy father had no other incumbrance than a rifle and sabre on his shoulder. The girls were quite pretty, and one had her naked toes protruding through her broken shoes; their hands, naked, and dripping wet. On loosening their packs, I was surpriz'd to find them so heavy, and remarked to the father, that it was a pity to make pack-horses of them. He said they had lost every thing, and finding a wagon of dry goods, had taken such articles as they needed, so that when they reached the settlements they could make up clothing for themselves. — A plate on the scabbard of the sabre was inscribed as a presentation, from a troop of cavalry in St. Louis to this Lieut. Irvine, as a tribute of esteem, &c. As I had discovered, in one of the wagons given to me, some articles of clothing, probably forgotten by the owner, I appropriated such things as would answer, to alleviate the situation of destitute travellers. So I gave each of these little girls a pair of yarn gloves, fine yarn socks, and a coarser pair, to draw over their shoes. They dried & warmed themselves, shoulder'd their packs and proceeded. The father seemed very grateful, and offered me pay.[25]

An old woman with a small boy came up, warmed and proceeded.

Late in the afternoon Lambkin moved on, with his cart and yoke of oxen.

The thaw, causing masses of snow to fall from the tall pines, crushed my large tent. Douglass proceeded ahead to join his comrades.

(*Merd. drizzly, very light wind S. Temp 40°   Sun Set flys clouds, light N.E. wind, Temp 40°*)

Seymour shot a fine buck, about ½ mile below the hill-top, and gave me a quarter of it, very kindly. We can now have bread & meat — as we have tough beef, and cold boil'd venison answers for bread. There are 2 families, with wagons, left at the government camp, a few miles back, They say they have their all with them, and will not abandon it, preferring to winter there, than lose their property.

Palmer, Genl. Wilson's guide,[26] is yet in Feather river valley, with a party, awaiting to be succored, it is said.[27] Lambkin return'd at dusk! I send notes & messages by the government men, for provisions and team, — at least a riding animal, that I may get in. This they promised faithfully to attend to, & see it done. Sick, all night.

A clear moonlight night.

[NOV.] 22nd   Commences clear, light wind. N. Temp 32°
    Merd.   ditto   ”   ”   36°
    Sun Set clear & calm,   ”   ”   33°

Poyle, this morning, assisted young Seymour, to bring up the remainder of the buck the old man hung up, on hill-side — and they kindly gave us a hind quarter.

After breakfast Willis & Seymour went back on the road, arm'd only with knives & pistols.

Caught Lambkin prowling around my camp, he said he was looking for a pack-saddle. I drove him off, with a threat. The hopes of his doing something for his child prevents me from treating him as he deserves. After he left, I found he had stolen 1 pack saddle and secreted another under a wagon. He said 1 ox had fail'd and he would have to pack the other. While this unfeeling wretch was going off, his little son cried for bread, & said his father would get him some. I told him I was afraid his father was a bad man, and would not bring him any bread. I gave him a spool of cotton to play with, and while unwinding it, he seemed to be reminded of home, of his mother, &c by the cotton; saying, "Mother's cotton, Mother's scissors, Mother has bread, and Mother has cake, and Mother has tea" &c. &c. Poor little creature! abandoned in a wilderness, by his father, to suffer, perhaps to perish! Thy mother will probably never again see her little boy! My compassion may prolong your sufferings, I cannot alleviate them much.

This has been a fine day, though it thawed little. Endeavored to secure things around camp from the pillagers. Cleaned up and arranged arms, and correcting my notes and drawings.

[NOV.] 23rd   Commences clear, light wind. N. Temp. 32°
    Merdⁿ Do   ”   ”   ”   40°
    Sun Set do   calm   ”   36°

Drying Harness, Saddles, bedding, clothing, &c. and writing. After breakfast Willis washed some clothing, and Poyle took a sack, and proceeded down the valley of Mill Ck. for edible acorns, for bread. Quite sick. Seymour's party went hunting, taking a mare along; the[y] proceeded to the S.E. down a deep vale, saw many deer, and late in the afternoon wounded 4, & killed 2 bucks, which they packed up on their mare.

At dusk P. returned, with about ½ peck acorns, but not the right kind. He amused himself shelling & boiling them.[28] The child has cried all day for bread.

I was so lucky as to find a bottle of peppers and about 1 pint of vinegar. By keeping near the fire all day, my cold & rheumatism are considerably relieved.

An ox-track around Vestal's wagon, and the contents over hauled considerably. — accounting for the lost pack-saddle, and Lambkin's return night before last. My camp is minus several axes, a rifle, and 3 pack saddles, since he last visited me. — He is doubtless associated with or employed by the *shingle-men*. Douglas met him the other day with an axe which once belonged to him, and the same which I took out of his wagon, and was using.

[NOV.] 24th Commences cloudy, with fine drizzle, light variable airs, Temp 34° Merd. clear, light wind N. Temp. 48° Sun Set clear and calm, Temp. 46°

Early in the afternoon a Mr. Roberts and his son, the former mounted, came up from the rear, in search of team to draw them up here — they had lost all their cattle.[29] As Seymour was just ready to move off, he could not loan his, so they proceeded for "Steep Hollow," about 10 ms. ahead.

Seymour's men lucky again at deer hunting, and as liberal as expert — gave me 2 sides, and 2 quarters.

About dark I was astonished by the appearance of a pointer dog at my lodge, and recollected that he was with Cox, and as Cox was last seen with Lambkin, some miles below, it is probable they are somewhere about this hill for plunder.

Seymour left here about the time Roberts did. I regretted much to lose such good neighbors. About 9 P.M. I heard footsteps in the snow, and taking my double barrel, charged with buck-shot, I crept cautiously out, in direction of the sound, keeping behind trees, till I spied an animal, about 60 yds. from me, could see only the shoulders as it moved, and fired; it sprang up, fell, and then sat up; I rapidly advanced a few paces, and gave it the other barrel, and on reaching it, found a very large yellow wolf, stretched out dead.

We experimented with the acorns. They were too bitter. We roasted about ½ gall. ground them in a coffee-mill, mixed with an equal quantity of flour, and added yest, — (some dry, in a bottle, which we dissolved with warm water) and set by to bake in the morning.

[NOV.] 25th Commences clear, light wind N. Temp. 40°

Merd^n clear and calm,   Temp. 56°
Sun Set " light wind, N.W. "   46°

This forenoon Mr. Henly and Burroughs,[30] with a horse and 2 mules, came up; they are going to the rear, a few miles, to a wagon, in which they had effects. They said a Mr. Shepherd [31] would be along to-morrow, with 2 yoke Oxen.

This morning we found our acorn-bread had risen, and put it in the oven, and baked it; producing a light, soft, & *brown* loaf, some what bitter, still it was bread. Curing our meat to-day.

At dark the two Roberts returned, and supped with me, on beef and coffee. They brought me a few pounds of flour, and a piece of salt pork, with a note, from Peoples, saying it was all he could send, R. informed me that the rains had inundated the Sacramento valley, cutting off all communication between Lassin's and the cities. He said he would bring his family here, & proceed 3 miles ahead, and there winter, as his daughter-in-law was in a delicate situation. Mrs. Roberts had walked many miles, in these mountains, to accommodate a wounded man in the wagon.

Latham & his comrades have engaged R. to complete the number of shingles they engaged to make for Lassen. They were to make 20 m. but *in consequence of turning all their attention to other matters*, have only got out 6 m. They say L. is to Pay $20 pr m for them. As we cannot get any better shelter in the settlements than tents, and living is enormously high there, R. thinks we are as well off here, if we can manage to keep in meat: My infirmities will not permit me to hunt, or even walk far, and unless succor is sent me from the valley, I am corner'd, for a spell. Roberts went back, about 10 P.M. to his camp. A beautiful moonlight night. Their Oxen came to my camp, in the night, anxiously looking around in the snow, for something to eat. I procured some old dry grass from a wagon, and took the straw out of an old pack-saddle pad, and fed them.

Just after turning in, about 11 P.M. heard a cry & scramble up a tree, close by, made by a catamount.[32] I got up, and sat out till chilled, without getting a shot at him, as he was in a tall pine of a thick group. So I gave him up & retired.

[NOV.] 26th Commences clear, light wind N.W. Temp. 44°
Merd.   do   do   do Temp. 48°
Sun Set — the same

About merd^n Mr. Shepherd came up with 4 oxen, on his way back to Henly. Gave him a dinner of beef & coffee. Acorn bread very satisfactory, sorry we have not a good store of it. About midnight I was awakened by the tread of a horse, and jingle of tin ware, and turned out to see what it was. My comrades accompanied me, and we soon discovered a yoke of oxen standing by a tree, which were recognized as belonging to Shepherd; they had a bag tied to their chain, which contained about 1 pck. green coffee, — this I deposited in our lodge. We looked about for the rattling affair, and then saw another yoke of oxen, to which was hung a large camp-kettle and numerous small tins, which had made the clatter we heard. Mr. Henly soon after came up on a mule, and stated that the oxen had got away from him some miles back, about dusk.

It commenced drizzling & we warmed & turned in, to sleep sound.

[NOV.] 27th   Commences with rain, moderate wind S.E. Temp. 42°
     Merd^n — same —
     Sun Set — do —   "   40.

We all slept late this morning, and then breakfasted on broiled venison & coffee. & H. proceeded. Henly said that when he had gone back, on the road, about 12 ms. at a wagon, he found a Mr. Smith & Scott (who were camped with Roberts, a short distance back) there; they had lost their oxen, and as the snow was about 2 feet deep, they could not carry 70 lbs of flour from thence to their camp; and told Henly & party that they could take it rather than suffering it to be lost, which Henly and his friend most gladly availed themselves of, and the 2 men who gave it to them returned to their camp. That when they (Henly, &c) had come on as far as Robert's camp, the Roberts' (Father & 2 sons) came out & claim'd the flour, and said they would have it, which he protested against; but his oxen had continued down the road, and he was compelled to follow them, and the Roberts' in chase, demanding the flour. He soon missed his mule, with the flour, and returned to the camp, & there found the mule, with pack gone, & lashings cut. Roberts denied having it, and he was obliged to come on after his oxen, leaving Burroughs & Shepherd to fight it out.

He also told me of seeing a dead ox dragged some distance, in the snow, by a grizzly bear, as he went back; and returning he noticed that the grizzler had dragged the carcass still further, and they found that one of the oxen Smith lost, had been killed, and devoured by a grizzler.

About Merd^n Messrs. Burroughs & Shepherd came up, very wet: They dried and warmed themselves. They were rejoiced to know that we had secured their oxen — They stated that besides the flour, the Roberts had robbed them of some coffee, the property of Shepherd. He demanded it, or half of it, in vain. Mr. Frink (his lady gone in under patronage of a friend) told him he would see that he got it, if it could be found, and he had better come on, as the odds was against them. So they came on, losing flour and coffee.

After a short rest they proceeded. Forepart of the night rain, and then, about midnight it cleared off.

[NOV.] 28th   Commences clear, Strong breeze N.W. Temp. 32°   Merd^n ditto, 42°   Sun Set ditto, 36°

In afternoon, Frink and his 3 comrades — Smith, Scott, & Co. with a cart & 3 yoke oxen came up & passed on —

Roberts' son with another man also passed. Late in the afternoon, Brown, who had lost his right arm, (belonged to Genl. Wilson's party) and 3 other men came along, on foot, and to rest here to-night.[33] Gave them apartments in a wagon with good bed clothes, and after supper they retired. We worked hard to-day, repairing our lodge against bad weather — Cut poles, rebuilt, and re-covered with wagon sheets the lodge, and repicketed the tents, and laid boards down to put our beds on. Drove sticks down & fasten'd a tail-board on it, for a table. Cut down & chopped up a small oak tree for fuel. Was told that Lambkin, and Cox were seen a few days ago, near here, and that L. said that Mrs. Cox would take the child, but I have not seen them, though he promis'd soon to come for him, with bread.

[NOV.] 29th   Commences clear, light wind from the N. Temp. 32° (much ice)

Merd same   ”   62°
Sun Set do   ”   46°

About 2 P.M. Roberts & son came up, from 3 ms. ahead, to go back on the road for the family. They had obtained 2 yoke of oxen. Stop'd 15 min. and proceeded. Procured fuel, mended clothes, cleaned and charged up arms, &c Poyle is an ingenious cook, he boils down the meat joints & bones reducing the meat & integuments to a jelly — which when cold is very fine and nutricious.

Wilson's men moved off early this morning, thanking me for a comfortable night's repose, and carried a note in, for me to the settlements, applying for provissions and team, or at least a riding animal. The emigrants have all gone by now, it is thought, except a man named White & 6 or 7 Germans, who were determined to winter on Pitt river, and near a cache of alcohol. — These folks have, ere this, been used up with alcohol, snow, indians, grizzly bears, starvation, and wolves.[34]

Beautiful night — full moon.

[NOV.] 30th   Commences clear, light wind & variable, Temp. 32°   (ice)
   Merd^n Ditto — 54°
   Sun Set, a few light clouds,   ”   42°

Willis had discovered an open cāche, near by our camp. I visited it to-day — A black travelling trunk was partly out of the hole; it contained carpenter's tools, books, papers and writing materials, all soaking wet. Finding it contained private papers of the owner, which might be of service to him, I took the trunk, with Poyle's assistance, up the side of the hill, about 400 yds. to my camp. We had to rest often getting up. In the bottom of the hole were 2 shovels and a pick-axe, wet & very rusty, of course. Among the stationary found some very neat pencil drawings, letters, &c. of Mr. Darach, an architect or carpenter, from Maryland, and a person I am acquainted with — I spread all out to dry, then carefully folded & tied up the papers &c and marked them so that the owner would stand a better chance of getting them.

This morning we baked our last loaf of bread, which is to last us 2 days, for breakfast only; & we have ½ pint flour, enough for a breakfast cake if increas'd with acorns. After that, unless relief is sent out, we must go it on meat alone.

DECEMBER 1st   Commences clear, light wind S. Temp. 42°
   Merd^n hazy, wind same,   ”   56°
   Sun Set do — do —   ”   44°

Hanging up pieces of clear beef to dry, & smoke, in our lodge. Getting water up from the spring, for to-morrow, — a troublesome job: have to descend a steep hill side ¼ mile, to the spring-hole, carrying large campkettles — This spring is a great resort for Grizzlers, & folks going down must look about them.

Willis talks of starting for the Settlements to-morrow, to obtain the aid I have so often applied for in vain. Late in the night some rain.

[DEC.] 2nd   Commences clear, light wind N.W. Temp. 32°
   Merd^n do —   do —   ”   39°
   Sun Set cloudy, Wind S.   ”   40°

Mr. Roberts and son, on a horse & mule, came up in middle of day & staid till dusk. They related their version of the *flour* affair, with Henly, &c. That Henly, Burroughs, & Shepherd, on their way to the rear, called at their camp, when they heard R. and associates talk of going back to the wagon for the flour, and desired to accompany them; & also expressed a wish to purchase some. All hand[s] proceeded, and while overhauling the wagon, Smith lost his oxen, and therefore his party could only pack a small quantity of flour on their backs: — leaving some 60 lbs which they said they would return for, and started for camp, leaving the trio busy spreading some wet *dry*-goods to dry. (The goods they had taken from a wagon which had been full, & left to be sent for.) Henly & co then took the flour, packed it on a mare, and loaded their 2 yoke of oxen with other articles; & came on. Arriving, late in the afternoon, at R's camp, where Smith suspected their intentions, was on the look out for them, and he, with young R. walked up & accused them of having their flour, which they admitted; and Smith then said he would allow them a fair proportion of the flour, for bringing it, or would sell them one-half of it: but half of it he would have, at risk of life. The holders of the flour retorted that they intended to retain all, and pay nothing. — While passing strong *mountain compliments*, the mare turned off towards the camp, which Smith perceived, followed her, and took off the flour. Henly & company had used a considerable portion — baked up much, and Mr. Roberts paid Smith 50 ct. per lb. for what he could spare him, for his family.

About 3 P.M. Joseph J. Petrie, (a Prussian by birth) with a pack of blankets & bread, and double-barrel'd gun on shoulder, walked up, from Davis' Rancho, bringing a note from Col. Davis to me, sending his & Col. Ely's compliments, that any assistance I needed, they would send to me, and desiring me to deliver such mules & other government property I might have, as they had purchased all of these from the government officers. Petrie also brought a note to Poyle, from his friend Allen, — who was writing for Davis. I desired Petrie to be at home in my humble mountain lodge, as well as he could. He said he met Denham, (or Denman) Latham, Dibble, & Hartmann, (the *Shingle-men*) with 3 wagons, heavily laden, having 5, 8, & 10 yoke of oxen drawing them, and several loose oxen. That Dr. Robertson was with them. That he also saw Roberts, who had a poney and mule, the latter had a government mark, but R. told P. that the government had loan'd him 2 mules, to assist getting his family in, and these he had given up. The mule he now had was a stray one, which Peoples said he could use if he found him. Mr P. told him that if he would ride in on the mule, to Davis', they could there and then decide what to do about it, otherwise he would be obliged to take the mule. P. intends, as soon as he can get down the Sacramento valley, to visit the City of Sacramento, so I shall avail my self of the opportunity to write down to friends there, and letters for home. Roberts & son are to meet Petrie & Poyle to-morrow morning in the N. hollow, (Mill Creek valley) to take a thorough search for mules & cattle; while Willis will hunt in the S. vale, for the same purpose.

Petrie most kindly gave us a large loaf of wheat bread, a piece of fresh beef, & some ground coffee. He is a clever worthy fellow, and very energetic. His benevolence has been liberally extended to unfortunate emigrants.[35] After dark some light snow fell, and snow during the night.

[DEC.] 3rd   Commences snow, strong variable wind. Temp. 29°
      Merd^n snow & sun shine, strong N. wind, Temp. 30°
      Sun Set flying clouds, strong gales from the N. Temp. 26°
Petrie & Poyle put on hard-weather coats, shouldered their guns, and started off. — They examined the deep vale of Mill Ck, for several miles; found numerous well beaten paths, and 2 very secluded old camping places, and at dusk returned, wet, hungry and fatigued, after a hard day's tramp through snow and mud, and over rugged rocks. They saw no animals. The[y] looked down into a southern gulch, which was full of snow. Poyle suggested to me the propriety of going in with Petrie, and securing at once that succor I so much needed, which had been so long deferred, and was now in reach, Mr. Willis objected to his going, thought that he (W) should go. "Very well," said I, it's important that some one goes, and you can, if you prefer it. So Willis & Petrie will start early in the morning, leaving us here, with the child. They cannot take the boy in, for it's quite a job for any man to get in with his blankets & rifles on foot. I mended clothing and washed some, to day. Sat up late at night, writing notes & letters. Strong gales and snow all night, causing our cotton castle to oscillate much, and we not only apprehended its blowing over, but had some concern about branches, limbs, & tree-tops, blowing down upon us.

The conduct of Willis seems to me rather singular; — he is busy gathering up every article of his own, and very carefully packing trunks & a chest, and piling them together — locking them, also. Here where every thing is in common, and has been so long; and cannot be disturb'd except in the event of our death, during his absence; when all his precaution would not save them from Indians, and wild beast. — And he is to return in three or 4 days at most.[36]

[DEC.] 4th   Commences clear, fresh breeze from N. Temp 22°
Merd   ditto   33° (ice plenty)
Sun Set   ditto   30°

At 9 A.M. my kind friends Petrie & Willis left, — taking a letter to Davis, with a statement of the manner in which I remained here, my indisposition, & other circumstances, and authorizing W. to make any arrangements for our speedy succour & deliverance.

As Willis shouldered his gun, to leave the tent, I pointed to the few pounds of smoked beef, hanging up in the lodge, and observed, "Willis, do you see that? — it is all the provender for 3 of us, till you return!" "Very well, Captain," said he, smiling, "I will certainly return, with supplies, &c. in 3 or at most 4 days." Petrie rejoined, "Yes, Captain, I will see that he comes back and brings you whats needed."

About 1½ P.M. Messrs. Henly and Burroughs came up; they were in search of Oxen, that Roberts told them had been driven down the N. hollow, to graze. They had been down and could neither find oxen or tracks of them. They had a piece of venison, & broiled it, to which I added Coffee, for their suppers, and gave them a bed.

[DEC] 5th   Commences clear, strong wind N.E. Temp. 28°
Merdn   do   do   42°
Sun Set   do   do   40°

Our guests moved off at day-break, intending to try another search in the deep valley. At night the wind still strong, occasionally blowing in heavy flaws, — the high mountains & deep gorges have much influence on it.

[DEC.] 6th   Commences clear, moderate wind S.W. Temp 34°
Merdn   do   do   48°
Sun Set   do   do   40°

Engaged mending clothes.

For a short time after dark the windy flaws increased. Feel much concern about the child, but if I procure a mule, I can carry him in very well. About 10 P M. some feline animal passed near our lodge, visited a dead ox within 50 yds of us, and made a considerable scratching on the hide of the old carcass. Poyle went out with his rifle, and heard it ascend the adjacent hill — Could not see it for the trees.

[DEC.] 7th   Commences clear, calm, Temp 26°
(The weather seems milder than the thermometer indicates, at least 10 degrees.)

Merdⁿ same, Temp. 39°
Sun Set do   "   32°

The ravens are numerous, and very loquacious, they are after the dead cattle scatter'd around, Oxen, mules, &c. that fell from exhaustion, during the travel through. Perched on the tallest pines, on stumps, and on the ground, croaking and chattering all day. They utter sometimes queer sounds, and I have often been deceived by them. I recollect that some time since, I was walking back on the road, when I heard some one, as I thought, calling to me, "Bruff, Bruff", the voice proceeded from the declivity of the hill, on my right, apparently about 50 yds. off. I answered, "Aye, aye!" — "What's wanted?" and turned down the hill, and soon saw a flock of ravens, on the ground, near a dead ox, & quickly discovered my mistake. To-day I distinctly heard a dog bark, as I thought, and called Poyle's attention to it, & he also thought it was the bark of a hound. — I went out, and proceeded in the direction of the sound some 300 yds. and listened, again heard it, a little further, and on going there, discovered it to be a raven, on the limb of a pine; and he seemed to be trying his imitative faculties — particularly of the barking of a dog.

There are several beautiful species of woodpecker here. The large red headed, small red head, red shoulder'd, a very minute dusky one, and another resembles much our male blue jay.[37]

Soon after dark it breezed up from the N.E. occasionally blowing in heavy squalls.

[DEC.] 8th   Commences clear, moderate wind N.W. 28°
    Merdⁿ   do   do   36°
    Sun Set —   do   strong N.W.   32°

Our fare to-day beef gelatine and tea. Last night a large saucy wolf had the impudence to come near our lodge, and serranade us, — rather too much *bass*. — This morning his tracks are very distinct, quite close to us, and of a large size. Busy getting things in order to move in. A raven, to-day, sat on a low pine limb, over our lodge, looking down with apparent curiosity at our movements, may be he thought we had some crumbs to throw out; if so, he missed it.

Fresh gales from the N.E. all night, and very cold: Occasionally was heard the booming sound of some giant of the forrest; and the heavy report, borne on the gale, swept up the deep gorges, sounding like the distant signal gun, at sea. Whilst the roar of the gale, through gorges and forrest, resembled that of the storm-lashed surf. Ever and anon we heard the howl of wolves.

[DEC.] 9th　Clear & strong breeze N. Temp 26°
　　Merdⁿ do light wind N.E.　　　　" 40°
　　Sun Set do. Moderate N.E.　　　　　" 32°

As our friends have been absent now 5 days, we are anxiously expecting to hear their voices every hour in the day.

Beautiful but cold morning. Broil'd salt ox and tea our rations to-day — the former causes frequent reference to the water pail. Poyle amused himself to-day boring sticks for pipe-stems.

[DEC.] 10th　Commences clear & calm, Temp. 23°
　　Merd. clear, light wind S.W.　　　　" 35°
　　Sun Set do calm　　　　　"　　　　" 32°

After an early breakfast friend Poyle shoulder'd his trusty rifle, and started back on the road, in search of beans, rice, or anything in the shape of provender, that might be left in some wagon. He proceeded 9 or 10 ms. and returned at dusk, quite fatigued. He said that about 2 ms. back, there was considerable snow; and all along the line of route there was a well-beaten trail, made by bears and wolves. These trails branched off right and left, in numerous places, leading down into the ravines & dells. A few miles further, the snow was about 3 feet deep, and broken only by tracks of bears, wolves, & panthers. The position of the dead cattle on the route, he easily discovered by the tracks to the hole in the snow, where they lay, and had been visited by the beasts. Found several wagons, and one seemed to have been left full of dry-goods, but pillaged by subsequent travellers, after the owners left. The wolves had dragged, tossed about, and torn, a large quantity of calicoes, pieces of cotton handkerchiefs, &c. &c. and in the wagon they had made a bed of such articles as remained, and it looked as though some of them lodged there every night. On returning, he found fresh grizzler tracks since he passed on; and in one place they had trampled and bloodied the snow in a large circle, as if dancing or fighting around a quarter of meat. Pieces of calicoes & cotton handkerchiefs scattered along the route, for miles, — some entire & compact pieces, & others loose. All wet & muddy. Some appeared to be drop'd by travellers, whose cupidity had made them attempt to carry off more than they could. He also saw 1 cast and 2 sheet iron stoves; Thousands of articles of every description buried under the snow. He said that the walking was very fatiguing in the deep snow. He packed in a coffee-mill, and some tools.

[DEC.] 11th Commences with flying clouds. Wind moderate W.S.W. temp 28° Merdⁿ cloudy, strong wind S.S.E. Temp. 32°　2 P.M. sprinkling snow.

Sun Set same, sprinkling snow, Temp. 32°. We feel some anxiety about Willis, fear he is sick, but trust it is some difficulty on road with team, occasions his detention this long. About Merdⁿ the 2 young Roberts and Mr. Clough, who was in their employ, as a teamster, called at the lodge; they are on their way back, as far as 30 miles, if they can reach there, to visit a wagon for some necessaries said to be there. They informed us that the old man (Roberts) had recently returned from Lassen's rancho; and that while there, a posse of emigrants, headed by Petrie and Willis, had gone in search of the *Shingle-men's* camp to identify animals, &c. of which they were very strongly suspected of having. — And that Lassen & Davis had with a train of wagons gone down the Sacramento valley for supplies, expecting to be absent 15 days. (5 days now since they started). The upper settlements nearly destitute of provisions, and the emigrants had to live on beef, at 50 cts. per lb. and coffee, at 75 ct. per lb. — no bread. Many had gone & were moving down the valley. And if we had bread stuffs sufficient we would actually be better off than those below. Mending clothes & tightening tents. Strong gales with snow all night (snow since 2 P.M.).

[DEC.] 12th   Commences with snow, Strong Wind S.S.E. Temp. 28°
Merd. do   do   ”   32°
Sun Set occasional snow, wind same.   Temp. 32°

Near Sun Set Messrs. Roberts & Clough returned, having gone only as far as my friend Poyle did. Last night they experienced an *interesting* time; huddled together, in a wagon, on wet rubbish, and covered with a wet coverlid, they had dragged out of the snow. Wet & cold they slept little, as might be supposed. They found it very difficult travelling going out, and worse returning. They were wet, fatigued and hungry. Broiled venison and made a hearty meal, rested themselves, & proceeded. At their camp below, they told me, they gave Henly 3 deer, for some service, and to sell for them; he sold all of it to some hungry emigrants, lower down, at 50¢ pr. lb. A few minutes before this party came up, I was astonished by the appearance, at camp, of 2 oxen, and was confident they were portion of a team Willis was bringing out for us; but they belonged to the Roberts, and had wandered up, looking for something to feed on. I cut up 2 pack-saddle pads, and a couple of horse-collars, and gave them the straw. Roberts had driven them down into the grass vale of Mill Creek, and nothing but fear of bears or wolves, could have induced them to leave a green valley, and toil up the steep ascent, in snow. Young Roberts said he would, in the morning drive them down again.

The snow, on a level, to-day is about 6 inches.

Made me a comfortable jacket of 2 old coats.

[DEC.] 13th Commences drizzly. Strong wind S.S.E. Temp. 32° All the forenoon drizzle and hail, with some snow. Wind the same, Temp. Merd. 33°

Afternoon same weather —

Sun Set cloudy, strong variable wind, Temp 32° (Although the thermometer indicates freezing temperature all day, except about 2 hours at meridian, it has thawed considerable, and the snow is quite wet.)

The smoke in our lodge is very annoying, my friend's eyes suffer much. None of the Roberts came to see to their oxen, and the poor things are hanging around the camp, freezing and starving, and we have nothing to give them. Regarding these people as clever neighbors I could do nothing to their prejudic, or to offend them; but really I think the meat of their oxen would be better appropriated for our benefit, than left, as they will be, for the benefit of grizzlers and wolves. — Who will assuredly nab them to-night. Our forage, for several days, has been boiled beef bones & tea — inducing constipation, thirst, and diuretic effects. A dose of rhubarb I found very beneficial. At supper we eat our last piece of venison. Repacked my collection of minerals and seed, I had collected on the route, hoping soon to get them in. Poyle thinks of hunting for deer to-morrow, for unless Willis returns in a few days, we will be in a *snap*. We give the child the largest share of food. Drizzling & hard rain, alternately, all night.

[DEC.] 14th Commences with fine sleet, and strong wind from the S.E. Temp. 30° Drizzles & snow all forenoon, Merdn snow, wind N. moderate, Temp. 32°

Sun Set flying clouds, strong N. wind, Temp 31°

After breakfast Poyle took my carbine, and a handful of cartridges, and started for a hunt, and will visit Roberts' camp, — 3 miles below. If unsuccessful in hunting, he may obtain some venison, or at least a gill of rice or flour, to put in soup, which we can make of beef liquor and bones. Roberts oxen are gone, doubtless devoured by this time. P. returned late in the afternoon, totally unsuccessful; and reports the Roberts folks have but 2 day's rations of venison, and out of bread-stuffs. The storm has driven the deer down the hills quite low. I found in a wagon a tin cannister containing about 1 quart of mustard or kale seed; and by beating an old flour-sack, obtained about $\frac{1}{2}$ pint of flour; with some extraneous matter, but could not afford to attempt separating it. We preserved the liquor in which venison and beef was boiled, so we had a chance for soup. Put about 2 galls. of the liquor in a camp-kettle, $1\frac{1}{2}$ gill of seed, and the flour, added pepper and salt, and produced delightful soup, and a hearty meal. I was attacked, shortly after supper, with excessive drowsiness, and weight or distension of the stomach and abdomen, which annoyed me for several hours. We are compelled to limit ourselves now, to 2 meals pr day, of the soup. If Willis has started out, he is most probably in difficulty on the road, and if he has not, he will have to remain for a more favorable spell of weather. Poyle and myself are speculating on the prospect before us, and of the ways and means to extricate ourselves. He could get in, but will not abandon me; I suggested the idea of his going in, and thereby be certain of succoring us, and releving the child & myself: but he observes that I am feeble, (with rheumatism) might have a very severe attack, and besides the indians in the gulch below, might visit me,[38] or a starved grizzler, or pack of wolves, might make a demonstration on me, — and fully regarding, the *five points of fellowship*, is resolved to share my fortune or fate. Snow all night.

[DEC.] 15th   Commences cloudy, light variable wind, Temp. 19°

Merd^n cloudy, moderate wind, W. Temp. 24°   Sun Set cloudy, strong wind from S.E. Temp. 20°

Made our breakfast of soup, which to-day is not so good, but it is 'Hobson's choice.' — we peppered it well, and had good coffee. The soup had the same effect on me to-day as it had yesterday, and with loss of strength. At dinner time (about Sun Set) Poyle over hauled the small store of smoked beef, found it all internally putrid; only an exterior of about $\frac{1}{4}$ inch thick, was sound, and that bitter with pyroliginous acid. After trimming it, find we have about 3 days very small rations, of 2 meals pr day.

After breakfast he took a musket & some cartridges, and went out hoping to shoot something, but about 3 P.M. he returned tired & luckless. The snow has obliterated all trace of the road, and so deep in hollows and in the forrests, as to change entirely the appearance of the country. The poor little child is failing, he is pale & weak, with sunken eyes, for want of bread and proper food. We shorten our rations in order to sustain him, as long as possible; as we can endure sufferings that so young a child should not feel, if possible to prevent it. We go to bed often, very hungry, when the child has a piece of meat laying by him, after eating hearty. He does not suffer from cold, except occasionally complaining of his toes, when he is immediately relieved. Poyle saw no living thing to-day, in his short excursion but ravens, and they were too cunning for him to shoot.

I found, under some rags, about $\frac{1}{2}$ lb. salt beef; we boiled and divided it. P. cut down a small pine & chopped logs for fuel. My mind is disturbed much with anxiety, about home, and apprehensions of unprincipled wretches writing there erroneous statements, as I know there are such wretches, who would seize with avidity the opportunity to take advantage of my present circumstances, to produce and unfavorable impression on those who did not know me, & to annoy my family, — I of course allude to some of the indifferent men we unfortunately had in the company I commanded. We drank tea, and went supperless to bed. We know where a red ox of Roberts died, about 12 days since, from exhaustion; ¼ mile beyond us, on the side of a hill. — Every night there has been frost since its death, and it is as safe as in a ref[r]igerator, if the wolves and bears have not found it. If we were located quite low down, near the Sacramento Valley, where we could be supplied with game, — deer, antelope, bear, &c we would be in a better situation really, than the emigrants in the upper part of the valley. But it is impossible to get down now. Willis has collected a large amount of good carpenter's tools, I gave him most of them, as they were left by the emigrants, or I found them in wagons — left & turned over to me. He is a carpenter, and these are important & valuable to him, and as he was known to have gone with Petrie, after cattle supposed to have been stolen, he will surely come out soon unless taken sick. I know that his animal propensities are strong, but I cannot think that he could abandon us, to what would appear to him, a certain fate, — for me at least. — I & the child are doomed, perhaps, if a very severe spell ensues, and as my friend Poyle is yet quite strong, there is much more chance for him. But W. must surely entertain a spark of gratitude towards me — I have protected him in the Company, and I have every way been his friend, and he appeared quite attached to me — or why did he volunteer to remain here with me? Unless ill, he will assuredly come out soon![39] Willis has been 12 days gone, and Lassen and Davis have been gone 9 days from their abode to Sacramento City: — they were to be absent from 15 to 20 days; and in the event of wagon travel being impracticable, they are to pack their supplies up, from thence and leave the wagons behind. So let it be as it may, we have 2 or 3 weeks before us, to sustain life by our wits, and Poyle and I are too philosophical to give up and die easily. Still the chance for us is very slender, in spite of our philosophy. I have a very severe cold, and inflamation in the eyes, particularly the right one, as well as the side of my face. Last night I applied tea-leaves to my eyes, which gave considerable relief. Heard trees fall at night.

[DEC.] 16th   Commences with a snow-storm; Wind S.E. Temp. 18° The gale has drifted the snow very deep in places. Merd. Gale abated some, wind veering to the westward, Still snowing, however, Temp. 20° Sun Set fine Snow & gales veering from S. to W. Temp, 20°

About 9 A.M. P. found some scraps of salt beef, and a small piece of dry beef, which he chopped up; then scraped & beat the dust & scales of flour out of 3 old sacks, which we stewed together, and had a good breakfast. We are rapidly approaching a crisis, when the last alternative, our dernier resort, will be, to find one of the ox carcasses, to subsist on. The green pine logs smoked so last night, that our lodge was full of dense acrid vapor, so that near midnight I awoke strangling & blind, and arose, gasping for breath, & thrust my head out of the aperture we used as a door, (covered usually at night by a flap of canvass) to get pure air. I staggered like a drunken man, and it was a convulsive effort that saved me. P. was nearly blinded, but the smoke did not settle so much in the opposite end of the lodge, where he slept. I had to keep my head some time exposed to the snow storm, for I was in a tremor, very weak, eyes inflamed & painful, and a severe headache. When I had recovered, my head & shoulders were full of snow. We had to roll the logs apart, and suffer our fire to go out. I then laid down, anticipating smothering asleep, and obtained the most miserable sort of broken slumber. — *Rather interesting!* I had to change my sleeping position, exposing my head to drip, for the balance of the night.

This morning Poyle procured the hounds & tongue of a wagon, which we cut up, and made a good fire, though some annoyance still, from the pine logs. Eyes to-day are very painful. Have to wash them frequently, & wet my head. Dinner to-day, a few ounces of dry, horney, and bitter salt beef. Our lodge, particularly the tent apartments, are much collapsed by the weight of snow. If it is increased, I do not know what we will do. Our lodge is thus, centre, a conical pole-lodge, covered with cotton wagon-sheets, in which is our fire. This connects a large and small tent. I sleep in the E. end, or large tent, in which is our table, and Poyle sleeps in the other end, — the small tent.

We are much concerned about the boy; he is pale, complains of pains, very weak, and bled at the nose & ears last night. We have continued to give him the larger share of the food, such as it is, and he eats with a good appetite. But he wants

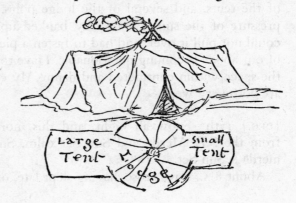

better food, bread, and exercise. He seems to be indolent, it may be weakness, and I am compelled to take him by the arms & walk him, rapidley to-and-fro, through our lodge, for exercise. Willis, nor any body else can get out to us now, unless on snow-shoes, and there are places on the road where they would be of no service. Old Crockett said, "It's an ill wind that blows no where," — so with the snow, for us, in one respect, — indians and beast cannot make much *headway* in it, to molest us. However, we have quite an armory here, some fourteen guns and pistols, all in order and charged; and any amount of ammunition.

The pine tree that P. cut down yesterday, is covered with snow now, excepting some small branches. The obtaining fuel, is now another difficulty. P. cannot go out far, without snow-shoes, (which we'll have to make)[40] then the tree is difficult to cut up, and transport; for most of the dry trees, & oaks near us, have been used up by the emigrants and all the fallen & loose stuff, of which there is abundance, is buried beneath the deep snow; and the wagons near us, are full of iron, and would be rapidly consumed; in fact are only fit for kindling, for which they must be reserved. We know, pretty near where carcasses of oxen & mules lay, and must soon refer to those larders.

After breakfast, a violent headache drove me to bed, where I had disturbed sleep, till called by my sincere & kind friend, Poyle, to eat my dinner allowance of the horney beef, & coffee.

Poyle cut down an adjacent oak tree, it was pretty large, and he cut up the limbs & branches, which we carried into the lodge to serve for the balance of the day and night: and we had a good fire. The scores were admirable for heat & light, when they became dry.

Night strong & heavy gusts of wind, veering from the S.W. to N.W. Heavy avalanches falling on our devoted habitation, the ridge and tent-poles of the tents, and several of the lodge poles, buckling & cracking, with the pressure of the snow; door way banked up, (the cover frozen so that we could not pull it over, and had to fasten a piece of cotton outside) Stability of our abode becoming questionable. Have to put up shores to sustain it. And the space within contracted and damp. My eyes still inflamed & painful. We are both very weak.

[DEC.] 17th Snow all night, and this morning the same, wind moderate from the S.E. Merdn and Sun Set calm. Snow all day, Temp. — Sun-rise, merdn & Sun-Set, — 28°, 32° 30°

About 8 A.M. we arose, having slept late, on account of loosing rest during the night, from smoke, drip, and noise of the elements, and we had just stirred up the fire, when a cracking noise drew our attention to the tent-poles, 2 of them buckled & broke with a considerable report, and we jump'd to them quickly & applied temporary supports against the immense pressure. All the other poles were much bent, & continually cracking. Times getting tighter every day. We took shovels, and dug our way out, to the wagons, which were within 8 feet of the lodge; he beat the snow down with shovels, to make a path. The snow was at least 4 feet deep here, where it could not drift. We cleared out 2 wagons which were so close together that a man could just walk between them. We then got our bedding out of the lodge, together with some arms, ammunition matches, &c. and put them in the two wagons. These being secured, we returned to the lodge, and piled up boxes & kegs, and with gun-barrels, spades, &c. so propped up the 2 tents, &c. that they could not settle down lower. Wood all buried, so we had a small fire, in a reduced space, all wet, and confusion. We boiled some pieces of beef, made coffee, and about 9 A.M. breakfasted Now we cannot enjoy a good comfortable fire; nor sit at our table, as the sides of the tent are pressed in on it. This is a great deprivation to me, about writing. Dinner at Sun-Set, same as the breakfast, and under the same cheerless circumstances. I fear my sight is seriously affected. O[u]r rations are shorter, and the child looks very haggard.

Poyle and I slept in the wagon, with the child at our feet. I took care to cover him in such a manner that he could not get uncovered during the night. I put a couple of rifles under the wagon-bows as standards, to support them against the snow.

All night it was dead calm, with very fine snow falling, temperature 30°

I am troubled with fever, and heat through my stomach and bowels, particularly about the navel. Slept badly, my mind much disturbed.

[DEC.] 18th Commences hazy & calm, temp 30° Forenoon & merd^n same, with occasional Sun Shine, Merd^n Temp 32° Sun Set clear, light wind N. Temp 28° Breakfast as yesterday We now prepare to get the dead oxen — "Nesesitas non habit legem." Making a sledge, and a pair of snow-shoes apiece. Poyle frames the shoes from wagon-bows, and I am to cover them, with canvass.

My eyes are a little better this morning.

Cut up a wagon to-day, selecting material for the sled & the remainder for kindling. Our dry beef will last, as we have been using it for several days, 2 days longer; but we are growing very weak on such insufficient and innutritious fare. By that time we will be ready to hunt for Robert's ox, and if unsuccessful in that search, we know certainly the exact spot of one, near a tall stump, and close to our lodge. I recollect very well of my complaining to Poyle, one day, that it was rather too odoriferous when the wind blew the scent towards us. By dusk we have nearly completed one pair of snow shoes, and framed another pair. Kept a small chip-fire all day.— More comfortable to-day, somehow, than I have felt for several days previous. — drink my coffee, and smoke my pipe, with considerable relish. — The meat lays very heavy on my stomach — is very indigestable, owing to the salt & pyroliginous acid, I presume. It also affected me with a sensation of great fullness, as though I had eat a very hearty meal, when it could [not] be much over 4 oz. If the wolves would come near we might nab one of them.

As the boy cried much during last night, and we had not sufficient space in the wagon, &c. I made a very comfortable bed for him in the next wagon. He sat all day in the lodge, by the fire, with things to play with, and to-night I wrapped him up in a coverlid, and carried him to the wagon, and there secured him comfortably, so that he could not get uncovered; and then fixed the wagon that if a bear or wolf should come along, and attempt to get in, it would awake me. (I always was very easy to awake — the slightest noise would at any time awaken me) A clear night, with light airs from the N.W. The boy cried nearly all night, and I slept none in consequence.

Another singular affection annoyed me to-night. — extraordinary iritability of the skin, as if covered with innumerable minute insects. Internal heat, and acrid taste; small scratches on my hands, healed over, and apparently well, as painful as bad sores; and on raising my knees, in bed, was astonished at the very strong and chorded pulsation of the artery over my knee, (the —) It was as strong as if a man was pressing his two hands on my knee, with force. — was quite annoying.

[DEC.] 19th Commences cloudy, wind moderate and variable, Temp. 28°

The disagreeable sensations I have lately experienced and am now laboring under, are symptoms of the putrid or malignant typhus fever, if I am not mistaken. — I mentioned this to my friend, and he concurs with me, and we conclude to use plenty of strong coffee, thinking it may be serviceable. We are careful to keep ourselves clean, frequently washing with warm water & soap, and change our clothing as regular as circumstances will permit. Willis has a puppy, a bull-terrier bitch, about 3 mos. old, born in these mountains, and which I have christened "Nevada". We have refrained from eating her, on her Master's account. As we all, and he, particularly, prizes her, and besides she is, of course, very thin, these considerations have so long saved her from making us a meal; but an extremity has come, and we are considering about killing & cooking her. — Poyle thinks if baked, with a tallow candle, she will make us a good dinner, and no more. — She has just recovered from a spell of distemper, so we will wait awhile, hoping we may save her, as her watchfulness is of great service. We support her by soaking & boiling old deer legs & hoofs, and an occasional bit of our very limited allowance. She sits by the fire and whines when we are eating, poor thing! But if we can all weather this spell out, and her master get here with succor, we will all get a good meal, and he will be rejoiced to see his poor little Nevada again.

We completed the snow-shoes, and late in the afternoon I tested mine. After a little practice under Poyle's direction, I soon got the hang of them, and could get along very well. Poyle has used them in Canada & the North part of Michigan. We procured some fuel, and corrected the straps on our snow-shoes. The wagons appeared to be high masses of snow. With axes we knocked a wagon bed of one of my old company wagon to pieces. My old comrade across the Continent, No 12, had now to contribute towards warming me; How could I have entertained such an idea, when, all hands full of glee, put in on board the Steamer Robert Fulton at Pittsburgh! We went over to the old camp of the *Shingle men*, and there obtained an ox-yoke, which I found standing against a wagon. I kept my eye on a very tall dead pine which was cracking in the gale, and fragments of his decayed limbs were being hurled to the ground by the breeze. The yoke was heavy, and I was weak, and found it quite a job to get 300 yds with it, on such unusual pedestals. — So we have a small store of dry fuel again. We could not afford to eat but one meal to-day, reserving one for to-morrow. Poyle covered one of his snow-shoes before dusk, and will complete the other to-night.

Gales and snow from about 8 A.M. and through the day, increasing in the evening, and at night strong gusts, from the S.W. veering around to the N.W. Temp. 32°

Found some medicine, and took 2 of Chapman's Antibillious Pills, and drank 2 cups of tea.

Our lodge is a complete wreck, the snow drifts in much through the N. side, and the opening at top. We have barely space to turn around in it, and do our little work. If we live to see the morning, we will have to dig our way in as we have to do at night, to get out. We have a few spermacetti and tallow candles: they are very useful, and we do not wish to eat them if we can help it. The dog eat a piece of common yellow soap to-day. Soon after dark, in order to economise fuel, we prepared to go to bed. — The yoke had been laid on the fire, and was burnt some, this we laid down flat, scraped the coales close to it, and covered them up with embers & ashes. Put a board over to keep the snow from putting it out, and another one at the side, to keep off the wind. Lit a lantern, put the boy in his wagon & secured him but, as usual, he cried much and late in the night. On going into our bed-chamber (wagon) the bedding was white with drift snow. We stood outside, at the back of the wagon, (snow level with the bed) took off our gum coats and laid them on the tail-board, then sat on them, and took off our leggings, (legs of old cloth pants, tied at the knee) and shoes, which we deposited in the corners, under our heads, shook the snow off as well as we could, got under cover, closed all the crevices we could with clothes, and hung the lantern up to a hook above. Poyle lay some time reading "De Toqueville's Democracy of America", while I wrote up my notes. Wind blowing in variable flaws, generally N.W. Our best repose was towards day-light.

[DEC.] 20th   Commences drizzly, wind light S. Rain & S. gales all day, & thawing much. (*Sun Set fly. clouds wind light & variable, Temp. 34°*)   I slept last night better than for several nights previous, and my comrade slept soundly. It thaws this morning. Found, among some medicines, a quantity of Snake-root, and we made tea of it for breakfast.[41] We have been in the habit, since we were first compelled to eat the tainted meat, to take a few drops of spirits of camphor after each meal, as a preventive of bad effects. Blood very hot in my veins, and head feels bad.

  We had to dig steps down into our lodge, this morning, through the snow. The interior looks like a damp cavern, or hermitage, abandoned by the poor anchorite who once inhabited it, but driven off by winter. The centre is an irregular circle, of about 8 ft. diam. — 3 ft. of the centre being occupied by the fire. A number of buckets & camp-kettles setting around, to catch the drip. After breakfast, of the last morsal, of *tainted* meat, I felt the usual effects, — a strange taste in the throat, and sensation of fullness, &c. Late in the afternoon P. completed his snow-shoes. and we went off to look for Roberts' old ox. — We proceeded about 400 yds, to near where we saw it dying: and searched around, probing in the snow, in a circuit of 100 yds. in vain. The soft snow yielded to our weight, and clogged the snow-shoes in such a manner as to fatigue us greatly, reduced as we were by hunger. The gales and weight of snow had prostrated numerous trees, broken down limbs, & branches, then covered all this with 4 feet of snow, and all we could distinguish around, was an irregular surface of snow, amidst the dark forrest. As the wind blew strong it was no small jeopardy to travel under, or near tall decayed trees, as they might fall, and large limbs, and heavy avalanches were continually falling. In fact one of the heavy pine cones, from 10 to 15 inches long, hurled down from a height of 200 feet, is no fool of a missile.[42] I have seen [a] piece of a dry pine limb, several feet long, and 3 or 4 ins. diameter, blown down, and striking into the ground a foot, and required force to draw it out. About Sun Set we reached our winter grot, very fatigued, and disappointed, as we know now, that only the dernier resort can save us. We found an ox yoke against a tree, and with that & some dry branches we had shouldered, we got up a good fire; by which we sat, drying, warming & resting ourselves, and chewing the cud of disappointment.

The snow had so changed the face of the country, and obliterated marks, that we found it impossible to hit on the exact locale of anything seen before the snow. We broke off some more wagon stuff, for kindling. We have nothing to eat to-morrow, but have reserved a piece of beef, about 4 oz: for the child. We think he has not suffered yet the pangs of hunger, but we have; and our rapidly depreciating strength warns us to make some extraordinary exertion to-morrow I boiled up some pieces of deer-skin, to feed Nevada upon. When we retired to our wagon-chamber, found the bedding quite damp, but an india-rubber blanket had been cautiously spread over all, or we would have been in another dilemma. — Hollows in it were full of water.

Fine rain & thaw all night, with a strong breeze from the S. Temp. 34°

Dropping of water occasionally, in our faces, during the night, was a little annoying.

I suppose that the thermometer is influenced by the height — elevation of our mountain-top, as a Barometer is, and hence it indicates a lower temperature than actually exists. (Willis absent 16 days)

[DEC.] 21st Commences with rain, and a strong S. wind. Temp. 34° Thawing rapidly, thank God! Snow soft, & has subsided several inches. I shot a raven for dinner; by hoky! another dinner! Our tramp yesterday put Poyle's snow-shoes out of kelter, and he is repairing them. I was again in luck; found about 6 oz: of smoked beef, which had fallen, behind a chest: this gives us breakfast, with coffee. "*Nil desperandum*"!

Divided the beef after boiling it; and with about a quart of hot strong Coffee, and our pipes, felt as though there was a chance yet for us. The weather of the morning was carried through the forenoon; Temp. 46°

Friend P. was thwo-thirds [two-thirds] of the day engaged on his snow-shoes. We think the snake-root tea is good for us. Found 18 small white beans (some one intended we suppose, for seed,) divided and eat them; the child cried for more; we then regretted we had not given him all. Afternoon misty, drizzly, & thawing, wind S. and light, during afternoon. Snow gradually subsiding. When P. finished his shoes, we had to go for fuel, occupying us till after Sun Set. We then built up our fire, stowed the fuel we had chopped up, and parboiled the raven, to cook for breakfast to-morrow.

Sun Set cloudy, strong wind S. Temp. 44° Kept the boy in the wagon all day, as the lodge is too damp and cold. — He is quite comfortable there. He cried much to get out, but I would not permit it. If we do not to-morrow find an ox, the poor puppy will have to go for one meal around. We sit up as late as we consistently can, conversing & smoking, to insure us the sounder sleep when we turn in: as watchfullness is one of the symptoms affecting us, besides the child cries regularly now, at least half of the night; what for we cannot divine.

[DEC.] 22nd Commences misty, light wind S. Temp. 46° We cooked and divided our raven, and with coffee, breakfasted. Our breakfast was a slim one. Lost ½ day vainly searching for an ox, and returned to our abode fatigued much. No wonder we are weak, when one day's rations for a man, as allowed in Service, is more than Poyle and myself have eat for a week. I found, under the sides of our lodge, a few leg-bones of deer, we had put there about 8 weeks since, to obtain oil from, for our arms [guns]. We roasted three of these shank-bones on the fire, and when they had obtained a *Boston brown*, chopped off the burnt muscle, &c. and cracked the bone and took out the marrow, of one, for the boy. P. & myself consumed what we could of the others, though we swallowed more carbon & burnt hairs, than nutritious matter: — This with coffee had to serve for dinner; are are very loath to kill Willis' dog.

Merd. flying clouds & calm, Temp. 48°

After *dinner*, we went to search for the ox carcase, within 50 yds of the lodge, which 6 weeks ago I had complained of, as odorifererous. We found one of our mark[s], a tall stump, the top of it forming a slight knoll of snow.— beside it lay the ox, ascertain'd by probing the snow with an iron rod. We dug away the snow, and soon exposed him; then P. descended into the hole, and with an axe, cut off the fore leg, at knee-joint: then cut around the fore-shoulder with his butcher-knife, and I held it up while he, with great difficulty disjointed it. We tied a rope to it, and dragged it to our lodge. Then secured a supply of fuel, and by the time we had put it away, it was dusk. We cut up about ¼ peck of the meat, in small pieces, boiled them nearly done, in salt water, then put the meat in an oven, added water, pepper, salt, and a handfull of moss from an oak; stewed nearly dry, and with coffee, once more filled our stomachs. The boy eat like a young wolf. This meat, when raw, was of a light lead color, blotched with reddish spots. We could detect no unpleasant taste, — if any taste at all. — The condiments were all the flavor we could determine. I[t] was very juicy, and as diuretic as water-melon-seed. Felt very full, (as we really were) and languid, after eating. We have now a larder, and must watch it, or the grizzlers and wolves will despoil us.

Sun Set clear, light wind S.W. Clear, Temp. 46°

I attempted to smoke my pipe before supper, but suddenly became very weak & giddy, and Poyle said, very pale. — After supper I smoked without inconvenience.

Soon after dark, and for some time in the night, cloudy, mistey & drizzly, with thaw. Had a sound night's repose, and our health extraordinary under such circumstances.

[DEC.] 23rd   Commences hazy, light airs from the S.W. Temp. 44°

We again have had a hearty meal of *ancient fresh* beef & with good strong hot coffee. After which we enjoyed our pipes, and a long chat, and consoling ourselves with the argument, that there are thousands in the world worse off than we are. We hear small birds singing quite merrily.

We, early this morning, took advantage of the good weather, shovelled away some of the snow from around and on our flimsy habitation, stretched the canvass tighter, put strong standards under the tents, and cleared away the pile of things we were compelled so hastily to prop them with. After which we had a general ablution, smoked our pipes & rested awhile.

Merd^n clear, very light S.W. breeze. Temp. 55°

Woodpeckers flying about, — chirping and crying, and "tapping the old trees. — Their boring often sounds like a woodman chopping wood. To-day I am very weak and nervous, with rheumatism in legs, but otherwise well. We have not desponded, nor will we, to the last, although we're *in a bad snap*. The spells of good & bad weather here seem to be pretty regular; — about semi-monthly alternations. Walked around some, for exercise, the snow, on a level, is about 3 feet deep, and very soft. I walked 100 yds. for a pole, sticking in the ground, and on reaching it was very weak, and worried myself in futile attempts to pull it up.

The wind had scattered about profusely dry branches of trees, and I gathered as many as I could shoulder, and took to the lodge. — I filled up our big coffee pot, sat it on the coals, and sank back against a box, perfectly exhausted.

P. busy clearing away snow, and we opend the lodge on either side for a ventilation, and sunning. — Done same to the wagons. Most of the wagon tops here are crushed down flat, the bows broken by the weight of snow on them. One has a large limb of a tree on it. It was well I thought of shoring up ours with rifles, as I did. Many tall trees were so bowed down with the weight of snow, that it will be some time ere they can recover their perpendicularity.

This afternoon I am afflicted with a severe pain in left breast. — This pain I have been subject to occasionally, and slightly, for several years; and I think it is rheumatism of the muscular portions of the heart. As they must have had several days fine weather in the Sacramento valley, and the lower spurs of the mountains are by this time divested of snow, it is strange there has been no attempt to reach us. Roberts' folks, also, are aware of our destitution, but I presume they have nothing to spare, and 3 miles travel up-hill in tolerable deep snow, (probably deep in hollows) would not pay to save us. The least depth of snow here has been 3 feet; and in some places, around, 6 feet. — It would likely average 4 feet. About 2 P.M. we dined heartily on broiled beef, with *mustard.* (found a small canister) pepper, and salt. I felt better after dinner. Clear & beautiful afternoon — thaw going on bravely. Sun Set clear, light wind W. — Temp. 48°

To night we can sit back in our abode, smoke, converse, and enjoy a fine fire of split oak logs and scores.

About 7 P.M. we had supper — broiled beef & coffee.[43] A beautiful & serene night. One evil we had to contend with, while the bad weather endured, was want of sufficient exercise.

We are exceedingly fortunate in having plenty of good coffee, condiments, &c. Bedding and clothing in abundance, arms and ammunition, matches, some spermacetti and tallow candles, a couple of good lanterns, 2 iron candlesticks, in fact we only needed provissions, a more secure protection from the weather, and fuel more convenient to get, in severe weather, and we would have laughed at the elements, &c. "and say, let the storm come down." We will get in a supply of our *preserved* beef.

A fine night & sound repose.

[DEC.] 24th   Commences clear, very light wind W. Temp. 40°

Another fine morning. About 9 A.M. looking out to the N.W. among the pines, saw 2 large grey squirrels run up a tree,[44] about 300 yds. off; jerked up my double-barrel, and went there, and soon brought a very large male squirrel down, his mate hid, — I did not see her after the first sight. — So we have a Christmas dinner sent us, by "that sweet little angle that sits up aloft, and looks out for life of poor Jack."

Poyle completed all repairs and improvements to-day.

Merd^n same weather, Temp. 60°

Exhausted by wading in the snow for the squirrel, with difficulty returned to camp; where I drank a pot of hot coffee, and threw myself down, for 15 minutes, drying my feet, and felt better.

A Dr. Caldwell left a wagon here, full of effects, trunks, &c. The cover of the wagon was tied down close, and buttoned together at both ends. This wagon had been often molested, at night, by unprincipled stragglers, and probably some *neighbors*, — when other folks were here; and I noticed that the contents had been reduced. Some time before the emigrants had all gone, I examined it, and found 2 trunks broken open. In one I found a considerable lot of very old cigars, maybe 1000. Some bedding, clothing, papers, saddles, &c. &c. and among some rubbish a small box, containing a fine gold chain and a large gold seal, with a topaz stone, cut with the initials A. M^{c}L. and as there were papers, &c. directed to Dr Allen McLane,[45] of St. Louis, I judge that these were some of his effects, and that Dr Caldwell was his comrade, and attended him in his last illness, if he was the person buried. and record of it on the [twelfth of October, 1849]

It was well I removed these effects, or pillagers and the weather would have used them up. The valuables, papers, &c. I put up in a package to give, if I get in, to Dr C. or dispose of them in such a manner as the relatives may obtain them. Coarse articles left in the wagon are spoiled, and the top is crushed flat.

The large trunk left by Mr Goodrich, had been pillaged by a squad I allowed to sleep in the wagons, but I found, among some children's clothing, an old silver Lepine watch, a draught on a gentleman in S^n Francisco, for $100, and a money-belt. Mr Goodrich had forgotten the draught no doubt; and the pillagers did not find that nor the watch, in the dark. These and several other articles, I put up also in a package, and marked, hoping some day or other to turn them over to their owner. The Vestal wagon was so repeatedly robbed, that little of consequence remained in it, but just before the snow set in, I packed all the contents close, and now a large branch of a tree by it, and snow together, have crush'd the top down flat. I have many articles, particularly papers belonging to people, that may be of service to them, if I can ever get them in. Many of these effects were left in my charge, for only 8 or 10 days, — to be sent for: and as they and I remained on the ground, I could not do less than take all the care of them in my power.

After dinner I walked about 400 yards, to find an ox carcass, of more recent date than the one we lately exhumed. I probed around in the snow, and found a red ox, and exhausted with the exertion, returned. — The weather looks unsettled again. — We must provide food while we have the chance to do so. — Unless we do so, such another storm as we recently experienced will consign us to the wolves. We had to procure fuel when I recovered sufficiently to walk.

Sun Set flyg clouds, wind moderate from the W. Temp. 48° At dusk we endeavored in vain, to turn the old ox, in the snow-pit, and though we chopped the neck through, we had not strength to turn him. So with my knife, I cut a camp-kettle full of bits & strips from the neck and along the vertebrae — sufficient for supper & breakfast. Soon after dark it cleared away, wind same, temperature milder.

Supped hearty and slept tolerably well. Boiled a kettle of meat at night.

[DEC.] 25th (*Christmas day*) Commences hazy & calm, Temp. 49°
21 days since the departure of Willis. Well, here's a Christmas for us, under *werry* peculiar circumstances. It is not [worth] while to recapitulate them. Poyle is an admirable cook, all he lacks is the *materiale*. But we should fare somewhat *luxuriantly* to-day, and he is trying to get up an *extra* breakfast. — He chopped up the fragments of the old ox, most of it integuments from the neck & shoulder; put it in a bake-kettle with water to stew slowly; adding the squirrel, cut up. (We had stewed it already, from dusk till midnight, last night) We now added 3 deer leg bones, cracked, — for the marrow, a gill of mustard-seed, pepper, & salt. Also some *dead* ginger we found. Stewed all about $1\frac{1}{2}$ hrs. made plenty of strong coffee, & had a noble breakfast. — We enjoyed this meal much. — Are there not persons, who to-day, who do not enjoy their breakfast, (surrounded by plenty and every comfort) as we do? At 9 A.M. old Sol shone out, and it continued clear, with light Wy airs, Temp. 49°

Our appetite for salt is great, — we use at least quadruple the portion we have been accustomed to under ordinary circumstances. We even use two teaspoonsfull to our pint of coffee. The red ox carcass I found yesterday is not the right one: P. says the one alluded to, is a black one, and lays close to the other. He went out, probed in the snow, and found it. So in the afternoon we cleared off the snow, and got a hind quarter. The meat looks more natural than that we have used, — is redder. — Roasted a piece and gave to the child. (Strange, this ox was one belonging to Lambkin) He said it was lost, but it actually fell and died with cold & hunger, from his neglect, when he first came up on this camp-ground. We put a large piece in the bake-kettle, and cut up a quantity to stew for breakfast. At $7\frac{1}{2}$ P.M. we dined on the baked meat; it was tender enough, but tasteless, & unnutricious.

Dined heartily, and with more satisfaction than many in better circumstances. After dinner we smoked our pipes, and speculated on the affairs of the world, our future prospects, discussed ancient history, policy of England; and lastly, enquired of each other and explained, how our friends at home were now enjoying themselves. — I spoke of merriment, mince-pies, egg-nogg, turkey, &c. and he, of roast surloin, plum-pudding, punch, ale, &c. We made some other improvements to-day, and one was the re-establishing our table, on which we dined. We cut up some running-geer of a wagon, and had a lively fire. "Well," says friend Poyle, "Cap, we are both philosophers, and may we not have some sort of a Christmas here?" "Yes," I replied, "but how?" — "Why," rejoined he "we can each sing a song, and tell a story; and then take a pot of coffee, and call it ale, egg-nogg, or what you please." — " 'Nough said," — and at it we went; — each sang 2 or 3 songs, and related several anecdotes, then smoked our pipes again, and thus enjoyed ourselves.

The child is doing well, and we can probably keep our pup, & let his master redeem him.

There seems to be a reaction to-day, in my system; better feelings, and strength increased; and mind more at ease. Probably the suggestion that succor may reach us in 48 hours, may have some influence on the mind. The snow has been several days rapidly subsiding; there are many bare spots, where the sun has had full influence, and the snow originally not so deep. Poyle is an excellent fellow every and any way. — Is an excellent Butcher, baker, & hewer of wood; robust, strong mind, energetic and obliging, & to sum up, he is a *true Brother*.

Our nightly visitors are about to night, — we have not seen them yet, but I think they are they lynxes, catamounts, or panthers. We apprehend they will interfere with our black ox larder. Beautiful night, temp. 41°. We ate too heartily, sat up too late, and the child cried a great deal, so that our sleep was much disturbed. Near day a slight drizzle of rain.

It is astonishing what immense quantities of this meat we can eat. 3 meals now, pr day, of not less than 3 or 4 lbs. each, besides a quart of coffee each — and occasionally a lunch during the day. We consume from 8 to 12 lbs of meat each, per day. — Hungry in an hour after eating, and find it very diuretic — (coffee we know is) Every day we cook a camp-kettle full, which contains more than a peck; and but few small pieces, if any remains for breakfast the next day.

[DEC.] 26th   Commences hazy with occasional drizzling rain, calm. Temp. 41°.

I arose early, and we breakfasted on Stew and coffee, with tolerable appetite. Pain in my left breast quite annoying before breakfast, but afterwards it subsided. My friend is afflicted with a severe cold, occasioned by going to bed last night, with wet feet: has a bad headache. We both feel too rusty and weak to exert our selves much to-day.

What can be the matter with Willis? He was aware of our limited provissions, for I called his attention to it, he knows that game has disappeared from these hills; aware that in a week after he left, a severe storm ensued, which could have no other effect on us than the most disastrious consequences; and he must think that if we have survived, the starvation we must have been subjected to, would render us too weak to attempt going in; and surely, humanity, if not friend ship would prompt him to take advantage of this favorable spell of weather. We cannot conjecture the cause of his delay.

Merd^n Same as commencement, Temp. 43°

I persuaded my friend to take a teaspoonful of camphor, and bathe his head with some, and lay down by the fire, and sleep; which he did, and it relieved him much. Hot coffee at Merd^n helped both of us, and I afterwards went out to procure a board, and on returning I was prostrated with weakness. —

We yesterday were busy all day, without food, then ate too heartily, and lost our repose. When one becomes debilitated for want of nourishment, every subsequent attack renders recuperation more difficult, and increases the requisite time. So that each spell is actually an increase of the original weakness, till nature has no sustaining power and the victim falls. —

Speculating on the effects of our food, I find it barely sustains life, but does not increase the streng[t]h because innutritious. So that nature is struggling with a false prop, which beyond a certain point will give way. And the food we are living on may have a tendancy to produce thyphus fever. My mind has been actively engaged meditating and conjecturing anxiously about the mysterious delay of succor. Still we are buoyed up with Hope, from day to day. Poyle and myself are too weak to walk far, and the absence of one would seriously jeopardize the life of the others, and risking his perishing on the road in a futile attempt to aid those he left behind. But if another violent and long storm comes over us soon, we are doomed; so we think that one or both had better try to-morrow to reach Roberts' camp, and there obtain a piece of venison or information, as some of them may have gone in, and returned. Or perhaps one of the 4 men there would go in for us, to Davis' rancho, and represent our critical situation, elicit immediate succor, and unravel the mystery about Willis.

Drizzles nearly all the forenoon, and till 3 P.M. when there was a smart shower. Dense fog in the adjacent valleys and gorges, and a rapid thaw going on. As regards work, (of which there is plenty to do,) [the day?] has been lost. No fuel laid in, nor additional meat procured, but we cannot help it. However, we trust that by retiring early and obtaining good repose, we will be much better enabled to-morrow to work.

The day closed with misty showers, tempt. 43°, and so continued through the night. We were so lucky as to find a vial of rancid olive-oil, which sprinkled on our broiled beef gave it quite a flavor. A wagon-wheel thrown on the fire, at night contributed to cheer us by the sacrifice of some good *fellows*, however. We crave some faranacious substance much, and fresh-meat, of any thing that walks, or moves, from an indian to a reptile, would be most acceptable.[46] I have shuddered at home at the accounts of the voraciousness and strong appetites of Russian soldiers, — eating train oil and tallow candles. — We would consider ourselves most fortunate to have a sufficient quantity of such rations on hand. We have already consumed several spermacetti candles, and 3 tallow candles, — fried with our beef, which I forgot to mention previously.

I was disgusted with the dirty broth of the Panak indian family, near F^t Hall, but now, it would be a very grateful morceau to us. We search about, in the snow and mud, for the deer-shanks we cast away 2 months since. — There's an old adage that "variety is the spice of life"; if so, we are now getting pretty well spiced.

The boy suffers for want of exercise; for it is only occasionally that we dare take him out of the wagon & put him in the lodge. He has as much of the food we have to live on, as he can eat, and he consumes as much as either of us. The exposure of carrying him to and fro in the wet would be pernicious; and in the contracted space in the lodge we have barely room to chop fuel, mend the fire, cook, &c. and when there he is constantly crying. And we never left him alone, for an hour, but on our return he was in some mischief, risking his life at the fire, or with gun-powder, &c. The poor little fellow has been so brutally treated by his father, and probably with a tincture of his father's composition, that he is exceedingly stubborn and artful. While we were present, he would feign perfect inability to stand or walk; and as previously mentioned, I have been compelled to take him under the arms, and run him across the lodge chamber, for exercise, when persuation, threats, &c. were inavailing to induce him even to stand: Yet finding things on the floor that we knew were out of his reach when we went out, we watched, to ascertain if he possibly could move about; and judge our astonishment, one day, to see him climb up in a chair, (we had several old rush bottom chairs, found in a wagon) get something down from a hanging shelf; and when he heard us, he ran quite sprightly, and seated himself by the fire! His abode, in the wagon, is the most comfortable one here; several blankets and coverlids under, and several others to cover him: and these aired and changed as often as we can. We give him plenty of meat, more than he can consume, coffee and water: And I frequently look in to see that he is as comfortable as circumstances permit.

It is strange, that when I had no idea of remaining here long, — expecting team, or a riding animal every day, that I should have put away and preserved my coffee and salt, instead of offering them to the travellers. The boiled coffee was always at their service.

[DEC.] 27th   Drizzly, misty, and calm, Temp. 43°
Merdn same Temp. 44°
Our breakfast to-day, is beef broiled with tallow candle basting. Our mid-day lunch, remains of the stew left from yesterday heated, with the remaining half of candle melted in it.

Hot coffee with one, and cold coffee with the other.

We were blest with good repose last night.

At about 4 P.M. while my friend was breaking up dead limbs for fuel, and I engaged tightening up the tents, judge my astonishment, to hear human voices, in the rear of our position, — in a N.E. direction. I was at first certain that a party of indians had arrived to give us our quietus; but was more astonished, on looking in the direction of the sound, to see 3 white men, on foot, with packs and rifles! I called my comrade. The strangers came up, weak and emaciated, and looked at me and around in a wild manner. The foremost one, a very tall fellow, wearing a soldiers great-coat, and having on his back a large pack or knapsack, and a long rifle in his hand, advanced, nodded his head to me, and faintly said "how do?" then threw off his pack and sat down, — with a deep sigh, on an adjacent wagon tongue. — The other two, nodded "how d'e do,' and also threw off packs, and sat down, panting with weakness and fatigue. Directly two others came along, and were lame, had to walk with staffs. — They acted like their comrades, and all appeared to be wild and lost. I asked where, in the name of Heaven, they were from? When the one who first came up, informed me. That his name was Elliot, and the grown lads with him, are his sons; they are Missourians. That he was engaged by the government as a teamster, from Fort Leavenworth to Fort Hall. He had sought that employment to obtain the means of completing the payment for his land in Missouri. — They could not send him back from Fort Hall, so the Quarter Master there advised him to go with a train, as teamster, to Oregon. He consented, and travelled ahead, of the train, with his sons, all mounted on mules, and where the Oregon and California roads fork, (near Goose Lake) he erroneously took the latter, and got too far on this route, to return and rejoin the train. He had quarrelled with the wagon-master. — While travelling in Pitt river valley, they fell in with a man named White, an Irishman,[47] and 2 Dutchmen — (White and the Irishman are the two who are here — follow'd Elliot) [.] And they all travelled together to Deer Valley. (These men are part of those who were reported to have determined on remaining all winter by the Alcohol càche at foot of the Pass). Here they had to leave the Dutchmen, being so badly frostbitten as to incapacitate them from travelling. They think that these, and 8 other Dutchment [Dutchmen], left at the Pass (alcohol càche) are undoubtedly dead, long ago.

Elliott says that they were paid up by the Qr. Master, armed, ammunitioned, and provissioned for 30 days, and mounted on good mules. When their rations were exhausted they eat their mules. That they have endured great hardships, feeding on carrion, ox-hide, moss, &c. — They found an ox skeleton, which the wolves had stripped of all the hide, except that on the forehead & face, which they cut off, broiled and eat. In deer-valley, he said that the snow was 8 feet deep, They made snow-shoes of ox-bows, covered with leather. Saw several indians; and in the basin of Little Goose Lake," (I judge from his description of the country, & distance) a party of indians tied a white horse and a couple of mules to trees, and concealed themselves within arrow reach, thinking that the whites would go up for the animals, and they would then shoot them. The decoy was perceived luckily. The indians caught fish in holes, in the margin of the lake.[48]

These men thought my establishment was the settlements, and were astonished when I informed them of its position, and my circumstances. They asked for provissions, and I referred them to my black ox larder, telling them that was my only food and depot. — "Such as I have, give I unto thee". — They immediately proceeded there, made a fire close by the carcass, and boiled a large quantity of the meat.

White recognized the child, had travelled with his father. Said Lambkin had abandoned him to perish. That the Elliotts and their comrade had plenty of gold coin, and he had a little. That he had been robbed 6 times. He seemed to be only about half sane.

Sun Set clear & calm, Temp. 44°

We were rather suspicious of these strange wild-looking men, and took all the precautions we could, in the event of any sinister attempt by them. At dusk White returned to our lodge, said the oldest son of Elliott struck him, and he was afraid of his life, with them, and wished to sleep by our fire. I told him we had no room, but I could fix him comfortably in a wagon. "Well," he said, "let me cook my supper here." I told him to go ahead. He held in his hand a very large and sharp Bowie-knife, took a seat near my left, and commenced mincing up a piece of the ox-meat, on a small piece of board, on his knee. He minced the meat very slowly, chopping it over and over, very fine, and ever and anon, looking askance at me from under his slouched hat, and feeling the edge of his large bloody blade. Now and then he'd pause, and barely cut at all, — seem'd absorbed in meditations. —Evidently deeply abstracted in mind. He thus sat about $\frac{1}{2}$ hour, cutting up $\frac{3}{4}$ lbs meat. During this queer performance, I cautiously put a pistol in my bosom, and moved off a little from him. He then put the minced beef in a small tin-kettle of water, & set it on the fire, after which he put a handful of wet ground coffee, from an old dirty handker chief, in another small tin kettle, with water, and sat that also on the fire to cook. He then laid his knife very carefully on the chair at his right, dropped his chin on his hands, with his elbows on his knees, and asked me many questions, without looking at me at all. Enquired the rates of provissions at Settlements, and often asking the same question over, after I had replied to the first. He ate his stew, drank the coffee, — about a qrt of each, and kept us up quite late, asking information we could not give, muttering inarticulate sentences, mingled with oaths & imprecations; and telling how the Dutchmen fattened and drove him before them, coming along in Pitt river valley, to make meat of him when it should please them to do so. He was much frost bitten, and greatly bloated with alcohol. I intimated our desire to retire, several times, and at last had to tell him, he must go, and I would conduct him to a wagon. He at length reluctantly got up and went to a wagon. He left a small greasy & bloody budget, kettles, and a large knife, in the lodge. I then closed our frail house as well as I could, and set a chair with tin ware in it, at the entrance so that it could not be entered without alarming us. We slept on our arms.

The Irishman is named Clark, and is miserable frost-bitten; has lost several toes, and a piece out of the side of one foot. I thought when in bed, how easyly these suspicious looking men, could destroy us; — and who would know our fate? — However, we slept soundly.

[DEC.] 28th Commences clear, moderate wind N.W. Temp. 32° Merd^n same temp. 56°

I urged White to start early, and get below the reach of severe weather but he intimated a desire to rest here, several days. However I started him off about 8 O'Clock with his naked and bloody knife, in hand, and muttering incoherantly, as he went. On first entering the lodge, this morning, he wept considerably; effects probably of imbecility. A short time after his departure, Elliott, the father, came up with his long rifle, and seated himself by my fire. Said he called to vindicate his character and his sons also, — as he suspected W. had been telling me a long and erroneous story about them. He stated, that last night, at *supper*, W. seated himself, as usual, *in the best position at the fire;* would bring no fuel, nor assist them in any manner; and accused his eldest son of *stealing his meat.* That the lad despised W. for his bad, worthless, and ungrateful character; and being of high temper, made reckless by hunger and sufferings, he struck him, and would have killed him, but for his (the father's) interference. He further said, that he had saved W's life, several times, and dragged his baggage, in a hand sled, for miles, to help him along, yet he was most ungrateful, mean, and lazy, and an inordinate gormandizer. (rather reprehensable under such circumstances) He then continued, "We are not robbers but honest people!" repeating this, with emphasis, several times. He expressed a doubt about getting Clarke off, on account of his feet. But I urged the necessity of getting him away, represented the sudden changes of weather here, and the advantages of reaching medical aid, and proper food; and that if left here, he would soon, inevitably perish miserably.

At near 10 O'Clock he arose, and said it would not be worth while to call around again, as he would soon be off, and bade me adieu. About 11 O'Clock I thought it would be well to walk down to the camp of these men, and see what they were about. When I reached it, I was surprized to perceive Clarke laying down under a tree, with a large camp-kettle full of boiled ox meat and a tin cup beside him, and Elliott & sons were strapping on their packs for a move. The old man said that they would have been off earlier, but C. slept so sound, poor fellow, he did not like to wake him; his feet had prevented him from sleeping at night; and they thought of going on a piece, and C. would follow when he awoke. I looked at the kettle of meat, and was convinced of their intention of leaving him here. But I insisted on his arising and accompanying them; expostulated and at last forced him to get up. When after much delay & grumbling, the party shouldered arms and proceeded. Clarke silent and sulky, evidently disappointed. We were further astonished to find by the fragments around the fire, that they had some bacon, dried apples, and breadstuff. We carried the kettle of boiled beef, some 30 lbs, up to our camp. Elliott and his sons slept in Vestals' wagon, previously throwing a number of articles out. The food leaves a queer insipid taste in the mouth: — it distends the stomach for a while, but strengthens not. — We do much better by eating often, and little at a time.

Sun Set clear, with strong wind from the N. Temp. 38°

Clear night, but soon after dark the breeze increased to quite strong gales. My mind suffers agony from anxiety. We are too weak to chop wood of any size for fuel, and have to content ourselves with small stuff. I slept well first part of the night, but tic-dol-ereuse [tic douloureux] annoyed me much afterwards.

[DEC.] 29th   Commences clear, Moderate Wind N. Temp. 34°   Pain in my face very severe. My mind much depressed, anxiety, weekness, and forebodings of evil. *My friend suspected me of discontent about his mode of cooking*, which very much increased my unpleasant state of mind. — I attribute it to his nervous state, as I never knew him to be petulent. I can never sufficiently appreciate his exertions, skill, friendship and magnaminity. Probably my weakness made me act as though fastidious, or most unintentionally made some remark about the meals; which he thought meant something else.

We cut up some cold boil'd beef, and fried it with a sperm candle. — it was very palateable. I have now lived 47 days on bad beef, and venison, and 8 on the slightest allowance of putrid smoked beef, and [8] days on ancient ox meat.

Merdⁿ hazy, moderate wind S.E. Temp 48°

We visited the ox carcass, and obtained the remaining fore quarter and some rib covering. We dined as we did yesterday. Poyle is very weak, with pains in his loins, and we are rapidly failing.

Sun Set clear, light variable wind, Temp. 44°

A large circle around the moon.

[DEC.] 30th   Commences clear, light wind S.E. Temp. 30°   Soon after sunrise hazy. Stewed beef with a tallow candle and eat heartily, after which we shouldered our guns and started off for Roberts' cabin. We were half a day getting there; the snow was hard, late in the afternoon. Roberts and family received us very kindly, and we saw the Elliotts there, who soon after went on. Roberts said that he had treated them well, and they had eat very hearty, yet they carried off considerable venison, leaving him and his family with but little.

One of Roberts' sons and Mr Clough, had been in to Davis' rancho, and only returned at day-break this morning. They saw Willis, who was faring well, and perfectly unconcerned about us. Davis had offered him mules & supplies, and ox team, and urged him to come out to relieve us, but he plead various excuses, and delayed till the severe storm set in, then could not; and evinced so much apathy about us, that Divis [Davis] and others became disgusted with him, and treated him in such a way that he left, and went over to Lassen's, where he obtain'd employment, as a carpenter. He told there that he was waiting for Lassen to return from below, to obtain team. Roberts told him of our desperate situation, when he replied that we ought to come in.

Merd^n cloudy, light wind S.E. Temp. 38°

Sun Set ditto. Temp. 36°   Heavy fog in the hollows, like thick white smoke.[49] This is a notable day with us, had a hearty dinner of fresh venison, *flour-cakes*, and coffee. We fed like hungry wolves. Mrs. R. gave me, from her small stock, about ½ lb. flour, for the use of the boy. They informed me of the difficulty and hardships to go in to, and come out from the settlements. — They had to wade deep cold streams — very rapid; and travel day and night, with sore backs from their packs. They paid for flour $1 pr lb; Coffee do, Tea $3, Salt $1, sugar do, Nails do. Beef 35 & 40¢ pr lb. — The only article plentiful, Whiskey 50¢ per drink.

Mr Clough accompanied, us back to our camp, and will assist us to-morrow to move down.

After resting, we procured fuel, boiled some beef, and with coffee, eat a hearty supper. Found the boy unusually still, chopped a piece of beef small, stewed & thickened it with flour, and on taking it to him, found him just recovering from a fit. — Occasioned probably by the state of his stomach. Mr. Clough is a hearty, robust, obliging fellow. We will, unless some accident prevents, move down to-morrow.

[DEC.] 31st   Commences hazy, moderate wind S.E. Temp. 35°

Merd^n ditto — Temp. 53°

Clough soon constructed a hand-sled, We stowed every thing compact in the Lodge; then put on the sled, a small tent, bedding, camp utensils, arms, ammunition, &c. and the boy on top, wrapped up in a blanket. I had a large knapsack, filled with note books, drawings, &c — a haversack with various articles in it, wore a belt with cartridge-box, hatchet and knife, Poyle's Pouch and horn, a small camp kettle, lantern, double-gun, and my pockets full of small articles.[50] Poyle and Clough fixed trace ropes to the sled, with loops, which they threw over their shoulders, and at 3 P.M. we moved away from the scene of pleasure and suffering. The sled was a heavy drag, and I heartily pitied poor Poyle. I could not assist them, for I had as much as I could stagger under. Ascending a hill was done by jerking the sled a few yards at a time, and were compelled to lighten our load, by dropping, ¾ m. from the cabin, coffee, salt, camp utensils, &c. We did not reach the cabin till 7 at night, and I fainted at the door.

Roberts' folks apprehend another storm, they have but 2 pieces of dried venison on hand. I proposed to these folks, that if they would furnish us flour for supper, and rations sufficient to carry my friends Poyle & Clough in, that they would go to the settlements, and bring out a supply, and I would return the amount with interest. — So they measured 7 tin-cup-fulls (about a pint each) of sour flour, a few slices of venison to broil, and a rib-piece to boil. P. with his usual alacrity & skill, soon baked 4 thin pan-cakes, and broil'd the slices of meat in the embers, while the ribs were boiling. — This with coffee afforded us another fine meal — delicious! We are exceedingly fagged down. Roberts had a tent standing near the cabin, and we threw our bedding in it, and put the child in. P. engaged after supper baking rolls, for the tramp to settlements. Good souls! — he and Clough, compassionating my situation, are resolved to go off tonight!

I wrote a note to Col. Davis,[51] and another to Mr. Myers [52] for Succor.

Sun Set same as commencement, temp. 40° The poor German is here. Has been taken ill, and R. made him a comfortable pallet before the fire. Child and self ill all night.

JANUARY 1st. 1850 Commences with snow storm, moderate S.E. Wind. Temp. 40°. My head violently affected; the younger Roberts yesterday, his father and myself, and the child, ill all last night, with violent pains & heat in the stomach and intestines. I obtained some relief from camphor. Roberts and sons took opiates. Our being simultaneously attacked with these violent symptoms, caused me to apprehend that we had been poisoned; and at first attributed it to the bad flour, but recollected that I heard Mrs. R. say that the substance she put in the bread, to lighten it, she *thought* was Sal Eratus; and I asked if it might not be something else, — of a poisonous nature. She submitted it to my examination, and from its character, and the effects of the bread on us, was convinced that the substance was *caustic soda!* — and threw it away.

Poyle & Clough started at midnight last night, assuring me of succor in 4 days, we shook hands, and I bade them God speed. P. insisted on my taking 4 rolls of bread last night, and I eat 2 reserving the other for the boy. We — the males here are very sick to-day, the old man worst.

Merdⁿ snow and drizzle, moderate wind S.E, Temp. 46°   Sun Set cloudy, wind same, Temp. 42°

Child's illness increasing, I endeavored to feed him with a little broth, Mrs. R. had kindly made for him. We done all we could for the poor little sufferer, but by 11 A.M. he was extricated from all the hardships of this life.

The German went in, I gave him a note to hand to Poile. We feel a little better this afternoon.

The extraordinary effects of the bread on us, has caused great anxiety about our good friends on their way down the mountains. I am very weak & stiff, in calves of legs & loins. I endeavored to go back ¾ miles for some effects we had to throw out when hauling our sled here, — but too weak, and staggered about over stones & snow in vain, and returned exhausted. Great headache at night, took camphor. I procured a piece of white cotton, stripped the boy, washed him with snow, and tied him up in the cloth, and secured the tent to prevent the wolves carrying him off. Great burning in my stomach & bowels, swelled body, acrid taste, and violent headache — laid on R's floor, in misery till near day, when I obtained a nap. The 3 Roberts also ill all night, with similar symptoms.

A clear night.

[JAN.] 2nd Commences with very light snow, light wind from the S.E. Temp. 34°

Boarding with Roberts, to return the amount of provissions in kind, on the return of my friends. We had a hearty breakfast of pancakes, venison stew, and coffee. Occasional light snow and drizzle all the forenoon.

Merdⁿ drizzly, light wind from S.E. Temp. 36°

At 10 A.M. I cleared away the fire, in front of my tent, within 5 feet of it, and assisted by young Roberts, dug a grave on the spot, and buried the boy, I then piled stones on the grave, procured a small piece of plank, made a head board, and sat up, with this inscription: —

WILLIAM,—
Infant Son of
LAMBKIN —
an
Unnatural
Father,
Died Jan. 1.
1850.

The calves of my legs are very rigid and painful, otherwise getting better.

Roberts' folks look out on the weather, and then to the meat, in the corner of the roof, and occasionally express the wish that Poile and Clough may have luck to procure the provissions & get out soon. Afternoon occasional snow and drizzles, with sunshine — to Sun Set — Wind light from S.E. Temp, 38° We had 3 meals to-day.

Ill at night again, the burning sensations and painful flatulency and swellings. — fear I have inflammation of the bowels. No sleep.

It snowed early in the night, for a short while. I took large doses of camphor and laudanum. In addition to all the other afflictions I have the hermarhoyds very bad.

[JAN.] 3rd. Commences clear and calm, Temp 30°

This morning early, I took 3 of Martins vegetable pills, — the only purgative I could obtain. — Their effects relieved me much.

Merd^n clear and calm, Temp. 43°

A small dinner to-day, a few very thin pancakes, of sour flour, fried with spermacetti. Coffee and stewed venison. After each meal the usual swelling, flatus, pain, and heat.

Sun Set same weather, Temp. 42°

Supped on soup and tea. And at night took a large dose of stale castor-oil, found since breakfast in an old box. Pain and extreme weakness of the spinal column. The oil relieved me greatly of the bad feeling in abdomen. I slept tolerably.

[JAN.] 4th　Commences cloudy, calm, temp. 30°

The dose of oil I took last night too large — renders me exceedingly weak this morning. A hearty breakfast of stewed venison, cakes, and tea.

Merd. Same weather, Temp. 40°

A deep seated pain in chest. Provissions are getting small. Mrs. R. is very kind: she is an excellent house wife, has been an experienced boarding-house keeper, at Galena.

About 3½ P.M. our ears were most gratefully greeted by the shout and song of our friends returning, and soon made their appearance, packs on backs. — Friend Poyle handed me a note from Messr. Davis Ely, & Green, — proprietors of the rancho & store. The[y] kindly wrote that as soon as the state of the roads would permit, they would send out for me and my effects. Clough had packed out, on his back, 50 lbs of flour, & Poile 40 lbs and a few dried apples, & some very dry fresh-beef. — He handed me a bill, as follows: —

50 lbs flour, ...a[t] $1 ¢	$50	..00
12 " dried beef . . . . " 75 "	9	..00
Board of 2 men	6	..00
6 drinks each, a 50¢	3	..00
Fruit (dried apples)	2	..00
6 lbs bread, .a[t] 75¢	4	.50
2 " coffee, ... " 50"	1	..00
2 " dried beef . . . . " 75"	1	..50
Board for Willis, 10 days ⎫		
at $3 per day ⎭	30	..00
		107 . .00 [53]

This reminds me of another circumstance of Willis' conduct. He had a pair of long boots, which he loaned to Petrie, and took the only pair of boots I had, without asking for them, when they [Willis & Petrie] left our old camp. I noticed it, but he was going to serve in a very important manner, for a few days and I therefore said nothing.

[JAN.] 5th   Cloudy, very light wind from the N.W. Temp. 33°. Snow, drizzle, and thaw all last night. About 10 last night we all looked out of the cabin to ascertain what made such a fuss close by, — screaming & tearing the trees. I found it was occasioned by two wild cats,[54] either playing or fighting: — they ran up the trees, within pistol shot.

8 A.M. 3 large wolves (grey) came near the house, but Roberts' dogs ran them off. After breakfast Roberts and one of his sons went hunting; Clough did also for me. R. returned about 3 P.M. with a yearling fawn, and C. at Sun Set, with a fine doe.

Merd. drizzly, light S.E. wind, temp 40°

Sun Set same, temp. 34°.

Set up my tent facing the one Roberts had lent me. Made our beds in one, and kept utensils, &c in the other. I gathered a quantity of spruce bark for fuel. Poyle is too weak to chop wood. More afflictions to-day for me: Swelling of body, severe tooth-ache, &c. Consequent probably on keeping feet wet all day, in the cold drizzle. Poyle cooked a couple of good meals for us to-day.

Wolves are very numerous here. — Yellow, grey, black, & *spotted*. There are 2 sizes of the former, small & great yellow, and same of grey; the largest grey wolf is often a very big fellow. Grizzlers go about here every night, but we do not see them. Our hunters saw several deer, but the cold rain confines them to the thicket.

I paid Roberts what flour he should say I owed him, giving him 7 cups that we had borrowed, and 6 he thought I owed him for board. = 13 cups, a severe reduction of my stock.

[JAN.] 6th Commences with spits of snow, & a strong S.E. wind. Temp. 33°

Weakness and great pain in my spine disturbed my repose much last night. Hermarhoids, and violent symptoms of indigestion produced, as I think from use of the dried apples & dried beef. Our breakfast a thin pancake and baked venison, with coffee.

Merdⁿ weather as [at] commencement, Temp. 35°.

Poile and Clough took sled and went back to our old camp, to procure some articles we needed, and see if it was undisturbed by beasts or indians. The three Roberts out hunting. The latter return'd at Sun Set luckless, followed by my friends, with a wagon cover, and the articles we were compelled to drop when we moved down to this place.

Sun Set drizzless [drizzles]. Wind S.S.E. temp. 34° Drizzles all night.

[JAN.] 7th Commences wet fog, & thaw, strong breeze Ey — soon bearing to S.E. temp. 38°. Warren G. Clough expressed a desire to join me, from motives of humanity alone. — He observed, that I was very much afflicted, and generally very weak, and my true and constant friend — Poile, had to hunt, — often at a distance, cut fuel, &c. and I was consequently left alone, at times. That the Roberts would soon move in to the settlements, and we would be troubled and jeopardized. His term of service with Roberts had expired, and he was in no hurry to go in yet. He had given Roberts a yoke of Oxen, and agreed to team a portion of the time coming out, from the States, for a term of months, which he had faithfully perform'd. And more; — had teamed nearly the whole distance through to this spot, had taken care of the stock, and in fact was the main stay of the party. For which services they were to carry his property, &c. They had treated him in the meanest way, yet he carried out honorably *his* engagements to them.[55] The women were clever and humane.

I told him that I could not expect him to remain in this wilderness, living in such a hard and precarious way; but if his benevolence insisted on it, I would allow him such per diem as the best mechanic commanded, or the average mining yield, in California, when we should get in, and I enabled to obtain the necessary amount. He was quite indignant that I should offer compensation for an act of humanity; and replied, "Capt. Bruff, I am a man with a heart in my breast, am an old hunter, and used to a rough life; I don't want to go in the sickly wet mines now, and when we get in, together, we can then cipher out a living together, and you may be able to befriend me in the country if I then need it. I ain't a man of larning, but I am a tolerable good rough Carpenter, and can turn my hand to most any thing. So this honest, benevolent, and clever old man joined us, in the most disinterested and magnanimous manner.

I slept tolerably well last night; though the pain and weakness in my back & loins were severe, which continues this morning. Venison, pancake, and coffee, for breakfast.

Clough intended to have gone below to-day, for the settlements; but the recollection of the recent and present wet spells, [which] had swollen the streams below, rendering them perilous to cross, caused him to defer it: So he and the young Roberts went hunting.

Heavy drizzling mist all the forenoon. Having given old R. a hint of his mean conduct in some particulars, he admitted *that he was selfish, and vindicated it as a virtue.*

Merd^n drizzly mist, Strong wind S.E. (thawing rapidly) temp. 43° Smoke is quite annoying. We boiled a piece of venison, and thickened the broth with flour, affording us good soup. Gloomy thick wet weather, continuing so all night.

[JAN.] 8th   Last nights' weather contin^d. Wind S.S.W. temp. 34°

We have to ration ourselves with the flour. A certain quantity, measured by a small tin cup, is made up in a thin cake, and tri-sected among us. Our piece of cake, stewed venison, and coffee gives us a good breakfast. Afterwards the Roberts' and Clough went hunting. Pain & swelling in my body, and tooth-ache, very annoying. Found a small sheet iron stove, which we have fixed up, to render us more comfortable in bad weather, when the wind will allow us to use it. We have scant 10 day's rations of bread & meat. Have written letters for home, to friends in San Francis° and to Davis & Ely. — ready, when they can be forwarded.

Merd^n continuance of bad weather, temp 42°

Afternoon Strong gales from the S.W. rain, continuing till Sun-set, temp. 36° Friend P. bent up a rusty piece of sheet-iron, and fixed up our little worn-out stove, and set it burning: — then hung a piece of old cotton to keep some wet out, and we became pretty comfortable.

The hunters returned unsuccessful. — Bad weather has driven the deer into the thickets.

The night rainy, with strong gales from the W. Our tents and *vestibule* to them, leaked much, dripping on our heads; we slept close together, and made the best of it.

[JAN.] 9th　Cloudy, light S.W. wind, temp 44°

Soon after 8 A.M. the sun struggled to shine out through the clouds. Swelling, pain, heat, and weakness, very bad, this morning.

Merd^n same, — glimpses of sun-shine, mod^e wind W. temp. 47°

Sun Set ditto,　　　　　　　　　　　　　　"　　46°

Showers and clear, alternately, during the night. I slept tolerably. Clough went out to-day, and returned, late in the afternoon, with a large buck. He was very tired, and hallowed for us, so we went out $\frac{1}{4}$ mile, and relieved him; he tied a stick to it, and had hauled it on the snow, a considerable distance. In the same way we dragged it to camp.

The Roberts' were unsuccessful hunting to-day. We gave the Roberts *ladies* a quarter of venison.

[JAN.] 10th　Commences with flying clouds, and light winds, varying from E. to W. temp. 48°

The Roberts, and my friend Clough went hunting.

Fine weather. I took advantage of it, for a thorough ablution, and felt much better.

(Poile related the difficulties, he & Clough contended with, going in to the settlements on the night of our arrival here. — He was very weak, from previous sufferings, and the poisoned bread had a severe effect on them: — symptoms similar to those we were attacked with, but not so strong, probably in consequence of the exercise they took. They had to wade through snow, and mud; exposed on naked elevated ridges to strong bleak winds, and rain; and crossing cold rapid torrents, — waist deep. P. the next morning after leaving us, was so exhausted, that he laid down in the wet, and begged Clough to beat him with a ramrod, to rouse and urge him on. Arrived at Davis' that night, both exceedingly exhausted and cold. — They were treated kindly. Spent a day there, when Clough with 50 and P. with 30 lbs. flour, &c packed on their backs, left at 10 A.M. travelled till dark, rested till 10 P.M. travelled all night & day, and reached this at 3 P.M. the next day. — A terrible tramp of 30 miles.)

Some light drizzles. Merd^n fly. clouds, light variable wind, temp: 50°

Sun Set the same, temp: 48°　Distant thunder after dark.

The hunters returned luckless. —

C. saw 3 deer at a distance. They were very wild. R & sons packed in about 1½ bushels of a blackberry called *mansaneta* — by the Spaniards. (little apple) This bush grows all over the mountains, except on the greatest elevations. — Smaller in size, and sparser, as it ascends. In favorable positions in deep valleys, and on low table-lands, it grows thick and large. I have seen it as tall as my head, — near 6 feet. Bark generally a dingy scarlet. Main stem short and thick, very crooked and angular, and numerous small branches. It is an evergreen. The berries, when ripe, are black, and under favorable circumstances, are as large as a ½ oz. ball. Are sweet, & pulpy, containing 3 or 4 hard seed, much like those of grapes. The stunted variety, growing on heights, seem not to produce full berries. Bears are very fond of them.

We tightened our tents, connected them on the bad weather side, and over head, with poles, & covered with the old wagon cover. Severe cold, and took rhubarb. We are projecting a plan of moving our effects down from the old camp, in readiness to transport, into the Settlements. Drizzles during the night.

[JAN.] 11th Cloudy, light wind S.W. temp. 37°
 Merd^n same, light wind W.   " 44°
 Sun Set ditto — — " 42°

My two friends went for berries, found they had nearly all fallen, but procured about ½ bushel.

Had to take laudanum and camphor to relieve me of bad sensations. Clough similarly affected, and took the same remedy. The Roberts went hunting, and returned with a doe & buck, and had killed 2 others, one of which, shot on the edge of a precipice, leaped down & was lost; the other they hung up in a tree. Mrs. R. tried experiments with the berries, to increase their stock of bread-stuff. Made bread of ⅔ flour, and ⅓ pulp of boiled berries, lightened & baked, a very palatable sweet bread. We procured a square of coarse iron wire screen, (one of the numerous articles dragged over the continent and abandoned) Sawed a candle-box through, so as to reserve a frame of the sides and ends, about 4 inches deep. over this we nailed the sieve-wire; and having boiled the berries, we put them in this sieve, and by rubbing and pressing, forced through all the available portion; leaving behind only seed and skin.

About 9 P.M. a large pack of wolves visited our settlement, and gratified us with a very distinct serrenade, — all their interesting notes, from the *fiest*-dog yelping of the small yellows, up to the gruff strong bass of the large grey and black animals. — The performance was 3 staves, of a long howl each, with all the variations and intonations peculiar to such music. It was dark, and we could not see our musical friends, but judged from their voices, that they were about 200 yards off, on the slope of a hill, among the pines. We listened, then set up an imitative yell, and they went off. Night cleared off.

[JAN.] 12th　Clear and calm, temp. 30°

I awoke at dawn of day and built up our fire. Feeling so much better this morning, I shouldered my gun and walked down a hollow, about $\frac{1}{2}$ mile: but very cold and fatigued on returning. We mixed up our flour and berry batter, for bread, and poured it in the oven, when it looked much like dark brown mud. It, however, produced a sweet palateable brown loaf of bread; and with venison and coffee we had a hearty breakfast.

Merdn clear, light wind W. temp. 43°

The Roberts brought in 2 deer to-day, — a young buck, and the one they hung up yesterday.

Clough also went hunting, and late in the afternoon P. went out to meet him — and brought us a fine large buck.

Sun Set clear and calm, temp. 42°

Night clear and serene, till after midnight, when it drizzled, followed by fine snow, and a light variable wind.

When Clough returned from the hunt, he brought 3 large pine cones, full of nuts, which I found very nice.[56] (*Drawing of them*)

[JAN.] 13th　Commences with snow, light variable wind, temp. 32°
Merdn — ditto　　　　　　　　　　　　　　　　”　　34°
A little sun shine during the forenoon.

After a merdn lunch, my friends went back to the old camp, on the hill.

During the afternoon quite a bustling little snow-storm, snow falling thick and fast, with a strong breeze, veering from the S.E. to N.E. with distant thunder.

Sun Set clear and calm, temp. 33°

A beautiful clear night, temp: at midnight, — 22°

About 3 P.M. my friends returned, bringing the articles they had gone for, and reporting the old lodge yet safe from interruption. The snow up there had thawed very little. — They were white with snow, cold, and tired, but I had a hot meal and coffee for them.

P. sat up late to-night baking bread for rations to carry him into the Settlements and probably down to Sacramento City, to carry my letters, &c.

[JAN.] 14th　Commences hazy, light wind W. temp. 22°
Merdn clear, wind same, temp: 34°

Sun Set snow, strong gales from N.W. temp: 26° Storm continued till late in the night.

My friends busy laying in a store of large fuel and baking bread, to travel on, and to leave me. Wrote all the letters and notes I intend — a letter to my wife, and several to friends in the cities below.

[JAN.] 15th Commences hazy, wind light, — W. temp: 28°
    Merd^n clear, wind same, temp: 40°
    Sun Set flyg clouds, light wind from the N.W. temp: 30°

I arose at day-break, made an early breakfast, and at sun-rise my two friends started to go in, — intending to travel some distance down a ridge to the left of the road, which they think is shorter, and not so rugged. Feel tolerable well to-day. Cleaned up our abode, and ran a number of rifle-balls (*Sketch of tents & boy's grave*)

[BRUFF'S NEW CAMP, NEAR ROBERTS' CABIN]

[JAN.] 16th Near morning a fine snow, wind N.W. — Sun-rise do. Wind light from W. temp. 28° Merd^n flyg clouds, wind same, temp. 34°. Sun Set clear, very light wind from N.W. temp. 30°

I have a bad headache this morning, but amused myself making a sketch of our habitation here. A clear beautiful night: the temp: fell, late at night, to 24°. Slept tolerably.

[JAN.] 17th Commences clear, wind light N.W. temp: 28° The bread P. baked and left for me, is of the berry mixture. — 3 loaves, about 10 ins diam: and 3 ins: thick, each, — to serve me 6 days. And nearly a whole deer. They carried a loaf of bread like mine, and a piece of venison with them. I am again troubled with tooth-ache, and pain & weakness in back, and loins.

Merd. flyg clouds, wind moderate, S.W. temp. 35°　I shot a raven.

Sun Set thick haze, strong breeze from S.W. temp. 32°

I cleaned my raven, found him quite fat, and put him in salt water, to soak. Disk around the moon.

[JAN.] 18th　Near day, fine snow & hail fell, for $\frac{1}{2}$ hour, accompanied with strong wind from the N.W.

Sun rise clear, Wind light, from the W. temp: 22°　Merd^n clear, moderate wind N.W. temp: 36°

A little after 11 A.M. while stewing my raven with some venison, the puppy ran up, from a hollow near by, where laid an old ox carcass, which he occasionally fed on: barking vehemently and exhibiting great alarm. I took a rifle, and proceeded down the hollow, a short distance, and soon got on the track, in the snow, of a large wolf. My pup followed, barking, whining, and hesitating occasionally, to advance.[57] I then, in 200 yds from my lodge, struck on the fresh track of a grizzly-bear; — He had travelled up from the South, along a ravine, — to the carcass, then continued up a snow rill, among bushes and trees, and up the hill to within 20 paces of my habitation, alongside of which, hanging on a large pine-tree, was my store of venison. I suppose that the pup was at the carcass, when the bear came up, and alarmed at the sight of bruin, he barked furiously & ran up, and the bear followed him, till he saw the smoke of my fire and heart [heard] me, then turned short round, and went up a high ridge, in the rear of camp. The bear, it would appear, caused a wolf to turn and retreat, who was going down to the carcass. So between the grizzler and wolf, my pup had a narrow escape.

On returning, I heard a wolf bark in the rear, on a ridge. I procured a store of red wood bark, for light and kindling.

Weakness in back, tooth-ache, chilblains, &c —

Sun Set clear, light wind, N. temp. 30°　Disk around the moon.

My puppy awakened me at midnight, and I heard an animal trotting past my tent, presume it is only a wolf, who wants my venison. — Some of these saucy intruders will catch a blue pill yet.

[JAN.] 19th　Commences clear and calm, temp. 22°

Merd^n clear, light wind W.　　　　　”　38°

Lumbago and weakness in loins very troublesome, and my mouth much inflamed. Shot one of those Jay-bird-looking woodpeckers.[58] I suspected that dampness had lodged under my bedding, and on examination, found such the fact. Removed the damp articles, & spread down some palm [pine?]-branches.

I have alleviated the pain in my back, by laying down before the fire, and exposing my back to great heat. A fine day, but cold. Saw the track, this morning, within 4 feet of where my head laid, in the tent, of the big wolf who alarmed my pup last night. — The poor little dog is afraid of these rascals.

Sun Set clear, light N.W. wind, temp. 29° Disk around the moon.

At 7 P.M. my good friends — Poile and Clough, returned from Lassen's rancho, bringing out 80 lbs of flour, — minus what they used on the road. It was sour, and $1 per lb.

[JAN.] 20th Commences clear, light wind N.W, temp: 24° Merdn hazy, wind same, temp. 39° Sun Set flying clouds, & calm. temp. 31° Disk around the moon, at night.

Strange conduct of Davis & Ely to my friends, hardly extended common courtesy to them; said, gruffly, they had no flour to spare. — So they [Poile and Clough] procured it at Lassen's, — of his Agent, — young Wilson, — who was as uncouth as a bear, using very unfeeling expressions about me, but telling my friends that they could have as much flour as they were able to pack up to me.[59] Lassin down the valley, endeavoring to get a steam-boat, with cargo of provisions up, to his landing. Provisions are scarce, and exceedingly dear, no cattle to be had, and the selfishness of the people such, that I have no hope of succor, but by a communication with some friends below, — in the cities. And P. says, good fellow, that it will be the best course to pursue, and that as soon as he can make arrangements, he will go down for me, find a friend, and render me that assistance, which seems cannot be expected here at all. Heard of Willis — who was eating & drinking well, and strutting around, unmindful of aught but self.

[JAN.] 21st Commences fine Snow, wind moderate, from the S.W. temp: 28°

Merdn same, temp. 30°

Sun Set flyg clouds, light variable wind, temp: 26° We have adopted an oeconomical mode of feeding, — taking the venison liquor in which we had boiled the meat, and thicken it with flour, adding a little finely chopped meat. — a kind of stir-about Stew, which we have christened — "Skillagalee" — (or rather friend Poile has thus named it).

Night occasionally hazy and cloudy. Disk around the moon.

[JAN.] 22d   Cloudy, Strong breeze from S.W. temp. 28°
  Merd^n   do   do   " 30°
  Sun Set   do   do   " 26°
  Clough went hunting.

Our little sled, we find exceedingly useful, in procuring fuel. P. made up a batch of berry-bread, — half-and-half.

C. returned after night, unsuccessful; saw several deer, and missed a fawn, by inadverten[t]ly snapping a cap merely at it: — had forgotten to charge the rifle. Slept well.

[JAN.] 23d   Commences with very fine snow, strong wind from the S.W. temp. 30°

We breakfasted to day, on *Skill*agalee, colored purple, with berry pulp, a biscuit each, of berry-bread, and coffee.

  Clough went hunting.
  Merd^n same as commencement.
  Sun Set   ditto. temp: 28°

9 P.M. C. returned, bringing a yearling buck, and while I was taking the pot off the fire, containing our last piece of venison. Collected fuel. P. baking biscuit, for travelling rations.

  Snow-storm all night.

[JAN.] 24th   Strong gales & variable, temp: 34°

Forenoon variable heavy flaws of wind, heavy mist, and occasional drizzles and fine snow.

  Merd^n a light variable wind, (thawing) temp: 36°
  Sun-set flyg clouds, variable wind, temp: 36°
  P. still biscuit-baking.

First part of night same as at sun-set, latter part, snow and sleet occasionally.

[JAN.] 25th   Commences with sleet, moderate wind from N.W. temp. 35°
Nearly all the forenoon showers, and some snow and sleet.

  Merd^n flyg clouds, light variable wind, temp. 36°
  Sun-Set calm, slight haze, temp. 35°

P. still busy, baking biscuit, — 10 day's travelling rations. About 9 P.M. we were quietly smoking our pipes, by the fire, when a couple of dogs at the Cabin, barked and chased a wolf and fox, running towards our camp; the latter ran, frightened almost among us, and I seized a rifle and hurriedly fired at the wolf, but missed him.

[JAN.] 26th   Comm^d cloudy, strong wind S.W. occasional hail;   temp 36°
Forenoon weather snow, hail, sleet; thaw, &c.

Roberts visited our camp, and desired us to loan or sell him 10 lbs flour.
We spoke of difficulty to procure more when our present small stock should
be exhausted, and that P. was on the eve of going in, to be absent some time;
and asked why he or his sons could not go in for a supply. This put the
fellow in a violent passion, and he abused us, as a set of rascals, &c. We
coolly informed him, then, that we would lend, *to the females not to him, or
for his use*, as much flour as we could possibly spare. He went off in high
dudgeon, but soon returned, in a more civil humor, and we agreed to sell
him 10 lbs. for which he paid us, $5 in silver, and a $5 note, of the Globe
Bank, of N.Y. We weighed it with Troy Scales and weights. C. hunted unsuccessfully to-day.

Sun Set flyg clouds, wind light, from the S.W. temp: 35°   Soon after a
slight mist, followed by a clear beautiful night.

[JAN.] 27th   Clear and calm, temp: 28°
11½ A.M. my friends strapped blankets on their backs, and started off
on a long hunt for deer. Merd^n clear, very light wind from W. temp: 56°
Sun Set clear, wind same, temp: 38°   Early part of night some flying clouds,
and light wind from the N.W. — then cleared off.

[JAN.] 28th   Commences clear, moderate wind from S.W. temp: 32°   Hearing R's dogs barking, I looked out, and discerned the cause; — A large grey
wolf was standing on the side of the hill, opposite the front of the cabin,
and about 150 yards from me. — He was looking steadily at the dogs, who
were standing close together alongside the cabin barking furiously at him.
I took a rifle, and fired, striking under him, and the [wolf] sulkily ascended
the ridge, occasionally looking around. Observing a raven, perched on the
limb of a pine, about 50 yds. distant, I sat my long rifle down, and took a
light one, and brought him down, with a broken wing, my puppy aided me
in catching him.

Merd^n slightly hazy, light wind S.W. temp: 50°   Venison seems to be
very diuretic, more particularly when we eat little or no bread. — If we
regard not the admonitions of nature, strong pains in the kidnies ensue, affecting the loins and back. I think that with myself there are inflammatory symptoms, being accompanied by great thirst.

Discovered that pine-smoke colors the metal of our arms; *Quere* — will not
pyreligenous acid brown gun-barrels? It gives a bronze color to brass, or
the tint of what is called *Princes' metal*.

Bathing my feet in warm water & salt, alleviated the chill-blains. Pains in my loins & back bad.

Afternoon flyg clouds, & moderate S.W. wind. — Thawing finely

Sun Set flyg clouds, Strong S.W. wind, temp: 38°   About midnight my friends returned, wet and cold, bringing a deer. Latter part of night drizzle, sleet, and snow.

[JAN.] 29th   Commences snow-storm, S.E. wind, temp. 34°   Merdⁿ rain & fine snow, Strong S.E. wind, temp: 38° — thawing. Raven and venison in our *skillagalee* breakfast & dinner.

About 1 P.M. a heavy fall of snow commenced, but decreased near Sun Set. Sun-Set fine snow, very light W. wind, temp. 34°   Soon after it cleared off.

[JAN.] 30th   Commences clear, light W. wind, temp: 32°

After Sun-rise, thawing.

Last evening Mrs. R. called Clough over to the cabin, and desired he would assist them to move in, soon. — When all hands would go in together, leaving me alone. Old Roberts told him, that when he abused our party, on the 25th, *he had no reference to him*; and that he believed I was only pretending infirmity, and if he was in his, (C's) place, he would see me d — d, before he would hunt and pack meat for me. C. and P. went hunting.

Merdⁿ clear, light S. wind, temp: 48°

Sun Set clear, wind moderate from the S: temp: 40°   About 7 P.M. my friends returned bringing a buck fawn. A short time before they arrived, I was startled by the barking of my faithful little watch, — Nevada, and heard the steps of an animal, in the snow; on looking out I caught sight of a large wolf, near my tent, he gave a low growl, and went away, around the tent. It was dark, and I did not bother myself about him. Pain in my back broke my rest much.

[JAN.] 31st   Commences clear, Strong wind S. temp. 38°   We are all weak to-day, more particularly myself. I had half an hour's repose this forenoon, which was serviceable.

Merdⁿ clear, modᵉ wind S. temp: 56°

Sun Set clear, light S. wind, temp: 42°   My friends took a nap in the afternoon, and afterwards procured a store of fuel. Clough wounded a raven with a rifle-ball, at 100 yds.

FEB: 1st. Commences clear, moderate wind S. temp: 42°

My friends are quite sick, particularly Poile, who slept till 11 A.M. My infirmities severe to-day. Clough went over the ridge, to the E. this forenoon, and back, found the snow deep, and no sign of deer.

Merd^n clear, same wind, temp. 58°

Old R. went in a S^y direction, with rifle and hand sled, to hunt deer. Clough brot in some pine cones, full of nuts. The coffee we brought from old lodge is out, and we had to dry the grounds and heat them in an oven, to make them serve again: This insipid beverage gave us acidity and nausea, — Found a pale green deposit in my tin coffee-cup, and a green fluid in Poile's, also: and on examining the old coffee-pot, found that the bottom was copper, — accounting for the green deposit, and nausea.

We took some buds, or tops, of the nut-bearing pine, and boiled them, for tea. A delightful aromatic-acid, much like the flavor of lemon-peel. — Believe that it would be an excellent substitute for lemonade, or punch, if we had the other ingredients.[60]

At about 2 P.M. the therm: rose to 64° in shade, and 92° in the sun!

Sun Set clear, light N. wind; temp. 42°   clear all night, the temperature falling very little below 42°

[FEB.] 2nd. Commences clear, light S.E. wind, temp: 42°   My comrades went hunting. A deers head, and a raven (found dead. — Supposed to be the one Clough wounded day-before yesterday. — I put in the pot for dinner to-day: — last of our meat.

Merd^n clear, light S. wind, temp: 60°

A little after Merd^n Roberts came in, with a large chest & keg on his sled. The meat of a deer he shot yesterday was in the chest. He found the chest in a wagon, about 1 mile ahead — on the road.

Sun Set clear, very light wind, W. by N. Temp: 46°   About 6 P.M. my comrades returned, bringing a buck they shot, 6 ms. from here. It required 4 hours toil to get it here, up steep rugged & brushy hill-sides. They wounded another one.

[FEB.] 3rd. Commences slight haze, very light S.E. wind: temp: 38°   I lent the Roberts some salt. R. left a deer he shot, in the wagon he took the chest from, while he hunted the other; and when he returned, found the wolves had carried off the first. (as he might have known.) We laid in a store of oak logs and pine-bark; when, about 11½ A.M. my comrades took the sled, and went off for the old camp. They will remain there to-night. When they return, some more fuel will be procured, and they then will proceed, — P. for the cities, and C. on an tramp for edible acorns, — near the valley.

I am very weak, and take all the exercise I can, in hopes it will strengthen me. Chopping wood, gathering bark, bringing water, cooking &c. afford plenty of work. Roberts is chopping fuel, to leave with his family, while he accompanies my comrades in to the settlements for some oxen he has bargained for.

Clough saw a large yellow fox this morning, and Roberts' dog started a grey wolf from the carcass a little below my camp. Painful swelling of abdomen, increased by pressure: had to rip my pantaloons open, in the back, and sew in a piece of stuff, 3 inches broad. The salt bathing has relieved the itching of the chill-blains, but my feet are sore and stiff.

Merd^n slight haze: very light wind from E. temp. 50°

The chiming of frogs, buzzing of flies, rise of sap, &c. indicate the approach or setting-in of spring. — No party of men can hail her arrival with greater delight, than ourselves. — We have had *tight papers*. A slight exposure to the inclemency of winter, when the common necessaries of life are at hand, is disagreeable enough; but situated and circumstanced as we have been, and thus exposed to its rigor, is a trial of all man's faculties.

I severely burnt my hand, by incautiously grasping the hot handle of a griddle. — I immediately clasped a handful of snow, and kept it in my hand till numbed with cold; — curing the burn in a short time. On a former occasion I burnt 3 fingers, so badly as to prevent sleep, and tied my hand up, full of snow, on again going to bed, slept soundly, and the burn was cured.

Severe headache this afternoon.

Sun Set some flying clouds, in the S.W. light E^y airs; temp: 46°

At night flying clouds, increasing, till latter part, it was all cloudy.

[FEB.] 4th   Commences hazy, wind light, from the N.W. temp: 39°.

About 11 A.M. my comrades returned; on reaching the old lodge, they found that the wolves had been there: — They had taken the ox-leg we left, half-consumed, near the entrance, carried it inside and there stripped it. They [Poile and Clough] brought some more coffee, salt, candles, clean clothes, &c.

Merd^n a thick haze, and very light N.W. wind, temp: 50°

Sun Set cloudy. Sprinkles of rain, very light & variable wind, temp: 42° Completed the preparations for the last mission in to settlements, before we finally quit the hills. — A store of fuel laid in; travelling rations of bread baked, &c. &c.

[FEB.] 5th   Commences hazy, light wind from the E. temp: 40°   An early breakfast, of *skillagalee*, broiled venison ribs, a roll of bread, & coffee. My kind and magnanimous comrades started on their mission. (about 9 A.M.)

(About midnight, last night, a pack of wolves, at the carcass, below my camp, treated me to another Serrenade, with all its symphonies: which elicited much barking & whining from Roberts 2 dogs, and my puppy; when silence resumed her sway, interrupted only by the monotinous hooting of an old owl, in a tree over my head.)

(Drizzles of rain during the last night.)

Merd^n hazy, light wind from S. temp. 48°   I repaired our broken coffee-mill. Sun-Set cloudy, with indications of rain, moderate wind from E. temp: 42°

Roberts and the females, begged Clough to go in, to Myers rancho, to get them some flour. For the sake of the females we consented,— *his* selfish, hypocritical, and abusive conduct, at first caused some hesitancy, on the part of Clough.

I furnished Poile with notes and letters.[61]

Through the night misty drizzles, easterly gales, and thawing rapidly.

[FEB.] 6th   Commences with misty drizzles, a moderate E. wind, temp. 38°

Last night's thaw exposed many spots of bare ground. Thaw continuous. A dense haze, occasionally affording us a glimpse of the struggling sun-beams.

Merd^n cloudy, strong E. wind, temp: 40° followed by hail. Pain in my left breast in the afternoon, and at night; which with the pup barking at the passing beasts, annoyed me much. This morning I noticed a flock of wild pidgeons, flying high, towards the N.W. And a large flock of a diminutive bird, like our thistle bunting, flew across the hill, low, chirping as they passed. They were swift, and close together.[62] 3 large vultures passed over.

My feet are very sore.

Sun Set drizzling mist, moderate E. wind; temp. 38°   some sprinkles of fine hail & snow, afterwards and then cleared off, with a light wind from the W. Thawing till late, a beautiful night.

[FEB.] 7th   Commences with slight haze & calm, temp. 34°   Merd^n clear, very light wind from N.W. temp. 46°   I boiled some vertebral joints of venison. — Near Sun Set a pair of bald eagles [63] soared over head.

Sun Set clear, wind as at Merd^n temp: 38°

[FEB.] 8th   Commences clear, very light wind from N.W. temp: 36°

R's dogs amusing themselves chasing wolves from the ox-carcass: — they do not like the idea of the wild beasts monopolizing it. Merd^n same weather, temp: 56°   Sun Set do, temp: 46°   Roberts shot a deer, about 4 miles off, brought half of it; and accompanied by his wife, brought the other half and his heavy rifle, afterwards.

[FEB.] 9th   Clear, light airs N.W. temp: 40°   Mrs. R. gave me some small pieces of boiled venison, and I returned the compliment with salt. (No salt to be had at settlements: — they have to eat without it there)   Merdⁿ occasionally a slight haze, light wind from E. temp: 56°

Sun Set clear, with light Eʸ airs, temp: 48°   At dusk Clough returned, bringing 20 lbs of flour for Roberts, and 3 pecks of shelled acorns for us. — These he gathered and shelled at night. He left P. on the 7th, at Sun Set to start the next day for Sacramento City. They put up at Mr Myers.' (Alcalde)

This afternoon I drew a pine stick out of the ground, driven in by falling from a tall tree. — It was 4 inches diam: 3 ft. long, and inserted in the earth ¾ of its length.

[FEB.] 10th   Commences clear, light wind S.W. temp. 53°   We cooked some acorns, broke and ground them, and with equal parts of acorn-meal  and flour, made good strong palateable bread. These acorns are the staff of life of the indians. They are very long and slender, without any bitter, in fact taste somewhat like chestnuts. The shell is of a light yellowish brown color, meat white.[64]

> The acorns Clough brought out, weighd at least 45 lbs
> The flour for Roberts ....   20 ”
> Kettle, rifle, &c. &c. ....   28 ”
> ───────
> 93 lbs

Packed 30 miles on his back, over a shocking bad road. Merdⁿ clear, Mod. wind from N.W. temp. 62°   Sun Set do temp: 50°   A clear night, with strong S.E. wind.

[FEB.] 11th   Commences clear, with a moderate N.W. wind, temp: 41°   10 A.M. C. went hunting. R. went also, but only brought in berries. Merdⁿ clear, light airs from the W. temp. 72! & 94°! in the sun.

Severe attack of weakness & hermarhoids. C. returned, near Sun Set, with a fine fat doe. Sun Set clear, very light wind from the N.W. temp: 54°   Set a snare to catch a wolf.

[FEB.] 12th   Commences clear, with very light airs from the E. temp: 51° Merd^n clear and calm, temp. 66°.

Last night Robert Roberts, one of the sons, arrived; he had been in the settlements and down the valley, some time. Yesterday morning the Roberts had made overtures to Clough, to induce him to abandon me. This morning they again called him to the cabin, after breakfast; and detained him till past meridian, and engaged him to assist them to move in, in 3 days time; and as they would be compelled to leave the bulk of *their property*, in the cabin till they could bring out team, they desired him on his return here, to live in the house, *but that I should not enter it!* He told R. that I was his friend, an honorable and unfortunate man, and that he would go no-where, where I could not. The females, and Robert — the younger son, spoke favorably of me, and reprimanded the old man for his harsh expressions towards me. After C. returned from the cabin, he went hunting. Young R.R. came up the Sacramento river in a steam boat, from Sacramento City.[65] — It had been overflown by an extraordinary freshet.[66] A rumor of the freshet having exposed gold, had attracted crowds of adventurers.

Sun Set clear, very light airs, from N. temp: 46°

Roberts and his eldest son went hunting. C. returned luckless. Boiled venison & acorn-bread our fodder to-day.

First part of night I slept well, latter part weakness and pain in back interfered. I told C. when he related old R's remarks, that he could not induce me to go in the cabin while it contained aught of his. That my cotton-house was just as good for me, as I had too long lived in a tent to care for a more substantial structure, and I would just as lieve die in my tent as in his log cabin.

[FEB.] 13th   Commences hazy, with light airs from the N. temp: 43°   (I either did not know when young R. went below, or forgot to note it)

About 9 A.M. my comrade started for the old camp, to obtain some necessary articles. He carried his rifle, hoping to get a deer on the route.

We breakfasted on a little broiled venison, and pot-liquor thickened with 1 part of flour to 2 of acorn-meal: and coffee. A large flock of wild pidgeons flew low over, towards the N.W. Visited the wolf-snare: — found it demolished, by a small wolf, who had, last night, got a choking, and stampeded with the noose and bait. I constructed it as I have often done, when a boy, —

on a small scale, by bending down a sapling oak, (no hickory here) by climbing up, trimming it, securing a new white 2 inch white rope to it, with a noose, and by swinging down, bent the head to the ground, with my weight: formed a pen, drove a notched picket in the centre, and hooked a baited crooked piece of wood to this, — holding down the springs, — adjusted the noose around the opening, and piled around roots, stones, and pine-branches, leaving only an opening for the animal to thrust his head in, through the noose. The labor of setting it exhausted me.

C. returned, in about $1\frac{1}{2}$ hours, leaving his rifle on the road, and bringing in a fat doe, which he shot through the heart, at about 200 yds. distance; a mile on the road back.

We lunched on *Skillagalee*, and he went on, to try it again. We have now 1 whole and the greater part of another deer, and 2 heads. I collected a considerable quantity of cedar and oak limbs.

Merd^n Same as commencement, temp: 58°

Troubled much with swelling & irritability of abdomen, and severe pains in the back. This is particularly the case at night. Near Sun Set young Roberts brought in a deer. At dusk my comrade returned, with a large bag, containing a large skillet & cover, a considerable iron pot, and a thick cotton wagon-cover. — He is a robust active man.

Sun Set clear, very light wind from the N.W. temp: 48°

Supper of fried liver and coffee. — Fried meat with a tallow candle.

[FEB.] 14th Commences clear & calm, temp: 43°
Merd^n ditto   ”   58°

As one of the tents I am using belongs to Roberts, he has demanded it. So I have been very busy all day, and in the night, taking it down, and removing mine about 20 ft further, on dryer ground. Sun Set same weather, temp: 48° Quite ill to-night.

[FEB.] 15th Commences clear, very light N.W. wind, temp: 40°
Merd^n clear, light wind E.S.E. temp: 58°

About 10 A.M. my comrade went hunting. I have been all day busy airing bedding, &c. and fixing my new locale. No wonder at pains in back, &c. for on moving, I found everything under my former bed wet and rotton: which I could not discover till I had removed the old hides, &c — strange that I never suspected it. Took 3 patent anti-billious pills. A little before Sun Set C. returned luckless. Sun Set clear, light airs from the N. temp: 48°

Severe hermerhoids afflicting me to-day. — result of severe cold.

[FEB.] 16th   Commences hazy, light S.W. wind, temp: 42°   About 10 A.M. Old Roberts and wife; eldest son, wife, and infant, Robert and Clough, all started, for the settlements, — C. asked me if I objected, was concerned about remaining here alone. — I told him to go, on account of the women & infant: that I was afraid of nothing, for a few days; had a lot of charged arms, and plenty of ammunition, provissions, &cc. that I knew he would not leave me longer than he could help. They carried a dog (pointer) with them, and left a pointer bitch, with pups, at the cabin. — Clough carried a tent, poles &c. and blankets on his shoulders, and the R. had rifles & packs, and the women, bundles and the infant

We had broiled venison & coffee for breakfast. I have some civilized creatures near me still: — my faithful little Nevada, and Roberts' pointer at the cabin, — 100 yds off. — These will at least warn me of approaching danger. The number and variety of wild beasts roaming about here day and night — particularly at night, is considerable. The indians cannot get near me without alarming the dogs; I do not fear them in the day time, and at night they cannot kill me, I think, unless they first kill my pup. I have so barricaded my bed, that they cannot shoot an arrow through, to hurt me while asleep. The stillness of the Camp may embolden them, as well as beasts, but I fear neither.

Merdⁿ slightly hazy, and alternately sun shine; a moderate S.W. wind, temp. 54°.

I set the snare again, with rope and a small dog chain. Boiled a kettle of neck-bone joints of venison.

Sun Set hazy, very light S.W. wind, temp. 49°.

I slept very well: — back not so painful. The wolves and dogs awakened me twice, with barking, yelping & howling.

[FEB.] 17th   Commences flyg clouds, moderate wind S.E. temp: 48°   Snare was sprung by a wolf again, — tracks around it. Fever and headache.

Merdⁿ occasional haze, light E. wind, temp: 62°

After breakfast I felt exceedingly drowsy; from losing so much repose by pain. Brought several back-loads of fuel, built a shelter, close to tent, for Nevada, and then went in, and slept soundly a couple of hours.

Sun Set cloudy, light N.E. wind, temp: 56°   Observed several musquitoes on the ground.

Set the snare again, hoping to catch Mr Wolf. Fever and weakness caused me to lay down near my tent, about Sun Set, where I got in a reverie on home, near 4,000 miles distant, all that is dear to me in life; my present forlorn situation, &c. and the low murmer of the evening breeze, through the majestic pines, and mountain gorges, and fell asleep, till my pup warned me of some straggling wolf intruding, and that the shades of night were gathering around my wild and lonely habitation.

[FEB.] 18th Commences hazy, light E. wind, temp: 48° Slept tolerably; had pain in loins and back. Snare, this time, untouched. My breakfast cake, this morning, I made of 5 table-spoonsful of flour, to 8 of acorn-meal. My right heel very sore from frost. Merd^n hazy, moderate E. wind, temp 57°. I mended the broken stock of my comrade's rifle. Feel considerably better to-day. My store of provender is yet fair: — I have about $\frac{1}{4}$ peck of boiled vertebræ to pick, and hanging to a tree, a hind quarter, part of the back-bones of two, 1 fore quarter, and some ribs: besides about 30 lbs musty flour, $\frac{1}{2}$ peck acorns, roasted coffee enough for 4 days, and 3 qrts. salt.

A large flock of gabbling wild geese flew over, low enough to shoot, but I was too weak, then went towards the N.N.W.

Sun Set thick haze & calm, temp: 50°   Beautiful night.

[FEB.] 19th Commences hazy, moderate S.E. wind Temp: 42° Awakened last night, 3 times by the dogs and wolves: the last about day-break. Pain in kidnies, back, and bladder, with frequent painful urinal calls — These sensations interfered much with my repose, last night. Snare yet unmolested. This morning I took 8 table-spoonful of flour, 10 of acorn-meal, and mixed up in a batter, with venison pot-liquor; seasoned it with pepper and salt, and baked it in the skillet; — accompanied with coffee, it was fine.

I found the oak I used as a snare, had lost its elasticity, and another idea struck me. — To find a short crooked tree, which I could easily get up on, or on a branch; put a rope over the arm, one end noosed, and set as before, the other end with a rock attached, — ran up the limb, while the bait-piece was secured, and the stone heavy enough to run up a large wolf. I found a short gnarled pine, on the hill side, about 300 yds in rear of camp, and spent nearly all the forenoon arranging and setting the trap. Rolling the stone 50 yards, hoisting it up, &c. completely prostrated me. I was just able to reach the tent & fall down on my pallet breathless. — Some time before I recovered.

Merd^n flying clouds, and mist, light variable wind, from S. to W. temp. 52° About 4 P.M. I noticed 12 vultures, soaring very high, in circles, over head, and moving towards the S.W. Sun Set clear, calm, temp: 44°.

The nearest dead ox — (or remains of him) is about 70 yds W. of my tent, & 2 S.E. of camp, about 150 yds. The grizzly bears and wolves visit these every night. The distant howl of a large wolf sounds much like the hooting of an owl, and the trinkling sound of a snow-rills is scarcely heard. The forrest is still, except now and then the fall of a pine cone, sounding like a stone thrown. At dusk, the howl of approaching wolves is heard, coming up the Western dell; but the dogs take no notice of them, till they are quite near. — They are accustomed to their howlings.

[FEB.] 20th Commences cloudy, strong S.E. wind, temp: 41°. All night geese, swan, and ducks were flying over, to the N.W. The usual noises and infirmities broke my rest much last night Soon after sun-rise the clouds thickened, and occasional gleams of lightning, fresh breeze from the E. Merdⁿ heavy flying clouds (scuds) and Easterly gales, Temp: 41°   I accidentally noticed the fall of few incipient hail-stones. — A tempest appears to be brewing, in the E. I boiled a kettle full of joints of venison

Strong gusts — blowing in eddies around my tent,: causing the smoke to annoy me. Tooth-ache, or tic-dolereaux, and inflamed gums.

This afternoon another thick flock of the small buntings, swept by me, chirping, and alighted on some low pines, to the westward. They are of an ash color.

About 4 P.M. fine snow & hail, for about one hour, then turned to fine wet snow, alone, and strong E. wind. Trenched around my camp, and secured tent against a storm. I chopped up much fuel.

Numerous vultures & eagles flying about. When a child, I was delighted to see the *"Welchman picking his geese"*. — Not so now. A little after 4 P.M. Clough returned. Sun-Set rain, and gales from the E. temp. 34°

Roberts paid Clough for his services, assisting them to get in, 15 lbs crackers at 50 cts pr lb . . — 3 pints molasses — $2 . . 50, and find himself.

Fine snow first part of night. Passed a very agonizing night: — pains in breast, sides, back, loins, kidneys, tooth, face &c. no sleep. — My sufferings are very severe, and importunate indeed.

[FEB.] 21st. Commences with fly. clouds & calm, temp. 33°   Gale last night sprung my snare, and a fox had been around and close to it, but renard was too cunning to put his nose in the trap.

Alternate sunshine & snow during the forenoon. Merdⁿ snow, moderate wind N.E. temp 32°

Afternoon snow, with a strong breeze veering from S.W. to N.W.

Sun Set hazy, and calm, temp: 33°   (snow 3 ins:)   Great luxury to-day, coffee, sweetened with molasses: — (Clough bro't out a canteen full of molasses, about a pint, for which he paid 75¢).

A very cold night, tent frozen stiff as sheet-iron. Dogs and wolves interrupted my repose.

[FEB.] 22^d clear and calm; temp: 24°

Acorn-cakes for breakfast, with skillagallee and coffee. Cakes baked with candle-grease. Feel better to day, except mouth, which is very sore. Merd^n flyg clouds, strong wind from the W. temp: 33°   Snare untouched. Coffee & crackers for dinner. Sun-Set flying clouds, light variable wind, temp: 44° Clough all day collecting fuel. At dusk cloudy, and spits of snow. Fine snow occasionally through the night. Slept better than for a long time.

[FEB.] 23rd   Continues hazy & calm, temp. 28°

Forenoon sun shine & fly clouds. C. proceeded back, to old camp. Merd^n fly. clouds, light wind S.W. temp. 38°   About 4 P.M. Roberts' Pointer barking vehemently attracked my attention, and looking towards the Cabin, I saw in front of it, 2 large grey wolves, — about 300 yds. from where I stood. Took a rifle, and proceeded some 50 yards towards them, without apparently disturbing them. — I fired, and struck so near the left one, as to make him leap and run up the hill; the other walked down the hill side, quite slowly, occasionally looking around at me. C. returned, with a small grindstone, some tools, and about ½ peck of coffee. Sun-Set clear, very light wind from S.W. temp 35°   Clear pretty night. Slept tolerably.

[FEB.] 24th   Commences clear, light wind N.W. temp. 34°   After 9 A.M. C went hunting. — half an hour after, I heard the crack of his rifle, and in half hour more, another, to the S. down a deep hollow.

Merd^n clr. moderate N.W. wind, temp. 44°. Many eagles & vultures soaring over head. — No doubt attracted by the ox carcasses. About 4 P.M. C. returned luckless, had fired at two deer, — beyond range. Sun-Set cloudy, moderate wind N.E. temp. 42°

Found it best to boil acorns in a brass kettle, the acid does not act so strongly on brass as iron: cooked them in 3 waters, — the 1st and 2nd. quite yellow.

When the sun was about 1 hour high, I observed in the S.W. a small inverted arc of rainbow, seeming very high. (*sun dog*, as sailors term it; and white clouds, tinted on their western edges, with irridescent hues. — (Friend C. says they portend bad weather.) A tolerable night's rest.

[FEB.] 25th Commences cloudy, moderate wind N.W. temp. 35° Thick flying clouds all forenoon. C. went hunting. Made light bread, with ⅔ acorn meal. — a pretty, sweet bread. Much saccarine matter in these acorns; boiled down some of the liquor till it formed a thin syrup. Merdⁿ thick haze, strong S.W. wind, drizzles, temp. 40° Fixing our camp against bad weather.

About 2 P.M. fine hail, & snow, and soon after quite a snow storm commenced; wind generally E. — but hauling, in heavy puffs, to S.E.[,] S.W. and N.W. Some cessation of the storm once and a while during the afternoon. Sun Set fine snow, rain, and mist; Strong wind W.S.W. temp. 34° About 7 P.M. my comrade returned, wet, cold, and fatigued, and luckless. His hair was full of snow, and froze to his cap. Shirt sleeves froze stiff. He shot 2 deer but they escaped in the brush; the storm & lateness of the hour prevented him from searching for them. I always have a good hot meal ready when he returns from a hunt, and the boiled venison & coffee, were particularly opportune this time. Snow'd nearly all night. — very cold. Pain in back very bad. C. related some incidents of his travels from the frontier of the states, told of a battle between Sioux and Pawnees, on the Loup Fork of the Platte. — Saw their graves and mode of burial. Met a war party of Pawnees mounted on fine horses, had been *licked*, — and consequently in an ill-humor. And that a Dr. Graham was drowned in the Platte, hunting for a ford. — got beyond his depth, and the current swept him off.

[FEB.] 26th Commences with flying clouds, and strong wind N.W. temp. 28° After breakfast C. started again to try for a *venison*, as he says. Sun shine and snow all forenoon. Merdⁿ flying clouds, wind light & variable. Temp. 35° Snow'd nearly all the afternoon. Put our last acorns, about 3 pints, on to boil. They are delightful, regret we have not a good store of them. — My legs and loins are very weak. Sun Set cloudy, light S.W. wind, temp: 26. Cooked our last piece of venison. About 7 P.M. my comrade returned, weary & luckless. — He had seen 11 deer, all very wild and beyond reach. Snow occasionally all night, night very cold, and so was the ground; and it seemed harder than usual. Pain in kidneys very annoying.

[FEB.] 27th Commences with snow, light S.E. wind, temp. 28° Had about ¼ lb meat left from yesterday. Chopped it up in a *skillagalee*, for breakfast. After breakfast C. started to try his luck again. 11 A.M. a strong gale from N.E. Merdⁿ snow and a modᵉ S.W. wind, temp. 31°. Had a singular dream last night, and as I recollect it perfectly, I shall put it down. —

Dreampt that a small dark brown hairless dog, with a sharp nose, and slim tail, and a string around its neck, came, in the forenoon of the day, to the tent; that I then called my comrade, pointed to the dog and said "there's some stranger about, probly a d — d indian." On looking out to the S.W. in direction of the road, saw a gentleman, in a blue military undress, frock-coat, approaching! he came up, and proved to be an old and highly esteemed friend.

We shook hands warmly, and he asked how I got on? I replied "bad enough." "Well," said he, get ready, "here's a pack mule train at hand, — coming up, with supplies, and to take you and all your effects down!"

Sun Set clear and calm, temp: 28°　About 9 P.M. poor C. returned, — cold, tired, and very weak, with another luckless tramp. Saw about 20 deer, and shot one thro' the body and broke one of its legs, yet it got off. He has travelled over the ridges & back about 10 ms.

[FEB.] 28th　Commences hazy, light E. wind, temp: 32°　I slept not, last night, till near the morning, caused by violent pains in back, loins, &c. Some spits of snow during the forenoon. Merd^n snow, strong variable wind, temp. 34°　Snow about 10 inches. A large flock of blue-herrons,[67] — sandhill cranes, flew over, a great height, going to the N.W. and croaking. C. building a shed over the fire. Sun Set light airs from the N.W. and clear; temp. 25°

Night clear, with a strong N.W. wind & very cold.

MARCH 1ST　Commences clear, with light S.E. wind, temp: 22°

C. split and chopped up wood, and about 11 A.M. went hunting. Merd^n clear, mod^e N.W. wind, temp: 40°　Very weak to-day, and loss of appetite. My poor comrade again returned disappointed. — Saw 3 deer, shot one through, and he got off — All the afternoon wind S. clear, and thawing. Sun-Set hazy, light N.W. wind; temp. 34° — Soon after cloudy & spits of snow, continuing through night, wolves and chillblains kept me awake all the first half of night: towards morning I slept well.

[MARCH] 2nd　Commences fine snow, Strong E. wind, temp. 30°　Chillblains annoying at night. 9 A.M. a snow gust of short duration. Cranes flying over, 11 A.M. heard a person whistling, and looking out, saw a man wearing a white hat, with a rifle on his shoulder, and thought it was Poile, and did not discover my mistake till close to him. We saluted, and he informed me that he had 3 comrades, coming along, with animals. They were from Feather river mines, had come up from the Settlements, and were *prospecting* for gold. They had plenty of bread but no meat. This person, and his friend, were Oregon emigrants, had lived there some time, but recently visited Cal[e] for gold. — Emigrated to O. in '47, from Illinois; the other 2 were young New Yorkers, and arrived in Cal. from around the Horn. The party had 3 horses.[68] They met the Roberts party, 7 miles this side of Davis' with 4 yoke of oxen they had purchased. These visitors slept in R's wagon. I gave them each a cup of coffee. They seemed to be clever fellows. Merd[n] snow, strong E. wind; temp. 35° Snow all the afternoon. Sun Set cloudy, Strong E. wind, temp. 32°

About 8 P.M. rejoiced to hear my comrade's song and report of his rifle. He brought in a fine buck fawn, which he shot at 200 yards distance, some 2 miles off. He wounded another deer. C. guided the strangers to a grazing place for their horses. They desire to-morrow to prospect for gold & hunt deer.

[MARCH] 3rd Commences clear, calm, temp. 29° C. and 2 of the strangers went hunting, and 2 of them remained in camp. Merd[n] clear.

Moderate wind W. temp. 40°. Thawing rapidly. The snare remains untouched.

My friend returned at dark unsuccessful. In half an hour after Mr Withers and his comrade Oregonian came in with a deer. They had left their horses in deer Ck. gorge. Sun Set clear, calm, temp. 35° A superstitious person would have thought the dream and appearance of these men was a singular coincidence. Withers certainly resembled in appearance, the figure of the man I dreampt of, on the 27th; — who said pack animals were coming. Clear night, strong gusts from the N.E.

[MARCH] 4th Commences clear and calm, temp: 25° Withers and a young man named Bargher, went prospecting. — They went to the N.E. in the hollow near old camp, and returned by 1 P.M. After a lunch, they started for a cañon to the S.S.E, — where their horses are. Merd[n] clear, light wind S. temp. 55° I have amused myself to-day cleaning my rifle, adjusting the sights, running balls, and firing at a mark. Though quite lame, I must take exercise. Parties returned at Sun-Set, and soon after. They bro't in a deer. Yesterday they shot one, and eat half, hanging the other half in a tree: To-day they found but one ham of it, the eagles & vultures had feasted upon it. They gave us a shoulder and head of deer.

(Night clear and cold).
Sun Set clear, light airs from the N.W. temp. 35°.

[MARCH] 5th   Commences hazy, strong gales from the E. temp. 34°   Venison & bread dust fare with coffee. We all sat up late last night, conversing, causing us to sleep late this morning. — Sol was peering on us before we turned out. About 10 A.M. Clough and the prospectors went exploring. Feel to-day badly. One of the strangers — a N. Yorker, named Schuyler, showed me specimens of gold he had obtained from Feather river, — of scales; and some from Trinity river, — irregular small lumps. Strange how we meet, in this world. The old Schuyler family of New York, and my Mother's family, were related, which has given that name to my only brother living, now in Baltimore Md. Old Genl Schuyler, of Revolutionary memory, and my maternal father, I think, were related.

Merd^n flying clouds & strong gale from the E. temp. 34°   some snow: till a regular snow-storm set in, for the afternoon, with strong Ey gales.

Sun Set do — temp. 32°   Soon after dark the wind hauled to the S.E. and blew fresh, with drizzles & fine snow. The strangers opened the Cabin and went in, to shelter themselves from the very inclement weather, for the gale blew all their fire away. Snow storm all night. I slept pretty well, but my poor comrade was up several times.

[MARCH] 6th   Fine snow & gales from the S.E. temp. 32°   We slept late this morning. We had our half-acorn loaf, broil'd venison & coffee. Merd^n rain & fine snow & sleet, fresh E. wind, 36°   Most disagreeable weather. All afternoon & Sun Set same, temp: 34°   Through the night the wind moderate, but occasional snow and sleet.

[MARCH] 7th   Commences with flying clouds, light S. wind, temp. 28° Merd^n cloudy, moderate S.E. wind, temp. 42°   All hands exploring for gold and meat. About 3 P.M. a snow squall of short duration — Withers and Schuyler came in early from stress of weather. — The others returned late, bringing the horses, who were very poor, — little grass there. Mahany is one of the Oregonians. Sun Set cloudy & calm, temp. 32°   All afternoon strings of sandhill cranes going over, to the N.W. — they fly exceedingly high. (have often distinctly heard their hoarse croaking, and looked up, in perfectly clear weather, and could not see them; beyond my vision. At dusk a large flock of geese flew over to the S^d My comrade did not return till after night, when he appeared, wet, hungry, fatigued, and luckless. He saw but

1 deer. The strangers most kindly gave me a tin pan full of crackers. — several pounds. I had no sleep last night, from chillblains and pain in the back. I gave Withers at his request, a government rifle, for and [an] old flint lock rifle, musket, and German double-barrel'd gun.

[MARCH] 8th   Commences cloudy, moderate wind N.E. temp. 24°. Cleared off soon after Sun rise. Our visitors packing their animals, to return. — About 10 A.M. these clever fellows bid us adieu. And C. went hunting down the western gorge. Forenoon Sun Shine & clouds   Merdn fly. clouds, strong N.E. wind, temp. 40

Withers related an account of theft & punishment in the mines, where he had worked. — A chap stole 2 bags of gold dust, from his employer and benefactor; — detected, tried, and sentenced to have his ears cropp'd, head shaved, and be whipped; but they only inflicted the latter, — well laid on with hickory gun-sticks, (cleaning-rods.)[69] a Doctor in attendance. After which, they recovered some of the gold, gave the fellow clothing, and started him off. —

A little before Sun Set, I heard the very agreeable sound of my friends successful chant, — ringing through the forrest and mountains — and he soon made his appearance, bearing a large buck on his shoulders. — He shot him at about 50 yds. seeing his head only, through the brush; about 1½ miles off. Sun Set flyg clouds, moderate N.E. wind, temp. 30°

Bathed my feet in warm salt water to relieve them. My pup wanted to follow the strangers away, and I had to tie her up. Little sleep from pains.

[MARCH] 9th   Cloudy, strong E. wind, temp. 34°   The fore part of last night, fresh gales from the N. and some wolf melodies.

R's pointer alarmed, C. went out, and saw a large yellow fox, sitting on the hill-side, near Cabin, apparently looking at dog. He fired his rifle at the fox, — about 200 yds. off, when it *jump'd* up, ran off, about 50 yd. and sat down again, alongside an oak tree. C. reloaded, but on again looking it had disappeared.

Merdn flyg clouds, light S. wind, temp. 45° — (70° in the sun)   Visited the snare, and between it & my camp saw the tracks of a young grizzler, a fox, and a large wolf. Sandhill cranes flying over, to the N. croaking distinctly, but out of sight. Also wild geese.

Sun Set clear, very light S. wind, temp. 38°   C. felled and chopped up a small oak tree, for fuel. Tried salt bath again, for chillblains. Severe headache, pains in back, breast, &c. Very little sleep.

[MARCH] 10th   Commences hazy, light wind E. 38°   Breakfast soup & remains of the crackers. About 10 A.M. Roberts arrived, with a young man he had engaged, from Davis' rancho, bringing 5 oxen: — had lost one on the road.

On finding that his cabin had been entered by the strangers, this old fool *shed tears*, swearing that they had robbed him, of clothing and valuable goods! He had accumulated a great quantity of plunder on the road, in the rear, before he came here with his family, and was constantly adding to it: — and was exceedingly nervous about it. I told him I did not believe that the party took an iota of his, they were doubtless an honorable set. He said that they had the greatest difficulty to get the team out here.

Merd^n a slight haze & calm, 46°

Roberts told me much. — Than [that] a meat ox, in the mines was worth $700. That the young man who had assisted him out with the oxen, was one of the party when Davis, Lassen & others (Myers & family) were lost in the snow in these mountains 3 years ago, coming in from Mo.[70] That now there was nothing to be made in the mines, and they were very sickly. He saw Willis, who had returned a week before, from Feather river mines. He also saw Poile, on his way to Yuba City. He met Wither's party, from here, 16 miles from Davis' this morning. The young man said that the people at the Settlements were much concerned about us, not only in regard to the weather, but they thought the indians dangerous. — They were known to be on the road not far off.[71] A mule, at Davis' is worth $200. At Feather river mines, $350, to $400.

R. loaded up his wagon, with piece dry-goods, cloths, cassimiry, silks, calicos, white cotton, and other valuable effects, & Packed bedding on a horse.

About 12½ P.M. Roberts & his assistant, started off their team, who dragged the heavy wagon up hill with much difficulty. The shouting, and whipping of the beasts was ringing some time in the forrest. On reaching the top of the hill, about ¼ mile, R. returned, secured his cabin, mounted his horse & rode on, without bidding me adieu. He also carried off the slut and pups. It will take him 3 days to get in to Davis'.

All afternoon calm.

Sun Set hazy, & calm, temp. 40°

A severe headache all day. C. went hunting this morning. At Sun Set, my pup barked & whined much, and I turned her loose, thinking she wanted to sup on one of the old carcasses below, but instead of which she streaked it up hill, on the road, as fast as possible, and, with a sigh, I gave her up, as lost. At dark, however, to my great joy, she returned, very tired, but with a full paunch. (Said to be an ox carcass 1 mile on trail)　C. arrived after dark, luckless; saw several deer, and shot one through, — but it escaped down a precipice. Back annoyed me much — allowing little repose.

[MARCH] 11th　Commences snow & drizzle, gales from E.S.E. — temp: 33° Annoyed much with smoke. Broiled venison, cake — 2 parts acorns to 1 of flour, and coffee. Heavy gales and snow, from the E.S.E. all forenoon — Disagreeable day.

Merdn do & rain, temp. 36°

The violent gusts of wind prevents us keeping up a decent fire; and the drip from tent & trees is annoying. Early in afternoon all rain — continuing late. (The first regular rain since the fall of the year)　The wind veering around occasionally, with violence, to the S.E. Near Sun Set, snow & rain. Sun Set, fine rain, & strong E.S.E. wind: temp: 33°

All day and night fever, chillblains, pain in legs & loins, and much weakness. Retired to bed early. Tent very damp. Drizzles & snow, latter predominating, all night.

[MARCH] 12th　Cloudy, strong E. wind, temp. 34°　Was quite ill last night; pains in abdomen, back, & shoulders, headache, fever, & watchfullness. Geese flying over. Breakfast cake, of $\frac{1}{5}$ acorn-meal, stewed venison & coffee. (We generally cook enough meat for dinner also. — At merdn lunching on the cold meat, — stew, &c. and at Sun-Set make a regular meal — similar to the breakfast.

At 9 A.M. old sol enlivened the scene for about 5 minutes, and at 10 o'clk it commenced sleeting. (Before breakfast I took 2 tablespoonsful of castor oil)　Forenoon strong wind from E. & S-E. I suffer depression of mind to-day. — very greatly.

Merdn fine hail, strong Ey wind, temp. 33°　A bleak wintry afternoon. Great thirst & little appetite — the oil has, however, relieved me some. My devoted friend Clough, is quite sick, — headache & diarohea; gave him 15 drops laudanum, and 10 do camphor. He slept after it & felt better. Sun Set, fine snow falling, fresh E. wind — temp: 30°　After night strong gales, increasing to heavy for several hours duration.

About 10 P.M. a wolf chant awoke me. I wish they would sing a little further off when I need repose so much.

[MARCH] 13th　Commences with fine snow, & strong E. wind, temp: 28° Acorns exhausted — Breakfast a thin flour cake, broil'd venison & coffee.

(Last night pains in shoulder, back, &c. severe.) Storm all forenoon. C. cut a piece of red-wood, and rived out some slats, 8 feet long, and formed a shelter for fire, and to keep the storm out of our abode.

Merd^n same weather, temp. 36°

Some 40 paces, in rear of our camp, stood a couple of large and very tall fur-trees. — They grew within 4 feet of each other, and some heavy gale, a year or so since, had started the roots of the larger tree, and it gave way, falling and lodging against the more slender one. — causing the latter to bend over considerable; and from about 50 feet above ground, the big tree pressed so heavily on the other, that from thence to their tops they lay perfectly close together. It was my friend's opinion that a few scores taken out of the lesser tree with an axe, would cause the two to fall to the ground. As their inclination was not in a direction near our camp, and they contained numerous dry branches, suitable for fuel, he determined on trying the experiment. He cut the tree, on the underside, about ⅔: & then nearly through, on the other, before it fell; when to our astonishment, the larger one remained, in its inclined position. The tree was slow falling, cracking and splitting up, some minutes. The toughest wood we ever saw. The larger tree inclined a little more when its support fell, and stretching out the long roots, they lifted the ground for many feet. This afforded us plenty of good fuel, close at hand.

Sun Set cloudy, strong S.E. wind, temp. 33°   While my friend was stripping bark off an adjacent cedar of large size, he found under it a common bat, such as we have home, but larger, and put it in our lodge, in an old lantern.

[MARCH] 14th   Commences again with light snow, wind light from the S.E. temp: 32° (snowed occasionally, all night)

My infirmities last night quarreled with Morpheus & drove him off. This morning C. attacked the big leaning fur-tree. He dug away the snow, to cut through what he supposed, were the supporting roots; but on laying them bare, found all of them near the surface, broken; and left him for the elements to overthrow.

We laid in a stock of the thick *fat* fir bark, so fine for light and kindling. My right eye is inflamed & swollen. We have a shoulder of meat yet uncooked, & about 32 lbs of flour. Bread is now forbidden fruit, — we must reserve our flour to thicken broth, make *skillagalee*. Spirrits much depressed to-day, cannot tell why. It may proceed from my circumstances, — very infirm, with rheumatism, &c. confined much to a smoky and damp abode, provissions very short, snow around, and falling. — bad enough. This is the 37th day since my sincere and kind friend, Poile, left us. (we daily expect him).

Of this time, there has been 20 day bad, stormy weather; and 8 cloudy, and bleak: leaving but 9 days of decent weather. —

At 11 A.M. though sprinkling snow, Clough shouldered his trusty rifle, and started off to obtain meat.

Merd^n cloudy, Strong E. wind, temp. 34° Diverted my mind, by inking over my pencilled notes. — numerous small pocket memorandum-books, and touching up sketches. Sun Set cloudy, moderate wind from E.S.E. — temp. 32° Pain (rheumatic) now has attacked my neck.

Late in the afternoon several flocks of geese passed over from the N. — sweeping around to S.E. and S.S.W. Soon after dark poor C. returned cold, jaded, and luckless. — Had been as low down as "Steep Hollow," — 7 miles; saw several deer, and shot one through, at 200 yds & lost him. No snow down there. Snowing and thawing all night. Pain in neck & back. Slept tolerably.

[MARCH] 15th Cloudy, light S. wind, temp: 33° Thawing. Broil'd venison and coffee for breakfast. C. cut up some fuel, cleaned his rifle, & started again for venison: — the last being now cooking.

C. told me, that yesterday evening, about 2 miles on the road, he saw 2 small yellowish grey wolves, in company with a large animal, somewhat the shape of a wolf. It was black, with brindled sides, slender tail, not bushy, but curled up like a hound's, and ears rather round. This, of course, was a large panther or cougar. It [he] was only about 50 yds. from it, and could easily have shot it, but thought best not to fire, as he saw tracks where indians had been ranging, and considering our circumstances, thought it more discreet to reserve his charge. I am certain that these mountains contain animals unknown, and undiscribed. There's the large spotted *wolf*, for instance.

On account of the recent numerous tracks of indians & grizzlers, C. has stuck a holster-pistol in his belt, and 6 cartridges in his pouch. Clough is as fearless a hunter, as indefatagable. — He has never shot a grizzler, and often remarked that if one came in range he would blizzen at him. And he is anxious to obtain the meat of one. I have protested against his molesting one of these Kings of the Sierra Nevada, assuring him that none but a practiced mountaineer can expect to fell him at the first shot, and if he but wounded one, his life would pay the forfeit of his temerity. He knows all the ridges, spurs, dells, gorges, &c. for many miles, and can, as he often has, find his way here, on a dark night, when a few miles off. Writing, &c. as yesterday. Wild geese flying over. Merd^n cloudy, Moderate S. wind, temp. 36°. About 1 P.M. a heavy fall of sleet, lasting 15 minutes only. Afternoon Sun & clouds Sun

Set flying clouds, wind strong, and veering from S.E. to S.W. temp: 34°. At dark geese flying over to the N. Heavy flaws of Wy wind. — Feel much better to-day than for some time. I kept the pot of hot meat, and the coffee by the fire, anxiously waiting the return of my friend. At 9 P.M. it hailed heavily for some time. Night dark & stormy; ever and anon the hoarse wolf-howl was borne on the gale. Hour after hour of anxious suspense, grew painful. — He doubtless had a long, ardious, and cold tramp; sleet and snow to wade through! poor fellow! He cannot be lost, if he has kept the ridge; but he may have attacked a grizzly bear, in some deep gorge, and there perished; mangled, bleeding, laying writhing in the cold and wet! Oh, if I knew where he was! lame and feeble as I am, I would take my lantern, and pistols, and endeavor to find & succor him! Perhaps he has fallen by the arrows of lurking indians!

There stands our kettle, containing the last meat! Thus cogitating, I sat, till past midnight, catching at every sound of wild animal or night-bird or falling branch, driven before the midnight breeze. — Drowsy, my last log on the fire, and chilled through, I rolled up in my blankets for repose. — Yet my concern for my friend, on such an inclement dark night, kept me awake some time. I was cold, and rheumatic pains were shooting through me, in all directions.

This was par excellence, an awful night.

[MARCH] 16th   I slept till sunrise, and sprang to my feet as soon as awakened. It was clear & calm, temp. 19°

Built up my fire, and heated the coffee and meat. My anxiety for the safety of my friend, increases every moment. Not only for him, poor fellow! but for myself, — what a lamentable situation, if an accident or calamity has befallen him! — I have no appetite for breakfast. $10\frac{1}{4}$ A.M. Great God! I hear his rifle! then his pistol! — he is safe, — coming up the W^n ravine! Still uneasy, — he may be wounded, and seeks my assistance! — In $\frac{1}{4}$ hour after the reports, I was entirely relieved, by his shout of success, — the deer song! I answered his shots by another, now shouted at the top of my lungs, and hobbled off to meet him. Never was sound more welcome to mortal's ear, than that shout of my devoted old friend! We met, about $\frac{1}{4}$ mile from camp, & C. had a fine doe, — dragging it with a stick. (she contained a male and female foetus, size of rats)   He shot her about 6 miles off, near Sun-Set yesterday, cleaned and shouldered her, and travelled till midnight: when the storm opposed his further progress. — He then descended into a hollow, where finding plenty of dry oak, he made a fire, cooked liver, heart, and tongue, made a hearty dinner, laid down, and slept well, till day-break this morning; when he started for camp. He saw 14 deer in the grassy deep valley of Mill-Creek, and he wounded one, which ran off. After his return, my appetite was rapidly revived, and about $11\frac{1}{4}$ A.M. we breakfasted heartily: then sat by the fire, smoked our pipes, and for a while thought we were happy. C. skinned, cut, and hung up the deer and gathered fuel. Pain in my back excessive. Bringing the deer over steep, rocky, and snow-covered heights, so far, and in a snow-storm, with loss of repose, has made my friend quite weak & sick; and last night's anxiety of mind, loss of sleep, &c has much enfeebled me to-day. C. laid down & slept. I had a good hot dinner for him when, at merd^n he awoke, and gave him, before dining a dose of rhubarb. He shot the deer in the shoulder, the ball ranged down the spine, and lodged in the rump, on the opposite side, — first passing through another deer at 200 yards. — They were close together.

Merd^n clear, light S. wind, temp. 40°
Sun Set same ” S.E. ”   ”   32°

My breast is weak & sore. Clough's feet are very sore. Broiled venison & coffee for supper. Pain in breast deprived me of appetite. Night clear and cold, young moon and stars are shining brightly: — calm. A fox passed near camp and barked.

With exception of pain in neck & back, I had little disturbance, and slept pretty well.

MARCH 17, 1850 - OCTOBER 9, 1850

Roberts' Cabin in the Sierra Nevada to the Honey Lake Region

MARCH 17 1850 Commences clear and calm; temp: 30°
Broil venison & coffee for breakfast.
Merd^n clear, light airs from the S., temp: 54° (in the sun 68°)
My friend now determined on felling the large inclined fur tree, which had withstood all other efforts to prostrate it. It stood at an angle of   ° with the horizon, was hollow, and burnt, at the base; and as before said, the upper roots were broken; yet was the wood so exceedingly tough, that he had to cut in, till but 8″ inches across the stump remained, when it slowly moved, cracked, splintered, and fell, with a tremendious crash: — dashing fragments of limbs and branches in all directions. Diameter of trunk, when cut, 4½ feet, length (perfectly straight,) about 200 feet.
Sun Set clear, light S.W. wind, temp. 36°
Dinner cold meat and tea.
(Clough related an anecdote of a dog, — that when they were on the Loup Fork of the Platte, he saw a dog, sitting by the grave of his master, who had been murdered by the indians. They brought the faithful animal almost to Fort Larimie, when he had fits & some one shot him.)
(*wolf-howl as we retired, about 10½ P.M.*)
Wild geese flying over at dark — Alternate clear and cloudy during the night, till near morning, when there was fine snow and strong N.E. wind.

[MARCH] 18th Commences fine snow, mod^e E. wind, temp. 33° C. saw a squirrel run up a sapling pine, but he eluded pursuit. Forenoon snow, and strong wind from N. and N.W. — temp: falling rapidly, to 30°. At Merd^n

clear, wind S.W. temp: 34° (60° in sun) In a few hours it fell again several degrees, and at Sun Set rose to 30° — Clear, with moderate wind from S.W. Night clear, with a variable wind, mostly N. Geese and cranes flying over.

[MARCH] 19th   Commences clear, light N. wind; temp: 28°
42 days of Poile's absence from here.
Broiled venison & tea breakfast —
Merd. clear, moderate S. wind, temp: 43°
About 11 A.M. Clough went hunting. 4½ P.M. he returned with a doe. He shot her about 2 miles off, in the W^n ravine. When he first saw her, she was laying down, in the sun, and he gained a position behind a pile of rocks, about 70 yards from her. He fired & missed her, owing to weakness & nervousness: — He re-loaded, and again fired, ineffectually, when she started, looked around, & commenced grazing. He re-loaded, rested his rifle on the rock, and fired again, and shot her through the heart. — He dragged her up on the snow. He observed several large wolves following, smelling along the trail, and says that we will get a serrenade to-night.
Sun Set hazy, light airs S.W. temp: 32°

[MARCH] 20th   Commences clear and calm, temp: 24°
Last night was very cold. Venison stew & coffee. Merd^n clear, light S. wind, temp. 45°   2 P.M. Cranes flying over. While the sun was shining, a small hail cloud passed, scattering small icy pellicles.
(*Laid down a thick bed of pine branches to sleep on.*)
Sun Set clear, light S. wind, temp: 34°
All night long, geese, cranes, and brandt were flying over to the North-ward.
Early in the night, we were amused with a considerable wolf symphony, followed by the *hoo,! hoo,! hoo!* of an old owl.
Our soft, elastic, and odorous bed, caused me to sleep remarkably well.

[MARCH] 21st   Commences clear, light S.W. wind, temp: 33°
Breakfast cold venison stewed up, and coffee. Cranes flying over, beyond vision. I am very weak to-day. Looking out for Poile.
Merd^n clear, light S. wind, temp: 50°
Sun Set flying clouds, same wind, temp: 44°
After dark hazy, then cloudy. Cranes, geese, brandt, and ducks, flying over all night, to the Northward. I slept very well, till near morning, when an

indiscreet pack of wolves, near the camp, started a thundering howl, for 15 minutes.

[MARCH] 22d Commences cloudy, fine snow & drizzle, moderate wind from the S.S.E. temp. 34°

Broiled meat and coffee. Merdn drizzles, Moderate S.E. wind, temp: 41° Thawing.

Sun Set cloudy, very light variable airs, temp: 38° Geese going over. A fox barked near us, at night. Rain throughout the night.

[MARCH] 23d Commences rainy, light variable wind, temp: 40° Thawing. Cold meat stewed, and coffee.

Merdn drizzly, and thawing, very light S.E. S.E. [sic] wind, temp: 47° Thawing and misty. We can always find plenty of work. — My comrade has been busy washing utensils, towels, &c. Fuel to gather, &c — and when I can do nothing else, I find a useful amusement in writing and drawing, when my infirmities admit. Severe pain in my body. About 4 P.M. a string of some 20 cranes flew over, quite low, when I threw a rifle-ball among them, causing great derange[me]nt, for a while, in their line of travel, & much croaking. (Pismires and flies are active, in the sun to-day, showing that spring is rapidly advancing.)

Sun Set calm and foggy, temp: 44° Occasional drizzles during the night, and thaw continuing. Slept tolerably, bodily. pains prevented sound repose.

[MARCH] 24. Commences cloudy, calm, temp. 44° — Occasional drizzles during forenoon.

Merdn same as commencement, temp. 52°

After breakfast my comrade went out for deer. The pains in my back are very severe. About 5 P.M. C. returned, luckless. — He saw 6 deer.

Sun Set cloudy, light S.W. wind, temp: 43°

Broiled & boiled venison & coffee to-day. Geese going over, to the Northward. Drizzles & showers all night.

[MARCH] 25th (*Last of Clough*) Commences with fine rain, & light S.E. wind; temp: 46° I hear frogs croaking, and small birds warbling. — Swarms of wild fowl constantly going over to the Nd all indicating that old winter is about to emigrate from here. About 10 A.M. my faithful comrade again started off to hunt deer: A light cool rain, however, may interfere with his success; but we have, after breakfast, only about 2 lbs. of venison, on a leg-bone. Our breakfast was cold boiled meat left from yesterday, and quite a scanty meal. My bodily pains are very annoying; — disturbed my repose much last night. When Clough was preparing to start, he observed that he might have to travel some distance for a *venison*, as he could not think of returning empty-handed; and if he should be luckless to-day, he would camp out, (make a fire & sleep by it) and try it again to-morrow. He proceeded about 10 paces, turned around, and observed to me, smilingly, "Cap, I wouldn't wonder if some of these times, in my wild rambles over these ridges and hollows, that some d — d grizzler or indian would pin me!" I replied, that the grizzlers would not be likely to molest him if he refrained from molesting them; and as for the indians, I believed them to be too infernally cowardly; yet it were best to keep out of the way of both, if he could.

Great weakness — perspiring with debility.

Merd^n a heavy shower of fine rain; light and variable wind, temp. 52° Sun Set wet fog, and calm, temp: 46°

I put my last piece of meat in the pot, and boiled it with the bone, which I previously cracked. — Dined, and left enough for my breakfast, if not hungry.

Night foggy and calm. Sat up late, threw logs on the fire, and retired to bed exhausted. The thaw and wet spell has undoubtedly swelled the streams below, and if Poile is at the rancho, he will have to wait till the waters subside some, ere he can come on. Wild geese flying over all night. Night clear. I slept badly.

[MARCH] 26th   Commences flying clouds, light and variable wind, temp. 41° Soon after sun rise, he shone out clear, — a beautiful morning; the birds singing and chirping in every direction. Stewed my meat, eat part of it, with coffee, for breakfast. Looking out continualy for Clough. Merd^n clear, light S.W. wind. Temp. 62°. Friend out yet! Sun-Set clear, light W. wind, temp. 50° 9 P.M. C. still absent! A beautiful night. Just after laying down I was attacked with a violent cholera morbus; took laudanum and camphor. Ill & awake all night. — Headache, fever, & prostration. — Took another dose of laudanum & camphor.

(*Bear visit*) In a feverish doze, near day, I was alarmed by the most vehement yelling of my pup, and crying as if in great pain, or fright. — I seized a carbine, and opening the tent, was looking in the face of an immense grizzly-bear, within 10 feet of me.[1] The fire between us was low, and my poor little Nevada was cowering & trembling with fright. We eyed each other, for full 5 minutes, very composedly, when he slowly turned his huge carcass around, and moved off, growling as he went. I was not alarmed; for I knew that if he was sent to wind me up, I had the consolation also to know, that it would terminate much suffering. — However, I thought that "discretion was the better part of valor" now; and I would not rashly commit suicide, by molesting him. He turned his head from me, when about to leave, — in such a contemptious manner, as to give me the impression that he thought me too contemptable to kill. When his rear was turned to me, I audably said "good morning," laid down and slept. Had I been well, and active, I might have had some amusement, and obtained a fine store of excellent fat meat. — For, with a pocket full of cartridges & caps, and a Hall's carbine, I could have dodged around the trees and mastered him. But I thought best to save my miserable life, for severer trials, and lose the meat.

[MARCH] 27th   Commences clear, moderate wind from the W. temp: 50° Quite ill this morning. Nothing to eat. Clough still absent; — I now concluded that my devoted old friend having chased deer far down, towards the settlements; and being so near in, he had determined to visit them, see if Poile was there, and return, with at least flour if no other aid. So I allowed 3 days for that; and if so, he will surely return to-night or in the morning. Well! I am now in a *snap* truly; without food, helpless, and subject to spells of prostration! How am I to sustain life? Another beautiful day. — Merdn clear, light S. wind: temp: 68°   Cranes constantly flying over to the Southward, out of sight — so high. Headache & fever, took a dose of Castor-oil, with camphor and laudanum in it, and drank a pot of tea. I put a musket & pair of pistols, with bag of cartridges, on top the cabin, to shoot the grizzler to-night, should he again visit me, and I am able to walk over & climb the corner of the house. Sun Set clear, very light airs from the W. temp. 58° High fever & headache all the afternoon. Am too ill to attend to bears or any thing else to-night.

[MARCH] 28th   Commences clear, fresh wind S.E. temp. 56°
   Headache and great prostration.
   Shot a very small blue woodpecker. — I took a small saucepan of water, put an inch of tallow-candle, the bird, pepper & salt, in; and boiled it; and made a pot of coffee — This is the first meal I have had in 48 hours. A strong variable breeze all morning. Mended my pantaloons, & procured fuel and water.
   Merdn clear, moderate & variable wind, temp. 72°   Feel a little better. Do not know where I am to obtain food, am perfectly perplexed how to sus-

tain life much longer. The birds are scarce, and very shy, and I am weak and nervous. — The wolves will not come close enough; and if they did, my nervousness will prevent me from taking correct aim at them. This afternoon the temperature rose to 74°. Near Sun Set hunger impelled, I took my double-barrel'd gun, and walked down the hollow ¼ mile, to hunt birds, and came suddenly on 4 deer, not 50 yds. off; fired, but too unsteady, to aim true and they bounded off. (Charge of buck shot) Saw several robins, but they were exceedingly shy. What a delightful day! if I could enjoy it; but fever and hunger interfere. Sun Set clear & calm, temp: 63° Wild fowl flying over all night. A clear beautiful night. Surely one or both of my friends will be out to-morrow. — If not, poor Clough is lost, and I must soon follow; for I feel myself sinking, in spite of all my philosophy.

[MARCH] 29th. Commences clear and calm, temp. 54° Hunger awakened me at dawn, and though exceedingly feeble, I must endeavor to preserve my life, [not] for its value to me at all, but for those who now little dream of my sad circumstances. I took my gun, and walked down the hollow again; the robins were crying & hopping about among the cedars, but flew before I could get near them. Saw a bald eagle and several vultures soaring over head. Fever and acid stomach. A flock of geese flew over to the Northward, — they were low enough to shoot, but I was too weak to raise my gun in time. The blue woodpeckers are as shy as the robins. Cannot get nearer than 200 yds. of either, and have no fine shot. — I am compelled to charge with heavy loads of buck-shot any how, in case of meeting deer or other beast. Returned exhausted: threw myself down, and rested. I then made coffee, drank a pint, put a teaspoonful of salt in ½ pint grounds, and eat that. I hunted around the cabin, and found several naked leg-bones of deer, long since stripped by the dogs and wolves; — these I gladly gathered, and carried to my abode. I cracked a couple, and found in each a yellow shrivelled string of marrow. I warmed some water, washed them some, & boiled them, producing a very *cheesy*-tasting broth. — This, seasoned with pepper and salt, I greedily swallowed, at 11 A.M. A large mixed flock, of geese & swan, flew over, to the N.W. —

Merdⁿ flying clouds, light wind W. temp. 76° About 12½ P.M. a small flock of dark cranes went over, towards the S.W. then swept around to the N.W. At 1 P.M. I put on belts, with pistols & knife, & shouldering my carbine, proceeded in a S.E. direction, over a low spur, for ½ mile, looking for deer, but saw none. With great difficulty I returned to camp, exhausted. About 5 P.M. a flock of wild pidgeons flew low, and very rapidly over. Sun

Set a slight haze, moderate breeze from the W. temp: 61°. Robins are chirping, but they are not for me to eat. At dusk a flock of geese passed, — going to the N. and flew high. — Their gabbling startled me, as has happened before. Geese and cranes, when distant sound very much like human voices, — and always sets my pup barking, as no doubt he is thus deceived also. — Must I eat my faithful watch? — My poor little Nevada, who has shared my sufferings? — for one meal, and then die regretting it? — I will not! Drank balance of bone broth. Have a few bones left for to-morrow; — when, if Clough is alive, he will arrive. I feel deep concern for his safety. — He may have killed a deer at a distance, and in the evening made a fire, cooked the liver, eat a hearty meal, after the fatigue of the day, and slept: — his fire grew low, and a grizzly-bear, scenting the meat, come to the spot, disturbed the brave old hunter, who combatted him, and fell, mangled; — his life dashed out! Perhaps, and most likely, that he hunted towards the Mill creek side, and down that vale killed a deer, supped and slept; the report of his rifle, and the light of his fire, attracted the infernal indians, from the gulch below; who stealing up, filled him with arrows. — He slept to wake no more! — Sacrificed in my service! Magnanimous, intrepid, and kind old man! Shall I ever forget thee? Never! Let my days be few or many, the grateful remembrance of thee will never leave my head and breast! — Thou wast a MAN! There are some true *men*, in this world. — Poile is another; and side by side with Clough, in grateful remembrance, shall he be likewise cherished, while memory retains her seat, or this heart continue to beat! What rare instances of nature's noblemen! And in such a community of extreme selfishness! The vain, superficial, sycophantical world cannot appreciate such men. One was a true *brother*, in kindness & humanity, the other was doubly a *brother. Oh, that all appreciated those tenets, inculcated by the highest principles that sublime truth ever enlightened man, with, and conformed thereto!*

Night clear and mild. — Wild fowl flying over all night. I got on the roof of the cabin, at night, with great difficulty, and lay there some time, looking for a grizzler to come along. The night breeze moans through the dells and among the tall trees; the howl of a distant wolf is heard, and in an adjacent tree, an old owl is hooting his monotonous ditty. All else is still, here, in this lonely spot. — Hush! I hear music! a sweet pathetic air, on the flute, &c! — Am I dreaming? No! There! I heard a cock crow! and a child laugh! What does all this mean? — Am I crazy? — certainly not. Pshaw! Of course there must be queer sounds here, caused by the various obstructions to the passage of the light breeze up these hollows, through trees, &c. I asked myself, audibly, (while peering around, with my hand upon my rifle,) if I was not too philosophical to allow my mind to give away, and sinking into imbecility, frustrate my struggles to save my life for the benefit of my wife and children? I rose, clinched my teeth, and said "Yes!" I was chilled; — walked over to lonely couch, and fell asleep.

MAR. 30. Commences clear, light W. wind, temp. 50°

A flock of geese just flew over to the N.W. Weakness and acid stomach annoying. If Clough does not return to-day, he is undoubtedly gone forever! I had a number of deer-skins hanging on a line, to dry. — I examined them, & found where the flesh side adhered, there were some very small strips of dry meat, and these places were full of worms; I carefully opened them, and with my butcher-knife, scraped out the *skippers,* and tore off the bits of meat; resulting in giving me about a gill of very *gamey* venison. This boiled with 2 old cracked leg-bones, and another inch of tallow candle, made me broth, which with coffee, had to serve for breakfast. I then shouldered my gun, and pouch, and started to go ahead, on the road as far as I dare, to look for game, and maybe to find the remains of my friend. I started several deer, many grouse,[2] and numerous small birds; — all seemed to know that I was a doom'd man: — Proscribed by Heaven! — An outlaw; and they must not allow me to come near enough to shoot them; must not contribute to support me, against the will of Heaven! — Such thoughts ran through my brain; I staggered, and sank against a huge pine. Here I fell in a trance, and thought I was most comfortable at home, — my little boy was at my side, and parting my long and matted hair, with his little hands. — Was brought to consciousness by a noise, and heard a wolf bark. — I now raised myself with difficulty; and retraced my weary feeble steps, to my melancholy-looking lodge, set my gun against the side, and threw myself down exhausted on my pallet; where I lay about ½ hour. I suppose I travelled about 5 miles. Geese and cranes going to the N^d Noticed an extraordinary fact, about the cranes; — that when a flock is flying out of sight of us, they have one lower, — within the reach of our vision, — who croaking, with a strong voice, guides the flock above, who respond to his *pilot*-notes: — he sees the land, while those above cannot.

Merd^n clear, strong W. wind, temp: 75° Found, at the cabin 2 dried pieces of deer ribs, which with a couple more, and last of the old gnawed leg-bones, made a pint of broth for my dinner. — It was a sort of rank meat *tea.* I also had a pot of coffee. There are plenty of deer, but not for me. — Were I permitted to shoot one, I could only bring a few pounds to camp, and the birds and beasts of prey would get the rest.

Sun Set clear, moderate wind W.N.W. temp. 56°

The road, as far as I went to-day is nearly clear of snow. The tracks of grizzly-bears and wolves, are thick upon it, going & coming this way, and some of them very recent. A grizzler must have gone on a very short time, on the road, before me. His track was perfectly fresh in the mud, and snow. Deer tracks in all directions.

I made coffee and eat the grounds, with salt, for supper.

At dusk I heard the husky howl of a large wolf, — approaching nearer and nearer, till his hoarse bark was near, and I seized a rifle, and went out to shoot him, but in [he] was in a brushy hollow, where I distinctly heard him ripping the hide of an old ox carcass, about 150 yds. off; but I was too weak to go down.

MARCH 31 — 7th day of Clough's, and 55 of Poiles' absence Commences cloudy, with light wind from the W.N.W. temp. 50° I slept little, but soundly last night — latter part, and this morning. Just before I awoke, this morning, dreampt of having just arrived at home, and embracing my family. Spoiled venison tea & coffee, for breakfast, and I again took my gun and went to try for game of any kind. — It commenced drizzling ere I reached 300 yards, and I found myself too feeble to proceed, so returned. I had proceeded about 50 yards when I struck the track of a large grizzly-bear, he had visited an old ox-carcass, turned it over, stove in the hide and ribs by a stroke of his sinewy arm, dragged it 50 yards, and drawn a horn off; — the prints of his teeth on it. — As the marks were all fresh, he must have been here while I was sleeping, this morning. I cut loose several of the old carion-ribs & took up to my starving dog. I found 4 deer-hoofs, and with an inch of candle and about an ounce of tallow, from the lantern, I made broth for dinner, seasoned it well with pepper and salt. — Also coffee, eating a gill or so, of the grounds with salt.

Merd^n a thick haze, and flying clouds, Strong E.S.E. wind; temp. 56° No wild fowl flew over to day, and the crows and ravens have abandoned me to what looks like a certain doom. I fired at a flock of small buntings, but too eager and weak — missed them. Raining all the afternoon. Supper, Coffee, and grounds. Found, on the road, yesterday, "James' History of Chivalry," — Family Library. — am drying it.[3]

Sun Set flying clouds, and showers, very light S.W. wind, temp: 46° — thunder. — Another day closed without succor. cloudy, & thunder at dusk, warning me of an approaching gale; and as I feared the falling of limbs and trees, I went into the Cabin, to sleep. — It was well I done so; for there came up, soon after, hail, rain, and strong gales from the N.W. with thunder, — which continued all the first part of the night. I was cold, and slept little.

APRIL 1st   The 8th day of Clough's mysterious absence! One, probably, that time will never solve! And the 56th of Poile's. I fear much that the former is gone to his long home, and the latter is ill, if not dead also!

Temp. fell, during night 16°

Commences clear, with light W. wind: temp. 30°

Hail lies thick on the ground. About daybreak I left the cabin, and went to my tent, to lie down, but was too cold to sleep much. I lay, hoping for repose, till sun-rise, when I built up my fire, made coffee, and warmed a pint of the bone-tea; but attending to the coffee, my kittle of broth fell over, and I thus lost my *last meal!* I picked up the pieces of bone & knawed them, drank my coffee, and eat a spoonful of the grounds.

(The thunder, last evening, was the first my pup ever heard, and it astonished and alarmed her much: — causing her to bark furiously, and run around, wildly looking about, and above. — The same occurred at night.

A little after midnight a grizzler visited my establishment, and I had to muzzle the pup, with a handkerchief, to prevent her irritating the huge beast, and causing our destruction. — I was sick and weak, hardly able to rise, but got up, and sat on a block of wood, in front of my tent, and threw pine-bark on the fire. The morose-looking old fellow came up, within 10 feet, snorted, eyed me about 3 minutes, and then slowly left. It is likely my fire saved me this time. Several large wolves soon after passed, casting a look at me, as they went by.)

Thus with infirmity, cold, dampness, — starvation, and yelping of my cur, and howling of wolves, I obtained hardly any repose, last night.

This morning I shall try to get on the road again, hoping to shoot something to allay the cravings of hunger, and preserve my life. General debility, and rheumatism in back and calves of legs, have hobbled me. Yet I must exert myself, or die at once; and, they say that "whilst there's life, there's Hope." Indeed, there is! And Sweet Hope, and a mind determined on surviving such a fearful trial, will yet save me, I think. Hope, and a resolve to triumph over difficulties, will bear one beyond them, and transport them successfully, through trials which seem insurmountable. — The human animal can bear more hardships and sufferings than can be described, if the mind be kept above water

I shouldered my carbine, put cartridges in my pouch, and started; — I proceeded about 2 miles, on the road, and then gave out. I saw 2 deer across a ravine, and numerous wild-pidgeons, grouse, woodpeckers, robins, crows, &c. But fate had marked me; — they knew it, and kept beyond my reach. After a lethargic rest, I retraced my painful steps, reached my lone shelter, and threw me, again exhausted, on my damp pallet. On recovering, the keen cravings of hunger warned me of the imperious necessity to procure food immediately. I recollected that Roberts had put a deer's head, under the eaves of the cabin, a long time since, where it became wedged in the logs, and he could not conveniently extricate it, to give the dogs: — This I sought. — Ha! I have food! I thought. On reaching it, I with much difficulty got it down, by the aid of a pole; and found it half decayed, and consumed by worms & insects. — However, I took it to a stump, near my tent, chopped it up with a hatchet, and cut out the shrivelled tongue. Gave the head and root of the tongue to my faithful pup, and put the small half of the tongue in a kettle to cook. While this was boiling, I overhauled the skins again, and found one, of a fawn, with the hoofs and fetlock-joints attached. — These I cut off, scraped out the worms, singed off most of the hair, and threw them also in the kettle. Then I made coffee, and thank God! had another meal, with some solid food; which possessed a queer taste; and would have been, probably, in different circumstances, quite disgusting! — Here, again, did I think of the Panak family's antelope-feet broth. Theirs was superior to mine, in every respect; certainly no filthier, and as certainly more nutritious, & agreeable to the palate. Well! I have dined again; *hoping* to find yet another meal.

Attacked with, what I at first conceived to be, a whooping noise, in my chest, on breathing, when walking; it annoyed me much, and I thought several times that it was the howl of a distant wolf. On walking out to day, this low wolf-howl haunted me, for go where I would, in every position, and in calm or breeze, still the same monotonous low howl of a wolf was heard; and though so low, as to sound like the voice of a wolf at least 2 miles off, yet it seemed to be near me! I tried my breathing, and ascertained that it was not thus produced! I reflected on it; what could it be? When at rest it rested also! I asked myself if I was becoming superstitious? or crazy? I then recollected that prolonged hunger produced insanity; and I reasoned with my own mind on that subject. Can I not stave off these dreadful consequences of starvation & weakness? Can I not rally my mind to struggle against such disastrous results? — "It must be done!" said I; — gritting my teeth and clenching my fist! — There is a reasonable and philosophical cause for this annoyance, this mysterious, and now painful sound. It shall haunt me no more! And I will be rendered miserable no longer, in mind, when I walk out, by this strange bogee of the winds! Could the breeze passing through my pouch-belt cause it? I walked a few paces, disproving that. Then I thought there might be something about my old felt hat: — No! Maybe there was something in my ear; I tried them, nothing in my ears! I sat down in a tremor of nervousness; could not rationally account for the irksome sound! My gun fell over, and that suggested the truth; — the air passing over the muzzle! — I arose, and walked, holding my gun at a trail, so as the breeze, or motion of walking would cause the current of air to pass obliquely across the muzzle. — This was the cause! — My anxiety was relieved; — it felt almost as serviceable as a good meal! I am not weak-minded! I am yet sane! — Thank God!"

Having *laid* the apparition, I will resume my journal. — My lower extremities are very weak and painful. Again tottered out, in quest of game, and soon returned again, enfeebled by the exertion. Merd^n flying clouds, moderate W. wind, temp. 46° Saw the track of last night's visitor — the grizzler, — along the road, up hill. Continually thinking about my two friends, expecting and hoping the return of one or the other: though Clough must, assuredly be lost![4] Sun Set hazy, a moderate W. wind; temp: 46° Growing so very feeble, and the stillness of the place, giving confidence to the beast[s], emboldening them, every day, more and more, I think that sleeping in the tent is unsafe; and by sleeping in the cabin, I can at least cheat the wolves for a while. So I took my bedding, arms, and ammunition, over and deposited them in the cabin. — Found plenty of old clothes & rags there, & soon had an excellent bed. Awakened 3 times during the night, with cold, and pain in the back, and each time had to replenish the fire.

Reflecting on the crisis, I see but one chance of saving myself. The impediment to attempt travelling in to the settlements, existed in disability to walk, from rheumatic pains in my spine & loins, and legs, — particularly the latter; to say naught about debility. At present, if I attempted it, prostration would leave me on the route, for the bears & wolves to devour; and there is as much chance to kill game here as any where. And there is nothing on the road to subsist on. Now, I have, in reserve, 2 tallow candles, and likewise a dozen acorns, which I had preserved for specimens. — These have just occurred to my memory. The candles will answer to travel on, when I can walk; and in order to relieve the pain in my legs, I shall, at once set to, and rub them, and continue to do so, every day, several times, with camphor and cayenne, both of which I am so lucky as to possess. I got up and prepared a mixture accordingly, and rubbed my back & legs, the latter several times; then laid down, and felt better.

APRIL 2^d Commences with flying clouds, & calm, temp. 38° Rubbed my legs well, and fancied it was beneficial. —Took a stroll, for birds; a cold and tedious exertion, of about 3 hours, on an empty stomach, and unsuccessful. — I yet had about a half pint of cold broth, in this I put the dozen acorns, & sat it on the fire, made coffee, and had a breakfast, if it could be called a meal. Procured some dry carrion for my pup. Saw where a grizzler had fed on the dry remains of an old ox-carcass, and then wallowed and rubbed himself between the roots of a large pine. Hunger has made these fellows, usually shy of people, approach me so impudently. There are no berries or fruit, and they have been compelled to eat what wolves cannot.

Merdⁿ Clear, light S. wind, temp: 60° Below my knees, my legs are very stiff. Rub them again. Still think the rubbing serviceable, and if no succor arrives, and strength & weather permit, I am determined to attempt going in to-morrow, let the issue be what it may. Now, I know, when I leave this, what I have to encounter, and how great is the risk; — at least 3 nights' exposure to cold, beasts, and indians, in my feeble condition; and liable also to be overtaken by a storm; but prudence dictates it as the last hope of salvation, from the imminent perils thickening around me, so I commenced making the necessary preparations. — Collected my note-books, & papers, — quite a parcel. — put ammunition, the 2 tallow candles, matches, flint & steel, a memorandum book & pencil in a haversack. A clean shirt, pair of socks, comb, towel, soap, pouch of tobacco & pipe — which I have not dared to smoke since I gave Clough up, as lost; my journal-books, my watch, one belonging to Mr Goodrich, and his draught; a gold chain & seal, found in Dr Caldwell's wagon, and a case of sewing materials, made by my wife, I put in a knapsack. I took the smallest quilt I could find, — one left by poor Dr Hearvy, rolled & strapped it up. Laid out my rifle pouch and horn, bowie-knife, pistols, and belt, and double-barrel'd gun, all ready. I transferred all our property, from the camp, over to the cabin, and stowed them up snugly, in a bunk. My pack, arms, &c. I fear much, are more than I will be able to carry.

Sun Set clear, & calm, temp: 44° I browned some coffee, ground it, and put it in a pouch, — about 1 pint. A small tin coffee-pot, capacity of about $1\frac{1}{2}$ pints, and a pint tin-pot, completed my equipment, for the attempt to reach succor. Oh! if I had but one good meal, to travel on! I am very weak! A clear night. I slept disturbedly, from cold & pains.

AP: 3^d Clear and calm, temp: 38° Scraped the hair off a piece of deerskin, stewed & eat it, producing a slight nausea. Gave some to my pup. Drank a pot of coffee. I am too weak to attempt travelling — Maybe I can shoot a bird; the least morsel of food will strengthen me. I therefore took my gun and went out for birds; saw plenty of robins, but they would not allow me to approach near them; so weak had to rest every 30 or 40 yards; at last shot a very poor and tough blue-bird, about the size of a brown sparrow. Had walked about 2 miles, and returned exhausted; cannot attempt going in to day. — Am done over. Found 2 old dirty flour-sacks, in the cabin; turned them, beat & scraped them, and obtained about 2 ounces of a very mixed compound, — of dark & yellow lumps & cakes of sour flour, hairs, cotton lint, & additions the mice had made. I picked out some of the extraneous materials, cut the wings off the bird, picked off most of the feathers, and gave them to the pup. Then the *flour* and bird, I made soup of, and thus, with coffee, had another and somewhat substantial meal; and reserved a little for breakfast to-morrow.

Merdⁿ flying clouds, Moderate S.W. wind, temp 56°

Laying down, on my pallet, about 4 P. M. — meditating, I was aroused by the very short bark & howl, of my pup, outside, as if hurt, by some thing! — I went out, with a carbine in hand, saw the pup, alongside the tent, whining and looking down the hill side, in the rear of my camp; and looking in the direction myself, discovered the cause of poor Nevada's alarm: — an immense grey wolf, — the largest I ever saw, and larger than I thought that animal ever grew. About 30 paces distant, he stood, alongside a large pine, looking first at pup and then at me. I took the best aim I was capable of, fired, and miss'd him; he snarled, growled. & snapped his teeth, and slowly trotted off, not over 50 yards, — where he joined another one, I had not before seen. I turned back, put my carbine in the cabin, and took out an old musket, charged with a large load of buck-shot, went out, and as they stood firm, side by side, I fired, at about 100 yds. The big fellow must have been touched, this time, for he leaped, and trotted off about 100 yds. further, and sat down beside a tree; his comrade turned, and moved off slowly and sulkily, as if he had half a mind to come down on me, for my temerity. I returned to the cabin, the excitement seeming to strengthen me, re-charged the carbine, put pistols in my belt. (I wore my large knife, always.) and went after these impertinent rascals. They had retired, up hill, apiece, and were standing by a pine, awaiting my arrival. — My pup barking now, with confidence; but refused to accompany me. — I had gone about 300 yards, and saw that I was rashly exposing myself, and becoming exhausted, at about 200 yards, discharged my carbine towards them. This started them to move slowly up the hill, and I returned, and charged up my arms. I can account for these villians coming so near. The large wolf, when I first fired, was near the grave of the child, which he had probably scented, or knew that it was a grave, having examined many on the road, maybe, and was going to it, when the pup heard him, and flew out of the tent, barking at him, which irritated him, and he ran towards the pup, frightening it and causing her to yell. — They had both been down some 100 yards lower, overhauling the dry remains of a carcass. The largest wolf seemed to stand 4 feet high, was very dark grey on the back, some white about his breast cheeks and face; and left the print of his feet, as large as those of a large panther; $4\frac{1}{2}$ inches across.

Sun Set clear, with light wind from W. temp. 44°
Pains in my back disturbed my repose much.

APRIL 4th   Clear, with very light wind from the E. temp. 38° Though frought with such iminent peril, I think I shall try to retreat from this position to-day. About $9\frac{1}{2}$ A.M. having mounted my knapsack, tied the quilt on my breast, and accoutred with belt & pistols, haversack, pouch, horn, &c. and gun on shoulder, assisted by a staff, I started on a very doubtful attempt to get in.[5] In ascending the hill, in front of the cabin, I found it steep and irregular, and exceedingly painful, gasping for breath, I had to halt and rest, on a rock or stump, every 30 or 40 paces. I perspired profusely, and expecting every moment to drop, but determined to keep on as long as nature would permit. My faithful little dog following & whining, occasionally looking up in my face, as if to enquire what I was endeavoring to do, or suggesting a fatal termination of my foolish attempt. Late in the fore-noon I reached "Steep Hollow", 7 miles from the cabin, and was astonished when I found that I had so miraculously travelled thus far. I had never been here before, but knew it by the description of travellers. There was a trail led to the right around a narrow curved ridge, — a good path, but I had forgotten that, and descended the long, steep, stony and rugged road, falling several times, and with great difficulty rising each time, and at length reached the deep seated narrow bottom, and sank exhausted, on the ground. After a short rest, I rallied, & got up to pursue my hopeless journey. — I had now a very steep and rugged hill to ascend, but shorter than the one I descended; this ascent was most trying, my breath and legs were constantly failing, and reached the top, by climbing 10 paces at a time, and resting each distance on a rock. Every time I sat down, my pup would walk a little ways ahead, and whine; as if remind me that I must not rest too long or too often, if I wished to get in. I then descended a long but pretty smooth hill, and at probably 300 yards from the crest, alongside a fallen oak, and close to the road, I fell down exhausted. When this passed over, seeing a black bird near, I rested my gun on the tree, and fired, the buck shot tore it to pieces. I then made a fire, and cooked some coffee, broiled the bird, and dined.

Merdⁿ clear, moderate S. wind, temp: 70°   Anxious to get as well down, as I could, and as soon as possible, while I had any strength, I rested till about 4 P.M. when I again set forward, and made, with the greatest difficulty, and at the slowest rate, about 3 miles more, and then sank to the earth. I was in a profuse perspiration, and tremor, and gasping for breath. — The last rays of the sun were on the hill tops. Sun Set flying clouds, light wind from the W. temp. 60°. No water at hand, and I am unable to walk twice my length. Had wet coffee grounds, about 1 gill, in my coffee-pot, I eat them. Gathered branches laying about, and piled them up for a barrier against the bleak night winds; made a fire, rolled up in my thin quilt, and laid down for the night, may be for ever. My knapsack answered for a pillow. Saw several deer to-day, but had not strength to take aim at them. Passed a sleepless night. — Back cold and full of severe pains, had frequently to get up & replenish my fire with brush. Near day a shower, damped my fire & wet and chilled me through. Wolves howled around and my 4 legged sentry barked.

APRIL 5th   Commences with flying clouds, light N.E. wind, temp: 53°   I am very lame, & enfeebled this morning. Must try to reach water, any how. Travelled about 300 yards, & found a small muddy rivulet. Threw off my pack, lighted up a fire, and made coffee. Drank a cup full, and shot another small bluebird. Gave the head, feet, and entrails to my pup, slightly grilled the bird, and eat it. Now, having had a *breakfast*, I proceeded, — exceedingly stiff & weak — very hard travelling; having to rest every 20 paces, on stones, &c. I had now to descend a very rugged & crooked road, to a stream, which I barely managed to cross without falling in: springing from rock to rock, by the aid of a pole. Then ascended a hill, on the Western side, about 300 yards, and in 100 yards more gave out, and fell. When I recovered so that I could set up, I thought of the candles, and got one out of my pack, — and eat about ¼ of it, with pepper & salt; it tasted bitter. (It was of that manufacture called the diamond candle)   Cut up a piece of raw hide & some leather strings, soaked and gave them to the poor pup to gnaw on. Gave her also the candle wick. Carcasses numerous, — merely skin-covered skeletons. About 11 A.M. it dropped rain. Merd. flying clouds, Moderate S.E. wind, temp: 70°   While resting, I adjusted the straps of my knapsack, which cut and chafed my shoulders much. There are numerous small black & white woodpeckers here, very lively, — noisy, chattering like parroquets, screaming & crying like crows, and, like the mocking bird, seem to be mimicking other birds. They are very shy.[6]

Nearly all the afternoon cloudy, with occasional sprinkles of rain. My pup chewed up & swallowed some of the hide, came & laid down by me, and drew a deep sigh! — it involuntarily elicited a responsive one from me! not only for the poor brute, but for myself! Found here a camp place, of about October '49, and where some seed had been spilt, I noticed a few very small sprouts of cabbages, lettuce, and reddishes, none over 2 inches long. I carefully gathered them, on my hands and knees, — procured about a gill, and eat them greedily, roots, and all — some grains of sand. I thought it was the sweetest cold salid I ever eat in my life.[7] Travelled on till again exhausted, and fell, near a wagon under a tree. Put my pack &c, in the wagon. Sun Set drizzles, and Strong S.S.W. wind; temp: 60°   Found a large piece of old oil-cloth, and covered my things in wagon, with it. I now made a fire beside the wagon, and crawled under the wagon out of the wet. Another sleepless night — lay in the wagon, wet and cold all night, and the howling of wolves, and my dog barking at them, awoke me when otherwise I might have slept.

[APRIL] 6th — Showers, and mists. Strong S.S.E. wind, temp. 50°   After great difficulty, on account of damp, and weakness, this morning, I made a fire. Hunted over the old camping-place, and procured about 2 oz: of the minute sprouts, of lettuce, &c. made coffee, drank it, eat the grounds and the sallad. Was wet and cold, took a couple of wagon-wheels, and laid on my fire, which after a while, burnt well, and I dried & warm'd myself. Boiled some bits of hide, in my coffee-pot, and gave to my pup, for her breakfast, poor thing. She is a mere skeleton, but as watchful as ever. While strapping on my pack, to pursue my ardious journey, a large yellow wolf came in sight, and howled, when Nevada jumped up, ran towards the wolf, some distance, and barked vehemently. — About 10 A.M. when I moved off, I called my dog, and left the wolf, on the side of a hill looking at us. I was lame, with the pains in my legs, and needless to say, excessively weak. — Shoulders much chafed with knapsack straps. I proceeded but a short distance, and reached a cart-body, on left of the road, when the hill descended rapidly to a deep brushy bottom, with a rill in it. The wind blew strong and cold, and I managed, some how, for I do not know what gave me the strength, to turn the cart-bed on its side, against a large granite rock, to break off the uncharitable wind. I sat my gun against the rock, dropped my knapsack, &c, and in this shelter was compelled to rest. I eat a piece of candle, endeavored to fix my straps so as not to gall my shoulders, and staggered on again. Merd^n flying clouds, and fresh gales from the S.S.E. temp: 62°

Thus I proceeded, perhaps 1½ miles more, halting at every stone and stump, where I could sit, and support my knapsack: every 20 or 30 paces at the most. Oak trees scattered about looking much like an old apple-orchard.[8] This was a sort of valley table-land, — on the right, about ¼ mile, the hill abruptly descended to a brook. I saw no place to shelter myself for the night, and it was drizzling, and threatening to rain heavy. Travellers had consumed all the ready fuel, and in my weak state, to be exposed all night to wet and cold, would assuredly incapacitate me from walking to-morrow. I crossed over, to the left of the road, intending to cut out a niche in a large bush I saw, to get in for the night, — as for sleep, I need not expect it, except that repose which is not disturbed by dreams. I threw down my packs, was about to draw my bowie-knife, when something caused me to look ahead, and on the left of the road, under a tree, I perceived a group of men, one in the act of charging a gun. — I at first thought them indians, and resolved to visit them, and obtain food, or die. I cocked my gun, and walked with considerable energy, some 300 yards, and reached the spot, found they were white men; I saluted them, staggered, fell, and asked in the name of God, for something to eat, that I was starving! One of them said he believed they had a piece of cold bread, and soon handed it to me, with a little salt pork grease. It soon disappeared. I now ascertained that this was a *prospecting* party, from neighborhood of Lassen's, bound to the vicinity of the Cabin: they were Messrs Barton, Collier, Darrow, Warren, Boston, O'Neil, and Bateman. It was about 3½ P.M. and they informed me that this spot is about 16 miles from Davis' rancho. So then I have travelled 14 miles: — 7 to "Steep Hollow,' and 7 this side of it. Surely my mind has dragged my feeble body on; physically alone, it were impossible! The rain prevented these men from pursuing their journey, and they fastened blankets up, for a sort of tent, to sleep under.

Sun-set cloudy, fresh breeze S.E. temp. 60°   At dusk I had the luxury of a pipe, but it rendered me so nervous, I dare not repeat it. Two of this party had known me, and also knew before meeting me, that I was in the hills. They huddled together under the shelter, from the rain, and invited me to do so, but there was no room, and I was satisfied to rest my weary head and shelter my shoulders only, between their legs. I gave my dog a pork bone.

Observed on the right of road, a grave: —

"C. Forman,
Died Sep: 25. — 1849,
Aged 21 years."

AP: 7th   Commences drizzly, moderate S.E. wind temp. 50°   The party dried their blankets, cooked breakfast, of flour cakes, fried pork, and coffee, inviting me to partake. — I needed not pressing to do so. They cut up, and equally divided the cakes, handing each his share. They, no doubt, eat a hearty breakfast, but it seemed to me, to be only a mouthful. I briefly related my recent sufferings, and that I feared much I had not sufficient strength to carry me in, *having nothing to eat*, and was growing weaker every hour. "Oh! Captain!" said one, "you can soon get in now; you need'nt be alarmed." And they shouldered their blankets and *sacks of flour,* said 'good bye Captain", and resumed their journey! It was about 10 A.M. when my *charitable* friends left me. I say charitable, for unless I had just then obtained such succor, I never could have survived that night. — Nature had done wonders, but she was exhausted. I rested some time after they left, & warmed myself. I thought how differently I would have acted toward one of them, had our positions been reversed. — They saw my pale & haggard face, and my weakness; yet not one said "here's a hand-full of flour, to go in upon." They hearty and robust, with 8 or 10 days full rations, and I an emaciated starveling! Such is human nature! Oh selfishness, thou makest wolves of mankind! I will not, however, be ungrateful — they fed me, and saved my life; — for this, I am very thankful. A small grey wolf, this morning early, came near camp, and Nevada run him off. In about half an hour after the party left, I resumed my toilsome journey — Saw, at about 200 yards, ahead, in the road, a large grey wolf, apparently awaiting my approach, I fired at him, and he sneaked off. I pushed on about 5 miles, to a deep dry hollow, ascended the opposite hill, about 100 yards, to where there was a ledge of rock, and some cut logs, for a fire. It was raining. — I was weak, sore, and full of pains, and could not possibly ascend the steep hill further. If I done so, I would reach the bleak top exhausted, and where was no fuel. So here I had to stop. —

Merd^n flying clouds, fresh wind from the S.S.E. — temp. 68°   I light a fire, and eat some coffee grounds, about $1\frac{1}{2}$ gills. (*Mill Creek Scenery*)   Deep down, about $\frac{1}{2}$ mile, was the roaring torrent of Mill Creek. But I could not reach it, and had no water to drink, or to make coffee with; and the salt pork had excited much thirst.

Occasional drizzles during the afternoon. Sun Set cloudy, with thunder, Wind still S.S.E. and strong, temp: 54°   I rolled up in my quilt, and laid alongside the rock, with the fire, mostly of brush, close to me. It rained soon after dark, and continuing all night. Had to keep up my fire, my quilt was soaking wet, but a small piece of oil-cloth, preserved the backs of my arms and my pack, from wet. Of course sleep was out of the question, and I passed the most wretched night I ever knew. I crouched by the fire; wet, but warm in front, every now & then groping around for brush, to replenish the fire. — The light attracted my old acquaintances, — the wolves, and they and Nevada barked all night. The night was intensely dark. With my face to the fire, the road ran up hill, behind me, about 10 paces. Occasionally I wrang the wet out of my quilt, heated it to smoking, and again enveloped myself.

APRIL 8th   Thank God! 'tis day! — commences (sun rise) clear, wind light & variable, temp. 50°. Just before day-break I heard steps, on the road behind me, going up the hill, my pup barked furiously, but it was all black darkness, away from the fire, and imagining it to be only a skulking wolf, going up, on the road, I paid no attention to it. I had a good brush fire, and I knew the varmints would not approach it too close.

Last night I fixed my coffee pot under a rock, to catch water, and it was full. Put in about a gill of coffee and boiled it. Drank the fluid, and eat the solid, for breakfast. Hung my quilt to dry. The sun must have been 2 hour's high before I proceeded. On striking the road, I was astonished to see, on it, the fresh tracks of an indian. He was pidgeon-toed, and I judge small. — Ah, ha! he it was, that passed before day, whose steps I heard, and who set my dog barking!

Oh! if I can only over take him! then will I have one hearty meal! a good broil! I examined my caps, they were good. I felt relieved, it gave me additional strength; to think I might soon get a broil off an indian's leg! I could not but laugh, when I thought of it, — the expressions I have heard, how people would starve to death rather than eat human flesh! Fools! how little could they form an idea of the cravings of hunger! Let them be placed in my circumstances, and see how soon they would discard such silly ideas! My mouth fairly watered, for a piece of an indian to broil! And I continued to look out sharper for one, than for any other game. The road was slippery with mud, and full of small round stones. Having attained the summit & followed it some distance, slightly descending, but going over several slight rises in it, after which a regular descent. As I came along, was compelled to halt, and rest, at every thing on which I could also support my knapsack. Feet quite sore, shoulders very sore, and would fail altogether, but for the hope of shooting an indian, to eat. Staggering, and resting every few paces, — on the indian trail still, at last reached "Dry Creek", at the base of the hills

8 miles, about, from where I parted with the company yesterday. This stream is rapid, appears to be not over 3 feet deep, and swollen by the melted snows and recent rains. The water is about 40 feet wide. On descending to the wagon ford, I loosened my packs & threw myself down, exhausted. On recovering, I eat my last small piece of candle: giving the wick to the poor pup. — She eats grass, just now eat a cartridge paper, and is busy gnawing a black leather strap. She occasionally runs to me, looks in my face, wagging her tail, and whining, as if upbraiding me for permitting her to starve. I am very drowsy, but cannot lay down yet. A fine day.

Merd^n clear, moderate S.W. wind, temp. 70°   Early in afternoon a strong cool wind from the N.W. After part N.E. Reached the creek about meridian. About 4 P.M. walked along the creek, — hoping to shoot a bird, or catch a fish: — for the latter I had bent a pin, to form a hook, and baited with a small black beetle, found under a stone. Made a fire first, and sat my pot on, with the last of my coffee, — about 3 dessert-spoonsful, to cook. On reaching a deep part of the creek where it was dammed up, & smooth water, I scared up two small indian dogs, and fired ineffectually at them. Laid some time on the rocks, with my line in the water, in vain, and gave up the fishing. Many small yellow-hammers[9] & sparrows, but they are very shy. Returned to camp, luckless. Drank half my coffee, eat half the grounds, and a common grey Lizzard, I was so lucky as to kill with a stick, and roasted. I now drew off my dirty socks, and threw them away; washed my feet well, and rubbed my legs, put on clean socks, and felt much better. Feet very sore, however. I indulged in a smoke, much to the discontent of my nerves. Saw numerous deer and antelope tracks on the latter part of road. The ground here appears to be dry, and having been deprived of so much sleep, trust I will get some to-night. Noticed some beautiful flowers.

Sun Set clear, wind moderate from N. temp: 62°

The drab proverb has just occurred to my memory: — "A gill of water is worth a mountain of gold, in the desert". — The same may be said of bread. The hearing of my pup is exceedingly acute, and the faculty is invaluable to us.

I forgot entirely to mention, that I related to the party of men I met, the strange disappearance of my friend Clough, and anxiously inquired if they knew, or heard aught about him? They replied in the negative; and also said, that they had conversed with Roberts, some time, and about me, and he would certainly then have mentioned it, if C. had come in. — An[d] he would have known if he had. I described C's equipment, &c. that they might identify his remains, and begged them to look for him. They promised to do so.

I collected brush, chiefly dead mansaneta bushes, built up a fire, and rolling in my quilt, slept in a small space between bushes. The cold awakened me often, and I then had to replenish my fire.

AP: 9th   Commences clear, with a light wind from N. temp. 44°   Warmed my coffee, drank & eat it, and prepared to ford the creek and cross the plains; some 8 miles, to the settlements. I am so weak, I fear I have suffered all this travel for naught, to give myself to the beasts & birds of the valley, instead of leaving my body for those of the hills. A little above the ford there were many large stones above water, but too far apart for any but an active man to cross on. I worked hard for some time, throwing in rocks to fill up, so as to enable me to cross, without getting in the cold stream. I dreaded the water, for it was cold as ice, and very rapid, and if I fell in, would assuredly perish. — I rested, and then attempted the passage, about 9 A.M. managed, by the aid of my gun, to get along on the stones about ¼ the way over, when I tottered, and slipped, but partially recovering, I caught hold of a rock, and found myself knee-deep, in water so cold as to feel like razors, cutting me. I proceeded right through it, in one place as deep as the seat of my pants, and gained the opposite bank. There, trembling with cold and weakness, I sat awhile, but knew that I must take exercise to warm me, and with difficulty ascended a stony inclined plane, of about 50 feet, and was fairly on the plain, in the Sacramento valley. It was extensive, and level, but the road was much cut up, and, like the rest of the plain, covered with loose red stones, of a small size. No large rock, no stump, nothing for me to sit on and rest! I could not sit flat on the ground with my pack, for I could not rise with it. And if I dropped it, I could not resume it, for there was no elevated object to support it, while I secured it across my breast, as I have always done, coming down. I was nearly exhausted, felt sick at the stomach, had a headache, and my legs pained me much. The sun shone out warm, and I proceeded, reeling and staggering, for about 3 miles, when I had to drop myself in the red mud, — a little left of the road. I looked around over the broad plain, not a living thing to be seen! I now loosed my knapsack, and knowing that I could send for it, if I lived to get in, — unless the indians found it, I put my quilt on it, and piled stones over all, forming a small pyrimid. — I also piled up a little pyrimid of stone, in the road opposite, to indicate the locale. After I had recovered, so as to proceed, I arose, by turning over, and rising on my hands. In a quarter mile more, I met a low square-built indian, very dark, and had slight mustache; he had just emerged from a deep gulch, on the left. He was nude, except a kind of fig-leaf, had a knife, a quiver full of arrows on his back, and a bow in his hand.[10] He was accompanied by a small black indian dog.[11] I spoke to him in Spanish, but he did not understand me. I then made signs that I was hungry — starving, and wanted something to eat, which he comprehended but gave me to understand he had nothing, and was on his way to Dry Creek, to shoot birds. My pup was following his dog, and I worried myself much to get her along; so glad was she to meet one of her own specie, I had to make signs to the indian to drive her back — beat her with his bow: — which he did. — While he was going off, I turned round, thought of eating him; he was then about 30 or 40 paces; but I could not shoot the poor wretch in the back: besides, he had done me a favor. So I proceeded. Could this have been a mountain indian? — the one I trailed, and wanted to eat? I dare say. I managed to get probably 2 miles farther, when I found the shrivelled carcass of an ox, on this I rested, looking to see if the indian visited my cāche, but he kept lower down, crossing the road some distance this side of it. While I rested here, poor, little Nevada was gnawing and pulling about the hard withered remains I sat upon. Arose, and continued on the muddy, rough, winding road, till I at length reached and crossed 2 small branches, and a deep dry bed of another, and soon after enter[ed] the oak timber, of Deer Creek bottom. I knew now, that I was 3 miles probably, from Davis' rancho, and that it was situated down the creek, below where the ford is. I nerve myself to persevere, by constantly exclaiming, "I will soon have plenty to eat! — bread, and meat, coffee, and milk! a house to sleep in! and an end of my sufferings!" Yes, yes, yes! — Saw a party of squaws, with large conical baskets on their backs, 2 men with them. I hailed them, the men came up, a dark wrinkled, and thin, old fellow, and a hearty-looking young man. I found they understood some Spanish; and asked for food. They pointed in two directions, telling me that Davis' was in that, and Lassen's in the other. — Hid from view by a forrest of oaks, &c. They gave me to understand, that they belonged to Lassen,[12] had nothing to eat, and the squaws were going to dig roots. So I left them, and went on. Soon after reached the banks of Deer Creek, at the ford; now a raging flood, a perfect cataract, and deep. (The indians were armed with quivers of arrows & bows, and long knives.

The stream here runs Westerly. I followed a path, keeping down, near the stream, turned an elbow, and reached a prostrate oak. I sat down, aching, feeble and weary, fell back, in the branches, fitting like the back of an easy chair; and fell into a lethargy, from which I would never have awakened in this world, had I remained undisturbed 2 hours. —

The bark of my pup aroused me, but I found myself unable to arise; and turning my head, beheld Poile approaching! He was as much astonished, and affected at my circumstances and appearance, as I was delighted to see him. After shaking hands, I asked for something to eat, when he handed me part of a hard ship-biscuit, which at once commenced devouring, like a starved wolf. — This devoted friend, this true *Brother*, was on his way out to the camp, to succor me. He had some flour and meal, and a piece of pork for me. Had failed seeing any one I wrote to; and intended to assist me till I could walk in. He was astonished to hear of the sad fate of poor old Clough. He wished to light a fire, make coffee, and broil a piece of pork; but when I learnt that Davis' house was only about 300 yds. off, around a point of timber, I resolved, with his assistance, to reach it. Poile assisted me, I arose, and went on, and in 15 minutes was at Davis' rancho, greeted cordially, by him, Col. Ely, Capt. Potts, Davis' sons, &c: but feeling faint, I was taken in the house: — and on recovering, eat a *very* hearty dinner![13] And Mrs. D. most kindly gave me a glass of toddy. My back was so weak and ached so much, that I could not sit up on a chair or bench, and had to sit flat, in a corner of the room. — I asked some person to get my pipe and tobacco out of my pouch, and filling my pipe, and taking a whiff, I said "Well! I'm not dead yet!" "Oh, No! replied the bystanders, "You're worth several dead men yet, Captain!" Col. Ely, most kindly mounted his horse, and brought in the knapsack & quilt, I left near Dry creek.

The bunks were full of lodgers, so Poile and I made a pallet before the fire, and there slept. — The soundest night's rest I have enjoyed for a long time. —

AP: 10th   Thank God! — I have safely passed a trying ordeal! My extreme sufferings are terminated, I trust. The people here, particularly Col¹ Davis' family, are exceedingly kind & friendly, and do all in their power to alleviate my misfortunes, and make me comfortable. A hearty breakfast, — Pan-cakes & molasses, rolls and fresh butter, stewed and broiled beef, coffee & milk! But I cannot control my voracious appetite, and I fear my uncontrollable imprudence will injure me. These good people have no more discretion than myself, in regard to my eating. — They only think of providing the provender, and smile at the manner in which I stow it away. After breakfast, my well tried devoted friend, my old mountain comrade, who true to the end, was going out on that rugged march, alone, to aid and succor me, and just in time to arouse me from what would have been my last rest, now shouldered his blankets and gun, to return to Yuva City, or the Feather river mines. He desired me, when occasion required, to address him at "Long's Bar."[14] He left for me, rather an incumbrance for him to carry, — a small quantity of meal, flour, salt, pork, and ground coffee. Most of my pains have gone, but I am yet tottering weak.

[APRIL] 11th　Another beautiful day. P. met Roberts, after leaving the *ranch*, and engaged him to assist, with a wagon, to bring in some of R's effects yet remaining at the cabin. His compensation the privilege of bringing down 100 lbs for himself. — Which the good soul undertakes more for me than for himself. So will bring down bedding, &c. I left in the Cabin. Mr McBride, who owns a wagon and plenty of team oxen, offers, when I have recuperated sufficiently, to go out, to my old camp, in rear of the last position, and bring in what effects may be found of consequence.

In the afternoon, accompanied by the family, I walked up the creek, a few hundred yards, to witness the skill of the indians in the water; carrying goods over. Mr. McB. and Davis' sons[15] are camped on the opposite side, killing & curing (jerking) beef, to take with them to the Trinity mines,[16] soon. The indian performances, in the swift waters of Deer Creek, cannot be surpassed by Otters.[17] After half an hour's amusement, — witnessing the aquatic performances of the indians, we returned to the house; and there, to my pleasing astonishment, I met Mr. Henry Wright, formerly of my Company. He rode up from Marysville, on business, and also to see Lassen about the Company property pledged at his *ranch*, by Brooks & Co. for their debt. He seemed very glad to see me, and noticed my haggard feeble condition. He gave me much information about the members, — our old associates in the long march: And kindly promises to send up any letters there may be below, for me.

The widow, 2 daughters, and son, of the Allford family are here. Glad to see me. They will go down the valley with Davis. Have a wagon.

The effects of *astonishing my stomach* and system, by the heartiest eating, of good food, has attacked me. — All the afternoon and night very sick; pain, acid eructions, flatulency, swelling, looseness, and drowsiness, but inability to sleep. At night took a dose of camphor and laudanum. One of the young Roberts called, and shook hands with me; he has recently returned from the City.

[APRIL] 12th　Mr Wright breakfasted with us. Indisposition continued. Cannot stand, or sit on an elevated seat long.

[APRIL] 13th   Wright still with us. My indisposition continuing, in the middle of the day I made some coffee, took a dose of laudanum, to alleviate the pains in my stomach, and drank the coffee. Mrs Davis would cheerfully have waited on me, but she had her hands full, and I could soon make the coffee, with little trouble. Col. Davis and his assistants cut down cotton-wood trees, and with these & parts of wagons, constructed a foot-bridge across the creek. A party of the young men rode down the valley for pleasure. A mile or so below, is a rancherea, or indian village, — an appendage of this *rancho*. About 2 miles below, but on the opposite side of the creek, stands Lassen's rancho. This was the first settlement Lassen made here. The house in which Davis lives, is like Lassen's, built of adobe, (vulgarly called *doby*,) and roofed with long oak shingles, and here stands the wreck of a mill old Pete constructed, to grind wheat, &c. This *ranch* has the indispensable appendage, of a large corral, for horses and cattle. It seems that when Lassen had selected the more favorable locale, on which he now resides, and improved it, he sold this, with certain grounds adjacent, to a man named Sill, — another old settler, from Mo.[18] Sill do [ditto] after a while and moved down south, & there marying a rich Mexican woman; and left this establishment in charge of a Dutch youth, who leased it for a short term to Davis. — This has expired, and the Davis' are making preparations also to move down south, I believe in the vicinity of San Josè.

Most violent dyspepsical paroxysms all night.

[APRIL] 14th   Am weak and filled with pains. About 3 P.M. Col. Davis called my attention to a pack company, of mules, crossing the plain, from the mountains, whom he said must be Myer's Company,[19] who several days since started for the hills, to *prospect*, — in the vicinity of my old camp — and lodge. We walked out to meet them, and sure enough it was Myer's party. I shook hands with Myers and another person I knew; and observed that the mules were all well, and carefully packed, most of them with full *cargoes*. I wished to enquire if they had seen any human remains, which I might conjecture could be those of poor Clouth [Clough]; and also, if they passed my camp on the big hill, to learn its condition. When lo! a negro was proudly riding around, with my sabre girt on, another man had my rifle, and my dragoon saddle capped a large pack on a mule. I at once demanded them, and they were given up; and the gentleman who knew me, said he had 2 saddle-bags, which probably were mine also, as they came from camp. They were, and contained several books, &c. and a *clean new pair of linen pantaloons*, of mine. Myers said, that he visited my camp, — knew that it was my camp by my name on a trunk, and other articles. (He knew previously where my camp was, just as well as I did) And that the indians had destroyed every thing. I enquired particularly about clothing, having left an extensive lot of clothing of every description there; and if here some would be of great service to wear, while I could sell the rest to very great pecuniary advantage. He said that there was not an article of the kind left: the indians had carried off all. I left those saddle-bags empty, how came my mineralogical works, and a pair of *clean* new pantaloons in them. How is it that if the indians had demolished the tents, and left the wreck of matter there exposed to the elements, that these things are fresh and uninjured? Why is not the rifle and sabre corroded & red with rust? And would an indian have left that sabre there? This party started out, to be absent a few days only, & consequently carried a small amount of provissions. — They have been absent as long as they intended, consequently can have very little, if any provissions left. — Now what have they found in their tour, of sufficient importance to freight their train with? And the largest packs are carefully covered with *pieces of tent-cloth.* This is J. J. Myer's party, and I doubt not have found pretty fair diggings! These met — had met Roberts and Poile this side "Steep Hollow", And [said] that while the party of Barton & Co. were hunting, the indians visited the cabin, and stolen all their bedding.

APRIL 15th Cloudy. Young Roberts is here, awaiting the return of his father. Wright is also here, and Messrs Hawthorn and Brookie: the former is the young man who went out to the cabin with Roberts, with the oxen. The folks here are very busy getting their effects across the creek. 2 strangers came here to-day. Roberts & Poile arrived in the afternoon; bringing me a tent, 1 blanket, 2 kettles, 2 coffee-pots, some soap, and a quantity of new rope, half of which old Roberts demanded for bringing. They stated that a party of 6 indians and a white man had robbed the cabin, and the party of 7, — Barton &c. had pursued them to near my old camp, 3 miles further. Can Clough be a prisoner among them? Oh no! Such a chance to escape he certainly would have seized.[20] A cold night. I slept indifferently.

APRIL 16. — The folks all moved over yesterday. I arose early, and waded across 2 streams, and crossed the tree bridge, to Davis' camp, and breakfasted. Shocking dyspepsia to-day. The party of 7 men returned. I noticed a double barrel German gun, a quilt, and several articles of mine, they brought down, but let them keep these as compensation for the pieces of bread they supplied me with, when they met me starving. I fried some cakes of flour and meal mixed, made coffee, and had a good dinner: but taken sick afterwards. (*View of Lassen's Rancho.*)

[APRIL] 17 — I crossed the creek, and breakfasted at the camp; then walked about 2 miles, down the creek, to Lassens,[21] introduced to L. and Satchel Woods,[22] by Col. Davis. Col. Woods, however, I had the pleasure to know in Washington, a short time before I left, and who kindly gave me much valuable information about the route. He had been over before; — and crossed again earlier than I did the last season. Capt Lassen pressed me to stay, and I slept here. Old Mr. Hough and son live here. Former book-keeper for Lassen.

[APRIL] 18th — Walked over early, to Davis' rancho, and discovered that I had been robbed. All my valuables, including those articles I had taken such care of, for other people; my duelling-pistols, a fancy belt-hatchet, presented to me by Ames, — the sword-cutler. &c. and all my flour & meal were gone. One of Col. Davis' sons said *that the indians must have done it*.[23] I made coffee, which with biscuit answered for breakfast.

[APRIL] 19 — Got 2 indians to assist, and moved my effects over to Lassen's. Saw Mr Vestal and his son — he enquired for me, and introduced himself and son. Said he was the proprietor of a wagon left with the Shingle men, and wished me to tell him if it was yet there. I told him the history of it up to the time I abandoned the old camp, and went to the cabin. Attacked with severe cholic. J. J. Myers slept here. We shall try to-morrow to visit the old camp, and I accompany the party, to see if I have any thing left. Lassen goes to bring in his shingles, and also Vestal's wagon, and 1 for me.

[APRIL] 20th   About 2 P.M. our party moved off, to revisit the old scene of my disasters. Lassen, Vestal, Young Hough, Campbell, & self; all mounted, and 4 indians, driving 43 team oxen: besides 2 mounted indians. We travelled 14 miles, and camped in a hollow. 9 oxen strayed off during the night.

APRIL 21. Reached the old camp by Sun-Set. Rested a short time at the cabin, and found that it had been pillaged, and also that Old Roberts had stolen many of my effects; and that he had made a cache of some of my things, and exhumed them on his last trip out. The old camp-ground was a scene of confusion, and wreck of what had remained. The cloth of the tents and connecting lodge, had been cut away, close to the ground, with sharp knives; trunks and boxes broken, and filled with dirt. Feather-beds & pillows which were in a wagon, had been cut open; and all around was ancle-deep in feathers and broken trash.

We made a large fire. At dusk ther was a grizzly bear at the spring, who alarmed our horses soon after dark. We kept guard. I had the first watch, and slept sound afterwards.

[APRIL] 22. — Loaded 3 wagons with shingles, and I gathered up what few relics I could find of any use, and some cooking utensils, and 2 or 3 old saddles.

We gathered yokes and bows, and chains for the oxen, and fitted them up. The oxen are very restive, and the horses are rather uneasy for want of feed; giving us much trouble. We cannot get away to-day. I turned over to my old friend Lassen, all the shovels, spades, scythes, snathes, tools, lead, &c. & a considerable quantity. Selected the wagons from those around, and loaded 3 with the shingles, or clap-boards; and 3 others with such articles as we had gathered. A horse ran away at night.

APRIL 23d   We arose early, and Vestal and myself saddled up, in order to drive the horses of the party in, as the men had to walk to manage the team and wagons. However, the band were hungry, and once on the road, were determined to get into the settlements, for grass, with all possible dispach. Mine ran rapidly down a considerable hill, and at the bottom tried to throw me. I dismounted, to ascertain if there was any thing wrong about the geer. I unsaddled, and he then broke away and ran off, snorting. I was too weak to hold him. Vestal rode on after the flying band, and I shouldered my saddle and blanket, and walked about ½ mile, to the cabin, and then awaited the arrival of the wagons.

The grave of the Allfords had been opened, at the head, 1st by *prospectors*, thinking it a cāche; and lastly by wolves. I pushed dirt in. I visited poor little Billy's grave, where my tent stood, near the cabin; that also had been opened by *prospectors*, followed by 4-legged wolves. The board at the head had been stuck down the reverse of the way I had fixed it. — Quadruped wolves would not likely attempt to readjust a head board to a grave, after knocking it down. On probing the hold [hole] at the head, I found that the body must be headless, and I then walked down the slope of the hill, about 50 yards, and there found the scull. I took it up with a stick, threw it in the grave, and filled it up again. I waited with hungry anxiety for the train, till past meridian, when 4 yoke of oxen ran down, went to hollow, drank, and ran up hill, on the road for home.

About 1 P.M. 2 wagons made their appearance, and came up. The oxen had broken the tongue of one wagon, axle of another, and capsized a third. The oxen I saw before, they had turned loose that they might graze in

"Steep Hollow". Sent 2 indians and Mr Hough to proceed there, and bring the oxen back in the morning. A little after 1 P.M. we *breakfasted.* — Coffee, ship bread & fried pork.

Lassen, Campbell, and 2 indians exam[in]ed a ravine for gold, but found none. They then returned on the road to refit the wagons. I, in the interum, burnt and ground some coffee. 6 miles in rear of old camp, the snow is from 3 to 4 feet deep. I lent my young friend Hough an over coat and musket to take to "Steep Hollow." The cattle, accustomed to plenty of good grazing cannot stand 48 hours fasting. Lassen knew there was no grass here, how easy to have brot some. At night the indians drove the oxen back, instead of permitting them to graze in Steep Hollow", the stupid fellows! I am very weak, and have strong pains in my back.

APRIL 1850 24th — I made my breakfast early; on coffee and crackers. The party went back on the road, with 13 yoke of Oxen, to bring down the wagons in the rear: leaving an indian with me, named *Shinbone.*[24] The indian and I loaded up a wagon with boards, &c. About $1\frac{1}{2}$ P.M. Lassen brought down 5 wagons. When we dined, on coffee and crackers. I was now compelled to walk. At $2\frac{1}{2}$ P.M. we moved on. Considerable trouble with the wagons getting them up the hill directly in front of the Cabin. A little before Sun Set we reached "Steep Hollow", & prepared to descend the long rugged hill. Locked the wheels, coupled 2 wagons together, &c. A wagon capsized about half down the hill. We camped in the bottom, by a rill, and had a cup of coffee. Meat & bread out, and unless we are successful hunting to-morrow, will suffer hungry times.

Lassen told me how he and young Campbell, in the morning, going back, from the Cabin, and about $\frac{1}{4}$ mile in the rear of it, came close upon 2 grizzlers. — They had no guns. — The bears were engaged eating some kind of plant at the time, looked around at the men, snorted, and walked away, across the road, into a hollow, on their left.

[APRIL] 25th — A breakfast of tea only. Lassen took his *old brown bess* — long rifle, and went back, to look for deer. He saw 13 deer and 2 fawns, down a ravine, about a mile from us, fired and missed. About 11 A.M. he returned, and found that another wagon, left last night, on the steep hill side, which they attempted to bring down this morning, was upset, & considerably crippled, about $\frac{2}{3}$ down hill. Old Pete now shot a white ox, and we were very soon feasting on savory broils. After breakfast we proceeded to the hill, set up the crippled wagon, and got that and another one down. I boiled a large camp kettle full of meat. We fixed all the wagons, loaded up, and commenced moving the wagons on the declivity down. Upset 2, righted and reloaded, moved on; then upset another, and by Sun Set got 2 down, and left the others. A good supper of boiled beef and tea. Cold night.

[APRIL] 26th   Cold morning: a strong W. wind. The hands endeavoring to get another wagon down hill, upset it: — turned it up, repacked, and got it down. Breakfast fried liver and tea. After breakfast went up to get the remaining wagon down. I am exceedingly weak, from the short fast I had, and working hard. About 11½ A.M. wagons all down. We now doubled team, and in about 2 hours reached the top of the hill — emerged from "Steep Hollow" — a most appropriate name. Near Sun Set we broke the tongue of one wagon, and the wild hungry oxen ran another foul of a tree, and broke an axle — 2 disabled. Reached deep hollow of Dry Creek, a very long, crooked and rough descent. Bro't 4 wagons to the brow, and took one down to the stream. A little ways back, on the ridge, a flock of deer and fawns ran rapidly across the road, when I fired my carbine, but I presume missed them. They were instantly lost amongs[t] brush, trees, and rocks, in the deep gulch below. The rear wagon was upset & left.

[APRIL] 27th — Being so weak, I volunteered to cook for the party, and prepared breakfast. After breakfast they went about getting the wagons down and over — Campbell and myself endeavored to drive the oxen across the stream, in order to hitch up and get the wagon over, but they were so refractory that we had to give it up for the present. Young Hough came down with the indians, and reported that they had broken the tongue of the rear wagon, against a rock. All hands, then, except Campbell and myself, went back on the road, to the rear wagon. I had just completed cooking 2 large camp-kettles of beef, and taken them off the fire, about 2 P.M. — when General Wilson's two sons,[25] a man named Fox, and another person rode down to us, from Lassen's house. We had been detained so long, lost the horses, and old Vestal had started some queer rumor, that they apprehended the indians had murdered all hands, and came out to learn our fate. They informed me, that a short time before they left the ranche, that Mr Windsor, and a party of my old associates, of the Company, with pack mules, on their way to the Trinity mines, had called at Lassen's, and not hearing of my escape from the hills, had turned off their road, for information, and the intention of coming out to relieve me. Our 4 visitors finding we were all safe, eat a lunch of beef, and returned, for the settlements.

Lassen repaired the damage, and late in the afternoon got the wagon up to brow of hill.

[APRIL] 28th — Before breakfast got 2 wagons down, after breakfast, (of boiled beef & tea) the other two, and hunted up the stray oxen. One of our indians ran off, for the settlements. — tired of hard work. Forded the stream, and with much difficulty got the train up a long winding slope. About Merdⁿ we reached the top of the ridge, halted by a tree and red wagon, on left of road, when I tried to sleep, in the rain, on the night of the 5th — We took this wagon along, and travelled a little ways, — 3 miles from the stream, and camped.

APRIL 29th   The principal cause of our trouble and delay, is with the oxen. No animal becomes so restive from hunger or thirst, as an ox. From the Sacramento, out to 5 or 6 miles in rear of my old camp, — about 40 miles stretch, there is no grass; except descending steep and rugged hollows. Besides, these oxen have been long accustomed to the soft carpet of the great valley, to walk on, and consequently the ardious travel over the roughest kind of hard ground & rocks, has lamed them, — made them very *tender-footed*. The indians, assisting to team, know little about it, and are indolent, and very careless.

We moved on to day about 4 miles, and within ¼ mile of "Dry Hollow". (On the rise of opposite hill I sat up all night of the 8th   Found our beef, laying on top the wagons, was spoiled, — perfectly green and offensive. It was dark when we reached this spot: and we were very thirsty. The hill descended abruptly, on right of the road, to the deep gorge of "Mill Creek". And Campbell and the indian Shinbone, each with a tin pail, went down the hill for water. Some distance down, it appears, they found a rocky basin, in which water had dripped from the bank above, and they suddenly there, ran down upon a large grizzler, drinking. The indian dropped his pail and retreated precipitately up hill, running into camp, with protruded eye-balls, and exclamations of horror: and told Lassen, in a mixture of Digger, Spanish, and English, that he saw a huge bear, that liked to have caught him![26] After a while Campbell made his appearance, laughing heartily at the trepidation and hasty retreat of Shinbone; but acknowledging that it was rather closer approximation for one not unprepared, than he cared about repeating. He brought the 2 pails half full of good water, excepting some vegetable matter thickening it. Said the bear snorted, and slowly descended the hill, much to his satisfaction, and he *mighty hastily scooped up the water & vamosed*. We cut out strips of the beef which *had the slightest tints of green,* roasted & eat them. — *rather strong game flavor.* Had a pot of tea each, a pipe smoke, and hearty laugh at the bear scrape, and slept soundly.

[APRIL] 30th — A *green* broil, pot of tea, puff of the pipe, and I shouldered my carbine, and started to get in, in advance, and send back relief to the party with the wagons. I was weak, but it appeared as if I travelled with extraordinary energy, over the distances I so painfully crept along, on the 9th and 10th. About $11\frac{1}{2}$ A.M. I was at Lassen's Rancho. I immediately dispached relief to the party, and found myself much exhausted. During the night the train reached the upper ford of Deer Creek — 3 miles above this.

MAY 1st The water was too high, and the train had to come down on the other side, and stop in a brushy field directly in rear of the ranch. My hands are very sore, have poisoned them.

Whites, and indians busy all day, transporting contents of the wagons over the creek.

MAY 2d. Mr Eastman — steam-boat engineer; and Colonels Woods & Wilson;[27] — the latter gentleman wish me to accompany them to the "Red Bluffs",[28] about 30 miles up the valley, to lay off a town there. They offer me 2 ounces pr day, and board, with a good riding-horse. Having previously engaged to lay off a town here for Lassen, whenever he is ready, and being under obligations to him, I can only go above, if he can wait till I return. But as I know he is not ready, I shall merely observe to him what I wish to start on to-morrow. We have no cook here, and have to scuffle along any how, to get a couple of meals per day.

[MAY] 3rd. Lassen objects to my going to the Bluffs, expects me to keep my previous engagement, and says he will get ready at once, for the survey here.

[MAY] 4th Woods & Wilson much disappointed. The former rode down the valley. Col. Wilson engaged me, for the company — Genl John Wilson, himself, and Lassen — proprietors of the Estate here, (Lassen having granted two-thirds of the lands and stock, for a certain amount to be paid him, in installments, *when they shall think proper to pay him,*)[29] to lay off the City of Benton,[30] assisted by Lassen, &c. and to make a plot of the same. I procured an old surveyor's compass, and 2 defective chains of Col. Davis, on credit, for $50. Commenced to-day drawing a guide plan of the town. My tent is under a large oak, 60 yards in front of the house, in this I sleep, on the ground. In it I have fixed the tail-board of a wagon for a table, and a trunk answers for a seat.

[MAY] 5th — Drawing and calculating. A party of Oregonian half-breed Frenchmen, camped close by, are on a *big drunk*. Sold a couple of pack-saddle trees to young Wilson, for $6.

[MAY] 6th — Completed plot of town. The Frenchmen all moved off, for Trinity mines. Lassen and party of indians engaged felling oak, sawing and splitting, to make pickets, for staking off the town.

[MAY] 7th   Flying clouds and a strong wind. Col. W. started early, on horse-back, for Sacramento and San Francisco. He kindly takes letters for wife, and to my friend P. Allan Brinsmade, Esqr. in Sⁿ Franᵒ making preparation for the survey. An indian attempted to cook, and give us a miserable dinner. Lassen & party making stakes. Other ranch hands, — the vacheros, are busy breaking colts.

McBride and young Davis, besides several strangers are here.

[MAY] 8th — Commenced the survey.[31] — The compass is a very indifferent instrument.

[MAY] 9th   A Coyoti, (small wolf of these valleys) jump'd into our band of sheep, which some one happened to observe, and gave the alarm: — I picked up a carbine, and gave chase, and got in shooting distance, when about ¼ mile from the ranch, fired, struck so near as to make him drop a young lamb, which on reaching I found was dead. Surveying.

[MAY] 10th   My hands very sore — Surveying — Old Pete interferes with it, thinks he can rectify the errors.

[MAY] 11th   Two strangers arrived, on foot, going to Trinity. To-day a young German, with a large pack and gun, came down the creek; he walked like as if a little intoxicated, came up, nodded his head, sat down on a bench, drew a deep sigh, and asked where he was? He came from the hills, reached the creek, forded it by the aid of an indian, and slept a little ways above, unawares of being in the settlements. When we informed him where he was, he burst into a flood of tears. He informed us that his name is Nicholas

Loux, a native of Hesse Darmstadt, but for many years of New York City, where he has left a wife and children. He started very late last season, for California, was caught with his comrades, in the snows at the Pass, and passed the winter in the neighborhood of "Little Goose Lake," and the great valley of Feather river, where the road traverses it. This we know from his description of the places, days' travels, &c. Two countrymen of his — brothers, were his companions in misfortunes. One of these was drowned, in attempting to descend Feather river, on a raft, — he was about 18 years of age. And the other one had accompanied him till within about 25 miles, (a little this side of the cabin) where total exhaustion prevented him from proceeding. He left him early yesterday. My old friend Lassen, who is a man of feeling, though a rough mountaineer, instantly had 3 horses caught and saddled; gave the poor German a hearty meal, and prepared to send succor to the poor fellow in the hills, and bring him in, very early to morrow. He [Loux] related his adventures in bad English. Said that they lived on carcasses, — oxen and mules. The indians of Feather river valley are a benevolent kind set of fellows. They compassionated the circumstances of these poor men. — gave them root-bread, small fish, and a wild duck, from their precarious supply of food. — Were afraid of the guns, desiring the whites to do as they had done, — throw down their arms. A tall aged man, they thought was a chief, came up, and made signs, and embraced them. He pointed up, and to them — indians & whites; and seem[ed] to say, that they were all common children of one God.[32] Much frost-bitten. About 40 miles back, (Deer valley, of the mountains) they came on 3 grizzlers grazing, one reared up and snorted, and the 3 bears approached them; when about 10 feet off, he threw down his pack, and cocked his rifle, when the bears suddenly turned, and went off. Nicholas too weak to ride. This morning, after breakfast, Lassen and myself going down the road, about 300 yards from the house, when a grey wolf crossed the path, 50 yds. in front of us. Lassen's interference with the survey, caused me to take my compass, and return to the house.[33]

[MAY] 12th   After an early and very hearty breakfast, the German mounted a horse, accompanied by Campbell, on another, with refreshments, and a lead horse, saddled, to bring in the unfortunate man.

MAY 13th   At Lassen's desire I resumed the survey. Campbell and Nicholas returned, this morning; found the young German, about 3 miles this side of where his comrade had left him. He was dead. — way [was] laying on his back, and at first they thought he was asleep. It seems, that in his dying struggles, he had worked down the gentle slope, some 6 feet, from a bush, where his cap lay: or maybe, a wolf had pulled him down, and was afraid to attempt eating him. Above him lay a handkerchief containing a little raw rice, and some clay pipe-bowls. Nicholas was superstitious about touching the dead, they had no implements to bury him with, and had not time to collect & pile stone on him, as they did not wish to sleep in the hills that night. So they turned and rode down, leaving the dead Dutchman for the benefit of the wolves. If they had buried him in the earth, or piled rocks over him, it would only have been useless labor; for the bears and wolves, would assuredly, have pulled him out any how.

About 3 P.M. the Steamer Jack Hays passed,[34] going up the Sacramento as far as she may be enabled to do.

[MAY] 14th — My old friend is so very perverse, and interferes with the survey so much, that I shall have to leave it. Late in the afternoon I had to quit work — At night 2 large wolves were prowling and howling around the ranch —

[MAY] 15th   The little steamer passed down stream this morning. I went down, 2 miles, to Myers' house (on town site)[35] in charge of Mr Brittle, — who is proprietor, agent, cook, &c. in absence of the Myers family. Mr Myers — the Alcalde, has gone to the Sandwich islands, on account of bad health, and Mrs M. and children are at Marysville. Lassen has cut a number of poles, and with the indians, will complete the survey, on the numerous angles established. He has the use of my chains and pins.

I dined at Myer's house, with Doct[r] Bowman, a Marylander, from the vicinity of the District of Columbia, and M[r] Brittle.

MAY 16th — Exceedingly weak to-day, from fatigue, and exposure to the hot sun, running lines, over these dry plains, through tangled brakes, thick with musquitoes, &c. Late in the afternoon Mr Darragh arrived, on his way to from Reddings,[36] to Feather river. He is an intelligent clever Baltimorian, and the person whose *cachè*, at my old camp was open'd, and his papers I had saved, in hopes of having the pleasure to return him. He had to take the will for the deed, as the prospectors, Indians, quadrupeds, and weather, had swept away every thing they could take or destroy therefrom. Mr. D. supped and lodged at the ranch.

[MAY] 17th — Darragh left for Feather river. a French man came up and breakfasted. Afternoon 2 New Yorkers came up, eat a meal & proceeded. Latham (one of the *Shingle-men*) came over from the other side of the creek, said he was looking about for establishing a ferry. Mr Wyman, an old friend, who accompanied the Fairchilds, came up, supped, and lodged.

[MAY] 18th   Mr Wyman handed me an order for Mr Goodrich, for the effects he left at the old camp. When I related under what circumstances I had travelled in, having an old silver watch of Mr G's, and his check & money belt, and how they were stolen from me by some person, at Davis' ranch. I presented him with a small rifle. He went down valley in afternoon; and Latham recross'd the Creek. I am very feeble, and have a severe head-ache.

MAY 19th   One of the young Davis' with 3 other white men, and several indians, came by, from Moon's Ferry,[37] 4 miles below, going to Davis' *ranch*. The New Yorkers are yet here. My headache continues. In the afternoon a young man, formerly of my company, (who had acted throughout the march improperly, and exhibited mutinous conduct, on the latter part; and for which I was prevented blowing out his brains, from the timely thought that his parents were good people; and I was bound by the *highest obligation* to his father,) came up, in company with a couple of sailor lads. The young man acknowledged, in a private talk, away from his comrades, that he had acted very rascally, on the route, for which he was sorry, and begged me to forgive him. I replied, that it would depend on his future conduct; and that I feared he was in bad company. They lodged here, camping under a tree.

[MAY] 20th   Byington & his associates left, for Trinity mines. The New Yorkers are machinest [machinists], and Scotchmen by birth: they obtained horses of Lassen, to ride up the valley. Petrie — the clever fellow who accompanied Willis in, when he abandoned me, came up, from Marysville. I accompanied him over to Davis'. Hapening to enter the room where I had been robbed, I noticed an adobe brick taken up, from the floor, and a spade standing by it. — An old indian observing me wondering what could have been cachèd there, and with signs, and a few English words, informed me that yesterday Dock Davis opened it, and took out a small package, tied up. — I thought of my being robbed here by the *indians*, while I slept at Lassen's and the same young Davis slept here. Petrie had met Col. Davis, as he came up, who told him that he left all his effects, tools, &c. (blacksmith) and an iron flask of mercury here, all safe, — in my charge! I had permission to sleep in a vacant room merely, and knew that Davis' folks carried away every thing of any consequence. Of course there was nothing to be found but rags and trash. Campbell ill, with a bone felon. We returned to Lassen's, & Petrie went over the ferry.

[MAY] 21st. Petrie, and the New York Scotchmen returned, this morning. Capt. McIlvaine and his son, — *compagnons de voyage* of mine, through the Sierra Nevada, in the fall, came up, with an ox wagon; — from Redding's, going down to Yuba City. Petrie & the Scotchmen jumped in & went down. I mended the stock of my fowling-piece. A very tall thin old man, on a very diminutive mule, without saddle, came up, late in the afternoon, drank, and moved off. Severe pains in face, — neuralgea —

[MAY] 22nd   This morning my eyes were greeted with the sight of ladies. — Mrs. Myers and Miss White, in charge of Col Woods, & Mr. Fox, passed, on their way to Myer's house, from Marysville. A Miss Hall, on the other side of the Sacramento river, about 3 miles below, is to marry Mr. Warren, (one of the 7 young men I met in the mountains when I was tottering in) to-morrow.[38] Mrs. M. sent up to Lassen, for a sheep, and her son, a boy about 14, on horseback, threw the lasso over a black ewe, put spurs to his horse, starting him at full speed, showing through the dust as he flew down the road, only his hat, and occasionally the ears of his horse; while a spiral string of dust in the road indicated the evolutions of the poor choked sheep.
In the evening I called to pay my respects to the ladies, was introduced and spent a pleasant hour, and returned to my tent. Cool night. Became acquainted with a clever little gentleman — Doct. Davis, of Missi:[39]

[MAY] 23. Cool morning. Dr. Bowman & Mr Brittle came to board at Lassen's. Forenoon I visited Myers' — Introduced, by Col. Woods to Mr. Thorn, a surveyor, whom he has engaged to lay of[f] the town at Red Bluffs. They mounted & rode off, for the Bluffs.

[MAY] 24. A cool morning. Spent afternoon at Myer's. A party from the wedding, and some other travellers, caught a ducking. Crossing a wagon, oxen and 6 men, in the scow, at Moon's Ferry, about 2 miles below Hall's, the oxen caused the boat to upset, and the men had to swim.

[MAY] 25 — Mr Hall, brother of the young lady recently married, came up. We are all projecting a prospecting expedition in the hills, where Lassen thinks gold can be found. I am ill, with rheumatic pains in my body, breast, &c. and severe dyspepsical affections. Passed a sleepless night, in consequence

[MAY] 26 — This morning Mr Hall went home. At noon Miss White, a very pleasant intelligent young lady, from Yuba City, called by, on horseback. A high fever. took 3 anti-billious pills. Mrs Myers & Mr Fox called. A party of Frenchmen arrived, with a wagon —

[MAY] 27 — Called at Myer's; Mrs M, in charge of Fox, started off for the bluffs [Red Bluff].

[MAY] 28 — Adjusting the sights of my rifle. 3 bullocks killed here to-day. Mrs. M. & Fox returned in the afternoon.

MAY 29 — I dined at Myers, with Mrs. M. Miss Elizabeth White, and Mr Fox. Mrs. M. has 3 children.

[MAY] 30 — Mrs M. invited me to dinner again, and as it was a scrambling for cooking at Lassen's, I readily accepted the invitation. Miss W. crossed the river on a visit to Moon. Heard that 2 packed mule parties, from Oregon, had passed Moon's, on their way down the valley.

[MAY] 31 — I walked over to Myers', for exercise. Saw there 4 men, from Trinity. — They report that there are too many people there, waters high, charges very high, and little made.

JUNE 1 — Doctor Bowman accompanied me on a visit to Myers', to see Col. Woods. The Col. & Mr Fox, soon after, started for the bluffs. Two strangers there. At night Mr Withers called at Lassen's; — he told me that Roberts had said that I accused him of robbing the cabin. His brother-in-law, and the New Yorkers, had sailed for Oregon. I have ascertained what caused so much apathy in regard to me, while in the hills. The story told by the men of my Company, who went out for the wagon[s], and by Willis and old Roberts, and the failure to deliver my notes, as well as Lassen's absence from the ranch. Old Pete told me, that had he been home, I would not have remained & suffered as I did.

[JUNE] 2nd. Preparations for the contemplated excursion in the hills. I am too feeble to travel yet. Mr. Parish and J. Queen, formerly of my company, with Mr. P's brother, who has lived in Oregon some time, and has a trading-wagon, came up, and camped close by; and they called to see me. Were glad to find me so well. I accompanied them to their camp. Supped there, and remained till late in the night.

[JUNE] 3rd. Mr Hough and son, Dr Bowman, Mr. Hall, and Campbell, nearly ready for the mountains.

JUNE 4. Two more of my old Company arrived from Trinity — Messrs. Marden & Slight. Parish & Co. are from below. The former very glad to meet me. A band of horses driven up, from below, on their way to Oregon.[40] Queen & Marden went off some where, on horseback.

[JUNE] 5 — To-day a lad, the son of Jno. Spence, an Oregonian French man, from their camp a short distance above, called & asked me for an emetic for his father, who was ill, — supposed to be billious. He had been drinking hard, and caught a severe cold. Dr Bowman was absent, and I had no other emetic than lobelia. Saw 2 bottles — of lobelia & composition powder, with full directions on them, measured out the doses, gave them to the lad, and told him very particularly how to administer them. He returned to camp, gave his father the lobelia first, and the composition tea afterwards![41] Excessive vomiting ensued, and I gave laudanum to relieve him.

[JUNE] 6th   Last night, at the rancheria, one indian shot another, accidentally in the knee, with a pistol. The boy, this morning reported his father dead — Died about 2 O'Clock this morning. Queen and Marden returned. About 9 A.M. the lad again called, requesting me to go to camp and prepare his father for burial. I went there, and found some superstitious ideas prevented the Frenchmen from laying out their dead comrade. I asked where the body was? When they pointed to a pile of brush, which they had piled over him. I threw off the brush, and found the old man much swelled, with dark livid spots on the neck and body. — His complaint must have been inflamation of the bowels. A large heavy man. I called for a blanket & packing needle to sew him up, when a blue blanket was taken from a tent, but thought too good for such a purpose, and therefore had to use the one he laid on. Sent across the creek for 2 indians, who dug a grave in a sort of Potter's field, under some oaks, in rear of Lassen's wheat field, 3 or 400 yards opposite the ranch, and ¼ mile from the Frenchmen's camp. (*Funeral of J. C. Spence.*)   Sent over & procured, from Lassen's, the running-gear of a light wagon, tied the body on it, a Frenchman mounted on a fine horse, with a lasso (called in California, a riato) fastened to the wagon-tongue, and to his saddle drew it along, while we followed, and pushed. Two Frenchmen, the son of the deceased, young Shively, and myself assisted. Buried him about 10 A.M. and I placed a board at the head of the grave, on which I had neatly pencilled the following. —

✝

In memory
of
John C. Spence,
of
Oregon,
Died June 6. 1850.
Aged 36 years.

Poor Spence was a worthy fellow, though addicted occasionally to a spree The Coyotes have burrowed holes in all the graves here   This spot is the resting-place chiefly of emmigrants of 1849. Side by side repose the remains of the brothers Plummings, Dr Marshall, and poor Hervey. There are a considerable number of graves here. Some have pieces of boards and sticks, at their head, rudely pencilled, telling who beneath, has ended his weary travel.

[JUNE] 7th   A party of chiefly Germans, bound on an exploration, came up and camped close by, they have a New York Negro for cook; and are well armed and equipped.

[JUNE] 8th   A pleasant morning, but strong breeze blowing. At dusk the Steamer Lawrence, Capt. Chadwick,[42] arrived at Lassen's landing, on the bank of the Sacramento, — 1½ miles below: with stores for a government party, now coming up, and destined for the vicinity of the Pass of the Sierra Nevada, to punish the Pautahs for the Murder of Capt. Warner, last year.[43] I went on board, introduced to the master, Mr. T. H. Tilghman — (in charge of stores),[44] and Mackintosh, a Cherokee chief.[45] I slept on board.

[JUNE] 9th   Breakfasted on board the Steamer, after which she left, — taking off Miss White, to go down as far as Moon's. Mr Tilghman has to go down the valley, and engages me to take charge of the stores, so I had my tent taken down, and pitched by them. In the afternoon Miss W. and Col. Woods arrived.

About Merd^n the prospecting party, of the Houghs, Dr Bowman, Campbell, & Brittle, started up Deer Creek, on their way to the head of Feather river. Late in the afternoon, my tent blew down, and I merely cleared it away one side, so as to use my pallet.

[JUNE] 10th   Still fresh breeze. — too strong to attemp[t] raising my tent, without assistance. Dust blowing about, very annoying.

[JUNE] 11th — Dr Drinker[46] and Mr Rowe, from Moon's rode up, and passed the forenoon with us. We amused ourselves at target-practice with rifles. I was introduced to these gentlemen. We also practiced firing pistols, in which Mrs Myers and Miss White participated, — Miss W. shot very well.

    In the afternoon Mr Rowe's brother, and several men, in a mule wagon came up, and remained all night. Cold night, cloudy, Strong breeze, and lightning.

[JUNE] 12 — Indications of rain. Strong breeze & cold. The Mounted Men and officers of the Military expedition arrived, and selected a camp-ground, about ¼ mile below. Soon after, to my very pleasant surprise, who should come up but Freiner, with 2 other gentlemen.

    Mrs. Myers, Miss White, and Col. Woods, in a wagon, left for Yuba City.

    At dusk a light shower. Tilghman slept at the Military Camp. Have a severe headache

[JUNE] 13 — Heavy flying clouds. The Quarter Master's men are packing provissions to transport on mules. I eat my meals, as I have done, since the arrival of the stores, at Myer's — 300 yards off. Severe headache all day.

[JUNE] 14 — The Quarter Master settled with me, for guarding the stores. — The men carried the stores, as fast as packed, over to the camp. The Quarter Master's clerk will take my effects up to Lassen's to-morrow. I shot a fine squirrel for dinner; gave it to the folks at the house —

[JUNE] 15th   Breakfasted at Myers', with Mr. Brown & Fox, and then got in a government wagon, with my tent, &c and returned to Lassens'. Introduced to Capt. Lyon, U.S.A.[47] Commander of the Military Expedition, who invited me very kindly to his camp, to tea; as he wished to obtain information about the route in the mountains. I supped with Capt. L. and his officers, and had the pleasure of making the acquaintance of Dr Dyerly, — surgeon of the command.[48] I took a note-book with me, — relating to the route in the Sierra Nevada. Capt L. has made up his mind, however, to proceed up this valley, and strike over on the Pitt river, by the way of Redding's, Cow-Creek, &c. below Tschastes.[49] Capt. L. is a kind gentleman, and insists on my remaining in Camp, so I slept in his tent.

[JUNE] 16 — Tilghman, having purchased a fine horse of Lassen, yesterday, rode down the valley this morning. I had the pleasure of breakfasting with Capt. L. and his gentlemanly officers, at a very early hour. Regret much that the Capt. is indisposed. We breakfasted at 4 O'Clock, and the command moved on their march at 6. In the afternoon Col. Wilson, & Dr. Cole,[50] his agent, arrived; bringing an Englishman and his wife to attend to domestic matters, at Lassen's ranch.

[JUNE] 17th — Col. W. engaged me to draw a plot of the town on a large scale. Tooms[51] and another gentleman came up.

[JUNE] 18th   Drawing a town plot. In the afternoon Lassen & Dexter, started out for the hills, a short distance

[JUNE] 19th. Dr. Cole ill. Du Cas, and the rest of the Frenchmen moved off, for Trinity

[JUNE] 20th   Mrs. M. and Col. Wood returned. A rumored discovery of immense deposits of gold, around a Lake, situate somewhere between the upper waters of the Feather & Yuva rivers.[52] Dr. Cole better. Finished drawing.

JUNE 21 — 3 travellers, going down the valley, rested here, and proceeded. I sat up, at night, with Dr Cole. The sheep got out of the pen, and were chased around the house, late at night, by the Koyotes — I went out & penned them up again.

[JUNE] 22. A party came up from below, with pack mules, who talk about the recent discovery of gold, and are anxious to go on an exploration for it. The place is called "Gold Lake", and described as being somewhere in the Mountains, E. or S.E. of Pitt river, or Tschastes.

[JUNE] 23. Another party of mule-packers, in search of Gold Lake, came up. 11 men.

[JUNE] 24. Attacked with severe cold, falling in my eyes — nearly blind, and very painful.

[JUNE] 25. Quite ill with pains in breast and eyes.

[JUNE] 26. Afflicted the same as yesterday.

[JUNE] 27. Same; took castor oil, & rhubarb. 6 Spaniards, with mules, called, rested, and passed on.

[JUNE] 28. My health a little improved. As Col. Wilson is about to visit San Francisco, I have written a letter home, for him to take down. Mr. Stout, the surveyor, came up, from Yubaville; dined and left. Dock Davis, McBride, Fox, and a half-breed Frenchman, came up. At dusk Jno. Young and Col. W. rode off, to go below. The last 4 days I have not eat one solid meal. Little sleep to-night.

[JUNE] 29. 4 men came up early. Headache, tooth ache, pain in eyes and breast, spoilt last nights' sleep. Lassen engaged me to attend to the store   One of the travellers told us that Dr Davis, — my amiable and esteemed friend, was drowned, a few days ago, in the Sacramento, attempting to swim over, near the Red Bluffs: Col. Wood's son in company with him.

I was also informed of numerous suicides, in the mines, from disappointments.

JUNE 30. 2 men rode in on exhausted mules, from the emigrant route, in the mountains. — 50 miles back, where they left their comrades, out of provissions. They belonged to some companies who had started across the plains too early, and had a great deal of wet to contend with. Had taken the advice of fools, — brought insufficient provissions and ammunition, and many had most foolishly abandoned their arms. In consequence they were reduced to starvation, & the Pitt river indians had killed several of the party, and stolen what animals the hardships of the travel had spared. These who arrived here, are from Ohio; supplied them with flour and pork, and then started back. They reported another company, they left on the Humboldt, whom they think must perish for want of provissions.[53] Very warm day.

There is a person here by the name of Clough, camped across the Creek, and commands a considerable company: who have spent upwards of a year prospecting, and is refitting for a summer campaign in the hills. He has so many titles, that I do not know which to apply — Captain or Doctor, or — However, he seems to have a good heart, though a conceited quack. He is perfectly illiterate   He lent the poor emigrants, who just left, 2 good horses, in place of their broken down mules; and arms & ammunition. In fording Green river, they lost their wagon, arms, &c.

JULY 1. Feel better to-day. Found out, in conversation with Clough, that my lamented friend, of that name, is his nephew: — He knew that he intended to come to this country, but did not before know that he had done so.

[JULY] 2. At day-break Lassen and Dexter returned, with 2 men of Clough's company. They had not seen my friends, Hough, & Co.

[JULY] 3. Lassen rode down, and crossed to Moon's, and returned with Dr. Drinker and another person. Dr D. keeps a shanty near Moons, (a sort of open shop) A St Louis Frenchman, by the name of Solomon, came in, from the emigrant road. Shot 3 beeves for the ranch and travellers. Lassen had some fine samples of gold he found. Late in the night, Capt Lysle arrived.

[JULY] 4. Fine morning. Several starved emigrants came in. One of them, on hearing my name, recollected seeing my card in the "Sarcophagus rock." They are from Ohio and Illinois. Jones is the name of one.

[JULY] 5. The emigrants straggling in. A party of them hurried off, and down the valley In the afternoon Messrs Burche & McCorcle of Washington City, the former of my company: came up from Marysville —

[JULY] 6. Campbell arrived this morning early. I crossed to Moon's to see Dr Drinker, and dined there. Returned in the afternoon, with the Doctor, and rode up, in Capt. Pott's wagon. The Houghs, Dr Bowman, Hall, & the German party, returned from the hills. Had been on Feather river. Dr Cole, Nicholas, and Jones all sick here, with typhoid, billious, and diarohea.[54]

JULY 7 — Myers and others who had been several days in the hills, return'd.[55]

[JULY] 8 — Straggling emigrants, ragged & starving, coming in. A party of 7 men, who had broken and thrown away their arms, as useless articles, were attacked on Pitt river, 6 killed, and 1 wounded, who managed to elude his pursuers by jumping in the river, and getting under a willow bush. 2 stragglers of Myer's party, came in.

[JULY] 9 — Emigrants, from the East, and some people with wagons, from Oregon, came in. Indians had stolen their animals, and murdered the emigrants. Emigrants had been reduced to eating horses, mules, dogs, &c. One of the emigrants told me that the grave of the Allfords was open, and bodies exposed, that they appeared very perfect.

Told that 10 miles back, on Dry creek, there was a party of 20 emigrants, perfectly destitute, and unable to proceed. Lassen sent them bread, fresh meat, liquor, and a horse to bring a sick man in upon. — This is the man, who was wounded on Pitt river, when his 6 comrades were killed. — One was his brother-in-law.

They brought this man in, and I examined his wounds, gave him Castile soap, lint, salve &c. and bandages. He has a tolerable bad wound, in his right breast, 2 in outside of his left thigh, and one inside of his right thigh. His brother-in-law made him throw away his pistol, telling him, that unless he done so, he would not travel with him. This happened the day before the murder. He met the Military on Pitt river, on the 3rd where they had been half a day. — 5 day's travel in from thence, on foot. — The indians had stolen, on Pitt river, 9 good horses, from the emigrants, and 4 mules from the troops. The latter fired on them. Starved emigrants came in at night. Attack of Typhoid, very severe, took pills.

JULY 10. Still sick. Some of the emigrants went below. Campbell returned without finding the reported sick man, but found his horse, and a *bloody* saddle. Suspicions strong against a certain Doctor, who was his particular comrade, and last seen with him. — The sick man had money.

The Houghs, Hall, and Dr Bowman gone down to Marysville, for stores.[56] Bowman is to let me have a horse. Retired early, with fever, which continued all night.

[JULY] 11. Ill with fever, took 4 more Lee's Anti-Billous pills. Dr Drinker administered an emetic, which relieved me some, but exhausted. Drs. Cole and Drinker, Clough, and Messrs Breed and Hoffman, are very kind to me. A great row between some half-breeds, vacheros, in which Fox figured largely. a tall indian suspected of stealing a saddle was tied to a tree and well whipped. And the great, heavy, brave Mr Fox beat a small indian who dare not defend himself. At night, what little repose, a lapse of the fever allowed me, was disturbed by a Blacksmith, who alarmed the whole settlement, because his charcoal pit was afire.

JULY 12   Am very weak. Mrs Parfitt, very kindly gave me some sago. Mr. & Mrs. P. were brought up from Sn Francisco, by Col. Wilson, to cook, and attend to the table, &c. They had recently arrived from Adelaide, N. South Wales. — Had a cargo of valuable goods, for the California market, and the vessel was run ashore at the Sandwich islands, causing them the loss of their property. I am preparing now, to join the parties going exploring for "Gold Lake".[57] I do not believe the story, but the excursion will be over a country very little if any known; and we may be so fortunate as to find a rich gold place, if not a Gold Lake. Bought 31½ lbs jerked beef, at 75 ¢ per pound.

Brittle and a German returned from a prospecting tour. I am very sick.

[JULY] 13. Better to-day. Shot several squirrels; mortally wounded many, but they escaped in their holes.[58] In that respect they are exactly like the prairie-dog. No matter how severely wounded, unless the head is shot off, they contrive to get in their hole, — or in some hole, — for the ground is bored full of them. There are two Russians, and a Dane, in the German party, and one of the Russians cannot speak or understand one word of English. I gave a Musket to Solomon, whom we have dubbed King Solomon. He wishes to accompany us prospecting. About 2 P.M. several men went ahead, to camp on the line of march — Young Wood very severely burnt with gun-powder, most imprudently pouring gun powder from a horn into the embers, to enliven them. *Morale* — Powder and fire will quarrel. Sultry to-day. Dr. Drinker has kindly offered me the use of his mule to pack pro-vissions on — as he cannot wait for me, and we have agreed to be partners,[59] in the expedition. At 4 P.M. Messrs Breed, Gibbs, and Adams, with packed animals, started for the hills. At Sunset Shively, Fox, young Marshall, Bat-tateaux (French half-breed) 4 indians, & 2 squaws, moved up creek a little. Dr Drinker attacked with fever, and I now had to attend to him. I was ill all night with fever myself. One of the late emigrants says he is a Mormon. — He is crazy, Mormon, or not.

[JULY] 14 — Lassen, with a large company, beef cattle, indians and squaws, pack horses, mules, &c started at 10 A.M. on the "Gold Lake" hunt Whilst I was absent a short time, from the ranch, a rogue called for my double-barrel'd Rifle, saying that Lassen sold it to him for 25 dolls. but Dr Cole would not let him have it.

At dusk Col. Woods and another gentleman, came up from Marysville, in a buggy. Fever left me to-night.

[JULY] 15 — Col. Wilson systematized things at the ranch. I had a singular dream, last night. — That I was home, in a room containing kegs of gun-powder, with loose grains on the floor. — Having thoughtlessly thrown a burning lucifer match down, was exceedingly alarmed, and ordered every one to fly instantly from the house; I rushed up stairs, where my family were, seized a child under each arm, and rushing down the stairs, told my wife to follow rapidly to secure her life. Expecting every moment to be blown up.

After breakfast, Col. Woods & his friend left for the bluffs. In the afternoon Mr Fitzgerrald of the Rifles, and Mr. Tilghman rode up. Capt. Lyons left an infirm soldier here. He sold me 4 squirrels for a dollar. Mr Alexander of my Company, sent word to me to go down to Marysville.

JULY 16. Early in the morning the Houghs, & Dr Bowman arrived. Mr. Fitzgerald & Tilghman left, for the cities, taking a letter for my family. Mr. Wright called & left —

[JULY] 17 — Busy preparing packs & pack saddle. Late in the afternoon young Hough kindly brought over the pack mule Dr Drinker loaned me. Mr. Hall came over. Dr Bowman kindly sold me a horse, on credit, for $150. — had his fore feet shod, costing $5. (I found the shoes and nails)   Slept little.

[JULY] 18. Near meredian before our little party were enabled to move off for our prospecting tour in the mountains. A sultry travel. Reached "Dry hollow", and I went down the steep hill with a comrade, to Mill Creek, for water. 15 miles from Lassen's. Our party is composed of Mr Hough and Son, Dr Bowman, Campbell, Hall, and self.

[JULY] 19 — We early led our animals down to water   After breakfast we traveled to my old Camp, 17 miles, and camped down the Mill Creek gorge, near the Spring. A cool pleasant night, we all slept sound.

[JULY] 20. Very early Mr Hough mounted his mare, and rode off in quest of our animals, which had strayed during the night, — leaving the rest of us asleep. Soon after I was awakened by a sensation of heat, and thought it was the rising sun shining on me, but soon found that it was the pine straws afire close to me. Jumped up and roused the party. — My packs of salt pork, and jerked beef, with other articles on them, were in a large blaze, near me. Rifles and guns, all charged, setting around a pine tree, had the flames flickering among them. We jerked powder horns & flasks up, and dashed them away; removed guns, &c. with dispach — but still suffered much loss, and caused delay. The breech of Mr Hough's rifle was much scorched, a powder horn was also burnt at the butt. A couple of pack-saddles much injured, a pack containing dried peaches, coffee, & salt, ruined, except part of the salt. — A haversack of mine, with packing needles & other useful implements;

a portable desk, and the greater part of my pork and beef consumed, the remainder much damaged — ropes, straps — &c.— &c — The log camp-fire was on the right of my head, as I lay on my back, about 10 feet, and when we laid down, was very low; but a breeze had fanned it, and the fire ran parrallel to me, turned, and came down towards my feet, and when it awakened me, was within a yard of my feet. Mr Hough returned with the animals, then he and his son & Campbell, mounted, and crossed over the hill to visit Deer Ck. gorge, to *prospect*, while we remained here to repair damages. They returned late in the afternoon, found no gold. By Sun Set we had all right again, for travelling. Found here the emaciated and sore-backed horse, of the supposed murdered emigrant, and Campbell brought him along.

[JULY] 21 — The Doctor and young Hough started early for the Doctor's and my horses, which had strayed off a little, and brought them in. Campbell's mare now ran off, and I lent him mine to catch her. It was near 10 A.M. before we all mounted & moved on. A hot ride, of 15 miles, to little meadow of a rill of Deer Creek. Afternoon I was attacked with chills and fevers, continuing all night —

[JULY] 22. Feel better this morning. Rode 10 miles to Deer Valley, lunched, rested, and moved on. Chills & fevers in afternoon — proceeded 8 miles to Butte Ck. valley, and camped. Plenty of grass. I saw a rackoon and 3 blue cranes. Am very sick, took 4 of Lee's pills. Snow-patches on the mountains to our right, — about 500 feet higher than this plain. Night very cold.

[JULY] 23 — Ice this morning. Feet ached with cold all night. We awoke early with cold. Animals chilled. Yesterday afternoon we passed the grave of a man who died late last October — Moved 12 miles, to the lower end of Butte Crk. valley. Noon 1½ hours, and moved on to Feather river valley, and camp'd on S. side of the first ford, (going out) and at the edge of a branch, — 4 miles. Plenty of good grass. Afternoon we continued, turning to the right, going E. over ridges and through timber till we reached a branch, a tributary of the Western prong of the N. fork of Feather river, and camped. During the afternoon — going through a bottom I saw the remains of Davis' wagon which he left here 2 years ago, when he thought he could enter the settlements by following Feather river down. The wagon could only be taken a few hundred yards further, when the rapid stream passed between abrupt hills. It is about 5 miles E. of the road. He abandoned the wagon, packed his oxen, and rejoined Lassen and others, on the trail above.[60] Some fever — very little sleep. Nervous excitement

[JULY] 24 — Sun well up before we rode on. In ½ mile we reached the river, — a N. Western branch, pretty deep, very rapid, and full of round and flat rocks.[61] Crossed about 40 yds over, to a little island, full of brush, crossed that, 20 yds, then the main branch, — rapids, full of rocks, and up to the saddle-skirts in places, — about 60 yards. All crossed safe — Now we rode over stony ridges, ascended a very steep stony hill, kept along a narrow crooked and elevated back bone, descended — over smaller hills, all rocky, with red earth, and white quartz, and talcose slate, till about 1 P.M. Crossed a wet narrow meadow, and nooned. 10 miles. Found holes of good water. About 2½ P.M. Myer's associates, with a train of mules they were taking back to the settlements, rested, and moved on — We moved on, ascended steep rugged ridges till we passed the apex, and descended on a lower range, where we met Lassen and 3 others, who had been out in the hills, away from their camp, and were endeavoring to regain it. Kept along the ridge till night overtook us, at the extremity, where it pitches down abruptly several thousand feet, to a cañon. Here we had to make a dry camp. — No water. Fallen pines afire near us, we passed numerous fires of this kind, and the hills are light with them. Prospectors & indians caused them. 9 miles — Lay down supperless. Severe headache all day & night, but fatigue answers as a sudorific [soporific] A fine vein of talcose slate runs over this hill.

[JULY] 25 — With hungry maws and dry throats, we packed and mounted early. Retraced last nights' march a short distance, turned to the right, down steep slaty ridges, over stony spurs, & hollows, with deep dust, till about 9½ A.M. we reached a very narrow valley, & deep-seated branch of Feather river, enclosed by very steep & high mountains. A northern branch. Some scattered grass, but best near the stream — Soda and sulphur springs in shelves of rock, some above & others below the water. Little current here — seems to be deep, and about 100 yds. over. Slate cropping out of the banks. Hills of the western side are very steep and high. Indian and deer trails plenty here — much travelled by them. Lassen and his comrades left the big hill before we did. His camp is some distance lower down this stream. We heard rifle-shot down there. Old man Hough is quite ill with fever. In addition to occasional fevers, I am lame with several biles [boils] — interesting predicament for riding all day over the roughest country that was ever piled up! Fire in the grass, and the cramp in one ancle awakened me just in time to prevent damage.

[JULY] 26th   Picketed 3 horses, loosed the others.
    The loose animals strayed off, last night, and we were much afraid of the

necessity devolving on some two of us, to ascend the steep mountain, in quest of the truant horses and mules; but they came down to the river, after having wandered up to the base of the hills a mile or two. Last night Campbell was attacked with chills: so that this morning we are equally divided, — 3 sick, and 3 well. About 10 A.M. Dr Bowman, Hough jr, and Hall, rode down the valley; leaving Hough sr, and Campbell, ill with fever, and I lame with biles [boils] on my leg, — to keep camp. — So, with smoking my pipe, and sketching, I whiled away the tedium of a solitary position. At Sun Set our well trio returned, accompanied by the worthy old Danish Sea Captain, of the German party. They reported having travelled, along the stream, 3 miles of rugged slate on edge, — most toilsome for the animals. In the afternoon 3 strangers, on mules, camped near us. — They have just descended on our trail, from the crest of the tall ridge. Looking up at this immense pile of pine-clad rocks, towering into the region of clouds, whose base is within rifle-shot of us, and think how we descended therefrom, most of the way mounted, rode down it! To those unaccustomed to such a country, and such travel, it would appear impracticable, to aught but beast and lizards! The strangers reported, that the old horse, Campbell picked up at my old camp, and who strayed off while we were descending the adjacent mountain, they saw, about half-way down. We now packed up, and moved down the valley, 3 miles, crossed the stream twice, and camped, in a pine grove. Trees had been nearly all burnt. Plenty of fuel, and tolerable grass. We divided the party in 2 messes. The Danish Captain and strangers, continued down lower. My partner, Dr Drinker, is with Lassen and party, and our stores, &c are divided, till we can meet. Hall took my horse and went back to look for the old horse on the mountain-side.

As we came along to-day, I noticed several bark lodges of the indians,[62] and burnt muscle-shells. Signs of deer being plentiful. The stream here, is very crooked, about 50 feet wide, and 2$\frac{1}{2}$ deep, stony bottom, and little current, except now and then short rapids. Large black ants are very troublesome here, as they are all over California, on oak-trees. Saw a small brown viper. The bottom, or valley here, is not over 500 yds. wide, and covered with fragments of talcose & micacious slate, white & ferruginous quartz. Prairie peas abundant, — cooked some, but they were too old & stringy. The hills subside here considerably; — on neither side are very elevated, but steep, and thickly *pined*. Orchard-looking oak scattered around.

Campbell ill, with fever and nausea: — I gave him a dose of Tart. emetic, which relieved him of much bile. 2 of my comrades tried a bar, in the stream, for gold, but found a mere *streak* only. Late in the afternoon, Lassen and 3

Oregon men, rode up, from their camp some miles below. — We tendered to them, mountain hospitality, — Supper was produced, and properly discussed, followed by the pipe, tales of the route, &c. — Kicked away the big stones, spread our blankets & saddle-pillows, & slept.

[JULY] 27 — Lassen and his comrades left us early. Some miles lower — a little above "Rich Bar,"[63] is a deep, narrow, and rugged cañon, where the stream tumbles through. Lassen related the perils of clambering through in, over elevated crags, and where they had to assist each other, and one of them came within an inch of being dashed to atoms. Animals have to ascend a steep range of hills before reaching the cañon — After breakfast, we packed, to move out of the valley. — While saddling up, 3 indians came along, from below. — An old dark-colored man, whose suit of clothes was merely a black-silk vest, and a black net around his hair.[64] — He had under his arm, a bundle of grass-looking weed, and said that it was "*boino por maslo*". (Good for sickness)   The 2 lads were slender, well-formed, of a light color, handsome features, and very lively. — They had quivers, bows, and arrows; and one, wearing a striped shirt, straw hat, and red ribbon, had an Allen's revolver [65] belted to his side. The other lad had a shirt tied around his waist, and wore a butcher knife and belt. We gave them bread, when one asked for "*Coffèè*" and "*Suuger*", which we also gave them: having some coffee remaining in the kettle. The old man wore moustache. About 9 A.M. we moved up the valley, preceeded by the naked legs. When we reached the hills, on the trail we descended by, we had an ardious time getting up. — Our course we had to scramble and drag our animals up by the reins. I grew very weak, with severe pains, and when we had left the tallest range, that we ascended from the valley, we dashed through brush, rocks, &c. and over fallen trees & stumps, —for a shorter cut, and arrived at the moist grass valley where we saw Myers and McBride, on the [24]. As much as I could do to keep in the saddle, during the last 2 hours, I was so ill and weak. It was about 5 P.M. when with the greatest difficulty, I dismounted here, unsaddle[d] my horse, and threw me on the ground, upon the smoking horse-blanket, and laid full two hours in a feverish lethargy, and exhausted. Mr Hall kindly unpacked my mule, and when they had prepared supper he brought me some strong tea. — This revived me. At dusk I felt nearly well again. My comrades are convalescent.

JULY 28. I had a tolerable night's repose — The morning cold, thin ice in the springs. Have a tolerable appetite, but headache and hermarhoids troublesome. Animals doing well. I Have taken blue mass, and laudanum. 9 A.M. Lassen came up, followed by Dr Drinker, — we were gratified to meet. Lassen & Drinker moved on, through the thick forrest of pines, &c, and we soon followed. After riding some distance, on undulating table-hills, and through pine forrests, and reached the ford of Feather river, with the island, in it, before described, (coming out) by 3 P.M. Two men stood there, waiting a chance to get over, by the assistance of travellers. (Many small parties going to and fro along here, prospecting, like ourselves) One of these men was sick; he wore a deer-skin mountaineer's suit, — both on foot. We lent them a horse, and they crossed. When we reached the little valley, on the other side, where Davis' wagon remains were, found a camp of Oregon men, also on the "Gold Lake" hunt. At about 5 P.M. we struck Lassen's Depôt Camp, in a grove of small pines, a short distance across the Emigrant road, about 3 miles below where it leaves this valley of Feather river, and ascends the hills, and half a mile above the ford of the river. The river sweep[s] around to the Westward of the camp, about 50 yds in our rear. The ground here is rather moist — Lassens indians, with their Squaws, and the Squaw of a half-breed Frenchman are here. Several sick persons are laying here, And the indians, under charge of a white man — camp-keeper, attend to the beef cattle and horses, grazing near by. Chills, fevers, and musquitoes, interfered much with my repose. Joined my partner — Dr Drinker, so we two are a mess of our own. The men here, are Fox, Battis, — the French half breed Oregonian; — he is called Battateaux, generally, and is brother of Capt Warner's guide, murdered with poor Warner. He has a Digger squaw, whom he alternately caresses and whips; — and is a poor drunken devil. Then Mr Messer Smith, (one of the late unfortunate emigrants) from Pa — German extraction — We call him Smith. — The two men we assisted over the river, The German party, 4 other white men, and a negro — (Andy). There are several others belonging to this camp, but they are out prospecting, hunting, &c. Just after we laid down to sleep, heard guns fired, and answered them by shots.

JULY 29. Cold and damp bed. Feeble and sore. Water fowl and cranes abundant — a humming bird's nest over my pallet, she is endeavoring to coax her young to attempt flying. Robins are also numerous Preparations nearly perfect, for the great "Gold Lake" hunt.

On the ride out, at the deep hollow, — some 20 miles from the settlements, the Frenchman's squaw, had to dismount, and cause a slight detention, while she gave birth to a child;[66] It was enveloped in a rag, and its mother mounted her poney astraddle, in half an hour, after, with the infant mountaineer, and rode about 35 miles, without any serious inconvenience. The child did not survive the ride, and was buried. — This shows the difference between artificial and natural folks. She is here, and very lively. A diarohea attacked me, and I had to take laudanum.[67] I wonder if I am to be persecuted to death, with all sorts of maladies? — Mr Hoffman, with Clough & others is campd above — H. is quite ill, has eat nothing for 3 days. About 1½ miles above is a trading party, with a tent, and camped there are Messrs. Breed, Gibbs, &c.[68] An ox shot for Lassen's party & indians.

[JULY] 30   Camp aroused at day-break. All the men fit for hard active service and ready, are now to start on the Lake hunt. At Sun rise they rode off, Lassen leading, and my partner Drinker accompanying them. Those left here, are Hough Sr. Campbell, Fox, Dexter, Nicholas, Battis, Marshall, — a lad, Hoffman, 3 other white men, Negro Andy, and about 12 indians — male and female. 6 of the whites, (including myself) are sick, and 2 indians. The Snow-Butte, or Mount St Jose, bears about W.N.W.

Little appetite, and severe headache & hermarhoids. Some one of Lassen's party said, that when first coming out, at the first water of deer valley, this side of my camp, near a wagon, on the road side, they saw the corpse of a grey-headed man, much decayed. Hoffman is very feeble.

Dexter, Fox, and Andy, on foot, went in a S.E. direction about 3 miles, prospecting Rheumatic pains are contributed to my afflictions. — What next? We assisted Hoffman on his mule, and he rode off for the tent. The three prospectors returned, reporting no oro. One of Clough's party, gave me an interesting account of the Snow Butte and surrounding country, where they recently travelled.

This snow-capp'd peak, is about 40 miles off. About its base, and some distance up, there are boiling springs, and crevices of volcanic action; shooting up columns of steam, smoke and gasses, from 50 to 100 ft. There are numerous holes, crevices, and fissures, the gasses and steam from which, makes a harsh rushing sound like that of a large steam-boat, blowing off steam.[69] Deer and grizzlers abundant there — they shot several of the former, and one of the latter.

A horse kept saddled & picketed by Lassen's camp, drew the picket, this morning, and ran away.

A cold night. The half-cured biles [boils] have changed to bad sores, on legs, which with headache, fever, and other pains, seasoned with considerable frost, on a light blanket, made for me, a very delectable night. Sleep vamosed.

JULY 31 — Plenty of ice, this morning.

Though sick and weak, I must help myself. Made a fire, and drew me
a pot of tea, and eat 3 or 4 oz: bread & meat   A French-half breed Oregonian, taken ill, with cholera-morbus, &c. and crazy. — He has eat hearty,
his comrade says, and "drank d — d hard." A party of prospectors came up,
— had been on all the head streams of Feather river, and were going in to
settlements, for provissions, and to return. Some of our indians, this forenoon,
amused me, by driving into camp, before them, a young blue crane, — with
it[s] long legs and neck, stood about as high as a common grown turkey. It
looked so very awkard, as running before the lad, through the grass, with
singular gait, looking right and left, and assisting its strides, by flapping its
young wings, like the ostrich. They found it in rushes in the river bottom.

A party of male and female indians crossed the river, and went back on
the emigrant route, some few miles, *prospecting* the old camp-grounds, and
returned ladened with old cotton-cloth, female apparel, &c. dirty, and damaged by exposure to 8 or 9 months' elements. Breed called to see me.

A pelican in stream,[70] but Andy fired at him in vain.

Pain in the back, head, &c. severe — again murdering repose.

AUGUST 1st   Awakened quite early by cold, headache, & Co. I walked down
to the stream, & washed. Feet ached with cold. Made a fire, warmed feet,
and laid down, and slept some time. On awakening again, I felt better, made
coffee, fried some cold bread, and eat a good breakfast — a pair of bald
eagles soared over the camp this morning. Negro Andy, kindly gave me a
skillet and lid, needed much to bake bread in. This he picked up on some
old camp-ground, emigrant road.

During the afternoon, I was awakened from a feverish sleep, by an outcry
among Lassen's indians, and on rising to ascertain the cause, I saw 6 mountain indians coming into camp. Of this party, 3 were the same who visited us
in the deep valley, and asked for coffee & sugar; they had each, spare bows
and arrows.[71] One of them made a speech, of some length, accompanied
with violent gesticulations, but Lassens indians, nor any of us, understood
the purport of it. A tall, thin, straight, dignified young man, among them,
wore moustache; he was of a light color, and spoke some Spanish: he frowned
much, and was very reserved. His comrade, also of a light color, was young
and lively, and quite loquacious, wore his "Allen's revolver"; — said, with a
mixture of Spanish & English, that we, (the Whites,) were good, but our
indians were bad. Their quivers were formed of the skins of a dark colored
fox, a mink, a small yellow wolf, &c. One was quite enamored with a squaw,

the wife of one of Lassen's indians; and offered the husband, all his personal effects and equipment, for her, which I explained to them, and they laughed heartily. One of our indians gave an old blanket, several strings of white shells,[72] &c. for a bow and number of arrows. An old man, of the mountain clan, had a yellow straw, about 2 inches long, thrust through the cartilage of his nose.[73] He had a tin pot of soup given him, and asked for "*salt*", and said "*Soupee*", distinctly. These chaps, no doubt were often among the miners.

On noticing the speech of the mountain indian, I told some of my comrades, that from the tone of the fellow's harrange, he was telling us some thing grave and important, I had no doubt. When a bystander remarked that maybe he alluded to the robbery of the loquacious one, a few days ago, by 3 of Lassen's indians. Enquiring into the particulars, I was informed, that the 3 indians were out exploring a few miles to the E. of this, and met this lone mountain youth, whom they immediately beset, robbed him of some dried salmon, and his bow, and several arrows, and threatened his life. That they had consumed some of the salmon, and had the rest hid. I told the person having charge of our indians, to make them give up the salmon, which after a while was done. 5 of the strangers seemed to be in good humor, but the moustached one, kept aloof and reserved, wearing a frown on his brow. I touched him on the shoulder, and spoke Spanish, but he jerked himself around, with a malicious smile on one corner of his mouth. — (*Feather river Indians plate*)

These mountaineers remained a couple of hours, and then proceeded up the valley.

A little before Sun Set, I was astonished at the appearance of 21 mountain indians, walking hastily in single file, approaching the camp, from above, (following the stream down). They gravely gathered around the remains of a camp-fire, under the pines; and I stepped back a few paces, and laid my arms, so that I could quickly handle them. There was one peculiarity I particularly noticed, of these wild fellows: — they were daubed with black, faces marked, and half painted over, streaks upon their arms and breasts. As I had never seen any indians of this country painted before, I at once concluded that it was a war symbol; They also had full quivers, knives, bows & three arrows in hand, and an extra bow in each quiver. — From the aged chief, down to boys, not over 12 years of age, it was the same. One old man, several middle-aged ones, 2 small boys, and all the rest hearty young men. All of a light color, except the eldest, well formed, and straight. Most of them looked grave, and several frowned; particularly the younger ones, including the boys. I admired these brave little fellows. — They were pretty, and stood erect and determined; I put my hand on the head of one, and he indignantly stepped aside, looked up at me and knit his young brows. When they had consolidated around the fire, a young man stepped forward, and commenced a speech. he spoke in an empassioned manner, with vehement gesticulation of the hands, for about 10 minutes, and fell back to the ranks. Our indian men had come up, and stood in a gaping group near. On the wild indian concluding his speech, one of our indian youths stepped forward, (the whites giving way for him) and also made a speech, intended for a reply, for they did not understand one another's language. His harange was of the same character, in expression, as the other. Then the old dark chief spoke, — in the same vehement style, and with much motion of the arms. It was most dusk, the whites, of our camp all sick but 3 men, and I thought it best to get rid of our visitors as speedily as possible. I told my comrades that these fellows came here to seek redress, for the robbery perpetrated upon one of them, or to kill Lassen's indians. I did not apprehend their harming any of us intentionally, but should they attempt to kill our indians, some of us might catch an arrow, when these missiles were flying over the camp. Our cowardly rogues had only returned a part of the salmon, and yet had a bow and arrows belonging to the mountaineer; and from signs the old chief made to me, I knew that was what they wanted. So the indians were made to produce the bow and arrows, which we handed over to the other party; upon which, the old chief, and several others simultaneously exclaimed "*buono*"! and quickly relaxed their stern features. — They now turned to go away, the chief and several others shook hands with me, and some of my comrades; and on getting off, about 100 yds. they raised a long and wild yell, mingled with shrieks — their "war-hoop" — and capered around, right and left, imitating a fight, drawing their bows, and brandishing their knives. Our poor indians were awfully frightened. It would have been all day with them, if we had not settled the difficulty.

The old chief wore a *crown*, of some thin red and black substances; it was a very tasty serrated diadem.[74] Most of them wore shirts and pants, some had beads on the neck and in their ears. Several wore a white bone or other white looking substance, thrust through the nose. The chief, or king, was blackened in the face, down to his nose, and across, to the tips of his ears. Others had large black circles around their eyes, some striped across the face, and most of them had marked their arms, bodies and legs.[75] Their "war-whoop" stamped[ed] our band of oxen, horses, &c. grazing about ½ mile off, causing them to scatter and run wildly some distance

After the restoration of the stolen articles, I approached the old chief, when he smiled, and extended his hand. He then pointed to each white man, around, and said, as he pointed, "*buono*", (good) and signified that we were all friends: but turning towards our indians, and pointing at them, he said emphatically, "maslo"! (bad!) Their village is about 6 miles above this, and it appears to me, that the small party, who first came to camp, called merely to ascertain if the guilty indians were here, and if protected by the whites. And the speech one of them made, was no doubt his address, informing them of their intentions to come and demand redress, and if dis-appointed, to slay all of Lassen's indians.

I am troubled with a kind of low typhoid fever, and ulcers very painful, and a severe headache.

This morning Gibbs rode down to see me, and kindly gave me some dough-nuts he had cooked for some sick comrades, and he promises me a little rice.

One of the wild indians, as he ran off, picked up the bloody head of the ox sloughtered the other day, and carried it off on his shoulders.

3 of Clough's party and 2 Oregon men rode up, after the indians left, rested, and proceeded up to their camp. I put my arms by my pallet, and slept, as well as fever would permit. A cold night.

[AUG.] 2 — Ice formed in a tin pan of water. I felt tolerable well, this morn-ing, but my knee was very sore. Breakfasted on beef soup and coffee. The Oregonians are camped about ¼ mile above us, and rather nearer the stream. Last night 2 horses & several of their oxen strayed off.

Our indians, I am told, slept very little last night, they were afraid of the yellow mountaineers. Yesterday afternoon, Lassen's men sent an indian boy off on a horse to search for some stray cattle, & as he has not returned, they think he has run off, for the settlements, or been killed by the mountain indians; I took a hearty drink of cream of tartar solution, to correct bad blood.

About 8½ A.M. the indian boy walked lazily into camp. He was at the camp above, a couple of miles, when the hill indians passed, and was afraid to return to his own camp. He left the horse there.

At Sun-Set, 4 men came up: one was mounted on a poney, the others a foot, — and they had a mule packed, with chiefly mining implements. — They were from the upper mines of Feather river, and bound for the settle-ments. Lassen's stray animals were found & driven in to camp. The Ore-gonians had sent a wagon in for stores. — it has just return'd, and they are establishing a trading-tent, with Whisky, flour, and pork, for sale. Slept tolera-bly, though cold.

[AUG.] 3ᵈ Awakened at day-break, with painful knee, sore hips and back, and a severe headache. I sat up, with a blanket around me, till chilled with frost, then lay down, and slept till the sun was half an hour high. — A severe headache on awakening the 2nd time. However, I made coffee, drank a pot full, and rested my aching body against a tree, in the shade. Sun very warm. The Oregon boys are a wild uncouth set of youngsters. They are continually racing their horses over the plain, and screeching and yelling like indians. Their horses are poor, and they poor riders.

A tall elderly stranger came into camp, and wished to buy some fresh meat. — He was informed that we had none to sell. He then said there was plenty, in camp, pointing to the staging at Lassen's camp, where beef was curing (being jerked) for the use of Lassen's party. They told him that it was not for sale, and besides, the person having charge of it, was just now absent from camp. This did not satisfy him; and he replied, that he did not come to beg, but was willing and ready to pay any price they demanded. He was very pertinacious, and continued to insist on their selling him some meat, till a person said to him, "old man, you can't get any, and you can talk just as much and as long as you please." After which he went off.

Some body found a plaster Phrenological Bust, at some old camp-ground, and brought it into camp, and sat it on a stump. Lassen's indians looked at it, exhibited disgust, and one told me, that it was *bad*, looked like a corpse, and ought to be buried. Some of them broke it to atoms, with a crow-bar.

This morning I noticed a man on horseback bring in a deer, taking it to a small camp above. In the middle of the day I walked up to get a piece of the meat. I stopped at the Oregon camp, — Several wagons, tents, booths; and men, women, and children as uncivil and uncouth as indians. About 100 yards beyond, found a camp of 5 men, in a pine grove, they were reclining in the grass, while one was reading a book. I was referred to the man reading for the purchase of a piece of venison. — He said that the deer was all their pro-vissions, but he would exchange a piece for a piece of pork, and gave me a neck piece, to make soup of.

Early in the afternoon, J. J. Myers, McBride, Moon, (proprietor of the Sacramento ferry) all mounted, with Mr Moon's *squaw*, astraddle a mule, and 10 of his indians a-foot, passed, on their way from the settlements to the upper Feather river mines.

Andy, the darkee, is very kind & obliging, — He baked me a nice little loaf of bread to-day. The Oregonians drove all their oxen by, and crossed the river, on the road.

Near Sun Set, a young man named Ray, rode into camp, he was quite sick.

— From the settlements, bound to the mines, to join Myers, & Co — He informed me that Capt. Lyons, with his command, had returned to Lassen's. He went in by the way of Cow Creek, & above the Snow Butte, the same trail he had gone out on.[76] He had a letter from the Capt. to John Avelyne, who is at Myer's Diggings', on the Feather, a few days ride from here. He wants the services of Avelyne, (who was one of Capt. Warner's party) to guide him to the spot where poor Warner fell, in order to look for his remains. When Avalyne joins the command, the troops will move out, on this road.[77] Ray knew me at Lassen's, but did not recognize me at first, I have so alter'd by sickness. Would have slept well to-night but for the music of owls and wolves.

AUG. 4 — Awoke early, and felt better. Prepared and eat a hearty breakfast, of fried venison, *light* bread, and tea.

After breakfast Campbell rode down the eastern valley in search of the old emigrants horse he picked up when we came out, and strayed off descending into the deep valley, some time ago. I lent him a spur. Feeling so much better, I walked around considerable, but it enfeebled me, and I took a nap. Lumbago affected me at night, and I took laudanum —

[AUG.] 5 — Slept late. Headache. No appetite. In the afternoon was attacked with fevers and some chills. Took quinine. At 2 P.M. 3 men, of Fox's party, came in, from the settlements, with stores. They reported that every body at Lassen's and the vicinity, were ill with fever, and that the military detachment were about to march out.[77]

I am very sick. Dew, at night, falling like a fine shower, and spiders, mice, lizzards, snakes, musquitoes, lumbago, fevers, &c. rather interfere with repose — Frost.

[AUG.] 6 — One of my old friends, Peck, — (a comrade of Poiles' on the march across the country), came in; said P. was close by, and in bad health. He had had no luck at the mines.

One of Fox's party kindly gave me half a cake of Chilian dried peaches. I stewed some, and they were very pleasant. I considered the damp ground here, was injuring my health — so constructed a kind of bedstead. — Cut away several sapling pines, so as to leave 4, to form posts of a bedstead. — lashed poles to these, about 2½ feet from the ground; for rails; then sewed a blanket over them, for a sacking, and thus had a magnificent bed.

At Sun Set I made my supper of bread soaked in tea.

At dusk, my ever dear friend, — Poile, called to see me, we spent several hours talking. Poor Fellow! he is ragged and luckless. I slept tolerably, excepting cold feet and legs. Headache.

[AUG.] 7 — Fox, and his party rode off, on a deer-hunt, very early, and returned at breakfast time, luckless. They saw several. Headache still annoys me. The entire afternoon I was kept too warm with fever. (*Mountain Hospital*)   A sick man lays under a tree close by, and appears to be nearly through his travel. All day a party has been playing cards beside him: and a little beyond, Lassen's indians are gambling, — their own peculiar game, with much noise;[78] an interesting hospital, this! Cooking, gambling, — horse-laughter, and strong virtuous exclamations. Still, ours is an orderly camp.

Poile again came and spent an hour with me. Chills and fevers all night.

AUG. 8   I feel better than I did last night.

Fox shot a steer he had, for meat.

Poile and Peck called, they said that last night and this morning were very cold. Some Oregonians, male and female, called to see the man so ill.

At meridian felt quite well, and dined on bread & coffee. I presented Andy, for his many little acts of kindness, a $5 Californian coin.[79] To-night I was blessed with accumulated affections — chills, swelled abdomen, headache, & cold.

2 of McBride's party passed, going in for provisions. Soon after, McBride himself came along, and visited us; he told extravagant stories about the gold found where he and Myer's party have located themselves, on Feather river.[80] One man had taken out 60 lbs of gold in one day. And several had accumulated all the fortunes they desired, in a few days, and left, to go home! — I considered this story to be worth just about as much as the *Traders* wished it to be.

[AUG.] 9 — Rose early, chilled and swelled up. — made strong coffee, and drank two pots of it, and eat some fried liver. At mid-day I was attacked with chills again, lasting till 4 P.M. when 2 hours hot fever succeeded. My kind friends, Poile & Peck, sent me a fine piece of venison, and Andy cooked some of it for me. I drank some of the broth.

Mr Dye came in,[81] from the mines, and contradicted McBride's statements about the yield. A very cold night, and I suffered some.

AUG: 10 — Awakened early with cold & pain in the back. I mixed quinine and blue mass, into a large pill, and swallowed it. Could not leave my patent bed-stead. Ice this morning. One of the men here bought 20 lbs of flour of the Oregonians, at $1 per lb. This man and his comrade, on mules, came in last evening; said they had been exploring from the American river, at its mouth, to its sources, had visited the Trucky river and lake, and along all the streams of the Yuva and Feather rivers, to this place, — travelling since December last. They were ragged, had been 10 days on one meal per day, and 4 days fasting. They have 6 comrades, camped below, about 6 miles, and are going down this branch of Feather river. They have accumulated nothing.

I had taken a nap, of about one hour, when, at 1 P.M. I was awakened by a fuss, — and looking over towards the road, saw the military expedition, moving on. — A colored man rode over to camp, for a drink, and I recognized him as Capt. Lyon's servant.[82] I sent my respects to the Capt. Capt. L. sent him back, saying he intended camping just over the ford, and would be glad to see me there; but I told him I was unable to do so. —

Lassen's squaws went out to dig roots. Pedro, one of these indians, is very ill, and his squaw, not over 15 yrs. of age, is exceedingly attentive to him, day and night. Andy made me a peach pie.

At Sun Set I was happy to see Capt Lyon, who kindly rode over to see me. He was quite indisposed, but I thought of the pie (a great luxury for us here) and we enjoyed a pot of tea & piece of pie. He told me about the route on which he first travelled out, and on which he returned to the valley. The trail lay along a series of fine valleys, no rugged steep hills to pass, a good road for wagons can easily be cut here — (This is where the emigration of '49 including myself, thought the road from the Pass went; and which I wished the company to let me hunt for, and they would not listen to *experiments*.)[83]   At dusk the Capt. proceeded to his camp   His command are now equipped properly for mountain-service — all on mules, and no useless, troublesome sabres.[84] 2 of Capt. L's command sent back to Deer Valley to look for a sack of papers the Capt lost there.

At night I took another blue-mass & quinine pill. After midnight I slept well

Avelyne came up, and joined the detachment —

[AUG.] 11 — Awoke this morning feeling quite well, comparatively. Made coffee & fritters and eat a good breakfast. Lieut. Payne[85] and a private, of Capt Lyon's command rode by, in company with one of Clough's party, who last night guided them out from Lassens. They went to the Oregon camp to get breakfast. The commissary's clerk & soldier, who were sent back to Deer Creek, returned. At 11 A.M. I gave them breakfast, and after they had rested themselves & mules, proceeded to join the command, moved ahead some 20 miles. Chills & fevers again attacked me.

Near Sun Set, Nicholas, Jas. Marshall, and Andy, rode off, to visit the indian village above. As they purchase whisky and drink along the route, it is probable that [they] will visit the indians drunk. They returned, at night, intoxicated, and tell how that they reached the village & found the males all absent, and caught a Squaw, who offered them roots, willow baskets, &c. if they would not molest her, but that they, successively, *did molest her!* This, if true, is villainous conduct. And it is such enormities which often bring about collissions between the whites & indians. Had chills, took quinine, a cold night.

[AUG.] 12 — Feel much better. Took a pill of quinin & rhubarb. Breakfast on broiled venison and tea. Evil consequences apprehended from the very reprehensable conduct of our trio who visited the indian village. A couple of men rode up, and we recognised each other as acquaintances in the settlements. They are part of a small company camp'd on the opposite side of the river, a few miles higher up. They had travelled all round the N. side of the Snow Butte, up to Mount Tschastes, then up Pitt-river, and down here, on the emigrant road, prospecting, but without discovering any gold. (I always thought that the two large peaks & their ranges were out of the gold district.) [86]

Attempted to smoke my pipe, but it so enfeebled me that I had to lay down. Another prospector, on a mule, came in, from Myer's Camp. He said that he was one of the early emigrants of last year; that he had accumulated much, and spent it all nearly, and managed to live only. They killed another steer, at Lassen's camp. The prospector who has just come in, is a very intelligent man. He said, that a few miles below, he met some fine-looking indians, who invited him to their village, where he went, and found a cleanly, lively, intelligent, and handsome set of indians. They possessed plenty of fine dried salmon, and gave him a couple. He offered them a couple of gay-colored silk handkerchiefs for a supply, when they offered him more than he could transport. He took only as many as were necessary. He says that he and his party, found a lake once, at the head of Cow Creek, which they think is the celebrated Gold Lake, for which we are all prospecting & bothering.

About 2 P.M. Messersmith, Battis, Young, Brittle, and several others of Lassen's expedition, rode in, as hungry as wolves, and their horses ditto, jaded and poor. They had travelled to Cow Creek, found a lake at its head, & several others; been around the Snow Butte, in a few miles of Pitt river, and struck on an indian village, and its inhabitants had vamosed, and found plenty of pro-vissions, which they much needed, — roots, root-bread, large quantities of very small fish, &[c]: They brought away some peculiar head dresses, quivers, beads, baskets, &c. &c. They were on a well-beaten trail, and these were doubtless Pitt river indians, as the trail lead [led] from the narrow valley in which the village stood, over a divide to Pitt river. A small lake in this valley

They said that Lassen, with 6 men would continue travelling to the East-ward for several days. And the rest of the party were coming on — close by. Drs. Drinker & Bowman had both been quite sick, with chills & fevers.

Late in the afternoon Drs. D. & B. [Drinker and Bowman] & several others came up. D. quite sick, and I made tea for us.

At night the Frenchmen got whisky, and had a regular spree. There were carousing, firing pistols, &c. &c. all the fore part of the night. — No one could sleep.

[AUG.] 13. Drinker and I awoke this morning with cold. Had a hurried break-fast, as the parties are catching their horses & mules to start off. One party goes into the settlements, for supplies; another is to visit the Tschastes coun-try, to find a lake Lassen did not see; and a third, is to prospect below, on the branch of Feather we visited. Lent my pocket compass to the Lake party. Poile goes in for supplies. After a considerable fuss, at catching horses and mules, packing & saddling, by 10 A.M they all moved off, on their different routes. My partner is quite sick to-day, while I feel quite well. I made up a batch of bread, and baked it. Peck brought his tent, and pitched it alongside of us.

Dr. had fever all day nearly, and took quinine.

Late in the afternoon a party of Clough's men rode by, and said that they had discovered good digging, on the branch of Feather river we visited. I doubt it.

Passed a good night; sound repose for once.

[AUG.] 14. Cloudy morning. My comrade is better. Breakfast broiled beef, bread, & tea.

Dexter, Smith, and others, rode down-stream, to prospect. Hazy and pleas-ant, till Merd. when the sky became overcast with clouds, and a strong Easterly wind in puffs. Some drops of rain. I feel well, except weakness & the hermarhoyds. The sick man, who a week since, I thought about to vamos from this life, is now walking by the aid of a staff.

My associates are very noisy at night — They and severe pains and weekness in loins and back, deprived me of repose, till near morning. Latter part of night cold.

AUGUST 15 — Arose early, and went to a camp-fire and heated my back there some time, which afforded me much relief. Dʳ D. is better to-day. We eat a hearty breakfast.

My comrade took resin from a pine, and stewed it with tallow, spread the composition on a piece of oiled linen, and applied it hot to my back. I winced, but it proved to be an excellent application.

About 10 A.M. 3 strangers rode in; one was mounted on the horse of Lassen's which ran off from here, some [16] days since. — He knew the brand, had caught him, travelled some distance with him, and on his way in, had now brought him to camp. My friend is improving. A very severe attack of hermarhoyds, after dinner, drove me to bed, where an hour's repose relieved me. Peck is quite ill. 2 mounted strangers camped above us. I took a dose of rheubarb. Battis whipped his squaw in the night. I was taken ill, with pains in the bowells, hermarhoydal pains, &c. till the rheubarb relieved me. So with the infirmities and fighting of Frenchman and squaw, I slept little.

[AUG.] 16 — The Dʳ and myself feel better to-day. Peck a little better. About 4 P.M. Dʳ Bowman, Hough jr, and co. came in, and soon after Hall & Henry Lining,[87] — (latter of the German party) from Lassen's party. No success. Hall & Lining returned for supplies, for Lassen &c. who is about 50 miles off, N.E. of this. Lassen lost a horse, by the indians. The two Oregonian Frenchmen are drunk whenever they can be. These half-breeds are a degraded set. Plenty of whisky, a horse, and a squaw, — no matter how ugly; any kind of food, — half cooked, or raw, and sleeping seems to be all they want in life. I did not sleep till near morning, and that nap was curtailed, at day-break, by a commingled melody of wolf-howl, and panther cry, in a willow jungle, not far off —

[AUG.] 17. Partner & self feel well, this morning, and breakfasted heartily, on stewed *jerky* (jerked, or dried beef, in strings) toast, & coffee. We are concerned about the safety of our friends in the Mountains, to the N.E. — The indians there are numerous and hostile, and the whites number only 4, — Lassen, Jones,[88] Isadore, (a Russian)[89] and an indian.

About 4½ P.M. Bowman came into camp a-foot, and severely bruised. — He had rode Hall's mare, (a wild mischievous brute) in search of his poney. The mare threw him, and trod on his breast, with both her fore-feet, but fortunately she was unshod, and the plain under him soft and yielding. I regret this exceedingly, he is a clever fellow, and a very intelligent man. Dr Drinker attends him. I am very weak from hermarhoyds, — pain in bowels, and little appetite. I almost despair of enjoying sound health again. At dusk the horses & mules were missing, creating much excitement; but were brought in after dark, having strayed over into another valley unnoticed. My infirmaties kept me awake till dawn.

[AUG.] 18 — At dawn I had to get up, and returning to bed slept sound, for a couple of hours. I attribute the most of my complaints to the effects of the blue mass I so imprudently took. Dr B. is quite sore and stiff, has to put one arm in a sling.

11 A.M. Hall, Campbell, Hough jr. and Edgar, (of the Germans) with packs of provissions for Lassen's party, rode away to join them.

Brittle and a comrade, came in from Myer's Diggings;[90] — Report, that on a bar there, the miners were taking out from 100 to 1500 dolls. worth, per day. — Shares selling for 10,000 dolls. each.

About half past 2 P M — our German friends came up, from the same locale. — (Danish Captain, 4 Germans, and negro.) They had all been ill with the fever. The old Capt and the negro too weak to stand. Dismounted & threw themselves on the ground, exhausted. Peck is better. The very sick man, at Lassen's camp, went to the Oregon camp, where under the kind attention of the women, he is rapidly recovering. Drinker and myself are slowly recovering. Brittle gives a very rich account of the mining, on Feather river — (such as are sent to the States for publication, for what purpose made, no one knows but the authors.) He says, that the ground on which Lassen & party, including himself, could scarcely find a trace of gold, was now yielding from 50 dolls. worth to 60 lbs weight of gold per diem![91] 3 men had, in 3 days, made an average of $2,000 each, per diem; sold their claims for several thousand dollars each, and gone home, — rich!

Thus the gold-stories run. — One, whose veracity you can rely on, tells you that a few only, are doing remarkably well, numbers are making about 1 oz: per day, and hundreds are not earning their salt. (the most likely) Whilst another, whose veracity you have no right to question, informs you that hundreds are very rapidly accumulating fortunes, — none making less than $100 per day, &c.

About 6 P.M. a man named Skinner, (one of early & unfortunate emigrants this year) who was with a party exploring for the "*Gold Lake*", came in; His mule exhausted, and him self much trepidated. — Informs me that they were riding towards a lake & several buttes, supposed on the Eastern slope of the Sierra Nevada, when menaced by a body of several hundred indians (must be Pautahs)   The indians drew up in line, and the small party rode towards them as if to charge, and finding the indians stood their ground, they retrograded. He says that as they cannot proceed for the indians, they concluded to return, & will arrive to-morrow. Our 4 friends, who started this morning, go in that direction. — They are well armed & as cunning as the indians, so there's no fear; and if they unite with Lassen, will be quite strong. Hope Lassen & co. are not used up. "*Prospecting*" over these hills sounds like a very easy thing to perform; But the best way of ascertaining its merits, — the wear and tear of men and beasts, perils, &c, is to make such a tour.

Small parties cannot operate with safety, in the vicinity of Pitt river, or over on the Eastern slope of these mountains. — The country is most favorable for the demonstrations of the villainous indians, and their [they] shoot their keen arrows, with strength and precission.

Skinner states, that their small party, when approaching the buttes, to investigate a lake at their bases, reached a morass, with tule (rushes) where the indians had some horses: Tubbs, — one of the party, thought he recognised Lassen's brown horse among them. The party camped here; and when they awoke, next morning, discovered 20 indians, with one horse, on the hillside, near them. That when they proceeded, they saw numerous trails, around their camp, made by large numbers of indians reconnoitring them during the night. The party proposed to charge up hill, on the 20 savages, and when almost in shooting distance, about 200 other savages arose from the ground, when the little party of whites fell back, and thought that in their way, they would attempt the capture of some of the horses in the plain: but there some 200 indians arose from the grass; the party then attempted to retreat on a known trail, but the savages anticipated that manouvre, and they turned to seek another egress, but here again the indians intercepted them. They now pushed for the lower end of the bottom, — the way they entered it, and the indians ran off, to head them there, but they had the start of the yellow-bellys, and escaped. Also, that when they were approaching this bottom, one of the party rode ahead, and ascended a small elevation, from which he saw several squaws, on the other side, not far off, digging roots, who perceiving him, ran off, into some hills, from which he saw smoke ascending, and supposes that the indians have a village there.

I passed a restless night.

AUG. 19. — At day-break turned out, with indisposition, followed by herma-rhoids — Turned in, and slept, a while, when awakened by the howl of a pack of rascally wolves, and yelping of foxes. Again slept, till my comrade awakened me to breakfast, of fried bread & coffee, Dr. B. Quite sore and stiff yet. Peck improving.

We are talking about getting up a party when Fox & co. return, to succor our friends and chastise the infernal indians. I amused myself running balls, while Drinker makes bread, at which he is very expert.

Near 10 A.M. 5 mounted men, 1 pedestrian, and a pack-mule, came up, from lower part of Feather river; enquired if this was Lassen's Camp? where he is? &c — and proceeded above —

Smith rode out about 1½ miles, in a S. course, up a ravine, for deer, and there found the hind quarter of a fawn, fresh and good. No doubt it had been wounded by some hunter, and the wolves had caught it. The marks of their very recent feeding on it were distinct. They had consumed every portion of it but that piece, which he brought in. Not a bone was left entire. My partner contributed a small can of preserved potatoes, and some bits of pork, and we soon enjoyed a fine stew.

Near half past 4 P.M. Tubb's party (Skinners late associates) rode in. — They called Skinner a deserter and coward; and said that when they were surrounded by the indians, he, (S.) lead off the retreat, at some distance, and quicker than the rest, thus giving the savages confidence, and caused them to chase the party several miles.

They all think that S. is a staunch believer in the "first law of nature." —

> "So when the fight becomes a chase,
> He wins the fight who wins the race."

They *did'nt diskiver nare a Gold Lake.*

It appears that poor S. became so bewildered, when the indians were aris-ing like Cadmus' teeth, from the ground, that he could only see his way out of the scrape, and his imagination supplied the defects of his hazy vision.

The party tell the story thus: — That when indians were discovered on the hill, while they were considering what course to take, S. moved on ahead of them; they did charge on the indians, — a large body of them, and they squandered [scattered]; at the same time the indians below, were busy running off the horses, and getting their squaws out of danger. The indians rallying, they fell back, and proceeded to leave the bottom, when about 100 indians, headed by one mounted, attempted to intercept them, & then pur-sued them some miles. They think there must have been about 200 savages. Skinner *put,* and they saw him no more till they reached this camp.

Organizing a party to succor Lassen and comrades. — Gathering provissions, arms, & ammunition. (Some of the men are very indifferently armed) Dr Drinker lent his horse, I lent mine, with the equipment, a rifle, pistols, pouch, horn, and balls; reserving a fowling piece, and one small pistol, for use or defense here. Felt very well to-day.

A clear mild night. Laid comfortably awake, till past midnight, when I fell asleep. — Near day-break severe pains, and the screaming of a panther awoke me. I wrapped a blanket around me, and sat up to listen to the music. — The moon was just sinking below the horizon. The Oregon camp is about 400 yards above, where, last evening they killed a beef. — Attracted by the smell of the meat, I suppose, the rascal came down, on the opposite side of the river, through tule swamps, to a point in rear of the Oregon camp, and about 200 yds from it. — The dogs there, and one here, barked furiously I judge from his voice, that he must have been a large fellow. He cried awhile, then paused about 10 minutes, and then gave a long hearty peal, sounding much like a combination of laughter and schreching, tapering off with a hoarse noise that sounded like the dying cadence of a mule's notes. He now slowly retired up the valley, occasionally crying, till, in the distance, it resembled the howl of small wolves. My associates were all soundly snoring, so having lost the music I laid down & joined them.

[AUG.] 20 — Feeling quite hearty, we breakfasted on venison stew, cold bread, and coffee.

After breakfast there was much discussion, and some perversity, on the ground, among the various parties camped here.

Dissentions in Camp. —

Last night, the party whose camp fire is near our pallet, were sitting around their fire smoking their pipes, and discussing the objects of the contemplated expedition, to succor Lassen, &c. — I laid, and listened to them. — A lank long-haired, loquacious Oregonian, — a very noisy bragging fellow, swore by G — d that Lassen was a d — d fool! — Knew nothing about the mountains, nor how to hunt gold; and that if the party contemplated joining L. after they reached him; he, for one, would not go! He wound up with long yarns of scrapes he had participated in, fighting the *Kiusi* [Cayuse] indians, in Oregon.[92] His vociferations, oaths, &c. impressed some green youths with the idea that he was *some pumpkins*, and was correct, and they acquiesced with him; the opposition to joining Lassen, now spread, among those who were too lazy, or afraid of arrows, and thus the contemplated force was reduced to a few staunch determined men. Tubbs, the leader, appeared to possess the requisite abilities. Preparations are going on, but the ungenerous perverseness of a few silly cowards, interferes much with the organization. The conduct of the opposition party is ungenerous, when it is well-known, that every man on this ground, came here either to go out at once with Lassen, or await his successful researches, and then realize the benefits of it.

The Oregonian's clamor was evidently the effects of fear. — for the burthen of his harangue was on the distance, and accuracy, of the indians shooting, their arrows, the great force, &c, and the great difficulties and sufferings one must endure if wounded, &c.

Passo tiempo: Camp entertainment

After supper groups are scattered around; some by the fires, and others laying about, on their blankets, in the dewy grass, or reclining against a tree.

One party listens to a comrade's travels, adventures, and indian scrapes, in Oregon; Another, to a Texian hero, (we have a Texian here, that Davy Crocket could not hold a candle to) his experience and exploits, with Greasers and Comanches, and a third are highly delighted with accounts of gambling, cheating, horse-stealing, Lynching, &c in the southern mines, &c. And, if there is whisky to be had, in a day's ride, there will assuredly be a fourth party, damning and screeching like mad, and singing the *chastest* songs.

Tubb's party tell a good anecdote of Andy, (the darkee). — That while they were retreating from the indians, Andy brought up the rear; and looking around, saw the mounted indians advancing rapidly upon him; when he leasurely drew a long brass-barreld pistol, from his belt; and quietly remarked to the person ahead, and near him, "I'm darned! old fellow! if you come much nearer, if I dont shoot you!" ——

The sick are rapidly recovering. My friend, Dr D. examined my knee, and discovered *proud flesh,* and applied blue-stone to it, and then ointment.

4 P.M. Fox & James Marshall came in, from the settlements, with stores, and brought my mail. — Sent up by Col. Wilson and Dr Cole. The first letters I have received from home, since I left Missouri. My mind greatly relieved by the news that they were all well. — dates up to April 3.[93] Dr Cole kindly sent me some figs, pipes, and tobacco. Poile returned at dusk Some men who accompanied Fox out, are camped above us, and carrousing till past mid night.

AUGUST 21 — After the noise of the drinking party permitted I went to sleep & slept soundly and late. I purchased 12 lb fresh beef, at the Oregon Camp, for 25 ¢ per lb. So we had a steak for breakfast. Considering the dampness of the ground here, and available fuel nearly consumed, and grass in adjacent plain, grazed off — We will move camp, — Lassen's company, ourselves, and most of the others who are camped here close-together — By going upon the trail which the prospectors take to descend Feather river, E. from this, $\frac{1}{4}$ mile off, is a slight ridge of pine forrest, for about $1\frac{3}{4}$ ms. when we keep a little to the left, and camp in the grassy river bottom   Smith has engaged an ox wagon of the Oregon folks. About 9 A.M. it came, and Lassen's camp was moved; then by Merd^n Hough's, the Germans, and ours followed. — Found fuel plenty, but trees afforded little shade. So we constructed a sort of one-sided booth, to keep off the sun, formed of an old rotten wagon cover, picked up from an old camp-ground. — Giving the D^r and myself a lodging place, of about 10 ft. square, between sapling pines. Between our position and the river, in front, about 40 yards, on its brink, is Lassen's camp, in a grove of pines, and willows. The trail runs close in front of our booth. All around is an open forrest of large pines. Nearly in rear of us — S.W. — 40 yds. is Hough & Dr Bowman's camp; and 50 yds. E. is the Germans. They killed an ox at Lassen's camp. Below are several camps of small parties — strangers   There is a good grazing bottom here. Attacked with one of those annoying nervous affections — watchfullness. Sat up all night, reading, & smoking. Some straggling travellers passed at night.

AUG. 22. About 2 A.M. I revived my fire, and drank a pot of tea. Soon after, the relief party commenced stirring, making fires, &c. 3 A.M. they had break-fasted, & in an hour after, the party, composed of 23 men, rode on. After they left I slept, till $9\frac{1}{2}$ A.M. when Drinker, having got up an hour since, made bread & coffee, and fricsied some beef liver called me to breakfast — which we both done justice to. Our four little camps contain 10 whites — and Lassen's indians. Little wind & warm. Slept tolerably well.

[AUG.] 23 — Indisposition again awakened me early. About 9 A.M. The Doctor and myself, feeling so well, took our guns, and walked down the banks of the streams, about $\frac{1}{2}$ mile, where we found an opened cachè. It had contained a wagon body, filled with every thing of consequence the pro-prietors could not transport in to the settlements. It was now a muddy hole, half filled with decayed & rusty rubbish. A very heavy and large force-pump, pieces of hose, wagon wheels, broken trunks, bottles, camp-utensils, books, newspapers, boots, shoes, clothing, &c. Not only in the pit, but scattered around for 200 yards. Doubtless some of the first prospecting characters this spring, discovered and opened it; as they opened also, all graves they found, to search for effects cached — by the emigrants of 1849. We found part of a large tent, and a wagon cover, ragged and rotten — but they would answer to screen off the sun from our temporary habitation, and we bundled them up & shouldered them. Smith gave me some ox ribs when we returned to camp, we had a roast dinner, and fixed up our *house*. We were fatigued, and retired early, but our sleep was disturbed by the Frenchman licking his Squaw, — cause liquor and jealousy.

AUG. 24 — We slept late. This morning early, 2 white men, and 12 indians, of Myer's company, passed by, on their way to the settlements. Soon after, a small party of Clough's men came in; they are from the hostile indian district, and were driven off by the savages.

A trading-tent has been put up — close by,[94] and I went over & bought

           1 lb. of rice   for $1..25
           1 ” dried apples   ” ”1..00

Dearahea weakened me, and I slept all the fore part of the day.

Poile and Peck called, and related adventures at the mines. — Reddings diggings, &c. (Northern mines) — They had to work with their rifles by them, & dare not sleep out of log defenses; — and if a man was compelled to sleep out, he had to hide him self among the rocks. The indians once swept off all the cattle, horses, &c. Would steal blankets, knives, provisions, &c. and shot miners while at work, and several asleep, at night. An acquaintance of theirs, was sleeping one night, in a hammock, between trees, with a blanket over him, the indians fired at him, when an arrow passed through the two sides of his hammock, piercing the blanket over his breast. The indians thus annoyed, harrassed, & murdered the miners, with impunity, because they were so selfishly bent on the accumulation of gold, that they could not spare the time, to go in a sufficient body, and chastise the Savages.[95]

A mild evening, and I slept well till midnight, when indisposition awaked me. Near morning it was cold.

AUG. 25 — We breakfasted as soon as it was light enough to see clearly. Poile favored me with another visit. I washed some clothing.

[AUG.] 26 — Cold and pains awakened me very early. This unprofitable leasure is quite annoying. — We are now well enough to travel, but dare not leave the ground for a few days, for fear that Lassen might come in, get supplies, and be off again, before we returned. And we do not know where he is now, so we must wait till the exhaustion of their provissions drive the party in. All the parties camped and close by, are awaiting the return of Lassen, to go out on the big and final hunt, this season, for the igneous faatius Lake. The time is wiled away, by reading, conversing, smoking, shooting, playing cards, — uchre and monte, & drinking.

At 3 P.M. 7 horsemen, from the mines below,[96] passed, going in.

Poile dined with us, and remained till night, and we sat up quite late, conversing on the past & speculating on the future.

AUG. 27 — The cold awakened me at dawn. I stirred around early, procured wood and water, prepared the breakfast, and wakened my partner to breakfast, near Sun rise.

4 pedestrians, with packs & guns, and a Newfoundland dog, came by, going below, on the river. They enquired for a stray horse. Soon after 5 others passed, with 3 pack mules, laden with bedding, camp utensils, & tools. — They camped a little below us; had been camped on the old ground, 2 miles above This last set of folks, after arranging their camp, (spreading blankets, and making a fire) commenced firing at a mark on a pine, with rifles, and like to have marked my friend, Mr. Hough. He walked over & asked if they did not know better than firing over a camp ground, on a level range?

At Sun Set, Dr Bowman and Mr Messersmith, rode in, supporting on a mule, Frank Pickering, wounded by the indians. — He belonged to Tubb's party. An arrow had passed through the fleshy part of his left arm, above the elbow, another had pierced his left side, between the 4th and 5th ribs, and a third had grazed his breasts. They rode 40 miles to-day. He was shot at half a day's ride beyond where the indians had chased off the party previously. — On the 24th they camped in a ravine — bottom, with grass, & a brook leading to a marshy lake. They picketed their horses close up, and put out 3 sentinals. In the 3rd watch, — a little after 2 O'clock, — some of the animals evinced alarm, — looking in the direction of a point of rock and brush, 50 yds. below: and a rustling noise was heard there. Poor Frank! being the sentry nearest the point, most imprudently walked down to within 10 paces of the suspicious ambuscade, when a volley of arrows was fired at him; he made an exclamation, fired his rifle, and the camp were up, with ready arms, and met him as he fell. They carried him up to camp. The arrows had penetrated through several folds of the Serapa he wore, when shot. — They found, in it, two obsidian points. Frank had drawn the arrows out of his arm and side, and dashed them away, when shot. The party next morning examined the ground, and picked up 15 arrows, — indicating the presence of at least 15 indians. They also found, where the indians had been, a knife, and a green hide halter; with which to cut the lariets, and lead off such horses or mules as they could steal. On the preceding day, they surprised an indian, and endeavored to persuade him to come up to them, but could get no closer than about 40 yards. He made signs to them, that the indians were numerous, and evil disposed, and that they must go away. The point where Frank was shot, is about 90 miles N.E. of this place.[97] This distance, over very rugged ground, they rode in 3 days. Frank is exhausted, and in great pain. — His comrades, who brought him in, are much chafed. Tubbs' party came back with them, half a day's ride, to escort them beyond the bad indian country. They [Tubbs's party] then continued their route, hoping in a few days to join Old Pete (Lassen) and party, or find their trail. They say, that the night before the attack, the indians set up a considerable wolf-howl, to stampede their animals; but only scared them a little, as they were, like themselves, familiar with wolf-music. A cool night and large camp-fire, with extraordinary news to discuss, kept us up late. I was awakened in the night by a pack of blackguard wolves.

AUG. 28 — Jack Frost swears I shall again rise early, — has been nibbling my toes. With Drs Bowman & Drinker, visited poor Frank, found him very pale, and thin, in great pain, and spitting blood. The Drs examined & dressed his wounds.

A very rough-looking christian, like any of us, came up, and enquired about Frank, we entered into conversation, and I found him to be a very intelligent man, and courteous manners. He has travelled much in the S.W. portions of the States, &c. He has a sick-comrade under a bush shelter, a short distance below.

Near Sun Set, a miner, from below, rode by. A call from Frank's tent, at dusk, for Dr Bowman, who, with several others went over, and found the poor fellow dead. A very short time previous he sat up, with his head reclined on his breast; and on being asked how he felt? replied "very bad!" He then laid down, straightened himself, drew his blanket up to his chin, and expired. A squaw entering, directly after, supposed him dead, and gave the alarm.

I bought 5½ lbs. salt pork, at $1 . . 50 per lb.

I retired early, and slept well.

AUG. 29 After breakfast, Frank's mess mates laid him out, and sewed him up in a blue blanket. Had a grave dug near by, under a large pine, and we gathered up the sojourners to bury of [our] friend. —

A considerable party of prospectors had just rode in, and the Oregon folks, — men, women, and children, assembled. At 10 A.M. the body was borne on poles, to the grave, 50 yds from his tent. In compliance with the requests of my associates I read to them, at the head of the grave, the following memorandum. —

"Our deceased comrade, is Francis Pickering, we think from the vicinity of Boston, Mass. He was about 35 years of age. — He was shot by indian arrows, over 90 miles, in an E. course from here. — He was of a respectable family, a worthy fellow, and highly esteemed by his comrades and acquaintances. — In a life so rude, and under such circumstances, it is often the case that the dead are committed to old mother earth, in a very hasty and imperfect manner: But on this occasion, the acquaintances of the deceased are gratified in being thus enabled to make a sort of funeral show, over their unfortunate comrade: — And we thank you all for your kind attention." We piled rocks on the grave, to keep out wolves, and I pencilled a board, and put at the head. —

FRANCIS PICKERING,
Of vicinity of Boston,
Mass:
Aged 35 Years.
Shot by indians, 90
miles E. of this,
died 28   Aug: 25. 1850.
Respected & esteemed
by
all who knew him.

Plenty of trout in the stream here.

G. D. Taylor, of the mounted party who came up at the time of the burial, is intending to go down Feather and Yuva rivers, and so on, down to the cities, but prospecting along the route.

German camp are fiddling, so we sit up late, to hear the musice [music]. After which, I slept well.

AUG: 30 — This morning they killed an ox, at Lassen's camp. At 9 A.M. Fox, Antoine, and 14 others, came in; leaving Tubbs, Dexter, Leining, and 4 others, pushing for a lake they had descried from an eminence. And they had seen nothing of Old Pete's party, nor their trail. They went on the emigrant route, going out, till within 10 miles of Pitt river.[98] The night after Frank was shot, they heard a whistle, answered by another, and followed by an imitation wolf-howl. The indians appeared to be very numerous around them.

The morning they came upon two, in a hollow, shooting squirrels with arrows: & took them prisoners. — A youth, and an old man. — They had several squirrels. Made them deliver their arms. Now arose a consultation, and dispute, whether or no they should kill these yellow devils, to avenge Frank. — It resulted finally, in giving the indians a hearty meal, their arms, and liberty. They found large quantities of grass-seed, gathered for food. On their return they met a party of 3 men riding out, in direction of the *infected district*. Afternoon hazy.

At night there was considerable disputation in camp, about the propriety of liberating the indian prisoners. — Some swore by — that they'd "blow'd h — out of 'em", and others said "d — n em, they might have been innocent." However, the majority were in favor of killing the indians.

Hall's mare, that hurt Bowman, and ran off [14] days since, came into camp, with the saddle still on her. She was as wild as a mustang, but caught & secured.

Severe pains in back, &c. interfered with repose some, and noise of carousing, by the return party, more.

AUG: 31 — The Oregon folks have ran ahead of time; they swear that to-day is the 1st September.

Shultz and some of his comrades, of the trading-camp, are going in to-day, so I wrote a letter for home.

The Oregonians also wish to go in, and are selling off their rum cheap, at only $3. per gall: — *its strength has not increased since they brought it here.* So those who have funds to spare, are going over, on foot and mounted, carrying kegs, jugs, canteens, &c. to avail themselves of so rare a chance.

Rheumatic pains, diarohea, & cold, spoiled to-night's repose for me.

SEP: 1. — 10 A.M. Shultz & co. Battis, and several indians, started for the settlements. Shultz kindly taking in a letter to my family. — And Dr Drinker, Poile, Fox, Andy, an Oregonian, and one of Fox' indians, and self, Rode down the valley to visit and explore a white quartz vein I discovered a day's ride E. of the ford. We proceeded on the trail, ascended the crest of a very high ridge, and descended to a small valley, about 10 miles, and nooned.

(We camped here on our first trip out) An hour's rest, and at 3 P.M. moved on 4 miles, reaching a valley of a creek tributary of the N. Fork of Feather river.

The Stream ran to the left[99] of the trail, some distance; and, as it was late, we sought water on our right, and wished also to prospect a gulch in this direction. It was dusk ere we found water, which was in a deep hole, in bottom of a ravine, leading from the gulch we intended examining. Watered our animals, filled kettles, &c. and camped about ¼ mile lower, in a grassy bottom. Here we found an accidental triangular breastwork, formed by 3 dead trees, and some stumps. Within this enclosure, we spread our blankets and adjusted our saddle-pillows. Tied our animals, close by, to limbs of the fallen trees, &c. Several large fires burning in the edge of the timber, on the hill-side, above the water-hole. We slept well.

SEP. 2 — Reposed till Sun-rise, and then eat a hearty breakfast. Fox contributing some sour krout, of which he had a small keg. We permitted our animals to graze till the sun was several hours high, when we saddled up, and moved on. — We travelled up a hollow, close on the right side of a small brook, turned to the right, where the gulch & stream made a bend, over stony spurs, ascending, till we were half way up a considerable range of hills. Stream, and several dry beds of torrents, lay deep-seated, on our left. We examined one of the dry gulches, but found no gold. We mounted, & now retraced our steps down, to the camping place, and struck from there, N. Westerly, over a pretty level valley, about 2 miles, over a stony plain, gradually ascending; and then across some awful stony and rugged ridges & spurs, — passing over some knolls & ridges exceedingly stony and brushy. Now descending the divide, down very steep, stony, and brushy, declivities; with deep dust, and loose rock; having to dismount & lead our animals. A well worn trail, however, made by prospectors & indians. Between ridges, we passed, obliquely, two dry stony gulches. We now crossed two dry and very stony beds of winter streams, and in about 4 ms. from our log-enclosed camp, we reached a small valley, watered by several branches of clear good water; thick willows along the banks, and oaks in the bottom. — All tributaries of the N. Fork of Feather r. Camp'd close to a bend of the stream, on a gentle rise of ground, under some large pines, and dined. Picketed our animals below, a short distance to graze. After resting, I accompanied 3 of my comrades, on foot, to prospect. We crossed the stream where a large island, several bars, and much drift were — crowding through the densest kind of scrub, stumbling over drift timber and branches, and occasionally getting in mud and water, till quite tired, and well scratched, we emerged on the other side, to our great relief. Examined several hollows, and at last I noticed a vein of white quartz, running over a spur, and cropping out the hill sides, for some distance. It was 8 or 10 feet wide, and superficially broken in blocks by the frost. Found minute crystals of quartz, and several specks of gold. In a lump of the rock, the size of a small biscuit, on one side I found needle crystals, and on the other, 2 pear-shaped nodules of gold, as large as robin shot. —

It being near Sun Set, we returned to camp: but went farther, and obtained a more convenient crossing, following a deer-trail to the bank, and through the creek bottom. We supped, and slept well, after the disturbance for several hours after dark ceased. Night cold. Some heavy animal, no doubt a bear, was in the brushy bottom of the branch, within 30 yards of us. Forcing his way through dry brush, breaking sticks & limbs, made considerable noise, but the thicket was too close to see him. Some sat up, in hopes he would emerge, but I lay down, and slept sound.

SEP. 3 — Arose early, breakfasted, and mounted. — On our route back to Depot Camp. — But to examine a range of hills, we first Rode N. up valley, crossed the branch about 3½ ms. above camp, then turned N.E. — in 3 miles more, commenced the ascent of a gradual but high slope, — being the Northern divide range. Reaching the summit of a long and high spur, thickly timbered with the largest growth of pines, and finding no indications of oro, we turned and retrograded on another spur. — These spurs are here spread out like the fingers of an extended hand. We now travelled a mien E.N.E. course, crossed numerous dry pebbly beds of brooks, in about 5 miles; and in ½ mile more, crossed 5 small mountain rills, divided by depressed stony ridges, each stream running through a narrow and marshy bottom, with fine grass, and thick willows. All the rest of the country timbered with pines of every variety. Lastly, down a narrow vale with marsh and good grass, and a fine brook through it, — water cold as ice. Here we noon'd. Bottom averages probably 50 yards broad.

My friend Poile, is quite sick, — chills & vomiting. Mike (Oregonian) and Andy, are also quite under the weather with chills and fevers. Here grows all sorts of pines, small oaks, willows, cedars, poplars, cotton-wood, sycamore, &c. Air fragrant with mint. Service-berries, currents, — black, red, & yellow; and several varieties of black & red berries we did not know. Rose bushes, and a beautiful scarlet flower. Innumerable black birds, woodpeckers, small hawks, doves, very large grey owls, &c — We rested here about 2 hours, and while pencilling my notes, fell asleep, till awakened to catch up my horse. — A pot of hot tea was beneficial to the sick men, and we mounted & proceeded. Course now westerly, over a succession of slight rolls, and intervening depressions, for about 6 miles, when, close to the brink of a precipitous descent to the valley of Feather river, not far from our old camp, noticed 3 conical dark ant hills, about 3 ft. diam: at base, & 4 feet high, each. A few hundred yds. beyond was the brow to descend. As we approached it, the scattered blocks of hard dark plutonic rock, gave us an ernest of the sort of declivity we must descend. The side of the boundary hills, to this valley, here, about 2 miles long, are inclined planes at an angle of 45°, covered with angular blocks of dark brown volcanic stone, deep sand, stumps, brush, logs, and trees. Of course we dismounted at the brow, and led our animals down, keeping one side, as well as the ground would permit, so that if a horse fell, he would not roll upon the man leading him. The trail down was necessarily circuitous, winding around large pines, rocks, and trunks of trees, probably 400 yds. We struck the plain safely, mounted, rode obliquely $\frac{1}{2}$ mile, to edge of stream, where it was broad & smooth, but shallow; — In half a mile more we reached the treble'd stream ford, and in crossing the first, or main stream, — broad & rapid, and full of sunk rocks, my horse put his left fore-leg in a hole, and fell, with his breast on a flat shelf, which gave me a considerable jar. The rapids are also annoying to the sight; you seem to be drifting against the current. Wet legs, however, was all the damage. Rode on, up valley, and over a low stony timber clad ridge, and about 5 P.M. reached the old camp; after an afternoon's ride of 10 miles.

About $\frac{3}{4}$ mile above the abrupt declivity, are a series of beautiful cataracts in the Feather river. At this part it is probably 200 yds. wide, and the falls are a series of many slightly inclined steps, the breadth of the river, breadth of the steps average probably 50 feet; and the fall of each may be the same. The roar of these cascades can be heard some miles in favorable weather — The fork of the stream our Camp is on, falls into this branch about $\frac{1}{4}$ mile above the falls.

We were tired and chafed, rode into the Camp of Lassen's party, where Messer Smith kindly invited us to supper; of course we respectfully acquiesced. We found the number of persons here, much reduced. — Many had gone in to the settlements, tired awaiting the return of Lassen and comrades, or giving them up, as gone cases, there being no news of him or his followers.

Rheumatism in back, face, & breast, all night.

SEP. 4 — An ox killed at Lassen's camp. A small party of Clough's men, rode in, from a prospecting tour, down the river; they rested awhile, and proceeded on, for the settlements. Rheumatic pains annoying me all day. Late in the night, a pack of wolves, accompanied by a panther, saluted us with a *hunter's chorus*. — From the sound of their melodious voices, I judged that they were on the opposite side of the narrow stream, in a willow jungle, the stream separating Lassins camp from them; and about 150 yards from us. The ox meat attracted them.

[SEPT.] 5 — A hearty breakfast of beef-ribs, bread, & coffee, I have a bad headache. At 12½ P.M. Tubb's & his party rode in, men and animals fagged out. Had been harrassed & threaten'd by the indians, night and day, to within 3 day's march of this. One night, about 10 O'clock, the savages approached their camp, with torches. They followed the party by day, and surrounded them at night, — often compelling them to sleep with their riatas (halters) in hand. Dexter returned my horse, — poor, chafed back, a swelled ancle, and tender-footed. They had seen no signs of Old Pete's party. At night,

> "The bright canteen,
>   In centre, front, and rear, was seen, —
> Driving fatigue away!"

I sat up late, by my camp-fire, with friend Poile, discussing Geology of the Gold districts, the Salt Lake establishment of the Mormons, &c. &c.

SEP. 6 — I was told this morning that a panther came to the bank of the river opposite a tent where hung some meat, river between about 60 ft. wide; and awakend the men there with his interesting symphony.

Who should I have the pleasure of seeing, but my kind old friend Seymour — who was my neighbor so long last fall on the hill now called "Bruff's Camp." He and his son, with 5 comrades, rode by, from below, on Feather river.[100] Our meeting was mutually gratifying. They went up stream 2 miles & campd

This party started from Yubaville, mined and prospected up the Uva, cross'd the divide, and followed Feather river up, — mining a little, and prospecting, as they came along. Late in the day, Avelyn, — Capt. Lyon's guide, rode in, and told me that the detachment were camped a little ways above the emigrant ford of the river, on the other side, — just returned from their expedition in search of Warner's bones; and were all sick. At Sun Set

I mounted my horse to ride over, when I was accompanied by several comrades, who were also going that way, above, to a trading-tent. On reaching the camp I found Capt. L. [Lyon], Lieut. Payne; and the command all down with chills and fevers, and typhoid. I regretted finding the Captain so sick. He looked badly, and was very feeble. The sickness rendered it necessary to transport some in wagons, hence they had to return by the road.[101] The Capt. informed me that he found only quadruped bones where poor Warner fell; these were the remains of the mule, probably. The spot where he fell, was marked by a pit, which on opening contained alternate layers of burnt pebbles, ashes, and charred wood.[102] — While he was camped in the valley at foot of the Pass, a band of about 50 indians came down from the opposite range of high hills, and formed a line, flanked by 2 horsemen. One of them fired a rifle several times, with some precission, and in good time. The Capt. sent 20 men out towards them, in column of 4, and when near musket range, they deployed into line, which manouvre caused the indians to break, and vamose up the defiles to the hills.

How can a wild indian, unacquainted with fire arms, correctly charge and fire a rifle? Who instructs them? May not some rascally white man be among them? The miners and emigrants assert that white men, for the sake of profit, are with all the troublesome indians, who murder and rob at the northern & southern mines; who murdered people and stole cattle and horses on the Humboldt, and here, on Pitt river. They think that such rascally whites, in this country, are chiefly Mexicans;[103] and on the Humboldt, are Mormons. I spent a couple hours with Capt. L. & returned

My partner — Drinker, is sick with chills, again. Wet my feet fording the river. At the ford, on this side, I saw the skeleton of an ox, and recollected the circumstances of his death. — When my company was fording the stream, this ox fell, in the lead of an ox team of a train that followed us; and was abandoned: A young man of my company coming up, curtailed its sufferings with a pistol-ball. I noticed the perforation in the white frontal.

On returning, I supped with Messersmith, Burton, &c. at Lassen's Camp.

A sneaking wolf to-night, came into camp, and approached a neighboring tent so close, that a man laying there, d — d him, and ordered him "begone!" like he would say to a troublesome dog; and Mr Wolf, (we have a Mr Fox) slowly retired, yelping and howling as he went

SEP. 7 — Pain in abdomen interfered with my rest last night, so I slept late this morning. My partner is better.

Capt. Lyon's detachment moved at 4 A.M. for the Settlements. At 8 A.M.

Clough's former comrades, left also for the settlements. Capt. Lyons told me that all the cāches on the route had been opened, except the one containing Genl. Wilson's Library, and that he found a mass of decay.[104] The Capt. spoke of this extensive grass valley of Feather river, as a good spot for an Indian Agency and Military Post. — An excellent idea. Here is excellent grass in abundance, and for winter use it can be cut and stored. Plenty of the purest cold water; timber for building-purposes, fuel, &c. abundant. Bear, deer, hares, &c. and water fowl. A post here would hold in check the Pitt river indians, and teach the good indians of this, and neighboring valleys, correct notions about matters & things.

There is only about 30 persons here now —

Ground squirrels, mice, gophers, and bugs crawl over us all night, much annoyance In the afternoon the traders, from above where the military were camped, came in, and camped below us, on edge of stream. They had a wagon load of effects, and pitched a tent.

Near Sun Set, Ford, McBride, and others,[100] with pack mules passed, on their way to Feather river mines, to bring up Moon, his indians, &c.

Drinker again sick. A fox barked near our *house*, at night.

SEP. 8 — 4 men from the camps here, rode down the river, in search of a mare, thought to have been stolen a few days ago, by a fellow who stopped here awhile, on his way down. The Doctor sick all day.

[SEPT.] 9 — Cloudy, indications of rain. We are tired of this inactive life, and wish to examine the white quartz vein below. So, at about 10 A.M. Poile, Fox, a comrade of his, and myself, mounted and rode on, with our blankets, &c. It soon commenced drizzling, and increased to steady rain. — We were thoroughly wet when near the ford, and became quite chilled, — Stiff with cold. The hills enshrouded in clouds & rain. So we returned. 2 P.M. Clough and some comrades, returned, from a short tour in the hills. Late in the afternoon, the clouds passed away, and exhibited the mountains to the N.E. of us, white with snow. Occasional drizzles during the night, wetting our legs. Diarohea, from the wet & cold. The Trader's camp, mountaineer style, gave Clough and his comrades, a return frolic.

SEP. 10 — Cloudy; wet mist. Merdn it cleared off —

My partner sick a-bed all day.

Great dissatisfaction in Camp, about lost time, advanced season, &c.

Dexter, Leining, Tubbs, & Burton, who went below, in search of a White mare of Hall's, came up, bringing the animal. — They had been as low as the first mines, and found her near the camp of the young man suspected of stealing her. He said that when he had gone some distance from here, he found her following him. Late in the afternoon two men of Moon's party passed, going in. Afternoon flying clouds. I procured a supply of fuel. Another spree, at the Trader's Camp. Poile and another man told me many anecdotes of the freshet at Sacramento City, in January last: I will relate some of these singular transactions, because they are authentic Boatmen were several times paid an ounce, ($16) to ferry a man across the street — Two boatmen were rowing up a street, when a man hailed them from a tent; — they pulled up, and discovered the proprietor setting on the counter, about a foot above water, with bedding, empty bottles, glasses, &c around him. He desired them to paddle in, and then to push the boat through the front room (a tent) into the back room, (another tent, against it) where they would find several kegs of liquor; and to bring one out to him. He desired them to take a *hearty pull*, and whenever they wanted a *horn*, to call on him. Having put the keg of liquor on the counter beside him, he said, "Now I'm all right again, and ready to serve any customer who comes along!" — The young man said, that he started to go in a boat, across the town; and besides other articles, she contained goods and a tent belonging to him, and 9 persons, a little beyond the town, the boat sank, the water rough and very cold. The people struck out for shore. He swam till tired, and returned, and stood on the boat, in water to his chin. He righted her with his feet, and she raised. — She drifted at the rate of 6 miles per hour. A negro who was in her drowned. Another boat picked them up. Every thing else was lost. — The waters rose so rapidly, that stores, tents, &c and stores of goods, were abandoned in haste. Barrels of meat, liquor, &c. were picked up, and stolen, and disposed of. Boatmen would row into the front door of a house, take what they desired, push their boat through the back door, and vamose.

This night cloudy. Showers near day. I slept well, but had to sleep in the form of G, to keep feet out of the wet.

SEP. 11 — Flying clouds and damp. After breakfast a meeting was held, of the persons assembled here, to send in to the settlements, for horse-shoes, nails, &c. to shoe our animals, preparatory to the long mountain ride we expect soon to start on. Fox and 2 others, agreed to go in for the articles. The Doctor is better to-day.

At Sun Set Hall, Isadore, Hough jr, and Montrose, rode in, and reported that Lassen, Jones, Campbell, &c. and indian John, were camped about 8 miles off, in the Feather river meadow, — emigrant route. Men half-starved and ragged, and the animals nearly used up. They had 2 indian dogs along, who had followed them, from the wild country. (Pitt river) They had been 40 miles N. of Tschastes, crossed Fall river, from thence travelled E. and S.E. about 200 miles Annoyed nearly the entire distance by the indians. The savages were near catching Capt Jones, (has been an East Indⁿ sea captain) in a cañon; and would have nabbed him, but for an extraordinary performance of his mule; who terrified by the pack of howling devils after her, leaped a deep-seated stream, about 40 feet from bank to bank. Young Hough, in the same interesting part of creation, a little previous, was with the Captain, in another snap. — They were riding in a sage-plain; were headed twice by large bands of these Arabs, but extricated themselves, by turning suddenly around, and ascended a steep rugged hill. — He says that 8 of these yellow skins came to their camp at dusk, and desired to sleep there — The party disarmed them till morning, and placed them under the surveilance of the sentinals. During the latter part of their travel, in the hostile region, (Eastern Slope of the mountains, and Pautah indians)[105] they came on a deserted village, (abandoned as they advanced) where they found several dress'd deer-skins, &c. baskets, beads, &c. One of their party took a couple of the skins; next day the savages stole one of Lassen's horses, worth $200, from a meadow near camp. In the afternoon, the indians on the crest of an adjacent hill, raised a cry, and exhibited on a tall pole, what they thought was a hide. No doubt it was the skin of Lassen's lass- [lost?] horse. The whites stole 2 deer skins; the indians retaliated, by appropriating the meat and skin of a horse. We sat up late, listening to the news, the capers of the yellow-skins, &c. It drizzled all night, and I slept well.

SEP: 12 — Cloudy. We slept late. Last evening Messersmith and Dr Bowman rode over to see Old Pete, and returned this morning. They say, that Lassen wants 20 days rations at once, for all hands who are to compose the party. — His camp here broken up, the indians, &c, sent in to the Settlements. Drinker thinks that I had better go, and he will accompany Poile, Peck, Fox, &c. down Feather & Yuva rivers. Equestrian performances are very common here. Lining has a dark grey mare, with very sore back, who either from painfullness of the back, or from perversity, has amused us just now, by some gymnastic feats, &c. He mounted her, when she reared, and then fell; repeated this performance, as often as he remounted. Some others persons tried her with the same gratifying results. — The last time she threw herself down, on her side, one held her head, while several, with sticks & thongs, beat her soundly. They now tried another saddle, with like results, and treatment. An Oregon half-breed Frenchman now mounted her, struck his big Spanish spurs in her paunch, whipped her furiously; and instead of falling down, she ran off, at full speed, 300 yds and returned.

Preparing pack saddles, provissions, &c — 2 P.M. thunder & lightning: — rain on the hills. — It soon cleared off, leaving the mountains white with snow again. Cliques, factions, selfishness, &c. exhibits the peculiarities of men. — Subject of private talks, whispering, and mysteficating as to who here, are to go on the expedition, and who should not; and how it is to be managed. — Antiphathy to the disgusting manners and dispositions of 2 men is the chief cause; and ignorance and selfishness completes it. They all firmly believe in the existence of this "*Gold Lake*" where each person can soon get his mule load; and they have explored around so that there is but a small circuit of country left to explore for it; and in that very circuit it must be! It will be well, here to give an account of my knowledge of this matter, and what has kept men and animals, all the summer, tramping down these streams, and over the rugged dividing ridges. And what impresses Lassen and his comrades, with the firm belief in the existence of such a Lake. — A young fellow named Gibbs, wearing *earrings*, from Boston, — nephew to a Surveyor employed by the government, accompanied his Uncle out, — up Sacramento valley, across Pitt-river, and continuing E. came to a deeply embosomed fresh water lake, about 5 miles long, on whose marginal mountains stood 3 buttes[106] — and that said lake basin was so full of gold, that he picked up pieces from the size of marbles to that of walnuts, along the edge of the stream, and washed them in his handkerchief. He thus procured, in a couple of hours, at ease, about $5000 worth. That the neighboring indians were hostile, and wounded some of their men. That the basin was so deepseated, that the lake could only be seen from the crest of the very steep mountain rim over it. The party *lowered down their pack-mules with ropes*. But they found an easier way to get out. That his Uncle returned to Boston and took him along, and desired Secrecy. — That he had the position of the lake, from an observation taken by his uncle, but he most unfortunately lost it on the Isthmus. His uncle is getting quartz crushing machinery made, to bring out next season; and as he (G's) is afraid some prospectors might accidently stumble on this Laguna del oro, he thought best to return, and anticipate such action of the outside barbarians. As the indians are very hostile there, and every man who goes is certain of speedily becoming a millionaire in a month or 6 weeks, it is indispensable that the party shall be strong, courageous, and honorable men. — A select party, of brave adventurous Gold Lake prospectors. Gibbs told me this statement, and related the same, with slight variations to others.[107] When explorers had used up animals and provissions, examining all the country between the head waters of Feather and Yuva, where he said the lake existed; and expressed doubts of its truthfulness; and the season had advanced, and all the benefit had accrued to the speculators who furnished outfits, then this fellow Gibbs, became alarmed at humbugging so many people, was taken very sick, and pushed down the Sacramento valley, to be rewarded for his ingenuity and zeal.[108] It may be asked, why did he not accompany a party and show them the way. He excuses himself by stating that he does not recollect the country he passed over at all, but can facilitate the search much better by giving all the information he can, and many squads, in various directions must find it, and he is continually unable to travel also   I saw through this affair at once, but thought that our party might find some rich deposits to compensate us for our trouble & expense. There was a young man who concurred with me, in the inconsistencies of the narration. All the rest implicitly believed Gibbs. — Every hollow the prospectors saw, must contain *the* lake; Every one or 2 buttes must be the *3 buttes*; and of course any of these features, with *hostile indians* to complete them, formed the exact country they sought; regardless of the character of the earth or rocks! It was amusing, and I've often laughed out, when I thought how easy it was to start such an excitement.

A late and hearty supper, last night, and probably a panther squeal, or wolf-howl, while asleep, causing me to dream the following. — Thought myself to be alone in an open forrest, of large low oak trees; the forrest was infested with numerous panthers; — I saw and heard several near me; and commenced mocking them, which I could do very accurately. One of these fellows, not being pleased with my imitativeness, took after me, and I ran for a tree, whose lowest branch ran straight out horizontally; under and close to which a canoe was suspended. I got in the canoe, and drew my legs up, to hide from Señor Panther; He sprang on the limb, looking for me, but one foot slipped into the canoe, which contained a number of sleeping wild-cats, as well as myself. A wild cat was hurt, and bit the panther's foot, a general screetching & clawing ensued, the fur flew, and I screeched too, and attempting to kick one of the cats off, kicked my partner in the ribs, causing him to roar out, and awaken me. I told him the dream; but he thought it were safer for me to pull off my heavy boots, and then the *heeling*-art, would be less objectionable. Rheumatic pains disturbed me much, at night.

SEP: 13 — Foggy; cranes and geese flying over to the S. portending the approach of bad weather. As I was ready for the expedition, except having no member to my mess; and as Old Pete was my particular friend, Messersmith, his Agent, now; invited me to belong to it. Jones came over, and returned my rifle & pouch & horn: the former *unimproved* by rough usage. And young Hough returned my Holsters and pistols. Clough, Tubbs, and 2 other men rode off, to visit the indian Village above, in search of stray mules. (5 or 6 miles up, towards the Snow Buttes)   All the unnecessary articles & utensils, we leave at the traders tent, as they will remain till we return. I lent Campbell a single shot gun and copper flask. My contribution to the expedition is 50 lbs flour, 10 of sugar, ½ of sal-eratus, & 2 of Coffee. Half of which belongs to my partner; and to secure a right in the Gold Lake diggings, or rather harvest, he is represented by the loan of a pack poney. — And the D^r insists that we remain partners, till we meet again, in the settlements; — half his earnings, and half of mine.

There was amongst us another or more agents for the Gold Lake speculators. — An individual knew a man, who not long since, travelling into California from the States, started with 5 comrades, from some where about the Mud Lakes, — leaving the emigrant road there, to reach the Californian settlements by a cut-off", — a diagonal *bee-line*, — And he found a Lake, deeply basined with high mountains, with plenty of golden pebbles, and hostile indians, near the head waters of the Yuva. He gathered about *$30,000 worth of oro*; his comrades were murdered by the indians, and he escaped. — He travelled at night, and hid himself by day. Cached $20,000 worth of dust, followed the Yuva river down till he reached Yubaville, taking *$10,000 worth of dust in there.* He is personally acquainted with the man, boarded in the same house with him, and can vouch for his veracity. This story clinched the matter; it fully corroberated Gibbs' statement!

There were other incidents, which I have forgotten, but the main points I have related.

Now let a person of common sense, who knows any thing about the rugged country, and the difficulties of travelling where that man is said to have gone; think how could this man have brought, destitute of food, on foot, and with a rifle alone,   lbs gold one or two day's travel, and   lbs about   miles further; and get along entirely at night?

Drizzly during the night. Indisposed at night, — with slight chills & fevers.

SEP: 14 — Cloudy; some drizzle. Awakened with headache. This morning we were to start about 4 O'clock, to join Lassen; but did not move off till about 3 P.M. Delayed by making up messes, hunting, talking about nothing, looking after stray animals; and lastly a big drink, at the Trading Tent. At last, 17 of us, with 3 pack animals, rode off; expecting to be joined by 5 more men, with 3 pack animals, in 24 or 48 hours. — Forded the river, and rode straight across the plain, W. of the road, crossed the slight rise dividing the valley; to the upper, or Grass-cutting wet valley, where the emigrants of last fall cut hay for the last 40 miles in. — Rode around its Western margin, on the road; till we reached old Pete's camp, on the other side, or head of it. — Found the old man well, with a blanket tent set up, about 5½ P.M. = 10 miles. At dusk we brought our animals in and tied them up. This is the very spot where my company nooned, last fall, on their march in. We supped heartily, spread our blankets by the fire, and slept, a few hours soundly; — till 11 P.M. when it rained hard, till morning; soaking us all most thoroughly. I had head-ache: And for the balance of the night, set against a tree, enveloped in two blankets, — like Ajax, defying the lightning. — It ran over me and through every thing. — I might then have well exclaimed, "Thou, thou, rains't in this bosom!"

SEP: 15 — Awakened at 2 A.M. by the rain; had enveloped myself in the blankets, and thought I could defy it, and take my sleep out, but it insinu-ated itself, and ran under me. I was well soaked, and compelled to get up. We made a large fire, and most of the company gathered around it, wrapped in blankets, and shivering with cold & wet. Some seated themselves on camp-kettles, and dozed, while others stood close to the fire, and sought consola-tion in smoking their pipes. As soon as day dawned, we prepared breakfast, and enjoyed it in the rain. Messersmith mounted, and rode back to the old camp, for an axe and some horse-shoes. Our horses and mules, grazing a mile below, are visited by deer, there are 3 among them. Sun rise disipated the bad weather, and we spread blankets, &c. to dry. People busy mending clothes, boots, &c. Burton shot a large brown hawk   My mess, (Lassen, Messersmith, Burton, & self,) formed a tent, of 2 blankets pinned together, and thrown over a ridge-pole, in 2 forked sticks, to protect us some to-night, in case of rain. Ducks and Geese are cackling and quacking in the stream, 300 yards off, and in the wet meadow beyond, large blue cranes are hooping. The wil-lows, tall grass, and marsh, protect them. Forepart of the night mild, with flying clouds: latter part clear and cold. We have, however, a fine log fire. Slept little till towards morning.

SEP. 16 — Ice this morning. The cold ducking, night before last, has affected me with cold and pains. Lassen awakened us early, and we struck our blanket shelter. At 9 A.M. we moved off. — Kept the emigrant road, to a narrow meadow, after crossing a dry grass plain. Crossed the upper end, and camp'd near the road, at 4 P.M. — 25 miles ride. I noticed, on the margin of the dry plain by the road, 2 vacant graves. — Clothing, muddy and decayed, lay scattered around one of them; the other was as clean as if just dug. Presume that prospectors had opened them, suspecting they were cāches, and the wolves afterwards, had little trouble in gutting them. Clear and cool night, and I slept well

[SEPT.] 17 — Frost. Aroused at day-break, and breakfasted at 6½ A.M. Some consultation and perversity. It appears, that a majority of this company had pledged themselves to Clough and two other men, that somewhere hereabouts they would wait 24 hours for them to come up and join us. Lassen was for pushing ahead, regardless of any thing else, for the reason that the season was late, and he likewise wished to have the benefit of moon-light nights in the hostile district. However, it was agreed to wait to-day.

The rock here is all fire-altered granite. — Blocks and Masses scattered about, and piled up on the adjacent hills. Considerable silver in these rocks. A party 4 rode back about 6 miles, to hunt deer. The 2 indian dogs with us, are of no use, and a great nuisance. — Though the men feed them, they will steal, and gnaw straps, bags, &c. just like wolves.

Small hornets, in these mountains are often a source of great inconvenience — When riding up to this camp-ground, and about 100 yards distant, a *yellow jacket* stung my horse about the nose, causing him suddenly to throw his nose between his legs, rear up, and then kick up behind, and dash off, at full speed, regardless of bit, to camp; expecting, as I flew through the timber, to get a leg tore off.

The meadow where we are now camped, is W. of the main emigrant road, about a couple of miles, I think; and is a camp road, for grass and water; while the other is on a dry timbered ridge. This road is probably in length, to junctions, about 5 miles. When my company passed last fall, we kept to upper road.

At 4 P.M. the hunters returned, luckless, and reported having met Clough, with 6 men, as they went out. — Soon after Clough, 6 comrades, and 2 pack mules came in. We organized our messes as follows.

No. 1. Lassen		No 2	Jones	Hough sr
Messersmith			Bowman	Hough jr
Burton			Hall	
Bruff			Campbell	

No 3	Tubbs	No 4	Edgar	No 5	Lyming
	Leining		Miroitz		Clough, Selby
	Dexter		Montrose		Fugitt, Stephens
					Capen, Gunion

Total 23 men, and 30 horses & mules. At night, some one in No 5 mess, fired a pistol at one of the dogs, caught stealing. He mortally wounded him; and the brute howled and whined a long time, after crawling off some distance. Pleasant night.

SEP. 18 — In saddle, and moving ahead, at 8 A.M. Struck and kept the main road some distance, left it, and proceeded Wy along the edge of the plain — which becomes more moist as we proceed, caused by numerous small branches, which sink in the sands below. We then rode N.W. over stony spurs, through pines, and sage bushes, till we again struck the road. By this route we have cut off about 8 miles — the road being that much further. Kept the road a few miles, left it & rode Westerly near a mile, and camped, at 4 P.M. in a deep narrow, rock enclosed valley, containing a brook & some good grass. The stream rises in several small and excellent springs, at the head of the hollow, about 50 yds above us. It is subteranean in ma[n]y short places. 200 yards below us is a very narrow gorge, where the stream passes, to enter Pitt river. Rode 28 miles. Scattered large pines in the bottom, and over the high hills on either side. Established regular guard duty. At dusk picketed our animals close to us, as the Pitt river indians might be *prospecting* up here to-night. 4 men on guard. When Capt. Lyon's detachment came out they camp'd here, and killed an ox.

On our way here, one of the party drew a revolver, from his holster, and killed the other indian dog. It is reported that General Taylor is dead; said to be in a newspaper, brought out by Clough, from the settlements.

I am on the morning relief.

SEP. 19 — As soon as it was light, we — sentinals, made a large fire, and warmed ourselves, on the plain above the valley where the camp was, as the animals had gone up after bunch grass. Drove them in, breakfasted, and at 8 A.M. were again on the road. Morning quite cold. In half an hour we gained the main road, and kept it. — Crossed a marshy tributary of Pitt river, and at 12½ P.M. halted in a narrow grass bottom, about ¼ mile E. of the road. This was a camping-place of the emigrants last fall. We determined to camp here, and selected a clear spot, beyond arrow reach of the willows, which grew around some spring holes and marshy places. These small spring lagoons supply streamlets, which unite from many branches, in a brook below, which turns S.W. passes through a cañon, and crosses the emigrant road where we crossed this morning. A short distance below, is where Tubb's party captured the 2 indians, before narrated — Rode but 12 miles to day. Very warm in middle of day. We disposed our blankets and saddles close together, forming a square, and piled pack saddles and packs around, to protect us while sleeping from arrows. My eyes much inflamed with cold. We picketed our animals close in, set guard & slept.

Night clear and cold. I was on the first relief.

SEP. 20 — At 6, this morning a drizzle in my face awoke me. About 8 O'Clock, while breakfasting, some one looked across about 400 yards, on the hill side, a short distance above where the horses & mules were grazing, and thought they saw a wolf, among the rocks & trees. We all looked in that direction, and saw an indian rise up, and run over a low ridge, and some saw others there. 3 of my comrades seized their rifles and ran across the plain, but the savages had vamosed. Capt. Jones jumped astraddle a horse and rode over the indentation the indian escaped by; but could not find then [them]. At 9 A.M. we mounted and moved on. A consultation now ensued about the leadership of the party, as there were several aspirants to that honor. So a vote was taken, those in favor of Lassen rode over to the right, and those in favor of Jones, to the left; resulting in the election of Lassen. We followed the road, crossed Fall Creek — a Pitt river tributary, (where last fall my company camped, and lost 2 mules) and ascended a very tall hill, the apex of the range bounding Pitt river valley on the E. On the top I turned around in my saddle, and beheld a magnificent view. — To the S.W. extended Pitt river valley and plains; green and dry grass, marsh, pools, and streams of water, in all the beautiful colors of a rich landscape. Then the hills rising from the level plain as if from the bosom of the calm sea, growing darker, bolder, and loftier, in all the tints of green, gray & blue, till they reached the majestic snow-crowned Tschastes. — A short distance, apparently, to the E. of the old sage, rises the dark forms of the Snow Buttes, with patches of snow about their tops, and light floculent clouds passing by them, sometimes seeming to cut them in half. Pitt river, in the warm sun, looked like a silver thread. And I could see where the head of the Feather river valley, of the branch we were camped on, extended. Here we left the road, travelled E.N.E. — crossed arid stony hills and hollows, say 5 miles, N.W. 2 ms. and then over very irregular ground, on the top of a long and very elevated range of mountains, thickly timbered with every species and size of the genus pinus keeping a mien E. course. Occasionally some opening through the trees, and gaps in the hills, afforded us a glimpse of Pitt valley, on our left. This is hard riding, for biped & quadruped. At length we descended, by a series of spurs, over all sorts of ground, rocks, & trees, into a long and very narrow grass valley. Having a deep cut bed of a winter's torrent running through it. We found in this gulch some water holes, containing enough water barely to make tea; so our poor beasts must wait till to-morrow, to quench their thirst. Drizzles all day. The grass here is tolerable. This gulch empties into Pitt valley. Lassen had picked up, on the route, an old rotten wagon cover, which we found very serviceable. This, our mess formed a sort of tent with, to sleep under, believing that we can sleep just as well under shelter, as if we were used to it.

This afternoon I am amused with chills fevers and headache; and on the 2d relief. Rain and cool at night. The first relief espied an indian in a cluster of willows, about 50 yds. from camp, and fired at him. We then drew the animals in, and picketed them close to camp. It rained all night, but I slept soundly after relieved from guard.

SEP. 21st   Up at 6 A.M. Hazy weather, but clear and warm a little after sun-rise. The rain had replenished the water-holes, and we led our horses and mules down to drink. It was 400 yards down to the principal hole we used. To procure water we had to get down into the ravine and descend it to the hole. The banks above, were lined with trees and rocks, and where the indians could easily shoot us. I carried a pail, to get water for my mess, & with my rifle, led my horse & poney to drink. Lassen had been over this ground before.[109] We emerged from this vale, and travelled N.E. riding over mountain spurs, descended steep hills, crossed several narrow flat arid plains, and through much timber and brush, winding around to the N. Two hour's ride brought us to a narrow grass vale, where I noticed a beautiful clear spring under a tree, and a bark lodge built over it, by the indians, in order to shoot the deer or rabbit who came to drink.[110] It looked much like a rustic spring seat at home. We now crossed several ridges and intermediate small plains; and descended a long spur, keeping more westerly, till we struck the head of a fine large grass valley. We descended this valley, keeping along the edge of a deep and narrow ravine, with willows and cotton wood. Occasionally saw places of clear cool water. No doubt that the greater part of this stream is subteranean, now a little streak of running water, and at last a considerable stream, — clear running-water in deep alluvial banks: and closely lined with willows. We continued down, seeking a place to water and ford. With some trouble we at last got our train down the bank and in the stream, knee deep, and one after the other scrambled up the steep grassy bank, through dense willows, on top the opposite side. It was quite difficult keeping seat in the saddle ascending here. A pack horse here gave us some trouble, by keeping in the stream, to browse the grass on the banks. We drove him up. About 200 yards lower down, we espied a naked indian. He ran out of the willows, and found that he could not elude us, squatted on the bank opposite, (side we crossed from) motioning with his hands, for us to go away, — not to shoot him. And then made other motions, indicating either that if we were hungry to go below — where he pointed, and they would feed us; or that he was up here to procure food to take there. Some one in the rear called to me "Shoot the d — d son of a gun"! — but I could not kill the poor contemptable, naked wretch, in cold blood. We wished to avenge poor Frank's death, but needed a sufficient pretext to do so. This indian was dark, thin, and elderly. We rode on, leaving the mahogany-colored wretch squatting on his haunches, and watching us. — We had only proceeded about $\frac{1}{4}$ mile after this, when we noticed several indians, — 2 or 3 running across from the willows we just left, following others ascending a naked hill, to our right, a short distance (to the N^d)

We now leave the stream on our left, and cross naked stony plains on a W. course; and about $4\frac{1}{2}$ P.M. reached a fine mountain stream, very deep seated, in alluvial banks; water clear and cool, quite rapid, — quite a creek. Dense willows & scrub oaks along the banks. — This stream is in a 2nd range of hills, parallel to those bordering Pitt valley, I think. — It comes from the N.E. where there appears to be another valley. This joins the southern one we crossed, and may be subteranean below. Camped on the plain, beyond arrow-shot of the willows. The South branch of the valley, runs S.W. and traversed by a stream: — It may empty into Pitt river, in 5 miles. Saw low down several columns of smoke indicating the presence of indians. Jones shot at 2 antelope. The North valley, runs N.W. at this time is an arid plain, and is separated from the former, by a short range of hills, below which they blend in extensive grass plains. Fine places these were, for the Pitt river indians to secrete and graze the cattle they stole last fall, from the emigrants.

At Sun Set we picketed our animals close up. I called the stream we forded, on account of the indians, "*Indian Creek.*" Dusk set guard, supped, smoked, and slept soundly. Night clear and cool, Wind S.W.

SEP. 22 — Awakened at Sunrise. Spread blankets, &c. to dry. Fuel rather scarce. Noticed basaltic lines of rock, running N. and S. over a small hill to the N.E. of camp. After breakfast, we proceeded, — on a S.E. course. Can see the Snow-Butte through an opening in the valley, on looking back, as we ascend higher in this gorge plain. Mt Tschastes appears baseless: — his white summit only, seen above the clouds. Snow Butte bears S.W. by W. and

Tschastes W. by S. The hills N. of us ¼ mile, are covered with long dry grass, & stunted cedar. Judging from drift, of twigs, grass, &c. that the stream we last camped on, which we chased up in the mountains, a long ways, is subject to overflowing the lower valley. The soft alluvial plain is cut into gulches, in all directions, by water. The Northern branch, which we have travelled by into the mountains, comes from the N.W. through a narrow stony gorge, about 5 miles, & then forks. The right hand branch sweeps around to the E. by N. and in about 2 ms. leaves a cañon, — which it may, from its source, traverse some distance. The main branch runs N.W. by W. sweeping around to the W^d through very narrow bottoms, between steep, stony, and thickly timbered ridges. Here is where we are travelling. We endeavor to follow the stream, but the timber, huge rocks, and the abru[p]t hill, on one side or the other, forces us occasionally, along very steep declivities, or crossing and recrossing the stream, throug[h] close and difficult brush. Just before entering the gorge vale, we crossed a dry plain of cracked clay, and minute fragments of quartz, pebbles, and stunted sage. — About 1 mile across. — I noticed that where grass had grown, the turf had been torn up, and removed by torrents. At 3 ms. above camp, this morning, Lassen wished to ford the creek, where the banks were steep. So in order to descend, he cut away the brush, and on his tall bay horse, descended, crossed, and ascended the opposite steep bank. 5 others, on horses and mules, followed, also successfully, but the 6th — Clough's, was an amusing affair. — He is a large man, and was mounted on a small black mule. His mule had ascended the steep clay bank, on the opposite side, about twice her length, when her hind feet slipped, she fell on her knees, and her rider sprang off; she made a somerset, and pitched into the stream and brush. — There she lay, floundering, much to the detriment of saddle, pistols, blankets, &c. when Clough descended, seized her bridle, *righted her*, as a sailor would say, and got her up, out of the scrape. She presented an interesting appearance after the evolution. Some ½ mile higher, and about 1 mile below the forks of the stream, the rest of the party crossed, where the banks were low, and no impediment. But we had more serious difficulties to encounter on the banks of the creek. The loose black soil was perforated with numerous sink-holes, caused by water settling, and undermining the sub strata. — Circular pits, from 18 inches to 3 feet diameter, and 2 to 4 feet deep; and hid by tall grass and rushes, which also grew all along. The path — an indian trail, ran close to the bank, where these sinks were; and on our right were stones and brush. My friend, Dr Bowman, riding about 10 paces ahead of me, when his mule put her fore feet into one of these hidden pits, fell, & after striking her nose, and rearing & scuffling, the D^r managed to get her out, without being unseated. — I thought to avoid this hole, and was anxiously looking over, to guide my horse safely by it, when down he went, — both feet in, and his breast and nose on the earth: I seized the loggerhead of the saddle (*Californian name — The pummel.*), and retained my seat. I jerked him up, touching the ground with my feet, and he floundered out. I looked around to my comrades, and pointed to the spot, that they might avoid it, but some pack mules not noticining [noticing] my warning signs, got in successively, and cut some fine capers; then a mule fell in, and pitched her rider a rod over her head; without any harm, however. — The balance of the train perceiving the many extraordinary feats performed ahead, avoided the enchanted spot, and that performance was closed.

We have not seen a Philistine to-day, but noticed numerous remains of willow lodges, burnt muscle-shells, and doubtless this is a favorite resort of theirs. At $12\frac{1}{2}$ P.M. we halted, in a narrow vale of dry grass, under a large spruce tree. This vale runs Westerly; the brook in it comes from the N. through a deep gorge. The Northern boundary hills are very tall. Under this tree, alongside a bend of the branch [of the stream] we camped. Two men rode up the Southern hills, while 3 ascended the tallest Northern one, in order to see the country beyond.

About 300 yds below us runs the branch, and the place is odorous with mint & wild rose bushes. Animals grazing a short distance below, on the banks of the stream, where it makes a sudden bend for the mountains. My horse is badly chafed by the saddle. Our party are variously employed, shoeing horses, baking bread, playing cards, &c.

While travelling over a dry plain, this morning, a hare afforded us some sport. Capt Jones pursued her at full speed, puss doubled, and crossed the trail, doubled again, and recrossed it, right through the train, when several others joined in the pursuit, quite a dust kicked up, and cracking of revolvers in vain; the hare hid somewhere, and nobody was hurt.

At $4\frac{1}{2}$ P.M. the explorers from the N. hill, came in. They had ascended its highest peak, but the dense forrest prevented their observing the country beyond. — They brought in a fine grouse. At dark, the other party returned, reported the same difficulty interfered with their prospects.

Squalls from the E. with showers and drizzles, late in the ev[en]ing, and all night. Here again, our tattered cotton-sheet became useful. — We quickly had a sort of tent, and covered the openings with blankets to keep the rain off our heads, any how. Squalls from the E. our shelter blew down, we sat it up as well as we could, and just as we got asleep, down she came again, conducting streams of water down my neck, and over my face. Once more we reestablished it, and once more had to repeat. Soil so loose that the pickets would not hold; and the same cause, kept the guard busy till day, catching the animals who had drawn their pickets, and tying them to large stones. Not very cold, and minus two hour's guard, and 3 tent casualties, I slept well. (At consultation, at dark, resulted in a decission to travel to-morrow in a N.E. direction.

SEP: 23. Cloudy and strong breeze from the S.E. Spread our wet blankets, &c. to dry. At 8 A.M. we mounted, and moved up the creek; it was very crooked, divided by rocky and brushy islets, in some places; and as we ascended, the gorge contracted, and the rocks and trees of the abrupt enclosing-hills encroached, so as to drives [drive us] from one side to the other; and looking, as we advanced, as if were about to get in a *tight place*. At last, finding a slight indentation, and plausable slope, we left the stream, and ascended a long slope of the mountain. — The stream comes from the westward. We crossed several hills, ascending, till we gained the summit of the range, — the tallest hills on the E. side of Pitt river valley. Here an opening in the heavy pine timber permitted us to look far down into Pitt valley. The isolated Butte, described and pictured, in my travels with the company, October 6th '49, and 180 miles N. by the road, from Lassen's Rancho, was in full view, looked blue, and appeared to be only about 15 miles distant, but might be much more.[111] It bears from here, by a pocket compass, S.S.W. We are probably about 10 miles from the edge of that valley. The eternal snow-capped Tschastes,[112] bears W.S.W. We rode along the narrow crooked ridge, northerly, in a cold drizzle and strong breeze, on our left the mountain was precipitous, and closely timbered with large pines and spruce. At length we gradually descended, and entered a very brushy hollow, with a rill, at right angles to our course; and which, no doubt, is the head of the creek we camped on, and followed so far up. This indentation is thick set with bushes and trees; Willows, plumbs, service berries, currents, goose-berries; and plenty of fine long green grass. We dismounted here, to rest and graze our weary animals; and all hands attacked the fruit bushes, and made quite a lunch there of. When we turned, to leave the creek below, and ascend the hills, Tubbs with a couple of comrades, kept up the creek gorge; this I did not notice at the time. We felt a little apprehensive about them. Steady rain, and a cold ride followed. At 4 P.M. we had descended into a deep narrow valley, with a brook, marsh grass, &c And camped on its edge, in the pine timber: and fixed up our tattered shelter, while the other messes made blanket shelters, to sleep under. The stream here, descends a narrow gorge about a mile E. of us, and probably the gorge, a little lower, contracts into a cañon. We procured logs and branches, and soon had large fires, and tea water boiling, and flour cakes cooking. Dried our bedding, by the fire, as well as we could, put sentinals on the animals in the meadow, smoked our pipes, and retired after supper to our damp beds. We had to sup in the rain, as there was not room in the tent. Tubb's men fired several shot, to guide him here, if in hearing distance   At dusk our anxiety was relieved by his answering shot, and he soon after descended to camp. On the opposite side of this vale, about 200 yards only, is a large trunk of a pine tree burning. —Set on fire by the indians. Night occasionally clear, and alternate drizzles. Picketed the animals close in. I forgot to mention, that while passing over a plateau, near the vale of berrys, a hornet stung my horse in the right flank, simultaneously with the application of my spur to the same spot. He kicked up, reared, and ran off about 200 yards, at full speed, through a thick forrest of pines, and descending. A pack mule, in the rear, was also stung. She ran off, broke some straps, and scattered her cargo.

SEP: 24 — Clear cold morning (ice) I had the morning watch, and my feet became very cold, standing in the half-frozen marsh. The weather soon clouded over again. After an early breakfast we moved on, — riding E. by N. — Crossed hills of every grade of character and elevation, several intervening dry pebbly and slaty plains; and dry rough torrent beds. Now ascended a troublesome hill; — steep and long; and covered with masses of dense mansaneta bushes, and angular granitic & basaltic fragments, and groups of rocks. Most tiresome and painful to our animals. — Had to rest them frequently. — Then we crossed, in a diagonal direction to its length, an elevated plain, of gravel, rocks, and sage bushes, alternating, with patches of dry grass; the course over it S.E. Reached the Eastern extremity, followed up a hollow in depressed hills, filled with poplars, willows, &c. — indicitive of water, turned left, from this valley, and ascended gradually, a slight depression, containing a ravine mostly dry; but in one part considerable fresh clear water. A little higher, we saw a place in the side of the ditch, where the indians had been dressing deer skins. — A stake, worn very smooth, driven in the clay, by a large circular hole.[113] As we advanced up the hollow, the tall grass[,] poplars, willows, &c. grew thicker, and we chased it up, — N.E. till we reached a shallow grassy basin, full of willows, near the apex of the hill. Searched around in vain, amongst the grass and willows for water; dismounted & rested, while Old Pete proceeded up about 300 yds. to the top, to reconitre the country. We lay here about 2 hours. Lassen, signified by a shot, that we had to mount, and retrace our steps to the water. So we retrograted about 1½ miles, and camped, by a little running water. (A stream here is mostly subteranean) Fine weather. On 1st watch, night cold (ice). On being relieved, and filling my pipe for a smoke, preparatory to going to bed, some wolves below, honored us with a serrenade. We picketed the animals close up, at dusk. The cold interfered much with repose —

SEP. 25 — Jack Frost, and wolves, awakened us early. A delightful morning, and beautiful scenery. The sun was about ½ hour high when we mounted. Rode on a mien E. course. Passed low table lands, and small grass plains. The hills on either side rise from the lowest grade and recede to moderate heights and here and there upon the upper range send up a singular knob or mount. The earth is tinted with the warm and rich hues of autumn. — Orange & bright yellow, — (of plumb bushes,) predominate in the plains, and on the lower slopes. Dark cedars are scattered about, and numerous thick groves of them.[114] At 11 A.M. we reached an elevated point, from whence I could just discern Mount Tschastes' white cap, — S.S.W. — Then we proceeded over a very rough volcanic country, about an hour's ride, and descended into a beautiful narrow grass-valley. Stream and holes of fine clear water, are along the S.W. side. This valley runs N.E. its breadth varying from ½ to 1 mile, and is several miles in length. The S.W. heights, where the spring-sources are, is about 75 yards above the camp. The springs, in our rear, are enclosed by rocks and cedars, and very tall grass.

The immediate boundary hills are quite low, but rise as they retire, to considerable eminences. A high range in the distant front, appears to run N.N.E. We camped at Meridian. Loosed the animals to graze below, and put a sentinal on them. A small party rode over, to gain a peak on the southern end of the high range in front, about 8 miles distant, to reconnoitre the neighboring country.

We dried blankets, &c. Smoked, played uchre, &c and I amused myself sketching.

Our camp is on a sloping meadow, about 15 feet above the level of the plain. Spring holes about 40 feet behind the camp: And a singularly split-rock, just above the spring, where masses of granite crop out. (*Split Rock*) The rock was split by frost, I suppose, and several years since. Bird-lime on the rocks, as hard as the rock itself. — This circumstance I have noticed several times. A few yards E. of this rock, on the slope of the hill, under 3 stunted cedars, growing close together, I saw where indians had recently camped. A bed of rushes & grass, sufficient for several persons to sleep on: coals, burnt bones, of deer, fish, and fowl, and broken obsidian arrow-points. Cedar-bushes had been piled around, to break off the cool wind. Near this cosey spot, I found a wolf's jaw-bone, roasted muscle-shells, piece of an arrow shaft, fragments of obsidian points; part of a stone lance-head, and on a stone the size of a bushel measure, lay a small one — about the size of a goose-egg, & fragments of obsidian around, proved this to have been an arrow-head manu-factory.[115]

This is another favorite resort of the Phillistines. One of these two-legged varmints arose from the grass below, and ran in the direction of a Cañon, — (shown in the view) and a smoke signal, in a peack, — like an extinct [vol-cano], warned us that we were watched by them. one of A party of 3, who had branched off S. on the way here, came in during the afternoon, one on foot, his mule ran away. Another one brought in a very large hare. At Sun-Set the explorers returned; reported the high mountains volcanic, (as I sup-posed) and a large lake on the other side, at the base of the tall peak. Brought me some brick-colored lava. Our Mess mate Burton, who is a good shot, brought in a large grouse. They saw the indian below, but it was late, and animals jaded, and they did not ride towards him. From 9 till 12 O'Clock, at night, our animals evinced uneasiness, but the sentinals were on the alert. A clear cool night.

SEP. 26 — Fine morning, and we were up early. Had the fore feet of my pack-pony shod. We started to-day, on a mien E.S.E. course over the low stony spurs in front of our camp, occasionally plains covered with stones and dry grass; then over mountain ridges, till about $3\frac{1}{2}$ P.M. we descended into an extensive basin, containing a large lake of very shallow water, sur-rounded by marsh, rushes, and tall grass. The rocky boundaries, at foot of the hills, showed that during the winter and early in the spring this was a con-siderable sheet of water. The soil around, is snuff-colored, — volcanic ashes and alluvial soil mixed. I judge that this basin is about 10 miles long, and from $2\frac{1}{2}$ to 5 miles broad. The firm grassy margin, is very narrow. We were all thirsty, but could not reach the lake, on account of the marsh.

Whilst sitting in the saddle, undecided which course to take next, Tubbs rode up to the N. over a low rocky ridge, in search of water. — He was gone about 15 minutes, when the crack of his rifle, and appearance of his mule soon after, without her rider, alarmed us; — and we dashed off in the direction, at full speed, — to rescue our comrade from the indians! However, we soon met him, and learnt that he dismounted to shoot a hare; and on firing, his mule ran off.

We rode along the N. side of the lake, a mile or so, turned left from it, proceeded over stony hills and hollows, till we reached a narrow valley, with a rapid creek, running from the S.E. and sweeping around to the N.E. This Creek has cut a deep bed in the black alluvial soil; Fine tall grass in the bottom, and vast quantities of rose-bushes line the margin of the stream. Their seed-pods are as delightful as conserve.[116] We ate many. — I called this, "*Rose-bush Creek.*" We continued up the valley looking for a good and secure camp-ground. At length we reached a narrow gorge, which appearing impracticable for us to pass, we ascended a large rocky hill to the right, and over its flat and elevated top, about 1 mile. This elevated plain was covered with sage bushes, and sprinkled over with fragments of beautiful white boytroidal crystals of chalcedony. — (Their concave faces are drusy.)

We descended, rather steep and long, through deep sand and sage bushes, into an L-shaped valley, — here about 400 yds. wide; turned left, and entered the lower branch of it; about 2 miles above the cañon, and camped, at 5 P.M. (Burton shot a grouse.) The stream here, is on the N. side of the valley, and runs N.E. The other branch from the S. I noted, this forenoon, while passing over a very stony volcanic plain, circles of angular brown volcanic stones. The most of these circles seemed to be about 20 ft. diameter. — Appeared to be pits, filled up with the angular fragments of rocks. The same kind of rocks were scattered over the plain, and occasionally in piles and masses, as if thrown there by cart loads; and those filling the circular pits, looked much fresher than the others.

SEP. 27 — After breakfast, 2 squads, each of 4 men, rode off, to reconnoitre the country beyond, — one proceeded for a peak to the N. and the other to another height, a little N. of E. A fine morning, light flying clouds. We had here to fix up our tent for a sun-screen. There were two groups of white conical rocks, in the hill sides near us; and I walked over to those N.W. of camp, — in a depression of the hill, about 1 mile from camp. They are a decrepitating white volcanic sand stone. The ground around, and all the hollows leading down from them, were white with the detritus of these groups. The soft hills have washed away and exposed them   On my way up, I picked up a long narrow blue quartz lance-head, pieces of red quartz lance-heads, and several black obsidian arrow-heads.

Found also, agatized wood, ligniformed quartz, semi-opal, calcedony, &c. On the slopes a fine powder of sea green earth, particularly on the edges of the numerous fissures, in the clay. (*Conical white rocks*)

At sunset we moved camp across the stream several hundred yards W. for better grass. At 7 P.M. the party, headed by Fugett, who went N. returned, and reported that all the surrounding country is rough volcanic formations. — They reached a very deep-seated lake, unexpectedly. — When arrived on the edge of a tall mountain, descending very abruptly to the water, before they discovered it. A tulè swamp surrounded the lake, but answers, in no other respect, the description of Gold Lake. This is about 12 miles off. — This is undoubtedly on the Eastern Slope of the Sierra Nevada —

SEP: 28 — Cold morning (frost)   About 7 A.M. Tubb's party returned. Had travelled N.E. about 14 miles, — all the country volcanic formations, and no lake. He saw, from an elevation, there, Mt. Tschastes — bearing, from a peak, — about 10 miles from here, W.S.W. And 2 miles further W. by S. We convened a council to determine our next course, and determined to go one day E. and from thence observe & determine the next, &c. At 10 A.M. we mounted, and rode on our E. course, following this branch up, several miles. — This, the main stream, comes from the N.E. with a few tributary branches on either side. — The gorges containing these branches, are grassy, and separated by high rocky ridges. The main stream now becomes pent in narrower bounds, till we can descry a cañon, from whence it runs.

We turned now, and rode E.N.E. over a hill, descended into a plain of dry grass. We turned left, to descend here, passing over a succession of small ridges, and descended by a hollow between long spurs. Now crossed some stony rolls of ground, and entered a basin or valley, of some extent, with a stream and good grass. — About 5 miles back, on a height, I saw the top of the Snow Butte, bearing S. by W. In the early part of to-day's march, Jones and 2 others, left the train, to pass through a valley, then S. of our course. Camped at 4 P.M. under a cedar tree, where the ground was slightly elevated above the surrounding plain. This stony spot was about 50 ft. diameter. Scattered sage plain above, and dry and green grass below us. Stream comes from the W^d runs Easterly; and may some where below, turn S. or W. Clear night. Several indian fires burning a couple of miles below.

[SEPT.] 29 — Clear, frosty morning. (on morning guard)   Breakfasted at 6 O'Clock. This valley runs E. and W. It extends below, to the E^d some distance, and in a E.S.E. direction, there arises from a range of blue hills, a remarkable sugar-loaf peak, and evidently a large rocky projection on its side, judging from the light and shade of the sun. This projection is vertical, on the S. side, and near the top, and white. It may be 30 miles off. W. of camp rises a tall conical hill, hollow at top, and doubtless an extinct crater.

I thought, after breakfast, of visiting this peak, equipped, and shouldered

my rifle to do so, but thought that company would be agreeable, and therefore asked my intelligent & energetic comrade, — Isadore Merowitz, if he did
not want an adventure? — I told him where; and he agreed to go, as soon
as he had completed his task of cleaning up the tin pots & platters, of his mess.
He equipped & shouldered his stout German rifle, and always wore a Circas-
sian creese at his side. The air is so pure, and the peak so dark, that I was
deceived greatly, about distance. I had no idea of the mount being over 2 ms.
distant — but it proved to be 5 or 6. We crossed the plain, ascended a gentle
but rocky slope, and reached a long ridge, at the other side of which, we
thought commenced the foot of the mountain; but we saw a considerable
extent of the most rugged and irregular ground before us, and intervening.
An earthquake could not have broken it up worse. —

It grew warm, and we put our overcoats on a large block of stone, to pick
up when we should descend. We however continued, crossed 2 branches of
the stream, over ridges composed of huge masses of volcanic angular rock;
piled or heaved up by volcanic action, and full of cavities. Saw several deep
funnel shaped holes, — had to pass through 2 of these. Bottoms flat & grassy,
sides steep and sprinkled with angular blocks, of stone. One was about 50
yds. diam: at bottom (sides at an angle of about 45°)   Scrambled over immense piles of large angular blocks, — having to leap from surface to surface,
over holes, and crevices. Now we commenced the rugged ascent of the volcanic mount, by following a narrow ridge up. He had several times to halt
and blow. At length reached a pile of rocks and cedars, on the rim of the
great crater; but could only see the walls on the opposite side; and wished to
go round on the rim, till we reached the highest point, on the opposite side;
to look down into the crater, and view the surrounding country. We could
discern the tree where the camp was, which we recognised by the smoke
Could barely distinguish some dark spots, which were the animals grazing. We stopped at the aforesaid pile of rock, & rested a few minutes, when
I observed to my comrade, "Well, Isadore, let's move on!" and at that moment something struck the hard ground on which we were about to step!
We paused, and I asked my comrade what it could be? He said, "a stone";
to which I replied, cocking my rifle, "it was thrown at us!" — Immediately
another, — an arrow, (as both were) struck in the ground, within 3 feet of
my friend! He exclaimed, "An arrow, by G — d!" wheeled around to the
right, and fired his rifle into the dark abyss of the crater: and then rapidly
retreated down the declivity of the hill. The inclination of the arrow showed
that it came from the ragged point on the other side of the rim, and about
100 yards from us. — The highest point, we were aiming to reach. If we had

gone but a single step from the cover which hid us from the yellow devils above, we would assuredly [have] been instantly sacrificed.

I called to Isadore, not to retreat so hastily, in face of foes, as it would give them confidence to pursue us; and probably there were numbers of them. I kept my rifle cocked, and slowly moved down the hill, looking out [expecting] every moment to hear if not to feel the arrows. We took a much smoother spur to descend on than that we ascended by. One of us wounded, would have involved the destruction of both, and probably several others of the party. For neither of us could have abandoned his wounded comrade; and on that exposed rim, we would have been excellent targets for the indians above, to fire at. The camp waiting for us to return, till night; when they could not make search; but early in the morning, a party would be sent up, who, if the indians had the sagacity, could as easily kill, from behind the rocks and trees, as they had us. So it appears that the rascals on the mount, stationed there to watch our camp, came pretty near nabbing us; and anyhow prevented me obtaining a fine view, and perhaps a sketch. We called at the rock, took our overcoats, and descended to camp, and related our adventures; creating much amusement; but Old Pete said we might *tank* our *Got*, we escaped so luckily.

Jones and his comrades had rejoined the company a little while before. He said, that last night they camped, on the trail, about 2 miles in the rear, among the hills, and that a large band of indians followed, on our trail yesterday, continuing down into this bottom. So that these same rascals had gone around, & ascended the mountain. (*View Old Crater*)

At 3 P.M. the exploring party returned, and reported nothing interesting except the fact that all the streams ran Easterly.

I found, on the ascent this morning, various kinds of lava, and other volcanic minerals; black obsidian, calcedony, agate, agatized & opalized wood. The night cold, and a little hazy, with a strong N. wind. Picketed our animals close up to camp, and kept our *eyes skinned*. The horses and mules evinced alarm several times, looking over to the foot of the ridge, on the N. side of the valley, ¼ mile off. I was on the 1st watch.

SEP: 30 — As the morning relief were driving up some mules which had rambled rather too far on the N. side, discovered tracks, and signs of the *Philistines*, showing that they descended the mountain and valley, late in the night, or just before day.

Ice this morning. Strong wind E. by N. At 8 A.M. we moved on, ascending from the valley at the point where we entered it: — to the S. and turned left on a very long inclined plain, ascending to the E. This plain is covered with dry grass and scattered stones; and at its upper end, — on a mountain, we could see down in the valley we just left, and had ascended parrallel with it, but separated by a narrow ridge, which descended abruptly to the valley About an hour's ride brought us to the top of the plane, and also of a tall mountain range, with several peaks at the summit. Rocks, dwarf-pines and cedars. Turned S. and in about 4 miles & reached a more elevated spot, where also we could [see] into the valley where we had camped, spread out like a map, and a large body of indians on our abandoned camp-ground. Continued on, over stony spurs, but in a very elevated region, till in 4 hours more while descending a hill, I caught sight of Mt Tschastes, and the Snow Buttes, — Former bearing W. ½ S. latter S.W. by W. Our mien course S. Trails and other signs of indians having recently passed, with horses and mules. We descended from the heights, and rode over a plain of rolls and hillocks of loose white sand; and through a thick sage covered plain, and at 4 P.M. we camped in the upper end of an extensive grassy basin. A water hole and spring, about 1 mile below. An indifferent imitation of the hooting of an owl, by indians, alarmd the animals at night. Warned the sentinals that the yellow legs were about. Night very cold.

OCT: 1st   Clear, with frost. At 9½ A.M. we moved on. A controversy about course to travel. I told them it was all the same to me, as every mile produced some new scenery.

We proceeded up the valley, about 1 mile S.E. Then S. 3 miles, over very rugged plains and ridges of black volcanic angular fragments, till at merdn found an indentation with marsh, and rill; here we watered and rested awhile, and had another consultation in regard to the course: resulting in electing Jones to lead; and we proceeded. We soon turned right, gradually descending, and at length entered a very remarkable Defile.[117] The bottom of this singular place, is from 40 to 60 ft. wide, covered with fine grass, and a large brook meanders through it: — the banks lined with willows and rushes. The walls are perpendicular, rough on the left, and as smooth & regular on the right side, as if of regular masonry as we descended. The walls are from 10 to 25 feet high, & of dark and very hard plutonic rock. The plain above is on a level with the top of the walls, and covered with small angular blocks, of the same kind of stone. From where we entered, this ravine & creek runs S. about 8 miles, then sweeps to the S.E. a mile or so, and meanders, to the N.E., as far as the eye can trace it, near the base of distant mountains. What renders it most remarkable is the fact of the entire right hand wall being marked over, on every space the size of a hat, with strange and *ancient Hie[r]oglyphical Symbols!*[118] — These were originally well cut, and on a surface which can only be so marked by a steel instrument & hammer. And must have occupied hundreds, — a long time. Under faces of projections, and other places that I could not conveniently reach, were all engraved. Yet so old are they, that those places most exposed to the action of the elements are partially, and some entirely obliterated. There are none on the left hand wall, as it is more ir-regular. This defiled branch may be 20 or 30 miles long, and is, I dare [say] marked all the way. We rode several miles in it, and those who had been ahead some ways, says they are all along. (*Hieogliphic Defile*) The creek was crooked, rapid, and in some places deep. And we had to cross & recross several times, — often. (*Lodge*) As I was about to cross, where the willows were very thick, I noticed a beautiful vine clad lodge, formed of pales & thatched with rushes and grass. It had a couple of small rocks within, for the indian hooter [hunter?] to shoot the deer or other animal which might come to drink near him.[119] I called this Hieoglyphic Defile & creek —

I pictured several of the most distinct groups of symbols, and some look much like the Egyptian; But was compelled to have a friend at my elbow, with ready rifle, to look out for the Philistines while I sketched. — The com-pany going on, and singing out to come on, or we'd catch a d — d arrow! At 3 p.m. we discovered a pile where the right hand wall had fallen. We spurred and whipped, and scrambled, up to the plain. Kept S. over a very stony plain, with scattered sage, and gradually descended to a meadow of grass & marsh, with rills and water holes. It runs along the base of a mountain range — to the S.E.

Here we camped, on a tolerable dry grassy place, alongside a marsh. The mountain range near us, rises to a very high peak, and a gap in the hills — which run E.N.E.

Lassen objects to travelling farther to the E. or Northward, from the facts that our animals are tender-footed,[120] provisions reduced, late in the sea-son; and ground to go over between here and the settlements, that in very bad weather would be impracticable for our animals, and we should therefore lose them, if such a thing happened, as a very wet spell of weather soon. Grouse plenteous This is all a volcanic country. — The earth dark brown, and very fine, cracked all over. About 5 p.m. we sat down to our dinner-supper. And 4 men, on foot, started to reach the peak near us. Fuel sage bushes. As we passed over a sage plain, I noticed several skeleton-willow lodges, and Indian as well as horse and mule tracks abundant — Lassen quite dissatisfied with the conduct of some of the party. At dusk the 4 men returned, could not reach the summit; but could see the Hieglyphic creek, pass E. through a gorge, and thence down a plain to the S.

This is so strange a country, and never before visited by whites, that I have drawn a panoramic view of the Scenery, from the camp [see p. 554].[121]

oct. 2. — After considerable talk, and much perversity and discontent manifested, — Jones agreed to conduct the party on a S. course, and at 8½ a.m. we rode on. We followed a ravine, S. of the camp, and leading in a mien S. course through rough hills, for about 6 miles. This ravine was very zig-zag, in consequence of descending spurs. A very rough route. He halted at a point from whence, to follow the gorge, now becoming very narrow & rough, would take us S.E. and Lassen now swore that he would proceed no further to the E. of South: and struck off to the S. leaving the company to pursue the gorge. Merowitz accompanied us. — Thus in the heart of a rugged hostile country, our little party of 5 men, with 7 horses, moved off.[122] The entire company were short of provissions, and on that score we were safer; but on account of the indians, I thought it rather hazardous. However, we had to be wide awake, and keep ourselves on the qui vive for the Philistines. We have grown nearly as cunning as they are, and if they dont cabbage our horses will make little out of us. The company promised, as we parted, to turn S. and overtake us in 24 hours. Our course lay now, over an elevated plain, covered and McAdamized with angular hard volcanic rocks, from the size of one's head down to minute fragments and detritus. Occasionally we passed considerable masses of it. In an hour we reached a depression, which led us into a long, crooked, narrow, brushy and rocky defile. Followed down, till the rocks closed in, and it became a cañon. Willows and cotton woods, and a rill in it. At length, in 3 or 4 miles, the huge rocks so impeded our further progress, and a very suspicious looking place, for indians to pick us off, that Old Pete thought best to get out. We had to retrace our steps to where we could extricate our selves, — at least 2 miles back. On reaching the stony plain again, we kept down, with the cañon on our left, our mien course being about S. by E. while the cañon ran about S.E. Occasionally we passed over patches of baked & cracked earth, of a mouse-color, and very fine. The rough plain extended about 8 miles, when it shelved off to a lower plain of the fine ash-colored cracked earth, and covered with a growth of large sage bushes. This plain was troublesome to cross, the horses and mules sinking fetlock deep, as if going throug[h] a crust of half-froze ground. Plenty of horse & mule tracks, and manure, not over 10 months old. Saw also a recent indian trail. In the midst of this extensive plain, we saw a large shooting-lodge of the indians, constructed with sage bushes, for the purpose of shooting the large hares from, which are so numerous here.[123] This plain, in the Summer time, or Spring, is no doubt a great hunting-ground for the savages. Noticed in the cañon that we left this morning, a white calcarious deposite on many rocks. And also, in patches, on the large sage plain.

At Sun-Set, we struck down, into the edge of a large oval basin, apparently covered with grass; but on entering the bottom, found it to be a level of dried mud, cracked, with narrow fissures, in every direction, — not one square yard uncracked. What seemed at a distance to be such beautiful green grass, was only weeds, — growing about 10 ins: high. This, in the wet season, is an extensive lake of water. Length appears to be about 5 ms. At the S. or lower end, it contracts into a long irregular valley, turning to the S.E. — but there is a slight rise of ground below, completing the form of the basin. We crossed this dried up lake, about 2 miles over. Here was a stumbling ride; for the animals sunk to their fetlocks, at every step. We ascended a gentle rise of ground from the bottom, scattered over with stones and sage, followed up the stony dry-bed of a winter torrent, for about $\frac{1}{4}$ mile, and camped. 2 men rode up the hollow, about $1\frac{1}{2}$ miles, to a green spot, of willows & grass, where they found a spring-hole, nearly filled with trash, and returned with a kettle full of a saturated solution of vegetable matter, to make tea with. We tied our horses to the big stones, scattered around. While descending, to the mud lake, we observed that the indians had telegraphed us. Their smoke signal appeared on the high peak in rear of our last camp, and it was answered below the lake basin; in a narrow valley, and from thence by another still lower down. We travelled about 18 miles to day. The party agreed to keep the guard hours unchanged. — I am to have the first, Burton, the 2d Messer-Smith 3d, Isadore 4th, and Lassen the 5th, or morning watch. (On leaving the company I lent my pocket compass to Jones.) Night cold.

OCT. 3 — Very cold, ice formed in a cup just used. Early this morning, Burton, Isadore, and myself mounted, and drove our horses up the hollow, to drink. We took a shovel and 2 kettles along, and had quite a job to clean out the hole, and procure, when it had triturated, our kettles half-full of pretty thick water. The horses had to suck mud; and after a stay of $1\frac{1}{2}$ hours, we drove them down to camp, & breakfasted. Our tea was, of course, *black tea*. The wolves this morning saluted us with a reveillee. A clear fine day. We will remain here to-day, in hopes that the Company will join us. Our tea contained ingredients, this morning, that are not usually added to that beverage; — but which, I have no doubt, are very nutritious. — Such as, bugs, worms, ants, moss, roots, grass-seed, pieces of straw, &c.

At 11 A.M. Smith, Isadore, & Burton, mounted and drove the horses up to water, I directed them to a green patch, larger than that where the mud hole was; it is higher up the hill, and about 200 yds S. of the other. So they went there, & found a good spring, and plenty of fine grass. The horses had here a hearty drink, and grazed an hour and a half, & returned to camp. After they had brought down the horses, the 3 men rode over N.E. to look for the company. About 2 P.M. I was busy writing an account of these smoke signals, and mentioned to Lassen, what I was writing, when he exclaim'd, "there's one!" and pointed a little to the W. of N. — the trail on which we were travelling yesterday morning. Sure enough, there ascended the tall spiry column of black smoke, then another S. of it, and also a 3rd, S. of that. Which I told Pete was done in reference to Jones' company; and that they then were passing that way at the time.

Indian Smoke Signals

Every one knows that the fire-signals of the celtic nations were of great antiquity. The Digger indians make them as follows: — The lookout, on some eminence, perceiving the approach of strangers, in their territory, catches up a handful of dry grass, or dry sage-leaves; and ignites it with *fire-sticks*; throws on more dry grass, or leaves, causing the smoke to ascend, (in fine weather,) in a slender spindle of white smoke. They then thrown on green grass, or leaves; and the column of smoke changes to black. Then the nearest point, in the vale below, where the nature of the country, is favorable, on perceiving the signal on the height, makes its signal, &c. in the direction to be watched, or where the intruders are supposed to be going. It gives them a chance of driving off cattle, removing squaws, children, &c. and also puts them on the look out, to beset the intruders, or steal horses.[124]

At night, fire answers the same purpose. The *fire-sticks*, are 2, in number, — one about 10 ins: long, and ¾ in: square, drilled full of conical holes, about ¼ in.: in diameter and depth, The other stick is about 18 ins: long, cylindrical, ¾ in: diameter, and pointed at each end. These they carry in their quivers. I saw several, on the route. To produce fire, the indian lays down the square stick,[125] inserts an end of the round stick, in one of the conical holes, drops in a few grains of fine sand, and some crumbs of dry rotten wood, then rapidly whirls the cylindrical stick around, with his hands, by rolling it with the palms, and then applies the whisp of dry straw, and in a few seconds has a blaze —

An hour before Sun Set my 3 comrades returned. Said that they rode to the E. till they could see a lake, and one which they think Lassen had previously seen in his first trip. At the E. in the distance, were numerous fires. The country they passed over exceedingly rough. Being already mounted, they drove the horses to water and grass. So we had a late supper-dinner. A clear pleasant night.

These indians crawl up on any thing, by keeping behind the rocks and sage bushes, will peep through a bush, and perceiving all quiet, move up to another bush or rock, and at each, lay flat on his belly. Thus they can noise[less]ly approach very close. In a predicament like ours, we must watch the horses, who are ever afraid of wild indians, or in fact any thing creeping towards them, at night. And as their senses are keen, they are the best guide for a Sentinal's conduct at night. — The horse or mule, always snorts, and points his ears, looking towards the object which alarmed him. We generally lay down, near one of our horses, listen attentively, and look around, but never get up, and expose ourselves. The sleepers have the packs and pack saddles piled around them, for protection against arrows. I was a little astonished in the latter part of my watch, to-night, walking along stooping, when suddenly a hissing, like that made by an old gander, arose from the ground, near me, and a sound like that caused by dragging a rope over the ground, and through a bush. It must have been a large snake, which I came near treading upon.

OCT: 4 — A clear fine morning, we arose early. 3 men took the horses up to water, and 2 remained to guard them, while they grazed; and the other, brought water for culinary purposes, and to drink — The sun was ½ hour high, when we made a signal, to the horse-guard, who then drove them down, and we breakfasted. At about 8 A.M. not seeing our friends coming, we mounted, and moved off, on, a course a little E. of N. gradually winding around very stony low ridges & inclined plateaus, to S. of E. on a well beaten indian trail.[126] In about 6 miles, we reached a depression in the hills, and through a gap on our left, discovered a white sheet of water.[127] (*view of Lake Derby* [see p. 552])   Soon after we met a small wrinkled old indian, crying out, as he advanced, "Pi-hi!" — "pi-hi", — "pi-hi!" This is one of the murdering Piutes, or Piutahs. He shook hands with us. Wore a white deer skin mantle over one shoulder, and had on mocasins of the same. Quiver, bow & arrows, and something tied up in an old white rag. He mentioned the Snake word "*tabbaboo*" — white people.[128] And by signs informed us he had seen some white people, (probably our friends, — Jones & co. We gave him a brass ring & piece of tobacco, and proceeded   Soon after, on the right of the trail, I noticed a stone breastwork, about 3 ft. high, in shape of letter C, about 10 feet diam. In the middle were burnt sticks. This, no doubt was a blind, to shoot hares from. Basaltes cropping out the hills, and fragments scattered about, over the slopes. Several ranges of basaltic rock, forming low parapets, around the hills, on our right, were crowned with blocks of stone, piled up, by the indians, to shoot from.[129] In a couple of hours, we entered a shallow pass, very rocky — the winter drein of the hills, into the mud-lake on this side. Hills on our left, abrupt & rugged, but more gradual slope on our right, but rising to a greater height. Riding down this irregular and steep gorge, after crossing the divide, we saw 2 grey wolves, on our left, not over 60 feet from us; and they turned around, with great assurance, and stared at us. — Lassen fired his rifle at one, missing it, when they turned, and ran up the stony cliff, close together, and hid behind rocks. This, to me was an interesting ride; — wild and beautiful, as well as remarkable country! — The gorge expanded, the descent became smoother, and the bold mountain promontories on either hand, as we were leaving the slope for the basin, were majestic. The latter part of the descent, was slaty, then clay and gravel, with sage bushes, and lastly, white volcanic sandstone.

Before us lay an extensive sheet of water, margined with green willows, rushes and tall grass, this encircled by a sandy plain, diversified with patches of grass and sage bushes, and sprinkled with blocks and masses of white stone: The opposite side was walled in with very elevated and precipitous mountains, the white rocks and earth showing in streaks, patches, and masses, through the dark pine forrest which clad them from the water line to their lofty summits.[130] On our left, the lake extended 5 or 6 miles, to its lower end and as the enclosing mountains receded they grew darker, and mingled with other ranges, in shades of blue. Small sand & rock islets, with willows, were sprinkled here and there in the bosom of the clear white water, and a narrow point of dark rocks, ran out in the lake a mile below; — on the extremity of which, there ascended a spiral of faint blue smoke, — the Indian's signal, that strangers were in their lake basin.

We passed through a large patch of wild mustard, stalks, as large as my finger, and their heads on a level with my shoulder, on a tall horse. I plucked some of the Seed, and found them quite pungent. This was on the last slight declination of the base of the hills, where we struck an indian trail, and about to turn on it to the right to follow the margin of the lake up, in order to reach its head; when a most extraordinary natural curiosity attracted my attention. (*Capital looking Rocks*)   I had seen large lumps of white calcareous rocks, as I thought; when I noticed a large and rude block of this stone, and beside it, another, — most symetrically formed, — resembling an Egyptian Capital of a Column; and appeared as perfect as if turned in a machine. I was so astonished, at sight of this architectural block, that I looked around, expecting to see other portions of some ancient ruins. I was not convinced of its being a mere freak of nature, till I rode up, and examined it; and found it rough, except on the side we first saw it; and that side is as complete as if chisseled. We proceeded, and in a short distance, on our right, saw numerous blocks of it — some very large with masses of earth, and other rock, forming a long point in the plain; — from the mountain spur, whose tall head towered above, in the back ground; and from some part of this mountain, the masses of stone below had rolled down.

Large hares and grouse numerous; and judging from the fresh foot prints, indians are equally so. Caught sight of a couple of the *Natives*, about 200 yds. ahead, on right of the trail, but only saw them for a moment. — They hid behind rocks and bushes. Some of the tracks were of small children. Travelled several miles, partly along the margin of the lake, and then on the banks of a creek that empties in it, on this side. The creek, here, is broad and deep, and very high perpendicular banks of rich alluvial earth; dense willows along its banks. We tried several places in vain, to descend & ford. This creek comes from the W. — heads perhaps 10 miles from where it enters the lake in the same mountain from whence we obtained water, on the other side. Is very sinuous; and a couple of miles above the lake, it occasionally expands, and contains islands, of every size. — All these, like the banks of the stream, have a very close growth of willows on them: In some places, where the creek is narrow, the shrubbery hides its waters. Ducks cranes, and geese, quacking and gabbling every where: — in the stream, on the lake, and flying over, in all directions. As we proceeded, saw smoke ahead, and soon perceived that it spread across the trail, and was continued above; and caused by the indians, burning the grass, to prevent us from ascending the valley, as they thought; — We continued to advance however, till we saw the flames, and observed that the combustion was carried from the creek, — 10 ft. on our left, towards the hills on our right, — several miles. And was being continued in each direction. Lassen was ahead, and I brought up the rear; and he cried out, for me to keep my eyes on the right side, while he looked out for the left. And thus, — with ready rifles, we moved on. — Reached the flames, after passing over considerable burnt space; I looked sharp, but could see no living thing, but our party. — The indians kept off, under cover of the thick black smoke. The dry grass, weeds, &c. snapped & cracked, and the flames flickered around and before us; causing our horses to snort, & hurry along. In about ¼ mile we got ahead of it. The flames and smoke had reached the foot hills, behind which the rascally savages were. We followed this creek up some 6 miles, looking for a ford; and as it was late in the afternoon, and we had to fortify our selves for the night, against the barbarous horde that infest this basin and its waters, and who have watched us all day; we determined to effect a crossing at the most favorable place, now at hand. We dismounted, and cut away the brush on the edge and sides of the bank, and also cut the bank, so that our horses could descend without falling. One man waded across, and [we] led our horses down, mounted them, and rode across, at the opposite side threw the riatas, (halter ropes) up, to the man on the bank above, who pulled, while we whipped & spurred up the steep bank. Drove the pack horses up. — We then in a few yards, reached a low broad island, by a well-beaten indian trail, and crossed this island, under a bower of willows, arched over head, and quite dark. This was a crooked passage, of about 50 yards through, and appeared to be a resort of the indians and *other beast* — Emerged from the bower passage and the creek bottom, and turned around to travel down on that side, to seek a camping-place. 5 Indians, in this covered-way, could have easily pierced each of us through the heart with arrows. We descended the stream about 2 miles, and reached an expansion of the creek bottom, with gentle steppes, leading to the edge of the stream, and full of tall green grass, and scattered Willow bushes, Rode to where the willows were large and very thick. on the brink of the stream. This spot we selected for our camp. We dismounted in a small semi-circle of large close willows, in a bite [bight] of the stream, unsaddled, and then led our horses out, and tied them to the surrounding bushes, to graze. We now chopped away some of the willows, to form a more secure nook, and in that recess, spread our blankets, and lay down our saddle-pillows, side by side; and across the front, piled the packs and pack saddles. Made a small fire, cooked, and supped; and near dusk, tied our horses close up. I took my rifle and sat behind a bush, and my comrades laid down to sleep.

Just after night closed in, the wolves commenced yelling, close by; which I thought sounded very much like an imitation; however, it was echoed & re-echoed, in the distance, around the basin. The horses expressed uneasiness, about the proximity of something unpleasant, and their attention seem[ed] directed to the point where we descended. When relieved, I told my friend to pay attention to the fact, laid down, and slept soundly. Very cold night.

OCT. 5 — Frost and ice. Wild fowl, innumerable, in the waters, and flying about, quaking and gabbling. Watered our horses early, and breakfasted. Yesterday morning, along lower part of this stream, I noticed several skeleton Willow lodges; and on the margin of the lake I saw many places where the indians had slept. — These are of fine grass, cut and laid down in a circular form, making a soft mat, on which these biped animals curl up, like a cat or dog, and sleep.

We had just concluded our humble breakfast; (jerky & tea,) when the approach of something, attracted our attention. — A couple of indians pushed aside the willows, and entered our sylvan nook. — One was a grey-headed old fellow, the other a young man. — They seemed to pay little attention to us; went to the fire, crouched by it, warmed their hands, and eyed us with a vacant stare. — "Hallo!" said I, addressing the old fellow; "Where did you come from, Pompey?" Seeing that I spoke to him, he made signs, that he was cold, and wished to warm himself; and that he had slept close by, last night, in the grass! "Oh, ho!" said I, to my comrades, — "that accounts for the uneasiness of our horses, all night." — The old man wore a scull-cap, of a dingy white color, with a tassel of braided grass attached. — And a mantel of rabbit or hare-skins. — This was formed of rolls of the skin, sewed together, and white deer-skin mocasins. His comrade was more indifferently clad, — having no other covering than a scant, and very dirty, dressed deer-skin, over his shoulders; he also wore skin mocasins. Both had quivers, full of arrows, and a bow. These they laid on the ground, close to their heels. Lassin gave them a handful of jerked beef; and while they were eating it, I sketched the old wild-boy. (*Pautah Indian*) We packed, saddled, and mounted; — the indians watching every movement. — We rode out of the bottom, leaving them to enjoy the jerky and fire. It was about 8 O'clock, when we emerged from the creek bottom, and struck a little N. of E. over the plain, for the head of the lake, on the other side; changed our course, and swept around to the S.E. over an irregular plain, of sand, sage, and grass; — and in about 6 miles, reached the upper, or S. end of the Lake. It was near noon, and our horse thirsty; so we resolved to halt and rest here, preparatory to climbing what looked much like an impracticable mountain. The spot we rested on, was about 50 yards from the lake shore, apparently about 20 feet above the water. Clumps of willows, and springs and holes of clear fine water by us; and all around excellent grass. We unpacked & unsaddled, and let the horses graze, while we lay in the grass, eat jerky, smoked our pipes, and rested.

(*Lake Derby*) Before us stretched this long and beautiful sheet of water. Just below, tall cranes waded about, and flocks of geese and ducks were swimming on its bosom, and flying over.

On the left stood the tall dark volcanic mountain,[131] on the other side of which we camped on the 1st, the same on which the indian's sent up their signal, of our entering the mud basin, and the same of which I pictured the profile (4th). Lower down, on the same side, I could discern the gap where we descended into the basin; and where now arose a signal, probably indicating that we are yet here. Below, the mountains retire in low blue distance. From thence, the boundaries sweep around to the right, rising as they approach, till on my right, they carry their crude and pine-clad heights in the upper air. Lassen thinks this Lake is 15 miles long; and is probably about 6 miles broad, at the widest part.[132] As this country has never been explored, — I shall take the liberty of naming this beautiful Lake, after my highly esteemed friend, Derby, of the U. S. Top¹ Engineers. (Capt. Derby is now engaged in surveying in the southern part of California)

A half hour's rest, and we saddled up, to leave this beautiful but dangerous place. Rode S. about ¼ mile, to the foot of the mountain, and commenced ascending by following a depression, which dreined the rains and melted snows, in the wet season. — Lower part dwarf oaks, interspersed with pines and cedars; all the trees above were pines and cedars, of every variety and size. The hollow contained willows, poplars, and thick undergrowth. Very steep ascent. Rocks are a decripitating sienite, feldspar predominating. This white rock presented every form and size. Square and angular blocks, rounded masses, and immense piles. The greater part however, were rounded, by the action of the elements, proving the rigor of the winters. It cropped out the hill sides every where, but on the crests of the hills, stood in bold masses. — The detritus whitened the hills, and it looked like sand. We soon struck an indian trail, and followed it. When we had ascended some distance, I caught a passing glimpse of the white lake, far below us. The hollow has now deepened, and contracted into a very rugged gorge, filled with immense blocks and masses of stone, and stately pines, besides dense scrub, and fallen trunks of trees. We had to ride cautiously, — with one hand promptly guiding the horse, and the other, as promptly changing the position of the rifle, that it might not strike a tree or a rock. It was also necessary to look out for the long horizontal arms of the pines, to prevent being *headed*, if not unhorsed. Occasionally we were compelled to dismount, and lead our horses. We were, at length obliged to scramble up the left hand hill, to extricate ourselves from what was rapidly becoming an impassable cañon. We now followed a crest, ascending gently, for a few hundred yards, and reached the small flat top, on which stood a number of huge square blocks of stone, resembling a promiscuous group of old castles. — We had to ride between a couple, — a narrow gateway, — where I drew my legs up on the horse, to prevent being jambed; passing them we stopped a while to blow. Lassen rode one way, and I another, to ascertain where we get out. In about 50 feet, I came to the brink of a precipice, some thousand feet, — all below masses of large rock, pines & cedars; the deep cañon at the base, was the head of the gorge we had ascended in. Lassen, on my right, 100 yards, found also a *"jumping off"* place; so, after much difficulty, — finding and driving our pack horses through the labarynth of huge blocks, and big trees, turned left, and in half an hour reached the summit of this steep and rugged mountain. The indian trail below, followed the gorge. We found the spring sources of the streams which ran down each side of this range. One N. empties into the lake, and the other, as far as we can see it, S. — These sources are not over 400 yds asunder. We descended the southern slope, in a marshy hollow, a few hundred yards, and camped. This is one of the most romantic camping spots I ever made, — a *tall* picnic. — I judge the altitude to be about 7000 feet. A large tree had blown down, and the roots torn out the soil, leaving a large deep hole; this was full of clear cold water. Rills, marsh, rushes and excellent grass, abounded. Willows, poplars, & cotton-wood trees plentiful; Around us, except to the S. the peaks rose 300 or 400 feet, — piled up with rock, and thickly timbered: while S. the hollow rapidly descended, thick set, with trees of a small size; and a gap there showing the clear sky. On a grassy slope, a little above the moisture of the bottom, on the W. side, beneath a large grey granitic boulder, we spread our blankets for repose; made a fire, (plenty of good fuel) and soon enjoyed our supper and pipes. (*Camp scene*)　I observed to old Pete, that I apprehended we might get the gout; "Why?" asked the old man; "because," said I, "we live so *high*." Plenty of rose-bushes here, and delightful pods. At dusk we drove our horses up, and tied them to the trees close by, and I laid close under a plumb bush, with my rifle, to guard my comrades while they snored. Night very cold: However, when relieved, I slept pretty well, though we had to douse the fire after tea.

ocт. 6 — Jack Frost pinched our toes, informing us that mountaineers should stir early, which we did. While I was concocting breakfast, Lassen proceeded down the gulch, to look for a deer; but returned to breakfast without one. At 8 a.m. we moved on, endeavoring to keep a S: course, but it proved to be a very devious as well as rugged line of descent. The rock, on this side, is darker than that of the other.[133] —

We passed over very steep & rocky ridges, through hollows, beset with granitic blocks and masses, fallen trees, and thick scrub. — During which, we had to dismount, and lead our horses, 6 times. About 3 p.m. we descended into a narrow valley, containing much long dry grass, dry-bed of a brook, and scattered pines and willows; but the heights on each side, were of the same character as we have just left behind us: rode up to the head of it, — a small semi-circle, surrounded by hight [high] & steep hills. — Here, close to the foot of a hill, we found a couple of water holes, — the resort of thirsty savages, and wild beast. Around was plenty of good grass. In the edge of the timber we camped. Watered our thirsty and jaded horses. Burton shot a grouse with his rifle, as he rode along, it was perched on the limb of a pine. (We saw plenty of deer tracks, but no deer. On descending to this mountain vale, we also saw the recent track of an indian.) We stewed our fowl, with some chopped up jerky, and had a fine supper. As usual, near dusk we drew in our horses and tied them up. Again I stood my first relief, and sat out my two hours between a couple of large pines, from whence I could see all around, and not be seen myself. The wind blew strong, sweeping in heavy gusts through the hollows and tree tops, but our deep nook could not be disturbed by it. During my watch, heard a rustling on the hill-side above, and a horse looked there; but it was too dark to discern any thing, and as the horses evinced no alarm, I presume it was only some sneaking wolf.

OCT. 7 — After an early breakfast, we mounted, in a drizzle, and rode down this vale, about ½ mile E. — then S.E. several hundred yards, and finally N.E. about 1 mile, and left it to our left, and crossd steep granite studded ridges and table-lands, and descended to a chain of very narrow meadows. — All the way in a bleak rain. About mid-day, entered a narrow vale, where we saw, a short distance ahead of us, a fire, and a figure moving about it. On coming up, found that it was a camp of indians; and from the light color, good looks and form of the young man, at the fire, judged that they were a party of Feather river indians. By the side of a large prostrate pine — blown down; was a fire of branches and bark. And a young indian, probably about 18 years of age, with a skin over his shoulder, was warming himself. On riding up, he made signs to us, that the rain was very disagreeable, and the fire was the reverse. — Of the truth of this, we had no doubt. A bark shelter had been formed over the long projecting roots of the tree, under which lay a skin of a brown bear. — This is probably the youth's chamber and bed. — At the other extremity of the tree, (40 feet apart) a larger bark lodge was constructed, over a limb; in which were an old man, a young squaw, 5 small children, bear-skins, quivers, bows, arrows, &c. I concluded that this was the family of the youth, and that the old cock was his daddy; and very likely the old fellow had sent the grandmother to wet her grey hairs in the cold rain, and dig roots, or catch small fish, in some brook. Lassen motioned the yellow lad to hand him a chunk, by which to light his pipe; when lit, he threw down the fire, and observed to us, as he turned his horses head from the fire, "let's push on." At which the indian said *"vamos?"* Now here was shelter and comfort got up on the spur of the moment. The body of the tree served to break off the wet cold gale, its limbs and roots furnished ready supports, the bark covered them in, and the rest of the bark, branches, &c supplied the fuel. — A very handy life! [134]

We bid adieu to the tree settlement, and crossed a very stony table-land, in a storm of rain, hail, and thunder. In course of an hour, the wind lulled, and it commenced snowing, with hail and rain; we were very wet and chilled through. Continued this most disagreeable ride, till near Sun Set, alternately in the valley bottom, and over low stony spurs. This valley runs up to the S. throwing out branch vales, on either side, and is traversed by a creek. [135] We ascended beyond the head of the stream, and 5 or 6 miles up on, over an elevated range, — destitute of grass and water; then had to retrace our steps, and camp near the brook, among pines & willows, about dusk. We judge that we have travelled, to this; not including the distance ahead, about 8 miles, to-day. The rock here, is granite, and compact red sand-stone, boulders of granular quartz, and masses of white quartz, — this extends some distance below. From the spot where the indians were camped, and perhaps for a couple of miles this side, the hollows gulches, and elevations, were covered with a detritus of a dark purple volcanic-rock, which no doubt came from the surrounding heights, which were crowned with masses and rows, like parapets, of such rock. — I examined some cubical and flat pieces, which I found were either sand-stone, or granular quartz, altered by fire. We were wet, and very cold, and therefore built a large fire, thinking it would be no more disagreeable to die by arrows, than to freeze to death. We set up our tattered *shelter*, I mounted guard, and soon my reeking comrades were snoring. Flying clouds all night.

OCT. 8 — Commences cloudy, with ice. My horse missing; I was alarmed, and we immediately instituted a search, and soon found him. — Last night, when our horses were brought up and secured, I tied mine to a large log, among the willows, and it appears that he had dragged his clog, and ascended the stream about 200 yards. After bringing him up, my pack-poney stumbled, and rolled into the brook, wedging himself lengthwise, in narrow boders [boulders?], — between the deep soft banks. Here was a fix! The pony jammed tight, head in the cold stream, and heels up! While one pryed under him with a lever, the others pulled on his halter, and giving several jerks, and finally a long pull, and a strong pull, and a pull all together, we extricated the clumsy brute from his droll position. After breakfast, we rode down the creek, about 1 mile, — left the bottom and crossed low ridges and mountains, descended to a small grass-plain, and ascended a narrow vale, with a brook, going S.W. Noticed sand-stone, white quartz, and basaltic rocks. 3 hour's ride took us to a jungle of willows and cotton-wood. We travelled on an indian trail. Old Pete being ahead, and about to enter the thicket, his horse *shyed* at something on the right, which we perceived, and turned aside to see what occasioned it. — About 10 paces to the right of where the trail enters the thicket, — surrounded by willows, was an indian's bark lodge, and embers burning in front of it. On looking in, we saw some deer-skins spread out, mocasins, &c. laying around, proving that the late occupant, on seeing us approaching, had fled into the jungle; And Lassen's horse saw him or her, vamose. We did not disturb any thing, but rode on, forcing our way through the thicket, — a scrub ride, of several hundred yards. — Emerging, the valley expanded. We kept in the bottom, on a course a little S. of W. and nooned, in the grass, near the stream, and a clump of willows: here we unpacked, and let our horses drink and graze, while we rested. We had eat some bits of jerky, and just lit our pipes, when an old indian emerged from the willows. — He came up, and squatted on him [his] hams by us; and made signs, (as Lassen explained them,) that in a day's march, in the direction we were going, there was plenty of gold, and miners at work there. For this information L. gave him an old check shirt, and a small piece of bread. — Lassen wished him to pilot us to the place, but he shook his head, and remained on the spot, on his haunches.

After we left the *bark-lodge thicket,* this morning, we rode across barren dry mud plains, sprinkled over with slaty fragments. Indian fires were burning on each side of the valley, in the skirts of the timber, and on our right, several bark lodges. On the same side saw a grey wolf. Hawks and ravens numerous. The valley will probably average about $1\frac{1}{2}$ miles wide, to this point. The stream runs Easterly. We now continued our march up the valley, rising imperceptably, and the valley contracting in width, and soon found that a dry grass plain, of such little elevation that we could only judge it was, by the fact, separated the waters running in different directions. — Now we are on the head of a stream running W — not 50 yards from the other. This we followed down, till the encroaching rocky spurs forced us to cross them, winding our devious course among large granite rocks, and pines, close above the rapid stream — which here becomes a large dashing roaring creek. We scrambled on, occasionally dismounting and leading our horses through difficulties, which might endanger the necks of both horse and rider, if mounted; and thus along the abrupt rocky declivity did we descend the gorge, till it became so very steep, and obstructed with huge rocks, that further travel, with horses, was impracticable. — Here was a large dam and Cataract, and about 2 miles below, the stream and Cañon bent suddenly to the N.W. We now rested, dug a hole, and washed for gold, but found none. So we had to retrograde, — retrace the troublesome trail ¼ mile, and about 4 P.M. camped in a grass plot in a small bend of the rapid creek, surrounded by willows. This is a very deep dell, — tall rugged pine clad peaks hem us in. Under a stunted pine we spread our blankets. The creek here, is about 20 feet wide, deep alluvial banks, and soft bottom, containing large granite boulders. It can only be forded about 1 mile above this. The hill on the N. side contains much white quartz. Burton went over, and brought back specimens of white and rose quartz. About Sun-Set, while we were securing our horses, for the night, we saw a small white indian dog descending the S.E. spur, and approaching camp. He walked up, pretty close; was a perfect skeleton, had red eyes, and open, frothy mouth. I thought the varmint was mad, and drove him away. — He went around, by the brink of the creek, and approached a mare, and smelt at one of her hind feet, while she was grazing. She suddenly saw him, and was exceedingly alarmed; — attempted to spring on him, with her fore-feet, and uttered a singular cry and snort. — The ugly cur dodged her, and ran off, down stream. Flying clouds and cool all day. Patches of snow surround us. Very cold night; freezing. During my, first watch, the skeleton dog re-appeared, and I began to think he must be "*Snarleyyow*". He approached a horse, and suspecting that he was but the *evant courier* of a biped cur, I levelled my rifle, and fired, but missed him; it was too dark to see through the sight of my rifle. He again appeared, in the 2nd — (Burton's watch;) and he blizzened, and missed him. — After which he disappeared. "D — n the dog!" cried old Lassen, when I fired, — "his master is close by, somewhere!" Poor wretch! it was hunger, no doubt, that induced him to visit the camp, so importunately. The dogs, of all these indians, are poor, and have to subsist like wolves; for their owners never think of giving them any thing but well-polished bones.

It was so cold, that I only slept about 3 hours, and with a blanket around me sat, drawn up, over a bank of hot embers, till light enough in the morning, to build up a good fire.

OCT. 9 — Plenty of ice, this morning. Jack Frost roused all hands very early, and we soon procured cedar logs, and had a large fire. Hot tea and cakes, with a smoke, by a good fire, were duly appreciated. We made an early start; — retraced yesterday's trail here, several miles, then struck over the hills, to the E. — very rocky. We then ascended a hollow, and crossed a plain, with a rill, grass, and sage bushes. — Still Easterly. Then struck a stream, and followed it down, till pent up in an impracticable gorge, like yesterday, and late in the afternoon. Here again, we had to retrace our steps. The hills are of a decripitating sienite, gneiss, talcose slate, Schistose rock, iron ore, quartz of various species, — some crystallized; calcedony, agates, carnelians, chlorite of iron, green fibrous talc, semi-opal, serpentine, feldspar — of every hue; brown hematite, — enclosing curiously formed crystals of feldspar.[136]

We saw a squaw, about a quarter of a mile below, apparently catching fish, with a willow-scoop. Lassen shouted to her, which on hearing, she ran up a hill & disappeared. Several indian fires below. This is a branch of Feather river. We forded the stream with much difficulty, on account of the willows, and camped S. of the Creek, ¼ mile, on a ridge, in pine timber, close to a hollow; with grass, and a rill that empties into the creek. Smith's (Messersmith) horse gave out, early in the day, and he had to exchange him for one of the pack-horses.

We had to ride about 40 feet through a marsh, and very close willows, forcing our way at the risk of being stripped of our breeches & dragged out of the saddle. — Then descended a steep soft bank & crossed, — in shallow water. This raised bed of the stream, was about 10 ft long, — above and below the bank the water was deep; and here, where we crossed, the descent to the deep water was sudden. The opposite bank was steep, thick set with dry & green willows, and about 20 feet high. We crossed, and reined up, at the brink of the deep hole, then dismounted in a scraggy bush, held on with one hand, and with the other, threw the halter-rope (riatta) up, to a man on the edge of the brushy cliff, who pulled, while the one below urged his horse up: and the rider followed.

We cut grass in the marsh and carried up to camp, till we had acquired a sufficiency, for our horses through the night: after which we drove them up, and secured them to the branches of a fallen pine, and gave them their grass. A very cold night, and we dare not have a bright fire. On guard, I noticed nothing particular, only a grey wolf, who made several circuits round the camp, and finding there was some one twigging him, went off, — down the hollow.

Awful papers! Such a night's repose! Jack frost pinched us.

OCTOBER 10, 1850 - JULY 20, 1851*

The Honey Lake Region to Washington City

OCT: 10th Cloudy, damp, cold morning. We drove our horses down to the wet hollow to graze, with a sentinel to watch them.

Lassen said that during his morning watch, a wolf descended the hill, and approached us: he took aim at him, but the moisture caused the cap to snap only, and the wolf then went off. Very cold rain. We are undetermined on the next direction of travel. After breakfast Isadore and Burton mounted their horses, to ride southerly, and endeavor to ascend a prominent peak in that direction, several miles, overlooking a cañon. They had not proceeded far, when heavy clouds obscured the peak and hills around it: soon after we were visited by squalls of snow, rain, and sleet, from the S.E.

At about 11 A.M. our Comrades returned; they had reached the peak indicated, from whence they could discern Lake Derby, bearing N. — and in the same direction three buttes: — and that S. about one day's ride, there was an extensive valley. — Below them, a little N. of W. was a deep cañon. When then [they] had proceeded about half the distance, they were overtaken by rain and snow, and the weather was so cold that they were compelled to dismount, make a fire, and wait there till the bleak storm passed off. On their return, they saw a bark lodge, with a fire before it, about 200 yards on their right, several miles from this. They did not visit it, but think it was the one from whence the very hydrophobical-looking dog evaporated.

Meridian, flying clouds and pleasant weather.

We saddled and pursued our travel, for the valley to the S. descried from the peak. We ascended the neighboring hills, and rode over them on a S.W. course; and descended into a narrow valley, with a branch, grass, and willows. Rode up the bottom — westerly, till 2 P.M. when we reached a cedar grove

* Excerpted from the 1853 version to complete Bruff's account.

on a slight hillock, near the creek, and where the valley is upwards of a mile broad; its bottom being a fine grass-plain; and camped. The weak condition of our horses, compelled us, thus early, to halt. Burton's poney gave out on the heights, since which he had driven him along.

South of camp, about 50 yards, meanders this sparkling branch of Feather river. Our position is on a very pretty spot, with the dark cedars, and masses of white rock, surrounded by light green grass and willows. Between us and the stream, on the slope of the knoll, ensconced amongst rocks and cedars, are the crumbling remains of Indian winter quarters. — Four crotched posts, — 4 feet high, and 5 apart, with poles, &c. exhibited the skeleton of a once good house. Deer skulls, horns and bones, were around the precincts.

In the afternoon the wind changed to the N.W. and blew cold: but the day closed with clear weather.

This is a very pretty valley. — The rocks, — scattered about, and cropping out of the hill-sides, and from the surface of the plain, are light and dark granite, and white and yellow granular quartz.

Dense pine forrests clothe the steep slopes of the enclosing mountains; and cedars darkly cover their bases.

We are now, certainly, far past the hostile region, and can indulge ourselves with comfortable fires. — Pine and cedar logs were soon gathered, and made us comfortable. At dusk, we drove up the horses, and picketted them within pistol-shot of camp: and kept guard, on their account. In the first watch, the horses evinced alarm at something on the N. side of us, at the base of the hills, about 400 yards distant: which I think was only some prowling wolf. Heavy frost.

OCT. 11th   The wolves sounded a grand reveillee, close to camp, about daybreak; which, with the intense cold, compelled us to arise, and replenish our fire. We saw several deer, about half a mile below, and Burton went after them; but they saw him, and fled across, to the southern hills. After an early breakfast, we mounted, and rode up the bottom about 2 miles, to the divide; — a transverse rise, of little elevation above the main bottom, but sufficient to separate, by a few hundred yards, two streams — running in opposite directions. We descended this western vale; which, unlike the other, is narrow and crooked. In a couple of miles it contracted so, by the obtruding rocking [rocky] spurs, on either side, that we had frequently to cross the stream. The bottom had much marsh, and numerous knolls, with clumps of cotton-wood, willows, and cedars. The stream was thickly bordered with the same growth. Hills stony and brushy; with open forrests of large pines over their lower slopes, and above heavily timbered. The brush, rocks, and narrow deep creek, occasionally forced us through portions of the frozen marsh, wading, breaking through the icy crust, and stumbling in holes, was irksome to horses and riders: this, alternating with clambering over rocky and scrubby spurs of the hills, and crossing and recrossing the branch, for about 6 miles, was tedious and unpleasant travelling.

The valley now had narrowed to a dell, and not far below us, became a cañon. So we ascended a steep rugged mountain, on our right (N.W. side). We endeavored to keep along the slope, and follow the stream, as far as we could. Rocks, loose stones, great pines, and prostrate trunks, impeded our travel much. One horse lost his pack, giving us much trouble to catch him, on the steep acclivity. — We were all compelled to dismount, and lead or drive the horses. — Isadore's little mare fell, — and rolled between a couple of parallel rocks, where she stuck for a while, *keel-up*, roots upper most, till extricated. We now ascended a stony depression, to reach the top of the mountain. — About 3 P.M. found moisture and willows, and continued further up, about 2 miles, to a circular hollow, with springs and branches, marsh, good grass, willows, and poplars: about pistol-shot from the crest of the hill. Around were dark rocks and a thick pine forrest. Here, alongside a great pine trunk, and close to a spring, we dismounted, to bivouack. A fine nook, for the purpose. Turning our weak and jaded horses loose, to rest and graze, we made a large fire beside the prostrate trunk. Lassen walked up to the crest of the hill, and on returning told us that there was a large valley W. of this, about one day's travel off. Within a couple of rods, are the remains of two bark lodges, built around pines, by the Indians. I passed several of them, while coming through the valley. I was so tired and thirsty, when I reached the springs, that on dismounting, I imprudently drank too freely of the cold water, which gave me a very severe attack of cholic, for which I took a dose of laudanum. When we had ascended the hill, about half-way, on looking through the creek gorge — to the West, I caught sight of the Snow Butte again.

The principal rock here is granite, but there is slate, white quartz, & chromate of iron, containing octahedral crystals. I stood guard with a severe headache; and when relieved, laid down with considerable fever, slept uncomfortably, and dreampt that I was abandoned by my family, my friends, and the whole world, because I had not found a gold mine.

OCT. 12. Clear and frosty. We arose from our white pallets, at day-break, had an early breakfast, and soon after were in the saddle. We rode across the marsh and rill, ascended a branch of the hollow, northerly, to a more elevated position, but where we might be enabled to descend on the other side. In this hollow we went several miles, trending around to the W. and we reached a gap, — from which we had a fine view of Feather river valley, and the Snow-Butte, to the Westward. We Here again we [sic] descended into another narrow vale, with brook[,] grass, and willows, and here again the encroachment of rugged spurs, forced us to cross and recross, several times. At length we were obliged to ride over a very rocky and steep spur. — Thick brush, and loose stones, rendered it irksome. The branch of Feather-river, at its base, descended a crooked, rocky, and brushy gorge, and then meandered through a narrow bottom. We had now to descend the rugged slope, and dismounted, to lead our jaded brutes down. We wound around the slopes of the hills, between rocks, and stately trees, till we reached a hollow, with a stream in it. We descended this, — alternately crossing spurs and streams, till it became a deep gorge, — occasionally expanding, and giving space to considerable bottoms, with long green grass, rushes, rose-bushes, several varieties of currents, oaks, sycamores, cotton-wood, cedars, and willows. Rocks, granite, white quartz — and talcose slate. We halted to try for gold, and dismounted in the bottom of the gorge, in a tangled thicket, of trees and brush, with tall grass & rushes. Barely sufficient level spaces to permit our horses a footing to graze. We dug a hole, and washed out the earth, but found *no oro:*

I have been quite ill, all day, with pains in the chest and bowels, accompanied with fever, for which I took a dose of laudanum & rhubarb.

After an hour's rest, we remounted, and rode on, down the tangled and rugged glen: and near Sun-Set reached a flat grassy spot, in a pretty valley of a branch of Feather river, and bivouacked.

The mountains on our left, are very tall, steep, rugged, pine-clad, and dark; with small patches of snow sprinkled over them.

While following an indian trail, — a short distance back, along the base of the hills, which were on our right, we passed two bark lodges, and a little further, another lodge of willows, covered with earth, close by which stood a tall, slender, willow acorn-crib. Between these was a miniature willow lodge, — about 3 feet high; perhaps made by children, or for some favored dog. The earth-covered lodge is a winter habitation, the others are for temporary purposes.

(The spot where we now are, is known, and is only about two day's travel from the old Depôt Camp, on Feather river, near the emmigrant route.[1]

We soon had a fine blazing fire, of logs, and supped. — A pot of hot tea relieved me much, as I had been ill all day. We chatted and smoked our pipes, and then slept soundly, though the night was frosty.

OCT. 13th   We breakfasted, and were in the saddle betimes, riding westerly, along the base of the tall hills, for some distance; over several hills, — the rocks of which were granite, quartz, and slate. Our course now W.N.W. over rough ground. The valley and stream increase as we descend, — on a well-beaten indian trail: though latterly much travelled by adventurers like ourselves. The prospectors call this stream the N. branch of the Middle Fork of Feather river. Here we made another examination for gold, and, as usual, without success. A cold rain and strong wind, made the ride disagreeable.

About mid-day we reached a part of the valley, which I recognized as a place we visited some time since, when I discovered the gold-bearing quartz vein. And in a little while after, I saw, hanging on the branch of a small tree, on the right of the trail, a pair of oval snow-shoes, formed of willow,[2] which I had before seen there. On the opposite side of the valley there is a large fire. Indian lodges are numerous in this valley, — composed of willows, rushes, bark, &c.

In the afternoon, our travelling was good, over slight elevations, narrow marshes, small rills, across several low hills, through a pine forrest, and near Sun Set, reached the rugged descent to the main Feather river valley, below the Cascades, — before described. This descent was bad enough when we achieved it before; but was worse now, on account of the jaded state of our horses, and their being so sore-footed. I was chafed much, and quite lame. About half down the devious rugged trail, while leading my horse, a stone on which I trod, — rolled, and I let go the bridle, and fell, and rolled over twice. On recovering, my horse was standing over me, and close behind him stood a pack-horse. I expected them to make a deep *impression on my feelings*, but they did not, and I escaped with some bruises, a fracture of my rifle-stock and loss of all the balls, from my pouch.

Passed the triple ford, without accident, crossed a plain, then over a stony elevation, through pine timber, across a marshy bottom, forded a brook, and reached the foot of the hills. Here, under a large pine, we pitched our ragged tent, and soon had a fine fire in front, against a large log. We were wet and cold, and the fire and hot supper were very grateful. We turned our jaded brutes loose, to graze in the wet bottom below, near a lagoon full of wild fowl. We are now but 3 miles from our old camping-place, but our animals are too jaded, to urge them there to-night.

Flying clouds at dark, but soon after it cleared off, and ice rapidly formed.

OCT. 14, 1850   The cold spoiled our nights' repose, and turned us out at day-break. We replenished our fire, soon after day break, had breakfast, from which had left a plate of stewed jerky; and a piece of flour-cake, — the last of our provisions. We had just arrived at these results when a good-looking Indian, of a light color, came to camp. He wore a blanket over his shoulders, which was tied around his waist: and had a deer-skin quiver, with bow and arrows. A dark cotton handkerchief was tied around his head, and small white vest buttons answered for ear-pendants. He made signs that he was going on a deer-hunt. We offered him the remains of our breakfast, which he tasted, and declined, signifying that he had breakfasted heartily at the Depot Camp. I explained, by signs, to him, how the Pautahs tried to kill me: which he seemed to understand; and in like manner, informed me that the Yuba Indians[3] once tried to shoot him, and one of their arrows penetrated through his blanket, wounding his left arm, and showed me the scar. The ducks were making such a quacking, in the lagoon below, that Lassen and Burton took their rifles, and proceeded — to shoot at some. They exchanged signs with the Indian, explanatory of their object, and he accompanied them. In the mean time, Isadore mounted, to visit our friends, and obtain some flour.

The range of mountains to the N. of this is not over 3 miles distant, and speckled white, with snow. — Wandering clouds are settling on the mountain peaks. My comrades returned, with 3 ducks, and the Indian went on his hunt. At 9 A.M. we mounted, to return to our old camp-ground. Within a mile of it, we met our estimable friends, — Jones, Bowman, and Hall. They had experienced much anxiety for our safety, till Isadore informed them of our return. The party had got in three days before us. Their animals were all broken down, and several completely exhausted. In the basin of Lake Derby the Indians stole a valuable horse from Dexter, which belonged to Lassen. After we separated, they visited a large lake, and saw a small one to the N. of it.

Our security, from molestation by those Indians, had consisted in the fact, of their attention being drawn to the larger party, and also in that they were making preparations for winter, in their mountain fastnesses.

The company were out of meat, and several men had already gone in to the settlements. On reaching the old ground, we sat our old ragged friend up against a large fir tree; and soon a large fire in front, and a hearty supper, consoled us.

Lassen purchased, of the traders, *25 lbs. flour, at $1. per pound*. Messersmith shot a couple of fine ducks.

A couple of half-naked indians came to camp, and we gave each of them a hot roll, as they promised to get us some *pish*, his queer variation of *fish*. Jones, and some others rode, rode up the valley, to look for stray mules.

We sat up quite late, at night, listening to yarns, and smoking our pipes, while a party played cards. After which we slept soundly.

[OCT.] 15th　Snowing. We arose early, and replenished our fire, and then enjoyed a fine breakfast; of stewed ducks, flour cakes, and tea.

Old Pete expressed a strange desire, to return at this season, to one of the Feather river valleys we passed through, to prospect, and pass the winter. He seems to entertain a great repugnance to returning to the old *ranch*. This morning he went, with a couple of comrades, to examine the adjacent hills.

Late in the afternoon, Jones & Co. returned, without finding the mules: and Lassen & Co. without discovering gold. Several persons are out hunting. After breakfast there were snow and sleet, for several hours; the day closed with drizzles. Lassen, Jones, and others have resolved to obtain provisions, and winter in a Feather river valley, two day's travel East of this.[4]

OCT. 16th. This morning the traders loaded up their wagons, and left, for the settlements. Lassen and others, who are resolved on wintering in the mountains, have made the following estimate, for supplies, to serve 10 men, 6 months: — 1200 lbs flour, 200 do pork, 100 do coffee, 10 do tea, 200 do salt, 200 do beans, 150 do rice, 400 do sugar, 100 do dried fruit, 150 do pickles, 100 do tobacco, 50 do soap, 4 do pepper, 6 do saleratus; 300 percussion caps, 1 keg gun powder, 1 bag duck shot, 1 gross matches, 1 doz: butcher knives, $\frac{1}{2}$ do tin plates, $\frac{1}{2}$ do. do. cups, 1 do knives & forks, 1 box candles, with quantum suficit of playing-cards, sewing materials, sail-needles, awls, twine, tacks, medicines, pepper-sauce, mustard, &c.

[OCT.] 17th　1850. Those intending to return to the settlements, prepared now to leave these regions; viz: — Messersmith, Bowman, Hall, Campbell, Isadore, Young Hough, and myself. At meridian, we mounted, and with our pack-animals, started for the Sacramento valley. We were soon on the emigrant road, travelled to Deer valley, crossed the first ford, and at dark bivouacked alongside the Trader's Camp, in the edge of pine timber; 20 miles.

[OCT.] 18th   Frost. We started early; crossed the next two fords, and the tall divide, passed 'Bruff's Camp," the Cabin, and 'Steep Hollow,' descended to the left beyond, and bivouacked about 2 miles from the road, at dark, in a deep hollow, with rill and grass. 25 miles. The ground here in [is] gravelly. We passed the trader's wagon, on the road. Gravelly beds and frosty night, did not aid our rest.

[OCT.] 19th   It was 8½ A.M. before we were in the saddle, this morning. our animals are nearly broken down. About Sun Set my comrades reached Lassen's rancho, but it was an hour in the night, before I could get in. 22 miles, or 67 miles, in 2½ days.

About two miles from Deer Creek, of this valley, I passed my pack-saddle and effects, on the road-side, with a card on them, desiring the trader's wagon to bring them in: as the poney had broke down. In a mile nearer I saw the poney, grazing. It was as much as I could do to get poor Bravo in, under me.

A very hearty supper, with good bread and fresh butter, was duly appreciated.

[OCT.] 20th   When Hall arrived, last night, he was informed of the death of his mother, — which occurred 10 days ago; and his sister's bridal was then awaiting his attendance. He, of course, hurried across the Sacramento, to their residence, about one mile above the ferry, and 4 from here. Mrs Hall, a widow lady, with two grown sons, and three daughters, emigrated early last season, from the States, purchased the tract they have improved, and on which the children now live. The brothers keep a well-known house of entertainment, called the "MINER'S REST",[5] on the great thoroughfare from Sacramento City to Redding's Diggings, and other neighboring mines. The two eldest girls are now married, leaving a very young sister single, and in feeble health. The Halls are enterprising intelligent, and clever fellows; and I am glad to believe that they are prosperous. Capt. Potts — formerly commander of the Wolverine Rangers, Squire elect for the county, officiated at the wedding.[6] A man named Wood, Commissary Clerk to Capt. Lyons, died here, of low typhoid, soon after the command came in.

[OCT.] 21st   We held a consultation about the requirements of our friends in the hills; and as we could not obtain a sufficient number of pack-animals to transport the estimated supplies, we resolved to send back two men, with provissions enough only, to bring them all in. So, at dusk, Isadore and Campbell, with 3 packed mules, rode down to the ford, — 3 miles above, to start early in the morning, for the hills.

[OCT.] 22nd   Col. Woods, Mr. Myers, and Mr. Stout, — a surveyor, lodged here to-night.

[OCT.] 23rd   Our general fare here, is about as follows: —

> Breakfast: — Stewed beef, bread, and coffee.
> Dinner: — Roast beef, bread, and milk.
> Supper: — (extra meal) Same as breakfast. $1.50 each

[OCT.] 24th TO THE 27th   Transcribing my notes, finishing sketches, &c.
  Col: Wilson has been absent, at San Francisco, several weeks; Dr. Cole — the energetic and gentlemanly agent of Genl and Col. Wilson, representing their share of Lassen's Estate, told me that several grizzly bears have been near this settlement: and more large wolves have visited this part of the Valley, than were ever before known. The Doctor has caught several Coyotes, (Jackalls) in beaver traps.

OCT. 28. 1850   I am attacked with cholera morbus, for which I took opium and camphor. As soon as I recover from fatigue and indisposition, I shall endeavor to get down to the cities.

[OCT.] 29th   30th   31st   Too unwell to descend the Valley.
  Many travellers pass frequently up and down the Valley: some rest here, obtain meals, &c. and many lodge for a night or two.

NOV: 1st   Cloudy and cold: fire comfortable. Geese numerous in the stream, and flying over. These were gabbling all night.

[NOV.] 2nd   Cold, with a strong N. wind. Dr Cole, this morning, rode after a coyote, ran him down, and killed him, with a club. The Doctor, has superintended the construction of a new and substantial horse-corral, and many other improvements about the rancho.
  Our fare has improved, and stands now: —

> Breakfast: — bread, beef, and tea
> Dinner — tea, beef, and bread. —
> Supper — dispensed with.

[NOV.] 3rd   A few days since I had the pleasure of becoming acquainted with Mr Dodge, of Yubaville, on his way down there, from Redding's; he introduced me to Messrs. Denton and Hamilton, and they all politely invited me to call, when I shall visit that town.

[NOV.] 4th McBride has very severely whipped a poor indian, and afterwards wounded him, with buckshot. I was informed, that a year ago, one of Davis' sons attempted to chastise this very indian, who resisted: and the young man then ordered the indian's brother to hold him, while he whipped him: this, of course, the Indian refused, when Young Davis shot him dead, on the spot. The other ran off, and kept himself secreted. — Some body said that the poor devil had sworn to be revenged for the death of his brother. Fearing ill-treatment, and perhaps death, from the Davis', this indian fled, to an indian village 10 miles down the valley: and remained there, till a few days ago, when he came up to see his relatives and old friends, at the ranch McBride and one of the Davis boys hearing it, went to the village, and captured him, tied him to a tree, and lashed him with a green hide thong till he swooned, and they left him hanging, with his head on his shoulder. The poor wretch recovered, and managed to extricate himself, and started for the village, when it became known, and McBride ran out, and fired upon him, and he staggered off wounded into the brush.

At night Lassen and the elder Hough came in from the hills, with a wagon. They left their comrades exploring. When leaving Feather river valley, they asked a couple of indian boys to come in with them, as Lassen was anxious to show these children of the mountains, our settlements, manners, (!) and to return them to their native hills when he went back. They understood his signs, agreed to come, and got in the wagon. They had advanced but a few miles, when three tall indians ran after them, overtaking the wagon, and one seized the reins, and they insisted on the boys getting out and returning. Lassen explained, as well as he was able, that it was not compulsory, and if they were permitted to accompany them in, they would be taken good care of, and safely returned in a few days. But the adults were strenuous in their refusal, and the boys got out, but they then signified to Lassen that for a couple of blankets, they could go; but he had not the articles to spare.[7]

Looking for tools, this afternoon, we discovered that Lassen's trunk, in a lumber-room, has been broken into, and robbed; but of what amount we do not know, not knowing what it contained. I had charge of the ranche for several days; and whenever we left the house, to visit another one, in rear of it, for meals, or otherwise I always locked the door. I now recollected, that two days since, Nicholas Loux, (the starving German emmigrant whom Lassen had been so kind to) came out of the door of this house, as I reached it, from breakfast: I had then locked the padlock, and turned it over with the key in. N. had an old trunk and bag in the aforesaid room, but lived 300 yards up the creek, in a tent, belonging to Lassen. He could, from his tent, see us all go to breakfast, and no doubt seized the opportunity to commit the theft, as there was no one else there, to do it. Conferring with Dr Cole, Dr Bowman, and MesserSmith, we agreed on a plan to detect him, and recover the property.

NOV: 5. 1850   An Indian told me that the poor creature, so inhumanly treated by McBride, was very ill, in a willow brake, on an island in the Creek, a short distance below. I engaged him to guide me to the spot, and we started, to visit the unfortunate savage. We walked down the bank several hundred yards, then along a narrow trail, through thick brush, crossed a branch of the stream, on a fallen tree, and then crawled and pushed through briars and wil-lows into the heart of a small low island; and in a clear space about 20 feet diameter, saw several indians. The poor Indian sat, drawn up, with his head bent over; and seemed from his groans and countenance, to be in great pain. A young squaw, his wife or sister, sat behind, supporting him; He was pale and haggard: In the rear sat an aged squaw, and another young one, with an infant, in her arms, and 2 small children standing by her, — one a pretty light colored boy, about 8 years old. The women had rueful countenances, and faces blackened with some substance, in token of grief, I presume. (As it is also, of war)[8]   An old blanket partially covered the sufferer. They spake not, but eyed me, and shook their heads. Remains of a small fire burnt close by. I examined the poor fellow's back, which was deeply scarred with the lash, and several of buck-shot wounds. One of the latter was below the left shoulder-blade, and a corresponding one was just below the left breast, as though the shot had gone through; but it could not have been so, or he would not now be alive.

I could render the unfortunate wretch little aid, but desired my guide to return with me to the house, and I would give him some medicine. The scars had all healed; and I judged, from the eyes of the Indians, that they had lost much sleep, in consequence of watching the young man, suffering acute pain. I gave the Indian a vial with $\frac{1}{2}$ oz: laudanum, and a pewter tea-spoon; and explained to him, to administer a tea-spoonful of the liquid to the wounded man then, half a tea spoonful at meridian, and one at dark; and to-morrow I would tell him what next to do. Perhaps the old woman was his mother, or his wife's mother, and she who sat beside her was his wife, with their chil-dren; while the female who supported him, was his sister.

When I related the incident to old Pete, he was deeply affected, and shed tears, observing to me, in a sorrowful tone, "Captain Bruff, that's his reward for speaking in defence of his murdered brother!" and told me that he knew the lad well, and he was an inoffensive clever fellow.

We told Lassen that he had been robbed, when he exclaimed, "Well, robbed again, of my honest gains, and hard work! — I owe debts, and don't care for my self, if I had not one dollar; but I do care for them I owe!" We consoled him, with the assurance that we knew the rogue, and would soon make him disgorge.

[NOV.] 6th   This morning, in accordance with our arrangements, we sent Messersmith, as sherrif, to arrest Nicholas, who soon brought the prisoner into the house, where about 15 persons were collected. He was accused of the robbery, and told that he was seen with the gold, and that unless he produced it, we would assuredly hang him in half an hour. A Yankee clock was pointed to, and he was desired to note the exact time. We had agreed to go as far as we durst, without injuring the fellow seriously: for there could not be a single doubt of his guilt. No other person had entered alone in my absence; and he had removed his trunk from where it was light, into a dark corner, on the one he had unquestionably robbed. Lassen says that the amount was considerable, and unless we extort it from the fellow, our integrity may forever after be doubted. —

We all looked very grave and solemn, and I told the accused that I thought it exceedingly foolish for a man to be hanged like a dog, rather than give up stolen property. — That we all regretted the awful necessity, but could pursue no other course here; and were compelled to be judge, jurors, and executioners. We previously applied to Potts, as a magistrate, to preside; but he declined, on the plea of not having qualified. We told the accused also, that the enormity of the crime was magnified by base ingratitude towards his benefactor; and we watched his countenance, which was down-cast; for he could not look one of us in the face; and he stammered, and told contradictory accounts of his visit to the room.

One of us then took down a raw hide riata, and greased the noose, before him; while some others spoke together in a low tone, but so that he might hear them, how to get it over the limb of a tree, and to place it around his neck. I now asked him, in a serious and pathetic manner, if he had not a wife and children, in the City of New York? He replied in the affirmative. I then said, that I thought he ought to address a few lines to them, concerning any thing for their benefit, and bid them an eternal farewell. He assented. — I moved the whisky-bottle and pewter cups to one side, and put writing materials on the counter, (an old wagon bed) desiring him to step up and write, and that after the execution I would direct and forward it. He pretended to cry, but it was a lame effort at imitation, and he walked up to the counter, and after some sniffling, and a pause, of a few seconds, said that he could only write German. We replied that German would not do, for we wished to understand what he might write. He then desired me to write for him, "such a letter as I would write to my wife, if about to be hung for roguery." So I indited the following epistle, but never expecting to be in such a fix, I cannot very well imagine myself standing precisely in his shoes:) —

> "Lassen's Rancho,
> Sacramento Valley, Cal:a
> November 6th: 1850 (9 A.M.)

"My Dear Wife and children,

"Long before this letter reaches you, my soul will be an inhabitant of another world, to answer for all my misdeeds in this. I am under arrest, on a charge of stealing a large sum of gold: I cannot prove my innocence; and as there is no regular law here, to aid criminals, the honest people have taken it in their own hands, and will hang me in 15 minutes. Attend to the matter of the money due me from Germany. I commend you to the care of Providence and kind friends.

> Fare well, for ever."
> Signed   Nicholas Loux

I read it aloud, and he signed his name   I then directed it, and told him that his time was very short. Some one in the room, said to him, "Don't be a d — d fool! but go, and get the d — d gold, and save your d — d neck!"

He now concluded that we were determined, and said that he had a paper in his tent which he wished enclosed to his wife. We told the sherrif to accompany him there, promptly, as the time had nearly expired. — On reaching the tent, Nick sat down, and M. told him of the certainty of his possessing the gold, and that it was equally certain we would hang him, in a few minutes, unless he gave it up. He studied awhile, after denying the theft, and then acknowledged it, and had hid the money close by. M. accompanied him to the bank of the creek, — (not 50 yds: off) and he pulled the buckskin bag from under a bush; and in 10 minutes time was returned to the house, with the bag of gold in his hand. I now counted the gold coin, and weighed the dust, the total amount of which was $1,398,,40 Lassen thinks that this is pretty near the sum he had.

The company, however, deemed it improper to allow this ungrateful rogue to go unwhipt of justice; and accordingly all the neighbors were collected, to sentence him. A judge was appointed, also counsellors for the commonwealth and the defence: and the others were jury men and witnesses. The guilt of the accused was sufficiently established, and it only remained for the jury to award the punishment. — After a short deliberation, the jury agreed to a very lenient punishment, in consequence of the prisoner's having for some time, and recently, had the chills and fevers; and therefore decreed that he be at once stripped to the skin, secured to a large oak tree, — opposite the door, and receive 20 lashes, well laid on his bare back, with a raw hide riatta (halter) And to leave this part of the country by day-light, to-morrow, under a penalty of 50 lashes per day, for each day he may remain longer.

The jury signed the sentence and handed it to the judge, who read it to the prisoner, and then approved and signed it, and the prisoner was immediately taken to the tree, and the sentence executed. But he in no wise seemed to like it.

A squaw told us, that on the morning I met Nicholas, coming out of the house, she saw him pass her, on his way to the tent, and he had a small heavy bag in his arm. I now, also, recollected that when I met him, that he had his hands thrust down into the pockets of his monkey-jacket. Indeed he told Messer Smith, that he brought the bag out of the house, in his right-hand pocket As the rascal's feelings were much hurt, Lassen, kind hearted fellow, gave him a big *horn*, to soothe him!

[NOV.] 7th   A hazy morning.

The older Hough related to me their first visit to Honey Lake, as they called it, from the sweet substance which they found exuding from the heads of wild oats in the basin. (I have named it L. Derby)   An aged Indian visited their camp, and they made signs to him that they were in search of a deep-basined lake, where there was gold; and they showed him a small lump of the metal. The old savage, then took a pair of macheres (large flat leathers, to throw over the saddle) and sprinkled sand over them, drew a model map of the country there, and beyond it, some distance. He heaped up sand, to form buttes, and ranges of mountains; and with a straw, drew streams, lakes, and trails: then adjusted it to correspond with the cardinal points, and explained it. He pointed to the sun, and by signs made them understand, the number of day's travel from one point to another. On it he had traced, (as I found on their explanation,) Mary's river, Carson river, Pyramid lake, and the emigrant routes, — above and below.[9] He moved his finger, explanatory of the revolutions of wagon wheels, and that white people travelled along, with guns, on the said routes. On his map, he had exhibited the lake they were then at, *and another in a deep basin, with 3 buttes beside it, and said that gold was plentiful there; and also, that 10 months ago the whites had visited it, and fought the Indians!* Thus apparently corroborating the story of Gold Lake.

At Sun Set, a company of two half-breed French oregonians, an American, and an Irishman, with 8 horses and mules, from Trinity, came down, and camped, to refit.

NOV: 8th   After dark, Jones, Isadore, Campbell, and Burton, came in, from the mountains, where they had travelled back to the "*deep-seated lake with 3 buttes;*" they had [been] beleagured by the pautahs, and saw amongst them, the horse stolen from Dexter. The lake described by the old chief on his map, — as being two day's travel from Lake Derby, on a certain course, they found; and both the distance and direction was correct. But the number of hostile Pautahs, in the vicinity, prevented them from reaching its shores.

On their return, they shot a black animal of the mink kind, the skin of which they traded off with the Feather river Indians, for *Cammas* roots.[10] So that Gold Lake may have a local habitation, as well as a name, after all.

NOV: 9th 1850   Three strangers on foot, with a horse heavily packed, passed, on their way to the northern mines. —

We have learnt that the cholera exists in Marysville

Lassen, and his comrades are busy preparing to return to the hills for the winter. They are fitting up a couple of wagons, to carry as far as practicable.

Several large wolves, and numerous koyotes, are howling and yelping around the ranche at night.

A couple of men came up, supped, and lodged for the night. — One of them I thought I recognized as an acquaintance, and was highly gratified to discover him to be a Mr   Roop, formerly of   , whose acquaintance I formed on board the Belle-Creole, ascending the Missouri, in May 1849. — I regret that his health is indifferent, but am glad to hear of his being successfully engaged in trading, at Redding's Diggings[11]   A very cold night.

[NOV.] 10th   Friend Roop is quite sick.

My fine old horse Bravo, which I obtained from Dr. Bowman, and for which I was to pay him $150, Now, that our explorations have resulted in more hardships than gold, he has kindly taken back, without any charge for the long and very hard use I have made of him, and which will incapacitate him for service for several months.

[NOV.] 11th   This morning I was glad to learn that Mr Roop is better, — and that with his comrade and Mr Myers, he had left, to ascend the valley. Mr Ford[12] arrived from the cities, reporting the cholera to be prevailing there alarmingly.[13]

[NOV.] 12th   I am preparing to leave this, and travel to Sacramento, in a wagon.

[NOV.] 13th   Lassen and his comrades packed two wagons, with flour, and provisions   Mr Hough shot a Koyote, this morning; he was after the sheep. They occasionally steal lambs, and the wolves carry off sheep.

[NOV.] 14th   A wagon and mules, with 5 men, from above, came by, on their way to Marysville. Here occurred an instance of Isrielitish fraternal regard. — My estimable friend Isadore, went to the wagon, in which was a friend of his, — a brother Israelite, whom he had previously served. He hinted to him his present situation, when the other offered him a purse of several thousand dollars, but he only took a small sum, to purchase some necessaries to carry out in the hills.

In the afternoon, another koyote was shot close by

[NOV.] 15th   At 10½ A.M. Lassen, Burton, Isadore, Jones, Hough Sr. Campbell, and two others, moved off, to winter in the mountains. — They drive a horse and an ox wagon, and are all mounted. They contemplate packing the oxen, &c. when they have drawn the wagons as far as practicable, and reserve the oxen for meat. They have stores on packed animals, as well as in the wagons.

Night hazy.

[NOV.] 16th   Morning hazy and cold. Last night a coyote got in the sheep corral, (enclosure), and devoured the greater part of a large lamb. — A steel-trap was set, alongside the hole he had entered, but he was not to be caught that way. These jackalls are very voracious: An old settler told me that he once knew one go towards a horse, which was picketted with a raw hide riatta. (A riatta is a slender rope formed of braided thongs, about 40 feet long, and very strong: one end is fastened around the neck of the horse, and the other is secured to a stake driven in the ground, — called Picketting)   He bit the riatta off, near the picket, and then deliberately chewed and swallowed several yards of it. At day-break the owner of the horse saw him walking off, led in this way by the jackall. A pursuit was at once commenced, and continued for some distance, until they reached a hill, and ascended it; but the jackall fell into a deep ravine, and the horse had to stop. On the pursuers reaching the spot, they found the beast disgorging the riatta, inch by inch, and shot him.

A friend of mine, camping alone, one night, in the hills, had wrapped a piece of venison up in a handerchief [handkerchief], and made a pillow of it — He was awakened by something pulling his hair, and scratching his head; and on raising up, his eyes met the glistening orbs of a large grey wolf; who quickly retreated, or he would have had a ball in him. On the recent visit of Jones and party, to lake Derby, they found there another tribe of the great family of Digger Indians, who call themselves 'Halla-loo.'[14] These were in the upper, or Southern end of the basin, and they pointed down to the lower end, with significations of dread, and said "*Shoshonee*". They also signified, by signs, that a line across the middle of the bottom and lake, separated the two tribes. Clough says, that in some part of the Rocky Mountains, there is a tribe of Indians who chant a song, the burthen or chorus of which are the words "*Halla-lu-jah*" As some of the symbols, in the Hieglyphic Defile, are very like those of the Egyptian, and the name of the tribe of pautahs at the lake, and the words of the song, sound much like Hebrew, I mention this statement for the sake of those who believe in an Eastern origin of the first people of this continent, About 10 O'Clock P.M. having occasion to go out of the house, I was astonished to see a jackall, standing within 10 feet of the door. The full moon was shining; and he stood and looked at me with as much indifference, as an old house-dog. I stepped in, and took out a rifle, but on hunting for him in the dark, I found him missing.

NOV. 17th 1850 Beautiful weather. To-day I received a newspaper from San Francisco, in which I read, with regret, the death of an estimable member of the Washington City Company, — Mr John Bates. In the afternoon Burton came in on foot, from the deep hollow, 20 miles off, in the hills, in search of two horses and a mule, that had strayed off from the party; he had tracked them all the way down, to the ford of Deer Creek. I sold a wagon, saddle, &c. &c. to Dr. Cole for $26.00

After dinner, I obtained four Indians, to carry my baggage, — a trunk, bag of clothing, bedding, and a couple of guns: and started, for Moon's ferry, to cross the Sacramento, on a visit to Hall's, preparatory to descending the Sacramento valley, for Sacramento City. The lazy Indians understanding that I intended to go to Hall's, took a path which I thought was a short cut to the ferry, and led me down to the margin of the river opposite Hall's house, and upwards of a mile above Moon's ferry. I was aware that Hall had lost the small boat he once kept there, and I had much trouble to make the Indians re-shoulder the luggage, and proceed to the ferry: and found it a still more troublesome job, to follow them through tangled brakes, along the thicket-covered banks of the river, by such a devious route, that the entire afternoon was consumed in getting through. At the ferry, I hallowed, for the scow, and at length the two Indian rowers came down, with the old patroon, and I was at length crossed. I supped at Moon's old ranche, and slept on the lower floor of his new unfinished house, a few rods above, spreading my blanket on the dirty boards, as the other men did, where we thought best. Geese flying over, and gabbling all night. Near me lay a thin pale man, suffering under an attack of severe cold. He was constantly coughing and spitting. He d — d the blasted headache and cough that prevented him from sleeping! He swore most sincerely, that he meant no harm, nor believed that he committed any sin, by these execrations, under the provoking circumstances: for, when he was well, he swore he was as religious "as the *next* man," (I hope he couldn't have meant me). He fell asleep, coughing, cursing, and moralizing.

The floor, overhead, was very open, and the upper apartment was occupied by the mechanics employed on the house. They conversed in a loud voice, and though the multifarious sounds were not conducive to repose, yet I was amused at some of it. "Have any of you seen the laws about Indians,?" asked some one above. "No!" responded several, simultaneously. — "Well," resumed the interrogator, "I have; — it's hung up at Neele's[15] ranch, where any one can go and read it for him self." "It says, first: — enacted; that if an Indian steals a horse, or a steer, he shall be whipped, with not less than 25, nor more than 39 lashes." — And if a white man does the same, he shall be imprissoned for several months, and fined $1,000."[16] — "Now, gentlemen, what sort of a law is that?" — "A d — d Digger to get off with 39 lashes, and a white man to be fined and imprisoned!" "I say *that* law wont work!" — "Who made these laws?" — "Why I'll tell you; — a set of d — d yankees, New Yorkers, Pennsylvanians, &c." — "Sich laws wont do here, no how you can fix it!" — "My uncle, — Jno: W. ——, of Louisville, Ky. is a great law-yer; he was twice in Congress; and when I was a boy, he made me read law, in his office; and I aint forgot what I read, neither: There's no sich d — d laws to be found in the laws of the United States!" To this learned harangue, — questions and answers: a fellow, in a gruff voice replied, "Well, stranger, if I catch an Indian stealing from me, I'll shoot him, by G — d!" A third person approved of the sentiment, and swore that he would shoot them in spite of any of their d — d yankee laws; and he'd like to see any d — d officer try to arrest him for it, by G — d!" This discussion and commentary upon the laws, lasted about two hours; when they came to the conclusion, that any other but Lynch Law, was a d — d humbug. The conversation turned now, to Grizzly bears, Coyotes, and wolves, and I fell asleep, dreaming of Lawyers and wolves, Grizzly bears, Indians, and other adventurers.

[NOV.] 18th   I arose early, and walked up, about 2 miles, to Hall's; and enjoyed the first decent meal I have partaken of in a year. A short distance above Moon's new house, is situated his *rancherea* — or indian village; the lodges being composed of poles and long mats, like those at Lassen's.

Hall sets a neat and excellent table. 25 travellers dined here, during the afternoon; and 15 animals were forraged, at the same time; and he sold considerable refreshments, besides, in his store.

The gabbling of the myriad of geese flying over all the evening and night, is exceedingly annoying. Strong wind and drizzles, during the night. The earth floor of the store-apartment, was completely covered with lodgers, as close as they could lie.

NOV: 19th   Rain, and strong S.E. wind. (Hall's youngest sister is quite ill.) High wind and drizzles, all day: and strong gales at night. Thus commences the winter, or rainy season, here.

[NOV.] 20th   I was awakened before the break [of day], by the loud exclamations of a man suffering severe pain, and his name was Payne, a person subject to paroxysms of acute heart disease. My friend — Dr. Bowman, is here, and administered large doses of opium and camphor. His groans, and cries, that his heart would break, while he rapidly walked the floor, striding over us, with his hands tightly clasped over his left breast, continued till 8 o'clock A.M. when he grew easier, and lay down. Flying clouds all day. Several travellers, on their way up the valley, dined here.

This morning I saw 5 deer quietly grazing to the west of the house and road, not one-fourth of a mile off.

The mountains are shrouded in heavy clouds, and I fear my old friends — Lassen and company, have a bad time of it.

[NOV.] 21st   Cloudy, Strong cold S.E. Wind, with occasional drizzles, all day. Travellers are constantly calling, and passing up the valley. A rainy blustering night. Wild fowl gabbling and quacking.

NOV: 22nd   1850   Bleak damp weather. Made the acquaintance of Mr Healy, a surveyor and civil engineer, and very civil young man. — His *ranche* is some distance down the valley, on the other side of the river.

Ten days ago Mr Hall's brother took a wagon down to Sacramento City, and a traveller has just arrived, who passed him on the road, a few miles below, looking for his stray cattle. They have sent oxen down to him. Another rainy blustering night.

[NOV.] 23d   Cloudy weather. At 10 in the morning, Dr Bowman accompanied me down to Moon's. he rode while I walked. It continued cloudy and cool till 4 P.M. and then cleared off for a while. In the afternoon I returned to Hall's, but had caught a severe cold. Hall is busy constructing bunks, to accommodate lodgers. Showers at night.

[NOV.] 24th   Cold, with flying clouds. Dr. Bowman returned, from Lassen's. where he saw Isadore, who had walked in, from the hills, to procure more animals. While the party were on the hill, where I spent that interesting winter, now known as "Bruff's Camp," their cattle ran off. — He left his comrades camped there.

Late in the afternoon Mr Hall arrived, with a wagon and packed mules, in company with gentlemen travelling up the valley with a pack-train. Mr. H. brought us some of the latest papers.

Many supped at the house, and several lodged here.

[NOV.] 25th   Clear weather. The packers, who camped alongside the house, breakfasted at the table, and then moved up the valley.

A very cold night.

[NOV.] 26th   1850   Cloudy. I settled my bill, — 8 day's board $16. And at 9 A.M. bade my kind friends and acquaintances, and old esteemed comrades, adieu. and sincerely wish the Halls, and Dr. Bowman, every good fortune. I threw my effects in a wagon, at the door, and jumped in, to travel down the valley. We drove 10 miles, to the "Lone House", fed the mules, and lunched. This cabin, stands upon a naked rise of ground, within 20 paces of the steep clay banks of the Sacramento. It is a slight frame structure, clapboarded with pine slats, and roofed with cotton cloth. Inside was a small cooking-stove, bedstead, a sort of counter, and several shelves, exposing for sale, whiskey, bread, and cakes. — By the stove sat two men, and the wife and a couple of small children, of one of them. Our train consists of three mule wagons. — My comrade, travelling in the same wagon, is Mr Chs: Feetum, an Englishman, who comes down from Redding's. He purchased two small rolls of bread, for 20 cents, and divided them with me.

After a rest of half an hour, we hitched up, and drove on, proceeding 15 miles more, to "Placer City" — which consists of two two-story frame houses, covered with slats and cotton, about 40 feet apart. In the first of these, I saw, to my great astonishment, Old Roberts and family. — Around the house several wagons were being loaded with effects, from the great piles of miscellaneous matter the old man had been accumulating for a year; — from Deer Creek, in the mountains, down to this place. They were about to vacate, and remove down south. Roberts told me that he had just sold the house and some extent of ground, for $8,000 cash. We were hungry, and the weather was bleak. Our teamster asked if we could obtain supper? And after several ifs and ands, Mrs. R. very kindly agreed to get us up a meal. We soon had a hearty supper, of flap-jacks, bacon, stewed apples, and coffee, after which R. offered us bunks, — in the front part of the house, for the night; which Mr. Feetum and myself gladly accepted. Mr F. is quite indisposed. The two Mrs Roberts' are sick with chills and fevers.

(*Indian Village*) Five miles back we passed an indian village, and 3 miles this side of it, the deserted site of another, and then an entire village of tumulii lodges. We slept soundly.

[NOV.] 27th Our teamsters awakened us very early, and we paid for the accommodations: — Supper $1,,50 each. We now drove 3 miles, to Marshall's, where we had a good breakfast, at $1,,25 each. Our teamster is the owner of the wagons and mules, and appears to be a worthy honest fellow. — His name is Samuel Cowell.

Passed a small cabin, before reaching Marshalls'. After breakfast we resumed travel, passed several cabins, and at 11 A.M. watered opposite to one. — At meridian we stopped to feed and water, at Taylor's *ranch*, — a very comfortable establishment, 18 miles from Marshall's. At the latter house I saw several skins of lynxes, wild cats, and otters. On the plains large droves of wild geese were nibbling the grass, like a flock of tame ones, undisturbed by the passing wagons. I also saw several coyotes. We next drove 14 miles, to "Salmon Bend," — quite a pretty place. — A level bottom, and oak grove, on the bank of the river, and several excellent new houses. There is also a fine brick store-house, and a house of entertainment, the former is Semple and Green's, and the latter is kept by Messrs Hendricks and bro: This is the *town* of Colussa.[17] On the opposite bank, hid from view by the willows, is the Indian village.[18] We passed several deserted sites of such villages. Occasional drizzles. We supped and lodged here.

NOV: 28th   1850   We had to wait some time for a very poor breakfast. Our meals, indifferent as they were, cost 1,,50 each. After breakfast, we drove 20 miles, to Johnstons, passing Sutter's Buttes,[19] on our left. — Johnston, the proprietor, is a clever, enterprising fellow, and his establishment is yet in embryo: consisting of only a booth, under an oak-tree, formed of plank and cotton, near which is a large tent. — The former contains the cooking-stove, liquors, &c. and the latter, a table, for the accommodation of travellers. Johnson has had a well dug, close by, 60 feet deep, with a windlass and bucket. Water clear and cool. He is receiving lumber to construct a large house. This place is about 12 miles east of the forks of the Coast range, and near 20, from the Buttes.

We fed the mules, and rested. Near this, I saw two coyotes, and fired at one of them, about 200 yards distant, striking his tail only. We proceeded, 14 miles, to "The Lone tree", so called, from a small scrub-oak, standing solitarily, on the edge of a deep gulch. Here we descended into the hollow, and crossed the narrow bottom, diagonally. — It was traversed by a ravine, containing pools of poor water. — It descends from the Coast range, and in wet seasons, conveys a considerable stream. In the bottom stood a place of entertainment; — a booth, formed of plank and cotton. — They had fresh meat, and liquor, for sale. We ascended the opposite bank, about 100 yards from the ensconced shanty, and found on the plain, near the brink, a very large new tent, stretched over a slight house frame; in which they were putting up a stove. We proceeded, and I fired at 3 coyotes, but hit neither. Road level and good. Night overtook us, two hours before we reached the place to stop at. — The last mile through oak timber, in a bottom. The weather very cold. Passed two wagons and a party camped in the woods, on the left. At 7½ o'clock we reached Mr Thomas Corcorans, on the edge of Caché Creek.[20] — 12 miles since last halt, and 46 miles to-day. Our mules were well "cared for." We had a hearty good supper, with some 20 odd persons. The proprietor appears to be an accommodating man. He offered me the only spare bunk in the house, but I yielded it to Feetum, who is in bad health, spread my blankets on the earth floor, before the fire, and slept soundly.

[NOV.] 29th   Cloudy, with indications of rain. Another hearty meal, which with supper, cost $2. (beef, rolls of bread, butter, pickles, and coffee)

Corcoran is enterprising, and rapidly improving the place. He had made a kiln, and burnt curved brick, for curbing a fine well, dug close to the house. — It is 50 feet deep, and cool excellent water. The original structure is an old log house — long and narrow, with large log fire-places at each end. This is the dining *saloon,* bar, and store-room. Against the E. end, a new 2 story frame house has been added recently, — not quite completed. About one mile above Corcoran's I saw a very neat little frame cottage, which I was informed, belonged to Messrs. Tyler and Parish, — Virginians. — They graze cattle and I sent my card to them.

This creek brings down the surplus water of Clear Lake, and is, in the wet season, a considerable stream; but now quite shallow. The earth banks are about 40 feet deep, and steep. The stream is about 40 feet wide, and 3 deep, with pebbly bottom. There is a good boat here, to cross in, during high water. About 9 A.M. we hitched up, and descended the inclined plane, cut for the purpose, forded, and ascended another steep bank, to the plain beyond. We now travelled about 5 miles through oak timber, 15 more, over a level plain, with the exception of 4 miles crooked road, of muddy swamp bottom, containing a dense growth of tall rushes, and reeds, and known as the *Tule* Swamp. (*Tulares* — bull-rushes)

Before entering the *tulare,* the dry plain was very extensive. Drizzly cold weather. Several mule-carcasses in the swamp-road. Reminded me of the long route. We have passed to-day, numerous travellers, going up the valley. — Large droves of oxen, many wagons, several long trains of packed mules, horsemen and pedestrians. About 2 P.M. we reached George-Town, — a considerable village opposite to Sacramento City:[21] and drove down to the ferry, to await the return of a small steam ferry-boat. — This is 24 miles from Caché Creek. What a sight for me! — A city, — steamers, ships, brigs, schooners, and all the bustle and appearance of our old Atlantic home! The shipping are very numerous here, at both banks of the river. We had to wait half an hour, for the boat, and then crossed. On landing, in Sacramento, we drove up the street (J Street) and stopped at the door of a restaurant, and deposited my luggage. I paid the teamster, fare $12; freight $4; and ferriage 25 cents. It was late, and I made a good dinner, on roast elk, potatoes, and coffee, for which I paid only 75 cents. After dinner I walked down the Street, turned, and proceeded a short distance on the front or water street, and had the pleasure of meeting my old friend of the long route, — Glynn, (formerly of the Colony Guards) He had a small store. While talking with him, who should pass, but my particular friend, Dr. Austin, (formerly surgeon of my company! We had a joyous meeting, and he insisted on my accompanying him at once, to his quarters which I did. On reaching the house, I found another acquaintance, from Washington, Mr. Drake.

The opposite landing of the ferry is 132 miles from Halls, which distance we travelled in four days.

I spread my blankets of [on] my friends' floor, and slept soundly.

[NOV.] 30th   The Doctor is a bachelor, and one of the tidiest house-keepers I ever saw. He possesses a snug travelling-case, containing a set of tea-pot, coffee-pot, sugar-dish, cups, and saucers, for two persons. In the morning we get up a breakfast, dine about town any where, and unite, and make our supper together. Dr. A. introduced me to Dr Hardenstein,[22] with whom he is studying the German language. In the afternoon Dr. O'Brian called to see us. — He told me of the death of Col. Ely, and also of Seymour, who travelled with my company,[23] from Grand Island, of the Platte. Dr. A. informed me that Farror and Foible, formerly of my company, had returned to the States: and that my estimable friend, — Fenderech, the artist, also of the same company, was ill, at St Jose [San José] of fever.[24] Dr. McDonald and family have moved down to St Jose. I presented my friend Austin with a very neat little rifle.

Cloudy and cool; streets inundated with mud.

DEC^R 1st. SUNDAY. I am attacked with diarohea.[25] Drs. A. and H. accompanied me down the street, when I was gratified with meeting my worthy and energetic guard-sergeant, — Riley, whose health, I regret to hear, is indifferent. Saw also Mr Coombs, of the company, who is engaged in a store. Pleasant weather, with flying clouds.

One-half the stores are open, and the numerous *hells* are in full blast. I passed, in the street, a tall straight mulatto man, with tattooed face, perhaps a Sandwich-islander. A Negro was shot in the street at night, for horse-stealing.[26]

[DEC.] 2nd   I received a letter to-day from my wife, which had lain in the Post Office one month. Met several acquaintances from Washington City. Fine weather. Messrs Jackson and McNairn called to see me. I am engaged lettering small signs, &c. I am engaged some what professionally.

[DEC.] 3rd   Ice this morning. Dr. Hardeinstein introduced Col. Fornet, a Hungarian. Some cases of cholera in town. Night cold.

[DEC.] 4th   Messrs Young and McNairn called. Ice plentiful this morning. Many strange scenes to be observed here: — An Irishman has just passed, driving a very diminutive donkey, which is surmounted by an immense tin can of milk. — Thimble-riggers are fleecing green 'uns, at the corners.

Passed the store of Pomeroy,[27] of Mo. who travelled up the Missouri with me.

DEC. 5. 1850   Ice again, this morning. In the evening we visited the salloons, to see the performances, and hear the music.

[DEC.] 6th   Ice again. Made the acquaintance of a very clever artist, — Mr Martin; he has several good pieces, at his studio: one large piece represents two *prospectors* on a mountain, looking and pointing down into a deep valley. —
I slept cold.

[DEC.] 7th   Ice. Learnt that Pope and Truman, of my company, have gone home.

[DEC.] 8th   Ice. Accompanied my friend McNairn, in a ramble. — We crossed the ferry, and walked down the river bank, about two miles, to a hamlet, and cultivated fields, part of which Mr McN. owns. Here is also, a good landing for hauling a seine. On returning to town, we dined at the Sutter House,[28] and then at Mr McN's room, where I found a letter from my wife, dated Octr 9th. and brought out by Colonel Fremont.[29] We now walked over to the back part of town, and visited the burial-ground, where I saw the long parallel lines of graves, of cholera victims. These mournful heaps of sand were the resting places of upwards of 1700 persons, who had fallen in 15 months; 900 of them were placed there in 3 weeks.[30]

[DEC.] 9th   A fine day. Saw a grizzly bear — hanging up in a meat-shop!

[DEC.] 10th — Cloudy, damp, and cool.

[DEC.] 11th — Clear pleasant weather. Rain at night.

[DEC.] 12th   Clear and pleasant. A wagon full of hay passed; stretched out on top of the hay lay a huge grizzler, killed a few miles from town, and brought in to sell to the meat shops.

At night there was a Squatter Procession,[31] with transparencies and a band

of music. On one transparency was this motto: — "Retrenchment and Reform." I called to see Mr Nevitt, whose partner[32] leaves to-morrow, on his
return to Washington City.

Occasional drizzles through the day, and rain at night.

[DEC.] 13th — Rain. Mud knee-deep in some streets. — The longest kind of
boots are in vogue here. Several cattle auctions in town, constantly selling
oxen, horses, and mules. Last night a young man in the store below us, shot
and killed a steer which was stealing flour from the platform Rain through
the day and all night.

[DEC.] 14th   Rain again. Mr Geo: Rowland (Nevitt's partner) kindly takes
charge of a small package and letter for home.

I walked down the street, and most unexpectedly had the pleasure of
meeting Dr Bowman and Mr Messersmith, in a refrectory. They had recently
come down on business for Lassen. They told me that 16 days after old Pete
and his comrades had last left the ranche for the hills, they — (B. and M.)
rode out, to bring the horses of the party into the valley, from Deer Valley,
— as preconcerted. But on reaching the cabin, they found the eight men there,
— minus every hoof of animal that they had carried out. They tracked them
down the hollow, and gorge of Mill Creek, to the spot where I had so often
watched the smoke from the Indian fires, and reached an Indian village. They
found one of the oxen dead, and full of arrows. — They attacked the Indians, killing several of them, and burnt the village. The party returned to
the cabin, and resolved to remain there while they thoroughly explored the
neighboring gorges. The next morning the Indians visited the cabin, and made
a treaty of peace.[33]

An election here to-day, for Municipal Officers. Much excitement; — four
sets of Candidates in the field: — Democrats, Whigs, Squatters, and Inde-
pendents. — Several processions, of the various parties, — on horses, in
wagons, and on foot; with music, banners, drinking and shouting. A white
flag hangs out from the Crescent City hotel, on which is painted, in black
letters: — "*Tom Spikens, the people's candidate*" — "*Tom's death on rats, —
Saved the mules, &c.*"

Tom, himself, stood there, harranguing the crowd and wayfarers. — Some
of his remarks attracted my attention. He said, that during the Mexican War,
he — with another man, had charge of a train of 10 ammunition wagons,
on the march to Cerro Gordo. — Genl Scott rode up, and asked him what
the wagons contained? "Ammunition, General," he replied. — "Then drive

on!" said the General. — "I was at the Battle of Cerro Gordo, Cherabusco, and Molino del Rey!" — "That Molino was hell!" — "T'was nothing else!" — exclaimed a by stander. Besides plenty more of such rigmarole, Tom said, that he could have easily sold the train to the Mexicans, for a load of money, but scorned the idea! He continued — "I am an advocate of an extensive importation of females, and reduction in the price of leather!" — "I have fought, bled, and (he was going to say died) for my country, Gentlemen; and I can do it again!" "I am the people's candidate!" — "Here's the right ticket, gentlemen, — I can put you through!" Such a string of balderdash the fellow kept pouring out, for some time, to the great amusement of the drunken loafers.

I had the pleasure of meeting Dr Stettinius, of Washington; he is an Assistant Surgeon, at the Hospital in the Suburbs, — Sutter's Fort.[34]

The Whigs triumphed!

Rain, drinking, drumming, and shouting, continued till late at night.

DEC: 15th SUNDAY I breakfasted with McNairn. Bowman and Messersmith left, for Lassen's rancho. I met Petri[e], — the clever German, who left my camp with Willis, when the latter abandoned us.

A fine day over head, but awful under foot.

At 10 A.M. I rode out with Dr. Stettinius, to the Hospital, and spent the day there, with him and Mr Cassen [Cassin], — formerly of my company. I found there, Mr Murphy, also of my company. — They are employed in the establishment The hospital is a large frame house, erected close to the old adobe fort, which is also another hospital. The former is cleanly and well regulated, and contains many patients The fort stands about 3 miles from the centre of Sacramento City. Like Larimie and Hall, — it is a quadrangular adobe structure, flanked with square bastions, at two angles. Its walls are in a very dilapidated state. Houses and small cabins are scattered around. It is within the city limits. Within a few hundred yards of the hospital, are several neat frame houses, one of which is a brewery, with a sign of "Galena Brewery"[35] on it. We tested their ale, and found it good. (paid 25 cents per glass, for it)

The suburbs of Sacramento City are a fair specimen of what the *City* was, in its primitive state. — Every description of temporary structures; log, slight frames, frame and cotton combined, frame and tarpaulins, do; tents of every size, shape, and hue, and in every stage of dilapidation. Painted signs, as multifarious.

The miners, so long accustomed to a celestial counterpane at night, still prefer their Gypsey camps and bivouacks. — Here and there, in the precincts, the blue smoke curls up, from their camp-fires, beside some stunted dwarf oak, an old stump, &c. while the hardy adventurers, regardless of damp ground and atmosphere, cook, smoke their pipes, and sleep soundly, on their sombre, well-tried blankets.[36]

At dusk, my friends hitched up the carryall, again, and soon set me down at Dr Austin's quarters. I had caught cold, was quite indisposed, and had to lay down.

Strong gales at night, increasing to a fresh breeze, with heavy gusts.

[DEC.] 16th　About 4 A.M. we were all aroused by a tremendous crash close by, and thought, at first, that it must be some part of our house; but which proved to be an unfinished two-story house, opposite, blown down in the gusty night. The frame was slight for so tall a structure; it had no lower floor laid, the upper one was; the roof shingled, and the 2nd story was weather-boarded. — So that it stood on many slender legs, and a heavy flaw of wind toppled it over, breaking the lower timbers. Two men slept on the upper floor, and escaped with only a considerable concussion. Our residence oscillated much. The manner in which they so rapidly run up houses here, is peculiar, and of course, very unsafe. — The platform is laid, as if for a wharf, several feet above the surface, according to the grade. — This is the first floor; on this sills are laid, and then the superstructure raised on them. Often the interior is sheathed, leaving the timbers exposed. The better kind of houses are lined within with cotton, callico, or paper.[37]

At day-break the gale abated, but a fresh breeze and rain continued all day, but the effects of the gale are visible all over town. At night the folks below shot another cow pilfering flour!

DEC: 17th　1850　Rain, gales, and mud. I dined with McNairn. Saw Mr. Shaw, of Washington. The friends of the man who owned the cow, shot last night, got up an excitement, and the marksman was arrested.

[DEC.] 18th　Clear morning. Met Mr Caruthers, another Washingtonian. Pleasant weather all day.

[DEC.] 19th　Fog and drizzles. 2 P.M. clear. Fine cool afternoon. Night very cold.

[DEC.] 20th　White frost and clear weather
At night a Whig Mass-Meeting, and a Democratic torch-light procession,

with banners, transparencies, drum & fife. The Whigs followed, with a similar show and fuss.

[DEC.] 21st   Cloudy: indications of rain. Election of Assembly men — Lyles — Whig, elected. Processions, &c. like yesterday. Pleasant, but hazy weather

[DEC.] 22d   A fine clear morning. I dined with Judge Young, at the "Missouri House."[38]

[DEC.] 23d   A fog early, after which clear fine weather.

Fifield and Hoyt, sign and ornamental painters, have their establishment near my residence. I have discovered that they travelled last year, on the Platte, when I did.[39] I met Mr Griffith, in the street, who was also in that emigration, and with whom I dined on buffalo veal pot-pye, near the lower ford of the Platte. Fine weather. I unexpectedly met Mrs. Chandler,[40] in the street. (the lady whose husband left her in charge of a military gentleman, — and who preceded her some time in the settlements, at the close of the emigration of '49) She kindly invited me to call and see them. Another member of my old company, Mr Marden, called to see me.

As yesterday was the Sabbath, there was a new species of gambling exhibited, as appropriate to the day — A fellow, in one of the streets, held in his hand a small neatly bound pocket-bible, clasped it and desired any of the by standers to bet such sums as they pleased, on the chance of inserting the blade of a penknife between the leaves, at a certain letter, named, which should be first at the commencement of the left hand page, when opened.[41]

A strong N. wind all day. Passing a corner, I observed a man put a small table on the platform, in front of a house, take a seat at it, and lay down three cards, and a handfull of doubloons and dollars. — Soon a crowd gathered around the table, and gambling commenced.

I was told, to-day, that a young man named Stephen Clarke, of Bladensburg, Md. — who travelled on the plains and in the Rocky Mountains, when I came over, was recently shot in the groin, at Hangtown, by a man named Rogers.

[DEC.] 24th   Clear and cool, Strong N. wind. I met to-day several acquaintances of the long route. — One of these told me that he had paid, for provissions, at Kelsey's diggings, on the S. fork of the American river[42] $212; and for the same articles, of better quality, in St Louis, but $9„25.

[DEC.] 25th, CHRISTMAS DAY What a contrast with the last! — I dined with Dr Austin & Major Fornet, at the Fremont House. Grizzly bear stake, Venison pie, fine vegetables, and delightful mince pie, garnished with wine. I discovered that a gentleman who sat next to me at table, was from Alexandria, D.C. and named Carson.[43] He came here via the Isthmus of Panama; has been unfortunate at mining, and is dissatisfied. After dinner we visited the saloons, to witness scenes and characters.

[DEC.] 26th Clear and frosty. Spent the day with some acquaintances who were endeavoring to get up a Panorama Company. Night frosty.

DEC. 27. 28. 29. 30. Fine clear weather, without and [an] event of interest. Mornings and evenings cold.

[DEC.] 31st Clear; frost. There is much anxiety on the public mind, for the safety of the Steamer Panama,[44] due some time since, from Panama
  Made the acquaintance of a Scotch Chemist, named Ramsay. He is a poet, and his genious much resembles that of Burns. He is an educated and intelligent man

JANY 1. 1851 A fine mild day. Several citizens have published cards, inviting the public to call and receive the civilities of the season.[45] I called on Nevill [Nevitt?], — found his house thrown open, and crowded, and a handsome collation on the table. Met there Dr Briarly of Va.[46] and Mr Sewell, of Georgetown, D.C. Dined at the Union Hotel.[47]

[JAN.] 2nd. Foggy till 9 A.M. when the weather cleared off

[JAN.] 2nd From this date to the 10th no incidents worth noting in my Journal. The weather in the meantime very variable. [Thus reads a slip, pasted over the original entries. On removal, appears: "Gratified to-day, by forming the acquaintance of two Doctors Caldwell, father and son. At night, returning to our quarters, I unexpectedly met Mr. Windsor, — formerly of my Company, who introduced me to Judge Turner, of Georgetown, D. C."]

[JAN.] 10th — Clear and pleasant all day

[JAN.] 11th — Same weather.
  There is considerable excitement here, amongst adventurers, about a golden discovery, recently, in a range of lofty bluffs, a few miles below the mouth of the Klamath river, on the coast. These auriferous cliffs have accordingly been

called the "*Gold Bluffs.*" And a company formed, called the "Pacific Mining Company," to work it, — *or* more correctly, to sell shares. Every idler is now talking of going there.[48]

[JAN.] 12th — Early this morning, it was damp and misty: Afterwards flying clouds, till Meridian, when it became clear for a few hours.

I saw four Chinamen travelling out of town, for the mines, — two rode on mules, and the other two walked, — driving a couple of packed mules. They evidently know little about the mystery of packing mules.

A poor sick man, begged at the Union Hotel, for a piece of bread and cup of tea, which the good people readily bestowed. Petrie called to see me.

[JAN.] 13th   Hazy and warm. Col: Overton has treated me most kindly, which I shall ever gratefully remember. Multitudes are flocking to the "Gold Bluffs." Had the pleasure of meeting Freiner, at the Orleans House.[49]

JANY 14th — 1851   At 2 P.M. I bade adieu to my kind friends — Dr Austin, Coll Overton, and Mr McNairn, and went on board the Steamer "New World," [50] for San Francisco. We touched at Benicia, on the way, and reached San Francisco, at 10 P.M. Became acquainted on the passage with Colonel Jenkins, an artist, traveller, and gentlemen. As I was a total stranger in the City, and anxious to get a supper and a place to sleep, I accompanied some others, to what, an agent of the house said, was a comfortable and convenient establishment, — the "Missouri House;" a 14th rate concern, inconveniently situated on a back half-graded street, nearly two miles from the boat. Cold beef, sour, heavy rolls, rank butter, and an apology for lukewarm coffee, answered for supper. After which, I was shown up to an elevated room, bunked around like the steerage of some large transport ship, and scrambled to one of the upper sleeping holes; but slept very well, except headache.

[JAN.] 15th. — Breakfast upon a par with the supper, except that it was hot. I paid one dollar each for the meals, and 50 cents for the bunk: and w[ent] down the street. In Montgomery Street I had the pleasure of meet[ing] Genl. John Wilson, who politely invited me to dine with the family, [at?] the St Charles Hotel.[51] I arranged to board at the Eureka Hotel;[52] o[n] Montgomery St. Called and shook hands with King — the banker, a[nd] saw his brother, also.[53] Was gratified with meeting several other a[c]quaintances: among whom were Mr Jno: Thaw, Esqr of the Customs, Mr Westcoat, and Little, of Washington, the latter on the eve of starting for home.

[JAN.] 16th. Genl. Wilson is president of the Pacific Mining Coy and invites me to [go to] the "Gold Bluffs" with them, in a steamer. The Bluffs are 25 miles N. of Trinidad, and 5 below Klamath rive[r.]

JAN. 17. 1851   Clear, with frost. I am attacked with severe cold, chills & fevers. Shouldered my blankets, carried them down Long Wharf, and put them on board the Steamer (propeller) Chesapeake,[54] bound to Trinidad. Had the pleasure of meeting Col. Collier, ex-collector,[55] on the wharf; and Mr McFarren of the Custom house.

[JAN.] 18. Mr Dorsey, formerly of my company, favored me with a call. Saw Mr Ager, an old acquaintance. Fine weather. Met Mr Breed, — a comrade of the "Gold Lake" hunt: and Capt. Schaeffer, U. S. Military Store Keeper.

The Steamer got under way at 4 P.M. Her commander a gentlemanly seaman, — Capt. Harding. Crowd of passengers and freight. A bad cold and the rolling of the vessel deprived me of sleep.

[JAN.] 19th. Awakened early. Course N.W. Shore about 10 miles distant. Hazy, with heavy fog-banks. Many of the passengers are sea-sick.

Deep swell, and slow craft, — rolling heavily. Latter part cleared off, cool, Wind N. I slept tolerably.

[JAN.] 20th. (*Capes*) A little rain at day-break. Afternoon hazy: with strong breeze from N. and considerable sea. Ship rolls heavily. Late in the afternoon, we passed Capes Gordo and Mendocina: at 9½ P.M. weathered the latter.

[JAN.] 21 — At sunrise entered Trinidad Bay; and at 9 A.M. anchored in the cove, a pistol shot from shore. About 10 o'clock (after breakfast) Genl Wilson, and other members of the company, landed in one of the ship's boats. — Soon after, another boat alongside, full of people, was in the act of pushing off; when a swell, and the carelessness of a man in her, forced an oar through her bottom, and she sank; fortunately no lives were lost, though one of the passengers made a narrow escape. Some property lost and damaged. At length I got in another crowded boat, and we landed on the beach, in light surf: and from thence ascended a small cliff, to the town of Trinidad. — Quite a thriving little place.[56]

Mr Lemon[57] (A Member of the Pacific Mining Co.) kindly invited us to his ranch, to dinner; and offered us a place to sleep.

(*Indian Village, Graves, &c* —)   I walked down one mile below the town, and visited the Indian village; it stands in a hollow, about 50 feet above the level of the beach.[58] Trinidad heights are several hundred feet high.

[JAN.] 22d   Breakfasted with our kind and polite host.

At 9 A.M. the pack mules, with bedding and provissions, being ready; and the two *greatest* men of the party mounted — (Generals John and James Wilson[59]) by way of contrast, on very diminutive mules;[60] and 10 pedestrians, including my humble self, took up the line of march, for the celebrated "Gold Bluffs." We travelled about two miles on the table-land of Trinidad; close on our left was the edge of the cliffs, over the beach of the broad Pacific.

We then entered a very irregular country, broken by numerous deep soft gulches, conveying brooks from the hills to the ocean. About 6 miles of such tiresome travel: — descending and ascending, by devious muddy paths, deep and brushy hollows; and rapid streams. After which we descended a long, steep, and exceedingly muddy inclined plane, and reached the beach. Now our travel was upon the beach, — soft, yielding, and irksome. — A heavy surf roared on our left, and perpendicular clay-cliffs towered high on our right. Alternate stretches of such beach-travel, from 3 to 9 miles, each; over tall, steep, rugged, and slippery promontories and points, and at length reached, at dusk, a cove, at the base of very tall and rugged promontory.

I was attacked, early in the day, with the most severe paroxysm of hemorrhoids, I had ever experienced, causing me frequently to prostrate myself, in agony, on the ground. The company passed on, of course; and left me, with a very kind friend, whom I had the good fortune to become acquainted with, on leaving the town: — Mr John A. Lewis: I told him to go on, and enjoy the advantages of provisions and blankets, but he magnanimously refused, and kept by me. We had travelled about 22 miles; cloudy weather, with a cool drizzle, and we were overtaken by night, without blankets, many many miles from our destination. Here we were, in a fix! To add to the disagreeable situation, the breeze blew the fine sprey from the surf over us. A slight nitche, in the face of a gravelly cliff, might protect our heads and bodies from rain, and this doubtful shelter we had to avail ourselves of. I threw myself down, with pain and fatigue, upon the wet gravel, while my generous comrade groped around the beach for drift-wood. He had a box of matches, and was so fortunate as to find a small piece of plank; — this we chipped up; and by the aid of a tuft of dry grass, obtained from under a shelving rock, we managed at length to get a fire! — This was a great consolation!

By degrees we introduced, and replenished our fire with larger billets of drift-wood, till we succeeded in making quite a bonfire. It now rained: and we unfortunate pilgrims, sat close together, on wet pebbles, against wet gravel and mud, reclining on one another, with the fire in front, which we had constantly to watch and replenish. — Alternately dozing, and gathering fuel, smoking our pipes, and soliloquizing, we passed the wretched night.

When the tide was at its full, we were confined to narrow borders, and entertained some apprehension of the heavy breakers reaching us. The night was intensely dark. Near day, awakened by cold, and wet gravel getting down my neck, I observed, to my comrade that I had once read, in some celebrated architectural work, that all sleeping apartments should be well ventilated; and asked him, if he did not think ours was?

[JAN.] 23rd   No other two men greeted the break of day more devoutly than we did, this morning. I felt much relieved from my attack, although ill from exposure and want of rest.

We passed yesterday, on the beach, many bones of whales[61] — vertebrae, ribs, &c. Numerous skate-fish, star-fish, &c. and indians and squaws going down. We saw an Indian slab hut.[62] Passed several long and narrow lagoons, — two of them being fresh water, from the mountains, containing numerous wild fowl.

As soon as it was fairly light, we left our marine grotto and bivouack, and returned down the beach, a short distance, to ascend the hills by an easy trail. Discovered the tracks of a large wolf, who had gone around the point of the cliff, just before day, and stood within 10 feet of us, eyeing us while we slept, I suppose. He no doubt thought that we were queer, miserable fellows, to sleep in a place which he would disdain. He had turned, and retraced his steps, on the trail we were following, to the hills. In about 100 yards from the cliff, we turned left, followed the base of the hills, and ascended by a slight hollow. — On top we found, in the path, several circular holes, about 2 feet deep through the alluvial, in which we could see and hear a clear cool subteranean rill. We drank; and in half a mile more, — through close long dry grass, weeds, and brush, over the hill-top, reached the declivity, — and by a long, crooked, and wet path, of black mud and slaty fragments, descended once more, to the beach. The greater part of this country is carboniferous, whether containing coal or not.

Three more miles of tedious beach-travel, brought us to where there was a low marshy place, containing a brook, in a clump of timber, about 400 yds. back from the edge of the beach. On a shelf of the immediately adjacent cliffs, stood a deserted Indian village[63] with its singular cemetary.[64] The slab lodges dilapidated, and the pallisadoes and ornaments around the dead, a mass of ruin. I am informed, that last summer, some Indians of this village, attacked a party of travelling miners, attempted to kill them, and wounded two. They had previously murdered several white men. The miners attacked the village, killed 7 or 8 of the savages, and the rest fled to the hills; and have been afraid to return.

We rested here a few minutes, and drank from an excellent spring, under evergreen trees: and then proceeded up the beach. In a few miles we reached an extensive lagoon, of fresh water, — called 'Red-wood Lake", — fed by several mountain streams. Where the narrow strip of beach joins the bold promontory above, the surf of the ocean breaks over it, mingling the waters, so that the lower portion of the lake is brackish. Occasionally the sea breaks through the slight sand-barrier, when it becomes an inlet. The beach is thickly strewn with heavy pine drift timber, — some of immense trees, which have come down from Oregon — The lake is quite deep, — in the Channel, with a rapid current. About 300 yards across, in a grove of trees, I saw a tent, where we knew they kept a raft, for the convenience of travellers, and we hailed them. The raft was soon after pushed off, with 5 men on it, two of whom propelled it with long poles.

On reaching us, one of the passengers jumped ashore, — and to our mutual astonishment and gratification, I met Mr Thos. Williams, formerly a member of my company. He was with two comrades, from the Klamath, on their way down to Trinidad. Lewis and myself got aboard the frail float, and the clever proprietors, — Messrs. Wilson and Brou [Bron?] (the former a son of Genl Jno: Wilson)⁶⁵ soon put us ashore at "Red Wood" — the wet mirky hollow, in which they set their tent, to attend to the ferry of the lake. It was near meridian when we reached the tent. These young ferrymen, of the wild and romantic Lake, charge travellers $2. a piece, to take them across. I washed, and felt better — Our friends were out of provissions; so that the breakfast they kindly got up for us, was only tough flap-jacks, and re-boiled coffee-grounds, yet we made a hearty meal. The company slept here, and had gone on about 2 hours before we arrived.

Innumerable wild fowl are in these waters. The evening was cold. About 20 persons crossed here, on their way down from the Klamath and Trinity rivers, to Trinidad. I was exceedingly fatigued, and as our blankets had been left, by our thoughtful friends in advance, we went in the tent and had a sound repose. Our relation of last night's adventure amused our hosts considerably!

JAN. 24th   1851   We slept late. About 8 A.M. the tent was hailed by three men, on the opposite shore, and the ferrymen pushed off with the raft. On returning, I was gratified to see, in one of the passengers, my friend Ramsay, from Sacramento City. A breakfast, similar to last night's supper, and at 9 A.M we left 'Red Wood,' for the Bluffs.

The path led through a deep, marshy, and tangled hollow, for about 400 yards, — very crooked, then by a slight ascent, of a fourth of a mile more, we reached the brow of a tall cliff, overlooking the sea-beach. The descent, like former ones, was over wet, blue, mud and slaty fragments. On reaching the beach it was apparently 50 yards broad, but increased in breadth, as we ascended it, while the cliffs grew higher and more abrupt; rising from 100 to 500 feet.

The flood tide was setting in, and as we proceeded the periodical return of the roaring breakers, often reached our feet. In about 6 miles, from Red Wood, we reached a point where the bold cliffs gave place to a deep woody gulch and stream; and turned the tall angle of the bluff, on a path, to ascend the lower side of the hollow for the cabins where our friends were. This is about the centre of the range of cliffs, called "Gold Bluffs."

(*Gold Bluff Station*)   The settlement is named the "Middle Station" of the company. We clambered up the soft steep sides of the hill, on a tangled path of brush, roots, and briars, and in about 400 yards from the beach, at 4 P.M. reached the Station — a couple of log houses, and two tents. We were kindly received by the Generals Wilson, and Messrs Burnell, Collins, and soon joined them at supper.

This position is too damp. The rays of the sun can hardly penetrate the thick pine forrest and dense undergrowth. The cabins stand upon a very small level space, with a good spring near them: In front, the hill and forrest rises, and in rear, the hill rapidly declines to the deep gorge and stream. Tall grass and ferns grow luxuriantly. Around the cabins are the stumps of the pines, where the trees were felled to construct them, and clear the space.

After supper we smoked our pipes, and related adventures, then spread our blankets upon palm [pine?] branches over the moist alluvial floor, and slept soundly.

[JAN.] 25th   Early in the morning hazy, but it soon cleared off.

(*Bluffs*)   After breakfast we walked up the beach, to the "Upper Station," about 1½ miles. At half the distance the cliffs are very tall: the base appears to be a recently formed blue sand stone, on which lies blue clay, and upper portions are of yellow and white clay. Large pines and firs crown their summits. Much pebble and gravel are on the beach — The Upper Station, like that we left, — is located on a plateau, above a dell and stream, and surrounded by hills, forests, and thickets — But the situation is more agreeable and healthy — for a larger space is cleared off, and the surface is more elevated. They are making a garden-spot.

The mountain-brook here, has cut its way through hills of clay and gravel, making perpendicular cliffs on the lower side, of great altitude, and it babbles through a deep and thickly-wooded cleft in the hills. The ascent to the station is also about 200 yards from the beach, over wet yellow clay and gravel. The accommodations are a good log house, a frame cook-house, with tent roof, and another small frame structure, for a sleeping place. And a good spring of water. A lot of handy fuel is cut and piled up.

The Steamer Chesapeake has arrived, and now lies opposite this station, about half a mile from the beach, in the day; but at night she will have to haul off considerably. She has stores to land, and will try to do so. The surf is a great impediment.[66] Midway between ship and shore they have anchored a buoy, from which a line extends to the beach. They float casks of goods to the line, and attach them by "travellers," and when ready, the people on the beach pull them ashore. By this process, the steamer landed, this morning, a covered zinc boat, full of goods; and by 4½ P.M. sent several large casks ashore. The zinc boat contained 700 lbs flour, &c. &c. Two of the casks were slightly bilged.

At SunSet we started for the other station. — The tide was up, and between the tall crumbling cliffs — on one hand, and the heavy bursting surf — on the other, we managed to get down, with wet feet only.

In the incipient sandstone, at the base of the cliffs, I noticed horizontal strata of large trunks of trees, slightly silicified. — The sand stone exhibits, in its formation, curves of water subsidence charged with silecious matter. At dusk we reached the station, and supped heartily. Wet feet and damp sleeping place, gave me a severe cold and sore throat.

[JAN.] 26th The cold and sore throat very bad indeed. Clear morning. After breakfast, Ramsay and several others left for Trinidad. The surf runs too high, to venture up the beach. Those who started to go down, returned, to await the ebb tide. After waiting an hour the tide subsided sufficiently, and we ran the gauntlet, up the beach. Remained there several hours, and returned.

[JAN.] 27th Drizzly cool day. A party proceeded to the other station, and returned at night. The ship landed some more articles.

[JAN.] 28th Hazy, with flying clouds. Surf light. Cold and rheumatism annoy me considerably. All hands are at the Upper Station, receiving stores from the ship. Several casks, containing bacon, were unfortunately lost. A large raft of lumber landed.

[JAN.] 29th   Rain, and a high surf. No one could traverse the beach until the afternoon. Mr Collins and 3 other persons came ashore on the lumber raft. A whale boat landed passengers, and returned successfully, to the ship. The steamer, yesterday afternoon ran up to the mouth of the Tlamath,[67] and this morning she passed, on her way down to Trinidad.

[JAN.] 30th   High surf this morning. The cliffs above, crumble, and fall occasionally, to the great peril of persons below. Drizzly all day and night. A working-party visited the Upper Station. Some men came down, from Tlamath river, on their way to Trinidad. They say that several vessels have been there recently.

[JAN.] 31st. Cloudy, with mist. High surf. A small party of Tlamath Indians visited us, and proceeded down, with the whites, some of them engaged to carry blankets for the latter.
   (*Upper Station*)   We all proceeded to the Upper Station, where I spent a very agreeable day sketching, and observing. —

FEB: 1. 1851   Cloudy, with mist. Packed mules arrived, from Red Wood, for the upper station, where they proceeded when the surf subsided.
   We shall be relieved from lying on the damp ground, as they are constructing bunks in the cabins of the middle station.

[FEB.] 2d   Fore noon clear and pleasant.
   I walked down to the lower station, which I hardly noticed when I came up, 2½ miles   It has just been abandoned, by the company. Mr Rowe, with three laborers, came up from Trinidad. Afternoon cloudy

[FEB.] 3rd   Clear. Rowe, with a comrade, left to return to Trinidad. High surf. A party of Tlamath Indians, among them squaws and children, visited us. They remained a short time, and then proceeded to the beach, and made a fire there, alongside a log.

[FEB.] 4th   Clear and cool. High surf —

[FEB.] 5th   Hazy before breakfast, afterwards clear. Very high surf —

[FEB.] 6th   Rainy. A party of miners, from Tlamath, on their way to Trinidad, breakfasted here, and proceeded.

Severe rheumatism in breast and shoulders, no sleep

[FEB.] 7th   Clear weather. Rheumatism very severe. no sleep

[FEB.] 8th   Rowe returned from Trinidad, accompanied by a couple of Indians, carrying his blankets, and baggage. Several miners and Indians proceeded up. Genl. Jno. Wilson, and Messrs Collins and Burnell, started for Tlamath. Clear weather all day.

[FEB.] 9th   Clear and pleasant. Went to upper station and returned in afternoon.

[FEB.] 10th   Clear and pleasant. Again visited the upper station. Many skatefish on the beach. Genl. Wilson and company returned, late in the afternoon much fatigued. They say, that a short distance below the upper station, an immense slide of the tallest portion of the cliff occurred, just before they reached the spot. Two men were within 20 yards of the avalanche of earth. Earth, rocks, and trees rolled down in a great volume into the sea; forming, above, a great loose ridge. The travellers hurried across the dangerous pile, and had just cleared it, when a second fall occurred, and in its descent obscured their foot-prints.

Once, while going up the beach, at time of high tide, a dash of breakers drove me close to the Bluff, when some small pebbles and bits of clay struck my head and shoulders, from the top of the perpendicular cliff, causing me to hurry from such a dangerous position. Several pebbles, as large as my fist, fell not far in my rear, and bounded into the surf. Had I been hit on the head with a large pebble, the next swell of surf would have swept me into the sea. A cold night

[FEB.] 11th   Clear cold morning. High surf. Genl Wilson, Mr Collins, and others, with myself, are preparing to go down this afternoon. At 1 P.M. we started, and reached Red Wood at dark. Cold night, with showers. I drank some brackish water, giving me a violent cholera morbus, and deprived me of sleep.

[FEB.] 12th — Our pack-mules strayed, detaining us, so that it was 11 A.M. before we got on the raft: — Quite a squad on it, submerging the little platform several inches. Of course we had wet feet. We had to stand very still, in the centre of it. It was a perilous passage, but we landed safely. The mules were towed, and swam over.

On the 9 mile beach we met several small parties of Indians. At one time, while I was engaged picking up agates, the company got considerably ahead of me, when I met a party of some 20 male indians, mostly young men, nearly naked, and each one armed with bow and arrows and very long knife, — hanging down the back. Their leader was a tall, thin, and dark elderly fellow — and carried an unusually long knife. He came up, and saluted me, as usual with them, saying "Ay-a-qui-ya?". (How do you do?) which I reciprocated, and shook hands. — The young men then gathered around me, and commenced dancing, squatting, and repeating the aforesaid expression, with grimaces and laughter. This was certainly intended as derision, and I became vext, but had no arms. —

At this juncture I saw one of my comrades returning from the company ahead, in great haste, with his rifle. He was an old miner and ranger in this region, and had fallen to the rear to rescue me from trouble, knowing the character of the savages, and that I was behind. I passed through the Indian party, and my friend seized my arm, and hurried me forward, informing me that those Indians belonged to a hostile mountain tribe; and that from their actions, and equipment, he believed they were bent on some deviltry; and considered that I was, for a while in great danger.[68]

At dusk, it rained, with a cold N. wind, continuing some hours in the night. Early in the night we reached Trinidad. I was fatigued and cold. Our kind friends gave us a good supper.

Latter part of the travel we passed many miners and pack-animals, bound to Scott river, &c.

A gentleman kindly allowed me to spread my blanket on the floor of a store room, and I slept a little.

[FEB.] 13th (*Trinidad*) Clear and cool. Made the acquaintance of Dr. Gatlin, a graduate of the Royal College of Surgeons, London, and a talented artist.[69] We walked together and made some sketches. I drew the bay, &c. I engaged a bunk at the house of Don Juan —, a very gentlemanly Spaniard from Havana. The Don's daughter is married to an Englishman, by the name of Smith, once a carpenter in the U.S.N. They are partners in a store and trading business; and Smith is a share-holder in the Gold Bluff speculation.

[FEB.] 14th. A clear fine day; and I am once more nearly clear of infirmities.

[FEB.] 15th Flying clouds. The Steamer 'Gold Hunter', from San Francisco, landed passengers, mules, asses, and stores.[70] Afternoon drizzly and cold.

[FEB.] 16th Rain, and strong S.E. wind; cold and disagreeable weather. The Gold Hunter got under way, for Oregon, and a schooner sailed for San Francisco. We are informed that the Chesapeake which started from Sn. Francisco, to come up, with passengers, mules, and stores, was caught in a gale, and sprang a leak, compelling her to throw most of the mules overboard, and put back.

Cold and cloudy all day. Clear cold night —

[FEB.] 17th Flying clouds. A party of horsemen came up from Union Town, Humboldt Bay.[71] We eat at a boarding-house kept by Mr. Harper, a clever gentlemanly young man. H. is son of [in] law of Col. Owen, of Independence, Mo. his trial for shooting a certain Lawyer is well-known.[72] A disagreeable drizzly day. At night rain.

A party of miners, not long since, found in the possession of some Tlamath indians, a gold locket, containing hair, of a mother and child, with a gold chain attached. The Indians at Scott river and the neighboring mountains, are mischievious, and often hostile.[73] Several white men have gone there, whose fate like that of many others in California, may never be known to their friends.

A few days ago, a small schooner, from this anchorage, attempted to run into the dangerous entrance of Humboldt Bay, during a gale and heavy surf: she struck and went to pieces, and all hands perished.

[FEB.] 18th Cloudy, and drizzly. One large and one very small schooner came in and anchored. Afternoon clear. A large schooner arrived at night. Rain during the night.

[FEB.] 19th Clear. Steamer 'Genl Warren',[74] arrived from San Francisco, and landed many passengers, a number of mules and asses, and some freight. Afternoon flying clouds. The steamer and a schooner left the harbor.

[FEB.] 20th Cloudy. This is a very muddy place. Another schooner sailed. Afternoon drizzly. At night rain, and heavy gusts.

Speaking to a miner, at Trinidad, about the large trees of the Coast-Range; — he took out his memorandum-book, and gave me the following dimensions, of an extraordinary Red-wood tree, which was felled by the traders, so as to form a bridge across a deep and rapid stream, called "Mad-Creek",[75] — in the Coast range, on the trail from the town of Humboldt, (H. Bay) to the upper mines, of Trinity, Scott-river, &c. In examining the diagram, I have drawn, of this immense vegetable production, it appears incredible, but I can not doubt it. Wagons and teams go across, on this huge trunk, without a rail to it. It happened, fortunately for their purposes, that the tree was a pretty flat oval, affording a nearly flat-surface, at the butt, of 15 feet wide. Embankments, were of course thrown up, forming inclined planes — to ascend and descend. The stump stood 3 ft. high. — The unbroken length, is 420 feet; long diameter of the oval 38½ feet; and short diameter, about 25 ft. at the butt end. — The small end, where it broke off, by the fall, is 2 feet 10 inches, diameter. The length required for the road-way was not over 100 feet. From the fragments, this magnificent tree was supposed to have been 600 feet in height!

The following Glossary of some words in the Language of the Trinidad and Tlamath indians, is derived from authentic sources, and is both curious and valuable: —

The village and spot occupied by Trinidad, is called '*Choli*', and those Indians call them selves '*Aliquois*'.[76]

Allumeth, — House.
Aich-quaw, — Sea-Lion.
Aloo-es, — Sick.
Augets, — Noon, or mid-day.
Augh-Colts, — Thunder.
Alcori-gaw, — A dip-net, or seine.
Bim! — a fire-arm (taken from the sound no doubt)
Con-nec-ti-can, — Bottle.
Che-wars, — Hands.
Chay-ger, — Froth or foam.
Car-taft, — Rain.
Cho-ho, — Good-Bye —
Che-way, — Give me.
Che-ah, — Give me, also.
Chen-aw, — Big
Chalice, — Knife.
Cah-Cah, — Sturgeon
Chi-Co-itzs, — To trade or barter.
Chesh-e, — Dog.
Chesh, — Mule.

Fer-gush, — Eagle.
Hip-e-may, — Pidgeon.
Horea, — Arrow.
Hok-koon, — Tobacco.
Hops-cul-waugh, — Large sinews.
Hoc-min-dugh, — Oak forrest
Hit-care, — morning (It often hits care by the bye)
Hit-care-waugh, — Evening.
Ish-ne-gaw, — To shoot.
I-equaw-ya? — How do you do?
Kal, — You.
Kegew, — Theft, or stealing.
Kuth-wow, — What's your name?
Kich-la-gaw, — Battle, or fight.
Kich-mike, — Dead, or the dead.
Ka-mala, — Bad.
Kel-lock, — Goose.
Kar, — Crow. (This also taken from the sound, — their cry)
Kah,-am, — Cloathes.

Kish-ne-waugh, — To-day.

Kit-taw-her, — Night.

Keg-rugh, — To the left.

Kag-taps, — To laugh.

Lep-ro, — Talk.

La-gent, — Buzzard.

Lep-ten-no, — Clouds.

Li! — Look here! or calling your attention.

Leptise, — Hair.

Lav-a-let, — Snake.

Mech, — Fire.

Mech-pa-ha, — Fire-water, or intoxicating liquor.

Mech-yoch, — Sail-boat. (As *Mech*, in the preceding, means fire, I suppose a steam-boat was the first craft that visited them.

Mar-wich, — Elk.

Ma-quit, — The male organ.

Me-gues-que, — Doctor.

Mur-rah, — Smoke.

Mow-wei-ma, — Chief, — Head of a tribe.

Marra-po, — A File.

Malt-co, — Head.

Ma-le, — Eye.

Ma-par, — Nose.

Mapes, — Tongue.

Mar-pith, — Teeth.

Ma-par-cho, — Whiskers

Mae-quire, — Breast.

Ma-jard, — Abdomen

Milch-paugh, — Legs

Match-car, — Feet.

Morgets, — Stars.

Ma-gaugh, — Tree.

Neck, — Me.

Nale-kish-la, — Let me see!

Na-ermit, — Duck.

Neck-wich, — Bear.

Napo, — Fish.

O-quer-tsha, — Mountains

O-taught-toase, — Father.

O-quack-ouse, — Mother.

Pa-gu-, — A Man.

Pa-poose, — Child. (This term has undoubtedly been introduced by the whites)

Paa-haa — Muscle. [Mussel?]

Pa-ha — Water.

Pop-Shaw, — Bread.

Poke, — Deer.

Pack, — Cog-ick, — Blood.

Quaw-er-term-er, — Shoulders.

Rep-ha, — Sugar.

Rep-sha-pa-ha, — Molasses.

Roree, — Snow.

Spa-ga, — Ears.

Scalt, — Earth, or dirt.

Smur-ote, — Scissors.

Slock, — Large vein

Spolts, — Vagina.

Ser-waugh, — 'Scott's river'.

Sco-ye-a, — Good

Skeen-aw, — Little.

Squir-gus, — Seal.

Schmact-er, — Bow.

Shraats, — Quiver.

Tine-Shaw? — What's that? — (or this?)

Tesh-a, — Beaver.

Taw-law, — Trace.

Tag-ōne, — Skin.

Vari-et, — Black.

Wors-ou-na, — Sky.

War-ki-li, — To see, Behold.

Winchuck, — Woman.

Wo-ga, — White.

Won-as-la, — Sun.

Yoch, — Boat. (How much like yacht!)

Yoch, — Papoose, — Small boat —

Koch-chu-wich, — one.

Nah-ah-wich, — two.

Nar-oh-wich, — three
Choar-nah-o-wich, four.
Maw-re-o, — five.
Cock-cher, — six.

Cher-vér-ser, — seven
Kera-ve-la-to, — Eight
Ker-mer, — nine.
Vio-la-mar, — ten.

Each village has its chief; the clan and village are of the same name, and are at enmity with clans and villages. *Rech-wa*, is the name of the village and clan on the N. side of the mouth of the Tlamath river; while that on the S. side, is called, '*Wilk-qua*'.[77] '*Shragon*', is the name of a village and tribe, 35 miles higher up the said river.[78] '*Oss-hragon*', was the name of the village and clan, which I spoke of, when near to the Gold Bluffs, as village deserted and from [which] Indians fled, after an attack from the miners

The up-river Indians, of the Tlamath, call those, at the mouth, in derision, "*Ulrucks*", — which the latter very much dislike, and contradict the aspersion.[79] The meaning of the term I could not learn, but it took much as if derived from the Russian Tartars.

FEB: 21ᵗ 1851   Rain and strong wind. Sea boisterous.

A brig and steamer arrived, landing more passengers, horses, mules, asses, and freight, — besides a full-blooded Chinaman, with broad-brim conical hat, blue nankeen unmentionables — of the most ample proportions, a pig-tail down to his heels, and a fine brown American frock. He is hired here, for a gardener: A schooner sailed, and a barque and two other schooners arrived.

[FEB.] 22 & 23ᵈ   Cloudy and cold, with occasional rain. Much gambling here.

[FEB.] 24th   Cold rain. The brig, and two schooners sailed. Night very cold.

[FEB.] 25th   Clear, with a white frost. I paid Don Juan, for the bunk accommodation $6, for the 12 nights. Was attacked by an ague followed with low fever. Dr Gatliff kindly attends me.

Capt Wells, commander of the barque, accidentally shot himself in the leg, with a small revolver. — In attempting to shove the boat off, the pistol fell out of his bosom, struck a stone on the beach, and wounded him severely, just below the knee. Dr. Gatliff attends him. Intelligence was sent off, to the captain's wife, who came ashore, and the mate then got under way with the barquee, for Umpqua river, Oregon. A good harbor exists there, as well as a flourishing settlement[80] —

[FEB.] 26th — Clear weather. Dr. Gatliff has extracted the ball from Capt. Wells' leg, in 4 pieces.

[FEB.] 27th   I continue very ill.
     At night the Chesapeake arrived.

[FEB.] 28th   Clear and pleasant. High fever all day and night —

MARCH 1. Clear fine weather. I am excessively weak —
     The Steamer Eudora,[81] arrived, from San Francisco.
     At 3 P.M. I accompanied Genl. Wilson and others, on board the Chesapeake.[82] At 5 P.M. we got under way, and at 9½ P.M. came to anchor off the bar, near entrance to Humboldt Bay.
     I did not sleep till near morning.

[MARCH] 2nd   Clear fine weather; but a thick fog in shore. About 7 A.M. weighed anchor, and stood down the coast, looking for the entrance and land-marks, to guide us into Humboldt Bay. When the fog cleared off, we found ourselves S. of the entrance; put the ship round, and ran up above the entrance, turned round again, and ran down — keeping close in to the breakers. The Captain saw the land-marks, but the surf was too high to see the passage. I saw the houses, apparently 5 miles off, and a gun was fired by them, to direct us in. We made several attempts, and in the last one came near grounding on the bar, in the midst of the tallest sort of breakers. At 11 A.M. considering the risque too great, we gave it up, and stood down the coast. 4½ P.M. passed Cape Mendocina, very close — many whale-spouts seen.

[MARCH] 3rd   Cloudy damp weather. Kept close to shore all day
     At night the ship rolled heavily. Kept off the land.

[MARCH] 4th   Clear, strong N. wind, and heavy sea. A pilot-boat from San Francisco passed us: hailed, and enquired if we wanted a pilot. At 9 A.M. ran in and secured to the wharf.
     On landing, I had the pleasure of meeting P. A. Brinsmade, Mr Lewis, and Dr Forrest; the latter of Washington. Evening cool

[MARCH] 5th   Clear and cool. Messrs James Barker and Stephen Culverwell, formerly of my company, favored me with a call. Mr. C. informed me that his father, whom I left at Grand island, Platte river, sick, remained there till perfectly recovered, and then travelled with a Mormon family, to Salt Lake, and from thence — with many others, accompanied some Mormons to come here, by a new southern route; and that his father and others perished on a desert.[83] I called to see Col. Fremont, but he was not in.

[MARCH] 6th   Clear. Messrs Peregay and Pollard have aided me much in obtaining drawing materials, &c. for which I am much obliged. Met to-day another acquaintance — Mr. Van Lone, a clerk in the Customs. Called on my friend Brinsmade — to whom I am under many obligations   Met Mr. F. Henderson.

[MARCH] 7th   Clear and cool. Called to see Stowell and Preston — and unexpectedly met my particular friend Lieut. Derby, U.S.A. just returned from surveying the mouth of the Gila.[84]

[MARCH] 8th   Met several old acquaintances. At 4 P.M. Genl. Smith left, in the Steamer Confidence,[85] for Benecia.

[MARCH] 9th   Clear and pleasant — Middle of the day the same.
   Walked around to-day to examine this singular city, of mixture, bustle, gambling, and trading, — Saw the celebrated Miss Amoy,[86] and several Bengalese — male and female, and 3 Chinamen, in full costume, with long *queue*, umbrellas, and paper fans.[87] The Israelites seem to predominate, amongst the small store keepers.
   This being Sunday, there are many stores closed, but the *Hells* and drinking-establishments, are in full blast. At night Opera and Theatre. Day ends cloudy. Met Mr Ennis, formerly of my company.

[MARCH] 10th   Clear and pleasant — At 5 P.M. I accompanied my friend, Derby and Capt. Andrews, U.S.A.[88] on board the Steamer 'New World', and reached Benecia at dusk.[89] Capt. A. politely invited me to his quarters. Lieut. Porter called. Made the acquaintance of Lieut. Williamson, U.S.T.E.[90] Capt. Wright, Lieut. Clarke, several other officers of the Army, and Mr Daniels. Had the pleasure of meeting Dr Dyerly U.S.A.

[MARCH] 11th   Clear and warm. This is quite a pleasant pretty place
   Cloudy and cold night, with a strong breeze —

[MARCH] 12th   Flying clouds and cold, with high wind
   Introduced to a gentleman from Stockton, who learning that I came from

the City of Washington, informed me that his friend, Mr Wm B. Cassedy, (of Washington) was recently killed by the southern Indians, after a long chase, in which it is thought that C. killed several of his pursuers. The savages overtook and killed him: then cut off one of his legs, cut out his tongue, and pinned it to his side with an arrow.

[MARCH] 13th — Flying clouds and cold, with high W. wind. Dr Dyerly and Mr. Bumford favored me with a call —

[MARCH] 14th　Weather same as yesterday. I visited Mr. Finch, took tea with him, and spent the night at his house —

[MARCH] 15th　After breakfasting with Finch, went on board a diminutive sloop called the "General Brady," to sail for Sonoma. — Head wind and tide; Half the day lost clearing the land at the town. Clear weather. After passing the entrance to Vallego, the wind was more favorable, and we sailed well in the afternoon. Dinner venison soup and *sea-cakes*. — Passed immense flocks of ducks, geese, and pelicans. — Entered the narrow creek, with the broad expanse of bull-rush flats on either side. Wind and tide strong against us. At dusk the strong breeze and tide, in a narrow reach, forced us to drop one anchor and swing alongside the muddy bank. Six persons, all told, on board. Venison and coffee supper. Two bunks and two counters to sleep on: the Captain very kindly gave me a place in the cabin, while he slept in the hold. At 10 P.M. the wind having moderated, and tide changed, we got under way, and sailed a little way up, and secured to the bank at the *Embarkedoro*, or landing.

MARCH, 16th　17th　18th and 19th　Looking around the place and vicinity.

[MARCH] 20th　(SUNDAY)　Circus, French Theatre, Gambling, drinking, and preaching

[MARCH] 21st　Clear and pleasant. Making arrangements for professional occupation.

[MARCH] 22nd　I have received numerous orders for drawings

[MARCH] 23rd TO THE 29th INCLUSIVE, busily engaged in drawing. —

[MARCH] 24th — 25th — ditto —

[MARCH] 26th — Fine clear weather — Political meetings & processions

[MARCH] 27th — Fine weather

[MARCH] 28th — Election for Civic officers. — Warm day. — Processions, and speeches, &c. — Whigs triumphant

[MARCH] 29th — Morning cold — day very warm, — night cold

[MARCH] 30th — A circumstance occurred, to-day, which shows the kind remembrance of an acquaintance, and our singular meeting. — I happened to step into the Exchange, and in the crowd a Mr Perkins recognized me. — About 5 years ago he was introduced to me, and visited my cabinet of minerals, and other curiosities. He has been nearly two years successfully engaged in this country in mining operations, and had with him, a unique specimen of gold in a quartz crystal, for me, which he kindly intended to forward to Washington City, from New Orleans, to my address, — supposing that I was still at home, and which he now presented to me. We had not met before since the introduction Last evening, while I stood within the door of the Union Hotel,[91] a Frenchman entered with a basket of boquets for sale — disposing of them readily at $1. each. He had belongd to the Garde Mobile, — and wore his fatigue-Cap, ornamented with a silver shell and flame.

A fat young man attracted some attention in the crowd; he appeared to be much bloated, with a very red face, and wore an enormous black straw hat. — He staggered to and fro through the room, constantly vociferating, in a voice hoarse with bawling, "Henry Clay, and the Union, by G — d!" and ever and anon, walked up to the bar, and drank — his friar-like sombrero being at the characteristic angle.

MAY 1 — & 2ᵈ   Cool. Met an esteemed friend — Pearce, the artist.[92]

[MAY] 3ᵈ   At a few minutes past 11 o'clock, at night, a fire broke out in Clay Street, above Kearney, on the E. side of the plaza, sweeping down and spreading, with fatal irris[is]tibility, till the principal portion of the city was in flames. I lodged in rear of the plaza, and was awakened at midnight, though I had heard the alarm before. I had barely time to rescue my papers and drawings, from the burning building on Montgomery Street, at much personal hazard. I assisted some French lithographers to save their effects, and in mistake they carried off a carpet bag of mine, containing notes, and other papers. I had then to hasten through the mass of people, goods, and vehicles,

&c. amidst smoke and cinders, some distance up a street, to find them, recovering my property, fortunately. My bedding, however, was burnt. After securing my few effects, I hastened down town, to assist a worthy friend, when I was knocked down by a dray, and stunned for some time: on recovering, I met the partner of the person I was on my way to serve, who had the books and papers of their establishment, under his arm, and he told me that those were all that they had saved from the fire. All else — a considerable amount of property was consumed.

[MAY] 4th — At 8 A.M. — completely exhausted by fatigue, I reached the Court House, where a couple of kind friends gave me lodgings, and slept soundly till 7 P.M. and after supper slept again[93]

[MAY] 5th   This morning, early, I walked through the smoking streets. — Already temporary structures were rising among the black and smouldering ruins. Forty-eight hours since, what a difference! — Compact streets, of neat, and very lofty and elegant houses; stores of every description, well filled with goods; and thronged with the gay and busy bustle of pleasure and business! Now, black and shattered walls, and heaps of smoking and burning ruins; confused piles of goods and chattels, and multitudes of houseless people! My bedding was burnt — Mr Thos McCalla, of Washington City, died.[94]

MAY 6th   1851   It is truly astonishing to see what numbers of buildings are up, and rapidly rebuilding. Many have resumed operations, on a more reduced scale, over smoking embers!

[MAY] 7th — Met an old friend, — Capt Alexander V. Fraser, U. S. Rev. Service

[MAY] 8th — weather cloudy

[MAY] 9th. — Cloudy and bleak morning. High wind, blowing clouds of blinding suffocating dust and ashes through the melancholy-looking city. Met another Revenue Officer, and old friend, — Lieut Tennison. — He is on guard duty, with a squad of marines, over the ruins of the Custom-House[95] and its vault of specie. Laborers are busy clearing away those ruins, in order to remove the specie. Tents and boot[h]s, with refreshments, have sprung up in all directions.

[MAY] 10th — Clear and pleasant — Busily engaged at my drawings. —

[MAY] 11th — Dined with Lieut Clarke, U. S. Cloudy bleak day; dust and smoke blowing through the ruined streets, gambling, rioting, and misery. Night drizzly.

[MAY] 12th   Cloudy, though pleasant weather, at 8 A.M. it cleared off. At 5½ P.M. I bade my friend Clarke, God speed, to his home; and the Steamer Carolina[96] bore him off, for Panama —

[MAY] 13th   Busy all day writing, — and drawing

[MAY] 14th   Pleasant weather. I met to-day several old friends and many acquaintances

[MAY] 15th   At 8 A.M. a considerable shock of an earthquake felt here. A fine day. The Steamers Northerner[97] and New Orleans[98] sailed for Panama. I saw a dwarf, in the exchange, who appeared to be about 35 years of age, and was not over 3 feet 8 inches high. The streets of the burnt district are nearly built up.

[MAY] 16th   Had the pleasure of meeting Col. Porter and other officers, of the Mounted Rifles, from Oregon, on their way home.[99]

At Sun-Set, in company with some friends, I embarked in a sail-boat, to cross the bay, for Contra Costa,[100] on a visit to some acquaintances. We reached the *ranche* on the beach, after night-fall, and became acquainted with Governor Alvarado,[101] and the two brothers Guiterez, of Manilla, clever Spanish gentlemen[102]

[MAY] 17th   Fine weather. Joined a party, to ride over the adjacent hills, on a visit to the Governor's estate. — There were 3 horses doubly mounted, and the same number with single riders. We started at meridian, crossed the hills, rode over a low marshy plain, — traversed by a brook — tributary of the Sacramento, and soon reached the pleasant vale, and alighted at the Governor's residence. Besides the buildings of the Governors, there are others close by, — of the brothers Castro.[103] The low white-washed adobe structures, and white pailings, and dark shrubbery around, have a pleasing effect. A gathering at the Governor's house, to elect Delegates to the Democratic Convention to be held at Benecia in a few days.[104] Besides the native Californians, there were Americans, Irish, English, Chilians, & Buenos Ayrians; inhabitants of this pleasant valley. At 5 P.M. we mounted our horses to return to the Bay shore. — In the plains were large herds of cattle and horses. A brook of fine clear water meanders near the Governor's house. At dusk we reached the beach *ranche,* and had a hearty supper.

[MAY] 18th   Rain and fresh breeze. Three of my friends — elected to the Convention, mounted their horses, this morning early, to travel up to the village of Martinez,[105] from whence they will sail across to Benecia. Weather cleared off, and I amused myself sketching and rambling.

[MAY] 19th, 20th AND 21st   Exploring and drawing.

[MAY] 22d   After breakfast I accompanied several friends, in a sail boat, to a rocky islet — a few miles off. It seems to be about 5 miles from the house. Of small circumference, but lofty and rugged. — It is one mass of iron, and its various mineral relations: — of which I noticed brown hematite, red and yellow ochres, and fine red chalk. Myriads of cormorants on its top. It is called the "Red Rock".

MAY 23   Fine weather. About 10 A.M. our friends — the delegates, returned from Benecia.

[MAY] 24th — About 11 A.M. I accompanied several of my friends, on board the sail-boat, to return to Sn Frano and bid adieu, for a while to those we had to leave. Fore part of the day light airs and calm. About 1 P.M. a breeze sprang up, soon increasing to a strong breeze, with heavy flaws. Tide very strong. We experienced much difficulty in threading the labyrinth of shipping before the city. — Ran foul of a ship's bow-sprit, and but for the prompt assistance of the hands belonging to her, some of us would have gone to Davy Jones' locker. The numerous obstacles and strong tide, drove us down to Rincon Point,[106] where we brought up, — all standing, — with great force, against a wharf, and secured the boat there, for the night, at about 4 P.M. We now soon enjoyed an excellent dinner, at that fine establishment — the "Hotel de Napoleon." and then looked in at the Masquerade ball at night.

[MAY] SUNDAY   25th   Dined, with my friends, at the "Hotel de Napoleon".

[MAY] 26th   I passed to-day, in one of the streets, a chinese female, in rich silk attire, with the celebrated diminutive feet. She was very pale, appeared to be in bad health; and hung on the arm of a swarthy son of the Celestial Empire, with his huge umbrella, fan, and long queue. — perhaps her husband. She hobbled along as if badly *corned.* This pair have just arrived.

[MAY] 27th   Pleasant day. While dining at a Restaurant, a lad and small boy also eat at the same table. — Noticing crape on the lad's arm, I enquired what relative he had lost? He replied that his father was buried on Sunday; — He had followed pedling, on Long Wharf, and at the fire exerting himself to save the property of a friend, he caught cold, and received other injuries, which hurried him to the grave. — The funeral expenses the boy said would absorb all that his father had made. He told me that he had a Mother and several brothers and sisters in Philadelphia; and that they had once been well off. He said that he meant to start for home on the 25th of next month. I asked him if the little fellow beside him was his brother? He replied in the negative, but said that he was "treating the poor little fellow, to a dinner."

[MAY] 28th   Pleasant weather. "The removal of the deposites," took place to-day. The car, containing the treasures, strongly guarded by armed men, and headed by the valliant Collector of Customs — revolver in hand, attracted considerable attention. It was carried from the vault of the burnt Custom House, up to the newly established one on the plaza.[107]

[MAY] 29th   I was much gratified to-day, to meet my worthy friend Fenderich, the artist, recently arrived from San Jose. My old comrade de voyage, has nearly recovered from his severe illness. At night I met Governor Alvarado, and at his request, introduced him to the Honl Mr Holmes of S. C. At 10 o'clock I returned to my room, and being rather unwell, took some laudanum, imprudently guessing, at the quantity: soon fell asleep.

[MAY] 30th   On awakening, I dressed for breakfast: and reaching the street, and finding the weather cool, I thought that it was early in the morning; but was astonished, on reaching the restaurant, to find that it was half past 4 P.M. A pretty far nap. Alarm of fire at night —

[MAY] 31st   Fine day. Night drizzly.

JUNE 1ST AND 2nd   at home industriously occupied. —

JUNE 3rd: 1851   Cloudy and cool. — I received a letter from my daughter — 8 years of age.

At 4 P M An alarm of fire. Amidst the cry of "fire"! "fire"! and rattling of Engines, through the streets, a great mob gathered around the Court House, where I then was: and rapidly increased every instant from all quarters. The cry of the inhabitants was "Bring him out!" — "hang him!", "hang him!"

I had just left my friend's room, in the 3ᵈ story, to learn what all this meant, when a party of police reached the floor, and quickly thrust a couple of men up through a trap-door, into the roof part of the house. — On seeing this, I was alarmed, thinking that the building was on fire; and enquired of them, if such was the case? — A policeman, apparently much excited, told me no, but that they were secreting a man to save him from being lynched! I descended to the next floor, and went out on the balcony, from whence I looked down upon a sea of excited human countenances, still vociferating "bring him out! "hang him!"

Several citizens addressed the mob, from the building; and it was near sun-set before they slowly dispersed, on the assurance that the prisoner, whom they sought, should have a speedy trial, and as promptly executed, if found guilty. During the addresses, the cries of the mob became more varied, and while some reiterated the demand to "bring him out," and "hang him!" others, as vociferously sang out "Hear him!" "hear him!" and "No! No!" — with cheering, laughter, and hissing, While the mob were dispersing, the police put the prisoner in irons, and sent him off to a man-of-war, for security.[108]

I was passing along Montgomery Street, and met 4 men bearing a wounded man on a cot, having his head badly cut, and very bloody. He had fallen from the top of a building.

Wind fresh during the afternoon, lulled at dusk for an hour, and then freshened with increased violence

[JUNE] 4th — Hazy and cool, with a strong wind. Night cold and boisterous: another fire-alarm, and a house burnt —

[JUNE] 5th   Hazy, but agreeable, weather.

[JUNE] 6th   Clear and pleasant   4th to 6th   Pleasant weather, without any incident to divert my attention from business.

[JUNE] 7th   Dined at the Toll-Gate,[109] with Col. Wilson and Dr Cole. Mr Ford, from the vicinity of Lassen's, is here. I learnt, with regret, that John Young, who left Lassen's some time ago, to return to Oregon, was poisoned, robbed of several thousand dollars, and died here, in the hospital: — and the perpetrators of the foul deed were unknown. — Doubtless they are some of the gang of English convicts, who have so long been committing murders, arsons, and robberies; but whom the good citizens are determined to get rid of promptly.

[JUNE] 8th — Hazy and pleasant — Met several old acquaintances again

[JUNE] 9th   Pleasant weather. 8th and 9th   To much engaged to hear any news

[JUNE] 10th — Late at night I was awakened by the tolling of the bell of the "Monumental Engine House", and proceeded to the plaza, where a dense crowd of people were assembled, having a prisoner to *finish off*.

[JUNE] 11th   At 2 A.M. The notorious Jenkins, — the burgler, murderer, and robber, paid the penalty of his rascalities; being hung by the populace, to the gable end of the old adobe, in the plaza, *"till dead*, "dead, dead."[110] A pleasant morning. The body of the hanged was laid out in the Engine House, close by, and afterwards removed to the police office. A considerable crowd lingering about the plaza all day. At 4 P.M. another crowd assembled in the plaza, who were addressed by some young lawyer. I was told that Jenkins had been transported for life, to New South Wales, some 14 years since, from England; and escaped from there, and arrived in this country about 2 years ago; since which he has led an industrious life of villainy, till it terminated, as it should have been, long ago. They say that he smoked a cigar on the way to the plaza; and when a minister of the gospel offered him spiritual consolation, — while the rope was around his neck, he repulsed him in the most rude and insolent manner. On searching his pockets, preparatory to running him up, they found 200 dolls. in gold, and enquired if he had any friends to whom it might be given? He answered negatively, and told them to scatter it among the mob. After death, they found that his ankles were callous, and marked by the long wear of shackles. While the culprit was hanging, a fellow in the crowd, sang out "Sarved him right, by G — d!" and he was instantly floored by a Sydney convict standing near; when the last named chap, was as promptly seized by the mob, decorated by the shackles which had just before graced Jenkins, and hurried off to the Police Office. A man who had hold of the rope — running Jenkins up to the beam, had his pocket picked of a small amount of gold, while thus engaged. (*Hanging Jenkins*.)

At 5 P.M. Another excited mob assembled in the plaza.

At night, in conversation with a Grand Juryman, he told me, that in the case of the notorious Lewis,[111] the Judge informed them, that as the term of the Grand Inquest had expired, they were no longer a legal body, and consequently could not act in the matter. — The State's Attorney then warned the Judge, that unless he assumed the responsibility of acting in the case, the people would assuredly take it in hand; and that too, in less than 48 hours. "His predictions", continued my informant, have been already verified; for in less than 24 hours, they have apprehended, tried, condemned, an[d] executed one of the villains; and are now anxious to mete out condign punishment to others."

[JUNE] 12th   Forenoon pleasant. At 4 P.M. the excited and restless populace gathered in the plaza again; and hearkened to several speeches, for and against Lynch-law.

Afternoon cool, strong breeze, and clouds of suffocating dust.

This afternoon, I met a grateful Irishman, who recognized me, as having done him some petty service, several years since, in Washington City. — "God bless, me!" "Sure, and how are ye?" — exclaimed he, on meeting me; I thanked him, and said that I was well, and enquired where he became acquainted with me? — "Oh faith! I'm the man that never forgets a kindness!" he replied: — and then reminded me of the circumstances. Shortly after, while conversing with a friend, near a corner, some one fired a pistol close by, which caused a large mob to assemble rapidly, about the spot. Gratified with meeting another estimable friend, — Met this afternoon another estimable friend, Capt. Kennedy[112] (son of the late Commander Kennedy,[113] U.S.N.) who has just returned from San Diego; having carried the initial boundary monument down, to be established by the Engineers.

[JUNE] 13th — Fine weather. Preparing to leave for Panama.

[JUNE] 14th — Clear, with a strong breeze. At 3½ P.M. I went on board the Steamer California. Lieut. Budd.[114] U.S.N. commanding. — (another highly esteemed friend)   Have charge of a trunk, and bag of packages, for Adam's Express.[115] The hour of sailing was 4 P.M. but in consequence of waiting for the U. S. Mail, the steamer did not leave the wharf till 6½ P.M. The mail-wagon brought down 64 bags of letters and papers. A great crowd on the wharves, to witness our departure, and I bade adieu, with inexpressable sensations, to numerous highly regarded friends and fellow travellers. for whose welfare, my warmest aspirations shall ever ascend. We have a large amount of *oro* on board. Capt. Budd made me acquainted with the Purser of the ship, — Mr Lott, to whom, and my kind acquaintances on board, I am, and shall ever remain indebted.

We supped at 8½ P.M. A heavy sea running.

[JUNE] 15th   At 8 P.M. we ran into the harbor of Monterey, and were detained half an hour, exchanging Mails, &c. and receiving on board, another kind friend,— Maj. Hobby, Asst. P.M. Gen[116] — who was sent out to regulate the mail-service. On putting out to sea, we had a pleasant run, fair wind and sea.

JUNE 16th   1851   (*Santa Barbara Passage*)

At 8 A.M. I came on deck. We are in the Santa Barbara Passage. Beautiful islands on our starboard side, and not far off. Smooth sea. My comrades du voyage are most agreeable company. Mr Wright, formerly of my company, is on board; from Marysville, bound to New Orleans.

Capt. Budd has engaged my services to draught deck plans of the ship's accommodations, and I have commenced measuring between decks.

[JUNE] 17th   At 4 A.M. we came too, for half an hour, at San Diego, Several officers of the U. S. Ship Vandalia,[117] lying there, were on board, amongst whom I had acquaintances.

A singular recognition occurred to-day. — Dr Crane, a fellow passenger, accidentally recognized me; had he not, I would never have known him, as the mere skeleton of a man — worn down by disease and want, whom I lifted out of a wagon, at my camp in the fall of 1849, when the Alfords were so unfortunately killed. — He is now a hale robust person, who can as easily throw me upon his shoulder as I before lifted his emaciated frame, out of the wagon. The worthy Doctor has, I am pleased to learn, an interest in a valuable mine, and is returning, for his family. He now enjoys better health than he has before for 20 years. (Measuring the ship).

Captains Moore U.S.N.[118] and Hunter, U. S. Rev: Marine, are fellow passengers   The coast on our larboard side can be discerned in the distance.

[JUNE] 18th   Delightful weather, and a fine run, — making 9 and 10 knots per hour. Passed between parallel chains of small islands —— those on the starboard side, about 5 miles distant, and the others more. (Busy measuring the ship)

Formed another valuable acquaintance — Dr Le Count, a gentleman, returning from a scientific tour, of several years.[119]

[JUNE] 19th   Smooth sea, and pleasant weather. The wind hauled around on the starboard bow, when the fore-sail and fore-topsail were handed. 6 P.M.

We passed Cape Lazarro, $2\frac{1}{2}$ miles distant. Going $9\frac{1}{2}$ knots. Drawing the deck plans. — My drawing-table is a door laid upon a couple of barrels, and my friends hold on, to prevent fetching away, while I manage to draw.

[JUNE] 20th   Misty and warm. Awnings hauled out. Smooth sea. At 1 P.M. running within 2 miles of the land: — Passed Cape St Lucas, — distant $1\frac{1}{2}$ miles: bidding adieu to Upper California, as the Cape receded astern. Sharks and dolphins are numerous. A good favorable breeze. All sail set.

[JUNE] 21st   Another fine day, and good run. — Wind on the starboard beam. Set the after wind-sail. No land in sight. — Meridian observation — Lat. 20° 46′   Very warm all day.

[JUNE] 22nd   Fine day and good breeze: — All sail set. At 8 A.M. we passed the Propeller "Commodore Stockton,"[120] on the larboard side, standing down also for Panama. — Exchanged the usual civilities, of ringing bells, and displaying colors. We very soon left her, — hull-down. The shore is about 5 miles distant, a lofty mountainous country; but appears verdant — continuing about the same distance from the land all the afternoon and evening. Breeze and sea increased. At 9 P.M. furled the Main sail and Spanker. Soon after, indications of squalls, — very warm. — All sail furled.

[JUNE] 23rd   Squally. At 3.45 A.M. heavy squalls of wind and rain, with sharp lightning, and pealing thunder. 8 A.M. strong breeze and rain, and head sea, Land about 8 miles distant, — high and rocky. 10 P.M. clear and moderate. Near the harbor of Acapulco. — Lights seen on the shore. The steamer, now turned, and ran out to sea, a mile or so, in order to bear down more advantageously for the entrance. Brought the vessel about, and ran for the land. At $10\frac{1}{2}$ P.M. we reached the inner harbor, and made fast to an old hulk. Shortly after, the Steamer Pacific followed us in. — The Steamers Columbia and Northerner are also here and the McKim, — laid up.[121]

JUNE 24th   Most of the passengers availed themselves of the hundreds of boats and canoes alongside, and went ashore early. The Columbia ran out of the harbor; followed by the Northerner. After the second breakfast, few of our passengers remained on board. At 1 P.M. a Chilian brig-of-war sailed out: and the Steamer Pacific ran out also. Several Spanish gentlemen, and some females, who came down with us, went on shore. Lieut. Gardiner, U.S.A.[122] and Mr. Connor, accompanies the gentlemen, across to the City of

Mexico, on their way home. 8 A.M. The Capetan del Puerto. visited us. Occasional showers, and exceedingly warm weather.

About 3 P.M. I got into a canoe, and went ashore. — Walked around the town. — A neat and picturesque place. — Tall cocoas, and other palms, — gracefully waving over the straw-thatched cottages and white-washed adobes. (*Cathedral*)   The new Cathedral is a long low Moorish-looking structure, — resembling more a great mausaleum than a church. The old one, — or rather its picturesque ruins, rise in shattered beauty, from a mass of stones shrubbery, and rubbish, in the central part of the town. — It was destroyed by an earth quake many years ago. The former stands on one side of a small plaza, opposite the landing, between which, and the barracks — on the opposite side, are the remains of a once pretty fountain. — An oval stone wall, about 3 feet high, and perhaps 12 feet longest diameter, was the basin, containing only rubbish and damp moss. — In its centre, stood a stone pedestal, with part of a small pipe, on top: — Once, no doubt, surmounted by a statue or some sea god.

While standing at the corner, engaged sketching the tomb-like Cathedral, a guard of a dozen black and bare-footed Soldados, carrying their muskets at a support, and headed by a mulatto Sergeant, came out of the adjacent barracks, and marched close by me. They successively stared at me, as they passed. I noticed, that upon the breech of each musket there was pasted an oval piece of paper, with the name of the soldier. These bravos wore callico shirts outside their pants, without coats or jackets: and tent-shaped blue fatigue-caps, edged with red. — Black leather belts and accoutrements; and had bright muskets and bayonets. In the wall, at the corner of each street, about 5 feet from the ground, was a small niche in which was painted a black cross, and below it the number. . . . Smut and grease showed that at times, lights were placed in them. They belong to the interminable ramifications of the established creed. There are said to be the 14 Stations, representative of as many incidents in the passage of Christ, from the Hall of Pontius Pilot, to Mᵗ Calvary. During the festival of Lent, a procession takes place, in which all the mummery, prescribed, for each event, is performed at the several stations, in succession. They also answer for penal Stations.

The Castle, or Fort, looks like a very neat fortification. Strangers are now allowed entrance to it, without the Governor's pass. — There is a good joke told, about this fortress. — During our War with Mexico, the Commadante fearing that it would fall into our possession, had the most of the brass guns taken out, and at considerable labor, transported to the neighboring mountains, and thrown into a gulch, where they remain, to this day, as the natives are too lazy to restore them.

The inhabitants appear to be friendly and accommodating, and many speak English. Indeed, several children cried out to me, as I passed, "How de do Sir"?

Observing a crowd gathering near a corner, I went up, to see what attracted it, and found that it was a cock-fight, going on, in a dirty vacant lot. — The pit, if it could be so called, was a rough dilapidated enclosure of wooden rails, within which several pair of ill-looking ragged Mexicanos, were pitting their fowls, and betting: Around was a crowd, of all sorts, looking eagerly on the sport. A Spaniard asked me, in excellent English for a light, from my cigar: — I complied, and observed to him, that he spoke good English. — He replied — "Yes, Sir, every body here will soon learn that." So I thought then a good deal of "inevitable destiny." Signs and placards, in English predominate over those in Spanish. The principal drinking establishments, are, of course, American and English.

Afternoon and evening rainy.

Purchased a bunch of very large purple grapes, for one *bit* — Small tables are set before the doors of the houses, as well as near the landing, exposing for sale, — bottles of lime-juice, eggs, vegetables, plantains, bananas, cocoanuts, pine-apples, oranges, limes, sweet-potatoes, grapes, and other fruits, and also brandy, rum, straw hats, grass hammocks, and embellished callabashes, besides very indifferent specimens of shells, corals, sponges, and corallines. All these articles, including bundles of horrid native cigars, are carried off to the shipping, in numerous boats and canoes.

While perambulating a narrow sandy street — at right angles to the landing place, & pleased with the simple reed-cottages — on either side, with their white-washed palings, — enclosing the large-brilliant foliage of the Tropics, and the tall feathery palms, bending over the happy and half naked group of urchins below, I heard vocal and instrumental music in one of these cage-like tenements, and walked around to its entrance in the rear. — A tall man, of a dark olive complexion, and well-formed, sat across the door, with a harp in his hands; negro, within, sitting on a block of wood, had a violin; and a dark female — with the usual large lustrous black eyes, of the clime and people, was reclining in a grass hammock. I approached, and saluted them, which they politely reciprocated, and asked me to enter — but I declined, and told them that the music had enticed me to make the intrusion. They then obligingly performed for me on their instruments, accompanied by the voice of the lady, in a very pretty Spanish Air. I thanked them, and said *Adios*. —

There are some Spaniards here, of a light color, many blacks, but the majority are a mixture, of the complexion which at home we call mulattoes. This is St. John's Day: hence there is great bell-ringing, church-going, cock-fighting, bathing, and display of fire-works, and happy countenances of the natives.

The beach, at the landing, is crowded with boats and canoes, with their white awnings, and tawny boatmen. They do a great business with the passenger vessels.

Near dusk, a gun fired from our ship, warned us to hasten on board, and I entered a canoe, with a friend, and in a few minutes reached her deck.

The children here, like those in the W. Indies, are great swimmers, and most expert divers. — The passengers found much amusement by throwing small pieces of money into the sea, for the colored urchins around, to dive after. It was really astonishing, to witness their activity and adroitness. — Of several hundred pieces of coin, thrown into the water, I do not think one piece was lost. — At least half the number were dashed quickly in, and sank out of our sight, — so deep that the divers descended below our vision also, in pursuit of them, invariably ascending to the surface, with the pieces in their mouths. They put them in their mouths, till full, and always exhibited to us, on reaching the surface, the last coin, between the thumb and finger, to show their success.

The steamer having taken in the requisite quantum of coal and water, at 8 P.M. got under way, to leave the prettiest harbor I ever saw, except that of Rio de Janerio. This harbor is perfectly land-locked, and there is but a slight difference of shade and height in the enclosing hills, to show where the entrance lies.

It was so intensely warm, below decks, that I could not sleep, until near morning; and not then, until after I put my mattress upon the deck, near the companion-way, to enjoy the consolation afforded by the wind-sail.

JUNE 25th   Light rain, and head wind. (Busy making the draught)   In the afternoon, a brig was descried, on the starboard bow, — standing to the southward. A lady in weeds, with her two daughters, came on board at Acapulco, where she had remained ever since the steamer of last month, brought the family from Panama. Her husband, — brother to our Consul at Panama, had caught the Panama fever, which compelled them to remain at

Acapulco, until he died. They were bound for San Francisco. The bereaved widow is in bad health, and absorbed in grief.

[JUNE] 26th　A fine day, Smooth sea, and head breeze, but our steamer makes very good head-way. Early in the forenoon we passed a steamer, — far out on the horizon; supposed to be the Columbus,[123] for Panama. (Still engaged drawing the deck-plans)　Average run to-day, 9 knots per hour. Night extremely warm, again.

[JUNE] 27th　Commences cloudy. Smooth sea, and head wind. Very warm. (Still drawing)　My comrades are lively, and find much entertainment, until late in the evening, spinning yarns, and singing. The night hot.

[JUNE] 28th　Cloudy, Wind E. by N. Course E.S.E. $\frac{1}{4}$ S. (I now complete the drawings)　"Mother Carews" chickens, in our wake. Heat interfered with sleep.

[JUNE] 29th　Heavy flying clouds. Our coal is indifferent, and we now make but 8 knots per hour. Middle of the day had the wind on the starboard beam. Set the spanker and foresail.

[JUNE] 30th — Commences clear. Course E.S.E. Light breeze from the N.W. All sail set. The land is in sight, — about 10 miles distant.

An act of kindness, this morning, by my generous friends, will never be obliterated from grateful remembrance.

Afternoon warm: the wind hauled, and the sails were taken in. The temperature has afflicted me sadly, with prickly heat, and I am compelled to discard under-clothing.

JULY 1st　Commences with light rain; at 8 A.M. it cleared off, and became very warm. Meridian, our course E. and nearing the land, till in half an hour, it was not over $2\frac{1}{2}$ miles distant. Beautiful country! — Mountains, hills, vales, and rocks, and thick forests, and shrubbery, of dark green. — Along the shore, are stripes of yellow beach; and here and there, breakers roll their lines of white foam over the reefs and projecting rocks, with an occasional cave, appearing like a good boat-landing. On the nearest hills and points, I noticed several spots, of a scarlet color, perhaps clay, or even cinnabar. The mountains, of the back-ground, are capped with clouds. Made sail on the ship again.

Some discontented steerage-passengers, got up an indignation-meeting, and paper, — signed by several, in order to publish, at home, they say, because the accommodations and fare, at the two ends of the ship are different. (Cabin passage $350, steerage $125.) The good accommodations at our end, and the accommodating gentlemanly manners of the Officers, elicited from us, a meeting and testimonial of an inverse character to that concocted forward. — Some of the steerage passengers signed with pleasure, our document.

At night, the ship changed her course, to the N.N.E.

JULY 2^d Flying clouds. At 6½ A.M. we entered the picturesque anchorage, of Tobago, amongst beautiful verdant islets. Tobago is a small town upon an island of the same name, and largest of the group. Here, bold masses and cliffs, of grey and brown rocks, start up from the midst of feathery palms, and dark green foliage — Bright green patches, on the slopes, — of plantains, oranges, bannanas, and spaces, speckled with brown and green, show cultivated patches.

The town, about ¼ mile off, from where we lay, looks exceedingly pretty. Thatched cottages of the natives, white-washed adobe structures of gentlemen, with their roofs of red tiles, some modern American-looking residences; the old monkish-looking church, and the graceful cocoa-nut trees, between and waving over them, produce a beautiful effect.

There are some fifty-odd vessels laying here; 6 large steamers, — the Constitution, Unicorn, Massachusetts, Carolina, New Orleans, and Fremont;[124] and the rest ships and brigs. The sea around is sprinkled with canoes. In the rear of Tobago arises a range of distant lofty blue, cloud-capped mountains, with many higher peaks. Received Mr Forbes[125] on board, and after a delay of half an hour, we proceeded, and reached the anchorage off Panama, about one mile from the shore, at 7½ A.M. Found here, one Propeller, 10 Ships, and 10 Brigs. A sensation of deep regret pervaded the company, on learning that Henry Tracy, Esq. Civil Engineer, and Agent for Law's line of Pacific Steamers, was dead: — a man of noble sentiments and character.

(*Panama.*) The celebrated City of Panama, from the anchorage, looks like most old Spanish towns, dingy and antiquated. The dilapidated walls are crumbling into the sea; sombre-looking rows of houses, with red-tiled roofs, numerous old churches; and in the midst, the tall towers of the Cathedral, whose lofty spires glisten in the sun, with coating of pearl-oyster shells, rise conspicuously. We brought down 205 passengers, — 54 of whom were in the Cabins; and 1,200,000 dollars, in gold.

Now is there excitement and confusion, on board: — getting out baggage, and leaving the ship. Swarms of boats and canoes, alongside; and a war of words, in many languages, with the English and Spanish predominating, in the Babal. My old companion, — Mr Wright, was exceedingly kind to me; he has a Californian wife with him. — We waited patiently, till the crowd and confusion abated, and then engaged a snug sail-boat: had our luggage put in, and bade adieu to the good ship California, — which has brought us so briskly and pleasantly down; and to her courteous and worthy Commander and officers, whom I sincerely wish long years of prosperity.

We raised a large sprit sail, and followed by a strong breeze, skimmed rapidly over the green waves. About midway, we were struck by a light squall and shower, which caused our little bark to bound more briskly, over the long swells. We had, however, to steer cautiously, to avoid the numerous sunken rocks in the way. Near the land, a small steamer ran athwart our bow, quite closely. — She plies between Panama and Tobago. We beached our boat, in light surf, in about 20 minutes, after leaving the ship. As soon as she struck bottom, the natives rushed into the water, — some assisting to draw the boat up, but the most of them, grabbing at the baggage, and passengers, to take them ashore. We had to order them peremptorily, to desist, till we were ready for their services. Three darkies now shouldered the passengers, — Mr. and Mrs Wright, and myself, and bore us up to the dry part of the beach. — Then the luggage was brought ashore, and piled up, and after that, the natives shouldered it, and we closely followed.

In about 100 yards, obliquely across the shingle and pebbles, we reached the entrance to the City, by a dilapidated gateway, through an arched passage, and then a narrow paved street, passing several very narrow transverse streets, till we at length arrived at a large portal, with a sign of "Entrance to the American Hotel". Entering we ascended a flight of broad stone steps, to a large hall, — paved with red tiles, in the back of which was a bar-room. Rooms were promptly assigned us, and our baggage accordingly disposed of. My quarters were a room on the 2nd floor, fronting the street, and opened into a balcony, floored over with red tiles.

Now came the tug of war! — About one dozen natives claimed pay for bringing up our baggage, though we had employed scarcely half that number. They gave us considerable trouble, to ascertain to whom we were actually indebted, and the just amount to pay. I got off by paying, $2,,50. When this was settled, I walked down to see the city.

There are many interesting ruins here. A detachment of bare-footed colored soldiers passed us, wearing only shirts and pantaloons, with bright arms, and drum and fife at their head.[126] I visited the Plaza, and examined the front of the great Cathedral; walked over to the guard-house and prison, in the rear of which, stood the stakes where a couple of criminals were shot, two days since. — A puddle of bloody sand was at the foot of each: and the wall of the prison, — some 10 paces, behind the place at which they sat was much cut by bullets.[127]

We ascertained, to-day, that there is no steamer yet, on the other side of the Isthmus, and in consequence, we must wait here, a day or so. After supper, Mr Wright told me, that early to-morrow morning, himself and wife, with a large number of the travellers, intended starting for Cruces; but I had to wait here till the local Agent of Adams & Co. — Mr Cover, had his packages ready, as he was to furnish me with mules.

The colored population seem to predominate here, and a large number are absolute blacks. I noticed a great many very aged females; but saw few handsome ladies. Clothing plentiful, and at reasonable rates. The fare at our hotel, is miserable; — for example, — Dinner, — fried ham, do. beef, boiled beans, molasses, and bread. — Dessert, — sliced pine-apple, and a table-spoon-ful, pr man, of bread-pudding. — Supper: — ham, beef, pork & beans, dry toast, bad coffee, and tolerable tea.

The Cathedral has been a magnificent structure, of the kind. There are many other large churches, a monastery and nunery, and ruins of the old Jesuit College. Most of these are in a ruinous state, covered with vines and moss. The walls and parapets of the City are alike ruinous; and the old stone turrets at the angles, are tottering over their foundations. The method of ornamenting the religious edifices, with pearl-oyster shells, was general, and when perfect, must have had a pretty and brilliant, if not appropriate effect. — Towers, spires, and gables, were thus enriched, the shells being arranged in regular forms, on stucco grounds, of various colors. I noticed a chain-gang, of criminals, sweeping a street, reminding me of my travels in South America.

There were but 8 deaths known in the City last week —

Here I had the pleasure of meeting Mr Wallach, formerly of Washington City, who has married a native lady, and is successfully engaged in the carry-ing business. I walked half a mile out of town, leaving the city by the land-gate, which has a bell-fry and bell over it, — to "Cocoa-Nut Grove:" where Capt. Hunter, and some other acquaintances have lodged them selves. Cocoa-nuts and other palm-trees, tropical plants, flowers, and birds, lend their charms, to this pretty spot — The American proprietors have built a neat two-story frame house, in the grove; where board and refreshments can be had; and pleasant repose, in grass-hammocks, under the tall trees, at night.

(*Nunery Gate*)   On returning to the City, I resumed my observation of it. — Walked upon the ramparts, which I reached by passing the entrance to the old nunnery, and ascended a small salient angle of the City Wall. — From this point I had an excellent view of the entire range, dedicated to St Francisco — the nunnery, convent, and ruined church. Below this long dingy row, stretched the broken walls of the city, and along its base, a strip of beach, full of canoes. — I sketched the scene, and resumed my travel, along the ramparts. Heat intense.

Reached an Angle of the walls, where lay several long heavy bronze guns, of beautiful proportions: none less than 100 years old. The natives aver that they are exceedingly valuable, on account of containing much silver in the composition; but which I doubt. I judge they are of the calabre of 32 pounders. — In the casemates, below, was a sort of arsenal; containing some mounted brass howitzers, and sundry piles of rusty shot and shell: — around which, lazy non-[com]missioned officers, with soldiers of various hues, were smoking their *papilletoes*. Rambling about all day, in the hot sun, gave me a severe headache; which, with the suffocating heat of the night, almost deprived me of repose.

JULY 3^d　At 8 A.M. Mr Wright bade me good-bye.

(*Gate &c.*)　In company with Capt. Day, U.S.A.[128] and Mr Seymour, U. S. Mail Agent, — (who were also passengers in the California, I walked up to the Porto Tierra, or Land Gate, and the Church of La Mercede, just within it: — both of which I sketched. On passing a window, I noticed, upon the iron bars, (no sashes here) a very large and brilliant beetle, — of a golden-bronze hue. On stepping up, to examine it, I saw that it was tied, by a leg, with a cotton-thread, and a handsome Spanish lady within, was watching me. — I saluted the lady, and enquired how I could obtain such a one? — She said that there were plenty in the country, but difficult to catch; and that this one was her pet, and she would not part with it. Small lizzards are quite numerous.

Great preparations are now going on, to celebrate our National Jubalee to-morrow; the civic and military authorities are participating　I noticed that the hairless dog, so common all over S. America and the W. Indies, is also common here.

From 6 to 9 A.M. Travellers, on horses and mules; and on Shank's mare, and long trains of heavily-ladened mules, were wending their way to the Land gate; a short distance beyond which the roads branch, — the left, to Gorgona, and the right, to Cruces.

JULY 4th   1851   Cloudy, and excessively warm. Native bands of music, have been, since day-light, practising our national airs of "Hail Columbia," and "Yankee Doodle," which they can perform very well. Children and youths are amusing themselves, and annoying every one else, with fire-crackers, and small rockets. A great bustle, making preparations for a parade, procession, and oratory. The flags of this, and our own Republic are fraternized. The "Panama Exchange," at the corner of the street leading to the Plaza, has a long pole projecting from the arcade, attached to which is a strip of cotton, thus inscribed, with black paint: —

> "Let Independence BE OUR BOAST,
> Ever mindful What it cost,
> Ever greatful for the prize,
> Let its Altars reach the skies."

At 10 A.M. the procession was formed, and marshalled, in the Plaza, opposite the Cathedral. — Native officers, with tri-colored ribbons and batons, were galloping about, and I forced my way through the crowd, to see the representation of Americans, in the affair. — Sure enough, there were 6 Yankee Naval uniforms, and friends of mine, and they insisted on my accompanying them; which I did, for a short distance, though I wore a light blouse. If several were surprized to meet here, unexpectedly, that of my friend Rodgers was the greatest, for we had not met before, since we parted in the Sierra Nevada, when he was attached to the Relief Party. Occasional showers, and exceedingly warm. A large party left to-day, for Cruces

I had forgotten to notice, yesterday, the detachment of returned Californians who marched out on foot, early yesterday morning, for Cruces. They were from two steamers. — Off they went, in a large body, with blankets and packs; rifles, pistols, and bowie-knives, and long mining boots. — They gave three hearty cheers, as they reached the gate. — This grotesque phalanx, of hardy adventurers, who are well acquainted with the *elephant*, would be tough customers to molest on the route.

At 11 A.M. I accompanied some friends, to the Government Hall, in the Plaza, and listened to an excellent address, by our Consul, which was followed by an explicatione, in Spanish, by a native general officer. The bands in the hall played our National Airs, and the banners of the two Republics were entwined. Salutes were also fired from the battery, and returned by the shipping

Our Consul, — Mr Corwine, gave a general invitation to the Americans, and at 7 P.M. there was a handsome entertainment at his house.[129] From 10 A.M. till 11 P.M. it was very warm, with light showers. Crackers, rockets, Bengal-lights, and other fire-works, with revelry and laughter, continued till late at night.

The people seem to be quite civil, and friendly. I heard a drunken soldier, in the street, sing out "Viva los Americanos!" — American signs are numerous, all over town.

I met a native, dragging a big snake along, tied by a chord around its neck. — The head was gone. It was about 8 feet long, and 18 or 20 inches circumference, at the largest part. It was of a mottled grey color, not unlike some of our rattle-snakes. The native showed me, that about 18 inches, including the head, was gone. I enquired what he intended to do with it? He replied that he would eat it, as it was very good. It came from the interior, where they are not uncommon. As our fare, to-day, has improved, I will notice it: — dinner; — Stewed fresh pork, fried plantains, tough fried beef, fried onions, and raw tomatoes. Dessert, plumb-pudding. The supper of hot cakes, cold meats from dinner, bad coffee, and tolerable fair tea. Some fights, at night, in the streets, — Yankees at the bottom of it.

I am informed that one of the pedestrian-adventurers, who started yesterday morning, for Cruces, a steerage passenger in the Columbus, walked across the Isthmus in long boots, red flannel drawers, loose red flannel shirt, felt hat, and rifle on shoulder — pretty warm work.

JULY 5th 1851 Awakened at 6 A.M. and started the baggage, for Cruces. At 8 A.M. all the remaining travellers had gone, leaving me alone behind, — awaiting for the agent to close his packages. At 11½ A.M., accompanied by Mr Leavett, (transit agent) we mounted our mules, and started for the gate. I could get neither holsters nor bridle; so tied my pistols together, over the saddle-bow; and hitched a piece of rope around the mules' lower jaw, to guide her.

It is well-known that the road, from Panama, across the Isthmus, was once paved, and some portions of the causeway still remain entire; but most of it, is swept away, or buried in mud. The paving is still good, some distance from the gate.[130] After leaving the gate about 200 yards, we turned to the right. On our left, there was an open space, containing a ruined fountain, and a dilapidated church, of stone, which seems to have been once of considerable importance. A little further on, we rode through a village, of two lines of houses, or rather huts, with mostly colored people. In a couple of miles further the road swept around to the left, being generally of red clay and sand.

The sun shone out with great power, and we spurred our mules, in order to compensate for the late starting. Occasionally we passed a native hut, on either side of the road, and mules returning from Cruces. Hairless dogs and half starved pigs were numerous.

We overtook a Spanish gentleman, on a mule, also travelling over, who spoke some words of English. He is going to New Orleans, to study the English language. Five miles from the City, we passed the train with the U. S. Mail, and I saw our pack-mules with it. — A little further, there was a muleteer reclining beneath a tree, with several packed mules, browsing around him: He hailed us, and on going up, we were informed, that two miles ahead, — at the entrance to a defile, three American brigands were stationed, and armed with revolvers, in wait for stragglers: which was the cause of his stopping, — to wait for more company. As there were three of us, also, we determined that the chances were equal, and proceeded.

The suspicious gorge was soon reached — narrow and deep; and a sort of covered way, of thick foliage. It was muddy, rocky, and sinuous: such a pass as three determined men, with revolvers, might occupy against superior numbers. In some parts, our knees were jostled against one or the other muddy cliff-wall; and I had, occasionally, to raise a foot, in passing a large rock or stump. The mules slipped, staggered, and leaped, through this interesting passage, of several hundred yards. I had sufficient, for hands and head, to preserve my equilibrium and seat; without thinking of banditti, after fairly entering the Pass.

On emerging from the gorge, we rode over small level spaces and undulating surfaces, enclosed by hills, for a short distance; and then entered another defile; — answering as a drain for torrents: it was full of deep pools of mud and water. This passage was, if any thing, more captivating than the first; — being just as crooked as numerous short bends, and right-angled corners, could make it. — Large prostrate trunks of trees lay here and there, — across the top, whose projecting branches and roots kept us constantly ducking our heads, to save our selves, from being unhorsed. — The reeking sides were from 8 to 30 feet high, and in some places, the passage was darkened by the overhanging and woven shrubbery.

Still ascending, About 1 P.M. it commenced raining, and soon after poured down, a perfect deluge, on our devoted heads; accompanied by such thunder and lightning, in blinding flashes and deafening peals, reverberating through the deep gorges and neighboring heights, as are rarely heard even within the tropics. The water ran off my arms and legs, in spouts and frisky fountains; and the old mule laid her ears back, and floundered through it, as if she thought her last hour was now surely come. My chief care, however, was to maintain my seat, and keep my pistols dry, both difficult achievements, under the circumstances of the case. The rain was of short duration.

We passed many return mules, driven by pedestrian natives. The sun occasionally glared upon us as from a reflector; parrots, macaws, and parroquets were constantly flying over, and hopping through the broad foliage, and chattering absurdly; and monkeys and other small animals were heard in the dank forests, alongside, engaged in similar garrulity.

Again we had to thread, narrow and rugged labyrinths: — in some places, so contracted, that it was a necessary custom to "halloo!" on entering them; — to warn travellers about to enter [the] opposite end of the pass. In several instances, where the walls of the pass were low, I had to throw my body forward, on my mule's neck, to clear a fallen tree, across the top. Fragments of the old Spanish paving, were scattered throughout the gorges; in confused masses; being now stumbling-blocks instead of facilities to the poor mules. Besides which, these narrow passages contained large rocks and huge masses of clay, — fallen from the cliffs; and the intervals were worn in deep round holes by the unceasing travel of mules.

But we shortly entered a gorge — intended to break the monotony of the preceding ones, by its new peculiarities. — The bottom was of that character, called, I believe, in some places, — a *corduroy-road*; — loose logs, laid helter-skelter, in mud, for about 50 feet, to the top of a hill. Then a descent, of the same distance, perhaps, but very narrow and crooked. — Steps of stones and earth, deep holes, pools of water, and deep lagoons of red mud; alternating with the loose logs below, and most unship-shape *cross-trees* above. Five resolute men, armed with revolvers, and stationed at some angle, in this peculiar passage, could discomfit and capture almost any number attempting to pass. — The foliage above was large and dense, where brigands could secrete themselves, while but one horseman could pass at a time below. In several spots, large masses of earth, rocks, and brush, stood in the centre of the gorge, like islands in the muddy water; — forcing the passage — (for road it could not be called) into branches on either side.[131]

Here and there, where the gorges of the route expanded, I noticed the reed cottages of the natives, with their thatched roofs, peeping from the thick brush and plantain groves, on the eminences. On the top of the *divide*, are three hamlets, some material distances apart, and each has a sign of "The true half-way House." At a native hut, on the left, perched on top of a bank, at the entrance to a defile, a man walked to the edge of the cliff, and asked us in English, Who were coming along? and how many travellers and trains were in the rear? I saw a couple of fellows behind him, and wondered what honest calling these Americans or Englishmen, could find here? What induce-' ment to live in an isolated indian hut, and feed on plantains, in such a climate.

Our Spanish comrade hurried ahead, on hearing interrogatories in English, from the cliff, and I told my companion that the case was suspicious, in which he coincided. So I told the fellow, on the bank, that there were many travellers, close in our rear.

Late in the afternoon, at an angle in the road, on the right, I passed a rude wooden cross, decorated with tinsel and ribbons, — opposite to which, on the branch of a tree, hung the sleeve of a white cotton shirt. A bare-footed native coming along, with a budget on his back, and a staff in his hand, — on reaching the cross, doffed his large straw sombrero, made a low bow to it, and proceeded. —

About 5 P.M. my comrade pushed ahead, in a Pass, as evening was closing around us, and he did not like to be caught in these suspicious gorges in the night. My mule was slow, but sure-footed, and I could not urge her to travel faster than she chose to do. At dusk, near the entrance to a deep and dark defile, on my right, about 50 feet high, upon the bank, I saw a reed hut, and the dark forms of several men crouching by a fire. I rode near the cliff, and hailed them in Spanish, asking the distance to Cruces? One of them replied, in Spanish, that it was 6 miles, and impossible for me to travel in the night! Another man cried out, "No possible, God d — n, you no can go Cruces esta night!" I replied, in a determined tone, "Si, possible, Carrahu!" and spurred on to the pass. I thought that those rascals might take a short cut, and head me at some dark turn in the gorge, but I was in for it, and there was no use in being skittish.

So I was soon within the walls of the narrow passage, where gloom amounting to darkness obscured every thing. — I had to close my eyes, occasionally, in order to observe the glimmer of the water beneath our feet, when I opened them. I knew not the ramifications of the black pass, but was sure that the mule did; so I dropped the substitute for a bridle upon her shoulders, and secured my seat upon her, by clinging to the saddle, before and behind. The faithful creature, however, went on, plunging, jumping, and stumbling; occasionally rubbing one of my knees against the muddy bank, but bearing me safely through darkness and danger. Had I been unhorsed, in that muddy cold glen, my situation would have been enchanting. I did not now fear robbers, for they could see no better in the dark than myself: and besides, it was not the hour for them to expect travellers on the road. We were rapidly descending; and at about 8 p.m. I was rejoiced to hear American voices, ascending from the town of Cruces. —

The gorge expanded, and I was no longer in total darkness. Soon the hill-sides became open space; and while listening to the sounds of laughter, in the town below, a rustle and cracking of sticks, on the cliff near my right, (25 or 30 feet high) caused me to look around, when a panther prowling there uttered so wild a cry, that my frightened mule laid back her ears, and ran down the mountain-slope, like Tam O'Shanter's mare, when closely pressed by the witches, — causing me to hold on the saddle, with might and main, like Johnny Gilpin, expecting momentarily to be projected far over her head, into the middle of next week. On reaching the plain, near the head of the town, I managed to catch the rope, and check her speed.

I had now only a short ride, of a few rods, and was about to turn, for a street, which was distinctly marked by a line of light, when a small black animal in the road, which I thought was a young bear, caused the mule to shy, and again start off at full speed, carrying me rapidly into the town; until I brought up at the "American Hotel," and dismounted, leaving half a dozen natives fighting about possession of the mule, though I told them who was the owner.

This so-called Hotel, is an American built frame house, rough and naked in the interior, and kept by a New Yorker. It was crowded, and among the sojourners I had the pleasure of again seeing Major Hobby and Mr Seymour, besides several other acquaintances.

I was weary and hungry, and obtained something to eat, for 50 cents, and then was shown up into a loft — or entire upper floor of the house, completely covered with cots and sleepers. For another 50 cents I had a cot, and sound repose: The night was drizzly, and cool enough to make a blanket comfortable.

I had put some rolls of bread in my pockets at Panama, but the rain had reduced them to soft pulp.

JULY 6th (SUNDAY)   Flying clouds, and very warm.

A miserable breakfast, and we could not tolerate the stuff they called coffee, so waited till a pot of tea was made. Another half dollar for this meal.

After breakfast I walked up the street, — and on the same side, a few doors above the hotel, I observed a man dead, within the door of a hut. On approaching the reed-formed tenement, I observed that he was extended on a table, in the centre of the room. He was dark, nearly negro; clad in a full dress-suit of black cloth, with black silk stock, white standing collar, and wore black patent leather boots, and his jaws were tied up with a broad black ribbon. On each side of him a candle was burning and several natives — of both sexes, sat around upon the earthy floor. They do not, it appears, use coffins here: but carry the body to the grave in a kind of coffin-bier. — (*Coffin*) One of these stood outside the door; — decently covered with faded purple velvet.

Silently leaving the house of mourning, I proceeded up the street to the church, which stands on an elevated plateau, at the head of the two principal streets, in an open space which I presume is called the 'Plaza.' Men, in rows, three deep, were kneeling in the broad doorway, which is the gable-end. These devotees were performing the usual genuflections, and whenever the priest at the altar rang a small bell, they bowed their heads in the dust.

When the services were concluded, a young man of olive complexion, who, as I was informed, was the Alcalde, convened all the males in front of the church, and read to them a long list of ordinances of the government, chiefly relating to duties, and transportation, on the routes. About a dozen men listened very attentively to him, and occasionally desired explanations of certain parts. When they dispersed, I walked into the mouldy old church, up to a long bench, which was placed mid-way between the Altar and Portal, and took a seat. Two creole women were at the foot of the altar, apparently doing penance. One knelt upon the lower step, with outstretched arms, audibly muttering her pater nosters. The annoying task imposed upon her, seemed to be, to repeat a certain number of Prayers, with extended arms. Her arms became fatigued, and gradually sank, and then she would raise them again, with a deep sigh, and occasionally bow her head, and kiss the dirty edge of the step before her.

It took her about 15 minutes to get through this ordeal, when she arose, made her obesience to a mutilated wooden image, in a cobwebby niche above, drew her serrappa around her head and shoulders, and walked off. Another female then entered, dropped a courtesey to another dilapidated figure full of rags, tinsel, and cobwebs; which appeared to me to have been the representation of some prelate. She then kissed a step of the Altar, blessed herself, and also retired. Being left alone, I walked around this very barn-looking church, to examine it and the mouldy remains of its decorations. The floor, was of earth, and sides and corners full of trash, such as rude frames for transparencies, palanquins, wooden crosses, mutilated wooden crucifixes, broken benches, and coffin-biers, rags, tinsel, and cobwebs. The Altar was chiefly of wood, and very dirty. Ragged common paintings, of Saints and the Virgin, dressed in cheap callicoes, which were dropping from them in moist decay, in unison with the *Irish drapery* [cobwebs?] around.

The plateau in front of the church, was once paved, about 20 paces wide to the front, where it broke off perpendicularly. Between the church and the front of the pavement, on one side, stood a rotten wooden rack or gallows, to which were suspended three very old, warped and split bells, of small size. One of them, was in fact, half gone, another had lost a large piece, and the third and best, was cracked. To ring them, a boy struck the best one with a pebble. The church is of stone, and stuccoed. — Roof of wood, open in several places, and threatening to fall in. The Buccaneers burnt this town once, when it was a considerable place, hence the unhappy condition of the bells.

The female who had performed the spread-eagle penance within, was now on the platform, outside. She hailed an adjacent house, and the boy whom I had seen ringing the cracked bell with a pebble, came out, bearing in his hand a pair of wooden clogs, which he handed to the penitent — when she knelt, took off her slippers, and strapped on these antique-looking sandals. The fore-part of the soles and the heels were several inches high, like those made for a person with a contracted leg; but taking her slippers in her hand, she walked down the street upon these mud dodgers, with much independence of manner. Another woman passing, looked down at her frail sister's feet.

On the pavement, on the opposite side to the bells, near the church, lay a couple of long and handsomely embellished brass guns, about the calibre of 6 and 9 pounders. One is French, and dated 1737; the other is Spanish, and dated 1809. Near these lay a very ancient looking iron anchor, half-corroded away with rust. — It might have once served a Galleon. About 40 paces in front of the church stands a very neat white stone structure, with roof of stone, and heavy iron door, resembling a large burial vault: but it is only for the temporary burial of English specie, on its way from Panama to England.

There are 3 long parallel streets, in this place, being the principal ones, which run down from the church, near the bank of the Chagres river. They are closely built up with reed and thatched houses, and there are a few transverse streets. The town, at a distance, looks like a tolerably symetrical arrangement of hay-cocks.

On my return from a short detour of observation, the defunct darkie was borne in procession, to the burial place, — nearly in the rear of the church. — The padre, with crucifix, led the way, followed by the bearers and crowd, in no particular order. On reaching the grave, they set the bier down, took off the cover, and then canted it so that the dead body rolled into the grave.

The bearers then jumped in upon it, and danced about, to straighten it, (perhaps to make sure of his death) and a bottle of wine or aqua-audenta [agua ardiente] was passed around, and the funeral ceremonies concluded with laughter and merriment. There are few white natives here. At night groups gathered around tables in the street, with candles burning, playing Monte, and other games. There is also a negro Billiard Salloon here, which no doubt contributes to the very refined sable sympathies of this miserable place. Heat oppressive, and the town a miserable place.

On awakening, and sitting up in my cot, I was astonished to see a young woman sitting up also in the next cot to me, and fastening the back of her dress; while all around were upwards of a hundred men perhaps, in every stage of rising and dressing. My evident astonishment compelled me to observe to her, that I thought it a very unpleasant predicament for a young lady to be placed in, and she replied that it was; but she had become accustomed to such inconveniences, having crossed the Isthmus several times! I was afterwards informed that she was the wife of the man who recently robbed a jeweller, and a priest, in Panama, and then fled across the Isthmus. She is still in search of him, and says that if she does not meet him in New Orleans, she will proceed from thence to New York. This lady's baggage, with some other, has been carried by mistake or villainy, to Gorgona, instead of being brought here; and th[e]y are going down the river in search of it.

There is much anxiety about our baggage, which, as well as the Mail and specie train, are still in the rear: and there is a report here, that a band of 30 brigands, well-armed, are on the road in wait for the latter.

At 1 P.M. our apprehensions were all allayed by the arrival of the mule trains; and a small party of us at once engaged a boat to descend the river. A good strong launch, with awning fore and aft, called the Gorgona, pulled by four yellow half-naked natives, and owned and commanded by a Long Island negro named Williams, is to take five of us and our luggage down the river to Chagres. Williams is a clever accommodating fellow; has served his three years in the U.S.N. and his boatmen are also very civil. We pay five dollars each —

My companion, of the Express, and two other passengers were acquaintances, and we were prepared to drift down as pleasantly as possible, — having to aid us in this particular, a box of ale, several bottles of claret, and a couple of Brandy, with crackers, cheese, cigars, pipes and tobacco. All hands were cheerful and agreeable, and we drifted down stream right merrily. Captain Williams handled the tiller, and had to steer clear of snags, sawyers, and sand banks, and guide us judiciously down rapids. The rowing was easy, or at least, appeared to be easily performed. We twice grounded, however, on banks, when each time the boatmen leaped into the water and soon shoved off again.

The river is exceedingly crooked, and enclosed between high hills, covered with thick forests and dense shrubbery, down to the water's edge. — Palms, bananas, rich vines, reeds, majestic plants, and beautiful flowers, crowd upon the stream in lavish luxuriance, and the reflection of this mass of verdure, gives the water a rich green and gorgeous aspect. Florid birds of the parrot kind, and others of brilliant plumage, are constantly flying over, and chattering, in their ridiculous Punch and Judy style of colloquy. I noticed several species of king-fishers, — some very small, and one of a large size. Herons, — blue, and white, and vultures with white shoulders, occasionally added to the diversity of the scene. Monkeys were holding their peculiar confabulations in the woods, at once screamy and expectorative. Saw a small alligator, and fired a pistol at him, causing him to grin horribly a ghastly smile, at my folly.

We passed several canoes and barges going up and late in the afternoon we reached Palenkena, where lay a very small steam-boat, just arrived from Chagres, full of California passengers, amongst whom were several wifes, with their little children, going out to seek their husbands. The passengers were taking boats to ascend the river. Soon another small iron Steamer passed, also filled with passengers, endeavoring to get higher up. These little steamers are called the "Milly" and "Swan".

JULY 7th   About 1 A.M. our gondola ran alongside the bank at Gatoon, — in the midst of a flotilla of barges, launches, & canoes: most of whom were bound up river. We rested here about two hours, and pushed off again. Our passengers, obtained some sleep, in such postures as we could best select for the purpose, where there was a little choice. At about 6 A.M. we reached Chagres, and hauled in to the bank, through legions of boats and canoes, and all sorts of people.

Quickly did we make our way ashore, in search of a breakfast, and was amazed at meeting so many acquaintances and fellow travellers The principal house of entertainment is called the "Irvine House", and fronts the landing, about 20 paces from it. Breakfast was nearly ready when we reached the house, and a crowd stood around the long table. At the raising of the hand-bell, they rushed into the seats, precluding us most effectually from any chance there, so we walked out and continued around the point to where we were told we could obtain a good breakfast. — We soon found the snug little shanty of old Joe Prince, and in a few minutes were regaled with an excellent and hearty breakfast, for which we paid 75 cents each.

The distances over the Isthmus,[132] are as follows: —

From Panama, to Cruces — 25 miles, mule travel.

By water { From Cruces to Palenkina,   20 do.
          ”   Palenkina to Gatoon   30 do.
          ”   Gatoon to Chagres —   10 do

                                Total   85 miles

After breakfast, I accompanied a few friends across the harbor, to the old town. Passing through the narrow dirty streets, I saw Mr Wright, who was waiting there, for the arrival of steamer for New Orleans. We were paddled across in a canoe. The main streets have once been well paved. The houses are similar to those of Cruces, except a few dilapidated adobes, and two or three American frames, of two storys. Many American & English signs indicative of eating and drinking establishments, such as "Jack of Clubs," "Davy Crockett," &c. Several Billiard houses, with black gamblers around the tables. We followed a street, nearly parallel with the water, to the foot of the tall hill on which stands the moss-grown old castle. Then turned to the right, — in another street, followed it a short distance, and then to the left on a moist and crooked path. The soil here is of the richest black loam. A slight ascent, of about one mile, along the margin of a deep tangled glen, brought us to a beautiful mountain brook. Our guide was my worthy friend Capt Hunter, U.S. Rev: S. — He had bathed in this place several years ago. The stream is in some parts 30 to 40 feet wide, but very shallow; and traverses a deep dell, fringed and oershadowed by rank grass and weeds, jungle, and damp forests of large trees, festooned with luxuriant vines, and clothed in mosses. A large number of parasitic plants are here. The bed of the stream is a soft sand stone, worn full of holes, some of considerable depth. The water is clear and cool; a perfect luxury in such a sultry climate. Moisture was weeping upon us from the thick tropical foliage over head; colored women were engaged at ev[er]y accessible part of the bank, washing clothes; and the slopes were covered with vestments of every kind. On returning, we met several male natives, with large machettas, apparently going up in the hills to cut fuel. At the end of the lower street, near the landing, I saw a treasure vault exactly like that at Cruces, and was told that it belonged to the same concern.

Quite a number of small craft are in the harbor: and boats and canoes innumerable. There were also several square-rigged craft, — mostly brigs. The Consuls all reside in the old town. The new town is almost entirely American, covering the narrow tongue of land which protects the harbor from the sea. At Meridian I transferred my small amount of luggage to a large row-boat, manned by Englishmen, and full of other return Californians. We pulled out about 2 miles from land, to the Steamer Brother Jonathan.[133] The swell increased till we reached the ship, where it was considerable, and required some adroit agility to get safely on board. We each paid the boatmen 2 dollars, and I paid for a cabin ticket in the steamer, 50 dollars. I was highly gratified on getting on board, to find my highly esteemed Comrades du voyage, on the other side, were also to accompany me in this voyage. —

There lays at anchor near us, the British Mail Steamer Trent, — a fine-looking vessel; and Steamer Alabama.[134] On looking down the coast, we saw, standing around a point of land, some 12 ms. off, a small steamer, — towing a brig; perhaps from Porto Bello. A barque is seen on the horizon; and an English cutter sloop lies near us.

The old castle, on the eminence, is a mass of grey stone and dark green moss and shrubbery. — The fortification and the hill on which it stands, are blended in a piece of grey stone and green verdure. Only here and there a short line of coping, an embrasure, or red tiles of a house-top, serve to convince one that there is any of man's work there. I regretted much that I had not visited the old castle. The ruins are exceedingly picturesque, and its history quite interesting. It was once captured by the English Buccaneer, Morgan, who managed to get guns upon the height in the rear, overlooking the castle, and thus reduced it. Since then the Spaniards fortified that height also, and the grey and moss-covered lines of that outwork are now all of apiece with the castle and hill. The Buccaneers first captured Panama, then crossed the Isthmus, burning Cruces in the way, and tearing up the paving, to prevent rapid pursuit.

The pedestrian party who left Panama on the 3d joined others already at Chagres, and they took possession of the old castle, to celebrate the 4th — They contrived to clean out several of the heavy old brass canon, fired a salute of 100 guns, and ran up the Stars and Stripes over the ruined walls, where they had never before been displayed. The authorities of the town expressed great indignation at this innovation of the rough Yankees.

When we had descended the Chagres river to where the water was brackish, our boatmen became thirsty, and pulled the boat into a deep glen on the left, where a delightful rill of pure water leaped sparklingly through the foliage, into the river. We entered a little cove, and the men drank from the brook. In the sandy bottom of the cove I saw several large crabs, with one immense claw, like the minute crabs familliarly known as fiddlers. Capt. Williams says that this stream is 3 miles above Chagres.[135]

I am informed that Major Hobby was robbed, at Cruces, of an over coat, and Capt. Moore, of funds, abstracted from his carpet-bag.[136] Capt. Squires, of the Brother Jonathan, informs me that robberies and murders are frequent at Chagres, and the Yankees have established Lynch law in consequence.

The Brother Jonathan is a good sea-boat, with a strong engine, but her accommodations are inconvenient and inappropriate for such service, in such climes: And no regulations usual on board such vessels are enforced. Her burthen is 1400 tons

> Commander Heber Squires,
> Sailing Master, E. McKeige
> H. Dennison — 1st Officer
> — Miller — 2nd Do —
> H. Sandford — Chf: Engineer
> Wm Mills — Purser
> Lemuel Wales — M.D. Surgeon

She has on board, 61 first class passengers, 7 — second class do, 156 steerage do — and 25 *uncertain* passengers: Total 249 passengers.

The officers of the ship are a very clever set of men. — Several steerage passengers exchanged their tickets — paying the difference, for places in the cabin.

My kind comrade across the Isthmus — Leavett, left the ship for shore, to return to Panama. About 3 P.M. we dined.

At 4 P.M. the swell increased, and the ship rolled heavily. A sail-boat brought on board our esteemed friend Judge Jones; and Judge Lyons, being in the boat, returned to shore, to await the steamer for New Orleans.

Many years ago, in my rambles over South America and the W. Indies, and Brazil, I had visited Chagres, in a Venezuelian Sloop of War, little dreaming of ever seeing it again.

About 6 P.M. we were heartily glad to find the steamer under way. At 7, the bell summoned us to supper. Hot weather, and a damp and dirty ship. Rain and lightning

A heavy sea, deep rolling of the ship, and suffocating heat below, entirely precluded all ideas of sleep, in the state-rooms:

About 11 P.M. passed a steamer, which from the color of her lights, is supposed to be the 'Crescent City'[137] going into Chagres.

I find that I remained too long in the cool stream at Chagres, and now feel the bad effects of my imprudence, by suffering pains in loins & breast, which compelled me to send to the surgeon for embrocation, in the night.

[JULY] 8th Commences with flying clouds, and heavy swell. Shoals of silvery flying-fish are skimming over the dark green waves, fleeing before our swift craft, no doubt immagining her to be some huge and voracious monster of the deep, in pursuit of them.

The trade-wind is quite fresh on our starboard bow. The exhalations from the lower decks of the ship are not very savory: No wonder, for I never saw a dirtier set of forward passengers, in any vessel; and their numerous monkeys, parrots, &c. and piles of tropical fruits, pealings, and shells, are sufficient to produce disease   enough to set up a perfumery establishment.

There is a great difference in this, the Atlantic, and the Pacific Ocean; at least near the land. This water is of a darker and clearer blue, and more lively and phosphorescent, than the latter. And it is also more susceptible of agitation than the Pacific from some cause or other.

Late in the afternoon the sea subsided a little, — the swells are longer and shallower than in the forenoon. There is no comfortable resting place here for the passengers. — Below, the heat is insufferable, in contracted apartments, subject to every kind of annoyance, many of the passengers being sea-sick. On deck, it is damp and dirty, or broiling hot, in the sun. Under the quarter deck and forecastle awnings, the steerage passengers have possession, and are rolling all over the decks. So a few of us have to avail our selves of the Captain's kind invitation, and hang around his little cabin, on Deck.

At night the sea increased, and all night the ship wallowed beautifully. In spite of the ship's motion, and the excessive heat, I managed to obtain 3 or four hour's sleep, before day.

[JULY] 9th Flying clouds, strong breeze, and heavy swell, and as heavy a roll of the ship as a moderate man could wish. At 8 A.M. set the fore sail, forestay sail, main-sail, and jib. — Squally, with light showers. Handed the stay-sail and jib.

Afternoon, light flying clouds, and strong breeze. — Ship goes ahead easier. At 5½ P.M. a sail on the lee bow: — a schooner, running before the wind, under main sail and two jibs. Our decks are very wet.

We have one lady passenger, an elderly and unreasonably homely Irish woman: — a forward passenger. — On coming out of the cabin, from the dinner-table, my attention was attracted to this unfortunate woman, by her outcries. — She lay upon a matrass, in a narrow passage, alongside the Engine-room — with several of the colored waiters around. — She was wringing her hands, shedding tears copiously, and swaying her body to and fro, while she moaned, and groaned, and with awful countenance, occasionally cried out, "I'm perishing for want of Support!" "Oh! I'm perishing for want of sup-port!" — I stepped up, and enquired the cause of her lamentations, and strange ejaculations? — She mournfully replied, "I'm very sick, and can eat noth-ing!" — "Have eat nothing for three days"! "Sure, and I paid two bitts for a bottle of Porter; and I asked them for a little rice-water, and they wont give me any; and I sent for the Dochter, and he wouldn't come! — Then she screamed out, again "Oh! I'm dying for want of support!" — I consoled her by the assurance that one of the boys should get her some rice-water, and I would speak to the surgeon. On reaching the upper deck, I enquired of the Doctor, why he treated the lady so ungallantly? He replied that all he knew about the dame, was that she had taken too much of what she called rice-water already.

Night set in cloudy, with a strong breeze. Took in the foresail. Exceed-ingly warm below. Ship rolls considerably

JULY 10th — Hazy weather. Sea ahead, and smoother; course N.E. $\frac{1}{2}$ E. — Took in sail. Sultry weather. About 9 A.M. land in view, on the lee bow, bearing N. by E. about 25 miles distant. — The dark blue tops of mountains can just be discerned, high, amongst clouds; below which, to the surface of the ocean, is a mass of vapor and dove-colored clouds. — This land is the high range on the Island of Jamaica. At 3 P.M. we were boarded by a canoe, under a sprit-sail, and received a negro pilot. We had made land about 25 miles to the windward of Port Royal, and had to run down for it. Steaming up the harbor of Port Royal, we were boarded by the Health Officer, which detained us a few minutes: and at 4 P.M. we hauled into the wharf, at Kings-ton.

The passengers leaped ashore as soon as they could, and I accompanied some friends ashore, just to see how the place looked since the slave emanci-pation: as I had visited it just before that notable event.[138] We made our way through a crowd of begging colored children, to the "Commercial Hotel," where we had an excellent supper, and as fine a Sherry-cobbler as any city in the States could produce, and refreshingly thick with Boston ice.[139] We then strolled through some of the principal streets, and returned to the Hotel, and slept soundly.

[JULY] 11th   Amused myself by examining the city and its characters. There is a constabulary police, uniformed in a sort of military fatigue suit, and carrying short heavy batons. All business is suspended here, daily, at 4 P.M.; after that hour the multifarious shades of colored blood, of both sexes, are dressed in their best, and loll about in the shade, or promenade the streets. Crowds of children beset you at the gangway, on the wharf, and along the streets, begging for "*dimes*". The females of the lower order, seem to have abandoned them selves entirely to dissatisfaction, and idleness.

We breakfasted at the Commercial, and bade our clever obliging host adieu. This is an excellent house, and worthy proprietors. About meridian our ship's gun summoned us on board, so we hurried down through the motley crowd, and reached her deck, no more to leave it, unless by accident, until we should jump ashore, at home. In about half an hour after, she backed out of the quay, with a considerable accession of trash, and fruit, to increase the nuisances already existing on board.

When off Port Royal, a boat visited us from the Admiral's Ship, the officer spoke to our purser, returned to his boat, and we proceeded. Night intolerably warm, and our ship rolling heavily. A little accident occurred, about 8 P.M. which if not so soon detected, might have resulted calamitously. — The friction of the wheel-shaft fired a portion of the wood-work which was improperly in contact with it. The fire was immediately extinguished.

[JULY] 12th   Clear, smooth sea, and light head wind. Very warm.

(*at 8 A.M. washed the decks*)   A brig on the starboard quarter — standing to the windward. 2 P.M. Cuba in sight, a little forward of the larboard beam. 6 P.M. opposite, and within 5 miles of Cape Maze [Maisí]: at 8 P.M. cleared it. A considerable swell, and the ship rolls much, in the trough of the sea. Lightning in clouds ahead of us. Set our three principal lower sails. The thermometer stands too high for me to sleep in the lower berth of the stateroom.

[JULY] 13th   Clear. Wind abaft the beam, and light: smooth sea; all sail set. Early in the morning abreast of Castle island, (Crooked island passage)   The islands on our starboard side are distant 8 or 10 miles.

9 A.M. Within 2 miles, abreast, of Fortune island, on which is a small town. 11 A.M. Clear of the land, and now have a clean run of 1000 miles to New York.

After dinner, took in all sail except the main-sail. A strong breeze on the starboard bow; temperature more agreeable than any since we left San Diego.

The night was clear and pleasant, and I sat up some hours after supper. Ship makes about 9 knots per hour, — A good night's repose —

[JULY] 14th   Clear, with very light airs, and smooth sea. Headway 9½ knots per hour. An abortive meeting of malcontents in the steerage: — they have cause of complaint in this ship, but if their fare is not so good as that of the cabin, they enjoy other privileges, — not inferior, that we would be glad to have — the entire decks are theirs   I was most agreeably surprised to recognise one of my old friends of "Gold Bluff" memory among the forward passengers.

   I P.M. light wind, on the larboard side. Set all sail. — A light shower of rain passed over us. At 5½ P.M. Small rain squalls blowing over, for a short time, then cloudy, with a pleasant breeze, and smooth sea; all sail set, and ship making 11 knots. At 9 A.M. a flaw of wind, carried away our fore-top mast. — It happened to be too small, and insufficiently stayed.

[JULY] 15th   Flying clouds, pleasant breeze, and smooth sea. — Making 10 knots. 9 A.M. a Sail ahead. — proved to be a hermaphrodite brig, standing to the S.S.E. and under all sail, except her topsail. Our course is N. Afternoon, breeze decreased. 6 P.M. a topsail schooner to leward, Standing to the N.W. A bark on our weather (starboard) side, standing S.S.E. At dusk a schooner on the weather bow. The breeze failing, and drawing ahead. Sails handed.

[JULY] 16th   Near day set sail. Course N. a slight haze in the morning. Two square-rigged vessels, with steering-sails set, ahead of us and standing N.N.E. Smooth sea, and light breeze; all sail set, on starboard side. Several vessels in sight, on both sides. — A brig on the lee bow appears to be standing to the N.N.E. A ship and bark standing in for land, and a small schooner standing to the Eastward.

   At Sun Set three sails were in sight.

   1851   JULY 17th   Hazy and nearly calm. Handed the sails. Many sails in sight, most of which are ahead an[d] in-shore of us. At 9 A.M. we passed a small schooner, on the opposite course. 10 A.M. Set the sails, with a light breeze, course N. ½ E. 4 P.M. light airs; clewed up the fore-sail. Barnegat and the Highlands in sight; — ahead. Sails numerous.

   Pilot-boat No 5, passed us.

   A paper, complimentary to the Officers of the Ship, and condemnatory of her arrangements and accommodations, and signed by the after passengers, was handed to the Captain. At 6 P.M. displayed our colours. At 7 P.M. a pilot-boat bearing down, took in sail and luffed. Confusion and vexation among the steerage passengers, on missing many Panama hats, &c. stolen by the hands of the vessel. The fore castle was searched, resulting in finding several of the stolen articles, and restoring them. Some rogue below pushed a panama hat through an air-port, while the search was going on. I have lost a pair of slippers and several other small articles.

Received our pilot, and stood up for the harbor of New York. Detained in the night, some time, off the Quarantine at Staten Island, waiting for the Health Officer: after his visit, we ran up, and after much bungling managed to get the ship in her berth, by 10 A.M. Some of the passengers became so impatient that they jumped into boats, and landed long before the ship was secured. On reaching the wharf, most of the passengers left. I would not trust the Express baggage and my own, to the set of characters who wished to get hold of them so determined to remain on board all night. I sat up late, conversing with a clever gentlemanly Inspector of the Customs, till near midnight, when I retired to my state-room, and slept very soundly, notwithstanding a large brilliant globe lantern near the door of my state-room, and loud talk and laughter of the servants.

JULY 18th   I arose at 6 A.M. awaiting Adam's Express car, for their baggage. At 7 o'clock I sent another Express car-man to tell Adams & Co. to send down their car. Soon after, several Agents of the Post Office Department came on board, and desired an examination of the baggage in my charge. After a casual investigation, they detained it, and I had to wait for their further action. At 8 o'clock the Express Car came down, but found that the baggage was then embargoed by Government Officials. Purser Miles politely invited me to breakfast with him. The P.O. gentlemen had the Express baggage and mine taken to the P. office, where I went with them. My own baggage was relieved from the dilemma, and sent to the Merchants' Hotel, where I went also. I felt greatly mortified at this procedure and the consequences, — rather an unfortunate winding up of my Agency.

On opening my trunk, to obtain money for some necessary purchases, I found that it had been thoroughly over hauled, and robbed, of every thing of value I possessed except my books and drawings. Those villainous hands of the steamer, had taken my trunk out of the state-room, carried it into another room, and examined it through, robbed it, and then put it back in my state-room, alongside of me. The night before, I happened to awake, at a late hour, and caught one of the servants just entering the room, who retreated on seeing me awake. It was my opinion that the same fellow and a barber were the rogues, for they were intimate, and of the articles stolen there were two razor-strops and a couple of good razors, leaving an indifferent razor in the trunk. I started down the street, intending to go on board the steamer, and have the suspected hands arrested, but had proceeded only a few squares when I met one of the passengers, who had also been robbed of several hundred dollars, — carpet-bag, and all. He told me that I might save myself the trouble of proceeding further — that the ship hands had left her, and it was all confusion on board — So I retraced my steps to the Hotel.

After dinner, when preparing to leave, for the cars, an officer served a subpoena on me, to attend the circuit court, as a witness, on the 5th inst. Of course, this must be in relation to the Express matter.

On my way to the Ferry, I had the pleasure of overtaking General Scott,[140] also on his way to Washington. Reached Philadelphia about 10 P.M.

[JULY] 19th   At 3 P.M. went on board a small steamer — which carried us to New Castle, Del. from thence we were conveyed, by R. Road, to the head of the Chesapeake Bay, and from thence, by steam-boat, to Baltimore; where we arrived about 10 P.M. and soon I had the pleasure of greeting the gentlemanly and accommodating proprietor of the United States Hotel.

[JULY] 20th. At 6 A.M. I breakfasted, and entered the cars for home, and in a little over two hours, was in the bosom of my family, after an absence of two years and three months. —

Never before did I so devoutly appreciate the heart-born ballad, "Home! Sweet home!", of my departed friend John Howard Payne, and none the less that I had "seen the elephant," and emphatically realized the meaning of the ancient myth — travelling in search of

THE GOLDEN *FLEECE*!

SKETCHES

FROM SUPPLEMENTARY NOTEBOOK A [P]
AND FROM THE HUNTINGTON
COLLECTION [H]

———————

ALL CAPTIONS are Bruff's, unless enclosed within square brackets. The wagons of the Washington City Company and sometimes one or two of its members afoot or on horseback are to be seen in many of the sketches. Some of the drawings extend across the double page.

————

[Bruff occupied his time from Feb. 13 to Feb. 20, 1851, in sketching in the village of "Choli," under Trinidad Head. The following notes are explanatory of these sketches.]

["The lodges of these Indians (Yuroks) are generally very well built; being made of boards riven from the redwood or fir, and of considerable size, often reaching twenty feet square. Their roofs are pitched over a ridge-pole, and sloping each way; the ground being usually excavated to the depth of three or four feet, and a pavement of smooth stones laid in front. The cellars of the better class are also floored and walled with stone. The door always consists of a round hole in a heavy plank, just sufficient to admit the body; and is formed with a view to exclude the bears, who in winter make occasional and very unwelcome visits" (Gibbs, "Journal," p. 140).

"It [the Indian cabin] is very much like a chalet, and they are every whit as clean, comfortable, and substantial as the Sennhütten, wherein is made the world-famous Emmenthaler cheese, for I have been inside of both" (Powers, *Tribes*, p. 46).

"A very characteristic thing about the more important Yurok villages is that the houses in most cases have names. . . . The house was a big thing in the life of the Yurok, and the house name stood for family standing and respectability" (Waterman, "Yurok Geography," p. 208).]

Grave of a Trinidad Squaw [P]   560

["On the death of a person, the friends assemble, and raise a peculiar cry or wail, which is caught up from one to another, and can be heard a great distance. The body is always kept over one night, before interment. If the deceased was one of any consideration, all the girls of the village unite in making baskets, to be placed round the grave; otherwise one only is staked down at the head, and another at the foot" (Gibbs, "Journal," p. 175). Gibbs and Bruff visited the Yurok in the same year, 1851.

"The graves, which are in the immediate vicinity of the houses, exhibit very considerable taste and a laudable care. The dead are inclosed in rude coffins formed by placing four boards around the body, and covered with earth to some depth; a heavy plank, often supported by upright head and foot stones, is laid upon the top, or stones are built up into a wall about a foot above the ground, and the top flagged with others. The graves of the chiefs are surrounded by neat wooden palings, each pale ornamented with a feather from the tail of the bald eagle. Baskets are usually staked down by the side, according to the wealth or popularity of the individual, and sometimes other articles for ornament or use are suspended over them. The funeral ceremonies occupy three days, during which the soul of the deceased is in danger from *O-mah-á* or the devil. To preserve it from this peril, a fire is kept up at the grave, and the friends of the deceased howl around it to scare away the demon" (Gibbs, quoted by Yarrow, *Introduction to the Study of Mortuary Customs*, p. 10).]

Sweating-House, Trinidad Indn Ville [P]   560

["Sweat houses. . . . Smaller than the dwelling and dug out over its entire extent. . . . The interior is neatness itself. . . . The door is in the middle of one of the long sides, and always faces the river or ocean. . . . A second door, used only as an exit, is at one of the small ends. . . . All winter long, and often in summer, men and grown boys slept in the sweat house, and passed the evenings in talk and smoking" (Kroeber, *Handbook*, pp. 80–81).

"The 'sweat house' is the oldest educational institution in America. A daily, five-hour course of instruction was given to all the boys. Attendance was compulsory. The curriculum embraced . . . law and religion, history and civics, music and morals, personal hygiene, private and public etiquette, public speaking, handcraft and scoutcraft" (Graves, *Lore and Legends of the Klamath River Indians*, p. 85).]

The grave of a chief. With feathers around pallisade & son kill'd by the Inds at Forks of Trinity & Tlamath — (the Eurooks) 100 ms. distant, & mountainous wooded road; from whence his squaw packed him down on her back in $2\frac{1}{2}$ days. Young chief named Largo — son of the Morweme (chief —)

In Feby 1850 — When Largo's wife brot in his remains, the Indians inform'd the whites at Trinidad & invited them to attend the funeral. His squaw ——, prepared the body for interment by washing & marking over it, many stripes of black — put his beads, wampum, &c. in his hands, envellop'd the body in skins; laid mats in bottom of the grave, after digging it herself, and assisted by the whites, laid the body on back, placing shells, &c &c — on breast — & cover'd it up. Women howling around, & old chief (the father) standing on sweat-house, directing.

———

[Colored manuscript map, now in the custody of the Archivist of the United States.]

Camp at St Joseph's (*Black Snake Hill*) Mo.

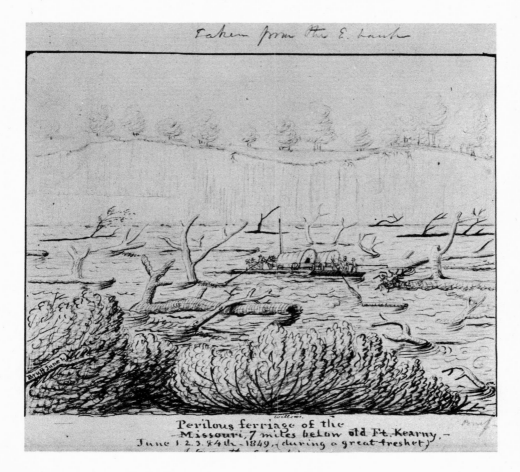

Perilous ferriage of the
Missouri, 7 miles below old Ft. Kearny,
June 1.2.3. & 4th 1849. (during a great freshet)

J G Bruff July 27 49

& Spurs of the Sweet Water Mts

Sweet-Water River & Rattle-Snake Hills, (Noon halt July 27.)
(½ mile above view plate A.)
(S. side river ½ mile below a cañon) 10½ Ms. W. of Devil's Ga

J G Bruff July 28 49

In the Bird Pass, a Gorge of Rattle-Snake Mountains, Sweet Water R.
(Noon halt on N. side of the stream)
N. side of the river

This modified dropping frying pan, kicking things over,
seizing arms, &c.

Eat a hearty supper, boys! To-morrow
you'll have to try Shank's mare!

Seeing Elephant No. 4.
The Buffalo Hunt   The Buffalo are not quite
so green as some folks think

green

sweet

Road

camp of the
Washington City
Company.

HENRY AUSTIN. M.D
JOHN BATES
CHS. H. MOXLEY

July 26th 1849). View of the sweet water River, the pl

534

meadows

mules & grazing

path – ind: trail – buffalo &c. also.

sand

er river

Poler Beh
Cincinati R....

Alfred Carter
...&c Hu...R...

John W. Smith June 1849
Thos. B. Brown. ...1849

G. B.
William Robertson. U...

Light

J. G. Bruff, Washington City Co
July 26th, 1849

The rock is a
coarse kind of
granite, feldspar
white, yellow, &
flesh color,
predominating

d distant Mountains, &c. from top of *Independence Rock.*

535

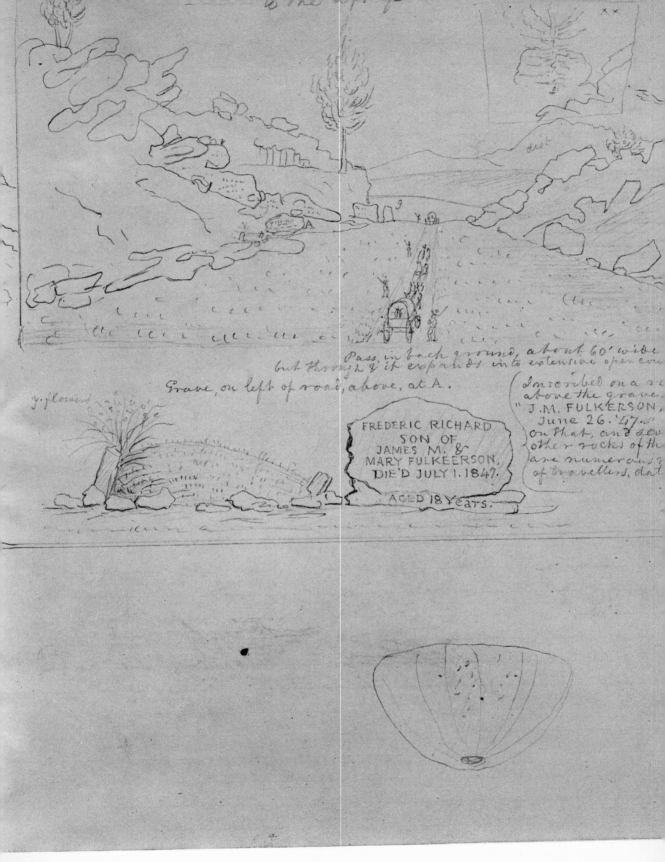

Pass, in back ground, about 60' wide
but through & it expands into extensive open cove

Grave, on left of road, above, at A.

y. flower

FREDERIC RICHARD
SON OF
JAMES M. &
MARY FULKEERSON,
DIED JULY 1. 1847.

AGED 18 Years.

Inscribed on a ro
above the grave.
"J.M. FULKERSON,
June 26. '47 —
on that, and sev
other rocks of the
are numerous 3
of travellers, dat

Terminus of the Greenwood
Cut off. — descent into Green
River valley —

CANTONMENT LORING.
on a small branch of Snake river, about
7 mi: S E. by E. from Fort Hall.
(Col. Andrew Porter Command?)

Commencement of a Cottonwood Stockade.

Bruff and comrades riding away.

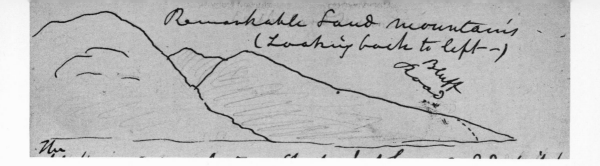

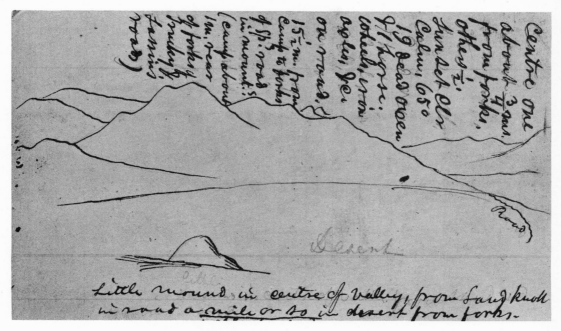

[THE LASSEN TRAIL AT THE TURN-OFF FROM THE HUMBOLDT]

THE RABBIT-HOLE SPRINGS,
(Wells in a desert.)

BRUFF'S CAMP, 9th 1849.

{ Camass which the author
   subsisted upon from 21st Dec? }

(straggling emigrant on passing)

{ Above the grave of the Allord
   is shown of the hill, left
   which they near the Indians
   their camp and the dead's grave. }

People making Snow-Shoe   Interior of Lodge

Winter in S. Nevada
Author on Snow-Shoes, seeking fuel

ROBERTS' CABIN IN S. NEVADA

Rear of the Author's Camp. Jan.ʸ 16. 1850.

Grave of Child

THE MIDNIGHT VISITOR

Mining

Road

thro' which
the Sweet Water R.
runs.

Sweet Water R.

Comrade ill, mule dead, provisions short, diggings run out, varmints & ingins down - time to put.

LASSEN'S RANCHO

CHO

Indians of the valley of Feather River
From life

Indians of Sierra Nevada. Feather River
Head waters of
From life

[Feather River] Indians – (N. branches)

Temporary Shelters

J. G. Bruff
1850

Acorn Crib
(of willow)

Habitations of the
Mountain Indians

Winter Lodge.
{Thatched willow lodge,}
{covered with earth –}

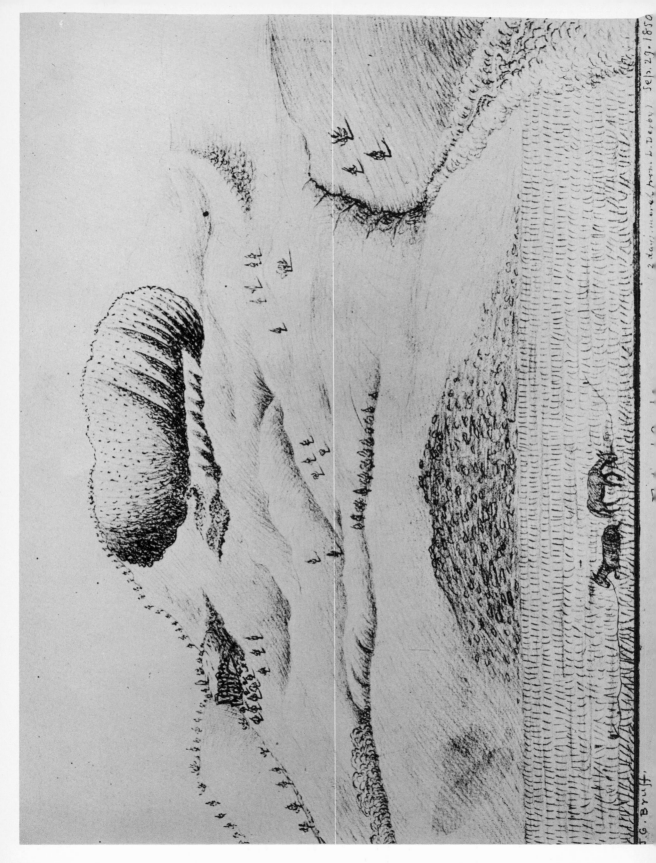

J.G.Bruff. 2 days march from L. Deep.) Sep. 29. 1850

Hieroglyphic Defile & Creek.

J.G.Bruff
Oct:1. 1850

common This detached pyramidal rock is charg'd
frequent all over with characters: front truly Ancient Hieroglyphics, —
represented.

The characters appear to have been chisel'd
in with a very hard and sharp-pointed instrument.

(basaltic formation)

(E" slope of Sierra Nevada.) Indian breastwork,

First view of Lake Derby.

552

³A Piute, Piutah, or Pauta, ━━

Of Young Lake basin

━━

(Knolli & Feachevous) 2nd

36 Prints
Oct. 5.
1850

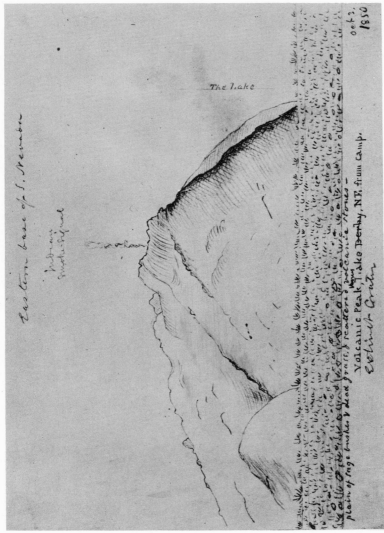

Eastern base of S. Newton

Indian
Individual

The Lake

Oct 3.
1850

Volcanic Peak Lake Denby, NE. from camp.

Extinct Crater

plain of sage bushes & dead forest, scatters volcanic stones

553

North part

The hieroglyphic Creek
is supposed to go thro'
this gorge & empty into
L. Bigby

J.G.Bruff

hieroglyphic beside a Cr.

plain cover'd with broken volcanic rock, hard & angular

Panoramic View of the irregular plain through which
Hostile

J.G.Bruff

(Extinct Crater & Indian Signal)

(Indian Signal)

Honey
Lake

554

Defile and Creek, scene sweeping round from E.N.E. to E.S.E.

(Extinct Crater on top this mountain,)
(at the rear, overlooking Lake Derby.)
Camp. for 24 hours.

north.

Oct. 1850

Eastern, or
lower end
of Lake

5 ms. long.)

Sketches the Dirt Lake;
Slough, or Scott's
Lake

Please observe name in memoirs
of S. Derby to Stony Lake, as the name is established

Oct.

Eastern slope of the Sierra Nevada.

Basaltic range. — part of S.W. boundary of the basin of Lake Denby. (W. side)

Peter Lassen lies asleep; beside him sits Bruff, smoking his pipe.

Trinadad N. C.

Pacific

breakers   breakers

sand

board

brown & g shrubs

buff sand

bright g shrubs
with some g
purple   bright g

br

Buff col'd sand
" beach

cedar

559

at Indn Village

The grave of a
chief - with ？
around ？ this
his sons ？
elsewhere ？
son kill'd by the
Inds at ？ of
? & ？lamestt
(the Crooks) 10
ms distant
mountains
wooded ？
from when
his squaw
packed his
down on her
back in ？
days. ？
? name
Largo
of the Mon
his Chief

Sweating-House, Trinidad Ind. Vil

In Feby 1850 - when Largo's wife brot in his remains the Indns
inform'd the whites at Trinidad & invited them to attend the
funeral. His squaw _____ , prepared the body for interment by washing & marking over it many stripes
black - put his beads, wampum, &c in his hands, en-
velloped the body in skins; laid mats in bottom of the
grave, after digging it herself. and, assisted by the
whites, laid the body on back, placing shells, &c in on
breast & cover'd it up. Women howling around, &
old chief (the father) standing on sweat-house, directing.

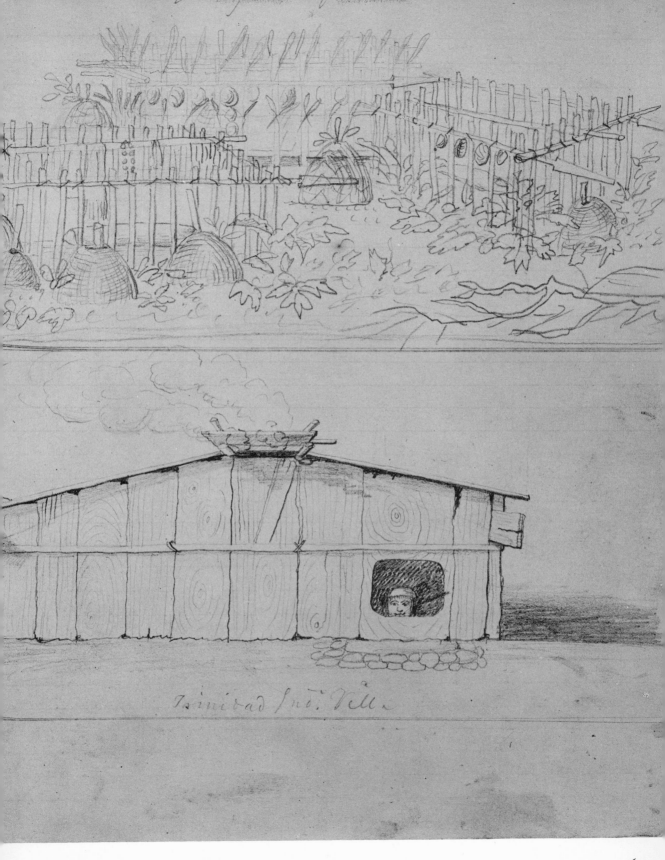

Trinidad Ind. Vill.

561

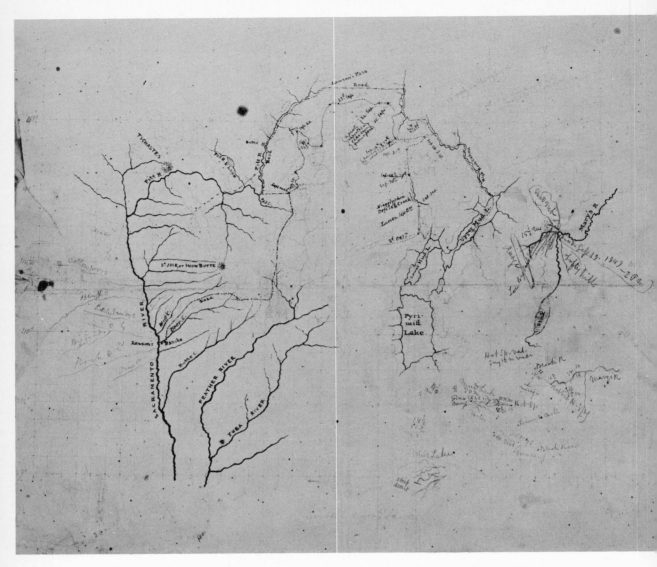

[BRUFF'S SKETCH MAP, SHOWING THE LASSEN TRAIL FROM THE
TURN-OFF ON MARY'S RIVER TO LASSEN'S RANCHO, 1849,
AND LASSEN'S GOLD LAKE HUNT, 1850]

Colored manuscript map, now in the custody of the Archivist of the United States.

NOTES

PI: APRIL 2, 1849—AUGUST 27, 1849

1. P 1 contains two accounts, April 2-May 10. As they give supplementary information, both are included.

2. Relay, Md., is about ten miles southwest of Baltimore. The Relay House was a hotel for the accommodation of passengers, near the Relay Bridge, or Thomas Viaduct, "one of the finest bits of railroad architecture within the entire land," built by Benjamin H. Latrobe, "a curving viaduct seven hundred feet long, of eight elliptical arches, each sixty feet in width and about sixty-five feet above the level of the stream. . . . Over a structure originally designed for the passage of six-ton locomotives with their small trains, there pass today, 300-ton locomotives, with the heaviest of steel trains, both freight and passenger. And this, with no alterations nor repairs to the original bridge, save, from time to time, the common upkeep of pointing its masonry fabric" (Edw. Hungerford, *Story of the Baltimore & Ohio Railroad* [1928], I, 166-67).

See *The Boston Herald*, Rotogravure Section, March 26, 1939, the "Coronation Scot, the crack train of England which will be exhibited at the New York World's Fair, and the American train, Royal Blue, photographed on a bridge at Relay, Md."

3. Known as the Washington Branch; that between Baltimore and Cumberland, Md., as the Main Stem. The first train was run on the Washington Branch Aug. 25, 1835 (Hungerford, *op. cit.*, I, 171, 269). The run from Washington to Relay took about $2\frac{1}{2}$ hours.

4. Washington *Daily National Intelligencer*, April 4, 1849: "Latest Despatches Baltimore, April 3 — 5 P.M. The California Mining Company arrived here from your city in the cars last evening, and put up at the United States Hotel. They appeared to be in fine spirits. They left this morning in the Western train for Cumberland. A large number of persons were at the cars to see them off."

5. Then the western terminus of the Baltimore and Ohio Railroad, about ten hours from Baltimore (or the Relay House). The first train entered the village of Cumberland Nov. 5, 1842 (Hungerford, *op. cit.*, I, 240).

6. "In the early spring of 1848, the trains known as the *Great Western Mail*, which left Baltimore at half past seven and Cumberland at eight o'clock each morning, passed one another and arrived at the opposite ends of the Main Stem at half past five o'clock the same evening. But, in March, 1848, . . . the *American Rail-*

way Journal" announced a second train each day each way. "The coaches upon the National Road will henceforth leave Wheeling regularly twice a day at 6 A.M. and 6 P.M. and Cumberland at the same hours, connecting regularly each way with the morning and evening boats at Brownsville" (Hungerford, *op. cit.*, I, 269). Bruff, arriving at Cumberland at 5.30 P.M., April 3, was able to step into a stage-coach leaving at 6 o'clock for Brownsville, but Brownsville was distant 72 miles from Cumberland, and Pittsburgh was approximately 40 miles by water from Brownsville. The customary duration of the journey from Cumberland to Pittsburgh was then about 24 hours, and it is difficult to see how Bruff, reaching Cumberland at 5.30, could possibly have arrived in Pittsburgh the same night. It is probable that there is here an error of one day and that he reached Pittsburgh in the evening of April 4.

7. Edwin Booth was playing in Pittsburgh: as Duke of Gloucester in *Richard III* that night, as Sir Edward Mortimer in *The Iron Chest* the following night. Pittsburgh *Daily Gazette*, April 3: "First appearance of the distinguished Tragedian Mr. Booth who is engaged for 3 nights."

8. *New-York Daily Tribune*, May 9, 1849: "We clip the following items from the [Independence, Mo.] *Expositor* of April 21: At St. Joseph there are now as many Emigrants as the Ferry will be able to cross, from now until the 1st of July, they having but one flat and making but two trips a day." May 22, 1849: "From St. Joseph. — The steamer Highland Mary, at St. Louis from St. Joseph on the 8th inst. reports that large numbers of emigrants were endeavoring to cross the river, preparatory to their final start for the Plains, and so great was the rush, that the two ferry-boats, though running all day and most of the night, were inadequate to supply the demand. . . . St. Joseph and the surrounding country is represented as being literally lined with wagons, teams and emigrants."

9. Old Fort Kearny, not the new Fort Kearny near Grand Island, on the Platte. T. H. S. Hamersly (*Complete Regular Army Register* . . . [1880], Part II, p. 139): "On the West bank of the Missouri River, fifty miles South of Omaha. Established in July, 1847, and abandoned in May, 1848." G. W. Cullum (*Biographical Register* . . . *U.S. Military Academy* [1868-79], I, 27): "a little north of Nebraska City, and 30 miles below the mouth of Platte River."

10. The wisdom of Bruff's choice of route is attested by many. The *New-York Daily Tribune*, June 1, 1849, quoting the St. Louis *Reveille*, May 22: "Latest from the Plains. From a letter written by a member of the Telegraph (St. Louis) Company to a friend in this city, and brought to the settlements by an officer of dragoons, who was on his way from Fort Chiles [Childs, or new Fort Kearny near Grand Island]: . . . 'The inconvenience which had thus far attended the traveling were much greater than the emigrants had anticipated. After one or two days' journey in the Pawnee country [i.e., soon after crossing the frontier in Missouri], they were continually stopped by creeks difficult to ford, where it became necessary to empty the wagons. This occurred generally once, and sometimes twice in

a single day, and was beginning to exhaust the strength and patience of the men.' "

11. Cholera scourged the country — East and West — in 1849. May 30, *Niles' Register* printed a symposium on the prevention and treatment of the disease, in part taken from the *Cincinnati Gazette*, through whose columns the great Dr. Daniel Drake had addressed the people of Cincinnati on this subject. Pres. Zachary Taylor appointed a day of prayer: "Official. A recommendation by the President of the United States. At a season when the Providence of God has manifested itself in the visitation of a fearful pestilence which is spreading its ravages throughout the land, it is fitting that a People whose reliance has been in His protection should humble themselves before His throne, and, while acknowledging past transgressions, ask a continuance of the Divine Mercy.

"It is therefore earnestly recommended that the first Friday in August be observed throughout the United States as a day of fasting, humiliation, and prayer. All business will be suspended in the various branches of the public service on that day; and it is recommended to persons of all religious denominations to abstain, as far as practicable, from secular occupation, and to assemble in their respective places of Public Worship, to acknowledge the infinite goodness which has watched over our existence as a nation and so long crowned us with manifold blessings, and to implore the Almighty, in His own good time, to stay the destroying hand which is now lifted up against us. Z. Taylor. Washington, July 3, 1849" (Washington *Daily National Intelligencer*, July 4, 1849).

12. R. B. Marcy (*Prairie Traveler* [1859], p. 326), cites Alexander Majors in praise of this road: "The military road from Fort Leavenworth crosses very many tributaries of the Kansas River, the Soldier, the Grasshopper, etc., etc., which are at all times difficult of passage. There are no bridges, or but few, and those of but little service. From Nebraska City [old Fort Kearny] to Fort Kearney, which is a fixed point for the junction of all roads passing up the Platte, we have but one stream of any moment to cross. That one is Salt Creek. . . . Upon the entire route there is an abundance of wood, water, and grass, and camping-places frequent."

A. B. Hulbert ("Crown Collection of American Maps," Series IV: *The American Transcontinental Trails*, Vol. I, *The Platte River Route*, original ed., nos. 51, 52): "The pathway [from Nebraska City, or old Fort Kearny, to new Fort Kearny] is depicted with accuracy . . . on the earliest surveys. Taken throughout its length, therefore, and backed by the assurance of accurate knowledge of its course, it appears the best illustration (known to the present editor) in American geography of brute and aboriginal cunning in practicing the science of the 'dividing ridge.' . . . Throughout its length, this trail on which the Nebraska City-Fort Kearney Road was first laid out, heads every stream which would be a hazard to big game animal or man (save Salt Creek only) and yet never leaves either man or animal out of easy striking distance of that imperative necessity of every traveller — water."

13. The "Robert Fulton" was advertised in the Pittsburgh *Daily Gazette*, April

4, 5, 6, and 7 to leave for St. Louis and intermediate points "this day"; the same paper April 6, 7 listed it under "Boats leaving this day." Presumably it did sail on the seventh. This would fit Bruff's account, allowing for his supposed error of one day in the time he reached Pittsburgh, since he says "3 days consumed at Pittsburgh in getting wagons together and on board the Steamer Robert Fulton" — April 5, 6, 7, supposing the boat to have sailed toward night.

14. *Niles' Register*, March 28, 1849: "*Collectors of the Customs. . . . James Collier*, San Francisco, California, (*new office.*)" "A collector has been appointed at San Francisco, under the act of Congress extending the revenue laws over California. . . . The collector proceeded overland, and advices have not yet been received of his arrival at San Francisco."

15. *New-York Tribune*, May 16, 1849: "The Washington City (D. C.) Mining Association (66) arrived at the same place [St. Louis] on the 14th of April." This, according to Bruff's record, was an error. An advance group appears to have reached St. Louis on April 13, and the remainder of the company, with Bruff, on the fifteenth.

St. Louis *Daily Missouri Republican*, April 16, 1849: ". . . Yesterday morning the steamer Robert Fulton reached this port with one of the best organized and equipped Companies we have seen. It is from Washington City, D. C. and is styled the *Washington City and California Mining Association*, with J. G. Bruff, as President and Commander. . . . This Company is in complete military uniform, consisting of gray cassimere pants and coats, surmounted with full rows of brass buttons, glazed caps, white shoulder straps and belts, cartridge boxes, canteens, &c. They are well provided with fire arms, cutlery, ammunition, &c. In the commissary and mechanical department, they are also amply furnished, having every thing for comfortable subsistence, and all the implements, tools, &c. deemed necessary for digging, smelting, and refining gold. From this they go directly by steamboat to St. Joseph, and from thence by the most secure and practicable route across the plains."

Washington *Daily National Intelligencer*, April 25, 1849: "A letter has been received in Georgetown, from a member of the Washington California Mining Company, under the command of Capt. Bruff, stating its arrival, without accident and all well, at St. Louis, on the 13th instant, which place they would leave in the steamer Alice on the 15th for St. Joseph's. Their wagons and harness were obtained in Pittsburg; their mules have been purchased on the Missouri west of St. Louis — first-rate animals, four years old, at $62."

This applied to a portion of the company only; H 3 (April 15, 1849): "Having preceeded from Baltimore across the Alleghenies to Pittsburg, and thence to St Louis, by the usual conveyances, I had transferred about two thirds of my men to the charge of my second in command [Gideon Brooke], to proceed up the river by the steamer Alice, already pretty full of California emigrants. Indeed the city was thronged with them; steamers arrived and departed almost every hour, with additional thousands, to swell the grand overland concourse. . . . In the midst of this bustle, din, and mud, I had much to do to complete my own preparations. Meal for our mules, had to be secured without delay, for news had arrived that the immense multitude of emigrants, men women and children, at St Joseph's, on the Missouri, though scarcely on the edge of the Indian wilderness, had already exhausted their supplies of corn. . . . The remainder of my men except eight, I sent up the Missouri in the Cambria, which like all the other steamers, 'bound up,' was crowded to excess."

16. *New-York Tribune*, April 19, 1849, from the St. Louis *Republican*, April 9: "The California Fever. — Hundreds of adventurers, on their route to California overland, arrive here every day. Our hotels, boarding-houses and steamboats are filled with them, and camps are formed in the neighborhood. The rush is tremendous. . . . If fairly set upon the route, the cavalcade might be made to extend the whole distance, from our western frontier [in Missouri] to the gold region. — It is not an extravagant calculation to say, that thirty thousand persons will leave for California, by this route, in the next three months."

17. An odometer (sometimes roadometer) is a contrivance for measuring mileage, based on the number of revolutions of a wheel of known circumference, not differing essentially in principle from the modern speedometer. Some were homemade (see Ashford's, Oct. 14, 1849, below), while others, like that of Bruff, devised by Jacob Blattner, instrument maker, of St. Louis, might be classed as instruments of precision, although the mileage measured was probably only approximate. Howard Stansbury computed distances by odometer, corrected by triangulation (Stansbury, *Exploration . . . of the Valley of the Great Salt Lake* [1853], pp. 293, 294, 296).

18. St. Louis *Daily Missouri Republican*, April 18, 1849: "For Weston and St. Joseph The fast running passenger steamer *Belle Creole*, . . . will leave for the above and all intermediate ports, on This Day, the 18th inst. at 12 o'clock M. . . . Persons bound for California, will find the accommodations for stock, superior to any boat running in the trade." *Ibid.*, 19th: "The steamer *Belle Creole*, left this city last evening, for the Missouri river, with between *three and four hundred passengers*, nearly all 'California' bound, with the 'gold fever.' "

H 3, April 17: "It was now the 16th day of the month, much of the baggage and stores of the expedition was still in the rear, our surgeon had not arrived, and yet we were to embark for St Joseph's next morning in the large class steamer Belle Creole. At 4 P.M. on the 17th we were on board amid such a dense medley of Hoosiers, Wolverines, Buckeyes, Yankees and Yorkers, including black legs and swindlers of every grade of proficiency and celebrity, as is seldom to be found together, even on our western rivers. The decks, above and below, exhibited an equally stupendous assortment of wagons, horses, mules, tents, bales, boxes, sacks, barrels and camp kettles; while every cabin and state room was an arsenal of rifles, fowling-pieces, bowie-knives, hatchets, pouches, powder-horns and belts. The river fell rapidly during the day, and the apprehension became general that the Belle Creole, would hardly reach her port of destination."

19. St. Louis *Republican*, April 25, 1849: "The steamer Belle Creole returned last evening from the Missouri river. On account of low water she was unable to proceed farther up than Camden, at which point, and at Lexington, she discharged her entire freight." At Camden, Bruff received word of the rest of the company (H 3, April 22): "The Steamer Cambria lay here, and her officers informed me that they had landed my men at St. Joseph's all safe and sound. They also reported all the Alice's passengers safely ashore at the same place."

20. H 3: "Anger and confusion prevailed on board. The passengers, as usual, resolved upon holding an 'indignation meeting,' on the hurricane deck, over which, in spite of my deferential declinatures I was called to preside, because it was supposed, however cool I might appear, I must be naturally and officially one of the most indignant passengers in the assembly. I mounted an axle-tree near the smoke stack and called the audience to order. . . . A committee of one from each state — represented on board, was appointed; who withdrew for ten minutes, and then handed in a scale or weight of the fare, freight, &c. they would agree to. — This was unanimously adopted: when the meeting adjourned."

21. H 3: "The town of Lexington is situated about two miles back from the river on elevated ground, the road to which is very crooked, and of red clay and mud. . . . The houses along the landing were dirty, and crowded with all sorts of inferior characters, so we turned some hogs out of a shed, and reversed the rough flooring boards as our best accommodation; and here we spent the bleakest night of the season."

22. "Meteor No. 3," Captain Turner, Master, was advertised locally.

23. Osborne Cross, leaving St. Louis May 10, 1849, to join the Mounted Riflemen at Fort Leavenworth: "It will not be out of place here to remark that the cholera was not only in St. Louis, but had spread through every town on the Missouri river, and in many instances had raged with great violence on board of several steamers" ("Report . . . March of . . . Mounted Riflemen to Oregon," *Report of the Sec. of War for 1850*, p. 128). Bruff, in St. Joseph (H 3, May 9): "A steamer arrived to-day, from New Orleans, — starting with 500 emigrants, 47 of whom died on the passage [of cholera]."

24. "Here I found two members of the committee, — whom we had sent ahead, from Washington, nearly two months before to buy mules. They had bought about sixty, which were near at hand, and as soon as they could obtain a few more were going to drive them on to St. Joseph's. The town Independence stands about two miles back from the landing, which is, itself, mostly an apartment of log-cabin liquor stores, one of which had the imposing title of 'Coffee House,' in block letters upon a tall perpendicular plank" (H 3).

25. "This tribe [Delaware] originally occupied a great part of the eastern border of Pennsylvania, and great part of the States of New Jersey and Delaware. No

other tribe on the continent has been so much moved and jostled about by civilized invasions. . . . From the Delaware to the lovely Susquehanna, . . . and to the base of and over the Alleghany Mountains, to the Ohio River, to the Illinois and the Mississippi, and at last to the west of the Missouri, they have been moved by treaties after treaties with the Government, who have now assigned to the mere handful of them that are left a tract of land, as has been done a dozen times before, 'in *fee simple, forever!*' . . . Mr. Catlin saw the Delawares on their reservation on the Kaw, now Kansas, River, in 1831-'32" (T. Donaldson, *George Catlin Indian Gallery*, issued as Part V, *Annual Report, U.S. Nat. Museum, for 1885*, p. 198). "For several years past the government of the United States . . . has been engaged in removing the Indian tribes, resident within the States, to tracts of wild but fertile land, situated beyond the verge of white population. Some of the tribes thus removed, however, when they came to hunt over the lands assigned them, encountered fierce opposition from the aboriginal tribes of the prairies, who claimed the country as their own, and denied the right of the United States to make the transfer. . . . This especially was the case, with the fierce and numerous tribe of Pawnees, inhabiting the banks of the Platte river. . . . These . . . laid claim to all the land lying between the Platte and Kansas rivers; a region comprising several hundred square miles. It had long been their favorite hunting ground, in which it was death for a strange hunter to intrude. This forbidden tract, however, had been granted by the United States to the Delawares" (J. T. Irving, *Indian Sketches* [1835], I, 9-11).

"They [the Delaware] are familiar with the languages, manners, and customs of their pale-faced neighbors; they are so feared as rifle shots that a host of enemies will fly from a few of their warriors, and they mostly lead a vagrant life, the wandering Jews of the West, as traders, hunters and trappers, among the other Indian tribes. . . . As hunters and guides they are preferred to all others by the whites" (R. F. Burton, *City of the Saints* [1861], p. 37).

26. Delayed by the mishap to the "Belle Creole," they were apparently eight days behind the contingent on the "Alice." Washington *Daily National Intelligencer*, May 7, 1849: "We have been favored with the following extract of a letter from a member of the 'Washington City and California Mining Association,' . . . 'In Camp of the Company, *St. Joseph's, (Mo.) April 20, 1849*. A portion of our company, twenty-two in number, arrived here yesterday, in the swift boat *Alice*, running ahead of all boats she came in competition with. We have with us all our wagons. The mules and the most of our outfit are with the balance of the party, whom we look for every hour. Immediately upon our arrival we pitched our tents for the night, and commenced camp duty. Lewis, Byington, Marden, Coumbs, and Donn were the sentinels of the first night. This morning we struck our tents, and again pitched them in a beautiful grove. Our fare is hard, considering what I have been used to at home, (having my every wish anticipated by my parents.) But to us every thing is made sweeter by our having hard duty to perform, in the

absence of two-thirds of our party. The health of our company has been very good."

27. H 3, May 4: "Next to exposure to bad weather, the mule-breaking-job comes hard on the 'boys.' — Most of them knew as much about mules, when they arrived here, as the mules did about them. And it is quite hard and vexatious work, to the most experienced. The enormous migration had increased the price of mules; and we could not afford to give, for the large number we required, the prices demanded in Kentucky and Tennessee. — Our agents were therefore compelled to purchase in Missouri and to get some that were too young. This threatening to subject us to mis-fortunes throughout; — beginning with the toil, hazard, and delay, of breaking; trouble in our first travel, and doubtless the failing and loss of many in the latter part. . . . Our excellent Blacksmith, Foy, has made a marking iron, and he is busy, with assistants, branding the mules."

28. Omaha. "This tribe of Indians lives at present . . . about 5 miles from Bellevue [Nebraska], on a small water course, called the Passio. This tribe is very poor; they have no annuity from government, except blacksmith and striker; . . . they are scarce of fire-arms, and suffer greatly from their inveterate enemy, the Sioux, who appear to be determined to exterminate the Omahas, Ottoes, and Pawnees. . . . These were once a considerable tribe, but from the ravages of cholera, small-pox and wars, they are reduced to but little more than one thousand" (*Report of the Com. of Indian Affairs for 1847*, p. 859). "In the absence of any written records it is almost impossible to fix dates, but it seems probable that the Omahas have dwelt near their present location for the past two centuries or more. . . . The westward rush of emigration brought much suffering to the border tribes, particularly to those who were trying to take on civilized life. . . . At the same time, these tribes became objects of distrust being regarded as faithless to ancient traditions, and consequently they were assailed by those Indian tribes who were determined to resist innovations" (A. C. Fletcher, *Historical Sketch of the Omaha* [1885], pp. 1, 5).

29. "The Omaha had a highly organized social system. The tribe was divided into 10 gentes called 'villages,' . . . each of which had one head chief. . . . Two of them . . . exercised superior authority. The functions of these chiefs were entirely civil" (F. W. Hodge, *Handbook of American Indians North of Mexico* [1910], II, 611).

30. "The potency of the medal was soon appreciated as a means of retaining the Indian's allegiance. . . . The result was the final adoption of a series of medals, each bearing on the obverse the bust of a president and on the reverse a symbol of peace. This series began with the administration of President Jefferson" (*Handbook*, I, 830, 835).

31. H 3: "May 1st. . . . I commence my guard system here [camp, St. Jo] that the men may become inured to it. I shall take my regular tour, as in everything, to set an example. I shall continue to stand guard, till we cross the river, and shall then have enough to do without such a gratuitous tax on my brief hours of repose.

The men grumble at it, as if it were a duty they had not expected." Posting guard was practiced by practically every company crossing the plains at that time, more or less faithfully. It was an essential precaution against Indian surprise attack and its importance was known to all, but it probably caused more friction in Bruff's company than any other one thing.

32. H 3: "A chap, who says that he once travelled '*across*', with Kit Carson, applied to us for employment as a guide. I told the members that we needed none; because in my opinion, instead of a slight trail, as we originally expected at best, they would find a broad road, and be seldom out of sight of travellers. But they thought differently, and desired a meeting, which I accordingly called; and they resolved to employ the guide. His compensation was to be, the use of a good riding horse, and equipment, exemption from guard duty, and $75 cash when we *got in*. The meeting also engaged the services of a man, at $1.50 per day, to co-operate with the guide, here, at breaking mules." Later, Bruff refers to this guide as "Stinson." The P 5 record, a leather-bound pocket notebook, is inscribed in the front "Presented to Mr *William Stinson* By G. v. Dycke of St. Joseph *Mo*". Presumably this was given to Bruff by the guide.

33. H 3: "To-day our surgeon, and two other members, whom we had left in the rear, arrived, bringing up the anxiously looked for tents, &c." This was "Henry Austin, Surgeon," and Bruff says that he was from Maryland. The Johns Hopkins University states (letter, April 7, 1936) that it is unable to identify this Dr. Austin, but suggests that he may have been Dr. P. H. Austin, who died at Baltimore Oct. 28, 1878. This Dr. Philip H. Austin (Austen) was born in Baltimore in 1822, "A. M. Yale, 1844; M.D. Univ. Md., 1845; D.D.D. Balto. Coll. Dent. Surg., 1849; Prof. Mechanism, Chem., Anat. and Physiol. and Dent. Sci., Balto. Coll. Dent. Surg., 1852-73" (Quinan, *Medical Annals of Baltimore*, pp. 59-60). Yale University believes (letter, Jan. 31, 1938) that this was Dr. Philip Hiss Austen, and knows nothing of his having crossed the plains in 1849. Henry Austin, of England, received his M.D. 1848, from Univ. Md., School of Med. (letter, Dean H. Boyd Wylie, Sept. 17, 1948). Morgan's *San Francisco City Directory*, 1852, listed "Austin, H. (M.D.) surgeon dentist, 136 Montgomery."

34. H 3: "One of our members, who is rather in bad health, left to-day, to return home: and a young man well known to the company, from St Louis, is elected in his place."

35. St. Joseph *Adventure*, May 4, 1849: "The company is encamped on a healthy position in rear of the town on Black Snake Hills and are busily engaged breaking mules and fitting up for the march; intending to cross the river today or tomorrow, all enjoying good health and fine spirits." A list of the company members follows, as also in the *Gazette*, same date.

36. H 3: "From our elevated camp-ground [Blacksnake Hill], we have an extensive and animated prospect. . . . Below us lies the town, from whence arises a cloud of dust, the buzz of the troubled throng of human beings, and the ceaseless

surge of animals and wagons. — The green fields and hills are sprinkled with the white tents of hundreds of camps; and every road and path is alive with people and wagons. . . . Sixty thousand souls, all bound for the land of gold, were — or soon would be thus encamped, preparatory to their entrance upon their immeasurable march."

37. H 3, April 30, June 6: "Nearer to us, on the same hill [Blacksnake Hill, St. Jo], was the camp of a company of Germans and Swiss, whose sons and daughters were said to have intermarried for the expedition. Their leader was a fine old Swiss, of most venerable and patriarchal mein. But there [were] young boys and girls among them whose laughter and songs rang out in exhilarating glee. . . . This morning my attention was attracted to my neighbor, — the silver-haired Swiss philosopher. — I approached, where he sat, beneath a live-oak, with a large clasped volume before him. — This book, he constantly carried under his arm. . . . His companion, the big tome, which I supposed to be the Bible, was in German text, and entitled 'The Philosophy of Nature'. . . . He told me at length that he was in easy circumstances, and not emigrating to acquire wealth; but to accompany his relatives, for the pleasure of travelling over such a country, and to find a quiet romantic spot, where he could satisfactorily end his days!" Months later, Bruff learned (Sept. 25, 1849) that old Mr. Abbott had died on the Platte. The book he treasured was probably a volume of Baron Alexander von Humboldt's *Kosmos*.

38. H 3: "The mass of emigrants, daily crowding down to cross the river, is astonishing. From the river bank, the road winds up a crooked clay road ascent, to a bridge, for a quarter of a mile; from thence, a street, perpendicular to the river, intersects the main street of the town, several hundred yards back. A dense line of wagons of every description, are seen crowding these avenues; horsemen & pedestrians; men, women, and children, are packed, from the water up to the main street. Inch by inch, they move down, whenever a scow takes off the lead-wagon; and the rear is supplied, from the parties continually arriving. *Day and night, has this been the case, for weeks;* and for several weeks more, it will continue. Wrangling and fighting for precedence in line is not unusual."

39. Given in detail, May 5, p. 3.

40. H 3: "At 11 A.M. I walked down to the 'line' and found that one of my wagons had, in due turn, got in the string just below the bridge; and the other one stood aside with its team unhitched. I asked the teamster of the ox wagon, ahead of mine, when he expected to get in the scow? He said 'Guess as how, if we have good luck, by 11 o'clock to-night.' This was fine prospect for my long train! For my company to cross, by this slow process, and experience all the disadvantages of the great delay, and separation, would not answer. I knew, too, that for some distance, the opposite shore was marshy, no provender to be obtained for our mules, and that in the great mass of emigrants there, the cholera was raging. I ordered the wagon out of line, to the great joy of the next teamster, who

promptly closed up, followed by the long string in the rear. Returning again to the camp, I at once convened the company and laid the facts before them. — I recommended our moving up the river, — on this side, — to Old Fort Kearney, and crossing there; stating that, in my opinion, there were many advantages in the Fort Kearney route, over the one from this crossing. — We could obtain corn for our mules, all through Missouri; would have no thronged ferry; and few streams between the Missouri and Platte rivers, unembarrassed by the petty annoyances of our frontier Indians. The company approved of my views, and unanimously resolved to go up the river."

41. H 3: "A steamer arrived with officers and troops for Oregon; they are going up the river. Among the officers I found several acquaintances." These were the Mounted Riflemen, from Fort Leavenworth, their point of departure for Oregon.

42. H 3: "Stowing the cargoes of the wagons, assures us of the fact, that we have a superabundance of stores, and will have to sell some. I furnished a member of the purchasing committee, with an estimate I had carefully and leasurely compiled; but this sage lost it, and purchased what he thought proper. There is also much superfluous weight, in useless articles. — I called a meeting, and we condemned for sale, some bacon, coffee, whiskey, salt, lead, and iron: and I dispatched 2 wagons with them to town, where they were sold at fair rates."

43. G. L. Cole, who crossed the plains in the spring of 1852 (*In the Early Days* . . . [1905], p. 15): "After two or three days at this point [St. Joseph], we drove up to the town of Savannah, where we laid in new supplies and passed on to the Missouri River, where we crossed by hand-ferry at Savannah Landing, now called Amazonia." Savannah is the county seat of Andrew Co., Mo.

44. *Stryker's Magazine*, III (July, 1849), 58: "The St. Joseph (Mo.) Gazette gives the following estimate of the number of emigrants and wagons that have crossed the plains *en route* for California: In making this estimate we give the number of wagons, and from this make our calculations as to the number of persons now on the plains. The wagons that crossed the river at this place, by ferry and steamboats, number 1,508; at Duncan's ferry, four miles above St. Joseph, 685; at Bonton, Savannah, and the ferries as far up as the bluffs, say 2,000. This makes the number of wagons 4,193. A fair average would be about four men and eight mules or oxen to each wagon. From this statement it would appear that there are 16,772 persons on the plains, besides 33,544 mules and oxen. A number of emigrants, anticipating some difficulty in getting through with wagons, went with pack mules, which would probably increase the emigration to at least 17,000, and the number of cattle and mules to at least 34,000." If the Duncan's Ferry referred to here be that visited by Bruff, the "four miles above St. Joseph" is an error, since Bruff makes the distance, by days' marches, to be more than fifty miles.

45. H 3: "The road soon descended to low lands and thick forrests, with much undergrowth, — the bottoms of the Nodaway river. Here great care was requisite,

but inattention cost us another broken axle, against a tree. Replaced it with a spare one, which, in 20 minutes after was also broken, and having no other spare axle, had to hew a substitute from a green tree, for present purposes." Nodowa is from "Nadowa. A name, expressing utter detestation, applied by various Algonquian tribes to a number of their neighboring and most inveterate enemies" (*Handbook*, II, 8-9). Lewis and Clark passed here July 8, 1804, and camped not far above "the mouth of the river Nodawa" (*History of the Expedition* . . . , J. K. Hosmer ed. [1903], I, 24).

46. There were several companies from Pittsburgh on the Trail, some of which seem to have gained an unenviable reputation. *New-York Tribune*, May 8, 1849, from the St. Louis *Reveille*, "29th ult.": "In St. Joseph there were about 1,200 or 1,500 Californians. Some disturbances had occurred in one of the Pittsburgh companies. . . . Dissatisfaction had ensued among several parties from Pittsburgh. A number had come to a determination to abandon the journey altogether, and were selling their mules, &c. previous to returning home."

47. H 3: "At 11 A.M. passed through the Village of 'Newark,' — the last collection of houses. This place is only a row of some 15 or 20 log houses, on either side the street — or rather the road. — A Wheel-right's and Blacksmith's establishments here, are very important, in such a district; where the roads are suffered to take care of themselves. — A piece of board over the door of a cabin, on the left, had chalked on it, 'DRY GOODS'; and a strip of home-spun carpet, nearly covering the front of the house, exhibited the fact, that even here the ladies could go a shopping."

48. H 3: "with some moist meadows. Near us are some scattered small farms, a brook runs by, which I judge to be a small branch of the Nodaway."

49. H 3: "In 13 ms: from Round Prairie camp, we reached a small deep branch of Tarkio Creek, — a tributary of the Missouri. . . . This is crossed by a very frail structure: — a diagonal bridge of loose sticks and logs." Little Tarkio River. Capts. Lewis and Clark passed here July 11, 1804: "After three miles' sailing we came to a willow island on the north side, behind which enters a creek called by the Indians Tarkio" (*Expedition*, I, 25-26).

50. H 3: "Kept by a man named Jackson, who is an acquaintance of our guide. — This is said to be 42 miles about St Joseph's, 15 below 'Duncan's Ferry', where we wish to cross the Missouri; and 250 miles from Grand Island, of the Platte. Mr P. Master Andrew Jackson, owns this tract and the improvements, and is a clever cute frontier man. . . . He sends the mails down every 2 months. . . . We are making up a more considerable mail for the Bluff P. Office trunk, than it ever contained probably before."

51. H 3: "Skirting the Missouri. A very crooked route in the forrest, where we passed a small cleared space and a couple of log cabins. Half a mile further we reached a point where the road descended a marshy bottom, through a thick forrest of gums, oaks, & walnuts, and at a turn on the left stood quite a neat new

frame house, — the tavern and store of Robert Hawk, of Ohio. . . . And we did not reach the bank of the river, at 'Duncan's Ferry,' till some time in the afternoon, though it was only a drive of 5 miles. . . . A group of neat log and frame houses here, were the residences of the proprietors, — Mesrs Duncan and M. A. Brannager, with their families. The former attends to the ferry; which is said to be 60 miles above St Josephs."

52. H 3: "The landing, or starting point, is about half a mile above. . . . Here, also, for the profits, Mr Brannager sets a table for those who choose to eat at his house. I find them to be worthy clever people. This place is called 'Hemmy's Landing', and is 45 ms: distant from Savannah. I spread my blanket between large trees upon the mossy ground, and composed myself for sleep, listening to the hooting of owls, the monotonous cry of legions of whippor wills, barking of foxes, the rushing of the mighty waters, and a musical party enlivening the night with 'Carry me back', or 'Dearest May,' ludicrously broken by the discordant braying of several mules. — "

53. H 3: "All the way from the Rocky Mts:"

54. H 3: "Some reader may not know exactly what is meant by a *sawyer*. — I will therefore explain. — A tree, which has fallen from the bank of the river above, drifts down, with the lower portion deeply immersed, by the weight of the stones, clay, &c. about the roots — Meeting with obstruction, in its downward progress, a sand bank, or logs and roots at the bottom, it becomes lodged there; and soon a deposite of mud, and logs, accumulate about the lower end, and securely moors it. — Then, according to its length, the depth of water, and the angle at which it becomes lodged, is it more or less above the surface — but always pointing up, — against the current. — There is a strong ripple around it, while the action of the current keeps it in constant motion. A *snag*, on the contrary, is more permanently lodged, and seldom appears above the surface."

55. H 3: "Oxen are admirable swimmers: — I witnessed their performances lower down the river, — where it was nearly two miles broad, with astonishment. — I saw one disengage himself from his yoke fellow, on the side of a scow, and swim across the rapid broad stream, get up on the bank, shake himself; look around, to see where he had come from, and the next minute, commence grazing, as complacently as ever."

56. H 3: "a large tributary of the Missouri. . . . not much current, and stream about 70 feet over. The scow was cordelled over, by a travelling line attached to a rope tightly stretched across." Lewis and Clark record July 14, 1804 (*Expedition*, I, 28): "a small distance above . . . is a river, called by the Maha [Omaha] Indians Nishnahbatona. This is a considerable creek, . . . and runs parallel to the Missouri the greater part of its course, being fifty yards wide at the mouth."

57. "Tarkio Ck" is in pencil, apparently inserted later. H 3: "a large branch of the Nishnabottony."

58. H 3: "This important information for the pilgrims, was certainly intended for some other location."

59. H 3: "Considerable trouble and loss of time, could have been avoided by taking the main road, further back from the river; but it was much longer, yet I now think we would have gained by travelling on it, in prefference to this. We were influenced by our *guide*, who professed accurate knowledge of these roads, and stated that the one we have unfortunately traversed, was good. The recent rains had increased the swampyness of the *Slew*, and though only about 2 miles across, it was a considerable obstacle. We were guided only by some wagon tracks and had to make for the firmest ground. Every wagon had trouble, the strong teams soon dragged through, but the weaker ones had to be doubled, and in 2 instances, the cargoes had to be discharged, and we were compelled to . . . put our shoulders to the wheel."

60. H 3: "An old fodder-house, of logs, and a large hay-pen are near the dwelling. Show [there] has been a farm here. . . . A small Mormon family are temporarily residing here. They have a wagon and oxen awaiting the arrival of the Mormon *train* as they call it, to proceed to Salt Lake. They also prepared indifferent dinners for several of my men, but gave us the best they had, and appeared to be clever folks."

61. H 3, same date: "The proprietor of the property [Lake House] arrived, with 3 young men, and told me that about 4 miles off, at the river bank, at a point 7 miles below Fort Kearney, he had ferry'd the river successfully, taking over several companies, before the freshet came down."

62. H 3, same date: "On examining the scow, we find her too low for the occasion   She has but 2 indifferent oars, with wooden thole-pins, and the steering-oar is insufficient every way. . . . Put a squad of mechanics, (we had some excellent ones, by good luck) on the scow, and to make, four good pulling oars and one larger for steering."

63. H 3, same date: ". . . the rest were formed into a pioneer party, and at it we went, to cut a road through the woods. Some handled axes and hatchets, and others used bowie-knives; and we worked hard, felling small trees, cutting away brush and brambles; and dragging logs and stumps out of the way, till, by Sun Set we had cleared a sufficient but necessarily crooked road, (on account of large trees, — standing and prostrate.) It was about three fourths of a mile through to the spot indicated by the ferryman. . . . I headed a large party, and went to the river bank, to cut a tow-path. — Through water, — in the edge of the river, sometimes waist-deep, over little projections of the bank, stumps, and logs, and through willow bushes and scrub; with axes, hatchets, and bowie-knives, did we steadily advance, and cut away the obstacles, for at least half a mile."

64. This crossing and "Indian Point," which Bruff gives as a few miles south of old Fort Kearny (Nebraska City), is believed to be the site of Bennets Ferry, established in 1852, in southeastern Nebraska. According to the Nebraska State

Historical Society, the crossing was at T. 7 N., R. 14 E., section 12. The Society estimates that the channel of the Missouri has here shifted so much farther to the east than in 1849 that the spot on the east bank from which Bruff's company crossed now lies in the stream near the west bank. There are "indications of Indian villages" on both banks at this point.

65. H 3: "The river is here over half a mile broad. . . . 2nd. We breakfasted very early, and emboldened by our experiment, I had a wagon and 4 mules put in the scow; and a sufficient pioneer party, to cut a tow-path in the face of per-pendicular clay cliffs above the landing, opposite; the usual tow path being sub-merged. . . . The scow was so low, and the drift so large, that when she was midway the boiling stream, we could only occasionally perceive the white wagon cover, and the heads of the men and mules and they appeared as if drifting down on the trees and logs. I went down and inspected the tow-line cut in the cliff on this side. Conceive, if you please, a range of perpendicular clay-cliffs, 50 or 60 feet high, their base washed and abraded by the boiling surge and drift timber; and about 10 feet above the flood, a path 2 ft. wide, cut, a distance of 300 yards, in the face of the cliffs; the wall cut down from above, to the inner edge of the path, and worn smooth by the elbows of the men — hauling the tow-line! It seemed to me perilous to walk even a short distance on it very carefully, without the incumbrance of a tow-rope. Over head hung roots and leaning trees, ready to join their brethren in the rushing torrent below. I was the first man to seize the tow-line, when it reached the shore, on the other side; and with it — over my shoulder, followed by the towing gang, wading and stumbling in the water, amongst logs and stumps of willows; and, it left me raw shoulders, and blistered hands, but it was nothing to the peril of the clay tow-path under the cliff, and I began to think my men would do."

66. H 3: "Thinking last night, about the crossing, it occurred to me, that some of my nautical knowledge might serve the company."

67. H 3: "a branch (Table Ck): of the Nemahaw." The company is now, of course, traveling on the western or righthand side of the Missouri.

68. H 3: "a brook tributary to the Mo." Lewis and Clark saw this stream July 20, 1804: "We passed at about three miles distance a small willow island to the north, and a creek on the south, about twenty-five yards wide, called by the French L'eau qui Pleure, or the Weeping Water" (*Expedition*, I, 31).

69. I.e., from new Fort Kearny on the Platte, to old Fort Kearny on the Mo.

70. Desertion was frequent, from the military posts and the marching Rifle-men. On June 6, three days' travel above Fort Kearny, Cross wrote: "Four men ran off last night, taking a complete outfit with them. This was not very unexpected to us, when we considered the material of which the regiment was composed, who merely enlisted, it is well known, for the purpose of getting com-fortably transported to California at the expense of the government, and not from any partiality for the profession of a soldier" ("Report," p. 144). On July

10, at "Devil's Gap," he entered in his diary: "The Colonel [Loring, in command of the regiment of Mounted Riflemen] issued a proclamation at Independence Rock, offering a reward of two hundred dollars for every deserter that might be brought back" (*ibid.*, p. 171).

71. H 3: "Thus, consecutively did we get all over in safety, by midnight. It was well done. By light of a lantern, I called the roll, and '*spliced the main brace.*'"

72. "*Milk vetch,* (*Astragalus.*) — A genus of leguminous plants, several species of which are used as food by the Indians of the Western Territories, and are commonly called Indian pea, pop-pea, ground plum, or rattle-box weed" (E. Palmer, "Food Products of the North American Indians," *Report of the Com. of Agriculture for 1870,* p. 419).

73. "Our old friends, the Pawnees, have had a hard time of it during the past Winter. When they returned from their hunting grounds, their trail could be followed by the dead bodies of those who had starved to death. . . . They have abandoned their old village 75 miles below us, on the Platte, and have commenced a new one at the mouth of the Saline, some 80 miles nearer the frontiers of Missouri. Their old enemies, the Sioux, are pressing them hard, which is probably the cause of this step" (letter, "Fort Kearney, Nebraska Territory, May 18," *New-York Daily Tribune,* June 14, 1849). "They are hunted (as you well know, sir) more eagerly than the ferocious wild beast hunts his prey; and it is not enough that they [the Sioux] are in pursuit of the Pawnees themselves, but they are determined to destroy every effort of the government and missionaries" (*Report of the Com. of Indian Affairs for 1847,* p. 929). The effect of this intertribal warfare between the Sioux and their neighbors was beneficial to the whites; I. J. Wistar, June 7, 1849, *Autobiography* . . . (1937), pp. 80-81: "Met numbers of Sioux this morning . . . very friendly. . . . There are several tribes of this great Sioux nation, and without their aid in keeping off the Pawnees, Cheyennes and Arapahoes, no whites could get through this country without a big army" (courtesy of Wistar Institute).

74. H 3: "Moved on, and camped near a rill and marsh, making 23¾ miles. Mr. Bennet, U. S. Mail Agent, from Fort Childs, accompanied by another person and an aged Pawnee chief, were on the ground when we arrived; the two former were going to Missouri." P. C. Tiffany, a month earlier, meets the mail from "Grand Island to St. Joseph," charge, 50 cents per letter (journal, MS, Coe Collection, Yale Library).

75. In H 3: "Very few of them are mounted, they are armed with bows and full quivers; and most of them have French flint-lock fusees, also."

76. Bruff, Supplementary Notebook A:

"The dark and savage Pawnees came, —
And asked for something to eat; —
But oh, how chang'd, & tame! —
They wanted bread & meat. —

"A dingy robe on the ground they spread,
And gathered, anxiously around; —
We gave them meat, and also bread, —
Where they sat on the ground.

"Then came a band of Cheyennes along,—	"And the murd'rous thieving Sioux,—
Darting, on horses fleet; —	Pursuing the fallen Pawnee foes; —
A very Arabic-looking throng,—	Who have little but lives to loose [lose],—
As e'er in desert you'd meet. —	Their race is near its close."

77. H 3, Bruff notes this chief's "Choteau medal." "The issuance of peace medals was not confined to the governments, as the various fur companies also presented to Indian chiefs medals of various kinds"; that of the Chouteau Fur Company of St. Louis (1843), "Silver; size 3⅝ in." (*Handbook*, I, 836).

78. Contrast Stansbury, same date: "Sunday, June 10 . . . it was discovered that three horses from our herd, and one from a neighboring encampment, had been stolen during the night. . . . The robbers were Pawnees. . . . Effective measures should certainly be taken to punish . . . a band of savages, who, although receiving a large annuity from the national treasury, take every opportunity to prey upon those under the protection of the government" (*Exploration*, pp. 22-23). Four days later (*ibid.*, p. 27) he records actual hostilities. As a matter of fact: "The Pawnees . . . have no annuity, and owing to their potent enemies, the Sioux, they still reside on the south of the Platte. . . . Their crops this season [1848] have almost been an entire failure, owing to the drought. Their corn in the Platte bottoms was literally burned up" (*Report of the Com. of Indian Affairs for 1848*, p. 466).

"This truly poor and persecuted people have suffered severely during the past spring and summer; besides the many attacks that have been made upon them by their enemies, the cholera has haunted them in their hunts, and swept them off 'like chaff before the wind.' . . . Should the Government do nothing for these poor and destitute Indians, in the spring a great portion of them must perish from starvation" (*Report of the Com. of Indian Affairs for 1849*, pp. 139-40).

79. For the first time. H 3: "(nearly opposite the mouth of the Loup Fork.)"

80. This was the village referred to June 8, 1849, n. 73, as having been recently abandoned on account of the hostile Sioux.

81. Gov. Alexander Ramsey, in the first report of the "Minensota Superintendency," of the Sioux and the Cheyenne: "Early in the period following the year 1600, a disruption of . . . geographical relations of all the tribes took place, consequent upon the settlement of the seaboard by the whites." The westward pressure reaching the Dakota, resulted in their abandoning "entirely, as a residence, the country of the extreme upper Mississippi and made them determine on proceeding to conquer new homes towards the setting sun. . . . The Cheyenne (Shian) Indians, living on the Cheyenne river, a beautiful tributary of the Red river of the north, . . . where there were 'plenty of buffalo,' were among those who experienced their power. The invading Sioux drove them . . . across the Missouri, and ultimately still further westward; for Lewis and Clark found them, in 1803, located in the Black mountains, at the head springs of the Cheyenne river of the Missouri. . . . The Indian agents for the upper Missouri report them as

now ranging between the Arkansas and north fork of the Platte river, and singularly enough, as staunch *allies* of the Sioux against the Pawnees. . . . In 1847, the agent for the upper Missouri reported them to have 530 lodges, containing five thousand three hundred souls" (*Report of the Com. of Indian Affairs for 1849, passim*).

82. The Indians believed themselves entitled to indemnification from the passing trains: "It is well known that the Indians of the Upper Platte and Upper Arkansas are all roaming tribes, . . . and live altogether by the chase. . . . What I now respectfully recommend to the department, . . . is at once, and without further delay, to have some understanding with them in regard to the right of way through their country. . . . This is what the Indians want, and what they are exceedingly anxious about, having been told long since, and so often repeated by travellers passing, (and who care little about the consequences of false promises, so they slip through safely and unmolested themselves,) that their 'Great Father' would soon reward them liberally for the right of way, the destruction of game, timber, &c., as well as for any kindness shown Americans passing through their country" (*Report of the Com. of Indian Affairs for 1850*, p. 55).

83. H 3: "We made this day nearly 18 miles, and camped at a spring opposite an island nearly 20 miles long. Shortly afterward, a couple of wagons with five young men came up and camped near us. After supper I walked over to my new neighbors, to see who they were, and they told me that the pawnees yesterday attempted to rob them of provissions: and had they not stood to their arms and exhibited determination, they would have been broken up. One of the men said that the Indians jerked a handkerchief off his neck, and ran away with it: And another young man said that while lighting his pipe with a burning-glass, a tall ill-looking Indian suddenly seized it, and ran off — I could not help laughing when he told me this, as I was the innocent cause of his loss. — I then told him, that I was lighting my pipe also with a sun-glass, which attracted a crowd of pawnees around me; and one in particular, answering the description he gave of the fellow who stole his glass, was exceedingly pleased with it, and offered to divest himself of his entire suit, to give me for it. While igniting my tobacco, he looked under and over it, felt, and tasted the glass, but could not comprehend its ardent qualities. I held it over his hand, and pointing up to the sun, endeavored to explain it to him. He cried 'ugh' and jerked his hand away. I explained to him that I had only that one, that we have travelled from the E. two moons, and had to travel W. 4 moons. I offered him a red pipe-bowl, but he cared nothing for it, and appeared quite disappointed & surly. He was resolved to possess the next glass he should see, and he obtained one sooner than I expected."

84. Of the Grand Pawnee, on the south side of the Platte "about thirty miles above the mouth of the Loup fork" (J. C. Frémont, *Report of the Exploring Expedition . . . in 1842, and . . . in 1843-'44* [1845], p. 78 and Map). J. T. Irving

describes it in its prime: "It is situate in the open prairie, at the foot of a long range of hills, and within about fifty yards of the Platte. . . . The lodges are numerous, and stand close together. . , . It was now humming with life. The warriors were collected in small knots of five or six, and, by their vehement gestures, were apparently engaged in earnest conversation. The children were rolling and tumbling in the dirt: the squaws were busily engaged. Some were bringing from their lodges large leather sacks of shelled corn; others were spreading it out to dry, upon the leather of their buffalo-skin tents, which had been stretched out upon the ground. Others were cleansing from it the decayed kernels and packing it up in small sacks of a whitish undressed leather, resembling parchment. These were then deposited in cache-holes for a winter's store.

"The *Cache*, is a large hole dug in the ground like a cistern. It is narrow at the top (about four feet in diameter) but wider as it descends, until its form somewhat resembles that of a jug. It will contain about one hundred bushels of corn" (*op. cit.*, II, 28-29, 44-45).

85. So young Lewis Dougherty found them, while the Pawnee were far from the winter comforts Bruff imagined they enjoyed: "I was sent to Fort Kearney in Nebraska to take charge of the sutler's store. . . . I spent my twentieth birthnight in the Pawnee Indian village, on the Platte river, December 7, 1848. . . . Owing to a very severe snow storm we remained two days and nights in the above-mentioned Pawnee village as, according to custom, they left their houses during the winter and followed the buffalo for meat. . . . There were hundreds of empty lodges in this village. They were very comfortable" ("Experiences of Lewis Bissell Dougherty . . . ," E. M. Withers, ed., *Mo. Hist. Rev.*, XXIV [1930], 363-64).

86. H 3: "I took out my pocket memorandum-book and found the name of 'Chiricherish,' among the old and principal chiefs of their nation (which I had obtained in St. Louis). When I pronounced the name, the chief was struck with astonishment & delight; and wished to look on the page as if he could read. We interpreted his signs to mean that he was the nephew of Chericherish, and himself a half-chief." The identity of Bruff's Sharitarish cannot be determined with certainty. In 1835 Sir Charles Murray describes the Sâ-ní-tsă-rish of his travels: "The names of the four principal Pawnee chiefs with whom I started were (*nearly*) as follows: — Sâ-ní-tsă-rich, or 'wicked chief,' grand Pawnees. . . . Nature had made him a gentleman, and he remained so, in spite of the corrupting examples around him" (*Travels in North America* . . . [N.Y., 1839], I, 183, 213). T. L. McKenney and Jas. Hall speak possibly of his sons, in 1854: "Sharitarish was principal chief, or head man of the Grand Pawnees. He was descended from a line of chiefs, and . . . succeeded his elder brother, Tarecawawaho. They were sons of Sharitarish, a chief, who is mentioned in Pike's Expedition under the name of Characterish" (*History of the Indian Tribes of North America* [1854], II, 163). But it would seem that Murray's own Sharitarish was active as late as Oct., 1848, and might

still have been living when Bruff passed: "Fort Childs, Nebraska Ter. Oct. 6, 1848. The Sioux and Pawnees are still actively employed in taking each others' scalps. . . . This is a war of 25 years' standing between these two tribes. . . . Old Si-re-chei-rish has been turned loose, and is again at his old amusements killing Sioux and hunting buffalo. [Signed] Nebraska" (*New-York Daily Tribune*, Dec. 28, 1848).

87. *Antilocapra Americana*, or prong-horned antelope. Geo. Catlin ("To the Reader," *North American Indian Portfolio* [*c*1844], p. 14): "The Antelope (Furcifer) of the Prairies and Rocky Mountains of America, . . . forms one of the most pleasing of living ornaments of the Western World."

88. Or (new) Fort Kearny, one of the government posts on the route. Every '49er noted these and divided his journey by them. The establishment of some of them that year and the march of the Mounted Riflemen to Oregon were long-delayed moves in an official program. When the wagon trains of 1842 and 1843 rolled out for Oregon the federal government had already taken steps for the protection of the Trail. The sites of Kearny, Laramie, and Hall were recommended by Frémont, after his two first expeditions (1842, 1843-44), but the Mexican War delayed the building of the posts. Kearny was established in May, 1848; Laramie in June, 1849; and Cantonment Loring, five miles north of Fort Hall, in July, 1849; and the regiment of Mounted Riflemen swung out from Fort Leavenworth for their long-deferred march across the plains in May, 1849. See 1st ed., pp. 490-92, for full discussion.

89. H 3, same date: "The oldest of these told me that . . . he had served in the Mormon Batallion in California, and was one of the first gold-diggers. He had been speculating in land warrants, and would probably go on to Washington. I wrote a pencil'd note by him."

90. Cross: "June 10. We met this morning a man from the Salt lake, who informed us that he had been robbed by a party of Crow Indians, who took from him his horse" ("Report," p. 148). "Crows. A tribe of 7,000, on the headwaters of the Yellowstone River, extending their hunts and their wars into the Rocky Mountains, inveterate enemies of the Blackfeet; tall, fine-limbed men, graceful and gentlemanly in deportment, and the most richly and tastefully clad of any Indians on the continent. . . . Mr. Catlin met the Crows at Fort Union in 1832, and again on the Snake River plains in 1854-'55" (Donaldson, *op. cit.*, p. 106). "In 1842, I found the Sioux Indians of the Upper Platte *demontés*, . . . with the failure of the buffalo; and in the following year, large villages from the Upper Missouri came over the mountains at the heads of the Platte, in search of them. . . . At this time [1843] there are only two modes presented to them, by which they see a good prospect for escaping starvation; one of these is to rob the settlements along the frontier of the States; and the other is to form a league between the various tribes of the Sioux nation, the Cheyennes, the Arapahoes, and make war against the Crow nation, in order to take from them their country, which is now

the best buffalo country in the west. . . . These [Crows] are the best warriors in the Rocky mountains, and are now allied with the Snake Indians" (Frémont, *Report*, pp. 145-46).

91. Lieut. Col. Benj. L. E. Bonneville, 4th Infantry. Born in France. Cullum, *op. cit.*, I, 157: left West Point Dec. 11, 1815, 2d Lieut. Light Artillery; served in Mexican War; "on frontier duty at Ft. Kearny, Neb., 1849." Retired 1861, but served during Civil War and in 1865 was made Bvt. Brig. Gen.; retired again in 1866. Hamersly, *op. cit.*, Part I, p. 308: died June 12, 1878.

H 3: "The kind and estimable gentleman, and old traveller in the Rocky Mountains—Colonel Bonneville commands the post: . . . Col: Bonneville kindly insisted on my being his guest while here, and I breakfasted with him. . . . Dined with my friends, at the fort. The colonel has related some amusing anecdotes, illustrative of the effects of the march on the pious gold pilgrims." Apparently Bonneville had then been at Fort Kearny only a few weeks. George Gibbs, traveling with the Mounted Riflemen, reached the post the latter part of May. May 30 ("The Far West," *The New York Commercial Advertiser*, July 25, 1849): "The command of this post has now devolved on Lt. Col. Bonneville, who arrived yesterday with Walker's company of the 6th Infantry, under the immediate command of Lt. Bootes. Major Chilton, with his company of dragoons, arrived on the 23d, and Lt. Davis, with Wharton's company, on the 28th; so that the post is now full."

Aug. 3, 1831, Bonneville obtained a two-years' leave of absence for a western expedition, undertaken with the mixed motives of fur-trading and exploration. According to his own statement (letter of Aug. 24, 1857, to Lieut. G. K. Warren, "Memoir," *Pacific Railroad Reports*, XI [1861], 33), he did not return to Fort Leavenworth until Aug. 6, 1836. Warren says (*ibid.*): "Captain Bonneville's long-continued absence after the expiration of his leave, during which time no news was received from him at the War Department, led to his name being dropped from the Army Register. He was, however, restored." Bonneville states (*ibid.*): "On the maps of those days the Great Salt Lake had two great outlets to the Pacific ocean. . . . It was from my explorations and those of my party alone that it was ascertained that this lake had no outlet; that the California range *basined* all the waters of its eastern slope without further outlet. . . . It was for this reason that Mr. W. Irving named the salt lake after me, and he believed I was fairly entitled to it." Warren refutes this claim (*op. cit.*, p. 34): "though called Lake Bonneville by Mr. Irving, its existence was well known to the traders and trappers on his [Bonneville's] arrival in that country, as was also that of the Ogden's or Mary's river." Time has reduced Bonneville's pretensions in this respect by limiting "Lake Bonneville" to the geological designation of a vast quaternary body of water of which the Great Salt and Utah Lakes are the residue.

Stansbury, on his way to the Great Salt Lake, makes only one reference in his report to Bonneville, whom he meets at Fort Kearny June 19, the very day on which Bruff broke camp and marched to the west: "Colonel Bonneville, whose adventures among the Rocky Mountains are so well known to the world. He received us very courteously, offering us every facility in his power in further-ance of our progress." Of the Great Salt Lake apparently not a word was said.

92. Levi C. Bootes. Hamersly, *op. cit.*, Part I, pp. 308-9: born in the D. of C.; private, Co. F, Mounted Riflemen, July, 1846; rose to capt. by June 5, 1860. Served with distinction in the Civil War, became Lieut. Col. 25th Inf. Jan. 1, 1871; retired Oct. 7, 1874.

93. Thomas O. Davis. Hamersly, *op. cit.*, Part I, p. 397: born in Me.; Dec. 30, 1847, 2d Lieut., 6th Infantry; May 15, 1851, dismissed.

94. H 3: "regularly arranged, to accomodate the command, stores, &c. . . . 55 ms: above the foot of Grand Island." Hamersly, *op. cit.*, Part II, p. 139: "Kearny, [Fort,] Nebraska. On the South side of the Platte River, opposite Grand Island. Established in May, 1848. Troops withdrawn, 17 May, 1871."

95. On Nov. 28, 1849, Adj. Gen. R. Jones to the Secretary of War (*Report of the Sec. of War for 1849*, pp. 185-86): "Fort Kearny, . . . three hundred and ten miles west of Fort Leavenworth, the first of the chain of posts to Oregon, was garrisoned at the date of the last annual report by two companies of the rifle regiment. These have since been relieved by one company 1st dragoons and two of the 6th infantry; but, as it may not be practicable to provide sufficient quarters for the troops the present season, the commanding officer has been authorized to order one of the infantry companies to Fort Leavenworth." *Niles' Register* (June 13, 1849, p. 369, from the St. Louis *Republican*) in a letter from Fort Leaven-worth, May 25, 1849, gives the disposition of various officers and men of the Mounted Riflemen and others on the Oregon route. Apparently these assignments were tentative, as some were later changed.

Maj. R. H. Chilton, 1st Dragoons. Cullum, *op. cit.*, I, 546-47: born in Va., grad. West Point July 1, 1837; served in Mexican War. "On frontier duty in Pawnee Expedition, 1849, being engaged in a Skirmish on Platte River, near Ft. Kearney, Neb., Oct. 29, 1849." Resigned April 29, 1861, and fought for the South in the Civil War.

Capt. Stewart Van Vliet, 3d Artillery. Cullum, *op. cit.*, I, 598: born in N.Y., grad. West Point July 1, 1840, 2d Lieut., 3d Artillery; served in Florida and Mexican Wars. "On Quartermaster duty, with Missouri Mounted Volunteers, building posts on the Oregon route, 1847-51 (Ft. Kearny, Neb., 1847-49, — Ft. Laramie, Dak., 1849-51)." Served in the Civil War as "Chief Quartermaster, of the Army of the Potomac, Aug. 20, 1861, to July 10, 1862." He became "Bvt. Lieut.-Col., Bvt. Colonel, and Brig.-General, U.S. Army, Oct. 28, 1864, for faithful and meritorious services during the Rebellion"; March 13, 1865, Brig. Gen., U.S. Volunteers; and on July 29, 1866, Lieut. Col. Deputy Quartermaster Gen. R. B. Marcy gives an interesting account of Van Vliet's mission when he "was sent to Salt Lake City to confer with the Mormon authorities" during the Mormon troubles in 1857 (*Thirty Years of Army Life on the Border* [1866], pp. 271-73).

Lieut. Charles H. Ogle, 1st Dragoons. Cullum, *op. cit.*, II, 221-22: born in Pa., grad. West Point July 1, 1848, Bvt. 2d Lieut., 1st Dragoons. "Served: on frontier duty at Ft. Leavenworth, Kan., 1849, — Ft. Kearny, Neb., 1849, — Scouting, — 1849, being engaged against Pawnee Indians, in a Skirmish near Ft. Kearny, Neb., Oct. 23, 1849, when he was wounded with an arrow, — and at Ft. Kearny, Neb., 1850. . . . Suspended, 1860–61. Dismissed, Apr. 23, 1861, under the 3d Sec. of Law of Jan. 31, 1823" (concerns accounts and accounting; see P 1, n. 292 on Lieut. Hawkins). Served in the Civil War; honorably discharged Nov. 24, 1862; died Dec., 1862, aged 37.

Lieut. Andrew J. Donelson. Hamersly, *op. cit.*, Part I, p. 409: born in Tenn., grad. West Point July 1, 1848, Bvt. 2d Lieut., Corps of Engineers; died Oct. 20, 1859. A grandnephew of Pres. Andrew Jackson.

"Dr Hammond   U.S.A." may have been John F., of S.C., 1st Lieut. Asst. Surg., Feb. 16, 1847; or Dr. Wm. Hammond, Jr., born in Md., appointed from Mo. Asst. Surg., March 2, 1848.

96. H 3: "equalized it to the standard quantum, of 50 lbs pr man. Much excitement among some of my men in consequence of having to abandon what they could not carry much further." This was the experience of all, the trail from about this point to the crest of the Sierra Nevada being littered with an amazing medley of discarded goods — foodstuffs, furniture, and personal property of many kinds. (See 1st ed., pp. 493-94.)

At Fort Kearny Bruff also left behind one member of his company who was too ill to travel — Culverwell, Senior. A compensation in money was voted him by the Co., and Bruff advised him to return home when his health improved and opportunity offered. Instead, Culverwell proceeded to Salt Lake City, where late in the fall of '49 he attached himself to a small party who followed Captain Jefferson Hunt's caravan on the "Southern" desert route. He was among those who left Hunt's leadership, dying in Death Valley. For a discussion of the Death Valley migration and the light thrown on it by the manuscript record of Nusbaumer (of Culverwell's party), see Introduction, pp. xlv–xlviii, and 1st ed., Appendix VIII.

97. H 3: "Encamped on the plain in front, and above and below the fort, were emigrant companies belonging to Boston, New York, Tennessee, Virginia, &cc. Was informed that Col. Porter, Genl Wilson, Indian agent, and Coll Collier (collector for St Francisco, Ca.) had all passed here many days ago; that Lieut. Woodbury U.S. Eng: had gone on to Fort Larimie, and Capt. Stansbury Top: Engs was daily expected."

Col. Andrew Porter, Mounted Riflemen, was already known to Bruff, who found him in command of Cantonment Loring near Fort Hall, on Aug. 19.

"John Wilson was a Missouri lawyer of large practice and more than ordinary ability. . . . From July 5, 1827, to July 25, 1828, he was editor of the *Missouri Intelligencer*, then published at Fayette, Missouri. . . . Wilson was an inveterate enemy of Thomas Hart Benton: wherever Benton spoke in Missouri, Wilson was almost sure to follow with a scathing address" ("California Letter of John Wilson," F. A. Culmer, ed., *Mo. Hist. Rev.*, XXIV [1930], 200). Pres. Zachary Taylor, newly elected, conferred with Wilson on cabinet appointments. March 30, 1849, he appointed Wilson Special Agent for the California Indians, "at Salt Lake, California." At Fort Leavenworth, Kansas, "Brevet Capt. Morris, Mounted Riflemen, with thirty men, awaits the arrival of Gen. John Wilson, Indian Agent for California, via Salt Lake" (*Niles' Register*, June 13, 1849). The General set forth from Fort Leavenworth June 5. Seven wagons and mules for his family carriage had been assigned him, and 8 teamsters with extras to drive ("John Wilson . . . Dec. 22d 1849. Report . . ." MS. Cited as Wilson, San Francisco Report). At Salt Lake, in late Aug., Stansbury (*Exploration*, p. 85) finds the Mormons difficult, since "It appeared, too, that their alarm had been increased by the indiscreet and totally unauthorized boasting of an *attaché* of General Wilson, the newly-appointed Indian Agent for California, whose train on its way thither had reached the city a few days before I myself arrived. This person, as I understood, had declared openly that General Wilson had come clothed with authority from the President of the United States to expel the Mormons from the lands which they occupied, and that he would do so if he thought proper. The Mormons very naturally supposed from such a declaration that there must be some understanding or connection between General Wilson and myself." H. H. Bancroft, *History of Utah* (1889), pp. 446-47: "On the 6th of that month [Sept., 1849], by order of President Taylor, General John Wilson, then United States Indian Agent, held a consultation with Brigham Young, . . . and others, with a view to the temporary amalgamation of the states of California and Deseret, in order to avoid possible difficulties on the slavery question. It was agreed that a memorial should be drawn up, . . . asking for a convention of all the people of Upper California, both East and West of the Sierra Nevada, for the purpose of consolidating the two states in one that should include all the territory acquired from Mexico. . . . John Wilson and Amasa Lyman were sent as delegates to California, and presented the memorial to the legislature; but . . . the legislature refused to entertain the memorial." Perhaps this Mormon liaison, and not the Indians, was the major purpose of Zachary Taylor's sending his kinsman to California.

New-York Tribune, May 11, 1849, from the St. Louis *Union*, May 1: "Col. Collier, who has been appointed Collector of the port of San Francisco, with his assistants, will be here to-day. They will leave as soon as possible for San Francisco, taking the route by Sante Fe, and following the course traveled by Col. Cook in 1846-7 [Col. P. St. George Cooke, commanding the Mormon Battalion]. These gentlemen are to have an escort from Independence, and will proceed rapidly on their route." This rapidity failed to materialize; T. H. Hittell, *History of California* [1898], II, 810-11: "On November 13 [1849], . . . Collier the new collector, after a long and tedious journey by the southern overland route, arrived at San Francisco."

Captain Stansbury arrived at Fort Kearny a few hours after Bruff left it.

Many companies camped here. Here converged various feeders of the Overland Trail, from Independence, Fort Leavenworth, St. Jo, making it natural to pause and reorganize for the long pull up the Platte Valley. *New-York Tribune* (June 14, 1849), from the St. Louis *Republican's* correspondent at "Fort Kearney, Nebraska Territory," May 18: "Every State, and I presume almost every town and County in the United States, is now represented in this part of the world. Wagons of all patterns, sizes and descriptions, drawn by bulls, cows, oxen, jackasses, mules and horses, are daily seen rolling along toward the Pacific, guarded by walking arsenals. Arms of all kinds must certainly be scarce in the States, after such a drain as the emigrants must have made upon them. No man but what has a gun and a revolver or two, and one fellow I saw, actually had no less than three bowie knives stuck in his belt. Many of the parties as originally formed in the States, have had dissensions, and are broken up, and each fellow is striking out for himself."

98. The days of the *Bison Americanus* were already numbered, although enormous herds still roamed the plains. J. J. Audubon and J. Bachman, *The Quadrupeds of North America* (1849), II, 40: "The roads that are made by these animals, so much resemble the tracks left by a large wagon-train, that the inexperienced traveller may occasionally imagine himself following the course of an ordinary wagon-road. These great tracks run for hundreds of miles across the prairies, and are usually found to lead to some salt-spring, or some river or creek, where the animals can allay their thirst." "Thousands are killed merely for their tongues, and their large carcasses remain to feed the wolves and other rapacious prowlers on the grassy wastes. A large Bison bull will generally weigh nearly two thousand pounds, and a fat cow, about twelve hundred" (*ibid.*, II, 43-44). H 3: "Our hunters succeeded in killing a buffalo cow, and brought in, at dusk a fine lot of the meat."

99. Audubon, *op. cit.*, II, 319, 320: "Spermophilus Ludovicianus. — Ord. Prairie Marmot-Squirrel.—Wishtonwish.—Prairie Dog. . . . It was probably only owing to the sort of yelp, chip, chip, chip, uttered by these marmots, that they were called Prairie *Dogs*."

100. H 3: "Formed the acquaintance of a very clever set of adventurers — a company organized on the same principle as ours, with mule wagons also, but the members were mounted on mules. They had also adopted a snug uniform, and were armed and equipped with U.S. rifles. — They are called the 'Colony Guards,' from New York City, commanded by Capt. J. McNulty. By invitation I dined with them on buffalo soup."

New York Herald, Feb. 14, 1849: "Ho! for California. Colony Guard — Overland Route, via St. Louis, Independence, South Pass, and Fort Hall, to California.

— Terms of membership, $400, which includes provisions sufficient to supply the company for the entire distance, and twelve months after arrival at the mines. To each member is furnished mining implements, clothing, arms, and ammunition amply sufficient for the use of the company during its existence. The Colony Guard is organized for 17 months, or for a longer period, at the option of the members. Experienced guides will be procured, one a member of the company. A physician accompanies the expedition. References required. For further particulars, apply at the office, 154 Greenwich Street." The Colony Guard went to Salt Lake City and the company apparently disintegrated on the march. Bruff met McNulty and a few others on the lower Humboldt (Sept. 17, 18). McNulty told him many had been left sick, in Salt Lake City, to proceed later to California under Mormon guidance. Among these was Edward Coker, a well-known figure in the Death Valley emigration. See W. L. Manly, *Death Valley in '49* [1894], pp. 373-76, for Coker's account, as given by him to Manly. Coker states therein that Culverwell, Senior (of Bruff's company), also a Death Valley figure, came from Washington City, where he had been employed as a writer in a government office. Although Bruff's first recorded meeting with the Colony Guard appears on June 22, after he had left Culverwell at Fort Kearny, it is entirely possible that Coker and Culverwell became acquainted on the Long Trail before this date. At any rate, Coker knew Culverwell well enough to recall, nearly fifty years later, these facts of his life. See Introduction, pp. xlv–xlviii.

Sept. 25, 1849 (H 1), Bruff, in the neighborhood of High Rock Cañon, met "some of the N. Yorkers." McNulty and others had apparently followed the Humboldt at the big bend, instead of taking the Lassen Trail turn-off, and had proceeded to California by the Carson or Truckee route. Capt. J. McNulty, in private life Dr. McNulty, reached Sacramento, whatever his route, in the fall of '49. Sacramento *Transcript*, April 18, 1850: "Dr. J. McNulty of New York City, would respectfully inform his friends that he has opened a Medical Office, on K street, third door from Front, and hopes by prompt attention to receive a share of public patronage." *Ibid.*, June 6, 1850: "For Sale — Shares in Ophir on the Feather river, and some of the most desirable lots in Pacific City, at the mouth of the Columbia river, Oregon — for sale by the subscriber, at his office, where a map of the above named towns can be seen. Dr. J. McNulty."

101. In contrast to the brevity of this entry, there are three elephant folios in H 3: "The morning was chilly and a little misty. . . . As the road was level and good, and the opportunity so fine for me to indulge in more excursive views than the trail afforded . . . I resolved to strike over the hills, shoot some game, and if too late to return to the company near where I left them, to keep along the base of the high land, and strike down on the road, and rejoin them by noon. I told my second in command, to take charge. . . . This relaxation from an ardious and troublesome charge, afforded me the opportunity for the free scope I so much enjoy." First he encountered a pack of prairie wolves, "a moving mass of dark

forms and pointed ears!" Buffalo were browsing on the hills, and he brought down an antelope. Farther off, where "not one white speck, indicating a tent or wagon, was to be seen," he encountered four Indians—either Sioux or Cheyenne— painted, feathered and armed, who caused him some anxiety before he escaped them. Next he captured alive a young wolf, about the size of a cat, and carried him along, struggling. "He was full of fleas, and very snappish." In the middle of the day, hungry, thirsty, and weary, he reached the wagons of some acquaintances and paused with them to rest. The young wolf he presented to one of the men. His own company was now well in advance, and apparently he did not rejoin it until the noon halt of June 23. Perhaps Bruff felt he had been guilty of imprudence, in exposing himself needlessly to danger, and might be considered blameworthy, in view of his responsibilities. There seems no other reason why the incidents do not appear in his pocket notebooks.

Bruff was not certain whether his Indians were Sioux or Cheyenne. He was in the midst of the Sioux country at the time. "Their vernacular name, Dakotah . . . is translated 'leagued' or 'allied,' and they sometimes speak of themselves as Osheti Shakowin, or the 'Seven Council Fires.' . . . "[The Teton] inhabiting the trans-Missourian prairies, and extending westward to the dividing ridge between the Little Missouri and Powder River, and thence south on a line near the 160° meridian . . . constitute more than half of the Dakotah nation. In 1850 they were numbered at 1250 lodges. . . . They follow the buffalo as chance directs" (Burton, *op. cit.*, pp. 95-97). "Several bands of the Sioux Indians have suffered severely by the cholera. This epidemic, they contend, was introduced by the whites, for the purpose of causing their more speedy annihilation. Superadded to this fresh cause of complaint, they, together with other prairie tribes, continue to remonstrate in threatening language against the destruction of their game, timber, &c., by the whites passing through their country, and the establishment of military posts by the government" (*Report of the Com. of Indian Affairs for 1850,* p. 49).

102. H 3: "nooned at a *slew;* opposite the upper end of 'Brady's Island' — This island is covered with grass and willows, about 10 miles long, and called after a trapper, named Brady, who some 14 years ago, being left in camp on this spot, with a comrade whom he had quarrelled with, was found dead, on return of his party, who had been out all day hunting: and it was thought that his comrade killed him. Buffalo numerous among the hills on our left; hundreds of bleaching sculls are scattered over the plain; their trails intersect it in all directions; and we are constantly passing their fresh wolf-gnawed remains. . . . camped on the river's bank, in long grass, the air thick with myriads of mosquitoes."

103. H 3: "nooned, on the edge of the Platte — The trail here runs within 5 feet of the brink, — banks 10 feet deep, soft earth, and white with nitrous crystallizations."

104. H 3: "Numerous small islands in the river. The valley, on this side, from

3 to 4 miles wide, bounded by a range of hills about 400 feet high — showing white streaks of probably sand or clay."

105. H 3: "A gentleman known to many of my men, came up, desiring to join the Company: I called a meeting, and he was permitted, on certain terms, to accompany us." This may have been E. Sanford Seymour, author of the now rare *Emigrant's Guide to the Gold Mines, of Upper California* (1849), who is known to have traveled with Bruff's company up the Platte and who gave Bruff an abstract of his guidebook for portions of the route ahead. Or Bruff may refer to one Hume Young, whom he later mentions as traveling with the company.

106. H 3: "I had the pleasure of . . . supping with the Orleaners, and my friend Bowen, on buffalo soup."

107. At Fort Kearny, when Bruff passed, L. B. Dougherty, college graduate and not quite twenty-one, was in charge of the sutler's store, owned by his father, former Indian agent of the Upper Missouri. He describes the forks of the Platte as Bruff must have seen them. "Both seem to head in the same place, paralleling each other so far, looking like broad streaks bright with silver in the sun and not pleasant to the eye when looked upon for long" ("Experiences," p. 376).

108. H 3: "on veal pot pie."

109. Marcy (*Thirty Years*, p. 344), quoting Gen. H. H. Sibley: " 'The chase of the buffalo on horseback is highly exciting, and by no means unattended with danger. The instinct of that animal leads him, when pursued, to select the most broken and difficult ground over which to direct his flight, so that many accidents occur to horse and rider from falls, which result in death, or dislocation of the limbs of one or both. When wounded, or too closely pressed, the buffalo will turn upon his antagonist, and not infrequently the latter becomes the victim in the conflict, meeting his death upon the sharp horns of an infuriated bull.' "

Note the characteristic carriage of the head in Bruff's sketch of bison (p. 533). This is apparently associated with the eye movements described by Catlin ("To the Reader," *op. cit.*, p. 6): "One of the most remarkable peculiarities of the Buffalo is the formation and expression of the eye, the ball of which is very large and white, and the iris jet black. The lids of the eye seem always to be strained quite open, and the ball rolling forward and down, so that a considerable part of the iris is hidden behind the lower lid, while the pure white of the eyeball glares out over it in an arch, in the shape of a moon at the end of its first quarter."

110. H 3: "At the place where I met my 2 mounted men, we turned down, towards the river, in a hollow between high sand hills, through which we could see the stream, about ¼ mile from the trail. Through the hollow there was fresh buffalo tracks, and on reaching the bank, found a beach, all broken up by the buffalos landing there, from the opposite shore [of the Platte]; looking across there were several at the water's edge, about to enter and swim over. A short distance below, as well as above, this small beach, the bluffs encroached upon the river, so that just here was a much used buffalo landing."

111. H 3: "At 7 A.M. my train as well as the others, moved off for the ford of the 'South Fork'. I told my *guide* to keep ahead and look out for the branch road leading off right to river and ford; as we must be close to it. I fell to the rear, to see a friend in one of the trains, and riding with him, was astonished at 11 A.M. at a halt, and that we were abreast of the ford! I had no horse, and my train had pushed on, keeping a well-beaten road, along the foot of bluffs, leading to other fords, higher up. . . . I looked forward, and could just see the rear wagon of my train 4 miles off, at least. My worthy surgeon and two other members of the Coy were with me, and we walked on, to endeavor to catch the train. . . . Met the guide, who, it appears, instead of looking out for the road, as I directed, took off among the hills, after a buffalo, and hence the error, which resulted in a separation for several days. . . . My men all went on however, except the Doctor, who remained with me."

112. H 3: "On entering this swift, but here shallow stream, (3 to 4 feet), and about 500 feet wide, at right angle with the shore; but we had to follow a pebbly sand bar, extending down stream at an acute angle with the shore, several hundred yards, and when well over, turn short up for about 200 yards more, keeping nearly parallel with that shore, till we reached the landing. . . . On the opposite shore there was discernible a long line of dust and wagons, and horsemen, coming up and moving down to the ford. . . . Looking across o[ver] the south shore, I saw the hills black with buffalo — a lar[ge] *stream* of them; extending from the brow of a hill down t[o] the river."

113. See the four grave inscriptions given by Bruff at the close of the entry for June 26. None of these, it will be noted, says "Died," and two give no cause of death — unusual omissions and perhaps indicating that these may have been caches, not bona fide graves. The "Dr. J. T. Boon" may be the same man who visited Bruff's Camp (Oct. 25, 1849). Bruff later records instances of these pseudo graves, as do other travelers.

114. Usually known as the Boston Pack Company; formed of the Granite State and California Mining and Trading Company, and the Mount Washington Company, both organized in Boston, having a combined membership of about seventy men, who agreed to travel to California together. Joseph Thing, a sea captain, Capt. Nathaniel Wyeth's second in command in the 1834 expedition overland to Oregon, piloted the Pack Co. Apparently Thing performed to Wyeth's satisfaction. In view of the experience of the Boston Pack Company (Aug. 22, 1849, and elsewhere), the most probable explanation is that Wyeth, an energetic and able man in any situation, directed his expedition without much assistance and never had occasion to test Thing's qualities as a responsible leader.

115. The Boston Pack Co. drove with them cattle for food. Kimball Webster, a member (*The Gold Seekers of '49* [1917], p. 38): "The horses, mules and cattle belonging to the two companies [which combined under the guidance of Capt. Thing to form the Boston Pack Co.] number more than three hundred.

. . . The cattle that we were driving were designed to furnish us with our principal dependence for provisions during our long journey." The company appears to have had trouble with its mules from the start; Bruff (H 3, June 27, 1849): "carry match trunks on their mules, which have very severely galled them." July 9, just after passing Fort Laramie, Webster records (*op. cit.*, pp. 57-58): "Before leaving Boston we had light, strong trunks manufactured — two for each pack mule — in which to pack our clothing, provisions, etc. . . . We now, after packing them about 700 miles, get a vote of the company to break them up and make bags from the leather coverings. . . . We have been packing thirty pounds of dead weight to each mule. . . . The first thought of packing these trunks . . . to California, was a sad oversight by Captain Thing, who suggested them."

116. H 3: "We noticed . . . about 2 miles off, in bold relief against the clear sky, a party of mounted Indians, proceeding Eastward. . . . I walked over at right angle to the trail, about ½ mile from it, and halted to observe. . . . The indians halted also and closed up. In a few minutes a single horseman rode down the hill side, and when upon the plain, dashed off at full speed towards me. He reined up within 2 feet of me, reached out his hand, and said "how do?" I shook hands with him. He was upon a pretty spiritted poney, and armed with a long brass-mounted rifle. He was a short, square built, fat, and merry-looking fellow. And as he sat on his poney watching the train, another horseman left the group, and in like manner dashed over the plain, reining up from full speed, when almost upon me. — He was a tall, thin, dark, and frowning character, armed with quiver and bow — He took my hand cooly when I offered it, and did not reply to my salutation, but sat reserved and frowning. In a few seconds, a third, also dashed off, and came up to me. They all wore white skin robes, leggings, and mocasins; and had some vermillion on cheeks, and about the eyes. Fine horses. The last one was also a young sociable fellow. By this time, there was a considerable crowd of our people come up around me: trying to talk with the Indians. The latter made signs that we could proceed, without molestation, supposing, I judge, that we had stopped, to know if we could do so! They spent about 15 ms. with us, then wheeled, and dashed on, to regain their party. On reaching them, they all collected in a close body, and, I suppose, received the report of their committee: soon after strung along on their way."

117. H 3: "Drove over a broken part of the range. Nooned about an hour, and continued on, and descended to a hollow and spring & camped. At Sun Set a magnificent view on the N. Fork some 20 miles, looking down ahead and on our right, from a very elevated point, a heavy column of light blue smoke was curling up from some indian camp-fire — deep and far off — and occasionally I could see the flickering flame, some where near 'Ash Hollow'."

118. H 3: "It was from my second in command, stating that they had crossed well, and getting along finely; to hurry up & join them soon. . . . The officers

of the colony guards hurrying with long marches, most kindly, to reunite me with my company. . . . The company will have to drive in the night in order to reach 'Ash Hollow,' where most likely my boys are. . . . By 9 P.M. struck into 'Ash Hollow and Creek,' . . . where we found the company, camped."

119. *Hosea B. Horn's Overland Guide* . . . (1852), p. 14: "south of river: — Deriving its name from a grove of ash trees growing in it; it occupies over 20 acres, and is surrounded by high bluffs." Dougherty, "Experiences," pp. 373–74: "We reach the brink of a hill near one-third of a mile high which we have to descend to reach the level of the hollow. . . . I cannot say at what angle we descend but it is so great that some go so far as to say 'the road hangs a little past the perpendicular!' "

120. H 3: "Here a little company of 3 wagons, several men, and 2 ladies desired to travel with us for security We took the little party under our wing, seem to be very clever people". A family named Thomas. They traveled with Bruff's Co. as far as Fort Laramie.

121. H 3: "Moved on after dinner 7 ms; making 16¼ miles to-day, and camped at a marshy rill, called 'Smith's Creek'."

122. H 3: "Our *guide* conducts us to bad camping places, and knows very little of the route."

123. Dougherty says of Court House Rock ("Experiences," p. 376): "After . . . entering Ash Hollow, you start up the south bank of the North Fork. Twenty miles up you will see Court House rock resembling a Missouri court house so much as to deceive many on their first trip. Father was once passing with a colored lad driving his vehicle. He had heard of this rock, and when opposite, the boy called father's attention to the rock saying, 'Court must be in session, there are so many horses hitched near the house.' There were cedar shrubs growing at the front."

124. "Feu de joie. — A discharge of musketry into the air, made in honor of a victory or other great occasion. It commences with the right-hand man of the line, who discharges his rifle, and is followed successively, at scarcely perceptible intervals, by the men on his left, until the extreme left of the line is reached" (Edw. S. Farrow, *Farrow's Military Encyclopedia* [1885], I, 631).

125. Wyeth, on his first Oregon expedition (*Correspondence and Journals . . . 1831-6* . . . [1899], p. 156): "9th [June, 1832] . . . arrived at the Chimney or Elk Brick the Indian name this singular object looks like a monument about 200 feet high and is composed of layers of sand and lime stone . . . it is scituated about 3 miles from the river."

F. V. Hayden, *Sun Pictures of Rocky Mountain Scenery* (1870), p. 47, gives an interesting account of the geological formation of this region: "The surface of the country is sometimes weathered by atmospheric agencies into peculiar fantastic shapes. The rock formations are entirely composed of the whitish and yellowish-white clays, marls and sandstones of the more recent beds of the great

Tertiary basin. The most striking examples are in the vicinity of Scott's Bluffs and Chimney Rock. . . . Chimney Rock shoots up its tall white spire 100 to 150 feet. The strata are perfectly horizontal and, therefore, we may infer that the surface of the whole country was originally on a level with the summit at least, and that these landmarks are monuments left after erosion."

126. For account of this Fourth of July celebration, see 1st ed., Appendix III. Other companies celebrated in a similar manner.

127. H 3, July 6, 1849: "Here the plain is broad, but in 10 or 12 miles higher up 'Scott's Bluffs' encroach on the river, and the road turns left and passes through a very singular formation. Drove 12 ms. [i.e., to vicinity of Scott's Bluffs] and nooned. . . . In a couple of hour's drive, from the noon halt, we entered an elevated narrow sand plain, with a sparse growth of sage. On our right are most extraordinary artificial appearances of the cliffs of which I took sketches. High sand hills and bluffs about 4 miles off, on the left. The trail follows the dry bed of a torrent for some distance —, westerly."

128. Described by Washington Irving from Bonneville's journals (*The Rocky Mountains* [1837], I, 45-46), and by many subsequent travelers. Supposed to have received their name from an unfortunate individual who died here, according to some versions deserted by his comrades. They form a bold escarpment, of the same marl and sandstone formation as Chimney Rock, rising up sharply from the river and thus forcing the Trail either through a pass traversing the center of the bluffs or into a detour around their skirts. Made a national monument in 1919, owing to the historic interest deriving from the Overland Trail, and to their scenic singularity. The highest point within the present state of Nebraska.

129. E. P. Howell, "Crossing the Plains, 1849" (MS, Bancroft Library), pp. 13-14: "Tuesday, June 19. . . . Six companies of a mounted Rifle Regiment of U.S. Troops with a train of about one hundred and twenty waggons, beef cattle mules etc. passed on a few miles ahead of us. Col. Loring is in command of this regiment, called the Oregon Regiment. . . . One soldier of Company I died this evening of Cholera."

130. H 3: "A Trading-post and Blacksmith's shop kept by one of the Robedeaux's of St Josephs, Mo. to trade with the Indians." The Robidoux referred to here appears to be Joseph E. (born in 1801 or 1802), son of Joseph, the founder of St. Joseph, by his first wife, Eugenie Delisle, who died soon afterwards. The boy was largely brought up at his father's trading post on Blacksnake Creek and from childhood learned to know Indians and Indian dialects. At an early age he was sent out to trade for his father on the plains. He is said to have raised two Indian families. "Young Joe," as he was known, retired from the Indian trade about 1857, married an Indian woman, and settled on the No Heart Indian Reservation near White Cloud, Kan., where he died about 1888. It was then said that he had traded with nearly every Indian tribe in the West and Northwest. (Information and identification of "Young Joe" by Mr. A. W. Toole, of St. Joseph, Mo., who is familiar

with the history of the Robidoux family.) See also Orral M. Robidoux, *Memorial of the Robidoux Brothers*. James D. Lyon (*Detroit Advertiser*, Sept. 10, 1849): "Near Scott's Bluffs there is a Blacksmith shop and store, owned by a Frenchman who says he has been there trading with the Indians for 14 years."

George Gibbs, Scotts Bluffs, June 19-20, *New York Journal of Commerce*, Sept. 1, 1849: "On ascending toward the road, we saw a little beyond us an Indian Lodge, and riding towards it, to our astonishment a log cabin. . . . It turned out to be the 'Fort' of an Indian trader, who, with his half-breed family had settled himself here, posted up a sign, 'Tinware, by A. Rubidue,' and occupied himself by doing blacksmith work for the emigrants in the interval of the trading seasons." This "A. Rubidue" is hard to reconcile with known facts. Antoine Robidoux, the only A. Robidoux, a brother of Joseph, the founder of St. Joseph, had been long identified with the trade of the Southwest and had established Fort Robidoux at the forks of the Uintah River. "In 1846 he accompanied Gen. Kearney, as interpreter and guide, to Mexico. . . . Returned to St. Joseph in 1849" (obituary, *St. Joseph Gazette*, cited by Burton, *op. cit.*, p. 75). In 1828 Antoine Robidoux is said to have married Carmel Genavides, of Santa Fe, daughter of a Spanish captain. He had no children save an adopted daughter. There is nothing in the history of Antoine Robidoux that fits into the picture of the Robidoux trader at Scott's Bluffs, with his Indian family. It is possible, of course, that Gibb's longhand notes were misread. Whatever the explanation, we believe that the trader of Scott's Bluffs was not Antoine, but young Joseph.

131. H 3: "The hollow where we now are [the pass through the Bluffs], is called 'Karante Valley.' " So designated by T. H. Jefferson, on his *Map of the Emigrant Road* (1849), often consulted by Bruff.

132. H 3: "skin lodges of the Sioux."

133. Bruff's is a typical sketch of Indian trade. "The degrading and demoralizing influence of intoxicating spirits upon the Indian was well understood. . . . They [private traders] were, however, allowed to take a certain amount on their expeditions for the use of their employes; but when it became apparent that the liquor so taken was most of it given (not sold, for that would violate the law!) to the Indians, . . . the importation of liquor into the Indian country was interdicted altogether. . . . But the efforts of the government were wholly ineffectual. . . . Liquor was the most powerful weapon which traders could employ in their struggles with one another. Its attraction for the Indian was irresistible, and by means of it he could be robbed of everything he possessed. There thus arose that stupendous practice of smuggling ardent spirits into the Indian country, which was a prominent feature of the entire history of the Indian trade" (H. M. Chittenden, *American Fur Trade of the Far West* [1902], I, 22-23).

134. About 10,000 feet in height. The tallest peak of the Laramie Mts., known then as the Black Hills (from the dark evergreens clothing them); not to be confused with the Black Hills of South Dakota and n.e. Wyoming, to which the name

was later restricted. Dr. W. E. Mendenhall, Director, Geological Survey, Washington: "One map of record prepared by 1st Lt. Geo. M. Wheeler of the Corps of Topographical Engineers in 1875 and published in 1879 to accompany a report names both the South Dakota and the Wyoming (Laramie section) 'Black Hills', while a second compilation by Col. E. T. Ensign, Forestry Agent of the Department of Agriculture, in 1885, names the southern group 'Laramie Mountains'. Hence it would seem logical to assume that the change in name took place between these years. It is not believed, however, that this change was a sudden one but came about gradually through the period 1875-85 and was occasioned largely through the medium of increasing usage of the new name on the part of local residents of that section of the country, this in an endeavor to obviate the confusion which must have become increasingly apparent through two nearby eminences bearing an identical name. It is only natural, too, that as this area at that time boasted of Laramie City (incorporated in 1869), Laramie Plains, Laramie River, and Fort Laramie, the logical name to be selected would be Laramie Mountains in honor of the original pioneer of the locality, Jacques La Ramie" (letter, Sept. 20, 1941).

135. Here applied by Bruff (see illus.) to the ground squirrel (*Citellus*) of the region, nearly related to the chipmunk. J. D. Godman (*American Natural History* [3d ed., 1836], I, 334) calls it the Federation Squirrel. *Ibid.*, pp. 318-19: "We retain the *specific* name first proposed by our distinguished countryman Professor Mitchill, derived from the number of stripes on the back of the animal, being the same as that displayed in the 'star spangled banner' of our federation."

136. H 3: "The deceased had served as a non-commissioned officer on the Rio Grande."

137. Often used as fuel. J. Q. Thornton, *Oregon and California in 1848* (1849), I, 72-73: "We used the *bois de vache*, this last resort of the traveler when driftwood, quaking asp, and dead willows, are not to be had to boil his tea-kettle or to cook his meat. As this was frequently our only means of making fires in many places in the subsequent part of our journey, it may not be improper to observe that it is the dry deposit of the bison, which furnishes to the traveler across the continent to the Pacific a very good substitute for wood, until he gets west of the Rocky Mountains."

138. The reasons are obvious. In the spring of 1847 the Rev. A. M. Blanchet, newly appointed Bishop of Walla Walla, left St. Louis to travel the Oregon Trail to his see. June 3, just beyond the Little Blue, Blanchet's company paused: "Ce fut un jour de repos pour les bêtes de somme. L'on profita de la circonstance, afin de dresser des règlements pour la sûreté du convoi. L'on forma six compagnies, chacune de dix hommes, pour faire la guarde; et il fut expressément défendu de tirer du fusil pendant la nuit, sans une nécessité pressante" (*Rapports sur les Missions du Diocèse de Québec*, "Mission de Walla-Walla" [1849], p. 15).

139. H 3: The friends of the man who was struck desired Bruff to try the case. "He [the offender] was a good guard-officer, and I much regretted the whole

affair." Farrow (*op. cit.*, I, 511), of a drum-head court: "A Court-Martial called suddenly by the Commanding Officer to try offenses committed on the line of march, and which demand an immediate example. This method is not resorted to in time of peace."

140. H 3: "I am told there is a long Mormon train there."

141. Noted by many. Stansbury, *Exploration*, pp. 20-21, 41: "We found the trees and stumps on its [Big Blue] banks carved all over with the names of hundreds of emigrants who had preceded us, the dates of their passing, the state of their health and spirits, together with an occasional message for their friends who were expected to follow. . . . The traces of the great tide of emigration that had preceded us [at Ash Hollow] were plainly visible in remains of camp-fires, in blazed trees covered with innumerable names carved and written on them."

142. Wm. Kelly, *An Excursion to California* (1851), I, 154: "a rapid little river, in which a Frenchman named Laramie [Jacques La Ramie] was drowned, yielding up his name both to the river and the fort."

143. H 3: "Fort Laramie (formerly Ft John) is to our left—S. W.—the road passes close by it, and then turns up westerly over the hills." Frémont, *Report*, p. 35 (July 15, 1842): "we came first in view of Fort Platte, a post belonging to Messrs. Sybille, Adams, & Co. situated immediately in the point of land at the junction of Laramie with the Platte. . . . A few hundred yards brought us in view of the post of the American Fur Company, called Fort John, or Laramie." Chittenden says (*op. cit.*, III, 949) that the latter post, built on the left bank of the Laramie in 1834 about a mile above its junction with the Platte, was named Fort William in honor of Wm. Sublette and came into the possession of the American Fur Co. the following year, being then renamed Fort John in honor of John B. Sarpey. Six or seven years later a second fort was erected a mile above and named Fort Laramie, Fort John soon falling into disrepair.

144. Nov. 28, 1849, Adjt. Gen. R. Jones to the Secretary of War, *Report of the Sec. of War for 1849*, p. 186: "The two companies of the rifle regiment, and one company of the 6th infantry, assigned to the second post in the chain [to Oregon], reached Fort Laramie in June, July and August. . . . This post is regarded as of great importance, being in the midst of several powerful tribes of Indians, the principal of which, the Sioux and Crows, have never been friendly to the whites. The Pawnees also have shown a hostile disposition on various occasions, but more recently by murdering two mail carriers on the road between Fort Kearny and Fort Laramie." Hamersly, *op. cit.*, Part II, p. 140: "Laramie, [Fort,] Wyoming. . . . Passed into the hands of the American Fur Company in 1835, and sold to the United States, 26 June, 1849." But Wistar, reaching Fort Laramie June 15, says Maj. Saunders with one Co. of Dragoons arrived June 16 to take over. June 17 he records: "The stars and stripes went up on the fort this morning, receiving our hearty cheers" (*Autobiography*, p. 85; courtesy of Wistar Institute).

145. Evidently the encampment of the personnel of the American Fur Co.,

who had recently turned Fort Laramie over to our troops. Crofutt says (*Crofutt's New Overland Tourist* . . . [1884], pp. 47-48): "The place [Fort Laramie], once a trading post of the Northwestern Fur Company, was purchased by the Government, through Brice Husband, the company's agent, for the site of a military post." Wm. Kelly, in May, 1849, before the occupation of the post by our troops, "found Mr. Husband, the manager, or governor as he is styled, a most obliging, intelligent, and communicative person. He offered us apartments to sleep in" (*Excursion*, I, 155).

146. Apparently an error for Simonson. According to Hamersly (*op. cit.*, Part I, p. 759), John S. Simonson was appointed Capt., Mounted Rifles, May 27, 1846; Bvt. Maj., 1847, for gallant and meritorious conduct at Chapultepec.

On the other hand, Bruff says, H 3: "I walked up to the fort, and introduced myself to the courteous & hospitable commandant — Major Sanderson, of the Mounted Rifles." *Niles' Register*, June 13, 1849, published part of a letter dated Fort Leavenworth, May 25, regarding the stationing of officers in the posts on the Oregon Trail: ". . . Major Sanderson stops at the first [new] post on the route, viz: Fort Laramie." According to F. B. Heitman (*Historical Register and Dictionary of the United States Army* [1903], I, 859), Winslow F. Sanderson was appointed Capt., Mounted Riflemen, May 27, 1846; Bvt. Maj., for gallant and meritorious conduct at Contreras and Churubusco, 1847; Maj., 1848; died, 1853.

Gibbs, who traveled with the Rifle Regiment from Fort Leavenworth, gives the disposition of the troops as arranged there, May 8, 1849 (*New York Journal of Commerce*, July 25, 1849): "Brevet Major Simonson with company B, Newton's, to which on reaching Fort Kearny, his own company, G, is to be added, proceed to Bear River, where he is to be stationed in command, and Bt. Lt. Col. Sanderson with company E, Duncan's, and C, Roberts', is ordered to Fort Laramie."

147. Hume Young and E. Sanford Seymour, the latter the author of the now rare *Emigrant's Guide to the Gold Mines of Upper California* (see 1st ed., Appendix VIII for Bruff's transcript of text). Both are known to have traveled with Bruff's company.

148. Lieut. Daniel P. Woodbury, Corps of Engineers. According to Cullum (*op. cit.*, I, 496-97): born in N. H., grad. West Point July 1, 1836; with 3d Artillery and Corps of Engineers alternately. "Served: as Asst. Engineer in constructing the Cumberland Road in Ohio, . . . as Superintending Engineer of the construction of Ft. Kearny, Neb., and Ft. Laramie, Dak., for the protection of the Route to Oregon, 1847–50." Hamersly, *op. cit.*, Part I, p. 875: "Died 15 Aug., 1864," aged 51.

149. H 3: "The Fort is about 130 feet square; walls 15 feet high. At the N.W. and S.E. angles of its walls are square bastion towers, — enfilading the walls. The principal entrance is on the S. side, in the centre; over which is a watch tower, loop-holed to defend it. The bastions have embrasures below and loop-holes above. The 2nd floor of the buildings have gallerys. In the centre of the N. wall is a gate also. It is much dilapidated. The well is under the main gateway."

150. "The shark of the plains," as Chittenden aptly terms the wolf, was frequently encountered.

151. John Torrey, "Catalogue of Plants Collected," Frémont's *Report*, p. 83: "From the forks [of the Platte] to Laramie river, a distance of about two hundred miles, the country may be called a sandy one. . . . Between the main forks of the Platte, from the junction, as high up as Laramie's fork, the formation consisted of marl, a soft earthy limestone, and a granite sandstone. . . . Above Laramie's fork to this place [mouth of the Sweetwater], the soil is generally sandy. The rocks consist of limestone, with a variety of sandstones, (yellow, gray, and red argillaceous,) with compact gypsum or alabaster, and fine conglomerates."

152. H 3: "to which a party of soldiers were attending, for the post of Larimie." Bruff is here quoting W. Clayton (*The Latter-Day Saints' Emigrants' Guide* . . . [1848]. *In* Loomis's *Journal*. . . . E. M. Ledyard, ed. [1928], p. 153): " 'Warm Springs,' Lat. 42° 15′ 6″. This is a very strong spring of clear water, but it is warmer than river water, at all seasons of the year." Frémont likewise: " 'the Warm Spring' " (*Report*, p. 46).

153. Pasteur had not yet dealt the deathblow to the idea of spontaneous generation, still defended by the distinguished chemist, Baron Justus von Liebig.

154. H 3: "On our left, about 35 miles distant, bearing W-S.W."

155. H 3: "Bitter Creek." Frémont's "*Fourche Amère*, so called from being timbered principally with the *liard amère*, (a species of poplar,) with which the valley . . . is tolerably well wooded" (*Report*, p. 48).

156. Frémont, *Report*, p. 10: "During our journey, it was the customary practice to encamp an hour or two before sunset, when the carts were disposed so as to form a sort of barricade around a circle some eighty yards in diameter. . . . At nightfall, the horses, mules, and oxen, were driven in and picketed. . . . Guard was mounted at eight o'clock, consisting of three men, who were relieved every two hours." For Bruff's sketch of his company thus encamped, drawn from the top of Independence Rock, see pp. 534-35.

Probably few of the emigrants — or the Army either — knew how old this custom was. Edw. D. Neill, *The History of Minnesota* (1858), pp. 449-50: "For many years the half-breeds of the Hudson Bay Company have subsisted by hunting the buffalo on the plains of Minnesota . . . and about the month of June they march forth to the plains. Their carts [A footnote states that in 1840 there were 1,210 carts engaged in such activities.] are truly primitive, having the appearance of being made before the days of Tubal Cain. Not a particle of iron fastens them together. The wheels are without tires, and wooden pegs take the place of iron spikes. Into the shafts an ox is harnessed with gearing made of raw hide, and with this vehicle they travel hundreds of miles. Women and children accompany the hunters, and, as they wind over the prairies in their gay hunting attire, they appear like bold crusaders on a pilgrimage. When they halt for the night, the carts are arranged in the form of a circle, with the shafts projecting outward, and within this wooden cordon the tents are pitched at one end, and the animals tethered at the other extremity — when danger is anticipated."

157. Clayton, *op. cit.*, p. 156: "The spring lays a little to the right of the road, at the edge of timber."

158. H 3: "(branch of Horse Shoe Creek)."

159. H 3: "We are now travelling over ground elevated about 5,000 ft above the sea, on one of the spurs of the 'Black Hills' — which rear their tall dark and irregular lines on our left."

160. H 3: "Tires are very loose, and all very tired. Tried a plan which succeeds very well — a wagon bow being split to half thickness, is taked around the wheel, the tire heated red-hot, is then put on, and after shrinking the screw-clamps are applied, — 3 to each wheel. These proceedings detained us, so that we made a late start."

161. *Phrynosoma cornutum.* J. E. Ware, *The Emigrants' Guide to California* . . . (1849), Princeton ed. (1932), p. 21: "La Bonte River. . . . The curious may here look out for toads with horns."

162. H 3: "Called Elk Creek."

163. "Mr. Pickering & lady" became friends of Bruff, through chance meetings on the Trail. H 3: "(Mr P. was an editor)." Pickering became well known in California for his newspaper and other activities. He died in San Francisco Dec. 29, 1892. Sacramento *Record-Union*, that date: "Born in Richmond, N.H., July 31, 1812. In 1832 he started West. . . . In 1846, at the age of 34, he entered the newspaper business in St. Louis, purchasing the Reporter and Missourian and subsequently establishing the St. Louis Union. In 1849 he started with his wife, who was at the time an invalid, across the plains for California. Here he spent a few months in the mines, but finally engaged in the mercantile business at Minerstown, a mining camp situated where Colfax now stands. In the latter part of 1850 he purchased an interest in the Placer Times, the pioneer paper of Sacramento. . . . In June, 1851, the Times was consolidated with the Transcript. . . . In 1855 he became part owner and editor of the Alta California, which he soon afterward sold. . . . In the following year [1861] he purchased an interest in the Evening Bulletin. . . . Six years later Mr. Pickering, in conjunction with Mr. Fitch and the late James W. Simonton, purchased the Morning Call. . . . During his life Mr. Pickering filled several responsible official positions. . . . In 1848 he was elected a director of the Bank of Missouri by the State Legislature, retaining that office until he left for the State of California in 1849. In 1852 he was appointed one of the Board of Commissioners, consisting of five members, to settle the State of California's interest in certain lands in San Francisco, an office he held until 1855." *The Sacramento City Directory* for 1851 ("Appendix," p. 91): "Pickering, Loring, Editor of the Placer Times"; *San Francisco City Directory*, 1852, under "Editors and Publishers" (p. 110 A), "editor Placer Times & Transcript, 152 Clay"; the authors of *A "Pile," or, a Glance at the Wealth of the Monied Men of*

San Francisco and Sacramento City, 1851, estimated the assets of Lawrence & Pickering, of Sacramento, at $20,000 — a figure not topped by many. Bruff explains elsewhere that Colonel Pickering and wife had with them on the Trail two colored servants.

164. H 3: "(Spring Ck)."

165. H 3: "Noon'd at a deeply embedded stream called La Préle River."

166. H 3: "In 8½ miles crossed Fourche Boise River and dry beds of streams."

167. H 3: "An immense and continuous camp, of emmigrants: hundreds of wagons and tents; and thousands of men, women, and children!"

168. H 3: "about 2 miles" from the ford over Deer Creek.

169. H 3, July 16: "This ferry is kept by 3 men from Iowa. They are emigrants, but think this a speculation worth their attention. . . . An inclined plane is cut in the bank on this side, for a landing, and the opposite shore is low. The animals are swum over." There seems to be some difference of opinion as to the construction of this ferryboat. Gould, of the "Boston and Newton Joint Stock Association," crossed here July 15 ("Diary of Charles Gould . . . in 1849," typescript, Newberry Library, pp. 37-38): "The boats are constructed of six 'dug-outs' fastened together, worked by oars. . . . the animals swam across." Stansbury, July 25 (*Exploration*, pp. 60-61): "The ferry-boat was constructed of seven canoes, dug out from cotton-wood logs, fastened side by side with poles. . . . This rude craft was drawn back and forth by means of a rope stretched across the river, and secured at the ends to either bank. . . . The charge for ferriage was two dollars for each wagon." Bruff shows eight canoes in his sketch and in his account. Also his wagons were ferried for one dollar each; possibly government then, as now, was costly.

170. Now known as the Laramie Mountains. Hayden, *Sun Pictures*, p. 63: "Some of the Peaks, like Laramie Peak, are quite lofty, but as a general rule they are low mountains, and for the most part composed of a nucleus of massive red feldspathic granites enclosed on either side with true gneissic strata."

171. P 2 notebook, inside the front cover, in Bruff's handwriting: "July 19th — Harry G. A. Allen, Canada James Young Myron Peck Wm Poyle." A bracket encloses the names, with a Masonic symbol before it. Against the name of James Young is penciled, evidently later, "dead in Cal." Wm. Poyle reappears, playing a heroic part in the Sierra Nevada in the winter of 1850, when he voluntarily remains with Bruff to assist him. Peck also reappears, as one of the horde of unlucky miners on the upper Feather River in the summer of 1850.

172. Stansbury, July 21, near Bitter Creek (*Exploration*, p. 57): "The road, as usual, was strewn with . . . immense quantities of white beans, which seemed to have been thrown away by the sackful, their owners having become . . . afraid to consume them from danger of the cholera. The commanding officer at Fort Kearny had forbidden their issue at that post on this account."

173. H 3: "Some of the Western States contributed immense companies to

this immigration: — one I knew from Iowa, which was laid off in divissions, —
8 or 10 wagons to a division; . . . the whole composed of many divissions."
Presumably this referred to the company of Col. Brophy and Maj. Haun (Bruff's
"Major Horn"). Mrs. Haun (Catherine Margaret Haun, "A Woman's Trip across
the Plains in 1849" [MS, Huntington Library]): "As it was necessary for safety
to travel in large caravans we reorganized by joining some of the emigrants who
were waiting here [Council Bluffs] for west bound companies. . . . After a sufficient number of wagons and people were collected at this rendezvous we proceeded to draw up and agree upon a code of general regulations for train government and mutual protection. . . . Each family was to be independent yet a part
of the grand unit and everyman was expected to do his individual share of general
work and picket duty. John Brophy was selected as Colonel. . . . Each week
seven Captains were appointed to serve on 'Grand Duty.' They were to protect
the camp and animals at night. One served each night and in case of danger gave
the alarm. . . . It took us four days to organize our company of 70 wagons and
120 persons." See also n. 177, this account, on the Spartan Band.

174. H 3: "An Irishman. . . . He had been *divided* out of some company."

175. H 3: "Painted and varnished wagon-covers were cut to pieces, while our
soft white ones were uninjured — owing to their elasticity."

176. H 3: "The banks below, at the Fords, and anthracite deposites, have
been cut away, in several places, and posts inserted, to lower wagons down by."

177. Trader's Point, now Council Bluffs. Prof. Fred W. Lorch, Iowa State
College (letter, Jan. 26, 1937): "The Spartan Band was one of the finest, best
equipped outfits I have any record of. . . . The Band numbered 57 wagons and
163 persons."

178. H 3, July 21: "Capt. Duncan, U.S.M. rifles, whom I left at Fᵗ Larimie.
. . . The Capt. was in citizen's garb. . . . He left Larimie on the 19th (3 days
ride of 138 miles)   He had most energetically pushed on, to this point, in so short
a time, but his horses were nearly used up. . . . I . . . ration the party for the
occasion." Thos. Duncan. Hamersly, *op. cit.*, Part I, p. 416: born in Ill., "1st Lieut.
Mounted Rifles, 27 May, 1846."

179. H 3: "This stream empties into the Platte opposite the Red Buttes. There
is a poisonous pond in this bottom." Frémont, *Report*, p. 54: "The river [Platte]
here cuts its way through a ridge; on the eastern side of it are the lofty escarp-
ments of red argillaceous sandstone, which are called the Red Buttes." Hayden,
Sun Pictures, pp. 61-63: "We see at a glance that these rocks are stratified, that
they hold a nearly horizontal position, that they stand out in the plains nearly
isolated. . . . Where are the intermediate portions of the rock out of which
these singular monuments have been carved by the chisel of time? These level
plains, covered now with grass and wild sage, were once on a level with the summits of these sandstones at least, while the vast mass of sandstone, which filled
up the general level has been swept away, who knows where? Who can estimate

the forces that have wrought this mighty work, or the immensity of the time that it required. How many myriads of ages have the winds and storms beaten against the sides of these rocks, gnawing out the cavities and giving the fantastic shapes they now possess? . . . These sandstones also afford a fine illustration of what is called irregular layers of deposition, and the materials are supposed to have been brought here and deposited in turbulent waters. . . . It seems to me it must have occurred as the surface was slowly emerging from the waters of the ocean. As the bottom of the ancient sea along the line of this mountain range slowly arose, the waters became shallow, and they would be more easily distributed by the winds and the erosive forces be proportionately increased, and if the rocks arose above the surface, the waves would dash against their sides and prove still more effective. The sediments would be wafted away and deposited in some other part of the ocean."

180. Marked on Jefferson's Map "Rock Defile." Horn, *Guide*, p. 21: "Avenue Rock: — The rocks here form a gateway, through which the road passes; several rocky ridges present themselves on the right." Clayton, *op. cit.*, p. 159: "Rock avenue and steep descent." According to information from the Wyoming State Library and Historical Dept., "Rock Avenue" is now known as Poison Spring Creek Pass, in the present Natrona Co., Wyo.

181. Perhaps on Clayton's authority: "Mineral springs and lake. Considered poisonous. No bad taste to the water, unless the cattle trample in it. In that case it becomes black, and is doubtless poisonous" (*op. cit.*, p. 159).

182. Apparently Bruff was here traveling by Clayton's *Guide*, using his naming of natural features and his recorded distances except for one obvious error. Clayton has (Ledyard ed., p. 159) "Mineral spring and lake . . . Rock avenue and steep descent. — $7\frac{1}{2}$ [miles] . . . Alkali swamps and springs 2 [miles]." Therefore the "Alkali Swamp & Spring" was 2 miles from Rock Avenue, but $9\frac{1}{2}$ miles, not $7\frac{1}{2}$, from the Mineral Spring.

183. F. V. Hayden (*Preliminary Report of the U.S. Geol. Survey of Wyoming* [1872], p. 30) explains the great quantities of alkali appearing in this region: "The entire mass [of Independence Rock], as well as all the granite ridges in the valley, may be called feldspathic; that is, the red and white feldspar predominate, while the mica occurs in very small quantities. It is quite probable that the vast quantities of this alkaline efflorescence were derived from the decomposition of the feldspars."

184. Apparently Clayton's "Small stream of clear spring water. — 4 [miles]. Good camping place. Plenty of grass, but no wood" (*op. cit.*, p. 159). Bruff's figure "$13\frac{1}{2}$" represents the correct total mileage from Mineral Spring according to Clayton ($2 + 7\frac{1}{2} + 4$); as Bruff gives the distances above, it would be $11\frac{1}{2}$ only ($7\frac{1}{2} + 4$). H 3: "A trying drive to-day, of $28\frac{3}{4}$ miles, the most of which was little better than a desert. A *guide-book* told of intermediate water, but it had evaporated early in the day's march — hence our suffering." Possibly a reference to Ware's *Emigrants' Guide* (Princeton ed., p. 22): "Five miles further [from Upper Platte

Ferry] brings you to a mineral lake and spring. Ten miles more will bring you to a piece of swampy ground, strongly charged with alkali. . . . To the north west, a short distance, you will find good water."

185. H 3: "Heard that there was a large Mormon train not far off in rear."

186. H 3: "At 11 P.M. Dr Austin volunteered to take water back to the wagons in rear, about 1½ miles, to the poor men; as for the mules they must suffer till to-morrow — So the amiable man, mounted his mule, and rode on, fairly covered with canteens of water. I accompanied him, though exceedingly jaded; for my bedding was in one of those wagons, and the night cold & clear. Aurora Borealis and Milky way exceedingly luminous, but the stench from the carrion — extending all the way from camp to the alkali pools, spoiled much of the poetry of the scene."

187. Most overland companies broke into smaller bands or became entirely disrupted long before this point. Bruff, as Colonel Bonneville had prophesied (see Introduction, p. xlix), was performing an arduous and thankless task in guiding his company and had accomplished no mean feat to bring them thus far with organization intact.

188. H 3: "a tributary of the Platte." Ware, perhaps contrasting it with the alkaline and sulphurous waters just passed, calls Willow Spring "a noble spring of cool, pure water" (*op. cit.*, p. 22).

189. H 3: "a deep vale, rill & marsh, called the 'Bad' slew, with sweet water, cool as ice."

190. H 3: "The few actually bad men in the company, have formed a faction, in accordance with that very truthful saying — 'Birds of a feather, &c.' and increase the difficulties of my ardious and thankless duties. It was well that I was preinformed of all this, and accordingly prepared for its development. Though vexed and worried, I have likewise been amused, to think what a party of men would do, if each had his own way. One set were prevailed on to countenance a division of the company, by two or three conceited aspirants for offices; another clique, who wished to travel perfectly independent of control, wished to divide and pack the mules, &c. but I was supported by a majority of the Company — a set of men truly of the '*right stripe*' in every particular. We overcame all these malign influences, and continued to roll on, more prosperously than any other similar company of many thousands. To these — my intelligent and worthy comrades, do I feel deeply indebted; and were I to go over the same route with many of them I would be happy." Guard duty was a powerful source of irritation to the members of the Washington City Co. Among the miscellaneous entries in the P 2 notebook are the following:

"Night 13th [July, 1849] Coumbs slept on post
      ”   ”   Cook   ”   ”   ”
   14th night refusing neglecting guard duty [names not given]

[Penciled lightly, under July 15:]
Donn & Truman refused guard duty as supernumerary.
21st   Burch repd [reported] Windsor
   "   Riley   "   Slye
22   "   "   Thaw refg [refusing] G. [Guard] duty
26th   Cameron & Capron refd duty
28th   Hillery refusing.
29th   Cameron reported Serg. Edmonston for sleeping on duty night before —
[and finally]
Aug. 6   Guard duty revised"

Other companies in '49 experienced similar difficulties. *California Star*, April 1, 1848: "Emigrating bodies should be especially guarded against the baneful effects of social discord. That unanimity of action is indispensable to their actual safety, let the fate of those who sank beneath the snows of Sierra Nevada [the Donner party, 1846] attest! In reviewing the history of those unfortunate people . . . it is shown that social harmony had long been extinct."

191. "In one mile from the last camp we ascended a high hill, from the summit of which is a grand prospect of the surrounding country, and hence it is named 'Prospect Hill' — From thence, looking ahead — westwardly, lay the valley of the 'Sweet Water' river, and bounded by the pale blue jagged line of the 'Rattle Snake' Mountains, enclosing it. On our right, or N. was a range of mountain peaks about 12 ms. distant, our rear was closed up with mountains of every shade and character; while deep below, on our left was the serpentine silver line of the Platte river, and rising in dark and bold grandeur beyond — to the South, the Black Hills walled in the scene" (H 3). Clayton (*op. cit.*, p. 159) names this " 'Prospect Hill' " and adds: "Pleasant view of the surrounding country, to the Sweet Water mountains." Horn, who here appears to follow Clayton closely, speaks (*Guide*, p. 22) of " 'Prospect Hill,' from which you have a beautiful view of the adjacent country."

192. H 3: "the last article was purchased by a wise man of the committee, *as necessary for blasting gold quartz in California!*"

193. H 3: "In one mile we ascended a long steep hill, the top of which was an extensive plain, — or rather inclined plane, for it declined to the southwestward. This extensive flat inclination is bounded on the W & N.W. about 15 ms. distant by the high dark range of the 'Rattle Snake Mountains,' which run off here at an angle of about 70° with the main range, valley and stream of the 'Sweet Water.' And through the gaps of this range, can be seen the far distant blue peaks of the 'Wind River Mountains.' "

194. H 3: "named from the grease-wood shrub, which covers large portions of this singular country, growing much larger than the common Artemesia — And being very resinous burns fiercely, with a crackling noise, like that of fat thrown

on a fire. . . . The creek is about 6 feet wide, and not over one foot deep. Is the last tributary of the Platte on this side." Bruff apparently consulted Clayton (*op. cit.*, p. 160): "Grease-wood creek, 6 feet wide 1 ft. deep."

195. H 3: "About 6 miles from last camp the trail passes between considerable Alkali lagoons, close to the smaller one on our left, and perhaps 2 miles from the large one — on the right. They remind one strongly of ponds of ice — dazzling white in the snow. Sal eratus encrusts all the mud and grass near them; and the main surface of it, is about the consistence and appearance of imperfectly frozen milk. My surgeon walked over to the large pond, where the Oregon emmigrants are in the habit of gathering sal eratus for the balance of their journey. He found the surface, about $\frac{1}{2}$ inch thick, of sal eratus, — over about the same thickness of pure glauber salt. In walking around the small pond, my feet looked as though I had been in white wash or lime water." Jefferson's Map shows "Soda Pond" on the left of the road. Clayton (*ibid.* p. 160): "Here gather your Saleratus."

196. The Sweetwater is said to have received its name from the fact that in the early days a pack mule, laden with sugar, fell into the stream. Chittenden remarks that the French form of the name, *Eau Sucrée*, and not *Eau Douce*, bears this out. July 8, 1847, the Rev. A. M. Blanchet, Bishop of Walla Walla: "Enfin, nous laissâmes la *Platte* pour ne plus la revoir, et la première rivière que nous devions rencontrer était l'*Eau-Sucrée* ou Sweet-Water, à 50 milles de distance" (*op. cit.*, p. 19).

197. Perhaps the most famous landmark on the Trail. Said to have been named by a party of trappers who visited it on July 4, 1830. The name was apparently well established at an early date. Wyeth, passing here on his first expedition to Oregon, notes in his journal (*op. cit.*, p. 157): "21st [June, 1832] . . . we arrived at Rock Independence at noon after a march of 15 miles." H 3: "It is covered over every accesable portion, with names, initials, dates, &c, in black and red, scratched and painted. It was only at the expense of marking over half obliterated names, that for the information of friends in the rear, and to gratify my men, I painted about 4 feet above the base — 'WASHINGTON CITY COMPY July 26. 1849.'" Hayden says, *Preliminary Report*, p. 30: "Independence Rock is really one of the granite ridges in this valley, and is a remnant of much larger mountains." Many described it in the days of the great migration, but none more succinctly than Bruff — "looks like a huge whale."

198. H 3: "We moved on, passing the foot of the rock [Independence] closely, and in $\frac{3}{4}$ mile, forded to the south side [of the Sweetwater], leaving the river on our right, and then travelled towards the S.W. over sand and sage — In about $3\frac{1}{2}$ ms. from the rock, reached the 'Pass' of the 'Rattle Snake Mountains, (an enclosing range at right angles to the valley boundaries) a beautiful and picturesque passage. — A grassy level, quite narrow, and probably only $\frac{1}{4}$ m. long, the trail straight through the centre of it. On either side hills and grey rocks, interspersed with dwarf cedars, plums, and currant bushes."

199. Not a grave inscription, but an emigrant's signature on the rock. James M. Fulkerson, born in Va., 1803; moved to Tenn., 1807, to Mo., 1817; married Mary Fuller, 1823; left for Oregon, 1847; in 1848, in Polk Co., Ore., married Mrs. Catherine Crowley, a pioneer of 1846. (Kindly verified by Mr. Lewis A. McArthur.) See Aug. 7 for grave of Mary Fulkerson.

200. Devil's Gate is in the present Natrona Co., Wyo. H 3: "The Sweet Water river runs through this immense and extraordinary gap. . . . At sunset I visited the gate (which is about 40 ft wide) and clambered on top a pile of rocks opposite the opening, and sketched the remarkable gap. . . . The rocks here are of dark grey, red and brown micacious sandstone, and marked in some places with evidence of volcanic action. . . . Vestiges of old camps all around, — and every inscribable lower portion of the 'Gate' is covered with names. The walls probably 400 ft high; N. side perpendicular　S side a little overhanging."

201. At eleven miles beyond Devil's Gate, his measurement, Clayton (*op. cit.*, p. 160): "Road leaves the river: Lat. 42° 28′ 25″. Road after this, sandy and heavy, and passes over a high bluff."

202. Clayton, at 10½ miles, his measurement, from where road left river, (*op. cit.*, p. 161): "High gravelly bluff. Left of the road, and a very good place to camp."

203. At 5¼ miles, his measurement, before the gravelly bluff where Bruff camped, Clayton (*ibid.*): "Sage Creek. . . . Doubtful for water, but Wild Sage plentiful." Four miles from Sage Creek he has "Creek, three feet wide. Doubtful for water, but the road runs close to the river." This is apparently Bruff's " '2d Ck.' of the 'Mormon Guide'."

204. Horn, *Guide*, p. 25: "12 feet wide."

205. Bruff says he nooned half a mile below a cañon, where the road leaves the river. In the afternoon the train traveled 8¾ miles, and in about one mile more the next day reached the "stone pile, looking like a ruined square tower." Jefferson's Map shows the cañon, the road circling out over the mountains, and, at a comparable distance to Bruff's 9¾ or 10 miles, a large oval, about a half mile to the left of the road, marked "Rocky Ruins." Named by Bruff in his sketch "Webb's Tower."

206. H 3, "Rattle Snake Mts." is corrected to read: "On our left in the lower distance the Sweet Water range of mountains appeared from 8 to 10 miles off, and the river is seen far below, in broken pieces, like bits of silver braid."

207. The second ford of the Sweetwater. Clayton, *op. cit.*, p. 161: "Road arrives at the river [from Bitter Cottonwood Creek]. — 6¼′ Leave the old road and ford the river. — ¼," making 6½ miles in all, as given by Bruff. Horn, *Guide*, p. 25: "Ford No. 2, Sweet Water: — 6 [miles]"; Ware, *op. cit.*, p. 24, likewise six miles.

208. H 3: "River and road now enters a Cañon — called the 'Bird Pass.'" So designated on Jefferson's Map. Clayton, *op. cit.*, p. 161: "Road turns between the rocky ridges"; Horn, *Guide*, p. 25, repeats this. Now known as Split Rock, in the present Natrona Co., Wyo. The two fords mentioned by Bruff here — "crossed and recrossed the stream" — are the 3d and 4th fords of the Sweetwater.

209. Bruff follows Clayton's wording (*ibid.*): "Ford No. 4 — good camping place. 8 [miles]   After this, the road leaves the river again, and you will probably find no water fit to drink for sixteen and a half miles." Actually the fifth fording of the Sweetwater, counting from that immediately after leaving Independence Rock. Horn, *Guide*, p. 25, correctly: "Ford No. 5, Sweet Water: 8 [miles] Here you will leave the river, and will probably find no more water for 15 miles."

210. H 3: "an extensive bog, sweeping around Westerly, across the trail, where the hill descends to meet it. Close to the northern base of the high land, in the bog, are the 'Ice Springs' — where, by turning up the sod, a couple of feet, we found ice in mass." Clayton, *ibid.*: "Ice Spring. . . . 5¾ [miles from "Ford No. 4" — actually Ford No. 5]. Horn makes the distance 6 miles. Dr. (T. G.?) Caldwell (journal, found in the Sierra Nevada and copied by Bruff; see 1st ed., Appendix XI), July 5, 1849: "After crossing here, we leave the river [Sweetwater] for 16 miles, on which stretch we pass the *ice springs* — & ice can be found in great abundance just below the surface. Good grass over it. As this is an alkali spg. of course a chemical action produces the ice. Emigrants afraid to let their cattle graze here, & justly too."

211. H 3: "the snow-capped peaks of the 'Wind-river' Chain of mountains, West of us some 40 odd miles." At about this point Jefferson marked on his Map, "First view of the Wind River Mountains."

212. H 3: "9½ miles from the 'Ice Springs'." Still traveling by Clayton (*op. cit.*, p. 162): "Steep descent from the bluffs. — 9½ [miles from "Alkali springs," which in turn is given by Clayton as ¼ miles from the Ice Springs]."

213. H 3: "fires & blue smoke, — curling up, travellers, dust, and surrounding mountains of every shade and tint!"

214. H 3: "We are near 'Uncle Sam's Back-bone' [the continental divide, here the South Pass]." Perhaps an echo from O. Johnson and Wm. H. Winter (*Route across the Rocky Mountains* [1846], Princeton ed. [1932], p. 22): "On the evening of the 7th [Aug. 1843], we left the head of Sweet Water, and in a few hours passed over the dividing ridge, through the Grand [South] Pass, and encamped by a marsh. . . . We slept here, on the great Backbone of North America, where . . . the Rivers . . . on the East and on the West, are only a few miles apart."

215. Still following Clayton (*ibid.*): "Ford of Sweet-water, No. 5. — 1 [mile]. Plenty of good grass and willow bushes. River about three rods wide and two feet deep." But Horn's "Ford No. 6, Sweet Water: 1 [mile]" (*Guide*, p. 26) is Clayton's and Bruff's 5th ford. Bruff's two fords near together follows Clayton (*ibid.*) exactly, and corresponds to Horn's "Ford No. 7" and "Ford No. 8."

216. H 3: "a tributary of the S. Water." Mentioned by name by both Clayton and Horn, but not by Jefferson.

217. Horn, *Guide*, p. 27: "Road leaves the River: — And winds through, around, and over steep, rough hills and hollows, which are dangerous to wagons. . . . [In one mile] Three Lakes, north of road: — These are about a quarter of a mile apart,

and have the appearance and taste of soap-suds." Apparently Horn is wrong, or else took a variant route here. Jefferson, in his Map, places three "Ponds" south of the Trail, which would correspond to Bruff's "Alkali lakes on the left."

218. H 3: "also a tributary of the Sweet Water." Jefferson lays down "Omaco Creek" on his Map here; Clayton and Horn do not mention it.

219. H 3: " 'Willow or Nokuti Creek." Clayton gives Willow Creek; Jefferson "Nokute C."

220. F. W. Lander's "Report" (*Pacific Railroad Reports*, II, 36) describes South Pass as "nothing but an extended plain, slightly broken towards the south into an undulating country. It is the first break down of the Great Wind River mountains at the north, among which is a summit of over 12,000 feet above the sea [actually there are five peaks in the chain which considerably exceed this elevation]. In this plain, and among these ponds and swamps, head the waters of the tributaries of the Grand Colorado, the Snake, and the Platte."

Through this great natural break in the mountains, approached by the long incline up the Platte and the Sweetwater Rivers, poured the emigration to Oregon and California, in the wake of Indians and trappers. The name derives from the fact that Lewis and Clark crossed the mountains to the north of this and that a belief persisted in the existence of a more southerly pass. It now appears that Astor's men passed here in 1812-13, but the South Pass did not come into general use even for trappers for some years after that date. Bruff's figure for the height of South Pass agrees with that given on his third and later map: "Table Hill 7489 ft." Frémont's estimate of 7,490 (by barometrical observation, *Report*, p. 128) was widely accepted and copied, although Clayton gives 7,085 feet, Horn "about 7,400," and Jefferson (*Accompaniment to the Map of the Emigrant Road*, p. 9) "7300 ft. above the sea."

221. H 3: Stinson, guide of the Washington City Co.

222. H 3, Aug. 2: "He had pursued the deserters some 20 miles down, on the Fort Bridger road; about 275 miles from Fort Larimie. I heard that Captain Stansbury, U. S. Top: Engn. and a surveying party, to explore the Salt Lake country, are no great distance in our rear." This was correct. Two days later Captain Duncan, traveling east, met Stansbury, traveling west, above Devil's Gate. Stansbury, *Exploration*, p. 69: "In the course of the day [Aug. 3], Captain Duncan, of the Rifles, who had passed us at Bitter Creek on the 19th of July, in pursuit of deserters, came into camp."

223. South Pass and Pacific Springs, despite the comparative tameness of the scenery, fired the imagination of early travelers. To Oregon emigrants and gold seekers alike these places symbolized the attainment of their objective, the holding of the Great West within their grasp. "This day we passed over the dividing ridge which separates the waters flowing into the Atlantic from those which find their way into the Pacific Ocean," wrote Joel Palmer in 1845 (*Journal of Travels over the Rocky Mountains . . .* [1847], p. 33). "We had reached the summit of

the Rocky Mountains. Six miles brought us to a spring, the waters of which run into Green river, or the great Colorado of the west. — Here, then, we hailed Oregon."

224. H 3: " 'Bog Creek', and is the fountain head, nearly, of the N.E. fork of Green River. . . . N. of this Valley, the ground ascends rapidly, in a distance of about 15 miles, to the peaked and snow-capped Wind river chain of the Rocky Mountains rising 2000 feet higher."

225. Inside the front cover of the P 3 and the P 6 notebook, is written, in Bruff's hand, and on the margin, against the entry, the words "Thornton says — ":

"Greenwood's cut off   July 20. Camp on Big Sandy   Cut-off of 40 miles commences here and ends at Green River. 22   Started early, filling kegs. Country lofty sand ridge, dust & sand very bad — a perfect desert (on road) generally level — Travell'd 20 m. & camp'd — little before Sun Set — near some ravines where there was very little grass. During day gave each ox 1 quart water   23 — 2½ A.M. rose, at 4 moved hilly & dusty; 3 P.M. arrived at 'Green River' — cross'd & camp'd". This is an accurate digest of J. Q. Thornton's *Oregon and California* (I, 143-44), under these dates.

Thornton belonged to the 1846 emigration and traveled much of the way in company with the Donner party, whom he left at the entrance to Sublette's Cut-off, they holding to the Fort Bridger road. *Oregon and California* was not published until 1849, affording another instance of Bruff's alertness in informing himself. Perhaps he borrowed Thornton's work from some fellow traveler; he says he "just obtained" the information. Caleb Greenwood, in '44, guided the Stevens-Townsend-Murphy party to California and is credited with having then led the first wagons over this cut-off, as well as over the Truckee pass of the Sierra Nevada. Thornton and Bruff indicate that he was actually the pioneer, but Wm. Sublette soon became identified with it. Ware, *op. cit.*, p. 26: "You save nearly five days travel by following what I have taken the liberty to call *Sublette's Cut Off*."

226. H 3: " 'Greenwood's Cut-Off', called here by the emmigrants, 'Soublette's Cut-off,' strikes due W. from where the usual road intersects 'Little Sandy,' crosses 'Big Sandy' and Green rivers, and strikes 'Bear river', at a prominent bend, about 60 miles below the 'Soda' or 'Beer Springs'. Soublette's old pack trail [Frémont's trace] cuts over to Fort Hall, from the neighborhood of 'Fremonts' Peak', a considerable distance N. of this, and probably now entirely obliterated." The Boston Pack Company, whom Bruff met at various points on the Trail (see June 27, 28) appear to have tried to follow this old pack trail. They became lost in the mountains and suffered considerably.

227. Gen. John M. McCalla. He "played an important part in the civic life of Lexington in the early part of the nineteenth century. . . . Distinguished in the actions of the 18th and 22nd of Jan. 1813. . . . A graduate of Transylvania University, Lexington, and practiced law in that town. Was an efficient political de-

bater. Later became a resident of Washington, D.C." (letter, April 30, 1937, from Kentucky State Historical Society). *Register of All Officers and Agents . . . in the Service of the U. S.* (1847), p. 18: John M. McCalla, 2d Auditor of the Treasury Dept., born in Ky., employed in Washington, salary $3,000 per annum. Bruff's "Visitors' Book," containing the autographs of many notable persons, has, Oct. 24, 1847, and elsewhere: "Thomas W McCalla Lexn Ky"; and "Wm R. Bradford Lexington, Ky". Col. Bradford appears to have been a descendant of Fielding Bradford, brother and assistant of John Bradford, first state printer of Ky., founder of the *Kentucke Gazette* in 1787, and author of the famous *Notes on Kentucky*.

228. "Major Horn" has been identified by us as Henry Peter Haun, born in Newton, Scott Co., Ky., 1815, admitted to the bar in 1839, practiced law in Ky., removed to Clinton Co., Ia. in 1845, helped to frame the first constitution of Ia., crossed the plains in 1849, represented Calif. in the U. S. Senate, 1859-60, being appointed by Weller to complete Broderick's term, died in Marysville, Calif., June 6, 1860. Bruff, being a Southerner, supposed the name "Haun" to be spelled "Horn." See 1st ed., pp. 510-15 for full discussion.

229. H 3: "the trail, — a dead level — smoking with dust and heat. . . . The men fixed blankets to the side of their wagons, to afford some shelter from the broiling sun, while they eat their dinner."

230. F. Piercy: "Notwithstanding the country had now been ceded to the United States, and the great influx of emigrants, no recognition had been made of the colony by Congress, either by providing for it a Territorial government or otherwise, the inhabitants, therefore, being chiefly L. D. Saints, were left entirely to the guidance of their ecclesiastical leaders, and justice was administered and enforced solely by the Church authorities. But the citizens were anxious that a civil government should be formed, and a Convention was called . . . which met at G.S.L. City on the 5th of March, 1849, for that purpose. This convention adopted a Constitution which ordained and established a Provisional Government by the name of the State of Deseret, with legislative, executive, and judicial powers. Brigham Young was elected Governor, and, with all other officers elected under the Constitution, took an oath to support the Constitution of the United States. On the 2nd of July the Legislative Assembly met, and elected A. W. Babbitt delegate to Congress, who was forthwith despatched to Washington with the Constitution and a Memorial to that body, . . . asking Congress to consider their interests, and, if consistent with the Constitution and usages of the Federal Government to ratify the accompanying Constitution, and admit the State of Deseret into the Union, on an equal footing with other States, or provide such other form of civil government as their wisdom and magnanimity might award. . . . On the 7th of Sept., 1850, . . . California, with a Constitution excluding slavery, was admitted into the Union as a State; and Deseret, under the Indian appellation of

Utah, and New Mexico, were erected into Territories" (*Route from Liverpool to Great Salt Lake Valley*. Illus. by Fdk. Piercy. Ed. by J. Linforth [1855], pp. 106-7, n.).

231. "Article VIII — *Declaration of rights*. . . . Sec. 3. All men shall have a natural and inalienable right to worship God according to the dictates of their own consciences; and the General Assembly shall make no law respecting an establishment of religion, or of prohibiting the free exercise thereof, or disturb any person in his religious worship or sentiments, provided he does not disturb the public peace, nor obstruct others in their religious worship; and all persons demeaning themselves peaceably, as good members of the State, shall be equally under the protection of the laws; and no subordination or preference of any one sect or denomination to another, shall ever be established by law; nor shall any religious test be ever required for any office of trust under this State" ("Memorial of the Members of the Legislative Council of the Provisional Government of Deseret, Praying for Admission into the Union as a State, or for a Territorial Government," 31 Cong. 1 Sess. Sen. Misc. Doc. 10, Dec. 27, 1849, pp. 8-9).

232. H. H. Bancroft, *History of California* (1884-90), VII, 165: "There were four denominations, two and a half, five, ten, and twenty dollar pieces. They were irregular in weight and fineness, averaging about $8.50 to the ten dollars." Piercy (*op. cit.*, p. 106, n.) explains that "The members of the renowned Mormon Battalion had now [1849] chiefly returned from the Mexican campaign, and a portion of them, who discovered the gold mines of California, had brought considerable gold dust with them, which was deposited with the authorities."

233. H 3: "so that often, in compassion, the men have put him in a wagon: . . . Far ahead, in the heat and dust, you can descry old 'Bull,' with drooping tail, moving on the even tenor of his way, resembling much a large yellow wolf. . . . I have, many a time been ahead, looking around for a good camping-spot to noon at, having made a long forenoon march, when 'Bull' would come up and whining look towards a stream, and bark at the train, as much as to say, 'halt here, — it is time'."

234. Mrs. Haun, wife of Maj. Haun ("Horn") of Col. Brophy's company, says (*op. cit.*): "We had several dogs with us but they were not of much use. . . . They suffered with tender feet and even those that were provided with leather moccasins were often lame and sore of muscle."

235. H 3: "we have probably seen the last buffalo," referring to the four seen that day. This was far west for buffalo. Jefferson wrote on his Map, north of Alkali Lakes, east of South Pass, "Last Buffalo seen here."

236. Both branches crossed Little Sandy and Big Sandy, but not at the same places or distances. Clayton (*op. cit.*, p. 164) places Little Sandy at 7¾ miles beyond the junction of the roads, i.e., the Fort Bridger fork. Horn, like Bruff following the Cut-off, places Little Sandy at 4 miles (*Guide*, p. 29). Bruff, H 3: "Our illustrious predecessors, on this trail [Sublette's Cut-off], must be legions, for it

is a broad and well-beaten road. . . . I found only 2 or 3 [notices] for the lower route, — all had gone on mine."

237. Refers, of course, to the historic symbolism of Freemasonry — "the symbolism of the Tabernacle set up in the wilderness by Moses."

238. H 3: "This is a suspected mound, — being too far advanced for cholera said to contain whisky."

239. H 3: "Probably the Sublette trail, but we kept the other — or main trail, on a S.S.W. course". Bruff here refers to "Soublette's old pack trail" (Frémont's trace), mentioned by him Aug. 2, presumably the route over which Capt. Thing tried to guide the Boston Pack Co. about this time.

240. Not the trader, Thomas, but a family who had traveled up the Platte with the Washington City Co. H 3, Aug. 4: "They left us at [Fort] Larimie." Four days later, Aug. 8, Bruff and a comrade, following their train on foot in the mountains above Bear River, note (H 3, Aug. 8): "Thomas' family party just left as we came down."

241. A Michigan company. "A company is forming in Marshall for California, to be called the 'Wolverine Rangers.' — Each member of the Association pays into the Treasury $85. . . . Independence, the starting point, where the company assemble on the 1st of May. . . . We venture the assertion that the wolverine boys will take care of the rocks as well as the most knowing ones. They have had some experience in mining, on Lake Superior, and know how to endure privations" (*Detroit Free Press*, Jan. 23, 1849). For Wolverine membership and other facts, see 1st ed., pp. 518-19. J. J. Baker was replaced, as captain, after ten days, by James D. Potts, whom Bruff meets later on the Trail and in California. For further information and meetings with Bruff's company, consult Index.

242. H 3: "By Fremont's map; . . . and I thought it highly probable, that midway, towards the foot-hills of the Wind-river Mts. we could obtain grass." Sublette's Cut-off itself is not, of course, given on Frémont's map, although Frémont's (or Sublette's) trace along the base of the Wind River Mountains, referred to above (Aug. 2, 4), is shown. Bruff's estimate of forty miles by Frémont's map from Big Sandy to Green River is close.

243. Haystack Butte, a few miles north of Farson, Sweetwater Co., Wyo., according to Mr. Joseph L. Bagley, of the Grazing Service, Green River, Wyo. Horn (*Guide*, p. 30) describes it as a "Clay mound, north of road: 3 [miles] — Resembling a bee-hive [skep]; 200 feet high."

244. H 3: "We made a wild dark-looking group around the bright flashing and crackling fire."

245. H 3: "A trifling accident would have precipitated wagon and team down the craggy steep, upon crude masses of rock below. . . . Wrecks of wagons told of disasters; and I was informed that two years ago, a wagon was precipitated down here, smashed to atoms, and two men, with the team, unfortunately killed. . . . Had an accident occurred in descending, I rather think the fellow [the guide]

would have been lynched." Horn (*Guide*, p. 31) refers to this and the succeeding hills mentioned by Bruff as "Long steep Hill. . . . Steep dangerous hill. . . . Most Difficult Descent. . . . Green River."

246. H 3: "This divide is a great branching spur of the Wind-river chain of mountains."

247. H 3: "To the N.W. was a pile of rock and scraggy cedars, reared up on the very edge of a tremendous precipice, and precluded any other view than that of the vacant sky beyond. This point must be about 8,000 feet above the sea. 'A nice place this, to take wagons down, Captain!' said a friend to me, on reaching the brow. — I answered, 'a very descent trail, sir!' A mile or so, N. of this, is a much easier descent to the river and a ferry, I am told; but here, as at the other declivity, our *guide* didn't know it! I shall get rid of him before we reach the Sierra Nevada." This is Horn's "Most Difficult Descent" (*Guide*, p. 31).

248. H 3: "the hardest drive we have yet had, of 43 miles in less than 48 hours. Ware, who is generally very correct, states the distance at 35 ms, meaning probably, only to the ferry above." G. W. Read, who used Ware's *Guide*, placed the distance from Big Sandy to Green River at 41 miles (*A Pioneer of 1850*, G. W. Read, ed. [1927], p. 70), but on arrival at Green River stated (*ibid.*, p. 71) that he had traveled 44 miles. Horn's mileage is considerably higher: at Big Sandy (*Guide*, p. 30): "you will find no more water for 49 miles," while his mileage to Green River totals 50. Other travelers report different figures recording, without doubt, variations in the route.

249. Camps of traders had been established in the vicinity for several years, doubtless for the purpose of trafficking with the Oregon emigrants. The Rev. A. M. Blanchet, Bishop of Walla Walla, records, July 30, 1847: "A dix milles de notre campement [on Bear River, north of Fort Bridger], le chemin *racourci* [Sublette's Cut-off] tombe dans celui que nous suivions. Nous y trouvâmes plusieurs loges de gens libres, venus pour trafiquer avec les émigres" (*op. cit.*, pp. 22-23).

250. A later account of this, with sketch, was published in the *Annual Report* of the Smithsonian Institution for 1872, pp. 409-12 (see 1st ed., Appendix VI). What event or victory it commemorates, we are unable to say. Inquiry, conducted through the kindness of Mr. William Hutton, Jr. and Mrs. James Chisman, both of Green River, Wyo., reveal that it is not known locally at the present time. However, Mr. J. L. Bagley, of the Grazing Service, has recently sent us photographs of similar scenes with the notation: "Pictures of Indian writings on Green River near Labarge creek and one mile from the old Sublette trail crossing." This is near where Bruff passed. Here were the haunts of the Shoshoni, in historic times, and all of these petroglyphs are within that period.

251. H 3: "a little tipsy."

252. H 3: "I wrote a note — directing it to the medical gentlemen who might pass, to pay some attention to Thomas, and we bade the poor fellow, and his son adieu."

253. H 3: "I think this, as well as the preceeding brook, are branches of Smith's fork of Bear river."

254. H 3: "We are on a part of the dividing range between the waters of the Great Basin and the Pacific. And the altitude of the hill we have just left, must be over 8,000 feet above the sea."

255. H 3: "The last stream must be a head branch of Ham's Fork of Green River."

256. H 3: "The level bottom, for 3 miles, was covered with vestiges of a large indian camp — or village. . . . I saw . . . pieces of green hide, skins, matting, and worn-out mocasins, strewn over the plain."

257. H 3: "Speaks little English, but excellent French and German: and all the Indian lingos of this part of the wilderness." The Greenwood family has long presented one of the minor puzzles of early western days. The father, Caleb Greenwood, was stated by Bancroft (*History of California*, III, 766) and by B. F. Bonney, who saw him as a child ("Recollections," *in* F. Lockley's *Across the Plains by Prairie Schooner . . . in 1846*, p. 3), to be a Nova Scotian. However, according to Charles Kelly (*Old Greenwood* [1936], p. 11), "it may be assumed that he was born in Virginia, of colonial English stock," although Kelly does say that according to family tradition Caleb was of French descent. All agree that Caleb Greenwood was a mountain man and a trapper, married a Crow Indian by whom he had several children, the two most often mentioned being Britain (Britten) and John. In '44, being then according to his own account over eighty, Caleb guided the Stevens-Townsend-Murphy party to California, the first wagons over Sublette's (Greenwood's) Cut-off and over the Truckee route. Bonney says that Sutter sent Caleb to Fort Hall to divert to California the Oregon emigration of '46, the Bonney family being among those who followed him. Caleb successfully headed the second Donner relief in '47, a hazardous feat. In '48 and '49 he and his son John were found by gold seekers in what was known as Greenwood's Valley (now the town of Greenwood), El Dorado Co., Calif. Bancroft speaks of Greenwood and "two sons, Britain and John," and adds (*op. cit.*): "It is impossible to distinguish between the 3, or to locate any one of them at any definite time." Kelly mentions the following children: Joseph, John, Britton, Bailey, William Sublette, James Case, Angeline, and Sarah Mojave, besides three more — Governor Boggs, Davy Crockett, and Sam — which he suggests *may* have been nicknames for some of those in the first list. Kelly adds (*op. cit.*, p. 127): "The oldest son, Joseph, is mentioned by two family sources, and it is said that he remained in Montana and never came to California. Nothing further is known about him." If, as Kelly thinks, Caleb married about 1812-13, or possibly a few years earlier, this oldest son, Joseph, would have been just about thirty-five years old in 1849, and the upper Bear River region would have been entirely within his range, from any place embraced under the term "Montana." Furthermore, Caleb Greenwood's son might well be in charge of a trading post for Bridger, old associate of Caleb. Therefore the most likely sug-

gestion would seem to be that the Greenwood encountered here by Bruff was Caleb's oldest son, Joseph. As to why Bruff thought him a Bavarian — beyond the fact that he may have had some knowledge of the German as well as of the French tongue and the Indian dialects — we are unable to say.

258. H 3: "on the conclusion of the performance, at about 11 O'clock, produced the brown jug, and we bade each other good night."

259. H 3: "a very delightful spring, in the hollow of a hill. Several paths led to it, and it was stoned around, and had a slab to stand upon. The work of Indians, no doubt."

260. Undoubtedly Shoshoni. "The country of the Shoshones proper is south of Lewis or Snake River, and east of the Salt Lake. . . . The Shoshones are generally at war with the Satsikaa, or Blackfeet Indians, and the Upsaroka, or Crows. The usual war-ground of these nations, is the country around the head waters of the Snake, Green, and Platte Rivers" (H. Hale, *Ethnography and Philology, U. S. Exploring Expedition. . . . Wilkes, VI* [1846], 219). "The main band numbers about seven hundred. The total number of the entire tribe is about two thousand" (*Report of the Com. of Indian Affairs for 1849*, p. 158).

The two published reports of John Wilson, Indian Agent for California, chiefly concern this tribe: "Among the Sho-sho-nies there are only two bands, properly speaking. The principal or better portion are called Sho sho nies, (or Snakes) who are rich enough to own horses. The others, the Sho-sho-coes, (or Walkers) are those who cannot or do not own horses" (Fort Bridger, Aug. 22, 1849, *California and New Mexico. . . .* 31 Cong. 1 Sess. H. R. Ex. Doc. 17 [1850], p. 184. Hereafter cited as *California*). Also a report from Salt Lake, Sept. 4 (*ibid.*, p. 109): "They [the Sho-sho-coes] usually draw most of their subsistence from roots and the black-mountain cricket, and are usually called root-diggers — (not *gold* diggers)." "How these people are to live or ever exist for any great length of time [Fort Bridger report, p. 185] I cannot by any means determine. Their support has heretofore been mostly game and certain roots. . . . The Mormon settlement in the Salt Lake valley has not only greatly diminished their former very great resource of obtaining fish out of the Utah lake and its sources, . . . but their settlement, with the great emigration there and to California, has already nearly driven away all the game, and will, unquestionably, soon deprive them almost entirely of the only chances they have for food."

261. "Snake Indians — a name loosely applied to various northern bands or tribes of Shoshonean stock, including Paiute, Bannock, Shoshoni and sometimes even the Comanche" (James Mooney, *The Ghost-Dance Religion* . . . [1892-93], p. 1056).

262. Probably Washakie. Despite economic straits, this tribe was uniformly friendly to the emigrants, held in check by their sagacious chief, and probably by Sacajawea, still living and revered among them — the "Bird Woman" guide of

Lewis and Clark. Wilson reports (*California*, p. 184): "The principal chiefs of the Sho-sho-nies are Mono . . . ; Wiskia, . . . Washikick (Gourd Rattle) with whom I have had an interview; and Oapiche." In speaking (p. 186) of the treaties he hoped to negotiate at Fort Bridger in 1850, he says: "I have suggested the matter of the great council to Washikick, . . . and he highly approves of the plan." "The Shoshones number fourteen tribes . . . ; the principal . . . is commanded by Washakie" (Burton, *op. cit.*, p. 474). "The Snakes (Shoshones) are more united than the Utes, and, according to Mr. Bean [G. H. Bean, guide and interpreter since 1849], a nation of more principle. . . . Their chief is Wasshekick, and he lives on Green river" (J. H. Simpson, *in Report of the Sec. of War for 1859*, p. 43). So stands their record under their great chief, proud, in his latter years, to show his credentials of 9,000 signatures from emigrants he had befriended. It would seem that Washakie visited Bruff (P 3, Aug. 18): "Yesterday, at meeting, while I was explaining . . . about the '*Cut-Off*'. . . . Elucidating the routes by a rough diagram . . . fastened on the side of a wagon, a tall, straight, elderly Indian, with much dignity, (had no other clothing than a worn out long blue frock coat, button'd up to his chin, strided rapidly through the semi circle of members, around me, pushed them aside, stepp'd up & extended his hand to me, and said "*how do?*" — I reciprocated the courtesy, and he plac'd himself on my right, standing very erect, with his hands folded on his breast, & his back against the wagon. . . . He was a chief, found I was, and holdg a council and desired a place in it.)"

263. In Wilson's Fort Bridger report (*California*, p. 184), there is mention of "a small band of Punnacks," with whom, together with the Shoshoni and Utah, Vasques and Bridger had traded "for more than 25 years." Their relations with the whites would seem from Bruff's account also to have been friendly. But they soon acquired another reputation: "The Bannocks were the most warlike of the Shoshone tribes except the Comanches. . . . They . . . had the reputation of being a sort of lawless banditti, frequently infesting the routes of travel and causing trouble to the emigrants. . . . The country of the Bannocks was the territory between the Great Salt Lake and Snake river, and it lay athwart both the Oregon and California trails" (Chittenden, *op. cit.*, II, 886).

264. H 3: "and afterward heard that the express rider was murdered, by the Pawnees." *New-York Tribune*, Nov. 5, 1849: "Fort Laramie, (Ind. Ter) Sept. 18, 1849. Those grand rascals of the Plains, the Pawnees, have again been embuing their hands in the blood of the whites. Two men — Thomas and Picard — carrying the U. S. mail from Fort Hall to Fort Leavenworth, were attacked by them a few days since, about half-way between this and Fort Kearney, and it is feared that both were killed. Lieut. Donaldson, on his way to this post, found the dead body of Thomas and the hat of Picard stained with blood. Before he reached the spot he met a war party of Pawnees. . . . Thomas's body had several arrows sticking in it." *Report of the Sec. of War for 1849* (p. 186): "The Pawnees also have

shown a hostile disposition on various occasions, but more recently by murdering two mail carriers on the road between Fort Kearny and Fort Laramie." Apparently Bruff met Thomas and Picard in the Bear River Valley Aug. 13.

265. H 3: "resulting in my re-election as *President*, of the civil association, and changing all the other officers. My friends, a considerable majority of the Company, heartily greeted me with their gratulations which of course were exceedingly gratifying to me, appreciating their friendly considerations as I did, though the office conferred no advantage, but rather imposed onerous duties. I continued the same able and energetic guard-officers; and abolished the adjutancy, though it increased my already severe responsibilities."

266. H 3: "(The fork above is named after him) [probably an error]. . . . In some wild adventure many years ago, his leg was badly broken, and he had no comrade with him. He amputated it with his own knife near the knee; then crawled in to camp, — a considerable distance, and dressed the stump. By good luck and an extraordinary constitution it healed He has fitted a wooden leg — (hence the appelation, by his comrades,) and a socket to the stirrup, permits him to ride as smartly as ever."

In *Hutchings' Illustrated California Magazine*, V (1860-61), 147-50, 420-21: "Thomas L. Smith, or, as he is better known. . . , Peg-leg; or, as he is familiarly called by the Indians, Tevvy-oats-at-an-tuggy-bone," was born near Crab Orchard, Ky., Oct. 10, 1801. At sixteen . . . he ran away from home, becoming a trapper and hunter. He joined Legrand's first trading expedition to Santa Fe; he became associated with such men as Antoine Rubedoux, Sublette, St. Vrain, and Platte. He became famous among the Indians by assisting a party of Utahs against the Snakes. In 1827, "while trapping for beaver on the head waters of the Platte, . . . he was standing conversing with his friend St. Vran [Vrain] . . . when he was shot by an Indian in the leg, a few inches above the ancle, shattering both bones; . . . and he sat down, calling upon his friends to cut it off! No one had the hardihood to undertake the operation." Smith then called upon the cook for his butcher knife and assisted by Milton Sublette cut it off himself. The party went into winter quarters on Green River, Smith being carried on a rough litter. Here they were joined by 40 lodges of Utah Indians, who treated and healed the wounded stump. The following spring (1828) "a rough wooden leg was fashioned for him by the most mechanical genius in the company, and he was dubbed Peg Leg Smith by his white friends, and Wa-he-to-co, by his red friends." In 1860 he was living with friends on a ranch near San Francisco, in which city he had become a familiar figure. "Any such [sunny] afternoon he is to be seen with his sound leg and one stump, dressed in some uncouth costume or other, . . . his white hairs stagging out from under a cocked wool or long-napped and slouching old beaver hat. . . . There is a something in the appearance of the old man, . . . that marks him out as a remarkable man. . . . For nearly half a century he lived in the wilderness, which stretches west and north and northeast of Santa Fé, as far as the mouth of the Colorado in one direction, and the Missouri in the other. . . . He became domesticated, as it were, among the plumed and painted warriors of the beaver and buffalo grounds; . . . but over the whole country, wherever bold mountaineers and brave leaders are in repute among the red men as well as among the white, from Fort Hall down to Albuquerque, and from Independence across to the plains overlooked by the white caps of the Sierra Nevada, the name of Tevvy-oats-at-an-tuggy-bone, is known and respected."

267. Most early travelers praise the taste of the springs in this vicinity. Nathaniel Wyeth is a refreshing exception; July 8, 1834 (*op. cit.*, p. 226): "to a place where there is soda spring or I may say 50 of them. These springs throw out lime which deposits and forms little hillocks of a yellowish colored stone there is also here a warm spring which throws water with a jet [Steamboat Spring] which is like Bilge water in taste." Burnett (*in* George Wilkes, *The History of Oregon* [1845], Part II, p. 82): "the Indians set a great reliance upon their virtues for a numerous class of disorders."

268. H 3: "Beer Spring Fork."

269. This name is mentioned by Joseph Williams (*Narrative of a Tour . . . to the Oregon Territory . . .* [1843], p. 15): "We next came to the soda springs. These springs seems to boil like a pot of water; but there is no heat in them, except one, that is just on the bank of the river, which is built in the form of a craw-fish hole, about three feet high, formed of sediment thrown up by the water, which spouts about three feet high every quarter of a minute. There is an air hole near it that makes a noise like a steam-boat, but not so loud." E. M. Ledyard, ed., L. V. Loomis' *Journal of the Birmingham Emigrating Company . . .* (1928), p. 65, n. 1: "The old Oregon Trail ran very close to Steamboat Springs. It was a favorite camp for emigrants and a famous bathing place for early settlers in this section. Steamboat Springs has been covered by the water of the dam built by the Utah Power and Light Company but the 'springs' may be seen bubbling on the surface of the water."

270. H 3: "After we had passed the main body, some stragglers came along, and among them I noticed an active old man accompanied by a very small boy on foot; the former about half, and the latter entirely nude. — Passing, I touched the child on the head and said, '*Good papoose*'; when, to my astonishment, the old man turned round, and said '*Yes, very good papoose, G — d d — nme!*' and smiled approvingly, as though he had paid me a considerable compliment."

271. H 3, Aug. 18: "This remarkable cliff is surmounted by a high round hill, studded with pines & verdure — Height 1000 feet. . . . Deep below, within these basaltic walls, the clear cold waters of the river rush and roar, hastening to mingle with the Salts of the Great Salt Lake, some 90 odd miles (S.S.W. from the bend.) A broken place in the bank, filled with detritus, permitted us, by a troublesome path, to reach the stream and dip up water." Frémont gives the height as 1,400 feet; it "is called the *Sheep rock* — probably because a flock of the common mountain

sheep (*ovis montana*) had been seen on the craggy point" (*Report,* p. 139).

272. H 3: "a new route, commencing ahead, where the Fort Hall road turns off to the right there, this proposed route turns left, crossing the neighboring mountains, and keeping along the Northern slope of the northern dividing range, in a drive of a week or so strikes down on the head waters of St Mary river. . . . This is averred to be only 120 ms. from these Springs to the intersection of the Fort Hall route, at head of Raft river. A few of the earliest companies this season took the Fort Hall route, and all the others followed the new trail. . . . I drew a diagram, with a fire coal, fastened it on the side of a wagon, and explained to them the Fort Hall road, and the supposed direction of the cut-off trail. — I told them that it could not be much shorter, and must be more rugged than the former. — That we could not tell what kind of a road it was, whereas I knew all about the other: and that the great argument in favor of the Fort route was the fact of the grass not being grazed off upon it, which could not be the case with the other. But, as before said, they must follow the rest, and so resolved to take the cut-off road."

In H 3, Aug. 18, Bruff inserted the length of the cut-off, by day's marches: "Having subsequently obtained the distances travelled by the company, while I was detached [at Fort Hall], measured by an excellent odometer, manufactured by Blattner, St Louis   I will here insert it, to show that the 'cut-off' was no cut-off at all. — The Forks of the road are about 5 ms: from the 'Soda Springs' — then, cut-off road — 18th — 19½ ms: 19th — 18¼ ms:

20th —	2¼ ms:	23d —	15¾ ms:
21st —	20 "	24th —	20 "
22nd —	18 "	25th —	14 "

Here, (head of Raft-river,) rested one day (26th) making the cut off route — from Beer Springs, to Head of Raft river, (intersection of routes) to be exactly 132¾ miles. And between the same points, via Fort Hall route, the distance has been computed at 134 miles." Other records confirm this estimate. Mrs. Margaret A. Frink, at the junction of the roads at Raft River, July 9, 1850 (*Journal . . . of California Gold-Seekers* [1897?], pp. 70-71): "When we came to the forks of the road [on Bear River], we decided to take the right-hand one, leading to Fort Hall, because of the advice and illustration given us by an old Indian at the Soda Springs. He raised up the bail of a bucket to signify a high mountain, and passing his hand over the top, said, 'This is Myer's Cut-off.' Then, laying the bail down and passing his hand around it, said, 'This is the Fort Hall road.' We were told afterwards that this was correct." Wagner, working on Lander's wagon-road survey, traveled this road in 1859: "we took *the old emigrant road, known as Hedspeth's cut-off, making* a complete survey of it. The road, in many places, is very rocky, the grades very steep, and there is one drive without water of 22¼ miles; the grass, in general, was good and sufficient" (F. W. Lander, "A Communication . . . ," 36 Cong. 2 Sess. H.R. Ex. Doc. 63 [1861], p. 21). Unfortunately the published report does not give the mileage.

This "cut-off road," as Bruff terms it, was known by various names — Emigrants', Myers', and Hudspeth's Cut-off. It was first used by emigrants in July, 1849, when James Hudspeth and J. J. Myers led over it a company they were guiding. Henry Mann, diary (MS belonging to Mrs. Adeline T. Cox), July 24, 1849: "Messrs. Hedspeth and Myers of the Jackson Co. Mo. Co. have just made their appearance through a gorge in the mountains. They left the main road at the point where we left Bear River, going west through a gap in the mountains. They intended to come out at the head of Mary's River, but not understanding their true latitude have struck the old road before it crosses the dividing ridge to the Basin. They would have made some 200 miles on the old road had they succeeded, but as it is they have made nothing. They were almost thunderstruck, when upon emerging they found they were only 70 miles from Fort Hall."

Bruff's mention of "the head waters of St Mary river" as the supposed terminus of the cut-off tends to confirm Mann's account. The failure of Hudspeth and Myers to attain their objective may explain what puzzled many thoughtful emigrants, including Bruff — that the reduction in mileage by this route was so slight. However, this cut-off became almost instantly popular with the emigration, and when Bruff arrived, it had clearly come to stay. On Oct. 7, 1849, Gen. Persifor F. Smith, commanding the Pacific division, wrote from Vancouver to the authorities in Washington (*Report of the Sec. of War for 1849-50*, p. 85), relative to the abandonment of Cantonment Loring: "If a post were established at Fort Hall to assist emigrants, it would be nearly useless, because they now follow a new route more to the southward" (i.e., the Emigrants' Cut-off).

273. Perhaps the most famous post on the Oregon Trail. Dr. Minnie F. Howard, associated with Ezra Meeker in 1916 in locating the site of Fort Hall, says ("Old Fort Hall as Related to Peace through Destiny," *Pocatello Tribune*, March 9, 1930): "More than two hundred thousand emigrants were gladdened by the sight of the old fort in the days between its building in 1834 until its final end in 1863. That was the year when there came such a flood as was not in the memory of Indian or white man. It razed the walls of the then abandoned fort, and for forty years no man save the Indians and a few pioneers knew where the fort had once reared its formidable walls." The post was built by N. J. Wyeth in 1834 as a necessary depot in his fur-trading enterprise, after the Rocky Mountain Fur Company (Fitzpatrick, Sublette, and Bridger) had refused to take goods ordered by them and brought across the continent by Wyeth. Wyeth subsequently sold the fort to the Hudson's Bay Company. On the settlement of the Oregon boundary question with Great Britain in 1846, Fort Hall lay within the territory allotted to the United States.

Today Fort Hall is a fugitive, ghost place, with little to remind one of the life that teemed there over the Trail a century ago — so lost in the waving grass of the Fort Hall bottoms that it takes an Indian guide to find it, although one approaches it, at the end, over the old trail. Bands of fleet, half-wild horses — some of them milk-white like Captain Bruff's Panack — graze and gallop over the bottoms, now part of the Fort Hall Indian Reservation; and copper-skinned Bannock and Shoshoni, descendants of those whom Bruff met, lift the speckled trout from the streams and drop the cock pheasant on the wing. Although the waters swept over it in the great inundation of 1863 and builders of the later Fort Hall "dobies," or stage station, three miles away (now marked by a monument), looted it for building material, while others have dug on the site for identifying remains, one may still trace the foundations of the walls, now raised only a few feet above the surrounding plain, the square bastions at the corners, the sunken entrance, pressed by so many feet in bygone days, the square rifle pits outside. The place is marked by a small stone shaft, without inscription, railed in for protection from the roving cattle, and the turbid Snake swirls by, now only a few rods away, its channel, it is said, having been changed in the great flood. The name Fort Hall is now also applied to a small settlement on Ross Fork, some miles southwest of old Fort Hall, which contains the headquarters of the superintendent of the Fort Hall Indian Reservation.

274. H 3: "a distance of 1,200 miles."

275. H 3: "between the waters of Pacific river and those of the Great Basin."

276. H 3: "Suppose this to be about 18 miles from the forks" (of the Fort Hall and Emigrants' Cut-off roads).

277. H 3: "the dark conical tops of skin lodges, pale spiry colums of smoke, and horses grazing, being seen."

278. H 3: "following the general course of the creek — on our left."

279. H 3: "The elevation of this pass [between the Bear and the Snake Rivers] is over 8,000 feet above the sea: and probably 2,500 feet above the surface of the plain at the forks of the road, — leaving Bear river."

280. Audubon, *op. cit.*, II, 306, 307-8: "The Cougar is known all over the United States by the name of panther or painter. . . . When the benighted traveller, or the wearied hunter may be slumbering in his rudely and hastily constructed bivouac at the foot of a huge tree, amid the lonely forest, his fire nearly out . . . he may perchance be roused to a state of terror by the stealthy tread of the prowling Cougar. . . . Lucky is he then, if his coolness does not desert him, if his trusty rifle does not miss. . . . For, be sure the animal has not approached him without the gnawing hunger — the desire for blood; engendered by long fasting and gaunt famine."

281. H 3: "We were now descending the western slope, and had left the sources of the Great Basin waters, and those of the Port Neuf, (Pacific) almost mingled at the mountain top." In other words, Bruff was heading directly into the Snake River plains. Before him, at a considerable distance, were the Three Buttes, while the Three Tetons were dropping behind him, in a northeasterly direction. The Three Buttes are visible here when the weather is not too hazy, and do resemble baseless islands, floating in the sea.

282. H 3: "Finding that Fort Hall, and the Military Post, were some distance apart, I desired the Indian to guide me to the latter" — Cantonment Loring, named in honor of the commanding officer of the Mounted Riflemen. Nov. 28, 1849, Adj. Gen. R. Jones to the Secretary of War (*Report of the Sec. of War for 1849*, p. 185): "The mounted riflemen moved westward from Fort Leavenworth, by detachments, in May. On the occasion of the march of this regiment to Oregon, instructions were issued according to the provisions of the 6th section of the act of May 19, 1846, and the original orders of the Secretary of War, of June 1, 1847, to establish two more of the chain of posts along the route to that territory — one to be at or near Fort Laramie, a trading station of the American Fur Company, some three hundred and fifty miles west of Fort Kearny; and the other at the trading establishment at Fort Hall, on the headwaters of the Columbia river, or somewhere on Bear river or its tributaries, near enough to the Mormon settlements, in the vicinity of Salt Lake, to draw supplies of subsistence and forage, and at the same time sufficiently near the direct road to Oregon to afford a stopping place for . . . emigrants." The Act also authorized the mustering of the Rifle Regiment.

Cantonment Loring's history is brief. Hamersly, *op. cit.*, Part II, p. 142: "Loring, Oregon. In a valley formed by the junction of the Pat Neuf with the Snake or Lewis fork of the Columbia River. Established in July, 1849. Abandoned 6 May, 1850." Wistar reached Fort Hall July 20; July 22: "The dragoon train has not arrived yet, but is daily expected" (*Autobiography*, p. 99; courtesy of the Wistar Institute). Bruff (P 3, Aug. 20, 1849) says Porter arrived Aug. 10.

The snow was unusually deep in the winter of 1849-50, and the little garrison suffered, but the deciding factor against this location was probably the increasing use of Emigrants' or Hudspeth's Cut-off. Although forever abandoned as an army post in the spring of 1850, the name "Cantonment Loring" persisted. Lieut. John Mullan visited it in Dec., 1853: "Cantonment Loring, so called in honor of Colonel Loring of the rifle regiment, . . . is located in a beautiful prairie section of the Snake River valley, and about five miles above Fort Hall." The property was then in the possession of Capt. Grant, former factor of the Hudson's Bay Company at Fort Hall. Mullan says: "we were most kindly received by Captain Grant, . . . who, inviting us into his house, spread before us all the comforts and many of the luxuries of life, and gave us a comfortable bed under his hospitable roof — all of which none more than ourselves could appreciate; and we thus passed the night once more near the abodes of civilization. Here Captain Grant is comfortably situated, surrounded by a happy family, and . . . lives as happily and contentedly as he so well deserves" (John Mullan, *Pacific Railroad Reports*, I [1853-54], 335). Today Indians who know the region can, it is said, point out the site, by certain pits and remains. To the ordinary eye it is not distinguishable on the swirling bottom land, broken by frequent sloughs.

283. Col. Andrew D. Porter, Mounted Riflemen, grandson of Col. Andrew Porter of the Revolution. *Appleton's Cyclopædia of American Biography* (1887-89),

V, 722: born, Lancaster Co., Pa., July 10, 1820, died, Paris, Jan. 3, 1872. "Entered the U. S. Military Academy in 1836, but left in the following year. He was appointed 1st lieutenant of mounted rifles on 27 May, 1846, and served in the Mexican war, . . . receiving the brevet of . . . lieutenant-colonel for Chapultepec, 13 Sept., 1847. Afterward he served in Texas and in the southwest [took part in the march of the Mounted Riflemen to Oregon]." Served in the Civil War, becoming provost-marshal-general for the Army of the Potomac. Mustered out April 4, 1864.

284. H 3: "before which was a fine fire, of cotton-wood logs. When I made myself known, the Colonel was pleasantly astonished, & desired me to introduce my comrades, and I begged to include the old chief among the guests. . . . 21st. The good old Panak who guided me in, last night, came up and bade me goodbye. I noticed, last night at supper, that he behaved at the table with perfect propriety, and the colonel explained his civilized conduct, by informing me that he had once visited St. Louis."

285. A note in Bruff's Supplementary Notebook A, barely decipherable, lists the following: "Officers at Cantonment Loring, — 5 miles below [above] Fort Hall on Snake River   Coll. Commandg Andw Porter, M. Rifles   Capt N. Newton, Dragoons Lieut. [?] S. K. Russell Commissy   Brvt Capt Gordon Granger 2d Lieut. G. W. Howland   A. Surgeon W. F. Edgar   Sutler John Owen, of Mo." *Noah Newton*, 1st Lieut., M.R., 1846; Capt., 1848; died 1853. *F.S.K. Russell*, 2d Lieut., M.R., 1846; in Mexican War; 1st Lieut., 1848; dismissed, 1852. *Gordon Granger*, 2d Lieut., 2d Inf., 1845; M.R., 1846; in Mexican War; various grades to Maj. Gen., 1862; died, 1876. *G. W. Howland*, cadet, 1844; various grades in M.R. and Cav.; retired, 1869; loaned by Stansbury to Brigham Young, to serve as adjt. in expedition against Indians (Stansbury, *Exploration*, p. 149). *Wm. F. Edgar*, asst. surg., 1849; maj. surg., 1861; retired, 1862; died, 1897. *John Owen*, ensign, Rangers, 1813; "Sutler in Oregon, Mar. 51." See C. K. Gardner, *A Dictionary of All Officers . . . in the Army*, 2d ed. (1860), *passim;* and Heitman, *op. cit., passim.* Of these officers two are diarists: Surgeon Edgar of the winter of '49-50 at Cantonment Loring, see Bancroft, *Chronicles of the Builders* (1891-92), VII, 361-63; and John Owen, *The Journals and Letters of Major John Owen*, S. Dunbar and P. C. Phillips, eds. (1927), I, 1: "The following year ['50] he established himself as a trader in the Bitter Root Valley. . . . He built Fort Owen."

286. Cantonment Loring's exact site remains to be established, marked, and measured in respect to the distance from Fort Hall. Cross, Aug. 8, 1849, places the post 3 miles above Fort Hall, and then 4 miles, but says it "is to be established" ("Report," pp. 190-91). Stansbury visited it Sept. 22: "We left Fort Hall on our left, and five miles beyond it terminated our journey, at Cantonment Loring" (*Exploration*, p. 93). Perhaps some allowance should be made for variations in route. The usual estimate is about 5 miles above Fort Hall.

287. Bruff saw the post in the making. H 3 adds: "with square bastions at the

angles, and all properly loop-holed." See Bruff's sketch of the Cantonment, p. 538.

288. H 3: "The officers can give me no information about the western end of our route."

289. This Co., according to Webster (*op. cit.*, pp. 65-71), did have a hard time between South Pass and Bear River: "August 1. . . . We left the road today with the intention of taking a straight course through the mountains to Fort Hall. . . . Captain Thing, our guide, states that . . . there is an Indian trail through which he thinks he can follow." Apparently he meant Frémont's old trace (Bruff's "Soublette's pack trail," see nn. 226, 239). Aug. 9 Webster records: "We found ourselves at the top of a peak of the Rocky Mountains. . . . Captain Thing says he was never before at this place and is at a loss to know what route to take to get out." Aug. 11: "We passed over places today on the sides of mountains along Indian trails which were about one foot wide, on both sides of which were steeps, almost perpendicular, for hundreds of feet on the one side up and on the other down." The next day the Co. quarreled: "Captain Thing . . . thought we had come too far north for the route he had taken eleven years previous [12 yrs. presumably]." By following the stream down to Bear River valley, they reached the emigrant trail "after having wandered in the mountains for twelve days," dubbing this course "Thing's Cutoff." H 3: "Thing was a trapper out here, when Fort Hall was first built; and thought that in the lapse of 20 years, he knew as much about the mountains as ever. He led a large company, by what he took for the 'Soublette Cut-Off' — starting from Fremonts' peak, at the source of the New or northern branch of Green river, — about 60 miles north of the 'Greenwood [Sublette's] Cut-off', from thence to proceed Westerly, across the divide, and so down the Snake valley. Well, my wagons, which the Boston packers passed, between the forks of the Platte, nearly 2 months ago, are now almost on the head waters of St Mary's river, in the Great Basin; and these unfortunate packers have just reached this point, exhausted and out of provissions."

290. An error. Thing was a sea captain, not a trapper. Fort Hall was, of course, built by Wyeth, for his own co., Thing at that time being in his employ.

291. Capt. Howard Stansbury, Topographical Engineers. *Appleton's Cyclopædia* (V, 647): born, N. Y. City Feb. 8, 1806; died, Madison, Wis., April 17, 1863; by profession a civil engineer; conducted various surveys with distinction. "He became 1st lieutenant of U.S. topographical engineers on 7 July, 1838, captain in 1840. . . . From 1849 till 1851 he was engaged in the Great Salt Lake expedition, his report of which gave him a wide reputation." During the Civil War years, until his death, he was "mustering and disbursing officer at Madison." Stansbury reached Cantonment Loring Sept. 22, just one month later. See n. 286, on Cantonment Loring, this account.

292. Lieut. George W. Hawkins, M. R. Cullum, *op. cit.*, II, 112: born, N. C., grad. West Point 1844, Bvt. 2d Lieut., 1st Infantry, trans. to M. R. 1846; served in Mexican War; 2d Lieut., M. R., 1847. "In garrison at Jefferson Barracks, Mo.,

1848; and in escorting Governor Lane to Oregon 1848-51. Dismissed, Jan. 27, 1853, under 3d Sec. of Law of Jan. 1, 1823." "Died 1854, in Warren County, N. C.: Aged 34."

In The Public Statutes at Large . . . R. Peters, ed. (1850), III, 724: "An Act concerning the disbursement of public money." The second section required the accounting of expenditures of public money, with all necessary vouchers, "within three months, at least, after the expiration of each successive quarter, if resident within the United States; and within six months if resident in a foreign country"; the third section provided for the dismissal from the service of offending officers.

In 1823, no one foresaw the day when U. S. Army officers would be escorting civil officials across the western half of the continent, nor the difficulties attending such duty as the escort of Gov. Joseph Lane and his party to Oregon in 1848-49. "The company which left Fort Leavenworth on the 20th of September [1848] numbered about fifty persons, including Lane, his eldest son Nathaniel, Meek, and Dr Hayden, surgeon of the detachment under Lieutenant Hawkins, twenty-five riflemen, with wagon-masters, teamsters, and servants" (Bancroft, *History of Oregon*, I, 778). The party went by way of Santa Fe, El Paso, Tucson, "and the Pima villages on the Gila River" — the Colorado River, and thence northwest to the bay of San Pedro in California, hoping to find a small vessel there "to take them to S. Francisco, and thence to the Columbia River." Our Army, returning from Mexico, had used up the forage. Hawkins therefore left his wagons and made the trip overland to San Pedro Bay with pack animals. He sailed with his party to San Francisco, and from there on "the *Janet*, Captain Dring. The vessel . . . after a tedious voyage of eighteen days anchored in the Columbia. The party to which Lieutenant Hawkins was still attached immediately took passage in a canoe for Oregon City, where they arrived the 2d of March, two days before the expiration of Polk's term of office" (after which Lane's appointment would have lapsed, had he not already been sworn in as governor of the territory — *ibid.*). Gov. Lane stated over his signature, Santa Fe, Oct. 18, 1848: "Lieut. Hawkins, who commands the escort, is a good officer, and has conducted the march well" (*New York Herald*, March 29, 1849).

Now, Aug. 22, 1849, Hawkins and his supply train from Oregon are long overdue at Cantonment Loring. Bruff encounters him, with his wagon train and his drove cattle, coming slowly up the Humboldt several weeks later. Colonel Porter had already been supplied from Fort Leavenworth. Stansbury, June 18 (*Exploration*, pp. 27-28): "We passed a government ox-train, laden with provisions for the new post about to be established in the neighborhood of Fort Hall. It consisted of thirty-one heavy wagons, four hundred oxen, (five or six yoke to each team,) and about forty men."

293. H 3: "This adobe quadrangular structure, is very similar to Fort Larimie — though much smaller, and appears to have more wood in its construction. The walls are in a very dilapidated state — and on the N.W. side are shored up with

timbers. The main entrance, in the South Eastern wall, is a large double gate, with a small gate within one of the others. My comrades crossed a hollow, half a mile beyond the fort, picketed their animals, spread their blankets, and got supper, while I visited the Old Mountain Fortress."

294. The Iroquois, were, of course, those of the eastern seaboard, living in historic times in New York. Many of them, siding with the British in the Revolution, went to Canada.

295. Grant was perhaps misinformed. Thing's well known defeat by the Blackfeet was recorded by Osborne Russell, one of Wyeth's men who helped build Fort Hall, May 31, 1835: "Captain Thing had started in April . . . for the purpose of establishing a trading post on a branch of Salmon River, but had been defeated by the Blackfeet, with the total loss of his outfit excepting his men and horses" (*Journal of a Trapper* . . . [1921], p. 19). "Satsikaa, or Blackfoot Indians. This is a well-known confederacy of five tribes, occupying an extensive territory in and near the Rocky Mountains, between the head-waters of the Missouri, the Saskatchawan, and the Columbia. . . . A few years since, the number and warlike spirit of the Blackfeet tribes made them the terror of all the western Indians, on both sides of the mountains. They were reckoned at not less than thirty thousand souls, and it was not uncommon to hear of thirty or forty war-parties out at once. . . . But in the year 1836, the small-pox carried off two-thirds of their whole number" (H. Hale, *op. cit.*, pp. 219-20). "Like all prairie tribes, the Blackfeet are wandering hordes, having no fixed habitations. They are generally found following the ever-varying migrations of the Buffalo. . . . The Blackfoot has always been regarded as a treacherous, blood-thirsty savage; this is a mistake. . . . It is true, they killed and scalped a great many of the mountain trappers. . . . They found strangers trespassing on their hunting grounds, and killing off the game upon which they relied for subsistence; any other tribe, or even civilized nation, would have done the same with less provocation" (Schoolcraft, *Historical and Statistical Information* . . . [1851-57], V, 686-87).

296. An error. The Hudson's Bay Company, London (letter of Sept. 23, 1938, of the Secretary, J. C. Brooks) has very kindly checked this for us: "With regard to the career of Captain Thing . . . we have to state that Captain Thing was never employed by the Hudson's Bay Company but was Wyeth's clerk at Fort Hall when this Fort was sold to the Company in 1837. We have ascertained from our records that in the autumn of 1837 it was Thing's intention to take a passage for the Sandwich Islands but we have no information regarding his subsequent movements."

297. H 3: "This conclusion, however, is somewhat improbable and altogether assumptive." It is understandable that Capt. Grant, being a man of acumen, might dislike a new cut-off which was certain to divert emigrant travel to the south of Fort Hall and thus disrupt a trade profitable to himself.

298. H 3: "I informed him [Capt. Grant] that I had the pleasure of knowing

Sir Geo. Simpson at Washington City, who desired me to use his name if necessary to him." *Appleton's Cyclopædia*, V, 537: Simpson was born in Scotland, 1796; died in Lachine, near Montreal, Sept. 7, 1860; Feb., 1820, "was selected to superintend the affairs of the [Hudson's Bay] company in America." He united the Hudson's Bay and Northwest Companies, long rivals; sent his cousin, Thomas Simpson, across arctic America, 1836-39; traveled around the world overland himself, 1841-42. "In 1841 he was knighted for his services in connection with the cause of arctic exploration."

299. "Between 1843 and 1846 there was considerable negotiation as to the boundary west of the Rocky Mountains, resulting in the treaty of 1846, which defined the boundary as far west as the Strait of Juan de Fuca" (E. M. Douglas, *Boundaries, Areas, . . . of the U. S.* [1923], p. 18).

300. "The Walla-walla Indians possess the country on the Columbia, near Fort Walla-walla, have large herds of horses and cattle, and are well armed, and friendly to the whites. They number 1,000. They cultivate the soil in small quantities, but live principally on fish, roots, and berries" (*Report of the Com. of Indian Affairs for 1849*, p. 160).

301. H 3: "I somehow missed the trail which ascends the Panack river, and leads to Salt Lake. Grant however, had advised me to ascend the 'Raft river' — in preference, and the oversight gave me no anxiety."

302. Travelers from Fort Hall, but not those using Emigrants' Cut-off, passed the American Falls, then a scene of great natural beauty. The Falls is now the site of a dam one mile in length, and one of the largest hydroelectric plants in the country. This dam backs the waters of the Snake River up over the Fort Hall bottoms to a distance of about twenty miles, but not over the site of Fort Hall.

303. H 3, same date: "to the N. we could just see what I supposed to be one of the celebrated Three Buttes, — of a very dim blue tint, about 85 miles distant." Probably Big Butte, the westernmost of the group which Bruff discerned in the distance, then to the west, as he approached Fort Hall over the divide. Now the Three Buttes lay to his north, and much more distant. Frémont, *Report*, p. 164: "at a great distance to the north [from the American Falls] is seen the high, snowy line of the Salmon river mountains, in front of which stand out prominently in the plain the three isolated rugged-looking little mountains commonly known as *the Three Buttes.*"

304. The Snake, the largest affluent of the Columbia. H 3: "The river, just above the falls is near 900 feet wide, but the plutonic rock piers have formed an irregular dam; and the basaltic walls of the river close in, below the falls, and continue to wall in the rapid stream, for hundreds of miles. A short distance below the falls, the southern shore is broken down, and the detritus & pebbles there form a large bank, gradually shelving to the water. On the opposite side the walls are high, and crowned with green hills." Cross, "Report," p. 193: "The right bank of the river along here rises to the height of at least fifteen hundred feet, entirely of

basaltic rock, and resembles very much the palisades on the Hudson river, a short distance above New York."

305. Named by Frémont, Sept. 26, 1843: "In about 4 miles we reached a picturesque stream, to which we gave the name of Fall creek. It is remarkable for the many falls which occur in a short distance; and its bed is composed of calcareous tufa, or vegetable rock" (*Report*, p. 165).

306. H 3: "21 miles below the Falls." *Rivière aux Cajeux* of the trappers. Ware, *op. cit.*, p. 30: "The distance from Fort Hall to Raft river, is about sixty miles. This part of the route is particularly difficult — in many places the wagons will have to be forced up the ascent or ravines, by manual force." Of course Bruff was here traveling without wagons.

H I :   A U G U S T   2 8 ,   1 8 4 9 – N O V E M B E R   5 ,   1 8 4 9

1. From the upper rim of the Great Basin, Bruff is here about to descend into its mighty bowl. "The contents of this Great Basin are yet to be examined. That it is peopled, we know; but miserably and sparsely. . . . Dispersed in single families; without fire arms; eating seeds and insects; digging roots, (and hence their name) — such is the condition of the greater part. Others are a degree higher, and live in communities upon some lake or river that supplies fish, and from which they repulse the miserable *Digger*" (Frémont, *Report*, p. 276). The name "Digger" is not generic, however, and is also the opprobrious term for the Indians of California. As applied to the Shoshonean bands, Mooney: "The northern bands of the Paiute are frequently included in the Shoshoni and others under the name of Snakes, while the others [Paiute] are often included with various California tribes under the collective name of Diggers" (*op. cit.*, p. 1048). Adam Johnston, Sub-Agent for the San Joaquin Valley: "Root-Diggers. . . . This name seems to embrace Indian tribes inhabiting a large extent of country west of the Rocky Mountains. . . . With these tribes, roots are, for the great portion of the year, their main subsistence" (Schoolcraft, *op. cit.*, IV, 221). A. L. Kroeber clothes the Shoshonean strain with unexpected splendor: "Actually this group is only part of a larger one: the Uto-Aztekan family. . . . The lowly desert tribes . . . are seen in a new light as kinsmen, however remote, of the famous Aztecs" (*Handbook of the Indians of California* [1925], p. 574).

2. Bruff first notes the signal fires so often to be mentioned.

3. Generally known as City of Rocks. Near the present town of Almo in Idaho. Horn, *Guide*, p. 44 and n.: "Pyramid Circle, . . . 5 miles long, and about 3 miles wide, level within the walls around, and studded throughout with numerous tall

white and green stones, from 60 to 150 feet high, and 10 to 20 feet in diameter at the foot. . . . Upon these stones are written, painted, and engraved, the names of many visitors, with the dates. This circle is entirely surrounded by the mountains, except an inlet at the east end of about 50 yards, and an outlet at the west end of about 20 yards." In 1849, as Bruff notes (H 3), a crossroads of travel: "Near the intersection of the Fort Hall, Oregon and California trails . . . at the intersection also of the 'Cut-off' trail."

4. H 3: "The stone . . . seems to be a fine sianite. . . . Deep hollows, caves, nitches, and cyclopean and fantastic forms. the ground is white with the detritus. . . . A block of this stone . . . proved on approaching it to be large enough for a habitation, being hollow with an arched entrance — and stooping I did enter, and found myself in a beautiful chamber, white as snow, with a shelf forming a seat along one side, and at the narrower end another small opening admitting light and air. . . . Five of us smoked our pipes in this delightful and singular grotto. . . . I sketched it under the title of 'Sarcophagus Rock.' "

5. H 3: "a sheet of paper folded into four pages, . . . entitled the 'Best Guide to the Gold Mines'. . . . I dare say it is tolerably correct. Its route crosses the Sierra Nevada, however, by the Carson or central route and I here transcribe it as, at least, a curiosity in travel: — . . . It commences with 'Steeple Rock' — (one side of the gateway outlet, from this singular valley, and about 2 miles ahead of us)". This "curiosity in travel," the "Mormon Guide" to the Carson, Mormon, or Battalion route, pioneered by a contingent of the Mormon Battalion returning to Salt Lake in 1848, is referred to in several contemporary journals (see 1st ed., pp. 547-48). Bruff recorded it, and it was first published in Appendix VIII of the first edition. From the descriptive text of Mrs. Sarah Royce, who also talked with its author, we have identified this Guide as that of "Ira J. Willes, GSL City"; from internal evidence his appears to be the guide used by Bennett C. Clark, Lorenzo Sawyer, Wm. T. Coleman, and P. C. Tiffany over the Carson in 1849, 1850. A complete text copied as "Way Bill of the distance, camping places Rivers hot springs &c in the rote from G.S.L. City To the Gold mines" (Bruff's begins at Steeple Rock) was found contained in the "Journal of Philip Badman of Warren, Pa." (MS, Coe Collection, Yale Library, which also has Tiffany's MS journal).

There are two special points of interest about the "Way Bill": (1) The route between "G.S.L. city" and "Steple Rock" (given at 173 miles) was that opened in the summer of 1848 by "Captain S. Hensly," and taken by the Battalion, who had met his pack train on the Humboldt (Aug. 27) and learned of this "route that he had found and just come" — thus cutting out Fort Hall (H. W. Bigler, "Diary of a Mormon . . . ," MS, Bancroft Library). I.e., Samuel J. Hensley opened this route from Salt Lake to the City of Rocks; the Mormons took over it the first wagons, in 1848. (2) Just beyond the Sink of the Humboldt, in 1849, those who trusted the "Mormon Guide" had difficulty in locating the "new track on your left that Childs intended to make last fall" (Badman), "The left hand, or Childs rout which is new . . . strikes 'Carson River' at about 45 miles" (Tiffany). Mrs Royce speaks in detail of the uncertainty of finding this left turn (*Frontier Lady*, R. H. Gabriel, ed. [1932], p. 34). In short, this direct line from the Sink to the Carson was not that of the Battalion, which reaching the base of the Sierra, "Left Carson River, traveled rather a N.W. course 25 miles when we struck the old trucky road" (Bigler), thence by it to the Sink. Sept. 30, '48, the Battalion met Joseph B. Chiles's train of 48 wagons headed west. Presumably, Chiles intended cutting straight across from the Sink to the Carson, and did so. I.e., from the Sink, one had a choice: the "Battaline route" to Truckee River (45 m.) thence to Carson River (25 m.); or the "new track" direct to Carson River (45 m.). D. H. Moss (letter, Sacramento City, Aug. 7, see *Missouri Statesman*, Nov. 2, 1849): "We left that place [Sink] . . . for a desert of 45 miles . . . ; we took a left hand road when we got some mile or two into it, called Child's route; it strikes over on to Carson river; that route does not touch Truckil river at all — most of the emigrants take the road we travelled." This route should be ascribed to Joseph B. Chiles, who brought his train into Sacramento Oct. 26, 1848, the first wagons from the east by the Carson Pass (date from Chiles's granddaughter, Mrs. J. H. Rea).

Willis' "Guide," complementing Clayton's *Guide*, credits to Mormon pioneering two routes continuous from "Winter Quarters" to GSL City, and thence "To the Gold Mines." See also Introduction, pp. xxxv-xxxvi. Later printed Mormon guides: that cited by F. Langworthy (*Scenery* . . . , May 5, 1850 entry); *Mormon Way-Bill to the Gold Mines* . . . , by Joseph Cain and Arieh C. Brower, G.S.L. City, 1851 (Coe Collection, Yale Library). This contains, among others, the Willis route.

6. H 3: "one of the sources of 'Goose Creek' ".

7. The Pioneer Line offered passenger service across the plains in the spring of 1849. *New York Herald*, March 8, 1849: "Pioneer passenger train for California — Overland by the South Pass. — The undersigned propose to organize a train of wagons expressly for the transportation of passengers and their baggage to California, in addition to their merchandise train, as early in the spring as practicable. . . . Elliptic spring wagons, covered and fitted up comfortably for carrying six passengers each, will be provided. Price of passage, including rations from the day the train starts, $200. 100 lbs. of baggage will be allowed each man — extra baggage, 20 cents per pound One half the passage money will be required at the time of signing the contract. For further information, time and place of starting, &c. address the undersigned (post paid) until the 20th of March next ensuing at St. Louis after that date, Independence, Mo. Turner & Allen, 32 Second Street, St. Louis, Mo." The first train left Independence May 9 with 20 passenger carriages, 18 baggage and supply wagons, and 125 passengers. A list of passengers, officers, teamsters, muleteers, and herders appeared in the St. Louis *Republican*, May 17, 1849; June 1 it announced a second train, to start by June 10. A. J. McCall, June 12, near Court House Rock, commented caustically (*The Great California Trail in 1849* . . . [1882], p. 35): "Some great stage men of St. Louis had or-

ganized this line of coaches, . . . promising to land their passengers on the Sacramento in about sixty days. . . . Their passengers were to be of the first class — grass-widows, *gamboliers*, bankers, brokers and young men of fashion." He adds (*ibid.*, p. 85): "The Grand Pioneer Line broke down on the Platte. Its passengers, without means, either worked or begged their way to the Pacific." McCall does not specify whether this was the first section or the second. The first appears to have gone through; it is noted in distress by fellow travelers at various points. And, Nov. 8, R. W. Hunt, on the Government Relief, Carson River route, reported: "[Oct. 15] we met the Pioneer train in quite a crippled condition, having lost thirty of their best mules the night before, by the Indians, and having been on short allowance for several weeks past" (*In* "Gen. Smith's Correspondence," 31 Cong. 1 Sess. Sen. Ex. Doc. 52 (1850), pp. 111-12. Cited as Rucker's *Report*).

8. H 3: "a N.E. prong at the head of Mary's river."

9. H 3: "after a separation of 14 days."

10. Better known as Thousand Springs Valley, although low divides separate this springy area, which aggregates some 50 ms. along the Trail between Goose Ck. and the headwaters of the Humboldt.

11. This river had many names before Frémont dubbed it "Humboldt" in honor of Baron Humboldt. Peter Skene Ogden visited it first in Nov., 1828, he being so far as known the first white man to examine it. April 8, 1829, he "reached the forks of Unknown River," his name for the Humboldt. June 2 he notes: "Unknown River is known as Swampy River or Paul's River," the latter doubtless for his trapper, Joseph Paul, who was buried on its banks Dec. 26, 1828. T. C. Elliott, editor of the Ogden journals, comments: "A few more names for this river, which should rightly be designated the Ogden river. . . . Maj. Chittenden and others speak of it being called Mary's river, which evidently was merely a trapper's story" ("The Peter Skene Ogden Journals," T. C. Elliott, ed., *Quart. Oregon Hist. Soc.*, X [1909]-XI [1910], *passim*). However, Bancroft also records this story, of Ogden (*Chronicles*, VII, 155): "To this stream [Humboldt] was applied the name Mary, . . . in honor of a Shoshone damsel whom the prudent trader married, that is to say bought." Bancroft elsewhere (*History of Nevada* . . . [1890], pp. 36-37) says that one of Ogden's trappers, "becoming enamored of a damsel native to that region, he married . . . her. . . . To the native woman . . . was given the name Marie, or Mary, who in turn gave her . . . appellation to the stream." Possibly this was George Nidever, who in 1832, it is said (*ibid.*, p. 40) started for Ogden River, "which he then called Mary River." Others, like Bruff, have said that the stream was named in honor of the Virgin.

The Humboldt heads in the mountain ranges bordering the Great Basin, winding creek-like, down the desert plains to its sink; it is nevertheless the great river of the region. Mrs. John Wilson sums it up neatly: "I was much disappointed in coming to the Marys or Humboldt — found it small and insignificant, course very winding, not sufficient water for a canoe but like the Platte will be fine for the construction of the railroad level, and I believe does not overflow" (San Francisco letter, Feb. 28, 1850; MS, Dr. F. A. Culmer).

12. Jefferson's Map, accompanying text (p. 9): "In the Buffalo region Indians are not apt to trouble oxen. Upon Mary river and the lower portions of Truckey river, the Indians steal oxen for food, and sometimes to secure them, shoot them with poisoned arrows." Also Ware (*op. cit.*, pp. 32-33): "From the forks of the river to the 'sink,' the mountains are peopled by a race of Indians of the most thievish propensities, requiring, on the part of the emigrant, untiring vigilance, to prevent their stealing and killing their teams, &c." Bruff distills all information in these words, scrawled across the Great Basin area of his large map: "Range of the Pah Utahs the original & most numerous class commonly called Mountain Diggers perfectly untameable & the lowest species of the genus Homo, next to them is the baboon."

A Paiute record in contrast: So-mit-tone Winnemucca, daughter of Chief Winnemucca, remembers "as a very small child when the first white people came. . . . My people were scattered at that time over nearly all the territory now known as Nevada. My grandfather was chief of the entire Piute nation, and was camped near Humboldt Lake, with a small portion of his tribe, when a party travelling eastward from California was seen coming. When the news was brought to my grandfather . . . he jumped up and clasped his hands together, and cried aloud, — 'My white brothers, — my long-looked for white brothers have come at last!' . . . The next year came a great emigration and camped near Humboldt Lake. The name of the man in charge of the train was Captain Johnson, and they stayed three days to rest their horses. . . . The third year more emigrants came, and that summer Captain Fremont, who is now General Fremont. My grandfather met him, and they were soon friends. Captain Fremont gave my grandfather the name of Captain Truckee, and he also called the river after him. Truckee is an Indian word; it means *all right*, or *very well*. A party of twelve of my people went to California with Captain Fremont. . . . When my grandfather went to California he helped Captain Fremont fight the Mexicans. . . . And all that time they were peaceable toward their white brothers" (Sarah Winnemucca Hopkins, *Life among the Piutes* [1883], pp. 5-9).

Edwin Bryant corroborates: "August 25 [1846]. This same Indian (Truckee) was the principal of the two who encamped with us twenty-five miles above the 'Sink' of Mary's river. He and his brother afterwards came over into California with a company of emigrants; and accompanied the California battalion on its march from Monterey to the Ciudad de Los Angelos" (*What I Saw in California* [1849], pp. 227-28). In 1849, Aug. 24, at the Meadows, McCall, who recalled and cited Bryant's account, had an equally friendly Paiute visitor (*op. cit.*, pp. 72, 77).

13. The *Sacramento Transcript*, Dec. 14, 1850, recounts the death of Bernard B. Light of Hedgesville, Va., perhaps the same man: "FROZEN TO DEATH — . . . on last Tuesday night week, a few miles north of Downieville."

14. H 3: "and other mineral pools and springs, in red and yellow clay all around this valley ford. They have much of the character of the Bear river Springs, except that sulphur water seems to predominate here."

15. Bancroft, *History of California*, V, 554: "Nearly one hundred adults, with some forty children, found their way in different parties, chiefly in 1848-50, to Utah" from California, after Brannan had brought back word that the Mormons were to remain in Utah. Brannan himself did not accompany this party, here encamped a little below the present Osino Cañon.

16. H 3: "We crossed the fork and ascended a considerable hill. There were a party of Snakes or Panacks here, on a hill. Some of them came down, to barter dressed skins for ammunition, as usual."

17. H 3: "Mr. Ths Rhoads, very kindly gave me much information I had long been seeking."

Thomas Rhoads was a well-known figure. According to Bancroft, he came overland to California in 1846 with his wife and twelve children: "He settled on the Cosumnes, and the visits of different members of the family are often recorded at Sutter's Fort in '47. . . . In that year Mrs. R. died. . . . R. subsequently went to Utah, where he died in '69 at the age of 77" (*History of California*, V, 693). Many other companies recorded meeting this Mormon train on the Humboldt, and it appears to have preached the gospel of California to all.

Rhoads's information as given in H 3 will be found in the 1st ed., Appendix VIII. What is perhaps Bruff's recording of it as he took it down, is in the notebook containing the P 3 and the P 6 records, and separating the two. It is entitled "Mormon Information": "The '*Truckey Pass*' — For 10 ms. this side the sink [of the Humboldt] there is very little grass, and none but sulphur water, which the animals, through necessity, will drink. At the '*Sink*' poisonous water and no grass. [For] 50 m. beyond, neither grass nor water — 15 ms. of which is heavy dry sand ⅓ up to the hubs. A southern road, or '*Cut-off*' made by the Mormons [Mormon, or Carson River route], will afford a little more grass & water, but the pass in the mountains is equal to the '*Trucky*', and this route carries you several hundred miles to the southward, beyond usual *Trucky* route. Has travell'd both routes. '*Lassin's, or Applegate's Pass*'. The renown'd Capt Applegate, in 1846, going to Oregon, turn'd the California Emigrants on this route, as being better than the southern ones. Lassin, last year, took numbers of emigrants through the same. —

"Hedgepeth, this season, did the like. Supposed that about ⅓ the emigration took it. — The most successful passage of wagons & stock, into California, has been by this route. — Few wagons got below top of '*Trucky Pass*' on Wn side, and very few animals: — most of them giving out before reaching top. Just this side of the *Sink*, are friendly Indians. — 100 ms. down from here are animal stealing & killing rascals. First part of Lassin's road, a desert of 40 odd miles — though with some springs in it. [Hudspeth and Myers were then (Sept. 5) on Pit R.]

"The foregoing is Information by Mr. Thos. Rhoads, of Brannon's Mormon party of 10 wagons Sept 5th & 6th 1849. Mr. R. had not travell'd *Lassin's Road*, but was intimate with many who had, and who communicated the foregoing account of it to him — and which, he said, could be relied on as correct."

18. It might appear that the choice of the Lassen Trail was a major error of judgment on Bruff's part, but examination reveals otherwise. Before leaving Washington, he had collected maps and guidebooks, and had found a letter from John J. Myers, to Brig. Gen. R. Jones, dated Fort Osage, Jackson Co., Mo., Feb. 13, 1849, bearing on this part of the route (see 1st ed., Appendix VIII). Myers came to California in 1843, according to himself, probably the Myers listed by Reading ("Journal of Pierson Barton Reading . . . P. B. Bekeart, ed., *Quart. Soc. Calif. Pioneers,* VII [1930], 176); was sergt. maj. and later lieut. in the California Battalion (Bancroft, *History of California,* IV, 751), with Lassen accompanied Com. Stockton to Frémont's court-martial, 1847. In his letter he claimed to know the California mountains and rivers, and to be able to guide any party from the Humboldt to the "head of the Sacramento," and thence to the main valley, "not over 150 miles" distant, and Bruff believed him to be the discoverer of the California end of the Lassen Trail. (This "150 miles," more or less, from the Humboldt to the Sacramento, was the greatest source of confusion to the emigrants of the Lassen Trail.) Rhoads's information (see n. 17 above) was favorable.

Lieut. Hawkins, whom Bruff met Sept. 8, must have further buttressed his decision. Aug. 23 Delano and his company had met Hawkins and his train fresh from Oregon via the Goose Lake junction of Applegate's and Lassen's Trails: "It was with much satisfaction that we learned that there was a good and feasible wagon road, leading from Goose Lake, beyond the Siérra Neváda, to California, which was opened last season; that the passage of the great mountain was not difficult, and that now there was grass and water all the way. . . . The best news of all was, that we should reach the gold diggings on Feather River in traveling a little over a hundred miles [from High Rock Cañon]" (A. Delano, *Life on the Plains . . .* [1854], p. 198). Myers, piloting Hudspeth's train, Round Valley turn-off: He had ridden to Lassen's in 1½ days. "But this road [Lassen's] was not made at that time." Unless "very crooked," he estimated 3 to 5 days (I. Hale, *op. cit.,* p. 128). In 1850 Myers walked it in 5 days, with a wounded man (pp. 365, 701).

19. Supplies designed for the use of the Mounted Riflemen, on their way to Oregon. Gen. Persifor F. Smith, *Report of the Sec. of War for 1849,* pp. 84-85, 106-7: "In compliance with instructions I had previously sent, a party, under Lieutenant Hawkins, . . . was sent [from Oregon] to Fort Hall, with provisions, to meet the rifles. They, however, took different routes, and did not meet. [Col. Loring followed the northern Oregon Trail; Lieut. Hawkins took the southern Oregon route opened by Applegate in 1846, through the Cascade Mountains, south to Goose Lake, and east to the Humboldt — the same route, as far as Goose Lake, which the Washington City Company was soon to traverse in reverse.] . . . Since

I began this report, I have received information of the arrival of Lieutenant Hawkins at Fort Hall [Cantonment Loring]."

20. The place of this attack was in fact a hundred miles east of the "headwaters of the Sacramento" (as the Pit River was then thought to be). Israel Hale, of several who noted the incident, gives succinctly the date, Aug. 25, the place, "Salt Valley" (the "Mud Lake" above Black Rock), and the circumstances ("Diary of a Trip to California in 1849," *Quart. Soc. Calif. Pioneers,* II [1925], 118, 120): "26th . . . We found a large number of wagons encamped, among others a train of the United States Troops . . . on their way from Oregon. . . . Yesterday they sent four men to search for a road from here to Humboldt, thinking that a better and more direct route could be had and more grass and water, but on the route two of the men went up on the mountain to take observations. While there they saw two Indians coming. They professed to be Snakes, but as soon as they came near enough they shot one of the men dead and wounded the other. The man that was wounded killed one of the Indians and the other fled. . . . 28th. By what I can learn the Indian that killed Garret was not much to blame. Garret was the first aggressor and I fear it will have the effect of enraging the Indians against the emigrants." The attacking Indians were, of course, not Pit Rivers — who were supposed at this time and for many years subsequently to be a "Digger" or Paiute band of the same stock as those of the Great Basin — but upland Paiute, then and later hostile to the whites.

21. H 3: "having an indian trail through it. . . . The Spring valley range is about 14 ms. long, terminating in a long and very stony descent to the river bottom, about a mile from a ford." Bruff's "Valley of Fountains" or "Spring Valley" took the Trail through the mountains to avoid Palisade Cañon. The Trail returned to the river just above Gravelly Ford. Here Bruff met Hawkins.

22. Bruff's Co. and the Rangers passed over the Trail about the same time. On Aug. 4, Bruff, then at the entrance to Sublette's Cut-off, noted that "the 'Wolverine Rangers', Capt. Potts, had been camp'd" opposite. Apparently, however, this was the first meeting between the two trains.

23. H 3: "All the emmigrants were aware of the fact, that the Mormons used every artifice to induce them to visit Salt Lake — The fact is, that the Mormons wanted wagons, oxen, and other property, at what they pleased to give; and furnished mules & other necessaries at the price they wanted for them."

24. In Elliott Coues's handwriting, on the margin, "*Bassariscus*" — of the raccoon family.

25. H 3: "Across the river a tall conical mountain and ranges of trap dykes on the next hill. The high bold range of the Blue mountains to the N.W. of us, about 30 ms. distant." The latter were the "Blue Mts" of the Jefferson Map, now the Hot Spring Range.

26. H 3: "The southern extremity of the isolated Blue Mountain range a few miles distant. On our front and right, the northern portion of that range arose

darkly, through the centre of which our road followed the river through a very deep and sinuous gorge, called the 'Pauta Pass.' "

27. Oliver Goldsmith, *Overland in Forty-Nine* (1896), p. 12: "When we organized we had adopted a set of by-laws. One of these provided for an election of officers when ten days out on our journey. This proved a very wise arrangement, for before that time had passed we made the discovery that our first captain was not a good one. . . . Our second choice for captain, Judge Potts, of Marshall, was made of the right kind of stuff and proved worthy in all respects of the confidence and esteem in which he was held, up to the last, by every member of the company." Bruff meets Capt. Potts in California in the spring and fall of 1850.

28. H 3: "The stream about 5 miles S. of us enters the deep dark gorge of the 'Pautah Pass' of the 'Blue Mountains.' About 6 ms. ahead the river makes a bend — doubling around nearly parallel with itself, — and then enters the Pass."

29. H 3: "Here also the south side road comes in. It appears that the long road around the bend, branches on the W. side of the Pass . . . while the main road turns around the point of the great mountain wall, and follows a narrow bank, along the stream, on the East side of the gorge. This latter we travelled upon; but I noticed a light horse wagon ascending the mountain trail. We had spent 3 hours to noon, and then forded the stream, and entered the gorge, before the long string of wagons came up. This, like most of the ranges in the 'Great Basin,' is an isolated one. . . . The mountain on the W. side very precipitous towards us, and elevated about 3,000 feet above the plain, was timbered with pine: — much basaltic ferruginous rock about it. The left, was a pile of rocky hills." "Paiuta Pass," between Preble and Golconda, through Hot Spring Range to Paradise Valley.

30. Biographical interest accrues to this "small map" because Jefferson was in close proximity to the Reed-Donner party and narrowly escaped their fate. Beneath the title, is the information: "This map is in four parts and represents the emigrant road from Independence, Mo. by the South Pass of the Rocky Mountains to California. The Author was one of a party of emigrants who travelled the road with waggons in 1846." Jefferson reached Fort Bridger July 25; on this day the Reed-Donner party also reached Fort Bridger. Jefferson pursued his way, across the desert (by Hastings' Cut-off), down the Humboldt, to the Truckee River, crossed the Truckee Pass Oct. 7, and reached Johnson's Rancho Oct. 20. Against Truckee Pass on the map he inserts: "It was six miles west of the Truckey Pass of the Cal. Mts. that Reed's Party in November encountered snow ten feet deep and half the party perished." Approximately Oct. 5, as Bancroft figures it, under the guidance of Hastings, "were the last parties to cross except the Donner party" (Bancroft, *History of California*, V, 529).

31. H 3: "From 20 to 30 miles W. of the Blue Mountains, there are 2 small ranges, running parrallel with the first — across the valley. This creates extensive transverse vales N. and S." Sonoma, and East Range.

32. The telegraph was a novelty in 1849. In 1844, only 5 years before, S. F. B. Morse "had dispatched the first long-distance message ever to be sent by electricity anywhere in the world" (Hungerford, *op. cit.*, I, 272). Dec. 20, 1847, telegraph service was extended as far west as the Mississippi: "the great wonder of the day — the culminating glory of the human intellect — the magnetic telegraph commenced operations on the Illinois side opposite St. Louis, and transmitted messages on the 'lightning wing' to the principal cities of the east" (R. Edwards and M. Hopewell, *Edwards's Great West* [1860], p. 398). Not until 1851, it is said, was the telegraph first used in railroad operation. The name "Magnetic Telegraph Company" reflects the popular interest.

33. Bruff is in error here, probably in transcribing from his original notes. He was at this point (Grass Camp) only 47 miles from the turn-off (pocket diary P 5, Sept. 15), and thus really about 185 miles from the Pass. See 1st ed., pp. 282-89, 621-24, and Appendix VIII. It was at this camp that Bruff copied the "Cherrokee Guide," a version of Jesse Applegate's "Waybill" of the southern Oregon route, and looked over his distances. As to Lassen and Myers, see n. 18; also Milton McGee, not Myers, led off with the first train, Myers and Hudspeth following, and Lassen (though met on the road at this time by Howell [*op. cit.*, Sept. 12] and others, guiding Lieut. Warner eastward) led his train over it in '48.

34. H 3: "The Dr was travelling with Brophy's Compy."

35. H 3: "A tremendous pile of mountains on our left." East, and West Humboldt Ranges.

36. H 3: "Through the great desert of Utariah — 82 miles perfect arid waste. — They suffered much, — reduced to the necessity of drinking their mule's urine — &c. The remainder of the Guards, with a considerable number of other emmigrants, under the guidance of some Mormons, would pursue a southern route from the Lake into California, a route, in my humble opinion which will consign many emmigrants and their animals to the wolves, and the rest to much suffering; and may throw a large amount of property into the Lake Settlement." The contingent above evidently traveled Hastings' Cut-off. On his large map Bruff marked a cross on the edge of the mountains forming the western boundary of the first great desert stretch due west of Salt Lake City, with the notation: "By my information, Capt [McNulty] & party found a spring here, after incredible suffering", signed in cipher "J G B". Those of the Colony Guards left at Salt Lake City were apparently to join Capt. Jefferson Hunt's party, most of whom left him and landed themselves in Death Valley. Edward C. Coker, a well-known figure among Death Valley Forty-Niners, was a member of the Colony Guards. Culverwell, Sr., a member of Bruff's company, left at Fort Kearny on account of illness, also wound up in Hunt's train, and perhaps on the Death Valley wanderings he and Coker were renewing an acquaintance formed when their original companies fraternized on the Platte. See Introduction, pp. xlv-xlviii, and 1st ed., Appendix VIII, for a discussion of the Death Valley migration.

37. H 3: "They will descend the river to its sink, and cross on the Carson route, or Trucky pass."

38. Bruff's "Visitors' Book" has, Jan. 31, 1848: "Jas. T. Ames (sword cutler) Cabotville, Mass." James Tyler Ames was born in Lowell in 1810, son of Nathan Peabody Ames, maker of dragoon sabres and navy cutlasses. He (the father) "had a contract with the United States Government as early as 1832 for furnishing dragoon sabres to the Army. His factory, which eventually became the Springfield Arms Company, marked his blades the first period as N P Ames Springfield. . . . He possibly handled more contracts for the American Government than any other maker between the periods of 1830-70" (letter from R. W. Bingham, Dec. 6, 1936). Upon the death of Nathan Peabody Ames, Jr., in 1847, Jas. T. Ames became head of the Ames factory, then situate in Cabotville (Chicopee).

39. Bruff's sketch map (p. 562) shows the turn-off in detail, and his outline drawing of the "sand mt" northwest of the Humboldt at this point supplies further data on a disputed point. Delano says (*op. cit.*, p. 179): "We left the Humboldt sixty-five miles above, where it disappears in the sands. . . . Our course was in a north-west direction, across the plain, towards a gorge, through which the road ran." Bruff specifies (H 3): "This turn is about 118° 30' W. and 40° 40' N. almost identically the latitude of New York City." See 1st ed., P 5 and annotations.

This, the southern Oregon route, was opened in June, 1846, by fifteen men from Polk County, Oregon, including Jesse and Lindsay Applegate and Levi Scott, who traveled southward by the Umpqua River cañon, Rogue River valley, Round Prairie, over the Cascade Range, by Klamath River, Klamath Lake, Lost River (supposed then to be the Sacramento), Tule Lake, and Goose Lake. They then went through the pass (called in '49 Lassen's, now Fandango), to Mud Lake, which they called Mud Springs, Black Rock, Rabbit Hole Mountains, and southward, striking the Humboldt near present Humboldt City. Going up the Humboldt to the Big Bend they returned across the desert in a more northerly course to Black Rock, rediscovering Rabbit Hole Springs, to be sure of the route. Their trail, from the bend of the Humboldt back through Rabbit Hole Springs, Black Rock, Mud Lake and Fandango Pass to Goose Lake, was followed by Lassen in '48, breaking the Lassen Trail. Lindsay Applegate's account ". . . Road into Southern Oregon," *Quart. Oregon Hist. Soc.*, XXII (1921), 12–45, gives many interesting details. See also "Way Bill from Fort Hall to Willamette Valley Signed by Jesse Applegate," 1st ed., Appendix VIII.

40. Others mention the post office; David Dewolf: "At the forks of the roads was a Post Office consisting of a large water cask" ("Diary," p. 47).

41. Bruff means here the Truckee or the Carson routes; not the southern Oregon route (Lassen Turn-off).

42. See p. 539 for this view.

43. Uncertainty exists as to the exact route of the Lassen Trail between the

turn-off and Antelope Springs. This seems peculiar. The Trail at the turn-off was a well-marked road as Bruff says, "broad and as well beaten as any travelled thoroughfare can be." Yet there may be a very simple explanation of this loss of the old Trail: Bruff here described to perfection the appearance and the characteristics of a playa lake — a level, sun-baked, sun-cracked surface in the dry time, a "sea of fine mud" in the wet season. Any wheel rut, anything discarded here, would tend to sink in deeper with every wet season that passed. Consider further that the Trail went up "ravines, gulches, & dry stony beds of winter torrents." The road — "pent up in lofty sterile mountains, — mostly naked dark rocks . . . became more contracted and rugged, — along the bed of what is, in the wet season, a torrent" — in other words, followed up an arroyo — this leading directly to the springs. A cloud-burst or two, with a wall of water sweeping down the gorge, would effectively bear away anything in its path. This is not to say that this part of the Trail cannot be located. The Dept. of Highways, of Nevada, has interested itself in charting early trails, where these lie within the state. Whether the Lassen Trail be found to go by Maud's Well, Rosebud Cañon, or elsewhere, a pretty problem awaits someone. Bruff's text, sketches, and detail map may prove to be the key.

44. Lindsay Applegate, *op. cit.*, p. 36: "From this point we could see what appeared to be a low pass through the ridge on the west, through which was a channel of a tributary of the Humboldt, now dry." Following this dry stream bed 15 miles, they came to what is now known as Antelope Springs.

45. Antelope Springs. In the present Pershing Co., Nev. "Thence they [the Applegate party] took a northwest course to Rabbit-hole Mountains" (Bancroft, *History of Oregon*, I, 558).

Lander, in charge of the Fort Kearny, South Pass, and Honey Lake wagon road, which followed the old southern Oregon road, or Lassen's Trail, from the Humboldt River to Black Rock, in 1859 (W. H. Wagner, engineer in charge) excavated both Antelope and Rabbit Hole Springs. Wagner found Antelope Springs to be "twelve miles distant from the Humboldt river" (Lander, "Maps and Reports . . . ," 36 Cong. 2 Sess. H.R. Ex. Doc. 64 [1861], p. 33). His men excavated the "solid slate ledge" and made a basin to hold an estimated 35,000 gallons of water.

46. H 3: "The 'Rabbit-Hole Springs'." Lindsay Applegate, *op. cit.*, pp. 31-32: "After traveling about fifteen miles [eastward from Black Rock] we began to discover dim rabbit trails running in the same direction in which we were traveling. As we advanced the trails became more plain, and there were others constantly coming in, all pointing in the general direction toward a ledge of granite boulders which we could see before us. Approaching, . . . we could see a green mound where all the trails seemed to enter, and on examining the place closely we found a small hole in the top of the mound, in which a little puddle of water stood within a few inches of the surface. . . . Digging down in this clay we

made a basin large enough to hold several gallons and by dark we had quite a supply of good pure water. . . . Great numbers of rabbits came around us and we killed all we wanted of them. This is the place always since known as the Rabbit Hole Springs." "The locality, . . . in a straight line, is distant from the Humboldt river about thirty-six miles" (Lander's "Maps and Reports," p. 32).

47. Catherine Margaret Haun, wife of H. P. Haun [Horn] ("A Woman's Trip across the Plains in 1849"), recounts the incident of baking loaves of bread for the animals before crossing the desert. Writing from memory sixty years afterwards, she erroneously places this incident on Bear River, instead of at Rabbit Hole Springs, where Bruff saw her.

48. It is particularly regrettable that Bruff, usually careful to note names, gives none to the Cherokee. There were several parties of Cherokee en route to the gold fields in 1849; most pertinent for us, and famous for blazing the Cherokee Trail, is the Company of Capt. Lewis Evans, of Fayetteville, Ark., to which, we surmise, Bruff's Cherokee belonged. The company of Capt. Evans, one-time sheriff of Washington Co., Ark., was the result of careful preparation. J. S. Vann, editor of the *Cherokee Advocate*, in his issue of Jan. 15, 1849, proposes a California company of Cherokee, to join that "now forming in Fort Smith." The Arkansans, on their part, may have seen, as Vann points out in his editorial of Feb. 12, that "there is one very great advantage in going with the Cherokee company. The Cherokees are on the most friendly terms with all the Indian tribes of the Prairies — consequently there will be no danger of attacks from our red brethren."

The Washington County Gold Mining Company, or the Fayetteville Mining Company, or "Cap. Evans' Company of 40 wagons and 130 persons, mostly from Washington county, Arkansas, set out for California the 20th of April, 1849 and took a route never before traveled. The company crossed the Neosho at the Grand Saline, Cherokee nation, and proceeded up between the two Verdegries almost a due northwest course, until it struck the great road from Independence to Santa Fe; the estimated distance being about 300 miles. No wagon had ever traveled this route before. . . . At the place we struck the Santa Fe road . . . we obtained a large stone and planted it in the fork of the road, and one of our cunning workmen cut these letters upon it: 'To Fayetteville, Ark, 300 miles — Capt. Evans' Cal. Com'y, May 12, 1849,' to apprise the prairie traveler of a new road" (letter of H. Davis, *Cherokee Advocate*, July 30, 1849).

From this point Captain Evans followed the trail to Bent's Fort, thence to Pueblo. At Pueblo, apparently, occurred the first split in the Company, for O. W. Lipe writes "Mormon City, Salt Lake," Aug. 15: "The packers who left us at Pueblo, had a man drowned in Green River. . . . We traveled from Pueblo by the following route: Fort St. Vrains on South Platt — crossed South Platt at the mouth Cache A La Pudre — up said stream thro' the mountains to Laramie Plains; thence crossed Laramie rivers near the mountain, crossed Medicine Bow river, passed Medicine Bow Mountains, crossed the North Park and North Platt, Green river, south of the South Pass, and intercepted the Independence road on Black's Fork, about 14 miles west of Green River. When we arrived at the Independence road, we Indians quit the company and went ahead. Since I commenced writing this, the others have come in, but in two separate companies, so we have put off starting until morning, and we go with one of the companies — so our train will be twelve wagons" (*Cherokee Advocate*, Jan. 21, 1849).

From Sacramento City, Nov. 20, Jos. A. Sturdivant, writing home, says: "I am now in camp with Wm Shores and Capt. Evans, who arrived here about three weeks ago with about half the Arkansas teams. *The balance of the train took the northern route on Humboldt River, and my team with them* [italics ours]. I learn from Lieut. Rucker who has been with supplies to relieve the emigrants that they had been caught in a snow storm, and have lost all the stock that belonged to the train" (*Cherokee Advocate*, March 11, 1850). These, then, were some of the Cherokee of Evans' party who "took the northern route on Humboldt River," whose camp Bruff first saw near Black Rock. It is perhaps not idle to speculate on the routes followed by some of the other Cherokee. Editor Vann of the *Advocate*, with the "packers from Pueblo" hired "Owen, a man that was once in Fremont's company" [Dick Owens], to guide them (*Cherokee Advocate*, Aug. 6, 1849), by the Truckee (St. Jo *Gazette*, Nov. 30, 1849). Dr. Jeter Thompson, leader of a group coming from Independence, writes ("Feather River Mines," Nov. 1): "Many we hear of still *on the road* all along for two hundred miles from the settlements, in snow three feet deep" — conditions which existed at that date only on the Lassen Trail. At least one member of Thompson's party, Senora Hicks, came in over it in time to go back with the first flying column of the Relief. Two others who traversed it were J. Mulkey and his son James (*Cherokee Advocate*, July 16, 1850). One might not go far wrong in surmising that Cherokee were among the first converts to take the north trail at the Bend of the Humboldt — a surmise arresting in view of its bearing there the name "Cherokee Cut-off," and the guide copied by Bruff that of "Cherokee Guide" (see 1st ed., P 5 [A], Sept. 15, 1849).

The Cherokee were renowned as pathfinders, sharing honors with the Delawares as guides. They were "A powerful detached tribe of the Iroquoian family formerly holding the whole mountain region of the S. Alleghenies, in S.W. Virginia, W. North Carolina and South Carolina, N. Georgia, E. Tennessee, and N. E. Alabama, and claiming even to the Ohio r. . . . , who were represented to have been driven southward . . . by the combined . . . Iroquois and Delawares. . . . Shortly after 1800, missionary and educational work was established among them, and in 1820 they adopted a regular form of government modeled on that of the United States. . . . Gold was discovered . . . within the limits of the Cherokee Nation, and at once a powerful agitation was begun for the removal of the Indians. . . . The removal was accomplished in the winter of 1838-39 . . . after the loss of nearly one-fourth of their number, the unwilling Indians being driven out by military force and making the long journey [to Indian Territory, the present Oklahoma] on foot" (Hodge, *Handbook*, I, 245-46). Large numbers of Cherokee had already crossed the Mississippi, settling in Arkansas. They were driven from Arkansas also. They adventured westward in quest of homes and many joined the gold rush. Ironically, it was Cherokee Indians who discovered and worked some of the richest diggings in Butte and Nevada Counties, which still bear their name; in Calaveras Co. and Kern Co., where they are forgotten; and some of Evans' Cherokee who, noting gold on Cherry Creek, returned later to bring about the founding of the city of Denver (Henry Villard, . . . *Pike's Peak Gold Regions*, Princeton ed. [1932], p. 5, n. 7).

49. H 3: "and black. — This is the great basaltic promontory of 'Black Rock,' — at its base, on the other side, is the great 'Boiling Spring' — grass, &c, and the end of the *hornadas*." Bruff here uses *jornada*, like Thornton and other early travelers, in its military sense of a forced march, usually to be performed by special exertion within a day, or at least without encamping.

50. Jas. D. Lyon, of the Wolverine Rangers (*Detroit Advertiser*, Feb. 22, 1850): "On the last 16 miles of this desert [Black Rock], there were nearly 100 wagons [abandoned]; and [dead] oxen, horses, and mules, were thick enough to have formed a complete line the whole distance. The road was completely lined on both sides, and the stench arising from them was almost suffocating. . . . As we passed along, we could hear the groans and moanings of the dying oxen, which had been left to perish from thirst and starvation."

51. H 3: "A short and very crooked, tedious trail, over this portion, brought us abreast of the great basaltic promontory of 'Black Rock', frowning in dark majesty over the dreary scene. . . . This terminates the frightful series of *hornadas* which so alarmed the Revd Mr Thornton, when, poor fellow! he imagined that the celebrated Capt. Applegate was piloting him to the infernal regions! He had a hard time of it, though." Thornton, later a noted Oregon jurist, was one of the first party of emigrants brought out from Fort Hall by Jesse Applegate's men in 1846 over this new southern Oregon route. He was extremely bitter against Applegate. These seems little doubt that both distance and conditions had been misrepresented by Applegate's men.

52. A guidebook is also mentioned by Delano at Black Rock, Aug. 18: "We find that we are on Applegate's route of 1846. . . . The Government of Oregon had a Guide book printed by Authority for the benefit of Emigrants on the route to Oregon which is in possession of some of the Emigrants. This we follow to the Sierra Nevada then turn to the left to the head Waters of the Sacramento & then down its Vally to the American Fork, unless McGee finds a route direct to Feather River where we prefer to go" (journal, MS, Coe Collection, Yale Library). Delano's statement of the proposed route is the clearest we know of, and may have been derived in part from Milton McGee, the pilot of this first wagon train, who, in '43, came down from the foot of Goose Lake to the Sacramento Valley by

the Pit River (long considered the Upper Sacramento) in the Chiles party. Yet there was "uncertainty and doubt . . . in camp" — there was no Way Bill for the route after it left the Applegate trail. Instead, the Way Bill, continuing to Oregon, called Lost River "Sacramento River" (following Frémont in this nomenclature) and reckoned the distance to it as only 80 miles from the foot of Goose Lake. No wonder the trains were confused.

Train after train in '49, from Black Rock Desert on, attempted to find the promised "Cut-Off" either to Feather River or to the Sacramento Valley — among them, McGee himself. Wm. H. Nobles' road from Black Rock Boiling Spring, by Granite Creek Desert, Smoke Creek Desert, Honey Lake Valley, skirting the northern sources of the Feather, over Nobles' Pass, and down to Cow Creek on the Sacramento accomplished one cut-off in '51 — 153 miles to the Feather River. The Chiles party had already blazed the cut-off from "Round Valley" on the Pit to the Sacramento in '43, followed by Frémont in '46, and attempted by Lassen in '48. But Lassen missed his way. The emigration of '49 followed, with imprecations, his "long, crooked *Lassin's*" road.

It is perhaps a reasonable query whether Lassen intended to send the emigration of '49 by his route of '48, or whether he tried to direct the trains to "Noble's" route. This was all that he claimed for his "Cherokee Cut-off" at the Humboldt Turn-off — "A cut-off to the Feather"; "A Middle Route between Lassen's Pass and the Truckee"; "running between Lawson's and Truckey's route." Lassen says he discovered it years before, and guided Nobles over it in '51 ("A Jaunt to Honey Lake and Noble's Pass," *Hutchings Illustrated California Magazine*, I [1857], 537).

There is a "Cherrokee Guide" transcribed by Bruff in his pocket notebook P 5 almost identical with one excerpted by Israel Hale in his "Journal." According to Hale his was from the *New York Herald*. The distance of 45 miles across the "dry stretch" from the Humboldt to Black Rock is given in both versions, and is also given by Delano. Bruff's transcript and Hale's version will be found in 1st ed., Appendix VIII. The original guide on which these are based — perhaps Delano's "guide book published by authority" — is the "Way Bill from Fort Hall to Willamette Valley," signed by Jesse Applegate, also in Appendix VIII.

53. Methods of making arrow points varied with materials available and tribal usages, which were ceremonial. An excellent description of arrow-making by Pit River Indians is given by Beckwith (this account, n. 101). The "hammers" seen by Bruff were used probably in the initial flaking up of larger stones into blanks. A variant method is: The stone to be worked was first heated; then, drop by drop, with precision, cold water was poured upon it. Flaking was automatic. A specially happy method for cleavage stones. (Information by the late John C. York, lifelong resident of northeastern California.)

54. A. M. Fairfield, *Fairfield's Pioneer History of Lassen County . . .* (1916), p. 6: "It was nearly thirty miles across the desert to the Big Hot spring west of

the Black Rock mountain, and five miles beyond that they found the first good grass since leaving the Humboldt river. They had jumped from the frying pan into the fire, and their troubles had only begun."

55. H 3: "the tall flickering flames lit up the adjacent hills . . . , enlivening the scene all around. Wagons, tents, men, women, children, oxen and horses formed the grouping of the high-toned picture, while the white earth, the tall grass, the sparkling brook, with dark banks and bushes, heightened its effects."

56. Late in 1843 Frémont came down from Oregon, accompanied by Kit Carson, Fitzpatrick, and others. On Christmas Day, 1843, he reached a lake to which he gave the name Christmas Lake (Lewis A. McArthur, *Oregon Geographic Names*, rev. ed., 1944: "probably Hart Lake"). On Jan. 10, '44 he came to Pyramid Lake, also named by him. His exact route between these two points remains to some extent a matter of conjecture, but there seems little doubt that he came down through Surprise Valley, perhaps entered High Rock Cañon from the western end, crossed from the eastern outlet to the Black Rock range — and rounded Black Rock itself, which he described as "a black cape, at the foot of which a column of smoke indicated hot springs" (*Report*, p. 213). Lieut. G. K. Warren, on the map compiled in 1854-57 from government sources to accompany the *Pacific Railroad Reports* — and Frémont's 1843-44 exploration was a government expedition — shows Frémont passing down the east side of Christmas Lake, east of the lakes in Surprise Valley, eastward through the mountains (presumably through High Rock Cañon, coming out just north of High Rock Lake), following the Black Rock range southeast, bending around Black Rock itself, then southwest to Mud and Pyramid Lakes. Frémont's description of High Rock Cañon and Black Rock supports this. Bruff, being a friend of Frémont's and having drawn all the maps for Frémont's *Report* (both expeditions), had in 1849 a fairly clear idea of the Colonel's route. Indeed the emigration had knowledge of Frémont's track here, though none of them seems to have followed it. Delano says (at Black Rock boiling springs, Aug. 17, 1849): "The only other outlet for us at this point is by way of Pyramid Lake & Truckees River by the route taken by Col Fremont which falls into the old road at the latter point & crosses the mountains on the usual pass" (journal, MS, Coe Collection, Yale Library).

On one of these "other peaks" crops out the rock named by Bruff "Frémont's Castle," in compliment to his friend, probably because he knew that Frémont and his comrades were perhaps the first white men who ever saw the Black Rock range. This supposition accords with the map in Frémont's *Memoirs*, "showing country explored by John Charles Frémont. From 1841 to 1854," and bearing the words "Black R. Range" by Frémont's trail at the appropriate point (although the name does not appear on the map accompanying the *Report*). Marcy (*Prairie Traveler*, p. 283) says of Black Rock point: "mentioned by Colonel Frémont in his trip from Columbia River in 1843-4."

57. H 3: same date, corrected to "Bentley." Bentley was shot and mortally

wounded on Sept. 5 by his partner, in an argument over common property. In his winter camp in the Sierra Nevada, 1849-50, Bruff found and copied the journal of a fellow traveler, and a fragment of another journal (for the text of these, see 1st ed., Appendix XI). Oddly, both these men were doctors and, both being in Mud Lake basin at the time, were called to attend Bentley.

58. Lindsay Applegate, July 11, 1846 (*op. cit.*, p. 29): "After a march of perhaps ten miles, came out on the east side of the ridge [High Rock Cañon]. Here we found a lake basin of several acres in extent, where there was but a little water and a great deal of mud, hence strongly suggesting the name of Mud Lake, which it has since always borne."

H 3: "This is the basin of the lower 'Mud Lake' called '*Salt Valley.*'"

59. Delano also saw the "Indian snare for catching hares" (Delano, *op. cit.*, p. 192). Howell passed this same "Indian sage fense for catching antelope" (*op. cit.*, p. 39). Isabel T. Kelly "Ethnography of the Surprise Valley Paiute," *Univ. of Calif. Pubs. in Amer. Arch. and Eth.*, XXXI [1932], 82) notes that this group of Paiute used to make brush deer runs.

60. Lindsay Applegate, July 10, 1846, approached High Rock Cañon from the west (*op. cit.*, pp. 28-29): "We came to a huge volcanic wall, varying in height from twenty or thirty to several hundred feet, extending north and south as far as the eye could reach and apparently without any gap through it. We divided at the wall so as to explore it both ways. The party going southward, after proceeding a few miles, came to a little stream, forming a beautiful meadow at the base of the wall, and flowing through a narrow gateway into the ridge. . . . We found it a very remarkable chasm, extending nearly due east. . . . The little bottom was grassy and almost level, and, indeed, a remarkable track for a road."

61. Evidently another split in the company, some preferring the Lassen route to the Carson or the Truckee previously determined on (Sept. 18).

62. Delano, Aug. 21 (*op. cit.*, p. 194): "the remains of fires, grass beds, and burnt bones, showed it to be the habitation of the miserable race of beings who dwell in these mountains."

63. Dec. 30, 1843, Frémont, like Applegate, coming from the west (*Report*, p. 213): "After following the stream for a few hours in a south-easterly direction, it entered a cañon where we could not follow; but . . . we searched a passage below, and entered a regular narrow valley. . . . On both sides, the mountains showed often stupendous and curious-looking rocks, which at several places so narrowed the valley, that scarcely a pass was left for the camp. It was a singular place to travel through — shut up in the earth, a sort of chasm, the little strip of grass under our feet, the rough walls of bare rock on either hand, and the narrow strip of sky above." This description is perfect for High Rock Cañon.

64. "July 11 [1846], we again entered the gorge [High Rock Cañon] and traveled ten or twelve miles to a place where the stream formed quite a pool. . . . Here another canyon comes in from the north, and at the junction there is quite

an area of level ground — perhaps two acres — mostly meadow, forming an excellent camping place" (Lindsay Applegate, *op. cit.*, p. 29).

65. The peaks of the Warner Range.

66. "In two miles' travel we came to the upper High Rock Canyon. As we came near the canyon we passed a spring of fine water. It came out half up the mountain and ran across the road" (Hale, "Diary," p. 121).

67. An error. "Little Mountain Pass" (Forty-Nine Cañon) leads into Surprise Valley from the east. It is in the western part of Washoe Co., Nev. See Sept. 30.

68. Upper High Rock Cañon. Hale, "Diary," p. 121: "Some of the rocks that we drove over were half as high as the wagon wheels. We also had to drive in a creek for some distance and cross it several times."

69. Hale, "Diary," p. 121: "In this canyon I saw the first trees I have seen since we left Fort Hall. It was quaking aspen or poplar and some of the trees were from four to six inches in diameter."

70. H 3: "the source of the cañon brook, which below the cañon receives the rill from the mountain spring."

71. H 3, Oct. 1: "This pass range is singularly pretty. — The hills are of a light olive green color; with vertical blocks and cliffs of a purple hue, (perhaps trap rock) and white sugar-loaf cones of volcanic sand-stone, perhaps, and some bright tints of clay. And here and there an isolated tree, or a clump of dark green cedars. We crossed a sage plain, and entered a circuitous dry glen, among the hills, driving on a mile or so, till we reached the foot of the pass. — This strange pass, was a very narrow part of the range, and a divide. — between the country we were leaving, and that on the other side — sloping westward. The little hill was quite steep, and covered with deep sand. A huge pile of decrepitating coarse sand-stone stood boldly up at the top, causing the road up to branch, right and left around it. — That on the left was a long straight ascent, and the right hand route was much shorter, and curved around to the left. — We followed up this, having to double team to several wagons. A level area on top, so small, that there was scarcely room, to accommodate 20 wagons. — An open growth here, of pines & cedars. A gentle curved trail led us down, on the other side, into a pretty and narrow vale, with a small brook in it."

72. H 3: "a fine view of some of the out lying hills of the Sierra Nevada, which were not more than 25 miles distant." This is a close approximation of the distance to the slopes of the Warner Range.

73. Topographical quad., "Painted Pt. 6378" feet. Southwest of Massacre Lake, Washoe Co., Nev.

74. Surprise Valley. Although he did not realize it, Bruff here entered California (at least as now constituted), this being the eastern part of Modoc Co. The Trail crossed between Upper and Middle Alkali Lakes, bore westward to the foot of the Warner Range, and northward for about six miles to the eastern end of Lassen's, or Fandango Pass, by which it passed over to Goose Lake Valley. Mrs.

Roxana Foster, *The Foster Family* (1925), p. 52: "north along the foot of the mountain 6 miles. . . . There is a large flat desert at the foot of the Sierra, varying from 5 to 8 miles, that is probably covered with water, some part of the year, but now dry and hard, making the best of roads." In May, 1939, there was considerable water even in Upper Lake, and the view eastward from the summit of Fandango Pass was breath-taking.

75. H 3: "It seems that the road which leads into the Sacramento Valley, is not the same as Fremont's trail; but a great deal longer; . . . that it follows the ridges of the Sierra Nevada a long way down South, instead of taking the direction we all thought it would." Again, Oct. 21: "Had the road been found, as I know it might, 200 miles back from Lassen's to run W., our company would now be at work in 'Redding's Diggings,' some 50 or 60 miles N. of this [Bruff's Camp], at the head of the Sacramento Valley." These were not afterthoughts, but stated again, Feb., 1850, in "Memorandum to Poyle" (1st ed., P 8 A). "My ideas, and so expressed, were, that I had been in favor of this *northern route*, and as described by Myers, in his letter to the Adjt. General, but coming into the Valley at its head — (not this long crooked *Lassin's* part of it)." Bruff's faith in the "Cherrokee Guide" (1st ed., P 5 [A]), with its airline to the Sacramento was undoubtedly due to this belief. Bruff had drawn the map accompanying Frémont's *Geographical Memoir upon Upper California*, published in 1848; this trail he indicates on his own field map, p. 562. Frémont's trail of 1846 led from the Sacramento, opposite Cottonwood Creek, "up one of the many pretty little streams that flow into the main river around the head of the lower valley" (Frémont, *Memoirs*, p. 478), thence in three days' time to Pit River (called Upper Sacramento), above Fall River, and on the fourth day to "Round Valley" (Big Valley).

In 1850, Capt. Lyon, in quest of Capt. Warner's remains, took this "Cow Creek" route, reaching "Round Valley" in three days. The Cow Creek route was, in fact, the one selected in 1849 by Gen. Persifor F. Smith "on information and advice furnished by Colonel Frémont" for Capt. Warner's own survey (*Report of the Sec. of War for 1849*, p. 83) — a route from which he too was deflected by Lassen (R. S. Williamson, *ibid.*, p. 17). H 3, Aug. 10, 1850: "The Captain [Lyon] described to me the route. . . . He said that the trail laid along a series of beautiful valleys, without any rugged or steep to cross; and where wagons can travel easily. This is where I thought the road ought to strike into the Sacramento Valley, from the valley of Pit river, below the Pass of the Sierra Nevada, when I crossed last fall." This is where Lassen, in '48, struck west "through a beautiful valley," to be defeated by a "mountain which could not be ascended except by some creature that had either wings or claws" (P. H. Burnett, *Recollections . . . of an Old Pioneer* [1880], p. 262). He did not thread the needle's eye.

76. Cedar, Warren, and Eagle Peaks, all between nine and ten thousand feet in height, are visible to a considerable distance and are snow-clad much of the year.

According to the Forest Service, "during years of normal precipitation Eagle and Warren peaks have snow patches the year round, but not Cedar peak."

77. Known today as Fandango Pass, the mountain as Fandango Mountain, and the valley west of the summit as Fandango Valley. C. S. Drew, "Official Report of the Owyhee Reconnoissance," *The Oregon Sentinel*, Feb. 11, 1865, says of the last: "A beautiful glade, putting down from a point about a mile and half from the summit of the old Emigrant Pass over the Sierras. This glade is known as *Fandango Valley;* so called from a night attack having once been made by the Indians upon a party of immigrants while they were celebrating the opportune arrival of friends with much needed supplies from California, and as is too often the case had neglected to guard their camp." Drew gives no date for this. Bancroft repeats the story, citing Drew (*History of Oregon*, II, 503-5). It appears, however, that the name had a different origin. Goldsmith, a Wolverine Ranger, states that "Fandango" originated with his company (*Overland in Forty-Nine*, p. 88): "After camping one night the weather grew so terribly cold that the men had to dance to keep warm, and named their wild camping place 'Fandango Valley.' It was a picturesque spot, lying at the foot of a long steep descent, from the summit of which Goose Lake could plainly be seen. The exhausted cattle, rendered weaker by the cold rains and scanty feed, were unable to rally enough after a night's rest to climb the hills. About half of them were left to die. The company, finding it impossible longer to keep together, split up into smaller parties, each making its own plan of getting to the end of the journey. The papers and records of the company were formally burned." Some of the wagons were used to feed the fires during the night, and their blackened remains, together with the abandoned cattle, may have given rise to the story of an Indian attack. Goldsmith included a drawing (facing p. 140), with the legend "They Danced All Night to Keep from Freezing." His account was written from recollection, nearly fifty years after the event and, as Cowen remarks, there is an "almost entire absence of dates." Some errors of fact appear, but his memory was vivid and the record is valuable. The name Fandango came into general use early. Capt. Nathaniel Lyon, in his second report, dated Benicia, Nov. 1, 1850 ("Report . . . of the Command Sent in Search of the Remains of Capt Warner. . . ."; unpub., Govt. files), writes "Fandango Valley." Wm. Swain (journal and letters, 1849-51, MS, Coe Collection, Yale Library), also a Wolverine Ranger, confirms the dissolution of the company at this spot and says they and another company held a "fandango" there that night. Simon Doyle (journals and letters, 1849-54, MS, Coe Collection, Yale Library) has, Sept. 18, 1849: "Drove 6 miles to Fandango Valey," correctly described, and in his "Waibill" enters "Fandang Encampment." Doyle's 1849 journal was apparently inked over and amended, as witness his entry of Sept. 2, 1849, apropos of Joel Palmer's advice to take the Lassen Trail, 100 miles farther, "but much better — It proved to be 250 miles longer and if it is better God have mercy on the poor Mortals & beasts that travel the other" — clearly information

not known Sept. 2, 1849. He made a second trip to Calif. in 1854 and might easily have heard the name Fandango then.

78. "From Surprise valley up through Fandango, or Lassen's, pass, the mountain looks a person in the face, and one would hardly want to go over the old road with a pack train" (Fairfield, *op. cit.*, p. 7).

79. H 3: "as we had done at the South Pass of the Rocky Mountains. — "

80. Israel Hale, Sept. 3, "saw a heavy laden wagon driven by ten yoke of oxen start rapidly down the mountain [backwards]. The chain attached to the tongue had broken just as they reached the Summit" ("Diary," p. 125).

81. Bruff here enters the territory of the Pit River Indians about whom little but their raids and massacres was known in 1849. "Diggers" or "Paiutes," they are commonly designated; and Bruff has a disquisition upon them as such (1st ed., Appendix IV). They are, in fact, an indigenous California tribe, of the Shastan family.

Pierson B. Reading, in 1843, gives perhaps the earliest account of these pits along Pit River which gave both river and Indians their name. About fifty miles from Goose Lake, on "Beaver Creek," the party "came to numerous pits lying across our path. They were about nine feet deep with small mouths covered with weeds. . . . We suppose the Indians made them for the purpose of entrapping game. . . . One of our company, Mr. McGhee [McGee], who was walking ahead a short distance very suddenly disappeared. In a few minutes we saw the top of his head rising in the path, he having met with the misfortune of stepping into one of these traps" ("Journal," pp. 187-88). With McGee in this Chiles-Walker party of '43 were his Missouri friends "Maj. S.J.H." and "J.M." ("Autobiography," MS, Native Sons of Kansas City, Mo.; courtesy James Anderson), whom we suppose to be Maj. Samuel J. Hensley and J. Myers, both listed by Reading. A Kentuckian, born in 1818, McGee is still honored in his adopted Kansas City. In 1849 he was piloting the first wagon train of the year along the Pit.

The two main divisions of the Pit Rivers, whose village-dotted valleys constituted the early trail for trappers and adventurers, and in 1849-50 a thoroughfare for immigration, were called in their own language the Achomawi and the Atsugewi. It is with the Achomawi, meaning "River Dwellers," that the narratives of 1849 are chiefly concerned, although the fringes of Atsugewi territory overlapped the Lassen route as it turned from Pit River up over the mountain spurs.

82. Capt. Wm. H. Warner, Top. Eng., killed by hostile Indians while leading an exploring expedition. Cullum, *Biographical Register*, I, 498-99: born in N. Y., grad. West Point 1836; served in Florida war, in evacuation of the Cherokee Nation to the West, in Mexican War, and on Brig. Gen. Kearny's expedition to California.

Gen. Persifor F. Smith stated (*Report of the Sec. of War for 1849*, pp. 83-84) the objectives of Warner's expedition: "The other point immediately demanding attention was opening a sure and easy communication by land with the Atlantic

States. The whole value of these countries [California and Oregon] to the United States depends on this. The route by the isthmus is too expensive and too insignificant for the number of travellers. The steamers can bring with propriety not three hundred a month, while the emigration by land, if divided throughout the year, would average three thousand a month. . . . A route across the interior is practicable, because it is annually travelled. But the way may be made better and more sure by careful explorations. As these can only be made in the summer and fall in the mountains, and Congress might be disposed to act at once, I determined to employ what remained of the proper season this year in having examined that one of the various traces within the limits of my command that seemed to offer most advantages. As the principal obstacle at this end of the road is the Sierra Nevada, the examination was confined for the present to the passage of that ridge from the low plains on this side to the high ones on the other. On information and advice furnished by Colonel Frémont, . . . I selected for examination a pass by the Cow creek, one of the headwaters of the Sacramento. Brevet Captain Warner . . . was charged with the duty, and an escort . . . accompanied him. They left Sacramento City in August."

Capt. Warner had been shot down by Indians, but the report was incorrect in other respects. He was killed Sept. 26, not Oct. 1; the place of his death was on the eastern side of the mountain range — afterward named Warner Range in his honor — through which Bruff had just passed by way of Fandango or Lassen's Pass. This spot was roughly one day's travel north of Fandango Pass — that much is correct. The guide, first reported wounded, was mortally so, dying within a few hours; and two soldiers were less seriously injured. See Oct. 5, for Bruff's fuller and corrected account; also June 8, Sept. 6, 1850, and n. 86 below.

83. H 3: "Large companies have parted into small ones, others entirely broken up, while few retain any systematic organization."

84. "This lake possesses the peculiarities of lakes in semi-arid lands. Dependent as it is on the winter snows of the Warner range, its volume reflects strikingly the variation of precipitation which occurs in irregular cycles. At present [1926] the lake bed is nearly dry. In 1875 it flowed into the Pit. In 1849 wagon trains passed over its dry bed [at the lower end]. According to one Indian tradition it has been dry five times. On the present dry bed are found heaps of obsidian chips which indicate at least some kind of dwellings" (F. B. Kniffen, "Achomawi Geography," *Univ. of Calif. Pubs. in Amer. Arch. and Eth.*, XXIII [1928], 309). In 1931 the lake was dry. In 1939 it was smaller in extent than in 1849. Stephen Powers, in 1874, spoke of it as "really an inland sea, fifty miles long and fifteen wide, roughly stated" ("A Pony Ride on Pit River," *Overland Monthly*, XIII [1874], 344).

85. Powers, "A Pony Ride on Pit River," pp. 344, 347: "A few miles south of Willow Ranch there is a bold promontory projecting into the lake on the east side; and, in 1854, the emigrants bound for Oregon [this route being practically abandoned for California travel] passed round the foot of this on the beach.

. . . Below the promontory the lake grows narrower, and the plains are of a vast width, almost on a dead level." In 1939 this "rocky point" was far removed from the waters of the lake.

86. P 5, Oct. 4: "Heard . . . that Capt — Warner was killed near head of this lake, on this side. Arrows flew like hail, party retreated, & saw savages cutting up the body of my lamented friend." Warner was killed on the eastern side of Goose Lake, but also east of the Warner Range. Lyon, sent in 1850 to recover Warner's remains, reported (2d Report, pp. 4-5): "As indicated on the map Capt. Warner, having crossed the eastern spur of the Sierra Nevadas to the North of Goose Lake, descended on the eastern side [of the mountains as well as the lake] in a South easterly direction, . . . and when near the base of the Mountains, took a Southerly course, which cuts at right angles the gullies & ravines, formed by streams from the Mountains. . . . It was in crossing one of these ravines at a favourable point, to which he had been lead by an Indian trail, Capt. Warner came upon a Rancherea, from which the Indians fled, and concealed themselves upon his approach, among the pedregral rocks on the side opposite that from which Capt. Warner and his party advanced, their arrows commanding the trail, as they came up the ravine on the South, when the Indians raised a simultaneous shout, and delivered their arrows with effect upon Capt. Warner & those of his party nearest to him."

Drew (1864), *op. cit., Oregon Sentinel*, Feb. 11, 1865: "it was at first supposed" that Capt. Warner was killed "in the main cañon putting into it [Warner's Valley] from the south. . . . John S. Drum, Esq., of Jacksonville, Oregon, who was connected with Capt. Lyon's command that went in search of Warner's remains . . . locates the point at which some of them were found a few miles south of the old Southern Oregon Emigrant Road, and consequently the fatal spot must be in Surprise Valley." Elsewhere in the same account Drew places the spot at 12 miles south of the Trail where it crosses Fandango Mountain. Yet Williamson, second in command when Warner was killed, in the map accompanying his official report of the expedition shows the location to be a little south of the 42d parallel, or roughly 25 or 30 miles north of Lassen's Pass. He also certified as correct Lyon's map of his route in 1850, superimposed on a map of Warner's route. The general map of the *Pacific Railroad Reports*, prepared in 1854-57 under the direction of the Army, likewise shows "Massacre of Capt Warner" at the point indicated north of the Lassen Trail. Sergt. Sheckels, of Warner's command, tells Bruff (P 5, Oct. 5) that Warner and Bateau, the guide, were killed and 2 men wounded on "[Sept.] 26th 30 ms. N. of [Lassen's] Pass in the Mountains." Against this contemporaneous evidence of principals, the statement 14 years later of a soldier of the punitive command seems hardly valid. Furthermore, Williamson says ("Report," p. 20) that when killed Warner was traveling "to the southward, *intending to recross the mountain on the Lassen trail* [Pass]" (italics ours). If Warner intended to cross by the Lassen Pass, he would hardly travel past it 12 miles farther south. Williamson's designation of Warner's death spot on the map accompanying his report (R. S. Williamson, "Report of a Reconnaissance of the Late Brevet Captain W. H. Warner, of a Route through the Sierra Nevada by the Upper Sacramento," *Report of the Sec. of War for 1849-50*, pp. 17-22) is accepted by the Government as correct.

87. H 3: "(Forks of the Oregon road here) Steep earth banks." Here the Lassen Trail left the Applegate or southern Oregon route. From the foot of Goose Lake the Trail showed variations. Some emigrants, like Bruff, struck directly south or southwest, coming in east of the present Alturas. Others crossed the bottom of Goose Lake and then went south or southwest across the Devil's Garden to Rattlesnake Creek, west of Alturas. Rensch, Rensch, and Hoover give only the western variant; Fairfield says both routes were used, but shows on his map only that coming in west of Alturas. Owen C. Coy's map (p. 145), shows the Trail as Bruff followed it.

88. Warner's second in command, Lieut. R. S. Williamson, born in N. Y., grad. West Point 1848, 2d Lieut., Top. Eng. (Cullum, *op. cit.*, II, 209-10). "Served: . . . on Surveys in the Pacific Division, 1848-53; in charge of Survey of Pacific Railroad route in California, in connection with the routes near the 32d and 35th parallels, 1853-54, — and of routes in California and Oregon, 1855-56; and on the Staff of the Commanding General of the Department of the Pacific." Also with gallantry in the Civil War. The official report of the Warner expedition made by him closes with a statement on the Lassen Trail in tabular form, but less detailed than this affixed by him to a tree for the benefit of the emigrants.

89. Comparing Bruff's "Cherokee Guide" (1st ed., P 5 [A]) with Williamson's table of distances this discrepancy of 150 miles stands out.

90. H 3: "Head of Pitt river."

91. H 3: "tributaries of Pitt river; and after crossing the ridge we reached a 4th."

92. Sheckels told Bruff (P 5, Oct. 5) that about "30 Ind[s] Killed Warner and Bateau (guide) instantly — with 11 arrows in W. and 9 in Bateau — through calfs of legs body, thigh, mouth — lascerating mouths & jaws much. wounded 2 men — 1 severely with 4 arrows, the other slightly, with 2." The injured man in camp here was George Cave, who died before reaching the Sacramento. The other, Henry A. Barling, reached Army headquarters at Benicia and eventually recovered. The guide was François Bercier (ordinarily called Battitu), "a very intelligent half-breed, born on the Red river of the north; had served some time with the Hudson's Bay Company in Oregon; had trapped in the rivers of the country we were about to explore, and proved himself to be a very valuable man" (Williamson, "Report," p. 17). Bruff adds (1st ed., Appendix IV): most of those [arrows] fired into Warner's party, were iron pointed," obtained by the Pit River Indians, according to him, "by the travel."

93. H 3: "This is, 'Cañon Creek', of Pitt river" (according to the "Cherrokee Guide").

94. H 3: "the main valley of Pitt river" — that is, of a tributary of the Pit.

95. "The Charlestown Mining Co. of Va. [now Charles Town, West Va.] departed from Charlestown on Tuesday last. They number in all about seventy-five — embracing some of the best and worthiest citizens of the town [a list of officers follows]" (Washington *Tri-Weekly Intelligencer*, March 31, 1849). E. W. McIlhany, a member of this Co., states that he reached Johnson's Ranch Oct. 1, 1849, by the Truckee route. So also did Dr. Wakeman Bryarly and Vincent Geiger, as recorded in their joint journal (*Trail to California*, D. M. Potter, ed. [1945]). This company, like some others, split, taking different routes.

96. This is on Davis Creek, one of the upper tributaries of the Pit. These singular rock clusters are to be seen today, a few of them damaged by road-making or other modern "improvements." Opposite, the eastern rim of the Modoc Lava Beds breaks into three towering "circular bastions" and long thick walls, as regular in appearance as though man-made.

97. Gen. Persifor F. Smith, then commanding the Pacific Division. According to Gardner (*op. cit.*, p. 417): born in Pa., later resided in La., becoming Adjutant General of the state; served in Florida war in '36, under Gen. Taylor on the Rio Grande in '46; made Bvt. Brig. Gen. in '47, and Maj. Gen. in '48. *New York Herald*, Oct. 29, 1848: "General Persifor F. Smith, who has justly earned the title the Hero of Contreras."

"As I was about starting for Oregon [Gen. Smith, Dec., 1849, to the Asst. Adj. Gen. (*Report of the Sec. of War for 1849*, p. 84)] the emigrants from the United States began to arrive. Hitherto a few hundreds had crossed annually, and had often suffered. . . . As the road this year was crowded with from five to seven thousand wagons, it was probable that the suffering would be beyond description among those who, coming last, would find the whole of the latter part of the route bare of forage, and in so many places everything burnt off by fire."

Bruff says, of the Relief (H 3): "To succor the emigrants in the rear; — particularly families." As to this, Gen. Smith continues: "Under these circumstances, I directed as many wagons as could be procured up the Sacramento to be despatched partly loaded with provisions, and to proceed in two parties by the two routes [Truckee and Carson] on which the emigrants were advancing; to issue provisions to such as were in need, and to send in the women, children, and sick in the wagons emptied. . . . Brevet Major Rucker, 1st dragoons, was selected to take charge of the train, and carry out these dispositions." Finding, however, that a great part of the emigration, enduring the severest suffering, was on the Lassen Trail, Rucker diverted to it a great part of the relief. It is a measure of the emergency that Gen. Smith appropriated from the Civil Fund $100,000 for the Relief (Fariss and Smith, *Illustrated History of Plumas, Lassen and Sierra Counties* [1882], p. 87, *passim*), trusting to Congress to support his action. Bruff met the relief train at some point between the present Alturas and Warm Spring Valley.

98. John H. Peoples, Rucker's chief aide in the distribution of relief on the

Lassen Trail. H 3: "(formerly a corresponded [correspondent] of the New Orleans papers, from the seat of war in Mexico)   Peoples was quite sick, with fever, and at my invitation, said if not better in a few hours would return to my company, for medical attention."

"Gen. Smith's Correspondence. California" (31 Cong. 1 Sess. [1850], Sen. Ex. Doc. 52, pp. 85-152), contains "Major Rucker's report of his expedition to the relief of the emigrants," sent to the Asst. Adjt. Gen.: "The general will recognize in one of the agents employed, (whose narrative I particularly recommend to his notice,) the energetic editor of the newspaper established in the city of Mexico after our entry — Peoplis [Peoples]" (Rucker's *Report*, p. 86). Library of Congress: "An examination of the American newspapers in our collection published in Mexico during the Mexican War identifies the following two with which John H. Peoples was connected. 1. American Star, no. 2. Semiweekly. Puebla. 1847., July 1 (Vol. no. 5) 8. Both of these issues bear the notation, 'Will be published . . . during the stay of the Army at Puebla, by Peoples, Barnard & Callahan.' 2. Daily American Star, daily., Mexico City. 1847-1848, Sept. 20-May 30." Peoples' report (contained in Rucker's *Report*) — the "narrative" referred to by Gen. Smith — will be cited frequently; invaluable in identifying Bruff's fellow travelers on this part of the route. Goldsmith (*op. cit.*, p. 81), states that Peoples was "from Lynchburg, Virginia." The *New York Herald*, Feb. 12 and April 16, 1849, letters from Peoples, commander of a co. from Corpus Christi to California: "We go by the Presidio Rio Grande, then travel up parallel with that stream to El Paso . . . ; then a little North of West, to and down the Gila to the Gold Diggins." "A large number of the men were unfit to go to California by any route, and will be unfit to stay there if they ever arrive, unless they get some situation in the shade, and in the neighborhood of a cologne lake." Peoples was drowned in Trinidad Bay, March 27, 1850, in company with Lieuts. Bache and Browning, of the Coast Survey, and two others, — a region visited by Bruff in the spring of 1851.

99. P 5 and H 3 both say "descended" into this (Warm Spring) valley, which is correct. The isolated butte is Opahwah Butte, known locally as Centerville, or Rattlesnake Butte. We are indebted to the late John C. York, of Susanville, Calif., for this identification. Bruff's contour sketch of the mountain (p. 180) is accurate today.

100. According to W. A. Chalfant, whose father, P. A. Chalfant, was a member of this company, it "started from Omaha with forty-five wagons, June 6th" (*The Story of Inyo* [rev. ed., 1933], p. 51). Chalfant also states that Col. Brophy and Maj. Haun (Horn, in Bruff's records) commanded the co., and that Rev. J. W. Brier, of Death Valley fame, was its chaplain. Chalfant believes the company entered California in the fall of '49 by the Beckwourth Pass, but says it followed the "northernmost" route, which would bring them where we find them, here on the Lassen Trail. For P. A. Chalfant's interesting recollections of his journey as a

member of this Co., see "A Boy in California in Forty-Nine," in W. A. Chalfant's *Outposts of Civilization* (1928), pp. 165-93. For a discussion of the route of the San Francisco Co. and of its connection with the Brophy-Haun party, see 1st ed., P 1, n. 252.

101. Lieut. E. G. Beckwith, in 1854, saw a Pit River Indian making his arrow-head: "One of them seated himself near me and made from a fragment of quartz, with a simple piece of round bone, one end of which was semi-spherical, with a small crease in it (as if worn by a thread) the sixteenth of an inch in depth, an arrowhead, which was very sharp and piercing, and such as they use on all their arrows. The skill and rapidity with which it was made, without a blow, but by simply breaking the sharp edges with the creased bone by the strength of his hands — for the crease served to prevent the instrument from slipping, affording no leverage — was remarkable" ("Report of Explorations . . . ," *Pacific Railroad Reports*, II [1855], 42). In his "Study of Bows and Arrows," Pope says of the finished point: "The California Indian makes the best aboriginal arrow of all the specimens examined" (*Univ. of Calif. Pubs. in Amer. Arch. and Eth., XIII* [1923], 374).

102. Dec. 12, 1849, Peoples, in Sacramento, reported to Rucker: "The next morning [Oct. 5], however, I made a forward movement, but before night was convinced that I would only delay my party by remaining with them; and having been kindly offered a place in Dr. Austin's wagon, and all the medical attention he could bestow, I started back on the morning of the 7th October, with the Washington City train" (Rucker's *Report*, pp. 117-18).

Peoples, like many on the Trail, was suffering from "mountain fever." Dr. R. R. Parker, P. H. Service, Rocky Mountain Laboratory, Hamilton, Mont. (letter, Jan. 16, 1942): "There are many references to 'mountain fever' in the literature of early days in the West. So far as one can judge, this term was used to cover a number of different diseases not then recognized as distinct entities. The designation likely included, among other diseases, Rocky Mountain spotted fever, but the one most frequently concerned appears to have been the tick-borne infection now known as Colorado tick fever. At present this occurs mostly in a strip of mountainous country extending from the eastern limits of the Rocky Mountain system in northern Colorado and southern Wyoming westward to include the Sierras in California."

103. The first cañon of the Pit, debouching into Big Valley. A marker, set to the right of the present road as it swings away from the narrow gorge, by the California State Automobile Association, reads: "Old Emigrant trail $5\frac{1}{2}$ miles. California State Historical Landmark 111."

104. Possibly; but also, considering its location, for smoking and drying fish.

105. "*Manzanita*, (*Arctostaphylos tomentosa*.) The *manzañita* of the Spaniards. It is a dwarf evergreen, producing a small fruit similar to the well-known bearberry, of an astringent taste. It also possesses acid properties, and by the early

Spanish settlers of California, Arizona, and New Mexico was called manzañita, or little apple, as, when not fully ripe, it tastes like an agreeably tart apple" (E. Palmer, *op. cit.*, p. 413).

106. This is Frémont's "Round Valley" (not to be confused with the present Round Valley north of Adin), now known as Big Valley. Frémont: "On the 29th of April [1846] I encamped on the upper Sacramento [Pit], above Fall River . . . ; the next day again encamped on it at the upper end of a valley, to which, from its marked form, I gave the name *Round Valley*" (*Memoirs*, p. 480). Beckwith, June, 1854 (*op. cit.*, p. 42): "a broad plain called Round valley . . . twenty miles or more in length, and ten or twelve in width; and several creeks flow into it, and overflowing form marshy lands of large extent. It is everywhere luxuriant in grass, and the mountains around it are heavily timbered. . . . In the west, Mount Shasta is a beautiful feature in the landscape; and to the southwest, other beautiful snow-peaks mark the western line of the Sierra Nevada." The haze and rain of the morning may have prevented Bruff from catching a glimpse of their snowy summits.

107. The last ford of the Pit, between Lookout and Old Bieber, near the present boundary between Modoc and Lassen Cos.

108. Toward the beginning of winter the "River Dwellers" returned from summer quests of game and wild foods in the mountains to their permanent villages in the valleys which, this fall of 1849, lay directly in the path of the oncoming emigrant trains. Here in Big Valley, a flourishing tribe of the "River Dwellers," calling themselves the "Valley Dwellers," lived. "The valley areas, in addition to their greater protection from winter snow and cold, offered an amazing variety of food. . . . The tule itself, in addition to its uses as material for the making of mats, shoes, twine, etc., is edible. . . . In addition are found in the marshy areas camass roots, a number of species of lilies, Indian potatoes, and seed-bearing grasses. . . . In the protected valleys are a number of fruit-bearing trees . . . the yew, manzanita, wild plum, and Oregon grape. Then in the less swampy areas or in the uplands adjacent to the valleys are found the epos root, wild garlic, wild turnip, wild buckwheat. . . . The western section of the area knows the oak with the acorn and all the accompanying technique. . . . As far east as Fall river the salmon was an important part of the food economy of the Pit Rivers. East of Fall river, suckers, pike, and trout were found and taken in abundance. In spring the northward moving waterfowl stopped at the little lakes and swampy areas. At this time of year ducks, geese, brant, and cranes were plentifully present. Sage hens and quail were shot, snared and netted. All the smaller animals, badger, ground hog, squirrel, rabbit, mink, and martin, were considered edible. . . . All these were in addition to the bigger game which naturally gravitated toward the water and the lush feed of the valleys: deer, antelope, occasionally elk, possibly a few bison, and bear" (Kniffen, "Achomawi Geography," pp. 301-2).

In 1855, Lieut. P. H. Sheridan, hurrying from Fort Reading to join Lieut. R. S.

Williamson, of Warner's ill-fated survey, noted a band of the Pit Rivers at the ford of Hat Creek, not far from Big Valley: "The Indians came to the bluff above the camp, and arranged themselves in a squatting posture, looking down upon Williamson's party with longing eyes, in expectation of a feast. They were a pitiable lot, almost naked, hungry and cadaverous. Indians are always hungry, but these poor creatures were particularly so, as their usual supply of food had grown very scarce. . . . In former years salmon were very abundant in the streams of the Sacramento Valley, and every fall they took great quantities of these fish and dried them for winter use, but alluvial mining had of late years defiled the water of the different streams and driven the fish out" (*Personal Memoirs* [1888], I, 44-46).

109. Peoples to Rucker, Dec. 12, 1849 (Rucker's *Report*, p. 117). Also· Williamson: "I met on Pit river a party under charge of Mr. Peoples. . . . He told me that several of his men, while hunting among the hills for some lost animals, had discovered a body of the Indians, which they estimated at five hundred strong" ("Report," pp. 20-21). Dr. Fred B. Kniffen identifies the "Digger Village" as probably "Sustadedje, at the hot spring 5 miles east of Bieber. . . . It seems hard to believe that they could muster 'several hundred' warriors, but this was unquestionably one of the major villages of the general region" (letter, Sept. 8, 1939).

110. Second Pit River cañon.

111. The lower Horse Creek ford, bearing today on scarred trees the marks of the ropes by which the emigrant wagons were let down. The upper Horse Creek ford, on the hill route, is equally notorious still as the "Wagon Trail Crossing." It is above Clark Valley (through which the trail passed and where many companies made camp) on what is now Bognuda Ranch, a mile or so east of the junction of the hill and the river roads (in accordance with P 5, Oct. 11).

112. A point (P 5, Oct. 8): "150 ms. from Lassen's & 13½ from turn off of road to hills," making the "turn off" 136½ miles from Lassen's. George E. Jewett reached the turn-off Sept. 18 ("Journal," MS, Bancroft Library): "There are two roads that come together the left is said to be very bad and 20 miles, the right 30 miles good. We concluded to take the right, drove 18 miles over some of the worst road I ever saw." Williamson, on this key point whence a real cut-off to the Sacramento Valley was practicable ("Report," pp. 19-20): "where the trail to Lassen's leaves the [Pit] river, it strikes into steep hills. . . . In the opinion of Captain Warner, the road should follow Pit River, or, by crossing over to the head waters of Cow Creek, follow down that creek to the Sacramento valley." Reading, McGee, Myers, and other "mountain men" had blazed this "Frémont's" or "Cow Creek" trail. Bruff wanted to try it; in 1850 Lyon took it; in 1851 Wm. H. Nobles (guided, it is said, by Lassen) made Cow Ck. the first link in his Nobles' Pass-Honey Lake-Humboldt road. Nobles, a "new comer," claimed all credit; under the misnomer — Noble, his identity has been lost to this day.

113. An early name for Lassen's Peak, which was also known as Mount Saint Joseph. Wm. H. Brewer, *Up and Down California*, F. P. Farquhar, ed. (1930) p.

334: "Lassen's Peak, and in fact that whole part of that chain, like Mount Shasta, is a gigantic extinct volcano, perhaps about twelve thousand feet high — a volcano not only much higher, but vastly greater in every respect of magnitude and effect than Etna. It is flanked by a considerable number of smaller cones, old volcanoes, from one thousand feet high, up to that of the main peak itself, many of these cones being much higher and greater than Mount Vesuvius." The volcanic nature of Mount Lassen was of course well understood; in May, 1914, it again became active, in a series of eruptions long to be remembered.

114. Jewett, having taken the right-hand road, wrote two days later ("Journal"): "4 miles to the junction of the roads. Think the other road the best."

115. H 3: "This brook is 'Pitt run,' going down N.W. to the river"; it sounds like the ford of Horse Creek on the left, or mountain road. A few miles from this point the right road, having forded "hair-raising" Horse Creek in turning from the Pit River Valley to the mountains, joined the left road. See 1st ed., P 5, pp. 318, 319.

116. Probably some variety of *ceanothus*, whose acutely serrated and often glossy leaves resemble those of the holly, forming with laurel, manzanita, and other shrubby growths the characteristic hillside cover of the Sierra and the Cascade ranges.

117. "*Umbellularia californica* Nutt., California Laurel. The California Laurel inhabits the Coast Ranges . . . and is also found on the western slope of the Sierra Nevada. . . . The native tribes roasted the nuts and used them for food" (W. L. Jepson, *Silva of California* [1910], pp. 243, 246).

118. H 3: "drawn by three yoke of oxen, and a yoke of cows." Bruff's sketch of his Camp, Oct., 1849 (see p. 540), shows the steamboat wagon in the right foreground.

119. P 5 (Oct. 11) says "2 mules lost," making no mention of Indians. This region, near Little Dixie Valley, was one of the strongholds of the hostile Pit River Indians.

120. The steamboat wagon.

121. Later, at Bruff's Camp, Bruff found and copied a diary of the Trail belonging to Dr. Caldwell, McLane's comrade, and a fragmentary record kept by McLane himself (Mud Lake to Fandango Pass). See 1st ed., Appendix XI.

122. Rucker's *Report*, p. 147: "Left camp [Feather River] this morning [Oct. 14]. . . . A short distance from camp met the Nodaway train; the men, women, and children were clamorous for provisions, but as I had ascertained from an undoubted source that they were supplied, and had been selling to the poor all along the road at high prices, I was constrained to refuse acceding to the demands."

123. Bruff's "Little Goose Lake" appears to be, by distance and comparison with other accounts, upper Feather Lake. Bruff himself says of the smaller pond, reached shortly (H 3), "This last pond is probably 'Feather Lake' of the mountaineers." Feather Lake or Lakes lie about 18 miles northerly from Big Meadows.

Mrs. Foster (*op. cit.*, p. 54), Sept. 21: "Passed on 4 miles to Feather Lake, merely a pond, without outlet; one mile farther passed another of the same character, great quantities of feathers around them, shed by the water fowl that frequent these waters."

124. Gardner, *op. cit.*, p. 390: D. H. Rucker, born in Mich., commissioned 2d Lieut., 1st Dragoons, 1837; held successive ranks; served in Mexican War; trans. Quartermaster's Dept. Aug. 1849. Rucker became a Gen. and later Quartermaster Gen. of the U. S. Army. In 1875 his daughter Irene married Gen. P. H. Sheridan.

125. H 3: "The hen-coop wagon is here. Ashford is also on the ground. . . . We drove 9 miles = 18¾ to-day."

126. Rucker (*Report*, p. 148), Oct. 15: "Before leaving camp this morning, supplied . . . Capt. Bruff, of the Washington city company, with some pork and bread."

127. Peoples, Rucker's *Report*, p. 118: "On the morning of the 16th of Ocober, the mountain fever having been broken on me by the skill of Dr. Austin, I started back towards the mountains with the party under your [Rucker's] immediate command, and continued with you until the 20th, on which day you deemed it advisable to return to Feather river valley, with a small portion of the provisions, as you had satisfactorily learned where the rear of the emigration was."

128. Not yet. H 3: "This is known as the large Feather river valley, and around, on the opposite side, some distance, is the place to cut grass for a long stretch at the terminus of the mountain road. This valley is 54 miles from the settlements; and in 14 more, we reach the altitude of 5,000 ft: above the Sacramento plain; and descend to it in 40 miles, by rugged ridge travel! . . . The clear creek — (a western branch of the N. fork of Feather river)". "Feather river valley" was later called Big Meadows. A large part of the valley is now flooded by the artificial Lake Almanor reservoir.

129. Henry A. Barling, "an emigrant & so was his more unfortunate comrade . . . : — Capt. Warner had engaged them on the road. . . . About 50 indians fired simultaneously on them. . . . They had not the chance to cover Warner with stones as first informed" (H 3).

130. Godman, *op. cit.*, I, 94: "*The Grizzly Bear.* Ursus Horribilis. — Ord. . . . This bear, justly considered as the most dreadful and dangerous of North American quadrupeds. . . . Gigantic in size and terrific in aspect." Chittenden, *op. cit.*, II, 822: "The king of American wild beasts was the grizzly bear (*Ursus horribilis*), the only animal which the hunter looked upon as really dangerous. . . . In size the grizzly bear averaged about six feet in length from nose to tip of tail, but they were often found to measure nine, and instances are mentioned of the enormous length of fourteen feet. A weight of five hundred pounds was common. . . . If thoroughly roused his strength and rage were terrible."

131. H 3: "Here it became necessary to convene the company into a court martial to try some offending members   a member for an assault; and also a man,

who had been permitted to travel with us, for slandering the company. Both cases properly disposed of." Hume Young was "discarded" and Owen punished.

132. "C[*eanothus*] *prostratus* Benth. Mahala mat. Prostrate plants, the branches thickly matting the ground, often rooting and forming dense mats 2 to 10 ft. broad. . . . Pine woods, 3000 to 7000 ft.: Sierra Nevada from Mariposa Co. to Mt. Shasta" (Jepson, *A Manual of the Flowering Plants of California* [1925], p. 624). Called locally squaw blanket.

133. Perhaps *Tamias quadrivittatus*, Missouri Striped Squirrel of J. S. Newberry. "In California, their subsistence is derived from the oaks and pines, and from the seeds of the everywhere abundant 'manzanita' " ("Zoology," *Pacific Railroad Reports*, VI [1855], pp. 54–55). Perhaps "*Sciurus Douglasii*, Var. California pine squirrel. This little fellow is everywhere known as the pine squirrel, though the name is not strictly correct, as it lives on almost all kinds of evergreen which furnish edible seeds. . . . Like the larger pine squirrel, their habit is to go into the tree and cut off and throw down a number of the cones, and then descending to tear them up at leisure. Unlike *S. fossor*, however, this squirrel has a burrow either under or in fallen logs, where the pine seeds are carried and stored for winter. By this habit, it is allied to the ground squirrel, (*Tamias 4-vittatus*,) which is its constant associate in the region which it inhabits" (*ibid.*, pp. 53-54).

134. H 3: "10 feet diameter, and 200 feet high, are common sizes, — and they are generally as straight as an arrow." "On some of the most elevated peaks over which we travelled [Sierra Nevada, Lassen's Trail] we found white pines 7 feet thick, 250 feet high, and as straight as the path of a christian" (James D. Lyon, *Detroit Advertiser*, Feb. 22, 1850). Jepson, *Silva of California*, p. 80: "The average age of Yellow Pine in mature stands in the Sierra Nevada is 250 to 350 years, according to Sudworth, although the longevity of occasional trees may reach 500 to 520 years. . . . The Yellow Pine . . . is particularly characteristic of the Sierra Nevada. . . . The largest trees most commonly grow along the ridges, and it is ridges which the trails ordinarily follow. Here the traveler may journey day after day, over needle-carpeted or grassy ground, mostly free from underbrush, amidst great clean shafts . . . of really massive proportions, but giving a sense of lightness by reason of their color, symmetry, and great height."

White, or sugar pines mingle with yellow: "The cones of this magnificent tree [*P. Lambertiana*] are from twelve to sixteen inches in length, and contain each one hundred or more seeds of the size and shape of the small white bean of commerce" (Newberry, "Zoology," p. 52).

135. P 6: "3 men on mules." Williamson, "Report," p. 21: "I here [Lassen's Rancho] sent back three men to carry provisions to the wounded [Cave and Barling], and to bring them back to Benicia."

136. *Cathartes Californianus* of Newberry. "As I sometimes recall the characteristic scenery of California, those interminable stretches of waving grain, with, here and there, between the rounded hills, orchard-like clumps of oak, a scene so

solitary and yet so home-like, over these oat-covered plains and slopes, golden yellow in the sunshine, always floats the shadow of the vulture" (Newberry, "Zoology," p. 73).

137. Like other companies, the Washington City and California Mining Association was finding the going hard and from twelve wagons and one spare "now have only five wagons, and imposed additional burthens on the packed mules" (H 3).

138. H 3: "5,000 feet above the valley of the Sacramento. (vide Official card)," referring to Williamson's note on the route posted near Goose Lake.

139. The ridge here becomes so narrow and the slopes so precipitous that one feels poised in mid-air. Anderson, approaching from the opposite direction (*Fighting the Mill Creeks* . . . , p. 66): "so at length reached the breaks of Mill Creek. From here we could see for miles over the wild regions of that great canyon."

140. Now known locally as the Narrows. In constructing one of their fire roads, which here follows the old Trail, the Forest Rangers found it necessary to widen the roadbed by filling. Consequently the rocks described by Bruff are no longer visible. Peter H. Burnett and his train from Oregon, who overtook and assisted Lassen on the Lassen Trail in the fall of '48, appear to have made the Trail at this point: "Old Peter Lassen insisted that our wagons should keep on the top of the ridges, and not go down to the water. . . . Our pilots . . . discovered a strip of ground, about thirty feet wide, between the heads of two immense and impassable ravines, and connecting the ridge we were compelled to leave with another. It was like an isthmus connecting two continents. Over this narrow natural bridge we passed in safety" (Burnett, *Recollections*, p. 266).

141. H 3: "elevated about 2,500 feet above the Sacramento Valley. — [Elsewhere "about 3,500." Actually, according to Forest Ranger W. J. Brokenshire, of Mineral, Calif., it is 4,000 feet.] The remainder of the road, down to the valley, — some 20 miles, is of the most broken and rugged character; and in very bad weather is impassable for team. . . . A spring, hollowed out of the bank — and the small rill from it, adds its waters with other similar sources in this deep gulch, to Mill Creek — which enters the Sacramento river, a few miles N. of Lassen's. It is about ¼ mile down, to the spring; but, as the emigrants say, (on account of the acclivity to climb) — 'half a mile up.' The top of this hill is a narrow flat surface — with very open timber on it, the greater part of the small oaks have been cut down, for the animals to browse on, the few oaks remaining being too large & troublesome to fell. . . . The hill is covered with tents wagons, oxen, mules, horses, men, women, and children; some camps are on either side of the road, for several miles back. Here also we rest awhile and feed our mules upon green oak leaves." This was the last command to halt ever given the company by Bruff, their last camp site selected by him.

142. This hill, where Bruff stopped for many weeks and where he acted as host to those of the '49 migration behind him on the Trail, became known, as

his marginal note indicates, as Bruff's Camp. Years later the name appears to have become corrupted into Bluff Camp, perhaps because of its location. In 1932 Mr. A. H. Clough, of Los Molinos, Calif., tentatively identified Bruff's Camp as Bluff Camp, stating that he had heard Bluff Camp called by both names. However, the location of Bluff Camp, as given on some maps, does not fit in relation to Black Rock, and in 1939 we relocated Bruff's Camp to our satisfaction about one mile farther back on the Trail. District Forest Ranger W. J. Brokenshire, long familiar with this region, aided in this and showed us Bruff's spring, then merely the dried-up bed of a mountain brook, the deepened scooped-out place where the emigrants filled their pails and the cattle drank being still discernible, the path to it dipping sharply over the hilltop into the Mill Creek slope. As a further check, Mr. Brokenshire kindly revisited the hilltop with Bruff's drawing of his camp, writing "there is no doubt but that we have located the camp. The site is correct as to topography and cover, and Captain Bruff's description fits the place perfectly."

This hilltop is a natural camp site and was doubtless used from the time the Trail was blazed. It was probably here that Burnett camped with Lassen in the fall of '48: "That evening [after passing the Narrows] a large portion of our party encamped on the summit of a dry ridge, among the intermixed pine- and oak-timber" (Burnett, *ibid.*). Broken pot covers, old trunk hinges and locks, wagon irons, and bits of rusted shovels and other implements rewarded our casual search. More recently the site of Bruff's Camp has been known as Barclay Cabin, or Barclay Spring, from a trapper who built a cabin there and gave his name not only to the immediate vicinity but to the mountain as well, Bruff's Camp being on the slope of Barclay Mountain. The Forest Service expects to erect a permanent marker here when funds become available: "BRUFF'S CAMP (Winter 1849-50) J. G. Bruff, Captain of the Washington City Company, made camp here October 21, 1849. His Company, with the few mules left, pushed on for the Settlements, Bruff remaining to guard the Company goods. At this camp he acted as host to the rear of the emigration, warming, feeding, and clothing many unfortunates. The emigration passed, deep snows came, and still Bruff remained, left by his company. Here and at Obe Field, aided part of the time by two chance acquaintances — William Poyle, a fellow Mason, and an old Missouri hunter named Clough — he passed a winter of exposure and starvation, finally making his way on foot to Lassen's Rancho early in April, 1850."

Bruff's Camp lies within the Lassen National Forest, but in one of those tracts which are privately owned. The magnificent pines, which were monarchs of the forest when Bruff saw them, may therefore soon fall before the lumberman, and the hilltop, undisturbed for the last century, be devastated.

143. These were probably rived from the sugar pines: "*Pinus Lambertiana,* or Sugar Pine. . . . Its grain is so straight and even, that thousands of houses in California are weather-boarded with shingles, which are merely split, without any

other expense or work" (J. M. Bigelow, "Description of Forest Trees," *Pacific Railroad Reports*, IV [1856], 21). The yellow pine is second only to the sugar pine in its straight cleavage and is used in the same way.

144. H 3, Oct. 22: "One of them is regularly stationed some 10 miles ahead, where there is a very deep hollow [Steep Hollow], and steep rugged hills; and it is thought that a trail exists around a narrow ridge — which enters the valley and thence up the gulch on the N.W. of us and reaches their camp, near me. Another is camp-keeper; a third goes back on the road a few miles, and assists the 4th, in driving cattle, horses, &c. down to drink, and afterwards to deep dells, known only to themselves." These fastnesses were the home of the Mill Creeks, or Yahi band of the Yana tribe of Indians — a band made famous in California history by the drama of their extinction — and this, so far as we know, is the earliest mention of their "stealing." "Yana territory stretches between two of California's best known streams, Feather River and Pit River. . . . The region abounds in cliffs and caves, and some of its gorges are picturesque in the extreme. . . . It was through this region, by the way, that a famous emigrant road to the gold-diggings passed. It was known as the Lassen trail (T. T. Waterman, "The Yana Indians," *Univ. of Calif. Pubs. in Amer. Arch. and Eth.*, XIII [1918], 39). In fact, Bruff's Camp was in the very heart of the Yahi territory, not three miles from Black Rock in the gorge below, and it was from Bruff's camp as a base that the destruction of the Yahi was later consummated. In Nov., 1850, the Yahi Indians did steal, from Lassen himself, when, in accordance with customary usage, their village in the gorge below Bruff's camp was burnt, and a number of them killed. That the survivors visited Lassen the next day and made a treaty with him is also recorded in this, the first authentic account of their long martyrdom (H 3, Dec. 14, 1850).

From 1857 to 1865 the Mill Creeks were relentlessly hunted. R. A. Anderson tells of the three successive attacks in which he took part, each launched from the pinery of "old Bluff Camp." "It is but just that I should mention, in closing, the circumstances which raised the hand of the Mill Creek forever against the whites. As in almost every similar instance in American history, the first act of injustice, the first spilling of blood, must be laid at the white man's door (*Fighting the Mill Creeks* . . . [1909], p. 86). "These events were considered at the time to have put an end to the Yahi people. The destruction however was not absolute. . . . They were on Mill Creek as late as 1894. Toward the latter part of their history, at any rate, they were living in the cañon of Deer Creek. . . . The next event is the breaking up of their village. . . . The episode begins with a survey of the lower part of Deer Creek cañon by a party of engineers for the Oro Water, Light and Power Company. . . . About ten o'clock in the morning [Nov. 10, 1908] they suddenly walked into an Indian encampment or village. Two Indians, running as if for their lives, were actually seen — one of them an old man, who was helped along by a middle-aged woman. They escaped over a rock 'slide' and vanished in the direction of the cliffs. This fleeting glance is all we know of these individuals. They have never been seen again. . . . Except for one individual, our account closes here. . . . Nearly three years later, at a slaughter-house four miles from Oroville, 32 miles away, very early one morning there suddenly appeared from nowhere a naked Indian. . . . He was thin, hungry, greatly worn, and of most unusual appearance. . . . For a number of years Ishi lived at the Museum [of the University of California]. Finally . . . he was appointed Museum Helper, so that for the last years of his life he was self-supporting. Here he served as a ready informant. . . . Ishi's life came to an end on March 25, 1916, as a result of . . . tuberculosis" (Waterman, "Yana Indians," pp. 53 *et seq.*). Waterman adds this tribute to the last of the Yahi: "He convinced me that there is such a thing as gentlemanliness which lies outside of all training, and is an expression purely of an inward spirit . . . an innate regard for the other fellow's existence, and an in-born considerateness, that surpassed in fineness most of the civilized breeding with which I am familiar."

145. "The native grape (*Vitis californica* [Benth.]) is often an enemy of individuals standing on stream banks. Climbing to the top of the tree, it sends its runners to the end of every branch and then proceeds to shroud the tree in a drapery of leaves, forming columns of foliage fifty to eighty feet high" (Jepson, *Silva of California*, p. 209).

146. *Cervus columbianus*, Rich., of Newberry: "Black-tailed Deer. Of the deer which I saw in California, living and dead, amounting to some hundreds, all were unmistakably of this species. The general colors, as given by Audubon, the black crescent on the forehead, the slender, dichotomous horns of the male, the tail black above and white below . . . carried down and invisible — all served to mark the species distinctly. . . . In size this species perhaps somewhat exceeds *C. virginianus*. . . . The average weight of the buck may be set down at one hundred and twenty-five pounds" (Newberry, "Zoology," pp. 69-70).

147. H 3: "Two of our five wagons have such weak team that they cannot draw them in to the settlements. Another wagon is so crippled, that I doubt its strength to surmount some difficulties 8 or 10 miles further ahead, which leaves but 2 wagons, with good team, that can possibly get in. The nearest settlements I am told, are a confused mass of thousands of emigrants, in the greatest disorder and suffering. Provissions are scarce, and command extraordinary prices; and the setting in of the wet season has rendered the weather most uncomfortable, while the travelling is horrible. — "

148. H 3: "I subsequently ascertained that only two of the wagons got in; one breaking down some 10 miles below. Their travel from here to Lassens, was accomplished in 3 days — reaching there on the 24th — 32 miles. A small squad remained there, and all the others hurried down the valley."

149. P 6: Lieut. George H. Derby (Top. Eng.), and Capt. Alexander V. Fraser (U. S. Rev. Serv.). Derby (Cullum, *op. cit.*, II, 145): born in Mass.; grad. West Point 1846; attached to the Ordnance Dept., then to the Top. Eng.; served in

Mexican War; was cited at Cerro Gordo, being severely wounded; served in "Department of the Pacific, 1849-52"; on sick leave Dec. 20, 1859-May 15, 1861, when he died aged 38. "Author, under the nom de plume of John Phœnix, of 'Phœnixiana; or, Sketches and Burlesques,' 1856, — and of 'Squibob Papers,' 1860." Member Benicia (Masonic) Lodge No. 5, from which he withdrew to help organize Sonoma Lodge, April 9, 1851 (*Fifty Years of Masonry in California*, I, 113, 130). At the time of Bruff's note, on way back from "Camp Far West," crossing Lassen's Trail Oct. 26. Fraser was sent to the Pacific Coast, commanding brig "C. W. Lawrence," under orders of Treasury Dept. Oct. 24, 1848, to "enter and examine all the different harbors which are now, or which may be, under the jurisdiction of the United States," the collector of customs for Oregon being his chief. Upon the arrival in late Nov. 1849 of Collier, collector for California (the same whom Bruff remarked on, on the Ohio River), Collier became chief. Congress having refused to "extend the naval laws over the [Revenue] service," Fraser lost practically all of his officers, forced to resign because of inadequate salaries and many of his men by desertion and otherwise (*California*, pp. 53-54, 58-59).

150. Fariss and Smith, *op. cit.*, p. 332: "a native of Denmark, and was born in the city of Copenhagen, August 7, 1800. . . . Apprenticed to the trade of blacksmith in his native city. In his twenty-ninth year he emigrated . . . to the United States, and arrived the same year in Boston. After several months' residence in eastern cities, he removed to . . . Katesville, Chariton Co., Mo. In the spring of 1839 he left Missouri in company with twelve others, . . . to cross the Rocky mountains into Oregon. . . . They arrived at the Dalles, Oregon, in October of the same year." Thence Lassen proceeded to California, landing at Fort Ross. "In the spring of 1841 he bought some land near Santa Cruz, where he built a saw-mill. . . . He sold out, taking one hundred mules for pay; and in the fall of 1842 he took them up near Captain Sutter's, and ranched them. He worked at his trade for Captain Sutter, taking his pay in stock. It was while in the service of Captain Sutter, in the summer of 1843, that Lassen, with John Bidwell . . . and James Bruheim, pursued a party of emigrants on their way to Oregon, overtaking them at Red Bluff, and recovering some stolen animals. The northern end of the valley was then entirely unsettled, and Lassen was so pleased with the country that he selected a tract of land, from a map of the region made on their return by Mr. Bidwell, and applied to Governor Micheltorena for a grant of land, which he afterwards obtained. In December, 1843, Lassen started for his new home, but because of high water in the valley he camped at the Buttes until February, 1844, when he arrived at his destination, and built the first civilized habitation north of Marysville. This grant lies on Deer creek, in the county of Tehama. From this time, though others settled around him, Lassen's ranch was the best known and most important point in northern California. It was from this place that Fremont started on his journey from the valley to Oregon, in the spring of 1846, and it was Peter himself who guided Lieutenant Gillespie, a few days later, in search of

the Pathfinder, and overtook him that memorable night on the bank of Klamath lake."

151. "The Wyandots belong to the Iroquoian Family of North American Indians. They are the descendants of the Tionnontates or Tobacco Nation of the Huron Confederacy. . . . In 1649 the Iroquois destroyed the Huron Confederacy. . . . The fragments of the broken tribes fled northward along the Great Lakes. . . . As they increased in strength . . . they gathered about Mackinaw . . . began slowly to descend the Great Lakes, and stopped at Detroit. Here they were Pontiac's best and bravest warriors. . . . On March 17, 1842, they ceded their Ohio lands to the United States. . . . The Wyandots left for the far West in July, 1843, and numbered at that time about 700 souls. . . . Here in the 'Indian Territory' they purchased the land in the fork of the Missouri and Kansas Rivers from the Delawares. They brought with them . . . a well organized Methodist Church, a Free Mason's Lodge, a civil government, and a code of written laws" (*The Provisional Government of Nebraska Territory* . . . , W. E. Connelley, ed., "Proc. and Col. Neb. State Hist. Soc.," [2] III [1899], 1-3).

William Walker, one of the original party to arrange for the emigration of his tribe, became, 1853, provisional governor of Nebraska. In 1849 he promoted the "Wyandott Mining Company," of which he left a record in his journals.

Two of the Wyandots were already in and camping with S. F. McCoy near Lassen's, having "been traveling in close proximity with us for several weeks, and with whom I pushed on ahead" (*Pioneering on the Plains*, J. M. Johnson, ed., 1929). The Wyandot miners, of whom a second company came out in 1850, have left their name to Wyandotte, Butte Co. "This place was first located in 1850, by a party of Wyandotte Indians, who were prospecting for gold. The diggings proved very rich. . . . In 1850, there were at least two hundred miners in the vicinity" (Harry L. Wells, *History of Butte County* [1882], II, 266).

152. H 3: "to E. [Edmonston] the one who carried my flour with him."

153. P 6, Oct. 27, says Boone was "a N. Carolinian, by birth, but a Missourian by adoption," and that "he graduated at Philadelphia." The Dean of the School of Medicine of the University of Pennsylvania writes (Dec. 24, 1935): "I imagine the Dr. Boone you are interested in was Dr. James H. Boon from Northampton, North Carolina, who graduated from our School of Medicine in 1843. . . . James H. Boon's name appears always without a final 'e' in our records. His graduation thesis was on 'Fractures.' In one old book, James H. Boon's address is given as Waterboro, Elleton District, South Carolina. This I believe was his address after he graduated, but whether just after he graduated or where he located years later, I do not know." Dr. Boone was probably accompanied by Dr. T. G. (?) Caldwell, who had joined forces with him a few days before, and whose diary Bruff later found and copied (see 1st ed., Appendix XI). *The Sacramento City Directory*, 1851, p. 44: "Physicians," "J. T. Boone."

154. P 6: "Oct 25th. . . . I took a cup of tea with the supposed pillagers. . . .

They said that Lassin had employ'd them to get out 10,000 shingles. . . . They had a poney, which they said Mr. Bryant (the traveller) had lost, & desired them to hunt for: after a great search, several miles back, they found the saddle; and a little further, the poney. . . . They had just brot him in, & *branded* him." There was only one Bryant "the traveller" to California gold seekers, Edwin Bryant, of Louisville, Ky., author of *What I Saw in California: Being the Journal of a Tour in . . . 1846, 1847*, by Hastings' Cut-off and the Truckee Pass. He captained his own company from Louisville (having returned East in connection with Frémont's court-martial) to California in 1849. His book, of successive editions, was the vade mecum of many a Forty-Niner, and a glimpse of his fast-moving pack train flashes from the pages of many a contemporary journal. Bruff's entry, arresting because it appears in one of his day-by-day unaltered diaries, seems to imply that Bryant traveled the Lassen Trail in '49. But he did not bring in his train by it. Bryant's route was from Independence, Mo., which he left May 8, by South Pass, Sublette's Cut-off, Fort Hall, down the Humboldt, over the Truckee Pass to Johnson's Ranch, which he reached Aug. 3, '49, "among the first to arrive overland this season" (*Alta California*, Aug. 30, 1849). See: Frankfort (Ky.) *Commonwealth*, Oct. 23, 1849, "Death of California Emigrants," recording the drowning of two members of "E. Bryant's California company" at the crossing of Green River; Louisville (Ky.) *Weekly Courier*, Oct. 20, 1849, letter dated "San Francisco, August 17, 1849." And still the Bryant pony in the Mill Creek gorges is left to be explained. It is possible that the freight wagons of Bryant's company might have taken the Lassen Trail, and with them his pony and his wagon containing a gold washer (1st ed., P 8 A, p. 741).

155. H 3: "Knoxville, O."

156. "*1838 — Oct. 12th.* The *Iowa Gazette* mentions the death of Black Hawk [Oct. 3], who was buried, agreeably to his own request, by being placed on the surface of the earth, in a sitting posture, with his cane clenched in his hands. His body was then enclosed with palings, and the earth filled in. . . . He was 71 years of age. . . . His denial of the authority of the men who, in 1804, sold the Sac and Fox country, east of the Mississippi, may have had the sanction of his own judgment, but without it he would have found it no difficult matter to hatch up a cause of war with the United States. . . . And when it broke out in the spring of 1832, the suddenness, . . . the great cruelties, . . . and the comparatively de-fenceless state of the frontier, gave it all its alarming power. . . . The battle of Badaxe annihilated his forces, and he was carried a prisoner to Washington. But he was more to be respected and pitied than blamed. . . . Like him [Pontiac] he sought to restore his people to a position and rights which he did not perceive were inevitably lost" (Schoolcraft, *Personal Memoirs* [1851], pp. 613-14). Black Hawk's remains were stolen, 1839, by a Dr. Turner, who seems to have caused them to be mounted as a skeleton. On protest of Black Hawk's sons to the gov-

ernor of Iowa Territory, they were recovered, but were destroyed by fire in 1855 (*Autobiography . . . of Black Hawk . . .* [1882 ed.], p. 140).

157. Dr. Hervey (sometimes Harvey) remained at Bruff's Camp about three weeks. Nov. 14 Bruff notes that he is "quite smart" now; Nov. 18 he leaves for the Settlements, urged by Bruff. June 6, 1850, Bruff visits the cemetery at Lassen's Rancho: "This spot was chiefly the resting place of the emigrants of last year [1849]. — Side by side are the graves of the brothers Plemmings, that of Dr Marshall, and near it that of poor Dr Harvey. . . . The coyotos (Jackalls), have burrowed into nearly every grave!" (H 3).

158. Rucker, Oct. 17 (*Report*, p. 148): "After starting, we did not get more than three hundred yards before we met eleven packers entirely destitute of provisions, . . . a few minutes after, I met Colonel Pickering and family, and having heard that he was entirely out of provisions, supplied him with some."

159. Henry A. Barling.

160. H 3: "(Old Grant's son was right, when he told me at Fort Hall, that on looking for the cut off trail, he found a considerable extent in the mountains burnt off)."

161. Probably Thos. H. Williams, M. D. Heitman, *op. cit.*, I, 1042: from Md.; Asst. Surg. March 2, 1849; resigned June 1, 1861; Surg., Confederate States Army, 1861-65.

162. Probably Chas. H. Smith. Hamersly, *op. cit.*, Part I, p. 765: born in Va.; Asst. Surg. 1847. Resigned April 25, 1861.

163. Peoples, reporting to Rucker Nov. 9, *Report*, p. 133: "A large camp has been established 30 miles from here, where a valley of grass has recently been found, and where an abundance of game abounds. The families there seem contented, and in no hurry to come in. I feel myself bound to do all I can to get in those I left, but can do nothing for those on this side of them."

164. Perhaps Wm. Russell Smith, landscape painter of note; brought to America from Scotland a boy of 7; worked first as a scene-painter, then on scientific drawings for Sir Charles Lyell and others; settled with his family near Jenkintown, Pa. His daughter Mary is said to have shown marked ability as a painter (H. T. Tuckerman, *Book of the Artists* [1867], 518-21).

165. H 3: "I met the Major and Mr. Hicks, (Cherokee chief) They hurried on." Rucker, sending Hicks in advance to warn and encourage the belated emigrants, gave him a "circular to the emigrants" stating: "The bearer of this, Mr. Hicks, has passed over the whole of the route to Lassen's in the valley of the Sacramento, and will give any information to the emigrants that is necessary for the preservation of their stock or their speedy progress" (*Report*, Oct. 13, 1849, p. 102). "Senora Hicks, who was employed by Maj. Rucker, of the U.S.A., to meet the near emigrants" (letter of J. Mulkey, *Cherokee Advocate*, July 16, 1850). The Mulkeys and Hicks belonged to the Cherokee party captained by Dr. Jeter

Thompson, dispersed by cholera. Apparently Hicks came over the Lassen Trail in an early train.

166. Of Maryland. H 3: "Poor fellow! he had buried his brother on this side the pass mountain."

167. Letter from the St. Louis Co., Rucker's *Report*, p. 105: "To General P. Smith, Commander in Chief in California, or any of his officers," as follows: "We, the undersigned emigrants, respectfully beg leave to represent, that on the night of the 19th October, the Indians drove off nearly all of our stock, oxen and horses, which places us in almost a helpless condition, as we were obliged to throw away a great deal of our provisions and clothing, to enable us to make some progress towards our destination; the season being so far advanced and danger of being caught in a snow storm. The able bodied men of the company feel themselves compelled to remain with the train to render all their assistance to the helpless women and children, of which there are twenty-five in number. The above robbery was committed upon us at Goose Lake, near the head of Pitt's River, on Lauson route. We would, therefore, earnestly solicit that the earliest help should be sent us from the settlements in teams and provisions, as otherwise we consider it impossible to reach the settlements." This was signed by "M. M. Bussard, Capt. of St. Louis Company. Archibald Henly, and family. . . . W. G. Clough. . . . Robt. R. Roberts, and family. . . . Wm. Roberts, and family . . . A. Shepard. . . . John Roberts." Peoples, in camp on Feather River, received this letter, commenting to Rucker (Rucker's *Report*, pp. 118-19): "If you recollect, I expressed to you my fears that the rear would lose their stock, but I never expected that in a company of thirty-two able-bodied men, a guard would be neglected." He ordered the company to hurry forward to his camp. He waited three days for them; they then refused to leave part of their wagons and keep up with his train, carrying their women, children and sick. "A few took my advice, and two or three wagons were left behind, but a majority seemed determined to get in, with mining tools, cooking utensils, beds, etc., or die with their wagons." Oct. 22, "Fourteen miles up Pitt River . . . The Indians swept the cattle off the rear, and the emigrants are in a devil of a fix" (*ibid., et seq.*). Bruff, H 3: "The St. Louis company were very badly treated by the Pitt river indians, who killed and stole all their cattle. The Indians are laying in their winter's supplies and I don't know that they act worse than some other people!"

168. The MS relief rolls for the Lassen Trail include the Ireland family: "Dr. Boskin's fam, Hight, Ireland, Kidwell, Cook (all with f) Tenn."

169. At Lassen's Pass.

170. From Bruff's spring a narrow trail leads down the ridge into Mill Creek cañon, undoubtedly very old and made by animals and Indians.

171. "*Æsculus californica* Nutt., California Buckeye. The California Buckeye is common throughout the Coast Ranges and foothills of the Sierra Nevada. . . . The color, size, and hanging position of the pods explain the name 'California Pear'

given the tree by the gold-seeking pioneers" (Jepson, *Silva of California*, pp. 262-63).

172. H 3: "and the small pidgeon-toed naked feet of an Indian." Bruff here hints again at collusion between the Shingle men and the Indians of Mill Creek in the traffic in animals carried on by the former at Bruff's Camp. It is entirely probable that the Indians were, as Bruff seems to imply, employed by the Shingle men for the purpose of herding their illicit droves.

173. A charming little valley known as the Savercool place, still lush with native grass and wild oats and today the ranch of a half-breed Indian family.

174. Black Rock, famous landmark on Mill Creek. Bruff's description is faithful and his sketch, although diminutive, truly delineates its outline as seen from downstream. It fails utterly, however, to indicate the immensity of the dark bulging bulk of the monolith, which, in spite of the sheer ridge carrying the old Trail above it and in spite of Round Mountain and other towering peaks of Mill Creek Rim on the opposite side of the gorge, dominates this part of Mill Creek cañon. The elevation of Black Rock above Mill Creek is 665 feet, and above the sea 2,662 feet (Forest Ranger W. J. Brokenshire). It was a place of ceremonial and the rallying center of the Mill Creeks, marking their chief village. It was probably here that Lassen fired the village and received tribute in 1850, and that the punitive expeditions of Moak and Anderson and Young extinguished the Mill Creeks in 1865.

175. Possibly *Elymus arenarius*, Linn. of Newberry. "Banks of Pit river, and in many other parts of California. . . . So high that, riding through it, it reached to the top of our heads while seated on our horses. It grows in all parts of California where there are deserted Indian lodges, and is, therefore, called by the inhabitants 'rancheria grass.' The seed is threshed out, and eaten by the Digger Indians" (Newberry, "Botany," *Pacific Railroad Reports*, VI [1855], 92). H 3: "Possibly wild oats." "The foothills and lower slopes of the Sierra for a distance of 500 miles, and the inner Coast ranges for a still greater distance, were likewise in the main carpeted with wild oats" (C. Hart Merriam, "Indian Population of California," *Am. Anthropologist*, n. s. VII [1905], 595).

176. H 3: "I found crushed cones of the pine (piñon), the nut bearing species: and some cracked nuts, where the Indians had been." This was not the piñon of the eastern slopes, but probably the Digger pine of the western foothills, "*Pinus Sabiniana* Dougl., Nut Pine, Digger Pine." "The seeds are as large as large beans and very palatable" (Newberry, "Botany," p. 41).

177. Similar fatal accidents are reported by others; not surprising when one considers that thousands of emigrants passed for miles through the virgin forest, camping in general where night overtook them and naturally taking shelter under the trees. The trail of the emigrants may be traced, in part, by the scarred blazes on the trees and the cuts in the tree boles of the ropes by which they let down their wagons at such places as High Rock Cañon and Horse Creek, while the black-

ened butt of many a stately pine on the Lassen Trail is a reminder of emigrant camp fires.

178. P 6 states that Dr. Boone "had never practised"; H 3, that "Dr Boone was present, and said that the hips and body were so crushed that it was impossible to do anything for them."

179. Dr. Ambrose Crane, who settled in Dubuque, Ia., 1837. "Dr. Crane had a decided inclination for surgery. His ability as a surgeon was soon recognized, and he secured a full share of that practice during the twelve years he remained. He removed to California in 1849" (Wm. Watson, "Early Medical Practitioners," *Historical Lectures* . . . , State Hist. Soc. [1894], pp. 7-8). Bruff, homeward bound on the "California" in 1851, was accosted by Dr. Crane, recovered, prosperous, and returning for his family.

180. H 3: "It is suggested that some persons may have kindly taken them to graze somewhere in the deep glen. . . . As relates to the cattle in the gorges, — I have frequently noted spires of blue smoke, at several points below and above; several miles apart. — A signal from this hill can be seen in those directions: and there are many narrow and deep ramifications of the long rugged gorge: so that it would be almost impossible to overtake any thing below, which had the proper warning from above."

181. Rucker, Oct. 30, at Lassen's Rancho: "Sent Dr. Austin back with instructions to Mr. Peoples to hasten in with the emigrants, telling him that Mr. Davis and others in the valley predicted an early snow-storm, and consequently there was great danger of his being caught in it" (*Report*, p. 150).

182. H 3: "The calamity afforded the demons who are prosperously speculating on the misfortunes of their fellow creatures, to run off an ox belonging to this family, as well as the cow and poney of the Alfords."

183. Dr. O'Brien and family named in relief rolls Oct. 25, as given mules. *The Sacramento City Directory*, 1851, p. 44: "Physicians" . . . "R H McDonald" . . . "J C O'Brien."

184. H 3: "Late in the afternoon I walked back, to visit the Fairchilds and Mrs. O'Brian's families. . . . I found the Fairchilds had a tent and a couple of wagons. — Their family consists of the parents, a son and daughter grown, and several younger children. I am much gratified with the acquaintance of these intelligent, educated, and kind people."

Rucker, Oct. 17 (*Report*, p. 148): "Met the train of Captain McIlvain, . . . and I gave to him, and to the family of Mr. Fairchild, and to several others, two quarters of beef and twenty pounds of bread." Oct. 25, *ibid.*: "issued a number of mules to individuals, to enable them to get their families into the settlement. . . . Amongst them were Dr. O'Brien, Mr. Hall, Mr. Jenkins, Mr. Goodrich and Mr. Fairchild." In the original relief rolls for the Lassen Trail, both H. Fairchild and R. Fairchild appear.

185. Peoples, Sacramento, Dec. 12 1849 (Rucker's *Report*, p. 122): "There was

scarce a tent or wagon to be found on the road [near Steep Hollow], which ten days before was literally lined with them. The few persons in the hills had determined to stay until they could get their wagons in, as they were satisfied no shelter could be obtained at Lassen's. Game was abundant all around them, and they were probably better off there, until the roads dry up."

186. H 3: "I have written by them, to Davis and Co. — stating my necessities, and asking aid." H 3, Nov. 5: "Rodgers [of the government relief] promised to come out soon, and succor me. — He took in a note for me."

187. H 3: "Which she told me, she had picked up on the road." Considering the difficulty of transportation, the overland emigrants started out with an amazing number of books, most of them discarded long before the journey's end. Among them Gen. John Wilson, often mentioned by Bruff, brought a legal library which he got as far as Fandango Valley. There he cached it, to the ruin of the books.

188. H 3: "being the remains of a once large Company. . . . I believe the company was called the Atchinson Coy."

189. H 3: "Hundreds I have had the pleasure of thus assisting. Indeed, I am kept busy, day and night, providing for the wants of the unfortunate. I keep up a large fire, have plenty of cooking utensils, axes, &c. and wagon-chambers for lodgers. I have no food for them, but plenty of coffee, and a good strong pot full is ever at their service."

190. H 3: "Mrs. G. once kept a Seminary in St. Louis, she is mistress of several languages & sciences, particularly botony, and is a considerable poetess, & author." The name appears several times on the relief rolls from "Mo.," but without initials or given name.

191. H 3: "late of the U. S. Mint, Phila". May be an error for "Robinson"; Rucker, Oct. 17 (*Report*, p. 148): "Also furnished Dr. Robinson, a gentleman lame with the scurvy, with a mule." The Mint at Philadelphia finds no mention of Dr. "Robertson."

192. H 3: "One of the travellers told me that he knew the Jenkins folks, and had travelled with them on the Platte". . . . "The Rev. Mr. L." tried to kill Jenkins, so as to "abscond with Mrs. J. and her daughter, and turn off to the Salt Lake settlement. . . . I pity the old gentleman, he has passed under the living[?] *arch*." All seem to have been touched by the miseries of the Jenkins family. Rucker, *Report*, p. 148: "Four miles on the road, met Thomas Jenkins and family entirely destitute of provisions; gave them a hundred pounds of beef, some bread and rice."

193. Thus Bruff made special efforts for the General's comfort — to which the General was doubtless accustomed. His arrival in San Francisco was awaited with interest in government circles. The fact that his was one of the belated trains in the Sierra gave impetus to the relief: "The military authorities were the more moved to this act of humanity because General Wilson, United States Indian agent, was among the sufferers" (Fariss and Smith, *op. cit.*, p. 87).

Nov. 1, Peoples reached the upper Feather River valley, "where I found all the rear of the emigration with General Wilson, family, and escort. . . . I urged the emigrants to move on, and also General Wilson. To the General I gave two mules to haul on his family carriage, and argued the propriety of his abandoning his wagons and packing his mules lightly. He did not agree with me" (Rucker's *Report*, p. 120).

It was not Wilson's first disagreement with the military. On Goose Creek he dismissed his escort, and under the guidance of Gen. Joel Palmer, of Lieut. Hawkins' train, took the Lassen Trail. In the first range of the Sierra he suffered the theft of 22 mules by Indians. To this point he had kept rolling his "waggons loaded with provisions & such of our substantial household property as we thought would have enabled us to go to housekeeping." In Fandango Valley he "caached" half his goods, among them his "Law Books." Now a second disaster: "That night," continues Peoples, "he lost all of his mules in the storm, whilst mine were safely sheltered in the valley." Wilson himself: "All died when we were overtaken by the snow . . . , leaving us on foot with part of our train 80 miles apart, . . . and we were left on foot & had to encamp till I sent my son [Wm. Henry] through the snow & rain to the settlements for animals to carry my wife & daughters." Here in a second cache was left the "balance of our goods."

P7: NOVEMBER 6, 1849–MARCH 16, 1850

1. Apparently Dr. Austin reported for Peoples to Rucker on the Relief: "Mr. Rogers and Dr. Austin will state to you many particulars which I have not time to put down" (Rucker's *Report*, p. 134).

2. Rucker, Oct. 25 (*Report*, p. 149): "Killed several beeves to-day, and issued to families who were in want, and to persons sick with scurvy, of whom there are a great many. Also issued a number of mules to individuals, to enable them to get their families into the settlement. . . . Amongst them were Dr. O'Brien, Mr. Hall, Mr. Jenkins, Mr. Goodrich and Mr. Fairchild."

3. M. M. Bussard, Capt., St. Louis Co., whose cattle were driven off by the Indians near Goose Lake, on the night of Oct. 19 (Rucker's *Report*, pp. 105, 118-19, 130-32). To this company belonged Warren G. Clough and the several Roberts families, who appear in our account later.

4. Part of the emigration brought in by the Relief. Nov. 9 Peoples reported to Rucker: "On the morning of the 4th I started with all the women, children and helpless men in the valley, and intended to reach Deer Creek that night, but . . . I was forced to encamp a mile this side of Bute Creek. . . . Here it snowed all

night, and the next day [Nov. 5] it was with the utmost difficulty that we could get over Deer Creek valley. Every man was on foot, including myself, and have been since our departure from Feather river, and not only the animals in use, but every man pushing against the hinder parts of the wagons. In that way, a few hours before night set in on the 5th, we ascended the big hill this side of the valley. . . . When I aroused the camp at four A.M. [Nov. 6], . . . I ordered every mule that could stand up to be saddled, and then called upon such women as could ride to mount and start ahead at once. . . . Eleven women and some half dozen children started with me, but the storm became so furious, and the snow so deep 'at the Springs in the road,' that, finding some abandoned tents and wagons, I caused all but six young ladies to dismount, as I saw it was impossible that the young ones could stand the ride. I left them with every particle of provision I had brought from the other camp, and killed a large beef, so that they could remain comfortable for ten days. Eight or ten miles from that camp, the snow suddenly disappeared, and gave place to a violent rain, which came down so fast, with an east wind, that we could neither see the road, nor drive the mule, and we were forced to encamp in the rain, without food for ourselves or animals" (Rucker's *Report*, pp. 132-33). Evidently they reached Bruff's Camp the following morning, Nov. 7.

5. H 3: "all on foot." James D. Lyon, a member of that company (*Detroit Advertiser*, Feb. 22, 1850): "The Rangers left all their wagons in the mountains between the dividing ridge and the valley."

6. H 3: "Some of these men had a scrape with the Pitt river Indians, — assisting Capt Peoples in an attack on a village, which they destroyed, and killed & wounded several of the savages." Probably the attack of Oct. 26. Peoples says (Rucker's *Report*, p. 119): "Early on the morning of the 26th [Oct.], so soon as it was light enough to distinguish objects, a band of Indians charged our camp [in Big Valley], and although fired upon by the sentinels, succeeded in getting off my whole stock of beef-cattle. Fortunately, the ground I had selected was favorable to us, and by mounting our animals without saddles or bridles, we recaptured them in less than half an hour. . . . The emigrant wagons [St. Louis Company] all came in before ten o'clock, and at 12 o'clock at night, the Indian fires blazed up simultaneously from every elevated point. Believing that they intended to make a grand and last effort to drive off our stock and that of the emigrants, and seeing them plainly around the nearest fire to us, I sent out a party to attack and drive them off. . . . Six were killed dead at the first fire of the rifles and carbines, and a considerable number wounded by the discharge of holster and revolving pistols. Those who escaped fled to the other fires with the news of their disaster, and soon all the hills were wrapt in a mantle of darkness."

7. H 3, Nov. 8: "(Mr Poile and his friend Allen will stay a day or so.)" This is the "small party" of the previous day.

8. Peoples to Rucker, Nov. 9, 1849: "Major, you can form no conception of

the road, for 20 miles back [from Lassen's and Davis' Ranchos], wagons are buried in the mud, up to the bed, and cattle [dead] lying all around them. It is impossible to ride the strongest horse along it, and if they deviate one foot from the road, they are irretrievably lost" (Rucker's *Report*, p. 133).

9. Lieut. Derby found the roads impassable: "We reached Sacramento City on the 2d of November, and encamped upon the outskirts during a tremendous storm of wind and rain. . . . The whole of the valley, I found upon my return, had been made a perfect quagmire by the recent rains, and several wagons had been lost on the same day in the attempt to go to Frémont from Sacramento City" (*Report of the Sec. of War for 1849-50*, p. 14).

10. Wm. Henry, the oldest son. He attached himself to a small party, one of whom was Wm. Swain, a Wolverine Ranger, who describes their travel (journal and letters, 1849-51, MS, Coe Collection, Yale Library): "Night found us on the Mts in a forrest of Mighty Pine & Fer." When morning came five of them set out with packs on back, "as fast a[s] cord and muscle would carry us, rising at very short distances elevation after elevation of the Mt Range, & passing, at every step, the remnants of once fine trains, fleeing, like ourselves, from the dangers of the increasing storm. Never shall I forget the scenes of that day. The clouds were dark, & lowering on the Mt tops. The snow descended, as it descends only in a Mountainous region & the thick foliage of the dark, Mammoth Fer & pines, were loaded, & bowed down, with snowy crescents. . . . Snow fell damp & melted fast, when fallen. . . . During the whole afternoon of that day our party waded through 2 ft snow with no path alternately leading an hour each, guided by the blazes on trees on the sides of the road while the fresh track of the Grizzly bear plainly told the character of our Mt Natives." The next day, as they descended the mts., torrential rains fell. Five of the party, including Swain and Wilson, camped that night on the Sacramento plain, wet and fireless. "We arrived at Antelope creek 8 ms from Lawsons at light we found it not fordable. . . . Gen. Willson's son Cannon & myself with our clothes lashed to shoulders forded the Stream with setting poles; none of the rest would attempt it; it was the hardest job I ever had, when I stepped onto the opposite shore I thought the flesh would drop from my bones as high the water came to my waist." This, the day of their arrival at Lassen's Rancho, Swain gives as Nov. 8. At breakfast time three days later, Wm. Henry is at Bruff's Camp, on his way back.

11. H 3: "A lady came up on a mule, she was thin and sallow, and had her head tied up in a handkerchief. — Who should it prove to be but the witty and pretty Mrs. Chandler, of Boston, whom I conversed with at the camp of the Wolverine Rangers, far back on the Humboldt."

12. Rucker, Oct. 19: "Before getting to our camp to-day, met several destitute families, whom I supplied with beef and bread, amongst them those of the widow Taylor, Mr. Gage, Mr. Henly, Mr. Mara and others" (*Report*, p. 149). "Archi-

bald Henly, and family" head the list of the St. Louis Company (*ibid.*, p. 105). This may refer to Capt. Henly or to his brother.

13. "Pinole is an Aztec word, and is applied to any kind of grain or seeds, parched and ground" (Bancroft, *Native Races of the Pacific States*, I [1874], 374).

14. H 3: "I am informed that the proprietors of many wagons, compelled to leave in the rear, till they can procure teams to haul them in, have found them rifled of their contents; and that the articles, principally clothing and dry-goods, are scattered for miles in wet and mud. Two men, known as belonging to a camp near mine, have been seen, a few miles back, to heavily pack mules and poneys, from a wagon on the road, and drive them down into the upper end of the Mill Creek gorge. The shingle men?"

15. H 3: "with some men of the Relief party." The family consisted of his wife, Wm. Henry, the eldest son, just returned from Lassen's, Micajah D., a law student (still in the rear), Bob, a lad of nine, and the two daughters, Mary Eliza and Susan, old enough to be in the social whirl of San Francisco that winter. His guide, Gen. Joel Palmer, and the 14 teamsters who comprised his escort, were no longer with him. The Wilsons had reached Bruff's Camp after much suffering. "On the 30th day of Oct at night," the General writes to Abiel Leonard in Missouri, "it commenced snowing and raining on us in the mountains. It snowed and rained alternately for 14 days and nights on us ("California Letter of John Wilson," p. 202). As for the animals brought back by Wm. Henry from Lassen's, "the roads being impassible they were of little use as travelling out there exhausted them so that out of 8 we lost 3 before we got to the settlement, & my whole family had to walk on foot, . . . some of us not having a 'change of raiment' to put on wading through snow 2½ feet deep, & roads with no bottom that a mule could reach, & remain head above ground" (San Francisco Report).

16. Cox, Symington's son-in-law, is mentioned by Rucker, Oct. 12: "The recipients [of beef] were the families of Messrs. Goddard, Cox, Bowen, Bell, Hanson, Mane and Burgess" (*Report*, pp. 146-47). See Sept. 4 for grave of Samuel A. Fitzzimmons, dead Aug. 25, 1849, of a bowie-knife wound inflicted by George Symington.

17. On Nov. 18, "the brothers Seymour" become "The Seymours. . . .The old man has been a Santa Fé trader: he has a son, 2 lads, a wagon & carryall; 3 oxen and a horse." These same Seymours, father and son, appear later (Sept. 6, 1850). The original rolls of those helped on the Lassen Trail in the fall of 1849 include "Mr. Seymour & party," "Seymour & f." Again, Bruff is told (Nov. 30, 1850) of the death of Seymour "who travelled with my company, from Grand Island, of the Platte." This was E. Sanford Seymour, author of the *Emigrant's Guide to the Gold Mines*, a transcript of which he furnished Bruff (see 1st ed., Appendix VIII). How long this Seymour traveled with the Washington City Company is nowhere stated. Again (July 3, 1851), Bruff mentions Mr. Seymour,

United States mail agent, who was a fellow passenger on the "California" for Panama. Apparently none of these Seymours are related except those comprising the party at Bruff's Camp.

18. Rucker, Oct. 18: "This morning, before leaving camp, issued to William Neal and family, Messrs. Lawrence, Vestry, Courtney, Fisher, and others, 120 pounds of beef and twenty pounds of bread" (*Report*, p. 148). Bruff's "Vestal" is probably the "Vestry" assisted by Rucker.

19. Nov. 9, Peoples, at Davis' Rancho, wrote Rucker asking for instructions. Peoples, waiting for orders, sent Todd: "On the morning of the 13th [Nov.] I started Mr. Todd, with five men and a wagon-master to bring in those whom I had left in the snow" (Rucker's *Report*, p. 121). Bruff says "Ford."

20. "The amount of suffering on the latter part of the route was almost incalculable. . . . Sights, the thought of which, would make the blood chill in any *human* breast. After I left the train [on the Lassen Trail, west of Fandango Pass], I saw men sitting or lying by the road side, sick with fevers or crippled by scurvy, begging of the passers by, to lend them some assistance; but no one could do it. . . . Consequently they were left to a slow lingering death in the wilderness" (James D. Lyon, *Detroit Advertiser*, Feb. 22, 1850).

21. H 3 almost gossips over the departure of the Shingle men, presumably for the Settlements: "One of their wagons passed, on the road, close by my camp: — it was very heavily laden, and drawn by 6 yoke of fine oxen. I was afterwards informed, that they drove another heavily laden wagon, drawn by 8 yoke of good oxen, . . . to the road beyond my camp; and some distance beyond, . . . they drove up several packed animals."

22. H 3: "I find much entertainment in transcribing my rough notes, and retouching my sketches."

23. From Joel Palmer's account of the wounding of Brown, of Wilson's escort, we infer that Micajah stayed behind with that unfortunate man, in the Feather River valley. H 3: "A son of Genl Wilsons came in from the rear. I addressed a note by him, to his brother, at Lassen's rancho, soliciting some provisions and 2 yoke of oxen by some convenient opportunity."

24. Nov. 19, '49, J. D. B. Stillman wrote from Sacramento ("Seeking the Golden Fleece," *Overland Monthly*, XI [1873], 297): "Now the roads are so muddy that wagons are abandoned where they are mired, by men who have come down from the mines for supplies for their companies, and are unable to return."

25. H 3: "Which I refused. — I told him that I was unfortunately beleaguered here for the present, with bad weather, severe rheumatic attacks preventing me from travelling any distance; and awaiting for team, to save my writings, sketches, instruments, minerals, &c. And as there had been an accumulation around me of numerous articles to alleviate the wants and sufferings of the emigrants, added to which were comfortable sleeping places, a good fire, and plenty of hot strong coffee, these were at their disposal. It was all I had to offer."

26. Wilson (San Francisco Report) says: "Before I separated from Capt M[orris], we both felt the absolute necessity of a guide on the waters of Goose Creek, some two hundred miles west of Salt Lake met Lieut Hawkins conducting a government train from Oregon to Fort Hall, there was with him a Mr Joel Palmer, who is perhaps the most efficient guide that has travelled the plains, whom Lieut Hawkins highly recommended & as he had just come over the road, we employed him."

Palmer, Wilson's new guide, was as notable and colorful a person as his employer. He was a Canadian by birth (1810), of Quaker parentage. As a young man, he migrated to Bucks County, Pa., where he married. Shortly he moved to Indiana, where he was farmer, canal contractor, and member of the state legislature. In 1845 he went to Oregon. The following year he brought out his family, in the same train with Thornton and Burnett, over Applegates' southern route. He was just in time to lend a hand in the Cayuse crisis, for the attempted adjustment of which he was appointed by the Provisional Government Superintendent of Indian Affairs for Oregon (1847). He also published that year his *Journal of Travels over the Rocky Mountains to the Mouth of the Columbia River Made during the Years 1845 and 1846*. 1848 saw him in Burnett's wagon-train from Oregon to California. It was this trip, by Lassen's road, and for the latter part of it in company with Lassen, that especially qualified Palmer to act as Wilson's guide over the same trail to the same destination, Lassen's Ranch. Palmer had returned, after mining on the Yuba, to Oregon, and in 1849 was guiding Lieut. Hawkins to Fort Hall when he met Wilson's west-bound company near Goose Creek, and turned back with the latter. He presumably had some part in the very sudden transference of two-thirds of Lassen's ranch to General Wilson and himself. He did not, however, become an active partner in the deal, but returned at once to Oregon. From 1853 to his removal from office in 1857, he was Superintendent of Indian Affairs for Oregon, and, with Governor Stevens of Washington Territory, negotiated important treaties with the northwestern Indian tribes. He was also a member of the state legislature. He died in 1879. (See Bancroft, *History of Oregon*, I, 359, *infra*; II, 82 *infra*; *Chronicles*, II, 553-57.)

27. From Palmer's own recollections in "Wagon Trains" (MS, Bancroft Library), he was not in the rear, but present in person, taking young Micajah down to his family. He says that after three weeks' stay with Brown, the injured man of Wilson's party, he "could not wait any longer. . . . The old lady [presumably Mrs. Wilson] had given me special charge about the boy and I had to take care of him. We just took our little duds, each of us with a blanket and some little grub and started."

28. "In most parts of California acorns were and still are the staff of life. They are pounded into meal, which is leached to take out the bitter taste and then boiled in baskets by means of hot stones, forming a thick jelly-like nutritious mush. Acorns are also made into bread. The yield is not constant, having cycles of

abundance and scarcity, but since in most localities half a dozen or more kinds occur together, and since all of these rarely if ever fail the same year, an absolute failure is probably unknown" (Merriam, *op. cit.*, p. 596).

29. Rucker's *Report* (p. 105) has a letter to "General P. Smith, Commander in Chief in California, or any of his officers," from the St. Louis Co., signed by the captain and 28 members of the company, among whom are "W. G. Clough," "Robt. R. Roberts, and family," and "Wm. Roberts, and family." It states that on Oct. 19, at Goose Lake, the Indians drove off most of the co. stock, obliging them to throw away food and clothing, that there are about 25 women and children in the company, and that they are in need of assistance.

The Roberts families passed on a few miles beyond Bruff's Camp and built a cabin, where they spent several months (now known as Obe Field). Bruff, almost in extremity, later joined them. Rucker's MS relief rolls for the Lassen Trail list "Rev. R. R. Roberts & Lady," and D. R. Leeper (*Argonauts of 'Forty-Nine*, . . . [1894], p. 72) speaks of "Reverend William Roberts and family," snowed in during the winter of 1849-50 near Steep Hollow. Apparently father and one son were ministers of the gospel — remarkable, considering their subsequent activities, as recorded by Bruff.

30. Rucker, Oct. 15: "Before leaving camp this morning, supplied the families of Messrs. H. Robinson, S. Burroughs, W. W. Ferguson, with a yearling beef, some bread and rice" (*Report*, p. 148).

31. A. Shepard signed the petition of the St. Louis Co. (Rucker's *Report*, p. 105).

32. *Felis Concolor*, Linn. The American Panther of Newberry. "The cougar is perhaps as common in California and Oregon as east of the mountains, and is essentially the same animal" (Newberry, "Zoology," p. 36).

33. James Brown, a Canadian by birth, said to have come to Oregon in '49; and to have lost his right arm in a gun accident on the way. Of this accident Joel Palmer, Wilson's guide over the Lassen Trail, in whose party Brown was: "On that trip was when this one, armed Brown lost his arm." Crossing a stream — the name forgotten — "Brown, who had a little short barralled shot-gun, shot himself. . . . A charge of shot went right through his arm" ("Wagon Trains"). In Feather River valley, Palmer and four other men, including Wilson's son, Micajah, staid with Brown, while Wilson's train went on. It was then late Oct. A month later, Brown and three attendants passed Bruff's Camp on their way to the Valley. Brown perhaps went on to Oregon with Palmer, who sailed from San Francisco. "One-Arm Brown" became a familiar pioneer figure in the Indian Service in Oregon, serving under Palmer, then Indian Supt.

34. See Dec. 27-28, for the arrival of White and party, hungry, frostbitten, and half demented, at Bruff's Camp. Peoples to Rucker, Oct. 24 (Rucker's *Report*, p. 129): "I sent a party yesterday to the St. Louis train. . . . There is a man by the name of White, who refused to leave with them. He was picking up everything that was thrown away, and having with him two years' provisions, will probably

stay at the foot of the mountains, and establish a ranch. Of course I shall pay no attention to him."

35. Bruff refers elsewhere to Petrie as a kind-hearted man, and apparently Petrie endorsed this idea. *The Sacramento Transcript*, Dec. 17, 1850, contains an amazing editorial, about a column and a half long, in which the relief of the emigration of '49 is credited to Petrie's personal exertions and private expenditures in entirety!

36. This was written the day before Willis' departure, when Bruff had no reason to doubt the man's integrity or faithfulness. As Willis deliberately betrayed his comrades by neither bringing nor sending the help which was essential to their safety, Bruff's relation would tend to show that his treachery was premeditated.

37. *Melanerpes Formicivorus* of Newberry. "This beautiful bird, the rival and representative of the red-headed woodpecker . . . is called '*carpentero*' by the Mexican and Spanish Californians, and is well known by the residents as the bird which pierces the bark of oaks and pines with holes, in which he inserts acorns, thus storing them up for future use" (Newberry, "Zoology," p. 90). The Downy Woodpecker (*Dryobates pubescens Gairdneri* [Audubon]), probably, the smallest of California woodpeckers, is Bruff's "very minute dusky one." From subsequent mention (Jan. 19, 1850), Bruff's jay was really a jay.

38. H 3: "He says, that only about three miles below, in the gorge, we know that there is a camp of indians. — Their character we do not know; and their tracks have been seen ascending the side of the gorge towards the camp, not half a mile off."

39. In the light of Willis' conduct, Bruff concluded later that the motive, from the beginning, must have been personal, material gain.

40. Bruff was not the first, of course, to be marooned in these mountains. The experiences of one such party offer striking similarities to his. In the late fall of 1844 the so-called Murphy, Stevens, Townsend party from Kanesville, piloted by Caleb Greenwood, reached the vicinity of Truckee (Donner) Lake. Moses Schellenberger, a lad of eighteen years, was left for weeks, sick, in the mountains, to be rescued later. He passed a terrible winter in his cabin. As he said, "I had two objects in life, one was to kill food, the other was to kill time. I thought the snow would never leave the ground, and the few months I had been living there seemed years, when, one evening, a little before sunset, about the last of February, as I was forlornly standing a short distance from my cabin, doing nothing (there was nothing to do), I thought I saw the form of a man coming toward me." This proved to be a comrade, returned to rescue him (W. F. Swasey, *Early Days and Men of California* [1891], p. 171, quoting Schellenberger, whom he knew).

41. "Seneca Snake Root. This root possesses more virtues than any one used in medicine. . . . It is now more than eighty years since its virtues were made known to physicians, by Doctor John Tenant, who learned its use from the Senagaroes tribe of Indians. By rewarding them liberally, he obtained their secret

remedy against the bite of the rattlesnake, which *he* called snake root on that account" (*Gunn's Domestic Medicine*, pp. 622-23). Bruff was familiar with this work, as a notation in one of his notebooks attests.

42. H 3: The cones are "of a spindle-shape," weighing from 2 to 6 lbs.

43. H 3: "It is astonishing what quantities of this peculiar meat one devours in a day. A camp-kettle is boiled with about ¼ peck of *boned beef*, for each meal; which we generally consume, and if any is left, it is eat intermediately, — for we are hungry in an hour after filling to distention. — So that I conjecture, . . . that there is the slightest nutrition derived from it; but it prevents the painful collapse of the stomach — called starving; and affords action, at all events, for the digestive functions."

44. "*Sciurus fossor*, Peale. California gray squirrel. This large and handsome squirrel inhabits the pine forests of all parts of California in which pine forests exist. . . . It is eminently a tree squirrel, scarcely descending to the ground but for food and water, and it subsists almost exclusively on the seeds of the largest and loftiest pine known, *P. Lambertiana*, the 'sugar pine' of the western coast. . . . These cones would be unmanageable by the squirrel in the tree, and he has the habit so common in the family of dropping them to the ground, where he can dissect them at leisure" (Newberry, "Zoology," pp. 51-52).

45. Dr. Caldwell, who came up to Bruff's Camp in company with Dr. Boone and wife on Oct. 25. Dr. McLane, Caldwell's comrade, died on the Lassen Trail, near Little Dixie Valley. Bruff apparently forgets that on Oct. 12 he passed McLane's grave and copied the inscription. See 1st ed., Appendix XI, for Bruff's transcription of Caldwell's journal from Missouri to California, together with a fragmentary record from Mud Lake to Fandango Pass by McLane.

46. Hunger is elemental, to a degree hard for us to comprehend, who know no more of it perhaps than the irritation consequent upon the occasional delay or omission of a meal. Emigrants and explorers understood better its driving force. "Every emigrant with whom I have conversed," wrote J. W. Revere (*Tour of Duty in California* [1849], p. 364), "admits that those who cross the Rocky Mountains, in emigrant wagons, with their families, undergo more hardships than they could ever have imagined possible. One of my company, who was a Rocky Mountain emigrant, once gave me an account of his terrible sufferings from hunger, during a period of twenty-two days. All that time he had nothing to eat except scraps of buckskin, and he never gave up his gun, and kept steadily on to the westward. He told me that at last, 'after looking hard for a buck,' he spied an Indian, and immediately gave chase. 'And, sir,' said he, 'had I caught him, I should have slain and eaten him, as soon as if he had been a deer.' " But Bruff was made of other stuff. See April 8 and April 9, 1850, for his reaction when put to the test. He could not even eat his dog. "Must I then eat my faithful watch? — My poor little Nevada, who has shared my sufferings? — for one meal, and then die regretting it? — I will not."

47. White and Clark, the Irishman, appear to have been two of the party referred to by Bruff Nov. 29, 1849: "a man named White & 6 or 7 Germans, who were determined to winter on Pitt river." "White & companions (footmen)" are on Rucker's list of those receiving relief. "T. Clark" also appears.

48. Pit River Indians, of the Atsugewi division, south of the Pit. There were few winter villages of this group among the mountains; but one is mentioned by Kniffen on a lake east of Cassel; and it is evident that a lake location afforded food that could not be found on the wind- and snow-swept plains that constituted the bulk of Atsugewi territory, descending from the Sierra crest to the east.

49. H 3: "Rises from the Mill Creek gorge."

50. H 3, same date: "We were securing our old abode, to prevent wolves entering it easily, when a dog belonging to Roberts, (which followed Clough up), looked to the rear, and barked.— And we saw a stranger approaching. — He had a heavy knapsack, a bundle on his arm, and a rifle on his shoulder. — He came up, and proved to be a German, and one of those whom Elliott thought must have died in Deer Valley."

51. Peter J. Davis, one of Lassen's party from Missouri in '48. Apparently Davis leased from Daniel Sill (who had previously purchased it from Lassen) the property known to emigrants at that time as Davis' Rancho. Bruff, H 3, April 14, 1850: "This place is a level open spot, on which are 2 low, narrow adobe houses, and a large corral or horse pen — Remains of a rude mill for grinding wheat, and a choked up well. — It was the first settlement Lassen made in the valley, some 14 [6] years ago — After which he built the houses in which he now lives, and disposed of this site for a valuable consideration, to a Mr Sill, (another old settler). — His agent leased it to Davis, and that lease has expired." Bancroft (*History of California*, II, 776) says Davis, a native of N. C., came to Calif. in '48 and mined on Feather River in '48-50.

52. Bancroft, *History of California*, IV, 751: "M. [Myers] (Wm), 1848, associate of Lassen in Tehama Co., who prob. came earlier; alcalde in '49." According to Bruff (March 10, 1850), Myers with his family accompanied Lassen on his return from Missouri in 1847 (1848), being of the first party to travel the Lassen Trail from Goose Lake southward, and succored by the gold-seeking Oregonians captained by Peter Burnett. "In 1847, Uncle Peter [Lassen], crossed the Plains to Missouri . . . and again returned (in 1848,) to this country, with several families, among whom was William Myers, the pioneer of Red Bluff, and now a farmer in this neighborhood" ("Peter Lassen. Supplementary Biographical Particulars," *Hutchings' Illustrated California Magazine*, III [1859], 512).

53. Prices in settlements and diggings were staggering to many. Stillman ("Seeking the Golden Fleece," p. 232) on the cost of living at Lassen's and thereabouts, Oct., '49: "Hundreds were coming in daily from the mountains, sick, destitute, and almost starved. They met here with harpies to prey upon them, and they were often compelled to sell their teams for food enough to last them down to Sacra-

mento City. Quinine was in great demand, and they charged $1 a grain!" The accompanying bill from Messrs. Davis, Green, & Ely, Jan. 2, 1850, shows no preferential treatment between Masons. "Friend Bruff, Your friends at this Ranche sympathise with you in your present misfortunes, and have returned to you, by our *brother* Poile, some immediate relief; and promise you, that as soon as the roads will allow, a team to travel, — that you and your valuables shall be brought in. In the mean time keep a stout heart, and believe us *worthily*

Your Brothers"

(Signed) Davis, Green, & Ely

54. *Lynx Rufus*, American Wild Cat of Newberry. "The wild cat is a very common animal in California and Oregon" (Newberry "Zoology," p. 36).

55. H 3: "He is robust and strong, accustomed from infancy to a hard life, and is an excellent rifleman: although well advanced in years."

56. The cones of the sugar pine (*P. Lambertiana*). "The seeds are edible. . . . Although very small they are more valued by the native tribes than the large seeds of the Digger Pine on account of their better flavor" (Jepson, *Silva of California*, p. 71). The sweet resin, for which this tree is named, they also ate.

57. Nevada, Bruff's "faithful little watch," through the long weeks in the mountains apprized him of the approach of dangerous animals and in his solitude afforded companionship not to be lightly discounted.

58. *Cyanocitta Stelleri*, Steller's jay, probably. Newberry says: "Steller's jay is, in size, form, and habits, the western representative of the blue jay (*C. cristata*) of the eastern States. . . . It is almost exclusively confined to the hilly and mountainous districts, choosing in preference those covered with forests of pine" (Newberry, "Zoology," p. 85).

59. Bruff's courtesy to the Wilson family (Nov. 12, 1849) had met with a thankless return. "Young Wilson" was Wm. Henry, Gen. Wilson's eldest son. The General, having purchased a third interest in Lassen's ranch the day after his arrival, set sail with his wife, daughters, and younger sons in a whaleboat for Sacramento (*Alta California*, Dec. 15, 1849), but "Wm. remained at our ranch" ("California Letter of John Wilson," p. 204).

60. John Boit, an officer on the "Columbia" under Captain Gray when he explored the Columbia River, records a similar experience ("Remarks on the Ship *Columbia's* voyage from Boston," *Proc.*, Mass. Hist. Soc., LIII [1920], 243): "We kept the Crew continually supplied with Spruce beer, and their breakfast and supper was Tea boild from the green *Spruce* boughs sweetned with Molasses. Perhaps this method kept the Scurvy off." Wm. Kelly, who reached "Middle Creek diggings" in Dec., 1849, found that "sickness prevailed to an alarming extent, particularly land scurvy. . . . An old mountaineer stepped into the gap, whose simple remedies, administered without fee or reward, brought about very beneficial and salutary results. . . . He interdicted the use of tea or coffee, allowing in their stead a decoction of sassefras and the leaves of the spruce, or (as it is there called)

the hemlock-tree, which made very palatable substitutes, and proved their sanitary efficacy in scurvy in every instance in which they were regularly used" (*Excursion*, II, 151-53).

61. Poyle was instructed to contact Capts. J. W. Schaumburgh, Geo. Derby, Alex. V. Fraser; Dr. Austin; Dr. Boone; Andrew B. Gray, U.S. Surveyor; Col. Frémont, and others. None of the letters appears in the Bruff papers we have examined, but the draft for all was carefully copied by Bruff into Supplementary Notebook B. The "small memorandum book of copious references" — P 8 A — is written in ink still bright and clear, only a portion of the inscription on the cover being obliterated, perhaps by the wet finger and thumb of Poyle, on his journey down the flooded valley of the Sacramento. The draft of the letter sums up his reasons for remaining in the hills, and his treatment by his company, both pertinent to the record:

"I hereby take great pleasure in introducing my worthy and well-tried friend, (& brother) William Poile. A series of circumstances & misfortunes have detained me here, and for upwards of two months, I have been too feeble to travel any distance. I am now much recruited, and hope in a few weeks being able to get in. Mr. P. can relate our trials together in the mountains, &c. He bears this in to seek aid for me as speedily as practicable; I trust in all confidence to his friendship, energy, & discretion, in any matters connected with this errand. The succor & friendly assistance I need, are — 1st — Sufficient provissions for 3 of us, for, say 2 months; means of transportation, or preferable — a team of Oxen. They could bring out the supplies, & then take in, when I can travel, my wagon, containing tents, bedding, saddles, clothing, arms, &c, camp utensils, books, papers, instruments, &c. and a mineralogical collection [followed by the words "through the route," crossed out]. Credit for the supplies & contingencies, and sum sufficient loaned, to purchase the team; or the loan of a sufficient [sum] to cover all. I owe Davis & Co. below, upwards of $100 for flour & expenses, at enormous charges, & Lassin & Co. $80 for similar. The great difficulty & hardships attending the labor of packing up supplies on the backs of my friends, their extraordinary prices, and the fact of uncertainty in obtaining more even under such circumstances; no team to be had at the upper ranches, all render it imperious on me, to make this application to some friends below, whom I feel assured will render me so important a service, extricating me from a very disagreeable exigency: and be assured that I shall embrace the earliest opportunity to liquidate the pecuniary obligation, while that of lasting gratitude will be cherished with the appreciation such an act of friendship must indelibly make on a grateful heart. I have in view some ravines & streams a day's march in from here, which doubtless are rich, and may, as soon as I can examine them, prove the realization of that hope which brought me across the continent; if so, you shall promptly be informed thereof. As a matter of course, many strange and false reports have been made, of the cause of my detention here, by malicious & ignorant persons. All kindness & accomodation extended to friend

Poile I shall appreciate as such rendered me — P.S. My regards to friends & fraternal remembrance to those of the *Order*".

Among those addressed by Bruff was "Col. Christy (in quicksilver mining)" [P 8 A]; according to Bruff's Visitors' Book (Aug. 20, 1848) "Jno G. Christie, Monterey, California." Col. Christie, arriving in S. F. from Honolulu Nov. 24, 1847, became "negotiating agent" for an association (including Thomas O. Larkin and Josiah Belden) to operate a quicksilver mine located on the Rancho de los Capitancillos, 6 ms. east of Los Gatos and 2 ms. north of the Almaden mines. Ownership, based on a grant by Juan B. Alvarado, became a subject of litigation, and the works were later shut down (information from Miss Caroline Wenzel).

62. Probably the Bush-Tit (*Psaltriparus minimus Californicus* Ridgeway). Bruff notes them again Feb. 20.

63. "*Hallætus Leucocephalus*. The Bald Eagle. The bald eagle throughout the far west reigns monarch of the feathered tribes," writes Newberry, adding, "The quills of this bird make better pens than those of any other bird I have ever seen" (Newberry, "Zoology," p. 75).

64. H 3: "The edible acorn, is only found in the valley of the Sacramento, bordering the mountains [erroneous] — The oak producing them, does not grow in the hills. They are the staff of life of the Indians, who construct large cribs, and fill them with acorns, for the winter consumption. My friend was lucky in obtaining them, for the Indians and bears very soon sweep off the crop, when mature. — The cup is small, but the nut part is very long and slender, (some attaining the length of 2½ ins: with a diameter of ⅝ in:)." The acorn described and sketched by Bruff is that of *Quercus lobata* Neé, Valley Oak (*Q. Hindsii* of Newberry, *Q. longiglanda* of Frémont). "This is the finest oak of California, and perhaps the most abundant. Its favorite habitat is on the slopes of the 'foot hills' and along the streams which traverse the valleys of that State" (Newberry, "Botany," p. 30).

65. Young Robert Roberts may indeed have traveled up the Sacramento River to Lassen's Rancho early in February, 1850, on the first steamboat ever to ply those waters. It is known that Lassen purchased a steamboat early in 1850 and brought it up the river: "In the spring of 1850, Peter Lassen, having disposed of one half his ranch and stock to Palmer [Gen. John Wilson, rather], took several teams of oxen, and went to Sacramento City to purchase provisions; and while there, conceived the idea of selling his cattle and buying a steamboat, which proved to him the most unfortunate speculation of his life. . . . Whilst Peter, with his purchase, (the little steamer Washington,) was cordelling up the river with his Indians, other parties were taking away and selling his cattle. The steamboat project proved a failure. . . . He accordingly sold to Henry Gerke, of San Francisco, his remaining interest in the place" ("Peter Lassen. Supplementary Biographical Particulars," p. 512). Bancroft (*History of California*, VI, 450) speaks of "the inauguration, in August [1849], of steam service by the *George Washington*" at Sacramento City. "On the 15th of August a scow was launched, and two days later the *George Wash-*

ington, the first river steamboat of California, arrived from Benicia" (*ibid.*). However, *Hutchings' Illustrated California Magazine* (IV, 4) contains an interesting statement in connection with this "little steamer Washington." It says that the "Lady Washington," a sternwheeler, was built at Sutter's embarcadero in Sept., 1849, that it ran on the upper waters, being the first to ascend above the mouth of the American River. According to this account, the little steamer struck a snag, sank, was later raised and renamed the "Ohio." If Peter Lassen purchased the "Lady Washington," and if, as *Hutchings' Magazine* states, it struck a snag, this might explain why Peter's steamboat venture was unlucky.

It is known that Col. Charles Lincoln Wilson became one of the partners in the Lassen Rancho. Bruff says (H 2, May 4, 1850): "Col. Wilson engaged me, for the company — Genl John Wilson, himself, and Lassen — proprietors of the Estate here, (Lassen having granted two-thirds of the land and stock, for a certain amount to be paid him, *in installments . . .*), to lay off the City of Benton." Perhaps Colonel Wilson purchased the share of Lassen's Rancho spoken for by Joel Palmer, but apparently never taken up by him. See H 2, nn. 21 and 29, for a discussion of this point.

In an obituary of Charles Lincoln Wilson, *The Themis,* Dec. 20, 1890, stated: "in the spring of 1850 [he] brought the first steamer that traversed the upper waters of the Sacramento river, to a point above the mouth of the Feather river and as far as Deer creek, where Peter Lassen had located. . . . After years had passed, the point of landing of Colonel Wilson's vessel became the Gerke ranch, and in later years has become the place where Senator Stanford planted and established the vineyard now of world wide fame — the vineyard near Vina. The little steamer of Colonel Wilson was freighted with goods for trading purposes, and at that time he purchased a league of land from Lassen, which he retained until his death."

Steamers in these waters previous to this time were unknown. Since Lassen and Col. Charles Wilson were partners, why not suppose this first steamer north of Sacramento City to have been jointly owned by the two men, or to have been owned by Lassen and underwritten by Charles Wilson? Lacking information to the contrary, this appears more plausible than that two steamers would have made an initial trip over these virgin waters at about the same date, independent of each other, and operated by two partners.

66. Stillman, who had established a hospital in Sacramento, with Drs. Morse and Higgins, wrote, Jan. 11, 1850 ("Seeking the Golden Fleece," pp. 299-300): "We are now witnesses of another act in the great drama of California adventures. . . . the calamitous flood that is now spreading destruction and death through the valley. We are all, about forty of us, in the upper story of our hospital: . . . We take only the sick, and none such are refused. . . . All sorts of means are in use to get about: baker's troughs, rafts, and India-rubber beds. . . . After dark we see only one or two lights in the second city of California."

67. *Ardea Herodias* of Newberry. "This bird is more common in California than in any portion of the eastern States with which I am familiar. . . . One is rarely out of sight of them" (Newberry, "Zoology," p. 97).

68. H 3: "The gentleman who first came up is named Withers, and his brother-in-law is along. . . . It [Oregon] is their home. . . . The prospecting party are, — Pendleton Withers, and William Matheny, of Illinois, and Nicholas Schuyler and Edward Bargher, of New York."

69. Flogging at this time was still incredibly prevalent. On Jan. 24, 1850, for instance, the Secretary of the Navy transmitted to Congress his "annual report of punishments in the navy" (31 Cong. 2 Sess. H. R. Ex. Doc. 26). This consisted of seventy-nine pages of fine print, mostly in tabular form, giving the name of the vessel, that of the officer ordering the punishment, the offense in question, and the punishment inflicted, which went as high as thirty-six lashes "with the cats." Commodore Stockton, then U. S. Senator from New Jersey, speaking in the Senate "on flogging in the Navy," Jan. 7, 1852, pleaded passionately: "Who, O Senators, is the American sailor, that he is to be treated worse than a dog? . . . Let me remind you that he has recently gained for his country an empire. Through perils by land and perils by water he has gained a golden empire. . . . You have neglected to give him even your thanks. And now, . . . would have him scourged" (S. J. Bayard, *A Sketch of the Life of Com. . . . Stockton* [1856], Appendix, p. 86). In California the absence of jails was a serious problem and contributed to flogging. Charles H. Shinn sums it up: "The entire absence of jails and prisons in which to confine criminals reduced available penalties to three, — banishment, whipping, and death. In practice the punishment awarded for theft was whipping for the first offence; but if repeated it was at the peril of the offender's neck" (*Mining Camps* [1885], p. 179).

70. Two years previous, not three. The incident is well known. The name of this young man is given elsewhere by Bruff (April 15, 1850) as Hawthorn. Burnett draws a very dark picture of Lassen and his party at the point where he overtook them, near Deer Creek Meadows (*Recollections*, pp. 264-65). This was on Oct. 20, 1848.

71. "We take the following from the *Sacramento Transcript: Difficulties with the Indians.* — The Rough and Ready Diggings are situated on Deer Creek, below the town of Nevada. The Indians in the vicinity have for some time back troubled the whites by stealing their cattle. . . . The whites are also continually stealing cattle and mules on the road. The last news was a rumor that the thieves [Indians?] had been found, and that twenty-five of the Indians had been killed" (*Daily Alta California*, April 15, 1850).

H 2 : MARCH 17, 1850—OCTOBER 9, 1850

1. H 3: "(The bear was a fine specimen, — not less than 9 feet long, and I judge would weigh upwards of 1000 lbs:)"

2. *Tetrao Obscurus*, the Dusky Grouse of Newberry. "The cock is decidedly the handsomest of all American grouse. . . . This bird inhabits the evergreen forests exclusively" (Newberry, "Zoology," p. 93).

3. G. P. R. James, the prolific writer of historical romances, was then British consul, stationed in Boston. His *History of Chivalry* appeared in 1830.

4. Clough was indeed lost, and the mystery of his death was never solved.

5. H 3: "My memoirs and drawings are securely packeted and directed, so that if they shall fall into the hands of civilized beings, they may not be lost, and my family stand some chance of obtaining them."

6. The Downy Woodpeckers before mentioned.

7. The effect of the Great Migration on the flora of the country would be an interesting study. Bancroft (*Chronicles*, V, 158-59): "They literally planted civilization as they went, for they left a narrow belt of flowering plants and familiar dooryard weeds from the Missouri to the Sierra. Wherever the wheels of their heavily laden wagons broke the tough prairie sod there sprang up the homely witnesses of their passage."

8. *Quercus Lobata* Nee, or Valley Oak of the Sacramento. "The trunk, rarely less than two, frequently seven or eight feet in diameter, rises eight, ten or twelve feet from the ground, and then divides into huge arms, which throw themselves out at right angles, and, bending low to the ground, cover a surface of one hundred or more feet in diameter. These trees are not thickly set, but usually scattered over the turf-covered ground in graceful groups of giants, whose branches touch each other with intervening open glades, sunny and smooth" (Newberry, "Zoology," p. 56).

9. The common name for the Boreal Flicker. The yellow feathers were much used for adornment by the Indians, wrought into their coronets, or thrust, sometimes the entire wing, through the septum of the nose.

10. Bruff's description is probably the first recorded of a Mill Creek Indian. The appearance of this foothill Indian doubtless approximated that of Ishi, the last of his tribe, and in view of contemporary comments on "Diggers," Dr. S. T. Pope's account of him may be of interest: "His skin is light, reddish bronze, soft, sparsely endowed with hair. . . . Bones small. Musculature is well developed. . . . The hair of his head is black, straight, and of medium weight. . . . He wears it over his ears, tied in a single brush down his back. . . . The teeth are all present . . . no evidence of decay. . . . Ears are well formed, of good size, and the lobes are pierced for rings. . . . The eyes are set straight. . . . The iris is dark brown. . . . The nose is strong and wide, the septum pierced . . . for the insertion of a small

stick. . . . The foot is a beautiful example of what the human foot should be. His method of locomotion is that of rather short steps, each foot sliding along the ground as it touches. . . . He progresses rather pigeon-toed, and approximates crossing the line of his progress each step. The hands are of medium size. . . . The fingers are gracefully tapered, pleasing in shape, with fingernails olivoid in outline, perfect in texture" ("Medical History of Ishi," *Univ. of Calif. Pubs. in Amer. Arch. and Eth.,* XIII [1920], 190-91). Bruff also notes, as a peculiarity, the mustache of this Indian; and later notes and depicts those of the Feather River (Maidu) Indians (July 27, Aug. 1, 1850, and *il*). As a rule, Indians the Continent over plucked out their usually scanty beard and mustache. But Dixon, on the Northeastern Maidu: "The mustache was sometimes allowed to grow" ("Northern Maidu," p. 163).

11. "The native dog of the Yahi was sharp-nosed, erect-eared, short-haired, of the shape and size of a coyote, but gentle and definitely domesticated. . . . It was used in hunting bear and deer, and was more or less fed on meat" (Kroeber, *Handbook,* p. 341).

12. All the great landowners, from Spanish times down, had attached to their persons and property such Indian villages as they were able to hold in a state of semisubjection. These Indians performed all the labor of the huge estates. The methods of Sutter in dealing with them, as described by T. T. Johnson, were also those of Lassen: "When he first settled in California he had much trouble with them [Indians], but he adopted, and has pursued steadily from the first, a policy of peace, combined with requisite firmness and occasional severity. Thus he had obtained all-powerful influence with them, and was enabled to avail himself of their labor for a modest remuneration" (*California and Oregon* [4th ed, 1865], p. 139). Lassen's Indians were of the same stock as Sutter's, the Wintun of the Sacramento Valley. "The Wintus are a nation or stock of Indians who before the coming of white men owned and occupied all that part of California situated on the right bank of the Sacramento, from its source near the foot of Mount Shasta to its mouth at the northern shore of San Francisco Bay. These Indians extended into Trinity County on the west, and still farther to the mountain slope which lies toward the Pacific. It is difficult to determine what the Wintu population was half a century ago, but . . . I should say that it could not have been less than 10,000. . . . At present [1896] there are not more than 500 Wintus in existence. The Wintus have suffered grievously" (J. Curtin, *Creation Myths* [1898], pp. 487-88).

On the left bank of the Sacramento also the Wintun claimed in its upper reaches all the valley to the foothills. From the mouth of the Pit downward to the tule swamps about Sacramento, a narrower and somewhat indefinite strip along the river was theirs. Redding was the site of one of their villages; at the mouth of the Feather was another, destroyed by Sutter; in the Sacramento marshes were many others. In Sutter, in Lassen, and in Reading the northern valley bands acknowledged their first white overlords. Adam Johnston, appointed Indian Sub-Agent for the San Joaquin Valley in April, 1849, writes (Schoolcraft, *op. cit.*, VI, 710): "The Indians of the Valley of the Sacramento are not a warlike people. They possess no war clubs, scalping knife, or tomahawks. . . . They are mostly indolent, docile, and tractable, but many of them are thievish; they . . . readily learn the more simple arts of agriculture." By 1849 they had settled into a tread-mill existence as herders and hands on the great valley estates.

13. P. A. Chalfant, a '49er on the Lassen Trail, recounts his pleasure on reaching Davis' Rancho, Oct. 24 or 25, '49 (*op. cit.*, p. 168): "We were at the Davis ranch, near Lassen's. . . . The man said we could have a square meal. . . . What a break-fast that was! A snow-white table cloth, sure enough queensware dishes; not a speck of dirt on one of them; biscuits and broad slices of light bread; coffee and cream and milk, beefsteak and milk gravy, and potatoes and butter — butter, for a fact. It was the climax of a civilized breakfast."

14. Long's Bar on Feather River, not that of the same name (sometimes called Long Bar) on the Yuba. The former was near the present Oroville.

15. H 3: "Col. Davis is about to emigrate to the valley of San Jose. His sons, McBride, and Capt. Potts, (formerly commanding the 'Wolverine Rangers',) are camped across the creek, jerking beef, preparatory to travelling up to the Trinity mines."

16. Gold was discovered on the Trinity by P. B. Reading, who gave the river its name. He states that this occurred in 1848, but some historians now place it, from contemporary evidence, in 1849. Wells (*op. cit.*, pp. 123-24) quotes him: "'In the month of July, 1848, I crossed the mountains of the Coast Range, at the head of middle Cottonwood creek; struck the Trinity at what is now called Reading's bar'. . . . Quite a number of miners gathered and worked on the banks of the Trinity in the fall of 1849." The Trinity was supposed to empty into Trini-dad Bay, this error being responsible for explorations opening up the adjacent coast and its tributary rivers to mining.

17. Of these Indians Stephen Powers wrote: "They are as remarkable as all Cali-fornians for their fondness for being in, and their daily lavatory use of, cold water. They are almost amphibious. . . . Merely to get a drink they would wade in and dip or toss the water up with their hands. They would dive many feet for clams, remain down twice as long as an American could, and rise to the surface with one or more in each hand and one in the mouth" (*Tribes of California*, Cont. N. Amer. Eth., III [1877], 233).

18. Daniel Sill, one of Lassen's neighbors in the Sacramento Valley. Bancroft (*History of California*, V, 720) says he was a native of Conn., who came to Calif. in '32. Like so many others, he worked for Sutter for a time and in '46 purchased a rancho from Lassen. Wm. Heath Davis (*Seventy-Five Years in California* [1929], p. 205) says Sill was a native of Ky. Bancroft says (*op. cit.*) that Sill "died in '62, at the age of 66."

19. H 3: "This party was led by J. J. Myers, whose letters and guidance had directed so many on the northern route. . . . Myers was astonished at seeing me." John J. Myers, according to Bancroft, came to California in '45, "one of Frémont's men." In the various lists of the Chiles-Walker party of '43, one may be considered authoritative, that of P. B. Reading. In his daily diary, Sept. 16, the day his party left Fort Hall for California, he sets down the 13 members of his (Chiles) division. Among them is "John Myers." Reading's list supplies no middle initials for any member except Joseph B. Chiles. J. W. Nesmith's "roll of 1843" of the Burnett-Chiles Cos. (*Trans., 3d Annual Reunion, Oregon Pioneer Assoc.* [1876], p. 50), lists "Jacob Myers." Milton McGee's "Autobiography" mentions his friend "J. M." from Mo. in the Chiles party, and asserts roundly that he (McGee) "is the first man that Discovered the head waters of Goos Lake," in their journey.

From Bruff's notices of "J. J. Myers" he was a "mountaineer"; Bruff credits him with the discovery of "Lassen's" pass; and Myers says in his letter to Brig. Gen. Jones (1st ed., Appendix VIII) that he has personally been over every pass of the Sierra Nevada. He also says he "was five years in the Country trapping for beaver and have examined every stream from South of the San Joaquin to the head of the Sacramento," which dates him as arriving in '43. Wm. Kelly (*Excursion*, II, 109-10), prospecting the Sacramento tributaries of the "western flank of the Sierra," in 1849, says they kept guard at night, "for Mr. Myers, the most experienced California mountaineer, gave us special warning of the treachery of the tribes of Digger Indians we were likely to meet." Myers might have been both a member of the Chiles-Walker party and "one of Frémont's men," for Frémont's men were never static. We incline to believe that Myers came to California with Reading and Chiles in 1843. Bancroft's notice (*History of California*, IV, 751) adds only that Myers served in the California Battalion. Myers appears last in Bruff's pages as discoverer of gold at "Myer's diggings," Rich Bar, July, 1850. What became of him does not appear.

20. In P 9 Bruff seems to credit these Indian tales, even to believing that a white man was with the Indians. "Think probably C[lough] is a prisoner with them," he concludes. But on second thought he adheres vehemently to views expressed earlier, on close acquaintance with the Shingle men, that the marauders were white. Delano speaks of renegade whites among the Indians (*op. cit.*, p. 309), and also of "organized thefts" of whites which were at first attributed to Indians in the winter of 1850-51 (*ibid.*, pp. 360-61). Hale, on the Humboldt, says of the theft of "a great number of horses" there, "I think some white man may be at the head of it. Horses are very valuable here." In 1850, in Scott's Valley — the region of the Trinity mines — Wistar makes a graver change: "The old circuitous trail," he says, "was at the time infested and watched by a lot of murdering white rascals disguised as Indians" (*Autobiography*, p. 254; courtesy of Wistar Institute).

21. Bruff finds here, besides "old Peter Lassen," new proprietors in charge of Lassen's Rancho, one being Gen. John Wilson, represented in the person of Wm.

Henry. It was on the day after his arrival there that Gen. Wilson bought a third interest in Lassen's ranch: "On arriving at Lassen's last fall I found old Uncle Peter Lassen with one of the best & finest ranches in California — containing about 18000 acres of as fine land as ever laid out of doors, 300 head of cattle, 260 of them American oxen, 250 fine fat horses & mules, 200 sheep, about 4 to 600 head of hogs, 12 waggons, a mill etc. & many other affairs. He put at me to buy an interest — finally myself and a Mr. Palmer of Oregon bought 2-3rds of the whole" ("California Letter of John Wilson," pp. 204-5). In a later letter (San Francisco, April 11, 1852; MS, Dr. F. A. Culmer), he writes: "Our whole ranch is one continued plain covered with oats, clover & grasses fine & nutricious to be mowed for hay if we want it. It looks like an old orchard with now and then a large branchy live oak making a shade for your stock in a warm day. It contains about 100000 acres, being the most lovely plain you ever saw with just inclination enough for the water to drean off to the river, & when I bought it which was the next day after I got into the country and the first ranch we came to or ever saw in California, it contained about 1000 head of cattle (as represented) say 700 or 800 — 250 head of horses, as many sheep etc. & I agreed to give 15000$ payable without interest in 1855, first day of Jany, for one third of the whole." The purchase was made in Nov., 1849. From the speed with which this bit of business was concluded, the terms, and the phrase "I found old Uncle Peter Lassen," it would seem fair to infer that Wilson and Lassen were old acquaintances in Missouri. No doubt another factor in the transfer to Wilson and Palmer was Palmer's prior acquaintance with both Lassen and his ranch, he having accompanied Peter Burnett from Oregon to California in 1848 in the train that overtook and extricated Lassen, in difficulty on his own road.

22. Sashel (or Saschel) Woods appears to have been a native of Ky., who early moved to Mo. and engaged in the Santa Fe trade. He was an associate of Peter Lassen, and in 1848 was one of Lassen's party from Mo. to Calif. They brought the charter for a Masonic Lodge, "to be located at Benton City, Upper California," issued by the Grand Lodge of Missouri, "Sashel Woods Worshipful Master, . . . and Peter Lassen Junior Warden." Bruff states in 1850 that Woods had twice made the journey to California: "The latter [an introduction to Saschel Woods], was reviving a former acquaintance I had had with Col. W. in Washington, a short time before I left for this country [i.e., California]. This last emigration, was the second time the Col. had crossed the continent." Fayette (Mo.) *Boon's Lick Times*, Dec. 21, 1844: "To Oregon Emigrants The undersigned, appointed agent by persons proposing to Emigrate to Oregon, next Spring, will be at Fayette on the 27 inst. He desires that all persons proposing to Emigrate to Oregon, from this section of the country, will attend at Fayette, on the above named day, and give in their names, and make such arrangements as may be necessary at the present time. Sashel Woods" (*Mo. Hist. Rev.*, XXXI [1937], 436). This may bear on the earlier journey referred to. Bruff depicts him also as one of the founders of the town of Red Bluff, Tehama Co. Woods opened the Masonic Lodge

at Benton City, Upper California, Oct. 30, 1849, the first to operate within the state of California, antedating California Lodge No. 1, long accorded priority, by 18 or 20 days. Woods was thus the first Master of the first Lodge in California (Western Star Lodge, No. 2); he was also the first Junior Grand Warden of the Grand Lodge of California. In 1852 he went by sea to Mexico to look after his interests, where he contracted chronic dysentery. Returning to San Francisco, he sailed for Crescent City early in 1853, locating the Gasquet Ranch at the forks of Smith's River. His illness soon rendered him helpless. The Masons of Crescent City brought him there and cared for him until his death on April 26, 1854. The Grand Lodge of the State erected a monument over his grave in Crescent City (*Fifty Years of Masonry*, I, 46-47, 48, 56, 84, 102, 191).

23. See May 20, when suspicion falls upon one of the Davis sons.

24. H 3: "One of Lassen's valley Indians."

25. Wm. Henry and Micajah, the latter just up from his winter's work in the Post Office at San Francisco and the passing of his bar examinations, to go mining with his brother ("California Letter of John Wilson," p. 204).

26. H 3: "Poor devils! no wonder they are afraid of these huge savage rascals, when they have nothing better than arrows to fight them with." One other weapon the Mill Creek Indians used — fire. "Ishi told us many times the methods he and his people used in killing bear. It was their ancient custom for a number of men to surround an animal, building a circle of fire about him. They then discharged arrows at him, attempting to shoot him in the mouth. . . . If the animal charged an Indian, he defended himself with a fire brand" (Pope, "Yahi Archery," *Univ. of Calif. Pubs. in Amer. Arch. and Eth.*, XIII [1918], 130).

27. This was Col. Charles Lincoln Wilson. *The Themis* (obituary notice, Dec. 20, 1890): "born in Maine, on July 11, 1813. He arrived in San Francisco in December, 1849, in the steamship Oregon. . . . In 1853 he built a plank road in San Francisco, from Kearny street, near Market, to the Mission Dolores. . . . In 1854, Colonel Wilson conceived the idea of building a railroad in this State, and went East. He was the pioneer of railroad enterprise on this side of the continent." He is credited with bringing Theodore D. Judah to California in this connection. "They [Judah and Wilson] projected a railroad from Sacramento to Marysville by a route crossing the American river near where the town of Folsom was subsequently located. Colonel Wilson transferred the road from Sacramento to Folsom to the Sacramento Valley Company, and took upon himself the construction of a road from Folsom to Marysville. In 1859 he completed the road to Lincoln, a town that he founded and to which he gave his middle name. . . . Circumstances compelled him to transfer his railroad property to the Central Pacific Railroad Company. . . . He was ahead of the times in which he lived. . . . To-day it is, and for years it has been, that colossal fortunes have been reaped through the foresight of Colonel Charles L. Wilson and T. D. Judah." See also the *History of Placer and Nevada Counties*, pp. 1042-45: "born at Topsan, Maine, in 1803, and died

at Lincoln, California, in 1890." As a young man, he made a fortune in the lumber business in Maine; served in the Mexican War, being commissioned Col. "He was one of the founders and a charter member of the California Pioneers of San Francisco. . . . Large of frame, courageous, with a clear intellect, Colonel Wilson was . . . in every way fitted to pioneer in the development of California" (*ibid.*). Colonel Wilson is said to have been a Mason.

28. Col. Wilson was not only part owner of Lassen's Rancho: he was also a partner, with Saschel Woods, in laying out Red Bluff. Bancroft (*History of California*, VI, 496): "Red Bluff was first laid out by S. Woods, and named Leodocia, it is said. The first settler was W. Myers, in Sept. 1850. *Hist. Tehama*, 18-19, says J. Myers erected a hotel here later in 1849, but this conflicts with the legal testimony, as recorded in the *Red Bluff Observer*, Jan. 13, 1866, etc." Bancroft (*ibid.*, p. 497): "With a large farming country around, with wool and lumber interests, and as a railroad station and county seat, Red Bluff became the leading town in the northern part of the valley." When Lassen refused to release Bruff to Cols. Woods and Wilson that he might survey Red Bluff for them previous to his survey of Benton City, Bruff notes regretfully (P 9, May 3, 1850): "Lassen objected to my servng [Cols.] W[ood] & Wilson as he had pre-engaged me on his survey here," adding elsewhere that he was engaged "for the company"—Gen. John Wilson, Col. Wilson, and Lassen — to lay out Benton City. Thereupon Col. Woods engaged another surveyor, Thorn, to lay off Red Bluff for himself and Col. Wilson.

29. Possibly Col. Charles Wilson purchased Joel Palmer's interest in Lassen's Rancho. Palmer appears never to have returned from Oregon to take up active partnership with Gen. John Wilson; and if Lassen retained a third interest, as Bruff states, it is hard to see how Col. Wilson could have acquired one-third of the ranch except by purchasing Palmer's share.

30. H 3: "Wilson & Lassen then engaged me, to lay off the town of Benton, on the East bank of the Sacramento, commencing at the mouth of Deer Creek, about 2 ms: below the Rancho." The pay, two ounces of dust per day. Named for Sen. Thos. H. Benton; though occupied for a time, it failed to survive. Fairfield, *op. cit.*, p. 169: "On the south side of Deer creek Lassen laid out a town . . . and erected several buildings. . . . He had a blacksmith shop, a gristmill, and a store." At this time seat of local government (W. Myers, alcalde).

31.The site of Benton City is now peaceful tree-shaded fields. A bronze plaque near the road commemorates it. The following excerpt from the *Sacramento Bee*, Aug. 11, 1930, gives perhaps the last chapter in the story: "About 200 people saw the unveiling of a marker which dedicated this spot as the end of Lassen's trail over the Sierra Nevada, and the site of the first Masonic Lodge in the State of California. Warren N. Woodson, father of Corning, was chairman of the fete, and in introductory remarks said there was no man in the history of California whose name was so monumental as was that of Peter Lassen. . . . Introduced to the audience was Mrs. George Williams, 88, whose husband owned and operated a general merchandise store at Benton City in the '60s. Plumber Edgar of Red Bluff was also introduced to the crowd. He had lived in Benton City in 1863, and with his sister sold peaches to passengers on the stages. . . . This trio is the only survivors of what once was the people of Benton City."

32. Of the mountain tribes of the Maidu. Whether mission-trained, or acting as the Paiute of Truckee's and Winnemucca's band did, on a tradition that whites and Indians were sons of the same great Ancestor, their kindness was not unique. E. S. Curtis (*North American Indian*, XIII [1924], 132) tells of the rescue, by the despised Pit River Indians, of a sick woman abandoned by emigrants to die, on the Lassen Trail. And when she died, they buried her. The dastardly reward, at the hands of Loux himself (Aug. 11, below), is, alas! equally typical. G. K. Godfrey, visiting these Indians and their habitat in 1851, says: "These meadows . . . are about thirty miles in length and from ten to fifteen miles in width. . . . Here lives a friendly tribe . . . of some two hundred souls" ("Lassen's Peak," *Hutchings' Illustrated California Magazine*, IV [1859], 299-300). "The region occupied by the Maidu . . . comprises, in whole or in part, the counties of Lassen, Plumas, Butte, Sierra, Yuba, Sutter, Nevada, Placer, El Dorado, and Sacramento. . . . The area just outlined divides itself topographically into several sharply differentiated portions. The entire western section lies within the broad, flat Sacramento Valley. . . . Eastward from this rich valley lies the long chain of the Sierra Nevada. . . . The forest in this section is quite dense. . . . The valleys of Honey Lake and its tributaries . . . present a sharp contrast. . . . We here come to the typical sage brush and alkali plains, and barren, treeless ridges characteristic of the Great Basin area. . . . From the year 1840 up to the time of the discovery of gold in 1848 [in Maidu territory], exploring parties (such as Frémont's expedition in 1844), and immigrants began to penetrate the region. . . . The sudden contact with the civilization of the mining camps quickly produced its usual effect. . . . Early in 1851 treaties were made by which the Maidu gave up all claim to their territory and were transferred, so far as possible, to reservations" (R. B. Dixon, "Northern Maidu," *Bull. Amer. Mus. Nat. Hist.*, XVII [1905], 123-27, 129-30). Of these reservations Kroeber says: "The first reservations established by Federal officers in California were little else than bull pens. They were founded on the principle, not of attempting to do something for the native, but of getting him out of the white man's way as cheaply and hurriedly as possible" (Kroeber, *Handbook*, p. 890).

33. H 3: "He is an honest old man, but ignorant, and exceedingly stubborn."

34. Thought to have been the first steamer to ascend the river above Lassen's. Advertised in the *Placer Times*, Sacramento, May 8, 1850, for Redding's Ranch, Red Bluffs, Bute and Placer Cities; "will leave on THURSDAY, the 9th inst., at 10 A.M. positively, for the above places, and all intermediate landings and ranches." *Ibid.*, news item: "Ho! For the Trinity! — The pet steamer Jack Hays leaves tomorrow morning for Reading, a town recently laid off by our fellow citizen Major

P. B. Reading, at the head-waters of the Sacramento, within forty-five miles of the Trinity diggings. . . . 'Reading' is located in the heart of a most extensive mining district — embracing as it does, Cottonwood, Clear, Salt, Dry, Middle, and Olney Creeks — besides its close proximity to the Pitt and Trinity Rivers. The departure of the Hays offers a desirable opportunity to all who are bound thither. It has been considered impracticable hitherto to navigate the Sacramento to this heighth." *Daily Alta California*, April 11, 1850: "She is named after the gallant Texan officer, our present Sheriff. The Hays is commanded by Capt. Moseby, late of New Orleans, who is part owner." According to *The Sacramento City Directory* (1851, p. 84), the "Jack Hays, 42 *Tons*. Moseby, Captain," was plying between San Francisco and Sacramento at that date. The initial trip, which Bruff records, was apparently not so successful as had been hoped. Bancroft (*History of California*, VI, 496), citing *Placer Times* May 22, 1850: "The *Jack Hays* steamboat came in May 1850 within 6 miles of Red Bluff."

35. H 3: "On the site of Benton City, is a very comfortable frame house, the residence of a Mr Myers [William Myers]."

36. These are the Diggings referred to bitterly by Bruff in H 3 on the day of his arrival at Bruff's Camp (Oct. 21, 1849), as between "fifty and sixty miles north," where, but for the crooked Lassen Trail, he and his company would then have been mining. Northernmost mines of 1848, they were the lodestone of many of Bruff's fellow travelers, where some — among them Hittell and McGee — were already at work. "Redding's Diggins proper," according to the MS journal of a Forty-Niner (Sept., 1849), were 25 miles from Cottonwood Creek, on Clear Creek. Wm. Kelly, early explorer for gold along the Sacramento (*Excursion*, II, 107): "I also visited an extensive mining settlement to the westward [of the Sacramento] called 'The Springs,' or 'Redding's Diggings,' said to be very rich." Bancroft (*History of California*, VI, 366, n. 31): "In the Reading district, centring around Shasta, or The Springs, a number of camps sprang up in 1849, along and near Clear Creek, among which Briggsville and Horsetown became the most prominent."

Reading came to California in 1843 by a route down the Pit River and its adjacent streams. By his own computations he reached the Sacramento near Cottonwood Creek, on which stream he located. He discovered gold on Clear Creek, at Briggsville, Horsetown and Shasta in 1848, and either in 1848 or 1849 the famous Redding's Bar on the Trinity. Then and later Redding's Diggings, Redding's Springs (Shasta), and Redding's Bar have been confused; possibly Redding's Diggings came to be applied to the collective finds. Bruff's estimate of distance from his Camp would seem to be to the Diggings proper. He was correct in this, as he was in his belief that a cut-off existed, from the Pit River basin to the Sacramento.

37. Bancroft (*History of California*, IV, 743-44) names him as William C. Moon, native of Tenn., coming overland with the Workman party. The story of his getting out grindstones in the Sacramento Valley is familiar. Bancroft says

he settled on a ranch in Tehama County and died there in 1878. Bruff often mentions "Moon's ferry" across the Sacramento.

38. Sacramento *Transcript*, June 1, 1850: "Munroes Ranche, Upper Sacramento May 24, 1850 Mr. Editor: Two days since I left Redding Springs, on my way down the valley, and last evening arrived at the 'Miner's Rest,' kept by Mrs. Hall, and was so exceedingly fortunate as to be just in season to participate in the wedding festivities of her eldest daughter, (Miss Antonia,) who was united in marriage to a gentleman by the name of Warren. . . . Mrs. Hall is from Mississippi. . . . And I could not help wishing that many of our eastern brethren who are so fearful lest slavery should be introduced to California, could call at Mrs. Hall's, where they would see the mother, two sons and four daughters, a family not to be out-done in refinement, all working with their own hands, although they came from Mississippi, where slavery is, doubtless, in as good repute as in any other State."

39. Also from the Deep South. Bruff, Supplementary Notebook A: "Dr O. P. Davis, Baton Rouge, La." *Fifty Years of Masonry* (I, 56): "O. P. Davis, *St. James* Lodge, No. 47, Louisiana," one of forty-four Master Masons present at a meeting held in San Francisco Nov. 17, 1849, to organize California Lodge No. 13, later No. 1.

40. H 3: "from Lower California."

41. H 3: "There was no other medicine at the house than what I had: and I could only find the Thompsonian emetic, lobelia." Samuel Thomson, the discoverer and patentee of Thomson's emetic and Thomson's composition powder, was the originator of a great American institution — patent medicines. According to his own account ("Narrative of the Life, &c., of Samuel Thomson," in Thomson's *New Guide to Health; or Botanic Family Physician*), he was born in Alstead, N. H., Feb. 9, 1769, where his father the previous year had carved a farm from the wilderness. Thomson says: "Sometime in the summer, after I was four years old, being out in the fields in search of the cows, I discovered a plant which had a singular branch and pods, that I had never before seen, and I had the curiosity to pick some of the pods and chew them; the taste and operation produced was so remarkable, that I never forgot it." This was *Lobelia inflata,* later named by Thomson "the emetic herb."

42. H 3: "(Benton City site)". According to *Hutchings' Illustrated California Magazine* (IV, 5), the "Lawrence" was a stern-wheeler, brought out by the New Bedford company, put together at New York on the Pacific, and put on the Stockton run in Nov., 1849, it being the first steamer to operate there. It was afterwards the first steamer to ascend the Feather River, making the trip to Marysville under Captain Chadwick. "We might mention *en passant*, to illustrate the large profits made by steamboats at that early day, that the Lawrence made a trip from Sacramento city to Lassen's Ranch, and received 30 cents per pound for freight on her entire cargo" (*ibid.*). This may well refer to the trip

Bruff speaks of, when Capt. Chadwick brought the "Lawrence" up with Capt. Lyon's supplies.

43. Unexpected obstacles had delayed the projected avenging of Warner's death (see Oct. 3 and Oct. 5, 1849). Nov. 13, 1849, E. R. S. Canby to Capt. A. J. Smith, "Upper Sacramento": "The commanding general has learned that the point at which Capt. Warner was murdered, is much more remote than was anticipated, when his instructions to you of October 25th were given, and that this in conjunction with the unusually early commencement of the rainy season will effectually prevent your accomplishing anything this season. He accordingly countermands the instructions then given you" ("Gen'l Riley's Military Correspondence," 31 Cong. 1 Sess. Sen. Ex. Doc. 52, p. 76). Feb. 26, 1850, J. Hooker, to Gen. Bennet Riley: "The time will soon be here in which the state of the roads and waters will permit the movement of troops, and must immediately be taken advantage of to chastise the Indians near Clear Lake, who have again committed murders there, and those who murdered Captain Warner. The same command may answer for both, for the second expedition cannot operate in the Sierra Nevada until June, when the snows have melted" (*ibid.*, pp. 83-84).

44. The *Register of All Officers* . . . , 1843 ed., lists J. H. Tilghman, clerk, Engineer Department, U. S. Army, born in Md.

45. John Mix Stanley, noted painter of Indians, wrote of Charles McIntosh [1843?], No. 23 in his *Catalogue of Pictures in Stanley and Dickerman's North American Indian Portrait Gallery* (1846): "A Cherokee half-breed, about 23 years of age, . . . he distinguished himself by killing a man upon the Prairies, by name of Merrett, an escaped convict." In 1843, McIntosh went to California, according to Bancroft (*History of California*, IV, 724) with the Walker-Chiles party. See "Journal" of P. B. Reading of that party, July 3, on the Platte: "One of the hunters, McIntosh, a half breed Cherokee Indian was badly wounded in the thigh and arm by the bursting of his gun" (p. 162); also McIntosh is mentioned as a member of the Walker wagon party, "killing a mountain sheep," on the way to Sutter's from Walker's Pass in Dec., '43 (*History of Napa and Lake Counties*, L. L. Palmer, historian [1881], pp. 388-89). But according to John Henry Brown (*Reminiscences*, Grabhorn ed. [1933], p. 4), McIntosh reached California that year as one of a band of Cherokee fur traders under the captaincy of Dan Coodey, of which party Brown also was a member. Bancroft notes him in 1845, "serving in the Micheltorena campaign in co. raised by Sutter. . . . Served in Cal. Bat. '46-7." In '48, this item (*St. Louis Union*, copied in *Saturday Morning Visitor*, Warsaw, Mo., July 29) appears: "Ft. Leavenworth, July 14, '48. . . . An express arrived at this place last night from Chihuhua. It was brought from Santa Fe by James Beckwourth, an old mountain man, Charles McIntosh, a half-breed Cherokee, and Henry Hamilton." Kit Carson was to have accompanied them, but was delayed (information from Dr. Kate Gregg). It would seem a safe conjecture that McIntosh knew of himself, or from Reading, Frémont, or Carson, the route up through

Cow Creek to Round Valley (Big Valley), and guided Capt. Lyon in 1850.

46. Dr. John Henry Drinker, great-great-grandson of Henry Drinker, the first white inhabitant of Philadelphia, who greeted William Penn upon his arrival. Dr. John Henry Drinker was born in Philadelphia Sept. 25, 1821; he attended Haverford College in 1838, but appears not to have graduated there. Where he completed his medical studies is uncertain. In 1849 he was one of a company of 60 men who chartered the ship "Mayflower" to carry them to California, sailing from New Bedford March 24. We are indebted to Dr. Cecil K. Drinker, also a descendant of Henry Drinker, for this identification.

47. Capt. N. Lyon, 2d Infantry. Cullum, *op. cit.*, II, 11-12: born in Conn., grad. West Point 1841; served in Florida and Mexican wars; "on frontier duty" in California, 1849-50; "Expedition to Clear Lake, Cal., and Russian River, 1850 [this refers to the first part of the expedition he is here continuing from Lassen's Rancho]." During the Civil War he served in Missouri, being for a time "in command of the forces for the Defense of the St. Louis Arsenal." Made Brig. Gen., U. S. Vol., May 17, 1861. Died in action Aug. 10, 1861, at Wilson's Creek (Springfield, Mo.).

48. Hamersly, *op. cit.*, Part I, p. 419: "Dyerle, Charles P." Born in Va. Asst. Surg., Feb. 16, 1847; died, Oct. 30, 1853. *Fifty Years of Masonry* (I, 113): "Dr. C. P. Dyerly, Surgeon U. S. Army at Benicia Barracks," member of *Benicia* Lodge No. 5, Benicia, with Lieut. George H. Derby and other Army officers. Served in Mexican War. *Stryker's Magazine* (I, 592) lists, among medical officers cited for merit by Gen. W. J. Worth to the Adjt. Gen., report from Tacubaya, Sept. 10, 1847, "Deyerle."

49. Frémont's route; the one Bruff was sure he could find, in 1849, from Round Valley (Big Valley) to the Sacramento.

50. *Fifty Years of Masonry* (I, 56): "R. E. Cole, *Marion* Lodge, No. 136, Kentucky," one of the 44 Master Masons who met in San Francisco Nov. 17, 1849, to organize California Lodge No. 13, afterwards renumbered California Lodge No. 1. Other associates of Lassen — Bruff, Meyrowitz, Leining, and Dr. O. P. Davis — were connected with this Lodge. In the absence of definite data concerning Dr. Cole, it seems reasonable to conjecture that he may have been this "R. E. Cole" — elsewhere "Rector E. Cole."

51. One of Lassen's nearest neighbors. Bancroft, *History of California*, V, 749: Albert G. Toomes, overland with the Workman-Rowland party from New Mexico. "He . . . obtained a grant of the Rio de los Molinos rancho in Tehama Co. . . . From '49 he lived on the place, became a rich and respected citizen, and dying in '73 at the age of 56."

52. In the late fall of '49 rumors began to circulate about a lake somewhere in the Sierra Nevada north of the Yuba and east of Feather River, whose shores were covered with lumps of purest gold. The author of this story is usually given as one Stoddard. Fariss and Smith (*op. cit.*, pp. 145-51) relate in detail several vari-

ants of the story, all culminating in the utter failure of Stoddard's expedition to locate the lake, and the disappearance of Stoddard. This expedition is said to have started from, and returned to Deer Creek, in June, 1850. All this is puzzling. On June 18 Lassen goes prospecting, returning to his ranch on July 2 with specimens he values. In June Bruff records in his diary the arrival of various parties who pause at the rancho on their way to seek the gold lake, and early in July a movement is afoot at the rancho for a great expedition to search for it. Bruff names one "Gibbs" as the author of the story, and this Gibbs is a member of the prospecting party which leaves the rancho on July 13. See Sept. 12, for a further account of Gold Lake.

53. In scattered entries below, Bruff records the arrival of starving emigrants at Lassen's Rancho. "The emigrants are coming in very early this season — they report great suffering. There has been several relief parties going out to meet them, both publick and by contribution of the citizens. I heard a gentleman say that enough had been sent out as far as the Humbolt to relieve 100000 persons" (San Francisco letter of Mrs. John Wilson, Aug. 15, 1850; MS, Dr. F. A. Culmer). Mrs. Wilson's husband, Gen. John Wilson, headed the San Francisco relief committee.

54. "I have already mentioned the deplorable mortality by one disease alone, diarrhoea . . . which has reigned epidemically in conjunction with a typhoid form of fever, during the last two months, throughout the whole valley of the Sacramento and its tributaries. . . . As to the causes which have induced this calamitous condition of health in California, we have only to reflect upon the great privation, fatigue, and exposure, which most of the immigrants, and particularly those who come across the plains, necessarily endure" (Thos. M. Logan [M.D.], "Letters from California," *N.-Y. Jour. Med.*, XVI, n.s. VI [1851], 281-82).

55. H 3: "J. J. Myers, and a small party, returned from prospecting. . . . He met Capt. Lyons' command, on Pitt river, on the 3rd, from thence they travelled in to the settlements in 5 days." Again the short route from Pit River to the Valley is noted by Bruff.

56. H 3: "For a prospecting tour."

57. H 3: "gotten up, in my opinion by a man who very gravely tells it, . . . for speculative purposes, in sale of provissions, &c."

58. "These squirrel colonies, composed of individuals of the species *S. douglasii* and *S. beecheyi*, are . . . all long-tailed, and more or less arboreal in their habits" (Newberry, "Zoology," p. 55).

59. A serious bond. "The early camps of California did more than merely to destroy all fictitious social standards. They began at once to create new bonds of human fellowship. The most interesting of these was the social and spiritual significance given to the partnership idea. It soon became almost as sacred as the marriage-bond. . . . The legal contract of partnership, common in settled communities, became, under these circumstances, the brother-like tie of '*pard*'-nership,

sacred by camp-custom, protected by camp-law; and its few infringements were treated as crimes against every miner" (Shinn, *op. cit.*, p. 111).

60. Bruff had already met another member of this 1848 party of Lassen's, named Hawthorn. See March 9, 1849, and April 15, 1850. Burnett, *Recollections*, p. 265: "The people that belonged to five of the carts had abandoned them, packed their poor oxen, and left the other half of the party a short time before we reached those that remained . . . with Lassen."

61. H 3: "A N. Western branch of Feather."

62. The bark lodges of the mountain Maidu.

63. Rich Bar of the east branch of the N. Fork of Feather River, not the Rich Bar then almost equally spectacular on the Middle Fork. The two were discovered in the early summer of 1850, in the wake of the Gold Lake delusion. The dangerous descent to the former is realistically described in the first of the "Dame Shirley" letters, which in their recent edition (*Letters of Dame Shirley*, C. I. Wheat, ed. [1933]) have revived the fame of Rich Bar. Dame Shirley gives July 20, 1850, as the date on which the news of the new Rich Bar reached Nelson's Creek on the Middle Fork (*Shirley Letters*, I, 40). George H. Baker, at Rich Bar on the Middle Fork, speaks of the recent excitement on the North Fork, forty miles beyond, "where a couple of men, a Dutchman and a Yankee, have taken out $22,000. It appears . . . that there are two extremely rich bars in the river" ("Records of a California Residence," *Quart. Soc. Calif. Pioneers*, VIII [1930], 67). It is interesting, though not conclusive, that Bruff mentions several times a party of German prospectors in this vicinity. Fariss and Smith (*op. cit.*, p. 248) quote Ripley C. Kelly as asserting that three Germans discovered the Bar.

64. Dixon says: "The older men, however, in the mountain area, often wore the netted cap known as wīká" ("Northern Maidu," p. 159).

65. C. S. Brigham, Director, American Antiquarian Society, writes: "The 'Allen's self-cocking revolver' refers to Ethan Allen of Worcester, who manufactured many kinds of revolvers. A sketch of his career is given in Charles G. Washburn's 'Industrial Worcester,' 1917, pp. 204-206, in which Mr. Washburn states: '. . . he invented the self-cocking revolver, which was widely known at that period, and subsequently during the Mexican War and the California gold discoveries.'" Leeper (*Argonauts*, p. 68): "Allen 'Pepperbox'. The revolver most seen in '49."

66. "Child-bearing falls lightly on the Californian mother" (Bancroft, *Native Races*, I, 391). Powers, in 1874 (*Tribes*, p. 280), tells of a baby born to a captive mother on the march in a snowstorm and plunged forthwith in the ice-cold creek. "Not only did the infant survive . . . but it grew excellently well. . . . Young [the captor] named it 'Snow-flake,' and it is living to this day, a wild-eyed lad in Tehama."

67. "Opium. Without this valuable and essential medicine it would be next to impossible for a physician to practise his profession with any considerable degree

of success: It may not be improperly called the monarch of medicinal powers, the soothing angel of moral and physical pain. . . . Laudanum . . . is nothing more than opium dissolved or steeped in any kind of spirits" (*Gunn's Domestic Medicine*, pp. 697, 702).

68. H 3: "The speculators in charge, are Messrs *Gibbs*, Breed, &c: the former is said to be in *bad health*."

69. "Mount Lassen and the Black Butte [Cinder Cone], its neighbor — volcanic cones both — are beautifully exposed, and tower higher than any mountain points in that direction until Shasta is reached, only seventy miles farther north" (B. P. Avery, "Summering in the Sierra," *Overland Monthly*, XII [1874], 179). Steam vents and boiling pools are characteristic of this volcanic region. Their activity may have been increased in the summer of 1850, preliminary to the lava flows from Cinder Cone the following winter. "Its last lava flow is not much older than the recent activity of Lassen itself, dating back to the winter of 1850-51 . . . when flaring lights, which persisted for many nights, were observed from various distant points" (*Lassen Volcanic National Park, California*, Nat. Park Serv. [1938], p. 10).

70. *Pelicanus Trachyrhynchus* of Newberry. "The white pelican. As one leaves the coast, penetrating the interior, on all the large rivers and inland lakes he will be sure to find it" (Newberry, "Zoology," p. 109).

71. Extra bows, with arrows ready in hand (see Aug. 1), were obviously for use! Of these Indian weapons Bruff notes, 1st ed., Appendix IV: "Obsidian is the favorite material with all the Inds. for arrowpoints, though they use all the other quartzose stones and iron likewise: — this last the Pitt R. Ind. have obtained by the travel. . . . All have their quivers filled with a short bow & arrows."

72. The medium of exchange in California, counterpart of eastern wampum.

73. "The septum of the nose was pierced only by men; and in the opening the usual ornament was a feather. . . . Instead of feathers, some wore a small piece of wood to which feathers were tied" (Dixon, *Northern Maidu*, p. 165).

74. Possibly of the feathers of the red-crested woodpecker, used effectively by the California Indians in dress and basketry for decoration. Sir Francis Drake described the crowns of the Indian chief who came to welcome him near San Francisco Bay: "In the fore front was a man of goodly personage, who bare the scepter or mace before the king, whereupon hanged two crowns, a lesse and a bigger, with three chaines of merueilous length; the crownes were made of knit work, wrought artificially with feathers of diuers colours" (Drake, *The World Encompassed*, Hakluyt Soc. No. 16 [1854], p. 223).

75. H 3: "I have since learnt, that those Indians only paint themselves for war; when they are, at the same time, solemnly consecrated, not to grant or take quarter, nor to permit their enemies to touch them." Curtis (*op. cit.*, p. 142) states that the men of the Pit River tribes used charcoal to blacken their faces in war. H. L. Abbot ("Routes in California and Oregon . . . ," *Pacific Railroad Reports*,

VI [1857], 64) says of the same: "They mark their faces with black, as a sign of mourning, and with red, for ornament."

76. The route followed by Lyon on his unsuccessful reconnaissance of June-July in quest of Warner's remains. From his MS map it is clear that in going out he struck north from Cow Creek, to follow the Pit, reaching the Lassen Trail at or near Horse Creek ford, and thence continued by it over the Lassen Pass. Returning, he came from Round Valley (Big Valley) approximately by Frémont's route, over to Fall River Valley and down Cow Creek.

77. That is, on Lyon's 2d expedition to seek Warner's death spot (N. Lyon, 2d Report).

78. P 10: "*Dommo* or gambling This game is play'd by 4 or any greater number — They sit flat in a circle, and the beginner has 1 black bone & 1 white one — which being envellop'd each in a bunch of grass (plenty being pull'd & cut short — distributed around — One has a bundle of slender sticks for counters — and begins by a low monotonous song — keeping time by quick movements of shoulders & head. The billet-holder dashes down the ivory invelop'd as they are, and puts more grass over them, pitchg them up &, mixing, — putting together & dividing, now in air & now on ground — while the others & [are] watching him closey, & now & then one guesses in which hand is the black bone — by pointing, and a quick ejaculation of *bak! — chuck! ah!* accompanied by clapping of hands, while the counter chap pitches a stick over to the successful guesser, and the enchanted bones are also thrown to him."

79. Bancroft, *History of California*, VII, 164-66: "Although gold-dust passed as currency, the demand for stamped coin became so imperative . . . that several private establishments began to coin money, from pieces of two and a half dollars to fifty-dollar 'slugs,' which found general circulation for some years."

80. H 3: "Rich Bar." See July 27, Aug. 18.

81. Another of Lassen's neighbors in the Sacramento Valley. Bancroft (*History of California*, II, 787) identifies him as Job Francis Dye, a Ky. trapper arriving in '32. "In '44 he got a grant of the Rio de Berrendos rancho, Tehama Co." (Antelope Creek), which he later stocked with cattle. He engaged in various enterprises and also in mining. In 1862, Brewer camped at Dye's ranch: "He was a fine old man. . . . But he had fallen into the hands of sharpers, and the sheriff was just attaching some of his property. I felt sorry for him" (*Journal*, p. 336; courtesy Yale University Press).

82. N. Lyon says (2d Report): "In compliance with instructions of August 3d, I moved from Lassen's on the 8th, & continuing on the emigrant trail, I arrived at Fandango valley, opposite the center and 10 miles to the east of Goose Lake, on the 19th." Two days' travel thus brought him to Lassen's Depot Camp.

83. By way of Cow Creek. See Aug. 3, 1850.

84. H 3: "or uniforms, to designate them as military."

85. N. Lyon (2d Report): "Lieut Paine Act'g Asst. Q. M'r. & . . . his Qr Masters

men." Paine was one of those attacked by illness, and was placed in charge of the other sick, the pack animals, and certain property of Gen. Wilson's, recovered from the cache, while Lyon pursued the search for Warner's remains. Hamersly, *op. cit.*, Part I, p. 676: Ferdinand Paine born in Maine. His service was all in California (1848-53); died 1854, aged 26.

86. Brewer explains this (*Journal*, p. 341; courtesy Yale University Press): "It [the Sierra Nevada chain] appears to have been upheaved, and then furrowed by water into great canyons, valleys, and 'gulches.' . . . Now, the lava flowed over this country *after* much of this denudation had taken place. Immense districts, which would otherwise be gold bearing, are barren because covered up by these lava deposits."

87. *Fifty Years of Masonry* (I, 56): "J. H. Leining, *South Memphis* Lodge, No. 118." Leining was one of the 44 Master Masons who met in San Francisco Nov. 17, 1849, to organize California Lodge No. 13, afterwards renumbered California Lodge No. 1. It was not mere chance that Meyrowitz, Leining, Bruff — and probably others of the fraternity — were members of Peter Lassen's Gold Lake party. The Masonic tie held.

88. Possibly W. E. Jones, "one of the early settlers of Plumas county. . . . Of Acomac county, Virginia, where he was born February 15, 1830. When a lad of fourteen he went to Philadelphia, and learned the plastering trade, which he followed till January, 1849, when he started for California, going by way of New Orleans to Galveston, and thence across Texas, New Mexico, and Arizona; his party being the first to go the southern route. They arrived at Mariposa mines September 15, 1849. . . . He mined at Hangtown and at Gold Run in Nevada county. From there, in company with seventy-five persons, headed by Stoddard, he started in search of Gold lake. The company disbanded. . . . He was in Honey Lake valley when there was not a house, and in Indian valley when Peter Lassen was hauling timber for his cabin" (Fariss and Smith, *op. cit.*, p. 263).

89. Isadore Meyrowitz, stated variously to have been a Polish or a Russian Jew. He was a Mason, one of the 44 Master Masons who met in San Francisco Nov. 17, 1849, to organize California Lodge No. 13, afterwards renumbered California Lodge No. 1 (*Fifty Years of Masonry*, I, 56). He is listed in the minutes of that meeting (*ibid.*) as of "*Fulton* Lodge, No. 198, Alabama." The same authority states (p. 47) that in 1851 he went to Indian Valley with Lassen and G. E. M. Felix and opened a trading post. "A few years later Bros. Lassen and Meyerwitz went to Honey Lake Valley, the first actual settlers of that region. Bro. Meyerwitz was drowned in the lake in 1856" (pp. 47-48). L. Fairchild (*California Letters*, J. Schafer, ed. [1931], p. 137), wrote from Monroeville, Dec. 25, 1851, that there was a food store there, "owned and attended by a Russian Jew, named Isadore."

90. Rich Bar.

91. Lassen was a singularly unfortunate man. He established the first ranch in

the Sacramento Valley north of Marysville, about 100,000 acres, "one continued plain covered with oats, clover & grasses . . . about 1000 head of cattle . . . 250 head of horses, as many sheep" (as described by the part purchaser, in 1849, Gen. John Wilson [San Francisco letter of John Wilson]), only to lose it. He bought one of the first steamboats to ply the upper Sacramento, but found the venture unprofitable. He went from California (with Stockton's escort) to Missouri in 1847, to secure a charter for a Masonic Lodge. Returning in 1848, he brought the first Masonic charter within the confines of the present state of California; yet by an error his lodge was numbered two, not one, and the error was never rectified. He prospected, none harder, in the Feather River country and eastward and southward in the summer, autumn, and winter of 1850; others reaped incredible fortunes in portions of this area, but he found none. The truth is, his heart was probably better than his judgment. Certainly many a starving emigrant had cause to thank him, though the old charge of profiteering motives in laying out the Lassen Trail recurs. Kimball Webster, in his original diary upon which his *Gold Seekers of '49* was based (kindness of his daughter, Mrs. George Abbott) says: "There was a man sent thro from Lassen's Ranch, to Mary's River — by Lasson, with instructions from him to report it as the shortest route; and as possessing many superior advantages over the old road . . . and he succeeded in decoying nearly one half of the large emigration into his snare, and realized several thousand dollars by the foul operation. I believe that he is now in fear of being shot by the exasperated emigrants — many of whom have threatened his life." T. H. Hittell (*op. cit.*, IV, 191) thinks Lassen moved to Honey Lake to escape the odium attaching to him for this behavior. Lassen managed his ranch well and handled his Indians kindly, according to the standards of the day. But when white men began to flood the country, he could not compete and gradually drifted away from them, first to Indian Valley in 1851, and later to the Honey Lake country. The very manner of his death contributes to the picture. The Black Rock Range was the scene of a silver mining excitement in 1858. According to Fairfield (*op. cit.*, p. 145), a certain James Allen Hardin, who had passed over the Lassen Trail in 1849, returned with a party nine years later to examine a deposit he had noticed at that time. He did not find the ledge in question, but the search for silver continued. In April, 1859, Lassen, who had gone with two comrades to prospect there, was shot and killed by Indians or by white men masquerading as Indians, thus meeting his death on or near the Trail he had opened, and indirectly as a result of the travel over that Trail. W. H. Wagner (1860): "At the foot of Black Rock peak" (Lander, "Maps and Reports, . . . Honey Lake Wagon Road," p. 37).

92. "The *Cayuse* Indians inhabit the country from the foot of the Blue Mountains to within 25 miles of Walla-Walla; they are a proud, haughty and overbearing people, as also very superstitious; . . . their band consists of about 800, 200 of whom are warriors" (J. Lane, Gov. of Oregon, *Report of the Com. of Indian Affairs for 1849*, p. 171). In the fall of 1847, this tribe became notorious by mur-

dering Dr. Marcus Whitman, his wife, and a number of fellow missionaries at the mission station of Waiilatpu. This massacre was avenged in a popular uprising, the "Cayuse War." Had it not been for the Cayuse hostilities, the new road to Oregon by Goose Lake might never have been laid out by Applegate in 1846 and the emigration of '49 to California might never have wound down Pit River, to arouse in the Pit River Indians like hostilities. Psychologically, this last was inevitable: "It [the Cayuse War] inflamed the minds of the Oregonians with a bitter and undying hatred of the entire Indian race. Carrying this feeling with them when they came to California, and indulging it freely by shooting the Indians on every favorable occasion, the latter soon came to regard these men as their special foes" (Henry Degroot, "Six Months in '49," *Overland Monthly*, XIV [1875], 343).

93. H 3: "They were taken from the Post Office at San Francisco, by Col. Wilson."

94. H 3: "about 100 yards below us, on the bank of the river, in a willow jungle."

95. H 3: "I am apt, however, to think that the origin of the trouble, was in some offence by the whites, as is generally the case. Whether the Pitt river Indians and the other Pautahs, of the Eastern slope, were first molested by the whites, or not, I cannot say: perhaps they considered the first incursion of whites, into their country to be hostile; and certain it is that the Indians are not alone to blame." The Indians of both Redding's Diggings and Redding's Bar were of the Wintun stock. When Reading, northernmost of American ranchers in the Sacramento Valley, first settled among them, in '47, his relations with them were entirely peaceable. They worked Reading's mines for him. Real trouble developed with the influx of miners, particularly of Oregonians who, "embittered against all Indians by reason of the recent bloody Indian wars into which they had themselves been plunged, protested against his Indian laborers" (Reading, "Journal," pp. 135-37).

96. H 3: "From the Feather river mines."

97. From P 10, Aug. 18, and this account, Aug. 19, the scene of these brushes with the Indians would seem to be in the heart of the Pit River country. See also Aug. 30. The party with Pickering, Bruff says, followed the Lassen Trail north "till within 10 miles of Pitt river," and then (H 3) turned eastward. "Ninety miles" from Bruff's camp of Aug. 19 would thus bring them into Dixie Valley, whose bands annoyed the emigrants of '49. Their valley was one of the most populous in the inhospitable volcanic terrain dipping down from the mountain flanks into the Madelin Plains. To Bruff, a Pit River Indian, wherever found, was a Paiute.

98. H 3: "Where they turned to the Eastward."

99. H 3: "or north."

100. P 11: "Seymour & 6 men came up from Nelson's Ck." "Among the hundreds who rushed into these mountains in the wake of the Stoddard party were two men named Nelson and Batterton. These two discovered diggings on a stream that was named Nelson creek. . . . Rich bar, on the middle fork a few miles

below the mouth of Nelson Creek, was discovered but a few days later" (Fariss and Smith, *op. cit.*, p. 287).

101. Capt. Lyon says (2d Report) that on Aug. 24 he arrived at the spot where Warner died but that the "feeble condition" of some of his men prevented his camping there and making an extended search and that he "moved by easy marches along the immigrant trail to Lassen's, where we arrived on the 11th September."

102. Lyon, 2d Report: "The map herewith appended shows the route taken, — the guides having lead [led] me astray on the 2nd & 3d days were successful on the 4th, (August 24th) in directing me to the spot where Capt. Warner was killed, at which place I arrived between 11 & 12 O'Clock of that day, & continued here searching with as much industry as the heat of the day (& place) would permit till between 3. & 4 O'Clock, P.M.; the ravine in which Capt. Warner was killed, was examined from the bed of the stream along the hill sides to their top, for about ¼ of a mile above and below the spot designated. Near this spot two bones were found, which were believed to be human, & upon which a difference of opinion seems to exist between the two Medical Officers (Drs Deyerle & Campbell), who have examined them; the gnawing & mutilations of the extremities by wild beasts, leaving but little clue to distinguish them. Several broken arrows, a piece of a broken kettle, a Spur & two small tin cans were also picked up, & with the two bones are now in my possession, subject to the wishes of the Gen'l Commanding, or of the friends of Capt. Warner. A pit was discovered near by, in which I conceived it possible the remains of Capt. Warner might have been burned, as the Pit was of a suitable size for the purpose, and had apparently been heated to a great extent, & filled with stone which from their previous heated condition, readily broke to pieces on being moved. Had this preparation been made for their own purposes of cooking meat, the Pit would have been reopened, but it was now full, & apparently undisturbed since having been industriously filled with heated rocks & combustible materials. Could I have encamped on or near this place, the search would have been protracted over a portion of the contiguous country, but being compelled to return on our trail six miles to encamp, the renewal of the search would have involved more hardship than (in the feeble condition of a portion of my men), the slight prospect of success would seem to justify."

103. N. Lyon ("Report," *Report of the Sec. of War for 1850*, Part II, pp. 78-79, 81-83; cited as Lyon's 1st Report), of the return from the Clear Lake expedition: "During our passage down Russian river an Indian was taken captive, who communicated some very unexpected intelligence — that some citizens (Spanish) had instigated the Indians against the Americans, confirming in this respect the hints previously thrown out to me by several persons." W. A. Chalfant ("The Bandits of California," in *Outposts of Civilization*, pp. 138-40) cites as a typical example Joaquin Murieta, the famous bandit, maddened by his wrongs, inflicted by American miners, these leading Murieta to swear, by his brother's grave, "that his soul

should know no peace until his hands were dyed with his enemies' blood."

104. Wilson made two caches of his numerous possessions, one just east of Goose Lake, and the other on Feather River. "I feel that the government ought to authorize me at their expense to send for my things left in the mountains which I caached. . . . Or if the government will not do that, I feel they ought to pay me for them" (Wilson, San Francisco Report). Accordingly Lyon was ordered to add to his duties of chastising the Clear Lake Indians for having killed some whites, and of identifying the Indians who attacked Capt. Warner and punishing them, the totally unrelated task of exhuming and transporting Gen. Wilson's "Law-Books." He says (2d Report): "on opening it [the cache in Fandango Valley] nearly everything in it was found to have been under water, & so much decayed as to be entirely worthless. . . . The property of the cache was exposed to the sun, & when dry enough to be moved, I selected about 50 volumes of such law books as were believed to be of importance, & not at present easily obtained." The scarcity of law books in California then made them invaluable. April 9, 1849, Gen. Persifor F. Smith wrote the Adjt. Gen. from San Francisco: "I cannot find a copy of the Laws of the United States in California, and they are of the greatest necessity" (*California*, p. 722).

105. Some of these may have been Paiute, although the region would seem to be in debatable country. Since the two stocks were on friendly terms, it is the more difficult to differentiate their boundaries. See, in this connection, Nov. 16, 1850.

106. H 3: "His partners, no doubt interested in the trading speculation predicated upon it, have been with us. . . . All this year, squads and parties, mounted and on foot, have been suffering and exploring the Sierra Nevada, in quest of such a spot."

107. See June 20, 1850, and n. 52 for an account of the Gold Lake rush, of which one Stoddard is usually the central figure. The Gold Lake excitement was further fostered by a belief prevalent at that time, that a fountain-head or source of gold existed high up in the mountains. "They [the miners] had noticed that the gold became coarser as they ascended the streams. . . . In many places around the old claims, generally in crevices, had been found 'pockets,' from which several hundred dollars were taken out in a few minutes, and it was not a violent assumption to think that 'farther up,' near or at the 'source of gold,' they could gather in twenty-four hours as much of the precious metal as could be carried away" (Fariss and Smith, *op. cit.*, p. 146). But this legend goes even further back than Stoddard's or Gibbs's time. See Degroot, *op. cit.*, for account of a Gold Lake expedition in May, '49, sponsored by Caleb Greenwood and son John; and E. C. Kemble, "Confirming the Gold Discovery," *Century*. n.s., XIX (1890-91), 538, for belief of Sutter's Indians in a demon-infested lake in the mountains, its shores lined with gold.

108. Bruff again intimates that Gibbs was in league with the traders who profited

by supplying the needs of the Gold Lake hordes — which is possible. "Perceiving an opportunity for profitable traffic, a number of merchants accompanied the eager throng with loads of provisions, which they sold at exorbitant prices, even killing the cattle that drew the loads, and disposing of the meat to the hungry crowd" (Fariss and Smith, *op. cit.*, p. 148).

109. H3: "In his last expedition." That is, in the summer of 1850.

110. This forms an interesting variation to the widely known method of the Pit River Indians of trapping their deer in pits.

111. Centerville Butte, in Warm Spring Valley.

112. Shasta, "a heaven-invading outguard of the world," is said to have received its name from Peter Skene Ogden. On Feb. 14, 1827, he wrote in his diary: "I have named this river Sastise River. There is a mountain equal in height to Mount Hood or Vancouver, I have named Mt. Sastise. I have given these names from the tribes of Indians" (*op. cit., p. 214*).

113. The dressed hide was softened by drawing it back and forth over the stake.

114. *Libocedrus decurrens*, here stunted from their customary porte.

115. A similar "workshop," described by Avery, is typical: "There is no reason to believe that any tribe permanently abode at great elevations in the Sierra Nevada, if anywhere within the deep snow-line. . . . But . . . they resorted to it regularly in the summer season . . . except where they were denisons of the great lower valleys, which supplied them with all they needed in every season. . . . Hence this region was the resort of Indians from both slopes of the range. . . . Along the summit of the Sierra Nevada there is scarcely any memento of them to be found, except the arrow-heads shot away in hunting or fighting, or the broken arrow-heads and chips from the same to be gathered at places which have evidently been factories of aboriginal weapons. The most notable find of this latter sort made by the writer was at the Summit Soda Springs — a most picturesque spot at the head of the northernmost fork of the American River. . . . On the rounded top of the ledge overlooking these foaming waters, on both sides of the stream, the Indians used to sit, chipping away with stone upon stone, to make arrow-heads. This was their rude but romantic workshop" (Avery, "Chips from an Indian Workshop," *Overland Monthly*, XI [1873], 489-92).

116. Also eaten by the Indians. In England, during the War, a conserve of rose hips was made especially for children, for its vitamin content.

117. Snowstorm Cañon. Bruff's Gold Lake route is probably irretrievably obscured. For the final nine days, through a country never before explored (unless by Lassen in his previous trip that summer) Bruff put down only one daily mileage, and gave few mean directions for the daily march. It may be said that he had here no such aim as on his overland journey — the writing of a guide for future travelers. Here he was looking for gold. Also, his was not the rôle of guide and pathfinder; that was Lassen's responsibility. Add to this that his compass was

loaned for part of the time to another section of the company, that Lassen perhaps alternately confused Shasta and Lassen's Peak — as Fairfield jestingly remarks
he often did (*op. cit.*, p. 7) — that Bruff's original notes for this part of his account are apparently lost, and the probability of error increases. What he does
give in compass readings applies to the innumerable twists and turns of a scrabble
up this hill or watercourse or down that. It is apparent, too, from checking these
readings, that he does not note every turn; for, following them, the reader has the
illusion of proceeding in a prevailing northeast direction, whereas Bruff must
actually have traveled a mean southeasterly course. This notwithstanding the
evidence presented in his field map which loses him, and Honey Lake as well, in
the limbo of the Great Basin east of the Sierra outpost ranges.

As to Bruff's general course we know (1) Bruff's immediate point of departure
and (2) his journey's end at a point also well authenticated. Thus we can guess
roughly the distance traveled in the intervening nine days' travel; and, from the
nature of the country and his own claims, notations, and sketches, make some
highly probable conjectures as to where he went. Helping us in this task is the
account of Lieut. E. G. Beckwith ("Report" [1854]) who traversed a part of the
same general region, taking seven days for approximately 100 miles. On Sept. 23,
1850, Bruff and Lassen, traveling northeast over hills to the east of the emigrant
trail of 1849, gained the summit of "the tallest hills on the E. side of Pitt river
valley," and looking back "far down into Pitt valley" saw the "isolated Butte,
described and pictured, in my travels with the Company, October 6th '49 . . .
about 15 miles distant," bearing S.S.W. This was Centerville Butte. Ten miles
N.N.E. (as Bruff guessed the distance) from the edge of its Warm Spring Valley
would place him on that day of 1850 in the vicinity of Alturas, a little to the south
of the emigrant trail. After nine days of travel, Bruff and Lassen arrive on the
shore of Honey Lake, having come down behind and around Shaffer Mountain
at about the pass of the present Alturas highway. For it is Shaffer Mountain that
Bruff pictures in his sketches of Oct. 4, 1850, first from his camp at its back in
"Secret Valley" and later from his bivouac facing it near the present Janesville on
the lake shore.

At what rate Bruff traveled is a matter of conjecture. We know that in one
instance he swung northeast a day's travel, and in another shifted west to throw
Indians off the trail. The distance from Alturas to the pass descending to Honey
Lake by today's very direct highway is about 90 miles. The distance that Lieut.
Beckwith traveled up Smoke Creek, 40 miles to the east of this pass, to the ford
of the Lassen Trail at Round (Big) Valley, 40 miles to the southwest of Bruff's
orienting point of Centerville Butte, was about 100 miles. He averaged around 13
miles a day. Counting that Bruff, in similar terrain, averaged Beckwith's mileage
each day, his mileage for nine days' travel would be 117 miles.

The northern section of Bruff's route, according to this theory, lies in the mountainous sources of the south fork of the Pit. East, across a wide valley, rises the

Warner Primitive Area, snow-crested in the Warner Range. Between, to the southward, runs a bold promontory tipped by McDonald Peak, jutting into the Madelin Plains. The bisecting area of these plains, east and west, is some forty miles in length by a varying width. At its eastern gate, guarding the pass through Smoke Creek to the Mud Lake basin, stands sentinel Observation Peak. South of this again is a broken transverse range stretched from Fredonyer to Shinn, with water courses, intrusive playas, and, to the west, dominated by Fredonyer, Eagle and Horse Lakes. One looks south from the eastern section of this range into the Secret Valley of the old maps, a playa watered, so far as Bruff traversed it, chiefly by Pete's Creek and by the creek running through Snowstorm Cañon on its northern edge to join that coursing through Ball Cañon on its southern confines back of Shaffer Peak, all tributary to Susan River. Only the range of Shaffer intervenes between Secret Valley and Honey Lake, pierced on the northwest by Willow Creek on its way to Susan River and Honey Lake.

In a semiarid country of fluctuating water levels in shallow valleys and seasonal water courses, it is hazardous to attempt to plot Bruff's route by lakes and streams. He does, however, mention three lakes which from his descriptions appear to be permanent features. One of these he himself identifies as Eagle Lake (1st ed., Appendix VII). Northeast of this the party skirts the northern shore of a smaller lake, which might be Horse Lake (Sept. 26, 1850). Traveling still northeast, up tortuous water courses (such as are to be found feeding Horse Lake) and onto an elevated plain, a reconnoitring party discovered, 12 miles to the north, a lake at the base of an abrupt mountain — possibly Blue Lake. This interpretation of the topography would place the camp of the following day (Sept. 28, 1850) to the east of McDonald Peak and W.N.W. of another landmark of the Madelin Plains, noted as we think by Bruff, namely Observation Peak. Bruff says: "This valley runs E. and W. It extends below, to the E^d some distance, and in an E.S.E. direction there arises, from a range of blue hills, a remarkable sugar-loaf peak. . . . It may be 30 miles off." Should this hypothetical location of the camp of the day be correct, the tall conical hill, hollow at top, west of the camp, which Bruff visited and pictured, must be McDonald Peak. From this region, the natural descent into Secret Valley would be by drains leading at will into either Pete's Creek or Snowstorm Cañon. The latter swings to the left, along the base of the range which forms the valley's northern wall; the former cuts through the valley southwest to join Willow Creek. Supposing Bruff's compass to be correct here, Snowstorm Cañon becomes the Hieroglyphic Defile. Bruff says of it in various places that its fountain head was a large spring in a gulch-head 28 miles from Honey Lake, that the volcanic rent commencing near the spring, shallow at first and bordered by low but perpendicular plutonic rock walls, became a defile with walls averaging twenty feet in height, the south wall being noticeably vertical "as of masonry," on which wall were inscribed innumerable petroglyphs; that the stream, a considerable brook bordered with willows, grass and trees, ran "in a general N.E.

direction diagonally across an extensive inclined sterile plain, covered with sharp angular blocks of a brown plutonic rock, among which, through this defile, the creek meandered." These specifications Snowstorm Cañon fulfills. Climbing out of it, the party headed in a southerly direction, passed over the divide to the east, and not that to the west of Shaffer Peak, and came down to the shore of Honey Lake between the base of Shaffer and the Boiling Springs. Photographs and explorations corroborate Bruff's sketches as to these locations adjacent to Shaffer Peak and on Honey Lake.

118. The petroglyphs of Snowstorm Cañon, which were such a source of wonder to Bruff, are characteristic of the Great Basin and its adjoining territory. Such adorn the rock shelters of Pete's Creek and Willow Creek, the sheer drops of Smoke Creek Cañon, the declivities of Ball and Stony Creek Cañons and, in fact, all the cañons of this, the western basin rim.

119. This was a typical California Indian hut of the Sierra, conical in shape, such as the Maidu might have built. Bruff makes a similar comment on the skeleton willow lodges he sees on reaching the plain that same day, in H 3 — "most probably erected to shoot hares and grouse from." Whether these latter were summer shelters of the Maidu, hunting and food gathering, or of the encroaching Paiute, whose abandoned willow lodges Bruff notes frequently in the Great Basin, one cannot say.

120. H 3: "Few of them have a shoe left".

121. Snowstorm Creek, of the "Hieroglyphic Defile," sinks seasonally in the dried floor of "Secret Valley" behind Shaffer Mountain. Through this long tableland a rough wagon road, still traveled "To Gerlach [Nev.]," as the signboard reads, traces the Nobles' Pass route opened in 1851 by Wm. H. Nobles, guided by Peter Lassen: the cut-off route from the Bend of the Humboldt to the Sacramento dreamed of by many a train-captain, including Bruff, in 1849.

122. This was perhaps not so disinterested as might appear. H 3: "Lassen . . . turned his horse's head to the S. . . . followed, of course, by his messmates, whose provissions were on one pack-horse."

123. More likely a summer habitation.

124. H 3: "This country of the Sierra Nevada is peculiarly favorable for transmitting intelligence by this method. Narrow dividing ranges, with numerous peaks and mounts: separating chains of crooked valleys, and basins. It seems that here, there are always suspicious look-outs on the heights, but whether they expect other Indians to invade their country, or have merely anticipated our approach in it, is uncertain. Their *modus operandi* is as follows. — The look-out man catches up a handfull of dry grass or sage-leaves, ignites it with his fire-sticks, and adds fuel till the tapering slender column of white smoke rises high in air: then, by throwing on green grass, or leaves, the color is changed to black. At night the varied blaze of fire answers the same purpose, and even minute information may be thus transmitted. This signal, on an eminence, is answered by the

savages sojourning in the vales below; and any of them in intermediate spaces can send up their smoke column, which, seen lower down, is there answered, as may be agreed on, or conventionally understood. The savages have thus time to secure themselves, secrete cattle, squaws, children & effects and be prepared to meet or annoy the invaders, long before they can reach them." Bruff was here in territory by legendary accounts in dispute between Maidu, Achomawi, and Paiute.

125. H 3: "Holding it with their feet."

126. H 3: "From the numerous answers to the smoke signal from the peak, we had good reason to suspect a considerable body of Indians there, and we therefore thought it safest to travel over into some other valley, from whence to proceed south. Accordingly, we rode up on a course a few points east of North in the direction our messmates had taken."

127. H 3: "looking like liquid silver, in the heart of tall, rugged dark mountains." This is an excellent description of the first view of Honey Lake when traveling south on the Alturas highway, which is approximately where Bruff entered the valley. Fairfield (*op. cit.*, p. 16): "Honey Lake and Honey Lake valley were named from the honey-dew found on the grass and some of the trees and bushes, but it is not certain who gave them the name. . . . It is also uncertain what white men discovered the valley, or when that event took place," thus positing three questions answered, we believe, by Bruff.

Bruff's entry for Oct. 4, 1850, in P 11 — a pocket memorandum undoubtedly carried with him — reads: "9 A.M. mov'd on E. of N. enter'd Honey or Hot Spring Basin & Lake." As regards the genesis of the name, there are two points of interest here. One is the use of "Honey Lake," and the other the words "or Hot Spring Basin & Lake." Fairfield thinks Noble or one of his party named Honey Lake in 1851 or 1852 (*ibid.*, p. 16), but Bruff's tiny entry gives an earlier date and other authors. In H 2 Bruff does not use the name. H 3 says (Oct. 5, 1850): "Lassen was here once before, — then for the first time, and some one of the party called it Honey Lake, from a sweet dew distilled from some plants they found in the bottom." Again, at Lassen's Rancho, Oct. 7, 1850 (H 3): "The elder Hough related to me their first visit to Honey Lake, as they called it, from the sweet substance which they found exuding from the heads of wild oats in the basin. (I have named it L. Derby)".

As to the Hot Spring, Bruff makes no mention of it in H 2 or H 3, a significant omission. Shaffer Hot Spring is too spectacular to have been passed over without comment had he seen it. I. C. Russell (*Geological History of Lake Lahontan*, U. S. Geol. Survey, Mon. XI [1885], 51): the spring "occurs near the northern shore of Honey Lake, . . . and discharges about 100 cubic feet of boiling water per minute. The ebullition is so energetic that the water is thrown in a column to the height of 3 or 4 feet," The steam is visible to a considerable distance. It therefore seems probable that Lassen had seen the Hot Spring on his first visit to the lake, and mentioned it, and the name "Honey or Hot Spring Basin & Lake," to Bruff at the time of their visit, Oct. 4-5, 1850, whereupon Bruff made the notation in his pocket record book — perhaps while the party enjoyed their noon rest in a clump of willows above the water, previous to their ascent of Diamond Mountain that afternoon.

Fairfield believed Isaac Roop the true pioneer of Honey Lake Valley. "Very few, perhaps none of the pioneers of this county went through Honey Lake valley before Roop came in here [June, 1853]. . . . It is hard to understand why F. and S. [Fariss and Smith] call Lassen and his five companions [Meyrowitz, Lynch, Hamilton, Lawrence, and Duchene] the pioneers of Lassen county" (*ibid.*, pp. 22, 28). In the light of Bruff's record it is obvious that Fariss and Smith were correct: Lassen, Bruff, and the other members of the little mess visited Honey Lake Oct. 4-5, 1850; and Lassen had been there earlier that year, naming it "Honey Lake." Peter Lassen was in and out of Honey Lake Valley from the summer of 1850 on, and some living knowledge of these facts must have prevailed. He was not only the pioneer of Honey Lake and Honey Lake Valley — he was perhaps their white discoverer.

128. Frémont wrote, Dec. 28, 1843, near Pyramid Lake: "Riding quietly along over the snow, we came suddenly upon smokes rising among these bushes; and, galloping up, we found two huts. . . . We had come upon them so suddenly, that they had been well nigh surprised in their lodges. . . . 'Tabibo-bo!' they shouted from the hills — a word which, in the Snake [Paiute] language signifies *white*" (Frémont, *Report*, p. 212). Pa'oi signifies *friend* (H. Hale, *Ethnography*, p. 583). Being undoubtedly members of Truckee's and Winnemucca's band — possibly one of the old men was Truckee — this Paiute and the two breakfasting in camp (p. 432) naturally expected a friendly reception. "The Pah Utahs . . . ranged over nearly all of what is now the state of Nevada, northeastern California, and some of southeastern Oregon and southwestern Idaho. Major Dodge reported in 1859 that there were between 6000 and 7000 of them. They lived principally along the rivers and around the lakes of the country belonging to them. When first known to the whites, 'Old' Winnemucca, or Po-i-to . . . was their head chief, and under him were many sub-chiefs. His headquarters were at Pyramid Lake" (Fairfield, *op. cit.*, p. 13). In H 3 Bruff adds this erroneous, but then accepted information: "This is one of the villainous Pautahs, or Piutahs, who inhabit all this country, from Klamath Lakes down to the divide between this and the sources of Feather river, and from the Great Basin over to the edge of the Sacramento valley, at its head. The murderous Pitt river savages are a clan of this tribe, as are also those who killed Capt. Warner."

129. H 3: "Whether built for war, or to shoot hares from, I am unable to determine, but judge that it was for the latter, as they are quite numerous here." Bruff was, as has been said, in Indian country run over, time out of mind, by rival claimants, most recently by the Paiute, thrust westward before the massed white immigration. The late John C. York, whose knowledge spanned two generations,

his father having been a pioneer settler of this region, and he having lived in it and known its Indians all his life, thought these circular enclosures, always in sightly spots, erected for fortifications; shelters not only from enemies but from the sweeping winds for the hill-watchers of the signal fires and the patrollers of the boundaries.

130. H 3: "On our left, — to the Northward, this beautiful, but shallow sheet of water, extended perhaps 5 or 6 miles, to its lower end, in which direction I think that Hieroglyphic creek enters it, and perhaps a little below that, the surplus water is carried off by a gorge, which can be traced indistinctly, in the blue mountains there". Actually, there is no outlet; no "upper" or "lower" end in that sense.

131. H 3: "On the western [northward] side, apparently 5 miles off, arose a dark extinct volcanoe [Shaffer Mountain], on the western side of which we bivouacked on the 1st: — and from which the Indians sent up the smoke signal, when we were descending to the dry lake-bottom, and the profile of which I pictured on the 4th. North of this, — in the same range, I could discern the gap by which we descended to this basin, and there arose another smoke signal, to indicate, perhaps, that we are yet in the basin. Below this, the mountains recede in the blue distance. From thence, they sweep around the foot of the lake, and range up its Eastern side, harsher, steeper, taller, as they approach, till on our right their rugged pine-clad heights soar up high in the upper air [Diamond and other peaks]." The sketch of Shaffer Mountain, to which Bruff here refers, was made from the vicinity of the present Janesville. His orientation is here revised to agree with his statement, H 3, Oct. 4 (n. 130, this account), and with actual topography.

132. Fariss and Smith, *op. cit.*, pp. 337-38: "It is a matter of considerable doubt as to who was the first member of the Caucasian race to pass through or come within the limits of this [Lassen] county." Walker's men, Beckwourth, and Greenwood are mentioned as possible but not probable early visitors; Frémont, in 1844, as very likely passing down Surprise Valley, a little east of the Calif. Nev. line. In 1848 "it is claimed that . . . they [Peter Lassen and Paul Richeson] visited Honey Lake valley." But Bruff says (H 3), at the time of his visit to Honey Lake (Oct. 4-5, 1850) in company with Lassen, that Lassen had been there earlier that summer, "then for the first time." Furthermore, it is known that Lassen went east in 1847 with Stockton; that he left Mo. for Calif. with a train of settlers in the spring of '48, traveling via Fort Hall (Bruff, P 3, Aug. 12, 1849), reaching the Sacramento Valley Oct. 31. Possibly Fariss and Smith's references to Lassen's explorations here may bear on those leading to the discovery of Nobles' Pass, claimed by Lassen, acting as Nobles' guide.

133. H 3: "And more decidedly granite."

134. Bruff's careful observations on the housing of the California Indians are valuable as dating from a time before the natives were uprooted and scattered. He understood the difference between winter lodges and summer lodges (Oct. 10,

12, 1850, and *il*), though prone to fancy the latter shooting blinds. His notes on Indians along the way (1st ed., Appendix IV) contain the following. Of the "Pau-tahs," a "band of Diggers": "As for their Lodges, all along Mary's R. in the thick willows, you can find these wattled willow Lodges, — some of them neat and snug Arbors, that would grace any gentleman's Garden Spot. Generally built of willows, interlaced with rushes & grass, & nicely carpeted with rushes"; of the Pit River Indians, then supposed to be also Paiute: "The Diggers W. of Mary's R. live in holes as well as rude wicker Lodges, and on Pitt R. these singularly excavated chambers were found & explored by some of my men—dug in the bank of the stream, among willows"; of the Valley Indians: "Those near the Settlements excavate an oval hollow in the earth, & construct their wattled rush lodge over it, leaving a small hole on one side . . . to crawl in by." His sketches of Yurok houses on Trinidad Head (pp. 558-61) are among his best.

135. H 3: "A head branch of Feather river, I am certain."

136. H 3: "We dismounted . . . , while a couple of men dug, and looked for gold, finding but a *trace*."

H 3 : OCTOBER 10, 1850–JULY 20, 1851

1. Probably Indian Valley. According to Hutchings, in 1854, it "is beautifully picturesque and fertile, and about twenty-three miles in length — including the arms — by six in its greatest width; being about fifteen miles southwest of the great Sierra Nevada chain; and, (like most of these valleys,) runs nearly east and west. Surrounded, as it is, by high, bold, and pine covered mountains of irregular granite. . . . This valley is well sheltered" ("Jaunt to Honey Lake Valley," p. 530).

2. "In the mountains, where the snowfall was heavy, snowshoes . . . were worn. The shoes were solidly fixed to the feet, and no heel-play was allowed" (Dixon, "Northern Maidu," p. 160).

3. Both Maidu tribes. The inter-village strifes of the Indians contributed to their undoing.

4. It is well known that Lassen was living in Indian Valley as early as the summer of 1851. This valley of a Feather River branch "two days' travel East of the meadows" might be Indian Valley.

5. "Her rancho is well located on the west bank of the Sacramento, on the road to Redding's Diggings. I am confident that all who stop at the Miner's Rest will be more than ordinarily satisfied with their entertainment, for I noticed that Mrs. H. gives her personal attention and labor, assisted by her daughters, instead of hiring domestics" (Letter signed "C," *Sacramento Transcript*, June 1, 1850). According to Bruff, Mrs. Hall died about Oct. 10, 1850.

6. Potts, upon his arrival in California, appears to have made his home in Red Bluff, where he died Nov. 5, 1886, "of paralysis of the heart. He was the last alcalde of this section of the state" (*San Francisco Call*, Nov. 6, 1886).

7. Reluctance perhaps due to well-grounded fear. "It has for years been a regular business to steal Indian children and bring them down to the civilized parts of the state, even to San Francisco, and sell them — not as slaves, but as servants to be kept as long as possible. . . . It is said that some of the kidnapers would often get the consent of the parents by shooting them to prevent opposition." So Brewer, in 1863 (*op. cit.*, p. 493).

8. To Lieut. Beckwith a Pit River Indian explained: "He performed a pantomime, to inform me of the cause of his cheeks and forehead being covered with tar. He represented a man falling, and, despite his efforts to save him, trembling, growing pale, (pointing from his face to mine,) and sinking to sleep, his spirit winging its way to the skies, which he indicated by imitating with his hands the flight of a bird upwards, his body sleeping still upon the river bank, to which he pointed. The tar upon his face was his dress of mourning" (Beckwith, *op. cit.*, p. 43).

9. Indian maps, on birchbark, skins, or sand, were the pioneers' earliest guides. "All Indians are great travellers. In any tribe, even in the deserts of Arizona, or the tribes of the plains, you will find guides who can lead you directly to the sea to the west, or the Sierras to the east" (Joaquin Miller, *Life amongst the Modocs* [1873], p. 239). McCall relates the making of a sand map by an Indian at Lassen's Meadows — an Indian, that is, of the same Paiute division as those found by Hough at Honey Lake, to which vicinity the tribe was even then migrating: "While at the Meadows I met a friendly and intelligent Indian who made for me in the sand, a topographical map of the route over the Nevadas. The sand was piled up to indicate mountains and with his fingers he creased the heap to show the canyons and water courses. To indicate wood and timber he stuck in sprigs of sage, and spears of grass where grass was to be found, and made signs to inform us where the Indians were friendly or dangerous. It was really an ingenious affair and he was well acquainted with the country" (*op. cit.*, p. 72).

10. "*Kamass root*, or *wild hyacinth*, (Camassia esculenta.) — This root resembles an onion in shape and a hickory-nut in size. . . . The Indians of Cape Flattery, the Nez Perces of Idaho, and those of Pitt River, California, are the greatest consumers of this article of diet" (E. Palmer, *op. cit.*, pp. 408-9).

11. Perhaps Ephraim Roop, brother of the better known Isaac N. Roop. Both brothers are mentioned as in business in Shasta (formerly Redding's Springs, of Redding's Diggings), where they had a hotel and store. This property having been burned, they settled in Honey Lake Valley in 1854. "Ephraim Roop died on the Isthmus of Panama while on his way to the East" in 1867 (Fairfield, *op. cit.*, p. 502). Susanville is the still-living monument to Isaac N. Roop, who is said to have named it for his daughter. He died there in 1869.

12. Another of Lassen's neighbors, probably the Henry L. Ford, who (Bancroft, *History of California*, III, 743-44) came to California in 1842-44, from N. H. or Vt. "In '48 he settled in Tehama Co., where in '51 he married Susan Wilson, and in '56 was accidentally shot and killed at the age of 33." "*Henry L. Ford — Susan Wilson.* Married: — On Monday evening, September 1st, by Rev. S. H. Willey, Mr. Henry L. Ford and Miss Susan Wilson, eldest daughter of Gen. John Wilson of this city" (*San Francisco Alta*, Sept. 3, 1851).

13. "On the 7th of October [1850], the steamer Carolina arrived at San Francisco, from Panama, and was reported to have had on board during her passage twenty-two cases of cholera, of which number fourteen had died. She was not quarantined. Since this period several well-marked cases and deaths of cholera have occurred at San Francisco. . . . In Sacramento City, . . . there is every reason to apprehend the worst" (Thomas M. Logan, *op. cit.*, pp. 282-83). "Our worst fears have been realized — for never, in the history of this cosmopolitan disease, . . . has any visitation been so destructive and appalling" (*ibid.*, p. 421).

14. Perhaps the Halil-li-pah Indians mentioned by Adam Johnston, Indian Sub-Agent for the San Joaquin Valley (*Report of the Com. of Indian Affairs for 1850*, p. 90) as living at the base of the mountains near Feather River. The Maidu Indians habitually hunted in the basin of Honey Lake. Or perhaps Pit River Indians, who also hunted there. They raided Indian Valley in the fall of 1851 ("Jaunt to Honey Lake Valley," p. 531). M. R. Harrington suggests that a Pit River Indian's answer to inquiry as to who he was would be "Yal'-le-yu," which means "man." Dr. A. L. Kroeber writes (letter, Sept. 10, 1941): "The people south of Honey Lake, and at enmity with the Paiute, were undoubtedly members of the large division which we call Maidu." There is today a tiny settlement called Hallelujah near Beckwourth Pass. Whoever these Indians were, their statement as to the boundary between themselves and the "Shoshonee" (Paiute) is important.

15. Samuel Neal was another of Lassen's neighbors in the Sacramento Valley; like many others, he worked for Sutter; he received a grant of land on Butte Creek in Dec., 1844. "In '46 he guided Gillespie up the Sac. Val. to overtake Frémont [that is, he accompanied Lassen on this undertaking]. . . . Died at his Butte Creek home in '59" (Bancroft, *History of California*, IV, 752).

16. "The legislature passed a special law April 22, 1850, for their [Indian] government and care, which confirmed them in possession of their villages, although owners of the land were at liberty to arrange with them for occupying some special section of it. A confined tenancy at most, for neither landed rights nor citizenship privileges were accorded. They might be hired to work under contract, and by special provision this was made to some extent compulsory by enabling the local authorities to arrest all whom they chose to denominate as vagabonds and beggars, and turn them over to the highest bidder for not exceeding four months. Any surplus wages, after providing the victim with clothes, was assigned to a mysterious Indian fund, unless relatives claimed the money. In cases of

crime juries might be demanded by either race, but white men could not be convicted on Indian testimony. . . . It was easy to charge any one with vagabondage, especially by enlisting the potent aid of liquor, and obtain his condemnation to forced labor. The impressment generally occurred toward harvest time; and this over, the poor wretches were cast adrift to starve, for their own harvest season was by this time lost to them" (Bancroft, *History of California*, VII, 477-78). Enactment 16 of these laws states: "An Indian convicted of stealing horses, mules, cattle, or any valuable thing, shall be subject to receive any number of lashes not exceeding twenty-five" (*Statutes of California*, 1850, p. 409). They were passed under California's first governor: "Peter H. Burnett, . . . who came to California from Oregon and had previously lived in Missouri, though by nature a humane man, seemed unable to see any good in the Indians or to think that they had any right to live" (T. H. Hittell, *op. cit.*, III, 899). His policy regarding the Indians was that reflected in the "new laws" and given in his Annual Message of Jan. 7, 1851: "Considering the number and mere predatory character of the attacks at so many different points along our whole frontier, I had determined in my own mind to leave the people of each neighborhood to protect themselves, believing they would be able to do so" (*ibid.*, IV, 58-59).

Supposing Gen. John Wilson, Indian Agent for California, had acted in that capacity, could he have brought order out of chaos in 1850? His instructions were merely to transmit "such statistical and other information as will give a just and full understanding of every particular relating to them [the Indians]" (*Report of the Com. of Indian Affairs for 1849*, p. 182). He himself says: "I found my office here in such a loco-foco state that I felt bound to resolve not to do anything till I could get instructions from Washington; those I could not get till the last of this month [April, 1850]" ("California Letter of John Wilson," p. 203). He had already resigned, Feb. 22, 1850. This left only one sub-agent, Adam Johnston, in all California.

17. Colusa was founded in 1850 by the Semples, in opposition to Monroeville. Bancroft, *History of California*, VI, 497: "Green, the editor, and Hicks were among the first occupants. . . . The place became in time the head of a large navigation." Green was Semple's nephew (*Fifty Years of Masonry*, I, 49): "Brother, Dr. Robert Semple, (an uncle of Hon. William S. Green, the proprietor of the Colusa Sun, a pioneer of 1849, and at present the United States Surveyor-General for California)." Swasey (*Early Days*, p. 63) says of Robert Semple, whom he knew in the Bear Flag campaign: "Dr. Semple was a more than ordinarily intelligent man, well read in history, and of varied accomplishments; in stature he was six feet eight inches, and very slim."

18. The Colusi, of the Sacramento Valley Wintun. "Their lodges are somewhat like low haycocks, being composed of a framework of sticks, thatched with the bulrush" (C. Wilkes, *Narrative of the U. S. Exploring Expedition* . . . , V, 192).

19. "By orders of the governor of California, Capt. Louis A. Argüello passed

up the Sacramento valley in 1820. . . . He discovered and named the Marysville Buttes, calling them *Picachos*. They were called the Buttes in 1829 by Michael Laframbois, a Hudson Bay Company trapper, and have since been variously denominated *Los Tres Picos*, Sutter Buttes and Marysville Buttes" (Fariss and Smith, *op. cit.*, p. 104).

20. The site of Yolo. "T. Cochran settled in Cacheville in 1849, and built a hotel at the creek crossing" (Bancroft, *History of California*, VI, 498). James A. Hutton later became host at "Hutton's Ranch," which won "the more expressive title of 'Traveler's Home' " (Tom Gregory *et al.*, *History of Yolo County* [1913], p. 51). In 1857 Yolo became the county seat, but later lost to Woodland. A place of fruit orchards and luxuriant meadows; now a sleepy village still shaded by primeval oaks.

21. Bruff here makes a curious error. Washington at that time was to Sacramento City roughly as Georgetown to Washington, D. C. Undoubtedly speaking of this settlement of Washington across the river from Sacramento, he names it Georgetown. Even on his route, sketched in on his large map, he inserts a dot across the river from "Sacramento" and labels it "Geo. T." Gregory *et al.*, *op. cit.*, p. 40: "Washington, afterwards renamed Broderick, was coming into being. J. C. Davis and J. B. and Kit Chiles had established a rope ferry between the place and Sacramento [Bancroft says, in 1848]." In 1850 (Bancroft, *History of California*, VI, 498): "the ferry . . . was . . . converted into a steamboat, *Alpha*, to suit the increasing traffic." "But to cut the matter short and give you a comprehensive description of the place, I will say that the town is about a quarter of a mile long, and fifty or sixty yards wide, in places; it has a town hall, a drug store, several groceries, gardens and hay yards, and a grave yard, out in the back ground" (letter from "Rambler," Feb. 28, 1851, in New Orleans *True Delta*, April 9, 1851).

22. *The Sacramento City Directory*, 1851, p. 90: "Hardenstein, Dr. Homœopathist, 12 K street"; *Placer Times* (Dec. 22, 1849), office in "Morris House," K Street.

23. E. Sanford Seymour, author of *Emigrant's Guide to the Gold Mines, of Upper California*. See 1st ed., Appendix VIII.

24. Fenderich's death was erroneously reported. Bruff met him the following spring in San Francisco. Although an artist of note, Fenderich left little mark in California (see Introduction, pp. xliv-xlv).

25. "This diarrhoea was so general during the fall and winter months [1849-50], and degenerated so frequently into a chronic and fatal malady, that it has been popularly regarded as the disease of California. . . . By nothing was this affection more distinguished than by its fatality. . . . I have no doubt that the number of deaths in California, from chronic diarrhoea of the character described, was greater than from any other disease" (Stillman, "Observations on the Medical Topography and Diseases [Especially Diarrhoea] of the Sacramento Valley . . . 1849-50," *N.-Y. Jour. of Med.*, XVII, n.s. VII [1851], 299, 300).

26. Dec. 3, 1850, *Sacramento Transcript:* "A Warning to Horse Thieves. — A gentleman who owns several horses and keeps them in a yard near some hay stacks in the back part of the city, discovered a man leading off two of them about ten o'clock on Sunday night last. The thief fled. . . . About two hours afterwards, he again discovered a man among his horses. He waited till the thief had untied the halters of three and was starting off with them, when he fired. The thief dropped, and was evidently badly wounded, as he groaned as if in great pain. The owner of the horses went for a light, and returned a short time afterwards in company with two of his friends, but no traces of the thief could be found, though he left his marks on the ground."

27. *The Sacramento City Directory*, 1851: Pomeroy and Peebles, merchants. *Sacramento Transcript*, Sept. 14, 1850: the City brought suit against Pomeroy and Peebles for obstructing the sidewalks; the firm was fined $5 and costs.

28. On Front Street, between K and L. *Sacramento Transcript*, Dec. 14, 1850: "The house has lately undergone thorough repairs, and the proprietors are now furnishing to their friends accommodations, not to be excelled in California. . . . Charges moderate — all shall be at home. Sweet, Dame & Aldrich Proprietors." *The Sacramento City Directory*, 1851 (p. 49): "Sutter hotel Dewey & Smith, 37 front street."

29. Recently arrived in California from Washington. *Sacramento Transcript*, Dec. 16, 1850: "confined to his house since his arrival by an attack of neuralgia."

30. "The cholera began its ravages on Oct. 20, and ended Nov. 12, 1850. . . . The two cemeteries were heavily occupied" (Bancroft, *History of California*, VI, 452, 453).

31. The Squatter party was an aftermath of the squatter riots which occurred in Sacramento in the summer of 1850. *Stryker's Magazine*, V (1851), 165: "A sanguinary conflict occurred at Sacramento city, between persons claiming lands under titles derived from Captain Sutter, and others, who had taken possession of them and refused to leave. Captain Sutter held them under his Spanish grant, the validity of which, so far as the territory in question is concerned, is disputed. Attempts to eject the squatters, in accordance with a decision of the courts, were forcibly resisted at Sacramento city on the 14th of August, and a riot was the result, in which several persons on both sides were killed, and others severely wounded. Several hundred were engaged in the fight. . . . Among those killed were Mr. Bigelow, mayor of Sacramento City, Mr. Woodland, an auctioneer, and Dr. Robinson, the president of the squatter association."

32. George Rowland (see Dec. 14). *Sacramento Union* (obituary, June 4, 1875): Rowland was born in New Haven, and in '49 went to California, arriving in June; in business with Joseph Nevitt, dealer in stoves and tinware, in Sacramento; 1861 appointed postmaster of Sacramento, which post he held fourteen years. He filled various other political and civic offices and was a member of the board of directors of the Society of California Pioneers in 1854. Died June 2, 1875, at Berkeley, Calif.

The Sacramento City Directory, 1851, p. 67: "Nevett & Co., No. 102 K street, between Fourth and Fifth streets, Dealers in Stoves, Hardware, Tinware, sheet iron, Tin plate, Miners' Tools, &c. Metalic Roofing and Job Work done to order."

33. This village of the blue smoke below Black Rock, watched by Bruff from his winter camp of '49, was the first and the last of the Mill Creeks' to feel the white man's vengeance. This is the earliest recorded clash in the Mill Creek valley.

34. Bancroft, *History of California*, VI, 450: "the firm [Hensley and Reading] withdrew from the fort, and concentrated their business at the more convenient landing. Others followed their example, giving a share to Sutterville, till the fort was deserted by traffic, and employed chiefly for hospital purposes." *Placer Times*, Jan. 5, 1850: "Sacramento Hospital. Under the care of Dr. Robert M. Stansbury. The undersigned having purchased the interest of Dr. Cragin and Mr. Abell in the Sacramento Hospital, near Sutter's Fort, are prepared to receive sick persons at the following rates: A patient occupying a room alone, $16 per day. . . . R. M. Stansbury, M.D. J. W. H. Stettinius, M.D. Charles E. Abbot Sacramento Hospital, December 24, 1849." *The Sacramento City Directory*, 1851, under "Benevolent Institutions" (p. 55): "Sacramento City Hospital, at the Fort. Established in May, 1850, . . . Dr J W H Stettinius, Assistant Physician." Probably "John W. D. Stettinius — Born 1826, D.C., M.D., 1848 Columbian. Died July 20, 1863."

35. "Brewery. The undersigned give notice to the public that they have opened a Brewery, making the best quality of Ale and Beer, opposite Sutter's Fort. P. Cadel & Co." (*Placer Times*, Feb. 16, 1850).

36. When Sacramento was laid out, Capt. Wm. H. Warner, whose death Bruff chronicled, made the survey. "The fort formed the nucleus of his operations; thence down to the embarcadero and along the river bank he laid out streets." Stillman, "Seeking the Golden Fleece," p. 228, fall of 1849: "this canvas city. Dust, men, mules, oxen; bales, boxes, barrels innumerable, piled everywhere in the open air. The trees were all standing — magnificent great oaks — and a crowd of ships were fastened to the trees along the bank. We pitched our tent on the west bank, to escape from the dust and confusion on the other side." Wm. Kelly, summer of 1849, *Excursion*, II, 48-49: "Sacramento city, as the embarcadero is called, was clearly visible from the fort, reposing on the plain in its white summer costume; the plains on both sides down stocked with cattle, mules, and horses, from which the ocean emigrants purchased their supplies, there being no animal market in San Francisco. For a mile out from the city, there was a suburb of snow-white tents of different shapes and sizes, erected amongst the fine open trees that skirted it, presenting a most pretty and unique appearance; and on entering the town I found nine-tenths of the houses made of the same material, nailed on very light frames indeed; the streets laid out with great regularity, and of a fine width, many of the majestic trees being permitted to remain." *The Sacramento City Directory*, 1851, pp. 78-79: "Oct. 1st, 1849, — The population of the city was about 2000. Wood buildings 45; cloth houses and tents 300, and about 300 camp-fires,

&c., in the open air and under trees. . . . By the first of December, 1849, the population was about 3500. . . . The present [Jan. 1, 1851] population of the city consists of about 7000 permanent, and 3000 transient people."

37. Gen. John Wilson (at the "fashionable" St. Francis Hotel, San Francisco, 1850): "All our partition walls in this country are cotton cloth hung up instead of lath & mortar, & then wall paper pasted on it. So all through the house we hear all that is said & can lie in our beds and talk to each other even at the distance of 4 or 5 rooms in ordinary tones of voice" ("California Letter of John Wilson," p. 208).

38. *Sacramento Transcript*, Dec. 23, 1850: "Lea's Missouri Hotel, J. Street between 3d and 4th, W. S. Long & Co., Proprietors. This establishment, having recently changed hands, the new Proprietors solicit the continuance of the public favor. . . . They will spare neither expense nor trouble in ministering to the comfort of their guests. W. S. Long, J. A. Cogswell, G. H. Peacock." *The Sacramento City Directory*, 1851, p. 47: "Missouri Hotel, No. 86 J Street, between Third and Fourth Streets."

39. C. S. Fifield and J. P. Hoyt, of the Granite State Co., part of the Boston Pack Co., reached Calif. in Oct., '49. Webster, *op. cit.*, p. 123 (Sacramento, Dec., '49): "Fifield has a paint shop and is doing a good business." *The Sacramento City Directory*, 1851, p. 93: "Painters, J street, between 7th and 8th. House and Sign Painting, Gilding, Graining, Imitations of Wood and Marble, and every variety of business in their line executed with dispatch and in the very best manner."

40. Feb. 14, 1850, Stillman, "Seeking the Golden Fleece," p. 302: "We had a visit this week from a lady — a Mrs. Chandler — who came to see one of our patients sick with scurvy [hospital, Sacramento]. It was the first time that I have spoken to a woman since I saw General Wilson's family in November."

41. *Sacramento Transcript*, Dec. 24, 1850: "Gaming on the Streets. — Dr. Spalding offered the following resolution in the council last evening, which was carried unanimously: 'Resolved, That the city Attorney be requested to draft and present to the common council, an ordinance to prohibit the exhibition of thimblerig, French monte, or other games of chance or skill, on any sidewalk, or in any street or public place in this city, to the inconvenience of the citizens thereof.'" *Ibid.*, Jan. 9, 1851: "It is to take effect from and after the 25th inst."

42. "About four miles east of Coloma was Kelsey's, one of the famous old mining towns" (T. H. Hittell, *op. cit.*, III, 75). E. G. Buffum (*Six Months in the Gold Mines*, . . . [1850], p. 129) saw a nugget picked up here in '48, weighing 27 ounces; Hittell mentions one "near Kelsey's in El Dorado county worth forty-seven hundred dollars" (*op. cit.*, III, 144).

43. Perhaps the James H. Carson noted by Bancroft (*History of California*, II, 747), who arrived in '47 from Va., was in the mines in '48, and "gave his name to several 'diggings,' and whose little book — *Early Recoll. of the Mines* — was

pub. at Stockton in '52. He died in '53, his wife and child arriving a little later, but returning to the east."

44. Of the Pacific Mail Steamship Co. Bancroft (*Chronicles*, V, 385) gives J. J. Watkins commander and tonnage 1,100. *Ibid.*, p. 381: one of the first three vessels constructed by the Co. for carrying the mails to the Pacific coast, under the agreement of Aug., 1848.

45. *Sacramento Transcript*, Dec. 31, 1850: "A Card," signed by 19 residents, inviting friends to call on New Year's Day, for "a period of social and festive entertainment," 10 A.M. to 2 P.M. at their respective homes. *Ibid.*, Jan. 1: "New Year's Calls. — Our New York friends have prepared to keep open houses to-day."

46. On Oct. 5, 1849 (H 1 account), Bruff, then on the Lassen Trail, mentions the Charlestown Mining Company of Virginia. Washington *Tri-Weekly Intelligencer*, March 31, 1849: the surgeon of this Co. was "Dr. Bryarly, of Baltimore." Possibly Bruff was here reviving an acquaintanceship of the Long Route. *Placer Times*, Sacramento, March 2, 1850: "Drs Deal & Briarly Office at Prettyman, Barroll & Co's, K street, between 2d and 3d. Will attend to all branches of their profession." May 3, 1850, *ibid.*: "Dr. Wakeman Briarly, Treas., Medico-Chirurgical Academy." Aug. 2, 1852, occurred a famous duel, in which Hon. James W. Denver killed Edward Gilbert, editor of the *Alta California*. Geiger was Denver's second, and Briarly (*Placer Times*) attended Gilbert on the field. See *Quart. Soc. Calif. Pioneers*, IV (1927), 72, for story of Washington, Geiger, and Long, of Briarly's co., at Shasta, making and selling peach pies.

47. *The Sacramento City Directory*, Jan., 1851, p. 49: "Union hotel, Roberts, Sutherland & Conley, 217 J Street."

48. About six months after the Gold Lake fiasco, the Gold Bluffs excitement swept California, and it is sardonic that Bruff should have been caught in both. In the spring of 1850, gold was discovered in the sandy beaches north of Trinidad. By fall hundreds of eager gold seekers had gathered there, and in Jan., 1851, following a voyage to Trinidad in the "Chesapeake," the Pacific Mining Company, a developing association, — our old friend, Gen. John Wilson, president — had been formed. What more natural than that Bruff, learning of these matters in Sacramento, should journey to San Francisco, possibly with a wild hope that in this new enterprise he might find a fortune; or what more natural than that the General should invite him to visit Trinidad, and that he should accept? Even before he left Sacramento City, the papers were full of the new El Dorado. *Daily Pacific News*, Jan. 11, 1851, printed an extended account of the Pacific Mining Co., ending: "There may be and undoubtedly is, an immense deal of 'black sand' at Gold Bluff . . . but the richness of it all is a matter of extreme doubt." *Ibid.*, Jan. 14, another feature article. *Daily Journal of Commerce*, Jan. 11, 1851: "The Gold Bluffs Excitement — seems to be on the increase in all circles." Soulé, Gihon, and Nisbet, *Annals of San Francisco* (1855), pp. 311-14, quoting a reporter for

the *Alta:* " 'In the spring of the year, after a succession of calms, the entire beach is covered with bright and yellow gold. Mr. Collins, the secretary of the Pacific Mining Company, measured a patch of gold and sand, and estimates it will yield to *each* member of the company the snug little sum of $43,000,000 [*say*, forty-three *millions* of dollars!] and the estimate is formed upon a calculation that the sand holds out to be one tenth as rich as observation warrants them in supposing.' . . . General John Wilson and Mr. John A. Collins, both of whom had been among the number of discoverers, frankly testified to the truth of these wonderful statements. The beach, they said, for a great distance, was literally strewed with pure gold. . . . No wonder people raved. . . . The ancient excitement of Mississippi and South Sea schemes was a bagatelle in comparison."

49. On Second Street, between J and K. "We beg to inform our friends and the public generally that we This Day open the RESTAURANT, where we will be pleased to see them. Every exertion on our part, will be made to procure the very best Fish, Meats, Game and delicacies that this market and San Francisco will afford. Our Wines and Liquors are of the very best quality. . . . Our Bed Room accommodation is ample. . . . We solicit patronage. Jos. Curtis, Manager Sac. City, 18th Dec., 1850" (*Sacramento Transcript*, Dec. 20, 1850). *The Sacramento City Directory*, 1851, p. 49: "Orleans house, Simmons & Curtis, 48 2d street"; *ibid.*, p. 50: "Restaurants. . . . Orleans house, A Bennusse, 181 J street."

50. Bancroft (*Chronicles*, V, 386): "Of other steamers running to Panamá, the Sandwich islands and along the coast at this early day [1851], there were the . . . *New World*, Captain Hutchins." Again (*ibid.*, pp. 134-35): "The *New World* was one of several steamers which . . . rounded Cape Horn, and plied either ocean or inland waters."

51. Not the St. Charles, but the St. Francis, "the only hotel at present where respectable ladies are taken in" (San Francisco letter of Mrs. John Wilson, Aug. 15, 1850). "This was the *fashionable* house of the day. Here the *élite* of the city either boarded, or were accustomed to congregate" (Soulé, Gihon, and Nisbet, *Annals*, p. 648). Commenting on gambling hells, "for nearly every public house is so (except the one we are at)" the General describes a gambler's death, overheard in this hostelry of cotton walls. Yet Bayard Taylor says: "The sleeping apartments of the St. Francis were the best in California" (*op. cit.*, II, 58).

The interim since the General stopped at Bruff's Camp had been busy, but not in Indian affairs. Having left Wm. Henry as deputy at Lassen's, he embarked from his own landing for Sacramento, thence continuing to San Francisco. His arrival is noted in the *Alta California*, Dec. 15, as of the previous Saturday (Dec. 8). His discouragement over the "loco-foco state" of his office ("California Letter of John Wilson," p. 203) may have been partially due to his failure in the confidential Utah mission entrusted him by Pres. Taylor. That his salary was uncertain also influenced him ("California Letter," p. 203). Considering that this was $1,500 a year, and expenses for traveling (including gifts to Indians) for the same period another $1,500 — all, and more, swallowed up by the expenses of the over-land trip — it is understandable that he should have paused in San Francisco. He turned his attention to his appearance before the legislature as delegate from Utah, to his law practice, his fellow citizens — he heads relief lists, serves on the Board of Education, presides at public meetings, is a director of the Pioneer Society — and his various business ventures: his ranch, his "*wash yard*" ("Don't let your aunt know that I have written you this," he admonishes his wife's Missouri nephew; yet at $8.00 a dozen, "double the wages of a member of Congress," as Bayard Taylor puts it, one can see it was a business), his chicken raising, his Sandwich Island cargo ("California Letter," p. 207), and apparently even more sub rosa his magnificent speculation of Gold Bluffs.

52. "On Montgomery st. stood . . . Eureka hotel (J. H. Davis & Co.)" (Bancroft, *History of California*, VI, 190, n.).

53. Born and raised in Washington, D. C., it is to be expected that Bruff would be acquainted with the Kings of Georgetown. James King of William was born in the latter town Jan. 28, 1822, grew up there, married there. He was a post-office clerk in Georgetown — as a government employee this would also have brought him into Bruff's circle — served with the firm of Corcoran and Riggs, and gained journalistic experience on the Washington *Daily Globe*. With the exception of one short absence, King lived in Georgetown until May, 1848, when he went to California by way of Panama and Valparaiso, reaching San Francisco in Nov. 1848. After a short essay at mining, he formed the banking house of James King of William and Co., which opened in San Francisco near the close of 1849. Reverses followed, and King threw his personal fortune in to meet the losses, also terminating an unfortunate connection with Adams and Company (the express agency) when that concern closed its doors in 1855. King then started the *Daily Evening Bulletin*, famous for its bold exposé of political evils in San Francisco. On May 14, 1856, he was shot and mortally wounded by James Casey, whose career King had sketched in his paper. King died six days later and his death resulted in the formation of the Second Vigilance Committee and the political housecleaning of the city for which King gave his life. King's older brother, Henry, was a member of Frémont's expeditions (1846-48), and his letters caused James King of William to start for the West. See *Dictionary of American Biography*, X, 407-8.

54. Bancroft, *Chronicles of the Builders*, V, 386: "Of other steamers running to Panamá, the Sandwich islands and along the coast at this early day [1851], there were the *Chesapeake*, Captain Ward." The "Chesapeake" had been purchased by the Pacific Mining Co. to make the run between San Francisco and Trinidad.

55. Collier's tenure of office as collector of the port of San Francisco was brief, and he seems to have retired under a cloud. Bancroft (*History of California*, VI, 673, n.) describes him as "a popular villain. . . . The govt brought suit against him for moneys not accounted for, the balance against him being $700,000. About half of this was paid up before suit was brought for the remainder."

Bancroft also charges that Collier had caused the seizure of foreign vessels, profiting from the sale of the cargoes. "These seizures fell principally upon French vessels, the gross claims presented by the French minister amounting to nearly $800,-000, which, with the other claims for illegal proceedings, aggregated over $1,000,-000. Of this amount our fine official paid $200,000, while the cost to the government was $300,000, after reducing the claims to about one quarter of their full amount" (*ibid.*). T. H. Hittell states (*op. cit.*, IV, 96) that in 1851 Collier was a candidate in the state legislature for U. S. Senator, but withdrew.

56. *Sacramento Transcript*, April 20, 1850 (from the San Francisco *Journal of Commerce*): "Trinidad City. — A company of gentlemen have located a site on Trinidad Bay, duly taken possession of the same according to law, and now make known the fact and locality of the spot. Several gentlemen who have seen the site, declare it the best spot in the whole region for a town. They say it is a good shelter for shipping, and sufficiently deep, a cable's length from the shore, to [fl]oat a frigate, and moreover that the surrounding country is both well timbered and [f]ertile. These advantages are all that are necessary to make a good commercial point on the coast; and now that the location is made, the new town will, no doubt, rival San Francisco in the rapidity of its growth." Bancroft, *History of California*, VI, 503: "The earliest site on this upper coast was that of Trinidad, selected during the first days of April [1850] by Captain Parker of the *James R. Whiting*. It was for a moment overshadowed by Klamath City. . . . Trinidad acquired the lead, soon counting 30 buildings, partly from its proximity to the Trinity mines, which, moreover, procured for it the seat of Trinity county, which in 1850 was created to embrace all this newly explored region west of the Coast Range. It received further impulse from the Gold Bluff excitement during the winter of 1850-1." See Bruff's sketch (one of the earliest), p. 558.

57. Probably George Frank Lemon, who came to California as lieut. in the N. Y. Volunteers. He resided in San Francisco 1851-53, and returned to New York. *San Francisco Alta*, Nov. 6, 1862: "At the outbreak of the rebellion he entered the army as Major and naturally attached himself to the California Regiment, raised by Baker and commanded by the lamented Matheson. . . . He was wounded in the leg in one of the battles before Richmond, and subsequently had the limb amputated. Our latest advices state that he has died from the effects of his injuries." *Ibid.*, Dec. 19, 1862: "He was for a long while connected with the business department of the Alta California, and for several years Secretary of the Society of California Pioneers. He was universally popular in the Army for his many generous traits of character, chivalric bearing and true qualities as a soldier."

58. Choli, according to Bruff's notes, Feb. 20; a hamlet of the coast Yurok. Col. Redick McKee, one of the Indian Commissioners immediately succeeding Gen. John Wilson, says, Sept. 1851: "They call themselves the Kori Indians, with Oqua as chief; are about fifty in number, and have always been friendly with the whites" ("Minutes . . . on the Expedition . . . through Northern California,"

32 Cong. Spec. Sess. [1853], p. 155). Wistar, in 1850: "Just south of the town [Trinidad] where the bluff was highest, there was a narrow bench somewhat more than half-way up the height, but a few feet wide containing a small *rancheria* or Indian village of three or four houses and a spring of water, through which a steep and rough Indian path . . . mounted the bluff" (*Autobiography*, pp. 200-1; courtesy of Wistar Institute). "Tsū'rai, translated 'mountain.' A town. . . . It lies near the white settlement of Trinidad. The white town occupies a flat . . . , with Trinidad head on the seaward side. . . . On the day of my visit, a cold wind was sweeping over the treeless flat about the white town, but in the Indian village, down over the bluff, the air was still warm and pleasant" (Waterman, "Yurok Geography," *Univ. of Calif. Pubs. in Amer. Arch. and Eth.*, XVI [1920], 271). "The Yurok inhabit a rather limited area . . . lying for the most part in Humboldt county. . . . They occupy the lower thirty-six miles of the Klamath river, from a short distance above the point where the Trinity enters it, to the sea, and a somewhat longer stretch of seacoast, reaching northward to Wilson creek, Del Norte county, and southward to Trinidad bay in Humboldt county, a distance of forty-two miles. . . . However, the Yurok actually occupied only the banks of the river and the ocean beach. . . . The hills lying back from the water they utilized for gathering grass seed, acorns, and for the pursuit of game" (*ibid.*, pp. 182-83).

59. Gen. James Wilson, born in Peterboro, N. H., March 18, 1797, educated at Exeter and Middlebury, admitted to the bar in 1823, practiced law in N. H. until 1841. Member of the state legislature for many years; 1820-40, served in the state militia, rising to rank of Maj. Gen. "In June, 1841, General Wilson was appointed by President Tyler surveyor general of public lands for the territories of Wisconsin and Iowa, which office he accepted and continued to discharge the duties . . . until 1845, when he returned to Keene. In 1847 he was elected to Congress, and was re-elected in 1849, and served until September, 1850, when he went to California, which had just been admitted into the Union as a state. He established himself at San Francisco in the practice of law, where he remained until 1867, serving for a time upon the Commission for settling private land claims. . . . In 1867 he returned to his old home." He died May 29, 1881 (*Cheshire Republican*, Keene, N. H., June 4, 1881). He is best known in California in connection with the Limantour land claim, he having been Limantour's counsel. T. H. Hittell, *op. cit.*, III, 697-98: "the most enormous and perhaps the most outrageously fraudulent of all these [land] claims was that known as the Limantour. It purported to be a grant of four square leagues south of California street, said to have been made on February 27, 1843, by Governor Micheltorena to José Yvez Limantour, a French resident of Mexico who was then a small trader to California, and an additional grant of Yerba Buena, Alcatraz and the Farallones Islands and one square league of land in Marin county opposite Angel Island, said to have been made on December 16, 1843. . . . These claims were filed in February, 1853, and confirmed

by the land commission. . . . Their confirmation had been especially and vehemently urged by James Wilson, . . . who had become the attorney for the claimant; . . . and he thus induced many persons, . . . to purchase quit-claim deeds from him as attorney-in-fact of Limantour. . . . Afterwards in 1858, when the cases came up on appeal in the United States district court, Judge Ogden Hoffman in rejecting them used very strong language. . . . As to the alleged grants themselves he pronounced them unquestionable frauds. . . . No attempt was made to appeal the decision. On the contrary Wilson, having staked whatever honor he may have had and lost, left the country." Limantour was indicted for perjury and jumped his bail.

60. Gen. James Wilson was a very tall man, " 'six feet and four inches tall and every inch a Whig,' as he often remarked" (obituary, [Keene] *New Hampshire Sentinel*, June 2, 1881). Apparently Gen. John Wilson was also unusually tall.

61. "The gifts of the sea which the Yurok talk most about were the sea mammals, especially whales. Whales, I think, were never hunted, for the Yurok have no whaling tackle. But the stranding of a dead whale was not uncommon and was considered a great event" (Waterman, "Yurok Geography," pp. 220-21).

62. See nn. and sketches, pp. 527-29, 559-61.

63. Bruff places his village between the northernmost lagoon and "Red-wood Lake." Oss-hragon, the name for it given by Bruff under date of Feb. 20, is similar to "Osegen" or "Ashegen," given by modern authorities (e. g., Waterman) to a town between the Klamath and Gold Bluffs. Gibbs says ("Journal of the Expedition of Colonel Redick M'Kee . . . 1851," *in* Schoolcraft, *op. cit.*, Part III, 133): "The Indians of . . . Gold Bluff [are called] Osse-gon." Bruff, as if in corroboration, explains that Oss-hragon was "near to the Gold Bluffs." Wherever it was, it is today a cluster of cellar holes.

64. See nn. and sketches of similar scenes at Choli, pp. 528, 529, 560-61.

65. Wm. Henry, Wilson's eldest son, who was at Lassen's in the early months of 1850, and who in April of that year started with his younger brother "Cage" and "quite a lot of Indians to work for them," for "the mines." "Wm.," his father remarks, "is just fitted for the mines, as to everything but saving and taking care of things" ("California Letter of John Wilson," p. 204). In the fall of 1851 his brief career terminated, "with Disentary, caught in the mines" (San Francisco letter of John Wilson).

66. This is a dangerous coast. In this vicinity, at a point roughly halfway between Trinidad and Crescent City, John H. Peoples lost his life in the spring of 1850. March 10, 1850, the brig "Arabian" sailed from San Francisco to Trinidad Bay, to locate "a new town in some good harbor midway between here [San Francisco] and Columbia river." March 27 Peoples, Lieuts. Bache and Browning of the Coast Survey, Capt. Connor, and six others left the brig in a whaleboat, "for the purpose of examining the shore." The *Alta* reported the accident, April 17, 1850: "Latest from Trinidad Bay. . . . The Arabian lost a boat and five people

four miles below Point George. Lt. Bache, U.S.N., Lt. Browning, U.S.N., Jno. H. Peoples, W. W. Cheshire, and John Purdy were the unfortunate persons drowned. . . . Lt. Bache is well known in California as the daring and successful commander of the steamer Senator, in her long and perilous voyage from New York to San Francisco. . . . Mr Peoples was well known as one of the previous editors of the Mexican War, and rendered important services to the emigrants who arrived late last season overland. He was an enterprising, intelligent and worthy gentleman, and is a great loss to California."

67. "The gold placers on the banks of the Trinity river were discovered in the spring of 1849, and it was soon found that the diggings were rich and extensive. In October and November a large number of miners had collected there, but they found the high cost of provisions to be a serious drawback to their profits. . . . They had heard of Trinidad harbor, and Trinity river had been named upon the supposition that it emptied into that bay. . . . It was under the influence of these ideas that two parties started from the mines of Northern California in the fall of 1849, to find a harbor and build a seaport on the coast. . . . One went by sea, the other by land. The former discovered the mouth of the Klamath river . . . ; the latter [led by Josiah Gregg] discovered Humboldt bay." The adventurers who came in the fall of 1849, in quest of a harbor to supply the needs of the mining settlements in the interior which radiated from the Trinity returned in the brig "Cameo" the following year (April, 1850) and landed near the mouth of the Klamath to explore. They were the discoverers of Gold Bluff and the founders of Klamath City, on the south side of the river, which they thought destined to reap a golden harvest from the mining activities. Thither a steady stream of sailing craft and even steamers came in the Gold Bluff excitement, as Bruff has noted. The first to enter the river was the brig "Sierra Nevada," in May, 1850, with supplies for the "Klamath Company," closely followed by the "Laura Virginia." "Klamath City was, but is not. . . . It has not even left a ruin for a memento. A lonely cabin may mark its site, but the tenants know nothing of the city that was, and was to be." So wrote J. S. Hittell in 1868 ("Story of an Unfortunate City," *Overland Monthly*, I [1868], 140).

68. Probably the Bald Hill, or Chilula Indians, of Redwood Creek, who were of an entirely different stock from the Yurok. "Chilula is American for Yurok Tsulula, people of Tsulu, the Bald Hills that stretch between Redwood Creek and the parallel Klamath-Trinity Valley. . . . The trails from Trinidad and Humboldt Bay to the gold districts on the Klamath in the early fifties led across the Bald Hills, and the Chilula had hardly seen white men before they found themselves in hostilities with packers and miners. . . . As a tribe they are long since gone" (Kroeber, *Handbook*, pp. 137-38). On the other hand, the salutation is that of the Yurok, with whom we have a definite record of hostility (Jan. 23, H 3). The knives worn served the double purpose of weapons and of cutting and cleaning salmon, seals, whales, and game. Powers, in 1877: "Another weapon made by them

is a sword or knife about three feet long, of iron or steel procured from the whites . . . a substitute for the large jasper or obsidian knives which they used to make and use" (*Tribes*, p. 52).

69. The Royal College of Surgeons of England has been unable to confirm this (letter, May 21, 1937, from the Secretary).

70. "The *Gold Hunter*, 175 feet in length and 26 feet beam, with two spacious cabins and berths for 100 passengers. . . . Her tonnage was 435" (Bancroft, *Chronicles*, V, 128, 129). *Hutchings' Illustrated California Magazine* (IV, 5) mentions "The 'Gold Hunter,' commanded by Capt. Branham, now [1859-60] the U. S. surveying schooner Active, was put on about this time [1850], but soon withdrawn." According to Bancroft (*op. cit.*, V, 450), the "Gold Hunter" was lost on the coast of South America.

71. Union Town, a site where, according to Bancroft, Gregg's unfortunate party had Christmas dinner in 1849, and to which, in April, 1850, some of the survivors returned to found a town. It became Arcata in 1860. Traffic with the mines, on which the success of the settlement was predicated, dwindled, it lost much expected trade through the shallowness of its harbor, and has grown only through farming the fertile bottom.

72. Connelley (*Doniphan's Expedition* . . . [1907], pp. 25-29) gives an account of this *cause célèbre:* John W. Harper, a clever but unprincipled young lawyer, "probably from Georgia," settled in Independence, Mo. "He paid court to Fanny Owens, then very young and very beautiful. His attentions were discouraged by Mr. and Mrs. Owens." However, Fanny Owens eloped with Harper. "The following spring a young man named Meredith came from Baltimore to make a trip across the plains with Colonel Owens. . . . A flirtation arose between him and Mrs. Harper. Harper became very jealous and determined to kill Meredith." He enticed the young man into his office and shot him dead. Harper fled, but was eventually returned to Missouri for trial, which was held in November, 1847. "Harper was promptly acquitted."

73. Here and along the base of the mountain which bears their name were the Shasta, whose extinction, with that of their neighbors, the Modoc, has been immortalized by Joaquin Miller's idyl, *Life amongst the Modocs*.

74. Bancroft, *Chronicles*, V, 386: "Of other steamers running to Panamá, the Sandwich islands and along the coast at this early day [1851], there were the . . . *General Warren*, Captain Thomas Smith." This vessel was lost in 1852. Bancroft (*ibid.*, p. 448) says: "In February 1852 the *General Warren*, Captain Thompson, was wrecked on the coast above the mouth of the Columbia, and forty-two lives lost." Soulé, Gihon, and Nisbet (*Annals*, p. 437) include it, as follows, in a list of vessels lost: "Jan. 31st, 1852, Clatsop Spit."

75. Mad Creek is associated with Josiah Gregg, leader of "a party which went by land to establish a seaport for the northern mines . . . who started from Rich

Bar on the Trinity River, on the fifth of November, 1849, with a dozen horses and mules, and provisions for ten days. . . . Some of their mules died of starvation, and they themselves narrowly escaped that fate. . . . They started to follow the coast southward. . . . At the mouth of Mad River, Gregg wished to take the latitude, but the remainder of the party did not care whether the place should ever be identified thereafter or not, and they refused to wait for him, whereupon he flew into a violent rage and cursed them. This incident suggested the name" (J. S. Hittell, "Story of an Unfortunate City," pp. 140, 144). It also led to the death of Josiah Gregg, whether through neglect, desertion, or even murder by his dissension-torn companions may never be known. At "Lat. 41° 3′ 32″ Barometer 29° 86′ Ther. Fah. 48° at 12 M. Dec. 7, 1849, J. Gregg" carved his name deep on a tree that told the world he had found Trinidad Bay. As its discoverer, as author of *Commerce of the Prairies,* and intrepid trader on the Santa Fé, he will be longer known than for Mad River, his pitiful epitaph. See also H. T. Dimick, "Reconsideration of the Death of Josiah Gregg," *N. M. Hist. Rev.,* July, 1947, pp. 274-85.

76. "They have no name for themselves other than *Olekwo'l* ('persons'), sometimes written *Alikwa*" (*Handbook,* II, 1012).

77. These were large and important towns in their day. The white settlement of Requa, with its salmon cannery, perpetuates the name of one. About both a few of the Yurok still live (Waterman, "Yurok Geography," pp. 231, 232).

78. "Sre'gon," as located by Waterman, is nearer twenty-five miles up the river. But the location may have been changed. "This place was not large; but its people were all related, and all excessively rich. Even yet, the Sre'gon people assume a rather overbearing attitude toward other Indians. . . . Everyone agrees that it has not been there very long" (Waterman, "Yurok Geography," p. 244).

79. From Bruff's legend beside his sketch of the grave of the chief's son at "Choli" (p. 410) it is evident that coast and river villages had their feuds. In itself "Ulruck," now spelled Yurok and applied by us to both upstream and coast divisions, means merely "downstream." The list of words is one of the earliest recorded of the coast dialect. The original orthography has been preserved.

80. Through the Umpqua Valley, in 1846, was made the road to the Humboldt, known thereafter as the Applegate or southern Oregon road — the same over which Bruff and his fellow travelers of '49 entered northern California — and here, at Scottsburg and its vicinity, were settled the pioneers of that road, Jesse Applegate, his brother Lindsay, and Levi Scott (Bancroft, *History of Oregon,* II, 568-72).

81. Wistar, in the spring or early summer of 1850, sailed "on board . . . S. S. *Eudora,* Barkman master, bound with a large freight and passenger list to Trinidad Head. . . . The *Eudora* was a barque rigged screw, and a large vessel for those days, with a tonnage of probably 1500 or thereabout" (*Autobiography,* p. 168;

courtesy of Wistar Institute). The ship encountered stormy weather, and Wistar and others ran it back to San Francisco and beached it off Rincon Point. Apparently it was refloated.

82. Bruff makes no comment, but his dreams of a fortune in Trinidad — provided he cherished any — were doomed. The Gold Bluffs excitement died as suddenly as it had flared up. The stock was put on sale by public advertisement on Jan. 10, by "John A. Collins, Secretary," "by order of the Board of Trustees." On Jan. 13 as many as eight vessels, advertised in the *Daily Pacific News* alone as sailing for Gold Bluffs, but toward the end of that month the bubble had burst. As for Gen. John Wilson, he appears to have had a boundless and abiding faith in the abundance and the ubiquity of gold in California. More than a year later, he wrote home to Missouri: "All the amazing stories of the richness of our mineral resources that have ever reached you, no odds how much they seemed to be exaggerated, are as far below the truth as the hill you live on is below the Sierra mountains. The truth is there is no known or by man a conceivable limit. There is gold everywhere & in every place" (San Francisco letter of John Wilson). But, like Bruff, Wilson made no lucky strike.

This is the last mention of Wilson in Bruff's pages. He died Feb. 2, 1877. San Francisco *Post:* "General John Wilson, the oldest member of the San Francisco bar, who died at Suisun yesterday, was a native of Tennessee. In early life he removed to Missouri where he became one of the leaders of the Whig party. In 1849 he came across the plains as Commissioner to Utah, and in 1850 [1849] he reached California, having been appointed Naval Agent [as well as Indian Agent] for this coast by his relative, President Taylor. Ever since he has been identified with most of the public interests of the State. He leaves behind him an aged widow, a son and a daughter. His funeral will take place this afternoon from St. John's Presbyterian Church."

83. See Introduction, pp. xlvi-xlviii, and 1st ed., Appendix VIII.

84. *Pacific Railroad Reports*, XI, 61-62: "Reconnoissance of the Colorado River, by Lieut. Derby, Topographical Engineers, 1851." See Sen. Ex. Doc. 81, 31 Cong. 1 Sess.

85. Bancroft, *Chronicles*, V, 133-34: "In 1851 the *Marysville* . . . ran twice a week between Marysville and Sacramento, and the *Miner* weekly between Marysville and San Francisco. The Union line also ran the *Confidence*, Captain J. P. Gannett."

86. Apparently "Atoy." Soulé, Gihon, and Nisbet, *Annals*, p. 384: "In 1851, there were only a few Chinese women in the city, among whom was the notorious Miss or Mrs. Atoy. Every body knew that famous or infamous character."

87. On Aug. 15, 1850, Mrs. John Wilson wrote home: "It is quite a curiosity to sit and look out upon the Plaza and see the great variety of people and languages that are here. The Chinese, the Malays, the Hindoos, the Turks, the New Zealanders, the New Hollanders, the Tahitians, and Sandwich Islanders, and from

every country in South America. You may truly say it is well to be cautious whom you associate with" (San Francisco letter).

88. Capt. George P. Andrews, 3d Artillery. Cullum, *op. cit.*, I, 122: born in Conn., grad. West Point July 1, 1845. Various frontier duties; served in Mexican War. "On voyage to California, 1848-49; on frontier duty at San Francisco, Cal., 1849, — Benicia, Cal., 1849-51." In Civil War in garrison in San Francisco harbor, and at other California points. "Retired . . . March 22, 1885. . . . Died July 2, 1887."

89. G. H. Q., Pacific Division of the Army and the Navy on the Pacific Coast. *Hutchings' Illustrated California Magazine*, IV, 10-11: "Benicia was founded in the fall of 1847 by the late Thomas O. Larkin, and Roland [Robert] Semple . . . upon land donated them for the purpose by Gen. M. G. Vallejo, and named in honor of the General's estimable lady." Bruff saw it in its heyday. It is today a town of a few thousand inhabitants.

90. Second in command of Warner's ill-fated expedition in the fall of '49. See Oct. 4, 1849, and *passim*.

91. "The first really substantial hotel [in San Francisco] was the Union, of brick, four and a half stories, opened in the autumn of 1850 by Selover & Co. . . . Burned in May 1851, and subsequently it became a less fashionable resort" (Bancroft, *History of California*, VI, 189, n.). *San Francisco Directory*, 1850, p. 110: "Union Hotel, Geo Brown, Pac b San and Mont."

92. Joshua H. Pierce. H. T. Peters, *California on Stone* (1935), p. 176: of New York and San Francisco. San Francisco, 1850, artist; 1854, lithographer. "Pierce did portraits, about 1841, for G. W. Lewis in New York." Associated with Pollard, as "Pierce and Pollard," in San Francisco "sometime about 1850."

93. The fifth great fire, according to Soulé, Gihon, and Nisbet, to devastate San Francisco: "May 4th [1851]. — The anniversary of the *second* great fire was signalized by the *fifth*, the ravages of which perhaps exceeded, in gross amount, those of all the fires together that had previously taken place in the city" (*Annals*, p. 329).

94. Mr. Robert Rea, Librarian, San Francisco City Library: "there is a record of the burial, or death, of Thomas McCalla on May 7, 1851. McCalla was a native of Washington, D. C., and was buried in Yerba Buena cemetery, San Francisco, grave no. 1118." According to Bruff's record, it must have been the burial which occurred on May 7. The *Register of All Officers* . . . lists (1847), p. 27, Thomas W. McCalla, employed in Washington, born in Ky., salary $1,000 per annum, one of the clerks of the surveys, Treasury Dept., Gen. Land Office.

95. This was built by Wm. Heath Davis (*Sixty Years in California* [1889], pp. 518-21; courtesy John Howell): "The first brick building erected in San Francisco was commenced in September, 1849, by the writer, at the northwest corner of Montgomery and California streets. . . . The bricks and cement, and other materials, were brought from Boston. . . . That building after it was finished, I

leased to the United States Government in June, 1850, for a Custom House. . . . In the great fire of May, 1851, the Custom House succumbed to the devouring element."

96. Of the fleet of the Pacific Mail Steamship Co. in 1851. Bancroft, *Chronicles*, V, 385: R. L. Whiting, commander; tonnage, 600.

97. Of the fleet of the Pacific Mail Steamship Co. in 1851. Bancroft, *Chronicles*, V, 385: Henry Randall, commander; tonnage, 1,100. "On the 5th of January 1860 the *Northerner*, Captain W. L. Dall, struck a rock at the entrance to Humboldt bay, and the vessel soon sank. The number of persons lost in effecting a landing was thirty-eight, and the treasure $14,000 in government funds" (*ibid.*, pp. 450-51).

98. According to the *Register of All Officers* . . . (1841), the "New Orleans," a ship of the line, was laid down at Sackett's Harbor in 1815 and work suspended before completion. In 1849 it was sold at public auction in New Orleans by the Navy Dept. (*Report of the Sec. of the Navy for 1849-50, p.* 461).

99. Early in 1851 the government ordered the Mounted Riflemen to return from the Far West. This change of policy was sudden. As late as by Act of June 17, 1850, Zachary Taylor had been authorized "To increase the Companies serving 'on the Western frontier and at remote and distant stations,' in the number of privates, to 74 each" (Gardner, *op. cit.*, p. 32). The accession of Fillmore on Taylor's death, however, caused a reversal of this policy, which materially affected Indian policies as well. "The Indians in California and Oregon having always appeared of an unwarlike character, and disposed to cultivate the good will of the whites, it was thought that the services of the regiment of mounted riflemen might be dispensed with on the Pacific. It was therefore ordered to Texas" (*Report of the Sec. of War for 1851*, p. 105). Gen. Persifor F. Smith seemed surprised at this reduction in an already small force. Gov. John McDougal, of California, was not only surprised; he wrote President Fillmore of his displeasure, March 1, 1851, declaring the troops originally sent, "considered in relation to the frontier to be protected, . . . totally inadequate" (*ibid.*, p. 138), and adding: "Protection by our people is regarded as their constitutional right; it is about the only benefit they can derive from their relation to the Federal Government, while their burthens are not light ones. It is not to be disguised that there is a feeling, and that a growing one, of dissatisfaction with the general Government. They are aware and feel that they have been taxed, but not protected" (*ibid.*, p. 139).

On April 30 Secretary of War Conrad replied to Governor McDougal: "Hopes were entertained, . . . that when the agents recently appointed to negotiate treaties with them [the Indian tribes in California] shall have accomplished their mission . . . that hostility which your Excellency considers as the necessary consequence of the two races being 'brought into sudden and close contact' would be avoided" (*ibid.*, p. 140). On May 3 of the same year the Secretary of War wrote Gen. Hitchcock: "You will use every effort to reduce the enormous expenditures of the army in California and Oregon" (*ibid.*, p. 142).

100. T. H. Hittell, *op. cit.*, II, 793-94: "Vallejo reported that in 1806 a military expedition marched from San Francisco against a tribe of Indians called 'Bolgones,' who were encamped on the western base of a mountain so-called, and that in the course of a fight, which took place there, an unknown personage, decorated with ornaments of extraordinary plumage, suddenly appeared on the side of the Indians. . . . The defeated soldiers, learning that the mysterious stranger made that place his home, supposed him to be an evil spirit, . . . so they named the imposing height El Monte del Diablo or the devil's mountain. . . . The good people who settled near it preferred a less irreverent and profane appellation for their country; and after a struggle in the legislature, the name Monte Diablo . . . was altered to Contra Costa."

101. Juan Bautista Alvarado was born in Monterey, Feb. 14, 1809, the scion of an old Spanish family, his grandfather being a settler of 1769. His mother was María Josefa Vallejo, sister of Mariano Guadalupe Vallejo; in 1839 he married Martina Castro, belonging thus by blood and marriage to the landholding Spanish families of California. In 1836 Alvarado staged a revolution to make California self-governing under Mexico; in 1838 succeeded Nicolás Gutiérrez as governor of California; in 1841, because of ill health, ceased to officiate; in 1842 finally relinquished his office to Micheltorena. He is known for his liberal policy toward the Americans. He is said to have "resided in Monterey until 1848, and afterward at San Pablo"; died July 13, 1882.

102. Whether of the Gutiérrez family to which Nicholás Gutiérrez, brief ruler of California with José Castro in the troubled interim of 1835-36, after the death of Gov. Figueroa, is unknown. The trade connections between San Francisco and Manila, under Spanish rule, were close, San Francisco having been visited first in 1775 and hailed as a safe harbor affording facilities for taking on wood and water, for the Manila galleons (G. H. Tinkham, *California. Men and Events* [1915?], p. 40).

103. To Francisco María Castro, father of the "Castro brothers," the rancho of San Pablo was granted in 1823 (Bancroft, *History of California*, II, 750). Francisco Castro was born in Sinaloa, Mexico, coming to San Francisco "before 1820." Apparently he was unrelated to the Castros who were already great landowners and political figures in California; but he took an honored place among them. Dying in 1831, he left San Pablo half to his widow and half to his eleven children, seven sons and four daughters. In 1851 the widow died, willing her share of the estate to her daughter Martina, wife of Gen. Alvarado. San Pablo on Contra Costa was an almost feudal estate, with its herds of four to five thousand cattle and one to two thousand horses, and its great house where the widow and her sons dispensed hospitality. It would seem that at the time of Bruff's visit Don Victor Castro was active in the management of the estate (Davis, *Seventy-Five Years*, p. 218). North of San Pablo were the ranchos of Gen. Vallejo, Petaluma and Temblex. At Benicia, on Vallejo's former estate, the Democratic Convention

was to be held; at Vallejo the General and his compatriots were to make a princely bid for the new capital of the new state of California. It was natural, therefore, that former Gov. Alvarado, nephew of Vallejo and husband of Martina Castro, should be at San Pablo at this time.

104. The first Democratic convention to be held in the state of California. According to Tinkham (*op. cit.*, pp. 96-97), the Democrats gathered in Benicia May 19, 1851, and the Whigs in San Francisco May 26: "The Benicia convention was composed of a solid body of Democrats who in after years became famous in state and nation. In their platform they censured the government because it had not, as they claimed, guarded the frontier against the Indians, provided postal facilities for California, nor built a mint at San Francisco." The Whigs built their platform on subsidies for ships and railroads, lands for farmers and miners, and financial aid for educational purposes. John Bigler was the Democrats' choice for governor and Pierson B. Reading the candidate of the Whigs, Bigler winning by a small majority.

105. "Situated in a lovely nook on the straits of Karquinez, nearly opposite the town of Benicia, is the wayside village of Martinez. It is quiet and sequestered, surrounded by romantic hills and shadowed by groves. . . . Martinez is a little over one year old" (*Daily Alta California*, April 3, 1850).

106. [Rincon Point] "A mile across from Clark Point. These two points presented the only boat approach [to San Francisco] at low water" (Bancroft, *History of California*, VI, 171, n.).

107. Wm. Heath Davis, *Sixty Years*, pp. 518-21: "The Collector retained possession of the premises for over a month, guarding the treasure which was saved in the vault, which proved to be thoroughly fireproof. . . . The removal of the treasure from the ruins of my building, to the new custom-house, Palmer, Cooke & Co.'s old banking house, northwest corner of Kearney and Washington streets, constituted a procession of about fifty armed men, which was headed by the Collector [Thos. Butler King] with a pistol in hand."

108. Soulé, Gihon, and Nisbet, *Annals*, pp. 339-40: "June 3d [1851]. — . . . This day one Benjamin Lewis underwent a primary examination on the charge of arson. As the evidence was being taken, the Recorder's Court began to fill, and much excitement to spread among the people. At this time, a cry of '*fire!*' was raised, and great confusion took place in the court-room, people rushing desperately out and in to learn particulars. This was a false alarm. It was believed to be only a *ruse* to enable the prisoner's friends to rescue him from the hands of justice. The latter was therefore removed for safety to another place. Meanwhile, three or four thousand persons had collected outside of the building, who began to get furious, continually uttering loud cries of '*Lynch the villain! Hang the fire-raising wretch! Bring him out — no mercy — no law delays! Hang him — hang him!*' Colonel Stevenson harangued the crowd in strong language, encouraging the violent feelings that had been excited against the prisoner. Mayor Brenham

endeavored to calm the enraged multitude. Loud calls were at length made for 'Brannan,' to which that gentleman quickly responded, and advised that the prisoner should be given in charge to the 'volunteer police,' which had been recently formed. . . . But when the prisoner was looked for, it was found that the regular police had meanwhile carried him out of the way — nobody knew, or would tell where." Probably no one dreamed that the quiet-looking little gentleman on the balcony above had just seen the prisoner thrust up through a trapdoor into the attic by the police!

109. The tollgate of the celebrated plank road from the center of San Francisco to the Mission Dolores. Early records tell of the streets of San Francisco and Sacramento being a sea of mud in the wet season. Plank roads were at that time a fairly new enterprise. *Stryker's Magazine*, V (1851), 251: "Among the many improvements in the means of communication which have been prosecuted in the last few years, plank roads are assuming a very important rank. It appears that the first plank road in Canada was laid down in 1836, and in New York in 1837, but it is only within the last four years that they have been much prosecuted." To Col. Charles L. Wilson (part owner of Lassen's Rancho, see May 4, 1850) belongs the credit of introducing this improvement to California. T. H. Hittell, *op. cit.*, III, 341: "Several sand ridges crossing Kearny street, south of California, had to be cut through, particularly one near Post street, where, as a point which could not be avoided, the toll gate of the road was established and for several years maintained." Dr. Cole was Wilson's agent at Lassen's Rancho.

110. The famous informal execution by which the Vigilance Committee began its reign. Soulé, Gihon, and Nisbet, *Annals*, p. 343: "June 11th [1851]. — The 'Vigilance Committee' is at last formed, and in good working order. They hanged at two o'clock this morning upon the plaza one Jenkins, for stealing a safe." *New-York Daily Tribune*, July 19, 1851: "Seen from the proper point of view, it is a manifestation — violent, it is true — of that spirit of Order which created the State of California, and while we regret the causes which induced it, our faith in the integrity of those who perpetrated it is nowise weakened." Jenkins appears to have been either an escaped convict, or a "ticket of leave" man. J. F. O'Connell, *A Residence of Eleven Years in New Holland* (1836), p. 69: "The 'ticket of leave' . . . is a conditional pardon. . . . Those sentenced originally for seven years, if convicted of no crime in New Holland [Australia], receive a ticket of leave at the end of three years; fourteen years' transports at the end of six; and *lifers* at the end of eight or ten." Recently T. Dunbabin, director Australian News and Information Bureau in New York (*New York Herald Tribune*, Oct. 14, 1947) claims that 20,000 Australians invaded California in the Gold Rush and that Hargreaves, a returned miner, initiated the Australian gold rushes that followed.

111. According to the *Annals*, Lewis was the man whom the police that day spirited away from the mob.

112. The Library, U.S. Naval Academy, identifies Capt. Kennedy (letter, June 9,

1938): "The 'Captain Kennedy' to whom you refer as having carried down the boundary monument in 1851, I find to be Lieutenant Charles H. A. H. Kennedy, commanding in 1851 the store ship Supply and at that time stationed on the Pacific Coast. His title 'Captain' would be a courtesy title given him as commanding officer of the Supply, a United States naval vessel." Born Va. Appointed N. C. Midshipman 10 Feb. 1819. Passed Midshipman 4 June 1831. Lieut. 3 March 1835. Commander 14 Sept. 1855. Dismissed from U. S. Navy 14 June 1861. Commander, Confederate States Navy, 25 June 1861. John B. Weller, "Commissioner for running the boundary line between the United States and the republic of Mexico," San Diego, Nov. 3, 1849, to the Secretary of State in Washington: "The monument will be placed five hundred feet from the ocean, and on a point of land forty-two feet above the level of the sea. Its precise latitude, as agreed upon, is 32° 31' 59". 58, which will make it about eighteen miles south of this town" (*California*, p. 87).

"This [the first monument] was an elaborate structure of marble, made in New York and brought to this coast by a naval vessel, landed in the bay, and hauled on wagons to its destination. It consisted of a pedestal and shaft of white marble, the whole 16 feet high, and resting on a foundation of brick laid in mortar. The cutting and polishing, as well as the inscriptions, were finely executed" (*Report of the Boundary Commission . . . 1891-1896*, 55 Cong. 2 Sess. Sen. Ex. Doc. 247. Part II, p. 173).

113. The Library, U. S. Naval Academy (letter, June 9, 1938): " 'the late Commander Kennedy, father of the above' we identify as Captain Edmund Pendleton Kennedy, who was born in Md. Appointed from the District of Columbia. Born in 1780. Appointed midshipman 22 November 1805. Lieutenant 9 June 1810. Commander 5 March 1817. Captain 24 April 1828. Died 28 March 1844, at Norfolk, Va. in command of the ship-of-the-line Pennsylvania, Receiving-Ship at the Norfolk Navy Yard."

114. Of the fleet of the Pacific Mail Steamship Co. *Shipping and Commercial List and New-York Price Current*, June 4, 1851, advertisement, "Steam Packet" "California," 1,050 tons. Bancroft, *Chronicles*, V, 380-81: "The contract for carrying the Oregon mail was let in November 1847 to Arnold Harris of Arkansas, who transferred it to William H. Aspinwall of New York. . . . Three vessels were constructed, namely, the *California*, *Oregon*, and *Panamá*, and the company owning them, styled the Pacific Mail Steamship company. . . . The *California* left New York October 6, 1848, and the other two followed at intervals of one month." *New-York Tribune*, July 19, 1851: "We are indebted to Mr. Chas. F. Lott, Purser of the Pacific Steamship California, and to Gregory and Co.'s Express, for the following report. . . . The California started from San Francisco 14th June, at 8 P.M., (the Propeller Commodore Stockton having started on the 12th June at 4 P.M., and the Propeller 'Columbus' on the 13th, at 5 P.M.) On the 22d June, at 9 A.M., passed the 'Com. Stockton,' on the 23d, at 10 P.M., arrived at Acapulco.

Took on board coal and water, and left at 8 P.M. 24th. Passed the Propeller 'Columbus' on the 26th, at 8 A.M., arriving at Panama on the 2d July at 7 A.M., making the passage from San Francisco in 16 days, 5 hours, allowing 30 hours for detention at Monterey, San Diego and Acapulco. . . . The following is a list of Passengers by the steamship California: J. L. Lecount   J. H. Wilson, W. L. Wilson   J. G. Bruff. . . ." E. W. Callahan, *List of Officers of the Navy* . . . [1901], p. 88: Thomas A. Budd, "Midshipman, 2 February, 1829. Passed Midshipman, 3 July, 1835. Lieutenant, 8 September, 1841. Resigned 29 April, 1853. Acting Lieutenant, 13 May, 1861. Killed in action 22 March, 1862."

115. T. H. Hittell, *op. cit.*, III, 444-45: "The original of this institution [Adams and Company] was an express company of Boston, Massachusetts, of the same name, at the head of which was Alvin Adams. In 1849 he sent Daniel H. Haskell as a resident partner to establish a branch house in San Francisco. . . . Meanwhile the California firm of Adams & Co. had added to its business as expressmen that of bankers. . . . Because of the confidence felt in the integrity and stability of the house, . . . and, as in the absence of proper or convenient mail facilities, it carried almost all the letters and money not only in California but between California and the east, it did a very large business." The consignment carried by Bruff was probably of considerable value, since he was accompanied across the Isthmus by the transit agent of the company. The postal activities of the company competed finally with those of the U.S. mail, which may account for the fact that on arrival in New York (July 18) postal agents visited the ship, embargoed Bruff's baggage and that belonging to Adams and Company and subpoenaed him to appear in circuit court as a witness in the case the government was evidently instituting against Adams and Company.

116. Selah R. Hobbie. Chas. Lanman, *Biographical Annals of the Civil Government* (1876), pp. 205-6: born Newburgh, N. Y., March 10, 1797. Practiced law Delhi, N. Y., "where he was soon appointed District Attorney and Brigade Major and Inspector." Rep. in Congress, 1827-29. Asst. Postmaster Gen., 1829-50, "when he retired on account of ill-health but assumed the duties of the office under President Pierce." Died Washington, March 23, 1854.

117. The *Register of All Officers* . . . , 1841 ed., lists the "Vandalia" as a first-class sloop, rate 20, built in Philadelphia in 1828. *Niles' Register*, May 30, 1849: Relaunched, "much improved," "at Portsmouth, Va., on the morning of the 26th inst." *New-York Tribune*, July 18, 1851: "The U. S. sloop-of-war Vandalia, Com. W. H. Gardner, was at San Diego, at anchor, on the 17th June. All well."

118. The Library, U. S. Naval Academy (letter June 9, 1938): "There was an officer named Moore serving in the Navy of the United States in 1851. His name was James H. Moore. Moore was born in New York State, was appointed from that state and held his citizenship in that state. He was appointed midshipman 10 February 1838. Appointed Passed Midshipman 20 May 1844. Appointed Master 5 April 1852. Appointed Lieutenant 7 January 1853. Died 18 October 1860. In

the years 1850 and 1851 he was assigned to Coast Survey duty and was given command of the Coast Survey vessel Ewing. The Ewing was assigned to duty on the coasts of California and Oregon during the years 1850 and 1851. He would be given the courtesy title of 'Captain Moore' because he was in command of a ship of his own, though he only held the naval rank of passed midshipman in 1851. There can be no doubt that he is the man referred to as there was no other officer named Moore in the United States Navy in 1851."

119. Probably John Lawrence Leconte; son of Maj. John Eatton Leconte, a zoölogist to whom Audubon, in his *Quadrupeds of North America* (New York, 1849?), acknowledged his indebtedness. The son was born in N. Y. May 13, 1825; graduated from the College of Physicians and Surgeons in 1846, "and while a student made several scientific journeys to the western states. He has since travelled extensively in North and Central America, for the purpose of scientific investigation, and has contributed many memoirs to the transactions of scientific societies and to journals, mostly upon the coleoptera of North America" (*American Encyclopaedia*, X [1883], 285-86). He was "the first biologist to map the faunal areas of the western part of the United States" (*Dictionary of American Biography*, XI, 89). Leconte contributed to the zoölogical sections of the *Pacific Railroad Reports*.

120. Bancroft, *Chronicles*, V, 386: "Of other steamers running to Panamá, the Sandwich islands and along the coast at this early day [1851], there were the . . . *Commodore Stockton*."

121. *New-York Tribune*, July 19, 1851: "The Steamship 'Pacific' arrived at Acapulco on the 23d June, at 10.30 P.M., 7 days, 6½ hours from Panama, and left for San Francisco at noon of the 24th." T. H. Hittell, *op. cit.*, III, 785: the "Pacific" was "one of the first regular Nicaragua steamers." *New-York Tribune*, July 18, 1851: records the steamer "Columbia" at San Francisco on June 12. The "Columbia" was one of three additions to the fleet of the Pacific Mail Steamship Company in 1851. According to the *Register of All Officers* . . . , 1841 ed., the "Columbia" was a frigate of the first class, rate 44, built in Washington in 1836. Bancroft, *Chronicles*, V, 450: "In August 1857 the *Columbia*, the first Pacific Mail steamer on the Oregon line, was lost in the China sea." *New-York Tribune*, July 19, 1851: "The steamship 'Northerner' arrived at Acapulco on the 23d June, at 6 A.M., 7 days 10 hours from Panama." *Hutchings' Illustrated California Magazine*, IV, 5: "The large propeller McKim, of about 400 tons burthen, was the next in rotation, and made her trip from New Orleans, through the straits of Magellan to San Francisco, in 1849, and took her first trip up the Sacramento, in the latter part of October of that year." Bancroft, *Chronicles*, V, 127: "She was sunk near Benicia in the summer of 1850, but was raised. . . . She was once beached in a gale at Crescent City, but floated gently off on the next tide."

122. Probably Lieut. Wm. M. Gardner, 2d Infantry. Cullum, *op. cit.*, II, 178: born Ga., grad. West Point 1846. "En route to California, 1848-49; on frontier

duty at Benicia, Cal., 1849-50, — and Camp Far West, on Bear Creek, Cal., 1850-51; on Coast Survey, Feb. 1 to Dec. 2, 1851." He fought for the South in the Civil War. Hamersly, *op. cit.*, Part I, p. 455: "Resigned 19 Jan., 1861."

123. Bancroft, *Chronicles*, V. 385: "The following steamers belonging to the United States Mail company, and known as the George Law line, were also running on the Pacific side in 1851, namely, the *Columbus*, Lieutenant John McGowan commanding." "Soon afterward [Jan., 1862] the *Columbus*, running from Panamá to Acajutla, was wrecked" (*ibid.*, p. 451). Wistar in 1850 shipped on the "Columbus" as a foremast hand from Panama to San Francisco: "The steamer had been built at Philadelphia to carry perhaps a hundred passengers of both classes [cabin and steerage] between that city and Charleston, South Carolina. By filling her entire between-decks and building four rows of standees, three bunks high, on her spar deck, 1100 passengers were crowded into her, with whom she sailed on her voyage of 3500 miles" (*Autobiography*, p. 164; courtesy of Wistar Institute).

124. Bancroft, *Chronicles*, V, 386: "Of other steamers running to Panamá, the Sandwich islands and along the coast at this early day [1851], there were the . . . *Constitution*, Lieutenant S. B. Bissell." By Act of Congress March 3, 1849, the "propeller steamer" "Massachusetts" was transferred from the War to the Navy Dept. It was thereupon "employed in the Pacific" (*Report of the Sec. of the Navy for 1849-50*, p. 461). The "Unicorn," of the fleet of the Pacific Mail Steamship Co. in 1851. *Niles' Register*, May 2, 1849: "Another Steamship for San Francisco. — The steamship Unicorn, formerly employed in the British Government mail service, sailed from New York for San Francisco, on Monday with 38 or 40 passengers. She stops on the way at Rio Janeiro and Valparaiso." The "Fremont," of the fleet of the Pacific Mail Steamship Co. in 1851.

125. Apparently one of the agents of the Pacific Mail Steamship Company. F. N. Otis, *Illustrated History of the Panama Railroad*, 2d ed., p. 149: lists Forbes and Babcock as representatives of the line in San Francisco.

126. T. T. Johnson, *op. cit.*, p. 51: "employed as guards to the immense amounts of specie and bullion sent across the Isthmus, and in various similar duties within the town."

127. *New-York Tribune*, July 18, 1851: "Two of the miscreants who were concerned in the murders on the Chagres River, were shot in the Cathedral Plaza of Panama on the 30th ult. Their names were Francisco Medrano & José Maria Radello." (Newspapers in those days secured news, in the absence of telegraph service, from passengers and officers of arriving steamers — in this case "The Brother Jonathan.")

128. Capt. Hannibal Day, 2d Infantry. Cullum, *op. cit.*, I, 250-51: born in Vt., grad. West Point 1823; served in Florida and Mexican wars. "On voyage to California, 1848-49; on frontier duty at Sutersville, Cal., 1849, — Bear Creek, Cal., 1849, — Camp Far West, Cal., 1850-51, — and Benicia, Cal., 1852-53." Served in

the Civil War. Hamersly, *op. cit.*, Part I, p. 398: "Retired 1 Aug. 1863. Brevet Brigadier Genl., 13 March, 1865, for long and faithful service in the army."

129. According to the Dept. of State, Washington, Amos B. Corwine of Ohio; appointed consul to Panama, Oct. 18, 1849. A Mexican War veteran.

130. E. L. Autenrieth, *A Few Words for the Traveller over the Isthmus of Panama* (1851), pp. 12-13: "It is stated that F. Pizarro, the conqueror of Peru, ordered the paving of this road, which was done with large round stones, sometimes a foot and a half in diameter. Since Panama sunk into insignificance, this pavement has been entirely neglected, and is now completely broken; and the big stones are lying loose and in great disorder, where formerly there was a pavement. . . . It is only astonishing that the mules are capable of passing at all over these loose heaps of round stones with a load on their backs. At the places where no pavement was needed, the rock is often excavated by the shoes of the mules in such a manner that a series of holes, sometimes more than a foot deep, have been produced, leaving a ridge of the rock between each hole. These are the most dangerous places for passing; the mule has to proceed with great caution, or he will fall."

131. Dr. Isaac Read wrote of the stretch from Cruces to Panama: "*Road* did I call this miserable attempt at a footpath? Do think the blue curtain of Heaven is not spread out over any thing so badly named, neither on the Moon, on the Earth, upon Jupiter nor any other planet. However we drove on against rocks, ditches, mudholes and all arrived 8 o'clock in the evening at Panama on the shore of the Pacific Ocean, covered with mud, worn out and sorely depressed in spirits, deeply lamenting the day we set out on this foolish journey" ("The Chagres River Route . . . in 1851," *Quart. Calif. Hist. Soc.*, VIII [1929], 13).

132. Bruff's record of 2½ days from Panama to Chagres is excellent, for the time. Toward the close of 1851, however, the first passengers were carried on the Panama Railroad from Navy Bay on the Atlantic side to Gatun, a distance of about seven miles, eastbound passengers from the next ship on the Pacific side being brought by rail from that point. This marked the beginning of the end of the old "Transit." By 1855 passengers were carried from ocean to ocean over the rails.

133. *New-York Tribune*, July 18, 1851: "The steamship Brother Jonathan, Capt. H. Squier, arrived at this port last night about 11 o'clock, from Chagres, which port she left on the evening of the 7th inst. She brings 238 passengers. The amount of gold dust in the hands of passengers is estimated at $465,000. . . . Previous to the sailing of the California, from San Francisco, on the 14th ult. buildings had been erected upon the greater portion of the 'burnt district.' . . . Passengers by the Brother Jonathan   J. G. Bruff. . . ." The "Brother Jonathan" was an unfortunate vessel. Bancroft, *Chronicles*, V, 452: "Another more terrible shipwreck was that of the *Brother Jonathan*, Captain S. J. De Wolf, July 30th [1865], near Crescent City. In open day and clear weather the vessel, which was heavily laden

with milling machinery for Idaho mines, and had a full list of passengers, struck on an unknown sunken rock, and in three-quarters of an hour had gone to the bottom. The wind being strong and sea rough, only one boat, containing sixteen persons, mostly the crew, reached the land; 150 perished. . . . Her officers all went down with the ship. Over this sad event there was general mourning throughout California and Oregon."

134. The "Alabama" was one of a number of vessels transferred from the Army to the Navy by Act of Congress March 3, 1849. It was then sold at public auction in New Orleans by the Navy (*Report of the Sec. of the Navy for 1849-50*, p. 461). J. M. Letts, in Chagres, Jan., 1850 (*Pictorial View of California* [1853], p. 197): "At 3 P.M. the Alabama moved off in the direction of New Orleans, crowded with passengers."

135. Letts, California-bound in '49, visited this spot: "There is a straight run of three miles. . . . We have now arrived at the bend of the river, and as here is a spring of excellent water, we make fast and fill our water-keg. Water is obtained here for the vessels in port, by sending up small boats. It can be obtained in any quantity" (*op. cit.*, pp. 17-18).

136. Dr. Isaac Read reached Cruces Nov. 24. "Put up at the American Hotel. . . . Here several had their Carpet-Bags rifled and my own was very near it but I happened to be awake and detected the thief under my cot and he slipped away" (*op. cit.*, p. 13).

137. One of the United States Mail Co.'s steamers on the Atlantic side. Bancroft, *Chronicles*, V, 408: according to her owners' estimate in 1857, she was built at a cost of $175,000. *New-York Tribune*, June 18, 1849: "The steamship Crescent City, Capt. Stoddard, arrived yesterday."

138. Cruelties, reprisals, and insurrection had preceded the unconditional emancipation proclaimed Aug. 1, 1838. "At nearly all the Missionary stations a funeral ceremony was performed at 12 o'clock, P.M. 31st July, over the 'remains' of slavery:

> Now Slavery we lay thy vile form in the dust
> And buried forever there let it remain
> And rotted and covered with infamy's rust
> Be every man-whip, and fetter and chain."

(E. Wooley, *Land of the Free* [1847], *passim*.)

139. The "Boston ice," had Bruff but known it, was a direct link with the Great West he had so lately left. When N. J. Wyeth, builder of Fort Hall (visited by Bruff Aug. 22, 1849) undertook his Oregon expeditions, he was associated in business with Frederic Tudor, ice merchant of Boston. After the collapse of his Oregon enterprise, Wyeth returned to the ice business and is credited with developing, together with Tudor, who had previously inaugurated the enterprise, a successful ice traffic with the West Indies.

140. Gen. Winfield Scott. Born in Va., 1786, died May 29, 1866. In 1841, by death of Gen. Macomb, became commanding general of the U. S. Army; in 1847 in chief command of the Army in Mexico. *Appleton's Cyclopædia*, V, 440-42: "A court of inquiry into the conduct of the war only redounded to the fame of Scott. In 1852 he was the candidate of the Whig party for the presidency."

INDEX

The symbol *il* or *ils* indicates a sketch or sketches by Bruff. The arrangement within the entries is in part chronological, in part geographical.